D1525216

Treasurer's Handbook

Treasurer's Handbook

edited by

J. Fred Weston
*Professor of Business Economics
and Finance
University of California,
Los Angeles*

and

Maurice B. Goudzwaard
*Associate Professor of Finance
University of Southern California*

DJ-I

Dow Jones-Irwin   Homewood, Illinois   60430

First Printing, September 1976

ISBN 0-87094-118-6
Library of Congress Catalog Card No. 75–39474
Printed in the United States of America

Preface

MANAGING FINANCIAL RESOURCES involves a broad range of activities in planning and operating a business firm. In the organization of the firm's finance department two major areas of responsibility are financing and accounting and budget systems. Both areas are integral parts of the planning and control system of the firm. The treasurer's office usually focuses on obtaining capital and allocating resources, while the controller's office concentrates on accounting control and budgeting. This Handbook emphasizes the responsibilities of the treasurer primarily in the area of financing and in the areas of his broad corporate responsibilities. There is also some overlap in the areas of financial planning and control shared with the controller.

The importance and complexity of financial activity have increased dramatically in recent years. The persistence of high interest rates and capital shortages makes it increasingly imperative to allocate corporate resources to their highest and best uses. Inflation places added importance on cost control in order to maintain profit margins necessary for an adequate return on assets. The increased instability in economic and financial markets presents new types of problems for treasurers. In such a turbulent environment the treasurer must both deal with financial stringency and avoid financial impairment of his firm. But the primary responsibilities of treasurers involve informing top management of the cash flow income and financial position implications of decisions in all areas of the business. The functions of treasurers have involved a broadening of responsibilities for effectively relating to other areas of the business and in so doing utilizing the increasingly sophisticated management concepts and analytical techniques that have become available. The purpose of this Handbook is to provide treasurers with the new conceptual materials and tools needed to carry out their broadened responsibilities effectively.

In recent years we have seen important new developments and new approaches to capital management. Some innovations emanate from researchers at the university level where financial management is viewed from a conceptual perspective. Other changes in the practice of financial management stem from innovative financial executives. One of the more significant changes in thinking concerning capital structure occurred with the publication of studies by professors Franco Modigliani and Merton Miller beginning in 1958. Their propositions have generated a host of empirical and theoretical studies enabling us to more clearly understand the determinants of financial structure. Their work has helped us sharpen our thinking regarding the impact of tax policies upon corporate financial decisions and the goals of value maximization. Financial managers have long grappled with the problem of defining business and financial risk and incorporating these concepts into financial decisions. In recent years, the development of the capital asset pricing model, associated with the contributions of Professors William Sharpe, John Lintner, Jan Mossin and Eugene Fama, has provided a framework for analyzing the relationship between market risk and return and the risk and returns of individual securities.

Other innovations have been developed by the business and financial communities. Tools and techniques such as linear programming, simulation, and computer application have been developed and expanded by financial executives in need of better methods to manage the massive flows of information. New financial tools and techniques are continuously being developed to accommodate changes in the economic environment and in particular the financing needs of firms.

This Handbook is written mainly by experienced business and financial executives for the practicing treasurer. Almost all of the chapters are original manuscripts prepared for the *Treasurer's Handbook*. The chapters represent recent thinking and current state-of-the-art practices of successful financial executives who actually face the day-to-day responsibilities of managing corporate resources.

One of the unique features of the *Treasurer's Handbook* is that the editors have developed an up-to-date compilation of additional information sources for each subject. The selected references correspond to individual chapters in most cases, but for broad subject areas developed in more than one chapter, the additional information sources are related to a group of chapters. There is no inference that the author drew upon these references in writing his chapter or sponsors the views contained in the additional information sources. The treatment in the references is generally more academic in nature and differences in views are encountered. In view of the divergent views in the references, the emphasis of this Handbook is to provide a framework by presenting the views of experienced, practicing financial executives.

Thus the chapters of the Handbook present a treatment of each subject based on successful experience to provide a foundation for further reading in existing and future literature. The Handbook thereby provides a useful place for the treasurer to begin his study of relevant concepts and techniques on any particular topic. The selected references merely seek to facilitate his effort if he wishes to do additional reading on any subject.

From one perspective we can look at the treasurer's function as asking and solving the "why" questions and the "how to" questions. The "how to" questions deal with the day-to-day problems of managing working capital flows, raising funds, meeting obligations, and so on. These problems are oriented to the short run and usually consume the bulk of the treasurer's time. Even more important in the long run, however, are the planning skills of the treasurer. The "why" problems are longer term in nature and force the treasurer to consider, for example, what required returns are appropriate for a capital projects, what the appropriate capital structure should be, and so forth. Each chapter contains examples of how successful treasurers actually apply the concepts and techniques of financial management in their operations. In most chapters copies of corporate forms and procedures are included as illustrative material. Our focus is on how successful financial executives actually employ sophisticated concepts and techniques and why these new and improved practices have been adopted.

The *Treasurer's Handbook* views the treasurer's responsibilities from several points of view. In Part I we look at the broad environment facing the treasurer and how he must cope with changes in governmental policies as well as the uncertain world in international finance and trade. In Part II we examine the treasurer's function from top management's point of view and explore the relation of that function to important external institutions. In Part III, we develop some conceptual perspectives on the treasurer's responsibilities. The topics include planning techniques for the corporate treasurer and the impact of recent developments in financial theory.

Part IV summarizes both new and old important tools and techniques of the treasurer. These include financial ratio analysis, cash forecasting, and the use of cost-volume-profit charts. In Part V we shift our focus to actual decision-making processes of choosing optimal investments. Particular attention is given to risk aspects of investment decisions.

In Parts VI and VII, ten chapters are devoted to working capital management and to short term financing. Important issues are cash management, trade credit policies, and inventory decisions. Optimal inventory policies are formulated for both manufacturing and retailing operations.

Part VIII takes up the subject of designing the capital structure. Here we view finance from the perspective of how financial theory influences managerial decisions. We investigate alternative models of corporate behavior and test these alternative approaches with empirical studies. Part IX focuses on problems of financing permanent capital needs of the corporation. The chapters analyze the alternatives of debt versus equity sources and forms of financing and the appropriate roles of each. A comprehensive treatment of leasing is presented. Financing instruments such as convertibles, warrants, and other options are also discussed in relation to the financial strategy of the firm.

Parts X and XI contain some of the more dynamic and innovative topics in the Handbook. These chapters discuss how and when to go public or to go private. New financing techniques such as project financing and the use of employee stock option trusts are fully developed. The problems of evaluating and financing corporate acquisitions are analyzed by businessmen with mature experience in these areas.

In Part XII, we view a range of financial responsibilities that will consume an increasing portion of the treasurer's time and energy in the future. These include communicating with the investment public and the responsibilities of corporate citizenship. The characteristics of the treasurer's enlarged responsibilities for pension fund management are also developed.

These contributions have been primarily the accomplishments of more than 50 contributing authors. Our work and theirs was stimulated by the members of the Editorial Advisory Board who were important initiators of this Handbook. In addition, we have had the help of consulting editors, who provided reactions to the drafts of these chapters and helped us make revisions and improvements.

Effective overall planning and guidance were provided by Professor Richard Vancil. We were aided in our editorial task by Woodrow Eckard, Maxwell Kaufman, and Susie Chen. Conscientious secretarial help was provided by Adelyn Hickman, Suzanne Bales, and Marilyn McElroy who also functioned as a coeditor.

We are hopeful that the joint efforts of this large group will help us succeed in our major objective of providing a practical and current guide to financial management. This Handbook seeks to update the treasurer on current practices and offers a new set of opportunities and challenges for the future. For there is one thing about which we can be certain—the next ten years of financial management will offer problems more difficult and more complex than they have been in the past. This Handbook seeks to provide a source to aid in preparation for meeting these new and enlarged challenges and opportunities.

Los Angeles, California   **J. Fred Weston**
August 1976   **Maurice B. Goudzwaard**

Contributing Authors

ANDERSON, R. A. (Chapter 14*)—Vice Chairman of the Board—Finance and Administration, Lockheed Aircraft Corporation

ANDERSON, W. D. (Chapter 21*)—Corporate Credit Manager, Control Data Corporation

ARNOFF, E. LEONARD, (Chapter 10)—National Director of Management Sciences and a Principal in the Management Consulting Services Division, Ernst & Ernst

BIANCHI, MARCELLO (Chapter 16*)—Sistemi Organizzativi S.p.A. and I.S.T.U.D. S.p.A.

BIEDERMAN, H. R. (Chapter 14*)—Senior Economic Adviser—Corporate Planning Staff, Lockheed Aircraft Corporation

BOWDITCH, RICHARD L. (Chapter 5*)—Vice President and Treasurer, W. R. Grace & Co.

BREWER, ROBERT E. (Chapter 24)—Vice President and Treasurer, S. S. Kresge Company

BROUDE, RICHARD F. (Chapter 46)—Member, Law Firm, Commons & Broude

BURTLE, JAMES L. (Chapter 5*)—Vice President, Economics Group, W. R. Grace & Co.

COPE, ROGER W. (Chapter 44)—Corporate Group Vice President, Planning and Development, Dart Industries, Inc.

DEBUTTS, JOHN D. (Chapter 6)—Chairman of the Board, American Telephone and Telegraph Company

EWERT, DAVID C. (Chapter 26*)—Professor, Georgia State University

EWERT, RUSSELL H. (Chapter 26*)—Vice President, The First National Bank of Chicago

FINDLAY, M. C. (Chapter 11*)—Professor of Finance, University of Southern California

FOSTER, ALAN H. (Chapter 13)—Vice President and Treasurer, American Motors Corporation

---

* Denotes coauthor.

GOODMAN, DAVID M. (Chapter 12*)—Chairman, Goodman & Mautner, Inc.

GOUDZWAARD, MAURICE B. (Chapter 2*)—Associate Professor of Finance, University of Southern California

HACKETT, JOHN T. (Chapter 4)—Executive Vice President and Chief Financial Officer, Cummins Engine Company, Inc.

HAYTHE, MADISON H. (Chapter 38)—Vice President, Morgan Stanley & Co. Incorporated

HERTZ, DAVID B. (Chapter 18)—Management Consultant, McKinsey & Company, Inc.

HOADLEY, WALTER E. (Chapter 7*)—Executive Vice President, Bank of America

HUSIC, FRANK J. (Chapter 51*)—Vice President, Alliance Capital Management Corporation

HUSTON, ROBERT L. (Chapter 42)—Senior Vice President, White, Weld & Company

KAPLAN, SANFORD (Chapter 12*)—Consultant and Director, Xerox Corporation

KAUFMAN, HENRY (Chapter 1)—General Partner and Member of the Executive Committee, Salomon Brothers

KELLY, PAUL K. (Chapters 33 and 41)—General Partner, Prescott, Ball & Turben

LEE, STEVEN JAMES (Chapter 48)—Financial Consultant, Bankers Trust Company

LoCASCIO, VINCENT R. (Chapter 9)—Manager, Peat, Marwick, Mitchell & Co.

LUDLOW, CHARLES H. (Chapter 19)—Vice President and Treasurer, Upjohn Company

McCAHILL, F. X., JR. (Chapter 50)—Director of Insurance and Safety, Bristol-Myers Company

MacDOUGAL, GARY E. (Chapter 45)—Chairman of the Board and Chief Executive Officer, Mark Controls Corporation

McGUINNESS, ROBERT J. (Chapter 34)—Vice President, Special Investment Services, Bateman Eichler, Hill Richards, Inc.

MAGEE, JOHN F. (Chapter 23*)—President, Arthur D. Little, Inc.

MEAL, HARLAN C. (Chapter 23*)—Head, Logistics Unit, Arthur D. Little, Inc.

MILLER, GENE I. (Chapter 39*)—Vice President, First Small Business Investment Company of California and Security Pacific Capital Corporation

MOBRAATEN, WILLIAM L. (Chapter 53)—Vice President and Treasurer, American Telephone and Telegraph Company

MOOR, ROY E. (Chapter 3)—Vice President and Director of Economic Research, Becker Securities Corporation

MURDY, J. L. (Chapter 17)—Vice President and Comptroller, Gulf Oil Corporation

QUACKENBUSH, W. B. (Chapter 21*)—Vice President and Treasurer, Commercial Credit Company

RANKIN, HARLEY, JR. (Chapter 27)—Treasurer, Continental Can Company, Inc.

---

* Denotes coauthor.

ROSSITER, BRUCE G. (Chapter 39*)—Vice President, First Small Business Investment Company of California and Security Pacific Capital Corporation

SAVAGE, ROBERT H. (Chapter 52)—Vice President and Director of Investor Relations, International Telephone and Telegraph Corporation

SEARBY, FREDERICK W. (Chapter 20)—Director, McKinsey & Company, Inc. and Manager of the Cleveland, Ohio, office

SHAD, JOHN S. R. (Chapters 40 and 47)—Vice Chairman of the Board, E. F. Hutton & Company

SHERIDAN, EDWARD P. (Chapter 36)—Senior Vice President and Treasurer, City Investing Company

SINNICKSON, LLOYD (Chapter 25)—General Credit Manager, American Cyanamid Company

SNYDER, NATHAN (Chapter 37)—Vice President, Acquisitions, CBS Inc.

SUGASKI, LLOYD J. (Chapter 7*)—Executive Vice President, Bank of America

SWEETSER, ALBERT G. (Chapter 22)—Professor of Finance, State University of New York at Albany

TAUSSIG, JOSEPH K. (Chapter 43)—President, J. K. Taussig & Co.

VAN CAMP, BRIAN R. (Chapter 8)—Member, Law Firm, Diepenbrock, Wulff, Plant & Hannegan

VERMILYE, PETER H. (Chapter 51*)—Chairman and Chief Investment Officer, Alliance Capital Management Corporation

VITALE, DAVID J. (Chapter 35)—Vice President and Treasurer, First Chicago Corporation

WELTER, PAUL (Chapter 16*)—Sistemi Organizzativi S.p.A. and I.S.T.U.D. S.p.A.

WESTFALL, STEVEN L. (Chapter 28)—President, Tradeline, Inc.

WESTON, J. FRED (Chapters 2*, 15, and 32)—Professor of Business Economics and Finance, University of California, Los Angeles

WHITE, FREDERIC ENOCH (Chapter 49)—C.P.A., Attorney, and Tax Manager, Arthur Andersen & Co.

WILLIAMS, EDWARD E. (Chapter 11*)—Vice President, Service Corporation International

WILLIAMS, GEORGE E. (Chapter 31)—Senior Vice President—Finance, Otis Elevator Company

WISHNER, MAYNARD I. (Chapter 29)—President, Walter E. Heller & Company

ZAKON, ALAN J. (Chapter 30)—Vice President, The Boston Consulting Group, Inc.

---

* Denotes coauthor.

Consulting Editors

CARR, ROBERT A., Professor, Chairman of the Department of Finance and Industry, California State University, Fresno, School of Business

DIETZ, PETER O., Professor, University of Oregon, College of Business Administration

DUNLAP, JAMES W., Dean, The University of Akron, College of Business Administration

FURST, RICHARD W., Professor, University of South Carolina, College of Business Administration

HASLEM, JOHN A., Assistant Dean, University of Maryland, College of Business and Management

HUSIC, FRANK, Assistant Vice President, Alliance Capital Management Corporation

JOHNSON, KEITH B., Professor, The University of Connecticut, School of Business Administration

LEDERMAN, HARVEY S., Vice President, Director of Marketing Services, Walter E. Heller & Company

LONGSTREET, J. R., Professor, Chairman of Finance, University of South Florida, College of Business Administration

O'DONNELL, JOHN L., Professor, Michigan State University, Graduate School of Business Administration

PINCHES, GEORGE, Professor and Director of On-Campus MBA Program, University of Missouri–Columbia, College of Administration and Public Affairs

RANDOLPH, JOHN M., President, Randolph Computer Company

RODRIGUEZ, RITA M., Professor, Harvard University, Graduate School of Business Administration

STEVENSON, HAROLD W., Professor, Arizona State University, College of Business Administration

SWEETSER, ALBERT G., Professor, State University of New York at Albany, School of Business

TRIVOLI, GEORGE W., Professor, University of Texas at Arlington, College of Business Administration

WEST, DAVID A., Professor, University of Missouri–Columbia, College of Administration and Public Affairs

Contents

Monitoring. Specific Responsibilities of the Treasurer: *Custody of Corporate Funds and Records. Budgeting and Accounting Responsibilities. Stock Exchange Requirements. Tax Responsibilities. Legal Compliance. Insider Laws. Securities Laws.*

PART VII SHORT-TERM FINANCING

PART VIII DESIGNING A CAPITAL STRUCTURE

and Debt Repayment Coverage. Leverage and Growth. Financial and Business Risk. Optimal Capital Structure—Constraints. Conclusions: Optimal Capital Structure. Conclusions: The Financial Executive. Appendix: *Derivation of Interest Coverage Equation. Derivation of Sustainable Growth Equation.*

of Stock Reacquisition Programs: *Delisting Possibility. Public Criticism. To Minimize Possible Abuses. How High a Premium Is Required?* Stock Reacquisition Approaches: *By Majority Shareholder Approval. Voluntary Reacquisitions.* XYZ Corporation Makes an Exchange Offer: A Composite Case Study. Soundly Structured Programs: Conclusions.

PART I

The New Financial Environment

THE DECISIONS of individual firms are made in relation to the general economic and financial environment. This is particularly true of the decision areas of corporate treasurers. Hence, this first section deals with the new economic and financial environments in which the treasurer functions. In the opening chapter Henry Kaufman discusses these developments with penetrating insights. He calls attention to changing credit markets characteristics, the new institutions and practices, the growth of debt, and the impact of international finance.

In the second chapter the editors seek to fill in some details of the general framework set out by Mr. Kaufman. In analyzing the background of inflation, we reach the conclusion that the nature of the environmental factors will cause the inflationary problem to persist over a number of years into the future. Hence, the implications of inflation for business financial policy require intensive and continued analysis. We discuss the impact of inflation on interest rate levels—past and prospectively—and on the increased external financing requirements. We assemble data showing the impact of inflation on financial reporting and on the financial conditions of business firms. We sketch how inflation has stimulated innovations in financing and has affected the traditional trade-offs in analyzing alternative sources of financing. We conclude by analyzing the impact of inflation on financial considerations in the pricing decisions of firms.

1

Since 1966, the U.S. and world economy has been characterized by increased turbulence, especially in the financial markets. This makes the timing of financial policy of increased importance. In Chapter 3, Roy Moor presents an analytical approach to decisions for timing the acquisition of funds and the selection of alternative sources and forms of financing under different economic and financial conditions. Dr. Moor first sets forth some general timing rules. He then analyzes the major influences on the equity markets, long-term debt markets and the commercial paper market. In a series of charts which portray the behavior of the economic variables that his research has demonstrated to be key influences, he provides evidence on developments in economic and financial markets that provide a basis for decision rules with respect to the timing of financial policy.

Of overriding importance in formulating financial policy have been developments in international finance. In Chapter 4, John Hackett begins an analysis of international influences by a discussion of the persistence of worldwide inflation. He shows the impact of these developments on capital requirements and debt levels of business firms. He indicates the liquidity problems that have been developing and calls attention to the need to redesign accounting systems to reflect the impact of inflation. Dr. Hackett then turns to an analysis of the use of the international money markets to obtain funds for corporate growth. He indicates the impact of future trends on the use of the international markets as a source of corporate financing. He then considers some broader issues related to the nature of financial reporting under inflation, the role of transfer pricing in the international operations, and environmental factors to consider in selecting countries for marketing expansion. He also analyzes prospective competition among multinational corporations and the requirements for the growth of U.S. corporations overseas.

In Chapter 5, Richard Bowditch and James Burtle deal with the operating management decisions of the corporate treasurer presented by the regime of floating exchange rates in the international financial markets in recent years. They treat two broad categories of foreign exchange management: transaction management and inflation management. They discuss two principal methods to avoid losses on foreign transactions through billing practices and "covering" practices. They then discuss the principles for taking statements originally presented in foreign currencies and translating them into dollars. They next discuss the issues involved in tax aspects of foreign exchange activities. Decisions and actions to avoid foreign exchange losses require some effectiveness in forecasting foreign exchange rates. Five methods are described with an emphasis on the use of lead indicators such as the money supply, relative price movements, and international reserve positions. They also discuss how an analysis of balance of payments developments can aid in assessing prospective foreign exchange rate changes.

The main factors describing the new financial environment in which the decisions of treasurers must be made are conveyed by these first five chapters. The central developments affecting the decisions of treasurers are persistent inflation and increased turbulence of the financial markets which impact both domestic and international markets. The new financial environment does indeed present new challenges to the treasurer in his important responsibilities for financial management.

Chapter 1

Forces of Change in the American Credit Markets

Henry Kaufman[*]

THIS INITIAL CHAPTER of the *Treasurer's Handbook* reviews the growth of the American credit markets with particular emphasis on money and bond market obligations. In addition, it describes the forces of change in these markets which constitute the environment in which the decisions of treasurers are made.

GROWTH IN THE CREDIT MARKETS

There has been a massive explosion of debt of all sorts in recent years and in turn, of course, an equal increase in financial assets. There cannot be one without the other. All outstanding debt encompassing the obligations issued by consumers, business, and our governments totaled over $2.5 trillion at the end of 1973 as compared with only $316 billion at the end of 1947. The growth of credit market debt was moderate in the early postwar period but gained momentum in recent years, averaging annually 6.2 percent in the 1950s, 6.9 percent in the 1960s, 6.6 percent in 1970, 9.7 percent in 1971, 10.1 percent in 1972, and 9.5 percent in 1973.

---

[*] Henry Kaufman is a general partner and member of the Executive Committee, Salomon Brothers, New York.

This chapter is based in part on original research developed by the Bond Market Research Department of Salomon Brothers, international investment banking and market-making firm.

4

The growth of the American money and bond markets has roughly kept pace with the growth of total credit market debt. The volume of outstanding bonds, including straight corporate debt issues, U.S. government coupon issues, and federal agencies and municipals, totaled $578 billion at the end of 1973 as compared with only $176 billion in 1947 and $231 billion in 1957. As shown in Table 1, the U.S. government coupon market had been the largest market in the aggregate for most of the postwar years. During the last decade or so, however, its size was surpassed by both the volume of outstanding corporate and municipal bonds. This development reflects not only the larger volume of corporate and municipal new offerings but also the reliance of the United States on the issuance of Treasury bills to finance its deficits and the rapid growth of federal agency financing.

The U.S. money market was also very small in 1947. The $4.3 billion in outstanding obligations shown in Table 1 consisted almost

TABLE 1
Volume of Outstanding Money and Bond Market Obligations for Selected Years from 1947–1973 (billions of dollars)

	1947	1957	1967	1972	1973
Money market					
Treasury bills (privately held)	$ 3.7	$ 25.5	$ 51.4	$ 73.5	$ 70.2
Commercial paper	0.3	2.7	17.1	34.7	41.1
Negotiable CDs	0	0	20.4	44.9	64.6
Federal agency discount notes	0	0	1.5	1.6	2.6
Bankers' acceptances	0.3	1.3	4.3	6.9	8.9
Total money market obligations	$ 4.3	$ 29.5	$ 94.7	$161.6	$187.4
Bond market					
Straight corporate bonds	$ 26.1	$ 66.8	$130.4	$209.5	$224.9
U.S. government coupon issues (privately held)	134.2	108.1	109.4	106.8	100.5
Federal agencies (coupon issues)	1.6	6.7	24.0	57.1	78.3
Municipal bonds	13.9	49.6	106.8	161.3	174.7
Total bond market	$175.8	$231.2	$370.6	$534.7	$578.4

entirely of Treasury bills. By the end of 1973, these obligations had risen to $187.4 billion, reflecting the growth not only of the bill market but, more importantly, of many private obligations. The continued rapid growth, moreover, in outstanding negotiable certificates of deposit (CDs) thus far this year has pushed the size of this market ahead of outstanding Treasury bills privately held.

Finally, in this review of the dimensions of the money and bond markets, we make rough estimates of the gross volume of activity in these markets. We calculated this volume by adding together the gross volume of new offerings, including refinancing and refunding, and the trading activity of the secondary market. These estimates are shown annually, monthly, and daily for 1973 in Table 2. In the

TABLE 2
Estimated Gross Volume of Activity for 1973 in American Money Market Obligations and Selected Bond Markets (billions of dollars)

	Annual	*Monthly*	*Daily*
Money market			
Treasury bills	$ 625	$ 52	$2.5
Commercial paper	370	31	1.5
Negotiable CDs	300	25	1.2
Federal agency notes	45	4	0.2
Bankers' acceptances	35	3	0.1
Total	$1,375	$115	$5.5
Bond market			
U.S. governments (marketable)	$ 265	$ 22	$1.1
Federal credit agencies (includes GNMA pass-throughs)	235	20	0.9
Corporate bonds	100	8	0.4
Total	$ 600	$ 50	$2.4

Note: Daily average is based on 250 trading days.

money market, the annual gross volume of activity was $1.3 trillion, or $5.5 billion per day. In the three taxable bond markets (U.S. governments, federal agencies and corporate bonds) it was $600 billion for the year and $2.4 billion per day. U.S. government securities led the activity in both markets, even though other obligations have increased rapidly in outstandings during the past decade.

FORCES OF CHANGE IN THE CREDIT MARKETS

Among the major forces that have contributed to the changing dimensions of the American fixed-income markets are: (1) the high rate of inflation; (2) the rising influence of monetarism; (3) the changing role of the commercial banks; (4) the removal of the money rate risk from important lending arrangements; and (5) the changing international monetary scene.

The Influence of Inflation

No force has had a greater impact on ballooning the size of the American money and capital markets than inflation. Because economic activity, both nominal and real, must be financed, the combination of a good volume of physical activity and increasing inflation in recent years has resulted in a sharp acceleration in credit creation and in a substantial unproductive debt burden. Based on the close correlation between total outstanding debt and the level of current dollar gross national product, we estimate that if there had been no inflation in the postwar years, the volume of outstanding credit market debt at the end of 1973 would have totaled roughly $1 trillion instead of over $2.5 trillion. In addition, without inflation, interest rates would have been at far lower levels in recent years.

The money and capital markets will continue to undergo vast and dramatic changes if inflation persists. Let me just enumerate some of the major credit and interest rate patterns that may be ahead under these conditions.

1.   Credit creation will continue to be excessive. If, for example, the yearly inflation rate is 8 percent and annual real growth is 3 percent during each of the next seven years, the volume of total credit market debt amounting to $2.5 trillion at the end of 1973, will total about $4.5 trillion in 1980.

2.   Virtually all commercial paper issuers rated below A–1 will be unable to finance in this market. All others will be forced to finance their needs through the commercial banks who will have neither access to the money market nor to the long-term market. The commercial paper market, however, will not contract but rather increase in size. It will be tapped as a source of funds by corporations rated A–1. Some are already issuers and others will also take the opportunity to arbitrage the financing cost spread between the prime and the commercial paper rate.

3.   With persistent inflation, the issuance of negotiable CDs will become more concentrated in the very large money center banks and the ability of other banks to use this source of funds will diminish. This development will enhance the strength of the large banks and diminish the role of medium and smaller banks.

4.   The quality of all sorts of credit will deteriorate. Insolvencies will occur quite frequently and the downgrading in credit ratings

of business corporations, now limited mainly to utilities, will spread to other industries. Consequently, investors will continue to favor high-quality obligations, and the yield spread between high-grade and medium-grade bonds will widen within time to above the 300 basis points briefly reached in mid-1970.

5.   The unwillingness of investors to finance the long-term issues of many medium and lower rated issuers will result in a substantial new volume of medium maturity offerings of notes and bonds, flattening the yield spread between medium and long obligations and leading eventually to a negative spread.

6.   All highly leveraged borrowers, other than medium or lower rated business corporations, such as banks and finance companies, will have to pay an increasing premium to obtain bond money over AA-rated business corporations and over the obligations issued by the U.S. government and its instrumentalities. This is because high-grade business corporations can offer substantial asset protection besides their earning power but financial institutions, being highly leveraged, cannot. In addition, industrial bonds will continue to benefit from their strong sinking-fund provisions. The U.S. government, of course, offers an obligation free of credit risk.

7.   The deteriorating credit quality of private borrowers will be accompanied by demands for governmental assistance. This will be provided through existing and many new federal credit agencies. The institutional framework is already in place. It is merely a matter now of lining up those who are to have access to this type of financing. With virulent inflation, denying governmental financing assistance will be difficult and resorting to it will be greatly appealing politically. The agency market, which is now dominated by housing financing institutions, will become quite diversified. In the process, however, the private sector will shrink and the role of the government will increase. Concurrently, the economic concentration in the private sector will also increase because the marginal and weak will either be absorbed by the government or large well-rated corporations.

8.   Governmental assistance to corporations in financial difficulty will not arrest the preference for high-quality obligations. The emphasis in these arrangements will be to maintain the public service aspects of these corporations and not to relieve immediately the plight of stockholders and creditors. In fact, governmental financial assistance will tend to raise the general level of interest rates and

increase the vulnerability of the marginal business in the private sector which are not receiving governmental support.

9.   The substantial volume of new offerings by the federal credit agencies will widen sharply the yield spread between these issues and those of the U.S. government while the yield spread between the agencies and high-grade corporate bonds will tend to be extremely narrow.

10.   In the high-grade bond market, the yield spread between deep and moderate discount bonds will narrow appreciably not only because higher interest rates will cause low coupon issues to sell off more than medium coupons but also because dealers will find it costly to carry deep discount bonds in an inflationary period in which dealer financing costs are likely to be high. Moreover, the yield spread between moderate discount bonds of utilities and industrial corporations will widen sharply. The latter will benefit from sinking-fund payments while the former will be hurt by rising interest rates and doubts about the ability of utilities to maintain their credit ratings.

11.   Investors may become reluctant to buy revenue bonds which do not have the direct guarantee of the state and local governments. The burden of inflation will force state and local governments to step up their direct financing which by itself would encourage enlarged "off-balance sheet financing" through revenue obligations. As inflation persists, however, the cost of services rendered by projects financed through these bonds may rise substantially. This, in turn, will require that these costs be passed on to the consuming public which may become highly irritated by the rapid rise in the cost of essential services and prefer a defusion of these costs through the tax route.

12.   Inflation will cut back materially the ability of Wall Street firms to fulfill their market-making and investment banking functions. The high cost of financing will force firms to hold down their positions, widen market-making spreads, decrease the number of issues in which active markets will be available, and concentrate this business in fewer firms.

These financial events will exert strong pressures to end the abuses that we have heaped on our economy and financial system. As they intensify, they will most likely continue to squeeze the economic excesses and lower the level of economic expectations throughout the country. In this sense, these pressures may be the first ray of hope for an eventual, although difficult, return to stability.

The Influence of Monetarism

The impact on our credit markets of attempts to follow a monetarist monetary policy in the United States is not as vivid at first blush as the impact of inflation, but it nevertheless has already been very profound. Indeed, if monetarism had been a manageable and effective approach, the inflationary rate would have been far lower in recent years and the volume of outstanding debt far smaller. Instead, attempts at monetarism were a convenient vehicle for our central bank to shift to a technical approach as a way of escaping some of its basic responsibilities as the inflation took hold in recent years.

Up until the latter part of the 1960s, the Federal Reserve followed a very fundamental strategy. The target of this strategy was reasonable economic growth and high rates of inflation were just unacceptable. While the Fed followed a money market strategy, the basic thrust in this effort was economic stability. There was no credibility gap between the market and the authorities. When the Fed raised interest rates and slowed the availability of credit, financial and economic participants moved to a conservative posture quickly, recognizing that the Fed meant to achieve its objective. Thus, this fundamental monetary policy, supported by a moderate fiscal policy, held credit creation and money supply expansion to reasonable proportions.

In the fundamental approach of years ago, all sorts of techniques were used to keep credit expansion reasonable. The Federal Reserve resorted to strong moral suasion efforts, open letters warning of disciplinary actions unless lending restraints were practiced by the banks, interest rate ceilings and, in wartime, even limits on housing and consumer financing. The frictional devices such as Regulation Q ceilings, may have been initially designed to hold down interest rates artificially, but they did serve to slow credit expansion and, in turn, to limit the level of interest rates. When these ceilings were reached in the past, they posed a barrier to rapid credit creation.

The unsuccessful attempts thus far at monetarism have, by definition, enlarged the volume of outstanding debt and have contributed to a substantial increase in interest rates. Unfortunately, the fail-safe devices that rescued monetary policy and prevented it from straying too far have been either modified or removed. Actually, the removal of the Regulation Q ceiling on commercial bank negotiable CDs (an action welcomed and strongly supported by monetarists) has created a structure among financial institutions that cannot function well in periods of restraint, although the removal was meant to improve the functioning of the market during tight periods. In 1969 and early 1970 commercial banks, mutual savings banks, and insurance companies experienced disintermediation. Now commercial banks, however, can bid for new funds through the issuance of CDs, but these other institutions cannot.

The Changing Role of Commerical Banks

It is also important to note that this monetary approach breeds several other unwholesome developments. The large disintermediation at nonbank institutions and the new intermediation role of the commercial banks in periods of restraint may actually make it technically difficult to slow the growth in the money supply as funds are transferred briefly from near-term money assets to demand deposits and then to time deposits. Thus, money rates rising sharply to high levels, which used to slow money growth, now may briefly spur money supply expansion. In addition, this new financial arrangement encourages borrowers to continue to finance in the short-term market in periods of tight money. Banks are able to buy the funds and recycle them mainly to short-term borrowers and, to a lesser extent, to other borrowers who are willing to pay the market rate. This is a process from which commercial banks cannot easily disengage themselves unless the Federal Reserve finds ways to slow bank credit expansion. The commercial banks are, after all, an integral and large part of a very competitive financial system in which size maximization has become a driving force.

If these problems are to be contained, controlling bank credit expansion must become a high objective of monetary policy. To be sure, other sources of funds, such as commercial paper, also serve as financing vehicles, but bank credit growth is still an excellent proxy for total debt creation. Commercial bank credit is a large part of each year's net new debt creation. During 1970–73, net new commercial bank credit was 40 percent of total net new credit market debt.

Removal of Money Rate Risk from Some Lending Arrangements

The significance of another fundamental force of change in the credit markets here and in Europe has been virtually unnoticed. It is the removal of the money rate risk from certain borrowing arrangements. Some may claim that these new financial arrangements are the result of the inflationary environment. I believe they also reflect the ingenuity of the marketplace. These floating interest rates are typified by our floating prime rate and by medium maturity financing in the Eurodollar market. In the latter, the lender, frequently a consortium of commercial banks, makes a loan for a fixed maturity but locks in his profit at a spread over the six-month interbank rate, thus eliminating the money rate risk and leaving only the credit risk in the transaction. The objective of the floating prime rate in the United States is the same except this lending arrangement is not yet as uniform or mechanical as the profit locked-in procedure practiced in Eurodollar financing.

What are the implications of the floating lending rates for the credit markets? First of all, the removal of the money rate risk serves as a strong stimulant to the lender to increase his loans substantially. The more loans he makes the more profit will accrue to him. This is because the lending spread, the profit due to the lender, is determined at the start for the entire duration of the loan. Second, the lending institution escapes part of the disciplining impact of monetary restraint. It passes it on to the borrower at rising interest rates. Under fixed lending rates, however, the profit margins of the institutional lender are squeezed as interest rates rise and the lender hesitates to borrow short and lend long because the liability costs will rise more quickly than the yield on assets. Consequently, the lender submits quickly to the objectives of monetary restraint, the slowing of credit expansion. This discipline is not present under floating interest rates which enable the lender to protect his profit margin whether interest rates are going up or down. I believe that a financial system functions best when the profit incentives for financial institutions encourage lower interest rates and when financial institutions themselves feel the pressure of tight money on their own profitability.

Impact of International Finance

Finally, the impact of international monetary and financial events on the American money and bond markets is probably far greater than we are able to quantify. The internationalization of credit flows is well underway, even though these flows may take circuitous routes at times. Indeed, the tendency is to think about these flows in very narrow terms. For example, weakness of the U.S. dollar is considered bullish for the U.S. government market because foreign central banks will use their newly acquired dollars to purchase U.S. Treasury obligations, while strength in the U.S. dollar may lead to the liquidations of U.S. issues by foreign central banks and pressure on the U.S. government market. Very little is ever said about the offset to these transactions. Dollars accumulate abroad for a variety of reasons, be it substantial American imports, or currency speculation or capital flows. When these transactions are financed, they exert pressure on the American credit markets. Our credit markets are influenced every day by a variety of international transactions engaged in by our multinational corporations, including the shifting of funds across national borders and decisions concerning the markets in which temporarily idle funds are to be invested. Our large American banks have not been solely domestic institutions for quite a while. They make loans directly to foreign borrowers and they also are aggressive participants in foreign markets through their branches and affiliates.

These interwoven relationships have complicated the problem of gauging the real significance of credit developments which in the past reflected mainly domestic conditions. Business loan trends, for example, used to reflect quite closely business inventory trends. In recent years, however, these loans have assumed an international flavor. Foreign corporations have borrowed here and American multinational firms have utilized bank borrowings for a variety of international and noninventory purposes.

There are dangers associated with the increasing linkages between the American credit markets and those of the rest of the world. Are these linkages to be used to accelerate inflation and debt creation both here and abroad or to help promote an orderly international economy? It is alarming to see in many places a great rush to finance huge balance of payments deficits, while few countries strive with fervor to return to stability. Even the procedure for financing many of these deficits may cause future problems. The machinery of the private credit markets is used to finance the deficits while the central banks around the world often watch passively.

IMPACT ON PORTFOLIO MANAGEMENT

The forces of change in our credit markets have had a dramatic and devastating impact on investment practices. They have made obsolete the approaches of institutional portfolio management which not too long ago were heralded as the wave of the future. From these changes, however, will come the lessons that will produce more balanced and comprehensive investment strategies.

The failure to perceive correctly the forces of change in our marketplace goes a long way toward explaining the recent difficulties of investment managers. To an extent, there was also an unwillingness to accept change even though changes in the marketplace were becoming evident. The easy investment life of the 1950s and early 1960s slipped by but the growing risks reflected in the broadest financial statistics were dismissed as irrelevant. The volumes of outstanding credit market debt, for example, competing with the equity market, which was moderate for much of the postwar years, began to grow rapidly and overwhelm the market value of outstanding equities. Total credit market debt exceeded the market value of equities by $241 billion in 1954, by $296 billion in 1964, and by $968 billion in 1973. I estimate that this spread exceeds $1 trillion at the present time, reflecting the additional increase in debt and the decline in stock values since the end of 1973.

A variety of debt obligations pushed their way into the portfolios of typically short-term investors or of investors restricted by legal requirements, but too rarely into the institutional portfolios with wide discretion. For a long while, the equity portfolio managers considered the rapid increase in all sorts of debt as a leverage technique that would enhance earnings per share and not as an encroachment on the welfare of equity investments. The rapid increase of debt raised the level of interest rates and provided new investment alternatives. It was a drastic departure from the 1950s when there were no negotiable CDs or Eurodollars, nor Government National Mortgage Association (GNMA) issues, nor bank debentures.

Why did so many portfolio managers fail to meet the challenge posed by the burgeoning debt market? I believe it was due largely to the high degree of specialization in American institutional portfolio management. The managers of fixed-income securities were waning in importance in the 1960s and the managers of equities were caught up in the glory of earlier successes. Specialization focuses on the narrow view and, as in other endeavors, people who specialize want to preserve and enlarge their importance. In investment specialization, the emphasis is on the development of in-depth knowledge of a small range of securities. There is a high concentration of effort devoted to finding a limited number of exceptional investment opportunities with the expectation that they will not only outperform others, but also withstand broad adverse developments. This just isn't so.

Faulty training must bear a good part of the blame for the inability of portfolio managers to perceive the changing dimensions of the credit markets. University training, in particular, has been at fault. During the past two decades, a plethora of textbooks appeared on equity investments and few, if any, on money and bond market portfolio strategies. Certainly, none have provided a comprehensive and integrated view of the investment field. The broad overview, if attempted at all, has usually been mechanical and deeply steeped in trend line extensions and reliance on econometric models that also depended heavily on forecasting the future through observations of past events.

IMPLICATIONS OF CREDIT
MARKET CHANGES

The financial decisions and portfolio strategies which will gradually emerge in the 1970s will not be simple but will reflect the problems of decision making in a complex and often trying environment. The management of securities will be replaced by the management of money. The allocation of money to a wide spectrum of securities will be based on relative value judgments. These allocations will incorporate judgments on the merits of short- and long-term, marketable and nonmarketable, credit quality differentials, and domestic versus international obligations. The most important aspects of these judgments cannot be computerized because they must deal with the implications of the changing economic and social forces both here and elsewhere on investment strategy.

The management of money, instead of securities, will also have a more objective view of portfolio performance. It will recognize more keenly that the fiduciary responsibility of managers has inherent in it a balance of objectives. The preservation of the nominal value of the funds managed is a worthwhile accomplishment in a deteriorating economic environment, but no large institutional portfolio can provide adequate safeguards against virulent inflation. We must recognize that portfolio performance is circumscribed by how well we as a nation manage our domestic and international affairs.

CONCLUSIONS

The treasurer's decisions must increasingly take into account the new financial trends. We should not forget the powerful destructive forces that engulfed this country as 1974 began. Double-digit inflation was rampant and expectations of continued high rates of inflation were common throughout the land. Business was obsessed with building and speculating in inventories. Backlogs of orders seemed endless. There were shortages in the midst of an economic recession. In the credit markets demands for credit were financed at a record-shattering pace in the first half of the year. In the commercial banking system alone, loans and investments rose at a seasonally adjusted annual rate of $95 billion or 15 percent, during the first six months. It was too late for fine-tuning or a moderate credit policy. The Federal Reserve had lost control over the banking system, and the only way it could regain authority was through Draconian measures.

This loss of control had its inception early in this decade when the Federal Reserve initiated measures and followed policies that automated the debt creation process, particularly in the banking system. It removed most of the Regulation Q ceilings for larger denominated CDs. This encouraged banks to bid for liabilities and to acquire assets with floating rates of return based on a spread over the cost of bank liabilities. The result was the removal of the money rate risk from banking transactions. This served to ignite a wave of debt expansion and sharp increases in loan commitments which the Fed found difficult to control through the setting of growth targets for the monetary aggregates. In fact, the automating of the debt creation process both in the United States and in other financial centers by the removal of the lender's money rate risk put financial institutions more in the position of entrepreneurs than fiduciaries of temporary funds and savings. It was only after the excesses of this process became evident and the Federal Reserve found a new Regulation Q device, namely bank capital adequacy, that our central bank again gained control over the banking system.

Consequently, the charges against our monetary authorities should not be narrowly stated in terms of the inept policies in 1974, but they should be made on broader and more fundamental grounds. The Fed permitted an excessive creation of debt. Its surveillance over the banking system was poor as evidenced by the problems of banks with a substantial volume of classified loans. In the overall picture, Fed policy is responsible for the large volume of bank liabilities and insufficient bank capital. At no time has the Federal Reserve or, for that matter, other bank supervisors rendered detailed reports on the health of the financial institutions under their jurisdiction. These shortcomings in monetary policy have now partially immobilized banks. Bankers have not only become unwilling lenders but also hesitant investors, an unprecedented development for the second year of a business recession.

Besides the ultimate difficulties caused by the removal of Regulation Q ceilings for negotiable CDs, the Federal Reserve did not focus on measuring the rapid growth of debt. Instead, it tried to monitor and control the growth of money supply (M_1), a rather small component of the American debt structure and of economic activity. I believe that the time has come to consider the obsolescent aspects of the money supply approach and to find a new and more appropriate monetary target. As shown in Figure 1, the money supply, consisting of demand deposits plus currency outside the banking system, is now a much smaller percentage of gross national product than a decade or two ago. It has drifted apart from GNP. A variety of money substitutes are now available, and high interest rates have produced great efforts to reduce cash balances to bare minimums. In addition, money supply growth does not lead economic activity consistently. The lead time is occasionally quite long and it is quite variable from cycle to cycle.

What I am proposing is that the target for monetary policy should be debt creation. I believe that it can be followed and measured

FIGURE 1
Economic Activity, the Growth in Debt and the Money Supply
(billions of dollars)

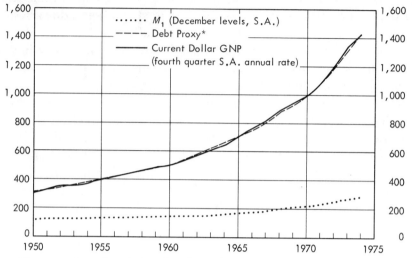

*Currency, demand and time deposits, and credit market instruments outstanding held outside of banks and other financial institutions.

reasonably well with only a small lag time through an effective proxy that encompasses a far greater financial base than money supply. This debt proxy would consist of the credit market instruments and deposits held by the private domestic nonfinancial sector (households, business and state and local governments). As shown in Figure 1, the relationship between the debt proxy and GNP (current dollars) is remarkably close over the period from the early 1950s through 1974. The debt proxy has moved contemporaneously with GNP over previous business cycles, periods of inflation, and widely fluctuating interest rates, thus giving considerable validity to the stability of the relationship. The level of the debt proxy is virtually equal to, and in exact alignment with, GNP. Regression analysis of quarterly changes of both series also shows behavioral consistency. Complete data on the debt proxy is available quarterly with a reporting lag of about six weeks. I have constructed a monitor that provides good interim estimates of the debt proxy. It is based on demand and time deposit data for the three sectors in the proxy together with estimates of the new volume of credit instruments bought by other than commercial banks and thrift institutions.

The intricacies of the current fiscal and monetary situation, posed against a backdrop of a troubled economy, can easily arouse a sense of frustration. We want to alleviate the economic suffering and move quickly into a new period of rapid economic expansion. This is an understandable human trait. Nevertheless, under the current circumstances, I know of no single initiative, or combination of policies, which immediately will be able to push the economy sharply ahead into a path of sustainable growth. Neither the expansionists nor the disciplinarians have solutions that deal adequately with the unusual problems confronting us today. The abuse of our economic and financial system has been too great in recent years. Governmental policies were not only inept but destructive. In the private sector, greed frequently overtook prudence, and we wasted a lot of capital. The cost of our extravagances is exacting its toll now. There are lessons here for all of us which we will not forget, at least for a while.

ADDITIONAL SOURCES

See Additional Sources at end of Chapter 2.

Chapter 2

Financial Policies in an Inflationary Environment

J. Fred Weston[*]
Maurice B. Goudzwaard[†]

A PERIOD of prolonged inflation has been experienced since 1966. Business has already made some adjustments in their financial policies and further innovations will be required. It is the purpose of this paper to place these developments in perspective and to provide a framework for understanding future probable changes as well.

The first questions are: What kind of inflationary environment will be experienced in the future? What will be its magnitude and duration? Will inflation have subsided within a few years? Or will temporary reductions in the inflation rate be followed by a resumption of persistent price-level increases in the range of 10 percent or more per year? To answer such questions requires a diagnosis of the causes of the present inflation that has persisted since 1966.

THE BACKGROUND OF THE INFLATION

A root cause of the U.S. inflation was our shooting some \$40–\$50 billions per year into the air in connection with the escalation of hostilities in Southeast Asia. This represented a decline in the real

[*] J. Fred Weston is professor of Business Economics and Finance at the Graduate School of Management, University of California, Los Angeles.

[†] Maurice B. Goudzwaard is associate professor of Finance at the Graduate School of Business Administration, University of Southern California, Los Angeles, California.

standard of living available to U.S. citizens that could not be made up simply by changes in financial policies as such. At the same time that the large expenditures in Vietnam began to be escalated in 1966, large increases in a number of domestic programs were also launched. These trends have reflected themselves in a continued pattern so that in the years 1966–68 federal deficits aggregated more than $50 billion. Again, to the extent that taxes do not finance these expenditures, inflation will result if they are financed by a large change in the money supply. The net result of inflation is a reduction in the standard of living.

Another fundamental factor affecting the price level is the impact of international trade and finance. With only minor interruptions, the United States was running deficits in its balance of payments from the mid-1950s through the 1970s. Many of the economic pressures that were developing in the mid-1950s were disguised by the overvaluation of the U.S. dollar in international trade. We were suppressing some of the underlying price increase trends by importing foreign-made goods into the U.S. economy. We did not pay for these foreign goods in cash but rather with credits in the form of claims on dollars that ran into the magnitude of $100 billion by the late 1960s. When the sheer magnitude of these credits became intolerable and it became apparent that the dollar as a store of value was weakening, the central bank authorities could no longer maintain the artificially low exchange rates.

Persistent deficits in the U.S. balance of payments resulting primarily from the Vietnam War eventually resulted in a formal devaluation of the U.S. dollar in 1971 and 1973. More freely fluctuating exchange rates brought about further revaluation of the U.S. dollar. To illustrate, the West German mark had been valued at 4 to the dollar or 25 cents for DM 1. By late 1973 the Deutsche Mark was valued at $2\frac{1}{2}$ to the dollar or 40 cents. Such revaluations have a considerable effect on the prices paid for goods. For example, a German product that needed to be sold for DM 400 to cover German costs of production at an exchange rate of 4 to 1 could be purchased for $100. At an exchange rate of $2\frac{1}{2}$ to 1 the cost would be DM 400 divided by 2.5 or $160, an increase of 60 percent. This represents a substantial upward pressure on U.S. prices. This devaluation of the dollar was not unique to the Deutsche Mark, but applied to other currencies as well. In 1974, about 10 percent of goods consumed in the United States were foreign made.

Some extraordinary conditions also contributed to high inflation in 1973–74. While the prices of foreign goods rose in general, the area in which the shift in the terms of trade occurred most dramatically, of course, was on petroleum. Oil which had been imported into the United States at $3 a barrel was raised in price through the actions of OPEC (Organization of Petroleum Exporting Countries). In a cartel action following the embargo launched in October 1973, the price of oil was increased to over $12 a barrel, more than a fourfold increase. This represented a tremendous swing in the terms of trade at which oil could be acquired in relationship to the values received for goods exported. In 1974, it is estimated that the additional outflows of dollars to foreign countries because of the price rise is $18 billions.[1]

The years 1973–74 were unusual, too, because the world experienced a decline in U.S. production of food while demand increased. This resulted in a large demand for U.S. wheat, soybeans, and so on with the result that prices rose. While it is alleged that the Russian wheat deal was primarily responsible for food price rises, the real cause was an overall change in the world demand and supply for food. In spite of these higher costs of production, agricultural businesses were able to take advantage of the situation and earn a higher than normal return. While it is true that prices to the rest of the population rose because of higher agricultural profits, farmers were better off. This differs from the case of petroleum where higher prices results in foreign interests being better off. The inflation that has been underway in the United States since 1966 reflects at least, in part, an unwillingness to face up to the reality of a decline in the rate of increase in our real standards of living. We must either face up to reconciling ourselves to a lower or even negative growth in our standards of living or improve our efficiency to produce goods and services. Governmental overspending aggravates inflation; it does not solve our fundamental problems of improving productivity.

The increase in money supply is a worldwide phenomenon. Beginning in the 1960s, aspiration levels increased throughout the world. The expectations of peoples throughout the world were raised by promises of full employment and high growth rates. These rising ex-

---

[1] "U.S. Balance of Payments Developments: Fourth Quarter and Year 1974," *Survey of Current Business,* 55 (March 1975), p. 31, Table D. Merchandise imports of petroleum and products into the United States in 1973 was $8.1 billion; in 1974, it was $25.9 billion.

pectations in the developing countries of the world were supported by our balance of payments deficits of the United States which began to be of substantial size by the mid-1950s. As dollar balances accumulated in Europe they were used as a basis for a multiple expansion of a borrowing and lending system. For the European countries it was called the development of the Eurodollar and Eurocurrency market. In general, Eurodollars represented the building up of foreign currency denominated liabilities to residents of countries other than the country in which the reporting bank is located. These external liabilities had reached a total of $217.7 billion by the end of 1973.[2] As a consequence, the world stock of money and purchasing power increased. One evidence of this was the increase in world trade from a volume of $518 billion in 1973 to $768 billion in 1974, an increase of almost 50 percent. While the increase of revenues by the OPEC countries increased from $43 billion to $133 billion to account for $90 billion of the increase, other trade still accounted for $60 billion. This marked change in the world stock of money and purchasing power planted the seeds for worldwide inflation. Since it was worldwide and since it represented an excess stock of money, it was very difficult to correct this condition by action of the U.S. monetary authorities. Whereas domestic monetary policy in previous periods took effect in relatively few months, in the 1970s it was less effective because the inflows and outflows of funds abroad could not be constrained as easily. Our persistent efforts to reduce inflation in 1974 resulted in interest rates that had risen to levels not experienced for decades. In fact, the continuation of tight money brought about a financial crunch and then an economic recession.

We might ask how tight money could cause a recession in the face of a world of excess money and purchasing power. The answers are as follows: (1) some segments of the U.S. economy are extremely sensitive to the availability of money; these are housing and construction; and (2) the continued inflation pushed individuals into higher progressive income tax rates. For corporations, traditional methods of accounting emphasizing the expiration of historical costs gave rise to a substantial amount of illusory profits. As a result, the increase in governmental tax revenues resulted in a significant transfer of purchasing power from the private section of the economy to the government sector. In fact, some argue that the rate of corpo-

---

[2] *Economic Report of the President,* February 1975, pp. 214–15.

rate taxation on real income is closer to 70 percent than to 50 percent. Another major reason was the transfer of domestic purchasing power to the OPEC nations.

The recession in the United States took hold with alarming sharpness and severity in late 1974. The impact was so great that action was taken to reverse the recession with fiscal policy. The tax law passed in the spring of 1975 provided for a reduction of $22.8 billions in taxes. Questions have been raised whether a tax cut of such magnitude will cause a renewal of inflation. A critical variable is the magnitude of the resultant federal deficit. When the $22.8 billion tax cut law was enacted, it was estimated that the federal deficit would run $60 billion. Later this estimate was raised to $75 billion. Subsequently, there was discussion that various spending plans would total to a deficit of over $100 billion. To the extent that capital raised to finance this deficit does not "crowd out" competing demands for capital from the private sector, the deficit need not be inflationary. To the extent that the federal deficit forces lenders to ration capital to the private sectors, it is inevitable that interest rates will rise. Monetary authorities are hard pressed not to increase the supply of money to finance both private and public demand, with the attendant result of encouraging inflation.

A critical factor, therefore, in the U.S. role as a part of the worldwide inflation process will be its ability to control the magnitude of the federal deficit. At a U.S. gross national product level running at the $1,400 billion level, a federal deficit of $60–$75 billion can probably be absorbed without undue pressure on the inflation rate and interest rate levels. But a federal deficit beyond $75 billion would raise serious questions about the renewal of inflation and, therefore, upward pressure on interest rates.

IMPLICATIONS OF INTEREST RATE LEVELS
ON EXTERNAL CORPORATE FINANCING

Prior to the onset of the 1966 inflation, price-level increases in the United States averaged 2 percent per annum for more than 100 years. Even the 2 percent average was brought about by price increases that took place in periods of war. It is extremely unlikely that the United States will return to such a low rate of price increase during the next decade. Sound management of our economic affairs would hopefully bring the price inflation rate down to the 4 to 6 percent per annum range. The implications for interest rates are depicted in Table 1.

Over a long period of years basic productivity in the U.S. economy has increased at about 3 percent per year. This has provided the basis

TABLE 1
Prospective Interest Rate Levels

	Percent
Basic productivity.	2–3%
Price inflation	4–6
Yield on government bonds	6–9
Risk premium on private debt.	2–3
Yields on corporate bonds	8–12

for the fundamental level of interest rates. The rate of productivity increase moved around the 3 percent level shortly after World War II, but in recent years has been below 3 percent. Hence a 2 to 3 percent range in the future is probable. With expected long-run price inflation of 4 to 6 percent, the yield on government bonds would range from 6 to 9 percent. A risk premium must be added for the yield on private debt. The resulting yields on corporate bonds would be in the 8 to 12 percent range.

Thus the level of the interest rates in the future will depend most heavily on the rate of price inflation. If we succeed in controlling it, interest yields on long-term government bonds could be held to the 7 to 8 percent range. If the inflation rate increases, yields on corporate bonds could move to the two-digit level.

Another important implication for financial managers is the prospect that significant amounts of financing will have to be raised externally. Some fundamental relationships for determining the extent of external financing are set forth in Table 2. Table 2 begins with a definitional statement of the degree of external funds required. This set of relationships can be generalized into expressing external financing requirements as a percentage of sales growth as shown in the final equation in Table 2.

The implications of the final equation in Table 2 can be shown by utilizing the relationships for all manufacturing corporations as of the end of 1974. The assets to sales relationship for all manufacturing is approximately 70 percent. The ratio of liabilities that increase spontaneously as a percent of sales is 20 percent. Thus, the financing required rate, I, is .50. A profit margin, M, of 5 percent and a divi-

TABLE 2
Determinants of the Extent of External Financing

Let:

$\dfrac{A}{S}$ = Assets that increase spontaneously with sales as a percent of sales

$\dfrac{L}{S}$ = Those liabilities that increase spontaneously with sales as a percent of sales

I = Financing required = Investment intensity = $\dfrac{A}{S} - \dfrac{L}{S}$

S_2 = Total sales projected

ΔS = Change in sales = $S_2 - S_1$

g = Growth in sales = $\dfrac{S_2 - S_1}{S_1} = \dfrac{S_2}{S_1} - 1$

M = Profit margin on sales

d = The dividend payout percentage $(1 - d) = b$ = Earnings retention ratio

R = Dollar amount of required external financing

$\dfrac{R}{S_1}$ = External financing as a percent of current sales = F

FS = Percentage of sales growth required to be financed externally

Then:

$$R = I(S_2 - S_1) - MS_2 + dMS_2 \qquad \text{Note that } S_2 = (1 + g)S_1$$

Hence:

$$R = (I - M)(1 + g)S_1 + dM(1 + g)S_1 - IS_1 \qquad \text{Divide by } S_1$$

$$\dfrac{R}{S_1} = F = (1 + g)(I - M + dM) - 1 \qquad \text{Substitute } b \text{ for } (1 - d)$$

$$F = (1 + g)(I - Mb) - I$$

$$FS = [(1 + g)(I - Mb) - I]/g$$

dend payout rate of 40 percent are utilized. When sales grow at a rate of 10 percent, the percentage of sales growth required to be financed externally is 17 percent as shown below:

$$FS = [(I - M + Md)(1 + g) - I]/g$$
$$[(.50 - .05 + .02)(1.10) - .50]/.10$$
$$[(.47)(1.1) - .5]/.10$$
$$(.517 - .5)/.10 = 17\%$$

When the inflation rate rises to 20 percent, it can readily be verified that the percentage of external financing required will move to 32 percent, as indicated below:

$$[(.47)(1.2) - .5]/.20 = (.564 - .5)/.20$$
$$.064/.20 = 32\%$$

The relationships set forth in Table 2 and the numerical illustrations are based on the relations for all manufacturing corporations and indicate the reasons why external financing requirements have increased.

This means that even if the firm produces and sells the same number of goods from one year to the next, the capital needs will increase. If the sales to asset ratio is constant, then inflation alone will create a demand for new capital. Just to stand still in an inflationary environment consumes new capital. In the short run, the fixed asset requirement does not change during inflation, but the working capital requirements for cash, accounts receivable and inventory do change.

In Table 3 these effects are illustrated. In the preinflation case, the cash balance is $50 and accounts receivable and inventory are each $100. With a 10 percent inflation, our current asset needs also rise by 10 percent, even if there is no change in the number of units sold. Therefore, our current asset requirements rise by $25. Our fixed

TABLE 3

Balance Sheet

Preinflation

Cash	$ 50	Accounts payable	$ 60
Accounts receivable	100	Notes payable	65
Inventory	100		
Current assets	$250	Current liabilities	$125
Plant and equipment	$150	Long-term debt	$100
Land	100	Common equity	275
Total Assets	$500	Total Capital	$500

After 10% Inflation

Cash	$ 55	Accounts payable	$ 66
Accounts receivable	110	Notes payable	65
Inventory	110	Current liabilities	$131
Current assets	$275	Long-term debt	100
Plant and equipment	$150	Common equity	275
Land	100	Deficiency	$ 19
Total Assets	$525	Total Capital	$525

assets do not change. On the liability side of the balance sheet accounts payable, our only spontaneous source of credit, increase by 10 percent or $6. Since we assume a zero profit, there is a capital deficit of $19. Liabilities or net worth must rise by this amount. If the firm is to maintain the same total debt to total asset ratio, then the $25 additional capital must be financed with $11.25 liability and $13.75 equity. Since spontaneous sources supplied $6—in this case, accounts payable—then $5.25 can be raised with notes and $13.75 with additional equity. If the total increase in funds from nonspontaneous sources is financed with short-term notes, then the current ratio declines from 2:1 to 1.83:1 and the total debt to total asset ratio deteriorates slightly to .47 from .45.

EFFECTS OF THE INFLATIONARY
ENVIRONMENT ON BUSINESS
FINANCIAL CONDITIONS

The impact of inflation is often pervasive and subtle. The financial officer must be aware of how inflation impacts the asset base and actual earnings position of his business. It is clear, for instance, that reported earnings overstate "real" or inflation adjusted earnings by a significant amount. It is estimated that for 1974 earnings as reported by major corporations may overstate real income by as much as 25–30 percent (see Table 4).

If we define income as a change in real wealth from one period to the next, then it is obvious that allowances for depreciations are too low because they are based upon historical cost data rather than replacement values. This can be partially overcome in the early years of an asset's life by using accelerated depreciation methods, but in total the depreciation will not sufficiently reflect actual current consumption of the asset. Similarly, the cost of goods sold is understated in the income statement because the cost is predicted upon old costs rather than replacement values. Use of Lifo valuation of inventories can help remedy this, but in most cases the remedy is incomplete. Still, the use of Lifo costing rather than Fifo can make a significant difference in net income and taxes (Table 5). It is estimated that about 40 percent of the major nonfinancial firms substituted Lifo for Fifo valuation methods in 1974. In some cases the impact was significant. For Standard Oil of California the difference in income

TABLE 4
Inflation-Adjusted Earnings All U.S. Nonfinancial Corporations (billions of dollars)

	Reported Pretax Profits	Taxes	Depreci- ation*	Inventory Cost†	Adjusted Pretax Profits	Adjusted After- Tax Profits		Dividends	Adjusted Retained Earnings Constant‡
						Current	Constant‡		
1965	$ 65.8	$31.3	$ 0.4	$ 1.7	$63.7	$36.1	$36.1	$19.8	$19.2
1966	71.2	34.3	1.4	1.8	68.0	38.0	37.3	20.8	19.4
1967	66.2	33.2	2.7	1.1	62.4	34.0	32.1	21.4	14.2
1968	72.4	39.9	3.6	3.3	65.5	31.4	28.8	23.6	9.6
1969	68.0	40.1	4.6	5.1	58.3	24.6	21.6	24.3	3.4
1970	55.7	34.8	6.6	4.8	44.3	16.8	14.0	24.7	-2.7
1971	64.1	37.5	7.6	4.9	51.6	21.9	17.5	25.0	1.3
1972	74.3	41.5	7.4	6.9	60.0	24.9	19.5	27.3	2.9
1973	95.3	49.8	9.1	17.3	68.9	23.7	17.6	29.6	0.5
1974	112.0	62.7	11.0	33.0	68.0	22.0	14.8	33.2	-4.5
Percent Change									
1965–74	70%				7%	-39%	-59%		

* Estimated current-cost depreciation minus depreciation used for income tax purposes.
† National income accounts inventory valuation adjustment.
‡ Deflated by GNP implicit price deflator, 1965 = 100.
Source: U.S. Department of Commerce.

TABLE 5
Impact of Switching from Fifo to Lifo Valuation of Inventory

Company	1974 Earnings per Share	Net Earnings Decrease from Lifo		1973-74 Earnings Change	
		Total (millions)	Per Share	With Lifo	Without Lifo
American Can	$5.48	$ 27.6	$1.56	53%	96%
American Cyanamid	3.24	26.0	0.54	36	59
American Standard	2.40	15.6	0.90	11	53
AMF	1.19	15.5	0.83	−62	−35
Cities Service	7.58	13.3	0.49	50	59
Clark Equipment	3.19	26.6	1.96	−21	27
Continental Can.	4.07	40.1	1.37	25	67
Crown Zellerbach	5.06	6.8	0.28	18	25
Dow Chemical.	6.35	141.5	1.53	116	168
E. I. Du Pont	8.20	145.0	3.02	−32	−7
Ethyl	7.41	6.5	0.68	48	61
General Tire & Rubber.	3.60	22.8	1.06	1	30
Hercules	2.21	19.1	0.45	1	22
Ingersoll-Rand.	5.62	8.1	0.45	15	24
Kennecott Copper	5.08	19.9	0.61	6	18
Kimberly-Clark	4.10	11.0	0.47	24	38
Martin Marietta	3.58	14.0	0.62	40	65
Owens-Illinois	5.74	18.6	1.34	22	51
Pfizer	1.93	9.9	0.14	11	19
PPG Industries.	4.51	17.9	0.86	1	20
Pullman	5.69	1.7	0.24	12	17
RCA	1.45	16.5	0.22	−39	−30
Reynolds Metals.	6.23	16.4	0.95	159	198
Rohm & Haas	5.83	13.2	1.04	13	33
St. Regis Paper	4.76	3.0	0.14	65	70
Scott Paper	2.00	16.3	0.47	23	52
Standard Oil (Calif.)	5.71	250.0	1.47	15	44
Texaco	5.84	196.7	0.72	23	38
TRW	3.05	13.0	0.47	3	19
Union Carbide.	8.69	14.3	0.23	82	87

Source: *Forbes*, March 1, 1975, p. 44.

amounts to $250 million, and for Du Pont the difference in income was $145 million. Not alone is net income represented more accurately in real terms, but taxes are reduced because of lower taxable income. So from a cash flow viewpoint, it is to the advantage of the financial officer to use Lifo rather than Fifo inventory valuation in periods of rising prices.

A changing price level affects not only inventory and fixed assets but all assets and liabilities. In order to understand these changes it is incumbent upon financial officers to obtain the real facts on their firm's financial statements. This means a complete restatement of the balance sheet and income statement to account for the changing value of the dollar. Some firms are already doing this. One prominent example is the Indiana Telephone Co. A comparison of their reported income and inflation adjusted income is shown in Table 6.

TABLE 6
How Price-Level Accounting Changes the Figures

INDIANA TELEPHONE CORP.

Income Statement, 1973

	Historical Cost (000 dollars)	Price Level (000 dollars)
Operating revenues	$12,495	$12,834
Operating expenses:		
Depreciation.	2,395	3,033
Taxes.	2,686	2,759
Other expenses	4,467	4,688
Operating income.	$ 2,947	$ 2,354
Deductions and credits:		
Interest.	(892)	(917)
Other.	235	238
Normal gain on retirement of long-term debt	16	17
Price-level gain on above.	−	50
Normal gain on retirement of preferred stock.	6	7
Price-level gain on above.	−	18
Price-level loss on other monetary items.	−	(209)
Net income	$ 2,312	$ 1,558
Earnings per common share	$4.55	$3.00

SHELL OIL CO.   BARBER-ELLIS

Income Statement, 1974   Income Statement, 1974

	Price-Level Accounting (millions)		Historical Cost Accounting (millions)		Replacement Cost Accounting (millions)	Historical Cost Accounting (millions)
Sales		$8,866.7		$8,493.0	$69.1	$69.1
Costs:						
Depreciation and depletion	$ 654.2		$ 502.9		$ 1.1	$ 0.8
Interest.	63.5		60.8		1.0	1.0
Taxes.	1,320.2		1,264.5		2.9	2.9
Operating and selling	6,317.3		6,044.3		62.1	61.1
Total Costs . .		($8,355.2)		($7,872.5)	($67.1)	($85.8)
Preliminary income .		$ 511.5		$ 620.5	$ 2.0	$ 3.3
Purchasing power gain.		111.9		−	−	−
Net Income . .		$ 623.4		$ 620.5	$ 2.0	$ 3.3

TABLE 6 (*continued*)

| | SHELL OIL CO. | | BARBER-ELLIS | |
| | Balance Sheet | | Balance Sheet | |
	Price-Level Accounting (millions)	Historical Cost Accounting (millions)	Replace-ment Cost Accounting (millions)	Historical Cost Accounting (millions)
Assets:				
Cash and accounts receivable	NA	NA	$12.1	$12.1
Inventories.	NA	NA	10.4	10.1
Prepaid expenses	NA	NA	0.2	0.3
Current assets	$2,161.7	$2,072.2	$22.7	$22.5
Investments	129.5	116.0	–	–
Property, plant and equipment	5,146.6	3,905.3	7.1	5.4
Goodwill and deferred charges	42.3	35.4	–	0.8
Total Assets.	$7,480.1	$6,128.9	$29.8	$28.7
Liabilities:				
Current liabilities	$1,272.6	$1,272.6	$13.5	$13.5
Long-term debt	976.6	976.6	4.1	4.1
Deferred taxes.	320.0	320.0	0.3	0.3
Total Liabilities.	$2,569.2	$2,569.2	$17.9	$17.9
Shareholders' Equity:				
Stock and contributed surplus	NA	NA	$ 0.6	$ 0.6
Retained earnings.	NA	NA	7.0	10.2
Revaluation surplus.	–	–	4.3	–
Total Shareholders' Equity	$4,910.9	$3,559.7	$11.9	$10.8

NA = not available.
Source: *Business Week*, May 5, 1972, p. 72.

For 1973, earnings per share was 34 percent lower in real dollars than in reported earnings. Shell Oil Co. and Barber-Ellis have also published data on the impact of price-level changes. It is not clear whether price-level or replacement cost valuation procedures should be used. There are practical difficulties in each method. If we adjust the value of an asset by a price index we need to know the acquisition date of each asset and each component of it. These data are not always available and in some companies it would be a herculean task to determine what the impact is of price changes. Using replacement cost would solve some of the data problems of price-level accounting, but it too faces some practical difficulties. For instance, how do we determine the replacement value of an asset which is no longer produced and which would need to be custom made to replicate the old asset. Obviously, this would be impractical since more modern equipment would be available. But should we use the values of the modern equipment as a surrogate for the old equipment when in fact the modern machine really performs these functions differently? Regardless of these practical difficulties, however, more and more firms must derive methods of representing their financial condition in terms of constant dollars so that management clearly understands the real financial posture of their firm.

In Table 7 some consequences of the inflationary environment are

TABLE 7
Changes in Financial Relationships for All Manufacturing Industries, 1966–1974

	1966†	*1974*‡
1. Percent fund uses from internal sources*	60.0%	54.1%
2. Total debt to equity	67.7%	88.1%
3. Change in debt to change in equity	116%	
4. Long-term interest-bearing debt to equity	23.2%	30.7%
5. Current ratio	2.22x	1.95x
6. Quick ratio	1.11x	1.04x
7. Cash plus marketable securities	0.29x	0.23x
8. Dividend payout	42.1%	33.2%
9. Times interest earned	13x	3x

* All nonfinancial corporations.
† Third quarter.
‡ Four quarters, ending third quarter.
Sources: Row 1. Henry Kaufman and James McKeon, *Supply and Demand for Credit in 1975* (New York: Salomon Brothers, January 1975), p. 2. Rows 2–8. Federal Trade Commission, *Quarterly Financial Reports 1966*, 1974. Row 9. *Business Week*, October 12, 1974, p. 55.

depicted. Developments that have taken place in nine areas of business finance are described. The percentage of internal financing has dropped from 60 to 54 percent. This is consistent with the model presented in Table 2. The ratio of total debt to equity has risen from 68 percent in 1966 to 88 percent in 1974. The situation is becoming one in which total assets are being financed in almost equal proportion by debt and equity. Indeed, during the period 1966 through 1974, the increase in debt was $196 billion while the increase in equity was $168 billion. The increase in total debt in the eight-year period was approximately 116 percent of the increase in equity. Thus the debt to equity ratio on the additional assets acquired by manufacturing corporations during the 1966 period was 54 percent financed with debt and 46 percent by equity.

Row 4 shows that the ratio of long-term debt to equity increased from 23 percent to 31 percent. When debt ratios are increasing it is generally true also that the current ratio will decline. Row 5 shows that the current ratio has dropped from 2.22 to 1.95 which is below the long-term banker's rule of thumb of 2:1. The quick ratio, which is current assets less inventories divided by current liabilities has declined from 1.11 to 1.04. The ratio of cash plus marketable securities to current liabilities has declined from 29 percent to 23 percent. As further evidence of a deteriorating liquidity situation, the time interest earned coverage ratio has declined from about 13 times in 1966 to a little over 3 times in 1974. This is due not only to higher interest charges on larger amounts of debt but also to lower levels of earnings.

As a consequence of the necessity for more external financing as inflation raises normal growth rates, coupled with the increase in debt and the reduction in liquidity, firms have altered dividend payouts. They have sought to reduce the dependence on external financing and particularly debt by reducing the dividend payout from 42.1 percent to 33.2 percent. Despite the decrease in dividend payouts which indicates that earnings retention has increased, the percent by which internal financing has been able to finance asset increase has declined, nevertheless, as shown in row 1. The percent of new capital raised from retained earnings has declined from 60 percent in 1966 to 54 percent in 1974. This is all the more significant when one realizes that the value of new equity issues has declined significantly. As recently as 1972 the amount of new common equity issues sold was $9.5 billion, but in 1974 it was less than half that at $4.2 billion. These nine ratios, then, depict the general patterns of pressures that have been developing on business financial conditions as a consequence of the inflationary environment.

Why has the use of debt increased? One general answer is that in a period of inflation it makes sense to use debt which can be repaid with cheaper dollars. However, lenders have the same view of the future and demand an interest premium to compensate for the loss in purchasing power. Even at 10 percent rates of interest it is not so high as to deter debt financing. Since all manufacturing firms on the average earn about 8 to 12 percent of total assets after taxes, financial leverage is still positive with an after-tax cost of debt at 5 percent (10 percent pretax). In other words, on average earnings on total assets still exceed the cost of debt either on a before or after-tax basis. Even at the high interest rates, financial leverage can still magnify gains (and losses).

Concurrent with rises in interest rates, earnings price ratios have risen as well. They have increased for the reasons that higher yields on bonds make equity less attractive and hence investors demand a higher return on equity. The expected growth rate of earnings has declined, and the expected variability on risk of equity is perceived to be greater. These factors are also reflected in the earnings price ratio. The earnings price ratio, is of course, the reciprocal of the price-earnings ratio.

One widely used rule of thumb is that the earnings price ratio on equity should reflect a capitalization rate equal to one and one half times the Aaa corporate bond rate. One and one half times a 4 percent bond rate represents a capitalization rate of 6 percent or an earnings multiplier of 16–17 times. One and one half times a corporate bond rate of 10 percent represents a capitalization rate of 15 percent or a multiplier of under 6–7 times. Thus, it should be readily perceived that the sharp decline in the multipliers on common stocks is directly related to the very sharp rise in corporate bond yields.

INNOVATIONS IN FINANCING

With the decline in the price-earnings ratios and a rise in debt ratios, some innovations in financing have developed. One trend has been toward the utilization of off-balance financing. One such arrangement is the documented discount note (DDN). Under this arrangement a trustee sells notes with payments guaranteed by major banks through a letter of credit. With the funds received from the guaranteed notes sold, the trustee buys equipment and takes title to it. The trustee then leases the equipment to business firms. Thus, the obligation is not directly on the balance sheet of banks, but is rather a contingent liability. The trustee has the note obligation, but the notes are backed by a guarantee. The user of the equipment does not have a balance sheet liability other than the guarantee. Trust and leasing arrangements have been utilized to finance oil inventories, timber cutting, construction as well as to finance power-generating facilities for public utilities. Under leveraged leasing, the lessor uses debt to finance the asset and leases the asset to the firm. Again, the debt is not shown as an obligation by the user of the equipment.

Another development has been "take or pay" contracts. The taker (user) guarantees that it will pay the debt service whether or not delivery or use of the facilities takes place. With such a revenue guarantee, a high rate of debt financing can be obtained by the entity with which the payment contract is made. Take or pay contracts have been utilized in connection with the financing of offshore oil ports, pipelines and oceangoing carriers. When the take or pay contracts are used in connection with vessels, they are referred to as "bareboat charters."

Another innovation generated by the inflationary environment has been the use of floating rate notes by the debtor. This provides protection to the creditor in the event that inflation causes interest rates to rise further. At the same time, it provides protection to the debtor in that if the general interest rate structure declines, the interest rate obligations on the notes also decline.

New common equity financing has been discouraged by the low price-earnings ratios. Even the use of warrants and convertibles is not attractive and therefore not used as much when the prices of equities have declined as substantially as they did during 1974. While the amount of capital raised through new equity is reduced, the amount of mutually preferred stock financing has increased. Sometimes the preferred stock is retired by the use of a sinking fund which matures in ten years or redemption may take place either at the option of the buyer or seller two to three years after the preferred stock has been issued. The use of mutually redeemable preferred stock enables a business firm to sell a form of equity in the sense that the principle and dividend need not be repaid. There are still the advantages of financial leverage because the dividend does not vary with operating profits. The chief disadvantages is that the dividend payments are not tax deductible. The buyer is protected against loss of principle by the opportunity of being able to redeem the preferred stock at par value or slightly higher.

With the financial crunch that has periodically developed in the United States, American firms have also utilized the International Financial Markets as a source of capital. The size of this financing reached several billion dollars per year. Part of the stimulus for utilizing these markets was the existence of capital controls by the U.S. government in the early 1960s. However, with the elimination of these controls in 1974, the use of the International Financial Markets by American firms became less valid because of the greater depth of the American capital market.

Despite the increased use of debt and innovated forms of financing, the financial pressure brought about by inflation has continued.

Of course, a prudent operating policy even in a noninflationary environment is to increase the productivity of assets. If the return on assets improves, then the need for financing abates. In recent years it has been increasingly difficult to improve asset efficiency because of the increasing internalization of social costs. Prominent of these is the cost of air and water pollution. In many ways the timing of these outlays was unfortunate. They were unfortunate in several respects. First, the necessity of making the outlays occurred in a year when there was a financing crunch and financing was so difficult to obtain, and second, the cost of replacing productive assets increased because replacement costs were greater than the allowance for depreciation on old equipment.

It was rather unfortunate that the requirements for pollution controls occurred with such rapidity. By requiring the installation of the equipment at such a rapid rate the dollar magnitude of the outlays was greater than it might have been had it been inserted at a more relaxed rate. Insufficient time was provided for the development of efficient techniques to accomplish valid objectives. As a consequence, the amounts to control pollution were larger than they otherwise would have been. The timing of the outlays were telescoped into a short space of time and the efficiency of the equipment utilized was reduced because not sufficient time was allowed to develop more effective equipment. It is estimated that about 11 percent of all capital spending in 1974 was for air and water pollution control. This amounts to over $10 billion. In the paper industry, for instance, about 24 percent of capital expenditures was for pollution controls. In the steel industry, pollution control expenditures represented over 23 percent of their total. While these expenditures are undoubtedly for the public good, the cost of these controls eventually are reflected in the price level. It is estimated that expenditures for pollution control accounts for about 0.5 percent of the inflation rate.

Other countries have provided government financing for such equipment. In the United States, some help has also been provided through the use of tax-exempt pollution control bonds and has amounted to about $4 billion through the end of 1974. The United States is behind other countries in permitting fast writeoff of capital outlays for pollution control equipment. The United States has also been behind other countries in the size of the investment tax credit allowed. Thus a change in tax policy would perform an important role in alleviating the financial problems of investing in equipment for environmental control while maintaining normal investment simultaneously.

Tax policy is a particularly important consideration because the ratio of fixed investment to gross national product within the United States appears to have fallen well behind those countries which have experienced rapid economic progress. It is estimated that for the period 1960–73, the ratio of fixed investment to GNP in the United States was 17.5 percent compared with a 35 percent rate in Japan and a 26 percent rate in West Germany over the same period of time. The United Kingdom, on the other hand, has a fixed investment rate to GNP at about the same order of magnitude as the United States.

INFLATION, FINANCING, AND PRICING

A problem of inflation affects not only financing decisions but those of pricing as well. Business firms use some variation of a return on assets or a return on investment measure as a checkpoint in corporate resource allocation as well as in pricing decisions. The use of a return on investment or return on asset measure is mandatory if firms are to earn more than the cost of capital and hence raise their net worth. The firm must price its products and services in such a manner that it can earn its cost of capital or it will not be viable in the long run.

An inflationary environment makes it difficult to use a return on investment or a return on asset measure as an appropriate measure of adequate profit. Since historical cost accounting understates current asset value and since profits as reported overstate real profits, the real return on assets is lower than it appears. What the firm must do is to calculate the current replacement cost as a measure of asset value and to compare the real income to it.

Furthermore, the cost of capital level itself must be adjusted upward as shown in Table 8. Many studies on the average cost of capital for business firms from the mid-1950s to the mid-1960s concluded that 10 percent is a pretty accurate rate. During this period interest-bearing debt represented about one fourth of financing and equity about three quarters. With an after-tax cost of debt at about 4 percent and an overall cost of capital of 10 percent, this implied a cost of equity capital at about 12 percent.

During the inflationary environment, however, the cost of capital must necessarily rise to reflect the impact of the inflation rate. Con-

TABLE 8
Trends in the Cost of Capital

	Proportion of Total Financing	After-Tax Cost (percent)	Weighted Cost (percent)
Preinflation Period–1966			
Interest-bearing debt	¼	4%	1%
Equity	¾	12	9
		Total	10
Inflationary Period–1974			
Interest-bearing debt	⅓	6	2
Equity	⅔	15–18	10–12
		Total	12–14

servatively, it may be estimated that the overall cost of capital is currently at 12–14 percent. With interest-bearing debt one third of total financing and costing 6 percent, this implied a cost of equity of 15–18 percent. These estimates of the cost of equity are consistent with the earnings price ratios observed in the stock market during 1974. This also implies that the earning rate on equity must necessarily rise to its cost in the market. Thus, one would expect under an inflationary environment that average levels on the return on equity would move from a 12 to 14 percent range experienced in the preinflationary period to at least a 15 to 18 percent range during the current inflationary environment. Yet, it appears to be extremely difficult for business firms to achieve prices on product and services that will attain these required rates of return in the current economic environment and political atmosphere. This aggravates the financial pressures that have increasingly beset business firms during the inflationary environment because investors do not find equity attractive enough to invest their capital.

CONCLUSIONS

The foregoing analysis demonstrates that business firms have been neither the cause nor beneficiaries of the inflation experience in the United States following 1966. Historical patterns of financing have been distorted. Financial ratios indicate that traditional standards of financial health of business firms have severely deteriorated. The financial problems facing business firms increasingly have been aggravated rather than mitigated as the inflation has continued.

Yet ironically, business firms have been blamed for inflation. But they have suffered from it and suffered severely. Thus, business firms, like the population generally, suffer from the fact that the quantity of real resources has been dissipated in war and has been invested in projects that do not yield increases in current returns. Outlays to improve the environment or investments in the Great Society programs that result in an increase in social welfare expenditures represent outlays that yield returns hopefully in the future, but do not help us in the short run. The decreases in real resources currently available accompanied by the shift in real resources caused by the general inflation and by the increase in the price of oil have simply resulted in a reduction in the quantity of real resources currently available for utilization in the United States as well as in other countries. Either a reduction in real resources available or an expansion in spending power beyond the increase in real resources have the same result. They result in too much spending power in relation to available goods. Both changes have occurred. The result is worldwide inflation. These are the basic causes. Until these basic causes are recognized and remedied, inflation will continue. Business firms, as other members of society, have suffered from the pressures and distortions caused by the continuing inflation. Their challenge is to adapt their operating and financial policies to cope with the inflationary environment of the 1970s.

ADDITIONAL SOURCES

Auerbach, Norman. "Switching to LIFO." *Financial Executive,* 43 (February 1975), 42–52.

Brinson, Gary. "How You Lose to Taxes and Inflation." *Financial Analysts Journal,* 29 (March–April 1973), 74–75.

Donaldson, Gordon. "Financial Management in an Affluent Society." *Financial Executive,* 35 (April 1967), 52–56, 58–60.

Elliott, J. W. "Control, Size, Growth, and Financial Performance in the Firm." *Journal of Financial and Quantitative Analysis,* 7 (January 1972), 1309–20.

Emminter, Otmar. "How Germany Beat Inflation." *Dun's* 104 (November 1974), 80–82, 84.

Harkins, Edwin P. *Organizing and Managing the Corporate Financial Function,* Studies in Business Policy, no. 129. New York: National Industrial Conference Board, Inc., 1969.

Harvey, John. "Curing Monetary Inflation." *Financial Executive* (February 1975), 22.

Jones, Reginald H. "The Challenge of Capital Attraction." *Financial Executive*, 41 (November 1973), 31–39.

Jones, Reginald H. "Capital Needs and Shrinking Profits." *Financial Executive*, 62 (May 1974), 44–48.

Jones, Reginald H. "Business Capital Requirements." *Financial Executive*, 41 (November 1974), 22–29.

Jones, Reginald H. "Financial Management during Inflation." *Financial Executive*, 43 (February 1975), 10–15.

Jones, Reginald H. "Why Business Must Seek Tax Reform." *Harvard Business Review*, 53 (September–October 1975), 49–55.

Konrath, Larry. "Accounting for Changing Price Levels." *Financial Analysts Journal*, 30 (November–December 1974), 50–56.

Lintner, John. "Presidential Address: Inflation and Security Returns." *Journal of Finance*, 30 (May 1975), 259–80.

Lowe, H. D. "The Classification of Corporate Stock Equities." *Accounting Review*, 36 (July 1961), 425–33.

Marek, Walter. "Reflections on Price-Level Accounting." *Financial Executive*, 42 (October 1974), 26–37.

Monroe, Archie. "Experimenting with Price-Level Reporting." *Financial Executive*, 42 (December 1974), 38–55.

Pohl, Hermann H. "The Coming Era of the Financial Executive." *Business Horizons*, 16 (June 1973), 15–22.

Russell, Alan. "An Application of Price Level Accounting." *Financial Executive*, 43 (February 1975), 21 and 78.

Schmitz, Robert. "Facing the New Normalcy in Corporate Finance." *Financial Executive*, 41 (November 1974), 14–21.

Seelig, Steven A. "Rising Interest Rates and Cost Push Inflation." *Journal of Finance*, 29 (September 1974), 1049–62.

Terborgh, George. "Inflation and Profits." *Financial Analysts Journal*, 30 (May–June 1974), 19–23.

Thorelli, Hans B. "A Consumer View of Inflation and the Economy." *Business Horizons*, 17 (December 1974), 25–31.

Van Horne, James C., and Glassmire, William F., Jr. "The Impact of Unanticipated Changes in Inflation on the Value of Common Stocks." *Journal of Finance*, 27 (December 1972), 1081–92.

Walter, James. "Investment Planning under Variable Price Change." *Financial Management*, 1 (Winter 1972), 36–50.

Weimer, Arthur M. "Ideational Items: Protecting Savings against Inflation." *Business Horizons,* 17 (August 1974), 48–50.

Weston, Frank T. "Adjust Your Accounting for Inflation." *Harvard Business Review,* 53 (January–February 1975), 22–24, 28–29, 146.

Weston, J. Fred. *The Scope and Methodology of Finance.* Englewood Cliffs, N.J.: Prentice-Hall, 1966.

Weston, J. Fred. "New Themes in Finance." *Journal of Finance,* 24 (March 1974), 237–243.

Wheelwright, Steven C. "Management by Model during Inflation." *Business Horizons,* 18 (June 1975), 33–42.

Wood, C. V. "Why It's Hard to Raise Capital Today." *Financial Executive,* 41 (November 1973), 21–30.

Chapter 3

The Timing of
Financial Policy

Roy E. Moor[*]

THERE are those who think of the timing of financial policy the way the late Vince Lombardi viewed winning: "it isn't everything, it's the only thing." But this attitude in this extreme form can lead not only to frustration but also to bad timing of financial decisions. A basic premise of this chapter is that perfect financial timing is impossible on any continuing basis. Unlike football, the individual participant in financial markets has essentially no control or even influence over the course of the game, and it is pure luck if he happens to be at the right spot at exactly the right time. Because perfection is unachievable, however, it should not be concluded that financial analysis is useless. This chapter is designed to help the corporate financial officer reduce timing mistakes. Financial analysis to prevent extreme timing mistakes is possible; it is also far more profitable in the sense of lowering financing costs than the illusory quest for perfect timing.

BASIC CONDITIONS

Timing considerations are most relevant to the financial officer in a company with certain characteristics, and the assumption made in

---

[*] Dr. Roy E. Moor is vice president and director of Economic Research of the Becker Securities Corporation, New York.

43

this chapter is that such characteristics are present. First, the company is growing and therefore has a need for funds for expansion, as well as a need to refinance maturing obligations. Second, the company will use internally generated funds initially to finance growth and only draw on external sources as necessary to supplement internal cash flow. Thus, this chapter deals with only the timing of raising funds among external markets, not the timing of investment of company financial assets in external markets. Third, the company has no overriding balance sheet constraints that prevent participation in any particular financial market. Fourth, the company has as its objective of timing analysis to minimize its costs of raising external funds over the long pull.

As indicated later, this chapter de-emphasizes reliance on forecasts. However, it is appropriate here to anticipate the general future financial environment in which external funds will be required. All corporate planning should, in our judgment, be based on the assumption that financial capital will be relatively scarce and difficult to obtain for as long a distance into the future as the planning envisions. (This forecast has the great virtue that if it is wrong, no one can make a mistake by having relied on it.) This forecast implies that the cost of financial capital in the future will be high by historical standards, regardless of the particular market or the particular time of financing. This condition, therefore, enhances the desirability of timing analysis in order to obtain as low costs as possible within this high cost environment. The forecast also implies that capital requirements will have to be met by involvement in as many alternative financial markets as possible. Thus, analysis must lead to decisions concerning the timing of movement from one market source of funds to another.

GENERAL TIMING RULES

Within these contexts, certain general rules can be postulated which should protect against extreme timing mistakes and improve the odds for beneficial timing decisions. These rules are not easy to follow, and they are not an ironclad guarantee of success even if followed. Rather, they are a set of mental disciplines that are superior to psychological feelings or urges. They are a means of controlling emotions rather than allowing emotions to control. They represent the first step toward objective financial decision making.

In a world where participants in financial markets are frequently blinded by emotions of the moment—during which times the worst financial mistakes can be made—the analyst with one eye on objective reality through a set of rules has a clear advantage.

Rule 1. Never Be Greedy. If conditions are favorable now for a particular type of financing, take advantage of it. Do not wait for an even better possible tomorrow. The best rule ever formulated for the stock market investor—and it applies equally to any participant in any financial market—was stated by Bernard Baruch: "Leave the first 10% and the last 10% for someone else."

Rule 2. Emphasize the Analysis behind Forecasts. Today's actual conditions are what is known, and none of us can be absolutely certain about the nature of tomorrow. Forecasts are useful if they reflect analysis, but it is the analysis behind the forecasts that must be examined and—if accepted—relied upon rather than the forecasts. Forecasts must be used, but it is essential to understand the qualifications to the forecasts; that is, the reasons why they could go awry. Also, there are ways as indicated below to minimize the role of forecasts in final decisions.

Rule 3. Do Not Be Dominated by Advice. Opinions by others reflect their own biases and attitudes that cannot be fully known and assessed by the user. You are the ultimate decision maker. You want your decisions to be based on facts and analysis—that may well be obtained from others—not upon hidden and uncomprehensible factors and influences. Advice is not analysis.

Rule 4. Never Be Afraid to Participate. It takes courage to take action, but "you can't win if you don't play." There are always imperfections among markets, and this means continual opportunities to reduce financing costs. Only the continual participant can be most aware of these opportunities and most accustomed to the procedures necessary to take advantage of them.

Rule 5. Participate over Time in as Many Financial Markets as Possible. There is no one market that is best for all times. Moreover, any balance sheet can be unbalanced by too heavy reliance on one market. As indicated below, it is easier to reduce "fixed" charges by moving between markets than by attempting to time changes appropriately within a market.

Rule 6. Maintain Continuing Data on Every Significant Money and Credit Market. As described in the following text, these data take little time to maintain and they help to meet all the rules above.

Data in the appropriate form can inform you whether conditions are currently favorable. Data are factual rather than futuristic, are not opinionated, and can provide current information about a number of markets and potential opportunities.

Rule 7. Rely on Long-Term Market Relationships. Market participants continue, as always, to be motivated basically by fear and greed. As the charts in this chapter show, patterns of behavior over many years repeat themselves again and again. The patterns are not perfectly smooth curves but they are sufficiently recurring so that they can be used as general signposts if not precise markers of turning points.

THE EQUITY MARKET

The highest long-term cost market—certainly for a growing firm—is the equity market. Nevertheless, virtually every company must utilize the equity market periodically for new funds. The reason for this is in order to place the company in a stronger position to minimize its financing costs in all other markets over the long term. Leveraging—trading on the equity by financing in nonequity markets—is acceptable practice in the view of the rating services so long as it is done in moderation. But the higher the fixed debt relative to equity, the lower the ratings and hence the higher the interest costs per dollar of debt. Moreover, the future is uncertain, and any company may at times find itself needing external funds and unable to draw upon the debt markets because of too heavy past borrowing. Thus, any company may be forced to issue new equity in periods when stock prices are low, and such financing is most costly. In effect, timing of new stock offerings must be controlled by the company, not controlled for it by financial conditions.

Table 1 shows how most companies have ignored equity financing and how it has hurt them. In the early years of the 1960s, while corporations were raising significant proportions of their externally generated funds from bank loans and bond offerings, they obtained only inconsequential amounts from new stock offerings. Then, in 1970 and 1971, when retained earnings and stock prices were both unexpectedly low, companies were forced to resort more heavily to equity financing. Since 1971, the proportion of total external funds raised in the stock market has again progressively declined, with the result that—at the end of 1974—overall equity coverage for total

TABLE 1
Percentages of Total Sources or Uses of Funds

	1963	1964	1965	1966	1967	1968	1969	1970	1971	1972	1973	1974
Uses:												
Plant and equipment	58.8	60.4	57.2	62.8	65.9	58.5	62.7	72.5	64.0	58.9	58.6	60.4
Inventories	6.6	8.1	8.6	14.8	7.8	5.6	5.7	5.5	4.2	6.6	7.3	5.4
Other*	31.6	31.5	34.1	22.4	26.4	35.8	31.7	22.0	31.8	34.6	34.1	34.2
Total uses	100.0	100.0	100.0	100.0	100.0	100.0	100.0	100.0	100.0	100.0	100.0	100.0
Sources:												
Retained profits	18.5	22.8	23.3	23.5	20.2	15.4	11.5	8.0	11.0	14.0	17.6	18.6
Depreciation	47.4	45.3	38.5	39.3	44.1	39.7	42.2	51.7	47.9	42.6	38.3	38.9
Total internal	67.5	69.8	61.9	62.9	65.4	54.3	51.4	57.3	56.4	53.2	48.0	43.7
Bank loans	5.5	6.2	11.5	8.5	7.0	8.5	10.0	5.3	3.7	9.1	17.4	14.8
Net new stock issues	0.0	1.8	0.0	1.3	2.6	0.0	2.9	5.5	9.5	7.4	4.2	1.9
Net new bonds	6.0	5.5	5.9	10.5	15.6	11.4	10.2	19.1	15.7	8.6	6.2	11.1
Total external†	32.5	30.2	38.1	37.1	34.6	45.7	48.6	42.7	43.6	46.8	52.0	56.3
Total sources	100.0	100.0	100.0	100.0	100.0	100.0	100.0	100.0	100.0	100.0	100.0	100.0

* Includes residential construction, receivables, and trade credit.
† Includes mortgages, open market paper, payables to U.S. government, other liabilities.
Amounts need not add to totals because of rounding.
Source: Board of Governors of the Federal Reserve System, *Flow of Funds Books.*

debt on the balance sheets of U.S. corporations was at a record post–World War II low. And this situation existed as they entered the highly uncertain business conditions of 1975.

Therefore, the first specific market timing rule is: *If a company needs—or even just expects to need—any external funds, it should always finance in the equity market when conditions in the market are favorable.* This is the least frequent form of financing because it is the highest cost. It is also the market where favorable conditions for financing occur least frequently. Therefore, analysis of the timing of financial policy should start with the analysis of the equity market and how relatively favorable conditions for financing in that market can be determined.

Figure 1 indicates one measure of the costs of equity financing;

FIGURE 1
Long-Term Security Yields

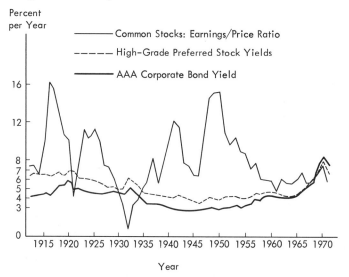

Source: *Historical Supplement to Federal Reserve Chart Book on Financial Business Statistics,* 1969; *Annual Report of the Council of Economic Advisors,* 1970; and *Federal Reserve Bulletin,* July 1971.

namely, earnings as a proportion of stock prices. Clearly, companies would like to issue new stocks when earnings are the lowest relative to stock prices; i.e., when the stock market is willing to pay the highest price relative to the earnings of the company. It can be observed in Figure 1 that while such earnings price (E/P) ratios are normally above yields or costs of other securities, they also fluctuate much more violently and are sometimes below the costs in other markets. Therefore, one desirable condition for a new equity offering is when stock market E/P ratios are below comparable costs in fixed-income markets or when your own company's E/P ratio is below the cost to you of long-term funds in other markets.

But the timing of equity offerings must also be influenced by the absolute level of stock prices. Thus, it would have been far better for most companies to have issued new stocks in 1972 than in 1970 or 1971. Earnings were higher but stock prices were also proportionately higher, and E/P ratios were still below costs in other markets. But when are stock prices "high"? Doesn't this judgment require a forecast of the stock market, and who can effectively do that? Isn't this just a counsel of perfection?

The answers to these questions are: first, the stock market is high only in relation to economic conditions. Therefore, a corporate financial officer must monitor those economic conditions that most directly affect the stock market. Second, "high" can be measured in terms of *existing* conditions and, therefore, avoid attempts to forecast stock prices. Third, as indicated earlier, stock offerings should be made when stock prices are high, but not necessarily highest because no one knows in advance what highest will be.

To help make this equity timing decision, every corporate financial officer should probably maintain a chart similar to Figure 2. This particular chart shows the Standard & Poor's 500 Stock Price Index, but whatever stock market index most closely conforms to a company's stock price can be used. Figure 2 indicates how the average S&P index in each calendar quarter was above or below a long-term trend for the market. Constructing such a chart is quite simple. The trend can be approximated by merely drawing a straight line through a long-term chart of the stock market and then measuring the difference between the trend value and the actual quarterly average value for the market in each quarter. It is important for financial analysis that a long-term trend (at least back to the mid-50s) be used and that quarterly average stock prices (rather than daily, weekly, or monthly) be used. The purpose of the chart is to accentuate the market cycle and the highs and lows in the market. Clearly, companies would be well advised to time their new equity offerings only in periods when stock prices are around high points

FIGURE 2
Standard & Poor's 500 Stock Price Index (trend removed)

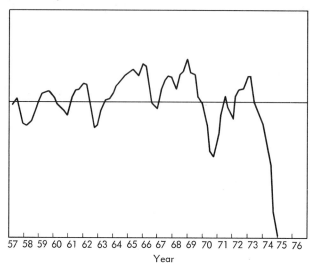

Year

Source: Becker Securities Corporation, *The Fundamentalist's Chart Book.*

in the market cycle and to avoid having to offer new stock around market lows.

Thus, the question in any future period is whether stock prices are near their highs in the market cycle. This question can be stated another way: Do present economic conditions suggest that the odds favor declining stock prices in the future? In effect, are stock prices (*a*) above long-term values and (*b*) rising, and (*c*) are economic conditions that affect the market beginning to deteriorate?

In addition to knowing where the market is in a historical perspective, therefore, it is necessary to monitor certain economic factors in relation to the market. These economic factors fall into two broad groups: monetary (which must be followed for other financial timing decisions) and nonmonetary (which can be analyzed in part through the company's own developments). All of these must be monitored. No one factor definitively determines a stock market high point, but enough of them in combination can warn a corporate officer that stock prices are more likely to be headed downward in the future than upward; i.e., that stock prices are "high" and that an opportunity for an equity offering is at hand.

The monetary factors fall into three categories: liquidity measures, interest rates, and the money supply. Each is a major influence on the stock market and each must be examined separately.

Figure 3 indicates the relationship between one measure of

FIGURE 3
The Market and Free Reserves (free reserves moved forward four quarters)

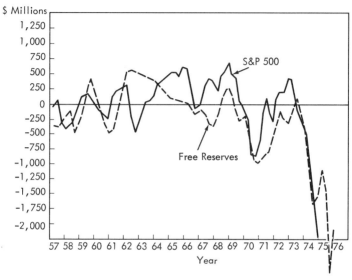

Source: Becker Securities Corporation, *The Fundamentalist's Chart Book.*

liquidity—free reserves in the banking system—and the stock market as shown in Figure 2. Two features of Figure 3 are relevant to corporate financial planners. First, liquidity in the banking system tends to go up or down on average about a year before liquidity in the corporate sector as measured by quick ratios. Second, the stock market is sensitive to corporate liquidity if it reaches too low levels. Therefore, the line for free reserves in Figure 3 has been moved to the right four quarters; e.g., the data for free reserves in 1973 are shown in the chart for 1974. This chart, which can be easily constructed from regularly published Federal Reserve data, informs a corporate financial officer that, when free reserves in the banking system decline from higher average numbers to the range of $100–$200 million, stock prices about a year later are likely to be adversely affected by concerns about corporate liquidity. No forecasts are needed for this analysis and no forecasts need be made about future stock prices. The corporate officer is merely informed that when free reserves are high, but declining, the time may be favorable for equity financing.

Figure 4 involves another financial market—the commercial paper

FIGURE 4
The Market and Commercial Paper

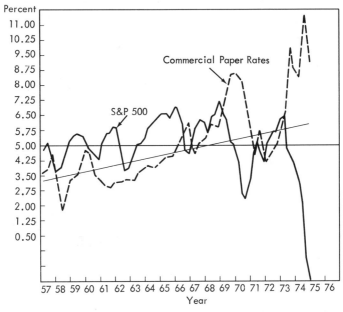

Source: Becker Securities Corporation, *The Fundamentalist's Chart Book.*

market—that corporate executives must carefully monitor independently as a source of funds as well as for its effects on stock prices.

The commercial paper market has exerted an increasingly important influence over interest rates in other financial markets such as prime bank lending rates and corporate bond rates, and the commercial paper market is also looked to ever more by corporations as a direct source of funds. In Figure 4, only the impact of commercial paper rates on stock prices is examined. The dashed line in Figure 4 indicates average commercial paper rates during each calendar quarter covered by the chart.

The key indicator in Figure 4 is the light straight line that trends upward across the chart. This line has been drawn to indicate the levels of commercial paper rates at various stock market "highs." Note that commercial paper rates were typically rising but below this line prior to stock market highs. In general it can be said that, since World War II, commercial paper rates rising above certain levels have tended to exert a negative influence on stock prices. The light line is an indication of what those levels have been in the past and how the levels have been themselves rising over time. Thus, again without any forecasts, a corporate financial officer is advised by maintaining such a chart that, if commercial paper rates are rising and approaching a level around the extension of the light line, the time for a favorable equity offering may be near.

The corporate bond market also exerts an influence on stock prices. However, these two markets have not been closely linked until relatively recent years. Therefore, the more long-standing relationships described elsewhere in this chapter—and which are the only type to use in determining financial timing decisions—are not as applicable in relating to the bond and stock markets. However, direct cost comparisons as indicated in Figure 1 are still useful. A company may choose either to compare average E/P ratios, e.g., for the S&P 500, against some appropriate corporate bond interest rate series, as is done in Figure 1, or the company's own E/P ratio can be compared to yields on bond offerings comparable to the company's rating. One warning: never use forecasted earnings for these comparisons, but rather instead actual trailing 12-month earnings. The timing implications of any such comparisons of E/P ratios and bond rates are, of course, that conditions are relatively more favorable in the lower cost market. Since rising bond rates do exert a negative influence on stock prices, periods when bond rates approach or exceed selected E/P ratios are appropriate times for considering equity offerings.

Figure 5 can be used in conjunction with the foregoing analysis of E/P ratios and also to incorporate into the equity timing decision another financial factor, the money supply. Changes in the rate of growth in the money supply—in this case, narrowly defined to include only currency and checking accounts—have been for years closely correlated in direction of change with stock market P/E ratios, and, therefore, inversely related to E/P ratios. Figure 5 shows the rate of change in a six-month moving average of growth rates in

FIGURE 5
Price/Earnings Ratio and Money Supply

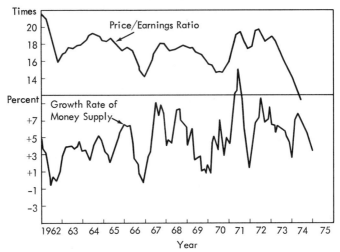

Source: Becker Securities Corporation, *The Fundamentalist's Chart Book*.

money supply. Thus, when the money supply is rising more rapidly than in a prior period, P/E stock multiples are likely to be rising, E/P ratios are conversely likely to be falling, and conditions are improving for an equity flotation.

There are a number of economic factors, aside from the monetary ones, that financial corporate officers must consider because the stock market is influenced by these factors. By all odds, the most emphasized of these factors is earnings. (In fact, earnings are usually greatly overemphasized relative to P/E multiples, although fluctuations in P/Es have a multiple influence on stock prices in comparison to earnings changes. The preceding paragraphs are significantly more important than earnings changes in judging when to make a new equity offering.)

Figure 6 indicates the way in which changes in earnings are related to stock price fluctuations. Two characteristics of this chart are important. First, stock prices tend to change in anticipation of earnings changes. The average lead of stock prices appears to be about six months, and the line reflecting earnings changes has been moved to the left by two quarters in Figure 6; e.g., earnings for the fourth quarter of 1974 is shown on the chart as the second quarter of 1974.

FIGURE 6
The Market and Corporate Profits (corporate profits moved
back two quarters)

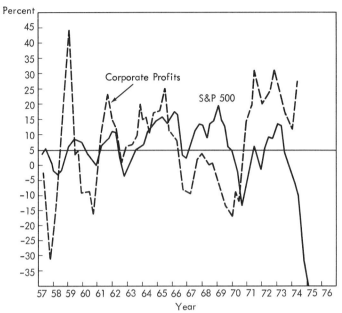

Source: Becker Securities Corporation, *The Fundamentalist's Chart Book.*

Second, stock prices are *only* sensitive to rates of changes in earn-ings, not the level of earnings nor whether they are rising or falling. For example, earnings rose throughout all of 1973. But they rose less rapidly in the latter half of 1973—shown on the chart as a decline in early 1973—and this slowdown in rate of growth was a negative influence on stock prices.

Thus, the corporate financial officer must consider, in thinking about the level of stock prices, future earnings changes. These are, of course, difficult to forecast. However, there are a number of ways in which the task can be simplified. First, the same relationship that prevails in Figure 6 between the overall stock market and aggregate corporate profits also is applicable for most company stock prices and earnings. The corporate executive must be primarily concerned about his own stock price. He also has the best forehand knowledge of factors affecting future earnings growth for his company, es-pecially over the next several quarters. Second, this analysis does not require a precise forecast of earnings per share in a future quarter. Rather, the only question that needs to be answered is whether current earnings growth rates can be increased, or are likely to slow. If prospective earnings are likely to be rising at lesser percentage rates than in the present or preceding quarter, an equity offering should be considered. The executive should know this before market analysts become aware of it. Third, as part of the preceding analysis, a corporate officer knows whether unusual or nonrecurring factors are favorably affecting earnings currently that will automatically result in slower growth in reported earnings in subsequent quarters. Finally, such analysis is only relevant in those periods when (*a*) stock prices are rising and above trend line, (*b*) corporate earnings are rising, and (*c*) quarterly earnings growth rates are improving. Within these periods, a good rule for equity offerings is to be conservative and, therefore, to be too early rather than too late.

One economic factor directly affecting both earnings and stock prices is inflation. The measure of inflation that is most relevant to the stock market—and, incidentally, to the bond market—is infla-

FIGURE 7
The Market and Inflation

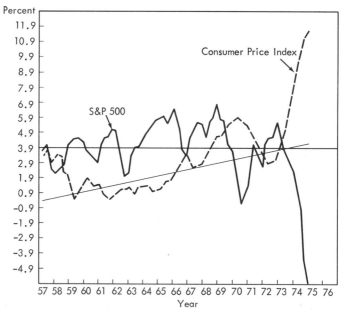

Source: Becker Securities Corporation, *The Fundamentalist's Chart Book.*

tion in consumer prices, the Consumer Price Index. Figure 7 shows a long-term relationship between inflation rates in consumer prices and stock market fluctuations. The chart can be used in exactly the same manner as Figure 4 on commercial paper rates. The light straight line indicates generally when inflation rates have risen to sufficiently high levels that they begin to exert a negative influence on stock prices. When inflation rates in consumer prices are around levels indicated by an extension of such a line and seem likely to rise in the future, the financial officer of a company should consider raising funds through the equity market.

There are a number of other economic influences on stock prices, but only two need be mentioned here because they both relate to a company's own business. In general, any corporation is involved in production primarily for either the consumer or the capital goods market. Demand in each of these markets affects stock prices and, since virtually every company is knowledgeable about demand in one of these markets, such knowledge can be a useful input in the timing of financial policy.

The consumer demands that most directly relate to major swings in stock prices are the demands for consumer durables, primarily autos and major household appliances. Figure 8 shows this relationship. Changes in stock prices only anticipate changes in rates of growth in consumer durable demands by about one quarter—probably because both are affected by similar psychological factors—and therefore the dashed line in Figure 8 has been moved only one quarter to the left. Thus, the producer of consumer goods—who can feel the beat of his customer before the stock market can—should be able to detect any softening in consumer demands and take it into account in his financing decisions before an equity financing opportunity is lost. Since consumer demands are always erratic, it is important that these be viewed in a fairly long-term context. If (*a*) stock prices are high; i.e., above trend line, and (*b*) consumer durable demands are rising strongly during a current quarter, and (*c*) is there any reason for wariness about the sustainability of future rates of growth in ensuing quarters? If these conditions are all present, they represent another justification for considering an equity offering.

The same reasoning applies to capital goods producers in looking at their future demands relative to stock prices, as shown in Figure 9. However, since capital goods expenditures, which are shown in

FIGURE 8

The Market and Consumer Durables (consumer durables moved back one quarter)

Source: Becker Securities Corporation, *The Fundamentalist's Chart Book.*

the chart, tend to be made after the appropriations, contracts, and installations have been completed, stock prices tend to change direction well before the actual expenditures. Thus, the dashed line in Figure 9 has been moved to the left three quarters. But capital producers have advance information about the plans of their customers and there are many surveys taken of capital spending plans, such as those by the Conference Board, McGraw-Hill, and the U.S. Department of Commerce. The company involved in a capital goods producing industry should have an exceptionally good feel about rates of growth of capital spending, and such information can be valuable in the timing of financial policy.

CORPORATE BOND MARKET

The next highest cost market for financing, after the equity market, is the corporate bond market. However, in contrast to the equity market, the bond market has two characteristics that make timing

FIGURE 9
The Market and Capital Spending (capital spending moved back three quarters)

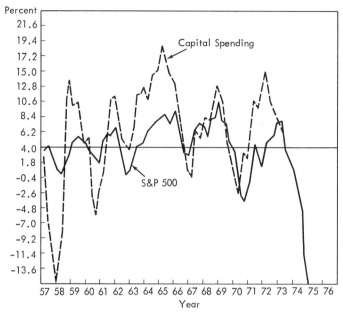

Source: Becker Securities Corporation, *The Fundamentalist's Chart Book.*

decisions much easier. First, the bond market tends to change direction only *after* monetary and economic conditions have altered. Second, the corporate bond market is the most relatively stable of all the various financial markets upon which a corporation may draw. (The stock market is the most volatile, hence the one where financing opportunities are the most difficult to predict.) Figure 10 indicates both the relative stability of long-term bond rates and also the extent to which the bond market fluctuates and therefore requires timing decisions. No attempt is made in this chapter, incidentally, to analyze changes in yield spreads or other fluctuations within the bond market, since data can be maintained by each company on how rates are changing for issues comparable to its own. As with all markets, the primary timing analysis must be in the form of longer term changes in direction of the entire bond market.

In addition to the interrelationships between the bond market and stock market described above, the specific rules governing bond

FIGURE 10
Long- and Short-Term Interest Rates

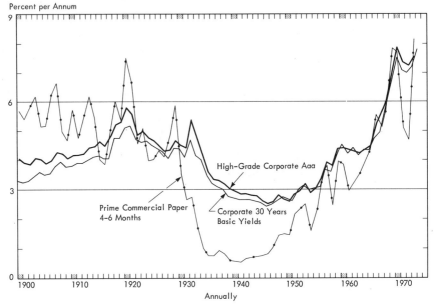

Source: *Federal Reserve Historical Chart Book*, p. 23

market financing are primarily related to the commercial paper market as a proxy for all short-term rates and sources of corporate funds. The fundamental choice, assuming that the conditions are not propitious for an equity offering, is between long-term and short-term borrowing.

A specific rule for bond financing is: *when commercial paper rates are below bond rates but have been rising and have come to within 100 basis points of bond rates, finance in the bond market.*

When short rates are above long-term rates, money supply conditions are usually tight in relation to market demand. The monetary policies, which helped to induce such tightness, historically have been associated with an ending of cyclical upturns. Thus periods when short-term interest rates are above long-term interest rates are likely to be periods of cyclical highs. Not only are long-term rates likely to be cyclically high at such times, but the conditions of offering are likely to be more onerous in such a period of tight money.

However, long-term rates have been trending upward since 1966.

Thus the decision as to whether to finance long or short when short-term rates are above long-term rates depends upon an assessment of the future trend of long-term rates, although the case for long-term financing under these conditions assumes that any future cycle in bond rates will be swamped by the long-term upward trend. However, if the specific rule for bond financing set forth is followed, then hopefully, the bulk of long-term debt financing will have occurred before short-term rates have risen above long-term rates.

The rule also has historical validity, as Figure 10 indicates. The rule is based on two concepts. First, bond rates are sensitive to short rates, not vice versa, and short rates will always reflect increasing demands for loanable funds before long rates. Second, as we indicated, financial capital is likely to be in short supply for an indefinite period into the future. Thus, arbitraging between financial markets will keep all rates in closer conformity than in the past. (The 100 basis point part of the rule is merely a general rule of thumb that may be varied up or down on the basis of personal judgment.)

The bond market is sensitive to a number of the other monetary and economic factors—in addition to short-term rates—that affect the stock market, but, as noted earlier, with a lag. If corporate liquidity as measured by quick ratios is declining, it is an indication that corporations generally are increasing their demands on financial markets. Such demands typically rise first in the short-term markets such as in bank borrowing, accounts payable, and commercial paper. Corporations always seem to borrow first—when their demands for external funds increase—in short-term markets. This is why short rates generally tend to lead—in direction of change—long rates. But such tendencies are reflected in corporate liquidity ratios. And these in turn are anticipated by declines in bank liquidity, especially free reserves. There is no consistent relationship between changes in free reserves and bond rates as there is with stock prices, but bank free reserves declining into negative territory on a quarterly average basis should be viewed as an advance indicator that corporations have increasing needs for borrowed funds and that these demands will fairly soon exert upward pressure on bond rates.

The influence on bond rates of changes in rates of growth of the money supply has long been debated by economists. Suffice it to say here that we believe there is an influence but that it cannot be quantified precisely. The nature of the relationship is closely tied to bank free reserves. As long as these are "adequate," even though declining in level, the money supply can rise rapidly and interest rates need not be materially affected. But let free reserves begin to become tight and the banks begin to raise their lending rates. This deters some borrowers. Thus the money supply begins to grow less rapidly, and the corporate borrowers are redirected by interest rates into the longer term corporate bond market. Hence, any slowing in rate of growth of the money supply should be received as a tip-off that bond rates will be rising soon.

Corporate earnings have an inverse relationship to bond rates, but again not a precise one. Generally, corporations resort to the bond market only when internal cash flow plus short-term borrowing cannot meet total capital requirements. Thus, a declining rate of growth of corporate earnings is usually reflected in a slower increase in cash flow and rising bond offerings. As with the equity analysis, therefore, a company management can either monitor rates of change in aggregate corporate profits or in its own earnings. But quarterly rates of change—not aggregate levels—remain the crucial factor to watch. Any slowdown in these rates suggest future increases in demands for long-term funds and rising bond rates.

Inflation is another influence on the bond market about which economists have long debated. Our view is that such an influence exists. However, the influence in our judgment is not precise and cannot be used as a basis for forecasting bond interest rates. Moreover, inflation should not be considered the only factor determining bond rates or even the single most important one, as this section attempts to indicate by emphasizing other factors as well. Inflation is perhaps the most general of the economic factors affecting the bond market. Nevertheless, certain characteristics of inflation should be watched by the corporate officer responsible for timing of financial policy. First, changes in the Consumer Price Index are more important to bond rates than other measures of inflation. Second, changes in average direction of inflation rates—not the level of inflation rates—are the relevant influence on the bond market. Bond prices tend to discount current inflation rates and, therefore, bond rates move higher with rising rates of inflation and lower with falling inflation rates.

Consumer demands are not particularly consequential to the bond market, even though they are quite germaine to the stock market. But capital spending is more relevant to the bond market than to the stock market, because such capital spending is relatively long term and is typically financed ultimately in long-term markets. However, the relationships between capital spending and the bond market have been changing in recent years and may well be changing further in the years ahead. Therefore, what we indicate here are the types of factors to examine in capital spending as part of bond market analysis.

First, there has been an increasing tendency by corporations in recent years to finance ever more fixed capital purchases in short-term markets. The one form of capital expansion that is still consistently financed—ultimately, if not immediately—in the bond market is new construction. Thus, the corporate financial officer is well advised to watch industrial—not residential—construction surveys. If these surveys show rising long-term plans to increase rates of construction for new industrial plant, it may be assumed that the corporate bond calendar will be rising in a subsequent period and exerting a depressing influence on bond prices; i.e., upward pressure on bond rates. For machinery and equipment purchases, the financing pressures are felt ever more in short-term markets and only as funds become less attainable in these markets do the demands for machinery and equipment financing impact the bond market.

Second, however, even construction of new industrial plant facilities only affects the bond calendar with a lag. The reason for this appears to be that an ever greater number of companies are using short-term construction loans to meet building expenses and then refinancing these loans in the long-term market after the construction is completed. The statistical series that most closely correlate with changes in the bond calendar is the new plant *expenditures* series published quarterly by the U.S. Department of Commerce. Other series referred to in "The Equity Market" section of this chapter, such as appropriations, plans, and contracts placed, anticipate this expenditures series because the expenditures are largely made after work has been completed. Therefore, the corporate financial executive, in monitoring free reserves in the banking system, can judge when capital spending for machinery and equipment is likely to shift toward the long-term bond market and, in monitoring the plant expenditure series, can assess when increasing capital outlays will be financed in the bond market.

A rising bond calendar represents—by itself—a depressant on

bond prices and a force toward rising bond interest rates. However, the calendar must be viewed in the context of the investment funds available—largely from financial institutions—for commitment to these new bond offerings. The financing available from financial institutions follows general long-term trends. These can be analyzed and the historical relations characteristic of each type of financial institution can be observed. However, these long-term historical relations must be adjusted to the impact of the particular conditions of the individual economic period under analysis. Thus, forecasting the cash flows of these institutional bond investors must utilize considerable judgment as well as the help from historical relationships.

One leading indicator of the willingness of these institutions to commit funds to the bond market—or to withhold funds from the market—is the private placement market. If interest rates in the private placement market are beginning to rise—and, even more significant, if funds are becoming less available through this market—the likelihood is that a rising bond calendar will be increasingly difficult to float in the public bond market. Analysis of industrial construction plans provides the earliest advance warning system of future increases in bond interest rates; a jump in private placement rates indicates that the swing to generally higher rates is already under way.

COMMERCIAL PAPER MARKET

In this chapter, we use commercial paper rates as indicative of all short-term rates. The reason for this is that the commercial paper market is the most sensitive of the short-term markets available for corporate financing and therefore tends to lead other markets in changing direction. This emphasis on commercial paper, however, is not meant to suggest sole reliance on this market by corporate financial officers. As indicated earlier, as many markets as possible should be drawn upon for financing needs and most corporations should move extensively among short-term markets on the basis of relative costs. Our emphasis on commercial paper does suggest, however, that short-term interest rates do tend to move together and therefore the opportunities are short lived for minimizing costs by shifting from one short-term market to another. Also, of course, we are here only considering timing decisions—essentially as between equity, bond, and short-term markets—and no considerations are given to such factors as the desirability of maintaining long-standing banking relationships. For timing analysis alone, commercial paper rates do tend to lead other short-term rates, and the corporate officer may wish to monitor these rates on a weekly or monthly basis as well as in terms of quarterly averages for purposes of comparisons with the equity and bond markets.

The specific timing rule for financing in short-term markets is: *finance in short-term markets whenever conditions in the long-term markets are not favorable.* In effect, therefore, all the conditions in the previous sections for the timing of raising funds in the equity bond markets are the conditions under which short-term financing should be minimized. These conditions include, of course, analyses of the liquidity requirements and prospective cash flow conditions in the company.

As is indicated in the charts earlier on the relationships between short-term rates and costs of money in other markets, in most periods the least expensive money is obtainable from short-term borrowing. The difficulty most corporate officers have is in moving at the appropriate times away from short-term markets, which is the reason so much space has been devoted to the monetary and economic disciplines that can direct financing into the longer term markets.

One negative point should be stressed concerning the analysis of short-term money markets. There is a sharp and almost complete separation of government short-term markets; e.g., Treasury bills, short municipals, and corporate short-term sources of external funds. The participants in the two types of markets are generally different, the forces affecting the two markets are distinctly different, and the direction of interest rates can be different for periods of time. Therefore, at no point in this chapter has the attention of the corporate executive been directed to government fiscal policy as such except to the extent that government fiscal policy has an impact on monetary policy and other factors reflected in the tables and charts presented.

We stress the point here because our experience suggests that corporate financial policy is too often based upon judgment or guesses about what the government may do—or, even worse, upon what someone hopes or fears the government may do. The problem with such an approach to financial markets is that it misdirects attentions away from the factors and forces, conditions and changes, within the private sector of the economy that are most significant to the corporation in its own financing. No political value judgment is required to recognize the fact that, in the United States at least, financial decisions made in the private sector of the economy far outweigh government fiscal decisions. This is certainly true in terms of the movement of private financial markets about which the corporate officer must be concerned.

Of course, changes in government fiscal policy such as the tax reductions made in 1975 in conjunction with related monetary policies may be able to change expectations and behavior in the private sector of the economy. Thus, general economic conditions can be affected and ultimately work themselves through financial decisions made in the private sector of the economy. Furthermore, the fiscal policies of the government are likely to be influenced by underlying conditions that are developing in the private sector of the economy. Nevertheless, the emphasis in this chapter has been on those factors in the private sector of the economy that have an historically established influence on private financial markets. The timing of financial policies of corporations aimed at the most favorable terms and costs of obtaining the use of funds must therefore concentrate on the analysis of these factors in the private sector.

ADDITIONAL SOURCES

Boudreaux, Kenneth. "Competitive Rates and Market Efficiency." *Financial Analysts Journal*, 31 (March–April 1965), 18–25.

Burton, J., and Toth, J. "Forecasting Long-Term Interest Rates." *Financial Analysts Journal*, 30 (September–October 1974), 73–85.

Cargill, Thomas F. "The Term Structure of Interest Rates: A Test of the Expectations Hypothesis." *Journal of Finance*, 30 (June 1975), 761–72.

Gibson, William E. "Price Expectations Effects on Interest Rates." *Journal of Finance*, 25 (March 1970), 19–34.

Gray, Jean M. "New Evidence on the Term Structure of Interest Rates: 1884–1900." *Journal of Finance*, 28 (June 1973), 635–46.

Kessel, Reuben A. *Cyclical Behavior on the Term Structure of Interest Rates*. New York: National Bureau of Economic Research, 1965.

Merton, Robert C. "On the Pricing of Corporate Debt: The Risk Structure of Interest Rates." *Journal of Finance*, 19 (May 1974), 449–70.

Norgaard, Richard L. "An Examination of Yields of Corporate Bonds and Stocks." *Journal of Finance*, 29 (September 1974), 1275–86.

Roll, Richard. "Evidence on the 'Growth-Optimum' Model." *Journal of Finance,* 28 (June 1973), 551–66.

Sharpe, William. "Are Gains Likely from Market Timing?" *Financial Analysts Journal,* 31 (March–April 1975), 60–69.

Van Horne, James C. *Function and Analysis of Capital Market Rates.* Englewood Cliffs, N.J.: Prentice-Hall, Inc., 1970.

Chapter 4

The International Financial Environment and Financing Decisions

John T. Hackett*

THE MULTINATIONAL CORPORATION AND WORLDWIDE INFLATION

DESPITE the many difficulties of international economics, the problem that has the most universal impact on the performance and management of multinational corporations is inflation. Yet, the multinational organization has also played an important part as a contributor to inflation. Therefore, managements must not only evaluate how best to manage their enterprises throughout a prolonged period of international inflation, but they must also achieve a greater understanding of the role they play in sustaining inflation, if it is to be contained. Obviously, the latter objective is more difficult and requires intricate working relationships between corporations, national governments and international agencies.

The current international inflation is a new and difficult experience for management for several reasons. First, unlike previous post–World War II inflationary periods, the current one is worldwide in

---

* John T. Hackett, Ph.D., is executive vice president and chief financial officer of the Cummins Engine Company, Inc., Columbus, Indiana.

This chapter is based in part on two articles that appeared in the *Financial Executive* in May 1974 and February 1975. Permission for the use of portions of those articles has been kindly granted by the Financial Executives Institute.

scope. Second, despite an economic recession in nearly all industrial countries, inflation continues to be a major economic problem. Third, the current inflation is more severe and less responsive to anti-inflationary policies than previous postwar inflations. Fourth, attempts by management to deal with the impact of inflation is rendered even more complex by severe problems with corporate liquidity and capital markets. Finally, the severity and length of the current inflation has tended to distort the financial information that management employs to measure and evaluate business performance.

No Industrial Nations Exempt

Unlike the inflationary periods of the late 1940s and 1950s, the current price spiral has affected all industrial nations. Therefore, alternative sources of supply for materials are restricted. In past periods of inflation, many corporations attempted to moderate rising costs by developing sources of supply among nations that were either experiencing lower rates of inflation or were able to price more competitively. For example, the expanded use of Japanese steel by U.S. and European manufacturers was a result of attempts to develop alternative sources of supply to combat rising costs. In addition, throughout most of the postwar period the timing of business cycles experienced by various industrial nations has tended to be offsetting and, thus, beneficial to multinational enterprises. As the United States was experiencing rising demand pressure on capacity and rising prices, other industrial nations were frequently undergoing a period of underutilization of capacity and unemployment. Therefore, U.S. companies were able to buy from foreign sources at lower prices or import from foreign subsidiaries at reduced cost. The aggregate effect of this business cycle balance and worldwide sourcing was to dampen the impact of inflation and afford greater price stability.

The simultaneous increase in worldwide demand that began in the early 1970s affected all industrial nations and there was no reserve of unused capacity to moderate cost increases. Furthermore, the rapid increase in demand for industrial products was reflected quickly in the demand for raw materials. In many cases, prices for raw materials from 1972 through 1974 exceeded price increases achieved throughout the entire decade of the 1960s. Consequently, there has been less opportunity to offset cost increases through development of new sources of supply.

Although the increase in demand that triggered the rapid rise in world prices was one of the most dramatic periods of industrial growth in recent history, it is apparent that most industrial nations began to encounter a significant decline in demand toward the end of 1973. It can also be assumed that the current economic downturn would have occurred even without the increase in oil prices, although not as rapidly. It is now apparent that a part of what appeared to be an increase in real demand was a combination of advance buying to avoid future price increases as well as outright speculation. But despite the recent decline in demand, manufacturers have experienced continued increases in labor and material costs. Thus, many companies face a period of declining demand and increasing costs that will result in severe reductions in both absolute profits and profit margins. Moreover, there is less benefit from the geographical diversification that many multinational corporations had hoped to realize as the trend toward declining demand and increased costs appears to be a worldwide affliction.

The current economic imbalance is further complicated by the fact that inflation is less responsive to restrictive monetary policies and other government policies aimed at controlling prices than has been the case with previous inflationary periods. Therefore, most industrial nations have maintained relatively restrictive economic policies despite the apparent slowdown in business activity and rising unemployment. The combined effect of these policies is a slower pace of recovery.

Inflation also accelerates corporate needs for capital to finance cost increases associated with working capital and plant and equipment expenditures. Working and fixed capital budgets as well as entire financial plans quickly lose their value as guidelines for management action as additional cost increases are absorbed. Pricing policies may be designed to offset cost increases, but in actual practice few corporations are able to institute price increases rapidly enough to maintain profit margins, due in large part to the use of cost accounting systems that are insensitive to inflation. Therefore, internally generated sources of cash provide less of the increased funds required to maintain corporate expansion and the reliance on external liquidity or external sources of funds is accelerated.

The corporate liquidity problem is further complicated by the fact that the current economic recession places ever greater pressure on corporate profit margins and cash flows. To add to this complication, a review of the balance sheets of many multinational corporations reveals a significant lack of financial flexibility.

Capital Requirements and Debt

During the prolonged expansion period of the late 1960s and early 1970s, many managements elected to borrow heavily in order to finance worldwide programs of expansion and acquisition. Increased financial leverage in the form of higher debt to capital and debt to equity ratios became a hallmark of sophisticated financial management, while more conservative guidelines regarding appropriate balances between debt and equity and fixed payment coverage ratios were rejected by many borrowers and lenders. In many instances, companies that enjoyed significant increases in price/earnings ratios and common stock prices were still unwilling to absorb the dilution associated with the issuance of additional shares of common stock in order to expand their equity base.

As growth in sales and earnings continued and prices rose, many multinational organizations became convinced that even greater amounts of debt could be absorbed without danger because of increased cash flow. In addition, diversification through acquisition was adopted widely as a means of achieving ambitious corporate growth objectives, and with newly acquired companies came capital requirements well in excess of cash generation. Multinational corporations that were not attracted toward diversification and acquisitions were often eager to expand their existing activities into new markets and new geographical locations which resulted in increased demands on corporate financial resources in the form of additional working capital, fixed asset requirements and start-up costs. As the rate of inflation accelerated, the amount of funds required to merely replace inventory and fixed assets also increased dramatically. Thus, the financing of inflation coupled with the financial demands of expansion soon exhausted both the internal liquidity and credit availability of many multinational companies.

As inflation spread throughout the international economy, a larger share of the worldwide efforts to combat price increases was assigned to monetary policy which was reflected quickly in reduced credit availability and unusually high interest rates.

Toward the end of 1973, many corporations began to rely more heavily on short-term borrowing to finance increased capital requirements. Corporate financial officers and bankers expected long-term interest rates to decline in the second quarter of 1974, therefore, funding of capital requirements was postponed and short-term credit was used until permanent financing was arranged. However, earlier predictions regarding interest rates, inflation and economic activity became suspect toward the close of the second quarter of 1974. It became apparent that the high rates of inflation were not responsive to restrictive economic policies and the continuation of inflation had masked a significant slowdown in economic activity. By midyear, equity markets began to decline rapidly. Common stock prices continued to retreat throughout the summer and early fall and reached a low price plateau by midpoint in the fourth quarter. By mid-1975 some improvement had occurred but equity markets remained uncertain.

Consequently, many corporations face one of the most severe liquidity problems in recent history. The combination of declining demand and inflation has significantly reduced net cash flow. Higher interest rates have limited the availability of cash for debt repayment of which a larger proportion is scheduled for repayment within one to five years. Many multinational corporations have relied upon short-term credit to avoid relatively high long-term interest rates. Others have been required to use short-term funds because of insufficient long-term borrowing capacity under negative covenants in existing loan agreements or unwillingness of investors to purchase the bonds of companies considered to have already exceeded prudent debt to capital ratios. The only recourse for many multinational corporations is an increase in equity via the sale of additional shares of stock. However, the recent decline in international equity markets and the apparent worldwide investor disenchantment with equity securities has restricted the use of this alternative.

The current corporate liquidity dilemma developed rapidly and it appears that many managements failed to identify the problem until it reached serious proportions. Failure to recognize the liquidity problem much earlier is due, in large part, to a combination of the distorting effect a prolonged period of inflation has on financial information and the hesitancy of management to adopt new accounting and financial reporting techniques that more accurately reflect current financial performance.

Most accounting systems, even in multinational corporations that are considered to have sophisticated financial management, are designed to measure income and value assets on a historical cost basis, rather than current costs and cash requirements. For example, until 1974, only a small number of major corporations had adopted Lifo (last in, first out) accounting principles as a means of determining material costs or valuing inventory. The primary reason for the lack of acceptance of Lifo was the negative impact on reported earnings and/or the refusal of the governments of several countries to permit Lifo accounting for tax purposes. The emphasis on maximizing reported income and historical cost determination is also reflected in the widespread use of accelerated depreciation for determining taxable income but continued use of straight-line depreciation, or historical cost, for income reporting.

Even more important, there is significant evidence that few corporations employ current cost data when establishing price policies. To assure that current costs are reflected in price policies, fixed asset depreciation and material costs should be determined on a replacement cost basis regardless of the technique employed for tax reporting or for public auditors' opinions. It is also reasonable to assume that most corporations have been underestimating the current cost of capital in determining costs and prices.

USE OF THE INTERNATIONAL MONEY MARKETS TO OBTAIN CORPORATE GROWTH FUNDS

Most large multinational corporations attempt to use worldwide capital markets when raising funds. Ten or 15 years ago, there was only one capital market in the world—the United States—where any sufficient amount of capital could be raised.

Today, however, a worldwide banking network exists. Many non-financial corporations follow a practice of borrowing funds in the currency that will be generated by the operation in which the investment is made.

If an American company builds a plant in Belgium but plans to sell the products in the United States, it may go to the Eurodollar market to finance the plant. The revenue from the sale of the products can then be used to repay the loan directly without any risk of loss in exchange rates. If, on the other hand, the company plans to sell all the products in Belgium, it may finance the plant with Belgian francs.

It is my observation that most industrial companies do not speculate in foreign exchange. Their business is manufacturing, selling and/or servicing products. If foreign currency loans are negotiated, it is usually for commercial reasons. That is not to say that the financial officers of industrial companies do not follow currency fluctuations closely; although they buy and sell foreign currencies for commercial purposes, they also try to make the exchange at the most opportune time.

Multinational corporations have been accused of engaging in speculative currency transactions. Its critics have claimed that the multinationals have helped destabilize exchange rates by moving in and out of currencies. But, in truth, commercial banks have been much more active in this kind of exchange rate speculation than have manufacturing corporations. Banks have a more valid reason —moving in and out of currencies is a legitimate banking purpose. Very few manufacturing corporations are actual speculators in currency. They buy and sell currency for commercial purposes.

In international markets, however, manufacturers usually lead the way and bankers follow. For example, an American corporation may enter into a joint venture with a Polish state-owned organization. The corporation may require loans to purchase machinery in the United States. A contract with a U.S. machinery manufacturer may be arranged who, in turn, will arrange an Export-Import Bank guarantee for 80 percent of the value of the purchase. The Export-Import Bank may arrange for the state bank of Poland to guarantee the payment of principal and interest.

These notes are discounted at a commercial bank by the machinery manufacturer. The machinery supplier will receive payment in dollars, and the U.S. commercial bank will hold notes from the joint venture in Poland guaranteed both by the Export-Import Bank and the state bank of Poland. As a result, the U.S. commercial bank is dealing in Polish currency and participating in Polish banking and financial activities. Therefore, the bank may promote opportunities in Poland among American corporations to help expand its Polish banking activity.

Future Trends in International Financing and
Business Arrangements

The Middle Eastern countries own significant amounts of hard currency because the price of their product has increased dramatically. The dollars, Sterling, Deutsche Marks and other currencies which these countries receive from the sale of oil create vast amounts of liquidity. As a result, many oil-producing nations have developed full-time staffs to invest their oil-based earnings.

In a naïve way, it was assumed that these countries would invest heavily in equities and might even buy the controlling shares of American corporations, particularly oil companies. It is now obvious that this investment pattern will not materialize. The Arab investors are concerned about how much equity they hold in corporations in the United States and other Western nations. They realize that ownership may have nothing to do with control, particularly if a company's host nation decides to intervene in the operation of the company. So they confined a large segment of their investments to direct loans, debt instruments and real assets.

In the past, OPEC nations have also conducted much of their business through the European banks, particularly the Swiss banks. Now, however, they appear to be developing their own banking capability. For example, in a recent discussion with a large bank that represents several Arab nations, it was requested that the Arab bank be permitted to participate in underwriting syndicates for U.S. corporations, particularly debt issues, in order to sell the issues directly to investors among its member nations.

International financial activity in the future will take a somewhat different direction, particularly with respect to equity markets. Many foreign owners of dollars were hurt badly in equity investments in the late 60s; today, they are more sophisticated investors and are more discriminating. They may even enter into direct loans. In the past, several countries in the Middle East were willing to make such loans. This trend has been accelerating and will probably continue to do so.

Mexico and Brazil are rapidly developing markets, Brazil particularly. Brazil is larger than the continental United States. It has many natural resources that we were not even aware of a few years ago, a population in excess of 100 million people, and a consumer-oriented population and economic system. Billions of dollars today are being invested in Brazil, primarily in extractive industries.

Comecon (Council for Mutual Economic Assistance) countries also want access to Western technology, and a few will consider joint ventures and license agreements. In most instances, the domestic markets themselves are significant.

A third emerging market is Africa. Many African nations have begun to present opportunities for Western businessmen, but they also present some new problems. Business techniques and policies that were successful in Japan 15 years ago or business policies in use in Mexico today may have no applicability in Africa. Many African nations expect to share in the equity and have a voice in policy determination. They may not accept wholly owned foreign subsidiaries operating within their national boundaries.

U.S. companies are also becoming more knowledgeable about the role of quasi-government financing agencies; for example, the International Finance Corporation and the Export-Import Bank. It is not uncommon for a U.S. company to use the Export Credit Guarantee Department of the Bank of England, the British equivalent of the Export-Import Bank, to guarantee payment on exports from plants in the United Kingdom to customers in Mexico.

As for GATT (General Agreement on Tariffs and Trade) and other international agencies, other than the World Bank, private corporations have little direct interaction with these agencies. Trade agreements among GATT member countries indirectly affect multinational corporations; however, the common market countries have gone their own way. Today there exists, among others, the Latin American Free Trade Area, the Andean Common Market, and there is consideration being given to an Asian Common Market. Common market groups may replace the GATT concept, in which each nation enters into trade agreements. Groups of nations or regions of the world may become principal negotiating blocs. The European Common Market may negotiate with the Andean group or LAFTA (Latin American Free Trade Association) or the equivalent of a Far East Common Market. There may be more interregional negotiation in world trade rather than the GATT-sponsored trade agreements.

Hopefully, we will return to some form of fixed exchange rate. Attempts to achieve worldwide agreement on currency stabilization have been disappointing. The biggest attraction to fluctuating exchange rates is that countries are not forced to deal with many of their internal economic problems.

Under the fixed exchange rate system, if a country permitted high inflation rates to continue unabated, external pressures were brought to bear on that economy. Under the flexible system that pressure is absent. We have to accept the concept that the entire world economy cannot expand at accelerated rates for extended periods without experiencing severe worldwide inflation. One way to achieve a more stable international economic environment is to establish a worldwide agreement on appropriate rates of economic growth and inflation and return to a fixed exchange rate system among world currencies.

The flexible exchange rate system was heralded as a means of solving many of our international financial problems. We have tried it, and I judge it to have been a failure. Corporations do not want the risks associated with a fully flexible exchange rate system. How does a corporation translate the value of foreign assets or income with constantly fluctuating rates of exchange? What is a reasonable basis for translating the value of foreign investments under a flexible exchange rate system? FASB (Financial Accounting Standards Board) *Opinion No. 8* has not solved this problem.

Flexible exchange rates also encourage speculation. Admittedly, some of the criticism of speculation has been naïve; limited speculation can aid stabilization. Some of the speculation we have witnessed in foreign exchange markets recently, however, has been destabilizing, and we now recognize that.

A CASE STUDY

With this general background, let me now describe the experiences of Cummins Engine Company and the lessons learned from its foreign capital ventures.

For those not familiar with Cummins Engine Company, it is the world's largest independent manufacturer of diesel engines. In 1974, worldwide sales reached approximately $883 million. The company includes ten manufacturing plants in the United States, six in the United Kingdom, joint ventures in Brazil and India, and license agreements in Japan and Mexico.

At the close of 1967, Cummins had a total long-term debt of $73 million of which $35 million represented a revolving credit agreement with two major U.S. banks. The revolving credit agreement had one year to run at the end of which time the company had the option to convert $25 million of the credit line to a three-year term loan. In addition, the company had approximately $12 million in foreign borrowing with maturities in the five-year range.

In mid-1968, it was decided that a portion of the revolving credit loan should be funded. The decision was based largely on a conviction that at least a portion of the intermediate credit represented a permanent addition to working capital. In addition, higher interest rates and reduced credit availability were expected during the next three years.

After evaluating various alternatives, the management elected to raise $20 million by issuing a 25-year subordinated convertible Eurodollar debenture. This was an unusual move for Cummins Engine Company in two respects. First, it represented the first public security issue by the company and it occurred in Europe as opposed to the United States. Second, the dollars were raised in Europe to refund U.S. bank borrowing. This was done by creating a Foreign Investment Company (FIC) which issued the Eurodollar debentures and used the funds to purchase shares in foreign subsidiaries from the parent company. Proceeds from the sale of foreign subsidiaries were then used to retire parent company bank loans.

The debenture was underwritten by both U.S. and European investment banking firms. It carried a 5 percent interest rate and the conversion price was 14 percent above the market price at the time of issue. The balance of the revolving credit loan was retired from internally generated funds by the end of 1968.

In early 1969, Cummins' management became interested in a proposal introduced by several merchant banking firms in London. This technique permitted U.K. subsidiaries of U.S. companies to issue Sterling denominated debentures that were convertible into the common shares of the U.S. parent company. The advantage and attraction to U.K. investors was the opportunity to acquire a security that could indirectly reflect the value of a U.S. corporate stock without being immediately required to pay the dollar pool premium. Although the exchange of Sterling for dollars ultimately had to occur if conversion was to be exercised, a British investor could hold the debenture and realize a profit from the rise in value of share price of a U.S. corporation by selling the U.K. debenture and avoiding the dollar premium.

In late 1968, Cummins had approximately $12 million in Sterling denominated loans with maturities ranging from one to five years and interest rates ranging from 5 to 8½ percent. In February 1969, Cummins issued a £5 million, 25-year, guaranteed, convertible loan stock (or convertible debenture) with an interest rate of 3¾ percent and a conversion price 17 percent above the market price to refund the Sterling loans.

As a result of the two European issues, $32 million of short- and intermediate-term debt was refinanced. The company was also able to significantly lower the annual debt service requirement as a result of both lower interest costs and longer maturities. Only the Eurodollar convertible issue has a sinking-fund requirement, which begins in 1978.

By mid-1971, nearly $15 million of the $20 million Eurodollar issue had been converted and OFDI rules required the replacement of the converted portion of the issue with new foreign borrowing. In October of 1971, an additional $15 million was raised via a Eurodollar convertible issue with a 6¼ percent coupon and a 12 percent conversion premium. In March 1972, a $25 million sinking-fund debenture with a 25-year maturity was issued in the United States. The interest coupon was 7.40 percent.

In retrospect, the first two issues were successful from the company standpoint whereas the third issue could have been placed with significantly better terms had the issue been delayed only 60 days.

Reasons for selecting the convertible debenture alternative rather than straight debt in 1968 and 1971 were associated with long-term corporate objectives and needs.

Demand for Cummins products has increased at an average annual rate of roughly 15 percent during the past decade. Demands for capital required that a fully leveraged capital structure be maintained. Under circumstances of rapid growth and full utilization of senior debt capacity, convertible securities offer an attractive means of acquiring intermediate-term debt at lower cost, issuance of equity at more attractive prices, and a means of adding to the equity portion of total capital to support additional senior debt when it is required.

The decision to raise capital in the Eurodollar market as opposed to the domestic capital markets in 1968 and 1969 was based on the more attractive interest and conversion rates available in the European market. In 1971, compliance with OFDI regulations was the basic reason. There was little difference in rates between European and domestic markets; however, there was a significant difference in terms between straight and convertible Eurodollar issues.

Involvement in foreign capital markets has also provided Cummins management with some insights into problems associated with these markets. For example, it is necessary to maintain a close and direct relationship with the European investors in order to understand market conditions and preferences. Only a few U.S. underwriters have established strong positions in foreign capital markets. They tend to rely heavily on advice from European correspondents. European investment bankers, particularly the Swiss and German underwriters, play a dual role of underwriter and investor. Therefore, advice to the issuer regarding terms may be biased in favor of the investor. As a result, the issuing company must be prepared to undertake a considerable amount of research and selling effort to acquire competitive terms.

The issuing company should insist on participating in the selling campaign to assure a successful issue. Some European underwriters may resist this approach because they object to a direct relationship between the issuing company and the investor. Nevertheless, for the European investor that is not well acquainted with American firms an explanation of the company, its products, markets and management can make a significant difference in terms and acceptance of the issue.

Another problem is the relative lack of a strong secondary market, particularly in the case of Eurodollar convertible issues. American and European underwriters traditionally have not maintained a strong aftermarket support effort in the Eurodollar convertible market. Therefore, the issuing companies should encourage underwriters to provide aftermarket support and conduct periodic briefings on company progress for European investors. This is necessary if the company desires to use the foreign capital markets on a regular basis.

As would be expected, the terms are heavily influenced by currency expectations. Furthermore, the European investor does not receive the same protection provided by the Securities and Exchange Commission (SEC) for American investors. The European investor is often more heavily influenced by subjective factors and fads. However, there is a growing institutional market in Europe that will help alleviate many of these problems. In Japan, it is entirely an institutional market. Terms on dollar denominated issues in Japan are similar to Eurodollar terms and a market for convertible debentures may develop.

SOME BROADER ISSUES

Business enterprise is not as innovative in the financial area as it ought to be. There is a tendency to conduct financial affairs as we did last year or the year before, or to raise capital by identical means. There is too much reluctance to accept new approaches or ideas.

New Trends in the World of International Corporate Financial Management

Several improvements must be introduced to improve capital markets. First, a more uniform system of reporting the financial results of corporations must be established. For example, there is much criticism of businesses regarding transfer pricing. The public does not understand how a multinational corporation determines the prices it pays for the components it buys from its wholly owned plant located in an African or a Latin American nation. Businessmen are frequently asked: "How do you really go about determining the price you pay? Are your transfer prices really fair to the nations involved?" Because transfer pricing provides a means for shifting capital between countries, businesses must be prepared to disclose the methods used to determine intercompany prices. The transfer price system, because it is complex, creates suspicion and mistrust. Even financial executives become confused when asked to explain transfer pricing policies.

It has begun to be understood that a corporation can use transfer prices to reduce the taxes it pays on a worldwide basis. Many countries have already begun to insist that transfer price policies be explained and justified. Multinational corporations will be required to prepare more comprehensive and understandable financial reports, publish annual reports in more than one language and provide more heavily documented quarterly reports. They must provide more detailed explanations regarding how profits were derived—and in layman's terms.

Financial reporting is an area in which American corporations are ahead of the rest of the world. A comparison between an annual report of a publicly held U.S. corporation with the statement of a European corporation demonstrates clearly the difference in reporting requirements.

Financial Factors Considered in Selecting Countries for Marketing Expansion

In selecting new markets or manufacturing locations, financial factors are not the most significant. The initial steps in a market evaluation include a determination of the demand for products and the technical capability and resources of the countries under consideration. The size of the markets, the ability to export from those countries, the impediments to bringing in components needed in the manufacture of the product all must be considered.

Financial analysis must consider the convertibility of the currency, the stability of the financial structure, the political stability of the country, and the availability of capital.

If a country has onerous tax rules, it may be better to continue to export to that country rather than manufacture there. If a government places severe penalties on the import of components, a company may elect not to enter the market. In most instances, it is best to reach agreement on operational conditions before any commitment is made. Once investments are committed the ability to negotiate is severely restricted.

There is also growing suspicion regarding the means by which multinational corporations make decisions regarding the manufacture of components in various countries. The governments of some developing countries believe that they are at the mercy of multinational enterprises because they do not produce entire products in their respective countries and the only party that really has control is the multinational firm. On the other hand, if entire products had to be manufactured in all markets, it would severely limit worldwide investment.

Competition among Multinational Corporations

The one commodity that the third world most desires from the United States is technology. Therefore, if as a nation we are to remain competitive, we must retain our lead in technology. Substantial investment in research and development must continue but it must be done in a disciplined manner. Investments in research and development should not be undertaken without a well-conceived plan. A significant amount of the commercial success of U.S. firms in the last 20 years is a result of our lead in technology. Not only do we know how to make electronic computers, aircraft, chemical products, machinery, and other products that the world desires, but we also know how to make them efficiently in terms of cost and performance. This is the only way in which U.S. industry will retain its commercial advantages.

The Growth of U.S. Corporations Overseas

The most serious impediment to the growth of U.S. industry abroad is the way in which it conducts itself as citizens in other countries, and secondly, what it contributes to those countries. If a corporation can provide a tangible benefit to a nation in terms of technology, employment and economic and social progress, the opportunities are unlimited.

The major opportunity lies in helping to create stable and equitable economic and social systems. There is a growing realization that the ultimate goal is not how much the gross national product increased last year. There are longer range goals that encompass issues regarding resource utilization, population, income distribution and the environment that may be assigned a higher priority than economic growth.

For example, what is the composition of the gross national product and does it meet the real needs of the citizens of a developing country? Do the underdeveloped nations in the world today require many of the products of the developed world? If existing products are not suitable for developing markets, industry must be ready to modify and redesign existing products, develop new products or decline to enter the market. The concept of "pawning off" obsolete products that are unsuitable for developing markets in order to recover investment on already fully depreciated machinery will no longer be tolerated by the developing nations. In the long run, the company that strives to serve these new markets as efficiently and aggressively as its home markets will be the successful competitor.

ADDITIONAL SOURCES

See Additional Sources at end of Chapter 5.

Chapter 5

The Corporate Treasurer in a World of Floating Exchange Rates

Richard L. Bowditch*
James L. Burtle†

SINCE THE ADVENT of floating exchange rates in March 1973, foreign currency management has become a greater challenge to company financial officers. Before there was widespread floating, decisions could be made on a perhaps quarterly basis as to whether or not a particular currency would be vulnerable to a one-shot devaluation or revaluation. Now, with the wide gyrations of exchange rates under floating, it is necessary to keep most currencies under constant surveillance since there are often quick reversals of upward or downward movements. An exchange rate that is rising rapidly may shift suddenly into a precipitant decline or vice versa.

This chapter surveys, first, the financial management techniques that can be used against a background of exchange rate volatility and, second, the methods that have been used for developing the exchange rate forecasts that are essential to effective international financial management.

---

* Richard L. Bowditch is vice president and treasurer, W. R. Grace & Co., New York.

† James L. Burtle is vice president in the Economics Group, W. R. Grace & Co., New York.

FOREIGN EXCHANGE MANAGEMENT

There are two broad categories of foreign exchange management: *transaction management* and *translation management*. Transaction management problems arise mainly because there are delays between when transactions are initiated and when payments are made. For example, goods are shipped from Italy to the United States and, as in the frequent practice, are not paid in lire until after actual arrival. Thus, there is a possibility of a foreign exchange loss or gain because the lira may appreciate or depreciate in the interim period between ordering and arrival. These effects of exchange rates on the outcome of transactions show up in profit and loss statements and in variances from budgets but do not result directly in balance sheet adjustments.

In translation management, on the other hand, exchange rate changes directly affect company balance sheets whenever these are translated from one currency to another. Thus, if there is a devaluation, a company obviously realizes losses when its cash holdings of the devaluing currency are converted into dollars. Also, it is standard accounting practice in reporting company earnings abroad to translate not only cash holdings but other balance sheet items and to consider translation gains or losses as part of reported company earnings. As discussed further on, the specific accounting methods are controversial and unsettled depending on the accounting system used.

Transaction Management of Foreign Exchange

There are two principal methods used in order to avoid losses on foreign transactions: (1) *billing* in dollars or in a currency not expected to change in value in relation to the dollar and (2) *covering* the transaction on forward foreign exchange markets.

The main objection to billing in dollars is that when the dollar shows signs of weakening, foreigners exporting to the United States will often refuse to accept payment in dollars. On the other hand, if the dollar is gaining in strength abroad, it may be overly conservative for U.S. importers to pay in dollars. This procedure would forego the gains that could be obtained as a result of the devaluation of the foreign currency in the period of shipment or otherwise carrying out a transaction. For example, if a shipment of goods from Italy is payable in lire on arrival and the lira is falling, the U.S. customer will gain if the billing is in lire.

In other cases, the U.S. importer billed in a foreign currency and concerned that the dollar may devalue will want to protect himself from an unexpected rise in the value of the foreign currency. (Or, conversely, if he is an exporter billing in a foreign currency, he will want to protect himself from a fall in the value of his export receipts.) For leading currencies this kind of protection can be readily obtained by buying or selling on the *forward* foreign exchange market instead of on the *spot* market.

The spot foreign exchange market involves trading in actual currencies; the forward foreign exchange market involves trading in contracts for the future delivery of currencies. Contracts are negotiated which provide that currencies will be delivered at a specific rate on a particular day regardless of what spot rate prevails on that date. Thus a company expecting to make a payment or to be paid in a foreign currency can guarantee the exchange rate it will receive by buying or selling on the forward market.

But operators in the forward market must, of course, be paid for providing insurance from the losses that would otherwise arise from devaluations or revaluations. The charges that are made for this service are known as *discounts* and *premiums*. When a currency is widely expected to devalue, traders will ordinarily provide it on a forward basis only at a lower exchange rate than the current spot rate. This difference is known as a discount. On the other hand, if a currency is expected to revalue, traders will be willing to sell it on a forward basis at somewhat more than the current spot rate. This difference is known as a premium. Premiums and discounts may be conveniently expressed as percentages. For example, if the spot market is $2, and there is a 10 cent discount for a three-month contract, (i.e., the former rate is $1.90) the percentage discount would be 5 percent; i.e., $0.10 ÷ $2.00. On the other hand, if the spot market is at 50 cents and is selling at a 2 cent premium on a three-month contract (i.e., the forward rate is $0.52) the percentage premium would be 4 percent. (Sometimes discounts or premiums are reported on an annualized basis. This means that fractions of a year are multiplied to put the discount or premium on a full-year basis. For example, a three-month contract at 4 percent would be annualized at 16 percent [12/3 × 4%], a six-month contract at 0.5 percent would be annualized at 1 percent [12/6 × 0.5], and so on.)

In some countries—because of exchange controls or well-known prejudices against trading forward in the currency of the area—forward cover is practically unavailable or the terms of forward currency contracts may be difficult to interpret or enforce. In such cases it is usually desirable to buy the relevant contracts outside of the country in which the company subsidiary operates. Sometimes, however, a considerable amount of searching will be required, especially for currencies of smaller countries, before such contracts can be found.

For major currencies, a company can cover transactions extending out for at least one year ahead on the forward market. Contracts are usually available for one month, two months, three months, six months, and one year ahead, and occasionally for longer maturities. But it would be a mistake for a company to attempt to cover all transactions. In some cases the cost of covering a transaction may simply be too expensive compared with the risk of losses from devaluations or revaluations. For a judgment on whether to cover the foreign exchange risk of a transaction, a company should set up a currency risk statement as shown in Table 1.

TABLE 1
Currency Risk Statement

Currency	Most Likely Revaluation (+) or Devaluation (−) over Next Three Months	Probability of Most Likely Devaluation or Revaluation	Expected Revaluation or Devaluation
Germany (deutsche mark)	+5.0%	75%	+3.75%
Japan (yen)	+5.0	75	+3.75
Switzerland (franc)	+5.0	50	+2.50
Netherlands (guilder)	+3.0	50	+1.50
Belgium (franc)	+3.0	25	+0.75
United Kingdom (pound)	−5.0	75	−3.75
Sweden (krone)	−5.0	75	−3.75
Norway (krone)	−5.0	50	−2.50
Denmark (krone)	−3.0	50	−1.50
France (franc)	0	−	−
Spain (peseta)	0	−	−
Italy (lira)	0	−	−

As indicated in Table 1, a key step in developing a currency management strategy is to calculate the *expected* revaluation or devaluation. Expected revaluations and devaluations differ from *forecast* revaluations and devaluations because an expected value is the forecast value (or series of values) adjusted for the probability of it (them) occurring. In the simplified hypothetical case in Table 1 each forecast of the most likely devaluation or revaluation is transformed into an expected value by multiplying it by the probability that the currency change will actually take place.

When the expected revaluations and devaluations are compared with percentage costs of cover on the foreign exchange market, coverage is usually desirable if the cost of cover is less than the expected loss from a currency change. On the other hand, if the cost of cover is more than the expected loss, coverage would ordinarily be considered too expensive.

Two simple rules of thumb can thus be set up as rough guidance for cover against devaluation or revaluation losses:

1. *Cover against losses from devaluation or revaluation when the most likely percentage currency change multiplied by the probability of the currency change happening (the expected currency change) is greater than the percentage cost of cover.*

2. *Do not cover against losses from devaluation or revaluation when the most likely percentage currency change multiplied by the probability of the currency change happening (the expected currency change) is less than the percentage cost of cover.*

Table 2 shows examples of when to cover or not to cover a foreign

TABLE 2
Some Examples of When and When Not to Cover a Foreign Exchange Position

(1) Forecast Devaluation or Revaluation	(2) Probability of Devaluation or Revaluation	(3) Expectation of Devaluation or Revaluation (1) × (2)	(4) Percentage Cost of Cover against Currency Change	(5) Cover if (3) Exceeds (4): Do Not Cover if (4) Exceeds (3)
12%	50%	6%	8%	Do not cover
12	25	3	2	Cover
7	50	3½	6	Do not cover
12	50	6	3	Cover
12	75	9	12	Do not cover
25	25	6¼	3	Cover
20	66⅔	13⅓	6	Cover

exchange risk. But it should be emphasized that these rules are highly oversimplified. First, it is stressed that both forecast exchange rates and probabilities are judgments that can easily go wrong since they depend on forecasts, as discussed further on. Only costs of cover are the sure part of the equation. Also, more sophisticated considerations of probabilities of devaluations or revaluations may involve probability distributions instead of a single probability. Moreover, in cases usually involving large transactions, where there is a low probability of a high devaluation or revaluation (as for example, from a political revolution of an election upset), a company's management may be willing to pay a discount or premium more than the expected amount of currency change in order to have total security against the shock of a big loss. This is analogous to the willingness of many companies to buy fire or burglary insurance at more than its actuarial value.

Translation Management of Foreign Exchange

Translation problems arise in foreign exchange management when items on the company balance sheet change as a result of devaluations or revaluations of foreign currencies in countries where the company has subsidiaries from the rates which prevailed at the time when transactions giving rise to the balance sheet accounts were recorded initially.

Problems of foreign exchange translation are complicated by different systems of accounting. Nevertheless, all accounting systems do have one concept in common. This is the concept of *exposed position*. An exposed position is the amount stated in local currencies on which a company will report gains or losses if there is a revaluation or devaluation. For example, if a U.S. company has an exposed position in British pounds, it will be affected by changes in the value of the pound versus the U.S. dollar.

There are two kinds of exposed positions: *long positions* and *short positions*. If there is a long position the company holds a foreign currency or claims on a foreign currency. If there is a devaluation, the company loses, and if there is a revaluation, the company gains. Short positions are the opposite of long positions: the company has an obligation to make a payment in the foreign currency. Thus, if there is a revaluation, the company loses because the U.S. dollar equivalent of debts becomes larger and if there is a devaluation the company gains because the U.S. dollar equivalent of debts becomes smaller.

As an example, consider the company holding a long position of $1 million in a French bank account denominated in French francs. If the French franc devalues by 10 percent, the company would lose $100,000. On the other hand, if the French franc revalues by 10 percent the company would be ahead $100,000. As an example of the contrary case of a "short" position the company might have an account payable of $1 million in French francs. Since it would be using less in dollars to pay its debt it would gain $100,000 from a 10 percent devaluation. Conversely, it would lose $100,000 from a 10 percent revaluation since it would cost more in dollars to pay off the debt.

While accounting systems agree on the effects of devaluations and revaluations on long and short positions, there is wide disagreement on what balance sheet items should be considered exposed. There are many variants of foreign exchange accounting systems, but, in this chapter, at the risk of some oversimplification, only two systems are discussed. These are the current/noncurrent system and the monetary/nonmonetary system. In the current/noncurrent system short-term items but not long-term items are considered exposed. In the monetary/nonmonetary system, as the name implies, monetary items are exposed, but physical items are not exposed.

Table 3 illustrates how the exposed positions can differ between the two systems.

TABLE 3
Example of the Calculation of Exposed Positions (all items in units of a foreign currency, in thousands)

	Amount	*Not Counted in Exposed Position*	*Counted as Exposed Position in Current/ Noncurrent Accounting*	*Counted as Exposed Position in Monetary/ Nonmonetary Accounting*
Assets				
Cash	30		30	30
Accounts receivables	30		30	30
Other short-term				
financial assets	20		20	20
Inventory	50		50	0
Fixed assets	100	100	0	0
Liabilities				
Accounts payable.	30		–30	–30
Long-term debt	140		0	–140
Net worth	60	60	0	0
Exposed position.			100	–90

In both systems cash, receivables and other short-term financial assets are considered exposed "long" positions since these are both short-term and monetary items.

In both systems accounts payable are considered exposed "short" positions since they are both short-term and monetary.

Fixed assets are exposed in neither system since they are noncurrent and a nonmonetary item.

Inventory is an exposed "long" position in current/noncurrent accounting since it is a short-term item but is not exposed in monetary/nonmonetary accounting since it is a nonmonetary item.

Long-term debt is an exposed "short" position in monetary/nonmonetary accounting since it is a monetary item but is not exposed in current/noncurrent accounting since it is a long-term item.[1]

Whenever there is a devaluation or revaluation net worth is adjusted (through the income statement) for foreign exchange gains or losses to bring the balance sheet into balance, but net worth itself is not considered in either system to be exposed.

As Table 3 indicates, the accounting system used can make a significant difference. What might be an overall short position under one system would be an overall long position under another system. In the example given, a company would be 100,000 foreign currency units long under current/noncurrent method but 90,000 foreign currency units short ($-$) under monetary/nonmonetary accounting.

In many cases long positions or short positions vulnerable to losses from revaluation or devaluation can be offset by making changes in the balance sheet.

Suppose that a company is in a long position and expects a devaluation, it will be able to reduce its long position if it can cut back on its holdings of cash or short-term assets by remitting these out of the country. In some cases companies may reduce their long position by borrowing and remitting the proceeds of the loan or by putting the loan proceeds into fixed assets or other nonexposed balance sheet items. Insofar as a company expecting devaluation has accounts receivable it may attempt to step up collection of these accounts, in order to increase remittances abroad. On the other hand, it may slow down the payment of accounts payable. Both of these strategies will tend to push the company into a short position.

If a revaluation threatens a company in a short position, it will follow strategies opposite to what is done with a long position threatened by devaluation. It may extend credit more readily since such credit is expected to be repaid at a higher exchange rate. The company will tend to repay debts (rather than extend its indebted-

---

[1] In October 1975, the Financial Accounting Standards Board recommended that companies follow the temporal method for translation international accounts. This method is essentially the same as the monetary/nonmonetary method; i.e., unlike in current/noncurrent accounting, long-term debt is exposed but inventory is not exposed.

ness as when devaluation threatens). If inventory is considered an exposed long position the company may build up inventory. All of these actions would be taken with funds brought into the country.

While it may be possible to follow all of the above methods for reducing exposure, some of these strategies may involve heavy costs, sometimes greater than the losses that might arise from devaluations or revaluations. Reduced working capital, including inventories, may be below what is required for the efficient operation of a business. Borrowing, of course, involves interest costs. Also lines of credit, required for other purposes, may be used up in covering exchange risks. Pulling in of accounts receivable may result in lost customers. Delayed payment of bills may jeopardize sources of supply. Thus in many cases a company may find that it is not practicable to eliminate an exposed position by changes in the balance sheet—sometimes called changes in the *natural position*. Under these conditions, as in covering the risks of transactional foreign exchange management, exposed positions can be covered on the forward foreign exchange market. Whether or not such coverage is worth the cost will, as in transactional management, depend on whether the expected value of the foreign exchange loss will exceed the cost of cover. As with transactional management of foreign exchange the general rules oversimplify many complications. Balance sheet items will be subject to change over varying periods and thus require cover in a wide range to contract maturities. In companies operating with a large number of subsidiaries abroad management strategy may find it advantageous to use intercountry adjustments in balance sheet positions. In some cases these relationships between company subsidiaries may become complicated enough to justify using computer programs to find the optimum management plan. Such a plan cannot, however, be much better than the exchange rate forecasts that are fed into it. Thus the somewhat lengthy discussion of exchange rate forecasting in the final section of this chapter.

TAX CONSIDERATIONS OF FOREIGN EXCHANGE ACTIVITIES

It is difficult to provide guidelines for assessing the tax considerations involved in the purchase and sale of forward currency contracts. The reason for this is that the tax rules, not only in the United

States but in other countries as well, which determine the tax treatment of gains or losses realized at the time a forward contract is liquidated, are not uniform. U.S.-based multinational corporations not only have the ability to take out contracts in the name of their U.S. parents, but if local exchange control regulations do not prohibit them from doing so, they can arrange for their foreign subsidiaries to take out such contracts as well. In many instances, companies which follow this practice arrange for contracts to be purchased by subsidiaries in countries where the income tax rates are lower than those in the United States. A gain realized by a subsidiary in such a country would, therefore, be subject to a lower tax than a comparable gain realized in the United States. However, the reverse is also true. A loss sustained in the liquidation of a contract taken out in such a country would provide a lower tax benefit than a comparable loss realized in the United States.

As far as the U.S. tax treatment of gain is concerned, a recent Tax Court decision in International Flavors & Fragrances, Inc., indicates that in the future the Internal Revenue Service will consider any gains or losses sustained on forward exchange contracts to be ordinary income transactions subject to a 48 percent tax rate as opposed to investments which give rise to capital gain or loss treatment at a 30 percent tax rate. The Internal Revenue Service reasons that the buying and selling of forward exchange contracts represents a normal business activity for companies operating in the international area and that, therefore, any gains and losses realized on the liquidation of such contracts is to be considered ordinary income or loss and, therefore, subject to ordinary income tax rates irrespective of how long the contract has been outstanding.

Thus, this case, which is currently being appealed, could modify the position taken by companies that when a forward exchange contract (considered a capital asset) ran for more than six months and then was liquidated, any gain realized on the liquidation was a long-term capital gain subject to the more favorable U.S. long-term capital gain tax of 30 percent. The same was true of losses where the contract had been outstanding for more than six months.

Another consideration which is often taken into account by a company purchasing a forward exchange contract is the degree to which a company wants foreign source income for U.S. tax purposes because of the availability to the company of foreign tax credits; i.e., tax credits resulting from taxes paid abroad and available to the U.S. company in question because of the remittance from abroad in the form of dividends, royalties, and so on of foreign profits which had previously been subject to tax in their respective countries of origin.

Contracts arranged through foreign banks by a U.S. company and then liquidated abroad create foreign source income or losses. For U.S. tax purposes the U.S. income tax can be offset to the extent that foreign tax credits are available to the U.S. company.

FORECASTING FOREIGN EXCHANGE RATES

An exchange rate is the price of a currency denominated in some other currency. Like all prices, exchange rates are not easy to forecast and this difficulty is compounded by the tendency of politicians to intervene in foreign exchange markets to an even greater extent than they interfere in many commodity markets. Moreover, since World War II, the actual floating of most currencies has been limited mainly to the period since March 1973. Thus there has been relatively little experience from which to develop theories explaining exchange rate movements. With more experience, better explanations may develop, but, at this early stage, most approaches to exchange rate forecasting are eclectic using a variety of admittedly imperfect methods. These seem to fall under five headings, one of which, the lead indicator method, is further subdivided:

1. Political methods.
2. Graphic, chartist methods.
3. Lead indicators:
    a. Money supplies.
    b. Prices, purchasing power parity.
    c. Reserves:
        i. Related to imports.
        ii. Related to money supplies.
4. Balance of payments analysis.
5. Econometric methods.

The Political Method of Exchange
Rate Forecasting

A rough and ready nose count of forecasters of foreign exchange rates indicates that the majority today are using an essentially political method. Exchange rates are viewed as determined mainly by the architects of monetary policy. It is, therefore, believed necessary to have a depth understanding of the personalities and decision-making processes of the exchange rate makers: central bankers, finance ministers, key civil servants, key legislators and sometimes heads of state. What are their prejudices, social goals, political alignments and attitudes under stress? How will they weigh pressures from conflicting interest groups? To what extent is monetary authority in a country tightly held or spread out among many officials? These and other questions are certainly important because over relatively short periods the monetary authorities can certainly influence exchange rates: they can sell their own currency to bring their exchange rate down and they can sell other countries' currencies to bring their rate up. But, while such interventions can delay a rise or fall in their currencies, cases have been numerous in which governments, although anxious to prevent devaluations or revaluations, were overwhelmed by market forces. In trying to resist pressures for a devaluation, as with the United Kingdom in 1967, they may risk losing all of their gold and foreign exchange reserves. In trying to resist pressures for revaluation, as with Japan in 1971–73, they may become swamped with a foreign currency inflow and consequent inflation. Thus, it is clear that political pressures, while often important to the short-run determination of exchange rates, are not always decisive over longer periods.

Graphic, Chartist Methods of Exchange Rate Forecasting

Graphic and chartist methods have only recently been applied to exchange rate forecasting though they have a long history in attempts to analyze stock markets and commodity markets. Graphic methods are exactly the opposite of political forecasting methods. Most advocates of graphic approaches believe that all political and economic considerations have already been discounted and that only the basic trend remains significant.

We believe that the chartist view of total discounting is an extreme exaggeration though, of course, some events are discounted. But the chartists do have two advantages in their favor. First, trends, as indicated by graphic analysis, tend to abstract away random movements. Second, at any point in time the most probable (though by no means certain!) next event is a continuation along the past trend. These tendencies are both evident in Figure 1 showing daily

FIGURE 1
Daily Values of the Mark, 1974 (U.S. cents per mark)

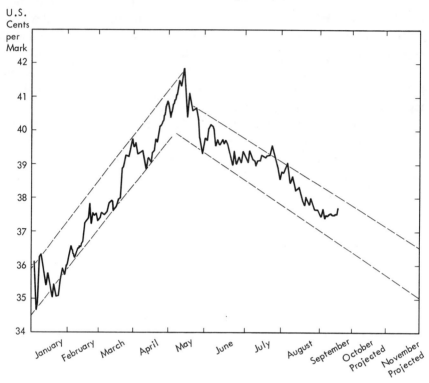

Latest date plotted: September 18.

movements of the value of the German mark from January 1 to September 18, 1974. In this case, as indicated by the bands around the trend, there is a tendency for random day-to-day movements to be within a 3.5 percent range. Also the trend within the band seems to show a clear direction either up or down for quite long intervals in the period covered. Figure 1 also indicates, however, that there was a turning point in the mark on May 14. Although some chartists talk about "resistance levels" and other somewhat opaque concepts, there does not appear to be any clear way by charting per se that will enable us to anticipate a turning point in a trend. But charting may nevertheless have a role in turning point analysis. Once a turning point is expected, on the basis of economic analysis, charting can help in more precisely isolating the area of the turning point. That area may arise when the trend changes direction and extends beyond the band—wherein direction changes are often of a random character. Toward the middle of May, for example, the mark broke through the band and reversed its direction. This analysis is, of course, not infallible since particular economic or political events can produce changes in direction that are not sustained even though they may temporarily break through the band. Nevertheless, graphic analysis, as a supplement to strong political and economic intelligence, can have a useful role in exchange rate analysis.

The need for more guidance as to when turning points are approaching brings us to a discussion of the important role of lead indicators in exchange rate forecasting.

Lead Indicators

Charting and graphic methods usually try to relate exchange rates to their own previous values. Lead indicators attempt to relate exchange rates in a particular period to some variable that has occurred earlier. Such a variable is known as a lead indicator. The main lead indicators can be broken down into two groups: (1) those which relate to the behavior of the general public of which money supply and relative price indicators are the most important and (2) those which relate to actions taken by governments and central banks of which the most important indicators are reserves in relation to imports (as a lead indicator of devaluations) and reserve changes in relation to money supplies (as a lead indicator of revaluations).

Each of these lead indicators will be considered separately.

Lead Indicators—Money Supplies

Of somewhat recent vintage but perhaps logically prior to other lead indicators is the idea of using total quantities of money as indicators of impending devaluations or revaluations. If the international money market is considered to be similar to a commodity market, currencies in excess supply are likely to have falling relative prices (i.e., devaluations of exchange rates) while currencies in short supply are likely to have rising relative prices (i.e., revaluations).

Relative currency scarcities may be indicated by relative amounts of money (including substitutes for currency such as bank deposits) in different countries, or, in a possibly more plausible form as relative rates of growth in money supplies. Countries with the most rapid growth in money supplies would be the most devaluation-prone as their currency becomes more plentiful. On the other hand, countries with slow growth rates in money supplies would be re-valuation-prone as their currencies become less plentiful.

In its strict form, the money supply approach is open to the criticism in that it pays no attention to the end purposes for which moneys are spent, whether at home or abroad, and, if abroad, whether for imports, or capital movements of foreign aid or other purposes. As a country's money supply increases (or decreases) its funds are assumed to spill over into (or be withdrawn from) the international money market without regard to the possibility that money may spill over (or be withdrawn) more rapidly for some uses than for other uses. Also, in practice, while varying rates of increase in money supplies will doubtless impinge on exchange rates, the time intervals between money supply changes and exchange rate changes do not appear to be uniform so, due to this varying lag, money supply changes tend to predict exchange rate changes too soon or too late.

Lead Indicators—Relative Price Changes (purchasing power parity)

An important lead indicator that focuses more on the consequences of money supply changes rather than on the money supply itself is the relative price level of a country, sometimes called its purchasing power parity. This is probably the oldest method of forecasting exchange rates; it was developed in its modern form after World War I in an effort to determine at what levels the then fluctuating exchange rates should be stabilized.

The logic of the purchasing power parity method is relatively simple. Countries with more rapidly rising prices will have more expensive goods and will sell less abroad. On the other hand, since prices abroad will be cheaper, the country with the greater inflation will spend more abroad. Thus currencies of higher priced countries will move in greater quantities into world money markets while, because of low exports, they will pull in very little money from abroad. The opposite will hold for low-priced countries. From this point onward the purchasing power parity theory is similar to the monetarist theory: currencies moving in greater quantities onto world money markets tend to devalue while currencies moving in smaller quantities onto these markets tend to revalue. But in the purchasing power parity theory the spillover of money onto world money markets is determined by relative prices while in monetarist theory the spillover is determined, though not fully explained, by the quantity of money per se.

Sometimes the monetarist and purchasing power parity theories turn out similarly because increases in the price level—affecting exchange rates in purchasing power parity theory—are often the result of the money supply changes which monetarists argue determine exchange rates. But neither the monetarists nor purchasing power parity theories stress enough the quite different reactions in different countries to changes in money supplies and prices. In some countries there may be a great liking for imports or other expenditures abroad so that as the money supply rises funds move abroad rapidly. In other countries as the money supply rises most of it will be spent internally. Likewise in some countries the demand for imports may be price inelastic; i.e., there is not much responsiveness to price changes. In other countries demand for imports may be price elastic; as import prices decline imports will increase more rapidly than the fall in import prices. Looking at it the other way around, some countries, usually manufacturers of consumer goods, export products with price elastic demand. Other countries, usually producers of primary products, export goods with price inelastic demand. In view of all of the variety of responses to changes in money supplies and relative prices, we can conclude that while these may be rough general indicators of exchange rate changes, it would be a gross oversimplification to depend on them exclusively.

Lead Indicators Pressuring Government or Central Bank Actions on Exchange Rates

Lead indicators based on money and prices are conceived in terms of the public's reaction to changes in money supplies or prices. Insofar as these indicators are involved in exchange rate determination, governments and central bankers do not play much of a direct role. Another approach to exchange rate forecasting, often used in conjunction with political forecasting already discussed, considers exchange rate changes to be determined by governments or central bankers reacting to economic pressures. The main pressure for devaluation is viewed as the threat of losing all gold and foreign exchange reserves and the main pressure for revaluation is viewed as the threat of inflation as an avalanche of funds moves into a country. A frequently used indicator of devaluation pressure is the ratio of reserves to imports—as this becomes lower, a country will tend to devalue rather than lose all of its reserves. An indicator of revaluation pressure is the reserve inflow in relation to the money supply. As this becomes greater the country will become more likely to revalue in order to stop inflationary pressures.

Neither reserve indicator would be meaningful in a world of perfectly free exchange rates and, in fact, they were of greater importance in the pre-1973 world of usually fixed exchange rates. Under perfectly free exchange rates governments stay out of foreign exchange markets so there are no reserve changes. But in reality, even under "floating" rates, governments do intervene in foreign exchange markets and in doing this they consider their reserve positions so the reserve indicators, considered in more detail in the next two sections, are not obsolete.

Lead Indicators—The Reserves-Imports Ratio

Clearly a country that is resisting devaluation will have to devalue when it has lost all of its reserves; i.e., its holdings of gold, foreign exchange, claims on the IMF (International Monetary Fund), and SDRs (Special Drawing Rights). This situation is like a family; it cannot keep on spending after it has run out of cash.

Ordinarily, governments will devalue before they have lost all of their reserves. A rough measure of reserve adequacy is the amount of reserves divided by annualized imports. As shown in Table 4, multiplying this percentage by 12 gives us the number of months of imports that reserves will pay for. Most countries become vulnerable to devaluation when reserves are less than enough for three month's imports.

Lead Indicators—Reserve Inflow-Money
Supply Ratios

The reserves/imports ratio is sometimes a good indicator of when a government or central bank will be obliged to let its currency devalue, but it is not useful as a lead indicator of revaluation. As al-

TABLE 4

Indicators of Devaluation Vulnerability, End-August 1974

Country	(1) Gold and Foreign Exchange Reserves ($ millions)	(2) Average of Latest Three Months C.I.F. Imports ($ millions)	(3) Ratio of Reserves to Imports*	(4) Months of Import Cover†
Switzerland	$ 7,253	$1,206 May–July	50.1%	6.0
Germany	33,131	5,879 June–August	47.0	5.6
Spain	6,335	1,419 April–June	37.2	4.5
Norway.	1,653	636 May–July	21.7	2.6
Japan	12,903	5,173 June–August	20.8	2.5
Netherlands	5,869	2,769 April–June	17.7	2.1
Belgium.	5,024	2,390 March–May	17.5	2.1
France	8,413	4,424 June–August	15.8	1.9
United Kingdom	6,842	4,067 June–August	14.0	1.7
Italy	5,363	3,624 May–July	12.3	1.5
Sweden.	1,670	1,250 April–June	11.1	1.3
Denmark.	815	782 May–July	8.7	1.0

　　* Column (1) divided by 12 × column (2).

　　† Column (3) multiplied by 12.

ready discussed, pressures to revalue a currency arise when a country's goods are too cheap and foreigners buy them in excessive amounts. The resulting inflow of foreign funds, converted into the country's own currency, swells the money supply and is thus an inflationary danger. Since most of the incoming foreign funds are converted by its central bank into the country's own currency, the inflow is reflected in the change in central bank reserves. As shown in Table 5, the change in reserves translated into the country's own currency indicates the buildup of the money supply from the foreign exchange inflow. The relative importance of this buildup is then shown by dividing through with the money supply. Higher levels of this ratio, possibly exceeding 10 percent on an annualized basis, are an indication that the government or central bank may be obliged to permit a revaluation in order to reduce inflationary pressures. (Because recent central bank reserves data are distorted by the effects of oil payments, revaluation indicators in Table 5 are shown for the first two quarters of 1972.)

Balance of Payments Analysis

For most observers of the foreign exchange scene it has become evident, especially since exchange rates began floating, that each

TABLE 5
Reserves and Money Supplies, Major Countries and Areas (millions of dollars)

	(1)	(2)	(3)	(4)	(5)	
			Increase/ (Decrease) in Reserves	Money Supply	Change in Reserves as a Percent of Money Supply, (3) ÷ (4)	
	End of First Quarter, 1972 ($ millions)	End of Second Quarter, 1972 ($ millions)	First- Second Quarter, 1972 ($ millions)	End of March 1972 (Seasonally Adjusted) ($ millions)	Actual	Annu- alized*
Denmark	$ 857	$ 786	$ −71	$ 5,710	−1.24%	−4.96%
Japan	16,664	15,844	−820	88,037	−0.93	−3.72
Italy	6,654	6,431	−223	62,852	−0.35	−1.40
Netherlands	4,361	4,388	27	10,385	0.26	1.04
Sweden	1,335	1,394	59	3,770	1.56	6.24
Belgium	3,673	3,844	171	10,726	1.59	6.36
Canada	5,890	6,218	328	19,360	1.69	6.76
France	8,469	9,398	929	51,862	1.79	7.16
Switzerland	6,744	7,018	274	14,247	1.92	7.68
United Kingdom.	7,074	7,725	651	27,703	2.35	9.40
Norway	1,209	1,289	80	2,889	2.77	11.08
Austria	2,370	2,486	116	3,607	3.22	12.88
Germany	20,027	22,940	2,913	36,585	7.96	31.84

* Actual multiplied by four.

of the lead indicators, discussed above, is too monistic an explanation of exchange rate changes. A more complete picture is needed in which all of the major elements affecting exchange rates can be brought into focus. Balance of payments analysis is one method of drawing such a picture.

A balance of payments, of which an example for the United States, 1973–74, is shown in Table 6, is simply a statement of a country's receipts and payments of foreign exchange.

In attempts to forecast exchange rates by means of balance of payments analysis we simply trace all of the inflows and outflows of spending into and out of a country. If total outflows exceed total inflows there is likely to be downward pressure on the exchange rate as more of a country's currency tends to move into international money markets. On the other hand, if total inflows exceed total outflows there is likely to be downward pressure on the exchange rate as a country's currency tends to be pulled out of international money markets. Thus, balance of payments analysis has something in common with the monetarist analysis already discussed, but, while the monetarist analysis assumes outflows and inflows to vary

TABLE 6

U.S. Balance of Payments, 1973; I and II, 1974 (in millions of dollars, seasonally adjusted)

Lines (L.)	1973-I	1973-II	1973-III	1973-IV	1974-I	1974-II
1. Merchandise trade balance	-954	-363	578	1,210	-74	-1,631
2. Other current account transactions, net	8	-577	184	427	51	-347
of which:						
3. Military transactions, net	-833	-763	-547	-58	-493	-636
4. Investment income from U.S. direct investments, abroad	2,194	2,210	2,323	2,688	4,619	4,449
5. Payments on foreign investment income in United States	-1,747	-2,100	-2,245	-2,602	-3,043	-4,492
6. U.S. government grants	-357	-645	-485	-447	-2,561	-1,395
7. Current account balance (L.1 + L.2)	-946	-940	762	1,637	-23	-1,978
8. Long-term capital transactions, net (L.9 + L. 10)	-52	-221	1,131	-2,268	1,809	-762
9. U.S. Government transactions, net	-371	94	-398	-862	1,343	388
10. Private capital flows, net	319	-315	1,529	-1,406	466	-1,150
of which:						
11. U.S. direct investments abroad	-1,815	-973	-710	-1,374	-627	-1,552
12. Foreign direct investment in United States	351	588	886	712	1,281	1,516
13. Purchase of U.S. securities by non-U.S. residents	1,718	489	1,173	670	687	397
14. U.S. bank claims on foreigners	-110	-239	227	-459	-26	-880
15. Basic balance (L. 7 + L. 8)	-998	-1,161	1,893	-631	1,786	-2,740
16. Recorded short-term private capital transactions, net	-5,104	540	413	2,367	-1,933	-3,768
17. Errors and omissions	-4,093	908	-364	925	1,209	1,979
18. Official reserve transactions balance (L. 15 + L. 16 + L. 17)	-10,195	287	1,942	2,661	1,062	-4,529

Source: National Foreign Trade Council and Bureau of Economic Analysis, U.S. Department of Commerce.

proportionally with increases in money supplies, balance of payments analysis disaggregates outflows and inflows into several components and makes a separate forecast of outflows and inflows in each component. As can be seen in Table 6, the overall balance of payments is subdivided into four different balances: the merchandise trade balance, the current account balance, the basic balance, and the official reserve transactions balance. (Other balances are sometimes used, but those discussed here are adequate for ordinary purposes.)

The *merchandise trade balance* is simply the difference between exports and imports. In the fourth quarter of 1973, for example, exports exceeded imports by $1.2 billion so the balance of payments was *favorable*. In the second quarter of 1974, on the other hand, imports exceeded exports so that the balance was *unfavorable* (as indicated by the minus sign) by $1.6 billion.

There are, however, a great many payments other than trade or investment which figure in balances of payments. These are the "other current account transactions, net" shown on line 2 of Table 6. For example, in the second quarter of 1974 this item was $347 million unfavorable. Important items in other current account transactions include military (−$636), investment income from U.S. direct investments abroad ($4,449), payments on foreign investment income in United States (−$4,492), and U.S. government grants; i.e., foreign aid (−$1,395).

The merchandise trade balance (−$1,631) and other current account transactions net (−$347) add up to the *current account balance* (−$1,978). This comprises all transactions except investments.

Long-term capital transactions, net, at $762 million unfavorable in the second quarter of 1974, is added to the current account balance for the *basic balance,* at $2.7 billion unfavorable in the second quarter of 1974. The basic balance is thus the overall balance of payments except for short-term capital movements which are often considered transitory and thus nonbasic. Long-term capital is distinguished from short-term capital since long-term capital comprises investments of more than a year's maturity as compared with short-term capital which has less than a year's maturity. In making this distinction it is assumed that direct investments and equity investments abroad will be long term. Among important long-term capital transactions are U.S. government transactions ($388) (usually foreign aid-type lending), U.S. direct investments abroad

(−$1,552), foreign direct investment in United States ($1,516), purchases of U.S. securities by non-U.S. residents ($397), and U.S. bank claims on foreigners; i.e. U.S. bank loans (−$880). Direct investments differ from security purchases in that the direct investment is controlled by the investor as in the case where a U.S. company sets up a branch or subsidiary abroad. In the case of security purchases, on the other hand, the U.S. investor will not have control over the management of the company abroad.

The *Official Reserve Transactions Balance,* at −$4.5 billion in the second quarter of 1974, was calculated as the sum of the basic balance (−$2,740), recorded short-term private capital transactions, net (−$3,768), and errors and omissions ($1,979). The official reserves balance represents the outflow of gold and foreign exchange from the United States plus the net buildup of claims of foreign central banks on the United States. In principle this item (−$4,529) should equal the basic balance (−$2,740) plus short-term capital transactions (−$3,768), but, since not all transactions are recorded, there is usually a large difference known as "errors and omissions" ($1,979).

From the above discussion of balance of payments analysis it must be evident that here is a more complete and analytically satisfying approach than any of the lead indicator methods for forecasting exchange rates. But this is cold comfort for most company treasurers and financial officers (except possibly in the largest companies) for whom an analysis of the overall balance of payments of major countries is far too costly in time and manpower resources. Usually a corporate treasurer or company economics department may attempt a balance of payments analysis of countries of key interest, but even this effort is likely to be lacking in the depth that would be ideal. A serious difficulty with balance of payments analysis is that it can easily open a "can of worms." The forecaster, instead of being faced with the problem of forecasting the exchange rate, is up against forecasting each item in the balance of payments—and some of these items, notable capital account components, are, if anything, more difficult to forecast than the exchange rate itself.

Moreover, as has been found by flow-of-funds analysts in forecasting interest rates, even if we do get a satisfactory forecast of every item in the balance of payments, this by no means guarantees a precise exchange rate forecast. Usually a forecast of an overall balance of payments deficit does augur currency depreciation and a forecast of a balance of payments surplus does auger a currency appreciation. But the extent and timing of these currency changes is by no means clear because, from balance of payments analysis per se, there are no clear indications of the extent and timing of the exchange rate changes that will tend to move the balance of payments toward equilibrium.

In the world of fixed exchange rates the problem of the timing and extent of exchange rate changes was of secondary importance. Outer limits of the possible length of time that a country could postpone a currency change, especially for devaluations, were often evident from reserve positions (though in some cases these were replenished by foreign borrowing). For the monetary authorities to make a one-shot currency change stick, it usually had to be greater than costs of cover. Under floating rates, however, there are no assurances whether currency changes will be large enough to justify the costs of cover. Also the timing by which market forces will close balance of payments surpluses or deficits remains a puzzle that is not made easier by the fact that, for most major countries, governments and central banks are also playing the market, often with the express purpose of squeezing bears and otherwise making life difficult for private holders of foreign exchange positions.

Econometric Methods

In principle, though this goal will not be attained easily and never perfectly, the basic requirement for forecasts of the extent and timing, as well as the direction of exchange rate changes, will be found in econometric models. Econometric models would relate the main components of balances of payments to key economic variables explaining them with specific numerical coefficients applying to each variable. For example, a country's imports might be related to its income and price level adjusted to exchange rate changes.

Currently available econometric studies give reasonably firm indications as to what variables are likely to be useful in explaining each balance of payments item. But on both a theoretical and applied level much work remains to be done on how balance of payments components, once forecast, tie in with exchange rates. There is a disconcerting tendency, when exchange rates are related to balances of payments, for the balances of payments to indicate more volatility in exchange rates than is actually observed. There appears to be a steadying element in the system that has not been fully identified.

As already stressed, complicated balance of payments analyses are out of reach for all but the largest companies, and the same point holds even more strongly for econometric analysis. As with much other econometric forecasting, it is likely, for exchange rates, to become the province of joint ventures, probably sponsored by consulting firms, and supported by a number of companies. But even with adequate resources available, it seems very unlikely that exchange rate forecasting, depending as it does on an entanglement of economic, financial, psychological, and political forces, will ever become easy.

ADDITIONAL SOURCES

Adler, Michael, and Dumas, Bernard. "Optimal International Acquisitions."*Journal of Finance*, 30 (March 1975), 1–20.

Aliber, Robert Z. *The Internnational Money Game*. New York: Basic Books, 1973.

Baker, James C., and Bates, Thomas H. *Financing International Business Operations*. Scranton, Pa.: Intext Educational Publishers, 1971.

Boyd, Winnett. "Business across the Border." *Financial Executive*, 41 (October 1973), 105–7.

Dawson, Steven. "Eurobond Currency Selection: Hindsight." *Financial Executive*, 41 (November 1973), 72–77.

Dent, Frederick. "The Multinational Corporation—Toward a World Economy." *Financial Executive*, 42 (February 1974), 42–47.

Dufey, Gunter. "Corporate Finance and Exchange Rate Variations." *Financial Management*, 1 (Summer 1972), 51–58.

Eiteman, David K., and Stonehill, Arthur I. *Multinational Business Finance*. Reading, Mass.: Addison-Wesley Publishing Co., 1973.

Folks, William R., Jr. "Decision Analysis for Exchange Risk Management." *Financial Management*, 1 (Winter 1972), 101–12.

Folks, William R., Jr. "The Optimal Level of Forward Exchange Transactions." *Journal of Financial and Quantitative Analysis*, 8 (January 1973), 105–110.

Fouraker, L., and J. Stopford. "Organization Structure and the Multinational Strategy." *Administrative Science Quarterly*, June 1968.

Franck, Peter, and Young, Allan. "Stock Price Reaction of Multinational

Firms to Exchange Realignments." *Financial Management,* 1 (Winter 1972), 66–73.

Franklin, W. H. "The Multinational Company: The Case against Trade Barriers." *Financial Executive,* 41 (December 1973), 58–61.

Gregor, William; Kirby, John; Robbins, Sidney; and Stobaugh, Robert. "Changes in International Capital Markets." *Financial Executive,* 41 (November 1974), 50–65.

Grossack, Irvin, M. "Multiple Currencies and Noninflationary Full Employment." *Business Horizons,* 17 (June 1974), 35–42.

Hackett, John T. "Raising Funds in International Money Markets." *Financial Executive,* 62 (May 1974), 20–27.

Hackett, John T. "New Financial Strategies for the MNC." *Business Horizons,* 18 (April 1975), 13–20.

Hackett, John T.; Seidler, Lee J.; and Patton, Arch. "Ideas for Action." *Harvard Business Review,* 52 (January–February 1974), 6–14.

Johnson, Keith, and Klein, Lawrence R. "Link Model Simulations of International Trade: An Evaluation of the Effects of Currency Realignment." *Journal of Finance,* 19 (May 1974), 617–30.

Korth, Christopher M. "Survival Despite Devaluation." *Business Horizons,* 14 (April 1971), 47–53.

Kreinin, Mordechai E. *International Economics: A Policy Approach,* 2d ed., New York: Harcourt, Brace, Jovanovich, Inc., 1971.

Lau, Sheila C.; Quay, Stuart R.; and Ramsey, Carl M. "The Tokyo Stock Exchange and the Capital Asset PRICING Model." *Journal of Finance,* 19 (May 1974), 507–14.

Lessard, Donald R. "World, National, and Industry Factors in Equity Returns." *Journal of Finance,* 19 (May 1974), 379–91.

Miller, Norman C., and Whitman, Marina V. N. "Alternative Theories and Tests of U.S. Short-Term Foreign Investment." *Journal of Finance,* 28 (December 1973), 1131–50.

Naumann-Etienne, Ruediger. "A Framework for Financial Decisions in Multinational Corporations—Summary of Recent Research." *Journal of Financial and Quantitative Analysis,* 9 (November 1974), 859–74.

Ness, Walter L., Jr. "A Linear Programming Approach to Financing the Multinational Corporation." *Financial Management,* 1 (Winter 1972), 88–100.

O'Connor, Walter F., and Russo, Samuel M. "Tax Consequences of the Currency Float." *Financial Executive,* 63 (January 1975), 48–52.

Olstein, R., and O'Glove, T. "Devaluation and Multinational Reporting." *Financial Analysts Journal,* 29 (September–October 1973), 65–69.

Petty, J. William, II, and Walker, Ernest W. "Optimal Transfer Pricing for the Multinational Firm." *Financial Management,* 1 (Winter 1972), 74–87.

Ravenscroft, Donald. "Translating Foreign Currency under U.S. Tax Laws." *Financial Executive,* 42 (September 1974), 58–69.

Robbins, Sidney M., and Stobaugh, Robert B. "Financing Foreign Affiliates." *Financial Management,* 1 (Winter 1972), 56–65.

Robbins, Sidney, and Stobaugh, Robert B. "Multinational Companies— Growth of the Financial Function." *Financial Executive,* 41 (July 1973), 24–31.

Rodriguez, Rita M. "Management of Foreign Exchange Risk in the U.S. Multinationals." *Journal of Financial and Quantitative Analysis,* 9 (November 1974), 849–58.

Rolfe, Sidney E., and Burtle, James L. *The Great Wheel: The World Monetary System* New York: McGraw-Hill, 1975.

Rolfe, Sidney E., and Damm, Walter, eds. *The Multinational Corporation in the World Economy.* New York: Quadrangle, 1973.

Root, Franklin F. "Public Policy and the Multinational Corporation." *Business Horizons,* 17 (April 1974), 67–78.

Santomero, Anthony M. "The Error-Learning Hypothesis and the Term Structure of Interest Rates in Eurodollars." *Journal of Finance,* 30 (June 1975), 773–84.

Shohet, Ruben. "New Investment Environment for the U.S" *Financial Analysts Journal,* 29 (September–October 1973), 26–33.

Smith, Don T. "Financial Variables in International Business." *Harvard Business Review,* 5 (January–February 1966).

Solnik, B. H. "The International Pricing of Risk: An Empirical Investigation of the World Capital Market Structure." *Journal of Finance,* 19 (May 1974), 365–78.

Stobaugh, Robert. "More Taxes on Multinationals?" *Financial Executive,* 42 (April 1974), 12–17.

Teck, Alan. "Control Your Exposure to Foreign Exchange." *Harvard Business Review,* 52 (January–February 1974), 66–75.

Toy, Norman; Stonehill, Arthur; Remmers, Lee; Wright, Richard; and Beekhuisen, Theo. "A Comparative International Study of Growth, Profitability, and Risk as Determinants of Corporate Debt Ratios in the Manufacturing Sector." *Journal of Financial and Quantitative Analysis,* 9 (November 1974), 875–86.

Upson, Roger B. "Random Walk and Forward Exchange Rates: A Spectral Analysis." *Journal of Financial and Quantitative Analysis,* 7 (September 1972), 1897–1906.

Verroen, John. "How ITT Manages Its Foreign Exchange." *Management Services,* January–February 1965.

Vaupel, James W., and Curhan, Joan P. *The Making of Multinational Enterprise.* Boston: Harvard Business School, Division of Research, 1969.

Walton, Horace. "Foreign Currency—to Hedge or not to Hedge." *Financial Executive,* 42 (April 1974), 48–55.

Weston, J. Fred, and Sorge, Bart W. *International Managerial Finance.* Homewood, Ill.: Irwin, 1972.

Wooster, John T., and Thoman, G. Richard. "New Financial Priorities for MNCs." *Harvard Business Review,* 52 (May–June 1974), 58–68.

Wright, Richard W. "Is the Multinational Firm in Danger?" *Business Horizons,* 14 (April 1971), 31–35.

Zenoff, David B., and Zwick, Jack. *International Finance Management.* Englewood Cliffs, N.J.: Prentice-Hall, 1969.

PART II

The Treasurer as Financial Manager

In Part II, we look at the various responsibilities of the treasurer. Part II begins with Chapter 6 by John deButts, who views the treasurer's function from the perspective of top management. He addresses himself not so much to the technical aspects of the treasurer's functions, but more to the treasurer's broader management responsibilities. These are described as financial support of corporate objectives, providing the financial viewpoint in management decisions, communicating financial information to the public, and enforcing ethical practices in financial matters.

In Chapter 7, Walter Hoadley and Lloyd Sugaski look at the treasurer's function from the viewpoint of commercial banking with whom treasurers are likely to have considerable and continuous contact. They point out that in smaller organizations, the treasurer is usually the chief financial officer and often the only financial manager. But among the larger companies, the division of top-management responsibility makes it more likely that the treasurer is involved in financial transactions rather than in financial policy and strategy exclusively. They describe "the ideal treasurer" from the standpoint of the banker. They are particularly enthusiastic about treasurers who systematically seek information and advice from many sources and then select the most appropriate financial advisers for their firm. The banker views the treasurer as the key information source on company developments and its prospective financing requirements. By working closely with his bankers, the

111

treasurer develops access to worldwide financial management services.

In Chapter 8, Brian Van Camp provides a broader perspective of the treasurer's responsibilities. He describes the basic objectives of government regulation as ensuring confidence in our economic system and enforcing the law so that all citizens are treated fairly. He describes regulatory activities in the areas of corporate criminal sanctions, licensing and surveillance, and monitoring. Specific responsibilities of the treasurer include custody of corporate funds and records, legal compliance, tax responsibilities, securities laws, insider trading, and stock exchange requirements.

Chapter 6

The Treasurer's Function as Viewed by Top Management

John D. deButts*

IN MOST COMPANIES the treasurer is responsible, to a large degree, for basic financial decisions—or, at least, for proposing viable alternatives to top management and then recommending the most intelligent and practical choice. But this function does not necessarily make the positions of treasurer and chief financial officer synonymous.

In many companies, including my own, they are not. Indeed, if there is a trend, it would appear to be in the direction of upgrading the voice and influence of financial management to the top levels of corporate decision making.

So it is mainly the duties of the *chief financial officer* that are to be considered in this discussion of the "treasurer's function." It is mainly what he must do, and be, as a full member of the top-management team, that most concerns me here. To that end, I should address myself not so much to the technical aspects of the treasurer's job, but to the broader management responsibilities which must be met by the top financial executive—regardless of title—in any corporation.

---

* John D. deButts is chairman of the board, American Telephone and Telegraph Co., New York.

There are four essential management requirements of any chief financial officer:

1. He has the rather obvious but not often easy duty to make sure that corporate goals are attainable from a financial standpoint.
2. He must contribute his financial expertise and viewpoint to management decisions.
3. He must serve as a communicator on financial aspects of the business to investors, employees, and the public.
4. Finally—and fundamentally—the chief financial officer must insist on corporate conduct that adheres scrupulously to ethical practices in financial matters.

These four requirements—assuring financial support for corporate objectives, serving as financial information input to management and output to others, plus enforcing ethical financial conduct—suggest the vital importance of the "treasurer's function" in modern corporate management.

Each requirement merits more detailed comment.

Financial Support of Corporate Objectives

There is no question nowadays that the financial executive is a key member of management; that his basic role in the decision-making process now is taken as a matter of fact in most corporate boardrooms.

As far back as 1962, *Fortune* magazine reported that "top financial officers now have a hand in everything from mergers and budgets to personnel and marketing." In 1970, half of more than 300 firms participating in a National Conference Board study said their chief financial executives were members of their boards of directors. A 1972 *Forbes* survey revealed that one third of the chief executives appointed by corporations in 1971 had backgrounds in corporate finance.

I suspect that the reason for this rather abrupt emergence of financial officers in the councils of top management is not that financing objectives had gained prime importance, but that achievement of overall *corporate* objectives in facing up to the social and economic challenges of the 1960s and 1970s had become vitally dependent on the certainty of financial support.

For one thing, terms such as "equal opportunity," "environmental protection," and "saving our cities" were becoming part of the discussion surrounding all major corporate decisions—and the financial implications were factors to be reckoned with at the highest level.

It also was becoming clear that a national shortage of capital was shaping up, and that financing of corporate growth through the 70s and 80s would be an increasingly difficult problem even if other concerns did not exist.

There have been many other factors, of course, in the growing corporate importance of high-level financial support planning. For instance, there is the new availability of decision-making data mined from computer applications in cost accounting; the greater interest of groups outside the corporation, including government and the investment community, in acquiring detailed financial information; the burgeoning complexities of taxes; the almost phenomenal new reliance on credit purchasing; the trend toward business decentralization; the growing number of mergers and acquisitions; the new forms of employee compensation—and the list goes on.

One other factor worth mentioning is that most industries, if not all, undergo changes over the years in which one or another management function takes on a critical importance. In manufacturing industries, for example, production overshadowed other functions until changing technology and emerging social demands put new emphasis on such areas as industrial engineering, pollution control, electronic data processing, and so forth.

The upshot of all this has been the greatly increased importance to business of having financial officers *within* the ranks of top management. It is not that financial considerations take precedence over broad corporate objectives in setting specific goals and policies; rather, it is simply that no company can serve the public well nor survive long unless it is financially sound. It is the financial executive's first obligation to understand corporate objectives, to participate in setting them, and then to develop his financial plan and alternatives accordingly as those objectives are translated into capital needs.

In no sense, however, does his first obligation to support corporate objectives financially imply that he would merit his job by merely taking orders—by just "digging up the dollars" at whatever cost!

The Financial Viewpoint in Management Decisions

The second necessary function of a chief financial officer thus becomes his contribution of special expertise and viewpoint as a full participant in the decision-making process.

Of course, fulfilling this function requires not just specialized knowledge in the financial area, but also the same wide familiarity with the business expected of other top-level managers. The financial executive must be, in short, a generalist as well as a specialist if his views are to carry their proper weight with his peers. Each of them naturally sees his own part of the business most clearly, and respects opinions which reflect understanding of his own goals and problems.

Since policy making belongs to the management team as a whole, its members must consider together possible alternative courses and probable results in terms of broad company goals. This includes financial policy, and the specific input of the financial officer—in all decisions—is to interpret the related impact on financing needs and the management of business funds.

He must, in fact, translate all corporate decisions into capital requirements and earnings needs because *he* holds the chief responsibility for acquiring capital funds, and for ensuring effective management of investment, revenues, and expenses to provide an adequate return on that capital.

In a very special sense, he is the investor's "ombudsman" in management—the particular person in the company who must appreciate the earnings requirements demanded by investors, and see that all policies adopted by top management are consistent with investor interests.

It almost goes without saying that meeting investor expectations is a key goal of every corporation because it is the only way to assure balanced financing and a continuing flow of capital funds to meet fundamental service or manufacturing objectives. So the chief financial officer must continually articulate earnings requirements to fellow managers and have optional financing plans on tap for every foreseeable situation.

Communicating Financial Information to the Public

The reverse of the financial executive's role as chief spokesman for the investor *within* the business is his obligation to communicate with investors, employees, and the public at large on financial aspects of the company. That obligation certainly includes *volunteering* nonproprietary financial information to those publics which have a special interest in it, rather than simply answering queries and complying with Securities and Exchange Commission regulations.

This is an age in which the public thirsts for information. Consumer groups, in particular, clamor for more complete disclosure of corporate financial policies. This puts the spotlight of public scrutiny directly on the financial officer. Inevitably, what is said and how it is said will influence public attitudes toward the company.

So the company's chief financial spokesman must not only be knowledgeable, but also an effective and articulate communicator. He must be able both in the practice of his profession and in teaching others who are less informed.

For example, it is obvious that the chief financial officer's job entails a multitude of contacts with bankers, securities analysts, share owners, rating agencies, professional associations, and so on. What may not be so obvious is that the larger public also is an important audience. There is no question in my mind but that much of the generally poor public opinion of business is due to plain ignorance of basic economics. The role of the investor in supplying capital to maintain and expand our nation's productive capacity, and the reciprocal role of profits in assuring the availability of investment capital, are badly misunderstood by most consumers. The financial officer must be concerned by this, and perform an educational function for the corporation.

The employee body is probably the most important nonfinancial audience or public the educational effort should reach. Broader understanding by the general public—of almost any corporate policy—begins with employee understanding. For instance, do employees have at least a general understanding why a company has difficulty raising equity capital when its shares are selling below book value? Do they understand why a company forced to issue large debt obligations at high interest rates faces a more difficult earnings situation? And do they understand, as they should, the relationship of inadequate earnings to their own job security? Or to the prices charged to customers?

Obviously, communicating with employees and other nonfinancial audiences requires an ability to talk in simple terms, to get rid of the jargon. This is particularly true in communicating with the public through the news media. Interpretation in layman's language must be provided—and is expected from the often-harried and perhaps less than sophisticated reporters covering your financial news.

Even if the chief financial officer may not personally handle all of the spokesmanship demands of his job, it is his responsibility to see that whoever does speak out for the company is qualified and prepared to do so.

Enforcing Ethical Practices in
Financial Matters

Finally, but certainly not least among my expectations of a chief financial executive, is his continuing obligation to assure—by edict and example and constant watchfulness—that the company conduct its financial affairs in a strictly ethical manner. For easy-to-understand reasons, money procedures tend to attract ethical as well as legal violations. Scarcely a day passes that the newspapers do not report some such trespass by someone in the business community, and we all suffer by association in the eye of public opinion.

Perhaps there is no area of any business where its public reputation for integrity, and the confidence of its share owners in the quality of management, can be destroyed more quickly than by unethical financial behavior. If one bad dream haunts top management, that is it.

Indeed, like Caesar's wife, it is not enough for a company to be above reproach in financial affairs. It must conduct itself in a manner beyond suspicion. This can be achieved only through constant internal vigilance by the chief financial executive.

In summary, the four major functions I have outlined as my basic requirements of the financial member of my own top-management team should apply, as well, to the chief financial officer of any business. The details of his job—the essentially professional requirements that his office demands—I have taken for granted in this overview. The following chapters will assess and define those qualifications and duties.

What I have tried to do is to set the theme I see as basic: that the financial executive is not a narrow specialist but a full-fledged member of the total decision-making process in top management, and that the importance of his contribution to that process cannot be exaggerated.

In the long run, any business will endure only so long as it serves the needs of its customers well, and behaves in the manner they expect. It can do this, and survive and prosper, only so long as it remains financially sound in fact and reputation.

ADDITIONAL SOURCES

See Additional Sources at end of Chapter 53.

Chapter 7

The Treasurer's Function as Viewed by the Banker

Walter E. Hoadley*
Lloyd J. Sugaski†

EVERY TREASURER who expects to be successful in the proper handling of his company's finances must have strong banking support. Similarly, no bank can hope to achieve a profitable relationship in marketing its financial services to any company without the treasurer's full support.

It follows that treasurer-banker relationships must be close and mutually beneficial to endure. This means far more than working together on important technical domestic and international financial matters, and includes a host of related planning, advisory, and confidential considerations when, in fact, close understanding is achieved. Moreover, truly effective treasurer-banker relationships will often develop into lasting personal friendships which add immeasurably to the satisfactions of all concerned.

The Treasurer's Role Varies Considerably

Any generalization about "the" treasurer clearly is fraught with danger because the treasurer's role varies considerably across companies and even within companies. In smaller organizations the

---

* Walter E. Hoadley is executive vice president, Bank of America, San Francisco.

† Lloyd J. Sugaski is executive vice president, Bank of America, San Francisco.

treasurer is usually the chief financial officer and commonly the only financial manager. Among the largest companies, particularly multinationals, the treasurer (or at times several treasurers) will regularly report to a financial vice president or chairman of the finance committee and is not the ranking financial executive. In these circumstances, the treasurer is more likely to be involved in transactional matters rather than financial policy and strategy. In addition, the largest organizations draw a necessary distinction between the accounting-controller function and the finance-treasurer function.

In these same substantial organizations, the relationships between the company and the many bank representatives servicing the firm are often channeled through a corporate "banking relationships officer." In practice this can impede or facilitate the treasurer-banker relationship depending upon the duties, authority, and personality of the banking relationships officer. From the treasurer's point of view, considerable time can be saved from routine calls by bank representatives soliciting business, seeking information, or servicing the account. From the banker's viewpoint, some time can also be saved in not having to queue up to see the treasurer. But, it is obviously more difficult to establish and maintain a close relationship with the treasurer or chief financial officer when the company banking relationships officer performs his buffer function.

The Banker Always Seeks the "Ideal" Treasurer

An experienced banker who has spent years meeting treasurers in their offices and his own understandably tends to rate or classify each treasurer relative to his ideal. Not too many treasurers probably qualify as ideal, but when they do, a mutually profitable working relationship is assured.

What does the banker look for in his ideal treasurer? First and foremost, he seeks outstanding native ability and "financial sense"; i.e., facility with numbers but also the capacity to see well beyond them to the many forces—economically, politically, socially, and psychologically—which impinge upon financial decisions. Next, the banker welcomes a knowledge of corporate finance or an open-minded willingness to be trained in the subject. And, highly important, the banker is on the lookout for the good administrator who has priorities, communicates well, and keeps on schedule.

It is still not unusual for company management to select as treasurer a man or woman who has progressed elsewhere in the organization and comes into the treasurer's office with little or no background for the work at hand. This situation often arises in smaller and medium-sized companies because the treasurer's staff tends to be limited and transactionally oriented, so that "growing your own" treasurer may be difficult. More commonly, the new treasurer is drawn from the accounting or controller staff, or from an outside source such as a CPA (certified public accountant) organization or financial institution.

The treasurer's background, the banker soon finds, makes a considerable difference in the approach to be taken in servicing the company account and in the results to be expected. Most treasurers are broad gauged, forward-looking individuals who eagerly seek information and advice from many sources before making their decisions and reward the bankers who are most helpful with profitable banking business. These treasurers, of course, are ideal for the banker. Too many treasurers, however, adopt a rather defensive attitude, attempt to conceal their lack of understanding of complex financial matters, unfairly and openly play one banker against another and ignore the practical consideration that the bankers servicing the account must show a profitable overall relationship over time. In recurrent times of tight money conditions, it should not be surprising to anyone that the banker will make a greater effort to provide assistance to those organizations and treasurers which have worked closely with the bank during times when money markets were easier.

The typical banker is always anxious to help a new treasurer get started well on his job. A great deal of helpful firsthand information and advice are available for the asking. Many banks sponsor treasurer visits to their headquarters, branches, or service facilities to assist in the practical training of corporate financial officers. In addition, bankers can readily introduce many treasurers to each other who might not otherwise have the opportunity to meet and exchange ideas. The "ideal" treasurer carefully evaluates the banker training aids which are offered and makes full use of the ones which seem most likely to be of assistance.

A seasoned banker knows from experience that the successful treasurer never forgets that his primary job is to facilitate the financing of his company's business. Finance is thus seen always to be the *means* to the end of profitable regular business operations and not as an end in itself. Treasurers—especially new ones—are tempted to try to build a record of short-term financial (i.e., borrowing and investing) results sometimes without full consideration to risk, liquidity, and longer term relations with credit sources. Obviously every treasurer has a responsibility to his company to obtain the lowest borrowing rates and highest return on investments possible, but commensurate with all the other variables which will affect his company's ability to command funds from financial markets whenever they are required. For, only as a treasurer can keep his company adequately supplied in funds at all times is he fulfilling his primary responsibility—at least from the banker's viewpoint.

What a young or inexperienced corporate financial officer may not readily recognize is the possibility of a fairly sudden corporate need for funds; for example, to meet a major new investment or to cover an unexpected loss. The ideal treasurer endeavors to establish a close understanding and rapport with his banker or bankers so that all the essential credit information for a loan is up to date and at hand. This continuing relationship also means a minimum of surprise in his requests and a constructive atmosphere for exploratory discussions of financial problems, policies, and programs long before final decisions have to be made. This is the essence of good financial planning for all concerned.

The competent banker welcomes—indeed, is disappointed—if he is not given a stream of challenges by the treasurer. The banker wants to prove that his organization can meet the test of difficult financial problems at least as well as his competitors.

It cannot be stressed too much that the treasurer-banker relationships which are enduring and most productive are those which produce a reasonable profit for both. One-sided deals seldom last very long and are resented. The treasurer should be aware that the company's reputation as well as his own are built relentlessly transaction by transaction through time and have a material effect on the eagerness with which an account is solicited and serviced even under the most intensely competitive conditions. Neither the treasurer nor the banker can forget the other's problems at any time.

The Treasurer Is the Banker's Key Information Source

Most bankers look to the treasurer as the principal source of information regarding the company and its banking requirements. It is quite natural for the banker's opinion of a company to be significantly influenced by the quality and timeliness of the information received. In the absence of the necessary tools to make a reasonable judgment, the banker inherently cannot be responsive or at least tends to become unduly conservative. The treasurer obviously knows when his banker is not responsive, but he may not be aware that the banker is being conservative because he knows too little about the company. One of the foundations of a good working treasurer-banker relationship is a steady flow of information to the bank and vice versa even when the company is not using bank credit.

The quickest way to jeopardize a good banking relationship is to inject the element of surprise unnecessarily. Bankers understand why they cannot have advance notice of botulism in a tuna cannery or of a sudden opportunity to effect a very desirable acquisition. However, they cannot be expected to appreciate an urgent request to fund an acquisition which the company has been negotiating for a considerable time without their knowledge, nor can they be expected to sympathize with an earnings report which is considerably worse than they have been led to expect.

Communications are, of course, simplest when a company has only one banker. In this situation, the company and the bank are almost always in close proximity, and it is unusual if several of the principal officers of each are not reasonably well acquainted. Each has an opportunity to follow the fortunes of the other in numerous ways other than through personal contact or the formal exchange of information.

The situation becomes more difficult when companies do business with several banks and especially when one or more of the banks is located at some distance. In these circumstances the treasurer must be concerned with developing proper techniques for dealing with multiple independent line banks or with several banks in consortium where one acts as agent. While it is entirely proper to confine initial discussions of financing concepts with lead or agent banks, treasurers should not allow plans to progress too far before soliciting input from all banks which would be affected. Bankers prefer to make their own analysis and not rely on another bank simply because the other bank has a larger share of the companys banking business.

Proper understanding of a business requires personal contact with the treasurer and frequently with other senior officers. All bankers, regardless of how small their participations in a credit may be, need access to key company officers to properly analyze credit requests and to effectively market other bank services. Every company should take advantage of the expertise which each of its banks has to offer. When a treasurer insists on dealing with all of his banks through his principal bank he can be certain that if the other banking relationships are not in jeopardy they are at least far from perfect. Therefore, representatives of each of the company's banks should be encouraged to visit the company from time to time, and the treasurer should systematically visit all his banks.

One technique which many companies employ successfully is to sponsor an annual meeting of representatives from all of their banks with the principal officers of the company. This meeting affords an opportunity to review the annual game plan with key functional division and subsidiary heads.

Treasurers should appreciate the fact that near- and long-term capitalization plans must be understood by the banker even though banking accommodations may be limited to short-term credits. For example, the bankers regularly should know the owner's objectives in a closely held company. Without information to the contrary, he will probably assume that growth will only be supported by retained earnings. If, on the other hand, he knew that a public offering of additional shares was planned, he might accept higher temporary leverage.

Bankers expect treasurers of publicly held companies and those which obtain long-term funding from institutional investors to work closely with investment bankers. In the absence of information to the contrary, the investment banker and the commercial banker each assumes that he agrees essentially with the other. It is incumbent upon the treasurer to satisfy himself that this is the case or to bring the parties together so that they can reach a meeting of the minds. This is essential to assure that long-term debt issues and the attending indentures are designed to be compatible with the company's short and intermediate credit requirements.

An experienced treasurer is always aware of significant changes in his company's production, marketing, and procurement plans. He knows that he must be privy to these in order to evaluate their financial implications. Still, most bankers can recall numerous instances where companies have strained their banking relationships by incurring increased credit needs well before consulting with their bankers.

The type and extent of company financial reports which a banker requires will vary greatly with the company, the industry, and the terms of the credit in question. If we assume that the banker's credit file contains adequate historical data, the banker then needs a forecast and subsequent reports which will permit him to follow the firm's progress. When applicable, special reports, such as certificates of conformity to loan agreements and collateral condition reports, will be needed. It is most important that the banker and the treasurer agree on what information is necessary and that it will be prepared carefully and submitted on time.

Credits of any size must almost always be supported by annual financial reports with the unqualified opinion of a CPA. In many complex situations bankers find it advantageous to have the treasurer arrange meetings of the banker, treasurer, and the CPA for the purpose of obtaining a better understanding of the financial statements.

It has been mentioned that bankers like to make their own analysis and not rely on the judgment of other bankers, and by the same token bankers often desire to make an independent analysis of the value of certain classes of a business's assets and not rely on the CPA. Accounting conventions simply do not permit the CPA to prepare a statement which reflects the true value of fixed assets in many cases. Judgments on how inventory should be treated when learning curves are involved and on the probable cost to complete a construction contract are always somewhat subjective. The past few years have brought an accelerated trend toward large asset write downs. These have resulted in serious capital impairment for many companies, and they have created an increased awareness on the part of bankers of the necessity to "get behind the figures." The banker should be able to look at a balance sheet and visualize the fixed assets as well as to understand the true nature of the inventories and receivables. Treasurers should recognize that in many cases the banker has a need for this firsthand knowledge which he can best obtain by visiting the facility and talking with various corporate officers.

The Treasurer Usually Controls His Company's Banking Relationships

The banker who endeavors to sell his bank's services to any company almost instinctively seeks out the treasurer to contact because experience shows that the treasurer generally has the greatest influence over which bank or banks will be used. Sometimes, of course, the selection of a bank will be made at a higher level, even by the chief executive officer if he feels it is advantageous to do so.

Nevertheless, the treasurer and his staff are the men and women who in fact determine how satisfactory any banking relationship will be on a day-to-day basis. Few treasurers are pleased to have some higher executive force them to do business with a bank. So, an enduring relationship really depends heavily upon a bank having smoothly functioning procedures and personnel operating on behalf of the company at all times.

From the banker's viewpoint, the treasurer is the customer, or in industrial terms the purchasing agent of the bank's services. Unless the treasurer buys what the banker has to offer there can be no sale and hence no possible profit for the bank.

Each banker realizes that the treasurer selects his bank or banks on the basis of potential helpfulness to the company. Except in the case of the smallest companies in areas where branch banking is not permitted, the treasurer will have a choice—often exceedingly wide—of which bank or banks to select. Accordingly, competition among banks is a strong fact of life. At the very least, therefore, the treasurer can compare services *offered* by various banks. In the common situation where two or more banks are used, the *actual* services can be compared and evaluated.

The banker soon learns that no creditworthy account can be taken for granted. Other bank representatives are always waiting to take over accounts which have any appreciable profit potential. The first step of success for any banker is to have a solicited company "open" an account. His subsequent success will be measured by how well (1) the account grows profitably in deposits, loans, service fees, and so on and (2) penetration increases in many of these same measures among all the competing banks serving the company.

A limited number of significant bank relationships is much to be preferred than a proliferation of smaller ones. This is simply because banks almost inevitably will assign their best talent to key accounts where it can be most effectively used. Moreover, the company concentrating its banking is certain to receive the best bank service and, especially to the extent volume permits, savings from lowest costs as well. Perhaps even more important, where there is established credit and a substantial treasurer-banker relationship, the company can expect first consideration when money is tight.

Some treasurers seem to look upon their bankers almost as competitors in handling funds rather than as part of their supporting team. Such treasurers constantly press extremely hard for a few "basis point" gains on every transaction but frequently overlook the far greater importance of a continuing mutually satisfactory working arrangement in which each side encourages the other to make its best effort for all concerned.

It is customary and important for new treasurers to reappraise all existing banking relationships. Frequently, the new treasurer assumes that his predecessor was a poor negotiator with bankers and seeks to prove he can bargain harder. No banker can properly object to this repeated "breaking in" experience with new treasurers. Nevertheless, there is a danger at times that the new treasurer will disrupt overall banking relationships by effecting dubious changes without a full understanding of prior considerations. But, unless the banker can satisfy each treasurer—new or old—and keep him satisfied, he knows his future is in jeopardy.

The Treasurer Negotiates for Bank Credit

The treasurer is the company's principal negotiator for bank credit. Conflicts often arise because each party fails to appreciate the other's real limitations on his freedom to act. The banker should be certain that the treasurer knows the bank's legal and any self-imposed lending limits as well as any particular policies or philosophy his bank has regarding term loans or loans to that particular industry. The treasurer then must be certain that his banker understands any company policies or any regulations imposed by governmental supervisory agencies which could affect the negotiations.

Loan agreements, while only occasionally employed as support for short-term lines of credit, are almost always required for term loans. When a term loan is approved, the banker has concluded that he is satisfied with the present status of the company but wants to be able to accelerate the maturity of the credit in the event there are adverse changes in the company's condition. Other than pricing, there is really nothing to negotiate except the definition of adverse changes.

The basic purpose of the loan agreement is not to constrain the company but rather to permit the credit to be renegotiated in the event of changed conditions. An agreement implies complete mutual understanding and should not be executed until that in fact is the case. Treasurers should not be reluctant to request amendments from time to time. Experienced bankers know that it is not possible to foresee all eventualities and generally will agree to reasonable amendments without pricing increases or other penalties.

The request for guarantees to support loans is in many instances puzzling to a treasurer. Everyone understands the banker's desire to have a strong parent guarantee the indebtedness of a weak subsidiary. But why might the banker want an owner to guarantee a loan to his corporation even though he has few assets other than the stock in that corporation? The answer is that it affords reasonable protection against the diversion of the corporation's assets to the owner. In some cases there are simply too many ways for such diversion to take place for the banker to rely on the rule of law which states that the debt follows the assets.

Frequently lenders ask that loans to holding companies be supported by the guarantee of the subsidiaries. When consideration for such a guarantee can be established, this procedure puts the lender on a par with the creditors of the subsidiaries. Without a guarantee from a subsidiary, the lender to the holding company can at best look to the equity in the subsidiaries for support. General partners are frequently asked to guarantee the debts of the partnership even though the general rule is that they are fully liable in the absence of a guarantee. The purpose of a guarantee in this instance is to enable the lender to proceed against the general partners in the event of default without first exhausting his remedies against the partnership.

There is a continuing need to establish a common view of collateral values. Sometimes collateral is taken as a means of limiting the borrower's potential for acquiring additional debt. Other times it may be taken to satisfy the bank regulatory authorities when credit is extended on a continuing basis without periodic cleanups. Generally speaking, however, collateral is taken to insure a means of collecting loans when companies fail. Therefore, the banker usually establishes collateral values by visualizing the company in liquidation rather than as a going concern. To understand the banker's approach to evaluating collateral, let us consider a few typical questions we might ask about certain classes of assets:

A. Accounts Receivable
    1. Are reserves for losses reasonable in light of the current aging?
    2. What is the sales returns and allowance record?
    3. Is the company selling to some of its suppliers thereby creating a right of offset?
    4. Do the sales consist of stock items sold under purchase orders or do they represent deliveries in partial fulfillment of production contracts?
    5. If the receivables represent construction contract billings, what are the rights of the assignee vis-à-vis the bonding company?
    6. Is the company liable to its customers under contract to service the merchandise which it sells?
B. Inventories
    1. What is the typical mix of finished goods, work in process, and raw materials?
    2. Do the company's customers have ready access to alternative sources?
    3. Is the raw material readily salable such as sheet steel of standard sizes, or is it highly specialized such as electronic components?
    4. Does the inventory include start-up cost which will only be recouped through long production runs?

Finally the banker is aware that if the company fails it might continue to operate under bankruptcy proceedings. In that event, collateral of any type may not be readily accessible and its value could diminish substantially before the bank can take possession and sell it.

The high volume of acquisitions during the past decade has resulted in numerous requests for loans supported by the stock of acquired companies. Many such loans have been made and repaid. Nevertheless, bankers view such collateral conservatively. The equity in a company is there to protect the company's creditors. When that equity also supports the parent's acquisition debt pending a favorable equity market, it is doing double duty.

There is a wide range of views on the proper role of subordinated debt in a company's capital structure. All too frequently bankers and treasurers view subordinated debt in almost the same manner as equity. Reasonable amounts of subordinated debt can be properly utilized in most companies. It is essential, however, that it be recognized for what it is, an obligation which must be serviced if the company is to remain viable. Good bankers and treasurers do not lose sight of the fact that holders of subordinated debt have the same recourse to the bankruptcy courts as do holders of senior debt.

As money markets and financial structures change, banks' attitudes toward pricing also change. Demand deposit balances are becoming a less important source of funds for banks. There is an accelerated trend toward banks' buying money and working on the spread. This provides banks with more flexibility in the matter of pricing and permits alternatives to earlier fairly rigid bank requirements which some treasurers have found objectionable. Banks are seeking a realistic yield on loan transactions and will tend to become more specific in pricing loans.

The Banker Seeks a Successful Portfolio of Accounts

The treasurer should recognize that the banker is most interested in the success and growth of his portfolio of accounts and that he and his colleagues have considerable experience to guide their decisions. When the banker observes exceptions to good financial planning and business practices, he cannot dismiss them lightly. Many of the serious problems which companies experience could be greatly diminished and possibly avoided if the banker's counsel had been given more serious consideration.

Banking is very competitive and most bankers from time to time extend credit even though they strongly disapprove of some of the borrower's financial practices. Fortunately for borrowers, as well as bankers, this tendency is becoming less prevalent, possibly because the credit crunches of 1966, 1969 and 1973–74 demonstrate that bankers can honor their convictions without sacrificing earnings.

A close study of the history of serious problem loans shows that such loans frequently were not the result of lack of recognition of poor company practices by the banker but rather the fact that the banker erroneously assumed that the company would soon abandon these practices, underestimated the magnitude of the potential problem, or underestimated the speed with which problems would materialize and become acute.

To ensure the greatest cost benefits, the treasurer should monitor all of the company's transactions involving the acquisition of bank services. He should be certain that his principal banks have the capability directly or through correspondents to provide all necessary bank services in an efficient manner. Poor banking and related financial advice can be costly at any time, but especially in present and foreseeable unsettled times.

Because of the multiplicity of banking services, it is frequently necessary for the company and the bank to establish numerous contacts at different levels. The treasurer and his principal bank contact should orchestrate the entire relationship in order to ensure that the company receives the most efficient, economic, and satisfactory service.

Banks Expand Worldwide Financial Management Services

Worldwide expansion in trade and investments has made the jobs of both the treasurer and banker more complex and necessitated a vast increase in financial services in all parts of the globe in recent years. The larger banks have both led and followed their customers abroad, but not without a great deal of negotiation with indigenous government financial authorities because of the pioneering work involved.

In many instances international bankers have taken the initiative to inform treasurers about money and related requirements for overseas operations which are all too often at variance from domestic requirements. In other cases, the corporate treasurers and other executive officers have directed their questions to bankers who in turn have had to seek reliable answers from their own staffs and authorities in many lands—Eastern socialist as well as Western democracies. The close association of the banker and the treasurer has been reinforced as their respective organizations have pursued new international opportunities in close cooperation.

The varying strength in the dollar and the rise of nationalism in most countries have presented many new challenges to all U.S. organizations with overseas operations in serving both indigenous national customers and U.S.-based customers. Treasurers have had to decide how much business they would do directly with local bankers and how much with and through their regular U.S. banking organizations.

Because of significantly different governmental regulations over financial transactions and institutions in different countries, the banker's ability to render financial services to the treasurer has also varied. In some respects, international banks have greater opportunities to service customers outside the United States than within our country. This is particularly true through affiliates dealing in investment or merchant banking. But on the whole, the strength of banker service to any company always rests with (1) knowledge of the customers needs—hopefully, well in advance—and (2) ability to marshal information, resources, and advisory skills from within and outside bank headquarters on a global scale.

Some of the greatest challenges to both the treasurer and the banker have resulted from the breakdown in the Bretton Woods post–World War II international monetary system. This has meant emerging greater flexibility and, hence, greater risks in exchange rates, changing currency parities through devaluation of the dollar and revaluation of many other currencies, enormous surging of international money flows, and a proliferation of government financial control measures. The problems associated with recycling the so-called petrodollars from the oil-producing nations and related balance of payments deficiencies of many developed and developing countries have only compounded the complexity of most international financial transactions. In addition, simultaneous worldwide inflation and recession have placed new stresses in global financial markets and institutions.

In these circumstances the treasurer's responsibilities have become much more exacting and his needs for professional financial expertise vastly increased. For example, so long as exchange rates remained essentially fixed against the background of a confident dollar, the corporate financial officer sensing an impending change in the value of some particular weakening currency could with minimum risk actively engage in the foreign exchange markets. In most cases, the unfolding events proved the treasurer to be correct and he showed a considerable profit for his foresightedness. Today, however, in the absence of fixed exchange rates and full convertibility of the dollar, the risks to the treasurer in direct dealing in the exchange market are infinitely greater. Such risks can prudently be accepted in fact only by substantial financial organizations which make a regular business of international money.

Prospects are for gradual resolution of international monetary reform and related problems over the years ahead. Hence, the specialized as well as regular services of the banker to the treasurer should become still more significant to the extent that worldwide banking organizations can in fact make an increasingly important contribution to the treasurer's international function in his company. Similarly, within the United States highly important changes are taking place across the spectrum of financial markets and institutions. Every treasurer will find it advantageous to keep abreast of all key developments because they may well influence his future relationships with banks and other lending-depository financial institutions.

Congress is expected to take some eventual action as a result of the *Report of the President's Commission on Financial Structure and Regulation* (1971) and a number of later recommendations for reform. The changes no doubt will come slowly, but may well affect, for example, the ability of lenders to make loan commitments, the freedom of corporate borrowers to acquire funds, and the relative competitive positions of financial institutions heretofore considered as principally serving specialized markets. Federal credit allocation laws are continually being proposed. Here again, it is evident that the treasurer and the banker have major common interests as well as a "seller-customer" relationship.

Bank holding companies and overseas financial institutions are in the process of opening a whole new horizon to worldwide financial services designed to assist the corporate financial officer and his team in carrying out their increasingly complex money management responsibilities. Bankers are obviously interested in selling these new services, but the key will always be to market them to meet the needs of individual companies in specific geographic, regulatory, and other environmental circumstances.

In most respects the new services of banks, especially in total money management across major currencies and maturities, have been developed because of specific needs of treasurers. Thus the close relationships which bankers have with many treasurers give rise to innovations in banking services to the mutual benefit of all concerned. Accordingly, it is clear that the treasurer should make his *potential* as well as actual needs known promptly to his banker. Concurrently, the banker has the challenge to help anticipate corporate financial service needs so as to be prepared to meet all needs promptly whenever and wherever they arise.

What complicates this matter of anticipating new financial service needs is the common experience that many treasurers are not included in the corporate planning process until a fairly late stage, and sometimes not at all. Obviously, this situation often leads to a scramble after important corporate decisions have been made to ensure that related financing and processing problems do not impede implementation of the corporate plans.

As seen by the banker, the treasurer must be called upon to do more financial planning. His banker must be still more helpful in the planning process. Banking and finance, especially on a national and worldwide scale, can only become more complex, demanding greater professional specialization and increasingly sophisticated technology. In these circumstances, banks and other financial institutions should be able to minimize risks for customers—including the largest—much more than the customers can do for themselves. That is why banks expect to remain a vital part of the economy over the years ahead.

Summary Observations

The most important question to be faced by the treasurer and the banker over the years ahead would seem to be how best they can work together in their mutual interest—of their respective organizations and their own personal relationships.

In current and foreseeable intensely competitive and uncertain domestic and global market conditions, the treasurer who can effectively manage his relations with banks and other financial institutions will have a continuing opportunity to acquire more competent financial assistance, not only in the United States but also in leading nations across the world.

Periodic acute money and credit tightness in the world's financial markets will necessitate more customer selectivity on the part of bankers and other lenders from time to time. This will be particularly true so long as overall worldwide capital requirements remain high and unsatisfied—which probably means for quite some time. Each treasurer accordingly, will find it highly advantageous to ensure continuing borrowing arrangements to obtain the funds he may need.

Monetary authorities seem increasingly concerned about lenders extending "excessive" credit during periods of restrictive monetary policy. Accordingly, it will be more than ever important for treasurers and bankers to do advanced planning to meet corporate financial requirements, rather than to assume that funds will always be available for creditworthy borrowers for whatever purpose may seem convenient.

Both treasurer and banker can expect to face an even more critical, not too well-informed, and impatient public whose day-to-day interests will always be under close surveillance of political leaders and candidates. The treasurer and banker must heed their common interests in helping the public better understand the role—long as well as short range—of private finance in increasing jobs, improving living standards, and promoting a higher quality of life within our system of enterprise.

The days of routine operational treasurer and routine transactional banker functions dominating corporate finance are rapidly disappearing. What lies ahead certainly are dynamic challenges filled with new risks and opportunities but inseparably linked to more sophisticated banking and finance at a time when human values will continue to rise relentlessly. Thus, the days of allowing finance to seem cold and impersonal are also over.

Only by working together can the banker and his treasurer customer—and the treasurer and his banker supporter—meet these challenges. There is really no other alternative. The past record of cooperation has been quite good, and we are confident the future will see more of the same.

ADDITIONAL SOURCES

See Additional Sources at end of Chapter 27.

Chapter 8

The Treasurer's Function as Viewed by the Government Regulator

Brian R. Van Camp[*]

AN EXAMINATION of the corporate treasurer's responsibilities to, and relationships with, governmental agencies at all levels should be preceded by a discussion of the basic relationship between the government, acting for the people as a whole, and the corporation or business entity. This is because most regulatory authorities impose few obligations upon the treasurer himself, but rather require certain actions by the corporation which are then assigned to the treasurer for performance or fulfillment.

GENERAL RESPONSIBILITIES OF THE TREASURER

In the broadest sense, the people of the United States and their governments at various levels look to the business community to provide for their economic needs, these being distinguished from certain social or spiritual needs. The business community has historically performed this function well. First, our founding fathers believed in the free enterprise system, and therefore left plenty of

---

[*] Brian R. Van Camp is a member of the law firm, Diepenbrock, Wulff, Plant & Hannegan, Sacramento, California. He was Commissioner of Corporations, State of California, 1971–74.

room and protection to the private entrepreneur. Also, over the years the business community has enjoyed the confidence of the public in both the basic quality of the goods and services produced and the fairness of the way in which business dealt with people as consumers, employees, and/or shareholders.

Business and Government

I suggest that today government has two basic premises for regulating the business community. First, it should attempt to ensure that confidence in our economic system will be retained (or regained, depending on your view of the current state of public trust in our corporate institutions), and second, it should exercise police powers to correct individual inequities or unfair treatment of citizens by the businessman. Naturally many governmental regulations serve both purposes, and, unfortunately, in my opinion, there are many which serve neither purpose.

In addition to these basic roles, modern critics of the business establishment have also suggested that the government should require that American corporations fulfill several other social responsibilities, such as providing jobs for all of our citizens, cleaning up the environment, reducing or eliminating racial discrimination and, of late, serving as an instrumentality of the nation's foreign policy through sales to or boycotts against certain other countries. Obviously, the scope of this chapter does not lend itself to a discussion of the legitimacy of these expectations, except to note that the role of the corporation in America is a changing one and, in keeping with its role in the nation's economy and social structure, an expanding one. (See Chapter 53 for further development of these themes.)

Simply put, however, corporations will continue to be the subject of attack as long as citizens perceive them as (*a*) not paying their fair share of taxes, (*b*) amassing a disproportionate share of wealth, (*c*) misrepresenting their financial state of affairs, or (*d*) defrauding or actually abusing their customers, investors, or employees. What cost, for example, to the confidence in businessmen have we seen as a result of the recent calamities brought about by the insider trading or dealing at Texas Gulf Sulfur and Geo-tech Oil and Gas Limited partnerships, the bankruptcy of the Penn Central Railroad, the frauds perpetrated by the Goldstein-Samuelson commodity option sham, the multilevel franchise schemes of the late William Penn

Patrick and Glenn W. Turner, and, of course, the granddaddy of them all, Equity Funding, involving 60,000 phantom life insurance policies? The public investor who was caught in such losses probably will sit out of the capital marketplace for a good while, having lost both treasure and faith in the system.

At the same time we all have a significant interest in the ability of business to form new capital to respond to our pressing economic needs. Immense amounts of capital are required today, for example, to attempt to become self-sufficient for our energy needs, for the continued modernization and expansion of our agricultural production, for the development and construction of modern transportation systems for both people and commerce, for the research and development of improved ways of delivering health care services to a broader spectrum of citizens, and even for the continued administration of our state and municipal governments. In order to meet any of these needs our citizens must have confidence that they can bring their savings to the capital markets without fear of unreasonable risk resulting from the misconduct or ill motives of either the capitalistic system or those who are responsible for husbanding the funds so invested. The governmental machinery established to regulate corporations and the capital marketplace is an attempt to secure that confidence.

Each level of government in our country has several different means of attempting to ensure compliance by the business community with its basic objectives, ranging from the simple business license ordinance at City Hall to the complex antitrust statutes of the federal government. In general, these laws fall into three categories: criminal sanctions, imposition of standards prior to entry into certain businesses, and regulation of ongoing financial and business activities. While the tax laws are not regulatory per se, their immense influence on directing business activity should also be noted.

Corporate Criminal Sanctions

In the area of criminal sanctions, the corporate official is governed not only by the traditional criminal statutes against fraud and theft, but also by some peculiarly white-collar statutes which prohibit activities such as embezzlement, misappropriation of corporate funds, insider dealing or trading of the corporate stock (which will be discussed later), or selling securities without a permit or license. In addition, corporate officials are subject to individual criminal prosecution along with the corporation if they violate certain non-financial regulatory provisions, such as the Environmental Protection Act, dealing with pollution; the Civil Rights Act, dealing with equal-opportunity employment; the Federal Campaign Practices Act, outlawing corporate contributions to political candidates; the antitrust laws, prohibiting anticompetitive practices; and, obviously, the Internal Revenue Code, just to mention a few.

Licensing

The second method of regulation in the governmental quiver is the requirement of securing a license or permit before entering into certain kinds of businesses or professions or before engaging in certain business transactions. Included among the former are the local business license, the state examinations required of attorneys, doctors, barbers, auto mechanics, and many other trades or professions. Other examples are the charter or license required of persons about to engage in certain businesses involving a finite public resource. These include common carriers, such as railroads, airlines, bus, ship and trucking companies or operating a radio, television, or telegraph business. In such cases permits, routes, tariffs or airwaves must be obtained from the Interstate Commerce Commission, the Federal Communications Commission, the Civil Aeronautics Board, state public utilities commissions or other appropriate bodies.

If a business will affect the public's funds, health, safety or morals it may also be required to obtain a charter or license. These are required prior to commencing business as a bank, savings and loan association, milk producer, bar, or—in some cases—a massage parlor. In each instance many states hold hearings to determine the "convenience and advantage" or "convenience and necessity" to the public of establishing that particular kind of business in the locale for which the application is made. Not only must the principals pass muster before the state authorities, but an express finding must be made that the needs of the public are such that granting the charter or license will not unduly dilute the marketplace or demand for such goods or services.

It has been well argued that this last style of regulation serves mostly the businessmen or professionals who want government to screen out competition from newcomers, rather than allowing new talent and the marketplace to determine whether or not goods and services should be offered to the public.

Examples of regulation of business transactions include the federal and state securities laws which require registration or qualification of a company's stock before it can be marketed to the public. In order to register with the Securities and Exchange Commission a corporation must conform to the "full disclosure" requirements which attempt to elicit all pertinent information about the company for the potential investors. Most states administer a "blue-sky" law which requires the finding that the public offering is fair, just, and equitable to the investor.

Surveillance and Monitoring

The third major regulatory thrust concerns the monitoring and review of ongoing financial or commercial activities for the protection of the public's investment or deposit in the company, or for the continued justification of a government-granted monopoly, as in the utilities area. In order to protect the savings of the public on deposit in banks, savings and loan associations, insurance companies, and similar institutions, both the federal and state bank examiners and other regulatory authorities examine the company's books to make sure that sufficient liquidity exists to meet the withdrawal demand of the customers. Also, the loan practices are reviewed to ensure the long-term health and safety of the company itself. The books and records of common carriers and utilities are similarly examined in order to test the legitimacy of the rate allowed by the government to be charged by companies holding exclusive franchises to provide certain transportation or communication services.

As the Securities and Exchange Commission moves toward an ongoing reporting and registration procedure for publicly held companies, the annual disclosure requirements are another example of government regulation of ongoing financial activities. A healthy capital market depends on a fully informed investment community. Laws and regulations requiring frequent reporting of the financial status of a company as well as unusual events, discoveries or occurrences affecting its position enhance the trust and confidence of the public investor in sharing his savings with the entrepreneurial community.

Again, due to the limited scope of this chapter, I will leave to others the discussion of the good and bad effects of the above-described regulation on the business community's ability to respond adequately to the economic needs of America and the world. I shall likewise leave to others observations on the appropriate role of corporate officials in the public dialogue which continuously modifies and reshapes the regulatory processes in response to a variety of emerging and changing problems, real or imagined. Suffice it to say, however, that simple and continued opposition to all governmental regulations is essentially a forfeiture of the opportunity to play a creative role in helping the government to attack the real abuses in the capitalist system. If business does participate in such dialogue, it can also point out the economic consequences of each new regulatory program proposed by social reformers.

SPECIFIC RESPONSIBILITIES OF
THE TREASURER

As an integral member of the corporate management team, and more specifically, as the officer most often trusted with the financial needs and opportunities of the corporation, the corporate treasurer has frequent brushes with many of the governmental regulatory authorities described above. Even so, he is not likely to be named by title in many statutes or governmental regulations. For example, the newly adopted California General Corporation Law provides in Section 312(a) thereof simply that:

> A corporation shall have a chairman of the board or a president or both, a secretary, a chief financial officer and such other officers with such titles and duties as shall be stated in the by-laws or determined by the board and as may be necessary to enable it to sign instruments and share certificates. Any number of offices may be held by the same person unless the articles or by-laws provide otherwise.

Nonetheless, corporate treasurers or controllers have, over the years, come to perform certain specific duties, many of which are not unlike the functions of a treasurer in many governments. This is not unusual, since the modern corporation is a direct descendant of the so-called Crown Trading Companies which were chartered by the king as a quasi-governmental agency which performed certain commercial and trading functions for the monarch and his people.

Custody of Corporate Funds and Records

In modern corporate organizations the treasurer usually performs responsibilities relating to the custody and supervision of corporate funds and assets, preparation of and attempting to require compliance with a budget, supervision of accounting to reflect the historical performance of the corporation, reporting of financial operations to management, shareholders and governmental agencies, and compliance with pertinent taxing and regulatory authorities. By the nature of his duties then, the treasurer will be in constant contact with governmental agencies.

In the matter of serving as the steward of the corporation's funds, the treasurer often deploys surplus funds into short-term investments. As the corporate officers are fiduciary agents for the shareholders, however, many states restrict the nature of investment which may be made by a corporation of its idle funds. In many cases certain standards of quality must be observed, and at the least the treasurer must not use the corporation's funds in such a way as to create a conflict of interest between the corporation's shareholders and another party who might be the beneficiary of the investment of the corporate funds. While this is more frequently a problem where the corporation is contracting with an entity owned by certain corporate officials or shareholders, it could conceivably arise if the treasurer were attempting to assist another enterprise in which he had a personal interest by lending corporate funds to such company in violation of the "prudent man" rule.

Another aspect of the custody responsibility arises where the treasurer is also the corporate secretary and is, therefore, charged with the responsibility of maintaining the stock record books. In such cases, however, his only obligation to the government itself pertains to the reporting of certain control persons' identities to the Securities and Exchange Commission (SEC), especially in the case of a secondary or nonissuer offering of stock by a controlling shareholder.

Budgeting and Accounting Responsibilities

The treasurer's responsibilities in the budgeting process are mostly internal to the company, but may become involved with a government regulator if the information from the budgeting process were leaked out in some form or were used as the basis for trading in the company stock in violation of the insiders' trading restrictions.

The accounting and reporting functions of a treasurer can be the most significant of the treasurer's responsibilities as they relate to governmental regulatory bodies. Whether financial statements are being submitted to the SEC for use in the annual report required by the SEC of a publicly held corporation, or for inclusion in the prospectus of a corporation making a public offering, the accounting methods will be closely reviewed for the fairness and accuracy of the statements in depicting the company's value and operating history. While the Securities and Exchange Commission has in its employ a chief accountant and a complete accounting staff, it has so far refrained from implementing or adopting precise or rigid accounting standards to be used in reports or prospectuses filed with it. Instead, such reports are reviewed for their accuracy. In addition, the accounting standards set forth by the newly created independent Financial Accounting Standards Board are relied upon heavily.

Stock Exchange Requirements

If the corporation is listed on a stock exchange it will have to comply with the accounting and reporting procedures and standards set forth by the exchange. Such exchanges have a quasi-governmental status, since they are authorized and regulated by the Securities Exchange Act of 1934 and by the SEC for fairness and accuracy of execution of public trading of securities. The board of governors of the respective exchanges attempts to instill as much standardization as possible in the financial reporting of their listed companies so as to better enable the public to make comparisons. Therefore, the several exchanges enforce particular accounting methods on their listed companies.

Other governmental agencies which attempt to impose a standardized accounting procedure include the rate-making bodies, such as the Interstate Commerce Commission, the Federal Power Commission, and the Civil Aeronautics Board. The standardization in those areas is more necessary and easier, since they are dealing in a homogeneous business community and are attempting to set rates based on the return on investment and profitability of the operations.

Tax Responsibilities

Finally, to the extent that the treasurer is involved in the preparation and filing of the corporation's income tax returns, he must be acutely aware of the accounting standards imposed by the Internal Revenue Service for income tax accounting. In such a highly complex matter which potentially involves a significant share of the corporation's earnings the treasurer who has other corporate responsibilities is well advised to engage an independent accountant to assist in the preparation of the corporation's tax returns. This not only brings needed expertise to the corporation, but frequently adds integrity to the return in the eyes of the Internal Revenue Service agent.

Legal Compliance

Under the general heading of "compliance," the treasurer is often charged with the responsibility of dealing with examiners if the corporation is an insurance company, bank, stock brokerage house, or other financial institution. If the corporation's liquidity is monitored, or if "return on investment" or profitability is subject to review as a condition of continuing to hold a governmental franchise, it is again frequently the corporate treasurer who is charged with filing the timely reports with the appropriate agencies. The appropriate form and reporting period as well as the content of such reports are all important aspects of the compliance functions of the treasurer.

Because of the rapidly expanding liability imposed by the courts on corporate officers and directors, it is worth noting in passing at least that failure to observe the disclosure requirements by delivering required information to the Securities and Exchange Commission and/or the shareholders can result in both civil and criminal liability at the instigation of either the SEC or shareholders or members of the public who are trading in the company stock.

It has long been accepted that the officers of a corporation occupy a special fiduciary relationship to both the corporation and its stockholders. The Securities Act of 1933 and the Securities Exchange Act of 1934, imposing statutory fiduciary responsibilities upon corporate officers, reinforce and emphasize that relationship. The requirements of those acts dealing with registration of securities, reporting requirements, solicitation and use of proxies, and the filings by insiders, are of special concern to all officers of corporations affected by them.

This need for protection of the investing public from abuse of power and knowledge by the corporate insider places a heavy burden on the corporate officer. It is the corporate officer who often will be penalized for failure to fulfill that need.

Insider Laws

One of the most important areas affecting corporate insiders in dealing with federal securities laws is Section 16(b) of the Securities Exchange Act of 1934 (Section 3b–2 of that act defines "insider" to include the corporate treasurer). Section 16(b) is designed to prevent the corporate insider from deriving primary benefit from insider information. It does this simply. It requires that any profit derived by the insider from a purchase and sale of his own corporation's securities within a six-month period must be turned over to that corporation. It does not matter that the insider does not make *unfair* use of inside information; the liability imposed by this section is absolute.

The second major area of concern to the corporate insider is Rule 10b–5 of the Securities Act of 1934. Primarily this section is concerned with disclosure. It places an affirmative duty on an insider who is part of a purchase or sale of a security to disclose material inside information relating to that sale or purchase. In the most well-known case under this section, *Texas Gulf Sulfur,* corporate insiders had purchased stock on the basis of material information not known to the investing public. The SEC successfully brought an action against the insiders to compel recision of those securities transactions. The court held that insiders must either disclose the material information or abstain from trading in the corporation's securities.

Securities Laws

The corporate treasurer as the chief financial officer of the corporation is usually involved in the security transactions of the corporation. In areas such as the registration of securities, reporting requirements, and the solicitation of proxies he is often called upon to render his opinion regarding the financial status of the corporation. It is his actual participation in these areas that will make him liable if violations of the securities laws result.

A good example of this was the *BarChris* case, which involved material misrepresentation in and omissions from a registration statement. One of the defendants was the corporation's treasurer who had signed the registration statement filed with the SEC. In finding the treasurer liable, the court found that he had not exercised "due diligence" in investigating information contained in the registration statement. Further, because of his intimate knowledge of the corporation, he was held liable for even the "expertised" portions of the registration statement prepared by others on specific aspects of the company's operations. The court found that because he had reason to believe those portions were in part incorrect, he could not rely on the attorneys or accountants in signing the registration statement. This case demonstrates the growing burden of investigation placed upon the officer of a corporation who participates in the corporation's security transactions.

SUMMARY

In sum, the corporate treasurer performs an important task in relating the corporation's activities to the regulatory agencies, the shareholders, and the public. The successful performance of these duties will not only ensure the good standing of the corporation before the regulatory agencies, but also will enhance the fuller understanding of the corporate activities by the shareholders. In the larger sense, the corporate treasurer can make a positive contribution to the confidence of the public, not only in his particular corporation but in the business community's role as a responsible, responsive, and productive element of the total society.

ADDITIONAL SOURCES

See Additional Sources at end of Chapter 53.

PART III

Financial Practice
from a Conceptual
Framework

PART III provides an overall framework for viewing the functions and responsibilities of business treasurers. Vincent LoCascio provides a conceptional framework of analysis for viewing the functions of the treasurer in a broad perspective. He characterizes the three major decision areas as fixed asset expansion, working capital expansion, and acquisition analysis. These result in an initial financing plan embodied in a set of related financial reports. Analysis of these reports provides a basis for evaluating financial strategy and information feedback in the original three broad areas of decision making. Concepts and principles involved in each of the steps of the financial decision process are set forth by Mr. LoCascio. This leads to a framework for evaluating alternative financing forms and sources.

Leonard Arnoff formulates the role of planning to aid the corporate treasurer in dealing with the increased turbulence of the economic and financial environment. He presents the principles of planning and illustrates their application with the aid of a case study. He shows the relation between planning and effective cost reduction. He emphasizes the importance of generating decision-oriented information systems for management to use in the planning process.

Important new developments in financial theory have taken place

149

in recent years. Edward Williams and M. C. Findlay summarize these developments and highlight their implications and applications, as well as their limitations. They begin with the basic concept of "efficient" capital markets. They next present the implications of portfolio theory for the capital budgeting decisions of the firm. They indicate how this leads to the capital asset pricing model and the capital market line, providing a basis for more systematic measurement of the risks of individual projects and of the risk of the firm as a whole. They explain the concept of covariance and "beta" as measures of risk. They point out the implications of these developments for capital structure policy, dividend policy, and the timing of financial decisions.

Chapter 9

A Conceptual Framework
of Analysis

Vincent R. LoCascio[*]

IN THE PRECEDING CHAPTERS we have put forth three views of the treasurer's function. Stated succinctly, the treasurer procures funds for the corporation (top management) from financial institutions (bankers) and in this pursuit must sometimes satisfy requirements of such governmental regulatory bodies as the Securities and Exchange Commission.

In the past, a complete study of this function would typically involve procedural and descriptive coverage of these relationships. More recently, the subject has been slanted away from the purely descriptive treatment and more toward the normative. Rather than treating the administrative and procedural intricacies of raising funds, the normative approach asks rather when should funds be raised, for which corporate purposes and from which sources so as to contribute most to corporate goals. Various tools of financial analysis can be used in determining the level of funds required for normal operations as well as for financing expansion. There is no real difference between the tools of analysis appropriate for management use and those which are of interest to financing sources. It is not uncommon especially for small- to medium-sized fast-growing corporations to develop long-range financial planning models first to indicate to themselves what their intermediate to long-term

* Vincent R. LoCascio is manager, Peat, Marwick, Mitchell & Co., New York.

growth capital needs are and, second, to present these findings to their bankers in order to secure the required funds. This is not meant to imply that the criteria of financial evaluation are the same for financing sources as they are for managers. The criteria of evaluation are defined on the basis of the relationship that the evaluator has to the corporate entity: short-term creditor, long-term creditor, owner, or manager. The short-term creditor will be primarily interested in solvency; the long-term creditor in safety; the owner in wealth maximization; and the manager, in achieving the best balance of solvency, safety, and wealth accumulation primarily but not solely on behalf of the owners.

The manager (in this case, treasurer) must negotiate with the various suppliers of funds by appealing to that which is of importance to each. Therefore, the financial analyses which his office will conduct must proceed along the following lines:

1. What is the proper level, scope, breath and nature of corporate activity that justifies the commitment of funds from the standpoint of the owners?
2. What combination of sources of funds in support of the above-determined level of activity is most desirable from the standpoint of the owners?
3. What other alternative liability structures may be necessary to satisfy the requirements of creditors?

In other words, determine first all undertakings which are worthwhile and commensurate with the risks that the owners are willing to incur; then, plan to fund this growth with the cheapest funding (again commensurate with acceptable risk levels); and finally, restructure the liabilities (or cut back on asset accumulation) to the extent that nonownership capital is unwilling to fund the planned activity. Often, for mature relatively stable industries, especially in firms with relatively conservative management philosophies, the third step is not really necessary.

Another view of this framework of analysis is given in Figure 1. The three boxes on the left indicate three different elements of corporate growth which will require financing. The mix of these three types of activity will dictate the optimal financing plan as represented in the box entitled "Original Financing Plan." The third set of boxes represent the financial reports which will reflect the plans discussed above. Bankers and other providers of capital will ex-

FIGURE 1
A Financial Planning Framework

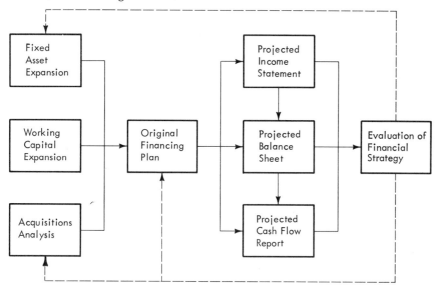

amine these financial reports in deciding whether to provide the desired capital, and at what price and under what conditions. The resulting evaluation of financial strategy will lead to feedback inputs into prior elements of the system, causing readjustments that work through the planning framework.

This framework for planning, by its very nature, requires looking more than one year into the future. Also, the analysis may require the aid of computer models where each of the boxes in the schematic in Figure 1 could be considered a module of the model. Once a grand design such as that suggested in Figure 1 has been developed, each module must be individually considered in terms of input requirements, outputs, transfers to other modules, and so on. The remainder of this chapter will be devoted to a discussion of each of these major areas required for a fairly comprehensive financial planning framework. Because of the many alternative approaches, the discussion will of necessity be general. The intent, then will not be to develop a specific approach to the analysis, but rather to describe the analytical processes which ultimately must be undertaken when a particular planning framework is designed. The objective will be to state objectives, sort out the significant from the insignificant considerations with respect to these objectives, and then formulate the skeleton of a financial planning system.

EVALUATING CORPORATE ACTIVITY

There are two corporate situations which require analysis: steady state operations and growth. In the steady state the financial decisions are involved solely with refinancing and changing the financial structure. At any given point in time assets equal liabilities and in the absence of asset accumulation the financial manager's job is mainly to review the methods of funding the operations as refinancing is required and to manage the disbursement of funds as cash flows are generated. Of course, since the treasurer is a key corporate officer he will play a role in any efforts aimed at increasing margins or in increasing turnover but these are not solely financial decisions.

The growth situation requires financial analysis of potential new investment. While it is true that analysis of new opportunities for investment will also involve production, marketing, and other executives, it also requires a financial evaluation not required in the steady state. In various firms, the responsibility for this analytical function may reside with the treasurer, controller or special analysis groups. Nevertheless, the determination of the proper level, scope, and breadth of corporate activity is an important financial function.

There are essentially three major forms of growth: (1) growth through fixed asset expansion, (2) growth through working capital expansion, and (3) growth through acquisition. Each of these growth situations, while similar, require somewhat different analytical tools and are discussed individually below.

GROWTH THROUGH FIXED
ASSET EXPANSION

This category of growth includes all capital expenditures for new fixed assets which are not undertaken merely to replace old fixed assets. It includes, therefore, expansion projects which increase the firm's production capability and also those which cut costs through the introduction of more modern technology.

When one is planning over a five-year planning horizon or so, the earlier years will invariably be less uncertain than the later years.

It might be possible for example, to specify all of the potential projects for the upcoming year, only two or three for the following year,
and none thereafter. On the other hand, as time passes, new opportunities for growth will be uncovered even though they are not
presently known. For planning purposes, it might be desirable to
group total capital expenditures (T) into three mutually exclusive,
all-inclusive groups: specified expansion (S), unspecified expansion
(U), and replacement (R). In formula form,

$$T = S + U + R$$

A knowledge of any three of the four will determine the fourth.
The breakdown into specified and unspecified is made to accommodate the observation made above, namely, that, some projects are
too small to be considered independently, and many opportunities
for future expansion are not presently known. Unspecified expansion
dollars will "fall out" of the above relationship, as in Table 1.

TABLE 1

Year	1	2	3	4	5
Total capital expenditures	100	110	115	115	125
Replacement expenditures.	30	35	40	45	50
Specified expansion	40	10	–	–	–
Unspecified expansion	30	65	75	70	75

$(U = T - S - R)$

Total expenditures can be projected from a knowledge of past
trends and normal growth assumptions as well as a specific knowledge of the future prospects of the firm and its industry. Replacement expenditures can be determined from a knowledge of the fixed
assets currently on hand and their economic life. Specified expansion will be determined on the basis of the normal corporate procedures (to be discussed in more detail below) for recommending
and approving such projects.

At any rate, as a basis for analyzing the effects of capital expenditures, it might be possible to determine average effects through a
detailed analysis of past capital expenditures. For example, $1 of
expenditure, on average, results in $0.35 of sales per year for eight
years and $0.05 of cost reduction for six years. Obtaining data for
such a determination is extremely thorny, and, in some cases may

be impossible. The alternative would be to state the effects on theoretical rather than evidential grounds.

The broad-based projections of expenditures discussed above are essential elements in fulfilling the treasurer's function. The evaluation of individual expansion projects is admittedly not primarily a treasurer's function. However, in the evaluation of major projects such as building or renovating entire plants where there are obvious financing implications, the treasurer should, and in many cases, does play a major role.

The financial analysis of the desirability of capital expenditure will, in one form or another, follow the traditional approaches to capital expenditure evaluation. This, of course, leaves much room for variation in specific approach. The evaluation can take the form of discounted cash flow rate of return, payback period, net present value, and so on. If risk analysis is desired, we can simulate results at various values for key variables, perform sensitivity analysis, employ probabilistic forecasts of variables, and so on. If the "portfolio effect" is considered important, still more complex analyses will be required. The portfolio effect refers to the interrelationship among projects. For example, while projects 1, 2, and 3 have individual risk-return characteristics, they are not additive; projects 1 and 2 might be complementary; projects 2 and 3 might act at cross purposes with each other; projects 1 and 3 might be mutually exclusive. If this effect is significant, it should enter into the decision process. (See Chapter 18.) In any event, the availability of data for each specified project will allow a rigorous analysis of one kind or another. The specific techniques of analysis will be treated in later chapters of this book.

WORKING CAPITAL EXPANSION

Working capital, as used here, refers to cash requirements for financing short-term assets. Generally, as the size of a firm increases, its need for working capital also increases. But this is not necessarily so. Changing margins, relationships with debtors and creditors, inventory turnover, and so on all combine to determine what the cash needs will be. The severest working capital management problems tend to occur when sales are not only growing but accelerating. This is typically faced by relatively new firms in new growth industries. Mobile home dealers, for example, in the late

1960s and early 1970s experienced accelerating sales demand. This, together with long-term sales contracts placed severe cash constraints on these small firms.

At the risk of oversimplification let us consider a company which pays cash for its inventory and also sells for cash. Let us further assume that the production process requires one month and that the profit on this product is 12 percent. Table 2 shows what happens during a 36-month period if sales grow at 20 percent for a period and then taper off to a 10 percent growth rate. Notice that even with a reinvestment of all profits in working capital, there is an ever building need for working capital that climbs to $463,000 by the end of the 24th month. It is only after the third year of operations that there is an ability to reduce working capital. Table 3 shows the even more drastic effects of an accelerating growth rate. By the end of the second year the firm will need financing of $3,589,900; by the end of the 32d month this will have grown to $8,863,300; but by the end of the third year, once the rate of growth in sales begins to decelerate rapidly, the funds required has been halved from its peak of four months earlier.

The potential fluctuations in working capital investment indicate that the more flexible the financing arrangements the better. Because of the availability of lines of credit and the shorter term maturity of debt instruments for working capital financing, the time horizon for planning is shorter than the time frame for fixed asset management. A two-to-three-year monthly forecast of operations is typically sufficient for flexible planning and management. Because of the number of variables, the complexity of their interaction, the tedium involved in the calculations and the desirability of planning for more than one set of future conditions, computer modeling can be helpful in analyzing working capital.

Of course, the individual characteristics of each individual firm will determine the level of detail at which they will perform this analysis. Some companies may feel the need to analyze by product line, others by plant, and still others by division. Some hybrid combination of the above is also possible. Forecasts of sales, cost of sales, inventory levels, receivables, profits, and so on are the cornerstone of effective working capital planning. Forecasting methodologies fall roughly into two major categories: fundamental and technical. The fundamental approach to sales forecasting would involve an examination of such key variables as share of market, total market,

TABLE 2
Working Capital Analysis, Example 1 ($ in 000)

(1) Month	(2) Growth	(3) Sales	(4) Cost of Sales	(5) Inventory	(6) (5)–(3) Cash Required*	(7) Cumulative Cash Required	(8) (3)–(4) Profit*	(9) Cumulative Profit
1.	0.20%	$ 100.0	$ 88.0	$ 105.6	$ 5.6	$ 5.6	$ 12.0	$ 12.0
2.	0.20	120.0	105.6	126.7	6.7	12.3	14.4	26.4
3.	0.20	144.0	126.7	152.1	8.1	20.4	17.3	43.7
4.	0.20	172.8	152.1	182.5	9.7	30.1	20.7	64.4
5.	0.20	207.4	182.5	219.0	11.6	41.7	24.9	89.3
6.	0.20	248.8	219.0	262.8	13.9	55.6	29.9	119.2
7.	0.18	298.6	262.8	310.1	11.5	67.1	35.8	155.0
8.	0.18	352.3	310.1	365.9	13.5	80.6	42.3	197.3
9.	0.18	415.8	365.9	431.7	16.0	96.6	49.9	247.2
10.	0.18	490.6	431.7	509.4	18.8	115.4	58.9	306.0
11.	0.18	578.9	509.4	601.1	22.2	137.6	69.5	375.5
12.	0.18	683.1	601.1	709.3	26.2	163.9	82.0	457.5
13.	0.18	806.1	709.3	837.0	31.0	194.8	96.7	554.2
14.	0.16	951.2	837.0	971.0	19.8	214.6	114.1	668.4
15.	0.16	1,103.4	971.0	1,126.3	22.9	237.6	132.4	800.8
16.	0.16	1,279.9	1,126.3	1,306.5	26.9	264.2	153.6	954.3
17.	0.16	1,484.7	1,306.5	1,515.6	30.9	295.1	178.2	1,132.5
18.	0.16	1,722.2	1,515.6	1,758.0	35.8	330.9	206.7	1,339.2
19.	0.16	1,997.8	1,758.0	2,039.3	41.6	372.4	239.7	1,578.9
20.	0.16	2,317.4	2,039.3	2,365.6	48.2	420.6	278.1	1,857.0
21.	0.14	2,688.2	2,365.6	2,696.8	8.6	429.2	322.6	2,179.6
22.	0.14	3,064.6	2,696.8	3,074.4	9.8	439.0	367.7	2,547.3
23.	0.14	3,493.6	3,074.4	3,504.8	11.2	450.2	419.2	2,966.6
24.	0.14	3,982.7	3,504.8	3,995.4	12.7	463.0	477.9	3,444.5
25.	0.14	4,540.3	3,995.4	4,554.8	14.5	477.5	544.8	3,989.3
26.	0.14	5,175.9	4,554.8	5,192.5	16.6	494.0	621.1	4,610.4
27.	0.14	5,900.5	5,192.5	5,919.4	18.9	512.9	708.1	5,318.5
28.	0.12	6,726.6	5,919.4	6,629.7	−96.9	416.0	807.2	6,125.7
29.	0.12	7,533.8	6,629.7	7,425.3	−108.5	307.5	904.1	7,029.7
30.	0.12	8,437.8	7,425.3	8,316.3	−121.5	186.0	1,012.5	8,042.3
31.	0.12	9,450.3	8,316.3	9,314.3	−136.1	49.9	1,134.0	9,176.3
32.	0.12	10,584.4	9,314.3	10,431.9	−152.4	− 102.5	1,270.1	10,446.4
33.	0.12	11,854.5	10,431.9	11,683.8	−170.7	− 273.2	1,422.5	11,869.0
34.	0.12	13,277.0	11,683.8	13,085.8	−191.2	− 464.4	1,593.2	13,462.2
35.	0.10	14,870.2	13,085.8	14,394.4	−475.9	− 940.3	1,784.4	15,246.7
36.	0.10	16,357.3	14,394.4	15,833.8	−523.4	−1,463.7	1,962.9	17,209.5

* Subtractions were made from exact numbers, therefore, figures will be slightly different from results using the rounded values shown in columns 3, 4, and 5.

TABLE 3
Working Capital Analysis, Example 2 ($ in 000)

(1) Month	(2) Growth	(3) Sales	(4) Cost of Sales	(5) Inventory	(6) (5) − (3) Cash Required*	(7) Cumulative Cash Required	(8) (3) − (4) Profit*	(9) Cumulative Profit
1	0.13%	$ 93.6	$ 82.4	$ 92.8	$ −0.8	$ −0.8	$ 11.2	$ 11.2
2	0.13	105.5	92.8	105.1	−0.4	−1.2	12.7	23.9
3	0.14	119.4	105.1	119.9	0.4	−0.7	14.3	33.2
4	0.15	136.2	119.9	137.9	1.7	1.8	16.3	54.6
5	0.16	156.7	137.9	160.3	3.6	4.5	18.8	73.4
6	0.17	182.1	160.3	188.3	6.1	10.7	21.9	95.2
7	0.19	213.9	188.3	223.6	9.7	20.4	25.7	120.9
8	0.20	254.1	223.6	268.7	14.5	34.9	30.5	151.4
9	0.21	305.3	268.7	326.3	20.9	55.8	36.6	188.0
10	0.23	370.7	326.3	400.1	29.4	85.3	44.5	232.5
11	0.24	454.7	400.1	495.1	40.4	125.6	54.6	287.1
12	0.25	562.6	495.1	617.0	54.4	180.0	67.5	354.6
13	0.25	701.2	617.0	773.0	71.8	251.8	84.1	438.7
14	0.26	878.4	773.0	971.0	92.6	344.5	105.4	544.1
15	0.26	1,103.4	971.0	1,219.7	116.4	460.8	132.4	676.5
16	0.26	1,386.1	1,219.7	1,531.3	145.2	606.1	166.3	842.9
17	0.25	1,740.1	1,531.3	1,920.2	180.0	786.1	208.8	1,051.7
18	0.25	2,182.0	1,920.2	2,403.4	221.4	1,007.5	261.8	1,313.5
19	0.25	2,731.2	2,403.4	3,001.1	269.9	1,277.4	327.7	1,641.3
20	0.24	3,410.3	3,001.1	3,736.1	325.8	1,603.2	409.2	2,050.5
21	0.24	4,245.6	3,736.1	4,634.4	388.9	1,992.1	509.5	2,560.0
22	0.24	5,266.4	4,634.4	5,724.6	458.2	2,450.3	632.0	3,191.9
23	0.23	6,505.3	5,724.6	7,037.4	532.1	2,982.4	780.6	3,972.6
24	0.22	7,997.0	7,037.4	8,604.5	607.5	3,589.9	959.6	4,932.2
25	0.22	9,777.8	8,604.5	10,457.6	679.7	4,269.6	1,173.3	6,105.6
26	0.21	11,883.6	10,457.6	12,626.0	742.4	5,012.0	1,426.0	7,531.6
27	0.20	14,347.7	12,626.0	15,134.6	786.8	5,798.8	1,721.7	9,253.3
28	0.19	17,198.4	15,134.6	18,000.3	802.0	6,600.8	2,063.8	11,317.1
29	0.18	20,454.9	18,000.3	21,229.3	774.4	7,375.2	2,454.6	13,771.7
30	0.17	24,124.2	21,229.3	24,812.8	688.6	8,063.6	2,894.9	16,666.6
31	0.16	28,196.4	24,812.8	28,723.6	527.2	8,591.1	3,383.6	20,050.2
32	0.15	32,640.5	28,723.7	32,912.8	272.3	8,863.3	3,916.9	23,967.1
33	0.13	37,400.9	32,912.8	37,307.0	−93.9	8,769.4	4,488.1	28,455.2
34	0.12	42,394.3	37,307.0	41,807.4	−586.8	8,182.6	5,087.3	33,542.5
35	0.11	47,508.5	41,807.4	46,290.8	−1,217.7	6,964.9	5,701.0	39,243.5
36	0.09	52,603.2	46,290.8	50,611.7	−1,991.5	4,973.4	6,312.4	45,555.9

* Subtractions were made from exact numbers, therefore, figures will be slightly different from results using the rounded values shown in columns 3, 4, and 5.

pricing structure, advertising, and so forth. In a modeling application, the analyst could either analyze these variables external to the model and then input the resulting sales forecasts, or, alternatively, generate the sales forecasts by programming the relationships among the key variables.

The technical approach relies on the stability of past patterns of behavior. A commonly used technical approach is time series analysis. In essence, a historical series of data is "explained" in terms of four types of movement: trend, cyclical, seasonal, and random. These patterns are assumed, then, to continue over the period to be forecast.

If the fundamental approach were to be applied to cost of sales, each of the major component expense items (labor, raw materials, and so on) would be examined separately. Such variables as changes in productivity levels, technology, wage rates, capacity utilization, general economic conditions, and a host of other factors would all be examined to come up with cost of sales projections. The technical approach, on the other hand, might attempt to identify a fairly stable past relationship between cost of sales and sales. This would more than likely involve regression analysis or some other such quantitative technique.

Each approach, fundamental and technical, has its strong and weak points. The fundamental approach asks "*why* has the past been as it was" and attempts to capture the essence of the actual cause and effect relationships at play. The technical approach asks merely "*how* has it been in the past" and attempts to describe that process itself. The former method is more ambitious, but the latter is far simpler—especially in modeling applications. And, of course, a degree of fundamental reasoning is applied in technical evaluations in the sense that the variables examined for relationships are ones that are known to have some rational relationship to each other.

Most analyses will incorporate both methodologies. For example, sales may be forecasted after careful fundamental analysis, and cost of sales projected through regression analysis as a function of sales and possibly one or two other variables. Inventory levels and accounts payable are known, fundamentally, to be related to future sales while accounts receivable are known to be related to past sales. Having made these determinations as well as necessary refinements for seasonal fluctuations and estimated lead and lag periods, technical analysis can be applied to quantify the fundamentals.

We mentioned earlier that these analyses could be on a product line, plant, or divisional basis. Depending on the degree of centralization or decentralization of the treasury function some or all of the detailed working capital projections would have to be aggregated in order to finalize the financial plan. And, of course, any final financial plan would have to integrate the analysis of working capital with the analysis of fixed asset expansion and the financial plan resulting from the analysis of acquisitions discussed in the next section.

ACQUISITION ANALYSES

In many ways, growth by acquisition can be considered similar to fixed asset growth. The traditional theory of valuation of a firm (used in acquisition analysis) is conceptually identical to techniques of capital budgeting. Specifically, a long-term asset (machine) or a complex of long-term assets (company) has a positive net present value insofar as the future cash benefit promised, after appropriate adjustments for risk and the time value of money, exceeds its present cost.

By the same token, there are also significant differences between fixed asset analysis and acquisition analysis that justify separate treatment. For one thing, the valuation of a company must go beyond the mere analysis of tangible assets. One must certainly consider the organization of the firm to be acquired and evaluate its strengths and weaknesses. If the acquiring firm has strong management, financial and marketing skills but are weak in research whereas the potential acquisition has the exact opposite strengths and weaknesses, then a mathematical addition of the independent expected results of the two firms may be misleading.

Another significant difference is the negotiating relationships that exist between owners, management and boards of directors of the acquiring firm and the acquired firm. Such complexities do not cloud the capital budgeting decision process. Most of the negotiations are going to involve the mode of payment and the form of combination each of which has its own constellation of tax and legal implications. These considerations will be discussed in a later chapter of this book and will not be discussed here where our major concern is defining the framework of analysis rather than the details of the substance of analysis.

The framework of analysis will involve a three-step process: (1) Developing corporate acquisition policy, (2) evaluating potential candidates, and (3) integrating the expected results of prospective candidates with the corporation's overall long-term financial plan. In the first step of this process the corporation will define the characteristics of companies it wishes to consider. One firm may seek to gain a larger share of the market in its current industry; another may attempt to capture a supplier thus accomplishing a vertical integration; still another firm may wish to expand into a related field for which they have the requisite management skills (horizontal integration); other firms such as the major conglomerates may not restrict themselves to any particular industry or groups of industries. Other policy goals that will form the basis of a firm's acquisition policy will include target growth rates in sales and profits, maintaining desired debt to equity ratios and determining the appropriate sizes of acquisition candidates.

Once a policy has been established, the job of searching out likely prospects begins. In addition to collecting data on and making forecasts of the operating characteristics and future potential of each candidate, the analyst must consider the form of combination and probable mode of payment that each acquired company may find attractive. In other words, the second stage of analysis (evaluating potential candidates) must be guided by the first stage (acquisition policy) so that when the projected analysis is integrated with the long-term plan of the company in the third stage, there will be less chance that a policy guideline will be violated. In essence, what we have described as the third stage of acquisition analysis is really broader than that: it ties all three areas of expansion analysis—fixed assets, working capital, and acquisition analysis into an integrated long-range plan. This is the subject of the next section and represents the bridge between the analysis of corporate activity and the more specific area of financing corporate activity.

ESTABLISHING AN ORIGINAL
FINANCE PLAN

At the outset of this chapter we organized the financial function into three broad categories (1) Determining the level of activity, (2) funding the level of activity thus decided upon from the standpoint of owners, and (3) adjusting the capital structure to satisfy creditors. In the preceding pages we have covered the first of these functions. In this section we will consider each of the remaining two functions.

Presumably, in the course of analyzing growth opportunities part of the analysis was devoted to a preliminary identification of the proper funding mechanisms. Because of the multitude of departments and individuals, each with their own objectives, who would have participated in that process, any indicated financing plan would have to be considered only a very rough first approximation to the ultimate plan. In fact, the integrating function we will be discussing here will itself be a cyclical process of establishing an initial plan, evaluating the projected financial reports that result from that plan and modifying the plan accordingly. As indicated by the broken lines in Figure 1, the nature of these modifications may be solely concerned with testing alternative funding sources or it may go further and result in a change in the activity levels themselves.

The primary basis for the original financing plan will have been dictated by the relative mix of capital expansion, working capital expansion, and expansion through acquisitions considered in conjunction with established corporate objectives such as the desired dividend policy and debt-equity ratio.

The desired debt-equity ratio will probably be a function of the industry and the tendencies of management toward either a conservative or aggressive stance with regard to financial leverage. An aggressive management may also be limited to the extent that suppliers of debt capital place restrictions on the degree of leverage. Once the debt to equity policy has been determined it becomes a guideline in evaluating expansion opportunities. But until the integration of all plans, one does not know if the policy will be violated. This is especially true in firms engaged in diverse multiplant, multidivisional operations where the integration step aggregates data from many different original sources.

Another key corporate policy influencing the financial plan is dividend policy. In many academic treatments of dividend policy there is the assumption of some target payout percentage of earnings. In practice, however, dividend policy tends to be more stable than this would imply. Most firms will not cut their dividend because of one or two relatively minor adverse years nor will they raise it during one or two extremely good years. Therefore, the firm may state its dividend policy as "maintaining our current dividend with intermittent increases to reflect growth." Now, if earnings are lower than expected while dividends remain unchanged, the debt to equity ratio will be higher than anticipated; conversely, if earnings increase at a faster than expected pace while dividends remain unchanged the debt to equity ratio will be lower than planned. Interrelationships between earnings, dividend policy, and leverage will cause an original financing plan, no matter how well thought out, to require one or more modifications during the development of the plan. This, of course, is in addition to the absolutely certain need to change and revise the plan during its execution.

While one must be aware that plans are going to change, he should not be dissuaded from establishing the best possible plan based on currently available information. This applies as much to the first draft plan as it does to the final plan. After all, the closer the original plan comes to a viable final version, the fewer cycles of modification there will be.

A first step toward developing a good original financing plan is to determine the proper financing instrument for major categories of assets. This chapter will not discuss all of the various considerations that must be addressed in choosing the most appropriate type of financing—they will be covered in subsequent chapters. However, a few very basic principles are necessary to a discussion of the planning framework.

The first concept is that the duration of the need for funds should be balanced by the maturity of the funding source. Therefore, a seasonal inventory buildup would not be funded by long-term debt. Why, however, would long-term assets not be financed by short-term debt that typically (but not always) carries lower interest rates? One reason is the costs associated with renewal. But perhaps the main reason is the risk that funds will not be available when refinancing is sought.

A second concept is that because of large relatively unpredictable swings in capital requirements, lines of credit may be preferred over debt instruments with specified maturity. This condition will occur, as we have seen, during a period of rapid sales growth. Erratic working capital growth patterns such as we discussed earlier would be appropriately financed through a line of credit. On the other hand, working capital growth resulting from fairly stable, normal growth patterns must be considered part of the firm's permanent assets, and should logically be financed with long-term debt and equity.

A third consideration must be the level of interest rates generally. When rates are high, they are typically high throughout the range of maturities. A shrewd financial manager may finance assets using shorter term securities than he otherwise would when rates are high and switch into a more appropriate matching of the maturities of assets and liabilities at some later point after rates have come down.

Still another consideration is the tax effect of alternative financing instruments. For example, preferred stock dividends are not tax deductible while the interest on long-term debt is. Tax considerations are especially important in the process of deciding the optimal financing of mergers. For example, the use of stock will avoid an immediate tax liability on the part of the owners of the acquired company. Beyond this there are a host of complex tax ramifications in the financing of acquisitions. The legal form of the merger will dictate allowable depreciation of assets, whether taxes must be paid on dividends from subsidiary to parent, and so on. And the legal form of the merger will be partially established by the financing mechanism.

By applying these and other appropriate financing guidelines, the financial planners will be able to establish the base plan. The integration of the financing plans and the activities financed will produce a projected income statement, balance sheet, and cash flow statement which can be evaluated to determine what changes must be made in either the expansion plan or the financing plan.

ANALYZING REPORTS

In order to establish a sound financial strategy, the financial manager must evaluate the projected effects of his expansion plans and his "first cut" at funding the expansion. We have, at this point, analyzed corporate activity in terms of identifying areas of potential fixed asset expansion, working capital expansion, and prospective acquisitions. Then, in the very broadest of terms, we determined the probable funding mechanisms based on sound, but nonetheless general, rules of thumb. The final goal is, at least conceptually, in sight; namely, to develop a fully integrated near optimal financial strategy which maintains control over levels of cash, the debt-equity mix, interest costs, dividend payout, and net earnings while considering a host of related nonfinancial corporate objectives, requirements, and constraints.

The first step in this process is to analyze the reports that are generated from the stages of analysis and planning that have been completed. In order to provide management with a reasonably complete picture of projected corporate performance, three key pro forma financial statements should be developed: income statements, balance sheet, and source application of cash.

The corporate income statement will be developed from a buildup and consolidation of product line, plant, or divisional income statements together with the inclusion of various corporate level accounts such as interest expense. Preliminary earnings per share calculations can be made to determine primary and secondary earnings and the various effects of dilution.

Some of the items from the income statement calculations will tie directly into the balance sheet. Net earnings, for example, after provisions are made for dividends, will be posted to retained earnings. Additionally, the provision for taxes, along with taxes due (calculated from a knowledge of various Schedule M items, such as depreciation, for example, whose tax treatment differs from the financial statements), will determine the taxes payable and deferred taxes accounts. In essence, then, the income calculations will normally result in increases to three entries on the right-hand side of the balance sheet. In addition, the original plan for funding the growth in assets will also have produced increases on the liability side of the balance sheet under normal growth conditions.

On the other hand, anticipated capital expenditures and working capital increases will have produced increases to the accounts on the left-hand side of the balance sheet. Since we have not developed a fully integrated plan as yet, these various effects all working simultaneously may produce a strange looking balance sheet. Table 4, shows what a typical result of this exercise might look like.

The cash account is a residual number. It results from having made a specific projection of each of the other accounts. We assume that a cash balance of $5,000,000 is the appropriate level of operating cash for the enterprise in question. The balance sheet in Table 4 indicates that new debt in the amount of $10,000,000 was raised in year 2 providing for amoritization of one-tenth per year. The balance sheet in Table 4 indicates that too much was raised in year 2 and for too short a maturity since there is a need in years 3 or 4 for more rather than less cash. If, instead of raising $10,000,000 in year 2 with a ten-year maturity, the following schedule of borrowing were planned, the results would be as displayed in Table 5.

TABLE 4
Balance Sheet Projections ($000,000)

Balance Sheet Item	Year			
	1	2	3	4
Cash	$ 5	$ 8	$ (7)	$ (3)
Working capital (excluding cash)	10	12	18	15
Fixed assets	30	35	45	45
Total Assets..................	$45	$55	$56	$57
Existing debt	$15	$13	$11	$ 9
New debt.......................	—	10	9	8
Other liability accounts	5	6	7	8
Capital........................	25	26	29	32
Total Liabilities and Net Worth	$45	$55	$56	$57

TABLE 5
Financing to Meet Cash Balance Requirements ($000,000)

Balance Sheet Item	Year			
	1	2	3	4
Cash	$ 5	$ 5	$ 5	$ 5
Working capital (excluding cash)	10	12	18	15
Fixed assets	30	35	45	45
Total Assets..................	$45	$52	$68	$65
Existing debt	$15	$13	$11	$ 9
New debt.......................	—	7	21	16
Other liability accounts	5	6	7	8
Capital........................	25	26	29	32
Total Liabilities and Net Worth	$45	$52	$68	$65

Seven million dollars with a 14-year maturity is raised in year 2. In year 3, $11,000,000 is raised with an 11-year maturity and $3,500,000 is raised with a 1-year maturity. Thus the amount of debt in year 3 is the $14,000,500 new debt raised plus the $6,500,000 remaining from the $7,000,000 borrowed in year 2. In year 4, $500,000 is repaid from the $7,000,000 as well as the $3,500,000 with the one-year maturity borrowed in year 3. This represents a reduction of $4,000,000 plus the $1,000,000 repaid from the $11,000,000 borrowed in year 3. Thus $5,000,000 is repaid in year 4 as compared with year 3.

This example is admittedly simplified for a number of reasons. First, we show no reduction in the growth of capital from Table 4 to Table 5. The differing debt levels in actuality would have an interest expense effect on earnings and thus on retained earnings assuming an independent dividend policy. Second, no mention was made of the various forms of either debt or equity securities which would have been considered in determining the optimum financing strategy. In other words, some of the obvious interactions are ignored and only the question "how much?" is answered; the concurrent question "of what?" is not addressed. In the final section of this chapter, we complete the loop by discussing the types of specific considerations one must pose in fine tuning the financing plan and selecting from among the alternatives.

FINE TUNING FINANCIAL STRATEGY

An analysis of financial strategy should be designed to treat all kinds of securities and their effects, perhaps broken down into convenient subgroupings such as: short-term debt, long-term debt, convertible debt, preferred stock, convertible preferred, common stock, and warrants. In addition, the analysis would not be complete without considering the other side of the coin: What should be done with permanent or semi-permanent excess of funds? Essentially the two key considerations would be dividend policy and purchase of treasury stock.

Later chapters of this book will deal with each of these issues in some depth. Here we are concerned mainly with the role that these considerations play in establishing a financial framework of analysis. They can conveniently be discussed in terms of the financing decision and the disinvestment decision.

The Financing Decision

The first decision that must be faced is whether the need for funds is short or long range. If short range, the option of using equity funding is effectively eliminated. The choice will boil down to selecting from among various short-term sources: trade credit, line of credit, commercial paper, secured or unsecured term loans. The criteria of choice will include (1) which are available (e.g., commercial paper is viable for only a handful of large firms and primarily only for those in a financing oriented business), (2) the relative carrying costs of each (mainly interest charges), (3) acquisition costs, and (4) degree of flexibility of repayment.

Within the context of establishing the broad planning framework we are discussing, however, financial planners should not spend an undue amount of time trying to project the mix of various short-term debt instruments the firm will employ. For intermediate to longer term planning purposes it is sufficient to estimate the amount and average cost of short-term debt.

On the other hand, an analysis of alternative funding for long-term capital requirements is appropriate to the planning framework. Here, the differences between sources are very significant involving a long-term commitment by the firm. The first and most significant decision is whether to use debt or equity. By equity, we are referring to new issues of stock rather than retained earnings which will also increase the equity portion of the capital structure. In practice, especially among the larger corporations, new stock issues are ordinarily not the favored method of raising capital.

The observed reluctance to raise equity capital is somewhat difficult to explain. After all, while the relative costs of alternative sources of capital may not be the sole criterion for this decision, it certainly should play a major role. Therefore, whenever the managers of a firm feel its stock is overvalued, they should seriously consider new issues as a cheap source of funds. Perhaps, the tendency not to use equity funding really reflects a reluctance to admit that the stock is overvalued. But that is exactly what is implied in a stock for stock acquisition at least on a relative basis. The acquiring firm is implicitly saying, "we believe our stock is overvalued relative to the stock of the acquired company." Explicitly, however, they can save face by making the statement in a more positive form "we believe the stock of the firm we have acquired is significantly undervalued."

Besides the use of equity in acquisitions, convertible securities and warrants were also used more and more during the 60s as a way of luring investors through the promise of equity participation. This is another way managers partially "disguise" the fact that they feel the stock is overvalued. By offering convertible securities they save in interest expense at the expense of risking dilution if conversion becomes desirable. This price would be too high if they believed the stock to be undervalued.

If managers are truly operating on behalf of long-term investors (not speculators) they should not be reluctant to consider equity financing as a bona fide alternative to long-term debt. Certainly at the height of prosperity when stock prices and interest rates are high, there should be a greater willingness to use stock in lieu of bonds to finance anticipated growth. This is especially true for companies in cyclical industries such as steel, heavy machinery, and automobiles. Not only would the equity capital be raised at higher prices, but as the economy swings in the other direction, the company will not be saddled with fixed interest costs.

The financial planning mechanism will serve as a tool for evaluating the effects of each method of financing. In view of the uncertainty factor, the analytical process should involve a simulation under various assumptions regarding operating levels, profits, and stock prices. The method chosen, in any event, should be significantly influenced by which source is cheaper for long-term investors based upon the prognosis of the financial managers. If based on this analysis, the choice is to raise long-term debt, the financial manager must also determine whether to issue bonds or secure a loan from a bank. Later chapters will cover in detail the criteria of choice between these two major categories.

In putting together a financial plan, however, the financial manager will be concerned primarily with projecting the expected cash flows. The cash flow will be similar whether a bank loan is amortized or a bond issue contains sinking-fund provisions; the cash flows for a nonamortized bank loan will be similar to a bond issue requiring no sinking-fund payments. In other words, the form of repayment is far more critical for planning purposes than the specific form of the debt instrument. By the same token, there are different costs associated with each form of loan which should not be entirely ignored in the process of choosing the most beneficial one for inclusion in the plan.

The financing decision at the planning stage, then, will involve, first, a choice between long or short term; second, for long-term requirements, a choice between debt or equity; and finally, a choice between various possible repayment schedules. In each case, the word "choice" is not intended to imply total control by the financial managers. The "choice" may very well be imposed by old debt agreements or negotiations with the new suppliers of debt capital.

The Disinvestment Decision

Disinvestment decisions are less frequently encountered in financial planning because they are associated with contraction rather than expansion. One method of disinvestment that goes on continually is the payment of dividends. It is normally not thought of as a disinvestment but rather as a payment to owners in the same way that interest is paid to creditors. Even the purchase of Treasury stock is not necessarily related to disinvestment since relatively minor amounts are continually being repurchased for granting stock options, or to support employees' stock purchase plans. Large amounts may be repurchased in order to recapitalize in favor of more debt. Disinvestment, therefore, is not the sole reason for dividend payments or repurchase of Treasury stock. It is, however, accomplished primarily by these two means. If a disinvestment situation is deemed to exist, the financial manager must choose between the two. If the stock appears undervalued, repurchase of Treasury stock becomes more attractive. This is especially true if the excess funds are only semipermanent. Also the repurchase will have a favorable impact on earnings per share calculations. In addition, the tax treatment is more favorable and it distributes the funds to the more marginal stockholders.

The financial planner will evaluate the cash flow impact of each form of disinvestment. An extra dividend has a one-shot effect; it permanently reduces the capitalization at a given point in time. An increase in the regular dividend will result in a stream of cash outflows and will become, in essence, a scheduled disinvestment over time. The repurchase of Treasury stock has the same initial impact as the extra dividend. It differs, however, in that it has the effect of increasing future cash flows over what they would have been, had an extra dividend been paid. This occurs because dividends will be paid on a fewer number of shares after the retirement. The financial manager will examine these cash flow patterns to see which integrates best with the rest of the overall plan.

SUMMARY

In this chapter we have been discussing the major elements of a financial planning framework. Schematically, Figure 1, presented earlier in the chapter, represents a concise overview of this function. Financial managers must, first, integrate the many forms and many levels of planned corporate activity. Second, based on the type of activity and an estimate of the timing and amount of funds needed, they must put together a "first pass" financing plan.

But this plan cannot be expected to produce a final product. Too many departments and individuals not having a corporate wide view will have been involved in identifying potential projects. A final plan will require an in-depth analysis of the financial impact of these myriad proposals. This will involve a projection and analysis of financial reports which when concluded will put the financial planning manager and other planning executives in a position to establish a firm, well thought out plan by which to guide future activity.

ADDITIONAL SOURCES

Ansoff, H. Igor. "Planning as a Practical Management Tool." *Financial Executive,* 32 (June 1964) 34–37.

Beranek, William. "The Cost of Capital, Capital Budgeting, and the Maximization of Shareholder Wealth." *Journal of Financial and Quantitative Analysis,* 10 (March 1975), 1–20.

Bibeault, Donald. "Corporate Growth: A Conceptual Framework." *Managerial Planning,* 24 (July–August 1975), 1–10.

Bierman, H.; Chopra, K.; and Thomas, J. "Ruin Considerations: Optimal Working Capital and Capital Structure." *Journal of Financial and Quantitative Analysis,* 10 (March 1975), 119–28.

Chambers, John C.; Mullick, Satinder K.; and Smith, Donald D. "How to Choose the Right Forecasting Technique." *Harvard Business Review,* 49 (July–August 1971), 45–74.

Gentry, James A., and Pyhrr, Stephen A. "Stimulating an EPS Growth Model." *Financial Management,* 2 (Summer 1973), 68–75.

Gershefski, George W. "Building a Corporate Financial Model." *Harvard Business Review,* 47 (July–August 1969), 61–72.

Gupta, Manak C. "Optimal Financing Policy for a Firm with Uncertain Fund Requirements." *Journal of Financial and Quantitative Analysis,* 8 (December 1973), 731–48.

Pappas, James L., and Huber, George P. "Probabilistic Short-Term Financial Planning." *Financial Management,* 2 (Autumn 1973), 36–44.

Weston, J. Fred. "Forecasting Financial Requirements." *Accounting Review,* 33 (July 1958), 427–40.

Chapter 10

Planning Techniques to Aid the Corporate Treasurer

E. Leonard Arnoff[*]

INTRODUCTION

THE ECONOMY has experienced some rather severe shocks during recent years. We have experienced rampant inflation as well as lingering recession. Unemployment reached high levels and corporate profits also fluctuated widely. The economy has experienced new kinds of influences and patterns.

Treasurers, as well as other executives, are searching for more effective ways to simultaneously face both inflation and recession. Executives are searching for more effective ways to cope with mounting financial problems. There are many sweeping changes that affect business and industry today. We want to be able to anticipate these changes—or, at least, be able to react to these changes in a timely and effective manner. We want to be able to influence and control our destiny much more effectively. To the extent possible, we want to turn these problems into opportunities.

We can do this through "planning."

To set the stage, let us briefly review what "Planning" is. PLANNING is a formal, systematic, managerial process to ensure the direc-

* Dr. E. Leonard Arnoff is National Director of Management Sciences and a principal in the Management Consulting Services Division of Ernst & Ernst, Cleveland, Ohio.

tion and control of the future of the enterprise. Change is the name of the game—and, stated simply: Planning is the management of change. PLANNING is a careful, thoughtful, time-consuming process of reaching agreement regarding the actions and resources required to achieve desirable future results.

PLANNING is a continuous process which addresses, and provides answers to, nine sets of questions:

1. Who are we? What are we? What do we want to be?
2. Where are we?
3. Where are we going?
4. Where can we go? Where do we want to go? Where should we go?
5. How do we want to get there? What's the best way?
6. When do we want to get there?
7. How will we know if and when we get there?
8. Who is responsible?
9. How much will it cost? How much is it worth?

These are fundamental questions—easy to ask, but difficult to answer in an effective manner. So, let us examine how we can assist in providing answers to these questions and, in turn, assist management in planning effectively.

In a general sense, the "key" to assisting management to plan effectively lies in greater, and better, use of mathematical models— that is, through mathematical representations of the process, system, or corporation. These models are used:

1. To answer all kinds of "what if . . . ?" questions.
2. To evaluate a host of alternatives.
3. To help define the organization's objectives and goals in an operationally meaningful manner.
4. To develop sound decision rules.
5. To answer the nine planning questions. (cited earlier)
6. To develop sound, well-conceived, and well-executed plans.

However, rather than discuss specific techniques which can aid the corporate planner, let us discuss the subject in the context of specific applications—that is, to illustrate how mathematical models can be used to make planning more effective.

CASE STUDY—PRODUCER OF
CONCRETE PRODUCTS

Consider a medium-sized company that has a cement plant and a number of ready-mix and asphalt plants, and extracts and distributes sand, gravel, and crushed stone in addition to cement, ready-mix, and asphalt products. Because these facilities are spread over a large geographic region, each functional group had been making decisions in its individual area. Often these decisions were made without sufficient consideration of their effect on overall company profitability. Even when the managers tried to cooperate on a decision, they were often unable to evaluate the effect of feasible alternatives on the entire company.

The major decisions company management makes include the following:

1. Extraction of Sand and Gravel. Should we invest in somewhat remote low-cost deposits which will not be worked for many years, or in more expensive deposits nearer our plants which can begin to produce in a few months?

2. Production of Sand and Gravel. Should we exhaust deposits as quickly as possible or at a more deliberate rate? (If we work a deposit—for example, over a four-year period—the *best* combination of plant, equipment and work force will be different from that required to work it over a two-year period.) We can choose which section of the deposit to work and which products to produce. Ideally, how long should we take to exhaust the deposit?

3. Marketing of Finished Product. The company bids on major jobs. These involve cement, sand, gravel, crushed stone, ready-mix concrete, and/or asphalt. How do we decide whether to bid on major jobs in total or on some parts of them? Which parts? At what price?

A team—including management science, industrial engineering, data processing, management accounting, and tax specialists, working with management—studied the problem of designing a planning system which would facilitate making these decisions. They determined that a planning model, a computer-stored mathematical representation of the company, was needed.

To oversimplify: A thorough analysis of the system was made; the system was flow-charted; and a corporate planning model was then developed. Further, the planning model was integrated with the company's accounting system.

This planning model expresses quantitatively the expected outcome, or outcomes, of different courses of action or of different values of the variables. Specifically, for each alternative, the model projects (1) income statements, (2) balance sheets, and (3) production results. (See Figures 1–4.) It also provides discounted cash flow

FIGURE 1
Project Level Profit Report

PRODUCT TOTS + UNIT STATS, PLANT NO. 14 NEW GRAVEL

	PERIOD 1	PERIOD 2	PERIOD 3	PERIOD 4	PERIOD 5
GRAVEL					
GROSS SALES . . .	0	204422	214767	225633	237049
DEDUCTIONS . . .	0	0	0	0	0
NET SALES	0	204422	214767	225633	237049
FIXED COSTS . . .	0	66160	61734	58066	55075
VARIABLE CS. . .	0	39663	41860	44183	46640
TOTAL COST . . .	0	105823	103594	102249	101715
OPR INCOME . . .	0	98599	111173	123384	135334
UNITS SOLD . . .	0	87360	89981	92680	95460
SALES PRICE . . .	0.0000	2.3400	2.3868	2.4345	2.4832
DEDUCTION/U . .	0.0000	0.0000	0.0000	0.0000	0.0000
NET PRICE/U . .	0.0000	2.3400	2.3868	2.4345	2.4832
FIXED CST/U . .	0.0000	.7573	.6861	.6265	.5769
VARIABL C/U . .	0.0000	.4540	.4652	.4767	.4886
TOTAL CST/U. . .	0.0000	1.2113	1.1513	1.1032	1.0655
NET MARGIN/U .	0.0000	1.1286	1.2355	1.3313	1.4177

analyses, as well as treatment of the common problems of transfer pricing and joint product costing.

The model permits management to evaluate alternative strategies; to ask "what if" questions; and to obtain answers based on overall corporate profitability rather than the profitability of individual operations.

In *procurement*, the model permits management to estimate the return-on-investment for various combinations of deposits. These

FIGURE 2

Plant Level Reports

COST DETAIL, PLANT NO. 14 NEW GRAVEL PLANT					
	PERIOD 1	PERIOD 2	PERIOD 3	PERIOD 4	PERIOD 5
FIXED COSTS:					
DIRECT LABOR ..	0	137280			
DEPRECIATION ..	0	221286			
TOT FXD COST ..	0	358566			
VAR COSTS:					
OPER SUPPLIES . . .	0	1847			
KILN BRICK	0	9233			
ELEC POWER	0	23294			
REPAIRS	0	33237			
ROYALTY	0	51702			
SHOP CHARGES ..	0	7386			
GRAVEL PURCH ..	0	80876			
MISC EXP	0	7386			
TOT VAR COST ..	0	214961			
TOTAL COST	0	573527			

PLANT INCOME, PLANT NO. 14 NEW GRAVEL PLANT					
	PERIOD 1	PERIOD 2	PERIOD 3	PERIOD 4	PERIOD 5
SALES :					
SAND	0	167918	176415	185341	194720
GRAVEL	0	204422	214767	225633	237049
FILL MATRL	0	58559	61522	64635	67906
TYPE I SACK	0	91260	95878	100729	105826
I C GRAVEL	0	199555	209653	220261	231406
TOTAL SALES . . .	0	721714	758235	796599	836907
DEDUCTIONS	0	0	0	0	0
NET SALES	0	721714	758235	796599	836907
FIXED COSTS	0	358566	334573	314700	298487
VRBLE COSTS . . .	0	214961	226862	239454	252771
TOTAL COST	0	573527	561435	554154	551258
OPRTG INCM	0	148187	196800	242445	285649

estimates reflect the interrelationships among existing reserves, existing equipment and plant, and present and future markets. Also, management can use the model to bid more effectively for new deposits.

In *production,* managers can now, for example, determine the profit implications of closing a high-cost plant and supplying the demand from adjacent plants. Or, they can now determine the best level of production, by plant, to achieve desired seasonal smoothing of the labor force.

In *marketing,* management can, for example, evaluate the return to be gained from expanding the ready-mix operations. They can also evaluate the profitability of bidding on a given major job at each of a range of prices.

By use of mathematical models, the company's managers now get informed estimates as to what the best overall course of action should be under existing or contemplated circumstances. The process of developing these alternatives and reviewing the output from the model yields a more thoughtful and realistic plan—and more effective results.

At this point, it is easy to conceptualize similar planning models for any process industry. In fact, the approach is perfectly general, and is applicable to virtually any company.

FIGURE 3
Area Level Summary Report

OPERATING SUMMARY, AREA 01

	PERIOD 1	PERIOD 2	PERIOD 3	PERIOD 4	PERIOD 5
PLANT 01	280211	251442	266468	280805	294453
PLANT 03	30657	32730	35611	41317	43245
PLANT 04	201112	0	0	0	0
PLANT 06	117611	134145	149651	162477	171631
PLANT 10	16606	17144	19173	22299	22793
PLANT 12	0	0	0	0	0
PLANT 14	0	148187	196800	242445	285649
TOT OPR INCM .	646197	583648	667703	749343	817771
AR SPRT COST					
ADMIN+SALES . . .	228161	233655	240433	250649	261595
TOT AD+SL EX . .	228161	233655	240433	250649	261595
TOT AR INCM. . .	418036	349993	427270	498694	556176
OPR. RATIOS . . .					
INCOME/SALES	17	14	16	17	17
PLANT ASSETS . . .	3569915	3419370	3297306	3220333	3174439
OVHD ASSETS	62471	62934	66620	70265	73164
TOT ASSETS	3632386	3482304	3363926	3290598	3247603
AVG ASSETS	2533934	3557345	3423115	3327262	3269101
PERCH R O A , , , ,	16.5	9.8	12.5	15.0	17.0

CONTINGENCY PLANNING

An important aspect of planning is that it must consider not only likely or desired conditions, but must also include plans for emergency or contingency conditions.

To illustrate: For many years, the frozen orange concentrate industry planned only for processing a *full* crop since, as they reasoned, the industry could *not* predict the specific timing and severity of crop-damaging freezing weather. And so, they waited until a freeze occurred; then they obtained revised estimates of the crop yield, and developed new plans for that season—but usually only after a substantial lapse of time.

FIGURE 4
Corporate Level Reports

CORPORATE OPERATING SUMMARY

	PERIOD 1	PERIOD 2	PERIOD 3	PERIOD 4	PERIOD 5
OPERATING INCOME:					
...AREA.01	418036				
...AREA.02	1947960				
...AREA.03	97451				
TOTAL....	2463447				
GEN. + ADMN.	238989				
EXPLORATION	14207				
OTHR ING+EXP	37015-				
PRFT SHRING.	264234				
TOT ADMN EXP	480515				
OPER INCOME	1982932				
INTEREST...	485042				
INCM BEF FIT	1497890				
FED INCM TAX	718987				
INVEST CRT..	331722-				
NET INCOME..	1110625				
PERCENTAGES:					
NT INC/SALES	11				
PERC R O A I	17				
NET INC/EQTY	18				
EQTY/ASSET	47				
AVG ASSETS	12013204				

CORPORATE CASH FLOW SUMMARY

	PERIOD 1	PERIOD 2	PERIOD 3	PERIOD 4	PERIOD 5
NET INCOME....	1110625				
DEPRECIATION..	948047				
SHT TRM DEBT..	0				
DEPLETION...	6080				
NEW L T DEBT..	3354000				
TOTAL AVLBLE.	5418752				
ASSET REPLMT..	448890				
PRPSED ASSET..	4290000				
SHT DEBT RTR...	300000				
SCH DEBT RTR...	1087846				
REC. REQUIREMNTS	477280				
INV REQRMNTS..	97734-				
LAND INVESTM...	0				
OTHER ASSETS	0				
ACCTS PAYBLE..	335271				
TAX LIABLTS....	0				
TOTAL RQRMNT...	6841553				
NET CASH FLW...	1422801-				
DEBT/ASSETS....	.53				
TOTAL DEBT....	6960254				
POLICY DEBT....	6717607				
AVAILABLE.....	242647-				

CORPORATE BALANCE SHEET

	PERIOD 1	PERIOD 2	PERIOD 3	PERIOD 4	PERIOD 5
CASH	1122801-				
RECEIVABLES	1566772				
INVENTORIES	420477				
CURR. ASSETS	864448				
PLT+EQUIPMNT	13637602				
ACUM DPRCTN	3941461				
NET PLT+EQUP	9696141				
LAND	2016370				
OTHER ASSETS	593920				
TOTAL ASSETS	13170879				
SHT TERM DEBT	0				
CRR PORT LTD	1168440				
ACCTS PAYBLE	664729				
FIT PAYBLE	0				
CURR LIABLTS	1833169				
LNG TRM DEBT	5127085				
TOTL LIABLTS	6960254				
OWNERS EQTY:	6210625				
LIABLTS+EQTY	13170879				
CURRENT RATIO	.5 .47				

CORPORATE OVERVIEW REPORT

	PERIOD 1	PERIOD 2	PERIOD 3	PERIOD 4	PERIOD 5
CURRENT RATIO	.5	.9	1.5	1.9	2.4
EQTY/ASSETS.	.47	.30	.35	.38	.45
TOTAL ASSETS	13170879	25191364	25247775	28770269	28953701
NT CASH FLOW	1422801-	819801	476423	1129449	1329290
AREA 01 P/L	418036	349993	427268	498695	556177
PERC R O A I	17	10	13	15	17
AREA 02 P/L	1947960	1550535	3495365	3978810	4356416
PERC R O A I	25	11	17	19	20
AREA 03 P/L	97451	106518	112772	116939	116016
PERC R O A I	242	148	190	219	227
NET INCOME BEF INT+TAXS	1982932	1664312	3438134	3904374	4262708
R O A I BEF INT+TAXS	17	9	14	14	15
NET INCOME	1110625	1205395	1114257	1603144	1552675

Now, however, at least one major processor plans for the full spectrum of possible crop yields, and develops corresponding contingency plans for each level of yield. Then, if and when a freeze occurs, it is fairly easy to get a revised estimate of the crop yield and quickly shift into the correct, previously designed, revised plan. Appropriate changes in labor force, in materials, in transportation facilities, and the like are then all smoothly carried out according to the predetermined plan.

PLANNING AND EFFECTIVE COST REDUCTIONS

Another important area—one that is directly related to the treasurer's responsibilities—is that of cost cutting. Since cost reductions are so important, I will emphasize several key thoughts:

1. Cost-cutting procedures *must* be part of a sound, well-conceived and well-executed plan. When cost reduction programs are launched without a sound plan—or when prior plans are set aside—cost reduction programs usually become ineffective, often costly, desperation moves.

2. Such plans, and corresponding cost reduction programs, can best be developed through the use of mathematical models and, in particular, through simulation models. Through mathematical models, conditions requiring cost reductions can be anticipated and the appropriate cost reductions can be carried out in a sound and effective manner.

3. The plans and mathematical models used to develop cost reduction programs can also be used to evaluate the effectiveness of these programs.

4. In many cases, we really should be considering *profit improvement*, rather than cost reduction. Such programs should be directed to achieving our objectives more *effectively*, rather than more *efficiently*. Again, mathematical models can be of substantial assistance, here.

DECISION-ORIENTED MANAGEMENT INFORMATION SYSTEMS

In planning, a key ingredient is the generation of *decision-oriented* information for management's use during the ongoing planning process. Accordingly, let us briefly discuss this topic next.

Effectiveness of MIS Work to Date

Today, "MIS" has come to mean all things to all people; it is a term of great glamour; and organizations have committed substantial sums of money to MIS. There have been some isolated reports of success—but, overall, the report card to date has not been good.

Too many attempts at MIS have been overconcerned with hardware; with the *quantity* of *data* instead of the *use* of *information;* with the mechanization of existing manual systems or the conversion from manual to card, from card to tape, from tape to disc, and so on. Managers have been inundated with computer printouts. All too often, designs of basic information systems are overconcerned with the flow of data and overlook the decision-making process and appropriate opportunities for optimization.

Too many management information systems are concerned with the rapid collection, processing and distribution of *historical* data. This, of course, puts the manager in a position similar to having to drive forward on a heavily traveled freeway looking only through the *rear*view mirror!

Too many MIS studies have been concerned with what the system *is*, rather than with what it *should* be. What good is an MIS if it restricts the manager to doing the same things as before, only now to do them faster? The real question, hardly ever answered, is what *should* the manager be doing? How best to do it? Too many MIS studies have proceeded *without* careful problem formulation, system analysis, and estimates of benefits. Too many MIS studies have been directed to the almost universal myth of cost reduction, instead of to profit improvement.

Too often, the MIS is designed on the assumption that all one has to do is give the manager all the information he could possibly need. Then what? The manager also needs decision rules and methods of solution!

Too many MIS studies have assumed that all you have to do is ask the manager to tell you his objectives and those of the organization. Managers can rarely state, *in an operationally meaningful manner*, the goals, objectives, and policies of their company!

Furthermore, you cannot assume that the manager will be able to tell you what information he needs—yet all too many MIS studies assume this, too. You cannot properly determine what kind of information is required, what kinds of measurements should be made, and what kinds of reports should be generated unless you know how the information and the reports will, and *should* be, used. The manager does not know this, and won't, until models have been developed and appropriate decision rules have been generated. In designing an information system, it is essential to know, and be responsive to, the true needs of the end user and to the end use of the information itself. Hence, a *decision-oriented* management information system is required. Most MISs have failed to meet this need.

Perhaps all this can be summarized—albeit rather harshly—by saying that too much emphasis has been placed on hardware and on software, and not enough on brainware. Consequently, it is not surprising that most of the results to date in the area of MIS have been, at best, unimpressive.

What Is Needed to Develop Sound, Effective Management Information Systems?

In brief, to design, develop, and implement an effective decision-oriented management information system, the management sciences constitute an essential ingredient. Through management science—through quantitative analysis of the alternatives and through some of the results of management science studies themselves—management can then define and specify, in an operationally meaningful manner, its basic goals, objectives and policies. Further, corresponding goals, objectives, and policies can be specified for each department (and other company units), and appropriate measures can be developed to determine the contribution of each unit to the total company.

Through management science (in concert with data processing, systems, programming, accounting, and many other company functions, both operating and staff), one can design, develop, and implement a highly effective *decision-oriented* management information system. To do this, one must sequentially determine:

1. What are the basic goals, objectives, and policies of the organization—in an operationally meaningful sense?
2. What decisions must be made to achieve these goals?
3. How *should* these decisions be made?
4. What information is needed to make these decisions? Hence, *then and only then,* can one determine:
5. What data must be generated and/or collected?

Stated in another manner, through management science, one can determine: Who needs what information? When? With what accuracy? In what form? to best contribute to the success of the overall organization. More generally, a sound management information system provides *decision-oriented* information—and, in turn, decision rules—for management's use in planning and in developing an effective planning system.

SUMMARY

For sound and effective planning, we need to be able to answer a wide variety of "what if" questions; that is, questions that ask *what* would happen *if* certain contingencies or contemplated events were to arise. Such questions are best answered—and corresponding plans best developed—by means of simulation models and other mathematical representations of the enterprise.

Further, to be sound and effective, such plans require: (1) that the objectives and goals of the organization be spelled out in an operationally meaningful manner; (2) that corresponding measures of effectiveness are specified; (3) that appropriate standards, targets, or budgets exist; and (4) that evaluation procedures are established *in advance.* For these purposes, too, the management sciences in general—and simulation and other mathematical models in particular—can be of substantial assistance and benefit.

The sophisticated executive will use mathematical models to supplement and augment that which has made him a manager—his knowledge; his skills; his perceptiveness; and his feel for opportunities, situations, people, and timing. As a result, much more effective planning will be achieved in an atmosphere of informed judgment, and far less management activity will be conducted in an atmosphere of crisis.

ADDITIONAL SOURCES

Adam, John, Jr. "What Kind of Management Control Do You Need?" *Harvard Business Review,* 51 (March–April 1973), 75–86.

Aines, Ronald. "Management–Planning–Tomorrow." *Managerial Planning,* 23 (May–June 1975), 1–4.

Breen, William J., and Lerner, Eugene M. "Corporate Financial Strategies and Market Measures of Risk and Return." *Journal of Finance,* 28 (May 1973), 339–52.

Brown, Gene. "Financial Forecasting by Corporations." *Financial Analysts Journal,* 28 (March–April 1972), 38–45.

Cleland, David I., and King, William R. "Organizing for Long-Range Planning." *Business Horizons,* 17 (August 1974), 25–32.

Crawford, C. Merle. "Strategies for New Product Development." *Business Horizons,* 15 (December 1972), 49–58.

Edwards, James. "The Corporate Planner and Creativity." *Managerial Planning,* 23 (March–April 1975), 12–19.

Forsyth, Willis. "Strategic Planning in the 70's." *Financial Executive,* 41 (October 1973), 96–104.

Gerstner, Louis V., Jr. "The Practice of Business: Can Strategic Planning Pay Off?" *Business Horizons,* 15 (December 1972), 5–16.

Gibson, D. W., and Butler, J. E. "Evaluation of Inventory Management." *Business Horizons,* 16 (June 1973), 51–60.

Ives, Brian D. "Decision Theory and the Practicing Manager." *Business Horizons,* 16 (June 1973), 38–41.

King, William R., and Cleland, David I. "Decision and Information Systems for Strategic Planning." *Business Horizons,* 14 (April 1973), 29–38.

King, William R., and Cleland, David I. "A New Method for Strategic Systems Planning." *Business Horizons,* 18 (August 1975), 55–64.

Lucado, William. "Corporate Planning—A Current Status Report." *Managerial Planning,* 23 (November–December 1974), 27–34.

Mancuson, Joseph R. "How a Business Plan Is Read." *Business Horizons,* 17 (August 1974), 33–42.

Meier, Arthur. "The Planning Process," *Managerial Planning,* 23 (July–August 1974), 1–5.

Merville, Larry, and Tavis, Lee. "Long-Range Financial Planning." *Financial Management,* 3 (Summer 1974), 56–63.

Meyers, Stewart C., and Pogue, Gerald A. "A Programming Approach to Corporate Financial Management." *Journal of Finance,* 19 (May 1974), 579–600.

Modak, N. "Corporate Planning and Security Analysis." *Financial Analysts Journal,* 30 (September–October 1974), 51–54.

Pappas, James, and Huber, George. "Probabilistic Short-Term Financial Planning." 2 (Autumn 1973), 36–44.

Schoeffler, Sidney; Buzzell, Robert D.; and Heany, Donald F. "Impact of Strategic Planning on Profit Performance." *Harvard Business Review,* 52 (March–April 1974), 137–46.

Singhvi, Surendra. "The Financial Planning and Analysis Function." *Managerial Planning,* 23 (November–December 1974), 35–40.

Tersine, Richard. "Forecasting: Prelude to Managerial Planning." *Managerial Planning,* 24 (July–August 1975), 11–17.

Tipgos, Manuel. "Structuring a Management Information System for Strategic Planning." *Managerial Planning,* 23 (January–February 1975), 10–16.

Vancil, Richard F., and Lorange, Peter. "Strategic Planning in Diversified Companies." *Harvard Business Review,* 53 (January–February 1975), 81–90.

Chapter 11

Financial Theory and the Treasurer

Edward E. Williams*
M. C. Findlay†

THE THEORY of finance has been expanding by leaps and bounds over the last decade. Much of it, however, has been expressed in such an esoteric mathematical form as to be inaccessible to the practicing financial officer. Our goal is to present some of the more useful aspects of this theory in a nontechnical way, pointing out implications, applications, and, perhaps most important, limitations as we go.

The basic concept which we employ is the hypothesis that capital markets are efficient. (We refer to this subsequently as the efficient markets hypothesis, or EMH.) An efficient capital market is, first of all, competitive, such that there are many buyers and sellers of stocks and bonds and no one of them can influence the price. It is also a market in which new information is rapidly transmitted and interpreted in an unbiased manner. Finally, it is a market in which taxes and transactions costs do not create gross distortions in the proper allocation of capital. These are the major attributes of the EMH which are important for our discussion, and there is a large

* Edward E. Williams is vice president, Service Corporation International, Houston, Texas.

† M. C. Findlay is professor of finance, University of Southern California, Los Angeles.

body of literature which indicates that they are satisfied at least to a first approximation.

The notion that capital markets are efficient has always had an intuitive appeal to classical economists. Nevertheless, the question as to whether or not any market is efficient is an empirical one, and the available evidence is almost uniquely confined to New York Stock Exchange listings. As a result, when one encounters discussions assuming the empirical validity of the EMH, it should be remembered that the primary security markets are generally not encompassed nor are OTC (over-the-counter) stocks and the smaller exchange listings. Additionally, the EMH relates only to the *capital* markets. Other markets, such as those for goods and services, labor, and plant and equipment are not included.

Granting the EMH for the moment, the major thrust of modern financial theory to the treasurer can be stated as follows:

1. An efficient market will only demand a risk premium (that is, an increase in the required rate of return) for the risk which it will actually have to bear (which we call *relevant risk*).
2. An efficient market will only pay a premium (that is, a higher price for shares or lower required rate of return) for actions undertaken by the firm when the market cannot do the same thing. In other words, the market will not reward the firm for doing things the market could as easily do for itself. Thus, for the firm, there is no such thing as a free lunch.

Both of these principles sound so straightforward we often wonder how anybody could dispute them. Yet there have been many bloody battles in print over them during the last 15 years. To initiate our discussion, it is necessary to consider the notion of *relevant risk*.

RELEVANT RISK AND INVESTMENT DECISIONS

Total Project Risk

Suppose that we organized a company for the sole purpose of drilling one wildcat oil well. Suppose further that the shareholders had put up every penny they owned or could borrow in order to buy the stock. In this case, the relevant risk both to the firm and to its shareholders would be the risk of obtaining profitable production from that one well. The total wealth of the firm and of its shareholders would be riding on the outcome of that one well and, since we are told that eight wildcats out of nine are "dusters," it is quite unlikely that many investors could be found to participate in such an endeavor. Note that we have said nothing about how profitable the well might be if it hit; we have merely suggested that eight chances in nine of financial ruin would be enough to dissuade most people, no matter what the potential gain.

Our oil example demonstrates three important points. Since almost everyone is averse to risk, he requires higher expected rates of return in order to undertake investments of greater risk. (David B. Hertz explores this point more fully in Chapter 18.) Second, this aversion to risk becomes extreme if there is any chance of total ruin; in other words, most individuals would not voluntarily undertake *at any price* a course of action which could result in disaster. Finally, the relevant risk to both the firm and its shareholders is the risk of the project *only if* the total wealth of both is invested in the project.

Throughout the last two decades, most advice given to practitioners about dealing with risk and uncertainty has reflected this thinking. Firms which viewed a project's risk as being measured by the variability of its cash flow stream (or, equivalently, by the statistical variance of its internal rate of return or discounted present value), and thus required higher discount or hurdle rates for those projects with greater variability, were implicitly adopting the "one oil well" approach. As long as the firm consists of more than one project, however, the risk of the project by itself is typically far greater than the increase in risk caused by adding the project to an ongoing firm.

Firm Portfolio Risk

To continue the example, suppose that our newly organized oil company is quite large and plans to drill 1,000 wildcat wells. The probability of hitting oil with any particular well is still one in nine, but the chance of finding at least some oil is now much improved. Although it is quite unlikely that we would hit oil in exactly 111 wells, the chance of not getting at least, say, 80 producers is quite small. Thus, the risk of drilling a given well if it is our 1,000th well is very different than if it is our one and only well.

Our expanded example illustrates the basic principle underlying portfolio theory. If some or all of the risk of a given investment is caused by purely random elements (that is, not affecting other investments), then by combining enough different investments into a portfolio these random elements will ultimately cancel one another. In other words, one investment may be doing much better than expected while another is doing much worse, but the combination of the two will be about on target. (This can also be viewed as an application of the law of large numbers.)

The portfolio approach to corporate investment decisions may be illustrated by Figure 1. If we were to take all possible combinations

FIGURE 1

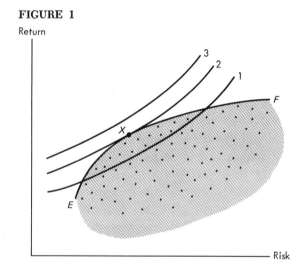

of all new and existing investments facing the firm, compute their risk and return, and plot the result, we would obtain the shaded area in Figure 1. Those capital budgets (or, if you will, portfolios of investment projects) with the highest expected return at each level of risk would form the curve *EF* (which is often called the *efficient frontier*) and the desired budget would be among them.

To select the best budget, we need to know the firm's (or its shareholders') risk-return trade-off function. Since we have assumed everyone to be averse to risk, we do know that higher levels of risk must promise higher levels of return to provide equal satisfaction.

A family of hypothetical trade-off curves is shown as 1, 2, 3 in Figure 1. All points on the same curve provide equal satisfaction, and the higher curves are more desirable than the lower ones. We can see that several capital budgets would fall on curve 1, budget X would fall on 2, and no available budget will fall on 3. Thus, from all the available investment plans, X provides the highest level of satisfaction and is the best choice.

The portfolio solution works well if the treasurer knows all projects the firm will face and can make a once-and-for-all determination. In most cases, however, a decentralized decision rule is desired that can be used over time as projects arise and at different levels of the firm. In sum, we desire the portfolio equivalent of the old-fashioned hurdle rate. To illustrate this, let us assume the firm adopted budget X from Figure 1 and was then confronted with a new project. The possibilities are shown in Figure 2, which is merely

FIGURE 2

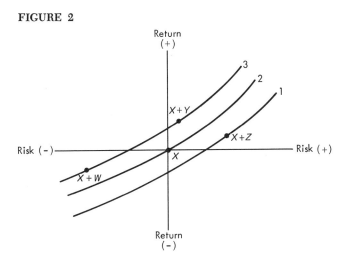

a blowup of Figure 1. We can see immediately that, if adopting the project would move us from X to Y, the result would be good; if it moved us instead to Z, it would be bad. The question then becomes how the risk and return of the project affect the risk and return of the firm.

The return part is relatively easy; the return of the enlarged firm will be a weighted average of the return on the old firm and the return of the project. The latter, of course, is measured in terms of the incremental costs and revenues to the firm resulting from the project's adoption. Thus, just as has been taught for years, acceptance of a project with an internal rate of return (IRR) above the firm's current rate will raise that rate. The risk of the enlarged firm will not in general be a simple weighted average, however. The change in firm risk will depend upon the *covariance* between the project and the old firm. Covariance is a statistical measure which includes the project's risk, the firm's risk, and the correlation between the two. The use of covariance instead of variability (that is, variance or standard deviation) gives recognition to the fact that some projects can be quite risky by themselves and yet add very little risk to the firm. Indeed some can even reduce risk! Consider the following:

> Why does any half-way bright treasurer buy fire insurance on his plant? Consider it as a capital budgeting decision. You invest some money (the premium) in return for a *very small* chance of a big pay-off. The risk is tremendous. And, worse yet, the IRR is negative (to account for the expenses of the insurance company). No capital budgeting proposal like that would ever pass muster.

The answer, of course, is that the "investment" in fire insurance is inversely correlated with the rest of the firm, in that it does well (pays off) when the rest of the firm does poorly (burns to the ground). Thus the covariance is negative and buying fire insurance reduces the risk of the firm. This reduction in risk reduces the firm's required return and justifies the acceptance of a lower (even negative in some cases, as the fire insurance) IRR on the project. Thus, if the purchase of fire insurance moved the firm from X to W in Figure 2 it would be justified (that is, it would place the firm on a higher trade-off curve), even though it lowered the expected return of the firm.

It might also be noted that another portfolio concept exists in this context. As the firm becomes larger and expands to several plants, it becomes increasingly unlikely that all of them would burn down at once. Thus, the relative size of any potential fire loss declines, as does the risk premium the firm is prepared to pay to insure against such a loss. Ultimately, the firm would reach a size where it would elect to self-insure against fire losses.

The analysis may be simplified at this point if (a) we may conduct the discussion in terms of IRR only and (b) we may assume that the firm has access to the capital market to borrow or lend at an interest rate of R. The data from Figure 2 may then be presented as Figure 3. The current firm is still at point X. If it holds additional

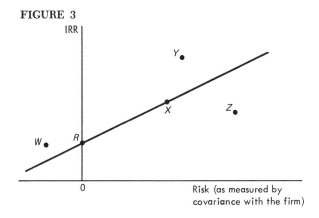

FIGURE 3

liquid assets its risk and return reduce down the line toward R (at R, the firm would be a money market mutual fund); if the firm issues debt at the rate R, its risk and return increase up the line beyond X. Thus, the line RX is the revised risk-return trade-off line for the firm, and any project which lies above it either increases return more than risk (project Y) or reduces risk more than return (project W) and, therefore, is desirable.

Systematic Market Risk

In moving from 1 oil well to 1,000, we allowed the firm to undertake numerous projects. We continued to assume, however, that all of the stockholders' wealth was tied up in the firm and, thus, that firm risk and shareholder risk were the same thing. For the final step, let us remove this restriction by postulating that there are many firms and that shareholders own diversified portfolios of stock in these firms. The operations of any one firm would then have a very small impact on the shareholders' portfolios. More to the point, the firm's risk would overstate the amount of risk relevant to shareholders.

The basic portfolio problem of the shareholder, as originally outlined by Markowitz and Sharpe (see Additional Sources at end of this chapter), proceeds in much the same way as the firm's portfolio decision which was discussed above. In theory, investors would take all possible combinations of available shares, compute the risk and return of the resulting portfolios, and derive their efficient frontiers (*EF* in Figure 4). If they borrow and lend at interest rate *R*, they

FIGURE 4

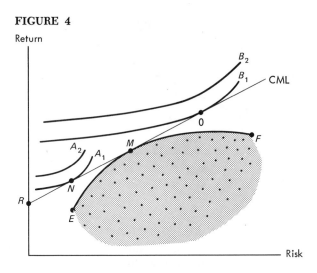

would then find the portfolio which provided the greatest excess return over rate *R* per unit of risk (portfolio *M* in Figure 4). If the investor were very averse to risk (such as Mr. A in Figure 4), he would then hold portfolio *M* in combination with riskless securities (depicted as portfolio *N* in Figure 4). If the investor were less risk averse (such as Mr. B in Figure 4), he would buy portfolio *M* on margin (that is, borrow against it at interest rate *R* to achieve the risk-return level given as 0 in Figure 4).

Although the shareholders' portfolio problem has little direct relevance for the treasurer, its ramifications do. To study them, we must temporarily make several more assumptions. Basically, they involve postulating that all investors are essentially alike; that they have similar expectations about the future; and that they have similar investment opportunities available to them. If this is the case, then all investors are confronted with *EF* and *R* in Figure 4 and, hence, they all wish to hold portfolio *M*. Since all shares must be owned by somebody, the only portfolio which everybody can hold is the market portfolio (that is, all securities in the market held in proportion to their market value—which is often approximated by an index like the S&P 500). In financial theory, then, the line *RMO* in Figure 4 is often called the *capital market line* and its slope (that is, the risk-return trade-off) is called *the market price of risk.*

If all investors hold the market portfolio *M*, the question then arises as to how individual shares would be priced. The theory would indicate that higher returns would be demanded for higher relevant risk. Furthermore, the increase in portfolio risk caused by adding the shares of a given company to an already diversified portfolio will depend on the covariance between them. We may therefore draw Figure 5, which is similar to Figure 3 except that the relevant risk to shareholders now is measured by the covariance between the return on the company's shares and the return on all other shares in the market. Line *RM* in Figure 5 is often called the *capital asset pricing line* (CAPL) and, in theory, all individual stocks and portfolios will lie on it if capital markets are in equilibrium and the EMH holds true.

By a simple transformation, risk in Figure 5 may also be deter-

FIGURE 5

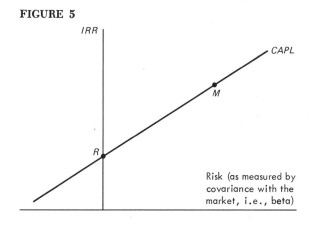

mined by the stock's "beta" coefficient. The use of beta as a surrogate measure of the riskiness of a firm has become popular in recent years, although there are those who are not convinced that the statistic is quite so powerful. The firm's beta coefficient is usually determined by a simple regression analysis. If we define "excess return" as dividend yield plus capital gains yield minus the riskless rate of interest (*R*), we can then collect these data for both the firm's stock and a market index (e.g., the S&P 500) over, say, a decade. Employing simple regression analysis, we would then estimate the values of α (alpha) and β (beta) for the equation: Firm excess return = $\alpha + \beta$ (market excess return). If the EMH held true, we would hope to find alpha approximately equal to zero. Thus, in a nontechnical sense, beta would provide a measure of the stock's sensitivity to overall market movements. In a technical sense, beta is merely the covariance discussed in the prior paragraph divided by the variance of the market's return.

The implications of the CAPL theory for the treasurer lie in the notion that a share merely represents a claim to future cash payments of unknown magnitude which are generated from investment in real assets. Any change in the firm's asset investment can alter the prospective risk and return of the firm's shares. We have assumed, however, that the market receives and interprets news of the firm quickly and that the CAPL presents the market price of relevant shareholder risk. Thus, any investment project which exceeds the market's requirements will increase the value of the firm and should be adopted.

As an example, suppose that the firm's shares currently plot at T_1 in Figure 6 and a capital budgeting proposal with risk and return

FIGURE 6

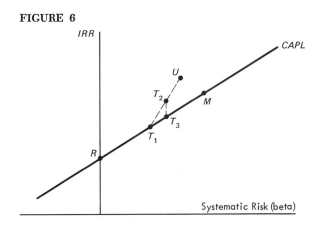

at U becomes available. Since U lies above the CAPL, we have suggested it should be accepted. Consider what would happen if it were. Any combination of the firm (T_1) and U will plot on the line connecting them; the exact position will depend upon the relative size of the project. Suppose that the firm, after adopting U, would lie at T_2. Capital markets would not be in equilibrium because the firm's expected rate of return would be too high at the new level of risk. The price of the firm's shares would be bid up until only the appropriate rate of return were expected; the firm would then plot at T_3 in Figure 6. The process of bidding up the price of the firm's stock would, of course, increase the wealth of current shareholders and, for this reason, we urged the adoption of U. Adoption of any other project above the CAPL would initiate the same process. Equally important, adoption of projects plotting below the CAPL would initially move the firm below the line and cause share price decreases as the firm moved back to equilibrium on the line.

A Recapitulation

Since risk averse investors will demand higher returns to compensate them for any increases in risk caused by capital budgeting decisions, this section has considered how this risk should be measured so that appropriate hurdle rates can be set. Our major contention is that the widely followed practice of measuring a project's risk in terms of the variability of its prospective income or cash benefit stream (or, equivalently, the statistical variance of its IRR or DPV) is simply wrong in most cases. As long as the firm undertakes more than one project, risk will be overstated by this technique and the implied hurdle rate will be too high. In extreme cases (which arise more often than one might think), projects can be made to look quite risky which would, in fact, reduce the firm's risk (reconsider our fire insurance example). Thus, firms should at least adopt a portfolio view of their operations.

Whether firms should move all the way to a CAPL view is, to us, an open question. The problem is basically an academic one unless the firm is substantially different from other issuers in the market. Nevertheless, it is interesting to note that financial theory would compel such a view only if (1) capital markets were absolutely perfect—which would include the assumptions that everyone held a perfectly diversified portfolio and could instantly remove any management team which was not maximizing shareholder wealth— or if (2) markets were merely efficient and managements were pursuing the sole goal of shareholder wealth maximization.

As a practical matter for most firms, it does not make a great deal of difference whether the CAPL concept is accepted once the port-folio view is adopted. If, however, a firm has a very low (or negative) beta and makes a "risk-reducing" (in the portfolio sense) invest-ment, it might think it was moving itself down the CAPL when, in fact, it was moving up (toward the rest of the market). Firms with very high betas face a somewhat different problem, as empirical studies seem to indicate that the CAPL may be rather flat in this region. Thus, although "risk-reducing" investment would move high beta firms down the CAPL, they might observe very little relief in their cost of capital. As a result, such firms might be able to reduce hurdle rates for such investments only slightly.

Our hesitation on adopting the CAPL in its entirety at this time can be traced to three problems:

1. Empirical evidence suggests that total firm risk (that is, firm portfolio risk), as well as systematic market risk (that is, beta), con-tinues to command a premium in the stock market. Such an effect could be explained by, among other things, the persistence of "pru-dent man" laws governing institutional investors and the inability (or unwillingness) of smaller investors to hold efficiently diversified portfolios. Whatever the cause, the implication is that firms which ignore their total risk to concentrate solely on their market risk do so at their peril.

2. Other evidence indicates that betas for individual stocks tend to be highly unstable over time and to regress toward unity (i.e., the average beta for all stocks). Thus, by the time one has collected enough years' data for a reasonably precise estimate of beta, the lat-ter has probably changed. Such instability is especially undesirable in budgeting or planning processes which extend many years into the future.

3. Finally, efforts to relate firm variables such as debt-equity ratios, variation about trend in income, and the like to beta have only been able to explain 20–30 percent of the variation in the latter. Much remains to be known about the link between the firm and the market.

> Many treasurers have been faced with the following plight thus far in the 1970s: they keep their financial statements in order; nothing very exciting has happened to their company; and yet they observe the Dow jumping all over the place and their own shares jumping even more. Being unable to raise funds in a depressed market, the treasurer approaches an expert:

> **Treasurer:** Why are my shares down with earnings up?
>
> **Expert:** Because they have become more risky.
>
> **Treasurer:** How is that?
>
> **Expert:** You have a high beta. Your shares move more than proportionately with the market.
>
> **Treasurer:** But the market is crazy.
>
> **Expert:** The market is efficient; it is as likely to jump up as down on any given transaction.
>
> **Treasurer:** Where I come from, that would pass for crazy; but I won't press the point. Why do I have such a high beta with stable financial statements?
>
> **Expert:** Financial statements are prepared by accounting rules and reflect the past. The stock price reflects the market's estimate of the future.
>
> **Treasurer:** But that hasn't changed! How can the market know more about the future of my own company than I do?
>
> **Expert:** Most versions of the EMH would presume you to have the superior knowledge.
>
> **Treasurer:** Then, if I use the CAPM in capital budgeting, I am starting with the market's current assessment of the firm (which I feel to be in error) in deciding which projects to accept? Couldn't that lead me astray?
>
> **Expert:** Unless you felt the market's judgment were superior, it certainly could.

From the above discussion, it might be concluded that a full-scale movement to "capital budgeting with beta" would be premature. Nevertheless, it should be clear that an astute treasurer of a firm whose stock has a very high, low or negative beta coefficient should certainly consider the CAPL effects of capital budgeting proposals. Woe be it to the treasurer of a gold mining concern (negative beta) who decided to "diversify" into another line of business (with a positive beta). He would be doing a disservice to his firm's stockholders, and his cost of capital would actually increase!

FREE LUNCHES AND FINANCING DECISIONS

Capital Structure Policy

There has been a very long and generally unproductive discussion in the financial literature during the last 15 years about whether or not the firm can advance the interests of its shareholders through the use of debt financing. In a very artificial world (which excludes taxes and brokerage fees), it can be shown that no premium will be paid for shares of levered companies if investors can obtain margin loans on equivalent terms against the shares of unlevered companies. By then recognizing the existence of taxes, it follows that leverage is desirable because of the different treatment afforded interest payments and dividends (i.e., interest payments are deductible from the corporate return, while dividend payments are not). If borrowing is to occur, it is clearly desirable that it be done at the corporate level so that taxes may be reduced.

Our synthesis of current thinking on capital structure policy may be presented in terms of Figure 7. It is generally agreed that a "pru-

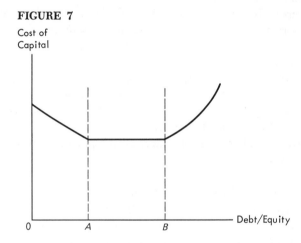

dent" use of debt will lower the firm's cost of capital (as shown by the curve from 0 to *A* in Figure 7), if for no other reason than the tax deductibility of the interest. It is also generally agreed that "excessive" amounts of debt will raise a firm's cost of capital (as shown by the curve beyond *B* in Figure 7); here it is often argued that financial distress has a cost and high levels of debt greatly increase the probability of distress occurring. Finally, it is often suggested that there may be a rather wide range of capital structures over which the cost changes very little (as shown by the curve between *A* and *B* in Figure 7).

The determination of prudent levels of corporate debt (in terms of the magnitude of distress costs and their probability of occurrence) will depend upon the nature of the business in which the firm is involved. Companies that face substantial business risk (caused by high levels of operating fixed costs and a volatile revenue pattern) might find it advisable to maintain a conservative capital structure. Railroads, for example, are very much at the mercy of the business cycle and have high levels of operating fixed costs. These concerns clearly should *not* engage in much debt financing, and the poor long-term results of many of the American railroads provides empirical testimony to such. On the other hand, firms that experience stable (or, at least, predictable) revenue patterns may incur above average nonfinancial fixed costs and still assume reasonably large amounts of debt.

As an illustration, holding companies involved in the funeral service industry have typically employed debt as an important source of finance, yet the inherent stability of funeral home revenues makes this one of the least risky types of business in the United States. According to *The Failure Record*, 1973, of Dun and Bradstreet, there were only three bankruptcies for funeral service companies out of nearly 21,000 concerns. This was the lowest failure rate for any industry.

It is also observed that bankers and/or the firm's own management may impose limits on the allowable amount of debt in the capital structure. If both groups place limits, the lower of the two would, of course, be controlling. It is interesting to note that, as long as this limit lies below *B* in Figure 7, the treasurer need not concern himself with determining the least cost (or, optimal) capital structure; all he needs to do is borrow to the limit. Only if the limit lies beyond *B* (which is unlikely in most cases), is it necessary even to consider the question of the least cost combination of debt and equity funds.

Dividend Policy

Paralleling the capital structure controversy has been a discussion of whether dividend policy will affect the value of the firm. In an artificial world similar to that discussed above, it can be shown that dividend policy does not affect value. Basically, we must assume that the firm has an investment budget which it will undertake in any event. Thus, any increase in dividends must be financed indirectly by a new issue of shares. It can then be shown, in efficient markets, that any change in dividend payments will be exactly offset by a change in stock value because of the dilution caused by issuing new shares. The recognition of taxes would tend to favor earnings retention, because shareholders would be subject to the more favorable capital gains rates and even then only upon sale of their shares. Adding brokerage fees might favor dividends, because stock sales would otherwise be necessary to provide current income. Thus, theory provides a rather unclear view of the role of dividend policy in valuation.

More traditional observers, who have been identified as "bird in the hand" followers, would disagree with the above analysis. They contend that the future is unknown, funds paid as dividends are not necessarily replaced with new issues, and investment budgets are far from immutable. They also argue that a dollar paid out in dividends is valued more highly in the market than a dollar reinvested within the firm which may or may not ever reappear in earnings.

In response to this argument, there has developed another view under the heading of "the informational content of dividends." The new theorists would not accept the explanation that dividends are valuable per se, but rather contend that dividends are increased because a firm's directors feel the higher level can be sustained. They then argue that it is this information about the company's future prospects, not the dividend itself, to which the market reacts. Both the traditionalists and the new theorists agree that dividend changes do appear to be associated with stock price changes in the same direction.

For a company that adopts the informational content of dividends view, it should be remembered that dividend reductions are usually met with a very unfavorable reaction in the market. The omission of a dividend can have an extremely severe impact even if the payout is restored in a short period of time. This is particularly true if the omission is unexpected or if the firm passing its dividend has many stockholders who have bought their shares to obtain current income. Consolidated Edison has undoubtedly paid a price in terms of market disaffection because of its abrupt dividend elimination even though a reduced payout was subsequently reinstated. On the other hand, if shareholders are convinced that a dividend reduction is necessary for the long-run health of the corporation, such might be considered a positive action. The recent cuts by General Motors and DuPont seem to have been accepted by most investors as prudent decisions in light of the current problems faced by both companies.

Another view of the dividend policy decision is that stockholders purchase shares in companies that have established records as either growth/low-payout entities or nongrowth/high-payout concerns. Stockholders in high tax brackets and those who prefer to accumulate capital gains buy the shares of corporations in the former category, while investors in low (or zero) tax brackets and those who are in need of current income purchase stock in firms evidencing the latter characteristic. This "constituency view" of dividend preference is accepted by many corporate directors as a part of the image their firm portrays to the outside world. Dynamic, successful companies attract stockholders of a similar nature and serve their constituents best by retaining earnings *so long as lucrative investment projects can be found.* Shares of conservative, mature corporations tend to be in the portfolios of eleemosynary institutions, the elderly, and others who very likely have a strong desire for dividends. High payouts would be advisable for these firms, especially if they lack lucrative opportunities for reinvestment.

Timing

The EMH has a rather interesting implication in regard to the timing of financial policies: timing doesn't matter. An efficient market already reflects all available information about the future. Thus, since long-term interest rates are assumed to reflect the market's best estimate of future rate changes, the treasurer could expect to earn no systematic gain by issuing bonds in lieu of notes or visa versa. Although theory often overstates the case, many treasurers have learned to their sorrow that techniques like "riding the yield curve" can produce large losses rather than guaranteed profits. For debt maturity policy, theory would suggest issuing debt: (*a*) in such a way as to minimize issuance costs and (*b*) of a maturity to cause the duration of the liabilities to match the duration of the assets as closely as possible to minimize risk.

When applied to stock, the EMH arguments may have even less intuitive appeal to treasurers: in an efficient market stocks are always "correctly" priced in relation to available information. Thus, treasurers' pleas like "we can't issue equity with stock prices so low" would be gibberish to EMH proponents. Non-EMH observers, following Keynes, might argue that even though everyone agreed prices were too low, they would not enter the market to bid them up because prices could go even lower (which is the EMH rejoinder). Thus, if the treasurer believes the EMH, it doesn't matter when he sells shares (or even, according to other EMH studies, how many shares he sells); he will always receive the "right" price. Nonbelievers, however, are advised to wait for booms.

CONCLUSIONS

It is now possible to bring the threads of our discussion together in terms of the CAPL, as illustrated in Figures 5 and 6. According to this theory, the firm should accept all investment projects plotting above the line and refund with or refinance by any financing opportunities which lie below the line. Because the capital market is presumed efficient, however, it is felt that financing opportunities would lie on the line and opportunities for gain through financing decisions would be limited and transitory. This view is reflected in the position of the new theory, expressed above, that capital structure policy (except for taxes) and dividend policy (except for information and transactions costs—which would include constituency effects) "don't matter" in determining firm value.

Since the CAPL theory does allow labor, goods, and other markets to be inefficient and, thus investment projects to plot above the line, a rationale for corporate investment behavior continues to exist even under the strong form of this theory. As the conglomerate merger involves combining shares which are already presumed to lie on the CAPL (and, thus, any combination will also lie on the CAPL), however, no rationale for this behavior is provided by the theory.

A technical distinction should also be made at this point. In traditional capital budgeting, the treasurer was advised: (a) to compute an IRR for the project before any financing costs; (b) to compute a cost of capital including the tax effects of debt and (since market rates were employed) the market's reaction to the firm's business and financial risk; and then (c) to compare (a) with (b). Since the CAPL depicts gross market yields, a slight modification to this procedure is employed. The marginal business and financial risk of the firm is treated automatically by the CAPL through dealing with individual investment and financing proposals. For example, a firm attempting to float a bond issue which exceeded "prudent" debt levels (one that would force the firm beyond point B in Figure 7) would find the yield on such bonds to lie well above the CAPL and abandon the idea. The required modification arises because market yields do not fully reflect the tax savings on debt. Thus, for CAPL purposes, the IRR of a project is computed to include any tax savings arising from the additional debt capacity available to the firm as a result of adopting the project. With this slightly changed definition, the above prescription (that is, adopt all investment projects above, and financing opportunities below, the CAPL) holds in theory.

Finally, we must note that theory, by definition, is an abstraction from reality. Nobody has ever suggested that the above can be applied blindly with favorable results. On the other hand, the general tendency to "throw out the baby with the bathwater" the minute one encounters a simplifying assumption that is viewed as unrealistic is equally ill advised. The test of any theory is its usefulness. We would suggest that the above theory is useful in at least three ways.

1. Financial theory, by simplifying reality to a few basics, makes the visualization of complex problems much easier and often serves to focus attention on the key elements.
2. To a growing extent, theory is becoming operational. Parts of the above framework (especially the portfolio risk concepts) are being implemented by advanced firms. And, as capital markets become more efficient over time, more and more of the theory becomes operational.
3. Finally, theory sharpens the treasurer's thinking by serving as devil's advocate. Many of the implications presented above (especially in the financing discussion) must be unattractive to the reader. The relevant question is: Why? We have presented our assumptions and logic; what are yours? The very exercise of going through the arguments to find the points of disagreement enhances the thought process and, usually, greatly narrows the area of disagreement—often all the way down to points which can be tested.

Thus, we would argue no matter how "practical" a treasurer may think himself to be, theory may suggest useful lines of thinking and analysis.

SOURCES

Selected Sources

For those interested in pursuing the topics covered in this chapter in more detail, the foundation of portfolio theory is to be found in:

Markowitz, Harry. *Portfolio Selection.* New York: John Wiley & Sons, Inc., 1959.

The groundwork for the CAPM and beta analysis are in:

Sharpe, William. *Portfolio Theory and Capital Markets.* New York: McGraw-Hill Book Co., 1970.

Results of empirical tests of the EMH are surveyed by:

Fama, Eugene. "Efficient Capital Markets: A Review of Theory and Empirical Work." *Journal of Finance,* 25 (May 1970), 383–417.

Jensen, M. C. "Capital Markets: Theory and Evidence," *Bell Journal of Economics and Management Science,* 3 (Autumn 1972), 357ff.

More "popular" versions of the above may be found in:

Modigliani, F., and Pogue, G. "An Introduction to Risk and Return: Concepts and Evidence," *Financial Analysts Journal,* 30 (March–April and May–June 1974) 68–80; 69–86.

Vasicek, O. A., and McQuoun, J. A. "The Efficient Market Model," *Financial Analysts Journal,* 28 (September–October 1972), 71–84.

Williams, E. E., and Findlay, M. C. *Investment Analysis.* Englewood Cliffs, N.J.: Prentice-Hall, Inc., 1974, Chap. 1, 15–20.

The "no free lunch" view of financing decisions originally appeared in:

Modigliani, F., and Miller, M. "The Cost of Capital, Corporation Finance and the Theory of Investment," *American Economic Review,* 48 (June 1958), 261–97.

Miller, M., and Modigliani, F. "Dividend Policy, Growth, and the Valuation of Shares," *Journal of Business,* 34 (October 1961), 411–33.

It has been synthesized in a recent monograph:

Fama, E., and Miller, M. *The Theory of Finance.* New York: Holt, Rinehart, and Winston, Inc., 1972.

Alternative views of financial policy are presented in:

Gordon, Myron. *The Investment, Financing and Valuation of the Corporation.* Homewood, Ill.: Richard D. Irwin, Inc., 1962.

Lerner, E., and Carleton, W. *A Theory of Financial Analysis.* New York: Harbrace, 1966.

Finally, the CAPM view of corporate financial theory has recently appeared in:

Rubinstein, Mark. "A Mean-Variance Synthesis of Corporate Financial Theory," *Journal of Finance,* 28 (March 1973), 167–82.

Weston, J. Fred. "Investment Decisions Using the Capital Asset Pricing Model," *Financial Management*, 2 (Spring 1973), 25–33.

Haley, C., and Schall, L. *The Theory of Financial Decisions.* New York: McGraw-Hill Book Co., 1973.

Additional Sources

Adler, Michael. "The Cost of Capital and Valuation of a Two-Country Firm." *Journal of Finance*, 29 (March 1974), 119–32.

Beaver, William, and Manegold, James. "The Association between Market-Determined and Accounting-Determined Measures of Systematic Risk; Some Further Evidence." *Journal of Financial and Quantitative Analysis*, 10 (June 1975), 231–84.

Black, Fischer, and Scholes, Myron. "From Theory to a New Financial Product." *Journal of Finance*, 19 (May 1974), 399–412.

Blume, Marshall, and Friend, Irwin. "A New Look at the Capital Asset Pricing Model." *Journal of Finance*, 28 (March 1973), 19–34.

Bowman, Robert G. "The Role of Utility in the State-Preference Framework." *Journal of Financial and Quantitative Analysis*, 10 (June 1975), 341–52.

Brennan, Michael J. "An Approach to the Valuation of Uncertain Income Streams." *Journal of Finance*, 28 (June 1973), 661–74.

Cooley, Philip L., and Copeland, Ronald M. "Contrasting Roles of Financial Theory and Practice." *Business Horizons*, 18 (August 1975), 25–31.

Cooley, Philip L., and Roenfeldt, Rodney L. "Decision Evaluation for Owner Wealth." *Business Horizons*, 17 (August 1974), 67–72.

Cooper, Richard V. L. "Efficient Capital Markets and the Quantity Theory of Money." *Journal of Finance*, 29 (June 1974), 887–908.

Elliott, J. W. "Control, Size, Growth, and Financial Performance in the Firm." *Journal of Financial and Quantitative Analysis*, 7 (January 1972), 1309–20.

Fama, E. F. "Risk, Return, and Equilibrium." *Journal of Political Economy*, 79 (January–February 1971), 30–55.

Fama, E. F., and MacBeth, J. "Risk, Return and Equilibrium: Empirical Tests." *Journal of Political Economy*, 81 (May–June 1973), 607–36.

Farrar, Donald. "Implications of the Martin Report." *Financial Analysts Journal*, 27 (September–October 1971), 18–20.

Findlay, Chapman, and Whitmore, G. A. "Beyond Shareholder Wealth Maximization." *Financial Management*, 3 (Winter 1974), 25–35.

Findlay, M. Chapman, III; Pettit, R. Richardson; McConnell, John J.; Sandberg, Carl M.; Bloomfield, Ted; and Ma, Ronald. "The Weighted Average Cost of Capital: Some Questions on Its Definition, Interpretation, and Use: Comment." *Journal of Finance*, 30 (June 1975), 879–88.

Friend, I., and Blume, M. "Measurement of Portfolio Performance under Uncertainty." *The American Economic Review*, 60 (September 1970), 561–75.

Gonedes, Nicholas J. "A Note of Accounting-Based and Market-Based Estimates of Systematic Risk." *Journal of Financial and Quantitative Analysis*, 10 (June 1975), 355–66.

Hakansson, Nils H. "Mean-Variance Analysis in a Finite World." *Journal of Financial and Quantitative Analysis*, 7 (September 1972), 1873–80.

Hayes, Robert H., and Nolan, Richard L. "What Kind of Corporate Modeling Functions Best?" *Harvard Business Review*, 52 (May–June 1974), 102–12.

Hogan, William W., and Warren, James M. "Computation of the Efficient Boundary in the E-S Portfolio Selection Model." *Journal of Financial and Quantitative Analysis*, 7 (September 1972), 1881–96.

Inselbag, Isik. "Financing Decisions and Theory of the Firm." *Journal of Financial and Quantitative Analysis*, 8 (December 1973), 763–76.

Kraus, Alan, and Robert Litzenberger. "A State-Preference Model of Optimal Financial Leverage." *Journal of Finance*, 28 (September 1973), 911–22.

Lintner, J. "The Aggregation of Investors' Diverse Judgment and Preferences in Purely Competitive Securities Markets." *Journal of Financial and Quantitative Analysis*, 4 (December 1969), 347–400.

Logue, Dennis E. "Market-Making and the Assessment of Market Efficiency." *Journal of Finance*, 30 (March 1975), 115–24.

Mayers, D. "Non-Marketable Assets and the Determination of Capital Asset Prices in the Absence of a Riskless Asset." *Journal of Business*, 46 (April 1973), 258–67.

McCallum, John S. "The Interest Rate under Capital Asset Pricing Theory: The Expected Holding Period Return, Uncertainty and the Term Structure of Interest Rates." *Journal of Finance*, 30 (May 1975), 307–24.

Merton, Robert C. "An Analytic Derivation of the Efficient Portfolio Frontier." *Journal of Financial and Quantitative Analysis*, 7 (September 1972), 1851–72.

Mossin, J. "Equilibrium in a Capital Asset Market." *Econometrica*, 34 (October 1966), 768–83.

Myers, S. C. "Procedures for Capital Budgeting under Uncertainty." *Industrial Management Review,* Spring 1968.

Pettit, R. Richardson, and Westerfield, Randolph. "Using the Capital Asset Pricing Model to Predict Security Returns." *Journal of Financial and Quantitative Analysis,* 9 (September 1974), 579–606.

Robichek, Alexander A., and Cohn, Richard A. "The Economic Determinants of Systematic Risk," *Journal of Finance,* 19 (May 1974), 439–48.

Roll, R. "Investment Diversification and Bond Maturity." *Journal of Finance,* 26 (March 1971), 51–66.

Schall, Lawrence D. "Asset Valuation, Firm Investment, and Firm Diversification." *Journal of Business,* 45 (January 1972), 11–28.

Sharpe, William. "Bonds vs. Stocks: Capital Market Theory." *Financial Analysts Journal,* 29 (November–December 1973), 74–80.

Sharpe, William F. "Imputing Expected Security Returns from Portfolio Composition." *Journal of Financial and Quantitative Analysis,* 9 (June 1974), 463–72.

PART IV

Tools and Techniques

IN PART IV, the key tools and techniques of financial management are set forth. In Chapter 12, David Goodman and Sanford Kaplan present a sophisticated treatment of financial ratio analysis to show how ratios can be used in making more effective decisions. They emphasize the selection and calculation of ratios relevant for the critical aspects of the decision process under consideration. They show how predetermined standard ratios and financial analysis facilitate comparisons between favorable and unfavorable performance. They describe how these standards may be formulated. They then demonstrate how the use of financial ratio analysis is adapted to the needs of four major different points of view: (1) the security analyst or investor, (2) the commercial bank loan officer, (3) company management responsible for planning, control, and operations, and (4) the board of directors. Their insights and analytical approach, based on successful experience, make financial ratio analysis come alive.

As described earlier, one of the consequences of the inflationary environment since 1966 has been to place increased pressure on the liquidity positions of business firms. Thus, cash forecasting has taken on increased importance. Alan Foster in Chapter 13 describes the techniques of cash forecasting including the illustrative format material. He describes variations in cash forecasting methods and how they influence forecasting for the short- and long-term planning horizons. Cash forecasting provides a basis for the temporary investment of cash beyond required levels. Mr. Foster describes the corporate policy considerations for determining the kinds and degrees of risk exposures. He then reviews the characteristics of a wide range of alternative short-term investment instruments. The mechanics of short-term investing are also treated.

Another important planning tool is presented by Roy Anderson and Harry Biederman in describing how firms use cost-volume-profit analysis. Mr. Anderson and Mr. Biederman bring important new insights to the use of "break-even analysis" in a broader framework and perspective. They present the results of a survey in mid-1974 showing how 358 industrial firms use "break-even analysis." In addition to describing the analytics of break-even analysis, they also illustrate how the concepts are used in industry.

Chapter 12

Financial Ratio Analysis

David M. Goodman[*]
Sanford Kaplan[†]

OUR OBJECTIVE is to describe techniques for deciding whether or not a business is earning a satisfactory return on the funds invested, or whether or not it is maintaining a sound financial position. Measurement of various returns on investments and market tests, such as earnings per share, price/earnings ratio, and dividend yield, are generally described in books on managerial accounting or finance which are readily available.[1] This chapter will concentrate on the common ratios employed in deeper financial analysis.

A ratio is simply one number expressed in terms of another number. It is found by dividing one number (the base) into the other number. A percentage is a ratio in which the base equals 100 percent, and the quotient is expressed as "per 100 of the base" or as a percent of the base. There are many ratios that can be computed from a conventional set of financial statements including a profit and loss statement and a balance sheet.

In using such ratios, most analysts do not compute mechanically

---

[*] David M. Goodman, chairman, Goodman & Mautner, Inc., Los Angeles, California.

[†] Sanford Kaplan, consultant and director, Xerox Corporation, Los Angeles, California.

[1] See Robert N. Anthony and James S. Reece, *Management Accounting Principles,* 3d ed. (Homewood, Ill.: Richard D. Irwin, Inc., 1975), Chap. 12; J. Fred Weston and Eugene F. Brigham, *Managerial Finance,* 5th ed. (Hinsdale, Ill.: The Dryden Press, 1975), pp. 19–53; and J. Fred Weston, *PLAID For Financial Management* (Homewood, Ill.: Richard D. Irwin, 1975), pp. 10–22.

all of the ratios known to mankind, but attempt to decide which particular sets of ratios are relevant for the kinds of investigation or analysis being made, and then compute selected ratios. In situations, such as loan analysis in commercial banks, key ratios (anywhere up to ten in number) are computed and compared regularly and periodically. In some large corporations, various numbers of ratios ranging from 11 to 15 are compared quarterly for comparison with budgeted ratios in the management five-year plan.

All financial ratios can be grouped into five general categories: (1) liquidity, (2) leverage or use of debt, (3) measures of asset activity, (4) measures of cost control, and (5) profitability.

Financial ratios involve the use of balance sheet figures and income statements, and the relationship between amounts taken from one or both statements. It is customary in tests of liquidity and profitability to compare the various percentages or ratios on an historical basis: monthly and/or quarterly, as well as annually.

The chief advantage in the use of ratios in financial analysis is that it permits making comparisons between favorable and unfavorable performance, depending on what standards are set. The ability to express the numbers on financial statements in relative terms is done through many ratios that can be calculated; though, as indicated, only a few are ordinarily used in connection with analyzing a given problem.

To best utilize ratios, it is essential to find standards or norms with which to compare actual performance over periods of time. Generally, these standards consist of: (1) goals or budgets set in advance of the statement period under review, (2) historical figures showing the performance of the same company in past periods, and (3) the performance of other companies as shown by their financial statements or by averages compiled from financial statements of a great number of companies by various financial services and trade associations. The American Society of Association Executives reports over 35 separate types of financial ratios that are compiled by more than 30 trade associations. Though none of these standards are perfect, and many allowances must be made for factors in the art of accounting which cause noncomparability, the use of ratios does give indications of questions that need to be answered and spurs on analysis which sometimes provides the answer. This chapter will be devoted largely to the application of ratio analysis to medium and small businesses, concentrating on manufacturing, service, or distribution.

The following statement is important in considering the use of financial ratio analysis:

> A ratio or series of ratios that are good in one year may become poor in succeeding years under poor business management. Managements are constantly changing in ability, ingenuity, aggressiveness and power, and in the relationship of these attributes as compared with competitive managements. A knowledge of the significance of important ratios will point out weaknesses and indicate whether a financial condition is wholly or partly good, questionable, or poor; but the great unknown is always management, which has the power to improve the condition or hasten the ruin of any business. It's not the ratio or ratios, *ipso facto*, that mean a business concern is out of line. The ratio is a symptom, like the blood pressure, or the pulse, or the temperature of an individual. Some managements can overcome or migrate the symptoms; other managements fail to recognize the symptoms or lack the ability, the aggressiveness, and the knowledge to do so.[2]

This chapter will place principal emphasis on visibility of operations, using the profit and loss statement and the balance sheet ratios now found commonly in use. We will attempt to utilize the classic financial ratios as they relate to four different major points of view with which one can regard the classical financial statements:

1. The security analyst or individual investor evaluating specific public entities.
2. The commercial bank loan officer looking to extend short-term or long-term working capital loans to the company. Since this is essentially credit analysis, we will also attempt to discuss the classical viewpoint of the credit manager or credit analyst considering extension of credit to the company.
3. Planning, control, and operations review by company management.
4. Financial visibility for the board of directors.

THE POINT OF VIEW OF THE SECURITY ANALYST OR INDIVIDUAL INVESTOR

The security analyst's position in using ratio analysis to study the relationship between major components of financial statements is in

---

[2] Roy A. Foulke, *Practical Financial Statement Analysis*, 6th ed. (New York: McGraw-Hill Book Company, 1968), p. 177.

some ways similar to that used by an entrepreneur or general manager attempting to use ratios in financial planning and control for profit. In fact, the techniques used by the security analyst and by the individual investor, depending on their degree of sophistication, are also very similar to those used by creditors or credit managers in assessing a company's financial position.

Table 1, Five-Year Financial Summary of Datascope Corp., and Subsidiaries, illustrates the use of financial ratios for the benefit of investors and security analysts. Such tabulations are coming more

TABLE 1
Datascope Corp. and Subsidiaries—Five-Year Financial Summary

		Fiscal Year Ended June 30, (000 Omitted)				
	Compound Annual Rate of Growth	**1974**	1973	1972	1971	1970
Operations Statement Data:						
Sales	68%	**$4,762**	3,132	2,176	1,063	603
Cost of Sales		**2,588**	1,570	1,126	594	331
Selling, General and Administrative expense		**1,019**	793	491	252	157
Earnings before taxes		**1,183**	798	557	208	107
Income taxes		**523**	362	267	100	51
Net earnings	85%	**661**	436	291	108	59
Balance Sheet Data:						
Current assets		**3,001**	2,159	1,787	599	450
Current liabilities		**868**	452	350	249	174
Working capital	67%	**2,133**	1,707	1,437	350	276
Plant & equipment (net)		**517**	256	97	73	54
Total assets		**3,724**	2,617	2,037	815	605
Stockholders' equity	75%	**2,748**	2,078	1,618	409	294
Weighted average number of outstanding shares		**733**	738	676*	638*	599*
Other Financial Data:						
Net earnings per share	73%	**$ .90**	$ .59	$ .43*	$ .17*	$.10*
Stockholders' equity per share	61%	**$3.87**	$2.95	$2.33*	$ .80*	$.58*
Gross profit margin		**45.7%**	49.9%	48.3%	44.1%	45.1%
Earnings before taxes as a percentage of sales		**24.8%**	25.5%	25.6%	19.6%	17.7%
Tax rate as a percentage of earnings before taxes		**44.2%**	45.4%	47.9%	48.1%	47.7%
Net earnings as a percentage of sales		**13.9%**	13.9%	13.4%	10.2%	9.8%
Net earnings as a percentage of stockholders' equity		**27%**	24%	29%	31%	28%
Current ratio		**3.5:1**	4.8:1	5.1:1	2.4:1	2.6:1

*After retroactive adjustment for 3 for 2 stock split effective December 1, 1972.

Source: Datascope 1974 Annual Report.

and more into common use in annual reports to shareholders of public companies.

Table 2, Analysis of Selected Over-the-Counter Companies, shows a working document used by an investment banking firm in monitoring small- and medium-sized public companies whose shares they have either taken public or in whom they have an investment interest. In looking at Table 2, one could determine some ratios of interest such as the price/earnings ratio, the sales volume as a percentage of total market value of the equity, and the percentage of return on the market value of equity.

Profit and Loss Statement Ratios

The security analyst is likely to assess any given company by the classical ratios, not necessarily in order of importance, but generally in order of review. In analyzing whether or not he wishes to recommend acquisition of securities in a public company, the typical security analyst's procedure is to first look at the profit and loss statement and to consider the following ratios as a percentage of net sales:

1. The cost of goods sold.
2. The gross margin of profit as a percentage of sales.

The next ratios which are reviewed carefully are:

3. The percentage of general and administrative expenses to net sales.
4. Marketing, sales, and service expense as a ratio of net sales.
5. Research and development or product development expenses as a percentage of sales.

The next significant ratio as a percentage of sales is:

6. The operating profit margin.

In reviewing these ratios, the security analyst tends to look for trends over recent periods of time, comparing quarterly and annual statements to see what changes in ratios have occurred, and if there are any significant trends, upward or downward. Ratios for any individual given company are then compared with other companies in similar markets or related fields. For example, companies making

TABLE 2
Analysis of Selected Over-the-Counter Companies

Company	Fiscal Year	No. of Shares (000)	Market 11/26/74	1974 Price Range	Approx. Sales Vol. 1975 (000,000)	1974E EPS
California Microwave	June	520	3½	9–3	10.0	0.62*
Computer Election System . . .	March	920	3⅛	5–3	7.5	0.77*
Data Disc.	Dec.	1,050	1½	7–1	10.0	0.25
Data Technology	April	1,225	2⅛	4–2	22.0	0.60*
ESL.	Dec.	760	5¾	9–4	27.0	1.15
Information Magnetics	Dec.	1,255	2⅝	9–2	22.0	0.40
Neutrogena	Oct.	950	5⅝	10–4	10.0	0.90
Microdata	Aug.	1,600	2¹⁄₁₆	6–2	18.0	0.24
Optical Coating	Oct.	1,100	4¾	23–4	22.0	0.75
Real Estate Data	June	1,050	3½	10–3	8.8	0.73*
Redcor	June	520	1⅝	1¼–1¾	4.8	0.30
Spacelabs.	July	680	4	9–3	12.0	0.12*
Wavetek	Sept.	860	3⅝	9–3	11.0	0.81*
					185.1	

* Actual.

electronic instruments will tend to be compared against results at similar sales dollar levels obtained by leading public companies in the same field. An instrument company in the $100 million sales level would be compared with firms such as Beckman Instruments or Hewlett-Packard, or Tektronix, Inc. A smaller instrument company in the $10 million to $30 million sales volume range might be compared to Fluke Manufacturing, Wavetek, Inc., Spectral Dynamics, or in the case of a $5 million to $10 million medical instrument company, to the Datascope Corp., data in Table 1.

The performance ratios as percentages of sales can be compared against published data in the annual reports of public companies, or offering prospectuses of new issues, and/or 10–K reports filed annually with the Securities and Exchange Commission. It is typical then that security analysts will compare classical ratios and profit margins with the most successful leaders in each field of activity as closely comparable to the company under analysis as is possible.

The more sophisticated security analyst will penetrate cost of goods sold in detail, analyzing percentages of labor, material and overhead, if such figures are available to him. The profit pretax may be a more important ratio than net after tax in most cases because of various tax charges in different companies. One obvious instance is

P/E 1974	1975E EPS	P/E 1975	Market Value (000)	Market Vol. Percent of Net Worth	Latest Net Worth	Short-Term Debt (000)	Long-Term Debt (000)	Current Ratio	Percent Return on Equity
5.6	0.85	4.1	1,820	65	2,800	–	–	3.01	11.2
4.1	0.95	3.3	3,105	65	4,759	–	–	1.86	16.4
6.0	0.25	6.0	1,575	33.5	4,700	1,500	100	2.10	5.5
3.5	0.90	2.4	2,600	55.1	4,720	12	200	1.88	17.8
5.0	1.35	4.3	4,370	87.2	5,014	–	–	2.75	16.9
6.6	0.50	5.3	3,294	78.4	4,200	5,500	383	2.20	11.8
6.3	1.00	5.6	5,344	179.2	2,982	–	–	3.60	29.5
8.6	0.35	5.9	3,300	64.5	5,120	3,000	600	1.75	7.4
6.3	0.40	11.9	5,225	57.8	9,043	–	2,500	2.50	8.9
4.8	0.65	5.4	3,675	81.6	4,502	74	708	2.57	18.7
5.4	0.60	2.7	800	53.3	1,500	–	–	7.30	13.1
33.3	0.70	5.7	2,720	92.9	2,927	2,500	–	1.49	–
4.5	0.90	4.0	3,118	59.4	5,250	750	1,000	2.81	15.7
5.56†		5.12†	40,946		57,517	13,336	5,491		

† Average.
Source: Hambrecht & Quist, Investment Bankers, 235 Montgomery Street, San Francisco, California.

the effect of tax loss carry-forwards on net after tax numbers. The comparison of profit pretax against relatively ideal standard ratios which the security analyst has derived from historical precedent is a common step.

Balance Sheet Ratios

In examining the balance sheet, the security analyst looks at liquidity. The most widely used measure of liquidity is the current ratio, which is an attempt to estimate the ability of a business to meet its current obligations. It is computed simply by dividing current assets by the current liabilities. The generally accepted rule of thumb figure of 2 to 1 is considered to be an acceptable current ratio. Of course, the major defect in the use of the current ratio is that it assumes that all current assets are liquid and can be converted to cash readily. Experience tells us that in the specific case of inventory and prepaid expenses this may not be true. Therefore, many security, credit analysts and others, investigating a company use what is commonly referred to as the "quick ratio" or the "acid test ratio" to measure liquidity. In this ratio, inventories and prepaid expenses are deducted from current assets and the remainder is divided by the current liabilities. The general rule of thumb is that a 1 to 1 "acid test ratio" is satisfactory. Bankers' loan agreements and indenture agreements for notes and debentures use a current ratio calculated with or without the prepaid expenses removed in setting loan default levels. For example, a loan or note agreement might read as follows: "The company must maintain a current ratio of at least 1.5 to 1. In computing this ratio, prepaid expenses are to be excluded from current assets."

A general word of caution applies to all financial analysis, but especially in security analysis; there is a tendency "to evaluate companies by use of ratios and rule of thumb figures without looking at the underlying facts. Many companies with a quick ratio of ½ to 1 or less are doing extremely well. Others with a quick ratio of over 4 to 1 are headed for bankruptcy,"[3] because their receivables are not collectible, and their products and services are unreliable.

One of the key indicators used by security analysts is the debt to net worth ratio, which tends to measure the degree of risk in a company. Generally speaking, the greater the stockholders' equity in relation to debt, the greater the protection to the creditors. However, the use of debt financing can increase returns to stockholders. Wherever "leverage" becomes favorable, the stockholders are bound to benefit. It is also true that "leverage" may be unfavorable if the return on investment tends to be less than the interest on debt. The security analyst working in rapid growth industries tends to disregard the old rule of thumb that there should be equal amounts of debt and equity. A stockholder is often far better off in a growth situation where the debt to equity ratio approaches 3 to 1, than when it is safe 1 to 1. (See Chapters 30 and 31.)

Relating Profit and Loss and Balance Sheet Items

A key ratio is the activity of inventories in relation to sales. In analyzing the net sales to inventory ratio, which is sometimes called "inventory turnover," manufacturing industries, service industries, and distribution companies, all have different ideal turnover ratios. Whether or not this ratio indicates that the company is carrying too

---

[3] Ralph F. Lewis, *Planning and Control for Profit* (New York: Harper & Row, 1961), p. 39.

much inventory in relation to its sales depends on the kind of business and whether or not the business is seasonal. Average inventory figures are generally used. Most manufacturing concerns expect a 5 to 1, or 6 to 1 inventory turnover ratio to be very satisfactory. Generally, the higher the inventory turnover the better for profits. Companies that manufacture to custom order against heavy backlogs or engage in defense contracts tend to have very low inventory turnovers, but still do very well as profitmaking investments.

Comparing the profit and loss statement to the balance sheet, the next most significant ratio to be calculated would be the return on equity. In most cases, the net return on tangible net worth is preferred, rather than calculating the return on assets employed in the business. One of the reasons for preferring return on equity rather than return on assets employed, is that the return on equity measures the results for the owners of the firm. Return on assets employed is still useful for planning and control purposes, especially by large corporations with investments in many subsidiaries and divisions.

In calculating the net profit to stockholders' equity ratio, the security analyst attempts to measure the return on the stockholders' investment in the firm. Here, the after-tax profit is commonly used, and even where companies have large tax loss carry-forwards, or for some other reasons pay an inappropriate amount of tax, it is common practice to assume a standard 48 percent income tax rate so that all companies' net earnings will be on a similar comparison level. Whether or not an individual company's return on equity is satisfactory depends on the industry that the company is in and whether or not the business is capital intensive. In some industries, a 10 percent return on equity is considered satisfactory—in others, a 25 percent return on equity is considered minimal.

Of the ratios discussed above, certain important ratios stand out as being the most useful. Depending upon the needs of management and the nature of the industry, very specialized performance ratios can be developed. The analysis of a railroad, public utility, or airline tends to be done with selected ratios not common to other fields of endeavor.

Use of Financial Standards

Because there are major differences in ratio values between industries, it is useful in evaluating specific companies against other companies in the field to consult some of the standardized ratios reported industry by industry and published regularly. These are sometimes used by security analysts, but generally, all of the 10, 14, or 15 classic ratios upon which the various services report are not as of great interest to the security analyst as to a loan analyst in a bank or the credit manager of a firm extending credit to customers. Such standard comparative data can be obtained, for example, from Dun & Bradstreet, Inc., in *Key Business Ratios,* a widely used source of comparative ratios for different industries. Dun & Bradstreet regularly computes 14 standard ratios for 125 lines of business. Data on comparative ratios for most industries and trades can also be found in *Statement Studies* published by Robert Morris & Associates. Other sources are the *Quarterly Financial Reports* of the Federal Trade Commission. There are also reports published by the Accounting Corporation of America and by various trade associations covering their specific industries for the benefit of their memberships.

In addition, certain research organizations, research bulletins produced by graduate schools of business, specific corporations, trade magazines, and trade papers also produce comparative operating ratios for specific industries. An example would be the study of department stores done, commencing in 1913, by the Bureau of Business Research, Harvard University, Graduate School of Business Administration. A specific study on all men's wear stores was done by New York University on a grant from *Men's Wear* magazine. Similar publications have authorized studies by graduate schools of management. The National Cash Register Company publishes annual expense ratios in 50 lines of business called *Expenses in Retailing.* Various sources of comparative operating ratios relating to financial statements can be obtained industry by industry from trade associations and from industrial trade magazines or industrial publishing companies, in addition to those regularly by the federal government.[4]

The one great trap in using these standardized sources of data and ratio analysis, in particular, is that though they can be valuable tools in gaining insights by comparative operations analysis of a business, both internally and externally, one must remember that all of these ratios are the product of financial statements. One must

---

[4] See *Ratio Analysis for Small Business* (Washington, D.C.: Small Business Administration, 1970), pp. 63–65 and 22–35, for a complete listing of sources and publications containing standard ratio analysis data.

be aware of the limitations of accounting statements and remember that accounting is essentially an art rather than a science.

The security analyst, in pursuing his comparison of companies to find the best investment for recommendation, once he has isolated a specific company that meets certain basic tests, will tend to use selected ratios as indicators for further investigation. He will then proceed to evaluate the market and management fundamentals of the company. The sophisticated individual investor also utilizes ratios as general indications of where each company stands in relation to its competitors in the same field of activity. The security analyst, as well as the intelligent investor, must use financial ratio analysis as a statistical indicator of problems or trends, and by no means as a final or accurate judgment as to the health of any particular firm in any specified industry.

THE BANK OFFICER OR CREDIT ANALYST USING FINANCIAL RATIOS

The commercial banking use of ratios to make short- or long-term working capital loans or to extend credit to customers differs somewhat from that of a credit manager and also from that of the security analyst or investor. The financial analysis functions within a commercial bank can be separated into two categories: credit analysis and loan analysis. To the loan officer, financial ratios are not magical numbers. For example, if the acid test ratio falls below 1 to 1, it simply signifies a greater reliance on inventory movement to provide liquidity. It does not mean that the loan is automatically canceled.

Point of View of Banks

Banks concentrate on the source of loan principal and interest repayment, and the quality of the repayment source within each company analyzed. Decisions with regard to loan availability are more related to trends than to what the ratio is calculated to be at a specific moment in time.

The credit analysis function within a well-organized commercial bank will run annual, semiannual and quarterly studies of shifts in ten or more critical ratios and pass these studies on to the loan department. Standard forms are available within most banks for periodic analysis of the income statement and the balance sheet.

These standard forms contain key numbers and ratios to be analyzed for each business. At the bottom of the standard operating analysis sheet in most well-run banks are a series of 10 to 12 ratios which are regularly calculated. Of these, approximately five or six are critical to the loan analyst who subsequently reviews these statement ratio analysis sheets.

The loan analyst in reviewing these studies is principally looking for the primary sources of the repayment of the loan. For example, suitable inventory turnover ratios are important, but they do not tell the whole story. The number of turns per year may range from 2 to 1, to 11 to 1, depending on the nature of the business.

In granting a loan or reviewing the extension of a loan, loan officers use a projection of financial statements prepared on a standard Robert Morris Associates form submitted by the company to the loan officer. This form is not too different from that used by most well-organized firms in preparing a budget forecast or a management plan for its own purposes.

A loan officer will use projected financial ratios in analyzing forecasts as a basis for making loans. The credit analyst within the same commercial bank can rely only on historical facts as reflected in financial statements. The lending officer weighs the credit analysis versus the company's own projections against "the risk." "The risk" really depends on the accuracy of the projections supplied by the company seeking the loan—do they or don't they meet their projections?

Financial Ratios Used

In making a historical review on a quarterly or annual basis from the operating statement or the balance sheet, the following ratios are generally used by most commercial bank credit analysts:

1. The current ratio.
2. Cash and receivables to current debt.
3. Receivables to average days' sales.
4. Inventory supply in days.
5. Total debt to tangible net worth.
6. Fixed assets to tangible net worth.
7. Net profit to sales.
8. Net profit to net worth.

9. Net sales to net worth.
10. Accounts payable turn in days.

Of these, the most critical are the current ratio, cash and receivables to current debt (the "quick ratio" or "acid test ratio") the receivables aging in average number of days, the inventory supply in number of days, and the total debt to tangible net worth. Another key ratio is the accounts payable turn in days. Though other ratios are often calculated, the ones set forth above are critical to the credit analyst, as well as to the loan officer in the commercial bank.

The following *Definition of Ratios* is one used by Lloyds Bank of California. This list not only gives the method of computation and the result of each ratio, but the principle on which the ratio is used. This series of ratios is reproduced in detail and is the best set of simple explanations of the use of ratios in financial analysis. Direct comparisons of these ratios by industry categories are available for most businesses in the United States.

DEFINITION OF RATIOS

Quick Ratio

Method of Computation. The total of cash, short-term marketable securities and net receivables divided by the total of current liabilities.

Result. The ratio measures short-term liquidity available to meet current debt.

Principle. Also known as the "acid test" or "liquidity" ratio, it is of particular benefit to short-term creditors, as it expresses the extent to which cash and those assets most readily convertible into cash can meet the demands of current liabilities. Any value of less than 1 to 1 implies a reciprocal "dependency" on inventory or other current assets to liquidate short-term debts.

Current Ratio

Method of Computation. The total of current assets divided by the total of current liabilities.

Result. The ratio is one measure of the ability of the firm to meet its current debt.

Principle. In comparing an individual company to the industry, a higher current ratio indicates that more current assets are free from debt claims of creditors and prompter payment can be expected.

Fixed/Worth

Method of Computation. The net fixed assets (plant and equipment less reserve for depreciation) divided by the tangible net worth.

Result. The ratio expresses the proportion between investment in capital assets (plant and equipment) and the owners' capital.

Principle. The higher the ratio, the less owners' capital is available for working capital. The lower this ratio, the more liquid is the net worth and the more effective owners' capital is as a liquidating protection to creditors. The presence of substantial leased fixed assets—off the balance sheet—may deceptively lower the ratio.

Debt/Worth

Method of Computation. The total debt divided by the tangible net worth.

Result. The ratio expresses the relationship between capital contributed by creditors of owners' capital—"what is owed to what is owned."

Principle. Total assets or resources represent the entire capital at the disposal of a given company and consist of net worth or owners' capital, and creditor capital—that provided by those outside the business for temporary use. The proportion existing between debt and worth—or leverage—records the debt pressure. The lower the ratio, the easier the pressure and the greater the protection for creditors.

Unsubordinated Debt/Capital Funds

Method of Computation. Total unsubordinated debt (all current plus senior long-term debt) divided by capital funds (tangible net worth plus long-term subordinated debt).

Result. The ratio expresses the proportion between senior creditors' capital and that provided by junior creditors and owners.

Principle. A common refinement to debt to worth which records debt leverage in relation to the capital base, sometimes referred to as the borrowing base. Gives recognition in the borrowing base to that capital provided by creditors whose rights are subordinated under instruments to other creditors. The use of subordinated debt capital does not altogether remove a corresponding amount of debt pressure from owners' capital, but it does provide an extra cushion for senior creditors who can then view leverage from this ratio.

Sales/Receivables

Method of Computation. The net annual sales divided by the total of trade accounts and bills receivable.

Result. The ratio expresses the relationship of the volume of business to the outstanding receivables.

Principle. A higher ratio—a higher turnover of receivables as it is sometimes called—indicates a more rapid collection of sales during the period and a greater liquidity of the receivables.

Days' Sales

Method of Computation. The total of receivables divided by the net annual sales for the group; this fraction is then multiplied by 360 (the number of days in one year).

Result. This figure expresses the average time (in days) that sales are uncollected.

Principle. A comparison of this figure with the terms of sale for the industry will show the extent of control over credit and collections. The greater the number of days outstanding, the greater is the probability of delinquencies in accounts receivable.

Cost of Sales/Inventory

Method of Computation. Cost of sales divided by the total of inventory.

Result. The ratio expresses the proportion between cost of sales and inventory at the end of the fiscal period.

Principle. The physical turnover measures merchandising capacity. The higher the ratio, the greater is the capacity and the more probable the freshness, salability and liquidating value of that inventory. Since profit has been eliminated, the cost of sales/inventory gives a more accurate measure of physical turnover than the sales/inventory. Other measures of physical turnover use average monthly inventory or an average of the inventories at the beginning and end of the period.

Days' Sales

Method of Computation. The total inventory multiplied by 360 and divided by the cost of sales for the group.

Result. This figure expresses the average length of time in days that merchandise inventory remains in the company before it is sold.

Principle. This number of days should correspond closely with production time.

Sales/Working Capital

Method of Computation. The net annual sales divided by the net working capital or excess of total current assets over current liabilities.

Result. The ratio expresses the turnover or annual activity of that portion of net capital not devoted to fixed or other non-current assets.

Principle. Net working capital represents the basic support for those assets undergoing conversion cycles (as inventory-receivables-cash) during the selling year. Relating sales to working capital suggests the number of turns in working capital per annum. A low ratio may indicate unprofitable use of working capital while a very high ratio often signifies overtrading—a vulnerable condition for creditors.

Sales/Net Worth

Method of Computation. The net annual sales divided by the tangible net worth.

Result. The ratio reflects the activity of owners' capital during the year.

Principle. Capital is invested in an enterprise in the hope of a substantial return. The probability of such a return is largely dependent upon a reasonable activity of the investment. This ratio is one measure of this activity. When the relation increases from year to year, it indicates that owners' capital is being used more frequently during the year. A very high ratio may indicate undercapitalization (lack of sufficient ownership capital) or overtrading.

Profits before Taxes/Worth

Method of Computation. The amount of net profit before taxes divided by the tangible net worth.

Result. The ratio expresses the relationship between the owners' share of operations before taxes for the year and the capital already contributed by the owners.

Principle. Capital is usually invested in a company in the anticipation of a return on that investment—in the form of a profit. This hope of a profit is the attraction for original and new capital. The higher the profit before taxes to worth, the greater is the probability of making appreciable addition to owners' capital after payment of dividends and taxes.

Profits before Taxes/Total Assets

Method of Computation. The amount of net profit before taxes divided by the total assets for the industry.

Result. The ratio expresses the owners' share of the year's operations before taxes related to the resources contributed by both owners and creditors.

Principle. The relationship indicates the net profitability of the use of all resources of the business.

Cash Flow/Current Maturities Long-Term Debt

Method of Computation. The net profits plus depreciation and amortization divided by the current portion of long-term liabilities.

Result. The ratio expresses the ability to retire term debt each year from cash generated by operations.

Principle. Cash flow or "throw-off" is the primary source of regular repayment of long-term debt, and this ratio measures the coverage of such debt service. Often much if not all of the depreciation will be needed for fixed asset replacements and expenditures, but similarly some part of net profits may be committed to dividends. Although it is misleading to think that all cash flow is available for debt service, the ratio is a valid measure of the optimum coverage and a very useful calculation in all considerations of term lending.

Accounts Payable Turn in Days

Method of Computation. Accounts Payable divided by purchases (if available from statement) then multiplied by the number of days in the period, or Accounts Payable divided by the cost of goods sold, then multiplied by the number of days in the period.

Result. Discloses trend of time taken to repay trade creditors.

Principle. To provide a statistical basis for comparing actual payment to vendors as opposed to terms offered. Can be compared to industry data provided. Key to whether or not company is taking discounts offered or, conversely, living off their vendors.[5]

These ratios are used in a judgmental way by bank loan officers as described at the beginning of this section. The ratios are used as a basis for reaching decisions on making bank loans. In his book, in *How to Finance a Growing Business,* Royce Diener states, in a section devoted to "Credit Criteria of Unsecured Loans" that:

> In order to qualify for this type of financing, a borrower must have a financial picture which gives certain assurances as to liquidity and general freedom from heavy debt and pressure from creditors. Credit acceptability is usually based on the following:
>
> 1. Debt to worth ratio.
> 2. Net current asset position.[6]

---

[5] Mr. Charles Martorano, assistant vice president (in charge of Credit Analysis), Lloyds Bank of California, Los Angeles, California.

[6] Royce Diener, *How to Finance a Growing Business,* rev. ed. (New York: Frederick Fell Publishers, Inc., 1974), p. 80.

Mr. Diener further points out that:

> From a realistic point of view, the current ratio is not as meaningful as the working capital position. Yet, partially because of custom and partially because it is such an easy fact to determine, the current ratio is almost invariably the first element of the Balance Sheet to be checked by analysts and lending officers.[7]

Diener observes that the fiscal year-end date may have no effect whatever on working capital and net worth, but it can definitely influence the current ratio and the debt to worth ratio.

Diener points out that the fiscal year-end date selected by the company should coincide with a lull which follows the annual peak of the business, because there it can make a significant difference in the ratios appearing on a financial statement prepared as of the date of greatest liquidity of the company in any year.

Financial Covenants

Commercial bank loan agreements will tend to vary rather widely in the use of financial covenants which the borrower must maintain in order to keep his line of credit. Following are three different clauses from three different loan agreements all issued from different headquarters or officers of a very large U.S. bank.

Agreement No. 1 is an annual agreement for one year on a $3 million revolving line of credit. Among the various terms and conditions of the loan, the following paragraph appears under the general heading of

Conditions:

Paragraph 3.   The following financial covenants:

a.   A current ratio of at least 1.4:1. In computing ratio, prepaid expenses to be excluded from current assets.

b.   Minimum tangible net worth is not to fall below $3 million. Tangible net worth to be computed as statement net worth plus subordinated debt minus intangibles and costs in excess of book.

c.   Debts/tangible equity ratio not to exceed 2.40:1.

d.   Minimum working capital to be maintained at $2,250,000.

Case No. 2 involves a $2 million revolving line of credit and among the conditions are the following:

---

[7] Ibid., pp. 82–83.

Paragraph 3. Borrower to maintain the following financial covenants:
  a. Minimum working capital of $1,300,000.
  b. Minimum current ratio of 1.9 to 1.
  c. Minimum tangible net worth less subordinated debt of $1,600,000.
  d. Maximum ratio of senior debt to tangible net worth plus subordinated debt of 1.2 to 1.

Case No. 3 involving a different office of the same bank contained in a loan agreement for a $4,500,000 revolving line of credit under

Conditions:
Paragraph 2. Borrower will maintain the following financial covenants at all times.
  a. Minimum consolidated current ratio of 1.40 to 1.0.
  b. Maximum consolidated debt (less subordinated debt) to tangible net worth (plus subordinated debt) of 1.50 to 1.0.
  c. Minimum consolidated tangible net worth of $150,000 less an actual at 9/30/74.

The three companies whose current loan agreements are abstracted above, are roughly similar in sales volume and area of business yet differ in some ways. Company No. 1 has a sales level of just under $20 million, has been unprofitable for the past two years, but is now operating profitably, having undergone extensive reorganization. Company No. 2 has a current sales level of $10 million per annum and has been consistently profitable for the past three years. Company No. 3 has a sales level in excess of $30 million per annum, has been profitable, was unprofitable last year, has just written off a substantial amount of obsolete inventory, and has turned profitable. Company No. 3 was unprofitable at the time the loan agreement was reached, but has been profitable for the last two quarters after signing the loan agreement.

Of course, the interest rates differ as do the percentages of receivables pledged; other conditions of the loan vary. However, the ratios used as conditional financial covenants are quite similar. Curiously, the company which is the most liquid and the most profitable must maintain the highest minimum current ratio, and the two firms that have recently "turned the corner" are down in the area of 1.4 to 1, and 1.5 to 1, rather than 1.9 to 1. This indicates a tendency on the part of some bankers to set current ratio minimums just below that current ratio which the company is now maintaining when applying for a loan, rather than to some predetermined standard of excellence, such as "2 to 1" as declaimed in nearly all of the standard texts. Also of interest are the differing debt to net worth ratios and the methods of calculating them. The more solvent and profitable company is limited to a 1.2 to 1 maximum ratio of senior debt to tangible net worth plus subordinated debt, whereas the less solvent, less profitable companies can extend out to 1.5 to 1, and, the company which has had two years of no earnings can go as high as debt to tangible equity of 2.4 to 1.

FINANCIAL RATIOS IN CREDIT ANALYSIS

Credit analysis is a field in which financial ratio analysis really has come to full blossom. The credit manager of a corporation, especially a small corporation, must make decisions on extensions of customer credit based upon sketchy information. In the small- or medium-sized company, it is essential that the credit manager make skillful judgments and decisions which can affect the future of the company. Though large concerns have adequate staffs and generally adequate financial information, managers of smaller companies tend to rely on less adequate information or reports from credit services rather than their own ability to analyze the statements of customers or vendors.

A classic text on cause and effect ratio analysis distinguishes between six primary "or causal ratios" and nine secondary ratios.[8] The six causal ratios are said to "reflect the relationships which directly influence the firm in its entirety." The secondary ratios are those which "yield important information about the financial structure and the competitive position of the company, but which do not individually indicate causes of strength or weakness."

Cause and effect ratio analysis is commonly used by credit managers. It has also been adopted by owners and managers to control their enterprises. Business firms knowing that their statements will be reviewed by credit managers, purchasing agents, commercial and investment bankers and security analysts have become familiar with standard financial ratio analysis techniques. Knowledge of financial ratio analysis by managers of small businesses particularly is important. Such knowledge can help management to control costs and

---

[8] Donald E. Miller, *The Meaningful Interpretation of Financial Statements* (New York: American Management Association, 1966), p. 20.

build profits in order to qualify for the best credit terms and working capital loans required.[9]

MANAGEMENT PLANNING, CONTROL, AND OPERATIONS REVIEW

Having defined in the sections above the various financial ratios available and the sources of financial standards against which individual company's ratios can be compared, we have described some fundamental tools of financial analysis. The use of financial ratio analysis by security analysts, investors, credit managers, and bank loan officers has been outlined.

To the company treasurer and chief financial officer, the uses of financial ratio analysis described in the first and second sections above, illustrate methods of reviewing a company's financial statement from time to time by people who are judging that company from the outside. There are a number of "publics" that will review a company statement (whether it is a public company or not) at periodic intervals. Stockholders of a public company generally rely upon security analysts to analyze and not recommend or recommend securities to them and to others. It gives the company treasurer an advantage to know what it is that the analysts are looking for.

Since security analysts, credit managers, and bank loan officers will be reviewing a company's financial statement at periodic intervals, it behooves the company treasurer and chief financial officer to see that the company itself pre-screens and ratio analyzes its financial statements before submitting them to outside review. There are very few managers of businesses who do not have to satisfy one or more of these "publics" on a periodic basis. Experienced managers use selected ratios to pretest acceptability of their firms' financial statements, as well as to compare them against the financial statements of competitive firms. It is better still to preplan and control the business activities of one's own firm by using financial ratio analysis for operating review at regular intervals. This has been a

[9] A useful text is Richard Sanzo's *Ratio Analysis for Small Business*, 3d ed., (Washington, D.C.: Small Business Administration, 1970). This handbook is available from any Department of Commerce Field Office or the Superintendent of Documents for 90 cents. A programmed learning instruction course that teaches "X-Ray Eye" financial analysis by use of standard ratios is also available. See programmed instruction course, *Analysis of Financial Statements*, Entelek, Inc., Newburyport, Mass. 01950.

common practice for some time in many businesses. For example, Figure 1 is a management memo abstracted from that actually produced by a computer peripheral equipment company (only the

FIGURE 1

VZI CORPORATION

Management Memo

15 January 1975

Third Quarter Budget

The budget for the last half of fiscal year ending 4/30/75, has just been completed and all Departments are operating on the new plan. The essential elements of the budget are scheduled below and the original budget is shown for comparative purposes. In addition, last year's operating performance is compared:

	Fiscal 1974 Operations ($ in 000)	Fiscal 1975 Original Budget ($ in 000)	Fiscal 1975 Revised Budget ($ in 000)
Orders	$ 7,300	$12,400	$10,400
Sales	6,200	11,000	9,500
Gross profit	3,300	5,800	4,600
Percent to sales	53%	53%	49%
Expenses	2,600	4,300	3,700
Percent to sales	42%	39%	39%
Pretax profit	700	1,500	900
Percent to sales	11%	14%	9%
Current ratio	2.0 to 1	1.8 to 1	2.4 to 1
Debt to equity	0.7 to 1	1.0 to 1	0.6 to 1
Employees (year-end)	186	269	223
Facilities (year-end)	31,000 sq.ft.	60,000 sq.ft.	49,000 sq.ft.

Plans are now being formulated for the preparation of the Operating Plan for Fiscal 1976. This activity will begin early in February.

S. O. Beich
President

names have been changed to protect the identity of the company, since it is not a public corporation).

Section 2, above, sets forth typical terms and conditions for bank loans. Company No. 2, described in that part of this chapter, has the same sales level and loan agreement as the company described in Figure 1 "Management Memo." Financial ratios are used as part of the summarized plan to compare fiscal 1974 operations with the fiscal 1975 original budget and the fiscal 1975 revised budget. The proposed current ratio and debt to equity ratio are now clearly within the conditions described in the company's loan agreement.

Note that the VZI Corporation accepted a profit pretax on sales and a gross margin on sales considerably lower than originally planned. This step was taken because the company found it necessary, during a period of falling order booking rate, to live within its means without further extending its bank borrowing. At the same time that the new order rate is slacking off, the company is required to develop new products which they believe will have substantial demand in fiscal 1976. The summary "Management Memo" illustrates the fact that VZI Corporation management is consciously dropping its gross margin, holding tight on its expenses in relation to sales and dropping its pretax profit margins, but staying well within a sound current ratio and a strong debt to equity ratio.

Table 3, following, shows the use of financial ratios particularly the use of percentages of sales for comparison purposes, in a company we shall call Advanced Nuclear Corporation. This table is a historical treatment for the first three years of the company's life and forecasts the next four years of the company's history. Advanced Nuclear Corporation provides products and services and, with four categories of products or services, is a bit more complex than the average small business. By using percentage analysis, the company is able to test the soundness of its management plan and compare it with other companies of similar size and in the same field.

The percentage of sales comparison concept permits managers to actually test the logical consistency and financial soundness of long-range plans and budget forecasts. For example, an analysis of the cost of goods sold in Table 3 indicates that the cost of materials as a percentage of sales will be steadily declining over the next four years. Labor costs as percentage of sales will also decline and overhead will vary slightly, but not significantly over the same years. The variations in gross profit and sales expense indicate that sometime in the fiscal year 1972 to 1973, greater emphasis was placed on sales. The company, which started as a regional supplier, planned to develop a sales force that would give it national market coverage by

TABLE 3

ADVANCED NUCLEAR CORP.
Actual and Pro Forma
Profit and Loss Statements
(in $000s)

| | 1969-70 | | 1970-71 | | 1971-72 | | | | |
	$	%	$	%	1st Qtr	2d Qtr	3d Qtr	4th Qtr	Total $
Backlog (Beginning)					174	140	163	180	174
New Orders:									
Industrial					65	75	85	100	325
Research and teaching					58	75	65	70	268
Large sources					15	30	30	35	110
Services					18	18	20	20	76
Total New Orders					156	198	200	225	779
Less: Shipments.					190	175	183	198	
Backlog (Ending)					140	163	180	207	207
Net sales (Shipments):									
Industrial					112	83	80	83	358
Research and teaching					55	55	60	65	235
Large sources					10	20	25	30	85
Services					13	17	18	20	68
Total Net Sales	226	100.0	385	100.0	190	175	183	198	746
Cost of Goods Sold:									
Material					49	45	47	49	190
Labor					35	33	36	37	141
Overhead					53	49	50	52	204
Total Cost of Sales	173	76.5	275	71.4	137	127	133	138	535
Gross profit	53	23.5	110	28.6	53	48	50	60	211
Selling expense	28	12.4	47	12.2	17	17	23	35	92
General and administrative expense	57	25.2	64	16.6	15	15	16	16	62
Operating profit.	(32)	–14.1	(1)	–0.3	21	16	11	9	57
Other expense.			2	0.5	2	2	2	2	8
R&D expense									
Special expense			4	1.0					
Federal income tax							1	2	3
Net profit (loss)	(32)	–14.1	(7)	–1.8	19	14	8	5	46
Receivable aging (days).	95		77		63	72	70	60	
Cost of Sales/Average Inventory	3.8		2.9						3.3

training a basic sales force with engineering and scientific qualifications to enter the field by the end of fiscal year 1972 to 1973. The following year, the company's own sales force would be combined with sales representatives, distributors, and wholesalers, very carefully selected.

TABLE 3 (*continued*)

ADVANCED NUCLEAR CORP.
Actual and Pro Forma
Profit and Loss Statement
(in $000s)

Forecast

1st Qtr	2d Qtr	3d Qtr	4th Qtr	Total $	%	$	%	$	%	$	%
		1972-73				1973-74		1974-75		1975-76	
207	240	290	345	207		365		465		815	
115	130	175	175	595		1,050		1,700		2,700	
80	100	100	100	380		450		700		1,500	
35	45	45	60	185		240		350		600	
23	30	35	45	133		160		300		600	
253	305	355	380	1,293		1,900		3,050		5,400	
220	255	300	360	1,135		1,800		2,700		4,800	
240	290	345	365	365		405		815		1,415	
97	115	140	175	527	46.4	990	55.0	1,500	55.6	2,500	52.1
70	80	90	100	340	30.0	440	24.5	650	24.1	1,300	27.1
33	35	40	50	158	13.9	220	12.2	330	12.2	500	10.4
20	25	30	35	110	9.7	150	8.3	220	8.1	500	10.4
220	255	300	360	1,135	100.0	1,800	100.0	2,700	100.0	4,800	100.0
53	57	64	90	264	23.3	338	18.8	480	17.8	900	18.8
42	44	51	60	197	17.3	330	18.3	435	16.1	750	15.6
54	58	65	75	252	22.2	412	22.9	565	20.9	1,090	22.7
149	159	180	225	713	62.8	1,080	60.0	1,480	54.8	2,740	57.1
71	96	120	135	422	37.2	720	40.0	1,220	45.2	2,060	42.9
40	40	45	47	172	15.2	216	12.0	284	10.5	528	11.0
17	18	20	23	78	6.9	112	6.2	156	5.8	240	5.0
14	38	55	65	172	15.1	392	21.8	780	28.9	1,292	26.9
2	2	2	2	8	0.7	14	0.8	20	0.7	40	0.8
6	9	10	11	36	3.2	90	5.0	120	4.4	240	5.0
2	11	22	27	62	5.4	144	8.0	327	12.1	521	10.9
4	16	21	25	66	5.8	144	8.0	313	11.7	491	10.2
60	57	60	60			60		60		60	
					3.6		4.0		4.0		4.0

Profit and Loss Statement Percentage Ratio Standards

The manager of a typical electronic instrument company beginning as a start-up venture can anticipate a standard pattern of statement results in the first year or two of existence. The founding company management will probably be happy to break even within the first two years. In order to achieve the profitability required for rapid growth, with increasing sales and profits, the manager will attempt to control company activities and direct them so that roughly the following percentage of sales ratios will exist in the third or fourth year of the company's history (see Table 4).

TABLE 4
Percentage of Sales Ratios for an Electronic Instrument Company ($2 million to $5 million sales volume)

Sales		100%
Cost of Goods Sold:		
Material	25%	
Labor	12	
Overhead	13	
Total Cost of Goods Sold		50
Gross Margin		50%
Expenses:		
General and administrative	7%	
Sales	20	
Product development	8	
Total Expense		35
Profit Pretax		15%

The above ratios are roughly typical of a successfully managed electronic instrument company at these sales levels.

Compare these ratios with those of a public electronic medical instrument company, Datascope Corporation, in the first section, above. You will note that for the year 1974, selling and general and administrative expense, as reported by Datascope, was approximately 21.4 percent of sales. In our sample company, total selling, general administrative expense came to 27 percent of sales. Earnings pretax as a percent of sales for Datascope in 1974 was 24.8 percent of sales, whereas in our sample Electronic Instrument Company earnings pretax were only 15 percent of sales.

By checking his performance against Dun & Bradstreet or Robert Morris Associates' standards, our manager will find he is in the upper quartile of companies reporting net profit on net sales, but this may not satisfy him or his investors. Knowing that someone else can do better in a public company, our sample company manager can then strive to set a higher goal than 15 percent pretax, for example, 20 percent pretax in planning next year's activity. He may even try to achieve profits of 25 percent pretax in two or three years. Datascope, in a different but closely allied product market, apparently was able to achieve these levels in 1973 and 1972. Using the Datascope example to spur him on, our electronic instrument company manager may decide to set higher goals. In future budgets he preplans his profit and loss statement by working over each item to see if he can improve it as a percent of sales. By improving purchasing activities he may be able to drop the price of material one or two percentage points with increased sales volume. By concentrating on direct and indirect labor expense he may be able to drop these costs as well. Decreases in the cost of direct labor, especially when accomplished by increased automation, generally have a tendency to result in higher indirect or overhead expenses, but lower net costs.

It is possible by preplanning and making careful decisions, adding specialized equipment for production, and lowering material cost, for the intelligent manager to preplan his gross margin to reach a goal of 55 percent—to do this he must lower his cost of goods sold to 45 percent of sales. In order to increase sales volume our company may have to increase sales promotion and advertising expense. With increases in sales volume, general and administrative expenses, if held firmly, will tend to decline as a percentage of sales. Management can then produce the statement below in percentage ratio

Sales		100%
Cost of Goods Sold:		
Material	23%	
Direct labor	10	
Overhead	12	
Total Cost of Goods Sold		45
Gross Margin		55%
Expenses:		
General and administrative	6%	
Sales	21	
Product development	8	
Total Expenses		35
Profit Pretax.		20%

terms of a typical electronics instrument company doing between $5 million and $10 million a year in sales.

A comparison of the above statement with the sample statement at the $2 million to $5 million sales level, will show that our sample firm has now achieved a pretax profit margin of 20 percent by tightening up material cost and direct labor, holding firm on general and administrative expense, keeping product development at 8 percent of sales (because at this level our electronic instrument company cannot afford to let competition outdistance them in new product development), slightly increasing sales expense to allow for the increased cost of advertising and promotion, and holding sales commissions at a fixed rate.

It has been assumed, for the purposes of this discussion, that our electronic instrument company will use established sales representatives who charge approximately 15 percent of sales until the company achieves sufficient sales volume to have its own direct sales organization. If the commission rate is 15 percent, the cost of backing up the sales representatives, providing them with factory sales support, literature, promotion material, and advertising will probably cost another 6 percent of sales, for a total of 21 percent. Sales representatives can be obtained in all major territories in the United States and in most market areas of the world. They are not paid their commission until 60 days after the merchandise has been delivered and the bills have been paid (these terms vary with the sales representatives). This helps the cash flow of a small but growing company. Once the company achieves a level of approximately $10 to $15 million, sales expense might be reduced slightly by negotiated changes on commission structure with sales representatives, or ultimately, by going to direct sales.

It is more prudent to use a sales representative network until such time as the company has achieved a substantial volume of sales; something over $25 million is the general rule. There may be other reasons why the company is forced to go to direct sales, but generally speaking, an effective network of electronic sales representatives, giving proper field service, can be built and supported economically.

The examples shown above can be varied as policies of management change. The next big step in achieving a wider profit pretax will probably be to go from a sales representative type of organization to company direct sales. This will lower sales expense with volume to approximately 15 percent of sales, which gives the company another 5 percent to be added to its pretax profit margin.

The reason for carefully looking at selling expense as a critical factor in percentage of sales analysis is that it is one of the key variables in comparing any company's plans and budgets with achievable reality. Total selling expense, including marketing, advertising, sales commissions, and promotion, is one of the key profit variables in all manufacturing enterprises. We have just demonstrated that an electronic instrument company, in its early stages of development tends to rely on established sales representatives and distributors to sell its product. This is true for many other industries as well, each has a network of sales representatives, manufacturers agents, and/or distributors, through which a new company can market its products.

The relationship between gross margin and selling expense can be controlled within every company, within known ranges for each industry, and vary with method of distribution. Computing and comparing percentage ratios to sales for these statement elements helps managers, planners, investment bankers, and others to evaluate management performance.

Where the starting company is an electronic component company instead of an electronic instrument company, another set of typical percentage ratios obtain. More fabrication is done in house than assembly and test of purchased parts. Material costs will usually tend to be lower as a percentage of sales, labor costs will tend to be higher than for our instrument manufacturer. For a typical electronic component company in the $2 million to $5 million sales class, ratios will be as shown below.

Sales		100%
Cost of Goods Sold:		
Material	24%	
Direct labor	14	
Overhead	16	
Total Cost of Goods Sold		54
Gross Margin		46%
Expenses:		
General and administrative	8%	
Selling expense	15	
Product development	8	
Total Expenses		31
Profit Pretax		15%

Moving up to a higher sales level, say $10 million, the well-managed electronic components company will try to achieve ratios to net sales as shown below:

Sales		100%
Cost of Goods Sold:		
Material	23%	
Direct labor	13	
Overhead	15	
Total Cost of Goods Sold		51
Gross Margin		49%
Expenses:		
General and administrative	6%	
Selling expense	15	
Product development	8	
Total Expense.		29
Profit Pretax.		20%

You will note in comparing the two sets of ratios at similar sales levels between the company manufacturing electronic instruments to the company manufacturing electronic components, that there is a wide difference in gross margins and a wide difference in selling expenses, but a similarity in profits pretax.

Sales representatives selling electronic components usually earn a commission of 10 percent or less, since they are selling a less complex product, even though they may be part of the same sales representative firm. By adjusting a great deal of his sales to distributor sales, rather than through sales representatives, the component manufacturer can achieve an even lower average commission. By use of volume discounts he can lower his average commission cost to somewhere in the order of 7 to 8 percent.

In any event, the one critical factor which determines how wide the gross margin must be to sustain a profit is selling expense. In the recent development of the electronics industry it became almost axiomatic that one could not build, sustain, and survive in a new venture in the electronic or computer markets unless one could plan a 55 percent to 60 percent gross margin in order to be able to afford the essential product development, selling, and service expenses inherent in this type of business. Another critical ratio is product development expense. In the early stages of growth of an applied science company it might need product development expenses of 12 percent to 15 percent of sales, declining to 7 percent or 8 percent of sales with increased sales volume.

Use of Financial Ratios in Managerial Control

Financial ratios described in earlier sections of this chapter are used as common statistical yardsticks providing relationships between two sets of numbers. Financial ratios may also be used to help control a business, as well as for longer range planning purposes. Financial ratio analysis can give management insights into operating efficiency and effects of marketing policy by observing periodic trends and the percentage relationships between cost of sales, marketing expenses, and product development expenses to net sales. The customary use of percentage financial statements, briefly illustrated above, has become an accounting practice in which additional columns on a financial statement show the percentage relationship of each item against the selected base. On income statements, the base is almost always net sales; on balance sheets it is almost always total assets or total liabilities.

By preparing percentage income statements monthly, and showing comparative data for prior months in the same year, or prior quarters in the same year, or preceding years, as well as years planned in the future, presentations can be made to management control groups, boards of directors, commercial and investment bankers. Use of percentage financial statements provides a picture of internal operations and financial changes which can be related to shifts in policies as well as permitting the observation of shifts from the relative size of the different elements of the statement. By doing this management can look at profit margins, the increase or decrease in selected items of expense, and the comparative importance of all elements on an income statement.

The use of the percentage balance sheet, though it is not as common as a percentage income statement, is sometimes a help in showing the relative significance of certain assets and liabilities which management wishes to carefully control. By using percentage financial statements the manager of any enterprise may illustrate the relationships between the key elements on his income statement and study them for internal consistency and balance. He also has the opportunity of comparing them against performance standards for other people in similar industries and other businesses, by using the average ratios for industries compiled by government agencies, trade associations, and published by Dun & Bradstreet, and Robert Morris Associates.

The availability of the percentage income statement and the percentage balance sheet to the financial manager, gives him tools that he can use for internal control and planning purposes, along with financial ratio analysis. Selecting key ratios with which the manager can test his company's performance against the outside world, will prepare him to discuss his company's statements with any banker, loan analyst, credit manager, or security analyst who wishes to understand the company.

General Liquidity and Solvency Problems

One of the best uses by management of financial ratio analysis is in predicting the future to determine the company's exact position in terms of liquidity and solvency. The expectation that companies may be unable to borrow money and obtain credit on the most favorable terms will lead the manager of an insolvent or near bank-rupt company to become conscious of the company's credit rating and debt structure. The sophisticated manager of a successful com-pany attempts to avoid this condition by frequently measuring and examining the corporate financial statements for evidence of any deterioration.

Investors also examine corporate financial statements and try to predict potential financial difficulties. In order to utilize financial ratio analysis, management should analyze each company's key ratios against at least three different standards: (1) The company's own historical experience in these ratios—this should be done on a quarter-by-quarter as well as annual basis to show seasonal varia-tions; (2) the ratios of similar companies in the same industry; and (3) the manager's model of a financially sound company. After making these comparisons, the manager or the investor, or the security analyst should all be equally concerned if trends in the ratios show a lower quality of profit performance. If a given com-pany's ratios consistently rank at the lower end of the range of in-dustry ratios for the same industry or similar industries, or compare unfavorably with leading corporations in this field, or if the ratios begin to violate the standards of soundness incorporated in the analytical model of a financially sound company in this field of en-deavor, then management can take action to avoid financial de-terioration. For example, the managers of our sample companies, above, in electronic components and instruments can compare their rates to lines 3671 through 3679 and 3811 in the abstract from Dun & Bradstreet's *Key Business Ratios*. These entries show the median and the interquartile range for 14 ratios (see Table 5).

Most financial managers will find that the nonliquid asset ratios are better predictors of serious financial deterioration than liquid

TABLE 5
Manufacturing and Construction

Line of Business (and number of concerns reporting)	Current assets to current debt	Net profits on net sales	Net profits on tangible net worth	Net profits on net working capital	Net sales to tangible net worth	Net sales to net working capital	Collection period	Net sales to inventory	Fixed assets to tangible net worth	Current debt to tangible net worth	Total debt to tangible net worth	Inventory to net working capital	Current debt to inventory	Funded debts to net working capital
	Times	Percent	Percent	Percent	Times	Times	Days	Times	Percent	Percent	Percent	Percent	Percent	Percent
3671–72–73–74–79 Electronic Components & Accessories (96)	3.41	3.41	9.85	16.22	4.29	5.87	42	6.8	27.0	30.8	64.9	62.3	62.0	28.0
	2.41	1.71	4.67	6.65	2.68	4.05	55	4.8	48.4	49.0	102.8	82.1	87.8	60.3
	1.79	(3.64)	(11.64)	(12.56)	1.89	2.87	71	3.4	79.1	77.3	160.4	107.4	128.5	92.6
3811 Engineering, Laboratory & Scientific Instruments (41)	5.18	5.83	11.40	15.43	2.57	3.36	52	4.7	28.0	15.9	47.6	54.6	34.9	16.7
	3.43	2.11	5.74	7.69	2.06	2.50	67	3.8	41.9	34.5	84.9	71.1	60.6	43.3
	2.31	(1.26)	(2.78)	(4.17)	1.78	2.16	86	2.8	61.1	65.2	136.0	90.8	81.7	70.1

Source: *Key Business Ratios* in 125 lines, 1970, Dun & Bradstreet, Inc.

asset ratios insofar as having superior predictive power both long term and short term. Among the nonliquid asset ratios that are best predictors are:

1. Cash flow to total debt.
2. Net income to total assets.

With regard to liquid asset ratios, any ratios using either net working capital or cash predict much more accurately than those involving current assets and quick assets. Generally speaking, quick asset ratios predict more accurately than do current asset ratios.

Managers using financial ratio analysis can predict and isolate the common characteristics of firms that are getting into serious financial trouble. These are:

1. A lower rate of sales growth.
2. Poor cash flow and net income position.
3. Higher level of total debt.
4. Less cash.
5. More aging of accounts receivable.
6. Lower current assets.
7. More current debt.
8. Unbalance or overextended inventory.

The use of financial ratios by managers in checking characteristics of approaching financial failure is only one aspect of their use in management planning. A more typical process is to use standard ratios against a model of success as illustrated above. One can do long-range forecasting and planning and five-year plans and spot-check their soundness by applying financial ratios much better than just by looking at the numbers predicted.

USE OF FINANCIAL RATIOS BY COMMITTEES OF THE BOARD OF DIRECTORS

Typically, committees of the board of directors (in public or non-public companies) have been established to provide smaller, more effective working groups of the board which, in its entirety, might tend to be cumbersome and unable to deal specifically with the variety of problems with which companies are confronted. The most prevalent type of board committees in an average size company would be the executive committee, the audit committee, and the finance committee. The latter probably lends itself more to a larger, more structured company than to a smaller one where the entire board would probably exercise the functions of a formal finance committee.

The audit committee would not, in discharging its normal functions, have much use for the type of financial ratios and analysis which have been discussed above. This committee is more typically concerned with the role and performance of the independent auditors and their relationship with the management of the company.

In this discussion we are dealing with the role and functions of the finance committee, whether as a separate committee, the executive committee, or the entire board of directors working as a "committee of the whole." The finance committee should make extensive use of financial ratios in determining the financial health of the organization, with a view toward ascertaining the capital necessary to sustain and grow the business. The committee examines in detail such areas as the forward product and marketing plans of the company, their impact on development, plant and equipment, tooling, working capital, and related expenditures necessary to support these plans. It must also consider the company's ability to generate the funds required to implement the overall plans. In other words, the finance committee is primarily concerned with the financial analysis necessary to determine the appropriate mix of capital and debt, for the long term and short term required to nourish operations.

Obviously, the types of financial analyses discussed previously would bear heavily on the finance committee's conclusions as how to best meet the financial needs of the enterprise. It goes without saying that such ratios as return on equity, debt to capital, inventory turnover, and collection cycles would bear heavily on final decisions made by the committee with respect to alternate methods of financing the enterprise.

This broad analysis function is performed in all well-managed companies, either as a formal finance committee, as an informal executive group, or by the entire board of directors. In our opinion a formal finance committee should be activated in every successful growth-oriented company, rather than allowing the functions of this committee to actually be performed by key members of the board as a part of their "normal responsibility" on a "catch as catch can" basis.

SUMMARY

The financial ratios defined and described in this chapter are used as common statistical yardsticks providing more than statistical relationships between two sets of numbers. Financial ratio and percentage analysis may be used to view a business from the outside, to control a business from the inside; for long-range planning and budgeting purposes; giving visibility toward decisions on program and policy matters at every level of management including the board of directors.

The proper use of financial ratio analysis can give management keys and insights into operating efficiency, marketing policy, liquidity, solvency, and profitability.[10] The judicious use of financial ratio analysis, tempered with experience and judgment can help the manager or owner to define periodic trends and to observe relationships between numbers on the income statement and the balance sheet and the relationships between financial statements.

The use of percentage financial analysis has been briefly illustrated. It has become accounting practice to show the percentage relationship between key items on income statements and balance sheets. The combined use of percentage analysis and ratio analysis by financial officers provides an extremely useful picture of company operations and fiscal changes which can be related to management policy decisions. Investors, security analysts, loan officers, credit managers, as well as company financial managers and representatives of ownership all have access to these management tools which, used with judgment and discretion, are extremely valuable and useful.

ADDITIONAL SOURCES

Altman, Edward I. "Financial Ratios, Discriminant Analysis and the Prediction of Corporate Bankruptcy." *Journal of Finance*, 23 (September 1968), 589–609.

Benishay, Haskel. "Economic Information on Financial Ratio Analysis." *Accounting and Business Research*, 2 (Spring 1971), 174–79.

Bierman, Harold, Jr. "Measuring Financial Liquidity." *Accounting Review*, 35 (October 1960), 628–32.

---

[10] See Thomas S. Dudick, *Profile for Profitability* (New York: John Wiley & Sons, Inc., 1972).

Edmister, Robert O. "An Empirical Test of Financial Ratio Analysis for Small Business Failure Prediction." *Journal of Financial and Quantitative Analysis,* 7 (March 1972), 1477–94.

Helfert, Erich A. *Techniques of Financial Analysis,* rev. ed. (Homewood, Ill.: Irwin, 1967).

Horrigan, James C. "A Short History of Financial Ratio Analysis." *Accounting Review,* 43 (April 1968), 284–294.

Horrigan, James C. "The Determination of Long-Term Credit Standing with Financial Ratios." *Empirical Research in Accounting: Selected Studies in Journal of Accounting Research* (1966), 44–62.

Johnson, Craig C. "Ratio Analysis and the Prediction of Firm Failure." *Journal of Finance,* 25 (December 1970), 1166–68. See also Edward I. Altman, "Reply," ibid., 1169–72.

Lev, Baruch. *Financial Statement Analysis: A New Approach,* Englewood Cliffs, N.J.: Prentice-Hall, 1974.

Theil, Henri. "On the Use of Information Theory Concepts in the Analysis of Financial Statements." *Management Science,* 15 (May 1969), 459–80.

Chapter 13

Cash Forecasting and Short-Term Investment

Alan H. Foster*

THERE ARE a few things to keep in mind concerning "Cash" itself before determining whether or not a company has enough, when more than enough, and how to invest it short term.

GENERAL OBSERVATIONS

Profits versus Cash

No one likes to invest in, or lend money to, a company that is not profitable. However, if any supplier or employee had a choice between a company having "Profits" or "Cash," both groups would rather be affiliated with a company that has cash to pay for its services than a profitable company that has used its cash for expenses or working capital and found itself in a nonliquid state. There are occasions during a down cycle, either for the economy or industry, where profits have to be disregarded in favor of cash.

The whole thrust of the corporation is to remain liquid. A case in point is Chrysler Corporation in calendar year 1975. Finding itself in a cash bind because of tremendous inventories, it decided to con-

---

* Alan H. Foster is vice president and treasurer of American Motors Corporation, Detroit, Michigan.

tinue a substantial rebate program to its customers without its competitors following. The rebate program was given, despite large losses and knowing full well that further rebates would contribute to its losses. However, it was a question of cash. If a company doesn't have cash, it is literally out of business because its suppliers will not sell to it and the company, therefore, cannot produce.

Cash Availability

The time that you need cash most is the worse time to raise it. A company treasurer should develop his lines of credit with banks when he does not need their assistance. This is the time when banks want most to lend to the company—exactly when the company does not need it. The price one pays for these lines of credit when they are not needed is small compared to the risk of not having them when you need them. The point is, credit should be in place before you need it and in such a manner that you are able to draw it down when *you* want it—not when the banks want to lend it.

Lenders of Cash

It is very wise to diversify as to those who lend you money. If your company is small, perhaps two or three banks are enough; but if your company is large, it should never rely on one bank or a small group of lenders but should diversify to spread their risk.

At American Motors Corporation, for example, there are 1,750 banks that supply wholesale and retail credit to 2,000 AMC dealers. However, corporate credit lines are from only 12 banks. In addition, AMC has developed a following of European banks so that the corporate credits extended to the company are evenly distributed between the domestic banks and the foreign banks.

Sources of Cash

When borrowing money, it is much easier to do so if you define a project for which the money is borrowed. A beneficial side effect is that it provides a diversification of sources of credit so that you are not borrowing from the same institutions all the time. For example, an office building should be financed by real estate money; working capital with seasonal lines of credit; plant and equipment with long-term debt; financing of consumer goods through commercial paper; overseas expansion with that country's currency from an overseas bank; and so on.

It is much easier for a financial institution to provide money if it knows the purpose. It is easier for a person in the financial institution to sell it to his loan committee.

There are many sources of credit and, therefore, cash. Each should be looked upon thoughtfully so that the treasurer is not restricted in his approach. Having alternate sources of cash also prevents the treasurer and the company he represents from wearing out his welcome by continually going back to the same bank or group of banks time and time again. There is a danger where banks feel they are overexposed. At that point they feel they have to exert some control over the organization. Also, however friendly the banks may be toward the company, they are prevented from lending by legal limit restrictions.

Determining Cash Availability

There are various ways of determining how much cash a company has available for its use. When American Motors Corporation acquired a company with $400 million sales, that company's balance sheet reflected no cash. When the figures were explored, those selling the company pointed out that the company was in a minus cash position. The reason was that the acquired company's treasurer had prepared but not issued checks drawn on the company. From his checkbook balance, however, he deducted the amount of all these checks even though the checks were still in the accounts payable department waiting his word for release. It was a strange situation, since that company's principal banks were very satisfied with the cash balances that the company kept with them. Conversely, the company showed a negative checkbook balance. The truth was that the company did have a substantial amount of cash in its bank accounts because it had never issued the checks.

Most companies have more cash than they think and are surprised when the bank statement arrives each month. The difference in what they thought they had and their bank statement is "float." It would be foolish not to deduct the amount of the check from the checkbook balance when a check is mailed to a supplier. However, until a supplier receives the check, its bookkeeping department makes the appropriate entry, and until it is deposited in the bank and credited through the bank clearinghouse, the money still remains in the bank account of the company that issued the check. This "float" should not be disregarded, but utilized. Banks utilize "float"; e.g., if a company deposits $1 million in a dividend disbursement account the bank disbursing the dividend checks has the use of the $1 million, or a part of it, until the dividend recipients receive their checks, cash them at their banks, and their banks collect from the issuing bank.

The ability to utilize "float" is being slightly diminished with the new systems that the banking community is installing. The old rule of thumb used to be that checks issued during the most recent two and one half days were available to the company as "float." To illustrate: with today being Thursday, half the checks issued on Monday would have cleared the system and were being debited to your bank account; but, the checks issued on Tuesday and Wednesday would not be charged against your bank account. In effect, those checks that you sent during that two-and-one-half-day nonclearing period, in dollar equivalent, could have been invested in short-term securities. On a rolling basis of two and one half days' "float" you could continually invest those funds.

The above technique in no way should be interpreted to mean that a company should or could issue checks without having the funds to cover them. The technique described above is just the opposite. You have the funds but you are getting the "float" of two and one half days' interest by investing those funds rather than letting those funds lay dormant in your checking account.

The Movement of Cash

There is a saying concerning cash—"get cash in fast and let it out slow." Lockboxes, for example, will get your cash in quickly; not prepaying your bills will let it out slow; drafting on your customer's bank for shipments will get it in fast; paying bills by covering only the drafts presented, lets it out slow; and so forth. The net result is, of course, to increase the cash available to your company and, hopefully, reduce your borrowing needs.

After discussing some broad thoughts on "Cash" itself, this chapter discusses the practical area of "Cash Forecasting" followed by a brief discourse on "Short-Term Investments" that are available for purchase.

CASH FORECASTING

Cash, because of its unique role as a liquid asset—but non-earning—must be managed very intensively. For liquidity purposes, the cash manager must be able to determine when disbursements are necessary and to highlight periods of cash shortages. Concurrently, because cash is a liquid asset and only contributes to earnings when utilized, he must be able to determine when and how to invest surplus cash in order to obtain an acceptable return in light of the risk.

To assist the cash manager in making these decisions, data, primarily a forecast of cash availability, are required. The forecasting objective is to project changes in the company's operations that have an impact on cash availability. A good forecast will provide the manager with information to permit the scheduling of disbursements and the investment of excess cash, as well as providing management data on a timely basis in order to correct any deficiencies. In addition, the analytical framework of the *forecast should give management the opportunity to observe all sections of the corporation on a consolidated basis* in order to make necessary operational changes. As a result, receivables and inventory levels, profit plans, and the short-term debt relationships can be collectively monitored from the cash forecast.

Format of the Cash Forecast

In general, the cash forecast takes three forms.

Short-Term Forecast.   This is the cash manager's working forecast which provides specific details on cash receipts and disbursements. This forecast usually is only three months in duration with the first month taking the form of an operational forecast, which contains the greatest detail with forecasted daily or weekly receipts and disbursements. From this operational forecast, the cash manager can analyze the schedule for disbursements and determine the excess cash available for investment.

A great amount of detail is not required for the remaining second and third months, since these tend to be planning forecasts, which give the cash manager a more general idea of his cash requirements so potential investments can be planned. This forecast should be updated weekly or biweekly in order to give the cash manager additional information and to permit him to adjust his cash strategy to accommodate changing corporate requirements.

Medium-Term Forecast.　With a duration of usually one year, this is a planning forecast. Its primary function is to provide input in order to finalize capital spending decisions and to permit time to arrange for necessary financing. Nevertheless, cash needs are presented often in as much detail as the short-term forecast. Normally, the forecast contains monthly detail and is updated each month.

Long-Term Forecast.　This is an extended forecast generally covering up to five years which is usually the maximum realistic forecast period due to the greater uncertainties involved. As a result, only a minimum of detail is presented. This type of forecast is useful in planning for major capital projects, acquisitions, and new financing. As an additional input factor, the state of the economy (i.e., domestic consumer demand, the money supply, foreign demand, and so on) must be expressly determined with these assumptions clearly spelled out and made part of the text of the forecast.

Cash Forecasting Methods

The receipt and disbursement method and the adjusted net income method are the two most widely used types of forecasting methods.

Receipts and Disbursement Method.　This forecasting method is less complicated than the adjusted net income method since cash receipts and disbursements are projected for any and all periods and from this the changes in cash balances can be determined. Because accounting data does not usually present information on a cash basis, this forecasting method is not useful for the medium- and long-term forecasts because of the great amount of additional analysis that is required to prepare the forecasts. However, this method does lend itself to the short-term forecast very effectively since most areas within a corporation have a good understanding of their cash needs and receipts for the next month and the necessary data can be compiled easily and accurately. The format is shown in Figure 1.

FIGURE 1

	Operating Cash Forecast Control No.____ Month of_____									
	Mon. (Date) ____	Tues. ____	Wed. ____	Thurs. ____	Fri. ____	Mon. ____	Tues. ____	Wed. ____	Thurs. ____	Fri. ____
Operating Starting Balances										
Receipts:										
Kenosha—Domestic cars										
—General										
Fleet sales										
AMPAC										
Detroit—Export										
—General										
Jeep										
Subsidiaries										
Zones										
Other										
Total Cash Receipts										
Disbursements:										
Kenosha—Vendors										
—Payroll										
—Other										
Milwaukee body—Other										
—Payroll										
Milwaukee body—Other										
—Payroll										
Detroit										
Toledo										
Payroll										
Real Estate, D.I.P. & Misc.										
Pension and Insurance										
Taxes										
S. U. B.										
Fleet repurchases										
Meyers Road										
Brampton										
Evart Products										
Can. Fab.										
Holmes Foundry										
Coleman Products										
AM General										
Charleston, W. Va.										
Total Disbursements										
Net Cash										

Types of receipts and disbursements generally include:

A. Receipts
   1. Cash sales.
   2. Cash from accounts and notes receivable.
   3. Sale of assets.
   4. Proceeds of financing.
B. Disbursements
   1. Payrolls (including all withholdings).
   2. Maturing debt.
   3. Interest.
   4. Large purchases such as raw materials and supplies.
   5. Capital expenditures.

Adjusted Net Income Method. This method uses accounting and budgetary data without modification and, therefore, lends itself to developing the medium- and long-term forecasts.

The adjusted net income method is simply a balance sheet or funds statement forecast. Net income is forecast with noncash expenses added back in. From this total, changes in the noncash items of the balance sheet are forecast with cash assuming the form of the balancing item. The format is illustrated in Figure 2.

The major problem with the Adjusted Net Income Method is that forecasts are limited to accounting periods, with the shortest period usually being one month. In addition, cash is a balancing item and is not forecast directly. If one does not work with the figures repeatedly, it can become confusing since deviations are used, not total figures.

Use of this method might include the following classifications:

Net Income
Plus Noncash expenses such as depreciation.

Sources of Cash
New finances.
Reduction in inventories or receivables.
Increased current liabilities.

Uses of Cash
Capital expenditures.
Debt retirement.
Increases in inventories or receivables.
Decreases in current liabilities.

FIGURE 2
1975 Fiscal Year—Cash Flow (dollars in millions)

	(Date) Account Balance	Actual 1st Qtr.	Actual 2d Qtr.	Actual (Month)	Increase/(Decrease) to Cash		Forecast			4th Qtr.	Total Year
					(Month)	(Month)	(Month)	(Month)	(Month)		
Profit/Loss after Tax											
Noncash											
Depreciation											
Tools											
Other											
Total Noncash											
Balance Sheet Changes											
1. Inventories											
Raw and in process–Automotive											
–Livingston											
–AM General											
–Other											
Finished stock –Automotive											
–Rent-A-Car											
–AM General											
Parts											
Total Inventories											
2. Receivables											
Domestic automotive–New Car Drafts											
–Rent-A-Car											
–Other											
International											
AM General											
Total Receivables											

3. Current Liabilities									
Automotive:									
Trade accounts									
Dealer rebate									
Sales allowances									
Dealer holdback									
Warranty/buyer protection									
Payrolls/payroll and miscellaneous taxes									
Pension and insurance									
Provision for income tax									
Rent-A-Car (buy/back)									
Other automotive									
AM General									
Total Liabilities									
4. Miscellaneous Changes									
Deferred tax benefits									
Prepaid expenses									
Other working capital									
Total Balance Sheet Changes									
Changes in Outside Financing									
AM general credit lines									
AM credit lines									
Construction financing—Southfield									
Total Changes in Outside Financing									
Capital Expenditures									
Capital budget (Assets, Tools, & D.L.)									
Southfield Building Construction									
Total Capital Expenditures									
Net Cash Flow									
End of period cash balance									

Note: Any adverse impact on cash would be shown in brackets which would indicate a decrease in cash due to an increase in assets and/or a decrease in liabilities.

These items are totaled and financing requirements in the form of cash shortfalls, or cash surpluses, can be determined.

This forecasting method presents information that can be readily used by management to monitor various corporate activities. Policies regarding receivables, inventories, borrowing, and so on, can be constantly reviewed and adjusted according to the current and projected corporate level of activity.

A similation cash forecast can aid in monitoring performance. By adjusting the individual parameters of the forecast, the effects of any change can be immediately isolated. From these results, management can take steps quickly to avoid possible adverse developments.

SHORT-TERM INVESTMENTS

Basic Considerations

Generally speaking, excess cash above an acceptable minimum level should be invested in marketable securities (or near-money investments) which provide attractive yields after due consideration is given to transaction costs, inconvenience, delay, and, of course, risk. Ideally, all excess cash (and this includes "float") should be invested in marketable securities whose maturity and liquidity could be adapted to anticipated needs for cash and could be liquidated to pay obligations as they mature. However, because of the uncertainties of the cash forecast and the inevitable delays in portfolio liquidation, short-term investing must be pursued cautiously if unforeseen cash shortages are to be avoided.

Corporate Policy Considerations

Historically, corporate treasurers opted for the safest near-money investments available, usually in the form of short-term government securities. The trend today, however, is toward maximization of income, which necessitates consideration of the full array of available near-money investments. Therefore, risk, which affects the amount of cash a company will receive upon portfolio liquidation, becomes a major factor in the investment decision. Risk for short-term investments generally takes three forms: default risk, liquidity risk, and maturity risk.

Default Risk. Although no security is entirely default free, U.S. Treasury securities are usually defined as riskless and are generally used as the standard for determining the risk premium for other securities. Yield varies with the default risk of other securities and the investment decision should be determined by the trade-off between expected return and risk. Obviously, for securities with identical maturities, the higher the return, the higher the risk.

To assist the portfolio manager in making short-term investments, other than in Treasury securities, the quality of corporate and municipal securities is graded by such investment services as Moody's and Standard & Poor's. Money market instruments such as certificates of deposits and commercial paper are graded by certain large investors and market specialists such as dealers and brokers.

Liquidity Risk. In addition to yield and safety of a security, consideration should be given to the ability to turn an investment into cash. Since it is possible to sell practically any asset in a short period if enough price concession is given, the lower the marketability of the security the greater the yield necessary to attract investors.

Maturity Risk. Generally speaking, the longer the maturity of the security the more subject it is to fluctuations in principal value as a result of changes in the level of interest rates. Thus, when interest rates are rising, fixed interest rate security prices tend to fall in order that the discount from face value will provide a yield comparable to the higher rate of other investments in the market. Conversely, when interest rates fall, the fixed rate security will command a premium because a purchaser can buy a security which offers a yield which is above that found in the marketplace.

Securities with longer maturities tend to experience greater discounts or premiums from par in the marketplace due to the fact that, while changes in price affect the total amount of discount or premium, the annual amount of discount or premium is affected by the number of years to maturity. Thus, the amount of discount or premium for longer term securities will be larger to compensate for otherwise smaller annual amounts accrued over a longer period of time. Although it is evident that maturity risk becomes less of a consideration if the cash manager is able to hold securities until maturity, most companies cannot afford the luxury of tying up capital for extended periods of time.

Skill of the Cash Manager

The cash manager should never take a passive stance when investing the firm's excess cash. Experience has shown that active and skillful management of the portfolio can increase yields. It should be noted, however, that active management alone will guarantee only that returns will be altered. Skillful management is the ingredient for success.

Generally, the skillful cash manager can increase the portfolio yields by anticipating short- and long-run trends in interest rate movements as well as taking advantage of temporary changes in interest rates brought about by supply and demand imbalances in the market.

In practice, *the cash manager would anticipate trends by keeping maturities short if he expects rates to rise or by buying longer term securities in the face of anticipated declining rates.* Care must be taken, and this approach should be governed by corporate policy considerations. Short-term changes resulting from market aberrations are often caused by technical factors such as exchange rate movements, changes in bank free reserve positions, and corporate tax payment considerations, to name a few. The cash manager should be provided with corporate policy from his treasurer as to his working parameters and then work for the best yield within them.

Major Types of Investments

Types of investments can be segregated into two major categories: public debt and private debt. Public debt, described in the following section, includes Treasury obligations, federal agency securities, and municipal funds; while private debt, covered in a succeeding section, is composed of money market instruments and long-term corporate obligations.

Here we are restricting our discussion to U.S. investments. Foreign "paper" is also suitable for investment, but one should be familiar with the country of origin, its banking system, and so on, so that he is as "comfortable" dealing in that country's paper as his own. Usually this occurs when a company is multinational with sales concentrated in a few countries.

Public Debt

Treasury Securities. Treasury securities are usually classified in terms of marketability. Marketable securities include U.S. Treasury bills, notes, and bonds. Nonmarketable Treasury obligations, which shall be omitted from this discussion because they are not actively traded, are composed of savings bonds, certain other nonmarketable obligations, and foreign series of notes and bonds.

Treasury Bills are highly liquid and very short-term and for these reasons, in conjunction with the strength and credit rating of the U.S. government, are considered by many to be riskless and serve as the standard for most short-term investments. Treasury bills are issued open face in a bearer form and are sold on a discount basis to pay par at maturity. One is able to convert the discount rate on a Treasury bill into the approximate yield of interest-bearing instruments through the use of statistical tables which are readily available. Income derived from the bills is subject to federal but exempt from state income tax.

New Treasury bills are readily available. Issues of 91- and 182-day bills are auctioned weekly, while bills maturing in one year are offered every four weeks. Tax anticipation bill (TABs) are sold when necessary to finance the Treasury's seasonal deficit. TABs offer the tax-paying investor a bonus of several days' interest, since they may be used at face value for tax payments; although they cannot be converted to cash until maturity, one week after the tax date.

Treasury bills enjoy the largest amount of secondary trading in the short-term money market due to their high quality, variety of maturities, and large volume of maturities outstanding.

Treasury Notes and Bonds. Securities in this group have original maturities ranging from 1 to 30 years. Notes are coupon obligations with maturities of 1 to 7 years while bonds have original maturities of from 5 to 30 years. Although there is a general 4¼ percent coupon limitation, issues up to $10 billion, as well as securities held by U.S. government accounts and Federal Reserve bonds, are exempt from this restriction. Bonds are obtainable in coupon or registered form while notes are usually, but not always, issued in coupon form.

Interest on both types is paid semiannually and is subject to federal, but not state, income tax. Purchases may be for cash or in exchange for existing obligations. With over $150 billion in marketable Treasury coupon issues outstanding a secondary market is assured.

Federal Agencies

The remainder of U.S. government public debt is composed of certain borrowings of federal agencies, which are owned by the government either in whole or in part. Originally conceived as instruments to attract capital to segments of the economy where flows were insufficient, federal agency credit programs have been greatly expanded in recent years.

Federal agency securities offer advantages similar to Treasury issues and generally provide higher yields. In addition, many securities are guaranteed directly or indirectly by the government. Income from all agency obligations is subject to taxation at the federal level.

The major federal agencies which issue securities or participation certificates in sizable amounts are:

Housing Credit Agencies

Federal National Mortgage Association (FNMA). FNMA is a privately owned association whose purpose is to assist home mortgages insured by the Federal Housing Administration (FHA), Veterans Administration (VA), and Farmers Home Administration, as well as certain conventional mortgages.

The sellers of these mortgages must, in return, purchase stock from FNMA in proportion to the amount of loans sold.

Financing is conducted primarily by sale of debentures and short-term discount notes. The debentures are in bearer form and are sold in $10,000 minimum amounts. The notes are similar to commercial paper in that they have 30–270-day maturities and are sold in $5,000 minimum amounts. Long-term financing is represented by mortgage bonds and government capital debentures. Mortgage bonds are guaranteed by the Government National Mortgage Association (GNMA) backed by the full faith and credit of the U.S. government). Subordinated debentures are general obligations which are subordinate to regular debentures and discount notes.

Short-term loans are also available to the FNMA from the U.S. Treasury up to $2.25 billion.

Government National Mortgage Association (GNMA). GNMA is a government-owned entity which is a division of Housing and Urban Development (HUD). It was created in 1968 to provide special assistance to FNMA with regard to mortgage functions and to manage and liquidate mortgages acquired from HUD and other federal agencies.

GNMA guarantees, with the backing of the U.S. government, mortgage bonds of FNMA and the Federal Home Loan Mortgage Corporation (FHLMC). These bonds have a maturity of 1–25 years and are issued in minimum denominations of $25,000. GNMA also guarantees principal and interest of pass-through securities issued by FHA approved mortgages. These securities differ from bonds in that principal and interest are paid monthly. Another variation of the pass-through security is the serial notes, which offer the investor a wider selection of maturities which can be tailored to specific needs.

Federal Home Loan Banks (FHLB). The Federal Home Loan Banks (FHLB) were created in 1932 to help finance the housing industry by supporting member institutions consisting of savings and loans, mutual savings banks, cooperative banks, insurance, and mortgage lending institutions. The association's borrowings are represented by bonds and notes. Bonds have maturities of one year or more with interest paid semiannually. Notes mature in less than one year with interest paid at maturity. Both bonds and notes are bearer instruments in minimum denominations of $10,000 and neither are callable prior to maturity. FHLB obligations are backed by the joint and several obligations of the member institutions.

Federal Home Loan Mortgage Corporation (FHLMC). FHLMC is a government-sponsored institution designed to further the development of the secondary market in home mortgages. It issues mortgage bonds guaranteed by GNMA in $25,000 minimum denominations and participation sale certificates, which are guaranteed by FHLMC although they are not backed by the U.S. government.

Farm Credit Agencies

Banks for Cooperatives. Banks for Cooperatives make loans to farmers' co-ops for working capital needs and fixed asset acquisition.

Funds are advanced through the Central Bank and the 12 member banks under the auspices of the Farm Credit Association. The banks finance their operations through consolidated collateral trust debentures sold through banks and dealers. All obligations are backed by the joint and several obligations of the 12 banks.

Federal Land Banks. The purpose of the Federal Land Banks is to provide long-term mortgage credit directly to farmers. Operations are financed by the public sale of consolidated Federal Farm Loan Bonds (FFLB). These bonds range in maturity from months to 15 years and are backed by the joint and several obligations of the 12-member banks.

Farmers' Home Administration. This agency makes direct government loans, insures privately funded loans, and extends grants in certain rural areas for various purposes such as housing, community facilities, and the development and operation of farms, land, and water resources.

Loans insured by them may be funded by local lenders or through the sale of insured loan notes to investors. In the latter instance, loans are advanced from revolving funds maintained by the agency, and the revolving funds are replenished when notes are sold to investors.

Insured notes may be purchased with maturities varying from 1 to 25 years. The underlying promissory notes are repayable at any time prior to maturity.

Blocks of notes held by them are offered periodically in lots of $100,000 to $500,000 to private investors through the use of an insurance contract. Both insured notes and insurance contracts are fully guaranteed as to payment of principal and interest by the U.S. government.

Federal Intermediate Credit Bureaus. This association is comprised of 12 district banks which make loans to, and discount paper for, various types of lending institutions. These loans, in turn, are used to finance short-term and intermediate credit needs of farmers. Financing is accomplished via consolidated collateral trust debentures which are issued to the public and have a maturity from nine months to five years. These securities are backed by the joint and several obligations of the 12-member banks.

Community Development Corporation (CDC). The CDC was created, as a division of HUD, to administer the guarantees by the secretary of HUD of the obligations of developers of new community development projects. The full faith and credit of the U.S. government is pledged to repayment of guaranteed securities, provided that income derived from such securities is subject to federal taxation.

Securities of Other Agencies

Other agencies which issue securities in various forms, maturities, and minimum denominations are:

Export-Import Bank of the United States
    Form: Coupon and registered.
    Current Maturities: 3 to 7 years.
    Minimum Denominations: $5,000.

General Services Administration
    Form: Registered.
    Current Maturities: To 30 years.
    Minimum Denominations: $5,000.

Maritime Administration
    Form: Registered.
    Current Maturities: To 25 years.
    Minimum Denominations: $1,000.

Small Business Administration
    Form: Registered.
    Current Maturities: To 15 years.
    Minimum Denominations: $10,000.

Tennessee Valley Authority
    Notes
        Form: Bearer.
        Current Maturities: To 4 months.
        Minimum Denominations: $5,000.
    Bonds
        Form: Coupon and registered.
        Current Maturities: Various.
        Minimum Denominations: $1,000.

United States Postal Service
    Form: Coupon and registered.
    Current Maturities: To 25 years.
    Minimum Denominations: $10,000.

Washington Metropolitan Area Transit Authority
    Form: Coupon and registered.

Current Maturities: To 40 years.
Minimum Denominations: $5,000.

Asian Development Bank
Notes
  Form: Registered.
  Current Maturities: To 5 years.
  Minimum Denominations: $1,000.
Bonds
  Form: Registered
  Current Maturities: To 25 years.
  Minimum Denominations: $1,000.

*Inter-American Development Bank**
Form: Registered.
Current Maturities: To 25 years.
Minimum Denominations: $1,000.

International Bank for Reconstruction and Development (World Bank)[1]
Form: Registered.
Current Maturities: 2 to 25 years.
Minimum Denominations: $1,000.

Private Debt

Listed below are securities often described as money market instruments and usually classified according to length of maturity:

Negotiable Certificates of Deposit. Negotiable certificates of deposit have been an important money market instrument since 1961 when commercial banks began issuing them and a secondary market developed to provide liquidity. The emergence of negotiable "CDs" represented an effort by banks to stimulate the growth of deposit balances and increases the stature of bank deposits in relationship to competitive liquid money market instruments. CDs were a switch on the part of the banks from asset financing to liability financing.

Banks issue negotiable CDs in bearer or registered form in minimum amounts of $100,000. Interest is payable at maturity and is calculated for the actual number of days divided by 360. CDs are generally issued with 30- to 180-day maturities but are also available for longer periods, allowing the investor to tailor the maturity date to suit his needs. Because corporations are the major

---

[1] Not agencies of the U.S. government.

customers, CD maturity dates tend to fall on dividend and tax dates when corporations normally need cash.

The interest rate that may be paid by banks on certificates of deposit is subject to Federal Reserve Regulation Q. This limitation, however, is often adjusted according to the Federal Reserve's desire to attract capital. With total CDs outstanding of approximately $70 billion, an active secondary market is maintained by dealers. Further, the secondary market is not regulated with respect to rates. Most secondary market transactions involve units of $1 million or more.

The interest earned on CDs is subject to federal and state taxation.

Eurodollar CDs. Eurodollar CDs are negotiable CDs expressed in dollars, which are issued by foreign banks or overseas branches of of U.S. banks. The major advantage to investors is that rates are not regulated and often yield a higher rate of return. On the other hand, this lack of regulation in conjunction with lack of disclosure and deposit insurance make Eurodollar CDs higher risk instruments. It is also necessary to make sure the issuing offshore bank is supported by the full resources of the parent bank and not merely by the offshore bank's net worth.

Bankers Acceptances. Bankers acceptances are drafts, accepted by banks, which are used in the financing of foreign and domestic trade. In effect, the bank substitutes its credit standing for that of the drawer. Most acceptances have maturities of less than 180 days and are generally of high quality. Rates tend to be slightly higher than that of Treasury bills of like maturities.

Commercial Paper. Commercial paper consists of short-term, unsecured promissory notes issued by finance companies and certain industrial concerns in order to raise working capital. Commercial paper can either be sold directly or through dealers. Maturities vary from 1 to 270 days. These notes are normally sold in bearer form on a discount basis with denominations starting at $25,000. There are three risk categories of commercial paper: prime finance paper, prime industrial paper, and finance paper.

Prime finance paper is generally issued directly by leading sales finance companies and certain large bank holding companies. The investor may specify the issue date and the maturity date so that funds will be available when desired, as for tax or dividend payment purposes. Prime finance paper is usually sold on a discount basis, although it can be obtained on an interest-bearing basis.

Prime industrial paper is issued by leading industrial firms through commercial paper dealers. Maturities are planned to meet the industrial firm's needs, and the investor can purchase only those maturities available on the market. The yields on prime industrial paper are slightly higher than on prime finance paper because of more restricted maturity dates.

Finance paper of less than prime quality carries a higher yield than either prime finance or prime industrial paper because the companies are not of the same high credit standing.

The discount earned on all three types of paper is subject to federal and state taxes on an ordinary (short-term) tax basis.

Repurchase Agreements. The repurchase agreement is a sale of short-term securities by a government security dealer to the investor, where the dealer agrees to repurchase the securities at a future specified time. The investor receives a given yield while he holds the security and may tailor the security to his own needs. Rates are related to rates on Treasury bills, federal funds, and loans to dealers by commercial banks.

Short-Term, Tax-Exempt Notes. Short-term, tax-exempt obligations issued by public bodies are investment vehicles of various risk and are ranked as to risk by rating agencies. Because the notes are exempt from federal income taxes, these securities offer the investor a superior tax-equivalent yield on funds not needed in current operations. They are particularly useful when timed to meet known cash commitments, such as dividend or tax payments, inventory buildups, and other predictable financial requirements.

There are four types of short-term notes: project notes, which are backed by the full faith and credit of the U.S. government; and tax, bond, and revenue anticipation notes, which are obligations of the issuing municipality or authority.

Project notes are issued in bearer form in minimum denominations of $25,000 with interest payable at maturity. Initial maturities range from 90 days to 1 year.

Tax anticipation notes (*TANs*) are offered periodically by municipalities to finance their current operations in anticipation of future tax receipts.

Revenue anticipation notes (*RANs*) are offered for similar purposes in anticipation of receipt of future revenues.

Bond anticipation notes (*BANs*) are offered in advance of long-term bond financing. These notes are available in bearer form in minimum denominations of $25,000. Generally, maturities extend from 60 days to 1 year with interest payable at maturity.

Municipal Bonds. Municipal bonds are distinguished by the security pledged to the payment of bond principal and interest. General obligation bonds, which bear a pledge of the borrower's full faith and credit, are backed by all of the borrower's resources and secured by taxes collectible on all taxable property within the borrower's jurisdiction, usually without limitation of rate or amount. From the basic types of municipal bonds there have arisen numerous variations, such as lease obligations or bonds having a limited claim on certain tax and/or revenue sources. It should be noted that municipal bonds vary dramatically in quality and yields depend upon the strength of the issuing municipality.

Revenue Bonds. Revenue bonds are secured only by the income derived from a specific public enterprise, as a water utility or parking facility. Assessment bonds, issued for a specific project benefiting a designated area, are payable from assessments levied on each piece of property within such area.

Long-Term Corporate Obligation

Because of their longer maturity and higher risk, corporate term obligations generally are not favored by corporate cash managers.

Mechanics of Short-Term Investing

Experience has proven that close contact with dealers who have a proven record of performance is valuable when investing surplus cash in short-term investments. A strong relationship with a number of good dealers allows the cash manager to "shop the street" for the best rate on comparably rated securities. Furthermore, it is a fact that rates do differ markedly on the same security. Although it is mandatory that the cash manager consider himself primarily as an aware investor who evaluates his own risks, sophisticated and concerned dealers can often reveal trends which might affect the value of a given security. Therefore, good dealer contacts can assist the cash manager in his choice of investments.

Choice of Investment

Because of their basic similarities with respect to price fluctuations, money market instruments do not readily lend themselves to diversification. As a result, the objective of the cash manager should be to maximize yields on similar instruments without compromising risk objectives or impairing minimum liquidity levels. The cash manager's task is further complicated by the cash flow peculiarities inherent in his own industry. In the automotive industry, for instance, the norm is to stay in high-yield, short-term securities. The average length of time to hold a security is about six months. Investments generally take the form of Standard & Poor's P–1 rated industrial or financial commercial paper.

As noted previously, prime industrial commercial paper carries a higher yield than prime financial paper because prime industrial concerns establish a maturity according to their markets, which do not always correspond to that of the prime finance companies and of large bank holding companies. On the other hand, finance companies are continuously in the paper market and, as a result, offer more liquidity to the investor.

When purchasing bankers' acceptances and domestic CDs, the norm is to purchase maximum maturities of 90 days from the 100 largest domestic banks. Often, CDs are purchased at a lower yield than commercial paper because of the company's willingness to further relationships with banks which have been helpful in providing lines of credit, dealer financing, or in other areas.

In the area of Eurodollar certificates of deposit, many cash managers are required to buy only from the top 50 world banks, usually on the basis of the most attractive yield. In this market, dealers are particularly useful since they are more rate sensitive and are able to batch requests and bargain on a collective basis for the highest rate. Furthermore, since the market is not regulated as closely as the domestic CD market, reputable dealers often alert the investor to adverse trends.

International Investment

Apart from Eurodollar CDs, international short-term investing is carried on since many multinational companies find themselves with surplus local currency that can and should be invested. The cash manager's primary decision should relate to whether the surplus should be converted to dollars and brought home, thereby avoiding any potential devaluation loss, or invested in high-grade local securities. Often this decision is further complicated by an anticipated increase in the local currency vis-à-vis the dollar. The decision, of course, must be made on an individual basis within the guidelines established by management.

Safeguarding Purchases

All purchases and sales of CDs purchased through dealers, commercial paper, and government securities should be done through a reputable money market bank and left there for safekeeping. These securities should be registered in the name of the purchaser.

CDs purchased directly from a bank are left at that bank with instructions to pay the principal and interest to a specified bank upon maturity. Acknowledgment of purchases and sales from the issuing bank should be mailed to the corporate cash manager.

Conclusion

"Cash" is *the* important element in any business. It is the end result. A treasurer must recognize what it is, where it is, and what he can do with it until it is spent.

ADDITIONAL SOURCES

Betancourt, Richard C. "Plan Your Own Cash Flow System." *Financial Executive,* 63 (January 1975), 28–30, 32.

Calman, Robert F. *Linear Programming and Cash Management/CASH ALPHA.* Cambridge, Mass.: M.I.T., 1968.

Horn, Frederick E. "Managing Cash." *Journal of Accountancy,* 117 (April 1964), 56–62.

King, Alfred M. *Increasing the Productivity of Company Cash.* Englewood Cliffs, N.J.: Prentice-Hall, 1969), chaps. 4 and 5.

Chapter 14

How Industry Uses Break-Even Analysis

R. A. Anderson*
H. R. Biederman†

BREAK-EVEN, or cost-volume-profit analysis, can play the role of obstetrician, pediatrician, and mortician in the life of a business. No less a matter than survival is often involved as this excerpt from a news item illustrates:

> S. KLEIN EXPECTED TO CLOSE 6 STORES. S. Klein the discount-store pioneer, is expected to close six of its suburban stores in the New York area because they are losing money, informed sources said yesterday. . . .
>
> Founded in 1906 by the late Sam Klein, the Klein stores were acquired by McCrory in 1965. Despite an aggressive expansion program in which 10 stores became 19 with the opening of large stores in suburban shopping centers, S. Klein suffered annual deficits from about 1959 through last year.
>
> However, the chain approached a break-even point in the late 1960's and early 1970's before lapsing into its biggest losses in the last two years. . . .
>
> In some cases, retail observers noted, the newer Klein stores proved to be too large—250,000 to 300,000 square feet—for a par-

---

* R. A. Anderson is vice chairman of the board—Finance and Administration, Lockheed Aircraft Corporation, Burbank, California.

† H. R. Biederman is senior economic adviser—Corporate Planning Staff, Lockheed Aircraft Corporation, Burbank, California.

ticular market, so that high operating costs turned potential earnings into losses.[1]

The problem of an adequate volume of business to pay both the
fixed and variable costs is one faced at one time or another by most
businesses. Break-even analysis relates changes in costs, revenues,
profits and losses to the *volume* of business. This is one of its distinguishing characteristics. The volume may be expressed in physical terms x, number of units sold; in value terms y, dollars of sales;
in capacity terms z, percent plant utilization. It may be a rate of
production or a cumulative quantity. In whatever manner volume
is expressed, costs, revenues, profits and losses are related to volume.

There are other names for break-even such as cost-volume-profit
or simply profit/volume analysis. These emphasize this essential tie
of performance to volume. They may also avoid the incorrect implication that this method of analysis is concerned exclusively with
the question of what is the break-even point. Although other names
may be more descriptive than break-even, we shall use that designation here. It is the easiest of the phrases to recall and is the most
popular. Further, the coining of the phrase break-even point by
Columbia University's Walter Rautenstrauch during the second
decade of the 20th century was in itself a breakthrough. Earlier
phrases like "zero profit point" and "profit graphs" were certainly
less felicitous.

More important than the name, of course, is the basic importance
of break-even. It emphasizes the importance of volume and as
Ernest Dale's management text reminds us, "The volume of sales is,
in fact, the key factor in all corporate planning."[2] Further, in evaluating a business the considerations that might be included are
demand, costs, pricing, profits, return on investment, and risk and
uncertainty. Break-even helps on most of these. It deals directly
with demand, costs, and profits. It may include risk and uncertainty.
Break-even does not encompass return on investment and its evaluation of capital investments is more rudimentary than those made
by sophisticated capital budgeting techniques.

It is true that a break-even chart is often an oversimplification,
but used with an appreciation of its limitations it can, in the words

[1] *New York Times,* June 1974.

[2] Ernest Dale, *Management: Theory and Practice* (New York: McGraw-Hill Book
Company, 1969), p. 320.

of Professor Warren Haynes, "cut through the complexity of reality and focus on the fundamental relationships."[3]

Is the technique used? To answer this question we made a survey in mid-1974 of 358 large- and medium-sized firms. These were, in most cases, firms with sales exceeding $100 million a year. The 116 firms that replied included representatives of manufacturing, construction, finance, transportation, utilities, retailing, and other industries. A copy of the survey form and a summary of responses is appended at the end of this chapter.

Seventy-two percent of those answering the survey were using break-even analysis. To help those answering the questions know what we had in mind, we briefly described the elements of break-even analysis. A slightly expanded description follows.

Definition and Place in Management Science

Break-even analysis is a technique for studying the relationships between revenues; fixed, variable, and total costs; and profits for a limited range of volume of business over a specified period. More briefly, it is a technique for analysis of revenues, costs, and profits as they relate to the volume of business. Still more briefly, the phrase cost-volume-profit is quite descriptive.

The qualifications of the longer definition are important however. The separation of costs into fixed and variable is a central feature of the approach. Further, the analysis is concerned with the consequences of limited variations in the volume of business during a specified period rather than with the effect of time itself on the evaluation. The whole question of the time value of money is not usually a part of break-even analysis; it is, of course, central to net present value and return on investment techniques which are discussed in Chapter 15 on capital budgeting.

Another important characteristic of break-even analysis is that it is usually summarized in a graph, in a break-even chart. Anything that can be said in a chart can be said in formulas and can be summarized in a table. But traditionally, an advantage of break-even analysis has been its ability to display the results in simple graphs. Rautenstrauch and Villers stressed this in their pioneering work. In their 1949 text they developed an example that involved reorganization of a firm to reduce overhead costs and revamping of manufacturing operations. At the end of that example, the authors re-

---

[3] W. Warren Haynes and William R. Henry, *Managerial Economics: Analysis and Cases*, 3d ed. (Dallas, Tex.: Business Publications, Inc., 1974), p. 202.

marked, "In a few minutes of chart construction, the important results of reorganization are revealed at a glance where many hours' calculation would otherwise be required, *and even then no visualization of results obtained*" (their emphasis).[4]

Since break-even analysis is a management technique it finds its place comfortably in this *Handbook* in a section on "Tools and Techniques of Financial Analysis." In textbooks it generally appears as a part of the discussion of costs or in a section devoted to planning and control. The relation to profit planning and in particular to profit contribution analysis, is frequently noted.

The Charts

Break-even charts can take on a variety of forms. Four of these are demonstrated below. The case is taken from a study of the petroleum refining industry performed by Stephen Sobotka and Company under the sponsorship of the Environmental Protection Agency in 1973.[5] As a result of their study of the industry they developed typical cost and revenue figures for a refinery producing fuel products, but no lubricants in the year 1971.

Here are the data used in the series of break-even charts that follow:

Price per barrel—$5.04
Capacity 25,000 barrels per day

Variable Costs	*Per Barrel*
Raw materials	$3.50
Fuel and utilities	0.26
Chemicals, catalysts, additives and materials	0.20
Total variable cost per barrel	$3.96

Fixed Costs	*Total*
Labor.	$ 6,250.00
Fuel and utilities	1,000.00
Insurance and taxes.	1,250.00
Interest	6,250.00
Depreciation.	6,250.00
Total fixed cost.	$21,000.00

---

[4] Walter Rautenstrauch and Raymond Villers, *The Economics of Industrial Management* (New York: Funk and Wagnals Co., 1949) p. 103.

[5] U.S. Environmental Protection Agency, *Economic Analysis of Proposed Effluent Guidelines for the Petroleum Refining Industry* (Washington, D.C.: Environmental Protection Agency, September 1973), p. 22.

The price of $5.04 exceeds the variable cost of $3.96 by $1.08. If enough gallons are sold this $1.08 per gallon will cumulatively equal and then exceed the fixed costs. Break-even would be at $21,000 (the fixed cost) ÷ $1.08, the difference between price and variable cost. This is at a volume of 19,444 barrels per day. The $1.08 difference between the price and the variable cost is often referred to as "the contribution to overhead and profits" or as the "unit contribution margin"—the contribution made by each added unit sold to covering the fixed costs or adding to profits. It is also called the "unit profit/volume (P/V) income."

As one of the editors of this *Handbook* has pointed out, "If a firm's costs were all variable, the problem of break-even volume would never arise, but by having some variable and some fixed costs, the firm must suffer losses up to a given volume."[6] In this case, there would be losses up to a volume of 19,444 barrels per day.

The break-even or cost-volume-profit charts that summarize these relationships can take many forms. Four of these are shown in Figure 1 (1A–1D). Figure 1A is the standard way of displaying the facts. The measure of volume of business is on the X-axis. In Figures 1A, 1B, and 1C, the volume is in physical terms—barrels of oil produced per day. In Figure 1A the fixed costs are shown as a horizontal line at $21,000. Variable costs are added—they start from the base line of the fixed costs and add $3.96 for each barrel produced per day. The distance between the fixed cost line and the total cost line is the variable costs at any given point. For example, at 10,000 barrels per day, the total cost is the $21,000 fixed cost plus 10,000 times $3.96 variable costs which adds to a total of $60,600 total cost. The total revenue line starts from the origin and increases at a rate of $5.04 per gallon. At 10,000 gallons a day, the $50,400 is less than the total costs and it is not until the break-even volume of 19,444 that revenues equal cost, both at 97,998.

Figure 1B is similar to 1A. The axes are the same and the total revenue line is identical. The variable costs are at the bottom of the two layers of costs rather than the fixed costs. The total cost curve is the same in both graphs. There is an advantage in stacking the fixed costs on top of the variable costs: the contribution to fixed

---

[6] J. Fred Weston and Eugene F. Brigham, *Managerial Finance*, 4th ed. (New York: Holt, Rinehart and Winston, Inc., 1972), p. 46.

costs and profits is more apparent. At any point prior to break-even, one can see the amount of fixed costs that are covered up to that point; and beyond the break-even point it is clear that all fixed costs have been covered and added volume is contributing to profits.

Figure 1C is a little more complicated. It treats fixed costs as a negative value that is overcome by the margin between variable costs and the selling price. The points that are plotted are found by multiplying the margin between variable cost and price—the $1.08, in our case—by the volume and subtracting the fixed cost. For example, at a quantity of 10,000 barrels per day, multiplying $1.08 times $10,000 = $10,800$. Next subtract the fixed costs of $21,000. The result is a negative $10,200 which indicates that the volume is not yet great enough to break even.

This profit/volume form of the chart is a revealing technique for comparisons of profitability of products, alternative combinations of labor and capital, and analysis of multiproduct operations.

Figure 1D is similar to 1A. The different feature is that the volume of business on the X-axis is expressed in dollars rather than in physical units. Figures 1B and 1C could also be redrawn with dollars instead of barrels on the horizontal axis. When a company produces a variety of products there may be no common physical unit in which to express the output. In fact, in the refinery example, there would be a variety of liquid petroleum products and we have implicitly assumed a constant mix of these different volumes.

When the volume of business is expressed in dollar terms on the horizontal axis, the total revenue line is a 45° line, if the scale on both axes is the same. If the volume of business is $100,000 one would find a point of $100,000 on the X-axis to indicate volume of production and the corresponding total revenue (or sales) figure would be $100,000 on the Y-axis. This assumes that what is produced is sold. The break-even point will, of course, be on the 45° production/revenue line since it will be at an intersection of the total revenue and total costs.

The example we have been working with is a real one for an industry but not for any one firm. It is a composite refinery based on a study of the industry. Figure 2 is an actual analysis for a plant owned by a corporation that replied to our survey. It summarizes key aspects of a one year's profit plan. A refinement with a message is the separate identification of some administrative and other fixed costs that are expected to make the difference between breaking

FIGURE 1
Four Ways to Depict Break-Even

A Petroleum Refinery with:
Fixed Costs. $21,000
Including depreciation   6,250
Variable costs . . . .   3.96 per barrel
Price. . . . .   5.04 per barrel

**1A. Standard Form with Horizontal Fixed Costs:
Volume in Physical Units**

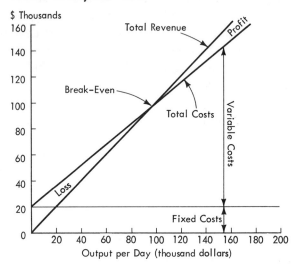

**1B. Contribution to Fixed Costs and Profits Form:
Volume in Physical Units**

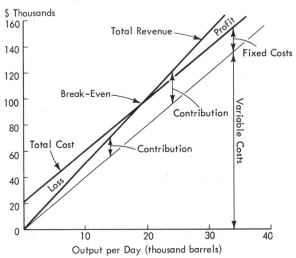

FIGURE 1 (*continued*)
1C. Profit-Volume (P/V) Form: Volume in Physical Units

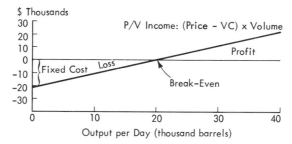

1D. Standard Form with Horizontal Fixed Costs: Volume in Dollars

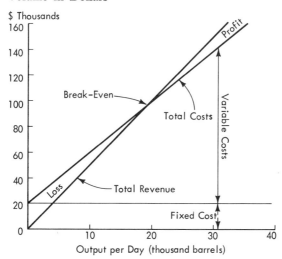

even and having a loss. These are mostly corporate costs that the plant has to help recover. The complaint, "The corporate allocation is killing us!" is a familiar one.

The cases we have examined have involved continuous production, rather than a limited production run. We have not emphasized cash as a matter of special interest. Further, we have not discussed strengths and weaknesses of the analysis. These and other matters will be considered as we turn now to a review of the results of the survey.

FIGURE 2

Containers, Optimum, 1974 (all cost increases covered by price increases)

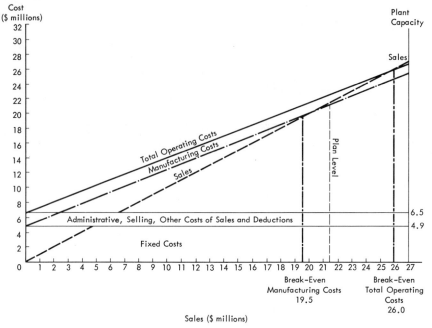

Prevalence of Break-Even Analysis

As noted earlier about three-fourths of the respondents to our survey use break-even analysis. That no doubt overstates the case since a firm that does not use the technique was less likely to reply to our survey than one that does. Several letters from firms that did not complete the questionnaire support this conclusion.

There was some indication of how intensively the technique is used although that question was not asked specifically. Four or five firms indicated they use break-even routinely. Sixteen wrote that their use was not mandatory or routine. For example, one reply noted:

> While I have stated we do use break-even analysis and that its use has grown, it is not considered a standard procedure that must be utilized. Our use of it comes about as one of several means of analysis where any one of our locations becomes marginal as to profit contribution. We could chart the factors to determine what dollar level of sales must be obtained to reach a break-even point. This

would assist in selling price determination or deciding if a facility of commodity should be terminated.

Have users tended to turn from break-even over the last decade? No, to the contrary, over a third have increased their use of the technique while most others have maintained about the same level of activity.

Sixteen firms said they "always" faced the question of what volume of business they had to have to make operations profitable. Only one firm replied that question never bothered them. Most were concerned with this basic break-even question frequently (41 firms) or occasionally (36 firms).

While the majority of the firms were acquainted with conventional break-even techniques, about a third replied that they had developed their own methods of analysis.

Although we have noted that a graphical representation is a central aspect of break-even analysis traditionally, detailed numerical calculations were much more popular with our respondents. Seventy-two used detailed numerical calculations, while 43 used graphs, 29 rough calculations, and 14 rules of thumb. Some used several approaches.

The small number stating they were using rules of thumb was unexpected. One television manufacturer used soft tooling if the quantity produced was expected to be less than 5,000. In another case, a restaurant chain operator wrote,

> We need a certain volume of gross sales to justify opening a new restaurant in a marketing area. Cost structure (operationally) is so simple that break-even analysis is not economically justified. Experience has proven our simple approach. Manager of each restaurant is aware of fixed and variable costs and all projections and actual results measure variation from norms.

These are cases of applications of rules of thumb, but few others were reported by respondents.

While most of the firms think of themselves as undertaking a break-even analysis when they do so, about 20 percent use other terms. For example, a number of firms associate the analysis with discontinuing an operation and think in terms of "phase out situations," "decisions to minimize losses," and "divestment, sale of a plant, or plant closing problems." Others think of techniques in terms of "incremental analysis," "cost analysis," "resource analysis," "profit feasibility studies," "earnings problems," "profit variance analysis," and "forecasting." These fit within the usual concept of break-even analysis. But there were others that relate break-even to capital budgeting and return on investment; these concepts should be differentiated.

Uses

The survey results showed the three most frequent applications of break-even analysis by a wide margin were to estimate profits and losses at various volumes of business (68), to decide on whether to undertake an operation (65), and to decide whether to shut down an operation (61).

At an intermediate frequency level were the examination of alternate pricing possibilities (45) and the analysis of the contribution being made by an operation to fixed costs and profits (43).

Less frequent applications included cash break-even (29), comparison of the profitability of segments of the business (25), product mix decisions (22), and operating leverage (19).

All of these applications were selected from a list supplied as part of the questionnaire. There was also a place for respondents to list other uses and some interesting ideas appeared there. One electric utility uses break-even analysis to help it make decisions on the type of generating capacity to build and another to schedule the use of auxiliary gas turbine generators. Here is an example of one of those replies:

> Although we do not use break-even analysis as described in the enclosure to your letter, we do utilize a form of that analysis to determine the least-cost alternative in an investment decision. One example of this would be in the selection of new electric generating capacity, where the capacity costs in dollars per kilowatt are fixed, and fuel, maintenance and operation are variable costs dependent upon the extent of utilization. By varying the percentage utilization of each type of capacity, we can develop ranges of most economical capacity type, based upon expected use.

Expansion has caused firms to expand the use of break-even. For example, one firm said break-even was used to check on the reasonableness of cost and profit projections for expansion. Another said it was used in acquisitions and expansion, and several required break-even data as part of the justification for capital expenditures.

Forecasting was mentioned by several respondents, and one firm said that it used this form of analysis as a monitoring device to detect and identify deviations from expense and sales plans. That firm also made occasional use of the technique to evaluate alternative strategic plans submitted by divisions and to compare profitability of different types of equipment.

A large manufacturer said it uses

> . . . break-even analysis techniques to also determine an "optimum volume level." This recognizes that fixed costs are not truly fixed, but increase in stages. Hence, there is a level of volume at which, considering all effects on variable profits, fixed costs, and operating environment, the firm can expect to achieve maximum profits and cash flow.

This idea of an optimum volume would be completely at home in economic cost theory. The total costs and total revenues are often nonlinear in that analysis and there is a point of maximum profits. This is where the difference between the total revenue and the total costs are the greatest and profits are at a maximum as shown in Figure 3. (Tangents to the curves are parallel at this point which

FIGURE 3
Nonlinear and Linear Break-Even

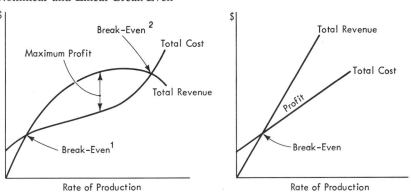

Rate of Production   Rate of Production

means that marginal revenue is equal to marginal cost, economic's prescription for maximum profits.)

Optimum volume is not a usual concept in linear break-even analysis since in the range of operations being examined the greater the volume, the greater the profits and there is no optimum volume. Of course it is possible to have nonlinear break-even analyses and semivariable costs introduce step functions. Figure 4 shows step effects on costs of both reduced material costs and adding work shifts. The introduction of nonlinear curves can lead to opti-

FIGURE 4

Semivariable Costs

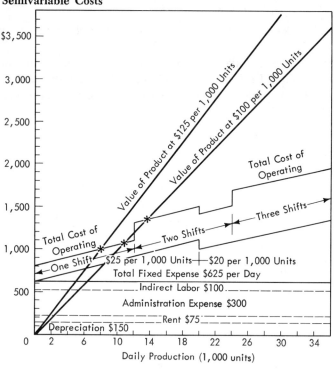

* Break-even points.
Source: Alvin A. Hass, "Profitability (or Loss) at a Glance," *Modern Plastics*, February 1972.

mum volume studies. However, we should recognize that linear cost and revenue curves are often realistic, especially when the time period is short and the variation in volume limited.

The questionnaire did not list as a possible use the most obvious one—to determine the break-even point. It did come reasonably close in what turned out to be the most popular use, to "estimate profits and losses at various volumes of business." A response from United Air Lines provided a good illustration of trying to find the break-even point. The approach is instructive since they start from a year's operating results and try to find the break-even point and then a break-even percent of total service provided.

The airline industry is concerned about the break-even passenger load factor. What portion of the seat miles flown must be occupied by fare-paying passengers for an airline to break even? A July 1974 common stock prospectus from UAL describes the calculation of break-even passenger load factor. These are essentially the steps. (A profit is assumed in this description, but the same approach can be used if there is a loss.)

1. Knowing operating revenues and revenue passenger-miles (RPM) in a given year, find the revenues per RPM. Assume linear relationships; that the revenues and costs per RPM are constant for all passenger volumes.

In most years operations will result in a profit or loss rather than just breaking even. The next step is to determine the number of RPMs in excess of (or short of) the break-even point.

2. Only RPMs beyond the break-even point yield profits. Those are called "incremental revenue passenger-miles," ΔRPM. The profits that are made on each incremental passenger-mile is the difference between the added revenue per passenger-mile and the added cost per passenger-mile. In other words, Profit = ΔRPM $\times$ (revenue per RPM — variable cost per RPM). It follows that ΔRPM = Profit/(revenue per RPM — variable cost per RPM). Figure 5, which is not to scale, depicts this situation.

FIGURE 5
Revenue Passenger-Miles Break-Even

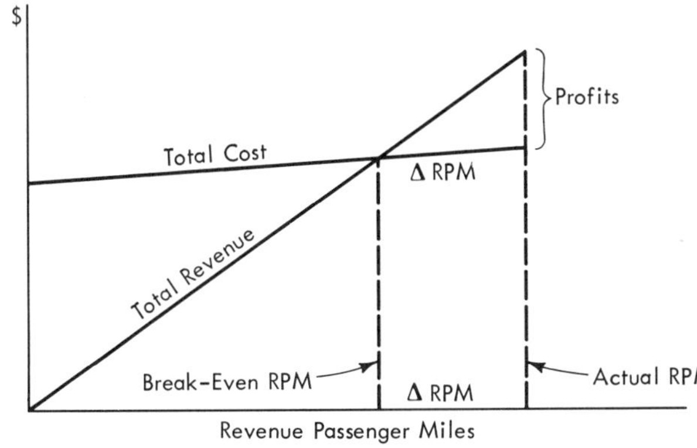

Revenue Passenger Miles

3. Subtract the incremental revenue passenger-miles from actual revenue passenger-miles. The result is break-even RPM.
4. To convert break-even RPMs into break-even passenger load factor, divide break-even RPM by total available seat miles actually flown.

In 1973, this calculation showed that the break-even passenger load factor was 50.5 percent while the actual load factor was 55.8 percent. The airline made money.

Cash Break-Even and Operating Leverage

Most of the break-even applications identified by the survey are fairly self-explanatory, but two may need further elaboration: cash break-even and operating leverage.

Cash implications of the volume of business are important and in some circumstances, critical. If you asked our company's finance staff for an L-1011 aircraft break-even chart in the early 1970s, the answer was, "Cash or total?"

There are noncash sums in both revenues and costs, but the most obvious item is depreciation. By excluding depreciation from fixed costs a first approximation of the cash impact of operations at various volumes can be observed. A firm may operate well below its break-even point and still be above its cash break-even. This form of the break-even chart is shown in Figure 6. It is based on the same assumptions as Figure 1. Excluding the $6,250 of depreciation from the fixed costs results in a cash break-even of 13,657 barrels per day compared to a profit and loss break-even of 19,444 barrels per day.

Operating leverage technically is the percent change in profits divided by the percent change in volume. It is a profit elasticity measure. But more generally, this concept is related to the substitution of plant and equipment for labor. The greater the use of fixed assets and the less of labor, the greater the operating leverage in most cases. This is because variable costs per unit of output typically decrease with the use of more capital equipment and less labor. An increase in volume will generally result in a greater increase in profits for the more capital intensive plant, than for the more labor intensive plant since variable costs will rise less for one than the other.

Figure 7 is an example of the application of break-even analysis

FIGURE 6
Cash Break-Even

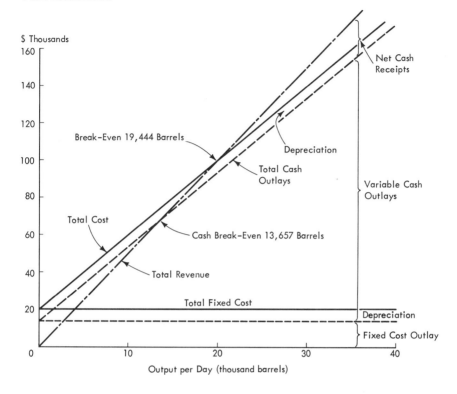

Output per Day (thousand barrels)

to the question of whether or not to substitute equipment for labor. It is a real problem faced by a military electronics equipment manufacturer several years ago. The circuit board component of a disposable acoustical device could be made manually or with an automated line. The manual assembly would require 25 employees and the automated assembly, only 6. The setup for the manual line would cost $25,000 and for the automated line an additional $50,000. To illustrate the principle of break-even in this situation, we can note that at a price of $14.50, break-even for the manual process was 36,000 units and for the automated system, 14,479 units.

The automated system costs less than the manual one at relatively low quantities and seems well worth installing. Frequently, the fixed costs required to automate involves an added risk. The investment will only be justified if there is a large sales volume. That is not a problem here. At relatively small volumes the automated system pays for itself.

FIGURE 7
Automated versus Manual Production

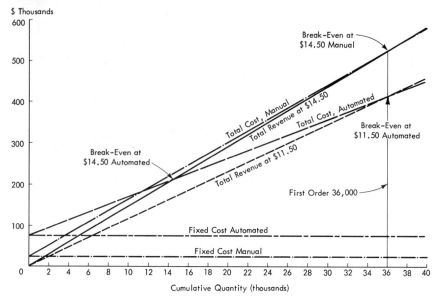

This conclusion is reinforced by the fact that in this case the whole cost of the automation is written off by the break-even point. Its full cost—not just its depreciation—is included in the extra $50,000. This is a limited production rather than a continuous production case as the volume is represented by cumulative quantity rather than the rate of production. This will be examined more fully later, but for now let us look further into the realities of this case.

The real problem was not to determine the break-even point under different manufacturing plans. It was instead how to compete for a contract for 36,000 units of the end item. The strategy was to bid less than $100 per unit for the devices. The circuit board as all other components were examined to see what they could contribute in cost savings. The intent was to break even on the bid for the contract of 36,000 and to make profits on subsequent contracts. The automated manufacturing of the circuit boards would permit the component to be made at a break-even cost of $11.50 rather than $14.50 and would help hold the price to less than $100. The decision was made to proceed with the automated production and the contract was won at a bid of $95. Plans went awry, however, when a decision to move the line to another location during production proved more costly than it would have been if the line had not been automated. And the follow-on contract was not won; so profits beyond the planned break-even point were never realized. A sad story!

Fixed and Variable Costs

In their *Managerial Finance* text, Weston and Brigham emphasize the importance of fixed costs to break-even analysis: "If a firm's costs were all variable, the problem of break-even volume would never arise, but by having some variable and some fixed costs, the firm must suffer losses up to a given volume."[7]

Participants in our survey were asked about the segregation of costs into fixed and variable and were unusually vocal in their response. Traditional accounts do not, of course, identify costs as fixed or variable, but a number of firms said their accounting system was now providing this information.

Two-thirds of the respondents recognized the division of costs into fixed and variable as essential for their break-even analyses. Most felt that the best way to separate the costs was by understanding the nature of each element and judging how it should be treated. Only 10 of those replying thought that the better approach was to correlate cost and volume of business statistically to derive a slope representation of variable costs and an intercept that would represent fixed costs.

There were three indicators in replies to the survey of the difficulty of identifying fixed and variable costs. First, given an opportunity to select, "It is a difficult and involved process," or "It is a relatively easy process," 22 said it was difficult, 28 said it was easy and more than half were silent. The second indicator was in answer to a question on difficulties in using break-even. The answer chosen more frequently than any other—on 43 of the replies—was "Difficulties in separating total costs into fixed and variable costs." A third indicator was written comments. A number of these said costs are often partially fixed and partially variable. Here are some examples:

> Too many costs are semi-fixed or semi-vairable. . . . Many costs are semi-variable. . . . Must recognize some costs are "semi-variable" or "semi-fixed." . . . It is our experience that no expense is

---

[7] Ibid., p. 46.

> 100% variable (there are plateaus for fixed expenses). . . . fixed costs are not truly fixed but increase in stages. . . . The biggest problems we have are in its use in the determination of the fixed and variable elements of a semi-variable cost. . . . [Break-even] is a difficult concept to get across to operating management and how they use it effectively. Each one sees fixed and variable costs differently.

Since in each of these instances someone close to the problem has taken the trouble to write of his firm's experience, it seems safe to say that the semifixed and semivariable nature of many costs is a prevalent difficulty. It may not be easy but this note suggests it is worthwhile. "I believe that the determination of the fixed and variable elements of costs of a product, division, company, or other entity are more useful in analysis than the break-even concept per se."

This comment is a reminder that break-even analysis is related to the broader concepts of marginal costs, opportunity costs, and contributions to fixed costs and profits. In the course of our survey these matters were not explored methodically but they did surface.

For example, two companies replied that since their businesses consisted of a succession of individual projects, they did not use break-even analysis. We shall discuss below break-even as it applies to limited production projects, but these replies raise a different question. Is there a plant break-even in addition to project break-even in a multiproduct plant? The answer is that there is a requirement to have enough work in a plant for it to have a base against which to charge its fixed costs. This is necessary if the plant is to recover its fixed as well as its variable costs and still quote competitive prices. This is a plant break-even concept that is separate from a product break-even.

A further question is what fixed costs should be charged to a new project being undertaken in a plant that has capacity that would otherwise be idle. The opportunity cost answer is that if there is no alternative use for the capacity, it is free to the project. Figure 1B illustrates the problem. Should management insist that the project reach the break-even point in such a case or should a project be accepted if it covers its variable cost and makes some contribution to fixed costs? Marginal reasoning would accept the project under certain circumstances. Some of the qualifications on (1) a project should not be accepted if there is a better use for the resources;

(2) it should not be accepted if it will "spoil the market" by having other customers ask for prices that will not cover full costs; and (3) a firm cannot survive without covering full costs in the long run. One of our respondents made it clear he felt the acceptance of such business was a mistake. "Let someone else have that business and its risks. The customers often come back to us in a short time anyway."

This issue was not a point of focus in our survey, nor can it be fully discussed here. But the division of costs into fixed and variable is a marginal approach. If relationships are linear, those variable costs are the added cost per unit of output just as the price is the added revenue per unit. This marginal cost information may be aimed at, and will surely permit, decisions based on marginal cost and revenue considerations.

Limited Production: Nonrecurring and Recurring Costs

Rate of production is the usual measure of the volume of production. It is appropriate when the production is expected to go on for an indefinite period and the quantities to be produced are essentially unlimited. Most manufacturing and service businesses are of this nature. But not all. Airplanes, special-purpose machines, cranes, elevators, ships, books, plays, and innumerable job shop orders for special items are examples of limited production. Here is what one economics text says of these cases:

> The traditional laws of production are oriented to the problem of infinitely continued production. . . . Many production decisions, however, involve a given volume or period of production. For example, the firm is to print 10,000 copies of a book or produce 300 planes of a certain type. . . . The traditional theory does not directly cope with production for a finite run. . . .[8]

Cases of limited production do lend themselves well to break-even analysis, but the relevant concepts are nonrecurring and recurring costs rather than fixed and variable costs, and cumulative production rather than the rate of production. In order to undertake a limited production of an item there are nonrecurring design and

---

[8] G. S. Stigler, *The Theory of Price*, 3d ed. (New York: The Macmillan Company, 1967), p. 171. Stigler credits Alchian and Hirschleifer in this section.

setup costs, most of which are accumulated before production starts. These must be recovered by sales if the operation is to be profitable. Recurring costs are expended during the production phase.

Figure 8 shows the break-even planning for an actual aircraft

FIGURE 8
An Aircraft Break-Even Analysis

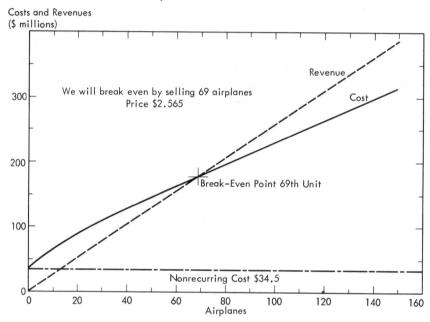

program. The nonrecurring cost of $34.5 million covers preproduction costs—those which are necessary to design, develop, perform tests, build mock-ups; provide production tooling. The recurring costs include not only manufacturing and procurement but support activities such as redesign and sustaining engineering and tooling.

Note the departure from our usual linear assumptions in the recurring costs. The curve shows that there are decreasing costs per unit as the cumulative quantity increases. Behind these decreasing costs is the "learning curve" or really a family of learning curves for assembly, subassembly, and various fabrication and processing stages in the production process. Learning curves usually take the form of a constant percent reduction in man-hours with a doubling of output. Thus an 80 percent curve is one that shows 80 percent of the original man-hours required in an operation as output increases from one to two planes or from two to four planes or from 200 to 400 planes. On an arithmetic grid the curve is a hyperbole; on a double logrithmetic grid it is a straight line.

While the nonrecurring cost curve in Figure 8 could be approximated by a straight line, the losses for quantities less than the break-even quantities would be understated and gains beyond break-even overstated if a linear approximation were used. There are similar discrepancies whenever linear approximations are used for nonlinear realities in break-even analyses, but the learning curve is so much a part of aircraft cost estimating that it is very likely to be included in break-even work.

The ideas of fixed and variable costs and nonrecurring and recurring have similarities, but are quite different in terms of costs included. Direct labor and material which are typically variable costs are included in both nonrecurring and recurring costs. Similarly, those overhead items that are usually fixed costs are included in both recurring and nonrecurring costs. The criterion for sorting costs in continuous and in limited production differs. In one case, the question is whether a cost element varies with volume. In the other it is whether a cost is related to the preproduction or production phase of the work. In both cases the question is whether the volume—rate of production in one case, cumulative production in the other—will be sufficient to overcome the hurdle of costs that do not vary with quantity.

In our survey responses, 34 firms indicated that they were engaged in limited production businesses while 69 were in continuous production. (This was out of a total of 92 since 11 firms had both continuous and limited run products.) With more than one third of the businesses engaged in limited production runs, recurring and nonrecurring approaches to break-even merit more attention than they usually receive.

Break-Even and Capital Budgeting

It was clear from the survey that very few in the financial community were confused about the distinction between break-even analysis and those capital budgeting techniques that discount future cash flows to arrive at a net present value or a return on investment.

Sophisticated capital budgeting techniques emphasize the present value of future cash flows over the life of a project. Break-even analysis of a continuous production product depicts cost, revenue, and profits related to volume of operations during a time of ongoing operations. It makes no attempt to describe the life cycle of the business. It is concerned with options during a short period of time.

There is, however, an interesting relationship between break-even analysis of limited production quantities and the most popular capital budgeting technique, payback period analysis. While a payback analysis usually does not explicitly discount cash flows, it is concerned with the *time* for a project to recover its investment. More exactly it is concerned with the time for net cash flow to recover from a negative position to zero. Break-even analysis, on the other hand, emphasizes the *quantity* that must be sold to break even. The two points are the same: the break-even quantity will be sold at the time the net cash position reaches zero. This is true in principle although some accounting reconciliations may be necessary.

Figure 9 is the same as the previous figure except for the overlay of net cash flow information. The small positive cash flow by the end of 1969 is due to prepayments that were expected by that time. The time scale is arbitrary prior to the delivery of the first ten air-

FIGURE 9
Break-Even and Payback Analyses

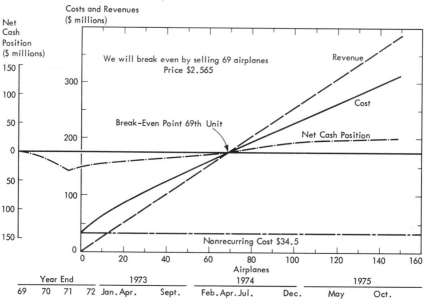

craft. After that, the time is keyed to the delivery dates of the aircraft. The fact that break-even and payback are different views of the same event in the case of limited production is well illustrated by this real case.

Problems and Limitations

Break-even analysis is, of course, not the one and only guide to business decisions. No single technique is. Fifty-five of those responding to our survey said that break-even is one of a number of interrelated analytical techniques that they use. Interviews with the 61 respondents that did not circle that item would probably reveal that almost all of them also rely on several approaches to managerial decisions. Especially clear replies on this subject came from two companies that provided information on their procedures for requests for capital appropriations. In both cases a break-even analysis was a requirement for dollar amounts over specified levels. But it was far from the only information or analytical technique used by either firm. For one of the companies it constituted 1 schedule out of 16; for the other, break-even filled 2 pages out of 164 in a manual of requirements.

Monsanto was one of the companies providing their break-even requirements and instructions. They have permitted us to reprint their break-even form (Figure 10). The definitions are particularly helpful though what is a fixed or variable cost for a chemical company may not be the same for a firm in another industry.

One firm expressed its feelings about the limitations of break-even in particularly strong terms:

> In capital-intensive industries in general, and ours in particular, problems of economic optimization abound. The problems are addressed with economic evaluation techniques considerably more sophisticated than break-even analysis as described (in your letter). They consider demand elasticities and cross elasticities, non-linear cost functions, use of equipment over alternative lives, and time value principles. Break-even analysis, per se, is seldom adequate for our market and cost problems.

In more detail, the problems with break-even analysis identified by those replying to the survey were first, as noted above, the difficulty of separating costs into fixed and variable (43 firms). Linear cost and/or revenue assumptions was the problem in second place (31

FIGURE 10
How to Prepare the Break-Even Analysis Summary

Monsanto	NUMBER: _____
	DATE: _____
Capital Appropriation Request	PAGE_____OF_____

ORGANIZATION:_____

PROJECT TITLE:_____

BREAK-EVEN ANALYSIS SUMMARY

Typical Year:_____

DOLLARS IN MILLIONS

% OF CAPACITY

FIGURE 10 (*continued*)

The break-even display need be computed for only one year. This year should be typical of operations, on a fully allocated basis, and contain no one-time charges such as obsolescence, dismantling, start-up, etc. The year should be noted at the head of the report.

Three lines are needed in the display:

1. *Total Fixed Costs*
   Costs which do not vary with production level. These should include straight-line depreciation. In reality, large fluctuations in production level (e.g., from 40 percent to 95 percent capacity) will create changes in fixed costs. Where these stepwise increases can be determined, they should be included in the graph. Where they cannot be established, the horizontal line should be set at the fixed cost level for the expected normal production range (e.g., 85–95 percent of capacity).

2. *Total Variable Costs*
   Costs which vary with production level (labor, utility charges, raw materials, supplies, etc.). Economies of scale may be possible with larger production levels. Accordingly, as these can be established, they should be included in the graphical plot. No one-time charges should be included.

3. *Total Sales Revenue*
   Total dollar revenue (internal and external) from sales during that year.

For common ranges of production level, this chart and Schedule I will show identical relationships. Outside this range, some differences may appear, as economics of scale and stepwise fixed costs have impact.

A verbal interpretation of this schedule may also be appropriate, as with the Sensitivity Analysis Summary and the Risk Analysis Summary.

When Required

Break-even analysis is required for projects on new product facilities and increased capacity on current product facilities whenever the new fixed capital request exceeds $1,500,000.

firms). In third place was the fact that the analysis fails to take account of the time value of money or to provide a return on investment (24). A number of people took the trouble to comment that this information was provided through other kinds of analysis.

The use of accounting inputs which are based on concepts that are not appropriate for the evaluations being made was tied for the next most frequently noted complaint (21). This is doubtless related to the difficulty of separating costs into fixed and variable. Two other items (1) inflation and (2) "ignores changes over time in technology, management, scale of fixed inputs, and product mix," were checked by 21 and 17 firms, respectively.

Fewer than seven firms selected from the questionnaire any one of the following items as problems in applying break-even: Interest, inventory levels, depreciation, taxes, or selling costs. Since some students of the technique have pointed to these as potential difficulties with break-even, this is informative. It is also interesting that nine of the firms using break-even said it presented no special difficulties.

Special weight should probably be given to those problems that were not among the multiple choices on the survey form but were mentioned independently by one or more of those replying. They included the following limitations:

1. Generally, break-even analysis is only valid for limited time over a relatively narrow range of quantity, for a fixed product mix.
2. Break-even is a "one-time" information tool.
3. Lack of accurate estimates of sales and costs involved in development projects.
4. Inadequate availability of cost and market data.
5. Difficult to achieve a diffusion of knowledge of evaluation techniques throughout the firm.
6. Not an adequate technique for pricing decisions; disagree with the theory of pricing based on marginal rather than full costs.

In attempting to overcome certain of these limitations firms have, as we have seen, included nonlinear relations in their analyses, and one firm noted that it is incorporating probabilities in its work.

Conclusion

Break-even analysis has earned a place among the analytical techniques of management. Without being a fad in recent years, its use has continued to grow supported by the development of marginal concepts in managerial finance and managerial accounting, the expansion of businesses into new fields, the increase in competition in some fields, and the growing use of computers.

Its limitations and difficulties are generally recognized by those using the technique. As a result it is usually only one of a number of approaches used in decision making.

While most emphasis in descriptions of break-even or cost-volume-profit has been on continuous production processes, a form of the analysis is also widely applied in limited production cases. The counterpart to fixed and variable costs in such cases are nonrecurring and recurring costs. While continuous production applications examine operations during a given period and do not attempt to trace the life cycle of an activity, limited production cases do cover cumulative quantities over the life or a major phase of the life of an activity. As a result, limited production cases have much in common with payback period analyses.

The ability of break-even to summarize costs, revenues, and profits in a way that permits an examination of alternatives and facilitates understanding of business essentials assures that this technique will continue to be a viable one.

Appendix: Survey of Break-Even Practices, July 1974

Note: Please refer to accompanying description of break-even. The technique emphasizes the relations between fixed costs, variable costs, revenues, profits, and volume of business.

Please circle the statements that come close to reflecting your views. You will find several statements you will want to circle in some sections. Do not let the space provided for comments inhibit longer answers. The more effort you are willing to put into views in your own words, the more valuable the survey. Again, many thanks.

Results

Replies received	116
1. We (use)	84
(do not use)	31
break-even charts; i.e., cost-volume-profit charts, and/or calculations in our business. (In either case, please continue to questions 2–10).	

2. We view break-even as follows:
   a. We know the conventional break-even techniques and apply them with care when appropriate........   66
   b. We face break-even questions and analyze them carefully using analytical methods that we have developed independently of the literature on the subject...   39
   c. We seldom have break-even questions and have not been concerned with this form of analysis...........   20
   d. The concept of some volume being required to justify an operation is basic and useful, but we have not made use of detailed separation of costs into fixed and variable categories, or formal break-even charts...   18
   e. Since our decisions are more frequently capital budgeting decisions than ones involving relations between output, costs, revenues, and profits, break-even has only rarely concerned us......................   18
   f. We have not given thought to the use of break-even analysis and are not versed in it...................   2
   g. We have tried break-even analysis and discontinued its use..   2
   h. At times we do face problems of determining if there will be adequate demand to make it profitable to continue to operate a facility or a piece of equipment. While these might be break-even problems, we don't call them by that name. We are more likely to regard them as _____........   19
   i. Other: _____........   5
3. We (always)   16
   (frequently)   41
   (occasionally)   36
   (rarely)   17
   (never)   1
   are faced with the question of what volume of business we must have to make an operation profitable. In our analysis of break-even problems, we make use of
   (graphs)   43
   (detailed numerical calculations)   72
   (rough calculations)   29
   (rules of thumb).................................   14

Results

We (do) 60
    (do not) 24
think of this in break-even terms.

4. We use break-even analysis to:
   a. Decide whether to undertake an operation.......... 65
   b. Decide whether to shut down an operation......... 61
   c. Estimate profits and losses at various volumes of business 68
   d. As one of a number of interrelated analytical techniques 55
   e. Analyze the contribution being made by an operation to fixed costs and profits...................... 43
   f. For *cash* break-even determination................ 29
   g. Help make product mix decisions.................. 22
   h. Examine alternate pricing possibilities............. 45
   i. Compare the profitability of segments of the business 25
   j. Evaluate an advertising budget................... 4
   k. Examine "operating leverage." We have used break-even techniques to examine the desirability of a more or less capital intensive process (including hard or soft tooling, automation, etc.) in light of changes in fixed and variable cost functions, the profit contribution of an additional unit sales, and demand expectations 19
   l. Other: _____ 12

5. Our use of break-even analysis has
   (grown) 44
   (declined) 5
   (remained the same) 56
   over the past 5 to 10 years. Comment _____
   _____.

6. The segregation of costs into fixed and variable:
   a. Is an essential step in our break-even work......... 77
   b. Has not been a preoccupation with us; we are concerned with total revenues and total costs and do not apply break-even analyses requiring a division into fixed and variable costs...................... 16
   c. Is a difficult and involved process................. 25
   d. Is a relatively easy process....................... 28
   e. Can best be accomplished by understanding the

nature of each cost element and judging whether it
is fixed or variable............................... 66

f. Can best be accomplished by time series analyses
that derive an intercept as a fixed cost and the slope
as variable cost................................. 10

7. In our business we are concerned with:

a. A continuous output process in which a certain level
of activity (e.g., rate of production or percent of
capacity) is necessary to make profitable use of a
fixed capacity................................... 69

b. A limited production run problem in which the
question is whether the cumulative quantity sold
will justify the initial and recurring costs.......... 34

8. The problems with break-even analysis that have given
us trouble are:

a. None 18

b. Linear assumptions when costs and/or prices do not
vary linearly with quantity....................... 31

c. Difficulties in separating total costs into fixed and
variable costs.................................. 43

d. The analysis fails to take account of the time value
of money or to provide a return on investment. 24

e. The use of accounting inputs which are based on
concepts that are not appropriate for the evaluations
being made.................................... 21

f. Changes in inventory levels...................... 5

g. How to deal with depreciation.................... 1

h. How to deal with taxes.......................... 1

i. How to deal with inflation....................... 21

j. The approach ignores changes over time in technology, management, scale of fixed inputs, and
product mix.................................... 17

k. How to treat selling costs....................... 3

l. How to deal with interest costs................... 6

m. Others such as _____. 8

9. I (am) 15

(am not) 87

able to enclose or arrange for you to receive under
separate cover an illustration of our use of a break-even
analysis. (No published use of such illustration will be
made without further approval.)

Results

10. Other comment (including the name and phone number of anyone that should be interviewed for further information) 21

Name: _____

Company: _____

Address: _____

ADDITIONAL SOURCES

Jaedicke, Robert K., and Robichek, Alexander A. "Cost-Volume-Profit Analysis under Conditions of Uncertainty." *Accounting Review*, 39 (October 1964), 917–26.

Jaedicke, Robert K., and Sprouse, Robert T. *Accounting Flows: Income, Funds, and Cash.* Englewood Cliffs, N.J.: Prentice-Hall, 1965.

Morrison, Thomas A., and Kaczka, Eugene. "A New Application of Calculus and Risk Analysis to Cost-Volume-Profit-Changes." *Accounting Review*, 44 (April 1969), 330–43.

Raun, D. L. "The Limitations of Profit Graphs, Break-even Analysis, and Budgets." *Accounting Review*, 39 (October 1964), 927–45.

Reinhardt, U. E. "Break-Even Analysis for Lockheed's Tri Star: An Application of Financial Theory." *Journal of Finance*, 28 (September 1973), 821–38.

Soldofsky, R. M. "Accountant's versus Economist's Concepts of Break-even Analysis." *N.A.A. Bulletin*, 41 (December 1959), 5–18.

PART V

Capital Budgeting

IN PART V we turn to the first of the major strategic financial planning areas discussed by Mr. LoCascio in Chapter 9. Chapter 15 begins by providing the basics for using compound interest relations. These concepts are then used to provide a survey of capital budgeting procedures as a foundation, especially for the following three chapters on aspects of long-term investment decisions. In Chapter 16, Paul Welter and Marcello Bianchi discuss how to appraise investment opportunities. First, they relate investment decisions to the strategic planning goals of the firm. In this context they review the standard methodologies for evaluating investment opportunities, including illustrative examples. This material is then related to broader considerations of investment strategy, where they discuss problems of measuring the cost of capital and the determination of the firm's financial structure. These techniques are then related to the total investment plan and the capital budget for the firm as a whole.

In Chapter 17, J. L. Murdy extends the analysis into the area of the administration of investment decisions. He effectively shows the interaction of business planning and capital budgeting decision processes. The determination of capital-funding capacity is described. The importance of the controllability of investment decisions is also developed. The procedural and timetable aspects of the capital budgeting decision process are set forth clearly. The relation of this process to investment decision criteria and capital proposal administration are also described with illustrative forms and documents. Finally, the importance of the company review process or post-audit of investment decisions is set forth.

It is particularly in the area of investment decisions that the inherent uncertainty of business decisions must be faced and dealt with. In Chapter 18, David Hertz presents a summary of his previous work, which has established him as a leading authority on this subject. He first analyzes and illustrates the nature of uncertainty and risk. The important concepts of utility, risk preference, and risk aversion are set forth and illustrated with specific examples. He then demonstrates the use and practicality of utility curves. Mr. Hertz also describes other decision methods and shows how to incorporate probability into investment analysis. He shows how the concepts are utilized in the formulation and development of an investment strategy.

Chapter 15

Some Techniques for Capital Budgeting

J. Fred Weston*

THE INTEREST FACTOR

FINANCIAL DECISIONS require comparisons among the alternatives of receiving payment immediately, periodically over a number of months or years, or at the end of a period of years. Therefore, sound decisions must take into consideration the influence of interest costs. The situations involving compound interest can be handled by utilizing a small number of basic formulas.

Annual Compound Interest Rates

Suppose that your firm is negotiating a sale. Two alternatives are being explored as to how the customer will pay for his purchase: either he will make one payment now, or one somewhat higher payment after a period of time. For example, suppose that you are offered $1,000 today or $1,200 at the end of the fifth year. Which should you take? We assume that if the company received the money

---

This chapter is taken from Chapters 10 and 11 in J. Fred Weston, *Programmed Learning Aid for Financial Management*, Learning Systems Company, Homewood, Illinois, 1975.

* J. Fred Weston is professor of Business Economics and Finance, University of California, Los Angeles, California.

immediately it could earn a 6 percent return on those funds. We can state the problem as follows:

$$P = \text{Principal, or beginning amount} = \$1{,}000$$
$$r = \text{Interest rate} = 6\% = 0.06$$
$$n = \text{Number of years} = 5$$
$$S_n = \text{The value at the end of year } n$$

The formula that applies is the compound interest formula:

$$S_n = P(1 + r)(1 + r)(1 + r)(1 + r)(1 + r) \qquad (1)$$
$$= P(1 + r)^n$$

Next the data are inserted in the formula:

$$S_5 = \$1.000(1.06)^5$$

We then look in Table A–1 in the Appendix at the end of this book to find that at 6 percent, a dollar over a five-year period grows to $1.338. Since the amount we would have now is $1,000, it is multiplied times the interest factor:

$$S_5 = \$1{,}000(1.338) = \$1{,}338$$

Therefore, if the firm can earn 6 percent with the money, it is worthwhile for it to receive the $1,000 today rather than $1,200 at the end of the fifth year.

Future Amounts and Their Present Values

There is an equivalent way of viewing the situation where a company is offered an amount to be received in the future. It is desirable to compare that amount with the value of whatever amount could be received today. This requires the computation of the present value of the amount to be received in the future. The determination of present values involves the same formula, except that it is solved for P, representing present value, instead of for S_n, which is known. By simple algebra the required formula would be:

$$P = S_n/(1 + r)^n \qquad (1.1)$$

Using our previous example, we determine S_n to be $1,338. Since the appropriate interest rate is 6 percent and the number of years is five, we would be dividing $1,338 by 1.338 to obtain the result $1,000.

But there is a simpler method. We can use a present value interest table (Table A–2 in the Appendix) which is the reciprocal of a compound interest table. In this case the formula is:

$$P = S_n(1 + r)^{-n} \tag{2}$$

We can now insert the illustrative numbers:

$$P = \$1,338(0.747)$$
$$P = \$1,000$$

Compound interest and present value computations are two different ways of looking at the same relationship.

The Present Value of an Annuity

Income flows are a series of periodic payments made over a span of time. This type of compound interest situation is probably the one most frequently encountered by a business firm. For example, a firm may sell some goods that will be paid for in three installments of $1,000, payable at the end of each year. At a 10 percent interest rate, what is the present value of those installment payments? The situation can be depicted as follows:

	End of Year			
	0	1	2	3
Present value of receipts		$1,000	$1,000	$1,000
$ 909				
826				
751				
Total $2,486				

Thus the present value of an annuity is the sum of the present values of the amounts to be received at the end of each year. But the present value of an annuity table (Appendix, Table A–3) will give the amount directly, which is convenient when more than two or three years are involved.

Consider the situation where the firm makes an investment from which it expects to receive a series of cash returns over a period of several years. At an appropriate discount rate, what would the series of future income receipts be worth today? The firm needs this information in order to determine whether it is worthwhile to make the investment. For example, the firm makes an investment promising the payment of $1,000 a year for 10 years with an interest rate of 10 percent. What is the present value of such a series of payments?

$$A_{\overline{n}|r} = \frac{a}{(1+r)} + \frac{a}{(1+r)^2} + \cdots + \frac{a}{(1+r)^n} \qquad (3)$$

$$= a \left[\frac{1 - (1+r)^{-n}}{r} \right],$$

where:

$A_{\overline{n}|r}$ is the present value of an annuity
a is the amount of the annuity
r is the interest rate
n is the number of years

Equation (3) represents the present value of an annuity factor of $1 at an interest rate, r, for n periods. Note that it is the sum of a series of present values of $1 expressions. Values for equation (3) can be found directly in Table A–3 for the designated interest rate and number of years. Since the expression in brackets is somewhat cumbersome, for convenience the symbol $P_{n,r}$ is used, where $P_{n,r}$ is the present value of an annuity factor for n years at r percent. Equation (3) above can, therefore, be rewritten as:

$$A_{\overline{n}|r} = a\,P_{n,r} \qquad (3.1)$$

Substituting actual numbers and using the present value of an annuity from the interest table (Table A–3), we obtain:

$$A_{\overline{10}|10\%} = \$1,000(6.145) = \$6,145$$

In other words, a series of payments of $1,000 received for 10 years, applying an interest factor of 10 percent, would be worth $6,145 today. Hence, if the amount of investment the firm were required to make was $8,000, for example, or any amount greater than $6,145, the firm would be receiving a return of less than 10 percent on its investment. Conversely, if the investment necessary to earn annual payments of $1,000 for 10 years at 10 percent were, say $5,000, or any amount less than $6,145, the firm would be earning a return greater than 10 percent.

A number of other questions can be answered using these same relationships. Suppose that the decision facing the firm requires determining the rate of return on an investment. For example, sup-

pose we would have $6,145 to invest and that an investment oppor-
tunity promises an annual return of $1,000 for 10 years. What is the
indicated rate of return on our investment? Exactly the same relationship is involved, but now the equation is solved for the interest
rate. Rewriting the equation gives:

$$P_{10,r} = A_{\overline{10}|r}/a, \qquad (3.2)$$

where r is the unknown interest rate.

We can now substitute the appropriate figures:

$$P_{10,r} = \$6{,}145/\$1{,}000 = 6.145$$

In Table A–3, where the present value of periodic payments received annually is shown, we look across the year 10 row until we
find the interest rate that corresponds to the interest factor 6.145.
This is 10 percent.

Now let us consider another situation. Suppose that we are going
to receive a return of $2,000 per year for five years from an invest-
ment of $8,424. What is the return on our investment? This is gen-
erally referred to as the internal rate of return on investment. It
is also sometimes referred to as the DCF, or discounted cash flow
approach to valuing an investment.

We follow the same procedure as before:

$$P_{5,r} = A_{\overline{5}|r}/a$$
$$P_{5,r} = \$8{,}424/\$2{,}000$$
$$= 4.212$$

Again, look for the present value of an annuity in Table A–3
along the row for year 5 to find the interest factor 4.212. We then
look at the interest rate at the top of the column to find that it is
6 percent. Thus, the return on that investment is 6 percent. If our
required rate of return was 8 percent, we would not find this investment attractive. On the other hand, if the required return on our
investment were only 5 percent, we would consider the investment
attractive.

Suppose that the firm has made an investment of $30,725 and will
be repaid in annual installments at an interest rate of 10 percent.
What is the annual amount the firm will receive for each of the
10 years? The general equation for this problem is:

$$a = A_{\overline{n}|r}/P_{n,r} \qquad (3.3)$$

Inserting the amounts given for the problem we have the following:

$$a = \$30{,}725/6.145$$
$$= \$5{,}000$$

The result is exactly $5,000. Suppose the question is, what amount should we have to receive $5,000 for 10 years at a 10 percent interest rate? In this instance we would solve the general expression for the present value as shown:

$$A_{\overline{n}|r} = a\,P_{n,r}$$

In this problem the annual annuity of $5,000 is given. The interest factor is determined by the knowledge that the interest rate is 10 percent and the annuity will continue over a 10-year period. When we insert the numbers, we have the following result:

$$= \$5{,}000(6.145)$$
$$A_{\overline{n}|r} = \$30{,}725$$

Compound Sum of an Annuity

We may also need to know the future value or future sum to which a series of payments will accumulate. The reason may be to determine whether we have enough funds to repay an obligation in the future. The sum of an annuity can be determined from the following basic relationship:

$$S_{\overline{n}|r} = a[(1+r)^{n-1} + (1+r)^{n-2}$$
$$+ \cdots + (1+r)^1 + 1] \tag{4}$$
$$S_{\overline{n}|r} = a\left[\frac{(1+r)^n - 1}{r}\right] = aC_{n,r}$$

where:

> S is the future sum to which an annuity will accumulate
> a is the annuity
> $C_{n,r}$ is the repeated event or annuity compound interest factor

Suppose the firm were to receive annual payments of $1,000 a year for five years and is charging an interest rate of 8 percent. What will be the amount that the firm will have at the end of five years?

We can solve this problem by consulting Table A–4 in the Appendix. Utilizing our equation we would have:

$$S_{\overline{n}|r} = \$1,000(5.867)$$
$$S_{\overline{n}|r} = \$5,867$$

The pattern of compounding can be shown by the following illustration:

End of Year

	0	1	2	3	4	5
Payments		$1,000	$1,000	$1,000	$1,000	$1,000
						1,080
						1,166
						1,260
						1,360

Compound sum $5,866*

* Difference due to rounding.

The calculation of the compound sum of an annuity is the sum of five single compound sum terms. (It will be observed that in this presentation we are assuming that the payments are made at the end of each year. This is called a regular annuity or a deferred annuity. If the payment is made at the beginning of the year, it is referred to as an annuity due.) However, these steps are performed for us in Table A–4, the sum of an annuity of $1 for n years.

The five payments of $1,000 each would accumulate to $5,867 by the end of the fifth year. Thus, if we had obligated the sum to repay a $5,000 obligation in five years, it would be able to do so. On the other hand, if the obligation were more, say $7,000, there might be a problem of insufficient funds.

Sometimes the same question is asked in a different way. Suppose that we need to have a specified amount of money, such as $5,867, by the end of five years. How much would we have to set aside each year at an interest rate of 8 percent in order to have that amount? We would solve the equation above for a, the annuity. We would have:

$$a = S_{\overline{n}|r}/C_{n,r} \tag{4.1}$$

Since we know that we need to have $5,867, we look in the interest table for the sum of an annuity, Table A–4 in the Appendix, to see what the interest factor is at 8 percent for five years. This is 5.867. Therefore, we would need to set aside $1,000 each year.

Now that the basic idea has been set forth, let us take a more complex example. Suppose the amount of money that the firm must have at the end of ten years is $29,000. The applicable interest rate is 8 percent. We wish to know how much we would have to set aside each year in order to accumulate the required amount. The general expression is:

$$a = S_{\overline{10}|8\%}/C_{10,8\%} \qquad (4.2)$$

Inserting the numbers given in the illustration we would have:

$$a = \$29,000/14.487 = \$2,002$$

It would be necessary to set aside slightly over $2,000 each year in order to have the required amount.

Overview

The following formulas have been used:

$$S_n = P(1 + r)^n \qquad (1)$$
$$P = S_n(1 + r)^{-n} \qquad (2)$$
$$A_{\overline{n}|r} = a\left[\frac{1 - (1 + r)^{-n}}{r}\right] = aP_{n,r} \qquad (3)$$
$$S_{\overline{n}|r} = a\left[\frac{(1 + r)^n - 1}{r}\right] = aC_{n,r} \qquad (4)$$

The two expressions for the compound future sum and for the present value of a sum that will be received in the future can be regarded as one equation. For annuities there are different expressions for the interest factor in calculating the present value as compared with the future sum. Thus, in total, only three basic equation relationships are involved.

These three basic equations enable us to solve at least 12 types of problems. We have three equations and we can solve each one of them for any of the four terms in the equation (present value, future sum or annuity, interest rate, number of years), given the other three. Thus, with a relatively small number of relationships, and the help of the compound interest tables, a variety of problems involving the time value of money can be handled. Before closing we will consider three variations on the basic themes set forth.

Compounding Periods within One Year

In the illustrations set forth thus far, the examples have been for returns that were received once a year (annually). For compounding within one year, we simply divide the interest rate by the number of compoundings within a year and multiply the annual periods by the same factor. For example, in our first equation for compound interest we had the following:

$$S_n = P(1 + r)^n \tag{1}$$

This was for annual compounding. For semiannual compounding (or m number of lines per year), we would follow the rule just set forth. The equation would become:

$$S_{n/m} = P\left(1 + \frac{r}{m}\right)^{nm} \tag{5}$$

where m is the number of compoundings during a year.

We may apply this to the first numerical illustration employed. The question originally was how much would $1,000 at a 6 percent interest rate accumulate over a five-year period. The answer was $1,338. Now we apply semiannual compounding. The equation would appear as follows:

$$S_{5/2} = \$1,000\left(1 + \frac{0.06}{2}\right)^{5(2)}$$

Thus, the new expression is equivalent to compounding the $1,000 at 3 percent for 10 periods. Looking in the compound interest table (Table A–1) for 10 years, the interest factor would be 1.344. The equation would read:

$$S_{5/2} = \$1,000(1 + 0.03)^{10}$$
$$= \$1,344$$

With semiannual compounding the future sum amounts to $1,344, as compared with the $1,338 we had before. Frequent compounding provides compound interest paid on compound interest, so the result is higher. Thus, we would expect that daily compounding, as some financial institutions advertise, or continuous compounding, as is employed under some assumptions, would give somewhat larger amounts than annual or semiannual compounding. But the basic ideas are unchanged.

The same logic is equally applicable to all categories of relationships we have described. For example, in the first illustration on the present value of an annuity, the problem was stated as the payment of $1,000 a year for ten years with an interest rate of 10 percent, compounded annually. If the compounding is semiannual we would employ an interest rate of 5 percent and apply the compounding to 20 periods. When compounding semiannually, it is also necessary to divide the annual payment by the number of times the compounding takes place within the year. Then, utilizing our previous example we would have the following expression:

$$
\begin{aligned}
A_{\overline{nm}|r/m} &= \$500(P_{r/m,nm}) \\
&= \$500(P_{10\%/2,10(2)}) \\
&= \$500(P_{5\%,20}) \\
&= \$500(12.462) \\
&= \$6{,}231
\end{aligned}
$$

It should be noted that with annual compounding the present value of the annuities is $6,145, but with semiannual compounding the present value is $6,231. With more frequent compounding, the results will be somewhat higher because interest is compounded on interest.

Calculations for a Series of Unequal Receipts or Payments

In all previous illustrations we have assumed that the receipts flowing in or the payments to be made are of equal amounts, which simplifies the calculations. However, if unequal receipts or unequal payments are involved, the principles are again the same, but the calculations must be extended somewhat. For example, suppose that the firm makes an investment from which it will receive the following amounts:

Year	Receipts	× Interest Factor (15%)	= Present Value
1	$100	.870	$ 87.00
2	200	.756	151.20
3	600	.658	394.80
4	300	.572	171.60
		PV of the investment =	$804.60

Using the present value interest table (Table A–2), at an interest rate of 15 percent we obtain the amounts indicated above. The interest factor multiplied times the receipts is the present value. The amounts for each year are then summed to determine the present value of the investment, which, in this example, is $804.60. This example illustrates how an annuity of unequal payments, which could not be computed directly from the present value of an annuity table, can be handled by breaking the problem into a series of one-year payments received at successively later time periods.

This illustrates a general technique that can be employed in using compound interest relationships. A particular business problem or decision involving the time value of money, no matter how complex, can usually be handled by compound interest methods. The technique is to take a complex problem and break it into a series of simple ones. Then the results of the simple problems can be combined to arrive at the overall solution.

The Determination of the Applicable Interest Rates

A number of sources can be used to determine the applicable interest rate in a particular business decision. One broad reference is the general level of interest rates in the economy as a whole. Individual interest rates in the economy generally differ by the maturity (the period of time over which the obligation runs), as well as the degree of risk of the obligation. Short-term U.S. government securities generally bear the lowest rate of interest, while the debt obligations of a small company with an uncertain future usually carry a relatively high rate of interest.

In addition, the levels of interest rates are affected by business conditions in the economy at a particular time and by economic developments in foreign countries. For guidance on interest rate levels in the economy, financial managers may refer to readily available publications, such as the *Survey of Current Business,* published by the United States Department of Commerce; the *Federal Reserve Bulletin,* published by the Board of Governors of the Federal Reserve System; *International Financial Statistics,* published by the International Monetary Fund; and *Economic Indicators,* available from the United States Government Printing Office. All of these publications are available at nominal subscription rates.

Another guide in the determination of which interest rate should be applied in making compound interest decisions is consideration of what the firm could earn if it used the money in some alternative investment opportunity. This is generally referred to as the opportunity cost of an investment. The opportunity cost of investments is the yield on the best alternative use of the funds.

THE INVESTMENT DECISION

Capital budgeting represents the process of planning expenditures whose returns extend over a period of time. Examples of capital outlays for tangible or physical items are expenditures for land, buildings, and equipment. Outlays for research and development, advertising, or promotion efforts may also be regarded as investment outlays when their benefits extend over a period of years. While capital budgeting criteria are generally discussed in relation to investment in fixed assets, the concepts are equally applicable to investment in cash, receivables, or inventory. Selection of the criteria for making such investments is the subject matter of this chapter.

Administrative Aspects

Investment decisions and their evaluation by capital budgeting analysis are important for a number of reasons: (1) The consequences of the decision continue for a number of years. Thus to some degree after making an investment decision, some flexibility for the future is reduced. (2) Capital budgeting requires effective planning, including accurate sales forecasts, to assure the proper timing of asset acquisitions. This means that capital assets should be available when needed, and yet not too early to avoid the extra cost of having them idle until required. (3) Since asset expansion involves substantial outlays, the required financing must be arranged in advance. (4) Since the dollar amounts of outlays on investments are large, the success or failure of an enterprise may result from excessive investments, inadequate amounts of investment, or undue delay in replacing obsolete assets within modern assets.

Individual firms usually have formal administrative procedures for reviewing capital budgeting requests. Small items can be approved by individual department heads, while larger dollar amounts require approval from officers at higher levels in the organizational structure. Major investment outlays require the review and approval of the company's finance committee or, in some instances, the board of directors.

The finance department generally coordinates its activities with other departments to develop systematic records on the use of investment funds. Records are also compiled on revenues and savings from equipment purchased. An important aspect of the record keeping are postaudits, which provide a comparison between the initial estimates and the actual results. The postaudits review past decisions to aid in improving decisions on new investment outlays.

Alternative Criteria

Three major methods for the evaluation and ranking of investment proposals are utilized. They are (1) the payback period (N), (2) the net present value (NPV), and (3) the internal rate of return (IRR). Each criterion will be defined, the numerical computation process will be illustrated, and the characteristics of the method will be described. For illustration, we will utilize Investment A, which provides cash flows (profit after taxes plus depreciation) of $300 for six years and requires an investment outlay of $900.

The payback period is defined as the number of years required to return the original investment:

$$\text{Payback period } (N) = \frac{\text{Initial fixed investment}}{\text{Annual cash inflows}}$$

$$N(\text{A}) = \frac{900}{300} = 3 \text{ years}$$

The main value of the payback period is that it provides information on the risk and liquidity of the project. The shorter the payback period, the greater the liquidity of the project and the less risky in terms of the number of years required before the investment is recovered. For a firm with cash flow or liquidity problems, the payback period may be given very heavy weight. The principal drawbacks of the payback period are: (1) It fails to consider cash flows after the payback period and consequently cannot be regarded as a measure of profitability. (2) It fails to consider the timing of cash flows during the payback period, ignoring the time value of money. (3) It is an incomplete measure of risk because, by focusing only on the expected outcomes relative to the original investment, it does not take into account the dispersion of possible outcomes. In the illustration, Investment A has a payback period of three years. In sum, using the payback method for evaluating alternative investments may lead to the wrong decision in that a project may be chosen which does not maximize the net present value of cash flows.

The second criterion, the net present value (NPV), is the present value of all future cash flows discounted at the cost of capital, minus the cost of the investment, which is also discounted at the cost of capital. Assuming a cost of capital of 10 percent, the calculation of the NPV for the project proceeds as follows:

$$\text{Net present value (NPV)}$$
$$PV(A) = 300.00(4.355) = \$1,306.50$$
$$NPV(A) = \$1,306.50 - 900.00 = \$406.50$$

The 4.355 for Project A represents the present value of an annuity of $1 at 10 percent for six years. The annual net inflows multiplied by the respective annuity factors gives the total present value of the flows for each. The cost of the investment is subtracted from the total present value to obtain the net present value of Project A, $406.

The three distinguishing characteristics of the net present value criterion are: (1) It accounts for the time value of money. (2) The present time is used as the reference point. (3) The NPV approach implies reinvestment at the cost of capital.

The third investment criterion is the internal rate of return. The internal rate of return represents the discount rate at which the net present value or net terminal value of all cash flows is zero.

The calculation procedure for internal rate of return (IRR) is: Equate net present values of revenues and costs and solve for r.

IRR(A)

$$900 = 300(P_{6,r}) \qquad (\text{use } r = 24\%)$$
$$900 = 300(3) \qquad (r \cong 24\%)$$

Equate net terminal values of revenues and costs and solve for r.

IRR(A)

$$900(1 + r)^6 = 300(C_{6,r}) \ (\text{use } r = 24\%)$$
$$900(3.635) = 300(10.980)$$
$$3,272 \cong 3,294 \quad (r \cong 24\%)$$

In equating net present values, we need to obtain the present value of an annuity factor of $1 such that the present value of cash inflows will equal the investment outlay. This is obtained by dividing the annual cash flows into the investment. For Investment A, the interest factor for an annuity of $1 for six years is 3.000, which represents an interest rate of approximately 24 percent. The same result is obtained by equating net terminal values. The procedure requires that the investment outlays be multiplied by the compound sum of $1, the interest factor for the appropriate number of years. These are equated respectively to the annual cash inflows multiplied by the compound sum of an annuity factor for the appropriate number of years. The interest rate that (approximately) equates these two streams is the internal rate of return.

The internal rate of return accounts for the time value of money. It implies reinvestment at the internal rate of return. From a practical or operational standpoint it has the value of providing a result expressed as a percentage factor or as an interest factor, which conveys meaning as a rate-of-return figure. A drawback of the IRR method is that if, after a series of net inflows has begun, in one or more years a net outflow occurs, multiple solutions may result. For this and other reasons the IRR criterion will sometimes lead to inconsistent results: that is, more than one discount rate may equate the present value of cash inflows to the present value of investment costs.

NPV versus IRR Criteria

To understand more fully the superiority of the NPV approach as compared to the IRR criterion requires the use of the calculation procedure when the amounts of cash flows each year are unequal. This will be illustrated for Projects B and D. The dollar amount of investment outlay remains the same, $900. However, the net inflows follow the pattern indicated in Table 1. The total amount received over future time periods is $1,200 for Investment B, with larger inflows in the earlier years. For Investment D, the total inflows are $1,300, with larger inflows in the later years. Because of the different time patterns of net inflows, the discount factor has a different weighting influence.

Table 1 illustrates the calculations of the net present values of Project B and Project D. The present values for each of the two

TABLE 1
Calculations of Net Present Values (C₀ = initial investment = $900)

Net Cash Inflows

Year	B	D
1	$400	$100
2	300	100
3	200	200
4	150	200
5	100	300
6	50	400

Interest Factor = 1%

Year	Percent	B	D
1	.990	$ 396	$ 99
2	.980	294	98
3	.971	194	194
4	.961	144	192
5	.951	95	285
6	.942	47	377
Present values		$1,170	$1,245
Net present values		$ 270	$ 345

Interest Factor = 9%

Year	Percent	B	D
1	.917	$367	$ 92
2	.842	253	84
3	.772	154	154
4	.708	106	142
5	.650	65	195
6	.596	30	238
Present values		$975	$905
Net present values		$ 75	$ 5

Interest Factor = 10%

Year	Percent	B	D
1	.909	$364	$ 91
2	.826	248	83
3	.751	150	150
4	.683	102	137
5	.621	62	186
6	.564	28	226
Present values		$954	$873
Net present values		$ 54	$ (27)

Interest Factor = 12%

Year	Percent	B	D
1	.893	$357	$ 89
2	.797	239	80
3	.712	142	142
4	.636	95	127
5	.567	57	170
6	.507	25	203
Present values		$915	$811
Net present values		$ 15	$ (89)

Interest Factor = 13%

Year	Percent	B	D
1	.885	$354	$ 89
2	.783	235	78
3	.693	139	139
4	.613	92	123
5	.543	54	163
6	.480	24	192
Present values		$898	$784
Net present values		$ (2)	$(116)

Interest Factor = 16%

Year	Percent	B	D
1	.862	$345	$ 86
2	.743	223	74
3	.641	128	128
4	.552	83	110
5	.476	48	143
6	.410	21	164
Present values		$848	$705
Net present values		$ (52)	$(195)

projects are first calculated. Since the net cash flows are different for each year, the calculations must be made for each year individually. Then the present value interest factor for each year and interest rate illustrated is multiplied times the net cash inflows for each year to obtain the present values of each net cash inflow. These present values are totaled for the six years to obtain the row labeled "Present Values." The net present values are obtained by subtracting the investment cost of $900 from each present value amount.

In Table 2 the net present values for Project B and Project D are

TABLE 2
Influence of Cost of Capital on Net Present Values

	Net Present Values for Various Cost of Capital Rates	
Cost of Capital	*B*	*D*
0.	$300	$ 400
1%.	270	345
9.	75	5
10.	54	(27)
12.	15	(89)
13.	(2)	(116)
16.	(52)	(195)

tabulated for all of the interest rates utilized in Table 1, which range from 1 percent to 16 percent. Note that at the very low interest rate of 1 percent, the present values of the inflows exceed the investment outlay by substantial amounts. At the 16 percent interest rate, the present values of the inflows are less than the initial investment outlay.

The net present values are calculated by subtracting the cost of the investment from the present values of the net cash inflows. The data in Table 1 demonstrate that the internal rate of return (IRR) is the special case when the net present value (NPV) is zero. For Project D the net present value at a 9 percent interest rate is $5, but at an interest rate of 10 percent it is a negative $27. Hence the net present value of Project D would be zero at slightly more than 9 percent. Similarly, for Project B at an interest rate of 12 percent the net present value is $15, but at an interest rate of 13 percent the net present value is a negative $2. Hence the internal rate of return for Project B is slightly under 13 percent. Table 2 shows that the investment worth of a project is measured by its net present value, which in turn depends upon the cost of capital appropriately used in discounting the net cash inflows. In addition, the net present values for a zero cost of capital are also included, simply representing the total net cash inflows less the initial investment of $900. At low costs of capital, the NPV of Project D is greater than the NPV of Project B. However, at higher rates of interest the NPV of Project D is less than the NPV of Project B. In general, the projects whose returns are largest in the earlier years will have higher net present values at higher costs of capital. Conversely, projects whose larger returns are realized in later years will have lower net present values at higher costs of capital. This is because the projects with higher returns in the later years are penalized by the lower values of the discount factors (the larger degree of discounting) applied in later years.

The foregoing relationships are depicted graphically in Figure 1.

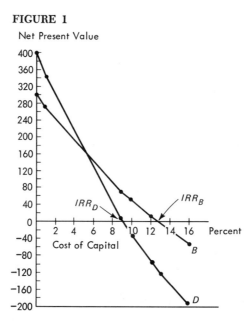

FIGURE 1

Net Present Value

At a zero cost of capital, Project D has a higher net present value. It remains higher until an interest rate of about 5 percent. At a higher applicable cost of capital, the NPV of Project B exceeds the NPV of Project D by increasing amounts.

Figure 1 also enables us to observe graphically the definition of the internal rate of return. The internal rate of return is the cost of capital at which the present value of a project is zero—the point at which the NPV lines cross the horizontal axis. In Figure 1 we can observe graphically that the internal rate of return of Project D is slightly above 9 percent and for Project B is slightly below 13 percent. However, we cannot say unambiguously that Project B is superior to Project D because its internal rate of return is higher. At a cost of capital of 4 percent, for example, the net present value of Project D exceeds the net present value of Project B; however, at costs of capital greater than 5 percent, Project B is superior. Only the net present value method provides an unambiguous rule for evaluating projects.

Using the NPV approach implicitly assumes that the funds generated during the life of a project can be reinvested at the firm's marginal cost of capital. The IRR approach implies that the funds generated by a particular investment can be reinvested at the calculated IRR. Note that the IRR is not a market return, but rather a "number" that results from the firm's evaluation of a given project. On the other hand, the firm's cost of capital is the market price the firm must pay for capital. Clearly it is much more realistic to assume that the firm can reinvest its revenues at a rate of return equal to that currently available in the capital market, rather than at a rate of return which happens to make the discounted net present value of a particular investment equal to zero.

Analysis of Replacement Decisions

A systematic procedure is set forth for the analysis of equipment replacement decisions. The concepts will be developed through the use of illustrative examples, data for which are set forth in Table 3. A tax rate of 40 percent is used to distinguish between the factor multiplied by $(1 - t)$ and the factor multiplied by t. For a small firm, an average or marginal tax rate of 40 percent is not unrealistic, but for a large firm a more accurate tax rate would be 48 percent. However, the aim is to make these illustrations relatively simple so that most of them can be followed by mental calculations. For actual situations, hand calculators or even computer programs can be employed. The aim here is simply an understanding of the principles involved.

In Table 4, a work sheet for the systematic analysis of replacement investment decisions is shown. The outflows are identified by refer-

TABLE 3
Facts for Analysis of Equipment Replacement

	Old Machine	New Machine
Purchase time	5 years before	This year
Cost	$10,000	$12,000
Estimated life	10 years	10 years
Expected end-of-life salvage value	0	$ 2,000
Sales level	$15,000	$16,500
Operating costs	$11,000	$ 9,500
Tax rate	40%	40%
Cost of capital	12%	12%
Current value	$ 3,000	$12,000
Book value at end of 5 years (straight-line depreciation)	$ 5,000	

TABLE 4
Analysis of Investment Replacement*

	Amount before Tax	Amount after Tax	Year Event Occurs	Present Value Factor at 12%	Present Value
Outflows at time investment is made					
Investment in new equipment	$12,000	$12,000	–	1.000	$12,000
Salvage value of old	(3,000)	(3,000)		1.000	(3,000)
Tax loss on sale	(2,000)	(800)	0	1.000	(800)
Total outflows (present value of costs)					$ 8,200
Inflows, or annual returns					
Benefits	3,000	1,800	1–10	5.650	$10,170
Depreciation on new (annual)	1,000	400	1–10	5.650	2,260
Depreciation on old (annual)	(1,000)	(400)	1–5	3.605	(1,442)
Salvage value on new	2,000	2,000	10	0.322	644
Total inflows (present value of benefits)					$11,632
Present value of inflows					$11,632
Present value of outflows					8,200
Net present value of inflows minus outflows					$ 3,432

* Straight-line depreciation used on both the old and new equipment.

ence to the time at which the investment is made in order to indicate the total amount of funds required to initiate the action. Thus the first item is the $12,000 outlay on the new equipment. If investment is made in the new equipment and a salvage value of $3,000 is realized on the disposal of the old equipment, the amount realized on the sale is $3,000. Since this would reduce the net amount of cash required to purchase the new equipment, the salvage value of the old machine, which is an inflow, is treated in the work sheet as a negative outflow. When the old equipment is sold at a price below its book value, a tax loss is established. Under the assumption of straightline depreciation, the book value at the time the old machine is sold is $5,000. The tax loss on the sale of old equipment, the third item of outflow, reflects a set of relatively complicated tax principles, the upshot of which is that a tax loss on the sale of capital equipment can be charged against ordinary income. Hence in the present example, the $2,000 tax loss establishes an after-tax saving represented by multiplying the 40 percent tax rate times the amount of the tax loss. Thus another negative outflow is the tax loss of $800.

Benefits and inflows are represented by an increase in sales and reduction of costs of $1,500 each or $3,000. It is clear that the benefits of $3,000 per year would be subject to the ordinary income tax of 40 percent. The amount of the benefit after tax would be obtained by multiplying the annual benefits by $(1 - t)$. Since the tax rate is 0.4, the value of $(1 - t)$ would be 0.6; when 0.6 is multiplied by $3,000, the amount after tax is $1,800. This is multiplied by the present value of an annuity factor at 12 percent, which is 5.650, to give $10,170.

Since the new machine has a depreciable value of $10,000 and a ten-year life, the depreciation is $1,000 per year. On the other hand, the undepreciated portion, or the book value of the old machine, will also be decreasing $1,000 a year for its remaining five years of life. Since the depreciation on the old machine is calculated over its remaining five-year life, it may be argued that the comparison is of a five-year flow for the old equipment and a ten-year flow for the new. While there are some technical niceties that might be explored here, the fact is that the new machine has a remaining life of ten years and the old machine of only five years. An equivalent annual cost analysis could be made, but would not be necessary in view of the margin of error to which the estimates of sales increases or reduction in operating cost are subject.

The reason that the after-tax depreciation amounts are included in inflows is that the depreciation expense results in a reduction of taxes. Since taxes represent an outflow, a reduction in taxes is a negative outflow and can be treated as a positive inflow. Just as the tax loss was multiplied by t, the tax rate, the annual depreciation expense is also multiplied by t (to determine the amount of the annual tax that is avoided or sheltered by the depreciation expense). The depreciation on the new machine of $1,000 is multiplied by 0.4 to establish a tax shelter of $400 per year for ten years. The depreciation on the old machine of $1,000 per year under a straight-line depreciation method is also $400; however, it represents a loss of a tax shelter extending over the remaining five-year life of the old machine.

The final item in the inflows section of Table 4 is the salvage value on the new machine. The new machine is expected to have a salvage value of $2,000 at the end of ten years. This amount is discounted over the ten-year period back to the present.

In this illustration, the sum of the outflows is found to be $8,200 and the sum of the inflows is $11,632. The difference represents a net present value of $3,432, at the firm's cost of capital of 12 percent, in favor of investing in the new machine to replace the old machine.

This work sheet method is a convenient procedure for systematically organizing the outflows and inflows, and is applicable to all types of investment decisions such as new product analysis, expansion decisions, and so on. The basic idea is to analyze the present value of outflows as compared with the present value of inflows obtained, utilizing the firm's cost of capital to discount both streams.

In the above example, straight-line depreciation was used to simplify the calculations. However, two accelerated depreciation methods are now widely used by business firms: either the sum-of-the-years'-digits method (SYD) or the double declining balance method (DDB). These two methods will be illustrated by reference to a machine purchased for $1,200 with an estimated useful life of ten years and a scrap value of $200 at the end of a ten-year period. Table 5 compares the depreciation changes under straight-line depreciation compared with SYD and DDB. The following discussion explains how each column is calculated.

The straight-line depreciation is simply the $1,200 outlay less the $200 salvage value which equals $1,000, representing the depreciable value of the asset. Its life is ten years. The annual depreciation over the asset's depreciable life is therefore $100 per year.

TABLE 5

Comparison of Depreciation Methods for a Ten-Year, $1,200 Asset with a $200 Salvage Value

		Depreciation Methods	
Year	Straight Line	Sum-of-the-Years'-Digits	Double Declining Balance
1	$ 100	$ 182	$ 240
2	100	164	192
3	100	145	154
4	100	125	123
5	100	109	98
6	100	91	79
7	100	73	78
8	100	55	78
9	100	36	78
10	100	18	78
	$1,000	$1,000	$1,198

Under the DDB method of accelerated depreciation, the annual straight-line rate is doubled and then applied to the undepreciated value of the asset as of the end of the previous year. In the present example, since the annual straight-line rate is 10 percent per year, the double declining rate would be 20 percent. The rules provide that the DDB rate can be applied to the full purchase price of the machine, not the cost less salvage value. Also, a company can switch from DDB to straight line whenever the straight-line depreciation on the remaining book value of the asset exceeds the DDB depreciation. For our example, the calculation under the DDB method would be as follows:

Year	DDB		Straight Line	Undepreciated Amount under DDB	
0					$1,200
1	.20(1,200) = $	240		$1,200 – $240 =	960
2	.20(960) =	192		960 – 192 =	768
3	.20(768) =	154		768 – 154 =	614
4	.20(614) =	123		614 – 123 =	491
5	.20(491) =	98		491 – 98 =	393
6	.20(393) =	79		393 – 79 =	314
7	.20(314) =	63	$ 78	314 – 63 =	251
8	.20(251) =	50	78	251 – 50 =	201
9	.20(201) =	40	78	201 – 40 =	161
10	.20(161) =	32	78	161 – 32 =	129
		$1,071	$1,198		

Check on the shift to straight-line method as shown in the table below:

Year	Remaining Book Value DDB Method	Number of Years Remaining	Depreciation
6.	$393	5	$79
7.	314	4	78
8.	251	3	84

In the sixth-year, shifting to the straight-line depreciation method would result in the same depreciation of $79 as under DDB, so there would be no advantage to shifting. In the seventh year there is an advantage of 78 less 63 which equals 15. There is no reason to wait until the eighth year to shift.

Evaluation Rules under Alternative Situations

Some additional distinctions are required to set forth appropriate investment ranking or selection rules. First, several different types of investment proposals are encountered. *Mutually exclusive proposals* are alternative methods of performing the same function. Examples would be a steel bridge versus a wooden bridge, or the selection of forklift trucks versus conveyor belts for moving materials in a factory. *Independent projects* are not related. For instance, the mechanization of a firm's accounting system, the purchase of loading docks, and the addition of power facilities are mutually independent proposals. *Contingent proposals* are those for which the consideration of one proposal is dependent upon first adopting a prior proposal. For example, a firm may need additional equipment, but has no remaining factory floor space. In order to purchase additional equipment, the firm must either lease or buy additional floor space—thus, the investment in additional equipment is contingent upon prior investments in additional floor space.

Second, we distinguish whether the situation is one of *capital rationing* or of no capital rationing. Capital rationing means that the firm does not have sufficient funds to finance all the proposals for investments that have been developed by the managers of the firm. In the extreme case of "strict" capital rationing, the firm may be unable to raise more than some specific amount of funds, for example, $10 million for a large firm or $200,000 for a small firm. In other words, at some dollar amount the firm is unable to obtain additional funds. Hence, under strict capital rationing, the total of investment outlays cannot exceed the absolute amount specified. If there is no capital rationing, the firm is able to raise all funds required for its available investment opportunities at its cost of capital. In the more realistic intermediate case, beyond some quantity of investments the firm's cost of capital curve is no longer horizontal, but begins to have a positive slope.

With no *capital rationing*, the acceptance of a single proposal and multiple independent or multiple contingent proposals is the same. The rule is to accept all projects if the net present value (NPV) or net terminal value (NTV), using the cost of capital as the discount rate, is positive. For mutually exclusive proposals, select the proposal with the highest positive NPV or NTV.

Under capital rationing, or a rising cost of capital curve, there is no simple selection rule. The theoretically correct result can be obtained only by the utilization of one of the mathematical programming techniques—linear programming, integer programming, dynamic programming, or variations on these basic types. The correct result under capital rationing, particularly if the projects are independent in time sequence, can be approximated by developing a ranking of the investment opportunities by their NPV's. This schedule is then related to the availability of funds at a range of costs of capital. Alternatively, the internal rate of return approach can be used. Projects can be ranked by their internal rates of return in order to obtain a marginal efficiency of capital schedule. This prospective investments schedule can then be related to the firm's marginal cost of capital curve.

ADDITIONAL SOURCES

See Additional Sources at end of Chapter 17.

Chapter 16

How to Appraise Investment Opportunities

Paul Welter[*]
Marcello Bianchi[*]

THE FUNCTION OF INVESTMENTS

EVERY COMPANY determines a set of strategic goals that it seeks to achieve through a series of operating objectives and bounded by a certain number of constraints. According to the socioeconomic context in which the company operates and according to who owns the company, its strategic goals may change. For instance, the business environment is drastically different in the United States and the Soviet Union. Even within the capitalistic system we find differences. The social constraints in Italy, for instance, are different from those in West Germany.

In order for any system to survive, whatever its final goal may be, it must create wealth. To create this wealth it is necessary initially to invest financial resources in capital goods that allow the company to carry out its activity. This in turn will create wealth to be reinvested in other goods to further develop the company. An industrial company will use its financial resources for producing one or more products for subsequent sale in the market. If the company's income which is derived from the sale of these products exceeds the direct and indirect production costs, the company creates wealth.

[*] Paul Welter and Marcello Bianchi are with Sistemi Organizzativi S.p.A., Milano, Italy, and I.S.T.U.D. S.p.A., Varese.

Two basic types of investment exist: maintenance and development. The first group of investments maintains the future efficiency of the company's actual wealth-creating capacity, while the second group increases its wealth-creating capacity. Whatever its aim, the investment is an actual cash outflow made to obtain a series of expected future cash inflows. Since the firm does not have an unlimited amount of cash, and as the use of cash bears a cost, we must evaluate each cash investment decision in order to choose those which allow the company to best achieve its goal.

INVESTMENT APPRAISAL

Appraisal Methods

Three categories of information are required:

1. The estimation of future cash inflows resulting from an initial investment.
2. The estimation of future cash outflows.
3. The discount rate which represents the company's preference for present cash over the future cash, a preference that may be also called cost of capital, or the minimum acceptable rate of return.

A project may be evaluated by calculating one of the following values, which are all part of the DCF (discounted cash flow) approach:

1. Net present value.
2. Discounted payback period.
3. Present value index.
4. Internal rate of return.

Each of these methods is intended to express the profitability of every investment in a single figure in order to permit a profitability comparison of each investment alternative. To calculate this figure, we must adjust the forecasted cash flows, which may differ in amount and in timing for each project. This adjustment is done by relating the various future cash flows to a specific moment in time so that the profitability figure may be expressed as a single measure—a value, a rate, or a ratio.

Net Present Value. The amount of $1,000 invested today at an interest rate of 7.18 percent compounded annually, that is, reinvested constantly at the same rate, will result in the sum of $2,000 at the end of ten years. Conversely, one can state that the sum of $2,000, obtained in ten years' time, is worth $1,000 today at a discount rate of 7.18 percent. If this procedure is applied to the expected future net cash flow, we obtain an amount which represents the *present value* of the cash flows. By subtracting the initial cash investment from the present value of the future cash flows, we obtain the *net present value*.

$$\text{NPV} = \sum_{t=0}^{n} \frac{C_t}{(1+k)^t}$$

where

C_t = Cash balance in t

k = Discount rate

$*C_0$ = Initial investment outlay, hence, negative

A positive net present value (NPV) indicates the additional amount of wealth created by the investment project. A negative NPV, on the contrary, indicates a loss of wealth which this investment would cause to the company. Note that calculation of the net present value assumes that values for the cash flows and the discount rate are known.

Example 1. The acquisition of a piece of equipment costs $50,000. It is expected to generate cash flows of $15,000 a year for five years. If the discount rate used is 10 percent, the net present value would be calculated as follows:

$$\text{NPV} = -50,000 + \frac{15,000}{(1.10)} + \frac{15,000}{(1.10)^2} + \frac{15,000}{(1.10)^3}$$

$$+ \frac{15,000}{(1.10)^4} + \frac{15,000}{(1.10)^5} = -50,000 + 56,862 = \$6,862*$$

Discounted Payback Period. By this method one calculates the time required to recover the initial investment from the future cash inflows that result from the investment, taking into account the cost of the resources that are tied up in the investment project.

$$\text{NPV} = \sum_{t=0}^{n*} \frac{C_t}{(1+k)^t} = 0$$

Here, we know the discount rate as well as the net present value, which by definition, equals zero. We also know the cash balances for every period, but we must calculate the period of time required to arrive at a NPV equal 0 (n^*). Consequently, this method does not consider those cash flows which the firm earns after the initial investment is recovered. It thus favors projects with early payoffs. It can easily be seen that the discounted payback period represents a variation of the NPV method.

For Example 1, the discounted payback period falls, between the fourth and fifth year:

Year	Discounted Annual Cash Flow	Cumulative Discounted Cash Flow
0.	−50,000	
1.	13,636	−36,364
2.	12,390	−23,974
3.	11,265	−12,709
4.	10,245	− 2,464
5.	9,315	+ 6,851*

* Difference is due to rounding.

Example 2. The acquisition of a new tooling machine costs $127,000; it permitted a yearly reduction of personnel costs of the tooling machine as indicated in Table 1. In addition, the residual value was expected to be $20,000. Considering that the company had fixed its minimum rate of return of 12 percent, the profitability of the project was calculated as follows:

TABLE 1
Acquisition of a New Tooling Machine

Years	Yearly Cash Flow	Discounted Yearly Cash Flow	Cumulative Discounted Cash Flow
0	−127,000	−127,000	−127,000
1	25,450	+ 22,723	−104,277
2	26,723	+ 21,303	− 82,974
3	28,059	+ 19,972	− 63,002
4	29,462	+ 18,724	− 44,278
5	30,935	+ 17,553	− 26,725
6	32,481	+ 16,456	− 10,269
7	54,105	+ 24,474	+ 14,205

It can be seen that the NPV of this project was expected to be $14,205 while the discounted payback period was six years and five months.

Present Value Index.   The present value index (PVI) is obtained by calculating the ratio of the present value of future returns to the initial investment outlay. The index indicates the present value of the actual increase in wealth for each dollar originally invested.

This index is useful because it allows a profitability comparison among different projects requiring different amounts of initial cash outlays. Thus, it enables us to neutralize an objection that is often raised against the NPV method. It is calculated in the following manner.

$$PVI = \frac{\sum_{t=1}^{n} \frac{C_t}{(1+k)^t}}{C_0}$$

For Example 1:

$$PVI = \frac{56{,}862}{50{,}000} = 1.137$$

For Example 2:

$$PVI = \frac{141{,}205}{127{,}000} = 1.112$$

Internal Rate of Return.   The internal rate of return (IRR) is the rate of discount that renders the NPV equal to zero—i.e., the rate at which the present value of future cash inflows is equal to the present value of current and future cash outflows. From a mathematical point of view, the terms of the preceding equation are the same, but in this case the unknown factor is the discount rate (k^*). That is,

$$\sum_{t=0}^{n} \left[\frac{C^t}{(1+k^*)^t} \right] = 0$$

For Example 1:

$$50{,}000 = \frac{15{,}000}{(1+k)} + \frac{15{,}000}{(1+k)^2} + \frac{15{,}000}{(1+k)^3} + \frac{15{,}000}{(1+k)^4} + \frac{15{,}000}{(1+k)^5}$$

k falls between 15 and 16 percent (15.24%).

Under some circumstances, the use of the internal rate of return will provide an incorect answer. One such instance is when there occurs in the cash flow pattern more than one change from the negative to the positive sign, or vice versa. This will result in multiple rates obtained for the present value of inflows and outflows, each of which will be mathematically exact. In other words, the project will have more than one IRR.

The IRR method is often recommended because it does not require a previous determination of a discount rate, which is often difficult to determine. A cutoff rate must still be known, against which the IRR of any investment must be compared. In reality, each company knows, precisely or imprecisely, consciously or unconsciously, its preference of the present over the future; i.e., its minimum rate of return or discount rate. Every opportunity compelling the company to clearly state this cost should be taken as it helps clarify to the whole company staff its financial goal and/or constraint.

Ranking Investment Projects by Their Profitability

While calculating the NPV or the IRR of a proposed investment, one takes into account, by discounting future cash flows, the cost of capital invested in the project at *any given period.* This periodic balance is the difference between the initial amount of cost outlays (investments) and the aggregate amount of the positive cash flows which have already occurred at each future period, and which may be regarded as "reimbursements." In order to be able to rank investment projects correctly, one should consider not only their NPV or IRR, but also how these periodically "reimbursed" sums are reinvested. In fact, differences in ranking by the NPV and the IRR may arise because of the difference in their assumptions concerning the reinvestment rate for the cash flows. The NPV implicitly assumes reinvestment at the cost of capital whereas the IRR assumes reinvestment at the IRR. The correct choice would, of course, depend on the actual rate the firm earns on the generated cash flows from the projects. One should remember that essentially, the company's problem is to decide how to use a given amount of financial resources available at present in order to maximize at a future moment the return on their investment.

To illustrate this concept, let us consider two investments: A and B.

Investment A. Assume that the company grants a $100,000 investment loan at an annual interest of 10 percent to be repaid (interest + capital) at the end of five years. This investment will increase the $100,000 to $161,051 at the end of the fifth year. At a discount rate of 7 percent, the NPV of this investment will be $14,827; the profitability index will be 1.14827 and the IRR 10 percent.

Investment B. As an alternative to investment A, the company may invest the $100,000 in an industrial project which will give rise to the following cash flow:

Time 0	−$100,000
Year 1	+ 20,000
Year 2	+ 40,000
Year 3	+ 35,000
Year 4	+ 25,000
Year 5	+ 5,000

The result of project B is:

NPV (at 7% discount rate)	$4,837
Profitability index	$1,048
IRR	9%

These data seem to indicate that project A should be preferred to project B. Before making our final appraisal, though, let us see what the situation may be at the end of year 5. In project A, the first and only "reimbursement," or "disinvestment," will take place in year 5; while in B the reimbursements (cash inflows resulting from the original investment) are spread over the whole period under consideration. Hence, we have the opportunity to reinvest these cash inflows. In order to ascertain which of the two projects is preferable, we should know what are the actual opportunities to reinvest the future cash generated by project B. If we are able to make these forecasts, we can then rank the investment projects.

The authors witnessed this situation in a company which was considering the acquisition of a new office building. As the available cash was limited, buying the building would have meant not investing in a plant expansion. Although the building project had a higher profitability index than the industrial project, it was not carried out. Indeed the company expected to have ready for introduction in the market a new product which would require heavy investments within two to three years. Hence it chose the industrial project because it generated cash immediately and because it had a lower profitability than the building project which had a low cash "reimbursement" pattern.

Determination of the Investment Project
Cash Flow

The DCF (discounted cash flow) method is conceptually very simple. Furthermore, the use of computerized models simplifies the calculation process problems which are often very complex. On the other hand, there are practical difficulties in forecasting the project's cash flow and the determination of the "term of comparison" or the cutoff rate.

The determination of the cash flow requires a great effort from those company functions that must forecast the value of certain variables which fall under their jurisdiction. In most cases any investment, regardless of its nature, involves more than one company function. For instance, expanding the production capacity for a given product is not a mere technical problem. In part, it requires from the sales department forecasts as to the salability of the new quantity to be produced; it concerns the marketing department which eventually must redefine the whole marketing strategy; it affects product planning, which must appraise the validity of the product in the future and study its effects upon existing and/or future products; it involves R&D, which might eventually modify its research and development program, and so on.

The viability of the expansion project must be determined on the basis of all its future effects on the company functions. This is why the project must be analyzed by all functions, each of which must forecast the basic information relating to its jurisdictional sphere; the interaction of all such information will eventually lead to the project's cash flow. The various company functions must draw on their specific experience and knowledge, which they alone have within the company. It is the role of the company staff—not an easy role, indeed—to coordinate all the information in order to attain the possibility of determining the potential significance to the company of giving, or not giving effect to a specific investment project.

The financial manager should be the coordinator. He must not only limit himself to collecting information, but must also check their cohesion and enlist the support of the various functions when necessary. He must present and comment on the results of the calculations and apply some sort of sensitivity analysis. He must stimulate a rethinking on the critical points of the information gathered and be ready to push ahead when additional information is provided. As the coordinator, though, he must *not* make forecasts exceeding his own specific responsibility area. Should he do so, he would produce a negative reaction from all other functions and this would jeopardize his efforts in coordinating all the information needed on which to base the investment decision.

It is important to recognize that this coordination job should not be underestimated. It is here that the most dangerous pitfalls are found. These dangers are not of a technical nature, for which a solution could easily be found, but rather they are psychological pitfalls of the most dangerous kind, as many companies have learned. In this context, the position of top management is very important: it must have accurate and clear ideas of the coordination function and let the other parties concerned know that it appreciates adequately its usefulness.

INVESTMENT STRATEGIES

Cost of Capital

The second difficulty in applying discounted cash flow concerns the choice of the appropriate measure of comparison. Because the goal of any investment is to increase the company's wealth and capital needed for such investments is a limited resource, the term of comparison must be the measure of the minimum profitability which the company wants to achieve through its investments. This minimum can be assumed to be the cost of financing to the company. It is difficult if not impossible to determine this *cost of capital* exactly; its calculation must reflect known conditions of the financial market as well as management's appraisal of less clear variables.

In the final analysis, for those companies whose strategic goal is a financial one, this goal may be expressed by a minimum rate of return. On the other hand, for those companies which institutionally have a nonfinancial goal, fixing a cutoff rate represents one of the constraints—and definitely one of the most important constraints—that must be complied with in the company's operations.

The cost of capital is the weighted average of the cost of the various financing sources used by the company. It must be emphasized that the cost of capital does not vary because of the particular source of financing used by the company when carrying out a particular investment. Usually a particular type of financing is not granted to a specific investment project, but to a company with its unique set of assets and liabilities.

Another consideration for the financial manager is to determine the impact of the particular investment upon the total capital budget as it relates to the cost of capital and overall risk of the firm. An additional project may provide a rate of return greater than the cost of capital and be deemed acceptable on conventional grounds. But if this project serves to increase the overall risk of the total firm, then its hurdle rate would exceed the cost of capital by the amount of risk premium demanded in the capital market for this kind of risk assumption. After defining the appropriate financial structure, it is necessary to determine (1) the cost for each of these sources, and (2) the proportion of each expressed as the ratio among the various sources.

The return on the investment must at least cover the cost of the financing required for investment; hence, we must evaluate the cost of the capital invested today. The problem is of relatively less importance with regards to long-term debts that are being contracted today, since their cost is fixed by contract for the whole duration of the contract. The problem becomes more apparent, however, in determining the cost of short-term financing (as, for instance, bank overdrafts), as this varies depending upon conditions in the capital markets. Consequently, to determine the average liability cost, the future evolution of the short-term liabilities cost must be estimated as well as the present and future ratio among the various categories of liabilities. It is important to realize that the cost of the debt to be considered must include not only the interest rate, but all the possible provisions and fees that are payable on these debts.

As far as the cost of equity is concerned, we may develop the following line of reasoning. A potential investor of funds in the financial market decides to buy stocks in a company to the extent he believes this company will give him a return on invested capital that compensates him for what he values to be the investment risk. In other words, this potential investor wants to receive the same return which he might obtain from a riskless investment, plus an amount that could be considered as risk premium. Of course, the quantification of this risk is a purely subjective evaluation made by the investor himself on the basis of the knowledge he has, or believes to have, of the company in which he is about to invest his money. It is thus clear that from the point of view of the company, there are as many risk evaluations as there are people investing in it.

Recent developments in the use of the *capital market theory* has stemmed from its usefulness in deriving an estimated required rate of return from given financial market data. The practical application of this theory, though, sometimes proves difficult to utilize to provide precise answers. Management may, therefore, be compelled to utilize theory to achieve a range of values, but use judgment to formulate an estimate of the company's cost of capital.

To illustrate this point, we present here an actual case in which the top management of an Italian company worked to systematically fix the cost of capital to be used for evaluating the company's investment projects.

Example 3.

Cost of Capital = Discount Rate

A.   Each investment project must cover at least the cost of the financial resources invested in it.

B.   The cost of capital to be employed corresponds to the weighted average cost of the various financial sources available to the company.

C.   To calculate this cost, one must:
   1.   Define the financial sources.
   2.   Determine the cost of each.
   3.   Determine the proportion among the different financing sources (i.e., the desired liability structure).
   4.   Estimate the percentage of the investments that are non-profitable by their own nature (company mess, ecological improvements).

D.   The above-mentioned problems may be approached as follows:
   1.   *Definition of the Financing Sources*
        The following financing sources are to be considered:
        a.   Equity funds (shareholder capital, reserves, profits).
        b.   Financial debts (bonds, loans, banks).
             Debts with suppliers are not included because the deferred payments to suppliers will be duly taken into account while determining the cash flow of each investment project.

2. *Cost of Each Financing Source*
   a. Financial Debts. Their yearly cost may be estimated at approximately 16 percent. This cost will likely increase to 20 percent to take into proper account the current inflation rate. Since the tax rate is 40 percent, the after-tax cost of debt is 12 percent.
   b. Equity Funds. The shareholders expect a return on their investment of at least 3 percent higher than the cost of financial debts. Consequently the cost equals 23 percent.
3. *Proportion among the Individual Financing Sources*
   The financial structure of the company needs to be strengthened in order to reach a leverage ratio of 1.5 interest-bearing debt to $1 equity funds in 1977. Considering also the desired operating efficiency and the evolution of the severance indemnity fund, the liabilities net of suppliers would appear as follows:

	Proportion		Cost		Weighted Cost
Equity funds	40%	×	23%	=	9.2%
Interest-bearing debts.	60%	×	12%	=	7.2%
Weighted average cost of capital.					16.4%

4. *Size of Investments That Are Nonprofitable by Their Own Nature*
   Investments for social purposes (ecological, etc.) amount to 7.5 percent of total investments. To take into account these investments, the cutoff rate must be increased by 7.5 percent as the profitable investments must finance those that are nonprofitable by their own nature. Estimated on the basis of current conditions, the discount rate to be used for evaluating the company's investments with the DCF is:

$$16.4\% \times 1.075 = 17.63\% \sim \underline{\underline{18\%}}$$

Determination of the Financial Structure

Having calculated or estimated the cost of each financing source, management must make another fundamental decision: it must decide on the financial structure by which to operate. This involves determining (1) the target debt ratio, and (2) the potential financing reserve.

Target Debt Ratio.   It is not possible to determine automatically, or through a mathematical formula, the maximum indebtness a company can bear. This is a function of the creditors' evaluation of the risk involved in their potential investment in the company, just as in the case of the potential shareholders. For instance, public utility companies usually show a high indebtness percentage on their balance sheet. This is due to the fact that the financial market considers an investment in such companies, or in such a market, a low-risk investment since these companies have a secure market—either because they operate in a monopoly position, or because they operate in a market that is stable and in which there is no keen competition. There are exceptions, of course. As an example, let us recall the difficulties encountered by the large American railroad companies and the financing problems of the public utility companies under inflationary conditions.

The maximum indebtness also depends on the situation existing in each market. For instance, a company operating in the Italian or Japanese market is allowed a higher degree of indebtness than would be acceptable for a similar company in the United States. But this is a consequence of a series of relationships in the economic structure—and in particular in the financial markets—which favor the tendency toward higher indebtedness.

Potential Financing Reserve.   In deciding on the appropriate financial structure for its company, it would be wise for the company management to consider not only the evolution of the market, the market's idiosyncrasies, and the company's image in the financial market, but also the necessity of maintaining a potential financing "reserve" and, the size this reserve ought to be. The amount of this reserve will, of course, be affected by the company management's evaluation of the risk inherent to the company operations. This reserve should, in fact, be large enough to constitute a safety margin against the possible absence of future profits; i.e., the future funds to be generated internally for reinvestment purposes.

Example 4.   In order to clarify this concept, let us consider two companies having the financial structure illustrated in Section A of Table 2. Let us assume that the two companies have fixed an identical

TABLE 2
Debt/Equity Ratio of Two Companies (in million dollars)

A. Normal Year	Company X		Company Y	
Equity	$ 5	50%	$ 3.5	35%
Debt	5	50	6.5	65
Total.	$10	100%	$10.0	100%

B. Year without Profits	Company X		Company Y	
Equity	$ 5	41.7%	$ 3.5	30%
Debt	7	58.3%	8.2	70
Total.	$12	100.0%	$11.7	100%

maximum debt/equity ratio of 70/30 (i.e., the overall debt is limited to a maximum 70 percent of the balance sheet total assets). Furthermore, let us assume that for the coming year both companies have a $2 million capital budget. Because of a temporary slowdown in general business conditions, neither company made a profit during the last year: they both just broke even. Thus, both companies may not be able to finance the investment through equity financing: internal sources have dried up and consequently, external sources would be fairly difficult to obtain.

In this situation, Company X can still proceed with its investment plan by increasing its debt, while remaining within the limits of its maximum debt/equity ratio. Its financial structure will result as indicated in Section B of Table 2. Company Y, on the other hand, may not proceed with its original investment plan. It can only use $1.7 million for new investments as constrained by its debt/equity ratio.

Company X, instead, was able to fully realize its investment plan in spite of a profitless year because it succeeded in maintaining a financial reserve equal to 20 percent of the balance sheet. This 20 percent is the difference between the acceptable maximum indebtness (70 percent) and the degree of indebtness at the beginning of the period under consideration (50 percent). Company Y, on the other hand, having maintained only a financial reserve of 5 percent, had to reduce its original investment plan as a consequence of a profitless year.

It is top management's responsibility to determine the minimum financial reserve needed to operate. The financial reserve is a function of the degree and the way in which the company management estimates the risks of the environment to the firm. Companies operating in a high-risk environment need a higher financial reserve than companies operating in a more stable environment.

Unrelated Investments

So far, we have restricted our analysis to companies operating in one country or market. Reality is usually much more complex, however. The distinction between two or more fields of activity is not always easy and clear. Of course, if a company sells pharmaceutical products as well as ice cream, the distinction is evident. On the other hand, if a company is engaged in oil prospecting and drilling as well as in operating a pipeline for transporting the oil from a known oil field to a known market, it is less clear where to draw the line between the two activities. Actually, these two oil activities are very different as far as risk is concerned. Oil drilling implies a higher risk than installing and operating pipelines.

Let us now consider a company which is considering investing in three different projects, A, B, and C, all in the same field of endeavor. These activities then, can be considered homogeneous as far as risk is concerned. In this decision-making process, the management may follow the reasoning described previously: using as a term of comparison the cost of capital, it will evaluate each single investment project alone and in conjunction with the total capital budget. It then proceeds to determine the investment plan's overall profitability and yearly ROI in order to evaluate its impact on the company's financial structure.

Let us consider another company which operates in many fields of activity with varying degrees of risk attendant to each group. We must remember, of course, that the firm's objective is to maximize its overall wealth position. The firm's wealth, in turn, is a function of the combination of return and risk of its investment projects. As it invests in different fields of business activity, it gradually builds up a portfolio: a combination of investments with its unique return and risk pattern. What management must consider is how the new investment activity affects the return and overall risk of the firm's existing portfolio of assets. If the new project's cyclical pattern is counter to the existing projects (negatively correlated), for example, the overall risk or earnings variation of the firm may actually decline. Such a favorable "portfolio effect" may lower the hurdle rate relative to the previous average cost of capital. It is the combination of risk and return added to the firm by the new project which is important. As the firm adds new projects, the required return on investment will vary according to the additional rate brought about by this project.

We recognize, however, that with well-developed financial markets, it is more efficient for investors to form their own portfolios than for a company to consciously seek to provide portfolios of investment projects for its creditors and owners. Diversification of investment projects by a business firm is justified only if the new projects added are, in light of its existing investments more profitable than if the same projects were undertaken by independent firms. The investment portfolio of the firm then has the potential of providing a return-risk combination that could not be achieved by an individual investor from his efforts in pure diversification.

Using as many cost-of-capital rates as there are risk groups permits one to avoid penalizing the future projects belonging to low-risk groups to the exclusive advantage of high-risk projects. In short, it allows a rational and well-balanced investment policy. Each new investment project, in fact, will be evaluated on the basis of the cost of capital relating to the project's risk group.

Before deciding what plan or plans should be carried out, management must consider the interaction in ROI terms. It must establish the overall annual ROI resulting from investments in different risk groups and calculate the overall ROI's impact on the company financial structure. It must repeat this as many times as there are the risk groups since there are as many cost of capital rates as there are risk groups. The goal, of course, is the desire for the additional project to add to the overall corporate value.

Example 5. This situation occurred in a company which had two different activities: real estate and electronic components. The risk inherent in the real estate business was considered low by banking institutions, which granted the company loans guaranteed by mortgages. The total amount of these loans represented 70 percent of the book value of the real estate. Banking institutions were less "generous" with the industrial activity: in fact all financial debt represented only 50 percent of industrial investments in fixed and current assets.

The company had set as a goal for remunerating its equity at a 16 percent level while the actual cost of mortgage loans was 8 percent and bank overdrafts 10 percent with a 50 percent tax rate. On this basis the company calculated as follows its cost of capital for each activity:

| | Real Estate Cost | | | Electronic Components Cost | | |
	Proportion	Cost	Weighted Cost	Proportion	Cost	Weighted Cost
Equity	30%	X 16%	= 4.8%	50%	X 16%	= 8.0%
Debts	70	X 4.0	= 2.8	50	X 5.0	= 2.5
Cost of capital			7.6%			10.5%

Thus the weighted average cost of capital for the industrial operation is higher than for the real estate activity. The real estate activity is able to utilize more of the low-cost debt with its tax advantage. In addition, the cost of debt is lower for the real estate operation. This illustrates why the appropriate cost of capital may be lower for one division than for another.

Minimum ROI

So far, we have examined the single investment and the overall capital budget exclusively in terms of discounted cash flow; i.e., in terms of its total profitability calculated according to a procedure that could be defined as "cash flow bookkeeping." This is in contrast to the "traditional accounting bookkeeping" which is the method used in the annual company financial reports presented to the outside world and the financial market. This latter forms the basis for calculating a ratio that summarizes effectively the efficiency of the business and expresses it in a single figure. This measure represents the ability of management in the past to properly use the tools or assets at its disposal. This ratio is the ROI (return on investment) which is calculated as follows:

$$\frac{\text{Net income plus interest costs net of their tax shield}}{\text{Total assets}}$$

Outsiders, and the financial market in particular, judge the company largely on the basis of its ROI. This future overall company ROI depends on the profit resulting from its present investment projects (i.e., from existing products) as well as profits that may result from future investment projects. Although relatively little can be done to affect the profit (and thus, also the ROI) relating to existing projects, management can influence the ROI resulting from the profits emanating from new investments. Company management should not limit itself to evaluating each single investment project strictly according to its own standards, but ought to appraise its significance to the overall investment plan. It must analyze the effects of this plan upon the company's yearly return on investment.

Thus, management must calculate—and in this context the use of the computer models is most useful—the performance of the yearly ROI on its new investments in order to see how this ROI affects the overall ROI. This will permit us to determine the yearly minimum ROI on new investments, which is a very important financial consideration that the company must take into account.

THE INVESTMENT PLAN OR THE CAPITAL BUDGET

Although the cost of capital represents the minimum acceptable return on investment proposals (i.e., the cutoff rate), it is essential, however, that the investment selection process based on this not be made automatically. The management may decide, indeed, to carry out certain investment projects below the established minimum profitability rate because they make it possible to achieve some specific short-term operative objectives. Yet, it must know how much this decision costs the company in terms of lost wealth.

In order to meet certain constraints imposed by the environment, the company must take into consideration a series of investments that could be referred to as "social investments" (for instance, the construction of a canteen, the acquisition of pollution-depurating equipment, investments aiming at improving working conditions, and so on). These investments have an indirect long-term profitability, which is extremely difficult to measure by a DCF method.

An improvement in working conditions, in fact, may result in an increase in productivity, or in a more favorable labor union relationship. Of course, it is extremely difficult to forecast when these improvements may take place, or to what extent they will increase profitability. Nevertheless, these investments must be made and, thus, be included in the overall capital budget of the company.

This capital budget, in turn, must be evaluated in DCF terms.

For instance, if the calculated NPV of the capital budget is positive, it means management chooses to invest in projects which create wealth for the company. This is all the more true if one considers that this positive value does not take into account the indirect profitability that may arise from the social investments. If on the other hand, the NPV of the overall capital budget is negative, then management must refrain from selecting certain projects, or they must be deferred to some future date when they will be profitable.

Thus, the projects selected must overcome a second hurdle which concerns the overall capital budget. Determining an investment's feasibility in this manner still does not mean that the plan must necessarily be carried out. In fact, management must now evaluate the effect of the overall capital budget on the company's financial structure.

In this context, the choice to enter one activity rather than another, may be studied in a more rational way; i.e., on the basis of its effect on risk and overall profitability as well as future financial liquidity. In fact, a current company activity having a low profitability, but a good positive cash flow, may induce the management to invest in a new activity bearing a higher risk, and corresponding potential high profits. This, of course, implies that the constraints regarding the yearly overall profitability are observed. Finally, the development of the company's total capital budget and its financial structure should allow it to obtain the financial resources it will require in the future.

ADDITIONAL SOURCES

See Additional Sources at end of Chapter 17.

Chapter 17

Managing Investment Decisions

J. L. Murdy[*]

No AREA of activity in a capital intensive business is more important than capital allocation and investment selection. These processes determine a company's long-term commercial patterns while necessarily eliminating a wide range of alternative possibilities which do not survive selective scrutiny. As a result, in most commercial organizations, capital allocation and subsequent specific investment decisions are extremely competitive internal activities.

Although capital investment choices go through an intensive internal selection process, their validity is finally tested and determined against the realities of commercial competition. Recognizing this, the need for effective capital budgeting controls and reliable investment decision disciplines must be set to ensure long-term commercial viability.

Commerce is as complex as any human activity. There are many reasons for success and these often defy definitive identification. However, reasons for failure are usually quite visible. Common among the most visible causes of failure are inept capital investments.

In the long run, solid business plans, brilliant product design, and aggressive marketing cannot overcome inefficient, poorly located

---

[*] J. L. Murdy is vice president and comptroller, Gulf Oil Corporation, Pittsburgh, Pennsylvania.

production and distribution facilities. Of course, the reverse is also true. However, the issue to be dealt with in this chapter assumes that these other aspects of commercial activity are functioning well. Our emphasis is to match these activities with effective capital budgeting and wise investment selection.

Glossary

To assist our treatment of this subject, the following glossary of terms will be used.

Capital Budget. A company's formal process (usually annual) of establishing approved appropriation and expenditure plans. Approval contemplates specific clearance by the board of directors authorizing executive management to implement the proposed pattern of capital replacement, renewal, and expansion.

Capital Projects. Investments in property, plant, and equipment and certain other activities such as exploration, major research, and new product development.

Appropriation. Overall project authorization.

Expenditure. Cash disbursements or liability accruals to outside parties in connection with executing a project.

Commitments. Contractual obligations for investment created in executing a capital project. Commitments generally will precede expenditures.

At this point, an example may help to illustrate these glossary definitions:

After extensive consideration, Company A wishes to build a new $50 million processing plant. This is the *capital project.* The plant will take approximately two and one-half years to build and become operational. Therefore, Company A wishes to obtain an *appropriation* for the entire project in the coming fiscal year. After the *appropriation* has been approved, Company A contracts for design and construction. These contracts are *commitments.* As third-party designers progress on their work, Company A begins to incur quantifiable third-party liabilities or disburses amounts for specific services. Such accruable liabilities or actual disbursements are *expenditures.* Sequentially, Company A first appropriates then commits and finally expends.

Now let's put this project into a *capital budget.* Prior to any outside commitments, Company A identifies a number of capital projects in which it wishes to invest. These are proposed to Company A's board of directors by requesting approval to appropriate $X for new projects with $Y to be spent in the coming fiscal year and the balance in subsequent years. $X constitute the *appropriations budget* and $Y constitute the *expenditure budget.*

FOUR MUSTS

Since the capital budget process is so crucial, a list of "musts" might be helpful to give a general framework to this discussion.

The capital budget (1) *must* be consistent with long-range strategic business plans; (2) *must* be compatible with financial capacities and management capabilities; (3) *must* be controllable; and (4) *must* be fully endorsed by executive management.

Consistency

The first "must" cited was that the *capital budget must be consistent with the company's long-range strategic business plans.* It takes very little reflection to understand that this first rule is particularly crucial.

Unless a company has valid long-range strategic plans, its capital budgeting process will most likely lack direction and cohesion. It is not an infrequent experience to find capital budgets distribute spending to areas and projects which are not critical to existing operations and do not create important expansion opportunities. In fact, without well thought-out, long-range planning, capital spending may be budgeted for separate projects which are mutually contradictory. Even with good long-range business planning, it is easy to find companies or segments of companies continuing to budget in fixed patterns based on prior year practices which are no longer desired by senior management.

Lack of consistency between the capital budget and long-range business plans will result in any number of examples of misspent capital funds:

1. Business plans call for expansion into new geographic areas but the capital budget allocates little or no funds to new areas.
2. Business plans call for reduction of investment exposure in certain geographic areas but the capital budget continues to allocate new project funding in those same areas.

3. Business plans identify needs for new product lines and distribution systems but the capital budget continues to limit spending to existing products within existing distribution channels.
4. Business plans call for caution in assessing changing conditions or new risks in an industry segment but the capital budget shows further heavy spending in that industry segment as if former conditions still prevailed and no new risk factors had arisen.

Assuming we are all convinced that consistency between capital budgets and long-range business plans is a "must," systems need to be developed to ensure that the capital budget will have this consistency. Approach in each organization will vary but following are some suggestions which have general applicability:

1. Long-range business plans need to be formalized and clearly communicated to personnel involved in capital allocation and capital project selection.
2. Business plans need to be sufficiently developed by the time capital budgeting is getting under way to give useful guidelines to that process in its earliest stages.
3. Throughout its formation process, capital project proposals should be regularly checked against critical business plan premises.
4. The capital budget should not be finalized until the formal business planning process has been completed and approved.

A graphic diagram (Figure 1) may be helpful to illustrate the critical interplay between business planning and capital budgeting.

Compatibility

The second "must" says that the *capital budget must be compatible with financial capacities and management capabilities.* This criteria for capital budget acceptability focuses on the practicality of capital plans.

First, the capital budget needs to be assessed within the context of funding capacity. Although funding capacity is not a simple concept, it does have a number of basic constituents. Each company needs to quantify its funding capacity at an early stage in the capital budgeting process. Such quantification begins with realistic

FIGURE 1

Interaction of Business Planning and Capital Budgeting

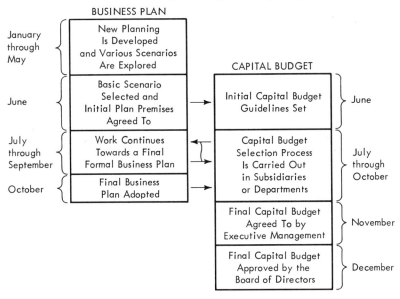

projections of operating cash flows. For this purpose, operating cash flow is defined in Figure 2.

FIGURE 2

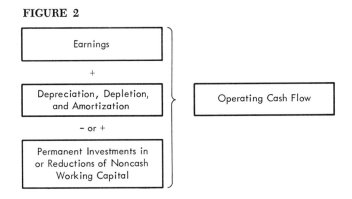

Earnings and depreciation, depletion, and amortization are commonly recognized as basic items in operating cash flow. However, the combination of these two elements is not a usable total until it has been appropriately factored by permanent changes in investments in noncash working capital. Since many operations overlook this last factor, they tend to overstate their cash flow generation abilities.

Noncash working capital consists of three basic elements: (1) Trade accounts and notes receivable; (2) inventories (raw materials, work-in-process, finished goods, and operating supplies); (3) current liabilities (trade payables, tax liabilities, payroll accruals and other similar short-term liabilities). Figure 3 adds two more factors.

Once operating cash flow has been reasonably determined, a company's fixed funding obligations should be matched against it. These fixed obligations will normally include: debt service (interest payments and mandatory principal liquidation), and annual cash dividend requirements.

At this point, a third major segment of the funding capacity equation can be addressed. This third segment includes special funding sources and uses which will normally show a wide range of fluctuation and content from period to period. Basically, however, special funding sources and uses will include:

1. Beginning cash balances in excess of continuing operating requirements.
2. Cash from sales of assets, major note collections, or other unusual processes.
3. Available unused long-term financing lines. (These specifically exclude short-term borrowing facilities.)

Each of these categories needs some further explanation since these are structured definitions which are not necessarily in common use.

Beginning cash balances in excess of continuing operating requirements would be that cash held by a company at the beginning of the budget cycle in excess of prudent liquidity needs or contractually required cash levels. For instance, following a particularly profitable period or as a result of significant asset divestitures, a company may be entering its budget period with cash balances substantially in excess of its day-to-day operating needs and substantially in excess of any unusual near-term liability exposures. In such circumstances, these excess balances can be considered available for new capital funding or accelerated debt retirement at the discretion of management.

Cash to be generated from sales of assets, major note collections, or from other unusual proceeds should be quantified and may be considered available for funding capital projects. Other unusual proceeds could include settlements from favorable litigation judgments, tax refunds, and so on.

Available unused long-term financing line is nearly self-explanatory. This quantification should include arranged credit lines plus conservative estimates of potential new equity and debt issues if such new issues would be prudent and viable in the light of overall business circumstances.

FIGURE 3

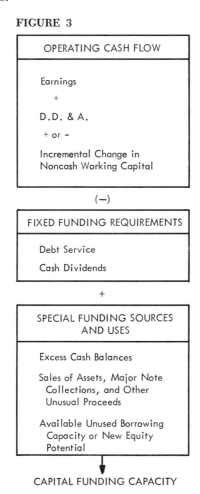

This key exercise in the capital budgeting process will necessarily involve considerable information input and evaluative judgment by the treasurer. He should be an early participant and needs to stay current with the thinking that evolves as each element is studied.

In many ways, assessing compatibility with management capabilities is more difficult than assessing funding capacities. Because evaluative techniques in this area are generally weak, it is probably the most vulnerable aspect of the capital budgeting process. In fact, assessing management capability is usually one of negative assurance rather than positive determination.

Essentially, the checklist to be gone through in this step emphasizes a proper matching of physical plant and equipment plans with the company's managerial capacities. Inherent in this matching process is the realization that management capabilities are limited in any organization. Management effectiveness in one industry or industry segment does not necessarily mean that existing management is capable of entering new industries. In a similar sense, imbalance of organizational skills may make expansion unwise. For instance, Company A may have exceptional engineering and production management skills and, therefore, designing, building, and running a major new facility may seem to be a logical move.

However, if those management capabilities are not matched with equally effective marketing management, expansion could prove to be an economic error. When such an organizational/management imbalance is recognized, capital budgets must be restricted until the problem is cured through infusion of new talent or until existing talent is upgraded.

Another operating management situation which should restrict capital expansion occurs when existing facilities are not running effectively. A case such as this is often found when marketing functions are extremely strong and the ability to sell significantly exceeds the ability to meet production schedules or to produce higher volumes consistent with product reliability criteria. Even though sales volume expansion may be realistically predicted, the unfavorable economic impact of another ineffective major production facility makes the project unattractive.

Although the techniques required to make such evaluations are usually controversial and hard to define, failure to detect critical management and organizational imbalances can severely cripple the entire capital allocation and budgeting process.

Before leaving this consideration, it is timely to again make the point that the capital budget is an intensely interactive process involving practically every significant element in management and severely testing each of these elements.

Controllability

Controllability is the third "must." And, as with the first two "musts," controllability has many aspects. To explore some of the most critical aspects, a basic concept needs to be identified. That concept is a truism of business.

"*Our business environment is continually changing so the best laid plans may turn out to be ill advised or ill timed.*" This realization requires that strong controls be built into the capital budget to ensure careful assessment throughout preparation and subsequent implementation. Although it is not feasible to catalog every possible control aspect, the following list serves to identify most common needs.

1. Capital projects should be separately categorized under two broad headings:
   a. Base level.
   b. Expansion.
   (These categories will be explained and discussed later.)
2. Major projects should be broken down into subphases providing a base against which to measure interim expenditures and physical progress.
3. Profitability criteria should be established for all expansion projects to facilitate optimum selection and priority ranking.
4. Appropriations should be time sequenced to ensure effective processing of planned projects through the evaluative and approval stages.
5. Projects already approved in the capital budget should be specifically and intensively reviewed prior to actual commitment of construction contracts or purchases later in the year.
6. Spending outlooks should be revised periodically to identify cost overrun situations which may necessitate rethinking the economic attractiveness or viability of a budgeted project.

The first step in establishing controllability in the capital budget specified the need for segregation between base spending and expansion. There are a number of synonyms for these two concepts. Some more commonly used are *necessary* and *economically desirable, required* and *discretionary, maintenance* and *growth,* and so on. Whatever the choice of words may be, they all recognize that some capital spending is required as an absolute to continue current operations while other spending is designed to expand current volumes or move into new products, industries, or areas.

In the first instances, management does not have a wide range of alternatives to consider. For example, a worn-out steam generator in a critical plant needs replacement. True, there may be a number of generator models from which to select (engineering alternatives) but management has no real capital budget alternative but to allocate sufficient funds for a new steam generator. Similarly, in a mining operation, each year new track and conveyor equipment is needed as mining faces move forward and existing facilities wear out.

In today's world, another type of investment has become as necessary as the two examples just cited. This is the antipollution facility. Unless installed, current operations will be shut down by governmental authorities for pollution infractions. Again, there may be engineering alternatives to meet environmental standards but the capital process has no real choice to ignore such demands.

Still another general category of necessary nondiscretionary spending can come from existing contractual commitments such as firm mineral sales contracts which will require developing raw mineral reserves. Of course, this assumes the contract is noncancelable and its requirements cannot be feasibly met by outside supply purchases.

A last instance of necessary spending may be caused by noncancelable or nondeferrable capital budget carry-overs from projects initiated in prior years. This does not mean to say that all carry-overs automatically qualify as base level or necessary. However, it does recognize that economic or legal penalties from canceling in-process projects may be so severe as to make cancellation an unreasonable alternative.

From these examples, a list of necessary base level spending definitions may be developed:

Base Level
1. Unavoidable and nondeferrable equipment replacement.
2. Facilities or equipment required to meet existing contractual arrangements.
3. Pollution control equipment required to meet regulatory demands.

4. Nondeferrable and noncancelable commitments on carry-forward capital projects initiated in prior years.

Base level determination is the keystone to the entire capital budget process. If well done, it results in cost effective capital renewal. If poorly done, it either short changes existing operations or allows existing operations to become "gold plated" thus cutting into valid expansion spending.

Base level determination is clearly a keystone to the third "must;" the need for controllable characteristics in capital budgeting.

In contrast to base level spending, expansion projects can be selected at management's discretion with engineering or technology playing a critical but secondary role. Expansion capital sets the pace for growth and diversification. Management initiative, imagination, and judgment come under possibly their most crucial test in addressing expansion concepts. How then is the expansion or discretionary part of the capital budget to be controlled? In answering this question, we need to go back to the funding capacity formula discussed earlier in this chapter. You will recall how an early step in capital budgeting works to quantify financing capacity in three major segments: (1) operating cash flow, (2) fixed funding obligations, and (3) special funding sources or uses.

This quantification solves to a total available for capital spending. Now, continuing with the logic of our process, base level spending is deducted from total funds available to come down to an amount available for expansion. This then becomes the control figure into which Company A's expansion planning must fit. Within overall financial constraints, expansion alternatives are considered and prioritized. From the long list of possible new projects, those with the most attractive economics consistent with long-range business planning can be identified and agreed to. Once this selection is made, the expansion project comes under the same extensive fiscal review and approval process as do base level projects.

By their very nature, expansion projects generally demand intensive attention from top management from their initiation through completion.

A well-controlled capital budget will be structured to give expansion projects high visibility. This necessarily requires more extensive detailed status reporting than is required to control base level spending.

Also, by their very nature, expansion projects are more prone to cost overruns and completion delays. Therefore, constant cost analyses and cost-to-complete reviews are necessities if proper control is to be realized.

Endorsement

The capital budget must be fully endorsed by executive management. The last "must" may have the ring of an overused platitude. However, unless executive management fully endorses the capital budget, its usefulness is substantially diminished and the entire process becomes suspect.

Executive management endorsement is required at each stage. Management must support the long-range plan, it must support the funding steps and management balancing steps highlighted as fundamental premises and, finally, it must live by the budget controls established.

Management endorsement is a complex interactive psychology which needs to be consciously developed. It may be possible to identify two key phases in this development: (1) consensus and conviction, and (2) action and discipline.

The consensus and conviction phase must be worked at from the start. Since good management is necessarily a strong-willed management, it is seldom easy to arrive at a consensus view of what a long-range strategy should be. Even when consensus seems to be reached on key strategic issues, further intensive effort must go into finding consensus on specific tactical plans within each strategy.

If worked properly, the struggle for consensus should have had the direct corollary effect of nurturing management conviction and resolved that the consensus judgments were the right ones and will be pursued with determination.

Indecision in strategy or hesitancy in tactics will become immediately apparent. Projects clearly contrary to long-term goals will be surfaced and not quickly discarded or previously discarded projects will continue to be resurrected because their sponsors continue to expect a change in receptivity. Signs of a lack of conviction may also be seen when preliminary designs or plans continue on projects or areas of investment which have theoretically been ruled out of the long-range strategy. Other symptoms of indecision and hesitancy occur when no specific designs or plans are initiated in new areas which have been highlighted for development.

Obviously, these are all qualitative observations which need to be consciously explored because no reporting system will automatically identify such problem instances.

To move forward, however, let us assume that a satisfactory consensus is reached and executive management clearly expresses its convictions as to the validity of that consensus. Now, we look for action and discipline. Action should be seen immediately as inappropriate projects and plans are stopped, staff direction changed and new initiatives undertaken. This step will often result in organizational and personnel shake-ups. Noncurrent, fixed idea subordinates will be set aside or removed when staffs are reorganized to place emphasis on priority areas.

Timetable

An obvious step in establishing the budget control process is to set its timetable. Earlier in this chapter, Figure 1 charted the interplay between the strategic planning process and the capital budgeting process and put this into a time sequence. Now let us elaborate on the details of that process (Figure 4). For this example, we have assumed Company A is a calendar year entity. If the board requires further revisions, a supplemental timetable would be established covering the need for additional adjustments and resubmissions.

The final characteristic of full management endorsement is discipline. Discipline has several manifestations. First, timetables should be set to see that projects are pursued aggressively with proper review and challenge. Second, approval mechanisms should be established to ensure effective delegations of authority and responsibility. Third, deviations from timing, cost performance, and quality goals should be quickly identified and corrective action taken. The organization should experience that fine balance of effective pressure and performance evaluation. All of this is simple to say, but terribly difficult to obtain.

Before moving into the next major area of discussion in this chapter, "Investment Decision Criteria," let us summarize where we have come to this point.

FIGURE 4
Capital Budget

	Week	Timetable
Mid-June	1	Obtain initial Capital Budget guidelines from the preliminary Business Plan. Approve Capital Budget instructions, format and timetable for subsidiary preparation and submittals. Disseminate instruction package and guidelines to subsidiaries.
	2	Subsidiaries receive guidelines and instructions and develop specific instructions to department and field locations.
July	3 4 5 6 7	Departments and field locations assimilate guidelines and instructions. Initial project selections are accumulated by each department and field location.
August	8 9 10	Department and field selections submitted to subsidiary headquarters. Submissions reviewed by subsidiary headquarters' staffs. Meetings held with each significant department and field location to review submissions and agree on an approved capital plan for each.
	11 12 13	Departments and field locations rework original submissions to conform to decisions taken in meetings noted in 10th week above. Final department and field location capital budgets resubmitted to subsidiary headquarters.
September	14 15	Subsidiary headquarter's staff consolidates department and field location submissions. Proposed subsidiary capital budget prepared and approved by subsidiary management. Proposed subsidiary capital budget submitted to corporate headquarters.
October	16 17 18 19	Corporate staff receives subsidiary submissions and consolidated initial capital budget proposals. Corporate management reviews consolidated submittals and forms initial judgments on appropriate base level and expansion levels or projects. Meetings are held with each subsidiary to review submissions and agree on makeup of final capital budget proposals 1. Consistency with long-range business plans. 2. Compatibility with financing capacity and management capabilities. 3. Control phases identified, and agreed to. 4. Management consensus obtained.
November	20 21 22 23	Final directives given to subsidiaries covering changes and deletions agreed to in review meeting with corporate management. Subsidiaries work out final capital budget proposals consistent with directives from corporate management. Final revised submittals received from subsidiaries.
December	24 25 26 27	Corporate staff consolidates final submissions from subsidiaries. Proposed consolidated capital budget reviewed with corporate management to agree on final proposal to the board of directors. Presentation to board of directors. Board approval obtained. Board approval or revision directives noticed to subsidiaries.

1. We have a formalized long-range strategic plan. Our tactical course has been agreed to, and we have the proper consensus and conviction that our strategies and tactics are valid.
2. We have accurately and realistically assessed our financing capacities. Similarly, we have a clear view of our organizational and managerial capabilities.
3. We have established effective control systems covering preparation, review, approval, and execution of our capital plans.
4. Executive management is of one mind in all of these matters and is determined to execute these plans as quickly and as effectively as possible. The organization is in place and authorities and responsibilities have been clearly set.

INVESTMENT DECISION CRITERIA

Once an appropriate list of proposed capital projects has been assembled, *investment decision criteria* become the heart of the capital selection process. These criteria are also often referred to as *profitability analysis*. Either label covers several types of calculations and review steps. Although academe and industry seem to consistently come forward with new decision selection determinants and approaches, it is generally more acceptable to have company management agree on a series of criteria which are commonly used and, therefore, hopefully, better understood. Consistent methodology over several years will have more utility than constant changes to new and "better" techniques. A representative list of usable calculations would be:

DCF-ROI (discounted cash flow-return on investment).

Impact on reported earnings.

Payout period.

Present worth.

A few years ago it was common to have heated debates as to which of these criteria was most meaningful. Today, general opinion seems to agree that no one calculation is "best" or totally indicative of a proposed investment's comparative merit. Rather, each calculation needs to be made and priority rankings then should be fitted to the circumstances of individual companies. For example, Company A may have substantial debt reduction scheduled in years four through seven. In such an instance, more rapid payout may be the determining factor when choosing from among a number of projects with similar DCF-ROI and present worth characteristics. In this case, choice of the quicker payout could help to avoid a liquidity crunch in the fairly short term. On the other hand, a company with ample liquidity is positioned to maximize rate of return if it so chooses and is, therefore, less influenced by short-term payouts. Another situation could find a company facing a severe temporary downturn in reportable earnings from existing operations. This company would do well to put comparatively higher premiums on those projects which will show a quicker bottom line contribution even if such projects are somewhat less attractive from a DCF-ROI or payout period perspective. Purists may argue that this last consideration corrupts the selection process since an economically less attractive project or program may be selected to the exclusion of more attractive economic propositions. Without contesting their theoretical objections, it should be sufficient to note that an effective project selection process cannot fully serve management if it ignores or attempts to rise above the very real exigencies of shareholder reactions and investment community critique. This is especially true when maintaining high stock value is a crucial premise in a strategic plan to grow through acquisitions.

In any event, the point of this discussion is to emphasize the broad scope of considerations that should go into the investment selection process. These examples also demonstrate that no single system of weighting these various measurements can be universally adopted.

Turning to another aspect of investment decision criteria, it is important to recognize that any empiric calculation is based on a number of critical assumptions and premises. Let's be candid. Sound business management techniques may make us better soothsayers than those who prefer to read a deck of cards or the entrails of birds, but the reliability of our projections are still intrinsically fallible. For this reason, it is presumptuous to express DCF-ROI on any basis other than in whole percentage points or to calculate payout in any unit shorter than full years.

In a similar sense, it is more realistic to look to various profitability criteria tests as better suited to detect the poor investment than they are to select the best. For instance, a project which shows high DCF-ROI but which carries more than a 15-year payout should generally be flagged as a poor proposition. Similarly, a program which appears to have good economic criteria but which could severely cripple reported earnings in the short term should be viewed very critically for the basic reason that disastrous near-term earning results could cause avoidable and unfortunate shareholder reaction against executive management's decisions.

An important further consideration in the capital selection process is to avoid the obvious tendency to establish cutoff measurements such as not approving any project which shows less than an X percent DCF-ROI or less than Y years payout. When such arbitrary cutoffs are set, capital project proposers seem to always find a way of working up their proposals to fit the corporate requirements.

CAPITAL PROPOSAL ADMINISTRATION

To conclude this chapter, let us take a project through the proposal administration process. To do this, it is necessary to outline an appropriate administrative process.

A. Standardized submissions:
   1. Common format.
   2. Specified content.
   3. Standard calculation formulas.
B. Specified review process:
   1. Comprehensive coverage:
      a. Financial (controller, treasury and tax).
      b. Planning (operations and long-range strategy).
      c. Legal.
      d. Other, depending on corporate staff makeup (engineering, estimating, research).
C. Formal approval authorities:
   1. Executive officer.
   2. Executive council.
   3. Chief executive.
   4. Board of directors.

STANDARDIZED SUBMISSIONS

Company A should have a capital budget manual which specifies submission procedures and explains their application. As part of this manual, Company A should include a common format to be used for all submissions. Such a format has several names such as authorization for expenditure (AFE), capital authorization (CA), etc. The AFE or CA should specify its content as follows:

1. Identify and describe the project from an operational point of view.
2. Summarize critical information such as geographic location, products, capacities, and tie-ins to other operational units.
3. Identification of budget category such as base level or expansion, and further designation within each category as to type of base level or expansion project. (Clear identification of any nonbudgeted project which may be submitted for approval.)
4. Listing of profitability criteria such as DCF-ROI, payout period, impact on reported earnings, and present worth.
5. Other crucial information appropriate to individual operating circumstances.

Company A's capital budget manual should establish specific formulas for each type of profitability analysis calculation. These formulas need to address the question of treating salvage values, current and deferred tax considerations, incremental noncash working capital requirements, inflation, currency exchange rates, and other factors which may be appropriate. As part of this step, arithmetic formulas also need to be detailed. Exhibit 5 provides an example of an AFE Form.

In practically all circumstances, the basic AFE will need to be supplemented with extensive backup materials such as marketability studies, supply analyses, engineering studies, covering facility construction and operation, contractual briefs, license agreements, and similar data. Supplemental data should also include an appropriate range of sensitivity analysis and risk analysis to quantify variable marketing and cost premises.

SPECIFIED REVIEW PROCESS

Company A's review process should be comprehensive and prompt. To assist in seeing that this is the case, a signoff schedule should be established by the controller department and should be specified on the AFE form itself. At the divisional level, approvals should cover appropriate operational, engineering, planning, finance and legal reviews as well as chief subsidiary executive endorsement. Depending on the corporate staff makeup, similar reviews should

FIGURE 5

AUTHORITY FOR EXPENDITURE AND PROFITABILITY SUMMARY

ALL DOLLAR AMOUNTS IN THOUSANDS

COMPANY & SUB-ELEMENT:	BUDGET DATA: ☐ BASE ☐ EXPANSION CATEGORY –	BUDGETED $ TRANSFER $ ADDITION $	SOURCE OF FINANCING:

NAME & DESCRIPTION:

BUSINESS PURPOSE:

CONTINGENT CONSIDERATIONS:

INVESTMENT ITEMS		CURRENT REQUEST	REQUIREMENT OVER LIFE
CAPITAL	NEW MONEY	$	$
	TRF'D ASSETS		
WORKING CAPITAL			
OTHER:			
TOTAL INVESTMENT		$	$

ECONOMIC INDICATORS	BASE CASE	EXPANDED CASE	INCREMENTAL CASE
RETURN ON INVESTMENT	%	%	%
PAYOUT PERIOD:			
INITIAL EXP. ( )	YRS.	YRS.	YRS.
START UP ( )	YRS.	YRS.	YRS.
DCF RATE	%	%	%

$

NET INCOME AFTER TAX

EFFECT ON CORPORATE NET INCOME (LOSS) AFTER U.S. INCOME TAX			AFE NUMBER
197___ $_____	197___ $_____	197___ $_____	

APPROVALS – ★ SPONSOR

★		FINAL APPROVAL

also be required, although hopefully, their reviews will not be duplicative in detail. Expressed in another way, corporate reviews should be from a corporate perspective of policy, direction and consistency rather than merely redundant exercises in arithmetic and grammar technique. To ensure promptness, Company A needs

FIGURE 5 (*continued*)

AUTHORITY FOR EXPENDITURE AND PROFITABILITY SUMMARY · PAGE 2   AFE NUMBER

BASIS OF CAPITAL ESTIMATE:

KEY ASSUMPTIONS & BASIS OF ECONOMICS:

ANNUAL RETURN ON NET INVESTMENT

SENSITIVITY ANALYSES:

INVESTMENT	ROI	PAYOUT (FIRST EXP.)	OPERATING EXPENSE	ROI	PAYOUT (FIRST EXP.)
DECREASE 10%			DECREASE 10%		
INCREASE 10%			INCREASE 10%		
INCREASE 50%			INCREASE 25%		
VOLUME			OTHER		
INCREASE 10%					
DECREASE 10%					
DECREASE 25%					
REVENUE					
INCREASE 10%					
DECREASE 10%					
DECREASE 25%					

a firm but not inflexible timetable that allows necessary review time (four weeks is normally sufficient) but does not allow a proposal to languish. Part of this process calls for identification of the poorly prepared proposal which should have its deficiencies quickly recognized and promptly returned to the field for correction.

FORMAL APPROVAL AUTHORITIES

Once reviews are completed, Company A should have a clearly established system of authority delegations differentiating between projects which may be finally approved at the executive, chief executive, or board of director levels. Timing requirements for review and approval will usually vary with the level of approval required.

SUMMARY

Capital budgeting and investment selection is a terribly important and complex matter which may only be superficially treated in a limited chapter such as this. Hopefully, however, this discussion has been helpful. As specific operating circumstances dictate, considerable elaboration could be sought out on each and every consideration, whether that be the tie-in to strategic planning, various profitability analyses or effective approval processes. In any case, the basic tenants of *thoroughness, common sense* and *practicality* should characterize Company A's approach to capital budgeting and investment selection.

ADDITIONAL SOURCES

Adler, Michael. "The True Rate of Return and the Reinvestment Rate." *Engineering Economist,* 15 (Spring 1969), 185–88.

Ang, James. "State-Preference Application in Capital Budgeting." *The Engineering Economist,* 19 (Spring 1974), 195–208.

Arditti, Fred D. "A Note on Discounting the Components of an Income Stream." *Journal of Finance,* 29 (June 1974), 995–1000.

Barnea, Amir. "A Note on the Cash-Flow Approach to Valuation and Depreciation of Productive Assets." *Journal of Financial and Quantitative Analysis,* 7 (June 1972), 1841–46.

Bernhard, Richard. "A Comprehensive Comparison and Critique of Discounting Indices Proposed for Capital Investment Evaluation." *The Engineering Economist,* 16 (Spring 1971), 157–87.

Bernhard, Richard H. "Mathematical Programming Models for Capital Budgeting—A Survey. Generalization, and Critique." *Journal of Financial and Quantitative Analysis,* 4 (June 1969), 111–58.

Bierman, Harold, Jr., and Smidt, Seymour. *The Capital Budgeting Decision.* 3d ed. New York: Macmillan, 1971.

Brigham, Eugene F., and Pettway, Richard H. "Capital Budgeting by Utilities." *Financial Management,* 2 (Autumn 1973), 11–22.

Burton, R. M., and Laughhunn, D. J. "On the Optimality of Single-Item, Incremental Cost Rules for the Make-Buy Decision." *The Engineering Economist,* 16 (Summer 1971), 227–46.

Cheek, Logan M. "Corporate Expansion: Predicting Profitability." *Financial Executive,* 63 (March 1975), 38–42.

De Faro, Clovis. "A Sufficient Condition for a Unique Nonnegative Internal Rate of Return: A Comment." *Journal of Financial and Quantitative Analysis,* 8 (September 1973), 683–84.

De Faro, Clovis. "On the Internal Rate of Return Criterion." *Engineering Economist,* 19 (Spring 1974), 165–94.

Doenges, Conrad. "The Reinvestment Problem in a Practical Perspective." *Financial Management,* 1 (Spring 1972), 85–91.

Dreier, Stephen. "Capital Expenditure Analysis with Time Sharing." *Financial Executive,* 41 (July 1973), 46–53.

Elton, Edwin J. "Capital Rationing and External Discount Rates." *Journal of Finance,* 25 (June 1970), 573–84.

Fogler, H. Russell. "Ranking Techniques and Capital Rationing." *Accounting Review,* 47 (January 1972), 134–43.

Fogler, H. Russell. "Overkill in Capital Budgeting Technique?" *Financial Management,* 1 (Spring 1972), 92–96.

Godfrey, James, and Spivey, Allen. "Models for Cash Flow Estimation in Capital Budgeting." *The Engineering Economist,* 16 (Spring 1971), 187–210.

Gupta, Manak. "On Intra-Firm Resource Allocation under Risk." *The Engineering Economist,* 18 (Summer 1973), 229–42.

Hastie, Larry. "One Businessman's View of Capital Budgeting." *Financial Management,* 3 (Winter 1974), 36–44.

Hawkins, Clark, and Adams, Richard. "A Goal Programming Model for Capital Budgeting." *Financial Management,* 3 (Spring 1974), 52–57.

Holt, Daniel. "Capital Budgeting." *Managerial Planning,* 22 (January–February 1974), 19–23.

Jarrett, Jeffrey. "An Abandonment Decision Model." *The Engineering Economist,* 19 (Fall 1973), 35–46.

Jean, William H. *Capital Budgeting.* Scranton: International Textbook Company, 1969.

Jean, William H. "Terminal Value or Present Value in Capital Budgeting Programs." *Journal of Financial and Quantitative Analysis,* 6 (January 1971), 649–52.

Jeynes, Paul H. "The Significance of Reinvestment Rate." *Engineering Economist*, 11 (Fall 1965), 1–9.

Johnson, Robert W. *Capital Budgeting*. Belmont, Calif.: Wadsworth, 1970.

Klammer, Thomas. "Empirical Evidence of the Adoption of Sophisticated Capital Budgeting Techniques." *Journal of Business*, 45 (July 1972), 387–97.

Ksansnak, James. "Measuring Productivity." *Managerial Planning*, 23 (November–December 1974), 15–21.

Leautaud, Lopez Jose, and Swalm, Ralph. "On the Fundamentals of Economic Evaluations." *Engineering Economist*, 19 (Winter 1974), 105–26.

Lee, Sang, and Lerro, A. "Capital Budgeting for Multiple Objectives." *Financial Management*, 3 (Spring 1974), 58–66.

Lerner, Eugene M., and Rappaport, Alfred. "Limit DCF in Capital Budgeting." *Harvard Business Review*, 46 (July–August 1968), 133–39.

Lewellen, Wilbur G.; Lanser, Howard P.; and McConnell, John J. "Payback Substitutes for Discounted Cash Flow." *Financial Management*, 2 (Summer 1973), 17–23.

Lockett, A. Geoffrey, and Gear, Anthony E. "Multistage Capital Budgeting under Uncertainty." *Journal of Financial and Quantitative Analysis*, 10 (March 1975), 21–36.

Mao, James C. T. "Survey of Capital Budgeting: Theory and Practice." *Journal of Finance*, 25 (May 1970), 349–60.

Merville, L. J., and Tavis, L. A. "A Generalized Model for Capital Investment." *Journal of Finance*, 28 (March 1973), 109–18.

Meyers, Stephen. "Avoiding Depreciation Influences on Investment Decisions." *Financial Management*, 1 (Winter 1972), 17–24.

Myers, Stewart C. "Interactions of Corporate Financing and Investment Decisions—Implications for Capital Budgeting." *Journal of Finance*, 29 (March 1974), 1–26.

Norstrom, Carl J. "A Sufficient Condition for a Unique Nonnegative Internal Rate of Return." *Journal of Financial and Quantitative Analysis*, 7 (June 1972), 1835–40.

Oakford, R. V. "The Prospective Growth Rate as a Measure of Acceptability of a Proposal." *Engineering Economist*, 15 (Summer 1970), 207–16.

Perrakis, Stylianos. "Certainty Equivalents and Timing Uncertainty." *Journal of Financial and Quantitative Analysis*, 10 (March 1975), 109–18.

Pettway, Richard H. "Integer Programming in Capital Budgeting: A Note on Computational Experience." *Journal of Financial and Quantitative Analysis,* 8 (September 1973), 665–72.

Quirin, K. David. *The Capital Expenditure Decision.* Homewood, Ill.: Irwin, 1967.

Robichek, Alexander A.; Ogilvie, Donald G.; and Roach, John D. C. "Capital Budgeting: A Pragmatic Approach," *Financial Executive,* 37 (April 1969), 26–38.

Robichek, Alexander A., and Van Horne, James C. "Abandonment Value and Capital Budgeting." *Journal of Finance,* 22 (December 1967), 577–90.

Rowley, C. Stevenson. "Methods of Capital Project Selection." *Managerial Planning,* 21 (March/April 1973), 33–40.

Sarnat, Marshall, and Levy, Haim. "The Relationship of Rules of Thumb to the Internal Rate of Return: A Restatement and Generalization." *Journal of Finance,* 24 (June 1969), 479–89.

Sartoris, William, and Spruill, Lynn. "Goal Programming and Working Capital Management." *Financial Management,* 3 (Spring 1974), 67–74.

Schnell, James, and Nicolosi, Roy. "Capital Expenditure Feedback: Project Reappraisal." *The Engineering Economist,* 19 (Summer 1974), 253–61.

Schwab, Bernhard, and Lusztig, Peter. "A Comparative Analysis of the Net Present Value and the Benefit-Cost Ratios as Measures of the Economic Desirability of Investments." *Journal of Finance,* 24 (June 1969), 507–16.

Schwab, Bernhard, and Lusztig, Peter. "A Note on Abandonment Value and Capital Budgeting." *Journal of Financial and Quantitative Analysis,* 5 (September 1970), 377–80.

Searby, Frederick W. "Return to Return on Investment." *Harvard Business Review,* 53 (March–April 1975), 113–19.

Shore, Barry. "Replacement Decisions under Capital Budgeting Constraints." *The Engineering Economist,* 20 (Summer 1975), 243–56.

Spies, Richard R. "The Dynamics of Corporate Capital Budgeting." *Journal of Finance,* 29 (June 1974), 829–46.

Spigelman, Joseph. "What Basis for Superior Performance." *Financial Analysts Journal,* 30 (May–June 1974), 32–45.

Unger, V. E. "Duality Results for Discrete Capital Budgeting Models." *The Engineering Economist,* 19 (Summer 1974), 237–52.

Vandell, Robert, and Stonich, Paul. "Capital Budgeting: Theory or Results?", *Financial Executive,* 41 (August 73), 46–57.

Van Horne, James C. "A Note on Biases in Capital Budgeting Introduced by Inflation." *Journal of Financial and Quantitative Analysis,* 6 (January 1971, 653–64.

Vickers, Douglas. *The Theory of the Firm: Production, Capital and Finance.* New York: McGraw-Hill, 1968.

Weaver, James. "Organizing and Maintaining a Capital Expenditure Program." *Engineering Economist,* 20 (Fall 1974), 1–36.

Weingartner, H. Martin. "Capital Budgeting of Interrelated Projects: Survey and Synthesis." *Management Science,* 12 (March 1966), 485–516.

Whitmore, G. A., and Amey, L. R. "Capital Budgeting under Rationing: Comments on the Lusztig and Schwab Procedure." *Journal of Financial and Quantitative Analysis,* 8 (January 1973), 127–36.

Williams, John Daniel, and Rakich, Jonathan S. "Investment Evaluation in Hospitals." *Financial Management,* 2 (Summer 1973), 30–35.

Young, Donovan, and Contreras, Luis. "Expected Present Worths of Cash Flows under Uncertain Timing." *The Engineering Economist,* 20 (Summer 1975), 257–68.

Zaloom, Victor. "On the Proper Use of Compound Interest Factors." *Engineering Economist,* 18 (Summer 1973), 257–64.

Chapter 18

Uncertainty and Investment Selection

David B. Hertz[*]

UNCERTAINTY AND RISK

An INVESTMENT's intrinsic worth is measurable in terms of the stream of values (including salvage) it returns to the investor over its useful life. The prospective worth of a capital investment, therefore, can be evaluated by the stream of net returns (in whatever form) that is expected to be forthcoming once it has been made. The investment inputs and returns usually (but not always, or necessarily) are measured in monetary units. As shown in Chapters 15 and 16, the times at which the various parts of the investments are made and at which the returns are anticipated need to be taken into account in order to compare the values of a dollar spent or received today with those that may be spent or received in the future. Discounting future cost and values at some suitably chosen rate of interest is used to relate a projected stream of investment costs to a projected stream of earnings in order to provide either: (1) a measure of the internal rate of return of the investment (DCR), or (2) a measure of the present value of the difference between the two streams at some chosen rate of interest (NPV).

---

[*] David B. Hertz is a management consultant, McKinsey & Company, Inc., New York.

376

The Nature of Uncertainty

However, virtually all of the elements of the DCR or NPV analyses are subject to the uncertainties of the unknown future. To illustrate the necessity for taking these uncertainties into account, consider a situation in which a company bids on a series of contracts. The costs of preparing and submitting a bid are known to be $10,000, and the possible (NPV) gross return (*ex* the bid cost) is known to be $50,000. In other words, the payoff is five to one, *if* a contract is obtained. Thus, if the chances of getting a contract are one in five (20 percent)—i.e., if one could bid five times on a similar contract (similar in size, payoff, and chances of winning) one or more of those should come through with reasonable certainty (but interestingly enough, there would be about a 33 percent chance—one in three—that even in five trials the bidder would win none). The actual rounded off chances for winning zero to five times work out as shown in Illustration 1.

ILLUSTRATION 1
Bidding Five Times, with a 20 Percent Chance of Winning Each Time—Total Cost $50,000

The Chance of Winning at Least	Is
No time.	0.3300
One time	0.4100
Two times	0.2000
Three times.	0.0500
Four times	0.0060
Five times	0.0003

The calculations for Illustration 1 are as follows:

Let $P(W)$ = probability of winning = .2 and $P(L)$ = probability of losing = .8. Two rules and the combination formula will be utilized.

Rule 1.   Multiplication Rule of Probabilities.

If the probability of event A is $p(A)$ and the probability of event B is $p(B)$ and the events are independent of each other, then the probability that both will happen is

$$p(AB) = p(A) \times p(B)$$

Rule 2.   Addition Rule of Probabilities.

If the probability of an event A is $p(A)$ and the probability of an event B is $p(B)$, and the events are mutually exclusive, then the probability that one or the other will happen is

$$p(A + B) = p(A) + p(B)$$

Combinations of M:

If M denotes the number of combinations of n things taken p at a time,

$$M = \frac{n!}{p!(n - p)!}$$

Calculations:

No time: $L, L, L, L, L = [P(L)]^5 = (.8)^5 = .32768 = 0.3300$

One time: W, L, L, L, L, etc. $= [P(L)]^4[P(W)] = (.8)^4(.2)$
$$= (.4096)(.2)(5)$$
$$= .4096 = 0.4100$$

$$M = \frac{5!}{1!4!} = 5$$

Two times: W, W, L, L, L, etc. $= [P(L)]^3[P(W)]^2$
$$= (.8)^3(.2)^2 = (.512)(.04)(10)$$
$$= .2048 = 0.2000$$

$$M = \frac{5!}{2!3!} = 10$$

Three times: W, W, W, L, L, etc. $= [P(L)]^2[P(W)]^3$
$$= (.8)^2(.2)^3 = (.64)(.008)(10)$$
$$= .0512 = 0.0500$$

$$M = \frac{5!}{3!2!} = 10$$

Four times: W, W, W, W, L, etc. $= [P(L)][P(W)]^4$
$$= (.8)(.2)^4 = (.8)(.0016)(5)$$
$$= .0064 = 0.0060$$

$$M = \frac{5!}{4!1!} = 5$$

Five times: $W, W, W, W, W, = [P(W)]^5 = (.2)^5 = .00032 = 0.0003$

If now we take the chances of winning as shown in Illustration 1 and multiply by the gross amount to be gained in each instance, we should find that the company approximately has broken even, since our payoff is five to one on odds of one in five (see Illustration 2).

ILLUSTRATION 2

Chance of Winning			Chances Times
At Least	Is	Gross Profit	Gross Profit
No time.	0.3300	0	0
One time	0.4200	$ 50,000	$21,000
Two times	0.2000	100,000	20,000
Three times	0.0500	150,000	7,500
Four times.	0.0070	200,000	1,400
Five times	0.0003	250,000	75
Total expected profit			$49,975

It will not matter how often the company bids; it still will have the *same* expectation of breaking even, under these conditions of uncertainty and payoff. When bidding once, there is an 80 percent chance that the $10,000 cost will be lost; when bidding five times, there is a 33 percent chance that $50,000 will be entirely lost. Although there is a chance (20 percent) that on one bid the investor will be rewarded with a return of 400 percent, most prudent managers probably would seek more than a 50–50 expectation of breaking even before going ahead. In other words, the uncertainty of winning (one chance in five) combined with the risk (80 percent) of losing the stake of $10,000 ordinarily would be too great to compensate for the size of the anticipated gain ($50,000). This simple situation illustrates why the prudent executive should seek to understand not only the investment stakes and the anticipated returns from a specific investment, but also the uncertainties and risks surrounding that investment.

The future always is uncertain. None of the expected events upon which the businessman builds analyses for investment decisions is absolutely certain. Of course, the amount or nature of the uncertainty will vary, depending upon the kind of event under consideration and the length of time before that event is expected to come to pass (tomorrow's weather is less uncertain than the weather on a specific date two years hence; next year's sales of a well-established product are far less uncertain than those of a new and untried product not yet out of the laboratory).

The end results of past business transactions are measured by a set of accounts that relate one to the other—sales revenue, costs of raw materials, manufacture, and overheads, to a specific product or a set of specific products, for example—providing profit and loss statements matched to balance sheet changes and giving a measure of return on investments related to those transactions.

The historical data that enter these transaction records, of course, are generally expected to be approximately accurate. Even they are subject to some uncertainty, but ordinarily this is not sufficient to call the results into question. The anticipated returns on future investments are evaluated by the same kind of accounting analyses as used to record historical operations. However, there is a very major difference: The data that purport to describe the expected transactions are now predictions or projected estimates. The actual outcomes of investment decisions based on such predictions and evaluations hinge on the particular combination of values that critical variables (e.g., sales volume or manufacturing cost) really do take in the future. And often the best that the manager can say about such variables as they are projected into the future is that they are likely to be wide ranging—in other words, highly uncertain. Knowledge of the uncertainties underlying the estimates used in such analyses is crucial information for the decision maker.

Two potential investments having the same "best (subjective) estimate" values for future profitability and return on investment are not equivalent if one has a much wider range of possible outcomes than the other—i.e., if the uncertainty surrounding the best estimates is very different. Thus, the decision maker should be able to differentiate among opportunities not only on the basis of their expected outcomes but also on the uncertainties surrounding these outcomes. If he does not have this latter information, he will not be able to judge adequately the nature of a particular investment risk. Therefore, the uncertainties inherent in the future surrounding each of the significant inputs in an investment analysis need to be understood clearly. The manager needs to have the uncertainties in these factors quantified. For example, the uncertainty of a sales estimate can be represented by either a table, a pie chart, a histogram, or a cumulative probability distribution (see Figure 1).

The forms most often used to express the uncertainties are the histogram and the cumulative probability distribution. The shape of the histogram reflects the certainty (or its converse, the ignorance) of the estimator as to the outcome of an event. For example, in a situation where manufacturing costs are significant, if cost estimates are well known from past experience to be reliable, the shape will peak sharply above the most likely value; but if there is con-

FIGURE 1

Four Ways of Representing a Probability Distribution

1. Table

Range of Sales (million tons per annum)	5 – 10	10 – 15	15 – 20	20 – 25	25 – 30
Probability of Sales Being in This Range	0.10	0.30	0.40	0.15	0.05

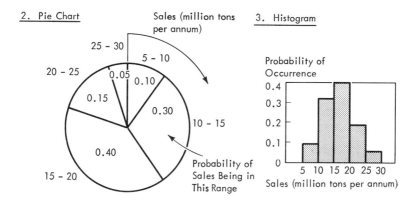

2. Pie Chart   Sales (million tons per annum)   3. Histogram

4. Cumulative Probability Distribution

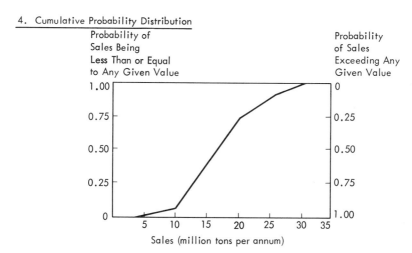

siderable uncertainty, the shape will resemble a plateau (Figure 2). In this way, explicit recognition is given to the uncertainty attached to a variable in the projected investment account. The histogram, or other form of distribution, provides a portrayal of the *specific estimated probabilities* within which the variable will fall, given ranges of values. Knowledge of the estimated uncertainties

FIGURE 2
The Shape of the Probability Distribution Reflects the Accuracy of the Estimate

A. Probability distribution of a cost that can be estimated accurately

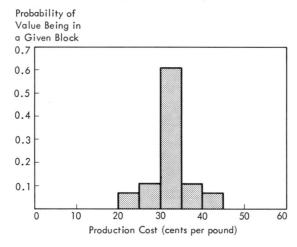

B. Probability distribution of a cost that cannot be estimated accurately

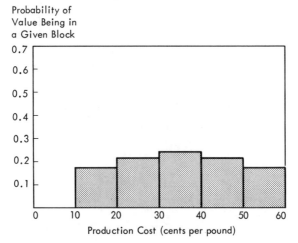

surrounding key variables permits better evaluation of the risks entailed by specific investment alternatives.

The Nature of Risk

A consensus of dictionary definitions of *risk* is "exposure to the chance of injury or loss, and the degree of probability of such loss." Managers are well aware of the fact that all investments involve a greater or lesser degree of risk—either by virtue of the size of the potential loss (a loss that could bankrupt a business will be viewed in a different light than one which simply could reduce earnings by a few percent) or because of the likelihood of such loss (the greater the size of potential loss, the more critical for the decision maker becomes the probability of its occurrence). And most businessmen, either intuitively or analytically, evaluate both of these elements of risk. But whether the executive, investor, or decision maker evaluates risk and takes it into account in making investment choices, if the risk *truly* does exist, then it is present whether he does or does not try to do anything about it.

Suppose that an investment whose price is $4,000 is expected to yield a $1,000 annual pretax return over out-of-pocket cost for seven years, given a 32 percent tax rate, straight-line depreciation and no salvage value, the posttax discounted internal rate of return (DCR) would be 11.6 percent. If the investment lasts only six years, instead of seven, then the return drops to 9.1 percent; if the pretax return turns out to be $800 annually, then the DCR falls to 6.5 percent, or only 56 percent of the original estimate. The variability of the return over ranges of uncertainty in the elements of the investment can be very significant.

For example, in a simplified conventional analysis of an investment, where the best guess estimates of the input elements are to be compared with the best (optimistic) and worst (pessimistic) cases, it should be clear that there is no way to make a prudent decision. Using a simple ROI measure, we obtain the following.

$$\text{ROI} = \frac{(\text{Price} \times \text{Unit sales}) - (\text{Costs})}{\text{Investment}}$$

	Best Guess Estimates	*Likely Ranges*
Price	$5.00	$5.00 to $5.50
Costs	$800,000	$700,000 to $875,000
Sales	200,000 units	175,000 to 225,000 units
Investments	$1,000,000	$950,000 to $1,100,000

Best Guess: $\dfrac{5.0 \times 200{,}000 - 800{,}000}{1{,}000{,}000}$ = 20 percent ROI

Worst Case: $\dfrac{5.0 \times 175{,}000 - 875{,}000}{1{,}100{,}000}$ = 0 percent ROI

Best Case: $\dfrac{5.5 \times 225{,}000 - 700{,}000}{950{,}000}$ = 56.5 percent ROI

What is significant here is not so much the fact that the possible ROIs range from 0 to 56.5 percent (although if the range were, say from 18 to 22 percent for the worst to best cases, the uncertainty involved probably would be acceptable) than that the chances a specific ROI will occur are completely unspecified. It should make a great deal of difference to the decision maker to know that 0 percent ROI has a 1 in 100 chance of occurring, while at least 20 percent ROI could occur 1 in 2 times and 56.5 percent ROI, 1 in 20 times versus 0 percent ROI at 1 in 15 chances, at least 20 percent ROI, 1 in 10 times and 56.5 percent ROI, 1 in 100 times. With the same ranges, the prospects for each of these investments would look entirely different.

Only the most naïve investors act as though there were no risk in every investment. At the very least they make one or more of the following adjustments to aid in their decision to make what they consider a risky investment, depending on their view of the risk:

1. Require a higher-than-normal return.
2. Require a shorter-than-normal payback period.
3. Adjust estimated return on investment to account for probabilities of varying results—e.g., assess the range of outcomes by using low, most likely, and highest values of factors to calculate result.
4. Adjust estimated return, or some of the input factors, on a purely subjective or intuitive basis.

There are two kinds of risks to be taken into account.

1. The risk implicit in the wider range of outcomes (the difference between the ranges 0 to 56 percent and 18 to 22 percent) is one of greater risk of low return coupled with *possibly* higher returns for the former, and a high degree of comfort or safety (i.e., freedom from risk) with the latter.

2. The risk of a greater probability of an unfavorable outcome (a

contract bid that has only one chance in three of not being won is inherently less risky—at the same bidding cost—than one that has four chances out of five of not being won).

In either of these kinds of cases, in order to understand the nature of the risks, it is necessary to attach some numerical probabilities to each of the outcomes in order to develop an average for these outcomes, weighted by the probability of their occurrence (see Illustrations 1 and 2). This average then will be the *expectation* or *expected value* of the particular investment. Thus, to calculate the expected value of the contract bids in Illustration 2, we should determine the payoff for each of the six possible outcomes, as shown in Illustration 3.

ILLUSTRATION 3

Bidding Five Times—Total Cost $50,000				
Chance of Winning Contract at Least	*Is*	*Gross Profit*	*Net Profit*	*Chance* × *Net Profit*
No time	0.3300	0	(−$50,000)	(−$16,666)
One time	0.4200	$ 50,000	0	0
Two times	0.2000	100,000	$ 50,000	$10,000
Three times	0.0500	150,000	100,000	5,000
Four times	0.0070	200,000	150,000	1,050
Five times	0.0003	250,000	200,000	600
Expected net profit				~0

This particular business opportunity cannot in the long run be expected to yield a profit and in the short run could yield a substantial loss. However, there is some probability of winning a contract that could make the investment attractive. That probability presumably will vary from manager to manager, depending on his "risk preference" or "risk aversion" viewpoints—in other words, on what is called his *utility function*.

UTILITY, RISK PREFERENCE, AND RISK AVERSION

In the situation described above, the cost of making the bid is $10,000 and the gross return is $50,000. This, of course, is equivalent to a lottery in which there is only one prize ($50,000) and in which a ticket costs $10,000. We have seen, as we would expect, that a one in five chance of winning leads to a break-even "expectation" along with a substantial "risk" of loss. This situation is equivalent to a capital investment that has been reduced to "certain" or "for sure" costs and returns, with only the chance of success remaining as the element that will cause management to decide whether or not to proceed. The net present value of the costs could be $100,000,000 rather than $10,000; the net present value of the returns, $500,000,000 rather than $50,000; the *basic* structure would not be altered (i.e., a manager would still have to decide what risk he would be willing to take—what probabilities of success would he require before he made a decision to proceed—and this could vary with the size of the business opportunity).

The Utility Function

Clearly, if the chances of achieving the estimated return (i.e., winning the lottery) were 100 percent (i.e., certain), the only issue would be whether there were some better return at equivalent risk that he might prefer. On the other hand, a one in five chance of winning *might* not appeal to him. So, how can one determine what probability of achieving a specific return would appeal to a given manager, knowing that this must be a matter of individual choice (one manager might require almost 100 percent certainty, another might be willing to risk a slightly better chance than one in five)?

A range of probabilities—from 20 to 100 percent chances of winning—may be considered to apply to alternative contract opportunities (see Illustration 4).

ILLUSTRATION 4

Contract	Loss	Probability of Loss	Return	Probability of Return
A	$10,000	0.8	$50,000	0.2
B	10,000	0.6	50,000	0.4
C	10,000	0.4	50,000	0.6
D	10,000	0.0	50,000	1.0

If these were four mutually exclusive choices, clearly the manager would rank them from D to A in descending order (i.e., D is a "sure thing," A has only one out of five chances of being successful). But, how can we determine, on a general basis, where the manager would choose *any* investment on the basis of the kind of data available here (known costs, returns, and probabilities of success)?

Consider any probability (P) of the successful $50,000 return on the investment. Then the probability of losing $10,000 will be ($1 - P$). Suppose that the manager already had incurred a debt of $5,000 to the contracting party and was offered the $10,000/ $50,000 contract *possibility* in return for cancellation of the debt. At what value of P would he *just* be willing to do this? Or, to put it another way, at what value of P would the manager not care *whether* he continued to owe the $5,000 *or* took his chances on losing $10,000 or winning $50,000? Suppose that he then concluded that P should be 0.3. This is equivalent to the statement that "The manager is *indifferent* between a sure loss of $5,000 *and* a 30 percent probability of grossing $50,000 along with a 70 percent probability of losing $10,000."

Now suppose that the manager is offered this contract and must choose whether to do it or not—what would he require P to be? Let us say at this point he says 0.6. Repeating this choice of P for other values of sure losses (debts), say $2,000, and sure profits of $4,000 and $10,000 against the basic contract, the results might be summarized as follows.

ILLUSTRATION 5

Debt or Profit	Choice of P in $10,000/ $50,000 Contract to Just Compensate for Debt or Profit
−$ 5,000.	0.3
−$ 2,000.	0.5
0 (doing nothing).	0.6
+$ 4,000.	0.8
+$10,000.	0.9

Note that a debt (sure loss) of $10,000 should be equivalent to a value of P of 0. And a sure profit of $50,000 could only be reasonably expected to require a P of 1. To describe these decisions in general terms, so that this manager's preferences for risk or gain can be applied in other situations, we derive the "utility" of each of these fixed gains or losses as follows.

To the sure loss of $10,000, arbitrarily assign a value of 0, and to the sure gain of $50,000 assign a value of 1. Then the utility of the combination of (1) the sure debt or profit (−$5,000) and (2) a 70 percent probability of 0 utility ($10,000) loss and a 30 percent probability of utility 1 ($50,000) gain is $(0.7 \times 0) + (0.3 \times 1) =$ 0.3. Thus, a sure (−$5,000) corresponds to a utility value of 0.3.

Similarly (—$2,000) corresponds to 0.5, 0 to 0.6, + $4,000 to 0.8, and $10,000 to 0.9.

ILLUSTRATION 6

Sure Loss or Profit	Utility Value
-$10,000.	0.0
-$ 5,000.	0.3
-$ 2,000.	0.5
0	0.6
+$ 4,000.	0.8
+$10,000.	0.9
+$50,000.	1.0

The "utility curve" to which these data correspond is shown in Figure 3. The units of the utility scale are arbitrary—any set of units from which the calculations for utility are made as described would serve (e.g., 0 to 10, 100 to 1,000). The units of utility often are called (arbitrarily) utiles and, *if* an investor is consistent, that is, follows the same curve for all decisions, can be used to discriminate among alternative risky investments. Also, the units of the horizontal axis can be of whatever values—e.g., DCR, NPV, ROI, ROS—that may be relevant to the investor's decisions and can span any range of values that may be useful. The utility scale itself is invariant under linear transformations. But the resulting utility curves must, of course, reflect a manager's relative preferences for greater or smaller gains or losses.

The formula for determining the utility (U) value for a specific sure loss or profit (say X) given that: (1) the utility of some value (Y) is agreed to be zero; (2) the utility value of (Z) is agreed to be 1.0; and (3) the probability (P) chosen by the decision maker that would make the attainment of X just equal for him of *either* getting Z with probability P or Y with probability ($1 - P$) is as follows.

ILLUSTRATION 7

(Utility of X) = P (Utility of Z) + ($P - 1$) (Utility of Y)

or

$$U_x = PU_z + (P - 1)U_y$$

FIGURE 3
A Utility Curve

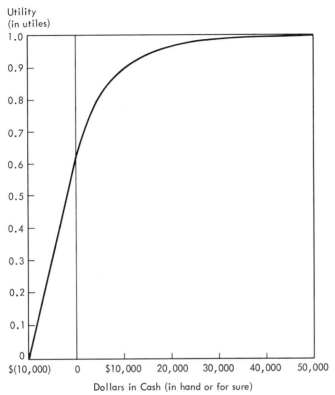

Dollars in Cash (in hand or for sure)

Risk Aversion and Risk Preference

The curve shown in Figure 3 is that of a highly "risk averse" investor. That is, the utility (to him) of avoiding a loss of $10,000 (going from −$10,000 sure to 0 sure 15) is 0.6 units greater, for example, than increasing to $50,000 for sure from a sure 0 (.4 units). This risk averse curve describes an investor who would require a probability of 60 percent or more of winning the $50,000 contract of Illustration 1 (at a cost of $10,000) compared to doing nothing (0 for sure).

A risk-preferring investor would simply require lower probabilities of success to make his trade-offs against doing nothing. Illustration 9, along with Figure 4, tabulates a different choice of probabilities in the −$10,000/+$50,000 situation (to just compensate for the sure debt or profit as before) and exemplifies the fact

ILLUSTRATION 8

It is clear that, from the curve

$$U_0 = (P - 1)(U_{-10,000}) + P(U_{+50,000})$$

Then,

$$.6 = (P - 1) + (P)(1)$$

$$P = 0.6 = 60\%$$

FIGURE 4
Utility Curve of a Risk Preferring Investor

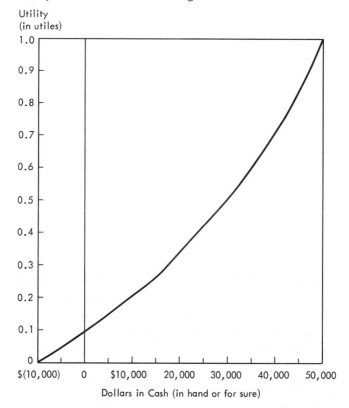

Dollars in Cash (in hand or for sure)

that a concave (Figure 3) utility curve is risk averting while a convex utility curve is risk preferring (Figure 4).

ILLUSTRATION 9

Sure Debt or Profit	Choice of P in –$10,000/ +$50,000 Contract to Just Compensate for Debt or Profit	Utility
–$10,000.	0.00	0.00
–$ 5,000.	0.05	0.05
–$ 2,000.	0.08	0.08
0	0.10	0.10
+$ 4,000.	0.15	0.15
+$10,000.	0.20	0.20
+$50,000.	1.00	1.00

This investor would accept the gamble on the −$10,000/ +$50,000 contract, rather than do nothing, at *any* odds above 1 in 10.

Using Utility Curves

Figure 5 illustrates a utility curve showing an investor's risk averse preferences for return on investment (ROI). In this instance, the investor equates a −5 percent yield with 0 utility and a 25 percent yield with a utility value of 1. Given a specific Ux (say 15 percent), if he chooses 70 percent as the probability which would leave him indifferent as between the sure 15 percent and the gamble of −5 percent/+25 percent, we can derive, calculating as before, a utility value of 0.8, as shown in Illustration 10.

ILLUSTRATION 10

$$U_{15\%} = PU_{25\%} + (1 - P)U_{-5\%}$$
$$U_{15\%} = (0.8)(1.0) + (0.3)(0) = 0.8$$

Given a correctly derived utility curve, the investor, if he acts logically and consistently, will rank his preference for investments in order of their respective utilities, and further the manner in

FIGURE 5
Investor's Utility Curve of ROI

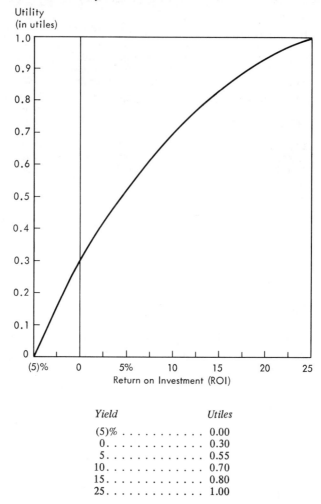

Yield	Utiles
(5)%	0.00
0	0.30
5	0.55
10	0.70
15	0.80
25	1.00

which the utilities are derived means that the utility of a *risky* alternative is equal to its expected utility.

Let us develop a decision-making example. An illustrative set of three alternative plant investments, the yield from each of which depends upon the growth of the market for the product under consideration, range from an $18,000,000 plant to $45,000,000 as shown in Illustration 11.

ILLUSTRATION 11
Return on Investment for Alternative Plants

Probabilities	Growth of Market		
	High ⅓	*Moderate* ⅓	*Low* ⅓
Investment			
1. $18,000,000 . . . . 5%		5%	5%
2. $25,000,000 15		10	0
3. $45,000,000 25		3	−5

The expected utility and his optimum course of action of each of these alternatives now can be determined, as shown in Illustration 12, from the ROI utility curve of Figure 5 and the probabilities of each of the market sizes indicated above.

ILLUSTRATION 12

For Invest-ment   *Expected Utility*

1. Expected $U_{(1)} = (\frac{1}{3} \times 0.55) + (\frac{1}{3} \times 0.55) + (\frac{1}{3} \times 0.55)$
   $= 0.520$ utiles

2. Expected $U_{(2)} = (\frac{1}{3} \times 0.84) + (\frac{1}{3} \times 0.7) + (\frac{1}{3} \times 0.3)$
   $= 0.613$ utiles

3. Expected $U_{(3)} = (\frac{1}{3} \times 1.0) + (\frac{1}{3} \times 0.45) + (\frac{1}{3} \times 0)$
   $= 0.480$ utiles

Thus, the expected utility of Investment 2 of $25,000,000 is the highest and would best reflect this investor's attitude toward risk at a particular point in time.

Practicality of Utility Curves

The derivation of this kind of utility curve is useful for analyzing the kinds of behavior managers may display in the face of risky capital investments. On the other hand, it is not a simple matter to obtain a consistent utility curve from a manager, nor is it possible to say that such a curve is stable over even short time periods. It should be obvious that the "state of the economy," the condition of a balance sheet, even a particularly satisfactory (or unfortunate) transaction might well change the manager's attitude toward risk.

Further, most managers do not feel comfortable in dealing with the idea of picking probabilities for gambles equivalent to sure results. One risky action may not be equivalent to another (although in [utility] principle they may be the same) in a manager's mind (e.g., a horse racing bet *versus* a new plant *versus* a government contract bid). A decision may be one that should reflect the preferences of multiple decision makers, but there is no simple or consistent way to combine these preferences into a single "corporate" utility curve. It is not possible to make consistent interpersonal comparisons of utility. Risky investments whose utilities *are* determinable do not combine additively unless the utility curve is a straight line. That is, the utility of an Investment A and an Investment B combined is *not* equal to the utility of Investment A plus the utility of Investment B in any of the curves above.

On the other hand, the derivation of utility curves may help determine what decisions are *so* risky that ordinary calculations of profit expectation do not provide straightforward answers. Where this is the case, an unraveling of policy considerations may result from the application of the ideas of utility curves and thereby permit better investment decisions to be made. These ideas provide the essential rationale for investment diversification. However, most capital investments are decided on the basis of their expected monetary value (EMV), plus such nonmonetary considerations that may be pertinent.

Diversification is most effective when the investor can choose more than one risky investment whose outcomes are significantly independent of one another. Illustration 13 shows two choices: either two investments together, or a single investment; the choice to be made by an investor with the utility curve shown in Figure 6.

Since B–1 and B–2 are independent investments, the probability of a $90,000 loss is (0.3×0.3) or 0.09, and the probability of a $30,000 gain (i.e., lose on either B–1 or B–2, gain on the other) is $(0.3 \times 0.7) + (0.3 \times 0.7)$ or .42, and the probability of a $150,000 gain is (0.7×0.7) or 0.49 (note, $0.09 + .42 + .49 = 1.0$).

ILLUSTRATION 13

Investment	Possible Loss	Probability of Loss	Possible Gain	Probability of Gain
A	$90,000	.30	$150,000	.70

Expected value$_A$ = $(-90,000 \times .3) + (150,000 \times .7) = \$78,000$

| B | B–1 | $45,000 | .30 | $75,000 | .70 |
| | B–2 | $45,000 | .30 | $75,000 | .70 |

Expected value = $-(45,000 + 45,000) \times 0.3$
$$+ (75,000 + 75,000) \times .7 = \$78,000$$

FIGURE 6
Utility Curve

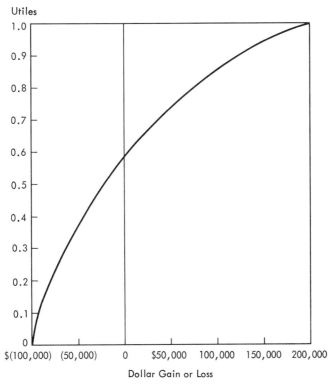

Dollar Gain or Loss

The utility for Investment A, from the curve in Figure 6 is:

ILLUSTRATION 14

$$U_A = U_{-90,000} \times 0.3 + U_{+150,000} \times .7$$
$$= (0.1 \times 0.3) + (0.95 \times .7) = 0.695$$

whereas, the utility of Investment B (with the same expected value as A, of \$78,000) is:

$$U_B = U_{-90,000} \times 0.09 + U_{+30,000} \times 0.42 + U_{+150,000} \times 0.49$$
$$= (0.1 \times 0.09) + (0.75 \times 0.42) + (0.95 \times 0.49) = 0.789$$

Thus, by diversifying between two smaller, independent investments, the investor does not change his *expected* gain, but reduces its variance—that is to say, takes less risk of making a loss, has a surer chance for a gain, although it should be noted that he has *reduced* his chances to achieve the highest gain (from 0.7 to 0.49). Since he is risk averse (a convex utility curve), it is to be expected that he would prefer the less risky situation of Investment B.

Other Decision Methods

For the investments discussed under the heading "Using Utility Curves," Illustrations 11 and 12, the risk averse utility curve gives the \$25,000,000 investment as the wisest choice, as we have seen. What if the investor feels that he would like to look at the *worst* that could happen (the *minimum* gain or *maximum* loss) and make his decision so as to do the best under these worst circumstances (*maximize* the *minimum* gain, or the *maximin* criterion, or its equivalent, *minimize* the *maximum* loss, the *minimax* criterion). Thus, reviewing the decision table (see Illustration 15) the worst

ILLUSTRATION 15
Return on Investment for Alternative Plants

		Growth of Market	
Probabilities	*High* $\frac{1}{3}$	*Moderate* $\frac{1}{3}$	*Low* $\frac{1}{3}$
Investment			
1. \$18,000,000	5%	5%	5%
2. \$25,000,000	15	10	0
3. \$45,000,000	25	3	−5

that could happen is for the market growth to be low, and the best decision under that circumstance would be alternative (1), yielding a sure 5 percent gain.

On the other hand, the decision maker might wish to *maximize* the *maximum* gain (the *maximax* criterion), which would lead to the optimistic conclusion that (3), is the best choice, with a one-third chance of achieving 25 percent ROI. Finally, the manager might wish to weight the odds on the maximum and minimum gains (i.e., multiply the maximum payoff for a given decision by a weight for that payoff and add to it the minimum payoff for that decision multiplied by a weight for that payoff) and provide a "mixed" (called Hurwicz) criterion for each investment that reflects his relative pessimism and optimism about the future.

Whatever choice he makes, there is a significant probability that the investor will wish he had made another; that is, he will regret the loss of opportunity that he had to do better. A criterion for making a decision that would minimize this regret or opportunity loss involves measuring the difference between the yield for a given decision and what *would* have been the yield for the best decision under a specific market growth (or state of nature). Thus, if the investor chose plant (2) and the growth turned out to be high, his regret would be the difference between the 25 percent he could have gotten by choosing (3) and the 15 percent he actually would receive under (2), or 10 percent.

Illustration 16 shows the values of the regret criteria.

ILLUSTRATION 16
Regret Criterion for Plant Investment

And the Choice of Investment Is	If the Actual Outcome Is		
	High Market Growth	Moderate Market Growth	Low Market Growth
1. $18,000,000	20%	5%	0
2. $25,000,000	10	0	5%
3. $45,000,000	0	7	10

Thus, the decision maker can see that investment (1) could give rise to the maximum individual regret, as well as the maximum expected regret or opportunity loss, while investment (2) provides the minimum expectation of such regret.

ILLUSTRATION 17

1. Expected Regret$_{(1)}$ = $\frac{1}{3} \times 20 + \frac{1}{3} \times 5 + \frac{1}{3} \times 0 = 8.34\%$

2. Expected Regret$_{(2)}$ = $\frac{1}{3} \times 10 + \frac{1}{3} \times 0 + \frac{1}{3} \times 5 = 5.0\%$

3. Expected Regret$_{(3)}$ = $\frac{1}{3} \times 0 + \frac{1}{3} \times 7 + \frac{1}{3} \times 10 = 5.67\%$

Summary

In general, the capital investment problem can be structured, at a given point in time, as a matrix in which *the investment choices* (I_1, I_2, . . .) are subject to future situations (S_1, S_2, . . .) in the world (e.g., "states of the marketplace," or the occurrence of specific events—in other words, *"states of nature"*) each with some assumed or estimated probability of *occurrence* (P_1, P_2, . . . , where $P_1 + P_2 + \ldots P_n = 1$) and yield outcomes ($O_1$, O_2, . . .) that depend on which state of nature actually comes about (Illustration 18).

ILLUSTRATION 18

States of Nature		S_1	S_2	-------------	S_n
Probabilities		P_1	P_2	-------------	P_n
	I_1	O_{11}	O_{12}	-------------	O_{1n}
	I_2	O_{21}	O_{22}	-------------	O_{2n}
Investments	–	–	–	(Outcomes)	–
	–	–	–	-------------	–
	–	–	–	-------------	–
	I_{1n}	O_{m1}	O_{m2}	-------------	O_{mn}

If the specific attitude of the investor toward risk can be determined (his utility curve), the outcomes expressed in consistent units, and the probabilities of the states of nature estimated, then the best course of action for him is to maximize his expected utility.

The investor's attitude toward risk can be used to help make choices when a utility curve is not determined—e.g., a maximax choice, a maximin choice, a minimum regret choice. These criteria exist because there is no *sure* way of dealing with the decision maker's attitudes, preferences, objectives, along with the uncertainties that inherently attach to the future.

If over the size range of the investment alternatives available his attitude toward risk is reasonably constant (i.e., he feels about the same—has the same relative preference for—about a sure loss of $-\$X$ as a gain of $+\$X$), then the maximization of *expected monetary value* (*EMV*) is a useful criterion. Using this criterion the investor chooses that investment strategy that maximizes his gain weighted by the (subjective or Bayesian) probabilities on the states of nature, or minimizes the opportunity loss or regret, weighted similarly. The EMV or Bayesian decision strategy will lead to the same result as the minimization of opportunity loss. For example, the alternative plant strategy chosen by the latter criterion in Illustration 16 was Investment 2 with a minimum opportunity loss of 5.0 percent. Under maximum EMV, the results will lead to the same decision.

ILLUSTRATION 19

$$EMV_{(1)} = (\tfrac{1}{3} \times 5) + (\tfrac{1}{3} \times 5) + (\tfrac{1}{3} \times 5) = 5.0\%$$

$$EMV_{(2)} = (\tfrac{1}{3} \times 15) + (\tfrac{1}{3} \times 10) + (\tfrac{1}{3} \times 0) = 8.33\%$$

$$EMV_{(3)} = (\tfrac{1}{3} \times 25) + (\tfrac{1}{3} \times 3) + (\tfrac{1}{3} \times -5) = 7.66\%$$

To represent either EMV or expected utility, the decision problem may be effectively structured by means of a decision tree.

DECISION TREES—INCORPORATING
PROBABILITY INTO INVESTMENT ANALYSIS

The decision path to a possible outcome under alternative states of nature or external events can be described by a *"decision tree."* The simplest case is one in which there is only one investment decision involving two or more alternatives and two or more states of nature—a single stage decision. Figure 7 illustrates such a case with the data from the alternative plant investments and market conditions in Illustration 11. The decision tree simply makes explicit the decisions and the uncertain elements facing the investor. The expected return (EMV) for each decision is calculated by tracing back the outcomes weighted by the probability of their occurrence

FIGURE 7
Use of Decision Tree to Analyze New Plant Investment Alternatives

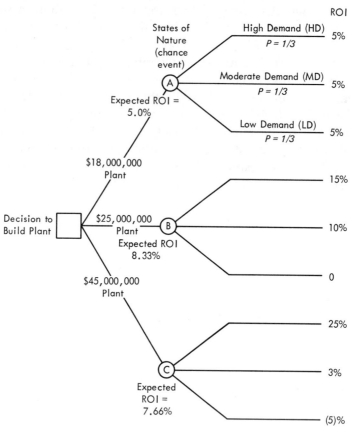

to each *"node"* where chance (e.g., a competitor's action) or nature (e.g., rainfall during a growing season) takes over.

Multiple Decision Stages

The same methodology applies to a multistage investment problem; i.e., one in which a series of decisions is required, the ultimate outcomes from which depend both on the various choices made, and the uncertainties of future events or states of the world. The method requires that the EMVs be calculated back from the end of the tree to each chance event node, with the decision yielding highest EMV at the node then being selected for the immediately previous decision stage. This decision stage then is treated as though it were the end of the tree and *"rolled back"* to the preceding chance event nodes, where the appropriate preceding decision is once again selected. The process is continued through all decision stages until all decisions but one have been eliminated. This one will have the highest EMV.

The possible decisions for a two-stage plant investment and subsequent expansion under conditions of uncertainty as to whether additional market share will become available are as shown in Illustration 20.

ILLUSTRATION 20

```
1. At first decision point
   A.  Large plant—$40 million investment
   B.  Small expandable plant—$25 million investment
   C.  No new plant—$0 investment
2. After three years—second decision point
   B-1 Expand plant (B)—$15 million investment
   B-2 Do not expand
   C-1 Expand plant (C)—$25 million investment
   C-2 Do not expand
```

There are two key uncertainty factors in the future: (1) under expansion, will the company capture a greater market share (probability estimated at 20 percent), or only maintain its present share (probability 80 percent); and (2) with no expansion, can the present product sales mix be upgraded to increase profits (probability 10 percent) or not (probability 90 percent)? Other questions include sensitivity of the present values of the alternative decisions to changes in these probabilities and to postponement of the decision to expand beyond 3 years. The completed decision tree for this two-stage investment decision problem is shown in Figure 8.

The first step in the calculation of the expected NPVs for the various decision points after having laid out all the alternative possibilities along the branches of the tree is to determine the net present value (or other criteria, such as discounted return on investment, or payback) that a manager may wish to use, using the accepted methods for determining that value (as described elsewhere in this handbook). Thus, there are 15 paths through the decision tree in Figure 8. Each one has its own NPV at the end of the tenth year, depending upon the decisions taken at the starting year and at the third year (decision points 1 and 2 on the decision tree).

FIGURE 8
Two-Stage Decision Tree for Plant Investment

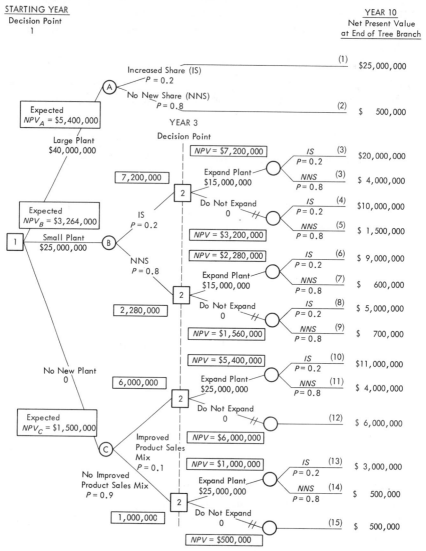

Thus, branch number (1) involves a $40,000,000 outlay for a large plant, the assumption that an increased share of the market would ensue and would yield an NPV (if the assumption held true) of $25,000,000. However, it is counterbalanced by the possibility of no new share of market, which would lead to overinvestment and an NPV of only $500,000.

ILLUSTRATION 21

Therefore, *rolling back* from these end points, as before, the expected NPV of a decision to build a large plant in the starting year is:

$$\text{Expected NPV}_A = (0.2 \times 25,000,000) + (0.8 \times 500,000)$$
$$= \$5,400,000$$

Similarly, for the small plant decision (B), working backward to decision point 2 (which did not enter into the calculation relating to the large plant since there was only one decision to be made), we find the expected NPV for the second expansion to be:

$$\text{Expected NPV}_{B-2} = (0.2 \times 20,000,000) + (0.8 \times 4,000,000)$$
$$= \$7,200,000$$

which must be balanced against no expansion at decision point 2, or:

$$\text{Expected NPV}_{B-2} = (0.2 \times 10,000,000) + (0.8 \times 1,500,000)$$
$$= \$3,200,000$$

Thus, if we had reached decision point 2 along the branches from a decision to build a small plant and had achieved increased share of market, the best decision (as we look at it in the starting year) would be to expand. Therefore, the manager can discard the no-expansion possibility (indicated by the two lines crossing that branch) and consider only the former. However, the increased share possibility only has a 20 percent chance of occurring; thus, the *no-increased share branch* also must be considered, one of its alternate possibilities discarded, and the best result combined with the $7,200,000 expectation at decision point 2. As Figure 8 indicates, expansion branches (6) and (7) yield an NPV of $2,280,000 whereas the no-expansion branches (8) and (9) result in only $1,560,000 and therefore are discarded.

The possibilities of the small plant expansion may now be combined to compare it with the other alternatives.

ILLUSTRATION 22

$$\text{Expected NPV}_B = (7,200,000 \times 0.2) + (2,280,000 \times 0.9)$$
$$= \$3,264,000$$

Similarly, for no new plant (possibility C), the expected NPV is calculated at $1,500,000. Thus, the large plant alternative has the highest expectation and should be chosen given a satisfactory degree of confidence in the assumptions.

The sensitivity of the decision to shift in the assumption of a 20 percent probability of increased market share can be checked by substituting larger and smaller values in the tree. It can be seen that any probability larger than 20 percent would increase the desirability of the large plant. And at 10 percent probability of increased share, the large plant still remains desirable. To determine the sensitivity of the result to the timing of either the first or second decision, additional branches can be constructed to this tree that represent alternative timing possibilities.

As many stages and alternatives may be included in such a tree as seem desirable and practical to the manager. Weak strategies (in terms of their expected yields) can be pruned out to simplify the calculations. But the basic methodology remains the same, no matter what the size of the tree: (1) laying out in sequence all the alternatives; (2) the chance events or states of nature that will affect them; (3) determining the payoff criterion at the end of each branch; (4) calculating the expected payoffs by rolling back through each chance event node to the relevant decision point; (5) selecting the strategies at the respective decision points with the highest payoff; (6) continuing to calculate through the chance event nodes; and to (7) the beginning of the tree.

A decision tree permits the evaluation and comparison of monetary expectations (EMVs) under the general circumstance that the number of branches leading from chance event nodes is relatively small (otherwise a decision tree may become impractically unwieldy). This means that the distribution of chance events at those nodes is represented by a few point estimates (e.g., 20 percent chances of increased and 80 percent chances of decreased market share). As a result, the decision tree EMV may not be an adequate representation of the average that would result if the estimated distributions of these chance events were taken into account. A more complete representation for each alternative investment decision, or strategy, would be a probability-type distribution of the payoffs (such as NPV, payback, ROI, and so on). Using these representations to compare business opportunities provides a more complete insight into the nature of specific risky investments. This method of incorporating uncertainty into investment evaluations is called *risk analysis*.

RISK ANALYSIS—DEVELOPING PROBABILITY DISTRIBUTIONS OF INVESTMENT OUTCOMES

Risk analysis combines estimates of the probability distribution of each factor affecting an investment decision (whether monetary or not—e.g., probabilities for varying amounts of rainfall might be used along with assessments of crop yields to combine with selling price probabilities to give estimates of cash crop possibilities) and then simulates the possible combinations of the values for each factor to determine the range of possible outcomes and the probability associated with each possible outcome.

Carrying Out a Risk Analysis

To carry out a risk analysis requires five basic steps as shown in Figure 9:

1. Describe in a flow chart the factors involved in the investment, over time, and their relationships to one another and to the period-by-period outcome of the investment from initiation to final disposal or to a chosen time in the future.

2. Estimate the range of value for each of the factors (e.g., range of selling prices, sales growth rate) and within that range the likelihood of occurrence of each value of the factor.

3. Estimate the relative dependence of the factors on one another, as shown in Figure 10—e.g., by dividing the range of the nondependent factor (e.g., price) into a small number (three or four) of categories and determining the type of estimates described by (2) above for the dependent factor (e.g., sales) for each of those categories.

4. Select at random from the distribution of values for each factor one particular value (Figure 11). Then combine the values for all of the factors and compute the payoff (ROI, NPV, or other criterion) from that combination. Where there are dependencies, as described in (3) above, select a value at random from the independent distribution using this value to determine the dependent distribution belonging to the particular category of the independent

FIGURE 9
Major Steps of Risk Analysis

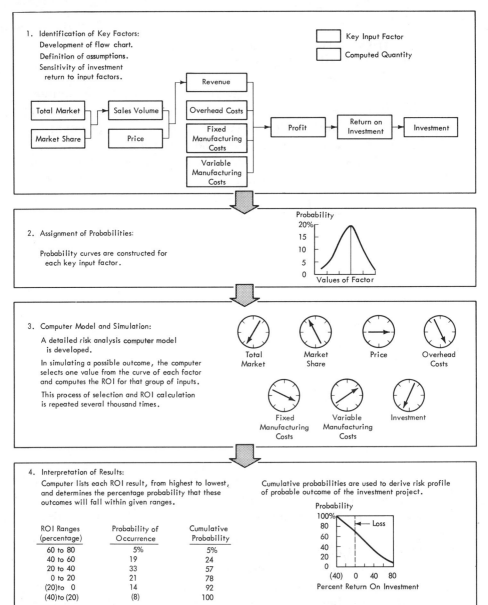

1. Identification of Key Factors:
   Development of flow chart.
   Definition of assumptions.
   Sensitivity of investment
   return to input factors.

   ☐ Key Input Factor
   ☐ Computed Quantity

   Total Market → Sales Volume → Revenue, Overhead Costs, Fixed Manufacturing Costs, Variable Manufacturing Costs → Profit → Return on Investment → Investment
   Market Share → Price

2. Assignment of Probabilities:

   Probability curves are constructed for
   each key input factor.

   Probability
   20% 15 10 5 0
   Values of Factor

3. Computer Model and Simulation:

   A detailed risk analysis computer model
   is developed.

   In simulating a possible outcome, the computer
   selects one value from the curve of each factor
   and computes the ROI for that group of inputs.

   This process of selection and ROI calculation
   is repeated several thousand times.

   Total Market   Market Share   Price   Overhead Costs

   Fixed Manufacturing Costs   Variable Manufacturing Costs   Investment

4. Interpretation of Results:

   Computer lists each ROI result, from highest to lowest,
   and determines the percentage probability that these
   outcomes will fall within given ranges.

   Cumulative probabilities are used to derive risk profile
   of probable outcome of the investment project.

ROI Ranges (percentage)	Probability of Occurrence	Cumulative Probability
60 to 80	5%	5%
40 to 60	19	24
20 to 40	33	57
0 to 20	21	78
(20)to 0	14	92
(40)to (20)	(8)	100

   Probability
   100% 80 60 40 20 0 ← Loss
   (40) 0 40 80
   Percent Return On Investment

FIGURE 10
Relating Factors to Each Other in Risk Analysis

Example: Sales to Price

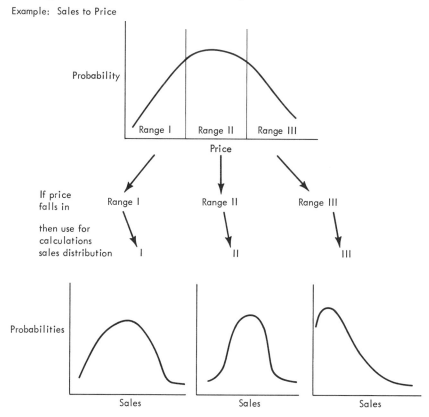

distribution in which the category falls and then select at random the dependent factor.

5. Repeat step 4 (usually with a computer) above, over and over again to provide a large number of outcomes that will define the odds of occurrence of each possible payoff value.

The process is one of simulating to the most practical extent the way events might unfold in the future. Clearly the most extreme events in each distribution would combine very seldom, having a low likelihood of being selected at the same time at random very often. Since literally there are millions of possible *combinations* of values in the usual investment analysis, the important point is to test the probabilities that various *specific* returns will occur. This is like finding out by recording the results of a great many throws of

FIGURE 11
Risk Analysis

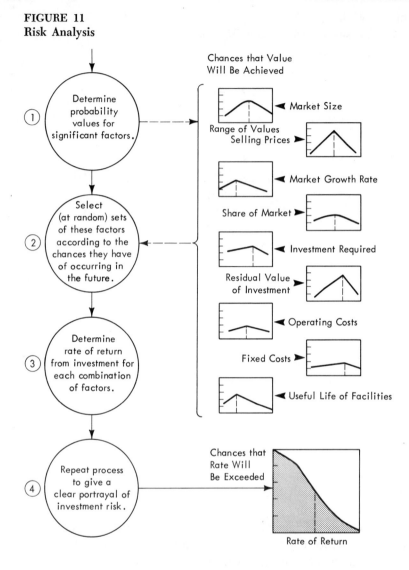

dice what percentage of "7s" (or other combinations) might occur.

The types of distributions shown in Figures 1 and 2 are used to describe the various input factors. These are combined, as shown in Figure 11, to give an output of probability that a given rate of return will be achieved or exceeded. Figure 12 shows the DCF outcomes from 500 repetitions of an investment project and the cumulative frequency distribution of those outcomes. Standard computer packages are available from computer manufacturers and from time-sharing services to run such risk analyses.

FIGURE 12
End Results from Risk Analysis of Investment Project

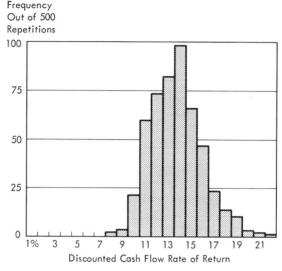

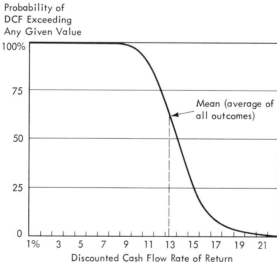

Isolating the Crucial Risk Determinants and Identifying the Key Factors

The first step in risk analysis covers the identification of the significant factors that affect the ultimate outcome of the project and determination of which of these can be quantified with certainty.

From the detailed flow chart of the economic process of the investment project that has been developed, the assumptions underlying
the major input factors are spelled out and checked for validity.
After the key input factors have been established, a nonprobabilistic
computer model is often constructed that provides early information on the sensitivity of the investment results to changes in the
input factors. By analyzing sensitivity at this early stage, decision
makers can gain valuable knowledge of the impact of each variable
on the total project and focus on improving the accuracy of the
most important factors.

Computer Model and Simulation

The detailed computer model that is usually used takes into account all of the significant uncertain input factors and the probabilities assigned to those factors as well as the factors that are known
for certain. As noted above, the computer selects at random within
the predetermined range of values one particular value for each
factor, combines the values, and computes the profitability of that
situation. The computer then lists the range of possible outcomes
in terms of such payoff measures as discounted cash flows, and payback, together with the percentage of situations falling within
given ranges. This information is put together in a risk profile of
the investment. This risk profile provides a manager with the expected value of the investment and tells him the chance the project
has of achieving each potential outcome, including the chance of
achieving various levels of loss.

Risk profiles are derived for each investment opportunity. By
comparing the shape and the relative position of these profiles to
each other, managers can determine the differences in expected
return, the possible variability of that return, and the relative risk
of alternative investment opportunities. On the basis of this knowledge, they then can select investment projects that best meet corporate objectives.

Advantages of Risk Analysis

Risk analysis adds a number of distinctive features to other approaches for evaluating investment alternatives.

Risk analysis provides more information about investment projects. Instead of single estimates or expected values, the approach

provides information on all the possible outcomes of a project ranging from total loss to the highest expected rate of return. At the same
time, the chance each value has of actually occurring is quantified
and described by the risk profile of the expected rate of return.

Risk analysis allows management to make comparisons between
investment alternatives with different risks and returns. Management is able to discriminate between investments by comparing the
risk profiles of investment alternatives:

1. The expected rates of return, based on weighted probabilities
of all possible returns, can be compared.

2. The shapes of the risk profiles provide information on the
likelihood of variance from the expected rates of return. A tight[1]
probability distribution, or risk profile, indicates a small chance that
the rate of return will vary greatly from the expected return.

3. The relative position of two or more risk profiles to each other
and to their axes indicates the degree of risk that each investment
project will incur a loss.

Risk analysis allows the user to ascertain the sensitivity of the
results of an investment project to each or all of the input factors.
This makes it possible to determine the effect of added or changed
information on the outcome of the investment project.

Comparing Opportunities

From a decision-making point of view, one of the most significant
advantages of risk analysis is that it allows management to discriminate between measures of: (1) expected return based on
weighted probabilities of all possible returns; (2) variability of return; and (3) risks.

Illustration 23 describes two alternate investments, A and B, between measures of: (1) expected return based on weighted probabilities of all possible returns; (2) variability of return; and (3)
risks.

When these investments are evaluated by risk analysis, the data
tabulated in the illustration and plotted in Figure 13 are obtained.

1. Investment B has a higher expected return than Investment A.

2. Investment B also has substantially more variability than In-

---

[1] The tightness of a probability distribution is characterized by the range between
the minimum and maximum value of that distribution. The smaller the range, the
tighter the distribution.

ILLUSTRATION 23

Comparison of Two Investment Opportunities (selected statistics)

	Investment A	Investment B
Amount of investment	$10,000,000	$10,000,000
Life of investment (in years).	10	10
Expected annual net cash inflow	$ 1,300,000	$ 1,400,000
Variability of cash inflow		
One chance in 50 of being *greater* than	$ 1,700,000	$ 3,400,000
One chance in 50 of being *less** than.	$ 900,000	$ (600,000)
Expected return on investment	5.0%	6.8%
Variability of return on investment		
One chance in 50 of being *greater* than	7.0%	15.5%
One chance in 50 of being *less** than.	3.0%	(4.0)%
Risk of investment		
Chances of a loss	Negligible	1 in 10
Expected size of loss		$ 200,000

   * In the case of negative figures (indicated by parentheses) "less than" means "worse than."

FIGURE 13

Comparison of Two Investment Opportunities

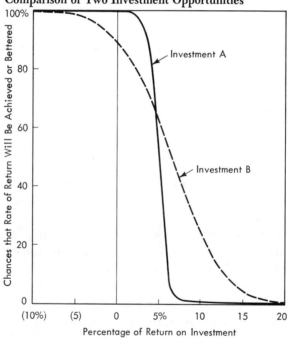

vestment A. There is a good chance that Investment B will earn a return which is quite different from the expected return of 6.8 percent, possibly as high as 15 percent or as low as a loss of 5 percent. Investment A is not likely to vary greatly from the expected 5 percent return.

3. Investment B involves far more risk than does Investment A. There is virtually no chance of incurring a loss on Investment A. However, there is 1 chance in 10 of losing money on Investment B. If such a loss occurs, its expected size is approximately $200,000.

Clearly, the risk analysis method of evaluating investments provides management with a maximum of information on which to base a decision. Investment decisions made only on the basis of maximum expected return are not unequivocally the best decisions, nor do they permit examination of the business opportunity in terms of risk averse behavior or preference of managers. Whether an explicit utility curve is available or not, the risk analysis profile permits direct comparison, at all points of the return distribution, of the probabilities attached to the alternative investments.

Combining Risky Investments—
Investment Strategy

An investment strategy may be defined as comprising a combination of individual business opportunities. The strategy can be described by the same attributes and in the same form as an individual risk opportunity. Thus, a strategy may be characterized by probabilistic profiles of profits, costs, and so on. To make strategies comparable for evaluation, investment and profit profiles should represent results over a common time period.

Since each of these characteristics typically is the sum of the corresponding characteristics of several opportunities, the combined attributes for the strategy can be assumed distributed normally (for statistical reasons) in the typical "bell-shaped curve." The expected value of the attributes for any strategy then will be the sum of the expected values of the corresponding attributes of the opportunities included in that strategy, and the variance will be the sum of the corresponding variances. On the basis of such profiles, a strategy may be represented as a specific outcome of the expected return for some specific capital investment.

Each strategy or set of opportunities can be described as a point

on a return/investment graph. This point represents the expected
values of the capital required and the returns generated as a result
of following that strategy. Each of these values has a probability
distribution associated with it. Combining these distributions and
representing the uncertainties attached to profits and investment for
a strategy produces an "oval of uncertainty" within which possible
outcomes of the strategy will fall (Figure 14). Specifying different

FIGURE 14
Strategy Definition on Investment-Return Graph

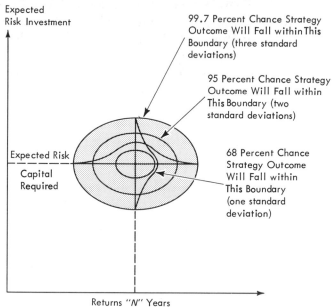

Expected
Risk Investment

99.7 Percent Chance Strategy
Outcome Will Fall within This
Boundary (three standard
deviations)

95 Percent Chance Strategy
Outcome Will Fall within
This Boundary (two
standard deviations)

Expected Risk

Capital
Required

68 Percent Chance
Strategy Outcome
Will Fall within
This Boundary
(one standard
deviation)

Returns "*N*" Years

levels of risk—e.g., one, two, or three standard deviations in the investment and profit dimensions—will result in ever larger concentric
ovals containing all possible outcomes of that strategy with roughly
68, 95, and 99 percent certainty, respectively. The decision maker,
by choosing levels of risk acceptable to him for both profit and investment requirement, then explicitly chooses a set of outcomes he
wishes to consider for a strategy.

Increased expected profits of a particular strategy or combination
of opportunities ordinarily will be directly related to higher investments. Additionally, both higher profits and higher investments
usually entail greater risks. Where this is the case, the oval areas of
uncertainty become larger for larger profit expectations.

Measuring variability, or risk, of outcomes in terms of the probability distribution over the values which are likely to occur makes the problem of choosing between alternative strategies more complex. Strategies are no longer as easily distinguishable as when they were characterized by a single set of estimates of expected profit outcomes and capital requirements. The risk versus return trade-off now must be considered in conjunction with the return versus investment amount choice that traditionally is made.

Management, of course, would like to select a strategy that both maximizes results (i.e., profits) at acceptable risk capital investment and minimizes the uncertainty or risk. Seeking additional returns, however, often entails accepting additional uncertainty— that is, risk. If two strategies produce the same average profit results, the one that involves a lower risk capital expenditure and/or involves less "variability" (or uncertainty as to the outcome) for the same yield clearly is a more desirable strategy. Conversely, of two strategies entailing the same risk, the one producing the higher expected profit return for equivalent risk investment obviously is the better strategy.

Based on this concept of suitable use of risk capital investment, a set of available strategies can be reduced to only those that promise the most attractive return for a given level of risk investment. A suitable strategy will belong to this smaller group.

Selection from the group of attractive strategies will be guided primarily by available risk capital. But, within any range of investment, several strategies may seem attractive. And these may not, in fact, be clearly distinguishable from one another, on the basis of expectation in the face of uncertainty. Then, the "intangible" factors that always enter into investment choice must be expected to prevail.

Summary

The process for selecting a strategy based on probabilistic representation of the uncertainties underlying investments proceeds as follows:

1. Generate possible strategies as combinations of the set of business opportunities and evaluate their associated return, capital requirements profiles over a specific period.

2. For any possible level of capital investment over the planning horizon, identify those strategies promising highest expected returns. Strategies identified in this way are attractive in their use of available capital.

3. From among the attractive set, select that strategy (or combination of exploration opportunities) that best meets expected goals at an acceptable risk level. If the corresponding expected required capital exposure is too high, trade-offs must be made. This can be done easily by moving down in expected profit to a strategy in the attractive set having a lower expected risk capital requirement.

The final choice between investment, returns, and risk of alternative strategies will not be determined solely by the presentation of these outcomes, but bringing out the differences and sharpening understanding of the trade-offs as this process allows will certainly lead to more consistent and better strategic decisions.

ADDITIONAL SOURCES

Adler, Michael. "On Risk-Adjusted Capitalization Rates and Valuation By Individuals." *Journal of Finance,* 25 (September 1970), 819–36.

Beenhakker, Henri. "Sensitivity Analysis of the Present Value of a Project." *The Engineering Economist,* 20 (Winter 1975), 123–50.

Bierman, Harold Jr., and Hass, Jerome E. "Capital Budgeting under Uncertainty: A Reformulation." *Journal of Finance,* 28 (March 1973), 119–30.

Blume, Marshall E. "On the Assessment of Risk." *Journal of Finance,* 26 (March 1971), 1–10.

Bogue, Marcus C., and Roll, Richard. "Capital Budgeting of Risky Projects with 'Imperfect' Markets for Physical Capital." *Journal of Finance,* 19 (May 1974), 601–13.

Brumelle, Shelby L., and Schwab, Bernhard. "Capital Budgeting with Uncertain Future Opportunities: A Markovian Approach." *Journal of Financial and Quantitative Analysis,* 8 (January 1973), 111–22.

Byrne, R.; Charnes, A.; Cooper, A.; and Kortanek, K. "Some New Approaches to Risk." *Accounting Review,* 63 (January 1968), 18–37.

Chen, Andrew H., and Boness, James A. "Effects of Uncertain Inflation on the Investment and Financing Decisions of a Firm." *Journal of Finance,* 30 (May 1975), 469–84.

Edelman, Franz, and Greenberg, Joel S. "Venture Analysis: The Assessment of Uncertainty and Risk." *Financial Executive,* 37 (August 1969), 56–62.

Grayson, C. Jackson, Jr. *Decisions under Uncertainty: Drilling Decisions by Oil and Gas Operators.* Boston: Division of Research, Harvard Business School, 1960.

Harvey, R. K., and Cabot, A. V. "A Decision Theory Approach to Capital Budgeting." *The Engineering Economist,* 20 (Fall 1974), 37–50.

Hayes, Robert. "Incorporating Risk Aversion into Risk Analysis." *The Engineering Economist,* 20 (Winter 1975), 99–122.

Hertz, David B. "Risk Analysis in Capital Investment." *Harvard Business Review,* 42 (January–February 1964), 95–106.

Hertz, David B. "Investment Policies that Pay Off." *Harvard Business Review,* 46 (January–February 1968), 96–108.

Hertz, David B. *New Power for Management.* New York: McGraw-Hill 1969, 66–105.

Hespos, R. F., and Strassmann, P. A. "Analysis of Investment Decisions." *Management Science,* 1965.

Hespos, Richard F., and Strassmann, Paul A. "Stochastic Decision Trees for the Analysis of Investment Decisions." *Management Science,* 11 (August 1965), 244–59.

Hillier, Frederick S. "The Derivation of Probabilistic Information for the Evaluation of Risky Investments." *Management Science,* 9 (April 1963), 443–57.

Hillier, Frederick S., and Heebink, David V. "Evaluation of Risky Capital Investments." *California Management Review,* 8 (Winter 1965), 71–80.

Keeley, Robert, and Westerfield, Randolph. "A Problem in Probability Distribution Techniques for Capital Budgeting." *Journal of Finance,* 27 (June 1972), 703–9.

Kryzanowski, Lawrence; Lusztig, Peter; and Schwab, Bernhard. "Monte Carlo Simulation and Capital Expenditure Decisions—A Case Study." *The Engineering Economist,* 18 (Fall 1972), 31–48.

Latane, H. A., and Tuttle, Donald L. "Decision Theory and Financial Management." *Journal of Finance,* 21 (May 1966), 228–44.

Lessard, Donald R., and Bower, Richard S. "An Operational Approach to Risk Screening." *Journal of Finance,* 28 (May 1973), 321–38.

Levy, Haim. "The Demand for Assets under Conditions of Risk." *Journal of Finance,* 28 (March 1973), 79–96.

Lewellen, Wilbur G., and Long, Michael S. "Simulation versus Single-Value Estimates in Capital Expenditure Analysis." *Decision Sciences,* 3 (1973), 19–33.

Lindley, D. V. *Making Decisions.* New York: Wiley, 1971.

Magee, J. F. "How to Use Decision Trees for Decision Making." *Harvard Business Review,* 42 (1964), 79–96.

Michelsen, D. L.; Commander, J. R.; and Snead, J. R. "Risk Allowance in Original Capital Investments." *The Engineering Economist,* 15 (Spring 1969), 137–58.

Miller, Stephen M. "Measures of Risk Aversion: Some Clarifying Comments." *Journal of Financial and Quantitative Analysis,* 10 (June 1975), 299–310.

Myers, Stewart C. "Procedures for Capital Budgeting under Uncertainty." *Industrial Management Review,* 9 (Spring 1968), 1–15.

Neave, Edwin H., and Rorke, C. Harvey. "Risk, Ruin, and Investment Analysis: A Comment." *Journal of Financial and Quantitative Analysis,* 8 (June 1973), 517–26.

Raiffa, H. *Decision Analysis.* Reading, Mass.: Addison-Wesley, 1968.

Riggs, James. "Acceptable Investment Diagram: A Perspective for Risk Recognition." *The Engineering Economist,* 19 (Spring 1974), 209–18.

Robichek, A., and Myers, S. "Risk-Adjusted Discount Rates." *Journal of Finance,* 21 (December 1966), 727–30.

Schlaifer, R. O. *Analysis of Decisions under Uncertainty.* New York: McGraw-Hill, 1969.

Schwendiman, Carl J., and Pinches, George E. "An Analysis of Alternative Measures of Investment Risk." *Journal of Finance,* 30 (March 1975), 193–200.

Stapleton, Richard D. "Capital Budgeting under Uncertainty: A Reformulation: Comment." *Journal of Finance,* 29 (December 1974), 1583–84.

Stewart, S., and Parker, G. "Risk and Investment Performance." *Financial Analysts Journal,* 30 (May–June 1974), 49–51.

Thomas H. *Decision Theory and the Manager.* London: Pitman Publishing, 1972.

Weinwurm, Ernest. "An Analysis of Applications of the Utility Concept." *The Engineering Economist,* 16 (Winter 1971), 131–40.

Weston, J. Fred. "Investment Decisions Using the Capital Asset Pricing Model." *Financial Management,* 2 (Spring 1973), 25–33.

Woods, Donald H. "Improving Estimates That Involve Uncertainty." *Harvard Business Review,* 45 (July–August 1966), 91–98.

PART VI

Working Capital Management

HAVING DIRECTED the firm into a set of product-market areas through its long-term investment decisions, we now turn to the day-to-day investment and financing processes of financial management. It is particularly in managing working capital, the subject of Part VI, that the treasurer performs a leading responsibility. In Chapter 19, Charles Ludlow provides an overview of "Managing Working Capital." He touches on each of the topics treated in the subsequent chapters on working capital management, showing how the individual decision areas relate to one another. He provides illustrative materials from direct business experience. An important emphasis of his presentation is his emphasis on integrating working capital management with overall corporate organization and operating performance. He also emphasizes working capital management planning for five- to ten-year time horizons. This provides an important framework for the short-run working capital management decisions.

In Chapter 20, Frederick Searby provides a comprehensive and imaginative treatment of how cash management can be used to help meet the capital crisis. He emphasizes the importance of effective banking relationships. Important insights are set forth in connection with designing the cash-gathering system and the mechanism for controlling disbursements. He points out how the cash forecasting process can be used to improve cash management. He concludes with a discussion of cash management in terms of its international dimensions. Thus, in a number of aspects the subject is developed within the framework set forth in previous chapters.

In the next two chapters the role of receivables in working capital management is discussed. Chapter 21 by W. B. Quackenbush and W. D. Anderson discusses trade credit arising from transactions between companies. The chapter takes the viewpoint of managing credit operations with reporting to the treasurer. The topics covered include organization, reporting, and credit policies and procedures. In Chapter 22, Albert Sweetser emphasizes what the treasurer, as contrasted to the credit manager and his staff, should know and do about receivables. The emphasis is on policy formulation. Policy building is discussed with reference to financial and structural considerations. The chapter concludes with the development of a criteria for the evaluation of the receivables portfolio.

Because of the large investment in inventories, the standards and controls for inventory management are of increasing importance. An authoritative framework for effective management of the investment in inventories is presented in Chapter 23 by John Magee and Harlan Meal. They describe the basic functions of inventories, the relevant costs in inventory analysis and the methods for formulating standards for inventory performance. The significance of the investment in inventory justifies the extended length of their treatment. Even so, the authors indicate that their coverage encompasses only the fundamentals of inventory management of greatest importance to the financial officer.

Applications of these general principles of inventory management are made in Chapter 24 by Robert Brewer, who focuses on retail inventory management and control. He first demonstrates the impact of inventory turnover on return on investment as it is conventionally measured. He then analyzes the factors that influence the turnover for a retail operation. Analysis of these factors provides a basis for the development of standards which may be used in developing retail inventory planning and control systems.

Chapter 19

Managing Working Capital

Charles H. Ludlow[*]

PERSPECTIVE ON THE PROBLEM

THE MANAGEMENT of working capital is one of the most important responsibilities of the treasurer. It involves the day-to-day funding of the corporate enterprise. It involves the timely management and investment of short-term assets. It involves the maximum use of available resources. And it requires an understanding of the entire corporate structure, its purpose, its marketing objectives, and its profit goals.

In recent years, the chief thrust of financial management has been directed at profit maximization. The result has been an undue emphasis and stress on the income statement. But times change, and now the balance sheet is gaining increasing attention.

The reasons are not difficult to discern. The economy has periodically undergone bouts of financial crises. Corporate liquidity has been badly strained by dwindling cash positions. As a result, the underlying financial health of the business organization has drawn detailed analysis—both internally and externally—to assure its *profitable* continuity. There is now taking place a return to the basics of financial management.

We must stress the critical role entailed in managing a corpora-

* Charles H. Ludlow is vice president and treasurer of the Upjohn Company of Kalamazoo, Michigan.

421

tion's working capital as part of the return to basics. The treasurer who understands the financial environment in which he has to work can better position his concern to assure (*a*) its financial survival and (*b*) its ability to remain flexible, competitive, and profitable.

This chapter will focus on an overview of working capital management; then examine in more detail how to deal with the problems of managing cash, receivables, inventories, and payables; and finally, discuss management philosophy and organization.

It is important at this point to have an exact idea of the terms we are using, and also the manner in which they are being applied. If we are talking about gross working capital, we are discussing *short-term* assets, those which as a general rule can be converted readily—or almost readily—into cash within a year's time. On a simplified balance sheet, they are represented by cash, receivables, and inventories—and usually in that order. The progression is a logical one, for it represents the degree to which the current assets can easily be turned into cash. Cash, after all, is the most liquid of current assets. Receivables are next, and inventories—ranging in order from raw materials to semifinished stocks to finished products—rank last.

Net working capital is the difference between current assets and current liabilities. The latter is represented by bills immediately owing or which generally are payable within a 12-month period. Included as a rule are short-term bank debts, current maturities of long-term debt, outstanding and unpaid supplier bills (otherwise known as payables), salaries, taxes, and, if they have been declared but not yet paid, dividends to a corporation's shareholders. Net working capital recognizes the broader approach, emphasizing the management of all current assets and current liabilities.

The Working Capital Cycle

Working capital management at the Upjohn Company emphasizes the control of the current assets and liabilities throughout the firm's natural business cycle. This cycle begins with cash, which is invested in raw materials and merchandise as well as various supplies and services. In any company a portion of this inventory investment is financed by suppliers through credit terms. The inventory investment is converted to accounts receivable investment as the merchandise is sold to customers. The cycle is completed when cash is received from customers as payment on the accounts.

The working capital cycle operates perpetually. Its length is dictated by a number of factors including problems involved in raw material acquisitions, trade terms offered by suppliers, the length of the production cycle, desired inventory levels, and terms of sale. The cycle will also reflect cyclical or seasonal factors affecting a firm's operations. At any given point in time, the sum of the components of the working capital cycle represents the firm's investment in working capital.

THE MANAGEMENT PROBLEM

The problem facing the treasurer in fulfilling his working capital management function is to ensure that the working capital investment is adequate to support business operations. He also has to be careful it is not excessive.

To be adequate, working capital should be sufficient to enable the firm to conduct its business on the most efficient and economical basis. Specifically, an adequate working capital investment allows the firm to maintain financial flexibility, and permit the carrying of inventories and extension of credit terms that will enable the business to satisfactorily serve the needs of its customers. An excessive working capital investment indicates a less than optimal use of capital funds, and lowers the company's return on capital. Symptoms of excessive working capital investment include: unusually high cash balances, stale or obsolete inventories, and a high percentage of past due or uncollectible receivables.

In performing the working capital management function the treasurer must attempt to achieve a balance between the production and marketing units—where there may be a tendency to increase working capital investment—against the financial goal of minimizing working capital investment. The key is in the systematic design of policies, procedures and organization which ensures the management of working capital in concert with overall corporate objectives.

To put it all in proper focus, it is necessary to view the management of working capital as the management of those assets of the corporation which are vital to its day-to-day operations. There is permanent capital, usually represented by equity contributed by the owners of the enterprise, long-term debt, and retained earnings.

As a rule—and mindful of the fact that all rules are made to be broken—so-called permanent capital usually is represented by investments in fixed assets. Thus, utilities, regarded as being capital intensive, are typified by enormous capital structures. On the other hand, a magazine publishing house, which contracts out for its printing services, can get by with a very narrow capital base, probably chiefly equity capital. Living off of subscription income, which typically arrives in *advance* of delivery of the publisher's product (in this case the magazine), the publisher can employ these funds to meet a good part of the investment required in inventories and receivables.

The differences, then, are represented by the allocation of capital. Permanent capital is best invested in fixed assets and the permanent portion of working capital. Use of short-term borrowings heightens the risk, not only because the availability of capital might not be there but also because the cost of such capital can vary widely depending on conditions in the money markets. As a broad general rule, financing long-term assets with short-term funds is a risky proposition.

At the start of this chapter, we noted in some detail that there has been an unfortunate narrowing in liquidity. But one test of efficiency of how a treasurer manages his capital is his ability to keep his funds fully employed. Like most things, such concepts get carried to the extreme and perhaps in large measure account for the deterioration discussed. Thus, idle funds—that is, cash—had for a long time been a hallmark of improper use of assets. But times change and so do markets.

Hence, when short-term money rates were yielding four to five percent, or less, an inordinate amount of cash on hand was cause for a raised eyebrow. The assumption was that such funds could more properly and more profitably be invested in the business. But then interest rates soared, the prime rate topped 10 percent and certificates of deposit and other "quality" short-term money instruments were bearing enormous yields. The treasurer who had managed to amass a small cash hoard and put it to work in the money market was widely acclaimed.

But all this basically underscores how easy it often is to miss the true significance of such epochs. The treasurer's job is to fully and profitably employ a firm's capital. And investing temporary idle cash certainly is one of his functions. The emphasis, though, must be on the temporary." A manufacturer of locomotives is not in the *money* management business, unless the board of directors of that concern in its wisdom determines that such is a proper course and alters its underlying capital structure to accommodate such fanciful enterprises. The management of cash to keep idle fund balances fully employed is an important responsibility of the treasurer. But such funds are to be invested not just for the return possible in the money market. They are to be managed primarily so that they support the business itself—and are available when necessary to expand inventory or accommodate a cyclical or seasonal growth in receivables. The funds must also be available to finance any new product development or marketing programs.

Likewise, excessive inventory investment in periods of slowing business activity represents tied-up capital, just as it is true that in those times when the economic expansion is quickening, inadequate inventories also can be costly. In periods of inflation a shortage in raw materials might mean purchases at relatively excessive going prices. Or, depleted levels of finished products might mean lost sales opportunities.

WORKING CAPITAL MANAGEMENT AT UPJOHN

Cash Management

Let us focus more closely on some specific aspects of the current assets and their management as they are handled at Upjohn. For example, cash management as a discipline has received increased emphasis as a result of inflation, high interest rates, liquidity crises and capital shortages. Although the cash manager's specific responsibilities vary widely from company to company, his duties will normally include: (1) cash flow mobilization, (2) bank balance control, and (3) investing surplus cash.

Cash Flow Mobilization. The function of cash flow mobilization is to accelerate the conversion of accounts receivable into cash. Although the first stage is the responsibility of the credit manager, as soon as the customer places a check in the mail, this conversion responsibility shifts to the cash manager who is responsible for transforming the mailed remittance into available cash as quickly as possible.

In performing the conversion procedure, the cash manager focuses on collection float, a measure of the investment resulting from remittances mailed but not yet collected as cash. Collection float has two components—mail float and clearing float. The former is a function of the mail time between the sending location and the receiving location. Some of the tools used by the cash manager to minimize mail float include: (1) lockboxes, (2) depository transfer checks, (3) automated depository transfer checks, and (4) regional concentration accounts. Clearing float measures the volume of remittances which have been deposited, but which because of the time required to clear the checks through the banking system, are not available for use. To control this form of float, the cash manager must be cognizant of clearing availability offered by a potential depository bank. Commercial banks play a big role in cash flow mobilization. In addition to being depository of remittances, they offer a variety of services aimed at reducing mail and clearing float and offer studies aimed at improving cash management systems. (See Chapter 20 for details.)

Controlling Cash Balances. The control of cash balances, as such, is a major function performed by the cash manager. The goal of this duty is to maintain the minimum cash necessary to meet the company's transaction need for cash and to meet compensating balance requirements. Cash must be available to meet the firm's maturing obligations including trade payables, payroll, taxes, sinking-fund payments, and loans. The size of the minimum operating balances obviously will depend on the firm's financial flexibility and the scope of its operations. Financial flexibility implies the ready availability of liquid marketable securities, credit line availability or access to the commercial paper market, all of which allow operating cash balances to be kept at minimum levels.

An important point needs to be emphasized. In managing cash balances, the cash manager must be concerned with *available* balances on the banks' ledgers, not cash balances on the company's ledger. Because of the leads and lags in the timing of accounting for collections and disbursements on the company's and banks' ledgers, only the banks' balances are representative of the firm's actual operating cash position. In addition, the effect of clearing float must be considered when the bank balances are being gathered. As a result, the cash manager must have an information system which provides timely data on available operating balances at his banks.

Investing Cash Surplus. At the same time, unneeded cash balances represent a wasted opportunity associated with capital funds being invested in nonearning assets. As a result, the investment of surplus cash is receiving greater attention, particularly since the opportunity loss associated with idle balances has risen, reflecting the climb in short-term interest rates experienced in recent years.

At the Upjohn Company, our investment policy hinges on three criteria, which in order of importance, are: (1) safety of principal, (2) liquidity, and (3) yield. The principle behind the first criterion is obvious. Any loss of principal is not acceptable. The second criterion follows the definition of the temporary investment function: funds must be available when needed to meet the requirements of normal business operations. The yield criterion ranks last in order and importance, but still is a key factor in the decision-making process. Within the constraints imposed by the safety of principal and liquidity criteria, the goal is to attain the highest possible yield.

Organization. Unlike receivables and inventory management, which lend themselves to the decentralized execution of corporate policies, the cash management function is most efficiently organized on a centralized basis. Fragmentation usually results in excessive idle cash balances, and ignores the economics of scale present in cash management and money market operations.

Accounts Payable Management

In managing working capital, a balance must be struck between risk and flexibility. But current liabilities are not to be overlooked as a source of capital. Proper management procedures might indicate that there is little in the way of flexibility when it comes to paying one's bills. After all, no corporate treasurer wants to be delinquent in meeting financial obligations, or a payroll, or seeing that taxes are promptly met. But it should be recognized that particularly in periods when sales volume slows down, the "payable" category—bills owed to suppliers—tends to lengthen. That is, instead of paying in 30 days the bills are paid in 35 days. Or, the checks to the supplier are drawn on a distant bank, so that it is often possible to pick up another two or three days in cash balances, since it takes that much longer for the check to clear.

If the corporation is on the paying end, it is one thing. But if it is on the receiving end—if it is the one that has to wait a week or more to collect the funds—then that is another matter. Then, the management of working capital requires adjustment so that there are funds available within the corporation to meet the necessary ongoing expenses. In such cases, inadequate cash balances can be crucial, perhaps even necessitating unexpected borrowings that will drive up costs.

The management of the payables function focuses on three areas: (1) taking advantage of the offered terms, (2) ensuring timely payment of trade creditors, and (3) ensuring that cash discounts are taken. On this first count, the firm is availing itself of the working capital financing provided by suppliers. To accomplish this, though, invoices must be paid on the discount or due date. Any early payment dilutes the working capital financing offered by the firm's suppliers.

By the same token, it is important that the payments also be made on time. Late payments or discounts taken after expiration of the discount period can damage the firm's credit standing and hurt a firm's relationship with suppliers. Capitalizing on cash discounts also is profitable. In most cases, providing working capital funds financing by passing up cash discounts is a very expensive form of financing. In the commonly used "2 percent/10, net 30" example, the cost of gaining 20 additional days financing by forgoing the discount is a very high 36 percent per annum.

Managing the Investment in Receivables

The broad category of receivables generally falls into two major classifications—accounts and notes receivable. Our basic philosophy at Upjohn is that a product is not sold until the account is collected. Based on that concept, collection of accounts is a shared responsibility between sales and credit management. In controlling the accounts receivable investment, concern must be directed in the following general areas: (a) terms of sale, (b) reduction of past due balances, and (c) extension of credit. Since terms of sale are generally dictated by competition, economic conditions, and marketing strategies, financial management must work very closely with the marketing staff to reduce the investment in accounts receivable through establishment of terms of sale.

Efforts also must be directed at reducing past due balances to favorably offset the accounts receivable investment. Past due balances can be controlled effectively by establishing written policy and practices as well as performance goals, and setting up a monitoring system. In extending credit, controls on potential losses involved in granting credit to high risk accounts should seek to avoid weakening the working capital position. Implementation of these requirements is required to achieve a system that will result in an optimal accounts receivable investment to the benefit of the overall working capital position.

Centralized and Decentralized Control of Receivables. The concept of managing and controlling the accounts receivable investment can vary based on organizational difference. For example, in an organization where accounts receivable are centralized, direct responsibility for follow-up and control is affected from one source. Hence, there is direct influence over policy, practices, and procedures; the investment can be well controlled and the account status is known at all times by the central authority. However, when the accounts receivable responsibility is decentralized, it can present control difficulties due to communication problems and differing management philosophies of the various entities. Decentralized functions can be controlled through centralized policy and practice, and by the centralized authority monitoring the decentralized functions' goals as compared to actual performance.

Control through Policy. Corporate accounts receivable and credit policies and practices should be established by a corporate authority (corporate credit manager) and endorsed by the corporate treasurer.

Formalized policy and practices aid prompt collections and improve the working capital position by requiring consistent follow-up, timely write-offs of bad debts, and referral of past due accounts for collection. Strict compliance by the decentralized credit functions and support of their local sales management will provide for improved collection experience and an improved working capital position.

Establishing and Monitoring Goals. Improvements in accounts receivable balances are also achieved as a result of establishing goals or objectives. These goals are established jointly by the Corporate Credit Management (central control) function and the decentral-

ized (business, division, subsidiary) function. In developing goals
it is most important that goals are realistic, strive for improvement,
and are comparable to industry averages. During the latter part of
each year, Corporate Credit Management requests goals from the
decentralized functions for the following areas: (1) accounts receivable month-end dollar balances, (2) estimated past due dollars by
month, and (3) estimated bad debts by month.

From these estimates, the corporate group calculates control
measurements (goals) as follows: day sales outstanding, accounts
receivable per dollar sale, past due percentages, and investment
in accounts receivable (A/R as percent of sales). These are calculated for the current periods (monthly) as well as for a 12-month
moving average, where applicable. The results are prepared and
forwarded to each division/subsidiary for its agreement. Once
agreed to, the goals become a target for the current year.

Establishing goals is merely the beginning. Improvement will
come only through monitoring and measuring actual performance
against established goals. To do this, the respective divisions and
businesses must report each month's actual performance. This is
done by providing the corporate group with monthly agings of account information regarding bad debt write-offs, and status and
activity reports. As information is received by the Corporate Credit
Management group, actual performance is calculated and various
reports and analyses are generated to reflect actual performance
compared to established goals. Corporate Credit Management reports are circulated to various levels of management for their review and comments.

Divisions or subsidiaries who are not achieving goals are contacted by Corporate Credit Management and its assistance is
offered to help improve performance or an explanation of variance
is requested.

In summary, a totally satisfactory accounts receivable control
system in a decentralized organization is a joint effort of the corporate group and the divisions or subsidiaries. The primary responsibility for achieving established goals belongs to operating
management. When these goals are not being achieved it is the
responsibility of the corporate group to work in concert with operating management to identify problems and related solutions and
assist in implementation of corrective action. These efforts in establishing and meeting goals and following corporate accounts receiv-

able and credit policies and practices will result in achieving the desired working capital position as it relates to accounts receivable.

Inventory Management

The management of inventory investment rests on the basic premise that inventory is created when the decision to acquire is made. Therefore, the time to manage inventory investment is at this point of acquisition. The size of the inventory is dependent on the decision of "how much" and "when." The *decision* to acquire inventory is a management decision. It must rest on an assessment of forecasted demand, manufacturing costs, the risk of short supplies and a balancing of alternative uses for the money invested in this working capital item.

There are three basic overall objectives in the managing of a company's investment in inventories: (1) to have adequate quantities of finished products on hand to meet sales requirements, (2) to have adequate quantities of raw and/or semiprocessed materials to meet production schedules, and (3) to have a minimum amount of money tied up in these categories.

In practice, it is necessary to alter these objectives because their relationship to one another makes it impossible to pursue one goal without throwing the other out of balance. Inventory management policy, therefore, must seek to optimize these relationships. While the objective is to balance cost on the one hand with potential opportunity loss on the other, it must be recognized that neither cost nor risk can be stated as precise numbers. To make them as accurate as possible, the department most qualified (and also accountable and responsible) must supply the factors used in computing this balance. None of the functional areas involved with flow of materials can be examined independently. They must be considered as a part of the total management system.

The actual flow of goods through various businesses differs widely. But the principles of materials management are the same. In a large, diversified company, control of inventory investment must be attained through the development of corporate policies, practices and procedures. The execution of these established policies is decentralized, with each of the business segments managing their flow of goods within corporate policy.

At Upjohn, a corporate unit under the treasurer has the responsibility for developing Corporate Inventory Management policies, practices and procedures in concert with line management. An overall inventory investment goal consists of individual goals by the various business segments. Inventory required to support sales and production varies by business for a number of reasons—type of industry, nature of the product, cost, marketing strategy, and management style.

The primary responsibility for achieving established goals belongs to operating management. When goals are not being achieved, it is the responsibility of Corporate Inventory Management to work in concert with operating management to identify problems and related solutions and to assist in implementing corrective action.

Inventory investment is necessary to support the desired sales level. The inventory-to-sales relationship is utilized to establish a realistic goal and also to aid in measuring performance. Average month-end inventory over the last 12 months was the investment maintained to support the sales for the past year—the "cents in inventory" to support "one dollar of sales." The determination of these guidelines compares this important segment of working capital to the revenue to be generated.

A PHILOSOPHICAL APPROACH

This brings us to a philosophical approach to working capital management that may very well be the most important consideration of a treasurer running the financial function. There are two principal considerations here. One is the integration of working capital management with the overall corporate organization. The other, since working capital management has long been a one-year-at-a-time proposition in keeping with the view that current positions are of only 12 months' duration, relates to working capital management planning for periods that stretch five or ten years into the future.

Let us take the last item first. We know that balance sheets are prepared presumably to provide a picture of a corporation's financial health at a given point in time. We know, too, that this presentation is somewhat artificial. After all, a business is a dynamic activity. It is an ongoing operation and a unique organization that enjoys, all other things being equal, perpetual life. The presentation of a working capital position then has to be viewed at a particular point in a corporation's cycles of activity. Consequently, there are both short- and long-term trends to consider.

The short-term factors relate largely to seasonal influences. A retailer's cash needs are vastly greater on October 31 than they are on January 31, after the important Christmas holiday season is over, and inventories have been liquidated, often with the help of year-end sales. A construction company may be affected by its order backlog, and its need to stockpile necessary parts to complete whatever projects it has under way. Thus, while not purely seasonal, there are timing influences peculiar to virtually every business. These must be taken into consideration with regard to planning working capital requirements.

As a rule, most treasurers recognize these short-run considerations and, in one fashion or another, plan for them. But what too often goes by the board is any blueprinting for working capital needs over the longer haul, say five or ten years. Yet if an organization is to grow, longer term requirements are no less crucial than preparing for immediate working capital needs. Naturally, there are differences. Looking ahead is fraught with all kinds of perils, since it requires making judgments about time periods in which the economic, financial, political, and social factors are at best uncertain.

But the vital point is that to a treasurer the presence of uncertainty should represent no block to planning. One can—and should—factor in assumptions, based on a variety of parameters. But the starting point must be a general knowledge of the direction in which the corporation is headed, particularly the aspirations of management with regard to marketing and product development, and with all that suggests in the way of plant additions or expansion, raw materials acquisitions, and enlargement of the working force.

There is, moreover, another factor to take into consideration—the international horizons. More and more, as the globe "shrinks," companies are reaching out to international markets. In foreign places, customs and modes of doing business are quite different from those in domestic markets. Payment periods may be longer, requiring great cash resources to finance overseas activities. We have found at Upjohn, for example, that financing international sales is more costly than domestic sales.

Similarly, the not-so-simple matter of currency devaluations or revaluations imposes other responsibilities upon the financial manager. Thus, hedging operations in the foreign exchange market may be indicated, or borrowing in local currencies may be desirable to preclude undue risks to working capital invested abroad.

This applies no less to forecasting the cash flow. In managing working capital, the treasurer is basically attempting to determine the corporate requirement for funds. The capital is important for what it can buy in the way of inventories and receivables. The efficiency with which cash is utilized relates to the collectibility cycle of receivables, no less than the turnover of receivables.

But cash needs have to be planned. And the only way that can be done is by anticipation of various operating levels based on different business scenarios. For example, at Upjohn we started planning our demands for cash because of growing receivables, expanding inventories, and because our capital requirements as projected were in excess of the cash we were generating. When a treasurer starts running out of cash, he starts looking for ways to conserve. And it does not take much calculus to visualize the effect of, say, a reduction of 15 to 20 percent in the average maturity of receivables. If there is $100 million invested in receivables, and if with better collections, more timely billing procedures, or perhaps appropriate discounts, the figure can be reduced by 15 percent, then that is $15 million less tied up in receivables or inventories.

The vital factor here is a constant monitoring of the plan. This requires regular evaluation of the underlying premises. And in fact it pays off in other less direct ways such as sharpening awareness of the many factors that come to play on working capital investments. Thus regular evaluation of long-term influences helps materially to heighten sensitivity to present forces, which, in turn, helps improve daily performance.

At Upjohn, for example, we noted over one five-year period, a surge in inventories and receivables that was outpacing our dramatic growth in sales. This huge increase in current assets caused Upjohn to step back and take a hard look at how working capital was being managed. In the process we discovered that the nature of our business had changed drastically. No longer were we solely a domestic pharmaceutical producer, but rather a large, international, multibusiness corporation. Hence, we changed our view of ourselves, a shift which fostered alterations as well in policies and operational goals all along the line.

In terms of the working capital management, it necessitated (1) the institution of new financial controls through a policy of strong but decentralized operations, and (2) a better definition of who is responsible and accountable for making the decisions that determine changes in working capital.

Here we come to the aspect of working capital management that is probably most important—the integration of the financial management function with the corporation as a whole. Upjohn's approach has been to develop a management system that basically controls the flow of goods from acquisition to the time of sale. In this plan, the treasurer exercises functional responsibility. With wide geographic dispersion it is impractical to have organizational control over all of the asset management functions. Thus, in the absence of organizational control, the treasurer must have policy—or as we call it, functional—responsibility.

However, we also feel strongly that the place to manage the asset is where the decision to invest in it is being made. The method of getting to that place is by defining the flow of goods. At Upjohn we traced the flow from the ultimate customer, back through marketing, distribution, production and purchasing. Once this flow was defined, we were able to determine who was responsible at each stage.

The flowchart at Upjohn would be depicted as follows: A forecast is made by marketing, followed by a production plan. Raw materials are acquired, production is scheduled and, as the plan is executed, value is added to the raw material. The product is packaged, sent to the distribution center, and finally delivered to the customer. All through this process, decisions have been made involving production, marketing, credit, and distribution. Thus marketing controls the acquisition of inventory, since it forecasts demand and establishes the customers' level of service.

Now let us take the situation one step further. The product is sold and becomes a receivable. The salesman is figuratively responsible for collection. The financial manager, though, helps him in defining parameters and risks. If the salesman cannot collect, the credit manager moves in and a plan is worked out to turn that receivable into cash. The credit manager also establishes limits on how much the client can owe.

Once this procedure of defining the flow of goods is established, financial management has to develop an information system on which reasonable decisions can be made with regard to forecasting sales, keeping inventories at adequate levels, seeing to the availability of raw materials and collecting receivables promptly. This information must be timely and accurate.

At Upjohn, we divided the various facets into modules—a forecasting module, a distribution module, a planning and scheduling module, and a control module. Information developed by the sales and production people in each area is fed into the modules. This encompasses not only major divisions, but each product as well.

This procedure underscores that the responsibility for the flow of goods does not belong to the financial manager alone. Marketing and production decisions greatly influence the levels of working capital. Therefore, they share responsibility for its management.

However—and this is the key—it is the treasurer that keeps it all together. He defines the flow of goods; develops material management systems to manage the flow; defines responsibility and accountability for decisions required in the system; and establishes goals and measures performances against goals.

In our view, the pivotal role of forecasting demand and establishing the customer level of service as well as the time of delivery rests with marketing. This is a very significant concept. For by extension it also is saying that from marketing flows the decisions with regard to production and inventory. Hence, if marketing determines production, it also ultimately determines levels of working capital.

And this is where the manager of working capital comes in. Most companies today are complex organizations, turning out a multitude of products for markets that may be diverse or allied. In this environment, the treasurer assumes a vital role. He makes certain that the responsibility and accountability for decisions required in the system are known. He also establishes goals and measures performances against these goals. The goals are little more than the corporation's objectives, and as defined in the policy manual, all decisions must be consistent with them.

The treasurer's role with regard to managing working capital becomes one of identification, monitoring, measuring, and, most critically, helping to make timely adjustments and connections. Based on this input and the centralized overview he must have—not only of the complex organization and its needs, but also the external factors relating to economic and financial forces—it is possible to chart a plan that will help assure the corporation's financial health.

The key in this arrangement is integration. For the treasurer to be sitting in isolated splendor, charting interest rates and measuring rates of return, is sheer folly. The necessity is to function as a member of the management team, but particularly one whose unique responsibility demands awareness and sensitivity.

To summarize, increases in the current assets—cash, receivables, and inventory—all represent uses of funds. Increases in fixed assets, and capital expenditures are also very large users of funds. But, for every use of funds there must be a source of funds. Increases in the current liabilities, accounts payable, and accruals are sources of funds, but the two most important sources are profit and borrowed money. Hence one cannot look at current asset management without also looking at current liability management. In other words, working capital management is a part of the larger job of financial management, which is defined as the total management of all sources and uses of funds.

If the management focus is only on asset management and the optimization of uses of funds, it could result in less emphasis on sources of funds, which could be to the detriment of the shareholder. The objective of management should be to optimize the value of the shareholder's equity. To achieve this objective, three elements must exist—organizational environment, information systems, and competent people.

Organizational Environment

Each employee contributes something different, but all must contribute toward a common goal or objective. Achievement of objectives requires that each job be directed toward the objectives of the business. In particular, each manager must focus on the ultimate success of the corporation. Results are measured by the contribution made to the success of the business.

In most businesses, managers are not automatically directed toward a common goal. For an objective to be meaningful, it must meet two criteria: it must be attainable and it must be measurable. Furthermore, it must be established at the top, and followed by the development of policies and a structure which will facilitate attainment.

Policy and structure must be developed in concert—not in conflict. In concert, managers must define:

What is to be managed and the results required.

What decisions have to be made.

When to achieve the required results.

Who is responsible and accountable for the decision.

How such decisions should be made.

And last, but not least, managers must participate effectively in the development of informational control systems which will permit measurement of actual performance against objectives.

ADDITIONAL SOURCES

Aigner, D. J., and Sprenkle, C. M. "On Optimal Financing of Cyclical Cash Needs." *Journal of Finance,* 28 (December 1973), 1249–54.

Beranek, William. *Working Capital Management.* Belmont, Calif: Wadsworth, 1968.

Cossaboom, Roger A. "Let's Reassess the Profitability-Liquidity Trade-off." *Financial Executive,* 39 (May 1971), 46–51.

Glautier, M. W. E. "Towards a Reformulation of the Theory of Working Capital." *Journal of Business Finance,* 3 (Spring 1971), 37–42.

Hunt, Pearson. "Funds Position: Keystone in Financial Planning." *Harvard Business Review,* 53 (May-June 1975), 106–15.

Knight, W. D. "Working Capital Management: Satisficing versus Optimization." *Financial Management,* 1 (Spring 1972), 33–40.

Ludeman, Douglas. "Corporate Liquidity in Perspective." *Financial Executive,* 42 (October 1974), 18–22.

Merville, L. J., and Tavis, L. A. "Optimal Working Capital Policies: A Chance-Constrained Programming Approach." *Journal of Financial and Quantitative Analysis,* 8 (January 1973), 47–60.

Pettway, Richard H., and Walker, Ernest W. "Asset Mix, Capital Structure, and the Cost of Capital." *Southern Journal of Business* (April 1968), 34–43.

Schiff, Michael, and Lieber, Zvi. "A Model for the Integration of Credit and Inventory Management." *Journal of Finance,* 29 (March 1974), 133–40.

Smith, Keith V. *Management of Working Capital: A Reader.* New York: West, 1974.

Smith, Keith V. "State of the Art of Working Capital Management." *Financial Management,* 2 (Autumn 1973), 50–55.

Stancill, James McN. *The Management of Working Capital.* Scranton, Pa.: Intext Educational Publishers, 1971.

Stone, Bernell K. "Cash Planning and Credit-Line Determination with a Financial Statement Simulator: A Cash Report on Short-Term Financial Planning." *Journal of Financial and Quantitative Analysis,* 8 (December 1973), 711–30.

Tinsley, P. A. "Capital Structure, Precautionary Balances, and Valuation of the Firm: The Problem of Financial Risk," *Journal of Financial and Quantitative Analysis,* 5 (March 1970), 33–62.

Van Horne, James C. "A Risk-Return Analysis of a Firm's Working-Capital Position." *Engineering Economist,* 14 (Winter 1969), 71–89.

Walker, Ernest W. "Towards a Theory of Working Capital." *Engineering Economist,* 9 (January-February 1964), 21–35.

Walter, James E. "Determination of Technical Solvency." *Journal of Business,* 30 (January 1959), 30–43.

Chapter 20

Cash Management: Helping Meet the Capital Crisis

Frederick W. Searby[*]

A FEW YEARS AGO, I wrote an article for the *Harvard Business Review* in which I had the fun of likening overlooked opportunities in cash management to the disguised value of the Maltese Falcon in the Humphrey Bogart movie of the same name.[1] The article pointed out that, just as the Maltese Falcon—a gold statue covered with precious stones encased in a black enamel—was passed from hand to hand for centuries without anyone's recognizing its true value, many businesses were overlooking internal wealth by not getting beneath the surface of their cash-gathering and disbursing systems.

Since that time, a number of forces have brought cash management to a noticeably higher level in both visibility and effectiveness. Corporate financial officers have turned aggressively to cash-gathering and disbursing systems to reduce mounting interest costs and help get through two worldwide liquidity crises. A number of relatively new cash-gathering and disbursing techniques have come into use, and the use of various short-term, cash investment vehicles has increased.

During this period, it has been particularly satisfying to watch

---

[*] Frederick W. Searby is a director of McKinsey & Company, Inc., and manager of the Cleveland, Ohio, office.
[1] Frederick W. Searby, "Use Your Hidden Cash Resources," *Harvard Business Review*, March–April 1968.

the dramatic, positive shift in the attitude of U.S. commercial banks toward cash management. From a largely defensive posture, banks have moved to enthusiastically promoting cash management assistance and taking a leadership role in innovating cash-gathering and disbursing techniques. The combined actions of U.S. corporations and commercial banks show up in the continued decline in corporate demand deposits in relation to overall activity as measured, for example, against the sales of U.S. manufacturing companies. In absolute terms, the secular trend of industrial companies' demand deposits is only slightly upward.

Notwithstanding this considerable progress, corporate financial officers face a new set of challenges in the cash management area. First, the second half of the 1970s and the early 1980s are likely to see fierce competition for capital which will lead companies back to a reexamination of internal asset reduction—particularly if the trend to declining returns on invested capital continues. Second, cash managers of companies with international interests are faced with the extra dimension of managing cash on a worldwide basis. Those who have ignored the need—not to say the opportunity—of integrating overseas divisions in their cash management (and overall financial planning) have felt the stinging penalties of higher than necessary interest costs and some dramatic currency exchange losses.

Finally corporate financial officers must deal in cash management with the same inexorable facts of life which confront all functions of a business; i.e., the need to respond to changing markets and technologies. Changing markets in the cash management context include shifts in: the scale and sources of remittances; prompt payment discounts given and applied; mailing time differentials; the services and charges of commercial banks; and the return, marketability, and safety of various vehicles for investing short-term funds. Among the technological factors which will force reexamination of even currently efficient cash management systems are: electronic funds transfer, increased use of noncheck/noncash payment mechanisms, changes in the structure and regulations of the Federal Reserve System (e.g., a revision to Regulation J, which governs clearing time allowances among commercial banks, and the creation of the Regional Check Processing Centers), and the increased cost effectiveness of the computer and high-speed data transmission channels.

Thus, corporate financial officers—whether they are currently operating effective cash management processes or not—find themselves with the same need for reexamination. And, as this chapter suggests, cash management in the late 70s and early 80s is likely to call for new responses and the application of proven approaches in both the establishment of an overall program and the execution of the major elements of the cash management job.

Establishing an Overall Program

Effective cash management begins with the recognition that it is an integral part of the overall planning processes of a business and must be carried out with the inputs of individuals in virtually all functions. The treasurer or his subordinate usually provides leadership and overall control, but many nonfinancial executives must contribute on an ongoing basis:

1. All major functions—engineering, manufacturing, marketing, data processing—in estimating the amount and timing of major receipts and disbursements (see discussion of cash forecasting below).
2. Marketing and credit personnel in providing intelligence and evaluating alternative credit terms and customer billing and collection procedures.
3. Purchasing personnel in providing intelligence and in evaluating alternative payment practices by vendors.
4. Data processing and accounting personnel in providing support for cash-gathering and disbursing practices and analyzing the economics of different configurations.
5. Field personnel—who may report through any one of several functions—in invoicing, billing, disbursing, and remittance processing.

Top-management involvement in cash management follows from this multifunction participation and the accompanying need to make trade-offs, some of which involve risk of one kind or another. Consider the following example.

A major U.S. oil company found that it was mailing each month $10 million in royalty payments 12 days ahead of industry practice and 15 days ahead of legal requirements in most states. Given the critical importance of maintaining good relationships with the production partners, the initial reaction of the production department to the possibility of changing payment schedules was understandably unenthusiastic. However, with the support of the company president, and after the legal department was consulted, the company began coding its royalty accounts so as to release computer-printed checks on an average of 12 days later than before. The recurring value to the company was nearly $250,000 a year based on the additional use of $10 million for 12 extra days each month.

Other points of risk which usually call for top-management review include vendor payment policies, selection of short-term cash investment vehicles, customer terms, currency hedging policies, and commercial bank relationships.

Top management may be specially concerned with the impact of cash management programs on commercial banking relationships. This is normal, since commercial banks are an increasingly important credit source for many companies and senior bank officers sit on many corporate boards as well as being influential in the business community. Thus, most treasurers ensure early on that they and their senior executives are in agreement concerning the basic posture to be maintained regarding commercial banks in general and individual banks which are particularly important.

The general philosophy which many cash managers have adopted toward commercial banks includes these specific characteristics:

Maintaining an Arm's-Length, Businesslike Relationship.   Most businesses favor a long-term relationship with an individual bank or a small group of banks based on mutual familiarity of needs and capabilities which this relationship fosters. While it is unusual to see any real evidence of major preferential treatment by the bank, it is not reasonable for either the company or the bank to expect a relationship which does not offer an attractive return to each party's shareholders in the long run.

From the company's point of view, this usually means maintaining a sense of competition among banks serving it and periodically making systematic evaluation of the competitive cost-effectiveness of banking services being used.

Being Tough-Minded in Evaluating a Bank's Services.   Few companies need all the services offered by the many banks with which they deal. Effective cash managers make selective use of banking services from the point of view of long-term full value of service as opposed to "cherry-picking."

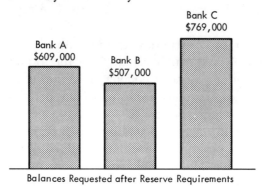

FIGURE 1
Balances Required to Support Uniform
Tangible Services
Can Vary Substantially

Bank A $609,000

Bank B $507,000

Bank C $769,000

Balances Requested after Reserve Requirements

		Bank A	*Bank B*	*Bank C*
1.	Unit activity costs			
	Checks deposited.	0.023	0.02	0.045
	Deposit slips	0.12	0.10	–
	Checks paid	0.065	0.06	0.09
	Wire transfers	1.75	1.65	1.65
	Reconcilement	0.029	–	$54 + 0.015
	Account maintenance	–	$ 1.50	$ 2.60
2.	Monthly activity costs	$ 2,952.00	$ 2,706.00	$ 4,332.00
3.	Earnings allowance	5.82%	6.41%	6.75%
4.	Balances requested			
	(after reserve requirements).	$609,000.00	$507,000.00	$769,000.00

Understanding the Full Economics of a Banking Relationship from Both Sides and Being Willing to Negotiate. Figure 1 illustrates the fundamental fact that banks' costs, earnings allowances, and terms are not fixed but vary from bank to bank. In the example used, Company X received a spread of over 150 percent in the bids made by three large, reputable banks for the same collection service. These terms are usually negotiable, but as in any negotiation, it is desirable to understand the economics of the banking relationship—*from the bank's point of view*—to identify points of leverage.

Thus, effective cash management begins with top-management support, companywide participation, and a well-thought-out philosophy toward commercial banks. With this as a framework, management is in a position to make appropriate decisions in the four major areas of the cash management job:

1. Designing the cash-gathering system.
2. Controlling disbursements.
3. Investing short-term funds.
4. Cash forecasting.

Designing the Cash-Gathering System

The cash-gathering system is defined by (*a*) the practices and location of billing processes, (*b*) the designation of remittance points, and (*c*) the mechanisms used for moving funds from the points at which they first enter the company's gathering system to the place where they are eventually used. Well-designed cash-gathering systems should not represent a single response but rather multiple solutions for dealing with different classes of trade, different billing patterns, different locations and, for multinational companies, different customs, currencies, and banking practices.

Getting the Bills Out. The starting point in examining a company's cash management processes is in the preparation of bills, where the company's control is quite high and there is frequently a sizable opportunity to free up cash. There is clear interface between receivables and cash, which explains in part the apparent legerdemain of companies which are able to extract more cash than they show on their asset statements. For example:

1. A financial services company, which reported cash balances of $8 million, took $18 million out and only slightly reduced its stated cash balances.
2. A transportation company that only showed cash balances of $9 million drew a total of $17 million out of its cash-gathering and disbursing system to help finance a major equipment acquisition program.

In each of these cases, the company was able to accelerate the conversion of receivables into cash available for use. Thus, a major part of the "cash" free-up actually came from the receivables account.

This sizable potential for cash free-up should lead treasurers to undertake joint ventures with controllers to accelerate billing, challenging where appropriate marketing shibboleths (e.g., "Our customers will go elsewhere if we ask them to pay earlier") or industry customs.[2] Some actions frequently fruitful are given below:

Accelerating Invoice Data. The American Telephone & Telegraph Company has led the way in using the computer and high-speed transmission of data over telephone lines to get credit card and collect call charges into billing centers. Smaller manufacturing companies frequently can speed the transmission of invoice data to billing sections by manual means. For example, a midwestern electric utility transports meter cards by truck each day from field offices to a central computer center.

Mailing Bills Promptly. This seems elemental, but a major U.S. railroad found that an accounting section was delaying the mailing of bills on interline settlements with other railroads by unnecessarily waiting to net their claims against the incoming claims of other railroads that sent out bills less promptly.

Identifying Customer Payment Locations. Many industrial companies centralize their accounts payable function for major vendors. This practice gives the vendor an opportunity to get paid more quickly by obtaining permission from local purchasing representatives to bill the customer directly at its central disbursement location, sending a "for information" copy to the local purchasing office. Agreements can also be made for follow-up audits to settle any points of difference. Some customers may object to this compression of the payable process. But surprisingly perhaps, many do accept direct billing—at least for trusted vendors—as a legitimate request and a way to reduce local paper work. Another version of direct billing which is coming into increasing acceptance is the presentation of bills by utility companies directly to customers' commercial banks. The system obviates the need for the customer to make periodic payments of routine bills, yet he retains the right to refuse payment.

Designing Creative Terms to Accelerate Bill Payment. The prompt payment discount is a classic means of encouraging customers to make their payment ahead of normal terms. Still some companies are able to be considerably more creative and have a higher impact than others with their credit terms. One electric utility

---

[2] As a caution, receivables which, measured in days of sales, appear quite reasonable, often mask levels of receivables for a particular class of trade, channel of distributor, geographic area, which are clearly out of line.

has been able to outperform the industry sales/receivables ratio by offering a small but enticing discount. In general, however, prompt payment discounts are an expensive and frequently unjustified means of accelerating payments.

Selecting Remittance Points. Most cash managers today have pushed past the point of automatically assuming that customer remittances have to be directed to accounting or credit centers or that gathering or concentration banks have to be placed in cities where the company has sales offices. Figure 2 shows a collection pattern used by a widely spread national manufacturer which incorporates local depository banks, regional concentration banks, and a central bank. The final determination of remittance points depends in large part on the mechanism used for moving funds to disbursing locations (see below) but the following generalizations can be offered about the selection of a concentration bank in a cash-gathering network:

a. The bank should be in the Federal Reserve city which is serving the collection area.

b. The bank should have access to the bank wire system.

c. The bank should receive a large percentage—over 90 percent— of deposited checks one day after they are mailed.

d. The bank should offer competitive earnings allowances, activity charges, compensating-balance requirements, and funds availability.

Moving Funds. Three mechanisms are useful for accelerating the movement of funds beyond normal check processing. Each of these impacts on the acceleration of funds flows in different ways and has a different cost. Various versions of these mechanisms are offered by individual banks.

Depository Transfer Check. This is normally the simplest and least costly way to move money and is used by companies whose customers remit to local sales offices. Daily, the local representative deposits the remittance in a local bank and then mails the depository transfer check to a concentration (intermediate) bank. This bank then credits the funds to the customer's account, putting the check into the clearing process. Although this process is automatic in that no action is required by the corporate cash manager, funds availability is limited by postal and clearing times.

A variation on this process is for the local representative to call in the amount of the daily deposit to the concentration bank, which

FIGURE 2
Cash-Gathering System—National Company Serving Several Classes of Trade

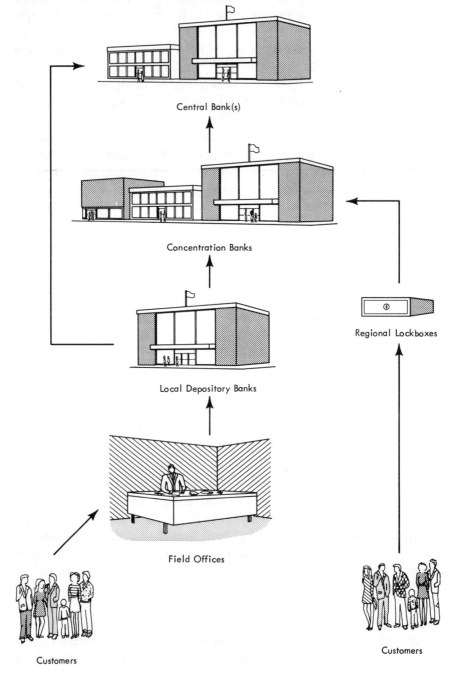

Central Bank(s)

Concentration Banks

Local Depository Banks

Regional Lockboxes

Field Offices

Customers

Customers

prepares and sets into clearing the depository transfer check. Thus, postal time is avoided.

Wire Transfers. A wire transfer of funds between banks provides a means of making funds collected at one bank immediately available for use at a bank in another city. Many banks offer a choice of several transfer systems, including the Federal Reserve Wire, Bank Wire, and TWX.

Obviously, wire transfers require that both the sending and receiving banks have access to the particular transfer system used. And, of course, wire transfers involve added costs. The economic trade-off is the value of accelerating the movement of funds over alternative, less costly means (e.g., depository transfer check). Generally, different cost/benefit trade-offs, plus the need to leave some funds in the gathering system for compensation purposes, encourages cash managers to use a variety of transfer means.

Wire transfers can be automated by leaving standing instructions with gathering banks for the automatic transfer of collected balances above the level needed to compensate each bank for its services. This procedure can be an effective way of managing complex cash-gathering systems, and the need for daily communication with remote locations or a formal, daily decision is eliminated.

Lockboxes. The processing of remittances can frequently be accelerated by the use of a post office box which is cleared directly by a gathering or concentration bank. The principal value to most corporate customers is in getting funds collected and available for use more quickly, because the accounting (updating of receivables) is done *after* instead of *before* cash depositing. The design of lockbox services varies somewhat among banks, especially in numbers of daily clearances and service charges. The administrative charges for this service by the bank usually approximate the cost of doing the work internally, and thus the economics of the lockbox decision depend largely on the value of accelerating cash collection.

Many banks will provide a tape or other input (ready for direct use) in the company's accounts receivable processing so that second handling of the remittances is not necessary. Banks will also separate and transmit to the corporate customer remittances which require special handling (e.g., complaints).

Monitoring the Cash-Gathering System. The analogy is often made that cash management is an inventory control problem. The funds in the gathering system—which for large companies can comprise hundreds of thousands of customers and several hundred banks —have a cost, as does inventory, and a flow and level based on both entries and withdrawals. Thus, up-to-date real data is essential. Effective cash managers focus on the high-volume leverage points in the cash gathering system much as an inventory manager may segment his inventory using an ABC classification. Automatic decision rules for funds transfers based on economics and projected activity levels are used by the cash manager the way the inventory manager uses automatic reorders based on EOQs (economic order quantities).

Without trying to identify their inventory equivalent, cash managers frequently find the following actions helpful:

Periodic Auditing of Actual Transfers by Gathering Banks against the Agreed-to Automatic Transfer Points. This is necessary to ensure attention and discipline in commercial banks' vast paper work/ clerically staffed operations centers.

Use of Actual Collected Bank Balances as a Basis for Transfer Decisions. This is necessary in cash-gathering as well as disbursing (see below) to get behind accounting fictions to discover real "inventories" of funds available to the business.

Use of Real-Time Communications to Track Available Funds. This is necessary to circumvent the increasing slowness of the U.S. (and most foreign) mail systems. Leased telephone lines and internal communications networks can provide a low-cost means for staying on top of cash availabilities in important but remote locations. For companies which do not have low-cost internal communications networks, outside service agencies (e.g., the National Data Corporation) will provide daily tracking data on what may be an economically attractive basis.

Periodic Auditing of Internal Cash Processing. This is necessary to overcome the persistent tendency of administrative and clerical people to worry more about the bookkeeping than getting the cash into use. Occasionally, even more highly placed personnel suffer from the same lapses as in the case of a vice president of a large chemical company who carried in his briefcase for two weeks a customer's check for $250,000.

By way of contrast, a diversified financial services company has established a separate priority process for opening, before normal business hours, mail addressed to its factoring operations which frequently have large, credit-sensitive remittances.

Controlling Disbursements

Potentially, controlling disbursements offers exceptionally high leverage for freeing up working capital in a short period of time.

A major U.S. wholesaler elected to delay its payments to its suppliers by one day. Receiving no adverse response, it then delayed its payments to its suppliers by an additional day, thereby freeing up some $12 million in cash. The second delay provoked a handful of inquiries but the wholesaler has been able to maintain his revised payment policy even in a period of some scarcities.

Naturally, payments policies are an area of some sensitivity; misapplied, they can produce friction with important suppliers or even affect a company's credit rating. One would like to think that for companies who systematically take unfair advantage of their customers, some chickens come home to roost in periods of shortages.

Beyond policy changes in accounts payable practices, cash managers have opportunities in the following areas: (1) control of disbursement practices, (2) matching disbursements with check clearings, (3) reducing the number of local accounts, and (4) use of bank draft payment mechanisms.

Controlling Disbursement Practices. It is not unusual for policy discrepancies to creep into payment practices. The policies are thought out in the top circles of a company while the practices are carried out in remote clerical staffs which may be characterized by turnover and an aversion to risk-taking. The former may lead to a lack of understanding of policy, while the latter usually encourages prepaying to avoid any risk of criticism. Most companies of any size have computerized the accounts payable function so that individual vendor accounts can be date-coded to trigger payment by the computer and facilitate mailing on the appropriate date. This is still an area which warrants periodic audit as well as review.

Matching Disbursements with Clearings. Figure 3 illustrates the phenomenon familiar to virtually all financial managers—actual cash balances in a disbursing account in excess of the book balances shown in the company's accounting records. The cash balances less checks in collection are the funds actually available for use by the company or (less reserves) by the bank. Using this float is entirely ethical and should not be confused with "kiting" checks—i.e., drawing checks for local payment on a deliberately remote bank in order to exploit collection times and/or—a variation on the famous "Ponzi"

FIGURE 3
Actual Funds Available while Company Y's Books Showed Zero Balances

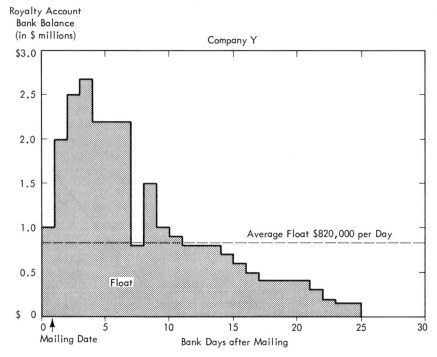

Royalty Account
Bank Balance
(in $ millions)

swindle scheme—maintaining funds deficiencies by depositing checks which are not backed by funds simultaneously in banks which are widely separated from each other.

Within ethical limits, companies can substantially reduce idle cash by effective matching of disbursements and check-clearing. This is undoubtedly a major element in the practices of companies like C.I.T. Corporation which, although it uses $1 billion of short-term money, "usually concludes a working day with no cash in its banks above the compensating balances needed to maintain credit lines."[3] Some useful techniques as follows:

1. Separation of major recurring disbursements into special-purpose accounts—for example, payroll, dividend, federal tax, and construction.
2. Periodic analysis of the clearing times on these accounts using

_____

[3] See the article written by the treasurer of C.I.T., Alfred De Salvo, "Cash Management Converts Dollars into Working Assets," *Harvard Business Review,* May–June 1972.

statistical techniques (many commercial banks provide this analysis as a service).

3. Establishment of zero balance accounts for all special disbursements. These accounts are replenished out of a central account so that it is not necessary to maintain a special reserve in each account.

Reducing the Number of Local Accounts.   Companies maintaining small working funds in field locations frequently find that the aggregate balance of these funds is quite large. Centralized disbursing and bank credit draft systems (discussed below) can reduce the amount of cash tied up in this fashion (several million dollars for one retail company operating in 25 states) while achieving better control and lower administrative costs.

Using Bank Drafts.   Bank drafts are receiving increasing use as a method of improving control and lowering administrative costs. The draft drawn by an individual—who can be a company employee or a vendor—is presented directly to the bank for payment. Obviously, this tends to compress the accounts payable payment time, but in return it reduces administrative costs and helps eliminate the need for multiple working balances. Under most plans, the company has the right to return drafts not meeting predetermined standards— amount, signature, or date—and the per item processing charges are lower than for checks.

Managing Short-Term Investments

Most companies have the opportunity to invest cash which cannot be permanently taken out of the system—i.e., by reducing debt or declaring a dividend—but is temporarily available. For large companies, even investing idle funds systematically over the weekend can produce a significant addition to annual income.

Cash investment opportunities can only be identified and implemented if a company has (1) rigorous control of cash-gathering and disbursing (discussed earlier in this chapter), (2) effective cash forecasting (discussed later in this chapter), and (3) an aggressive, detail-oriented attention to cash balances.

The choice of investment instrument depends in part on the mechanism for effecting the conversion from demand deposit to investment and back to demand deposit. Since this involves use of funds already on deposit, it is often logical to select investment vehicles marketed by commercial banks: certificates of deposit, U.S. Treasury certificate, or repurchase agreement.

The decision to consider a range of other investment alternatives including direct or dealer-placed commercial paper depends in part on the yield, risk, and liquidity of the particular instrument in question. Many U.S. companies have moved from a policy of U.S. Treasury bills only in the late 1950s and early 1960s to a more aggressive investment policy; in the early 1970s this policy was revised when a combination of failures and near-failures of some major paper issuers redirected attention back to lower risk borrowers.

For companies with large short-term investments, it is useful to take a portfolio approach by segmenting investments according to their purpose, such as (1) certain near-term obligation (e.g., tax payment); (2) certain medium-term obligation (e.g., construction work-in-process payment): (3) uncertain business fluctuation cushion (e.g., to maintain dividends or capital expenditures during earnings downturns); and (4) opportunities or crisis fund which may be held for years. With this structuring, different liquidities can be bought, offering at the less liquid end a higher rate of after-tax return (e.g., purchase of preferred stocks which have a low effective tax rate).

Cash Forecasting

Most companies today use computer-based financial simulation models for projecting their cash flows. These forecasts provide useful perspective, but frequently are not in fine detail and describe accounting rather than cash flows. Fortunately, effective cash forecasting for cash management purposes usually rests on some fundamental requirements such as planning horizons, detail, and participation.

Planning Horizon. This can vary by type of business and preference, but frequently forecasting one month by day, two months by week, and one year by month provides a sufficient and reasonably realistic look ahead.

Detail. Major receipts and disbursements should normally be forecast individually for major flows (say, 1 percent or more of sales) and collectively for all other (preferably the smallest 20 percent). The timing of large receipts and disbursements should be individually forecast where possible and "spread," using a historical, statistical analysis for nondefinable flows.

Participation. Responsibility for forecasting the timing and amount of large receipts or disbursements should be assigned outside of the financial department to the executive best able to control or anticipate each major flow.

The key to effective cash forecasting rests not in the sophistication of the procedure, but in making integrated, thoughtful assumptions about a relatively small number of variables. Doing this requires the collaboration of executives throughout the company. As suggested below, it is important for multinational companies to make forecasts for each one of the currencies in which they trade or maintain a position.

International Cash Management

The expansion of U.S. companies overseas has converted cash management from a two-dimensional checker game to a three-dimensional chess game.[4] The stakes are large and, for companies with significant international business, there is no option not to participate.

A medium-sized Ohio manufacturer whose announced policy is "not to speculate in foreign currencies" borrowed $5.5 million in Swiss francs for its European operations. In the next three years, as the Swiss franc rose against the dollar, the company wrote up its dollar obligation for this loan by over $1 million.

The unlucky speculations of some U.S. commercial banks have made headlines, but hidden are the considerable implicit speculations such as the Ohio company described above. Companies that genuinely want to remove themselves from international currency speculation must, as a minimum:

1. Determine precisely and periodically their exposure by country in terms of receivables, payables, and other assets and liabilities.
2. Decide on the amount of exposure they want to protect against—e.g., all exposures or only selected risks such as current-year foreign currency-payments and receipts.
3. Design the cash-gathering and disbursing system to provide as much control and flexibility as possible.

---

[4] For a fuller discussion of the requirements of international cash management, see the article by my two associates, John T. Wooster and G. Richard Thoman, "New Financial Priorities for MNCs," *Harvard Business Review*, May–June 1974.

4. Evaluate the most cost-effective means of reducing risk, such as currency hedges, overdrafts, discounting letters of exchange, and interdivisional transactions.
5. Install controls for continually monitoring covered and uncovered exposures and ensuring that down-the-line employees are following company policy.

There is considerable evidence to suggest that worldwide control of cash-gathering and disbursing is necessary, just as two decades earlier companies saw the need to centralize cash management on a national instead of a divisional basis.

Cash management in the decade beginning in the mid-70s enters a new era of challenge and visibility. Cash managers have never been more sophisticated or had such sophisticated tools at their disposal. Success in a period where use of capital is likely to receive more attention than ever before will depend not only on effective use of these sophisticated tools, but also on the old-fashioned virtues of judgment, attention to detail, and discipline.

ADDITIONAL SOURCES

Budin, Morris, and Van Handel, Robert J. "A Rule-of-Thumb Theory of Cash Holdings by Firm." *Journal of Financial and Quantitative Analysis,* 10 (March 1975), 85–108.

Daellenbach, Hans G. "Are Cash Management Optimization Models Worthwhile?" *Journal of Financial and Quantitative Analysis,* 9 (September 1974), 607–26.

Pinches, Christine. "Lock Box Banking: Key to Faster Collections." *Credit and Financial Management,* 69 (June 1967), 16–21.

Rayburn, Gayle. "More Effective Management of Cash." *Managerial Planning,* 23 (May–June 1975), 15–19.

Searby, Frederick W. "Use Your Hidden Cash Resources." *Harvard Business Review,* 46 (March–April 1968), 74–75.

Sethi, Suresh P. "A Note on Modeling Simple Dynamic Cash Balance Problems." *Journal of Financial and Quantitative Analysis,* 8 (September 1973), 685–88.

Stone, Bernell. "The Use of Forecasts and Smoothing in Control Limit Models for Cash Management." *Financial Management,* 1 (Spring 1972), 72–84.

Chapter 21

Credit Management

W. B. Quackenbush[*]
W. D. Anderson[†]

THE NEED for sound, efficient management of a company's investment in accounts receivable has become increasingly apparent as the total economy grows. According to the "Quarterly Financial Report for Manufacturing Corporations" prepared by the Federal Trade Commission—Division of Financial Statistics, between 1965 and 1973 aggregate receivables of manufacturing corporations increased from $63 billion to $141 billion with $41 billion of this increase occurring between 1970 and 1973. During the past 25 years receivables have grown at a more rapid pace than either inventories or sales. The increase in trade receivables (which generally ranks 1, 2, or 3 in size on a company's balance sheet) has caused an increase in the attention given to their quality and quantity by senior management. The timely collection of receivables represents the principal source of internally generated cash to be used by the treasurer in providing all or part of the day-to-day financing for his company's operations.

By far, the great percentage of all sales of good and services are made on a credit basis. Trade credit is a very important tool in moving goods within the U.S. economy. And while the use of credit in connection with overseas sales is secondary to letters of

---
[*] W. B. Quackenbush is vice president and treasurer of Commercial Credit Co., Baltimore, Maryland.

[†] W. D. Anderson is corporate credit manager, Control Data Corporation, Minneapolis, Minnesota.

credit or other vehicles of selling, it has continued to be used on an increasing basis as exports and imports grow.

This chapter deals with and discusses *trade* credit which is confined to receivables arising from transactions between companies, as contrasted to consumer credit which is extended to individuals. Trade credit is also distinguished from bank credit in that it is usually not extended as a profit-making tool per se but rather as an aid in selling goods or services at a profit.

The role of the credit executive has become of prime importance in affecting companies cash flow, financing needs, and balance sheet. His efficiency is reflected in all of these areas and, in turn, directly can affect the profitability of the company. In short he has become an important part of the financial management organization of his company.

Some of the benefits that result from competent and efficient credit management are: (1) protection of corporate liquidity; (2) safeguarding of a major investment; (3) profit enhancement; and (4) marketing assistance.

This chapter takes the point of view of the management of credit operations which is subject to control by the treasurer. The subsequent chapter describes the role of the treasurer in his managerial responsibilities for the credit department.

ORGANIZATION AND REPORTING

Staffing

Peculiarities of the specific business such as product line, geographical coverage, seasonal influences, terms of sale, competition, and profit margin all contribute to the staffing of a credit department. Additionally, centralization versus decentralization has an important bearing.

It is, therefore, difficult to portray a standard organization. Most companies, however, have a credit manager who devotes full time to the credit and collection function of the company. Typically he will have an assistant or one who is training to become his successor.

The remaining staff is dictated by the needs and may well include several credit analysts or credit specialists, collection personnel, plus secretaries, and clerical personnel. A multiline or multiproduct company may find it most appropriate to staff based on product line because of special considerations or peculiarities in specific areas.

Staffs may also be based on geographical considerations or exposure considerations.

Reporting

Credit and collection activities or management of trade receivables both carry virtually the same meaning and are considered a part of the financial organization within a company. As a result, the function usually comes under the direction of the treasurer.

The total performance of the function, however, does cross lines of authority in that the basic product managed (trade receivables) involves working with customer ledgers. Control of these ledgers generally is under the direction of the company controller. Occasionally, the credit function will be considered a selling tool and will come under the marketing operation. As a practical matter, however, the best interests of a company are served when there is a "check and balance" system operating and thus, two reporting structures: one, marketing; the other, the credit department functioning through the treasury organization of the company.

The credit department may have either line or staff responsibility. Generally, it has line responsibility for the granting of credit, collection of accounts, customer relations or contact as it pertains to credit matters, band debt losses and doubtful account analysis, and management of the accounts receivable ledgers.

There should be a close relationship and/or sharing of responsibilities on the part of marketing in collection of accounts and customer contact. Where there may be operating units or divisions, the management of these may well jointly share responsibilities with the credit department and each have a common set of goals.

If a credit department is limited to that of a staff responsibility, the company normally will be a large, diversified one. In this situation the credit department will be responsible for formulating and updating policies and procedures as well as monitoring and reporting receivables individually and collectively regarding quantity and quality.

Centralization versus Decentralization

Certain advantages or disadvantages accrue to centralized operations and quite naturally the same is true for decentralized operations. The final decision, however, must be the needs and goals of the company. For certain functions, it is more economical to operate on a centralized basis. Policy making, credit investigations, and credit approvals are better handled centrally. The major advantage is uniformity but, in addition, economies result from size alone.

Centralized credit operations typically provide credit services for all units of a company regardless of size or location. Centralized operations can entail only the policy making, credit investigations, and credit approvals, with the collection function on a decentralized basis. This helps to eliminate one of the primary disadvantages of a centralized operation; namely, the timely and efficient servicing of accounts located at considerable distances from the centralized offices.

Decentralization occurs along divisional, product, or geographical lines. It can mean centralized credit approval and decentralized collection or vice versa. Decentralization is used by companies having a substantial volume, wide range of products and/or wide dispersion geographically. Some of the advantages are: closer rapport with the customer, physical proximity enabling more timely reaction and awareness to local situations and a closer relationship with the marketing department.

If, in fact, a company has separate and distinct profit centers, decentralization along those lines enables a better distribution of credit department operations and allows costs to be more clearly identified.

Domestic–International

As geographical distances become less influential with today's transportation systems, and as more companies tend to direct expansion into foreign markets, staffing for handling international receivables has become more important. Again the key is the method by which a company is organized. Some have centralized foreign headquarters, others operate through distributors, some have foreign subsidiaries, and finally there are those that sell direct. Each, as would be apparent, has different staffing requirements; however, for consistency the policy making and general guidance should come from a centralized location and person.

POLICIES AND PROCEDURES

Policies express the basic strategy and philosophy of a company's management through long-range goals and intentions. They also provide a framework of reference or guides in carrying on a company's activities. Written statements of these policies not only enable the broadest dissemination, but also provide consistency in handling continuing transactions, eliminate the need to rely on memory, and assist in the decision-making process. Procedures on the other hand represent the more detailed plans, methods, and actual basic instructions for accomplishing the intent of the policies.

Any company will have a variety of policies, some applicable to the entire firm, and others to certain functions or units within the company. These secondary policies should complement the overall policies or philosophy of the company. As an example, the credit policy should be in concert with the company's marketing policy. The importance of policy coordination rather than policy conflict should not be minimized. Therefore, all policies should be reviewed and approved by one individual in senior management or by a policy committee.

Elements of a Credit and Collection Policy

As outlined earlier, a secondary policy will carry the tone and intent of the company's basic business objectives. The major objective of the credit and collection function focuses on efficient management of the investment in trade receivables.

Therefore, some of the elements of the credit policy will include:

1. Granting credit, including the assignment of lines of credit and classification or identification of risks.
2. Terms of sale.
3. Security.
4. Monitoring and analyzing receivables.
5. Handling delinquencies.
6. Counseling.

Terms of sale will vary greatly, depending on line or type of business. The Credit Research Foundation publishes information by industry reflecting the generally used terms of sale. The terms of sale used by a company can have an important bearing on its receivable turnover and thus represent a key in not only the credit policy but the company's total policy as it relates to internal dollar turnover and cash management.

Samples of typical large company credit policies and implementing procedures are shown here.

APPROVED POLICY ON CREDIT AND COLLECTIONS

Purpose

The purpose is to outline the requirements and procedures necessary to ensure the least amount of loss of exposure to the enterprise consistent with maximum profitability in its pursuit of business growth.

Policy

It is the company's policy to grant credit terms in contracts with its customers, sufficient to enable the normal conduct of business activities, providing that extension of such credit is consistent with sound business practices. All sales of goods and services must have credit approval.

It is the company's policy to pursue the collection of its accounts in accordance with the terms of payment in its contracts on the premise that when the company has performed in accordance with the requirements of its contracts, it can rightfully expect the customer to observe his obligation to pay.

In the administration of its credit policy, it is the company's intention that its financial dealings with customers be so conducted as to foster the best possible customer relations, while at the same time not imposing an excessive financial burden on the company.

Scope

This policy shall be applicable to all divisions and subsidiaries of the corporation.

Responsibility

Credit Approval

A. The responsibility for credit approval rests with the general credit manager. It is a staff function which may be delegated only with the written approval of the vice president of finance or company owner.

B. All orders shall be approved or rejected by the general credit manager or his designee. In the event of disagreement on a credit decision, the matter shall be referred to the treasurer for resolution.

C. Payment terms other than standard, may be granted on an exception basis only with the specific written approval of the general credit manager, or his designee.

Collection

A. Responsibility for collection activity will be delegated using procedural guidelines established in the approved procedure on collections. The general credit manager will monitor the entire accounts receivable activity and provide counseling and/or collection assistance.

B. Collection objectives and responsibility shall be established by the company management based upon recommendations of the general credit manager and line management. Assigned collection objectives will be a specific component of the performance objectives of operating units.

C. The general credit manager shall establish overall corporate procedures for the administration of the collection activities.

D. The vice president of finance or company president is responsible for the maintenance and final interpretation of this policy.

APPROVED PROCEDURE ON CREDIT APPROVALS

This procedure should be used to implement the company credit policy.

General Information

All orders for products and/or services shall be reviewed for acceptability of credit prior to order acceptance, except as follows:

a. Orders from government agencies other than those involving extended payment terms.

b. Orders other than those involving extended payment terms from companies previously identified as "unlimited credit" by the credit department or its designee.

c. Orders other than those involving extended payment terms of individually small dollar amounts, $300 or less, provided the customer is not on a COD status.

To avoid unnecessary selling and technical effort, preliminary credit approval should be obtained for prospective customers, with an undetermined ability to pay, prior to preparation of a proposal. An early credit review in such instances will permit determination of any limitations on such prospects' credit and/or development of a financial plan for inclusion in the proposal accommodating the specific situation.

Well-established companies will usually require much less time for credit action. Nevertheless, sufficient time must be allowed for updating existing credit files or securing additional information, if such is required. Therefore, credit checks should be requested sufficiently in advance to avoid delay to contract and/or purchase order acceptance for that reason.

Recognizing the many products, services, facets and lines of business within the total company structure, this procedure will encompass these operations, using the assumption that prospective customer information is available.

In the case of certain operating units, credit approval authority may be delegated in writing and within certain limitations by the vice president of finance. Also, for purposes of further clarification within certain operating units, more detailed procedures may be written and implemented. These must be signed by the vice president of finance.

Specifics

Responsibility	*Action*
Line management	1. Advise credit when a potential customer (prospect) reaches 50 percent in the prospect cycle or when an order for goods or services is expected within a short period of time. All prospects and/or confirmed orders or contracts must have a credit review, except as noted in paragraph one under "General Information."
Credit	2. Perform credit investigation and analysis.
	3. Advise line management of approval, restrictions or the need for additional requirements.
	4. On a continuing basis, reappraise the credit-worthiness of existing customers.
Line management	5. Communicate credit decision to the appropriate personnel within their organization.
	6. Ensure that credit has been approved prior to providing any goods and/or services.
	7. Ensure that future orders are within established limitations.

APPROVED PROCEDURE ON COLLECTIONS

This procedure should be used as a guideline to operating units in developing their individual procedures in implementing the collection phase of the company credit policy.

General Information

The responsibility for collection of all accounts rests with the operating units who have been assigned that responsibility by the company management.

The general credit manager will provide counseling, assistance and support to ensure that corporate and operating unit objectives are met. At the request of the responsible operating unit and on its behalf, the general credit manager may perform its collection functions.

This procedure is the recommended method for accomplishing the following:

1. Performing the collection function.
2. Interfacing with the credit department.
3. Making monthly reports.

Responsibility		*Action*
Operating unit	1.	Maintain the customer's aging report of accounts receivable. This will contain at a minimum an open item listing by customer. Invoice amounts are aged as follows: current, 30 days, 60 days, 90 days, 120 days from date of invoice. Partial payments are shown.
	2.	Update the aging report on a monthly basis or more frequently as appropriate.
	3.	Send collection notices (letter, telegram, phone, personal call) to delinquent customers in accordance with the following schedule, starting at a specific date from date of invoice and at desired intervals thereafter.
	4.	Distribute collection letter copies as appropriate to all parties concerned with collection of the account.
	5.	Resolve in a timely manner any internal problems which are resulting, or could result, in payment delays.
	6.	On a monthly basis, provide credit department and the responsible line management/executive with a detailed explanation of primary collection problems and key accounts.
	7.	Refer to credit department (except where total credit responsibility has been delegated in writing by the vice president of finance) all accounts which could result in: a. Litigation. b. Bankruptcy. c. Notes. d. Special payment schedules. e. Collection agency assistance.
	8.	Submit to credit department at month end the following: a. Copy of accounts receivable aging. b. Current month's billing. c. Calculation of accounts receivable delinquency.
	9.	Based on assigned objectives, and on the same time schedule as (8) above, any operating unit not meeting its objectives must report to its line manager/executive and credit department action plans, including time frames, for attaining objectives.
Credit department	10.	Provide counseling and collection assistance.
	11.	Perform collection function under conditions noted in (7) above.
	12.	Prepare summary reports monthly and special reports when appropriate.

Communicating Policy and Procedures

To be effective and useful, a policy must be known by any person or department that has a "need to know" or who is directly affected. Certainly any member of a credit activity, be it centralized or decentralized, must have thorough understanding of the policies related to credit and collections.

Policies are and should be disseminated and made a part of the company or department operating manual. They can also be transmitted or disseminated by oral communication at meetings or other group sessions.

Customers should be advised of credit policies as the need dictates. However, it is generally good practice to obtain basic understandings which follow the company credit policy at the time the account relationship is established.

Revision

While there is no set recommendation for timing of revisions, a company's activities, the business climate, economic conditions, and so on will normally make it practical to review and revise credit policies on a regular basis, annually or biannually.

The responsibility for creating and revising the credit policy rests with the company treasurer. Substantial input and influence can and should also come from the vice president of finance as well as the credit manager.

COMMUNICATIONS

One of the real keys to a successful credit operation is communication. Communications must be a continuing ingredient within the department, within the company, between customer and the credit department, and with other companies.

Within the department, the credit manager must clearly communicate the following:

1. The policies and procedures as they relate to or affect the credit operation.
2. The established standards of desired or expected performance.
3. Tried and tested methods for performing the credit and collection function.
4. Evaluations of performance with individuals in order to promote growth and professionalism for each individual.
5. Company or departmental practices.

Within the company, the credit manager must communicate to those in a "need to know" position the policies and procedures in order to effectively carry out levels of performance expected of the credit department. The success of the department is in part dependent on cooperation with or action from certain other areas. A sales or marketing manager must convey the need for timely action on the part of his salesman when the sales department is asked to participate in obtaining payments from customers. This will occur either on a direct or indirect basis as customer contacts are made. The billing department must react to, and resolve on a timely basis, problems reported or discovered on a specific billing to a customer.

Communication within a company can be written, by telephone, or in person. Obviously, the proper mix of all three will be most ideal. Personal contact, however, cannot be overemphasized. Such contact provides for better understandings between people and enables individual analysis of methods for accomplishing tasks. Personal contact via group sessions or meetings also is desirable from an efficiency standpoint.

Outside the company, communications from the credit department are usually written, although the telephone is also used extensively. Certain customers, such as large accounts and problem or risk accounts, should receive personal visits regularly in order to establish the proper rapport between the individuals involved.

There are many needs for communications outside the credit department and company in addition to the customer. Banks, either one of the company's or the customer's, can provide valuable information which will enable the credit department to better understand its customers and thus provide cooperation as necessary.

Mercantile agencies, such as Dun & Bradstreet Inc., credit associations, and credit interchanges all provide various types of reports on customers and all require some type of communication from the credit department.

ACTIONS AND METHODS TO ACCOMPLISH TASKS

The methods and skills with which a credit executive and his department personnel carry out their task (i.e., efficient management of receivables) has a pronounced effect on the company's liquidity.

The skilled credit man must exercise good judgment, be constructive and imaginative, complement the sales force, be an able customer counselor and action oriented. As has been pointed out earlier, he and his department are charged with efficient management of one of the three top investments of the company.

Credit Approvals

Extending credit to customers probably has more long-range effect on the company's receivable levels than any other single factor. The credit grantor must be able to develop sufficient information to make a sound decision as to the amount of credit to extend, often referred to as a line of credit. Sound decisions in establishing new account lines of credit or revising existing lines can be regarded as preventive maintenance to avoid problem accounts that are likely to result in future losses.

The credit approval cycle normally starts with a sales prospect. Companies have a variety of ways to identify potential customers. Here is where communications again plays an important role. The earlier the credit department is involved, the better can be the final credit approval decision. Also support can be supplied to the sales department at an earlier stage, and generally the relationship with the customer can get started with clearer understandings and closer rapport.

Sources of Credit Information

Among the principal sources used in gathering credit information are reporting agencies, banks, competitors, public records, trade publications, credit associations including industry groups, and the customer.

The value of information obtained from the customer again points up the need for the credit department to be involved early in the order cycle. Such things as company history, officer or owner backgrounds, operating information, financial statements, and projections, including revenue, cash flow, and expansion, all should be available from the customer. More and more companies are cognizant of the need for information on which to base good sound credit decisions. The benefits accrue to both the customer and the seller.

Probably the widest used outside agency for credit information is Dun & Bradstreet, Inc. It provides credit ratings on millions of firms throughout the world in the form of periodic reference books and detailed reports on companies.

Dun & Bradstreet, Inc., rating keys (Figure 1) are frequently used by companies in establishing guides for the extension of

FIGURE 1

Key to Ratings

ESTIMATED FINANCIAL STRENGTH			COMPOSITE CREDIT APPRAISAL			
			HIGH	GOOD	FAIR	LIMITED
5A	Over	$50,000,000	1	2	3	4
4A	$10,000,000 to	50,000,000	1	2	3	4
3A	1,000,000 to	10,000,000	1	2	3	4
2A	750,000 to	1,000,000	1	2	3	4
1A	500,000 to	750,000	1	2	3	4
BA	300,000 to	500,000	1	2	3	4
BB	200,000 to	300,000	1	2	3	4
CB	125,000 to	200,000	1	2	3	4
CC	75,000 to	125,000	1	2	3	4
DC	50,000 to	75,000	1	2	3	4
DD	35,000 to	50,000	1	2	3	4
EE	20,000 to	35,000	1	2	3	4
FF	10,000 to	20,000	1	2	3	4
GG	5,000 to	10,000	1	2	3	4
HH	Up to	5,000	1	2	3	4

CLASSIFICATION FOR BOTH
ESTIMATED FINANCIAL STRENGTH AND CREDIT APPRAISAL

FINANCIAL STRENGTH BRACKET	EXPLANATION
1 $125,000 and Over 2 20,000 to 125,000	When only the numeral (1 or 2) appears, it is an indication that the estimated financial strength, while not definitely classified, is presumed to be within the range of the ($) figures in the corresponding bracket and that a condition is believed to exist which warrants credit in keeping with that assumption.

ABSENCE OF RATING DESIGNATION FOLLOWING NAMES LISTED IN THE REFERENCE BOOK

The absence of a rating, expressed by two hyphens (--), is not to be construed as unfavorable but signifies circumstances difficult to classify within condensed rating symbols. It suggests the advisability of obtaining a report for additional information.

EMPLOYEE RANGE DESIGNATIONS IN REPORTS OR NAMES NOT LISTED IN THE REFERENCE BOOK

Certain businesses do not lend themselves to a Dun & Bradstreet rating and are not listed in the Reference Book. Information on these names, however, continues to be stored and updated in the D&B Business Data Bank. Reports are available on such businesses and instead of a rating they carry an Employee Range Designation (ER) which is indicative of size in terms of number of employees. No other significance should be attached.

KEY TO EMPLOYEE RANGE DESIGNATIONS

ER 1	Over 1000 Employees
ER 2	500 - 999 Employees
ER 3	100 - 499 Employees
ER 4	50 - 99 Employees
ER 5	20 - 49 Employees
ER 6	10 - 19 Employees
ER 7	5 - 9 Employees
ER 8	1 - 4 Employees
ER N	Not Available

© *Dun & Bradstreet, Inc.* **1974**

99 Church Street, New York, N.Y. 10007   18B-7 (730801)

credit. As an example, a company with a rating of 5A1 may be authorized unlimited credit whereas a company with an EE2 may be authorized $500 either set on a per order or total balance basis.

Local credit associations, generally a part of the National Association of Credit Management, often have formed industry groups and have periodic meetings for verbal interchange of information as well as trade reports outlining a company's payment habits with various suppliers.

Lines of credit or credit limits, when established, then set the stage for accepting orders within the lines set. Most companies also establish levels of authority within the credit department and on up the various levels of management. A regional credit man may have authority to accept orders up to $25,000, the credit manager to $500,000, and any order over that amount must be approved by the treasurer or vice president of finance. The above represents only a possible limit of authority. Product lines, size of normal order, and many other factors will determine the proper level of authority within any company organization.

Collections

There are generally two important questions to answer in determining the collection practices of a company. First, recognizing the terms of sale, the best time to begin the collection effort for payment of the overdue balance must be determined. Second, a collection method must be selected; e.g., letters, sales force, or some other manner.

The diligence and timeliness with which accounts are followed for payment of balances due or overdue will have a bearing on the rate of turnover and the size of the investment in receivables as well as the amount of bad debt losses.

Most companies will begin their follow-up on overdue accounts 10 to 15 days after the balance is due. The most widely used method is a series of reminder letters forwarded at specific intervals (ten days to two weeks). If a payment has not been received after three or four computer-generated or form-type reminders, then the credit man will compose a personalized letter. In contacting overdue accounts it is always wise to involve the salesman, if only to provide him with a copy of the letter for information purposes. In many instances the salesman will have information which explains the reason for the delinquency.

Size of account, identified marginal accounts, and certain risk factors each may require a different approach in the collection activity. Earlier follow-up, more frequent reviews, and telephone or personal calls all may be desired to ensure adequate coverage and protection against nonpayment of overdue accounts.

There will always be some accounts that do not pay even after many requests or contacts. Some companies involve their own legal staff in collection, but most likely an outside collection agency is involved. Placement with an outside agency usually means that future business with that customer should be other than open account; i.e., cash in advance or COD.

Collection agencies vary in quality and effectiveness. Experience will highlight the performers. From a control standpoint it is best to utilize only a small number of agencies. One of the factors dictating the number will be geographic coverage.

Security in Account Transactions

Frequently it may be in the best interests of a company to deal on other than an open account basis. A brief description of types of security to be considered is in order.

Guarantees. Guarantees may be personal guarantees from individuals, bank guarantees or guarantees from other companies. They should always be in writing. The strength of the guarantee is only as good as the financial strength of the guarantor. Therefore, investigations must be conducted to ensure that the guarantee is of adequate substance. Bank guarantees must be signed by an officer authorized to bind the bank. Similarly, a guarantee from another company should not only be signed by an officer of the company but also be accompanied by a resolution of the board of directors acknowledging the guarantee.

Letters of Credit. Letters of credit are often used in foreign transactions. They should be irrevocable and drawn on a bank of mutual agreement by the customer and seller. Wherever possible they should also be *confirmed* irrevocable letters of credit. Letters of credit require precise and exacting document handling in order to receive payment against the letter of credit. It is very important to be totally familiar with all requirements.

Escrow Accounts or Deposits. As the name implies, escrow accounts represent funds set aside in an account in favor of the supplier. These agreements should also be in writing and all details clearly spelled out to enable the supplier to draw on the escrow account without complications should the need arise.

Financing Statements. Secured transactions are a complex subject and contain many technicalities. It is best to seek the advice of an attorney or one skilled in the subject. Security interests and financing statements are one method of retaining a legally perfected interest in equipment, merchandise and/or proceeds from the sale of same, if such documents are filed timely and properly.

Secured transactions and financing statements fall under the broad legal subject, Uniform Commercial Code, Article 9.

Other. Certain other types of security are used from time to time in dealing with customers. They are subordination agreements, liens, trust receipts, bailments, deeds of trust, pledged instruments (collateral notes or bills of lading) and warehouse receipts.

MEASUREMENTS

Numerous methods are used in measuring the performance and effectiveness of receivables management; i.e., the credit and collection department. The method or methods used are tailored to fit the internal needs of a company after considering the overall policy (strategy) regarding credit and collection. Probably the one most consistent with senior management's analysis of all operations is the return on investment in receivables or return on assets. Often management goals are geared to a certain percentage return on assets, which includes all assets employed, including receivables.

Another frequently used method is aged-days index or the number of days sales in receivables. This can be computed either by working back from the end of the month or on a month-by-month comparison to sales. It can also be an average of the last three months. Finally, it can be based on a 12-month moving average. The latter will not highlight changes as they occur but rather will emphasize trends. When aged-days index is used, it is measured against established internal goals and also industry standards or comparisons. The Credit Research Foundation publishes such figures by all manufacturers as well as by industry groups.

Still another measurement rather new and not widely used is

the percentage of delinquent receivables, measured against sales, generally for prior months. These can be total delinquencies as well as delinquencies beyond a specified aging. Since this is a fairly recent method of measurement, industry comparisons are not known to exist. Therefore, any measurement must be against established goals. These goals can best be set by a review of past percentages.

A credit executive's skill in managing trade receivables is also reflected in the company's accrual for doubtful accounts and bad debt write-offs (losses). Businesses expect to sustain a limited amount of losses in the normal course of doing business. These expected or planned losses vary depending on the line of business as well as economic conditions.

Once the standard of acceptability has been established, a comparison of actual losses to the internally set goals, as well as industry gathered figures, will provide a basis for gauging the success of the credit manager and his department.

REPORTS

On a regular basis the credit manager should provide management with reports which analyze and evaluate the trade receivables of the company. This not only keeps management constantly updated but also enables the credit manager to perform evaluations on himself as well as the people making up the credit department.

The following are some typical reports submitted and their frequency of submission.

1. Weekly. Status report on high dollar and/or high-risk accounts.
2. Monthly. Comparative agings or delinquency reports for each subunit within the company.
3. Monthly. Internally generated reports from levels of credit to the credit executive.
4. Monthly or Quarterly. Analysis of trade receivables.
5. Quarterly. Industry reports reflecting aged-day information, past-due information, and bad-debt information.
6. Quarterly. Bad debt and doubtful account analysis.

The monthly or quarterly analysis of trade receivables can take on almost any format, depending on the desires of management. Certain comparisons are more appropriate and meaningful than others. Total investment in receivables shown by aging category, both dollars and percentage as against last month and one year ago, provide meaningful data to show trends. In addition, days sales in receivables can be shown for the same periods, again reflecting trends or changes. Reports should contain commentary in sufficient detail to point out significant changes, trends, problem areas or unusual situations which could affect the company's investment in trade receivables. Management should also be advised how its company compares with others in the same industry. These industry reports are available on a quarterly basis.

BAD DEBT AND DOUBTFUL ACCOUNT ANALYSIS AND ACCRUALS

One of the primary methods for evaluating the performance of a credit operation are the losses sustained in the form of bad debts. Certainly, the company's policy relative to taking or rejecting risk business is the key determinant of expected losses. Once the policy is established, then it is the responsibility of the credit department to evaluate credit risks consistent with the policy and the potential exposure can be defined.

Therefore, certain factors have a direct bearing on the level of bad debt expense:

1. The investment in receivables related to terms of sale expressed as the number of days sales outstanding. The larger the number the greater is the exposure to possible bad debts.

2. Effectiveness of collection action. If payment does not occur as a result of numerous contacts, the account should be referred to a collection agency.

3. The quality of accounts approved for open account, which depends on the company policy.

Bad debt losses as a result of uncollectible accounts are handled either one of two ways. They are written off indirectly, against previously established reserves for doubtful accounts, or as a direct expense as they occur.

Most firms establish a reserve for doubtful accounts which enables the company to charge expected losses from bad debts against the income of the period in which the sales took place. This procedure eliminates unexpected expense items as a result of a sudden charge off, and it more clearly reflects the true value of the receivables as reported on the company's balance sheet.

Reserves for doubtful accounts can be established in two ways: (1) by making an account-by-account review and analysis (i.e., establishing the reserve to the doubtful accounts ledger on an identified account basis), or (2) by accruing a certain percentage of sales as expected losses. The latter must periodically be reviewed against actual write-offs to ensure that the reserve is sufficient or that it is not too large.

ADDITIONAL SOURCES

Benishay, Haskel. "Managerial Controls of Accounts Receivable: A Deterministic Approach." *Journal of Accounting Research,* 3 (Spring 1965), 114–33.

Benishay, Haskel. "A Stochastic Model of Credit Sales Debt." *Journal of the American Statistical Association,* 61 (December 1966), 1010–28.

Brosky, John J. *The Implicit Cost of Trade Credit and Theory of Optimal Terms of Sale.* New York: Credit Research Foundation, 1969.

The Conference Board Inc. *Managing Trade Receivables.* Conference Board Report No. 540., 1972.

Greer, Carl C. "The Optimal Credit Acceptance Policy." *Journal of Financial and Quantitative Analysis,* 2 (December 1967), 399–415.

Lewellen, Wilbur G. "Finance Subsidiaries and Corporate Borrowing Capacity." *Financial Management,* 1 (Spring 1972), 21–32.

Lewellen, Wilbur G., and Edmister, Robert O. "A General Model for Accounts-Receivable Analysis and Control." *Journal of Financial and Quantitative Analysis,* 8 (March 1973), 195–206.

Marrah, George L. "Managing Receivables." *Financial Executive,* 38 (July 1970), 40–44.

Mehta, Dileep. "The Formulation of Credit Policy Models." *Management Science,* 15 (October 1968), 30–50.

Mehta, Dileep. "Optimal Credit Policy Selection: A Dynamic Approach." *Journal of Financial and Quantitative Analysis,* 5 (December 1970), 421–44.

Moore, Carroll G. "Factoring—A Unique and Important Form of Financing and Service." *The Business Lawyer,* 14 (April 1959), 203–27.

Reisman, Albert F. "What the Commercial Lawyer Should Know about Commercial Finance and Factoring." *Commercial Law Journal,* 79 (May 1974), 146–56.

Shapiro, Alan. "Optimal Inventory and Credit Granting Strategies under Inflation and Deflation." *Journal of Financial and Quantitative Analysis,* 7 (January 1973), 37–46.

Sisson, Roger L., and Statland, Norman L. "The Future of Computers in Credit Management." *Credit and Financial Management,* 67 (May 1965), 13–15, 40, 44.

U.S. Federal Trade Commission. *Quarterly Financial Report: U.S. Manufacturing Corporations.* Washington, D.C.: U.S. Government Printing Office.

Smith, Jerome J. "Factoring." *Manhattan Mind,* 3 (Winter 1974), 53–73. (Published by the Borough of Manhattan Community College, 134 West 51st Street, New York, N.Y. 10020.)

Vancil, Richard F. *Financial Executive's Handbook.* Homewood, Ill.: Dow Jones-Irwin, 1970.

Wrightsman, Dwayne. "Optimal Credit Terms for Accounts Receivable." *Review of Economics and Business,* 9 (Summer 1969), 59–66.

Chapter 22

Management of Receivables

Albert G. Sweetser*

THE OBJECTIVE of this chapter is to discuss what the treasurer, not the credit manager and his staff, should know and do about receivables. Management of receivables can be broken down into the areas of policy determination and operating procedures. It will be assumed here that the latter lie within the competence of a capable credit manager and need not command direct attention by the treasurer. While a good credit manager can and should rise above procedural responsibilities by comprehending their financial implications, it is nonetheless the responsibility of the treasurer to formulate financial policy and to oversee its implementation.

POLICY BUILDING: FINANCIAL CONSIDERATIONS

In building general policies governing trade receivables, the treasurer must consider not only the direct costs involved but also the potential effects upon the company's financial position; against these he must weigh advantages in the form of increased sales and profits, and he must consider the ways in which he may wish to use receivables in his borrowing program.

---

* Albert G. Sweetser is professor of finance, State University of New York at Albany.

The Costs of Trade Credit

Three factors enter into the costs of creating, carrying, and liquidating receivables: (1) those related to operations of the credit and collections department, (2) those related to providing the capital required, and (3) those related to assumption of the risks involved. On an incremental basis, only the last two would be pertinent. Methods of measuring these elements of cost are of no importance here. For each it is possible generally to use either the company's own experience and calculations or the costs or having various functions handled externally.

Effects of Receivables Policies upon Financial Position

At first glance it may seem difficult to realize that to create and carry receivables requires capital, since no direct outlay of cash or assumption of debt is involved. Yet, to delay payment of a sale creates a capital requirement just as though cash had been paid out. The magnitude of this requirement is influenced not merely by the amount involved, but also by the length of time that elapses before collection, just as man-hours are used as a measure of labor input rather than merely the number of workers involved. For instance, the impact of receivables upon capital requirements could be doubled either by creating twice as many in dollar amount, or by allowing them to remain outstanding twice as long. The former is under the control of the seller while the latter is less subject to his influence.

Part of the elusiveness of this capital requirement is demonstrated by a need for cash to be used not in connection with the receivable itself, but for buying operating assets needed to replace those used in the sale that gave rise to the receivable in question. Thus, since capital requirements created by the carrying of receivables generally appear to be related to other causes, it is easy to underestimate their importance.

Even though receivables are classified as a near-cash form of asset, the applicability of the "so near and yet so far" adage is inescapable. Growth in receivables results in corresponding reduction in cash; carried to extremes the liquidity of the company is affected, and ultimately its solvency may be threatened. In guarding against these dangers, the treasurer stands alone, viewing projections of increased profits in terms of what must be sacrificed to achieve them.

The profit potential of a sale is exceeded many times by the amount of capital needed to produce that profit. For example, if a series of sales amounting to $10,000 each were expected to yield a net profit after taxes of 10 percent each, and to require periods of two months for collection, there would have to be a series of ten such sales to generate, through net profits earned, enough new capital to carry the necessary receivables. To make these sales would require an initial capital of $100,000 that would be reduced by 10 percent each 2 months as earnings accrued until the operation becomes self-sustaining in terms of capital 20 months later.

Obviously, the treasurer should not refuse to approve all such proposals. The danger lies, not in any one such project, but in an unwise combination of too many such projects. Growth, the factor that often is looked to for company success, can be its downfall if too much is attempted too fast.

Effects of Receivables Policies upon Net Profits

Departures from established policies in connection with receivables generally must be approved by the treasurer. In most instances, the inducement is expectation of greater net profits, to be achieved through increases in sales volume or better handling of inventories and production schedules.

Sales-Oriented Considerations. A classic area of controversy that is found in most companies involves the treasurer and the vice-president in charge of marketing. This conflict arises from the treasurer's interest in controlling credit to minimize bad debts and the marketing vice president's interest in expanding credit to increase sales. Obviously, it is essential that the treasurer be at least equal in bargaining power to his colleague in sales (in matters to be decided by the board of directors) or that he command effective veto power over all proposals that involve uses of capital.

Almost all proposals coming from the sales area will be aimed at increasing the company's share of the market. Occasionally these will take the form of requests for general changes in terms of sale or selling limits. But more often they will center around some specific project for market penetration in connection with:

1. A particular product.
2. A particular geographical region.
3. A particular group of customers.
4. A particular level of the trade, such as mail-order customers.
5. A special deal designed to introduce new products or to induce customers to handle the company's full line.
6. Penetration or development of foreign markets.
7. A favored customer.
8. An advertising campaign.

Production-Oriented Considerations. Another type of request for exceptions from regular policies governing receivables may come from the vice president in charge of production, sometimes supported by his counterpart in marketing. These will include proposals centering around special terms of sale for:

1. Out-of-season shipments to permit level production throughout the year.
2. Inventory clearance and job lot sales.
3. Orders in quantities related to mill capacity.
4. Shipments made in anticipation of shutdowns resulting from strikes and other causes.
5. Shipments in truckload, carload, or barge lots.
6. High-volume customers.

In evaluating such proposals the treasurer must be aware constantly that most of them involve additional capital requirements and thus are in competition with many other compelling demands. Decisions cannot be made upon the absolute merits of any proposal, but must be made only upon a comparative basis after careful examination of all considerations involved.

Effects of Receivables Policies upon Borrowing Capacity and Methods

The treasurer should recognize that general policies governing the creation and handling of receivables can be of considerable assistance in the company's borrowing programs, especially for short-term and seasonal needs. A company's ability to borrow fully, easily, and economically upon the basis of its receivables will depend upon their form and quality. Little can be done about these characteristics after the receivables are created, so optimum borrowing ability depends upon careful forethought. Consideration must be given to: (1) the type of lender and loan arrangement that will be used, (2) the amount that may have to be borrowed, (3) the duration or seasonal pattern of the loan, and (4) the degree of flexibility desired. In anticipation of the need to use receivables for borrowing, the treasurer should consider the factors discussed below.

Choice among Types of Lenders

When looking into the possibilities of using receivables to support his company's borrowing, the treasurer normally will consider first the lender that is most convenient; usually this will be the company's traditional bank of account. If the company's requirements exceed the lending limit, the bank may offer to arrange participation with correspondent banks. In other instances, the treasurer will go directly to one of the company's larger banks, even though this involves handling transactions at some distance. This may not be suitable if use of receivables involves a continuous series of small transactions such as exchanges of collateral. If the company's needs require the services of specialists in the making of loans on receivables, and particularly if they have characteristics that make them less than attractive to a commercial bank, he may approach a finance company or a factoring organization. While most of these institutions can handle any type of loan based on receivables, it is nonetheless true that some of them are better suited to certain types of loan arrangements than others.

Choice among Types of Loan Arrangements

Unsecured Loans. Probably the simplest type of loan arrangement based in whole or in part upon the value of the company's portfolio of receivables is an unsecured loan. Almost always this is obtained from one or more commercial banks. While such loans are based upon the general credit standing of the borrower, it would be a mistake not to recognize how closely banks scrutinize the quality and, especially, the expected maturity schedule of the outstanding receivables. After all, this is the principal source of cash inflow that will enable the borrower to repay the loan. One disadvantage of this type of loan arrangement, however, is that the full loan potential of the receivables is seldom utilized: the maximum amount of loan available generally is determined by the anticipated proportions of various items in the company's balance sheet after accounting for the loan and the subsequent disbursement of the borrowed funds by the company.

Discounting of Notes and Trade Acceptances. A far more effective method of borrowing fully upon the value of some or all of the receivables held is possible if they are in the form of promissory notes or, better yet, trade acceptances. Then it is possible for the bank to buy these from the borrower, with full recourse in event of nonpayment for any reason, at their full maturity value (including interest to be accrued on the face amount, if any) less a slight discount to cover interest charged by the bank to the borrower. There are many advantages to this form of borrowing. Since the "paper" that has been bought by the bank from the company usually is payable through the customer's own bank account, and in fact is treated as a cash item just like a check on maturity date, it can be sent for collection through other commercial banks or the Federal Reserve System and presented locally through interbank clearings. Not generally known, however, is the fact that notes and acceptances presented in this fashion are given priority in payment over checks if the customer's balance that day is not adequate to cover all items presented, and that further preference is given to a note or acceptance bearing a rubber-stamped symbol indicating that it has been discounted by, and hence is the property of, another bank. A related advantage to the borrower is that his bank generally applies a charge for collecting notes and acceptances owned by the depositor, but that this charge does not apply on items already discounted by the bank. Often the interest cost will be no greater than the collection charges would have been, and thus use of borrowed funds is obtained without extra cost.

One of the greatest advantages of having receivables in the form of bills rather than accounts is the much greater certainty of payment by the customer on maturity date; further, prompt payment generally takes place without the need of a collection effort by the company or its bank. This makes feasible much closer forecasting by the treasurer of his cash inflows if he owns the bills until maturity, or it eliminates entirely his need to repay loans if they have been discounted.

Advantages accruing indirectly to the company that offers its bills to the bank for discount include the fact that banks prefer this type of collateral to accounts receivable. With a bill receivable in hand, the bank has a specific claim upon a third party for payment at maturity date and thus does not have to look primarily or exclusively to the borrower for repayment; because of this it is described as "two-name, self-liquidating paper." In instances when the borrower would be unable to reduce or repay loans on schedule the lending bank is able to liquidate its loan position as the purchased bills mature without placing any strain upon the borrower. Still another advantage to the bank of holding discounted customers' B/Rs (bills receivable) is that they can be rediscounted at the regional Federal Reserve Bank if the bank needs funds. Although this process has not been used during the last 30 or 40 years, it is still available.

When a company borrows by discounting its bills receivable, the arrangement is described as an "advance," not a loan. The reason is that the bank is anticipating or advancing the date on which the borrower normally would receive payment from his customer. It is not a loan in the sense that a loan consists of a payment of money to the borrower by the lender on one date in return for the borrower's promise to repay an equal amount, plus interest, on a later date. The process of making advances to merchants and manufacturers of their anticipated future revenues from sales already made is one of the traditional functions of commercial banking.

In summary, there are many advantages to companies, especially in times of capital shortages, establishing use of trade acceptances as their regular terms of sale or insisting upon getting promissory notes to cover each month's billings where the terms of sale are long or where payment habits of customers have been observed to achieve the same result. To the extent that this could be accomplished, either by industry groups or by individual accounts, many problems in effecting collections might be avoided. In any case, it is recommended that the treasurer of a company that chronically needs working capital follow a policy of discounting with his local commercial bank, immediately upon receipt, all bills receivable regardless what other types of loan arrangement also are used. The treasurer should recognize that he must take the initiative in adopting terms of sale involving trade acceptances and promissory notes, since the credit manager seldom sees great need to move in this direction.

Collateral Loans Based upon Pledge of Receivables. An alternative method of borrowing upon bills receivable is to offer them as collateral, or security, to a bank loan. This requires a specific pledge agreement that can be included as a separate clause on the face of the promissory note executed by the borrower (thus making it a secured or collateral note) or it can be in the form of a general pledge agreement that has the effect of converting all such notes into this category. It is simple for the bank to obtain an effective lien in this way since it will hold, as collateral, instruments that of themselves have value. For firms whose receivables are a substantial portion of financing needs, the pledge of receivables provides a flexible method of financing related to the varying levels of the firm's requirements.

The disadvantage of this method of borrowing is that the bank probably will be willing to lend only some portion (possibly 80 percent) of the face value of the bills, whereas in discounting the same instruments it would be willing to advance almost the entire maturity value.

To use accounts receivable as collateral to loans (from either commercial banks or finance companies) is somewhat more complicated than to use notes or acceptances receivable since there is no specific piece of property in tangible form that can be held by the lender as evidence of its security interest. Since the borrower cannot pledge the receivables themselves, he must pledge his ownership interest in those receivables. This is done by execution of a hypothecation agreement which differs from other pledge agreements in that it covers intangible property not in direct physical possession of the lender. To establish public record of, and to preserve the lender's security interest in, pledged accounts receivable it is necessary to file in the appropriate public offices one or more financing statements. Also it may be necessary that each ledger sheet be marked with a notation that the account has been pledged to a certain lender, or that signs to this effect be posted conspicuously in the room where the ledgers or the computer records are kept, processed, or available for inspection.

But the really cumbersome aspect of such loans are two requirements placed upon the borrower by the lender in order to preserve the validity of his security interest in the accounts receivable serving as collateral and in the proceeds of collection of these receivables. To accomplish the former the lender must insist that the borrower provide detailed weekly reports on the status of and all changes in each account pledged. To accomplish the latter it is often required that all proceeds of collection on these accounts be turned over directly to the lender in the very form in which they are received. Checks received from customers may not be deposited in the borrower's bank account, nor may cash received be deposited; both the checks and the very same cash that is received from each customer must be turned over to the lender intact and identified with a particular account. Obviously, these detailed requirements place great burdens upon the borrower's clerical personnel and upon officials who must ascertain that these procedures are followed meticulously.

Another drawback in pledging accounts receivable as collateral to loans is that these extra burdens of complying with the lender's requirements fall upon the bookkeeping department, which is less likely than the credit department to be under direct control of the treasurer. This may lead to problems in coordination which would not arise in connection with borrowing on bills receivable. Another problem arises if collections are received at many different company offices or branches or through outside agents such as banks using lockbox plans. In such cases, it is virtually impossible to arrange that the exact proceeds of collections be turned over to the lender.

Other disadvantages of borrowing from a commercial bank through pledge of accounts receivable include the following:

1. The lender may insist that all accounts be pledged, even though the amount to be borrowed is much less in amount and the loan is not continuous.
2. The lender may insist on notification to customers, and require them to make payments on account directly to the lender.
3. The percentage of loan to collateral value may not be higher than 50 percent, depending upon the quality of the portfolio as evaluated by the lender.
4. The arrangement is somewhat complicated to set up, and consequently is practical only when fairly steady borrowing is contemplated.

Borrowing on Accounts Receivable from a Commercial Finance Company. Many of these disadvantages can be avoided by borrowing on pledged accounts receivable from a commercial finance company rather than from a commercial bank. The commercial finance company generally will insist on receiving from the borrower each day a schedule of assigned receivables, supported by copies of sales invoices and other documents—such as bills of lading on which the customer's signature acknowledges receipt of the goods —to verify the facts of the sale. Advances, running up to 80 percent of maturity value of pledged accounts receivable, will be made immediately, with the balance to be credited when the customer makes full payment. In the meantime interest will be charged on the advance on a daily basis at a rate that typically is 5 percent above prime. All collections received by the borrower must be deposited directly in a local bank account carried in the name of the finance company. On his balance sheet the borrower shows an equity of about 20 percent in his total accounts receivable and adds a footnote to disclose his contingent liability on the remainder that will be charged back to him about 90 days after maturity if it is still unpaid. If his bank wishes to participate in the loan, the commercial finance company will handle the entire account and pay to the bank interest on its share of the advances made to the borrower. While somewhat costly, this type of borrowing is flexible, does not involve notification to customers, and often is about the only source of working capital available to a company that has good prospects (and often rapidly growing sales) but that is temporarily in a condition in which adequate funds cannot be obtained from commercial banks.

Sale of Accounts Receivable without Recourse. An expensive and seldom-used method of realizing the value of receivables in any form is to sell them to a finance company without recourse. Generally, this is a measure of last resort when a company is under pressure to "clean up" its balance sheet by elimination, for once and for all, of part or all of an excessive and embarrassing position in receivables. (It should be noted that when receivables are sold in this way there is no need to include a footnote to the balance sheet to indicate the presence of a contingent liability, which should be done when receivables have been discounted with recourse.) More likely than not such pressure comes from need to repay some other creditor or to improve balance sheet ratios sufficiently to enable the company to qualify for some other form of loan. If the treasurer has to consider this type of action it is a sure sign that there is something basically wrong with his policy (or lack of policy) on receivables.

Borrowing against Proceeds of Factored Sales. One of the simplest and most effective ways of borrowing against the proceeds of sales is to have them factored and then borrow from the factoring organization or from a commercial bank on the basis of the account receivable from the factor. This entire process will be treated later in this chapter.

Summary

An effective borrowing program for short-term needs almost always depends directly or indirectly upon the value of receivables, and also upon the form in which they are held. Not only will a well-planned portfolio, in terms of risk exposure and control over delinquencies, reduce need for borrowing, but also it will create a more acceptable borrowing base. To attain this objective, thoughtful development of policies on limits, terms, form, and supervision of receivables is necessary; this is a responsibility that falls ultimately upon the treasurer.

Adaptation of Receivables Policies to Changes in Business Conditions

Policies on creation and handling of receivables must be responsive to changes in conditions external to the company. These can be related to the industry or industries in which the company operates and may take the form of a different competitive environment, cyclical changes in patterns of demand, or problems related to availability and costs of raw materials. On a wider basis, factors such as shortages of capital, higher interest rates, periods of boom and depression, wars, strikes, and higher levels of taxation all can call for changes in the company's policies on receivables. Almost inevitably, such matters command the attention of the treasurer.

POLICY BUILDING: STRUCTURAL CONSIDERATIONS

In addition to financially oriented policy decisions, the treasurer also has to determine the basic structure of the department or departments in which credit and collection functions will be handled.

Centralization versus Decentralization

The most fundamental decision is whether, and to what extent, handling of credits and collections will be on a centralized basis. First, it should be noted that it is not necessary to handle the creation, servicing, and collection of receivables in parallel fashion. Record keeping may be combined with other similar functions and supervised by the controller. The routine aspects of collections may be the responsibility of some other branch of the treasurer's division concerned with management of cash. Neither of these functions needs to be handled by the credit department itself to enable it to operate efficiently in its function of making decisions as to extension of credit and collection of slow accounts. It is, of course, imperative that systems be established to keep credit men in touch with the accounts they manage and to enable them to obtain up-to-date information on any account on virtually an instantaneous basis. Development of computerized systems with companywide communications networks in continuous operation makes it possible for each aspect of the management of receivables to be performed in the manner most suitable to it without reference to the ways or locations in which related functions are handled.

With progressive improvements in communications systems freeing credit men from the need to be situated within walking distance of the receivables ledgers, treasurers should reexamine periodically their basic philosophies on centralization of the judgmental processes of credit-granting and collection of slow accounts. Strong arguments can be given for a centralized operation that is large enough to support and encourage a high degree of professionalism, that may benefit significantly from economies of scale, that achieves uniformity of policy implementation throughout the company, and that may be sufficiently removed from any particular situation to permit detached judgments.

The extent to which centralization in handling credits and collections is carried out may vary considerably. Some companies may concentrate the entire process, while others may apply the principle only to accounts that run over a certain amount; still others may permit credit judgments to be made locally but subject them to periodic review and analysis by the central staff. Other variants would be to distinguish between local and national accounts or to separate the functions of approving requests for credit from collecting slow accounts. Generally, collections are more decentralized than credit approval, a logical arrangement since collections may require more frequent and closer relationships with certain customers and better understanding of and consideration for local conditions.

Arguments in favor of decentralization are based on closer contact with the company's marketing division at points of sale; on ability to service accounts more quickly and to achieve closer rapport with the customer; on the differing needs of various divisions resulting from variety in product lines, types of customers, geographical locations, and sizes of accounts; and on ability to allocate costs more equitably to various profit centers.

Handling of Foreign Receivables

Determining the appropriate degree of centralization in handling receivables from sales made to customers in other countries probably will be influenced by considerations differing from those arising domestically. Essentially the structure will depend upon whether sales are made by the company itself as exports from the native country: through foreign branches or divisions; through foreign subsidiaries that may be owned wholly, in the majority, only in part, or jointly with other companies, foreign or domestic; or through distributors, including selling agents, franchisees, and dealers. Overriding considerations will be limitations imposed by foreign laws and the ability to repatriate the proceeds of collections or the net profits of overseas operations. In view of wide disparities in business procedures in various countries, it is likely that there are stronger arguments for decentralization of the processes of granting credits and collecting slow accounts when selling abroad than at home.

Use of Captive Finance Company to Handle Trade Receivables

Although wholly owned sales finance companies generally are organized to handle customers' receivables originated by the company or by its dealers, especially when they are in the form of notes or serial payment contracts, their use has spread in some instances to the handling of trade receivables as well. This came about first in the automobile and appliance industries through handling of the dealers' own notes arising from the carrying of inventories of new goods, a process known as floor planning or wholesale financing. There have not been many instances in which companies have had their captive finance companies handle their receivables in the form of accounts, but possibly this is a procedure that should be investigated by treasurers.

Elimination of Receivables through Factoring of Sales

Probably one of the most generally misunderstood financing operations is factoring. Almost always it is confused with, or considered to be the same as, the financing of receivables by a finance company. The essence of a factoring arrangement is complete separation from the selling process of the entire procedure for creating, servicing, collecting, and assuming credit risk in connection with the receivables generated. The factor participates as an original party to the sale, making the decision involving approval of the buyer's credit-worthiness. The buyer becomes indebted directly and immediately to the factor. The factor does not get the receivable from or through the seller, nor does the factor make a loan against it. The seller never becomes the creditor, even for a brief instant. The only responsibilities assumed by the seller arise under his expressed or implied warranties of sale; i.e., his obligations regarding claims arising in connection with such things as defective goods or services, shortages, failure to meet specifications, or defective title to the goods delivered. The seller assumes no responsibility for any loss that may arise if the buyer is unable to make payment or if there are delays in payment.

The factor handles the entire process of servicing the receivable, including all invoicing, bookkeeping, record keeping, correspondence, and collection. Sales are made on the regular terms of sale used by the seller. Once a week the factor sends a statement to its client (the seller) showing all of that client's sales in which the factor has assumed the receivables, including their amounts (less any trade discounts) and their maturity dates, after which 12 days are added to allow time for the buyer to make payment and the factor to collect payment on the buyer's check. This weekly report is a statement of the factor's obligation to the seller.

Each week the seller receives from his factor a check for the amount of all sales made 72 days earlier (where the terms of sale called for payment in 60 days), less whatever amount is needed to leave with the factor a reserve to cover claims that might arise under the seller's warranties. Except for this temporary retention of reserves, payment to the client (the original seller) does not depend upon payment by the buyer to the factor of the amount owing.

The overall effect of having sales factored is that the seller never holds receivables representing amounts owed to him by his customers; instead he holds one receivable only, called *due from factor*. This appears in his balance sheet where it can be evaluated by the seller's banker as support for an unsecured loan. Also it can much more easily and effectively be pledged to the banker than can a large group of individual receivables that are changing constantly.

Although factors are willing to make advances to their clients of the full amounts of their obligation to them (less the retained reserve), they prefer that clients borrow from their own commercial banks. The reason for this is that factors are essentially not lenders; they do not have large reservoirs of capital obtained from depositors, as do banks, nor do they have sufficient funds from equity or long-term debt sources to permit them to make loans to their clients in substantial volume. As a convenience, however, a factor will make advances to clients (sometimes reluctantly) and charge them interest at a rate about 2 percent above prime per annum. Actually this may result in lower total cost than borrowing from a commercial bank on an unsecured basis at prime, since there are no requirements for compensating balances, annual cleanups, or continuation of the loan for agreed periods of time such as one, two, or three months.

The costs of having sales factored are negotiated individually between factor and client. They depend upon the volume of sales, the expected quality of the receivables to be generated, the amount of handling cost anticipated, and the loss ratio estimated. The cost is applied as a percentage calculated on the entire volume of sales handled and often amounts to not more than 1 percent. Almost always factors require that all sales made by their clients be included in the factoring arrangement. If the factor rejects a particular credit transaction, the client may still make the sale, on "client risk," in which event the factor will still handle all procedural details, but not assume any of the risk of nonpayment.

In making the decision whether to have his company's sales factored the treasurer must realize that he is eliminating all future costs of operating a credit department, maintaining records of receivables, collecting them (routinely or otherwise), and all risk of bad debts (except the risk of the factor's own insolvency). In many instances factors can operate so much more skillfully in managing receivables than can some companies that the total cost of the factoring arrangement may not exceed the amount of bad debt losses that otherwise would be sustained.

In essence, therefore, the decision of whether to have receivables factored is similar to a make-or-buy decision with respect to items entering into the manufacturing or merchandising processes. It is also similar to the decisions whether to lease or buy fixed assets, and whether to handle the company's own advertising or to contract it out to an agency. It is a decision that should be faced by treasurers who are interested in reducing the complexity of their companies' operations and the multiplicity of risk exposures.

Summary

Although the treasurer should not concern himself with internal operations of his credit and collections department, he cannot avoid responsibility for making certain basic decisions determining the structure within which these operations will be carried out. The fundamental choice is whether the company should handle these functions itself or contract them out to a factor. Unfortunately this question seldom is faced explicitly since factoring generally is not recognized as a viable alternative and since its adoption would destroy many vested interests within the company. The second choice is to spin off credit and collections to a subsidiary finance company. Again, this represents sufficient departure from traditional methods to generate resistance based on inertia rather than analysis. The third area of choice involves the optimum balance between centralization and decentralization of operations. In this area also all persons directly involved are certain to have built-in prejudices. Thus, it is essential that the treasurer, from his vantage point outside of the operation itself, make the ultimate decisions involving structure.

EVALUATION OF THE
RECEIVABLES PORTFOLIO

Regardless of how much confidence the treasurer has in the credit manager and his staff, it is essential that he be able to evaluate performance of the department. Generally, this will be done in terms of the quality of the receivables portfolio. This cannot be done by using absolute standards, however, since handling of trade receivables requires consideration of the trade-off between increased profits and increased risk of bad debts generated by credit expansion. Ownership of trade receivables is not an end in itself (except to a financing organization) and any income generated through interest collected should be regarded as an offset to costs and not as an independent contribution to revenues. Furthermore, any advantage of holding receivables in terms of their use in connection with borrowing is more than offset by the capital requirements generated by the fact of their existence. It must be remembered at all times, therefore, that trade receivables are created and held only to assist in the making of sales.

Ratio of Bad Debts

The most obvious measure of the value of a receivables portfolio is the percentage of bad debts experienced. As a measure of effectiveness of the credit department, however, this is simplistic and almost completely misleading. The purpose of the credit department is not to identify and reject all doubtful credit risks; instead it is to increase sales volume by selective penetration into groups of less-than-satisfactory credit risks in such a way that net profits earned on such sales more than offset costs associated with handling expense and risk involved. Any credit manager who aims too single-mindedly at maintenance of a low ratio of bad debts to sales should be replaced, just as should the small-town librarian who boasted that all but nine books entrusted to her care were present and accounted for.

Use of the bad debts ratio to compare the effectiveness of credit managers handling different product lines or selling to different classes of trade is equally unfair. A company selling machinery to farmers, building contractors, and governmental units should expect quite different results in terms of collection periods and ultimate payout.

From the point of view of a lender, however, the bad debts ratio is a useful indicator of the quality of a receivables portfolio.

Aging of Accounts Receivable

The treasurer should always receive an analysis of receivables according to how their ages are distributed, dollarwise, by months from date of creation. Comparisons of such distributions on month-to-month and year-to-year bases call attention forcefully to any deterioration in collections. Other ratios used by financial statement analysts who have no access to more detailed information, such as the average collection period or the average number of times that receivables turn over into sales volume in a year, are of little value to persons with statistics on aging except for comparisons with other companies. The treasurer also may ask for supplemental information in the form of names and amounts of all accounts seriously past due, and other data that may show whether deterioration is occurring in a particular product line, company division, or geographical area.

Size Distribution of Receivables

Another presentation of receivables should distribute them by size and should be accompanied by a listing by names and amounts of the largest accounts. Also attention should be called to any accounts that have increased in size significantly since issuance of the last periodic analysis. Totals for product lines, company divisions, industries, classes of customers, geographical areas, and other pertinent groups should also be included. The treasurer should be aware of the dangers of too much concentration in any one account or group. The number of accounts in each size group and any changes in these numbers can be important indications of trends. When evidence of mounting concentration in certain groups is noted, explanations should be sought. In some instances it may be appropriate to call for detailed analysis of the credit standing of certain customers or for the making of special studies of industries where the company's commitments are growing. Obviously, any conclusions drawn will be tempered by knowledge of expected seasonal fluctuations. Periodically, the treasurer should call for the credit files on certain accounts that appear to be running heavily or slowly for the purpose of checking on the up-to-dateness of information, its adequacy, and other indications that the account is being followed in an appropriate manner. In situations that appear to have gotten out of hand, he should inquire what special precautions have been taken, possibly in the form of strengthening the company's position with promissory notes, collateral, guaranties, subordination agreements, endorsements, and the like.

ADDITIONAL SOURCES

See Additional Sources at end of Chapter 21.

Chapter 23

Inventory Management and Standards

John F. Magee*
Harlan C. Meal†

INTRODUCTION

TREASURERS and other financial officers should be vitally interested in inventory management despite the complexity of the subject. A substantial fraction of the assets of the firm are invested in inventory, although that fraction, naturally, varies from industry to industry and among firms in any one industry. If the chief financial officer of a firm is to assist manufacturing and marketing management constructively in the management of these assets, he must understand the functions to be performed by inventory assets, the methods by which these assets may be managed or controlled and the standards against which inventory performance should be judged.

We cannot, of course, describe here all the methods available for inventory management. We have concentrated on the fundamentals of inventory management which we believe to be most important to a financial officer. First, we describe the basic functions of inventories and the costs which are relevant in inventory

* John F. Magee is president of Arthur D. Little, Inc., Cambridge, Massachusetts.
  † Harlan C. Meal is head, Logistics Unit, of Arthur D. Little, Inc., Cambridge, Massachusetts.

economics. Second, we outline the basic problems of inventory control and the ways in which these problems have been addressed most successfully. Finally, we describe methods which can be used to set standards on inventory investment levels and on inventory performance.

INVENTORY FUNCTIONS

In the management of inventories it is essential to understand the functions served by those inventories. Also, in setting inventory standards, the function to be served will influence the desirable level of the standard.

Inventories serve to decouple successive operations in the process of making a product and getting it to consumers. Also an inventory is required because of the time required to accomplish an operation. Thus, inventories make it possible (or are required) to process a product at some distance from the customer or raw material supplies, or to perform two operations at different places. Inventories make it unnecessary to gear production directly to consumption or, alternatively, to force consumption to adapt to the necessities of production. In these and similar ways, inventories free one stage in the production-distribution process from the next, permitting each to operate more economically.

The essential management question is: How much inventory is economic in performing the decoupling function? To arrive at a satisfactory answer we must first distinguish between (*a*) inventories necessary because it takes time to complete an operation and to move the product from one stage to another; and (*b*) inventories employed for organizational reasons; i.e., to let one unit schedule its operations more or less independently of another.

Movement Inventories

Inventory balances needed because of the time required to move stocks from one place to another are often not recognized, or are confused with inventories resulting from other needs—e.g., economical shipping quantities (to be discussed in a later section).

The average amount of movement inventory can be determined from the mathematical expression $I = S \times T$ in which S represents the average sales rate, T the transit time from one stage to the next, and *I* the movement inventory needed. For example, if it takes two weeks to move materials from the plant to a warehouse, and the warehouse sells 100 units per week, the average inventory in movement is 100 units per week times two weeks, or 200 units. From a different point of view, after a unit is manufactured and ready for use at the plant, it must sit idle for two weeks while being moved to the next station (the warehouse); so, on the average, stocks equal to two weeks' sales will be in movement.

Another example is the material tied up in processing. A drying or curing process may require ten days. If the average usage rate is 300 units per month, 100 units will, on average, be tied up in the process. Similarly, if a complex machining operation takes 6 hours per piece and the lot size is 40 pieces, the batch will require 240 hours to complete—three weeks, if two 40-hour shifts are worked each week. This will also require a three-week movement inventory.

Movement inventories are usually thought of in connection with movement between distant points—plant to warehouse. However, any plant may contain substantial stocks in movement from one operation to another—for example, the product moving along an assembly line. Movement stock is one component of the "float" or in-process inventory in a manufacturing operation.

The amount of movement stock changes only when the sales rate or the time in transit is changed. Time in transit is largely a result of method of transportation, although improvements in loading or dispatching practices may cut transit time by eliminating unnecessary delays.

Organization Inventories

Most of the management attention devoted to inventories is concerned with the inventories which reduce the amount of organization or organized effort required in an operation. The larger the interstage inventories the smaller the amount of coordinative effort required to keep the operation running smoothly.

Contrariwise, if inventories are already being used efficiently, they can be cut only at the expense of greater organization effort—e.g., greater scheduling effort to keep successive stages in balance, and greater expediting effort to work out of the difficulties which unforeseen disruptions at one point or another may cause in the whole process.

Despite superficial differences among businesses in the nature and characteristics of the organization inventory they maintain, the following three functions are basic:

Lot size inventories are probably the most common in business. They are maintained wherever the user makes or purchases material in larger lots than are needed for his immediate purposes. For example, it is common practice to buy raw materials in relatively large quantities in order to obain quantity price discounts, keep shipping costs in balance, and hold down clerical costs connected with making out requisitions, checking receipts, and handling accounts payable. Similar reasons lead to long production runs on equipment calling for expensive setups, or to sizable replenishment orders placed on factories by field warehouses.

Fluctuation stocks, also very common in business, are held to cushion the shocks arising basically from unpredictable fluctuations in consumer demand. For example, warehouses and retail outlets maintain stocks to be able to supply consumers on demand, even when the rate of consumer demand may show quite irregular and unpredictable fluctuations. In turn, factories maintain stocks to be in a position to replenish retail and field warehouse stocks in line with customer demands.

Short-term fluctuations in the mix of orders on a plant often make it necessary to carry stocks of parts of subassemblies, in order to give assembly operations flexibility in meeting orders as they arise while freeing earlier operations (e.g., machining) from the need to make momentary adjustments in schedules to meet assembly requirements. Fluctuation stocks may also be carried in semifinished form in order to balance out the load among manufacturing departments when orders received during the current day, week, or month may put a load on an individual department which is out of balance with long-run requirements.

In most cases, anticipating all fluctuations is uneconomical, if not impossible. But a business cannot get along without some fluctuation stocks unless it is willing and able always to make its customers wait until the material needed can be purchased conveniently or until their orders can be scheduled into production conveniently. Fluctuation stocks are part of the price we pay for our general business philosophy of serving the consumers' wants (and whims!) rather than having them take what they can get.

Anticipation stocks are needed where goods or materials are consumed on a predictable but changing pattern through the year, and where it is desirable to absorb some of these changes by building and depleting inventories rather than by changing production rates with attendant fluctuations in employment and additional capital capacity requirements. For example, inventories may be built up in anticipation of a special sale or to fill needs during a plant shutdown.

The need for seasonal stocks may also arise where materials (e.g., agricultural products) are *produced* at seasonally fluctuating rates but where consumption is reasonably uniform; here the problems connected with producing and storing tomato catsup are a prime example.

INVENTORY ECONOMICS

The basic management question with respect to inventories is the selection of the inventory level which provides the best balance between the cost of carrying the inventory and the operating cost which is (presumably) reduced as the inventory increases. This balance is perhaps clearest in the case of lot size inventories. Each time a production lot is made a setup cost is incurred; also, an investment is made in inventory. The larger the production lot, the smaller the annual expenditure for setup costs but the larger the average investment in inventory.

Similarly, with fluctuation stocks, the larger the inventory investment, the lower the cost of shortages or expediting or schedule changes. These trade-offs are usually not simple, directly proportional, relationships. In some cases a significant analytic effort will be required to determine the relationship. However, determining the trade-off relationship is only part of the analysis required to establish the desired inventory level. In addition, to make an economic choice, the manager must know the costs of carrying the inventory and also the operating costs which are influenced by the inventory level.

Inventory Costs

Characteristically, the costs which influence inventory policy, are not the costs recorded, at least not in directly available form, in the usual industrial accounting system. Accounting costs are derived under principles developed over many years and strongly influenced by tradition. The specific methods and degree of skill and refinement may be better in particular companies, but in all of them the basic objective of accounting procedures is to provide a fair, consistent, and conservative valuation of assets and a picture of the flow of values in the business.

In contrast to the principles and search for consistency underlying accounting costs, the definition of costs for production and inventory control will vary from time to time—even in the same company—according to the circumstances and the length of the period being planned for. The following criteria apply:

The costs shall represent "out-of-pocket" expenditures; i.e., cash actually paid out or opportunities for profit foregone. Overtime premium payments are out-of-pocket; depreciation on equipment on hand is not. To the extent that storage space is available and cannot be used for other productive purposes, no out-of-pocket cost of space is incurred; but to the extent that storage space is rented (out-of-pocket) or could be used for other productive purposes (foregone opportunity), a suitable charge is justified. The charge for investment is based on the out-of-pocket investment in inventories or added facilities, not on the "book" or accounting value of the investment.

The rate of interest charged on out-of-pocket investment may be based either on the rate paid banks (out-of-pocket) or on the rate of profit that might reasonably be earned by alternative uses of investment (foregone opportunity), depending on the financial policies of the business. In some cases, a bank rate may be used on short-term seasonal inventories and an internal rate for long-term minimum requirements.

Obviously, much depends on the time scale in classifying a given item. In the short run, few costs are controllable out-of-pocket costs; in the long run, all are.

The costs shall represent only those out-of-pocket expenditures or foregone opportunities for profit whose magnitude is affected by the schedule or plan. Many overhead costs, such as supervision costs, are out-of-pocket, but neither the timing nor the size is affected by the schedule. Normal material and direct labor costs are unaffected in total and so are not considered directly; however, these, as well as some components of overhead cost, do represent out-of-pocket investments, and accordingly enter the picture indirectly through any charge for capital.

Primary Cost Elements

Among the costs which directly influence inventory policy are (*a*) costs depending on the amount ordered, (*b*) costs that depend on the magnitude of shortages, (*c*) costs of changing production rate, and (*d*) costs of storing and handling inventory.

Costs That Depend on the Amount Ordered. These costs include, for example, quantity discounts offered by vendors; setup costs in internal manufacturing operations and clerical costs of making out a purchase order; and when capacity is pressed, the profit on production lost during downtime for setup. Shipping costs represent another factor to the extent that they influence the quantity of raw materials purchased and resulting raw stock levels, the size of intraplant or plant-warehouse shipments, or the size and the frequency of shipments to customers. Shakedown or learning costs appear whenever quality or quantity is below standard at the beginning of a production run. These must be taken into account. They can be treated as setup costs.

Costs That Depend on the Magnitude of Shortages. Upward fluctuations in customer demand will occasionally exhaust the inventory provided to protect the production operation from such fluctuations. When this happens, the operation may incur additional cost. It may be possible to meet the demand by producing the required amount on overtime or by purchasing it from the outside. The cost or foregone profit in these cases are straightforward to estimate. In some cases, neither of these is possible and the demand must be backordered or lost. There are both short- and long-term costs involved in these cases. The short-term costs are the paper work costs of handling the back order and expediting costs (overtime and/or premium freight) to fill the back order quickly. The long-term costs are the loss of customer goodwill and potential long-term loss of sales as a consequence.

Costs of Changing Production Rate. These are the costs of overtime and undertime, of hiring and firing, of low productivity as a consequence of hiring and firing and of any other steps taken to adjust the production rate in response to a change in requirement. Since such rate changes imply the availability of sufficient plant capacity to accommodate the change there may be a cost associated with that capacity. If additional capacity is bought in order to be able to make such changes, the cost of the plant and equipment is a rate change cost. If the capacity is in place and cannot be liquidated, there is no incremental cost of capacity.

Normal or standard raw material and direct labor costs usually do not vary with the run length, the production rate, or changes in the production rate. They do enter the inventory problem since they strongly influence the magnitude of the inventory investment, as discussed further below.

Costs of Handling and Storing Inventory. This group of costs which are affected by control methods and inventory policies includes expenses of handling products in and out of stock, storage costs such as rent and heat, insurance and taxes, obsolescence and spoilage costs, and capital costs (which will receive detailed examination in the next section).

Inventory obsolescence and spoilage costs may take several forms including: (1) outright spoilage after a more or less fixed period; (2) risk that a particular unit in stock or a particular product number will (*a*) become technologically unsalable, except perhaps at a discount or as spare parts, (*b*) go out of style, or (*c*) spoil.

Certain food and drug products, for example, have specified maximum shelf lives and must either be used within a fixed period of time or be dumped. Some kinds of style goods, such as many lines of toys, Christmas novelties, or women's clothes, may effectively "spoil" at the end of a season, with only reclaim or dump value. Some kinds of technical equipment undergo almost constant engineering change during their production life; thus component stocks may suddenly and unexpectedly be made obsolete.

Amount and Cost of Capital Invested in Inventory

Evaluating the effect of inventory and scheduling policy upon capital investment and the worth of capital tied up in inventories is one of the most difficult problems in resolving inventory policy questions.

The *amount of capital* invested in inventory is the out-of-pocket, or avoidable, cash cost for material, labor, and overhead of goods in inventory (as distinguished from the "book" or accounting value of inventory). For example, raw materials are normally purchased in accordance with production schedules; and if the production of an item can be postponed, buying and paying for raw materials can likewise be put off.

Usually, then, the raw material cost component represents a part of the out-of-pocket inventory investment in finished goods. However, if raw materials must be purchased when available (e.g., agricultural crops) regardless of the production schedule, the raw material component of finished product cost does not represent avoidable investment and therefore should be struck from the computation of inventory value for planning purposes.

As for maintenance and similar factory overhead items, they are usually paid for the year round, regardless of the timing of production scheduled; therefore these elements of burden should not be counted as part of the product investment for planning purposes. (One exception: if, as sometimes happens, the maintenance costs actually vary directly with the production rate as, for example, in the case of supplies, they should, of course, be included.)

Again, supervision, at least general supervision, is usually a fixed monthly cost which the schedule will not influence, and hence should not be included. Depreciation is usually a fixed monthly cost which the schedule will not influence, and therefore should not be included. Depreciation is another type of burden item representing a charge for equipment and facilities already bought and paid for; the timing of the production schedule cannot influence these past investments and, while they represent a legitimate cost for accounting purposes, they should not be counted as part of the inventory investment for inventory and production planning purposes.

In sum, the rule is this: for production planning and inventory management purposes, the investment value of goods in inventory should be taken as the cash outlay made at the time of production that could have been delayed if the goods were not made then but at a later time, closer to the time of sale.

The *cost of capital* invested in inventory is the product of three factors: (*a*) the capital value of a unit of inventory, (*b*) the time a unit of product is in inventory, and (*c*) the charge or imputed interest rate placed against a dollar of invested cash. The first factor was just discussed. As for the second, it is fixed by management's inventory policy decisions. But these decisions can be made economically only in view of the third factor. This factor depends directly on the financial policy of the business.

Sometimes businessmen make the mistake of thinking that cash tied up in inventories costs nothing, especially if the cash to finance inventory is generated internally through profits and depreciation. However, this implies that the cash in inventories would otherwise sit idle. In fact, the cash could, at least, be invested in government bonds if not in inventories. And if it were really idle, the cash very likely should be released to stockholders for profitable investment elsewhere.

Moreover, it is dangerous to assume that, as a "short-term" investment, inventory is relatively liquid and riskless. Businessmen say, "After all, we turn our inventory investment over six times a year." But, in reality, inventory investment may or may not be short term and riskless, depending on circumstances. No broad generalization is possible, and each case must be decided on its own merits.

The cost of the dollars invested in inventory may be underestimated if bank interest rate is used as the basis, ignoring the risk-bearing or entrepreneur's compensation. How many businessmen are actually satisfied with uses of their companies' capital funds which do not earn more than a lender's rate of return? In choosing a truly appropriate rate—a matter of financial policy—the executive must answer some questions:

1. Where is the cash coming from—inside earnings or outside financing?
2. What else could we do with the funds, and what could we earn?
3. When can we get the investment back, if ever?
4. How much risk of sales disappointment and obsolescence is really connected with this inventory?
5. How much of a return do we want, in view of what we could earn elsewhere or in view of the cost of money to us and the risk the inventory investment entails?

INVENTORY POLICY CHOICES

We have already seen that the cost of capital invested in inventory is a matter of financial policy. Often this is described as a "policy" choice rather than an economic choice because the choice involves both long- and short-term factors and the magnitudes of the costs are uncertain, regardless of the amount of cost analytic effort which goes into the cost determination.

In much the same way, the costs of shortage or the costs of failure to meet a customer demand are difficult to measure. The effects are both long and short term and may be largely intangible. Faced with this situation it may be most effective to establish a customer service policy which describes the fraction of the customer demand to be satisfied within a specified period of time after order receipt. In some situations the stock out or shortage frequency provides a more useful policy description.

It is possible to arrive at an "economic" choice of the customer service policy if the costs of shortage can be established. The cost of a shortage includes the cost of the extra clerical effort involved in processing back orders and the potential cost of premium freight in the event that the item back ordered is shipped by a faster, more costly mode. It may also be only one of several items ordered and may incur freight rate penalties by being shipped separately from the other items ordered.

These costs, while difficult to determine, can be estimated with satisfactory accuracy by standard cost analytic methods. There are problems with joint costs, but these are much the same as those which are encountered in estimating setup and ordering costs.

The primary problem in the customer service area is that of the effect of poor customer service on sales. The effect may or may not be immediate. A customer may shift his business to a competitor offering better service and the marginal loss of gross margin can be determined from an estimate of the lost sales. However, the loss in sales may not be so immediate and dramatic. Instead of transferring all of his business to competitors, the customer may reduce the fraction he places with your firm. Also, it may be a less profitable fraction, the items of which he can afford to carry larger inventories to protect against your delivery unreliability.

This may have long-term deleterious effects on the firm which cannot be quantified. Somehow, however, the management must make the policy choice. As was pointed out in the introduction, the easiest way to handle this policy choice is by displaying the trade-off or balance between inventory investment and the level of service provided. Both of these can be, and should be, measured routinely. Even though management may not have a satisfactory "cost" relationship between the two, they should have a good business sense of how much service they can "afford" in terms of the required inventory investment.

A typical customer service trade-off curve for one single item carried in a field warehouse is shown in Figure 1. As the shortage

FIGURE 1
Customer Service Trade-off Curve for a
Single Item

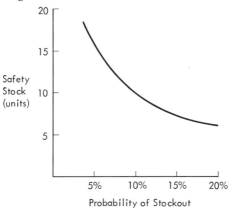

rate increases the fluctuation inventory decreases. Although it is very difficult to determine from such a relationship what the correct service level should be, the aggregate relationship for all the items in a warehouse may provide the needed information. Such an aggregate relationship is shown in Figure 2.

FIGURE 2
Aggregate Customer Service Trade-off Curve

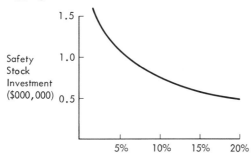

The methods to be used in calculating such trade-off curves will be described further in subsequent sections. They are mentioned here as an alternate to detailed and difficult cost analysis in establishing inventory policy.

A third inventory policy choice is concerned with the frequency and magnitude of production rate changes. If production levels are changed frequently, in response to changes in the customer demand rate, there will be very little accumulation of smoothing or anticipation inventory. Similarly, if output levels are changed seasonally to match a seasonal demand pattern, there will be no seasonal anticipation stock.

Such a policy involves costs of changing production rate. These costs are even less tangible than the shortage costs just discussed. Costs of hiring and firing are difficult to measure, especially since the cost of the hiring activity may not change much with the hiring rate. Some layoff costs are reasonably direct. Unemployment insurance premiums rise with layoff rates and the effect can be estimated; clerical costs of termination can also be estimated. The difficult cost consequence to estimate is the effect of labor force instability on productivity. In some industries a great deal of training is required before a new worker achieves the output rate of an experienced worker. If the firm has a reputation as an erratic employer it may not be able to attract high-quality production labor even with premium labor rates.

Thus, the inventory investment required to provide a particular stability in the production rate may be compared with the stability provided, even though it may not be possible to compare directly the "costs" of inventory and of instability. Such a comparison will facilitate the selection of an inventory policy even though there is no reliable way to establish that it is the "economic" policy choice.

This can be done parametrically for the anticipation stocks required to smooth production in the face of varying customer demand. Such a trade-off curve is shown in Figure 3. In this case the control number relates the fluctuations in production rate to the fluctuations in demand rate. With a control number of one, the production fluctuates just as much as the demand; with smaller values of the control number the production fluctuations are reduced relative to the demand fluctuations until finally, with a control number of zero, the production rate is held constant at the

FIGURE 3
Production Stability Trade-off Curve

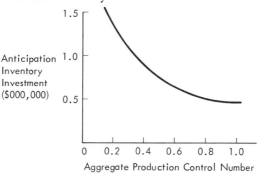

Anticipation
Inventory
Investment
($000,000)

Aggregate Production Control Number

average demand rate and all short-term fluctuations in demand must be absorbed by the anticipation inventory.

Such a parametric representation is not possible in the case of anticipation of a seasonal demand. In such a case several optional plans should be prepared, showing both the production rate variations and the inventory implications of each. In this way management can select a policy or strategy with full knowledge of the implications or consequences of that selection.

INVENTORY CONTROL METHODS

Level of Detail

In nearly all operating situations we find that both *aggregate* and *item* control decisions are made. An aggregate decision will determine the total production of a group of items during some planning period and then detailed decisions will determine the amount of each item to produce. For example, a chemical reactor produces a number of different grades and specifications of a synthetic polymer. An aggregate decision will determine the running rate of the reactor; detailed decisions will determine the quantities of each different polymer to produce each planning period. In another example, an aggregate decision will determine that it is time to begin production of a lot of electronic instruments of a general type. This may be a basic instrument with many optional variations. At the same time, or possibly at a later time, the lot must be allocated among the individual optional configurations.

Characteristically, the aggregate decision deals with the *rate* at which a production unit operates. By determining that rate the total output of all the items made by the unit is determined. The unit may be as small as a single machine; e.g., a screw machine, or a numerically controlled machining center, or as large as an entire plant, in which there is substantial interchangeability of the productive capacity (men and/or machines) among all the items to be produced by the plant.

Also characteristically, the item decisions are batch decisions, determining the quantity and timing of lots of each item to be produced. Of course, these lot decisions are constrained by the aggregate rate decision. Lots must be planned to use all (but not more than) the capacity provided.

There may be more than two levels of detail. A plant level decision may determine the total work force (and output) level for the plant; a shop level decision will allocate the work force available in the plant among the shops in the plant; an item level decision will allocate the capacity among the items produced in each shop.

Note that decisions can be made about aggregates only if there is substantial interchangeability of capacity among the subunits (items or shops) in the aggregate. If a plant makes electric motors and motor controls with no significant interchangeability of machines or manpower between the departments producing these two product lines, it is not sensible to talk about the aggregate output rate of the plant. In such a case the aggregate rates for the two departments must be set separately and independently.

There may well be subdivisions within a production unit producing a single product line; for example, a parts fabrication department and an assembly department. In such a case, the aggregate levels of the two departments must be set in a coordinated, consistent fashion. If they are not, the parts inventory will be either too large or too small to support the assembly schedule.

The importance of the aggregate decision in inventory management is often overlooked. Many inventory problems are the result of attempting to control item inventories with a detailed decision-making process which is treated as though it were independent of the aggregate decision process. A common consequence of this approach is a manufacturing order backlog which fluctuates a great deal, many missed delivery promises and parts inventories which are out of control, with excessive stock levels and shortage rates.

Making the item decisions without adequate consideration of the constraints which result from aggregate level decisions, leads to decisions which are infeasible and parts plans which are not matched to assembly requirements.

The level of aggregate investment in inventory is determined as much by the skill and judgment applied to the aggregate level decision as it is by the sophistication of the detailed decision-making system. Often it appears that the problems of controlling many items have made clear the need for a sophisticated system approach to item control even though the total production unit output is determined by an intuitive assessment of the market potential or the availability of skilled labor. If the total finished inventory investment is too high, it is necessarily the case that *total* plant output has been too large, regardless of the precision with which item control decisions have been made. The general management of the firm and, especially, the financial managers must be aware of this relationship if they are to be helpful to the production and marketing managers in making inventory management decisions.

Kinds of Decisions

In most inventory control systems, separate but related subsystems control the several types of inventory. For example, in a simple warehouse replenishment system, the lot size or order quantity decision is made by one subsystem and the safety stock or order timing decision is made by another subsystem. In describing the inventory control methods in common use and the inventory which results from their application, we will separately describe the methods used to control different kinds of inventory.

Even though there is no way to decide which unit in the warehouse resulted from which control rule, it is essential to understand the workings of the several control rules which influence the inventory of a single item. At any time the inventory on hand may include components of cycle or lot size stock, safety stock and production smoothing stock. Thus, to tell whether the inventory on hand is too high, too low or about right, one must know how much inventory was planned for each of these functions and the relationships or interactions there may be among the different inventory functions.

We will not attempt to describe all the different forms of control rules needed in the wide variety of operating situations which exist in industry. Instead, we will describe examples of the different kinds of control rules, illustrating the principles involved in developing these rules.

The most fundamental difference among rules arises from the need to observe capacity constraints in some cases. In most production or manufacturing situations, the total output of the manufacturing unit constrains the production quantities of the individual items. Since this is not usually the case when items are purchased, we designate the capacity constrained rules as rules for *manufactured* items and the unconstrained rules as rules for *purchased* items. Even though there are no production capacity constraints which influence purchased item inventories, there are multiple item factors which must be taken into account when several items are purchased from a common source. Although these are similar in some respects to capacity constraints, we will describe them under the heading of purchased item control methods.

Control System Approach

Inventory and production control systems can be divided according to the method used for scheduling the review of item status and the placement of replenishment orders. Review may be *continuous* (i.e., following immediately every inventory transaction), or *periodic*, taking place at a specified calendar time, regardless of the number or size of transactions which have taken place since the status was last reviewed. The overwhelming majority of the production and inventory control systems in use today are periodic review systems. This has come about largely because the inventory record posting and status reviewing tasks are much easier in both manual and mechanized systems when the transactions are batched for processing. In addition, production schedules are normally issued periodically (weekly, biweekly, and so on) and there is no point in reviewing the status of an item unless some action can be taken as a result of the review.

In a *periodic review system,* the amount ordered at the time of a review, should an order be required, must be at least enough to last until an order placed at the next review can be received. Since no order can be placed until that next review, no earlier replenishment can be obtained. The amount ordered must provide both the amount required to satisfy expected demand during the review interval and also the amount needed to protect against demand fluctuations during the time until the next possible replenishment, the review interval plus the replenishment lead time. The amount required to protect against demand fluctuations is commonly referred to as safety stock. The amount ordered to provide for the expected demand during one or more review intervals is the order quantity which leads to cycle stock. In a periodic review system, the order quantity decision is constrained to take on values corresponding to the usage during an integral number of review intervals.

In a *continuous review system,* the order quantity has no corresponding constraint. The lot size can have any value. In such a system, the situation is reviewed after each transaction and an order can be placed at any time. The order must be placed early enough to provide adequate assurance that the replenishment will arrive before the supply is exhausted. The amount of stock provided in excess of expected demand is safety stock.

These two basic systems have slightly different ways of determining cycle stock and safety stock, but the factors involved in determining these inventory components are the same in both systems. The cycle stock is determined by the balance between the cost of placing an order and the cost of carrying inventory. The safety stock is determined by the uncertainty in requirements during the replenishment lead time and the service policy to be met.

CONTROL RULES FOR PURCHASED ITEMS

Lot Size of an Independent Item

This classic formula, often referred to as the "economic lot size formula," the "Wilson lot size," or the "square root lot size," was developed many years ago. It has been widely used, often inappropriately. It has many variations, reflecting modifications needed as a consequence of one or more changes in assumptions from the basic case.

The simplest form of the result is:

$$Q = \sqrt{\frac{2AS}{c}}$$

where

Q = Order quantity (pieces or units)
A = Order cost or setup cost per order (dollars)
S = Annual usage or sales (pieces or units per year)
c = Cost to carry one piece or unit in inventory for one year (dollars per year)

This result can be derived in a number of different ways. It rests on the following assumptions:

a. The cost of a lot Q is given by

$$B = A + bQ$$

i.e., by a fixed cost A independent of the order quantity plus a constant marginal cost per piece times the order quantity.
b. The resupply *rate* is very high relative to the usage rate; i.e., a batch arrives essentially all at once, as in the receipt of a shipment at a warehouse.
c. The usage rate is constant or may vary around a constant average.
d. The individual withdrawals are small relative to the replenishment quantity; i.e., usage is continuous.
e. The costs of ordering and carrying this item are independent of the ordering decisions made for other items. (This is required for assumption (a) to hold.)
f. The cost to carry the inventory is proportional to the quantity in inventory (c per unit) and there is no relevant upper limit on the amount to be carried in inventory.

Given these assumptions the inventory will vary with time in the sawtooth pattern shown in Figure 4. The average value of the inventory level is $Q/2$.

FIGURE 4
Inventory Time Plot for Lot Size Determination

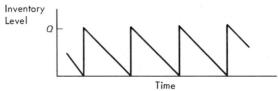

There will be S/Q orders per year. The annual cost of purchasing and carrying inventory will be:

$$C = \frac{S}{Q}(A + bQ) + \frac{Q}{2}c$$

$$= \frac{SA}{Q} + Sb + \frac{Qc}{2}$$

Differentiating with respect to Q and equating the result to zero to find the minimum cost order quantity we have:

$$\frac{dC}{dQ} = -\frac{SA}{Q^2} + \frac{c}{2} = 0$$

$$\frac{c}{2} = \frac{SA}{Q^2}$$

$$Q^2 = \frac{2SA}{c}$$

$$Q = \sqrt{\frac{2SA}{c}}$$

Although this result has only limited applicability in this form, the development illustrates some important fundamental concepts in inventory management. The average cycle inventory is half the order quantity and the cost to carry the cycle inventory increases in direct proportion to the lot size. The annual cost of ordering declines in inverse proportion to the lot size.

The limited applicability of this formulation results primarily from the lack of independence of the item. In many cases the item will be ordered in combination with other items. As a result the inventory and ordering costs of any one item must be considered together with those of the other items ordered with it.

Lot Sizes for Items Ordered Jointly

The most common reason for grouping items for ordering is that such grouping allows assembling a *total* order large enough to obtain a price discount from the vendor or a lower freight rate from a carrier. If this benefit were obtained by ordering items singly much larger orders would be required and much larger inventories would result. By ordering the items jointly the benefits from quantity ordering are obtained with minimum cycle inventories.

The economic lot size formulation developed for an independent item may also be used for a group of items to be ordered jointly. This is appropriate when the quantity to be ordered, as a result of such a formulation, is larger than the quantity required to obtain the maximum joint ordering benefit (minimum price or freight rate). In that case, the ordering cost becomes, in general, a cost to place the joint order plus a charge for each item on the order (a header cost plus a line cost). The usage rate to use is the total of the item usage rates. The item inventory carrying cost is replaced by a weighted average inventory carrying cost, the carrying cost of each item being weighted by the item usage rate.

This leads to the following result for the joint order quantity,

$$\Sigma Q_i = \sqrt{\frac{2(A + \Sigma a_i)\Sigma S_i}{\Sigma S_i c_i / \Sigma S_i}}$$

where

ΣQ_i = Total order quantity to be placed

A = Ordering cost (header cost) resulting from the fact of placing the joint order (does not depend on the number of items)

a_i = Ordering cost (line cost) resulting from the fact of adding item i to a joint order

S_i = Usage rate of the ith item

c_i = Inventory carrying charge per year for the ith item

This rule does not determine the individual item order quantities. The total order quantity may be allocated among the items in a number of different ways. If all the items are ordered each time a joint order is placed, the average order quantity of each item will be in proportion to the item usage rate, $Q_i = S_i \Sigma Q_i / \Sigma S_i$. If the items have substantially different usage rates, it may be advantageous to order the slow moving items less often than once each joint order cycle. This will lead to a different allocation rule and average inventory.

Whatever the general allocation rule to be used, usually each order placed will be allocated among the items so as to adjust the inventory to some desired set of ratios among the items. Thus, the specified item order quantities will not be calculated with the rule given here but with an allocation rule which takes into account the current inventory position of all the items and the desired inventory balance or mix. Such allocation rules are described in a later section.

The formula given above is satisfactory only if the order quantity developed in that way is larger than the amount required to obtain the maximum joint ordering benefit. If this condition is not met, a modified approach must be used. Because of the discontinuities in the price-quantity relationship, an analytic formula cannot be developed. Instead, the total cost of acquisition (ordering cost and purchase price including freight) and of inventory carrying must be calculated at each of the price break points. The price break point yielding the lowest total cost determines the joint order quantity to be used in most cases. In a few cases, an order quantity calculated with the square root formula given earlier will yield a still lower total cost of acquisition and inventory carrying. This should also be checked in finding the correct joint order quantity in quantity discount situations. In all of these cases, care should be taken to calculate the inventory carrying cost so as to reflect the possible effects of quantity discounts on the purchase price.

Exactly the same procedure should be used to find the correct order quantity for an independent item which may have quantity discounts available. Of course, the appropriate ordering and carrying cost factors must be used. The situation was not described there as its most common occurrence is in the joint ordering situation.

Safety Stock for Purchased Items

Safety stocks protect a supplying process from uncertainties in demand (equally, they protect a user from supply uncertainties). In a distribution warehouse enough stock should be on hand to cover unforecasted demands which are larger than expected. Characteristically, provision is made to cover most, but not all, of the expected fluctuations. Thus, to set safety stocks efficiently, we need to: (1) determine the statistical characteristics of the demand fluctuations, or, more rigorously, the forecast error distribution, (2) establish the fraction of those fluctuations to be covered, and (3) devise a control system which will use the statistical characteristics of demand to carry out the established service policy.

In examining requirements for safety stocks we find that there are two basic forms of control system and that the role of safety stocks is different in each. In an *order point, order quantity* (*OP-OQ*) system, a replenishment order for a fixed or constant quantity is placed each time the stock available falls below a specified order point. In a *periodic reordering* system, the stock position is reviewed at regular intervals and (normally) an order is placed at each review. The quantity ordered will vary from order to order but the order interval is fixed while in the *OP-OQ* system, the order quantity is fixed but the time between orders varies from order to order.

Safety Stock in an *OP-OQ* System

The objective is to place an order whenever the available stock is just sufficient to meet the demand during the time required to obtain additional stock—the replenishment lead time. An examination of the history of demand for an item will show that the demand during the lead time varies a great deal. The *pattern* of variation may be very stable, however, and if the distribution of demand during the lead time looks like Figure 5, we may plan

FIGURE 5
Probability Distribution of Demand during a Lead Time

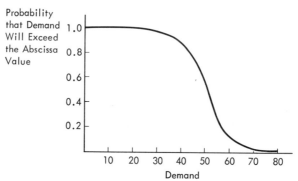

our replenishment on the basis that the demand during the next lead time will be distributed in a similar fashion. From the diagram we see that we can expect, one time in ten, to run out prior to receiving the replenishment order if we place the order when the available stock is 60 units. Put differently, the probability that there will be a stock out (a shortage of one or more pieces) is 10 percent if the order is placed when 60 pieces remain available. The available stock level at which the order is placed is called the *order point.*

Other order points will provide different levels of assurance of no shortage. An order point of 50 yields a 50 percent chance of stock out prior to obtaining replenishment, an order point of 66 reduces this chance to 5 percent and so on.

The control system which obtains the prescribed level of protection against stock out must have two basic elements. It must have a way to examine the stock level frequently to determine whether or not the available stock is equal to or less than the order point. When that happens, a replenishment action must be taken. It must also have a way to estimate the distribution of demands during the lead time in order to determine what the order point should be.

Most *OP-OQ* systems review stock levels frequently, much more frequently than orders are placed. In some cases the situation is reviewed after each withdrawal transaction. (This can often be accomplished conveniently in connection with the transaction posting system.) In other cases the situation is reviewed weekly for all those items which had transactions during the week.

The distribution of demand to expect during the replenishment lead time is usually estimated by developing the historical distribution and demonstrating that it has been stable (or reasonably so) in the past. All this requires is collection of a history of demands during time periods which are as long as the lead time. Since that can be rather awkward to do, most systems collect a history of demand during a unit time (week, month, or quarter) and adjust this upward or downward as needed to reflect the actual duration of the lead time.

The usual way to estimate the distribution is to conduct an analysis of distribution shapes every year or so or when there is an indication of a change and then measure a parameter of that distribution; e.g., the standard deviation or the mean absolute deviation of the individual observations from the average. This allows maintenance of accurate order points with reasonable economy in data collection and processing.

Any practical *OP-OQ* system will have many additional features as well, but the core of the system is just these three elements:

(1) measurement of the average usage during a unit time and a lead time, (2) measurement of the deviations of demand from that average, and (3) a method to compare frequently the stock level with an order point calculated from the two measured parameters and the desired service standard or policy.

Safety Stock in a Periodic Reorder System

In a periodic reorder system, the objective of the replenishment system (at least, the objective of the part of the system concerned with safety stock) is to order enough stock to provide the desired level of protection against stock out until the next order can be placed and the goods received. This is illustrated in Figure 6.

FIGURE 6
Inventory-Time Relationship in a Periodic Reordering System
(reorder times indicated by arrows)

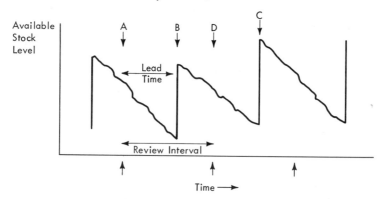

An order placed at time *A* will arrive at time *B*. Together with the available stock at time *A*, the order must provide enough stock to last until time *C*. The order which will arrive at that time will have been placed a lead time earlier at time *D*. Thus, in placing an order at time *A*, the inventory controller must recognize that he is vulnerable to stock out through the entire period until time *C*, a review interval plus a lead time later.

We proceed in exactly the same way as in the *OP-OQ* system to determine how much stock should be provided. The distribution of demand during the review interval plus the lead time is estimated from historical data. Such a distribution might also look like Figure 5. There is only a 10 percent chance that demand will exceed 60, a 5 percent chance it will exceed 66, and so on. If we wish only a 5 percent chance of stock out, we will have to order enough stock to bring the available stock up to 66; e.g., if we have 18 on hand, we should order 48. Note that even though an *OP-OQ* system and a periodic reorder system may have the same replenishment frequency, the periodic reordering system requires more safety stock. This comes about because the situation is not examined during the review interval. At the time of any review, the stock level may be much lower than expected. In the *OP-OQ* system, the stock level is frequently reviewed so there is substantially less uncertainty in the stock level at the time of review.

On the other hand, the *OP-OQ* system generally requires substantially greater clerical or data processing effort to execute than does the periodic reordering system. Just reviewing the records in a system controlling many thousands of parts may be so time-consuming that it should be done only periodically instead of after every transaction.

Measure of Service

Under various circumstances and conditions, it is desirable not only to set different levels of service, but also to measure service differently. Thus far, we have described service only in terms of probability that a stock out will occur (or not occur) during the time the operation is vulnerable to stockout. This time is the replenishment lead time in an *OP-OQ* system and the review interval plus the replenishment lead time in a periodic reordering system.

The stockout probability is one measure of service. It is appropriate in those customer service situations which require a high certainty that no stockout will occur because of the high costs of a shortage. This is often the case in processes which supply assembly operations. A shortage will interrupt assembly and the magnitude of the resulting costs may not be particularly sensitive to the amount of the shortage.

In a retail or wholesale operation, the magnitude of the shortage and the total amount of the shortage may be the best measure of the impact on the business of the shortage situation. In most cases, the magnitude of the shortage should be related to the magnitude of the demand. This leads to the use of the *fraction of demand short* or *fraction back ordered* as convenient measures of service.

To measure the fraction back-ordered, the expected magnitude of the shortage must be compared with the usage of the item between potential back order or shortage occurrences. Thus, the replenishment quantity enters into the determination of the service measure. The larger the replenishment quantity the larger the expected shortage can be and still meet the service objective. In the probability of stockout measure, the service is independent of the replenishment quantity.

Although the two measures described here are the ones most commonly encountered in practice, other measures of service are sometimes used. The number of stockouts per year, the fraction of orders filled complete (when multiple item orders are received), and the delay time in filling orders are examples of service measures found in practice. In implementation of any service objective, the basic task is to set up a system which will achieve a particular probability of stockout which is derived from the service objective and other factors such as the replenishment frequency, the number of items per customer order and so on.

Service Policy

In many cases, it seems that it should be possible to establish the "economic" service level, the level which minimizes the total cost of carrying inventory and of shortages. However, the costs of shortage are usually so difficult to determine and are also a combination of immediate, short-term costs, such as lost profits from lost sales and the costs of handling back orders, and long-term costs, such as loss of customer goodwill and, therefore, future sales, that most firms find it most effective set the service policy without evaluating shortage costs.

The easiest way to arrive at a service policy is to examine the consequences of optional policies as described earlier. Considering a trade-off curve of the type shown in Figure 2 usually will allow selection of a service policy which reflects a reasonable balance between the cost of carrying inventory and the service provided to customers.

Material Requirements Planning (MRP)

The description of safety stock requirements shows that the amount of safety stock required depends directly on the magnitude of the forecast errors which are expected. Note that it is not the *variability* in demand which leads to a requirement for safety stock, but the *uncertainty* or lack of perfect forecasts of demand. In many manufacturing situations, highly variable requirements for parts can be known accurately (or nearly so) well in advance of the time the parts must be ordered.

This happens because the parts demand is a consequence of assembly schedules. These assembly schedules may be frozen so far in advance that there is time to order the needed parts (for purchase or fabrication) after the assembly schedule is frozen and still obtain the parts before they are required by the assembly process. Thus a perfect forecast of requirements is available.

Since many assembly processes are very irregular, with assembly of a production lot of one item and then a lot of another, the demand or requirement for a particular part may be extremely irregular, even though it is known exactly. This is the case for parts which are used in many finished products as well as those which are used in only one finished product.

In such a situation, it is possible, in principle, to have available a perfect forecast of a highly variable demand and, as a consequence, to carry no safety stock of the item in question. To carry this out in practice, however, requires careful management of a large amount of information. Prior to the availability of inexpensive mechanical or electronic information processing, this careful management was feasible in only a few instances. Today, however, the data management required can be accomplished at a reasonable cost by nearly all the firms which have this sort of operating situation.

Two basic data processing operations must be accomplished:

1. *The bill of materials* or list of parts required to assemble one of each of the finished products must be maintained current. This is sometimes referred to as engineering data base maintenance.

2. There must be a way to *explode* or transform the finished product assembly schedule into a parts (or material) requirements plan.

In addition to these two data processing requirements, there is a critical operational requirement—the assembly schedule must be frozen far enough into the future so that parts can be ordered and obtained within the frozen period. If this is not the case, the perfect forecast is of very limited value. Knowing what parts should have been ordered two weeks after they had to be ordered is only a little better than knowing it two months after they had to be ordered, especially if demand is highly variable.

On the other hand, if demand can be known closely, in advance of placing a parts order, still further advantages can be obtained. The *quantity* to be ordered can be matched to the requirement in a way which markedly reduces the inventory remaining after assembly requirements have been withdrawn and until the next receipt takes place. If order quantities are calculated using the formulation developed at the beginning of this section, assuming that the demand has a constant average rate, they will often be poorly matched to the actual requirements. The result is often a substantial carry-over stock, from one assembly requirement to the next, which is insufficient to meet the next assembly requirement and, as a consequence, requires ordering another "economic" quantity.

Finding the correct order quantity to use in this situation is not a simple direct task. Several different approaches have been recommended. Under the not often encountered situation that demand is known exactly (or nearly so) for several order cycle intervals into the future the Wagner-Whitin algorithm provides an optimal choice of order quantity.[1] The Silver-Meal algorithm, however, provides nearly all of the benefit of the Wagner-Whitin method in those circumstances and does so with substantially less computational effort.[2] In addition, it is superior in dealing with the commonly encountered situation of increasing uncertainty in the demand beyond the period covered by the parts order to be placed.

Detailed descriptions of the MRP method and its strengths can be found in Orlicky[3] and in Plossl and Wight.[4] The approach was

---

[1] Harvey M. Wagner and Thomson M. Whitin, "Dynamic Version of the Economic Lot Size Model," *Management Science,* 5 (October 1958), 88–96.

[2] Edward A. Silver and Harlan C. Meal, "A Heuristic for Selecting Lot Size Quantities," *Production and Inventory Management,* 14 (Second quarter 1973), 66–74.

[3] Joseph A. Orlicky, *Material Requirements Planning: The New Way of Life in Production and Inventory Management* (New York: McGraw-Hill Book Co., 1975).

[4] G. W. Plossl and O. W. Wight, *Production and Inventory Control: Principles and Techniques* (Englewood Cliffs, N.J.: Prentice-Hall, Inc., 1967).

first suggested by Magee.[5] We will not describe the method here but will illustrate it with an example.

Suppose that the assembly schedules for three different circuit boards are as shown in Figure 7. Board CKT–1 requires five 3N32 transistors, board CKT–2 requires three of the same transistors and board CPT–3 requires two such transistors. If the parts are required two weeks prior to assembly completion, the demand for the 3N32 transistors will be as the requirement schedule shown in Figure 7. Although this demand is very irregular, it is also known exactly once the final assembly schedule is fixed.

FIGURE 7
Assembly and Requirement Schedule

Assembly Completion Schedule																
Week	*12*	*13*	*14*	*15*	*16*	*17*	*18*	*19*	*20*	*21*	*22*	*23*	*24*	*25*	*26*	*27*
CKT–1			25	25		25	50	25				50	50	100	50	50
CKT–2			40			40			40			40			40	
CKT–3	25			25		25		25		25		25		25		25

Parts Issuance Schedule																
Week	*12*	*13*	*14*	*15*	*16*	*17*	*18*	*19*	*20*	*21*	*22*	*23*	*24*	*25*	*26*	*27*
CKT–1	25	25			25	50	25			50	50	100	50	50		
CKT–2	40			40			40			40			40			
CKT–3		25		25		25		25		25		25		25		

Requirement Schedule																
Week	*12*	*13*	*14*	*15*	*16*	*17*	*18*	*19*	*20*	*21*	*22*	*23*	*24*	*25*	*26*	*27*
Transistor 3N32 . . .	245	175		170	125	300	245	50		420	250	550	370	300		

If the parts demand is known at least a parts procurement lead time into the future, the materials manager has a perfect forecast of that demand. This forecast will allow him to support the assembly operation with very little inventory. The only inventory there will be is the pipeline or transit inventory for the time required to accomplish the receiving, inspection, and issuing operations, plus any cycle inventory resulting from procuring more than one week's supply in one order to obtain quantity discounts or other savings. On the basis of this planned requirement, the materials manager or purchasing agent can schedule replenishments as he needs them and provide for no safety stock or carryover from one week to the next.

---

[5] John F. Magee and David M. Boodman, *Production Planning and Inventory Control* (New York: McGraw-Hill Book Co., 1966).

This example illustrates both the strengths and weaknesses of the method. If demand is highly variable but known accurately, substantial inventory reductions (relative to methods requiring minimal data processing) can be achieved. On the other hand, if the master assembly schedule is not frozen far enough into the future (and marketing management often objects strenuously to the resulting rigidity in schedules) or if parts lead times show significant uncertainty, only small advantage may be obtained from the data processing effort expended to obtain a "deterministic" requirements plan.

Control methods under material requirements planning are only slightly modified from those used for independent item management. We have already mentioned two modified lot size calculation approaches. These provide greater benefit (relative to the simpler methods described earlier) as the variability (not uncertainty) in demand increases.

Safety stocks should be largely eliminated by materials requirements planning. If, however, there is substantial uncertainty in parts fabrication lead times or in vendor delivery times, safety time (which leads to safety stock) must be provided. The replenishment order must be placed early enough to provide the desired assurance that the replenishment will arrive prior to the time required. The procedure for assuring this is exactly the same as that described in the section on safety stock except that the uncertain variable is the vendor delivery lead time rather than the user (assembly) demand.

Thus, although providing substantial opportunities for inventory reduction in those cases where assembly demand is well known and vendor delivery times are reliable, MRP does not entirely avoid the problems of dealing with uncertainty and does require substantial amounts of data processing effort to obtain its advantages.

CONTROL RULES FOR
MANUFACTURED ITEMS

We have (rather arbitrarily) divided inventory management problems into two groups—purchasing control and manufacturing control. Further, we distinguish between those two by the absence or presence of capacity limits or constraints. If there is no meaningful operational limit on the amount of an item which can be ordered (and obtained) at any one time, we treat this as a *purchasing* control problem; if there are operational constraints on the rate at which the needed material can be obtained, we treat this as a *manufacturing* control problem.

In nearly all cases the rate or capacity constraints are on the aggregate output of a manufacturing unit (shop, department or plant) which produces several (or many) items instead of on the output of a single item. This means that, in the control of manufacturing inventories, we must control separately, but in an integrated or coordinated way, the aggregate output of a manufacturing unit and the output (inventory) of each of the items produced by the manufacturing unit. The primary determinant of the total finished product inventory is the way in which the aggregate output of the manufacturing unit is controlled. The detailed or item control procedures determine primarily the mix of the aggregate inventory among the items. The quality or sophistication of the item control procedures determines the minimum inventory with which the firm can operate but the average inventory investment required in excess of that minimum is determined by the aggregate control procedure.

Item control procedures have received a great deal more attention in the business, trade and academic literature than have aggregate control methods and procedures. For this reason, we will concentrate here on aggregate control methods and their consequences, describing the item control procedures only briefly. Readily available sources will provide additional information on item control procedures.

Aggregate Control by Horizon Planning

The name "horizon planning" arises from the use of this method in planning production to meet a seasonal sales or demand requirement. If the cumulative forecast of demand is plotted against time and to that is added the desired inventory level at each point in time, the resultant curve looks like a hill to be climbed by someone standing at the beginning inventory position. As he looks up this hill, he eventually sees a "horizon," the point at which a line from the beginning inventory position is tangent to the cumulative requirements curve (see Figure 8).

This line has special characteristics. It describes the cumulative

FIGURE 8

Anticipation Inventory Accumulation with Constant Rate Plan

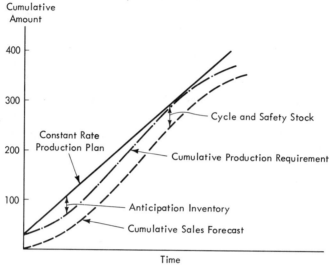

production which will meet the cumulative requirements with the lowest maximum production rate. (The production plan with the lowest maximum production rate to meet any requirement target is the plan with the *same* rate at all times which just meets the requirement.) Such a plan has a higher inventory requirement than a plan which adjusts the production rate from time to time to match that rate more closely to the current demand and the cumulative production more closely to the cumulative requirement. Figure 9 illustrates the differences. It shows a production plan with three different production rates, yielding substantial reductions in the anticipation or seasonal inventory requirement.

Here we see that the aggregate production plan has a substantial impact on the total amount of inventory required in the system. Within the available production output many different item control procedures can be used and *not influence the seasonal inventory in the slightest way*. These item control procedures will, of course, determine the minimum amount of inventory with which it is possible to operate. This minimum becomes a target level at the season end but, since it must be present at the end of the peak season, it must be present during the rest of the year in addition to the seasonal inventory.

FIGURE 9
Anticipation Inventory with Varying Production Plan

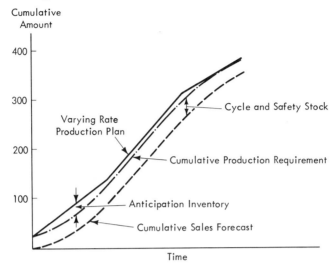

The horizon planning approach can also be applied to non-seasonal situations. Aggregate demand fluctuates from time to time even though it seems to have a stable or nearly stable expected or average value. In such a situation it is often preferable to have a production plan which is more stable than the demand, not following the week-to-week or month-to-month demand fluctuations.

One way to do this is to establish a planning horizon of, say, four to six months and plan production each month so that any current inventory excess or deficit will be corrected at the end of the planning horizon. If a four-month horizon were used, one quarter of any inventory deficit relative to objective would be made up in the first month of the plan.

The following month the process is repeated. Since demand fluctuates from month-to-month, an expected inventory deficit may have been transformed into an inventory excess position. The same rule is still followed; a fraction of the excess is planned to be worked off in the first month of the plan.

As the planning horizon is lengthened, the production plan becomes more and more stable. However, it requires more and more anticipation inventory to assure that customer service will be maintained in the face of fluctuating demand and (reasonably) stable production. Similarly, shortening the planning horizon leads to a more responsive and "nervous" production operation.

This approach to production control is described in Magee and Boodman as *control number planning*. The control number is the fraction of the inventory difference from standard which is to be liquidated each planning period. Control number planning is equivalent to horizon planning (in the nonseasonal case) with the control number equal to the reciprocal of the planning horizon.

Magee and Boodman have developed expressions for the amount of anticipation inventory required to smooth production by varying amounts in the face of demand fluctuations of different sizes.[6]

This is a simple, powerful technique for control of aggregate production levels. It is probably the most widely used aggregate control technique today.

Aggregate Control by Linear Programming

Mathematical programming, especially linear programming (LP), has been used in a wide variety of operating situations. It is perhaps most widely used in the planning and control of refineries and chemical plants of various sorts.

The use of an LP formulation of the aggregate production level decision problem has the advantage that the complex trade-offs among inventory levels of each of many items and operating costs of many kinds can be handled rigorously in detail and an optimum plan derived. One can take into account the costs to change production rate, overtime costs, detailed capacity limitations, and almost any other factor which influences the cost of production.

However, there are often severe difficulties with the application of LP methods to aggregate planning problems. The biggest single problem is that of determining the cost to change production rate. Overtime and undertime costs are usually easy to estimate. However, it is not easy to estimate the effect on the work force and on productivity from frequent layoffs and rehires. Without a good estimate of these costs, the LP system cannot make a reasonable estimate of the optimum production plan.

The second drawback to the use of LP in production planning is the inability of the LP system to handle demand uncertainties in a satisfactory way. In some cases, this is not a problem and one

---
[6] Ibid.

can deal with changes in forecast and with the forecast errors by simply developing a new plan each month. This is a good control technique in any event. However, when demand uncertainty leads to a need to take explicit account of it in planning, different approaches must be used.

The LP formulation of an aggregate plan minimizes the costs of production (including overtime, and any other rate dependent costs) and the costs of inventory carrying. By expressing these costs in terms of the amounts of each item to produce during each planning period, the minimum cost plan which will satisfy the demand can be found.

One can also include more than one stage of manufacturing and distribution in an LP model. This is very difficult to handle in a satisfactory way with a horizon planning model. We can summarize the conditions under which it is desirable to use LP as follows: LP is needed when the factors to be taken into account are too complex to handle by horizon planning methods. Such factors include:

1. Overtime costs.
2. Shift premiums.
3. Costs of subcontracting.
4. Multiple stages of manufacturing and distribution.
5. Multiple plant planning.
6. Assignment of warehouses to plants.

For further information on the use of this approach to aggregate planning, standard texts on the subject should be consulted.

Other Approaches to Aggregate Planning

A number of other approaches to aggregate planning have been developed. One of the best known is that of *linear decision rules* which was developed in the late 50s. It has not been used much in practice because of difficulty in developing the needed cost inputs. It was developed before computing hardware and software were available to make economic the solutions these problems by linear programming. With the availability of economic linear programming solutions to large problems, the linear decision rule approach has not been further developed.

The *heuristic programming* and *management coefficients* methods are extensions of the basic notions of control number planning. In both of them, damped response rules are used to correct not only inventory positions but also other variables as well. These include the work force, the amount of overtime, the amount of subcontracting and so on. The basic approach is the same as in control number planning but more factors are included. These methods have not been widely used because their added complexity does not seem to lead to sufficient improvement in planning.

Anticipation Inventory Requirements

In either the horizon planning method or the linear programming method, application of the method will yield an estimate of the anticipation inventory which will be accumulated in addition to the inventory required for lot sizes and for item safety stocks. In most cases of seasonal stock accumulation, the only way to compare optional aggregate plans is to try them "on paper." With horizon planning this may require a substantial amount of clerical effort to get the item information aggregated, but the analysis of optional plans is simple and easy to accomplish.

Computer systems are required to use the linear programming method. Since they are required for solution, computer files are set up for the aggregation of the item data. Once those files are established, several different aggregate plans can be run economically. Each plan will have an inventory profile and characteristic costs as well as intangible advantages and disadvantages as a consequence of the particular plan. The production manager can then readily find that plan which best accomplishes the objectives of the firm and can review the options with general management, showing them the expected consequences of optional choices.

If the horizon or control number planning method is used in nonseasonal situations, the expected anticipation inventory can be found directly from the demand characteristics and the control number. This relationship and its development is given in Magee and Boodman.[7]

Item Control Rules

Once the aggregate level of production has been established, the next task of production control is to determine how much should

---

[7] Ibid.

be produced of each item, or, put differently, decisions must be made which divide the available production capability among the items to be produced. There are, perhaps, as many ways of doing this as there are manufacturing firms. Usually, this process is referred to as *production scheduling*, a field rich in its complexity and variety of methods.

There are, however, two basic approaches to the scheduling problem. These are *run out list* and the *allocation* methods. In the run out list method, a schedule is prepared with fixed size lots to be made of each item, roughly in the sequence the items are needed to prevent run out. The time at which any one item will be produced will depend on the amount of the available production time which will be used by the items which are more urgently needed.

In the allocation method, the production capability of the manufacturing unit in a planning period is allocated among all the items to be produced by the manufacturing unit. The production lot sizes of the items are adjusted so as to use all the available capacity during a planning period.

Most scheduling systems employ features of both these methods. Any practical system is likely to be essentially a run out list method with allocation features or an allocation method with run out list features.

Run Out List Scheduling

In scheduling with a run out list "fixed" lot sizes are established for each of the items to be manufactured. This is done with the same general formulation as that described earlier for purchased items. The ordering or setup cost must include the costs of manufacturing setup as well as the cost of the clerical work involved in placing the order.

A frequently required modification to the formulation adjusts for the effect of a production rate which is not a great deal larger than the sales or usage rate. If the usage rate is large compared to the production rate a significant fraction of the production lot will be used during the time required to produce the lot. Thus, the cycle inventory investment will not be as large for a given production lot size as it would be if the production rate were very high. This is illustrated in Figure 10.

FIGURE 10
Inventory-Time Relationship with Finite Production Rate
(production quantity = Q; production rate = p;
usage rate = S)

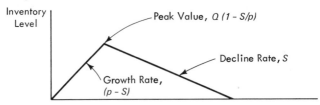

A time Q/p is required to complete a production lot of size Q. During that time the inventory usage amount is $S(Q/p)$. Thus, the net inventory increase is $Q - QS/p = Q(1 - S/p)$. As a consequence the average cycle inventory becomes $Q(1 - S/p)/2$. Usage of this in the cost-minimizing relationship yields the following expression for the economic production lot size including the effect of finite production rate.

$$Q = \sqrt{\frac{2AS}{c(1 - S/p)}}$$

where

Q = Economic production lot size (units)
A = Setup cost per order (dollars)
S = Annual usage rate (units per year)
c = Inventory carrying cost (dollars per unit per year)
p = Production rate (while producing) (units per year)

There may also be families of items which share a major setup cost, which, after it has been incurred, permits production of any member of the family with little additional setup cost. This leads to the use of the economic lot size formulation given earlier for items grouped for ordering. This formulation may also be modified to account for the effects of finite production rates.

In order to prepare a run out list schedule, we need to establish the production lot quantities as just described and also determine when each item will run out. Since some time is required to accomplish the production paper work preparation, the production itself and to move the product to where it is next needed there is some vulnerability to demand uncertainty. Also some delay may be encountered in commencing production because two or more items may be running out at about the same time. To protect against these demand or usage uncertainties "run out" times are commonly calculated as the times the stock level is expected to reach the safety stock level. This safety stock level is calculated as described earlier to provide adequate protection against stock out prior to replenishment.

After the run out times have been calculated, the items are sorted into run out sequence. The schedule is prepared by ordering a lot of each item in sequence until the total amount ordered is sufficient to use all the available production capacity.

Commonly the amount of capacity available will be greater than required to schedule the items so they are expected to run out at the time they are scheduled. The amount by which the schedule is ahead of run out time is the current amount of anticipation stock available. This can and should be used as an aid in control. By monitoring the amount of anticipation stock relative to plan the production controller can determine whether the aggregate capacity should be adjusted.

The cycle inventory and safety inventory required by this system are given directly by the lot size and safety stock rules.

Allocation Scheduling

Very few pure allocation systems exist. There are many production units which spend most of their time producing a few items, each of which is produced every planning period, but very few which produce *every* item every period. In most production periods, there are a few items to produce which are produced in large enough quantities so they will not be produced again for some time.

For this reason, most allocation scheduling systems include a large group of slow-moving items which are produced each time they run out. However, this production usually occupies only a small fraction of the available production time. The remainder of the production time in a production period is allocated among the items to be produced each period.

A number of different allocation methods are used. The basic idea is usually to allocate the production among the items so as to maintain as nearly as possible an optimum mix of inventory. The optimum mix criterion will vary according to the objectives of the firm and the function being served by the inventory. If seasonal stock is being accumulated, the best allocation may be one which uses the available production time while minimizing the investment in inventory. On the other hand, if the peak selling season is drawing to a close and the seasonal stock has been exhausted it may be best to allocate the production in a way which will provide the best customer service. The way in which this is done will depend on the measure of service.

In any allocation method one must first determine the requirements for each item to the end of the planning period. The amount by which the total production capability exceeds the aggregate requirement is a good measure of the current level of anticipation stock. This level can be used as described under run out scheduling to control the aggregate production level.

In an allocation system, item safety stocks must be determined in the same way as described earlier. Each item inventory is vulnerable to demand uncertainty through the period being planned and until production can be received in the next production period. The safety stock level required for each item is calculated in the same way as safety stocks for purchased items as described earlier.

Item lot sizes have not been considered here. In many allocation scheduling situations, the item lot sizes are determined by the scheduling or reviewing interval, rather than by manufacturing set up costs. However, it is appropriate to examine the manufacturing set up costs and the cycle stock consequences of the scheduling interval to estimate whether the scheduling interval should be substantially lengthened or shortened.

INVENTORY STANDARDS

With well-designed production and inventory control systems, it seems as though the inventories of raw materials and purchased parts, of work-in-process and of finished product, both at the factory and in the distribution system, should always be at just the right level. If this were the case, one would need no independent monitoring of system performance and of inventory levels. Of course, many things happen to cause inventories to be different from plan. The actual demand may be substantially more or less than forecast, there may be production interruptions because of equipment failure or employee absence, or vendors may be early or late in shipping ordered material.

The production and inventory control system is supposed to react to these circumstances and restore the inventory to the desired level. Sometimes, however, special management intervention is required. Also, in order to make sure that the system is performing as planned, it is well to compare periodically the actual inventory with a standard. If there is a substantial difference between the actual and the standard, further investigation to find the source of the difficulty is indicated.

Several different sorts of standards are needed. The financial manager is first interested in the total inventory investment. He should not, however, concern himself only with the total investment. That total is made up of inventories accomplishing the widely differing functions described earlier. Testing each major component of inventory against a standard may be more important than testing the total. Significant differences from standard in one component may be masked by offsetting differences in other components in the total.

Even though there are aggregate decisions which determine the aggregate production level and, hence, the aggregate inventory, ultimately the inventory investment is the result of individual item decisions. A decision was made to purchase some quantity of a particular part at a specific time; a decision was made to ship some quantity of a particular item to a field warehouse at a specific time. The consequence of all these item decisions is the magnitude, mix, and location of the inventory investment. Even with standards on the total inventory and its major components, a manager needs standards for each stock-keeping unit to test performance and to assist in finding difficulties.

In establishing standards for inventories, we must start with the stock-keeping units. There is no way to tell what the correct (or standard) inventory should be for an aggregate or group of stock-keeping units without knowing the correct inventory for *each* stock-keeping unit. From the stock-keeping unit standards, we can build up the aggregate standards.

Standards for Variable Quantities

One of the difficulties with inventory standards is that inventory levels are supposed to vary with time. The organization inventories described earlier are supposed to decouple successive stages in the operation in order to reduce the need for coordination and the costs which result from close coupling of successive operating stages. For example, a manufacturing lot may be much larger than the usual customer order. The finished product inventory of the item will rise rapidly when the manufactured lot is completed and then will decline more slowly as deliveries are made to customers. Any finished inventory level between the desired minimum just before receipt of the manufactured lot and that minimum plus a lot size is within "standard" limits.

The "minimum" itself is variable. Fluctuation stocks provided to cover variations in customer demand are supposed to fall and rise in response to demands which are greater than or less than forecast.

Thus, we must set standards which are not single valued but which have an acceptable range. That range may be very broad relative to the usage rate of the item for a single stock-keeping unit. If the item is produced annually, the finished inventory level will increase by a year's supply with the completion of the lot. The standard inventory for that stock-keeping unit must reflect that variability.

As we develop aggregate standards, this problem diminishes. As the inventory of one item increases, that of another decreases, so the total inventory varies much less (relatively) than does the inventory of individual stock-keeping units.

Cycle Stock Standards

For an individual stock-keeping unit the cycle stock standard is given by the replenishment lot size rule. If the lot size is Q, then the cycle inventory should lie between zero and Q and have an average value of $Q/2$. However, this formula is valid only if the production rate is much higher than the usage rate. If the production rate is not more than about ten times the usage rate, the average cycle inventory will be $Q(1 - S/p)/2$.

For a large number of items in a particular stockroom or warehouse, the standard cycle inventory will be the sum of the standards for the stock-keeping units.

$$I_c = \frac{1}{2} \sum_i Q_i(1 - S_i/p_i)$$

The actual cycle inventory should be very close to this standard as long as there are no cycling effects which tend to have a large number of the items near their maximum or minimum levels.

The standard deviation of the cycle inventory around this standard is

$$\sigma_c = \sqrt{\frac{\Sigma Q(1 - S/p)}{12}}$$

Thus, a cycle inventory with a standard value of $1 million should have a standard deviation about that value of only $400. Thus, the actual inventory will have only a small chance of being more than $1,000 in excess of the standard for random reasons.

This may seem to be an unrealistically narrow range on the cycle inventory standard. Most firms find that their inventories are much further away from their plans than this would indicate. The reason for this is that the primary determinant of variations in the aggregate inventory level are a consequence of variations of the aggregate demand from the forecast, and of the way in which aggregate production levels are set in response to those variations. This is discussed further below.

Safety Stock Standards

The safety stock standard for an item is given by the rule established from the measure of service and the characteristics of the demand and forecast uncertainty. In most cases, the safety stock for an item is set equal to a multiple of the standard deviation of the forecast error distribution. Thus, the safety stock is

$$SS = k\sigma$$

where

k = A safety factor
σ = Standard deviation of the forecast error distribution

k and σ are determined separately for each item. Of course, the actual safety stock of an item, the amount on hand just prior to arrival of replenishments, varies considerably around the expected value. In fact, the distribution of actual safety stock values is just the same as the distribution of demands during the lead time or of the forecast errors. Thus, we may use the analysis of the forecast error distribution to assist in estimating standards for safety stock.

For many items or stock-keeping units, the aggregate standard is obtained by summing the individual item standards. Thus, the aggregate safety stock standard is

$$I_{ss} = \sum_i k_i \sigma_i$$

As with cycle stocks the expected variation around the aggregate standard is small relative to the standard. The standard deviation of the aggregate safety stock is approximately

$$\sigma_{ss} = \sqrt{\sum_i \sigma_i}$$

This estimate neglects the effect of shortages or back order. This is satisfactory for high customer service objectives.

In calculating the standard, it is usually simplest just to sum the item safety stock *objectives* directly. With mechanized files and data processing this is not a difficult task.

In most cases, the *actual* inventory cannot be divided into cycle inventory and safety stock. Instead the total for each item or for the aggregate must be compared with the sum of the standards for cycle stock and safety stock. If there is any anticipation stock in the system that must first be subtracted from the on hand total.

Anticipation Inventory Standards

Anticipation inventory is usually accumulated as a result of the aggregate production plan, not as a result of the item production schedule. The aggregate production plan will show the planned aggregate anticipation stock, but will not provide directly the amount of anticipation inventory accumulated in each item. Thus, one must first look at the aggregate anticipation stock and then look at individual items. The scheduling method will normally show how anticipation stock has been allocated among the items.

In the case of seasonal accumulations no analytic form of the standard anticipation inventory is available. That must be taken directly from the plan itself.

The variation about that plan or standard depends on the demand or forecast uncertainty and the method by which the aggregate rate is controlled. If production is controlled relative to plan with a control number planning method the standard deviation of the anticipation inventory about its planned value will be

$$\sigma_A = \sigma_D \sqrt{\frac{1}{2k - k^2}}$$

where

σ_D = Standard deviation of the *aggregate* demand forecast error per period

k = The control number $(0 < k < 1.0)$

From this we see clearly that the primary variation in the total inventory comes from variations in the anticipation inventory. This is true for both a seasonal accumulation and for the production smoothing situation. Even with a control number of unity, the standard deviation in the anticipation inventory is equal to the standard deviation of aggregate forecast error. This will almost always be much larger than the standard deviation of the cycle inventory or safety inventory.

Other Inventory Components

We have discussed standards for only the major components of the organization inventories. Two other inventory components should be mentioned.

Transit inventory standards present no problem. They are equal to the aggregate amount in transit which is equal to the aggregate flow rate on each link times the average transit time.

Obsolete inventories are always a problem even though setting a standard for them may not be difficult. A standard should be set and inventories measured against that standard. This will help identify problems early enough to take effective corrective action.

Standards on Total Inventories

From the foregoing, it is clear that standards on the total inventory can be built up from the components. These components exist in each of several different forms including raw materials, semifinished parts, finished parts and subassemblies and finished products. By building up standards on each of these, a standard can be developed for the total inventory.

ADDITIONAL SOURCES

Bradley, Steven P.; Hax, A. C.; and Magnanti, T. P. *Applied Mathematical Programming.* Reading, Mass.: Addison-Wesley, 1976.

Brown, Robert G. *Decision Rules for Inventory Management.* New York: Holt, Rinehart and Winston, 1967.

Driebeek, Norman J. *Applied Linear Programming.* Reading, Mass.: Addison-Wesley, 1969.

Greene, James H., ed. *Production Control Handbook.* New York: Mc-Graw-Hill Book Company, 1970.

Magee, John P., and Boodman, David M. *Production Planning and Inventory Control.* New York: McGraw-Hill, 1966.

Orlicky, Joseph A. *Material Requirements Planning: The New Way of Life in Production and Inventory Management.* New York: McGraw-Hill, 1975.

Plossl, G. W., and Wight, O. W. *Production and Inventory Control: Principles and Techniques.* Englewood Cliffs, N.J.: Prentice-Hall, 1967.

Silver, Edward A. "A Tutorial on Production Smoothing and Work Force Balancing." *Operations Research,* 15 (1967), 985–1010.

Silver, Edward A., and Meal, Harlan C. "A Heuristic for Selecting Lot Size Quantities." *Production and Inventory Management,* 14 (Second quarter, 1973), pp. 66–74.

Wagner, Harvey M. *Principles of Operations Research—With Applications to Managerial Decisions.* Englewood Cliffs, N.J.: Prentice-Hall, 1969, chaps. 9, 19, and Appendix 2.

Wagner, Harvey M., and Whitin, Thomson M. "Dynamic Version of the Economic Lot Size Model." *Management Science,* 5 (October 1958), 88–96.

Chapter 24

Retail Inventory Management and Control

Robert E. Brewer[*]

IN A RETAIL OPERATION the major *controllable* investment is the merchandise inventory. Basic management decisions on land, building, and fixture investments are fixed for relatively long time periods. The major short-run investment decisions a retailer makes are those affecting the level of inventory to be carried. Generally, the land and buildings are leased and frequently even the fixtures are also. Regardless of whether the fixed assets are owned or not, proper inventory management is critical to a retailer's profitable operation. Obviously, it is with the turnover of the inventory investment that the revenues are generated to pay for the fixed assets. Sufficient revenue must be realized from the sale of merchandise to provide an adequate return on the *total investment* including the inventory, land, buildings, and fixtures.

INVENTORY CONTROL AND RETURN ON INVESTMENT

The relationship between inventory turnover, profit margin on sales, and the amount of the investment determines the return on investment. Table 1 shows the relationship between profit margins,

---

[*] Robert E. Brewer is vice president and treasurer, S. S. Kresge Company, Troy, Michigan.

TABLE 1

Desired ROI	Profit Required per $1,000 Investment	Sales Necessary at Various Net Profit Margin Rates			
		3%	4%	5%	6%
10%	$100	$3,333	$2,500	$2,000	$1,667
15	150	5,000	3,750	3,000	2,500
20	200	6,667	5,000	4,000	3,333
25	250	8,333	6,250	5,000	4,167

sales, and return on investment (ROI). If the desired ROI is 10 percent, then $100 per year in net profit must be realized for every $1,000 investment. That means when net profit is only 3 percent on sales, then sales must total $3,333. However, if net profit is 6 percent on sales, then $100 in profit is realized on only $1,667 in sales.

The relationship between the inventory investment and the other required investments such as fixtures, land, and buildings, is very important in determining the profit required on the inventory alone. Table 2 indicates that if $1,000 of fixed asset investment is required

TABLE 2

Ratio of Inventory Investment to All Other Investment	Profit Required per $1,000 of Inventory Investment at Various ROI Percent Objectives			
	10%	15%	20%	25%
1:1	$200	$300	$ 400	$ 500
1:2	300	450	600	750
1:3	400	600	800	1,000
1:4	500	750	1,000	1,250

for every $1,000 of inventory then a profit of $200 is required to realize 10 percent ROI on the total investment. However, if it takes $4,000 of additional investment for every $1,000 of inventory, then it would take $500 of profit for every $1,000 of inventory investment to provide a 10 percent ROI on the total investment of $5,000.

The balance between merchandise investment and total investment largely determines the sales level and profit percentage required to provide a satisfactory return on investment. The more elaborate and expensive the fixed assets, the greater the burden placed upon turning inventory into sales and profits. The newspaper boy does not require very much profit per paper to cover his investment in fixed assets, but the high fashion dress shop in an elegant boutique with expensive decor must recover that cost on a relatively few units of sales. The sales required at various net profit percentage levels to provide a 10 percent return on total investment is shown in Table 3. When the inventory to all other assets ratio is one to one,

TABLE 3

Ratio of Inventory Investment to All Other Investment	Sales Required at Various Net Profit Ratios to Provide a 10 Percent Return on Total Investment			
	3%	*4%*	*5%*	*6%*
1:1	$ 6,667	$ 5,000	$ 4,000	$3,333
1:2	10,000	7,500	6,000	5,000
1:3	13,333	10,000	8,000	6,667
1:4	16,667	15,000	10,000	8,333

and net profit is 3 percent on sales, then sales of $6,667 are required for every $1,000 of inventory if a 10 percent ROI is to be achieved. However, if the inventory to other asset ratio is one to three, it would require a 6 percent net profit on those same sales in order to earn a 10 percent ROI.

One obvious way retailers minimize their investment in inventory is to arrange payment terms with their vendors which allow for selling part of the shipment before the goods are paid for by the retailer. Some vendors of highly seasonal products such as air conditioners will ship several weeks in advance in order to alleviate a warehousing problem and offer a delayed billing until well into the selling season. This, of course, allows the retailer to generate some cash ahead of the payment date, and reduces the amount of working capital he must put into the business himself. The relationship between payment terms and the inventory turnover rate is an important operating factor to study. For example, in many industries it is common for vendors to allow 30 days for the payment of goods shipped. Ideally, a retailer would like to sell all of the shipment before he has to pay the vendor. Table 4 shows the relationship

TABLE 4

Inventory Turnover Rate per Year	Number of Days Supply on Hand	Number of Days Carried by Retailer	Percent of Total Carried by Retailer
4	90	60	66.67%
6	60	30	50.00
8	45	15	33.33
12	30	0	0

between various turnover rates and the amount of inventory carried by a retailer who has 30 days payment terms.

Assume that a retailer has annual sales of $5 million and the retail markup on inventory is 25 percent (33⅓ percent over cost). The significance of turnover can be seen in Table 5.

TABLE 5
(dollars in thousands)

Inventory Turn- over Rate per Year	Retail Inventory Value	Cost of Inventory	Percent of Inven- tory Carried by Retailer	Cash Re- quired by Retailer
4	$1,125	$844	66.67%	$563
6	833	625	50.00	313
8	625	469	33.33	156
12	417	313	0	0

The difference between zero inventory investment and over $500,000 is clearly a pretty significant fact of life for a retailer. Those businesses where little investment is required usually have a lot of potential retailers going into (and frequently out of) business. The clever paper boy in my neighborhood collects monthly in advance, and pays for his papers weekly in arrears. At the other extreme is the furniture store that allows up to 90 days to pay without a finance charge. Many retailers have an investment in display fixtures, delivery equipment, and office furniture in addition to their investment in inventory. Some even own their own building. The purpose of making an investment in these assets is hopefully to earn a return on the investment that is greater than putting the money into the bank or buying some bonds at a fixed interest rate.

Assume that the retailer in Table 5 had invested $500,000 in fixtures over and above the merchandise investment. Further assume that he earned a 5 percent pretax profit margin on the $5 million in sales, or $250,000. The total investment and return on that investment at various inventory turnover levels are shown in Table 6.

TABLE 6

Inventory Turnover Rate per Year	Total Investment	Return on Total Investment
4	$1,062,528	23.53%
6	812,500	30.77
8	656,234	38.10
12	500,000	50.00

The nature of your particular sector of retailing will determine whether it is practical to achieve 12 turns or not. Also, the vendor payment terms indicate the relative benefit of various turnover rates. Within any given sector of retailing, however, there is a considerable difference between the turnover levels achieved by the highest and lowest performers. Turnover per se is neither good nor bad. It is only when it is put in context with sales, gross margin, net profit, total investment, vendor payment terms, and so on, that it becomes meaningful. A retailer who gets 12 turns and is out of stock on 50 percent of his SKUs (stock-keeping units) is much worse off than he would be at a lower turnover level with a 90 percent in-stock position.

Turnover is very important to achieving a good ROI percent, however, you "can't sell from an empty wagon." On the other hand, "an overloaded wagon breaks down." The key is to determine what range of turnovers is practical for your store. Then try to reach the upper end of the range without letting the other important operating figures deteriorate. Set realistic goals and work toward reaching them within a reasonable time frame consistent with the constraints of your organization and merchandising system.

STANDARDS FOR CONTROL OF RETAIL INVENTORIES

There are several factors which influence the final turnover of any retailer. Many of them are strictly related to the nature of the particular type of retail store being operated. However, there are some universal factors which should be considered by all retailers when trying to set turnover goals for a particular retail store. These are discussed below in no particular order of importance.

Organization. The age, experience, and capacity of an organization affect the final turnover results. A seasoned and competent organization should be given a higher goal than a newer organization.

Sales Level. Generally the large volume stores can achieve a higher turnover than a smaller volume store carrying the same merchandise.

Sales Mix. A significant shift in sales mix between high and low turnover SKUs will cause variations in the final turnover. For example:

	Sales Mix	Item's Annual Turnover	Weighted Average Turnover
Store No. 1:			
Item A	50%	4.0	2.0
Item B	50	8.0	4.0
Combined	100%		6.0
Store No. 2:			
Item A	60%	4.0	2.4
Item B	40	8.0	3.2
Combined	100%		5.6

Store No. 1 has not necessarily done a better job than Store No. 2 of controlling inventory. The sales mix is different between the stores and more analysis is required to determine which mix is more desirable.

Methods of Distribution.   By warehousing a portion of the inventory it should be possible to increase turnover in a multiple store chain. However, just the opposite result could be experienced. If a sufficient improvement in cost of goods sold is realized by warehousing it could provide a greater return on investment, even with a drop in turnover. For example, assume that a retailer could improve net profit by 2 percent on sales after paying for all warehousing costs:

	Sales	Average Inventory	Annual Turnover	Net Profit to Sales	Net Profit	Return on Inventory
A	$1,000	$200	5	4%	$40	20%
B	$1,000	250	4	6	60	24

Even though in B above the turnover was lower than A and the inventory investment was $50 higher, the additional $20 profit brought the ROI up 4 percent on the total inventory. Note that the extra $50 inventory investment earned a 40 percent ROI. ($20 net profit ÷ $50 inventory).

Buying Practices.   Buying from overseas suppliers versus domestic sources generally means a slower turnover, but hopefully a correspondingly higher gross margin to pay for it. Even the choice of domestic suppliers could affect turnover by their distance from your store and the reliability of delivery schedules. Buying a six month's supply of an item when appropriate purchase discounts are available could reduce turnover, but improve profits and ROI percent. Obviously, a careful analysis is required to determine if the discount covers the full cost of carrying the larger time supply. Also, it is important to avoid crowding out other purchases of needed items to make room for a lopsided supply of special purchases.

Operational Standards. Generally management determines what mix of merchandise will make up the inventory assortment and strives to maintain a high in-stock position. It is not practical always to be 100 percent in-stock on a wide variety of SKUs. Therefore, an acceptable level that provides the desired sales, gross and investment results is established. Whenever management pushes too hard for high turnover, the inevitable result is a lower than desirable SKU assortment, resulting in lost sales and possibly a lowered average gross margin. Training and supervision can help maintain the proper balance.

Package Quantities. Suppliers may be inclined to push for larger package quantities for their own economic reasons. However, even at a higher cost it is often worth trying to get them to provide smaller package quantities to keep store level investments down.

Freight Costs. With the transportation industry's labor and energy costs escalating it may be reasonable to accept a lower turnover in exchange for larger more efficient shipments. Small shipments are costly for truckers to handle, and their tariffs discriminate against them. Some vendors offer free delivery when a certain weight or dollar level is reached. The larger inventory investment and lower turnover must be compared with the rapidly rising freight costs when placing orders.

Inflation. In a period of rapidly rising inflation turnover will go down, because higher prices are reflected first in inventory levels and then subsequently in sales. A new shipment of winter clothes, for example, may cost 10 percent more than last year's. This shows up immediately as the inventory is 10 percent above the prior year at the beginning of the season (assuming the same unit level of inventory).

Sales increases over the season would be 10 percent higher eventually if they were all sold at the higher price. However, as inflation escalates, the lag between sales increases and inventory increases causes the dollar turnover to go down. The opposite result occurs when deflation takes place.

Various inventory valuation methods such as Lifo (last in, first out) and Fifo (first in, first out) are used for financial reporting purposes, but internal operating reports are usually kept on a Fifo basis. A discussion of the various inventory valuation methods is beyond the scope of this paper.

Abrupt Economic Change.   A sudden change in demand such as occurred in the fourth quarter of 1974 when gross national product dipped over 10 percent causes the inventory-to-sales ratio to become seriously out of balance.

Shortages.   During the 1974 energy crisis a shortage of antifreeze for automobiles caused an incalculable increase in turnover on that product. Each small shipment was immediately sold out upon being put on the sales floor. Generally the entire inventory was sold before the invoice could be processed for payment, providing an ideal cash flow situation.

Special Situations.   When Easter is late in April the March inventory figure is usually considerably higher than in those years when Easter is earlier. Turnover is generally calculated by taking month-end inventories and averaging them for dividing into sales.

Obviously, a high inventory at the end of March would compare unfavorably against a lower inventory when Easter sales fall largely in March. A similar situation occurs when Labor Day and Thanksgiving shift to different dates. The month-end book inventory figures are distorted for comparative purposes. To some extent the Halloween and Christmas holidays shift to a different accounting period from year to year for some companies who use a fiscal month ending on, say, the fourth Saturday of the month.

COMPANY CHARACTERISTICS THAT INFLUENCE THE INVENTORY PROGRAM

Retail inventory control is a complex problem. It requires a thorough knowledge of your company and the peculiar factors that are unique to it. No two companies are directly comparable because of the many variables that influence inventory levels. Even two stores within the same company chain will have significant differences in the mix of variables that go into producing the resulting turnover. Each store does have its own record of performance from year to year, and if proper attention is given to the significant difference between years, a reasonable comparison can be made.

When you have gained an insight into the factors affecting your company's turnover you can then set about to design a program to control it. This may take the form of a plan to *increase* inventories. Usually inventory control programs are thought of in the context of a reduction of investment. Optimizing profits and return on investment should be guideposts used in the design of any inventory control program. This generally means reduction in inventories for most companies.

ADDITIONAL SOURCES

See Additional Sources at end of Chapter 23.

PART VII

Short-Term Financing

PART VII takes up the subject of short-term financing. Two major sources of short-term financing are trade credit and unsecured bank loans. In Chapter 25, Lloyd Sinnickson discusses the role of trade credit as a source of financing. He describes what suppliers require as a precondition for extending trade credit. He lists the sources of information used by suppliers in making credit decisions. Mr. Sinnickson emphasizes the value of developing good supplier relationships. He provides guidance on the effective use of trade credit as a financing source.

In Chapter 26, we go to an analysis of unsecured bank loans. Russell Ewert and David Ewert discuss the evaluation, structuring, and pricing of credit requests as viewed by a commercial banker. The subjects of cash forecasting and the cash budget previously developed in Chapters 13 and 20 are now discussed in the context of the preparation of a loan request or loan package. Of particular value to the treasurer is the section of this chapter showing how banks look at profitability of an account and their basis for the calculation of service charges.

Earlier, Chapter 7 had discussed how the banker looks at the treasurer and his firm. In Chapter 27, Harley Rankin turns the coin over and discusses how the treasurer selects a commercial bank. Key dimensions are the financial condition of the bank, the quality of its management, and the nature of the services offered in relation to the needs of the firm. Of particular interest is a presentation of the account analysis report which in Chapter 26 is viewed from the standpoint of the bank and in Chapter 27 is viewed from the standpoint of the corporate treasurer. A formal evaluation of the quality of banks is proposed to indicate the quality of services as well as the degree of interest the bank is likely to have in working with the company.

Since inventory is a major use of corporate investment funds, it is useful to analyze inventory as a source of financing as well. In Chapter 28, Steven Westfall begins by indicating that the unused inventory credit capacity of business firms in the United States as of May 1974 was about $140 billion. The status of inventory and inventory financing under the Uniform Commercial Code is set forth. The major forms of inventory financing are described and the alternative sources of inventory financing are discussed relative to the different circumstances and needs of borrowers. The procedures for obtaining an inventory loan are set forth in a step-by-step fashion. This discussion is supported by use of illustrative forms and documents. The chapter concludes with a discussion of the costs, cautions, and opportunities in connection with inventory financing.

Chapter 25

Obtaining Trade Credit

Lloyd Sinnickson[*]

What It Is

TRADE CREDIT arises from goods or services delivered to a business enterprise without advance payment, with the understanding that payment will be made at a specified future time. For the recipient of the goods or services it is a source of operating capital which, if not available from suppliers, would have to be obtained from loans or additional investment.

The time specified for payment usually is determined by the invoice terms. In most lines of business the terms of payment shown on the seller's invoice are customary among all sellers and accepted by buyers. They are subject to competitive pressures, just as prices are. Examples of frequently used terms are:

Net 30 days.   Payment due 30 days from invoice date.
1 percent 10 net 30 days.   1 percent discount may be deducted from the invoice amount if payment is made in 10 days from invoice date; otherwise the full amount is due 30 days from invoice date.

Further examples might serve only to create unnecessary confusion, as there are at least several hundred variations in terms of payment

---

[*] Lloyd Sinnickson is general credit manager, American Cyanamid Company, Wayne, New Jersey.

used in trade credit in the United States. A large corporation with numerous product lines may use dozens of different terms, being guided by the established custom among sellers of each product line.

The terms have a considerable influence upon how much credit a firm can obtain from suppliers. However, there are other factors, as will be shown later. First, it will be helpful to review some of the things which influence suppliers in extending trade credit.

What Suppliers Look for

The key to obtaining trade credit is the confidence of suppliers. This confidence can be earned and maintained in a variety of ways, none of which is any problem for a well-established, successful enterprise. Among the favorable things suppliers look for are:

1. A consistent record of earnings over a period of time, with at least a portion retained in the business.
2. A good ratio of current assets to current liabilities (a very old but still useful rule of thumb is a minimum of 2 to 1, but this may vary with the line of business).
3. A strong equity position in relation to debt. This will reflect the initial capitalization and the retained earnings.
4. A record of prompt payment of suppliers' bills.

Each of these points is helpful to the supplier in judging the probability of being paid within terms. The first three give clues to the firm's ability to pay, now and in the future.

A company which has been operating profitably is more apt to do so in the future than one which has been losing money or breaking even, or has had a spotty record of gains and losses with no real progress. Even if operations have been consistently profitable, if all of the earnings have been paid out in dividends or withdrawn by the owners in some other form, the business is not gaining financial strength or improving its creditworthiness (assuming that no additional capital investment is made). On the contrary, if its sales are increasing its financial strength is declining, because additional sales require additional working capital in the form of inventory, receivables, and cash balances.

If this increase in working capital is not provided by retained earnings or new investment it can only come from increased debt, which will impair the current ratio and the ratio of equity to debt. Payments to suppliers may fall behind if increased trade credit is used as a source of funds to finance increased receivables and inventory. A good current ratio will give suppliers confidence that the firm will be able to pay its bills as they fall due. A strong relationship of equity to debt protects the solvency of the firm, and the interests of its creditors, by providing a cushion against adversity. What these ratios should be varies somewhat, depending upon the line of business. Robert Morris Associates, an organization of bank credit officers, and Dun & Bradstreet, Inc., compile ratios by industry.

How Suppliers Get the Information

In the case of a publicly held corporation, financial information will be available to suppliers and potential suppliers through data filed with the Securities and Exchange Commission and published in financial journals, newspapers, and Dun & Bradstreet reports. The paying record will become known to suppliers through their own experience, or the experience of others as disclosed by trade credit groups or Dun & Bradstreet reports.

A privately owned firm's financial data can be made available to suppliers by sending copies of annual audit reports to Dun & Bradstreet, who will publish them in their reports and use them in arriving at the firm's rating in their rating book. Most trade credit grantors subscribe to the book and make a practice of looking in it for an indication of the size and financial responsibility of a prospective customer.

Many companies make a practice of sending copies of audit reports, or at least the balance sheets and income statements, to major suppliers. If the information is favorable, they want suppliers to know about it. Even if it is not, it may be to their advantage to keep suppliers informed.

Developing Good Supplier Relationships

It is no problem for firms with strong balance sheets and good earnings to obtain trade credit. They have no need to cultivate their suppliers' credit managers. It is a different situation with new, struggling companies, those which have experienced losses, or companies which may be very profitable but have grown so rapidly that even though all earnings have been retained, the equity has not kept pace with the growth in sales. These companies have a greater need for supplier credit than most, but greater difficulty in getting it. There is an old saying that bankers like to lend money to people who do not need it. Trade creditors are no different. There is nothing surprising and nothing antisocial about this. They must be reasonably sure of getting their money back on or close to schedule, without extra costs. If they extend too much credit that turns out otherwise they will be in trouble themselves.

When a company's ability to operate profitably has not been demonstrated, or it has no working capital, or its total debt exceeds its net worth, or it is late in making payments to suppliers, some suppliers, at least, will need a lot of reassurance to induce them to provide the company's requirements. Yet, it can be done; it is done every day. The key is earning the confidence of suppliers by dealing with them frankly, by showing them realistic plans for improving the situation, and by keeping commitments made to them.

A classic case is that of W. T. Grant Company. Grant had an operating loss in their fiscal year ended January 31, 1975 of $177 million. Yet, suppliers continued to extend trade credit, some for hundreds of thousands of dollars, a few for $1 million or more. Retaining the confidence of suppliers despite the disastrous losses became a major preoccupation of Grant's top management. They were remarkably successful in doing this by announcing changes in the policies which caused the losses, replacing some key management personnel, offering some security in the form of an inventory lien and, most important of all, paying suppliers' invoices promptly.

It was only after another six months' loss of $111 million that Grant was compelled to file a petition for an arrangement with unsecured creditors under the Bankruptcy Act. Their experience illustrates the point that even a company with poor operating results and a weak financial position can obtain trade credit if proper attention is given to relations with suppliers.

It is important for a debtor who wishes to get maximum cooperation from suppliers to be frank about his situation. Even when it is not good, the actual facts may not be as bad as the supplier will imagine if he learns them for himself, a little at a time. Along with the facts about the situation, the supplier should be told the plan for improving it. This, of course, compels the debtor to formulate some plan other than praying or hoping for the best. The suppliers may even help to improve the plan, or to implement it successfully.

Another vital point in obtaining trade credit is never to make a commitment which cannot be kept. Broken promises destroy confidence even faster than bad operating results. The moral factor is as important as the financial. It is better to give a supplier a commitment with which he is not entirely satisfied, and honor it, than to give him one that pleases him greatly until he finds out that it has not been met.

Dependence upon Trade Credit

The degree of dependence upon trade credit varies considerably among different lines of business. *Annual Statement Studies* published by Robert Morris Associates lists balance sheet and income ratios compiled from the financial statements of thousands of businesses. The 1975 edition indicates that for manufacturing firms, trade credit typically represents 10 percent to 15 percent of total liabilities and net worth. However, in one line of business (furs) the composite balance sheet for the 19 manufacturing firms shows 29.3 percent of total liabilities and net worth due to trade creditors. In another line (brick and structural clay tile) the percentage for the 35 firms included is only 4.9. These composite statements include a breakdown into four different size categories, in addition to the totals for all companies in the line of business. In any given line, the smaller firms usually have much higher percentages (are much more dependent upon trade credit) than the larger firms.

Among wholesalers, the percentage due to trade creditors tends to fall between 15 and 25, although 61 wholesalers of tires and tubes owed trade creditors 45.5 percent of total liabilities and net worth. For 27 tobacco leaf wholesalers, the percentage was only 10.9. Here, too, it is usual for the smaller firms to depend more upon trade credit than the larger ones in the same line.

For retailers, the percentage is as high as 29.5 percent for 132 retailers of floor coverings and as low as 6 percent for 2,169 retailers of new or used automobiles. (Short-term debt to banks was 40.5 percent of total liabilities and net worth for auto retailers, who do not get much trade credit from the manufacturers.)

It is clear that for most businesses, trade credit is an important source of operating funds. In the aggregate, it is a tremendous force in the U.S. economy. At December 31, 1973 it totaled $252.2 billion, which exceeded total commercial bank loans to business outstanding on that date by $92.3 billions according to the SEC *Report on Working Capital of U.S. Corporations.*

Effective Use of Trade Credit

Trade credit as a source of operating funds has an obvious advantage over bank loans or other interest-bearing obligations, as there usually is no interest charge. Moreover, it may be easier to obtain than the proceeds of a stock issue, and there is no dividend requirement or dilution of ownership. However, there are some limiting factors to the profitability of using trade credit in preference to other sources of funds. One limiting factor suggested earlier is that the supplier will be influenced in granting or refusing credit by the prospective customer's balance sheet if he sees it, or by what he assumes it may look like from his evaluation of the information he does obtain. He will be concerned about the ratio of current assets to current liabilities and the ratio of debt to equity. A company which tried to obtain all its operating capital from trade credit would have great difficulty finding suppliers willing to extend credit. It almost surely would find it impossible to pay within terms, too.

Assuming that a supplier is willing to extend credit on his normal terms, the amount of credit made available depends upon what the terms of payment are. If the customer buys $50,000 worth of material a month on 30-day terms, and pays within terms, the credit made available is $50,000, but if the terms are 60 days the customer has a $100,000 line.

In most cases the buyer has little influence upon the terms. They are fixed by the seller, usually in accordance with custom in the industry or product line, and are applied by the seller to all sales to all creditworthy buyers of the product. For the seller to extend different terms to comparable buyers might put him in violation of the Robinson-Patman Act, which forbids discrimination in price or terms or conditions of sale among buyers who compete with each other. If the buyer looks for longer terms he is apt to find that they are uniform for all the sellers because the terms offered by the most liberal seller were met by the others.

The buyer in our example above who requires $50,000 worth of material a month payable in 30 days may be under great pressure to obtain; e.g., $150,000 credit, rather than $50,000. His available working capital may not be adequate to permit payment 30 days from the supplier's invoice date. The time required for him to receive the material, process it, sell it, extend credit to his customer, and receive payment may be 90 days. There is a gap of 60 days or $100,000 between his cycle of turning the material into cash and the terms offered by the supplier. Some of the alternatives are:

1. Investing an additional $100,000 cash in the business to increase working capital. The cash may not be available.
2. Borrowing $100,000 from the bank. The bank's credit line may be fully utilized already, or the interest cost may be more than the profit margin on the transaction can bear.
3. Paying the supplier 60 days late. This may jeopardize the continuity of deliveries, as the supplier may not be willing to accept a unilateral decision to take 90 days for payment, or may become concerned about the customer's ability to pay. It also may result in the imposition of a late payment charge, or service charge, of 1 percent or 1½ percent per month which may exceed the cost of borrowing at the bank.
4. Discussing the situation with the supplier to see whether he will agree to accept payment 60 days late, after all the facts are presented.

Discussion with the supplier will serve the buyer's interest better in the long run than simply taking the extra time. There may be circumstances which provide an acceptable rationale for 90 days, such as a longer than normal transit time for the material, a seasonal pattern of use, the fact that the buyer can render a superior service as a distributor of the seller's materials, or the fact that the buyer is developing a new use for the seller's material. The buyer may be able to demonstrate that within a short time he will be in a position to pay promptly on regular terms. The supplier, in any event, is apt to react more favorably to a 90-day commitment that is met than to a 30-day commitment which is not.

Seasonal Arrangements

In some product lines whose use is highly seasonal, such as lawn and garden supplies, sellers offer extra time for payment of material bought in advance of the active use season. In order to get their products out of their plants and warehouses and onto the shelves of the retail stores before the heavy demand, they may offer to ship material in January and February to be paid for as though it had been shipped in March or April, for example. This arrangement benefits both buyer and seller.

Abuse of Trade Credit

There are risks in keeping pressure upon suppliers for all the traffic will bear in the way of extra time for payment. One risk is that the supplier will come to look upon the customer as less desirable than those who pay in accordance with terms. The slower payer will be a less profitable customer because he compels the seller to make a greater investment in receivables per sales dollar for him than for prompt-paying customers. Consequently, the seller may offer the buyer less in the way of services. When materials are in short supply the slow-paying account may not receive the same priority in allocation of material as the prompt payer. At such times, the slow payer may have to give up the extra time hitherto taken for payment. Having geared his financial planning to excessive use of suppliers' credit, he may find it difficult to obtain the funds necessary to satisfy suppliers. If he does succeed in getting additional funds, it probably will be expensive, because at such times interest rates and the cost of capital are apt to be at their peak.

ADDITIONAL SOURCES

Edmister, Robert O., and Schlarbaum, Gary, G. "Credit Policy in Lending Institutions." *Journal of Financial and Quantitative Analysis,* 9 (June 1974), 335–56.

Herbst, Anthony F. "Some Empirical Evidence on the Determinants of

Trade Credit at the Industry Level of Aggregation." *Journal of Financial and Quantitative Analysis,* 9 (June 1974), 377–94.

Herbst, Anthony F. "A Factor Analysis Approach to Determining the Relative Endogeneity of Trade Credit." *Journal of Finance,* 29 (September 1974), 1087–1104.

Schwartz, Robert A. "An Economic Model of Trade Credit." *Journal of Financial and Quantitative Analysis,* 9 (September 1974), 643–58.

Chapter 26

Obtaining Unsecured Loans

Russell H. Ewert*
David C. Ewert†

ONE OF THE treasurer's primary responsibilities is obtaining properly structured, properly priced credit availability for the firm. Unsecured bank credit is both a convenient, flexible source and one of the least expensive financing alternatives available. This chapter examines the evaluation, structuring, and pricing of credit requests as viewed by a commercial banker.

EVALUATING THE CREDIT REQUEST

The first question the treasurer usually wants to know when borrowing money is how much should be borrowed? Is it the total of the bills and operating expenses? Is it based on some relationship of debt to equity? Should the request be increased in anticipation of the banker's automatic, arbitrary reduction of the request? The answer is that a proper loan request meets two tests: (1) Will the loan be sufficient to finance the corporate needs? (2) Can the loan be repaid?

The first test is measured by comparing the corporation's financial needs with the magnitude of the loan. Surprisingly, many

---

* Russell H. Ewert is vice president, The First National Bank of Chicago.
† David C. Ewert is professor, Georgia State University, Atlanta, Georgia.

treasurers have not analyzed their firms' financial needs in detail before requesting a loan. The danger of underestimating the size of the loan can be every bit as dangerous as overestimating from the viewpoint of the treasurer and the lender.

Failing the first test is relevant because there is no rationale for a banker to finance an endeavor that is not fully viable. If the need is to provide working capital for a seasonal buildup of inventory and accounts receivable or to provide for the introduction of a new product, the banker needs assurance that the project is fully financed. The financing can include the use of internally generated funds, trade payables, long-term debt, and additional equity, as well as bank loans. It is unwise for the banker to finance a project that is not complete and equally unwise for the treasurer to accept that loan.

The second test is measured by whether the loan can be repaid and, if so, when and from what sources. There are four basic sources of repayment: (1) profits, (2) reduction of assets, (3) external financing, and (4) foreclosure.

Profits

The profits generated by the successful operation of the business are the ultimate continuing source of repayment. A continuing source of repayment is important because the banker wants to develop with the treasurer an ongoing relationship accommodating a borrowing pattern that develops over the years. There is less interest by the banker in financing a single transaction that will not lead to a continuing relationship.

A caveat when evaluating the repayment prospects from profit deals with the critical distinction between profits and cash flow. Profitable operations do not necessarily generate cash. This is why it is important to look at the income statement, the balance sheet, and the cash budget. The typical life cycle of a successful business is an initial period of profitable growth including a growth in inventory and receivables as well as plant and equipment, all of which absorbs cash. This is a period when additional financing can be required and with faster growth the likelihood of external financing increases. The next stage is a slowing of growth allowing the profitable business to generate enough cash not only to support itself, but also to provide for debt service and dividends. The last stage as the business declines (the inventory is sold and not replenished and more receivables are collected than created) substantial amounts of cash can be generated with little or no profits.

The practice of taking the profit after taxes from the income statement and adding noncash charges, principally depreciation, to determine the cash flow is likely to be an oversimplification in many instances. The practice does not take cognizance of the effects of: (1) changes in assets, such as inventory buildup and the sale of a fixed asset, (2) changes in liabilities, such as repayment of a bank loan and the amount owed the supplies, nor (3) changes in net worth, such as the sale of additional common stock and the payment of dividends.

Reduction of Assets

Funds can be obtained from the reduction of assets or the orderly liquidation of assets. The key word is orderly which means the reduction occurs in the normal course of business. An example would be the sale of seasonal inventory or the collection of accounts receivables. This is the most common method of repaying short-term loans. Of course, the banker has a preference for a continuing relationship with the treasurer. Thus, a banker may find little attraction in financing a seasonal working capital need even though it can be repaid easily through the orderly reduction of these items if there is little prospect of the business being profitable over the longer run.

External Refinancing

Refinancing through another bank loan or another external source, either debt or equity, is a means of repaying the short-term loan. However, in the absence of a firm commitment by a substantial financial source, a "take out" is not a reliable repayment source. Many lenders view the possibility of refinancing a short-term loan to be so risky that they are extremely reluctant to rely on this source of repayment.

Foreclosure

The forced liquidation of assets is usually unreliable and unpopular to both the treasurer and the banker. This method of repayment is typically a distress situation when the borrower is otherwise insolvent. The value of the assets is reduced considerably if the borrower is no longer a going business. At best, forced liquidations of a business are expensive, time consuming and not reliable, regardless of whether the debt is secured or unsecured.

USE OF A CASH BUDGET

In order to answer how large a loan is required and how and when the loan will be repaid, a cash budget is essential. Using a cash budget will show the total cash requirements, the timing of these requirements and the repayment schedule. The statement is based on assumptions concerning sales levels, expenses, receivable collections and numerous other items. The accuracy of the assumptions depends on the history, size, and nature of the business. If the result of the cash budget based on the first set of assumptions demonstrates that the firm's needs cannot be financed by the banker, then one must seriously question the assumptions. Possibly the firm's sales growth is too ambitious, the early acquisition of some of the assets is premature, and so on, given the financial strength of the firm at this point. Alternately, the growth prospects could be very profitable allowing the treasurer to entice others besides the banker to fund the growth. In either case, a second set of assumptions needs to be made and a second cash budget developed. The completed cash budget also provides a good plan to measure actual performance.

THE LOAN PACKAGE

The preparation of the cash budget is the first step in the treasurer's preparation of the loan request or loan package. After the treasurer is satisfied with the assumptions and the resulting cash budget, it is still incumbent on the treasurer to document the validity and attainability of the assumptions. To accomplish this the loan package should contain:

1. A description of the company, its history, products or services, its industry, its competitive position and, most importantly, the management.

2. A statement of the loan request including amount, terms, uses of proceeds, repayment sources, and repayment schedule. Alternative repayment sources should be available and listed.
3. The cash budget. The set of assumptions used to derive the cash budget should be stated.
4. The income statements for the past three years and the most current interim statements.
5. The balance sheets for the same periods. These statements should have an unqualified opinion by a reputable Certified Public Accountant and should be the complete submission by the CPA, including all footnotes and supporting schedules. If appropriate, the consolidated and consolidating statements must be presented.
6. Any other information, including stockholder releases and reports to governmental agencies such as the Securities and Exchange Commission.

STRUCTURE OF A LOAN

Maturity

A loan with a maturity of less than one year is referred to as a short-term loan. The short-term loan is traditionally made to finance seasonal or temporary increases in accounts receivables and inventories. A longer term loan is usually required to finance the acquisition of fixed assets, another company or other long-term project. The financing needs of a business could be graphed as shown in Figure 1.

The graph portrays the financial needs of a firm which is growing and experiences a seasonal pattern with its sales. The treasurer has accomplished the financing of the firm by balancing equity, long-term debt, and short-term debt. Initially, equity was invested in the firm before creditors could be attracted. The equity bears the greatest risk and, correspondingly, contains the greatest profit potential. Long-term debt has been used in conjunction with equity to finance the initial needs of the firm and its growth in permanent assets. The treasurer employed short-term debt only to finance the seasonal fluctuations in the firm's financial needs. Short-term debt has not been used to finance growth or the permanent increases in receivables and inventory but only the temporary increases in these

FIGURE 1

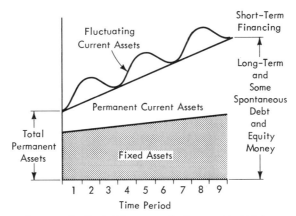

Source: J. Fred Weston and Eugene F. Brigham, *Essentials of Managerial Finance,* 3d ed. (Hinsdale, Ill.: Dryden Press, 1974).

items which occur seasonally. The short-term debt is completely eliminated periodically which is referred to as the cleanup.

The absence of a clean-up period converts a short-term note to a long-term obligation. A term loan creates a greater risk than a short-term loan. The term loan locks a bank into a credit without the possibility of review. Therefore, when a term loan is analyzed, all of the significant factors such as management, profits, and general economic conditions must be viewed for a longer period. The lender assumes a greater risk of loss by making a term loan and should be paid more. It is essential that the banker recognize when the loan is a term loan and analyze the loan as a term loan and price the loan as a term loan. A common problem is the 90-day note that is renewed at maturity. The face of the note would suggest a short-term note, but the lack of a cleanup indicates a term credit.

The short-term note can be for a specific period of time (e.g., 90 days) or on a demand basis. The demand basis empowers the bank to call the note at any time. A demand loan can be used when the source of repayment is certain, but the timing is not. The banker may also want to use a demand note in a work-out situation so if the borrower's condition warrants, the bank can move quickly without waiting for a maturity date. The demand note can be flexible and useful to both the treasurer and the lender, but the use requires confidence of both the treasurer and the banker.

There is reluctance on the part of the banker to use demand notes because both the treasurer and banker lose the discipline provided by the time note for the opportunity of review at each maturity. The time note is frequently written with the thought of renewal at maturity. If the financing project requires nine months, the treasurer may borrow a portion of the total amount for 90 days. At the maturity of that period, the borrower may renew that note for a second 90 days and borrow the remaining amount for 90 days. After the second 90 days, the borrower may reduce the indebtedness partially and renew the balance for the last 90-day period. This enables the treasurer to tailor the amount of money borrowed to the amount of investment required.

For example, if the treasurer has financing needs for a period of nine months that will peak during the middle three months at $1,500,000, the initial borrowing could be a $500,000 note for 90 days. At the end of 90 days that note could be renewed and increased to $1,500,000 by a second 90-day note. At the end of that 90-day period, the treasurer may wish to pay $800,000 and renew $700,000 for the remaining 90-day period.

Interest Rate Quotations

The interest rate can be quoted as a fixed rate or a floating rate.

1. *A fixed rate* for the life of the loan has the effect of transferring the risk of rate fluctuation to the bank. The bank is bearing more risk and may charge a premium rate.
2. *A floating rate* is tied to some other rate, typically the prime rate. As prime rate goes up or down, the rate charged the customer correspondingly goes up or down. This transfers the risk of rate fluctuation to the customer.

The treasurer should recognize that today the banker is more profit oriented than ever before. It is significant to distinguish a change in attitude from a banker of a decade ago who spoke as a caretaker of the depositor's funds. Now a concurrent, though not exclusionary, obligation to the stockholders is recognized.

The safety of the loan portfolio is, and has been, paramount. Nothing said here would detract from that. However, there is now an additional emphasis on profitability. This transition changes the relationship between the bank and the borrowing treasurer. The treasurer laments, "The loan will be repaid, what more does the banker want?"

More is a better return to the bank. There are a variety of ways this return can be improved. Fundamentally, banks buy and sell money. The return to the bank can be improved by increasing the interest rate charged by the bank when the bank sells money. The return can be improved if the price the bank pays when it buys money is reduced. Banks pay for the money bought either in cash (interest rate) or by providing a service.

1. Banks buy money by paying an interest rate on savings accounts or certificates of deposits.
2. Banks buy money by providing checking account privileges. This is one of many noncredit services the bank performs where the bank can be compensated if the user maintains excess balances in the checking account.

HOW BANKS LOOK AT PROFITABILITY

Bankers examine checking accounts to determine the profitability of the account and availability of excess balances to support additional credit or noncredit services provided by the bank.

This examination is done by completing an analysis similar to the simplified one that follows:

Gross balances — Uncollected funds = Collected funds

Collected funds ×

earnings credit — service charges = Profit/loss on account

$$\frac{\text{Loss}}{\text{Earnings credit}} = \text{Additional balances required}$$

$$\frac{\text{Profit}}{\text{Earnings credit}} = \text{Free balances available}$$

1. *Gross balances* are the balances on the bank's books. This may be at variance with the balance on the treasurer's books because of checks disbursed but not presented for payment or deposits sent but not received by the bank.
2. *Uncollected funds* are created by checks recently deposited

that have not been collected from the bank on which the check has been written. The collecting bank does not have the use of the funds and, therefore, does not give the customer credit for these uncollected funds.

3. *Collected funds* is the difference between gross balances and uncollected funds.

4. The *earnings credit* is set by each bank and bears some relationship to the current money rates and the earnings credits set by competing banks.

5. *Service charges* are made based on the type and volume of services performed at a rate that varies considerably within the banking system. The services performed include processing deposits and honoring checks drawn on the account.

6. Either a *profit* or a *loss* is possible in an account. If the account analysis shows a loss, the bank can ask the treasurer to increase balances, decrease activity (checks written and items deposited) or pay a fee. The banker, however, may consider this to be a loss leader and absorb the loss because of other relationships with the customer. This is a marketing problem similar to that faced by other businessmen. If the loss is to be eliminated in the particular account, the banker can calculate the additional balances required assuming no reduction in the activity of the account.

If a profit is shown in an account (as the balances currently maintained are in excess of those required to compensate the bank for the services performed), it is converted to free balances available to support other services or the extension of credit.

Table 1 below examines a customer's account which has an average gross balance of $100,000. There is $30,000 of uncollected funds, thus, the collected balance available for the bank's use is $70,000. The earnings allowance given is 6 percent which this bank computes by using the average U.S. Treasury bill auction rate.

The customer uses the bank to deposit 250 items at a $0.03 unit charge and wrote 375 checks at a $0.108 unit charge. The monthly activity charge is $48 and the annual charge is $576 which requires collected balances of $9,600 ($576/6% = $9,600). Since the customer has collected balances of $70,000 and needs $9,600 to support activity, there is $60,400 available to support additional activity or to satisfy compensating balance requirements for any loans. For instance, the customer might need to borrow and a 20 percent compensating balance might be required. The approximately $60,000 of free balances would provide the requisite balances for a $300,000 loan ($60,000/20% = $300,000).

It is difficult for the treasurer to determine which bank is pricing checking accounts most favorably. The bank that gives a higher

TABLE 1
Corporate Customer Account Analysis

	Quantity	Unit Price	Amount	
Average gross balance.				$100,000
Less average·uncollected funds				30,000
Average collected balance				$ 70,000
Earnings allowance at 6%				
$70,000 × 6% = $4,200				
Activity charges				
Items deposited	250	$0.03	$ 7.50	
Checks written	375	0.108	40.50	
Monthly charge			$ 48.00	
×			12	
Annual service charge			$576.00	
Balances required to support activity				
charges $576/6%				9,600
Balances available to support credit/				
other activity				$ 60,400

earnings credit may have correspondingly higher charges for its services. The bank with the lower service charges may have a lower earnings credit.

A suggested method for quickly evaluating various earnings credits and charges is for the treasurer to get a quote from various banks reflecting the dollars of balances necessary to support a given level of activity; e.g., what level of collected balances are required to clear 1,000 checks or how many checks can be cleared with $1,000 of collected balances?

Banks sell money by extending credit or the availability of credit. The banker computes the interest rate to charge for credit by the interplay of the following factors:

1. *Cost of funds* is the largest factor and the most volatile. The funding of banks has been changing from demand deposits to greater dependence on purchased funds. As this change occurs, the cost of funds is becoming more expensive and more volatile.

2. *Risk of default* is included by allocating the expense of some loans not being collected. The charge to all borrowers must cover these bad debts. Strong credits which are thought to have a lower probability of loss are charged less which is similar to the life insurance practice of charging a lower premium to the actuarially healthier policyholder.

3. *Cost of administration* can be reduced by either a volume discount reflecting the economy of handling one note for a large amount rather than numerous smaller notes from several borrowers or eliminating the complexities of handling collateral (see Chapters 28 and 29 dealing with secured borrowing).

4. *Profit margin* is included as some measure of profit is necessary for the bank to continue to serve its customers.

5. *Market conditions* at any point in time may be of critical importance. Competition has a very pervasive impact which can, especially for short periods of time, override the other rate determining considerations. The actions of the government regulatory authorities can affect the freedom of the market place to determine rates.

PRIME RATE

Prime rate is the lowest rate quoted by a banker to its biggest and best customers. The biggest relates to the lower cost of administration of fewer borrowers and the absence of monitoring collateral. Only the strongest borrowers can obtain credit on an unsecured basis and, if collateral is required, it indicates the underlying financial strength of the borrower is weaker. Occasionally even a borrower with an impeccable credit record can pledge excellent collateral, such as government securities and obtain a lower interest rate than if an unsecured loan was granted. The best customers present little credit risk or have a lower risk of delinquency and default because of their financial strength.

The concept of a prime rate started in the 1930s and the rate itself moved very slowly and in small increments until 1966. Since 1966, the prime rate has changed frequently, which is a reflection of the volatile money markets and the dependence of the banking industry on purchased money.

The uniformity of virtually all banks establishing identical prime rates at the same point in time has led to the charge that the prime rate is administered collusively. In part due to this criticism, some banks recently have adopted what is known as formula prime rate which is based on the cost of funds such as the cost of certificates of deposits. The formula prime also demonstrates the dependence on general market conditions for short-term money.

In addition to the interest rate charged by the bank, the borrowing treasurer can benefit the bank by keeping free balances in the checking account. In recognition of this benefit, the bank may reduce the interest rate charged. Historically, the practice of keeping free balances to compensate banks for making loans is so common that interest rates are quoted with a compensating balance requirement as an integral, often unstated, component of the borrowing rate.

The interest rates quoted and the effective rates charged on loans vary directly with the compensating balance for the treasurer is to pay a higher rate if balances are maintained which otherwise would not have been. This is demonstrated in Table 2.

TABLE 2
Effective Rate Charged

Balance Requirement	Quoted Rate					
	7%	8%	9%	10%	11%	12%
10%	7.78	8.89	10.00	11.11	12.22	13.33
15%	8.24	9.41	10.59	11.76	12.94	14.12
20%	8.75	10.00	11.25	12.50	13.75	15.00

Compensating balances should be free balances—balances over and above those required to maintain the activity in the checking account. If the same balances are used for activity compensation and for borrowing, the banker is deluded by this double counting in making the profit analysis. The double counting of balances must be made up elsewhere in the banking relationship if the banker is going to obtain a competitive return.

Compensating balance requirements are computed on an average basis and are not frozen funds in an account. The treasurer may draw the balances below the agreed figure if the balances are satisfactory on average. If the treasurer agrees to keep 20 percent of the loan in the checking account, the bank will analyze the balance maintenance on monthly or seasonal averages. If average balances do not meet the agreed level, the banker has a marketing decision to either charge a fee for the deficit balances, increase the interest rate on future borrowings, ignore the deficiency, or refuse further borrowing accommodations. Realistically, much of this decision is dependent on the behavior of competing banks or on market conditions. If it is a period of tight money when the banker must ration his scarce resource, compensating balance agreements are monitored very closely.

The rationale behind requiring compensating balances comes from the historical practice of customers keeping balances in their checking account in excess of what is required as working balances. The bank benefits from the use of these funds and shares this benefit by reducing the interest rate on loans. However, the corporate treasurer, through careful cash management (ironically with the expertise of cash management advisory staff of many banks) and the investment of excess funds (ironically through the bond department of many banks) has, in many instances, diminished or even eliminated any excess balances.

Banks survive these reduced deposits by substituting purchased money, for example, in the form of negotiable certificates of deposit, commercial paper, and Eurodollars. The net effect is that banks have to buy the money that had been in checking accounts. The increased cost of purchased funds and the volatility caused by purchasing funds in a market atmosphere has been reflected in higher and more volatile interest rates for loan customers.

It is widely accepted that the practice of compensating balances is anachronistic and will not be as prevalent someday. Nonetheless, they are a real fact of life today and especially with tight money are of primary importance to the banker.

ADDITIONAL SOURCES

See Additional Sources at the end of Chapter 27.

Chapter 27

Selecting a Commercial Bank

Harley Rankin, Jr.[*]

THE SUCCESSFUL and profitable relationship between a company and its commercial banks depends in large part on the proper selection of those banks. The banking industry's dramatic growth in resources in the last decade has encouraged banks to offer more complete financial services to its customers. The advantage to a company of these expanded services is evident; however, at the same time the selection of a commercial bank has been rendered more difficult because of the wider assortment of services from which to choose. A mitigating factor in this situation has been the new professionalism of bank managers which has enabled most banks to better understand corporate needs.

Before a decision can be made to use a particular bank, the corporate treasurer must analyze carefully the company's banking requirements. Closely related to the treasurer's own clear understanding of the company's needs will be his determination of the type of bank that will be most able to meet these needs.

Generally speaking, corporate banking relationships involve three principal types of banks. First are the money center banks on which many large companies depend for most of their credit needs and other important banking services. The second type is made up of regional banks which offer many of the services of the money center banks but operate over a more limited geographic area. Finally,

[*] Harley Rankin, Jr., is treasurer, Continental Can Co., Inc., New York.

there are local banks which tend to cater to the financing needs of smaller businesses and local plants or branches of larger corporations.

Once the corporate treasurer has identified the specific banking requirements of his company and the type of bank needed, the process of selecting the proper institution begins. Although there are many variables involved in the decision to use a particular bank, the principal ones are: the financial condition of the bank; the quality of its management; the willingness and ability of a bank to meet a company's financial requirements; the location of the bank; its reputation in the community and banking industry; and the nature of services offered.

FINANCIAL CONDITION

One of the major factors to be considered in selecting a commercial bank is its financial condition. Every financial officer has a responsibility to ensure that the banks he selects for the company's depositories are financially strong. Although all banks are supervised and examined regularly by various state and federal bank authorities, this in itself does not guarantee the financial strength and safety of a bank. Further, although most banks are insured by the Federal Deposit Insurance Corporation to the extent of $40,000 for each depositor, the insurance feature has no relationship to the financial stability of the bank. At the very least, a financial officer considering opening or maintaining a corporate account in excess of $40,000 should determine the financial soundness of the institution.

Financial Review Methods

Most companies make some effort to review the financial condition of their banks, including prospective depositories, but the frequency and extent of the reviews vary widely. Some firms are content with an occasional reading of bank annual reports and interim statements. Others, however, prefer a more careful study, involving a thorough analysis of bank statements and other published financial data.

One of the prime considerations in analyzing a bank's statement is the degree of protection afforded the depositor by the capital structure, for the ultimate strength of a bank lies in its capital funds. A strong capital structure in relation to a bank's deposits and volume of business is an obvious sign of financial strength.

In recent years, however, capital ratios of the banking industry have declined. Several factors have contributed to this contraction. Liquidity positions, particularly at money center banks and to an increasing degree at regional banks, have been declining because of a major shift in the banking industry's source of funds. The proportion of funds obtained from the deposit market (excluding large negotiated certificates of deposit) has fallen in the last ten years. At the same time, banks have increased their short-term borrowings as a percentage of total lending resources.

The reduction in liquidity positions has been compounded by the entrance of the industry into nonbanking activities. The 1970 amendments to the Bank Holding Company Act have made possible this evolution of banks from traditional deposit and loan institutions into broadly based financial intermediaries. In some cases, however, the rapid pace of holding company expansion has added new risks in nonbanking areas and, by increasing the industry's leverage through use of short-term money market instruments, has magnified the threat to a bank's own assets.

The dramatic change of the last several years in the financial posture of the commercial banking industry is a major reason for every financial officer to conduct a thorough financial analysis before selecting a new bank. A wide range of statistical techniques exists to aid him in this task, including the following:

Growth of Capital Funds and Reserves. Capital growth generated from retained earnings and which compares favorably with the rate of growth of similar sized competitors would indicate sound operating procedures.

Capital Ratios. Besides analyzing capital growth trends, there are various ratios which also serve to test a bank's capital adequacy. These ratios include total capital to deposits, total capital and reserves to total capital assets, senior debt to total capital, equity capital and reserves to total assets, equity capital to risk assets, and equity capital to total loans.

Risk assets generally comprise those assets not included in the "liquid" category. In most cases, this means loans, securities other than governments, and other invested assets. A more refined variation of the capital/risk assets ratio would be to weigh risk assets according to the approximate amount of risk of each asset.

A recent variation of the equity capital to loan ratio is to relate equity capital not to total loans outstanding, but to past loan loss experience. Forty times the average loan losses of the previous five years is a standard often cited for well-managed banks; i.e., the loan to loss ratio should be below 2.5 percent.

Profitability. An uneven or deteriorating earnings record should be considered significant in terms of increasing the degree of financial risk for a particular institution. Any change in profit margins (gross income as a percent of operating earnings) should also be evaluated. Other ratios which measure the earnings performance of a bank include return on equity capital, return on total assets and the net interest margin.

Loan-Loss Record. An increase in this category could indicate indifferent management or an existing competitive situation which is forcing the bank to make higher risk loans than normal. If the information is available, the mix of loan maturities and rates should also be considered. An equally important ratio is the relationship of profits to loan losses since profits tend to be the first line of defense against loan losses after use of normal reserves for such losses. The suggested rule of thumb for well-managed banks is that profits should be at least twice the actual loan losses expected to be incurred.

Liquidity. The most common liquidity measurement relates banks' cash and U.S. government security holdings to total deposits and other liabilities. The definition of "liquid" assets is not universally accepted; some calculations include loans insured by the U.S. government or, in some cases, municipal bonds. In measuring liquidity, one should remember that a portion of U.S. government bonds may be pledged to secure government deposits.

Other factors which should be considered are the ratio of loans to deposits, potential volatility of the deposit structure, and the change in short-term borrowings of a bank as measured by the relationship of "other liabilities" (all liabilities except for deposits, loan-loss reserve and long-term debt) to net worth.

At Continental Can Company, the general practice with regard to analyzing financial statements of prospective banks has been to emphasize those measurements which test a bank's capital adequacy. Recently, we have also stressed analysis of a bank's profitability in judging its soundness.

Interpreting bank balance sheet ratios requires some standards of comparison. Rather than attaching specific importance to the actual numerical value of any ratio, comparison should be made with standards based on some broad aggregate of banks, such as the average for all Federal Reserve member banks, all insured banks, or all banks falling within certain size categories. Measurement according to size is particularly important since banks of dissimilar size tend to face different problems with regard to liquidity and other factors. Any pronounced departure from the aggregate or average bank standard should lead to closer analysis. A few banks, of course, will deviate from the norm for various acceptable reasons.

Ratio analysis, however, should not be used as the final determinant in considering the opening or maintenance of a deposit relationship. Numerous variables such as seasonal fluctuations exist which may influence ratios at particular times.

Frequent criticisms of the use of ratios are their failure to adequately assess the capability of a bank's management, their limitations in measuring the quality of bank loans and investments and their dependence upon information appearing in published reports which may make suitable comparisons impossible. This last factor is indicative of the tendency of banks to report certain items differently. For example, as previously pointed out, some banks include in liquid assets Federal Reserve stock, loans insured by the federal government and municipal bonds while others exclude these longer term Treasury obligations.

Despite its limitations, the statistical analysis of banks is generally regarded as having some practical value for corporate treasurers in that it provides objective, quantitative information on which the analysis of a bank's financial condition can be based.

Sources of Banking Data

What sources of information are available for a company that wishes to examine the financial health of a prospective bank? The major sources are the annual and interim reports that banks themselves issue to their stockholders. Most banks have summaries of these reports published in business journals. It is primarily from these reports that the necessary data for statistical analysis can be obtained.

Most banks also submit detailed information with respect to earnings, deposits, loans, investments, new services, personnel changes and other factors. If necessary, a treasurer should feel free to request banks to make available additional information not ordinarily contained in the stockholders' reports.

A second major source of information are the annual reports that banks must make to the Comptroller of the Currency, if they are federally chartered, and to state banking authorities, if they are incorporated under state law. A detailed statement of assets, liabilities, and capital funds is also included in these reports.

In the case of larger banks, other substantive information is available through various investment houses, including pertinent data such as loan and investment yields, net operating earnings and forecasts and analysis of various capital ratios. In addition, bank or bank holding companies whose shares are publicly traded must file financial statements with the Securities and Exchange Commission every year.

Information on banks is also available from a number of financial publications. Those best known are Moody's *Banks and Finance Manual* and Polk's *World Bank Directory*, which are updated annually; *Banking*, a monthly magazine; and *American Banker*, a daily banking newspaper. The latter publication discloses, on a semiannual basis, the leading banks in the United States and the world as ranked by deposits.

QUALITY OF MANAGEMENT

A second major factor in the selection of a commercial bank is the caliber of a bank's management. Since this is an area that does not readily lend itself to precise measurement, it is best to have as wide a range of contacts and references as possible so as to be able to assess accurately the character and ability of a bank's directors and officers.

A treasurer's contacts with individuals who have had personal or business associations with a bank's officers can be helpful in gaining insight on the competency of management. Many corporations with representatives located in a bank's geographic area rely on these individuals' assessment of the quality of a bank's management. These representatives can often provide specific items of interest obtained from local newspaper sources about a particular bank, as well as information about the general reputation of the bank's officials in the community. Officers of correspondent banks can also be helpful sources of information on the caliber of a bank's management.

The most direct approach, of course, is to interview representatives of the bank itself. It is often possible at this time to identify those banks with an aggressive new business policy who are particularly interested in helping local business interests. In the final analysis, the financial results of a bank's operations and its reputation among its peers in the banking industry also provide an indirect but fairly reliable measurement of the quality of its management.

FINANCING REQUIREMENTS

A business that borrows from a bank must take into account the institution's willingness to grant the loan, its ability to meet the company's financial needs, the flexibility of arrangements that can be made and the costs that will be incurred. For a company that has substantial borrowing needs, the willingness of a bank to lend is obviously a prime consideration. Even when borrowing is not contemplated, it is wise to be familiar with a bank's lending philosophy in case future expansion or acquisitions call for additional funds.

When a company is in need of extending its credit, it may find it useful to associate with banks of high standing in the community and banking industry. The fact that a well-known and respected bank is willing to lend to a company often can enhance the firm's prestige and credit standing.

In addition to considering the willingness of a particular bank to lend, attention should also be given to the size of the bank. Since there are economic and legal limits to the amount of credit which one bank may advance to a single borrower, a company should use a bank that is capable of accommodating its needs for credit. A company often gets better service from banks whose typical customers receive loans that are comparable in amount to that which the company is likely to require. Large companies may find their choice is limited to relatively few institutions, particularly because of legal restrictions on the size of the loan a bank may grant. Most banks are limited by regulations to granting loans up to a maximum of 10 percent of their combined capital and surplus to any single borrower.

If the bank is too small, the loan request assumes undue importance. For this reason, a large amount of national lending tends to be done by a few big money center banks. At Continental Can Company, for instance, the seasonal nature of the business and resultant borrowing requirements tend to make lines of credit which are less than $500,000 impractical.

On the other hand, a relatively small company will sometimes receive little attention from a large bank. Even worse, a small firm that is not in strong financial condition may have trouble finding a bank willing to grant a loan.

The type of financing required is also an important factor. Certain types of borrowing best suited for a given corporation may not be available at all banks. For example, some banks do not have the inclination or facilities to service specialized loans such as borrowings based on assignment of accounts receivable, inventory field warehousing agreements, or discounting of notes receivable and trade acceptances. More recently, some banks have promoted lease financing, industrial revenue bonds and pollution control financing. Because of the unique nature of these credit arrangements and the specialized skills that must accompany them, many banks still do not offer them to customers.

Because banks will differ in their lending policies and in their familiarity with various industries, the lending requirements of some companies may best be served by a bank which has specialists with knowledge of the technical aspects of a firm's operations. Normally, this type of expertise is associated with large lending institutions.

LOCATION

Location can be a major factor that may affect the choice of a bank in several ways. Since corporate banking relationships involve dealing with money center, regional and local banks, the importance of a depository's location will vary according to the type of bank sought.

Depending on its size, a company may use any number from a few to hundreds of banks. For a large company with numerous banks, its most valued relationships are normally with those large banks located in New York and other money market centers. In these cities, banks are generally selected not only on the basis of their financial condition and quality of management but also on the factors of lending ability, convenience and range of services offered, together with the cost of such services. Larger banks usually offer a broader range of services and are better equipped to handle the volume of business associated with large corporations. Because of these additional attributes, location is a relatively less important factor in choosing a large bank.

In addition to money center banks, most large companies will have need for regional banks, which may provide many of the same important services offered by large depositories and which may also be particularly useful because of their strategic location in servicing a network of banks in a common geographic area. For example, regional banks often act as concentration banks for collection of accounts receivable or in handling disbursement functions for a particular area. Location becomes more of a factor here since a company is looking for a qualified institution to represent its interests in a specific area.

A company's choice of a local bank is usually based on the location of its plant or retail branch, besides the more general factors of financial condition, caliber of management, and standing in the community. Location assumes major importance when considering specialized services offered by local banks such as payroll preparation, reimbursement of a plant's petty cash fund, or check cashing facilities for its employees. In this regard, the plant or retail branch manager's preference as to a particular local bank usually carries additional weight.

Similarly, less substantial businesses which are located in smaller communities and which lack the substantial credit requirements of larger firms tend to gravitate to the smaller banks located in their area.

Local banks are also selected based on a corporation's desire to maintain a good relationship within the community in which an important facility is located. Even though a company has no need of a banking association, it will sometimes maintain a small fixed or "dormant" deposit account in the local bank as an indication of its interest in a beneficial and long-term relationship with the community.

REPUTATION IN THE COMMUNITY AND BANKING INDUSTRY

Respectability and creditability are important for any financial institution; however, determining a bank's reputation in the community or among similar institutions in the banking industry can often be as difficult as appraising the quality of bank management.

At Continental Can Company, several factors are looked at in considering a bank's reputation. Primarily, during selection of a local or regional bank, we attempt to evaluate the institution's standing in the community. As in judging the quality of management, we often rely on firsthand reports conveyed to us by our managers in the field. When there are two leading candidates in one geographic area, we sometimes follow a policy of splitting banking functions between banks.

The reputation of the bank among its peers in the banking industry is also a major determinant. In the case of nonmoney center banks, the recommendation of a bank's larger correspondents can be extremely valuable. Information on such items as general financial condition and creditworthiness, caliber of calling officers, aggressiveness in promoting innovative services and capability of "backoffice" operations can be obtained. Additional sources of useful information also can be found in various financial journals and newspapers. Particularly useful is the *American Banker*, which although directed to the banking industry in general, is probably one of the most current and complete sources of banking information available. Knowledge of the general character of a bank's customers is also beneficial. Information of this type can usually be gained from bank correspondents. An awareness of a bank's reputation among one's suppliers and customers can also be valuable.

SPECIAL SERVICES OFFERED

The dynamic growth of the banking industry in recent years, paralleled by increasing competitiveness within the industry, has led banks to offer many services at home and abroad never offered in the past.

In addition, the 1970 amendments to the Bank Holding Company Act have provided a major stimulus for banks to expand into nonbanking but financially related services. In general, the amendments permit bank holding companies to own more than one bank, and to be in any business the Federal Reserve Board deems "closely related" to banking. At present, banks have been able to diversify by acquiring finance and leasing companies, to sell insurance, to provide data processing and travel services, to engage in factoring, mortgage banking and investment management, and other assorted financial activities.

Because of this growth in resources, together with a new concern about marketing bank services, companies now have a wider assortment of services from which to choose. As such, the determination of which banks are most suitable for serving a company's financial needs is often based on the nature of services offered.

Most banking services can generally be divided into two broad areas, although the characteristics of some are not always so clearly defined.

The first area is operational requirements. Major specialized services included here are cash mobilization systems, such as administering a company's network of lockboxes, transferring funds, processing of federal tax payments, payroll preparation, freight payment plans, and automatic reconciliation of payroll and payable accounts.

A bank may also act as trustee of pension funds, as commercial paper and dividend disbursing agent, as registrar and transfer agent for capital stock and as escrow agent. Often a bank will also offer a variety of conveniences such as guaranteeing signatures, giving letters of credit and letters of introduction, and providing for bank money orders, certified checks, cashier's checks, draft collection, bond coupon collection and safekeeping facilities.

Some corporations favor using a smaller bank for operational or back-office services since the bank generally has less volume to handle and thus can devote more personal attention to assuring relatively error free service. Smaller banks are also introducing services that, while not new to the banking industry, formerly were offered only by large money center or regional banks. These include products such as payroll preparation, lease-buy analysis, and cash management services. Often a smaller bank's merger into a bank holding company already offering a wide array of services has permitted this expansion into new products.

The second broad class of banking service is financial advice. Banks are selected on the basis of availability of specialists for counseling in specific areas such as cash management, merger and acquisition analysis, and domestic and international financing. Also incorporated in this category would be investment advisory services, including pension fund management, money market investment services, and credit information services. Advice of a more generalized nature might include economic forecasts, international business counsel, including trade data, and foreign exchange information.

Some large banks currently have an advantage over smaller banks in that their customers can obtain financial advice through the use of remote terminals. Such a system permits the flexibility of changing input information so that a customer may experiment with a variety of assumptions. Computerized advice can be made available for forecasting working capital requirements, developing short- or long-term financing plans, scheduling cash flow needs, evaluating capital budgets, and so forth. Normally most smaller banks do not have the necessary computer equipment and expertise to offer this type of service.

There are also many intangible services to be considered. Obtaining home mortgages and stock option loans, use of relocation services and the availability of bank facilities to company employees for cashing paychecks can be valuable to any firm. Banks often are able to assist in promoting company sales through contacts with other customers in the bank. In many cases, bank credit assistance to valued customers may prove extremely beneficial to a company.

Most treasurers will agree that the variety and multiplicity of services offered by banks sometimes make it difficult to select the proper institution to meet one's requirements. The most important factor is that the service offered should satisfy a particular need of the business. In addition, there are several other criteria which can be of value in selecting a particular bank's service. At Continental Can Company, a needed service is usually evaluated on the basis of four factors: quality, reliability, cost, and the bank's willingness to offer the service.

Quality and reliability are of particular importance for operational services. The cost of services is important, but we will sometimes forego incremental savings if it is felt a greater degree of quality and reliability can be obtained. Equally important is one's assessment of a bank's ability and dedication to providing the service at an agreed standard of performance.

The majority of companies pay for most of their banking services through compensating balances. These are funds a corporation leaves on deposit with its banks to enable them to earn a profit for maintaining a line of credit, handling the firm's checking accounts and performing other functions required by the company in managing its finances.

In recent years, however, a growing trend has been to compensate banks for certain services through fees. Banking services supported by fees seldom include general accounts or related activities, such as the transfer of funds through bank wire services. Generally speaking, the average daily deposit should be sufficient to compensate the bank for activities such as these. Fees tend to be established for those services that require banks to handle clerical functions in large volume. Such services usually include payroll preparation, account reconciliation plans, trust and escrow services, dividend and debenture payments, and stock transfer and registrar services.

REVIEWING BANK RELATIONSHIPS

Having selected a bank to meet a company's financial requirements, a treasurer must take care to ensure that the institution continues to perform according to the company's expected standards. If a banking association is to be valuable and ongoing, both the company and the banks should periodically reassess the relationship. A company whose financial needs call for dealing with many banks has an even greater challenge to determine, on a recurring basis, which banks are giving it the best service. It is especially important for a large company to be able to judge the performance of its principle money center banks.

There are several ways to evaluate bank relationships. At Continental Can Company, four principal methods are utilized. The first, and traditionally the most favored approach among financial executives, is to evaluate banks on the basis of personal contacts with their officers. Usually this is the easiest and most convenient method for corporate treasurers to keep up to date with their bankers. A treasurer normally has many opportunities for such contacts. A company's major banks will make scheduled calls during the year plus additional visits to introduce a new service or simply to resolve a specific problem. Likewise, many corporate treasurers will call on banks, although on a less frequent basis. From these meetings and discussions, a treasurer can often learn about the bank's performance and current problems as well as gain a first hand impression of the quality of management. The importance of such contacts should not be underestimated for, as previously pointed out, a company can sometimes acquire valuable knowledge about other banks as well as learn about its own bank.

A second major way to evaluate bank relationships is through use of the account analysis report.[1] An increasing number of corporations now request these reports which show the breakdown of activity and the charges applicable to the different services rendered. In addition to summarizing account activity, the report also shows the

---

[1] Cf. the discussion of the use of the same report form in connection with Table 1 in Chapter 26 from the standpoint of a bank.

earnings value assigned to average collected balances. A copy of the account analysis form used by Continental Can Company is shown in Figure 1.

The starting point of the analysis is the company's average daily

FIGURE 1

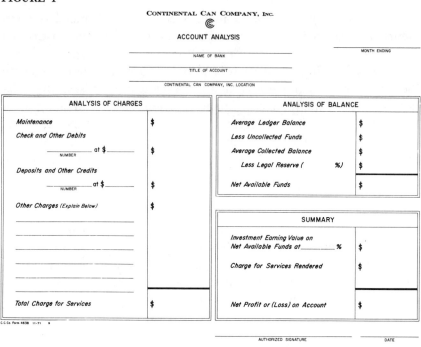

ledger balance for the month. Subtracting the amount of uncollected funds, representing checks deposited but not yet cleared, gives the average collected balance for the month. From this figure is deducted an amount representing the legal reserve which must be kept by the bank. The net result is the balance of funds available for loans or investment by the bank. Applying the average earnings rate to this net figure produces the bank's estimated gross profit on the account, from which is subtracted the cost of providing the specified services to the company during the month. The difference represents the net profit or loss on the account.

Use of analysis reports enables a corporate treasurer to note differences in prices that various banks charge for their services. These charges and the earnings credit allowed may vary widely, particularly among smaller banks.

Surveys conducted by corporations among their subsidiaries or field representatives on the relative value of bank services is another method used to assess bank relationships. At Continental Can Company, various field representatives in contact with major credit line banks are requested, on an annual basis, to rate the quality of services of each bank in their area on a scale of *A* through *D*. Services rated include expertise in processing lockbox receipts, sharing of credit information, interest in lending financial assistance to customers and assistance to company employees. The results are then analyzed for any significant findings. We have found the system valuable in providing a rough indication of not only the relative quality of routine and clerical services performed by a particular bank but also the degree of interest the bank has in working with the company.

A fourth method of evaluating bank relationships is through the use of special studies involving one or more particular bank services. Probably the most common of these specialized reports is the lockbox study which analyzes and evaluates a company's collection system. One of the major conclusions of a study of this type is a listing of those depositories producing the minimum total collection time for company receipts for a specific area. Of growing importance recently have been disbursement studies which attempt to isolate those banks most suited to maximizing a corporation's collected balances through disbursement activity.

SUMMARY

We have examined the principal factors which a company treasurer should use in selecting a commercial bank. At the outset, it is important that a company identify as accurately as possible which specific financial needs a prospective bank will be expected to satisfy. Such requirements could include additional credit facilities, specialized services such as merger and acquisition assistance, international financial consulting, and domestic cash management services.

The financial condition of a commercial bank is of primary importance in the selection process. As noted, the decrease in capital in relation to other balance sheet items for the banking industry in general in the last decade underscores the necessity of frequent and thorough analysis of a bank's financial status.

The quality of a bank's management and its reputation in the community and banking industry are two additional factors which a corporate treasurer should investigate in determining a suitable bank for his company's use. Because of the imprecise nature of both these factors, it is essential that the treasurer examine as many reliable sources of information as practical. These will include his own acquaintances and business associates, his company's representatives in the field, officials of correspondent banks, personal interviews, and various financial publications.

The willingness and ability of a bank to meet a company's borrowing requirements is a fourth selection factor which should be carefully reviewed by the corporate financial officer. Attention must be given to the size of a prospective bank in relation to the magnitude of the company's financial requirements.

Location is also important in the choice of a commercial bank. The degree of significance of this factor will depend in part on the type of bank that a company treasurer is seeking. The location of a regional or local bank is generally of greater strategic importance to a company than that of a money center bank.

In addition to being a depository and lending institution, a bank offers a variety of other financial services, any number of which can be crucial to the selection of that institution by a company treasurer. The dramatic growth of resources of the banking industry in the last several years, aided in particular by the 1970 amendments to the Bank Holding Company Act, has stimulated the variety of innovative services offered by banks. In addition, many of these services are now being promoted by smaller banks.

Finally, we have seen that continuation of a successful corporate banking relationship requires a periodic reassessment of the relationship by both parties.

ADDITIONAL SOURCES

Abraham, Alfred B. "Factoring: The New Frontier for Commercial Banks." *Journal of Commercial Bank Lending,* 53 (April 1971), 32–43.

Baxter, Nevins D., and Shapiro, Harold T. "Compensating Balance Requirements: The Results of a Survey." *Journal of Finance,* 19 (September 1964), 483–96.

Crane, Dwight B., and White, William L. "Who Benefits from a Floating

Prime Rate?" *Harvard Business Review,* 50 (January–February 1972), 121–29.

Harris, Duane G. "Some Evidence on Differential Lending Practices at Commerical Banks." *Journal of Finance,* 28 (December, 1973), 1303–11.

Hayes, Douglas A. *Bank Lending Policies: Issues and Practices.* Ann Arbor, Mich.: Bureau of Business Research, University of Michigan, 1964.

Hayes, Douglas A. *Bank Lending Policies: Domestic and International.* Ann Arbor, Mich.: University of Michigan, 1971.

Nadler, Paul S. "Compensating Balances and the Prime at Twilight." *Harvard Business Review,* 50 (January–February 1972), 112–20.

Nadler, Paul S. "The Territorial Hunger of Our Major Banks." *Harvard Business Review,* 52 (March–April 1974), 87–98.

Shay, Robert P., and Greer, Carl C. "Banks Move into High-Risk Commercial Financing." *Harvard Business Review,* 46 (November–December 1968), 149–53, 156–61.

Stone, Bernell K. "The Cost of Bank Loans." *Journal of Financial and Quantitative Analysis,* 7 (December 1972), 2077–86.

Chapter 28

Inventory Financing

Steven L. Westfall[*]

BORROWING to finance inventory requirements is anything but a simple financial transaction. The first problem the prospective seeker of inventory loans finds is that few bank loan officers are experienced in granting this type of credit, with the result that many bankers are uncomfortable with anything but meager percentages of advance against total inventory value. The second problem is that inventory financing is a highly specialized form of credit, and when properly administered it has what appears to the borrower to be very stringent compliance requirements.

For many businesses, however, inventory financing is an extremely important source of continuing credit, and for others it is a large source of untapped credit capacity. The purpose of this chapter is to inform financial officers who are considering inventory loans as a source of credit for their business about sources of such credit and the lending procedures that usually apply.

What Is Inventory?

Most of us have a pretty fair idea of what sorts of assets are included under the heading of "Inventory." But lest there be any doubt, the Uniform Commercial Code, which has become the law of the land in every state except Louisiana on the subject of secured credit defines inventory in some detail.

---

[*] Steven L. Westfall is President, Tradeline, Inc., San Francisco, California.

The principal test to determine whether goods are inventory is that they are held for immediate or ultimate sale. Implicit in the definition is the criterion that the prospective sale is in the ordinary course of business. Machinery used in manufacturing, for example, is equipment and not inventory even though it is the continuing policy of the enterprise to sell machinery when it becomes obsolete. Goods to be furnished under a contract of service are inventory even though the arrangement under which they are furnished is not technically a sale. When an enterprise is engaged in the business of leasing a stock of products to users (for example, the fleet of cars owned by a car rental agency), that stock is also included within the definition of "inventory." It should be noted that one class of goods which is not held for disposition to a purchaser or user is included in inventory: "Materials used or consumed in a business." Examples of this class of inventory are fuel to be used in operations, scrap metal produced in the course of manufacture, and containers to be used to package the goods. In general it may be said that goods used in a business are equipment when they are fixed assets or have, as identifiable units, a relatively long period of use; but are inventory, even though not held for sale, if they are used up or consumed in a short period of time in the production of some end product.[1]

What this definition tells us about inventory is that an extremely wide range of goods, many of which are not commonly thought of as inventory assets, come under the legal definition. The overriding principle is that inventory consists of goods which are consumed in a short period of time. Further, the definition makes no restrictions on either possession or condition; thus, finished goods on consignment, raw materials purchased but not yet received, goods in transit, and work in process, all qualify as inventory. Assets of this kind, as well as raw materials, finished products, and supplies held on the borrower's premises, represent assets which are financed through inventory loans.

The Potential for Financing Inventory

Inventory financing has come to be regarded as an important area of credit for three fundamental reasons. First, the need to finance inventory is inescapable; no one has found a way to do away with

---

[1] *Uniform Laws Annotated, Uniform Commercial Code* (St. Paul, Minn.: West Publishing Company, 1968), p. 73–74.

the need to acquire and hold inventories. Second, the numbers are large—the aggregate dollar value of manufacturing and trade inventories mid-1974 stood at $240 billion, and in recent years has shown annual increases on the order of 10 percent, or some $24 billion a year. Third, by arranging secured financing on inventory collateral, borrowers have found they can greatly increase their credit capacity, often up to three or four times their unsecured borrowing capacity.

Nationally, there is a tremendous untapped credit capacity hidden in unfinanced inventory assets. Of the outstanding $250 billion in bank and commercial finance loans to commercial and industrial firms in 1974, it is estimated that less than $50 billion is to support inventories. Using the standard that the loan value of inventory averages around 60 percent of the inventory book value, the total inventory credit capacity of U.S. commercial and industrial firms stands at $140 billion—or some 2.8 times the present loan level.

Who Borrows on Inventory?

Today there are few industries or products which do not meet the criteria for inventory loans. Industries such as steel, aluminum, tires, consumer electronics, fertilizer, paper, farm machinery, plastics, building materials, and petroleum are using outside credit sources to finance their growing investments in inventory.

In 1974, a representative distribution of the estimated $50 billion in inventory loans outstanding was:[2]

		($ billion)
1.	Wholesale trade	$20.0
2.	Manufacturing	20.0
3.	Retail trade	5.5
4.	Services	1.8
5.	Construction	1.3
6.	Transportation	0.9
7.	Mining	0.4

Businesses that use inventory loans generally are typified by one or more of the following characteristics:

---

[2] This distribution is based on data from Lawrence Systems on the mix of secured loans controlled by Lawrence Systems.

1. Their manufacturing and/or distribution pattern is such that there are extended periods between receipt of raw materials and sales of finished goods.
2. Inventory is a major current asset (as in the case of wholesale and retail trade businesses).
3. Alternate sources of financing are inadequate for current needs.
4. Major increases in inventory occur sporadically in the normal course of business due to special purchase opportunities or variances in deliveries, production, or sales.
5. The business is highly seasonal, requiring large purchases or accumulation of finished goods that do not result in sales until a specific time of year.
6. The company is anticipating rapid growth in sales that requires an even larger anticipatory buildup of inventory.

Inventory Financing and the Code

Inventory financing is the extension of credit to a borrower from a lender in which, in the event of default on the part of the borrower, the lender has recourse to the borrower's inventory as a source of debt repayment. Because of this recourse feature to a specific asset or class of assets, inventory financing is a specialized form of credit that falls under the more general subject, secured financing. While it is unnecessary for a borrower to know the many legal steps and considerations taken by an experienced lender in a secured loan transaction, he should be generally aware of the law that governs that transaction—namely, the Uniform Commercial Code.[3] Specifically, Article 9 of the Uniform Commercial Code deals with secured financing and defines "security interests" as existing whenever goods serve as collateral for the payment or performance of an obligation. Thus, a lender making an inventory loan in which he requires a recourse to inventory or inventories will arrange this transaction pursuant to the requirements of Article 9 of the Code.

Unsecured Loans and Secured Loans

In an unsecured loan, the lender does not take the steps to assure that the assets being financed will be available to satisfy the indebtedness, if needed. In a secured loan transaction, he does.

---

[3] In all states except Louisiana.

Unsecured working capital loans to finance inventories and other current assets are becoming increasingly rare. Unsecured loans of this type are loans which are made on the sole basis of the general creditworthiness of the borrower and are generally restricted to large corporations with long histories of borrowing and profitability, and where the amount of unsecured working capital credit is small relative to the company's net worth. Occasionally, unsecured working capital loans to finance small amounts of inventory are made where long-established personal relationships exist between borrowers and their local banks. In these cases the loan amounts are typically under $100,000 and the loans are treated more as personal loans than as business loans.

A secured loan is the customary instrument for inventory financing. While lenders seldom enter into a loan transaction with the idea that their source of repayment will be the liquidation of assets, those lenders that have not provided adequately for that contingency take a perilous and unnecessary business risk. The fact is that it does not take many loan losses to completely wipe out the meager return on assets that is characteristic of the banking and commercial finance business. Today, the best of lenders, and the most aggressive ones, see to it that they have the protection and security of assets behind their loans.

In setting up a secured credit for inventory as well as receivables, the lender has two objectives. First, he must *create* a security interest. Second, he must *perfect* his security interest.

To *create* a security interest, the lender will:

1. Prepare and have executed between lender and borrower a security agreement which describes the assets which are to serve as collateral, describes the amount and terms of indebtedness, specifies the maintenance and proper insurance on the financed assets by the debtor, and prohibits any other liens on the same assets.
2. Obtain from the borrower his statement that he has ownership or assignable rights to the collateral.
3. Prepare and have executed a loan agreement giving value to the borrower.

In order to enforce his security interest against third parties, such as other secured creditors, other unsecured creditors, or a trustee in bankruptcy, the lender needs to *perfect* his security interest. To do this, he will take one of two steps:

1. He will take possession of the pledged collateral by taking possession of a negotiable bill of lading or warehouse receipt, or a similar nonnegotiable instrument assigned to the bank.
2. Where the possession of this type is impractical, the lender will record his secured position with the secretary of state with a financing statement (Form UCC–1, See Figure 1) and take steps

FIGURE 1
Sample UCC Financial Statement with Instructions

STATE OF FLORIDA
UNIFORM COMMERCIAL CODE — FINANCING STATEMENT — FORM UCC — 1

Reorder from: Ferris Ptg. Co. 146 West South St., Orlando, Florida 32801

Any forms used for filing with the Office of Secretary of State pursuant to the Uniform Commercial Code must be approved by Richard (Dick) Stone, Secretary of State, State of Florida.

INSTRUCTIONS:

1. PLEASE TYPE this form. Fold only along perforation for mailing.
2. Remove Secured Party and Debtor copies and send other 3 copies with interleaved carbon paper to the filing officer. Enclose filing fee of $5.00
3. If the space provided for any item(s) on the form is inadequate the item(s) should be continued on additional sheets, preferably 5"x 8" or 8"x 10". Only one copy of such additional sheets need be presented to the filing officer with the first three copies of the financing statement. Long schedules of collateral, indentures, etc., may be on any size paper that is convenient for the secured party. Indicate the number of additional sheets attached. Enclose filing fee of $2.00 for each additional sheet.
4. If collateral is crops or goods which are or are to become fixtures, give the legal description of the real estate and name of record owner or record lessee.
5. When a copy of the security agreement is used as a financing statement, it is requested that it be accompanied by a completed but unsigned set of these forms. An additional fee of $3.00 is required.
6. Please sign this form with a ball point pen. Signatures must be legible on alphabetical and numerical copies.
7. If filing with Clerk of Circuit Court consult Chapter 28, F. S., or local clerk for proper fees.

THIS FINANCING STATEMENT is presented to a filing officer for filing pursuant to the Uniform Commercial Code:

3. Maturity date (if any):

1. Debtor(s) (Last Name First) and address(es)

2. Secured Party(ies) and address(es)

For Filing Officer (Date, Time, Number, and Filing Office)

4. This financing statement covers the following types (or items) of property:

All inventory now owned or hereafter acquired, wherever located, including but not limited to ____________________

5. Assignee(s) of Secured Party and Address(es)

6. The secured party(s), whose signature(s) appears below, states that the stamps required by Chapter 201, Florida Statutes, if any, have been placed on the promissory instruments secured hereby, and will be placed on any additional and similar instrument that may be so secured.

This statement is filed without the debtor's signature to perfect a security interest in collateral. (Check ☒ if so)
☐ Already subject to a security interest in another jurisdiction when it was brought into this state.
☐ which is proceeds of the original collateral described above in which a security interest was perfected:

Check ☒ if covered: ☒ Proceeds of Collateral are also covered. ☒ Products of Collateral are also covered. No. of additional Sheets presented:

Filed with:

By: ____________________ Signature(s) of Debtor(s)

By: ____________________ Signature(s) of Secured Party(ies)

STANDARD FORM — FORM UCC–1

Approved by Richard (Dick) Stone, Secretary of State, State of Florida

(1) Filing Officer Copy - Alphabetical

to assure that the pledged collateral is always available in sufficient quantity and quality to satisfy the obligation. In the case of receivables, such assurances would also include the validity of receivables and the handling of collection proceeds.

Techniques of Inventory Financing

By "techniques," we mean the various devices used by lenders to secure and administer their inventory loans. The techniques of inventory finance have undergone major change in the past decade, but surprisingly few bankers have kept pace. As a result, it has become increasingly important for the borrower to understand the credit tools at his disposal and take a more active role in structuring his own inventory loan. New data processing services, new laws established by the Uniform Commercial Code, and the growing use of collateral guarantees have greatly facilitated the development of flexible secured lending practices that are tailored to the modern manufacturing, distribution, and sales patterns of today's companies.

Collateral Certificates. Bank financing on the basis of collateral certificates is the newest and most popular inventory financing technique. A collateral certificate is a periodically prepared statement issued by a third party certifying to the existence of inventory quantities pledged as loan collateral. These certificates are issued to the bank weekly or with whatever frequency the borrower or lender requires. They provide the lender with guarantees that inventories represented on the collateral certificate do, in fact, exist and will be available to the lender if required. An example of such a certificate used for a combination inventory and receivables loan is shown in Figure 2.

The popularity of bank financing on the basis of collateral certificates is ascribed to its flexibility and simplicity of application. The flexibility of the certificate approach to inventory financing lies in several areas. First, the certificate can be used to cover all forms of inventory in various stages of processing. Unlike warehouse receipts that require physical segregation and possession, collateral certificates can be used to cover work-in-process, inventories of large numbers of diverse items, and goods stored in open areas. Second, because the principal control feature of this technique is the maintenance by the certificate issuer of a *minimum amount* of inventory that is to be on hand at all times, a great deal of freedom in the movement of goods can be worked out with the borrower in advance. Third, as can be seen in Figure 2, the collateral certificate approach can tie the borrower's inventory financing directly into a receivables financing plan to provide for a smooth flow of financing as inventory

FIGURE 2
Inventory Certification

LAWRENCE SYSTEMS, INC.

[COLLATERAL CERTIFICATE]

ISSUED TO: (LENDER)   FIRST NATIONAL BANK OF ANY TOWN

40020

AT REQUEST OF: (BORROWER)   ABC COMPANY, INC.   DATE: 9/5/74

REP TYPE	REG CODE	REC. LOCATION NO.	INV. LOCATION NO.	HOLDER NO.	PERIOD	
R	23	7007A	7007B	H913	8/28/74	TO 9/4/74

LAWRENCE CERTIFICATION

1. CERTIFIED ACCOUNTS RECEIVABLE
   - A. BALANCE LAST REPORT (Line 1G) .... $ 190,000.00
   - B. PLUS NEW ACCOUNTS RECEIVABLE .... $ 40,000.00
   - C. LESS DEPOSITS .... $ 22,000.00
   - D. LESS NON-CASH CREDITS .... $ 1,600.00
   - E. PLUS DEPOSITS - NON-CERTIFIED .... $ 2,100.00
   - F. ADJUSTMENTS - PLUS (MINUS) .... $ 3,400.00
   - G. TOTAL VALUE OF OUTSTANDING ACCOUNTS RECEIVABLE .... $ 211,900.00
   - H.   LESS ACCOUNTS RECEIVABLE OVER   60   DAYS. .... $ 32,931.00
   - I.   LESS CONTRAS REPORTED BY BORROWER .... $ 1,345.00
   - J. NET ELIGIBLE ACCOUNTS RECEIVABLE FOR THIS PERIOD .... $ 177,624.00

2. CERTIFIED INVENTORY
   - A. INVENTORY LAST REPORT (Line 2E) .... $ 278,000.00
   - B. PLUS INCOMING INVENTORY .... $ 92,000.00
   - C. LESS OUTGOING INVENTORY .... $ 30,000.00
   - D. ADJUSTMENTS - PLUS (MINUS) .... $ (1,500.00)
   - E. TOTAL CERTIFIED INVENTORY FOR THIS PERIOD .... $ 338,500.00

NOTE: LAWRENCE SYSTEMS, INC. certifies to the validity of the Accounts Receivable shown on Line 1G and to the inventory as shown on Line 2E. This certificate is not assignable and is issued in accordance with the terms of a Certified Accounts Receivable Agreement three party and/or Certified Inventory Control Agreement three party among Lawrence Systems, Inc. lender and borrower. Lawrence assumes no responsibility for any representation contained hereon to anyone other than the lender above.

LAWRENCE SYSTEMS, INC. Manager(s):

LOAN REQUEST

3. LOAN VALUE OF ABOVE COLLATERAL
   - A. RECEIVABLES   90   % OF LINE IJ ABOVE .... $ 159,861.60
   - B. INVENTORY   80   % OF LINE 2E ABOVE .... $ 270,800.00
   - C. F/W & CIC-S.I. INVENTORY $
         % OF ABOVE AMOUNT .... $ N/A
   - D. TOTAL COLLATERAL LOAN VALUE THIS PERIOD .... $ 430,661.60

4. LOAN BALANCE LAST REPORT (LINE 7)
   - A. LESS DEPOSITS, LINE 1C ABOVE APPLIED TO LOAN
   - B. PRESENT LOAN BALANCE .... $ 307,000.00

SAMPLE

5. EXCESS (*DEFICIT*) - SUBTRACT 4B FROM 3D .... $ 123,661.60

6. PLEASE INCREASE (*DECREASE*) OUR LOAN BY THIS AMOUNT .... $ 103,000.00

7. NEW LOAN BALANCE THIS PERIOD (LENDER AGREES TO NOTIFY LAWRENCE SYSTEMS, INC. IF THIS AMOUNT IS INCORRECT) .... $ 410,000.00

Borrower hereby authorizes lender to apply any balance in the cash collateral account necessary to decrease the loan as required on Line 4A or 6; remaining balance of $ -0-   to be transferred to borrower's regular checking account. If request for loan decrease exceeds cash collateral account balance please charge our regular checking account $ -0-

BORROWER'S AUTHORIZED SIGNATURE: Title

LENDER ACKNOWLEDGEMENT

8. LENDER AGREES that all previously issued collateral certificates are hereby cancelled and superseded and that Lawrence's liability shall be limited to collateral certified as set forth in 1J and 2E above.

LENDER: FIRST NATIONAL BANK OF ANY TOWN   AUTHORIZED SIGNATURE:

DO NOT ACCEPT IF ANY ERASURES APPEAR HEREON

assets are converted to receivable assets in the normal course of business.

In addition to covering a wide range of goods with flexible controls, the lender and borrower can greatly simplify their loan administration and compliance procedures by relying on the certificate issuer to perform many of the control and administrative functions. Typically, the certificate issuer will:

1. Do price extensions using inventory prices which have been agreed to by the borrower and lender.
2. Maintain on hand at all times a minimum inventory figure to secure the loan (the "Minimum Hold Figure") and/or limit the value of inventory released within a given period of time ("Delivery Authority").
3. Limit the type of inventory to be reported to specified classes of inventory and provide separate reporting on the movement of special items.
4. Calculate the borrower's unused credit capacity and loan position under the terms of the loan agreement on a weekly basis.

Some specific examples of inventory credits that have made successful use of collateral certificate financing include the following:

Business	*Assets Financed*	*Approximate Credit Line*
Fruit packing	Receivables, fresh fruit, cans, work-in-process, finished goods	$10,000,000
Beer distribution	Beer in case lots	$ 100,000
Wine making	Fruit, bulk wine, bottled wine	$ 750,000
Petroleum refining	Accounts receivable, raw materials, and finished petroleum products	$ 2,000,000
Lumber mill	Cut logs, lumber	$ 1,200,000
Steel wholesaling	Structural steel, accounts receivable	$ 750,000
Garment importing	Sport-type clothing	$ 5,000,000
Appliance dealer	Washers, dryers, refrigerators, TVs	$ 200,000
Wholesaling	Motorcycle parts and accessories	$ 500,000
Importing	Sporting goods	$ 80,000

Field Warehousing. The oldest technique of inventory financing still in use is bank advances against field warehouse receipts. The field warehousing approach to inventory lending can be historically traced to the financing needs of seasonal industries. Some 60 years ago field warehousing was a financing innovation that provided lenders with the possessory security of a warehouse receipt and provided the borrower with the convenience of storing his inventory on his own premises.

A field warehouse is a segregated area of the borrower's facility that houses the pledged inventory. A third-party field warehousing firm controls these segregated areas and issues its warehouse receipts for the warehoused goods. The warehouse receipts issued in connection with this type of storage are accepted as valid loan collateral by lenders (see Figure 3).

FIGURE 3
Sample Field Warehouse Receipt

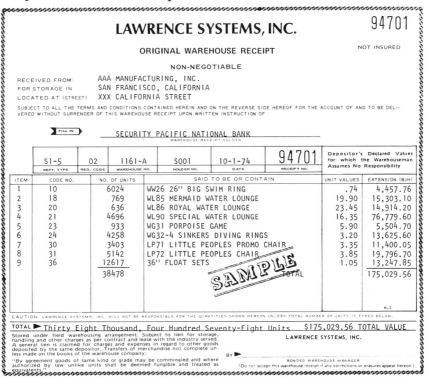

The elements of field warehousing that still make it an important inventory financing technique are: (1) the increased security it affords through third-party possession (the field warehouseman) of the goods being financed, and (2) its ability to qualify inventory loans for eligible bankers' acceptance financing (discussion follows). The disadvantages are that only goods that can be segregated and stored in a limited number of locations can qualify, and the control requirements at the borrower's location are rather stringent.

Today, field warehousing is limited in its use to specialized, large transactions such as commodities loans, cattle financing, and bankers' acceptance loans, and where banks simply are unaware of alternative techniques.

The operation of a field warehouse is simple and straightforward. The borrower engages the services of a field warehousing company to take custody, on the borrower's own premises, of the goods that are to be pledged as collateral and to issue, usually to a specified lender, warehouse receipts evidencing goods held by the servicing firm. Field warehouse receipts naming a specific lender are non-negotiable receipts while those with no specified lender are negotiable, meaning that they can be freely bought and sold. Because the risks of fraud on negotiable warehouse receipts are greater for both lenders and warehousing firms, the nonnegotiable receipt has become the more popular form.

In theory, the warehouseman releases goods from his field warehouse only when he receives specific instructions to do so by the receipt holder (the lender). However, it is impractical in most businesses for borrowers to obtain written releases for each and every delivery out of the field warehouse. Therefore, it is customary for the warehouse receipt holder (usually a bank) to give the field warehouse company written authority specifying a certain maximum dollar amount that can be delivered (or released) within a given period of time.

When releases are made from the field warehouse, a "Confirmation of Delivery" is submitted to the receipt holder accompanied by the borrower's check in the amount equal to the amount of the loan made on the goods delivered. In place of such a check to cover an appropriate loan reduction, accounts receivable generated from the sale of inventory are very often substituted as collateral for the inventory loan. In some instances a collateral certificate summarizing both receivables and warehoused inventories is used when the loan is on inventory and receivables.

In addition to these individual transaction documents, the lender receives periodic summary reports such as those shown in Figure 4. These reports show all movements of goods into and out of the field warehouse during the period, and summarize the values so that the current inventory figures are readily available.

FIGURE 4

Samples of Field Warehousing Data Processing Report Forms: Recap—Detail
—Summary

PAGE 1

AUGUST 31, 197–

LAWRENCE SYSTEMS FIELD WAREHOUSING
CODE SUMMARY REPORT

0504

ACCOUNT – A B C APPLIANCE CO INC
ANY TOWN STATE

HOLDER – 1ST NATL BANK OF ANY TOWN

REGION – MAJOR CITY

7007

CODE U/M	DESCRIPTION	BAL. FWD.	RECEIVED	RELEASED	BALANCE	UNIT PRICE	BALANCE VALUE
				95	85	40.00	3,400.00
				10	20	90.00	1,800.00
AX-49 EA	GARBAGE DISPOSAL	180	0	50	50	60.00	4,000.00
AXR02 EA	HOTSTOVE ELECTRIC RANGE	30	0	0	100	600.00	60,000.00
AY-49 EA	GARBAGE DISPOSAL	100	0	0	50	30.00	1,700.00
A2950 EA	29 CUFT COML REEFER W/AUX PUMP	100	50	250	60	50.00	3,500.00
BA-63 EA	PORTABLE BLENDER	50	50	30	70	200.00	12,000.00
BC-52 EA	BUILT-IN BLENDER	260	0	80	60	200.00	14,000.00
B57L EA	BRONZE MOD 57 REEFER LEFT HAND	100	50	100	70	200.00	16,000.00
B5TL EA	BRONZE MOD 57 REEFER LEFT HAND	90	110	100	80	200.00	18,000.00
B5TR EA	BRONZE MOD 57 REEFER RIGHT HAND	60	110	90	90	600.00	60,000.00
B5TR EA	YELLOW MOD 57 REEFER RIGHT HAND	70	180	290	100	600.00	18,000.00
	COLDCO ...ICE MAKER	200	120	90	30	600.00	54,000.00
		70	25	15	90	600.00	32,000.00
		20	80	10	40	800.00	8,000.00
		25	0	40	10	800.00	
		50	0		955 ***		306,400.00 ***

TOTALS

LAWRENCE SYSTEMS FIELD WAREHOUSING
WAREHOUSE RECEIPT DETAIL REPORT

0504

ACCOUNT – A B C APPLIANCE CO INC
ANY TOWN STATE

HOLDER – 1ST NATL BANK OF ANY TOWN

REGION – MAJOR CITY

7007

PAGE 1

AUGUST 31, 197–

CODE U/M	DESCRIPTION	RECEIPT #	ITEM	DATE	REL. #	RECEIVED	RELEASED	BALANCE	UNIT PRICE	VALUE
BA-63 EA	PORTABLE BLENDER	34011	1	4/15/7–						200.00
				8/10/7–	7	10			30.00	300.00–
							10			100.00– •
BC-52 EA	BUILT-IN BLENDER	34011	2,	4/15/7–				0 •		2,500.00 •
AXR62 EA	HOTSTOVE ELECTRIC RANGE	34011	3	4/15/7–		50			50.00	2,700.00
				8/10/7–	7	30		50 •	90.00	900.00–
							10			1,800.00 •
2950X EA	29 CUFT COML REEFER W/ICE MAKER	34011	4	4/15/7–		20		20 •		
370R5 EA	37 CUFT COLDCO REEFER 5 HP RT HAND	34011	5	4/15/7–		20		20 •	400.–	
				8/ 3/7–	6					
				8/17/7–	8					

370L5 EA 37 FT COLDCO REEFER

PAGE 1

LAWRENCE SYSTEMS FIELD WAREHOUSING
RECAP REPORT

0504

ACCOUNT – A B C APPLIANCE CO INC
ANY TOWN STATE

HOLDER – 1ST NATL BANK OF ANY TOWN

REGION – MAJOR CITY

7007

913

02

AUGUST 31, 197–

DATE	RECEIPT #	REL. #	RECEIVED QUANTITY	VALUE	RELEASED QUANTITY	VALUE	BALANCE QUANTITY	VALUE
7/31/7– BAL. FORWARD			1,355	291,600.00			1,355	291,600.00
8/ 3/7–		6			70	18,000.00	1,285	273,600.00
8/ 7/7–	34017		280	80,000.00			1,565	353,600.00
8/ 7/7–	34018		150	29,500.00			1,715	383,100.00
8/11/7–					325	11,300.00	1,390	371,800.00
8/11/7–		7			170	40,000.00	1,220	331,800.00
8/17/7–		8					1,420	391,800.00
8/18/7–	34020		200	60,000.00			1,420	391,800.00
8/20/7–	34019V				270	82,000.00	1,150	309,800.00
8/24/7–		9						
8/30/7–	34021	10	145	87,000.00	210	54,000.00	955	306,400.00
8/30/7–		11			130	36,400.00	955	306,400.00
8/30/7–					1,175	241,700.00		
TOTALS			2,130	548,100.00				

Order Bills of Lading. An order bill of lading is a negotiable
shipping document issued by a common carrier evidencing his
custody and delivery responsibility for goods-in-transit. Since the
order bill of lading provides that whoever presents the bill at the
point of destination can take possession of the transported goods, and

since it is freely assignable or salable, it is acceptable as collateral for loans on goods-in-transit. In cases where a large number of bills of lading are to be pledged on a revolving basis or when nonnegotiable bills are involved, the lender may require that the bills of lading themselves be placed in the custody of a field warehousing firm with instructions that receipts for the actual goods be issued to replace the bills of lading as shipments are received.

Trust Receipts. A trust receipt is a receipt given to the lender by the borrower himself that passes title of pledged goods to the lender and represents that the borrower will physically hold those goods as the lender's trustee. The legal and control pitfalls of this form of loan security are well recognized and thus this technique has become limited to use as a supplemental protection on loans to firms that would generally qualify for unsecured credit. Where it is used, it requires specific identification by serial numbers of receipted goods—a constraint that is infeasible in the majority of inventory financing situations.

Sources of Inventory Loans

Banks. The best source of credit to finance inventory is from your own bank—the one with which you presently do business. Bank interest rates are about the lowest you will find, and faced with the possibility of otherwise losing your account to another bank, your present banker most likely will try very hard to accommodate your credit request. If your own bank won't help, try another bank, but try to pick one that is comfortable with both the nature of your business and the size of your credit request.

Bankers' Acceptances. One form of inventory financing that is particularly popular with banks during tight-money periods is bankers' acceptances. A bankers' acceptance is a draft bill of exchange drawn on and accepted by a bank to finance the shipment and storage of goods. Eligible bankers' acceptances are bankers' acceptances which are eligible for rediscounting at the Federal Reserve. Eligible bankers' acceptances can be sold by the accepting bank in the open market as a general bank obligation to raise the needed funds for the transaction without affecting the bank's liquidity.

In acceptance financing, the bank is essentially using its own name and balance sheet to help create short-term commercial paper for a preferred customer who is unable to do so for himself. Because of the open-market nature of raising acceptance funds, these loans generally involve amounts of $1,000,000 or more.

Acceptance financing is an established finance tool which is regulated by Sections 13 and 14 of the Federal Reserve Act and by Regulation A of the Board of Governors of the Federal Reserve System. Section 13 of the act specifies that, when warehouse receipts are issued for the goods being financed, an acceptance can be created which is eligible for rediscount with the Federal Reserve. The transaction is thus exempt from the usual bank reserve requirements that normally restrict the total amount of loans a bank can make.

Eligible bankers' acceptances supported by warehouse receipts may have maturities up to six months and can be used to finance almost all types of raw materials and manufactured products in storage or in transit. Bankers' acceptances are also a popular method of financing imports, and field warehouse receipts have been successfully used to extend the period of eligible acceptance financing to cover that period of time for which the landed goods are held prior to ultimate sale.

An example of how this inventory finance technique can work is shown in the case of a West Coast tuna packer who sought to borrow $5 million against an inventory of canned goods. At the time this loan was sought, the lending bank was facing a shortage of lendable funds and decided to raise the capital through the bankers' acceptance market. Separate drafts were drawn up for each specific lot of canned goods, the bank co-endorsed these drafts, discounted them, and then sold them to third-party investors or brokers. The bank, in turn, took warehouse receipts for each specific lot, and through that receipt held possession of the lot until the corresponding draft was paid. In instances where lots were not sold within the maturity period of the bankers' acceptance, the bank simply made a conventional inventory loan on the goods, and applied the proceeds of that loan to repay the acceptance draft.

Supplier Credit. One of the most frequently overlooked sources of inventory financing is from the supplier of those very goods you wish to finance. Suppliers are excellent sources of working capital credit to support inventory for two very important reasons: (1) there is an extraordinarily large profit incentive for a supplier to help one of their dealers expand his business, and (2) in the event that he has to look to the inventory to satisfy the indebtedness, the supplier is perhaps best equipped of anyone to handle the resale of those goods at the going wholesale market price.

The fact that many major U.S. corporations offer extended payment terms, and in effect perform a banking function for inventories, is not widely recognized. Moreover, where this type of credit can be obtained, it usually results in 100 percent financing at very low financing cost. Financing costs, which often include only inventory certification charges paid to a field warehousing or collateral control company, and in some cases nominal servicing charges paid to the suppliers, seldom amount to much more than 3 to 4 percent per annum on the amount of credit extended. Examples of industries where this form of financing has been used successfully include: appliances, industrial air conditioning, tires, carpeting, marine engines, recreational vehicles, auto parts and accessories, and construction materials. A list of major U.S. companies that have made secured credit of this type available is shown below in Figure 5.

FIGURE 5
Examples of Major Firms Providing Secured Credit to Dealers and Distributors

Admiral Corporation	Armstrong Furnace	Continental Can
Allis-Chalmers Mfg.	Company	Company
Co.	Bethlehem Steel	Adolph Coors
Aluminum Co. of	Corporation	Company
America	Blatz Brewing	Copeland
Amana Refrigeration,	Company	Refrigeration Co.
Inc.	Borg Warner	Crown Zellerbach
American Brass	Corporation	Corp.
Company	Boise Cascade	Dow Chemical
American Can	Brunswick	Company
Company	Corporation	Dura Corporation
American Cyanamid	Bryant Manufactur-	Dunlop Tire &
Company	ing Co.	Rubber Co.
American Distilling	Chrysler Corporation	Durkee Famous
Company	Colorado Fuel &	Foods
American Machine &	Iron Corp.	East Asiatic Co., Inc.
Tool Co., Inc.	Columbia Records	Fairchild
Ampex Corporation	Company	Semiconductor
Anheuser-Busch, Inc.	Container Corp. of	Fedders Corporation
Armco Steel	America	Fibreboard Products,
Corporation		Inc.

FIGURE 5 (*continued*)

Firestone Tire & Rubber Co.	National Union Electric Corp.	Sears Roebuck & Co.
W. P. Fuller Paint Co.	Norge Sales Corporation	Seiberling Tire & Rubber Co.
General Electric Co.	Owen-Corning Fiberglass Corp.	Shell Chemical Corporation
General Motors Corp.	Peterbilt Motors Company	Sony Corporation
General Tire & Rubber Co.	Philco Corporation	Stanley Building Products Co.
Gibson Refrigerator Co., Inc.	Phillips Petroleum Company	Stewart-Warner Corporation
Glidden Company	Pittsburgh Plate Glass Co.	Stromberg-Carlson
Goodyear Tire & Rubber Co.	Purex Corporation	Sylvania Electric Products, Inc.
Holly Sugar Corporation	Raybestos Manhattan, Inc.	Tappan Stove Company
Hupp Corporation	Reichhold Chemicals, Inc.	Trane Company
International Harvester Co.	Revco, Inc.	United States Plywood Corp.
Kaiser Aluminum & Chemical	Revere Copper & Brass, Inc.	United States Rubber Co.
Lennox Industries, Inc.	Reynolds Metals Company	Westinghouse Electric Corp.
Mercury Record Corp.	Rheem Manufacturing Co.	Weyerhaeuser Company
Monsanto Chemical Co.	Schenley Industries, Inc.	Whirlpool Corporation
Motorola Corporation	Seagrams Distillers Co.	York Division Borg-Warner
National Lead Company		

The procedures in establishing a line of secured credit from a supplier are virtually the same as in the case of a bank. Field warehousing, collateral certification and trust receipts are control and security devices that suppliers use as well.

There are two basic forms in which supplier credit is found. The first is a consignment sale in which title to the goods remains with the supplier until the final sale is made. The second is a secured sale in which title passes to the wholesaler or dealer and the supplier takes a security interest in the goods as his protection on the receivable due him.

Finance Companies.   If bankers and suppliers fail to meet your credit needs, try a commercial finance company. The larger ones are highly reputable; they know a lot about inventory financing, and they are accustomed to lending large amounts of money against modest equities when assets are available as security. Financing charges of commercial finance companies generally run from 4 to 8 percent per year above the prevailing prime lending rate.

Obtaining an Inventory Loan

Application for inventory financing is not unlike application for other types of loans, except that additional, specialized information will be required by the lender. Before a lender will grant an inventory loan, he will have to ascertain four basic facts:

1. That the borrower's financial condition is such that he is likely to repay without the necessity of liquidation.
2. That the lender can perfect his security in the inventory and thereby withstand the challenge of any other creditors in the event of bankruptcy.
3. That the liquidating values of the goods pledged are sufficient to meet the lender's inventory value-to-loan ratio.
4. That an adequate system exists to assure the lender that the inventory is properly controlled.

The Required Data.   The borrower should be prepared to present data corroborating these facts when he makes an inventory loan application. Some preparation may be needed to assure the lender as to the borrower's strength and the viability of his operations. The borrower will be asked to demonstrate, in addition to the normal balance sheet data, the adequacy of his systems (inventory handling, record keeping, and so on), his storage facilities and his pricing structure. In addition, of course, full details on present inventory and purchase commitments should be available in an organized form.

Most borrowers will want to extend their credit capacity by negotiating an additional line of credit secured by the receivables generated from the sale of inventory. For this reason, historical data concerning customers, payment experience, bad debt percentages, discounting policies, and the like should be prepared for submittal. The lender will also want to review the borrower's shipping, invoicing, and collection procedures.

If there are prior filings against any of his inventory, the borrower should present details of these obligations to the lender, along with his plan for either paying off these obligations or limiting his loan request to specific inventory and receivables which are free and clear. In the latter event, a separate bookkeeping and control system will be required to ensure that the assets securing the various loans do not become commingled.

Proof of Value. The onus of "proving" the liquidating value of the pledged inventory is normally on the borrower. Of course, where the inventory credit is from a supplier, this is usually not an issue. Although inventory loans are being granted on an ever-widening class of goods, they are not being granted (and probably never will be) on highly styled inventory such as fashion goods, perishable foods stuffs that are end products useless in any other form, or any inventory of a similarly specialized nature that would limit its ready marketability. In evaluating and itemizing his inventory to be pledged, the borrower should eliminate all goods of inadequate marketability and prepare pricing and market data which clearly demonstrate the value of goods of doubtful marketability.

The treasurer should also be prepared to provide data demonstrating that none of the goods to be pledged would involve an inordinately high cost of sales in the event of forced liquidation. Some types of inventories, such as crushed stone for use in road construction, are prohibitively expensive to transport, and therefore they would only be available to local buyers, at whose mercy the lender would be in a forced sale situation. At the very least, the lender will assign a cost factor to conducting an auction *unless* the borrower can clearly demonstrate a ready market for the goods. A central commodity exchange would suffice, of course, but so might identification of several buyers each of whom would have need for all or a majority of the goods, thereby ensuring a competitive market and a quick, uncomplicated sale: The best situation would be a standby purchase or repurchase agreement from a financially sound customer or supplier.

Business Systems. Finally, the secured lender will demand a workable and verifiable inventory control system to protect himself from inventory shortages. Few lenders will trust this control and reporting function to the periodic checks of a CPA firm. Even though the lender can perfect his lien by filing, banks are painfully aware of the inadequacy of such protection if shortages occur, whatever their cause. Hence, most lenders insist on adequate inventory control and reporting systems.

If the borrower determines that a third-party inventory certification service will be needed, he can usually expedite the loan transaction by working out the certification arrangement *before* he makes his initial loan application. A certification firm will survey the borrower's inventory, inventory handling systems, business systems, pricing, and so on, and make appropriate recommendations for any modifications needed to satisfy potential lenders. These are all functions that the lender will need to understand in any event, so the borrower can take advantage of these free advisory services to properly prepare his loan proposal. In many cases the collateral certification firm can benefit the borrower at the outset by recommending alternative sources of inventory financing.

Conditions and Costs

In assessing the potential of inventory financing, the treasurer should remember that he will not be able to borrow funds from a bank or finance company equal to the full value of his inventory. The lender will evaluate such factors as the borrower's financial conditions, product marketability, and cost of sales to determine the "true" value of the inventory. After applying his own loan formula to this reduced value, a lender will agree to a percentage advance that can vary anywhere from 30 percent to 90 percent of the book value of the inventory. The variance in this advance ratio has as much to do with differences between lenders as it does to different types of inventories. Generally, however, the higher the percentage accepted as collateral, the higher will be the interest charge.

FIGURE 6
Representative Interest Rates on Inventory Loans (interest plus certification charges)

Product	Percent of Advance 30–50% of Inventory	Percent of Advance 50–85% of Inventory
Large Companies, Large Bank Loans		
Readily marketable, stable prices	Prime plus 1%	Prime plus 3%
Propriety products, no established market	Prime plus 3%	Prime plus 6%
Small Companies, Small Bank Loans		
Readily marketable, stable prices	Prime plus 4%	Prime plus 6%
Propriety products, no established market	Prime plus 6%	Prime plus 8%

As shown in Figure 6, the total financing charges (interest plus certification and security charges) vary not only with the prime lending rate but also with a number of other factors. Large firms borrowing small amounts on readily marketable commodities pay relatively low-interest charges. Small firms borrowing large amounts on specialized inventories pay relatively high rates of interest. The financing costs shown which vary from 1 percent to 8 percent over prime are representative of national averages, and some variation can be expected among different geographic regions and types of industry.

Cautions and Opportunities

For some companies, such as those with few fixed assets, those experiencing rapid growth, or those in highly seasonal businesses, inventory financing is often the only practical financing method. Under certain conditions, however, inventory financing can be the poorest source of working capital. Classically, these conditions exist when a company's inventory has widely fluctuating values, when a company cannot control its own inventory, or when there is a high risk of obsolescence as in stylized goods or perishables.

The problem with inventory financing is that it results in firm liabilities of magnitudes normally much greater than the borrower's net worth. If inventory values drop dramatically, or if through lack of control substantial amounts of inventory turn up missing, or if the quality of inventory assets being financed otherwise is seriously diminished, the actions on the part of the lender are usually precipitous in putting the borrower out of business. In this regard, it should be remembered that inventory financing usually results in substantial debt leverage which can work to the borrower's disadvantage if there is a significant downward change in the quality of assets being financed.

In a great number of applications, however, inventory loans can be creatively used with little risk. One good example is the case of an importer of Japanese autos who worked out a method of financing his purchased goods from the time they were loaded on ship at the port of origin until they finally arrived at dealer showrooms across the United States. To accomplish this, the auto importer negotiated a loan with the financing bank, initially pledging his shipping documents as collateral. The bank avoided the necessity of handling the shipping documents by having them sent from Japan directly to a third-party collateral certification firm at the port of entry. The certifier issued a warehouse receipt for the documents and the bank then advanced funds for payment to the Japanese manufacturer soon after the shipment left the originating port. The importer's advantage in arranging early cash payment was the realization of substantial cash discounts from the manufacturer.

When the shipment arrived, the autos were placed in a yard under the certifier's control. The bank released the warehouse receipt on the documents and accepted inventory certificates covering the actual automobiles. From the bank's approved list of dealers, autos were released to public carriers for overland transport and the bank received an inventory withdrawal report and a copy of a draft drawn on the dealer's bank, payable to the bank financing the importer's inventory when the autos arrived at the dealer locations. The entire transaction secured the bank's interest in the inventory during all phases of shipment, even though the inventory was physically out of the possession of both the importer and his dealers.

Inventory financing is very different today than it was just ten years ago, because it has adapted to new business methods and needs. The simplification of secured lending procedures and the liberalization of thought in the banking community on what constitutes appropriate inventory for financing have made the inventory loan an attractive source of business credit. Properly used, it can be an important and continuing part of any treasurer's financing program, and in some cases, an avenue to substantially increased credit capacity.

ADDITIONAL SOURCES

Adler, M. "Administration of Inventory Loans under the Uniform Commercial Code." *Journal of Commercial Bank Lending*, 52 (April 1970), 55–60.

Clines, T. "There's a Way to Finance That Inventory (Field Warehouse Receipts)." *Bankers Monthly*, 77 (March 1960), 42–44.

Daniels, F. L., Legg, Sidney C., and Yuille, E. C. "Accounts Receivable and Related Inventory Financing." *Journal of Commercial Bank Lending*, 52 (July 1970), 38–53.

Eisenstadt, M. "Finance Company's Approach to Warehouse Receipts." *Robert Morris Associates Bulletin*, 49 (December 1966), 35–47.

Haley, C. W., and Higgins, R. C. "Inventory Policy and Trade Credit Financing." *Management Science,* 20 (December 1973), 464–71.

Jacoby, Neil H., and Saulnier, Raymond J. *Financing Inventory on Field Warehouse Receipts.* New York: National Bureau of Economic Research, 1944.

Rogers, R. W. "Warehouse Receipts and Their Use in Financing." *Robert Morris Associates Bulletin,* 40 (January 1958), 105–13.

Silberfield, E. S. "Financing Purchase Money Paper." *Journal of Commercial Bank Lending,* 55 (May 1973), 25–30.

Versagi, F. J. "How Money Gets to Market: Explanation of Inventory Financing." *Air Conditioning, Heating and Refrigeration News,* 96 (June 4, 1962), 34–35.

PART VIII

Designing a Capital Structure

IN PART V principles of longer term investment decisions were described. In Part VI investment in various types of current assets were described, and in Part VII some major sources of short-term financing were detailed. We now turn to sources and forms of longer term financing in their overall aspects. In Part VIII fundamental issues of designing the capital structure for the firm are discussed. In Chapter 29, Maynard Wishner provides a useful transition from short-term financing to long-term financing. He summarizes alternative sources of short-term financing including topics that were not covered in the previous chapters. He then provides an overview of long-term financing sources which provides a framework for the capital structure discussion in the following two chapters and for the chapters on individual forms of long-term financing presented in Part IX. Mr. Wishner concludes his chapter by using a quantitative analysis to compare the costs of short-term versus long-term financing.

In Chapter 30, Dr. Alan Zakon presents a stimulating discussion of how finance can interact with the planning and operating strategies of the firm to enhance its growth, profitability, and competitive strength. He begins with a discussion of the nature of leverage extending the concept to include dividend coverage and debt repayment coverage as well as interest coverage. He demonstrates both theoretically and empirically how specific companies have improved their profits and growth by the creative use of debt. He demonstrates the relationships between the sustainable growth and the profitability rate of the firm.

Mr. Zakon considers constraints on the use of leverage, classifying them into the categories of liquidity, pragmatic and conceptual constraints. He points out that the literature of finance theory which argues that the use of leverage does not affect the cost of capital of the firm fails to take into account the interaction between the influence of financing decisions on the decision to invest. The central theme of the chapter is the responsibility of the financial executive to take an active role in using financial strategy to mesh with, and indeed stimulate, improvements in the operating performance of the business.

In Chapter 31, George Williams develops some additional aspects of the effective use of financial leverage. He presents materials to show how leverage can increase the return on equity. He demonstrates how under different circumstances buying shares and selling debt will increase earnings per share while under other circumstances the reverse strategy will also increase earnings per share.

Utilizing data based on an analysis of the *Fortune* "500" list of industrial firms, Mr. Williams finds that the companies with the highest achieved return on equity had the lowest leverage. These facts plus the risks of excessive debt leads Mr. Williams to conclude that prudence suggests a degree of leverage in the direction of "better too little than too much." The emphasis of this chapter diverges from that of the previous one. Since neither the theoretical nor practical literature has established a basis for a general unanimity on the issues involved, it is useful to consider both points of view.

The materials in Chapter 32 are included in the *Handbook* to discuss how the use of leverage or the choice of capital structure may affect the cost of capital of the firm. Procedures for measuring risk are also set forth, utilizing the capital asset pricing model discussed in Chapter 11.

Chapter 29

Analysis of Alternative Types of Financing

Maynard I. Wishner[*]

THE TREASURER AND THE CREDIT FUNCTION

JUST AS QUALITY and production control can make the crucial difference between an efficient and marginal operation, similar consequences of success or mediocrity can result from the competence or the lack of skill with which money is attracted, managed, and used. All businesses, no matter what the nature of their products or services may be, have in common the use of one basic raw material: money. The opening entry on a balance sheet, the one that reflects the very first act of the incorporators, generally involves the investment of some amount of cash. Even when the initial investment is in property of varying kinds, its appearance on the balance sheet is always measured in terms of money. At the same time each company has its own dynamics in the process of manufacturing and distributing. Its founders typically bring to the effort such particular talents as design or production know-how, or a flair for selling. But it is a rare entrepreneur who also brings to the business a similar flair for dealing with money—money which is not only the basic resource, but also the reason for the entire game: a bottom line result in profitability which in turn bears some relation-

* Maynard I. Wishner is president, Walter E. Heller & Company, Chicago, Illinois.

ship to the investments made and the risks taken to get the enterprise started. Not ordinarily being financiers, these entrepreneurs frequently lose sight of the operational essence of money.

The company "treasurer," whether he bears that title or not, plays an indispensable role. His fine hand in understanding and using the most efficient, flexible, and reliable sources of this raw material is a modern-day necessity for corporate success. A treasurer is no longer a mere custodian of funds; he is more than a mechanic of record keeping and preparer of routine reports. He has, in practice, become a manager: a decision maker of considerable talent. Indeed, he may exhibit all the artistry of a virtuoso, playing the financial keyboard like a concert pianist.

The tests which the treasurer applies in the administration of money are essentially the same as those applied elsewhere in the company. Efficiency in the use of money pays the same rewards as minimizing waste in the usage of raw materials and efficiency on the assembly line. A treasurer seeks to have on hand just about as much "material" as will be needed; he knows what his sources of supply will be in the event of an unexpected surge in cash requirements; he endeavors to buy it at the least possible cost. As with other corporate purchasing, this financial "buyer" looks not merely for price, but for real cost; not simply for availability of sources and methods, but for their suitability.

This chapter concerns the various options available to the financial manager in acquiring credit. An attempt will be made to analyze the cost factors involved in utilizing these various sources of funds.

SHORT-TERM FINANCING

Trade Credit

If cost were to be the primary ingredient, certainly the use of trade credit would appear on its face to represent the most advantageous source of "outside" money, for it is the use of other people's assets in a business. Goods are delivered and the time for payment is postponed. Interest as such is not generally charged by the seller, at least not at this time. However, there are certain cautions to be observed. Most obviously, the use of trade credit beyond the date of cash discount has a clear and measurable cost. For example, consider the selling terms of 2/10 net 30. In effect, the supplier is telling the buyer that if he pays in 10 days, the buyer will receive a 2 percent discount for sacrificing the use of his money for the 20-day period between the discount date and the date the full amount of the invoice is due. That rate of discount is the equivalent of earning approximately 36 percent on a per annum basis if he simply lends out his money for the 20-day period. The effect of a 36 percent return on a loan which has no risk since it is made on the buyer's own credit represents a tempting corporate opportunity. Thus, if it should be necessary to borrow in order to take advantage of cash discounts, the cost of borrowing, even at interest rates significantly above the record high prime rates in effect in 1975, should be measured on a net cost basis against the possibility of earning at the 36 percent rate.

The other alternative for the buyer is to forego the discount and also to ignore the due date. The "stretching" of trade payables would appear to be cost free for as long as the supplier's tolerance holds out. This is a dangerous assumption. The generous supplier who traditionally lets his receivables run beyond due dates without pressing for payment is doing so at a considerable cost which has to be passed on in some way. Heavy reliance on such suppliers by company purchasing agents deprives the firm of the advantages of shopping for sources of supply. Furthermore, the company may not get the favorable treatment and service provided those who are paying in accordance with the required terms. The consequences of limited purchasing opportunities may be higher purchasing costs and an inability to compete effectively in the market. The cost of being saddled with such price differentials can be translated by the treasurer into an "interest cost" equivalent and should be measured accordingly. More difficult, of course, is the determination of the implicit cost resulting from the lower credit rating of the slow-paying company. Most threatening of all, however, is the plight of the company that traditionally leans heavily on trade payables hit by a period of material shortages. It should come as no surprise that suppliers will choose to sell to customers who pay most rapidly.

In summarizing, there is no questioning that trade credit is the largest source of "nonbank" credit, both in availability and actual use. Like any other form of credit, it has cost ingredients to which the treasurer should be alert. He should quantify these cost factors so that the "excessive" use of trade credit can be measured against other forms of financing where costs are expressed in more direct terms.

Unsecured Bank Credit

Unsecured bank credit is the most conventional source of short-term accommodations. This form of financing has become crucial to American business and plays a basic role in our system of commerce. The company which can obtain its cash requirements through properly priced unsecured bank borrowing obviously will use the bank. The benefits are generally those of cost and convenience, but these advantages do not obviate a cost analysis by the treasurer.

Two ingredients beyond the expressed interest charge for the accommodation must enter a cost analysis here, and both relate to the maintenance of compensating balances. The first factor is that funds which remain on deposit, whether just lying idly or covering a compensating balance requirement, represent a cost in terms of lost earning opportunities. For example, some of the money might be used to purchase quality commercial paper of major U.S. corporations, which is available in 1- to 270-day maturities. The second factor in the analysis is the matter of borrowing in excess of actual need to support compensating balances. It is illusory to express the cost of borrowing in terms of the face amount of interest if the company is permitted to make use of only 80 percent to 85 percent of the amount of the loan. Interest is paid on the total amount of the loan. Therefore, under a 20 percent compensating balance requirement, the interest cost of the borrowed money which is actually put to use in the borrower's business is 125 percent of the expressed rate of interest. There is even another cost factor when the required balance must be maintained during times when the line is not being used. When balance requirements can be met from the normal minimum cash reserves which a well-run enterprise ought to have available for its daily needs, we are not dealing with the additional costs described above. However, the artificial maintenance of balances to meet borrowing requirements is, without question, a real cost ingredient.

Apart from the above cost considerations, there is the matter of timing involved in periodic "cleanups" (paying off the loan). The question is whether the bank accommodation fully serves the company when these requirements are imposed. They can create diffi-

cult "short-term" problems for the treasurer in terms of his requirements for cash. For example, if the cleanup is made at the expense
of leaning on trade credit for the period involved, the cost and
relationship factors referred to earlier in this chapter come back
into play and should be analyzed.

Another aspect to this concern is the time basis for charging
interest. This factor is frequently overlooked when a seemingly
favorable rate is proposed to the borrower. An analysis should determine the extent to which the company actually makes use of its
borrowed money.

In the typical company, the requirements for borrowed cash are
not at a constant level. There are periods of the month which are
characterized by heavy cash demands, such as the classic challenge
of meeting the payroll. There are other periods during which the
inflow of collections operates to relieve cash pressures. Similarly, in
many businesses there are seasonal characteristics which impose
requirements for borrowed funds at sharply differing levels during
the course of the year. If a chart is prepared to show the need for
borrowed cash on a daily basis it will appear as a series of peaks
and valleys, the slopes of which will vary greatly depending upon
the type of business. In contrast, a bank borrowing generally will
appear as a flat amount for a stated period. In analyzing this type
of straight bank loan, it should be recognized that the face amount
of interest will not be the sole determining factor in costing it out
against alternative forms of borrowing. One of these alternates is
secured borrowing where charges for the use of money are made
on a daily basis. These charges are at a higher *expressed* rate of
interest than is normally charged on unsecured bank loans. The
following process may be used to obtain a fair comparison of the
true costs of these two types of short-term borrowing.

To begin, note the amount of the bank loan. This is generally
arranged to cover both the company's peak requirements during a
60- or 90-day cycle and the required compensating balance. Using
the expressed per annum rate, compute the actual *dollar* cost of
interest for the full loan period. That amount may now be measured
against the cost of borrowing only the *actual daily funds required*
during the period, without having to maintain compensating balances. To compute that cost, determine the amount of actual funds
required for each day and total them. Divide the total by the
number of days in the cycle, and the resulting figure will represent

the average daily loan amount *required* by the company for the period. Apply the interest rate which would be charged on a secured loan for the period to the average loan amount and the result will be a dollar cost which can be compared to the dollar cost of the unsecured bank accommodation. The higher of these two figures obviously represents the more expensive borrowing. In many cases the program which expresses the highest annual rate will not be the most expensive in actual cost.

Secured Lending

There are times, however, when despite a favorable cost analysis, the company will not be able to obtain its working capital requirements through an unsecured bank loan. The bank may turn down the loan because it does not feel comfortable with a company's debt to net worth or working capital ratios, or its prospective ability to repay the loan within the short term. Much importance, of course, is attached to the company's record of earnings, so it is more difficult to arrange for bank credit coming off a loss period. Generally, all of the bank's considerations boil down to the requirement that it would not be making a "permanent" investment in the company; that it would be providing only an accommodation for periodic needs during the normal cycle of business activity. While generally familiar with the activities of his customer, the unsecured lender is not usually in touch with day-to-day developments. He needs to feel the assurance that upon the maturity date the company's position will be substantially as predicted, and that it will have generated sufficient funds out of operations to repay the loan.

The secured lender is in a much different position than the unsecured lender, as can be demonstrated with a familiar example. There are relatively few individuals who could walk into a lending institution and obtain a $30,000 loan for 25 years on their signature only. But these same potential borrowers might have relatively little trouble in obtaining a $30,000, 25-year loan secured by a mortgage on a new home. While the character and creditworthiness of the customer is the same in both cases, the ability of the mortgage lender to grant the accommodation lies in the fact that he is secured by a mortgage. Whatever vicissitudes may lie in wait for the borrower, there is the home, carefully appraised as to value, which should support the financing and assure the lender that he will be repaid. Thus, we see that the difference between being able or not being able to grant a loan may well be determined by the security which supports it. It should come as no surprise to the treasurer to find that lenders who specialize in providing secured business loans are comfortable in extending larger amounts of credit because they have adequate collateralization. They are not necessarily "high risk specialists." The typical business possesses different types of acceptable collateral it can offer to secured lenders. Generally, these consist of the accounts receivable and the inventory of the company. Secured term loan accommodations also are available, possibly as part of a "packaged" program, to include borrowings on machinery, equipment, and real estate owned by the company. With the protection of this viable collateral, the secured lender need not look primarily at net worth for his credit judgment, and he will not be unduly troubled by a situation which shows that the company has distended payables and has difficulty in meeting its obligations. Actually, the tools the secured lender brings to bear may help relieve these problems. Having the comfort of adequate collateral, he is prepared to work very closely with the borrower to achieve a program that will foster improvement or growth. Naturally, he will consider the prospects of the company since he does not want to become involved in a situation that will require liquidation. He must also have faith in the ability and dedication of the company's principals and a conviction that a secured financial program will have mutual economic feasibility.

Loans secured by business assets have characteristics that may make them attractive to the borrowing company. For one thing, funds are made available against assets of the company which are expected to increase in size as its business activities grow. Receivables, for example, frequently make up the largest portion of a company's current assets and they are also the primary collateral source for secured short-term borrowing. These receivables represent goods which have been shipped and to produce them the company had to invest in labor and materials. Since the company must grant competitive terms as a seller in the marketplace, it therefore needs the ability to carry its investments in these receivables to the point of collection. The secured lender is able to convert that investment into immediate cash, generally amounting to 80 percent of the acceptable receivables. The fact that the volume of the borrower's receivables may be growing does not present a problem to the lender. As a matter of fact, the secured lender generally seeks growth situations where his accommodations to a company may increase.

Similarly, the acquisition of additional inventory materials to produce increased amounts of goods provides an asset base for the secured lender. Usually he can lend funds to bridge the time between their purchase and conversion, first into receivables and then ultimately into cash. Most often, inventory loans are secured by raw materials or finished goods that are already in stock. These loans can also be arranged in advance to buy materials, which will then serve as collateral after their purchase and receipt.

Borrowings against accounts receivable, and perhaps supplemental inventory financing, normally provide a company with enough cash for current operations, but unusual financial needs are apt to arise in any business. To meet these needs, the secured lender can provide loans on machinery and equipment as adjuncts to the firm's basic financing. Actually, equipment loans are available to firms even when they are not financing their receivables, but inventory loans, alone, are seldom made by secured lenders. Equipment loans may be made on equipment already owned and in use or for the purchase of new equipment. In addition, the secured lenders offer a wide variety of leasing options as another means of acquiring new equipment.

The secured short-term loan is an accommodation which has certain of the characteristics of a long-term loan. When a straight bank note falls due, it must be repaid or rolled over, but in any event it must generally be "cleaned up" at year's end. However, a secured loan may constantly revolve and continue until the parties to it decide to conclude the arrangement. In effect, the secured lender has a new loan each day because his accommodations are being retired and re-extended on a daily basis as mature receivables are collected by the borrower and new ones are created. His inventory loans also revolve with ins and outs as inventory is consumed and supplies are replenished. Moreover, the term loans which the secured lender may provide against machinery or other chattels can frequently be serviced by retirement of debt in amounts equivalent to depreciation expense reflected on the profit and loss statement.

As previously noted, the secured lending device provides funds on a daily need basis in relation to the ebb and flow of business activity. The client uses funds only as he needs them and pays on the basis of a daily usage formula. This has provided many companies which have experienced sharp growth or contraction periods in their life cycles with funds that would not have been available from other sources of financing. Furthermore, the lender is content to stay with the arrangement for as long a time as the relationship is mutually satisfactory. If the secured loan is no longer needed, it can be replaced by other types of financing that seem to be more appropriate at the particular stage of the company's life cycle. While there is a minimum term stipulation, it is nominal under almost all circumstances.

Who are the secured lenders? Historically, they are represented by the commercial finance industry, which comprises a small group of major national companies and a somewhat larger number of smaller companies operating regionally throughout the country. In recent years some banks have begun to offer secured lending as a regular service.

SPECIAL-PURPOSE LOANS

There is a specialized "short-term" capability of commercial finance companies: the financing of acquisitions, buy-outs, and mergers. These situations often do not fall within the parameters of bank financing. The commercial finance companies, on the other hand, have developed unusual and very productive techniques in this area of financing. Briefly stated, they are generally able to use the assets of the company being acquired as collateral to provide a loan which covers a substantial portion of the purchase price. Moreover, the financing can be arranged to provide continuing operating funds for the new or merged concern. These deals are normally very complex in their structuring. Literally, they may be "one of a kind," so only general reference is appropriate here. It should be noted, however, that a substantial number of these transactions are a direct result of the growing trend toward reversing the conglomeration process started in the 60s and "going private."

FACTORING

There is another way of financing which should be mentioned with any listing of "short-term" methods: factoring. While it serves some of the purposes of short-term borrowing, factoring is primarily a specialized, professional *service*. It is not simply another way of lending money. Factoring can include an arrangement to accelerate cash flow, but this is only an optional service which a factoring client may elect to employ.

Factoring versus Pledging of Receivables

Because of the increasing use of factoring as a form of financing, a detailed discussion of this service is provided. Hopefully, this will serve to clarify a common misconception. Quite often, one hears people refer to commercial finance firms as "factoring houses." By this, they are implying that everything these firms do is factoring, and are incorrectly applying the term to both *lending* against receivables and the *purchase of receivables*. Only the latter relates to factoring. Lending against receivables is a fundamentally different service known as accounts receivable financing or *pledging of receivables* which has been extensively discussed earlier.

There are some general observations which should be made before beginning a detailed description of factoring. First, factoring is suitable and productive for manufacturers and wholesalers; its use is widespread in lines of business ranging from lumber mills to steel tube welders, toys to scientific instruments, and textiles to electronics. Second, the service benefits, alone, have special appeal to well-financed, established firms who do not need the cash advances which are available, if wanted, before maturity of the accounts. Third, because of the service aspect, factoring relationships tend to continue over long periods of time.

Factoring is a very specialized, professional service, and not necessarily a method of obtaining money. Many businessmen are not aware of this *service* versus *lending* distinction. While factoring can include an arrangement to accelerate cash flow, this is only an optional service. The following description, however, explains what the factor does when he supplies both service *and* advance payment so that the entire story is told. It begins with a reference to the cost of factoring.

What a company pays for factoring may be no more, and often may be less, than what it would cost the company to perform all credit and collection functions on its own. If the company handled its own credits, it would be required to buy credit information, pay collection and attorney fees, incur inevitable bad debt losses, and absorb a variety of other miscellaneous overhead items. Specifically, what does the factor do? He establishes lines of credit for the customers of his clients and allows shipments up to those amounts at the factor's credit risk. When shipments are made, the factor will, at the client's option, immediately advance up to 90 percent or so of the net invoice value to the client. This is merely an advance payment for goods or services sold since the factor has actually purchased the accounts. It is in no sense a loan which must be repaid. The factor then ledgers the receivables and collects them. The 10 percent or so of the net value of unpaid receivables is retained by the factor only as a reserve for protection against merchandise disputes, the risk of which he does not assume. If this reserve exceeds 10 percent of the outstanding receivables, it is refunded at the end of each month or more frequently, if desirable.

"Old-Line" versus "Maturity" Factoring

The combination of services and quick payment is known as "old-line" factoring. Without the early advance, it is called "maturity" factoring. Under a maturity arrangement, the factor performs all of the service functions and takes the same risks as in old-line factoring, but does not advance money at the time of shipment. Instead, the factor pays for the receivables around the time of their average maturity date. Hence, there are no interest charges in maturity factoring.

In both types of factoring, a charge is made for the factoring services; that is, setting the credit lines, ledgering the receivables, collecting and assuming the credit risk. This charge is called the factoring "commission." In old-line factoring interest is charged for the period between the date of the advance at the time of shipment and an agreed-upon date after the maturity of invoices.

A factoring relationship can involve a loan as a supplement to the basic services provided. For example, firms in lines of business with heavy seasonal demands may need funds to build inventory. Most factors, and particularly those who also do commercial financing, will provide loans for this purpose. Additionally, factors will also make equipment loans or meet other unusual cash needs of their clients. These loans, however, are not part of the factoring process. They are handled separately, and most often provided merely as an accommodation to the client.

Because factoring is not a loan, its effect on the client's balance sheet is unlike that of any other type of financing. For example, assume that a company has a current ratio of about 2 to 1, is not factoring and has current assets and current liabilities as follows:

Current Assets:		Current Liabilities:	
Cash	$ 10,000	Payables	$160,000
Receivables	100,000		
Inventory	200,000	Net worth	150,000
	$310,000		$310,000

Now suppose that the same company is factoring its sales, with a 90 percent advance, and is able to reduce its payables because of accelerated cash flow. The balance sheet changes to reflect a current ratio of better than 3 to 1:

Current Assets:		Current Liabilities:	
Cash	$ 10,000	Payables	$ 70,000
Due from factor.	10,000		
Inventory	200,000	Net worth	150,000
	$220,000		$220,000

Companies which use factoring think of it as a sales-minded service. This capability has to be carefully developed by a factoring firm. Its credit staff has a delicate job. The factor must master the art of making credit judgment and collecting in a way that not only avoids customer dissatisfaction, but also develops growing, profitable users of the clients' products. This necessitates bringing credit lines to the customers' full credit capacities, as well as paying special attention to increasing the buying power of customers or prospects with marginal credit standings. It does not mean that factors are foolishly liberal with credit. Their credit staffs do develop expertise and special advantages that are not usually shared by the credit people of the normal business firm. Factors have wide-ranging experience in the industry served by the client, augmented by frequent trips out in the trade to keep abreast of industry trends. The availability of the factor's own tremendous store of current credit files on business firms also is beneficial. The result of all this, of course, is that credit becomes an important sales tool for the client, to the advantage of both the client and the factoring firm.

It is interesting to note that the reader is closer to factoring than he or she may know. Each time a personal credit card is used, the holder is participating in a form of factoring. The cardholder is the "customer," the store or restaurant is the "client," and the credit card issuer is the "factor," who does the credit checking, bookkeeping and risk-taking. The store or restaurant is charged a "commission" for those services.

Export Factoring

The factoring of exports is a very specialized capability of this service developed over the past ten years or so. It has become worldwide in usage as a simplified method of distributing goods across national boundaries. Many manufacturers do not export because they are apprehensive about foreign credits and collections. Others hold back because they think it involves too much red tape. Both concerns are largely unfounded, and if businessmen let export opportunity go begging, they are shortchanging themselves and their communities. Through export factoring, companies can open up new opportunities for expansion. They have the convenience of selling overseas on open account without credit risk. Along with it, they can facilitate their selling job by increasing the number of foreign firms they can do business with, and the amounts they can sell to individual customers.

The traditional credit instruments such as letters of credit are practical for the export of major capital goods and other materials purchased infrequently in large lots. They are not entirely suitable for the export of consumer and small industrial products, which have lower unit prices and are normally reordered on a continuous basis. For such transactions, letters of credit tend to be cumbersome and their use is less attractive to foreign buyers than open account terms. Thus, the simplicity of export factoring is one of its most compelling features. A hypothetical case will illustrate how it works.

A Chicago-area manufacturer wants to sell to a distributor in the United Kingdom, so he enters into an arrangement with the Chicago office of an international factoring firm which, in turn, asks its overseas subsidiary in England to furnish an approved line of credit on the potential buyer. With that in hand, the manufacturer begins shipping to his English customer, watching only that the amount of his shipments to the customer does not exceed the credit line. The exporter submits to the factor invoices and evidences of shipment. The factor previously has agreed to pay him 100 percent on a certain date. As far as the Chicago manufacturer is concerned, that is all there is to completing the transaction. Furthermore, the manufacturer does not participate in the credit risk. He has no chores in connection with credit or collection. His only obligation is to ship acceptable goods, as ordered. Since the invoices have been purchased by the American factoring firm, it takes on the collection functions, through its British counterpart, and assumes the bad debt risk. For this service, the manufacturer pays a factoring commission.

If the exporter also desires immediate financing, often an important consideration, the factor is ready to advance up to 90 percent of the invoice amount at the time of shipment. On such advances, the factor will charge interest for the period of time between the advance and the mutually agreed-upon regular payment date. The latter date is generally dependent upon the exporter's selling terms.

In a real situation, the factoring arrangement will not be a one-shipment deal, as the example implies. It will have a much broader scope, in both the number of overseas customers served and the number of countries involved. The manufacturer undoubtedly will have other customers in the United Kingdom, and a credit limit will be established by the factor for each of them. Furthermore, the exporter will usually request credit lines on prospective customers, as well. These same export factoring services may be used for open account shipments to most of the industrialized countries around the world.

American exporters, large or small, will no doubt have little difficulty understanding the value of open account selling as a sales tool, especially if they seek a broader base of overseas customers. It is no trick, as far as credit is concerned, for the exporter to sell to the counterparts of Marshall Field and Sears, Roebuck in other countries, or to regular customers with whom he has already established a good credit relationship. With the availability of factoring, however, it is a new ball game. Now the sole concern of the exporter is selling. His markets are immediately expanded to the productive and profitable hinterlands of foreign countries. The credit facilities of the overseas factor reach out to firms in small cities as well as in major centers. Factors are strictly in the credit business, and have intimate business knowledge of the countries in which they operate. Consequently, they may tend to grant larger credit lines than would be available from other agencies. Also, factoring techniques often make possible sales to companies with marginal credit ratings, thereby maximizing the sales penetration of the exporter.

As noted earlier, the particular domain of export factoring is consumer merchandise and low- to medium-priced industrial goods. Both involve short-term sales and the expectation of getting frequent re-order business. Rarely would it be appropriate in selling major capital equipment. The point here is that the essence of factoring, in domestic or export trade, is the development of a continuing, sales-oriented relationship between both the factor and his client, and the client and his customer. To that end, the factor makes it his business, through the application of credit as a sales tool, to create a climate that is conducive to increasing his client's sales.

Perhaps the case for export factoring, as presented here, will dispel the credit bugaboos that have inhibited many would-be exporters. Yet, it is disquieting to learn from a recent survey, that many manufacturers have not even tried to export because they are "too busy" or lack "vision" or "sales energy." Perhaps, they will someday become a little hungrier for business and decide to go after the "plus" sales volume obtainable overseas. Other firms, sincerely cautious about exporting in the past, but anxious to get started now, will do well to follow the advice of the Department of Commerce. It is moving on a broad front to assist smaller and medium-sized firms, literally taking businessmen by the hand and leading them to export markets.

LONG-TERM FINANCING

Venture Capital

Venture capital and conventional long-term borrowings are alternates to stock issuance as sources of capital funds. A typical method of venture capital financing is to provide a long-term loan to the company, generally subordinated to the obligations to other creditors. The loan agreement carries privileges of conversion into equity, directly or by the exercise of warrants. The scenario of the venture capitalist is to be on board a good growth situation with the idea of "taking the company public" when it shows improved earnings and dramatized potential. Going public is the occasion to cash in on warrants or conversion, and to show a return which combines both the interest on the original loan and the multiple of earnings the equity will enjoy in a prosperous market. Recent developments in the equities market have seriously limited the venture capitalist's optimistic outlook for "cashing in." A natural consequence has been a disappearance of the significant funds that were available to growing companies from these sources.

Government-backed and licensed small business investment companies (SBIC) are another source of venture capital. They are permitted by the Small Business Administration (SBA) to take actual or potential ownership of stock in the businesses they serve. SBIC also make straight loans, but all of their financings must be arranged for at least five years. The additional restriction that they may deal only with small businesses works to no real disadvantage for the SBIC because a huge segment, perhaps 90 percent of the nation's total business establishments is included in their approved market. A firm is "small," according to the SBA standards, if its assets do not exceed $9 million, if its net worth is not more than $4 million, and if its average net income after taxes for the preceding two years was not more than $400,000.

Is SBIC financing a viable option for the treasurer? That is a difficult question to answer because of the variation in policy and credit judgment which surely exists between SBIC companies. Most of them are privately owned by small groups of local investors. However, the stock of a substantial number is publicly traded and many are partially or wholly owned by commercial banks or larger, parent corporations. As with any other financial option, the treasurer should make a careful comparative cost analysis of SBIC versus other forms of financing.

The Small Business Administration provides financial assistance in other ways than sponsoring SBICs. It prefers to work toward government-guaranteed bank loans, but it sometimes makes partial or complete loans on a direct basis. As the SBA announces in its own published material, "If a small businessman needs money and cannot borrow it on reasonable terms, SBA often can help." Although the SBA normally is not a financial vehicle for most corporate treasurers, the occurrence of catastrophic events such as storms and floods provides certain occasions for such assistance.

Conventional Long-Term Sources

Conventional long- and medium-term borrowings from sources such as insurance companies and pension funds are a possibility, and banks are displaying a growing willingness to make term loans.

Clearly, when this type of financing is needed to provide a physical facility which will be amortized over a significant period of time, there is a good possibility that credit can be obtained. The lender can see the servicing of that debt over the useful life of the property as a reasonable program that is comparable to the payment of rental on a current basis. The comfort from brick and mortar may be sufficient to attract his investment.

In other situations, it may be more difficult to obtain an unsecured long-term loan. Ratios are a basic part of the analysis and their maintenance will frequently be required in the covenants the borrower must give the lender. As a result, there will be borrowing limitations in relation to net worth, as well as a requirement to maintain certain working capital positions. The borrower must accept the fact that these covenants will shape the direction in which his company is able to move during the term of the loan. Unfortunately, what seems reasonable for a borrower to agree on today in the way of restrictions may be onerous and expensive when unforeseen opportunities come along tomorrow.

To attract long-term credit, a company may have to meet tougher standards than imposed by commercial banks for extending short-term credit. After all, the long-term lender commits himself to be on board for a much longer period of time. He cannot pull back in 90 days and decline to renew the note since he is lending for 10, 15, or 20 years. He has to have such complete comfort in the history and prospects of the borrower that his money is unavailable to many who would have an appetite for it. With insurance companies, there is another credit hurdle. They are generally required by state regulations to confine their loans to business firms with profit histories that meet certain favorable standards. This virtually eliminates credit to a newer, growing company that has excellent present earnings and profit prospects, but does not have a profit history. For the same reason, there is little chance that credit will be granted a firm that has successfully turned around from a loss to profit picture, but at the same time is plagued with a poor profit history.

TIMING[1]

The guessing game of whether "now is the time" to commit for long-term funds is an endless one for the treasurer. The universal

---

[1] See Chapter 3 for a full development of this topic.

financing problem defies solution here because it varies with both company and capital market conditions. What the treasurer can consider, however, is whether available short-term funds can bridge a period when long-term rates appear to be "too high." Short-term borrowings may enable him to bide his time until money market conditions are more favorable.

The Use of Leverage

The appropriate use of financial leverage is a topic dear to the hearts of all treasurers. Its use has been particularly dramatized in the real estate industry. Essentially, it operates on the understanding of the usefulness of borrowing in order to create an asset which can produce more revenue than the cost of borrowing. The results of leverage can be illustrated in a simple way. When the cost to service a mortgage, or any kind of debt, is less than the income produced by that asset, the net difference flows down to the bottom line and is referred to as "positive leverage." Conversely, if the financing cost is more than the revenue produced, the company has a "negative leverage" situation which, if left unchecked, will drain the operation of its life blood. However, financial leverage is not employed appropriately in a simple way. The borrower who seeks to apply it must determine the optimum mix of equity and debt in their many, varying forms.

COSTS OF SHORT-TERM VERSUS EQUITY FINANCING: AN EXAMPLE[2]

At this point, let us consider how to choose among alternate forms of financing and, particularly, how to measure their cost. An example of such an analysis appears in the following tables. They illustrate how a method of short-term borrowing can be economically employed to obtain larger stockholder earnings per invested dollar than would be effected from the combination of bank borrowing and the sale of stock. This example happens to turn out best for secured short-term financing ("secured money"), though it will not always turn out that way.

The conclusions are as follows:

1. Plan 1 returns much less earnings per dollar of stockholder money than if secured money were used exclusively as the

---

[2] This section is an introduction to the analysis of the use of leverage, a subject developed more fully in the following two chapters.

source of funds as shown in Plan 3. Further, in Plan 1 the new stock issued comes to 26.7 percent of the total final amount outstanding and, therefore, the cost of the capital is 26.7 percent of the after-tax earnings each year thereafter.

2. Plan 2 also returns less earnings per dollar of common stockholder money than if secured money were used as the source of funds, and carries with it the continuing burden of preferred dividends.

3. Plan 3 gives the greatest return per dollar of shareholder money. It also has the advantage that the cost of borrowing the secured money will shrink since secured advances are not debts with due dates which increase a company's liabilities. They are *self-liquidating, revolving funds* that provide the assets required to finance the sales.

Problem. Company needs $350,000 additional operating funds.

Balance Sheet and Earnings of Company Used as Example

Cash in bank.	$ 25,000
Accounts receivable.	275,000
Inventory.	400,000
Fixed assets	300,000
Total Assets.	$1,000,000
Sales of this size company	$3,000,000
Profit before deductible interest and taxes (12%).	360,000

TABLE 1
Analysis of Cost of Capital and Stockholders Earnings per Dollar Invested (using various sources of money on which to operate)

	(1) Using Bank Money and Common Stock	*(2)* Using Bank Money Plus Preferred and Common Stock	*(3)* Using Secured Money Only
Usual current liabilities.	$ 100,000	$ 100,000	$ 100,000
Bank loans at 9%	150,000	150,000	–
Secured money at 13%.	–	–	350,000
Preferred stock	–	150,000	–
Stockholders' money.	750,000	600,000	550,000
Total Liabilities	$1,000,000	$1,000,000	$1,000,000

Notes:
  In Plan 1 the corporation's common capital of $550,000 has been increased by $200,000 through the sale of additional common stock.
  In Plan 2 the company has had to sell an additional $50,000 in common stock to be able to sell $150,000 in 7 percent preferred stock to investors.
  In Plans 1 and 2 the company has been shown as borrowing $150,000 from a bank at 9 percent.
  In Plan 3 the company is shown as getting all of its needed money, $350,000, through secured borrowing at 13 percent.

TABLE 2A

Plan 1.   Using Bank Money Plus the Sale of $200,000 Additional Common Stock

			Interest Amount	
Source of Funds	Amount	Interest Rate	Deductible	Nondeductible
Usual current liabilities.	$ 100,000	–	–	–
Bank loan	150,000	9%	$13,500	–
Stockholder money.	750,000	–	–	–
Total.	$1,000,000			

Earnings before interest	$360,000
Less deductible interest	13,500
Earnings before tax.	$346,500
Less tax at 48%	159,820
Net after tax for stockholders.	$186,680

Stockholder earnings per $1.00 invested . . . . $ 0.249

* Tax computed at 48% less $6,500 surtax exemption: $346,500 × 0.48 – $6,500 = $159,820.

TABLE 2B

Plan 2.   Using Bank Money Plus the Sale of $50,000 Additional Common Stock and $150,000 of 7 Percent Preferred Stock

		Interest and Dividend Rate	Interest and Dividend Amount	
Source of Funds	Amount		Deductible	Nondeductible
Usual current liabilities.	$ 100,000	–	–	–
Bank loan	150,000	9%	$13,500	–
Preferred stock	150,000	7%	–	$10,500
Stockholder money.	600,000			
Total.	$1,000,000			

Earnings before interest	$360,000
Less deductible interest	13,500
Earnings before tax and preferred stock dividends	$346,500
Less tax at 48%*	159,820
Net after tax before preferred stock dividends	$186,680
Preferred stock dividends	10,500
Net after tax for stockholders.	$176,180

Stockholder earnings per $1.00 invested . . . . $ 0.294

* Tax computed at 48% less $6,500 surtax exemption: $346,500 × 0.48 – $6,500 = $159,820.

TABLE 2C

Plan 3. Using Secured Money Only

Source of Funds	Amount	Interest Rate	Interest Amount Deductible	Interest Amount Nondeductible
Usual current liabilities	$ 100,000	–	–	–
Secured money	350,000	13%	$45,500	–
Stockholder money	550,000	–	–	–
Total	$1,000,000			

Earnings before interest	$360,000
Less deductible interest	45,500
Earnings before tax	$314,500
Less tax at 48%*	144,460
Net after tax for stockholders	$170,040
Stockholder earnings per $1.00 invested	$ 0.309

* Tax computed at 48% less $6,500 surtax exemption: $314,500 × 0.48 – $6,500 = $144,460.

SUMMARY

Money is the common basic raw material and measuring stick of all business, yet it is a rare entrepreneur-founder of a company who brings to the business a flair for dealing with this primary and essential commodity. It is the treasurer, therefore, who has become indispensable to corporate success, since efficiency in the use of money pays the same rewards as efficiency in operations or marketing. No longer is he a mere custodian of funds; rather, he has become a practiced decision maker who often exhibits considerable artistry in handling corporate financing.

Various options are always available to the treasurer when he seeks to acquire credit. They include secured borrowing which, on a dollar cost or other economic basis, may be more advantageous than straight, unsecured, bank borrowing. Similarly, these short-term, secured loans may be an economic alternative under certain money and capital market conditions to long-term borrowing and equity financing. This means that particular attention should be given to the cost-and-use analysis of secured loans in comparison to the utilization of other types of financing. As is true in all types of business purchasing, the tests for economy and effectiveness in financial "buying" are real cost rather than price, and suitability as opposed to simple availability.

ADDITIONAL SOURCES

Berger, Paul D., and Harper, William K. "Determination of an Optimal Revolving Credit Agreement." *Journal of Financial and Quantitative Analysis,* 8 (June 1973), 491–98.

Boness, A. James; Chen, Andrew H.; and Jatusipitak, Sam. "On Relations among Stock Price Behavior and Changes in the Capital Structure of the Firm." *Journal of Financial and Quantitative Analysis,* 7 (September 1972), 1967–82.

Boot, John C. G., and Frankfurter, George M. "The Dynamics of Corporate Debt Management, Decision Rules, and Some Empirical Evidence." *Journal of Financial and Quantitative Analysis,* 7 (September 1972), 1957–66.

Brown, Bowman. "Why Corporations Should Consider Income Bonds." *Financial Executive,* 35 (October 1967), 74–78.

Cory, Patrick. "An Alternative Approach." *Financial Executive,* 41 (November 1974), 73–77.

Donaldson, Gordon. "In Defense of Preferred Stock." *Harvard Business Review,* 40 (July–August 1962), 123–36.

Elton, Edwin J., and Gruber, Martin J. "Asset Selection with Changing Capital Structure." *Journal of Financial and Quantitative Analysis,* 8 (June 1973), 459–74.

Gordon, Myron J., and Halpern, Paul J. "Cost of Capital for a Division of a Firm." *Journal of Finance,* 29 (September 1974), 1153–64.

Klein, Melvyn. "Comparative Cost Analysis." *Financial Executive,* 41 (November 1974), 78–90.

Martin, John, and Scott, David. "A Discriminant Analysis of the Corporate Debt-Equity Decision." *Financial Management,* 3 (Winter 1974), 71–78.

Chapter 30

Capital Structure Optimization

Alan J. Zakon[*]

Introduction: Liquidity, Profitability, and Growth

THE CLASSIC DILEMMA in optimizing the capital structure is the trade-off between liquidity and profitability. Clearly, a company with no fixed interest charges is in the best possible position to weather a storm, while one with a heavy load of debt runs the risk of embarrassment should earnings fall to the level of the interest charges—or below. The pure equity company will have a higher cash flow in poor times and can meet an unforeseen need for funds more easily by turning to debt than can a company which already has debt on the balance sheet.

In the context of capital structure, "liquidity" may be taken to mean the firm's ability to raise money when an unforeseen need arises. The all-equity capital structure can incur a given amount of debt with a resulting lower debt/equity ratio and higher fixed charge coverage than can a company with debt already existing on the balance sheet. At the extreme, the all-equity company may well be able to borrow funds when the high debt company is wholly foreclosed from the debt market or faces a cost of money that is highly onerous.

While the all-equity capital structure maximizes liquidity, as in all things, there is a price to be paid for flexibility. That price is

[*] Dr. Alan J. Zakon is vice president, The Boston Consulting Group, Inc., Boston, Massachusetts.

profitability. As funds are borrowed and employed at a return higher than the interest cost, the organization makes more dollars than the all-equity capitalized company and the owners earn a higher percentage return on their equity. This, of course, is simply leverage. Leverage, however, is a powerful tool in generating the maximum return to the owners' equity.

The classical capital structure problem, then, is balancing liquidity and profitability or, stated differently, the risk of financial embarrassment against the maximum return on equity. This balance, however, is only part of the capital structure problem. The next element and, perhaps, the critical long-term problem, is the relationship between the capital structure and growth.

In the long term, the corporation must generate adequate funds to grow. Essentially, there are only three sources of funds: the profit margin, debt, and new equity. Dilutions to growth ability are interest on the debt and dividends on the equity. The balance to be struck is one which allows the corporation to generate funds to support its growth within some overall constraints of risk and cost.

The corporation financing growth only through retained earnings and new equity sales generates a problem. The immediate cost is the continual dilution of ownership through the sale of new equity. The risk is that in bad business years when profit margins are reduced more new equity is needed. Yet it will be exactly those years when stock values are most depressed. This means that it will be more difficult to raise funds at all. The act of selling more equity will probably depress stock values even further, and the ensuing shareholders' dilution will be at a maximum. For example, 1975 profit margins and price-earnings ratios were badly depressed relative to historical norms. However, the five-year outlook in most industries was for shortages. This meant that adding capacity at high rates of growth would most probably result in bringing the capacity on stream when the market was there. Selling shares at four to six times earnings, the modal range for the New York Stock Exchange, meant that those funds had to earn 25 percent to 17 percent, respectively, after taxes, to overcome the shareholders' dilution. The further question exists as to whether large amounts of equity money could in fact be raised in this environment.

The addition of debt to the capital structure generates a further source of growth capital, and one which enhances return to owners' equity, rather than subtracting from this return. The risks are clear, again taking the 1975 context. The cost of debt ranged to record levels, with major corporations facing interest costs of 9–15 percent and with the availability of debt being in question. The interactions among reduced profit margins, high costs of debt, the ensuing diminution of interest coverage, the resulting bond rating, and the absolute unavailability of debt without a strong bond rating, are complex. An additional complexity is whatever depressant debt might exert on the equity price.

These are essentially the major considerations to be developed in this chapter. After discussing each of these, the problem then remains as to the decision rules in optimizing the capital structure. Finally, this chapter will conclude with an elaboration of the capital structure decision in the context of the nature of the company. That is, there are profound differences between concentrated companies and highly diversified companies and between high and low growth companies. While the same principles should be applicable to all corporations, these are best illustrated by examples of various kinds of corporations.

Leverage

Simply stated, leverage is the practice of borrowing funds at a low rate and employing them at a higher rate. Let us take the example of two companies in identical businesses each earning 10 percent, after taxes on their assets, and each capitalized differently. If both companies have total assets of $1 million, each earns 10 percent on their assets, or $100,000. If Company A has a capital structure of all equity, its $1 million in assets is financed by $1 million in equity and the company earns $100,000/$1,000,000, or 10 percent on equity. Thus, the return on assets equals the return on owners' equity. Company B differs only in that its capital structure has a 1 to 1 debt/equity ratio; that is, its $1 million in assets are financed by $500,000 in equity and $500,000 in debt. At a 10 percent interest rate, interest charges would amount to $50,000 per year (10 percent of $500,000) and, after 50 percent taxes, would reduce earnings by $25,000. Thus, Company B only earns $75,000, after interest and taxes. This is, however, a 15 percent return on the owners' equity—$75,000/$500,000. (See Table 1.)

It is clear that Company B earns 50 percent more than Com-

TABLE 1
Leverage

	Company A	Company B
Total assets	$1,000,000	$1,000,000
Earnings	$ 100,000	$ 100,000
Return on assets.	10%	10%
Debt	0	$ 500,000
Equity	$1,000,000	$ 500,000
Interest*	0	$ 25,000
Earnings after interest	$ 100,000	$ 75,000
Return on equity	10%	15%

* 10 percent interest, or 5 percent after taxes.

pany A as a percent of equity and that Company B will earn 50 percent more per share of equity if each financed their equity with shares sold at equal price-earnings ratios.

The arithmetic of leverage is clear and, so too, are the advantages. Before it is pointed out that Company A earns $100,000 and Company B earns only $75,000, it should be noted that Company B would earn $150,000 *if* it invested as much equity as Company A *and if* it earned the same 10 percent on the additional assets.

Leverage and Interest Coverage

The question is how far to increase leverage in pursuit of attractive financial results. Table 2 expresses returns on equity at

TABLE 2
Debt-Equity Ratios and Return on Equity

Return on Assets (percent)	Debt-Equity	Return on Equity* (percent)	Interest Coverage†
10%	0	10%	∞
10	10/90	11	20.0 times
10	30/70	12	6.7 times
10	50/50	15	4.0 times
10	70/30	22	2.9 times
10	90/10	55	2.2 times

* Assuming interest at 10 percent, or 5 percent after-tax.
† Earnings divided by interest charges.

varying ratios of debt to equity and their concomitant interest coverage.

Again, return on equity rises as leverage increases but financial risk increases as interest coverage declines. With a 1 to 1 (50/50) debt-equity ratio, earnings would have to decline by 75 percent in order to just cover interest payments.

Earnings would have to decline by only 55 percent to threaten interest payments at a 9 to 1 (90/10) debt-equity ratio. Table 3

TABLE 3
Debt-Equity and Interest Coverage

Debt-Equity	Return on Assets* (percent)	Coverage†	Maximum Possible Decline‡ (percent)
0.	10%	∞	∞
10/90.	10	20.0 x	95%
30/70.	10	6.7 x	85
50/50.	10	4.0 x	75
70/30.	10	2.9 x	65
90/10.	10	2.2 x	55

* After-taxes.
† After-tax earnings divided by after-tax interest.
‡ Percent decrease from on-trend 10 percent return on assets for earnings to just cover interest charges.

summarizes the relationship between debt-equity ratios and interest coverage.

The ratios in Table 3 are, perhaps, surprising. The table indicates that very high debt ratios can be supported by companies with only moderate earnings stability. For reference, the *Fortune* "500" had an average capitalization of 35 percent debt and 65 percent equity for the 1972–74 period. This is a debt-equity ratio of 35/65, or .54 to 1, and with an average after-tax return on assets of 9.5 percent, a coverage of 5.4 times. This means that earnings could have fallen by 81 percent before interest charges would not have been covered.

A first reaction is that American companies are conservatively financed. This is probably true. However, the relationship between earnings and interest charges is only part of a considered analysis. Interest is only one claim on earnings. Debt repayment, dividends, and growth requirements are other claims.

Before moving to broaden our analysis, it would be well to consolidate the concepts developed thus far. Leverage has been expressed in terms of the debt-equity ratio. The operational impacts of increasing the debt-equity ratio are two; positively, as the ratio increases any given return on assets is levered to a higher return on owners' equity and, negatively, higher debt-equity ratios produce lower coverage ratios at any given return on assets. The consequence of a lower coverage is that the corporation must have stable earnings to ensure meeting interest payments.

If the example of a company with a 1 to 1 debt-equity ratio, 5 percent after-tax interest rate, and a 10 percent return on assets is used, an interest coverage of four (4) times results.

Since leverage is commonly expressed in terms of debt-equity ratios, an equation[1] relating coverage and debt-equity ratios can be written as:

$$\text{Coverage} = \frac{R\left(\frac{D}{E} + 1\right)}{i\,\frac{D}{E}}$$

Where:

$$R = \text{After-tax return on assets}$$
$$\frac{D}{E} = \text{Ratio of debt to equity}$$
$$i = \text{Interest rate, after taxes}$$

Using our example above,

$$R = 10\%$$
$$D/E = 1$$
$$i = 5\%$$
$$\text{Coverage} = \frac{.10(1 + 1)}{.05(1)}$$
$$= \frac{.2}{.05}$$
$$= 4 \text{ times}$$

Examining the coverage equation suggests strongly that simply looking at debt-equity ratios tells us very little about the impact of leverage. A company with a high return can use more debt *with more safety* than a company with a low return. Compare, for example, two companies, one with a high return and a high debt ratio and another with a low return and a moderate debt ratio:

[1] For derivation of this equation, see Appendix at end of chapter.

	Company A	Company B
ROA	20%	7%
D/E	2:1	.4:1
i	5%	5%
Coverage	$\dfrac{.20 \ (2+1)}{.05 \ (2)}$	$\dfrac{.07 \ (.4+1)}{.05 \ (.4)}$
	6 times	4.9 times

The high return, high debt company has a better coverage than a low return, low debt company. Thus, measuring leverage by debt-equity ratios alone is quite misleading. Properly, we are looking to a margin of safety concept, not a static ratio concept. Coverage tells us much more than debt/equity, and the equation,

$$\text{Coverage} \ = \ \frac{R \left(\dfrac{D}{E} + 1 \right)}{i \left(\dfrac{D}{E} \right)}$$

expresses this margin of safety concept within the traditional debt-equity format.

Leverage, Dividend Coverage, and Debt Repayment Coverage

As indicated earlier, dividends and debt repayment represent additional claims on the earnings stream which must be provided for. Technically, the dividend is not a fixed charge. Pragmatically, however, few managements are willing to pursue an aggressive debt policy to the point where the dividend is threatened.

For this reason, this chapter will treat dividend payments as *having priority over* interest payments and debt repayment in terms of management long-term decisions and, hence, in terms of capital structure policy. That is, capital structure decisions must be part and parcel of overall financial strategy *including dividend policy*. One aspect of dividend policy is the dividend level. Another is the commitment to the stability of the dividend. Again, pragmatically this suggests that financial policy will include a commitment to a maintenance of the dividend—even in adverse business years. This means that capital structure policy must normally include this commitment as prerequisite.

Thus, a dividend policy oriented to a 50 percent of earnings payout has a sharp impact on effective coverage. Our company with a 10 percent return on assets and a 1 to 1 debt-equity ratio had a coverage of four (4) times, assuming a 5 percent after-tax interest rate. If that company had a 50 percent of earnings payout policy, coverage would look as follows:

Assets.	$100
Debt	$ 50
Equity	$ 50
D/E.	1:1
ROA	10%
Profit before interest	$10
Interest.	$2.50
Coverage	4 times
Profit after interest	$7.50
50% dividend	$3.75
Total fixed charges	$6.25
Effective coverage	1.6 times

Since dividend policy is normally premised on earnings after interest, this means a dividend payment for our example of $3.75. This means that total fixed charges are $2.50 for interest and $3.75 for dividends, or $6.25. Dividing this into the $10 available for interest and dividends provides an effective coverage of $10/ $6.25, or *1.6 times* versus *4 times* with no dividend.

In a real sense, then, dividends are destructive of debt capacity. A 1.6 times coverage means that an earnings decline of only 37 percent will leave no margin over interest and dividends. It is perhaps not surprising that high dividend companies were the prime acquisition targets of highly levered conglomerates in the 1960s. The high dividend represented great debt capacity for the conglomerates who had nominal dividend payouts themselves.

If the assumption is made that our company borrows on average 20-year terms, then on the average, 5 percent of the debt must be repaid or refinanced annually. In an adverse year in which refinancing is not practical, provision must be made to repay 5 percent of the debt. Adding this in to our example looks as follows:

Assets.	$100
Debt	$ 50
Equity	$ 50
D/E.	1:1
ROA	10%
Profit before interest	$10
Interest.	$2.50
Dividend	$3.75
Debt repayment.	$2.50 (5% of $50)
Total charges	$8.75
Coverage	1.14 times

This company's four (4) times coverages has melted, then, to about no coverage taking all charges together. Thus, a first blush reaction to leverage is "borrow." A second reaction indicates the requirement for a considered look at the stability of earnings and both the probability and severity of adversity. Again, this chapter is using adversity to mean a year of reduced earnings when access to the capital markets is limited such that debt repayments cannot be refinanced and must, then, be considered as a fixed charge.

This perhaps, states the classical liquidity versus profitability dilemma. This chapter, so far, has evaluated the liquidity analysis. The clear problem is that a careful enunciation of all the risks tends toward a highly conservative capital structure. The profitability side of the equation—the price of flexibility—remains to be examined. An introduction to this section is well served by an anlysis of the Dow Chemical Company as compared to Du Pont (Table 4).

TABLE 4
Dow Chemical and Du Pont ($ in 000,000)

	Dow Chemical*		Du Pont*	
	1964	1973	1964	1973
Sales	$1,077	$3,068	$2,761	$5,276
Income	94	271	471	586
Debt†	239	1,226	–	250
Equity‡	762	1,446	2,015	3,550
Return on assets	10.4%	13.3%	23.4%	15.9%
Return on equity	12.3%	18.8%	23.4%	16.5%
D/E	.31	.85	–	.07:1
Marginal D/E	–	1.44:1	–	.16:1
Compound sales growth	–	12.3%	–	7.5%
Compound income growth	–	10.9%	–	2.5%
Compound asset growth§	–	11.5%	–	7.3%

    * All data from Value Line.
    † Funded debt.
    ‡ Including preferred stock.
    § Debt + equity = assets.

Perhaps the most striking comparison that can be made between these two companies is their debt policy. Dow Chemical now has a debt-equity ratio of .85 to 1. This is high, compared to the *Fortune* "500" average of about .5 to 1, in an industry that might be viewed as less stable on a year-to-year basis than major corporations on the average. Even more interesting has been Dow's marginal debt policy. For the 1964–73 period, $1.44 in debt has been added for each $1 in equity. Interestingly, this marginal rate has been relatively consistent annually, suggesting a consistent capital structure policy. Du Pont, alternatively, has virtually no debt and has followed a minimal debt policy.

This striking difference in philosophy shows in two major measures of performance—return on equity and growth.

In 1964, Dow levered a 10.4 percent return on assets to a 12.3 percent return on equity, using a debt-equity ratio of .31 to 1. By 1973, the .85 to 1 debt-equity ratio enhanced shareholders' returns from 13.3 percent to 18.8 percent. Thus, while return on assets increased by 28 percent over ten years, the shareholders' return increased by 53 percent.

In contrast, Du Pont earned 23.4 percent on assets and on equity in 1964. By 1973 the return on assets was still higher than Dow's, at 15.9 percent, but minimal debt usage levered this return only to 16.5 percent. Thus, while Du Pont was able to achieve a substantial higher return than Dow in an *operating sense,* the Dow shareholders earned a significantly better return on their invested equity.

Leverage and Growth

Dow's leverage, additionally, provided the funds to grow at a faster rate than Du Pont. Dow was able to compound its assets at a rate of 11.5 percent annually, between 1964 and 1973, while Du Pont was able to grow only at 7.3 percent per year. While debt does not create growth, investment is required to provide asset growth. Growth funds are available from three sources only: (1) reinvested equity; (2) new equity; and (3) new debt. Neither Dow nor Du Pont sold any meaningful amount of common stock during this period, thus they financed growth fully through reinvested equity and new debt. Further, asset turnover (sales ÷ assets) remained constant for both companies, so that asset growth was directly translated into sales growth.

Thus, each company's ability to raise funds to support growth was a function of:

> Earnings
> Less: Dividends
> Plus: Incremental debt

Since earning power (return on assets) and debt interact to produce return on equity, we can develop the relationship between debt, dividends, return on assets, and growth. At a given level of return, earnings are equal to assets employed times the return earned on these assets.

$$\text{Earnings} = \text{Return on assets} \times \text{assets}$$

Corporate growth will equal the rate of return on assets if all earnings are reinvested; that is, if no dividends are paid, and no debt is used. In Table 5 the rate of growth is clearly 10 percent, where the return on assets that supports it is 10 percent. Notice that since no debt is used, the return on equity is also 10 percent (Table 5).

TABLE 5
Growth and Rate of Return

	Year 1	Year 2	Year 3
Total assets	$100.00	$110.00	$121.00
Equity	100.00	110.00	121.00
Return on assets	10%	10%	10%
Profit	$ 10.00	$ 11.00	$ 12.10
Dividends	0	0	0
Debt	0	0	0
Reinvest	$ 10.00	$ 11.00	$ 12.10
Return on assets	10%	10%	10%
Return on equity	10%	10%	10%

If debt is introduced into Table 5, the results change dramatically. Assuming a constant debt-equity ratio of 1 to 1 and after-tax interest costs of 5 percent, the net return on assets drops to 7.5 percent (reflecting interest charges), but the *rate of growth* and *return on equity* increase to 15 percent (Table 6).

TABLE 6
Growth, Debt, and Rate of Return

	Year 1	Year 2	Year 3
Total assets	$100.00	$115.00	$132.25
Equity	50.00	57.50	66.12
Debt	50.00	57.50	66.12
Debt/equity	1:1	1:1	1:1
Return on assets	10%	10%	10%
Profit before interest	$ 10.00	$ 11.50	$ 13.23
Interest	2.50	2.88	3.31
Profit after interest	7.50	8.62	9.92
Dividends	0	0	0
Net return on assets	7.5%	7.5%	7.5%
Return on equity	15.0%	15.0%	15.0%
Equity reinvestment	$ 7.50	$ 8.62	$ 9.92
Additional debt	7.50	8.62	9.92
Total new investment	15.00	17.25	19.85

A critical impact of debt, then, is not simply levering a lower return on assets to a higher return on equity, but *more fundamentally* allowing a firm to generate funds to sustain higher rates of growth.

Note that Table 6 provides for a constant debt-equity ratio. That is, no provision is made for debt repayment; rather, it is assumed that the firm will maintain its debt-equity ratio to support its growth rate, once a proper ratio has been determined.

The earlier discussion noted that dividends erode debt capacity through their impact on effective coverage. Dividends further impact on the growth rate by diverting equity funds from reinvestment and, therefore, *growth funds also*. The impact of dividend policy is introduced in Table 7. The result of a 50 percent payout is a halving of the growth rate, although returns on assets and equity remain at the earlier level. Whereas with zero payout, a 10 percent return on assets is levered to a 15 percent return on equity and rate of growth; the 50 percent payout introduced in this example drops the growth rate to 7.5 percent, thus nullifying the leverage effect. Note that this in fact takes place despite the 1 to 1 debt-equity ratio. If no debt were used, the 50 percent payout policy would result in only a 5 percent rate of growth. (Verify this by introducing

TABLE 7
Growth, Rate of Return, Debt, and Dividends

	Year 1	Year 2	Year 3
Total assets	$100.00	$107.50	$115.56
Equity	50.00	53.75	57.78
Debt	50.00	53.75	57.78
Debt/equity	1:1	1:1	1:1
Return on assets	10%	10%	10%
Profit before interest	$ 10.00	$ 10.75	$ 11.56
Interest	2.50	2.69	2.89
Profit after interest	7.50	8.06	8.67
Net return on assets	7.5%	7.5%	7.5%
Return on equity	15%	15%	15%
Dividends	$ 3.75	$ 4.03	$ 4.34
Retention percentage	50%	50%	50%
Equity reinvestment	$ 3.75	$ 4.03	$ 4.33
Additional debt	3.75	4.03	4.33
Total new investment	7.50	8.06	8.66

a 50 percent dividend with the example in Table 5.) (See Table 7.)

The net result of this sustainable growth analysis is to demonstrate that the high debt, low dividend company can grow much more rapidly than the low debt, high dividend company—*at the same return on assets.* Importantly, it also means that his company can outperform its competition even with a lower return on assets— if the competition chooses a less than optimal debt policy and/or a higher than optimal dividend policy.

Tables 5–7 can be restated by a simple equation[2]:

$$\text{Sustainable growth} = \frac{D}{E}(R - i)p + Rp$$

where:

$$D/E = \text{Debt/equity}$$
$$R = \text{Return on assets, after taxes}$$
$$i = \text{Interest rate, after taxes}$$
$$p = \text{Percent of earnings retained}$$

This equation assumes that all depreciation is reinvested to keep earning power constant and that no new equity sales or retirements are made.

Returning to Dow Chemical and Du Pont, we can insert their 1964–73 figures into the sustainable growth equation:

	Dow	Du Pont
Incremental debt/equity, 1964–73 (D/E)	1.44:1	0.16:1
Average return on assets (R)	10.8%	15.1%
Interest rate (i)	3%	3%
Retention percentage (p)	50%	32%

For Dow,

$$\begin{aligned}
\text{Sustainable growth} &= \frac{D}{E}(R - i)p + Rp \\
&= 1.44(.108 - .03).5 + .108(.5) \\
&= .056 + .054 \\
&= \underline{11.0\%}
\end{aligned}$$

For Du Pont,

$$\begin{aligned}
\text{Sustainable growth} &= \frac{D}{E}(R - i)p + Rp \\
&= .16(.151 - .03).32 + .151(.32) \\
&= .006 + .048 \\
&= 5.4\%
\end{aligned}$$

---

[2] For derivation of this equation, see Appendix at end of chapter.

Comparing these with the actual growth rates for 1964–73, results show:

	Dow	Du Pont
Sustainable growth calculation	11.0%	5.4%
Actual growth in:		
Assets	11.5	7.3
Sales	12.3	7.5
Earnings	10.9	2.5

The calculated sustainable growth works out about right for Dow and undershoots for Du Pont. This underestimate is primarily caused by a 1971 equity increase over and above retained earnings. Again, the equation assumes no external equity purchases or sales. To the extent that this external equity was preferred stock, it should properly be considered as debt.

Dow, then, has been able to outperform Du Pont in terms of growth and, by 1973, shareholders' return, through a mixture of more aggressive debt policy and a higher retention of earnings. While relative dividend policies have had a significant impact, if we neutralize this by plugging a 50 percent retention rate into the equation for both Dow and Du Pont, the resulting sustainable growth rates are:

For *Dow,*

$$
\begin{aligned}
\text{Sustainable growth} &= \frac{D}{E}\,(R - i)p + Rp \\
&= 1.44(.108 - .03).5 + .108(.5) \\
&= .056 + .054 \\
&= \underline{11\%}
\end{aligned}
$$

This mean that 5.4 percentage points of Dow's growth was accounted for by its unlevered return, after dividends, and 5.6 percentage points of growth were provided by borrowed funds.

For *Du Pont,*

$$
\begin{aligned}
\text{Sustainable growth} &= \frac{D}{E}\,(R - i)p + Rp \\
&= .16(.151 - .03).5 + .151(.5) \\
&= .010 + .076 \\
&= \underline{8.6\%}
\end{aligned}
$$

Again, if Du Pont had Dow's dividend policy, only 1 percentage point of growth would have been generated by debt and 7.6 percentage points by its unlevered return: This means that Du Pont— with a much higher basic return on assets (50 percent above Dow's on an average), would still have been in the position of being able to sustain a slower growth rate.

Financial and Business Risk

The faster the rate of growth in industry demand, the higher the rates of return and the profit margins on sales must be to sustain that growth. If demand grows at 20 percent per year, the industry as a whole must earn 20 percent just to generate the funds necessary to add capacity to meet demand growth—this means that, with a once annual asset turnover and no debt, profit margins on sales *after tax* must also be 20 percent.

The magnitude of these numbers have critical implications for management. Despite a 40 percent profit margin, a business that must grow at 20 percent per year

1. Cannot generate funds for dividends.
2. Cannot spin off cash into other businesses, either for corporate earnings enhancement or for investment hedges against obsolescence.
3. Cannot finance growth in *excess* of the 20 percent industry average.

The risks are obvious and compound one another. While some managers and some, but fewer, shareholders have come to realize that the real value of a business derives from its *potential* ability to pay dividends, the demand of a high growth business push that potential farther into the future. It is very easy to imagine growth industries in which firms show very high profit margins and report rapidly growing earnings, but which can *never realize* these earnings for the shareholder in the form of dividends.

For example, many of the firms in the germanium transistor industry reported annual earnings increases of 25–50 percent per year during the early growth phases. But *all* earnings were required for investment to keep up with the growth in demand for the product.

The risks in this situation are that a firm will *not* reinvest earnings and, therefore, erode their future competitive position, or that they *will* reinvest earnings in assets that never pay out. The net result of a heavy investment program must be an asset base that allows the firm to be competitive in future markets and, hence, repay the owners for the use of their money or one which cannot generate funds to repay itself. Many semiconductor firms built up substantial levels of retained earnings that represented noncompetitive assets or assets employed in a business that was becoming obsolete. As a result, none of the reinvested earnings were available for dividends.

Retained equity, built up during the rapid growth phase of a business, can be distributed to shareholders in dividends *only* when annual earnings plus depreciation exceed reinvestment needs: This is likely to occur only when any of the following conditions are met:

1. The firm's capital structure and cost structure will sustain required *growth* and allow payment of dividends.
    a. Industry-high debt levels.
    b. Industry-low cost levels.
    c. At least maintenance of market share.
2. The firm *liquidates* its market position by growing more slowly than the industry and thereby generates more funds than it reinvests.
    a. A growth company can be liquidating itself by shrinking its market share even though it grows at a rapid rate.
    b. High profit margins may generate reported earnings but erode market share.
    c. Slower than average industry growth can generate cash at the expense of future production costs, relative to the competition.

When a growth company reinvests earnings it is betting that it can establish a position in a market such that the earnings from that business will *ultimately* be dividendable. This means that the firm must concentrate *first* on establishing its competitive position in terms of production costs and capital structure.

This means that growing less rapidly, on trend, than competition will erode market position and, ultimately, profitability relative to competition. While a business may not choose to fully utilize its debt capacity, this choice implies a high- and increasing-degree of business risk. The properly levered competitor can grow faster than the more conservatively financed company and, like Dow versus

Du Pont, with lower required rates of return. The ultimate risk of overconservatism is increasing business risk if competition is aware.

Clearly, the coverage analysis shows that financial risk (liquidity risk) increases rapidly as debt usage increases. Equally, business risk increases as a company strives to grow in competition with a more properly levered competitor. This risk is the long-term one of eroding market position and the shorter term one of being outpriced in the marketplace as the conservative firm attempts to grow primarily through the profit margin by striving for ever higher price realizations.

Determination of optimal capital structure, then, is one of maintaining minimal risk with maximum return in a *total business dimension*—not a financial liquidity dimension alone. Financial analysts focus on liquidity risks primarily. This is dangerous and misleading. Competitive risk is, in the long term, the more profound risk facing a firm. Financial strategy, then, involves the total corporation and its competitive interactions, rather than financial and liquidity analysis only.

Optimal Capital Structure—Constraints

The benefits of higher debt usage in the capital structure have been addressed, as has the liquidity risk from debt usage. In addition to liquidity, which will be reexamined in later sections of this chapter, two additional constraints exist: one pragmatic and one conceptual.

Pragmatic Constraints.   Pragmatically, financial officers, analysts, and institutions, equate debt with risk and risk with debt-equity ratios. A great deal of financial literature is concerned with the need for an equity base for debt and analysis of industry-average debt-equity ratios. Yet, on the other hand, the post–World War II American experience has been that New York Stock Exchange firms have been *net buyers* of common equity. No new equity, on average, has been required by these firms in almost 30 years. While some of this phenomenon is the result of the introduction of accelerated depreciation and the investment tax credit, a major part is due to increased debt usage. In the past ten years, the average debt-equity ratio of the *Fortune* "500" has gone from .35 to 1 to over .5 to 1, or a 50 percent increase. Perhaps it is not surprising that interest rates have steadily increased over this period.

The net result of this gap between financial perception and business reality is that capital structure optimization must be approached on a logical, analytical basis. This chapter noted earlier that the debt-equity ratio had no meaning in terms of coverage without being viewed together with the trend rate of return on assets.

Further, coverage ratios have little meaning without being viewed in terms of stability of earnings.

Just as the high return company can sustain high debt-equity ratios with high resulting coverage, the stable company can enjoy low coverage ratios with great safety.

For example, *Overseas Shipholding Group* (OSG) has had the following history (Table 8).

TABLE 8
Overseas Shipholding Group

Year	Sales ($ millions)	Debt ($ millions)	Equity ($ millions)	D/E	ROA	ROE
1968	$ 45	—	—			
1969	53	$ 88	$ 36	2.44	9.5%	19.1
1970	65	98	55	1.78	9.8	18.5
1971	70	116	67	1.73	10.4	17.8
1972	85	136	91	1.49	9.6	16.4
1973	127	164	110	1.49	11.2	18.4
1974	185	215	139	1.55	14.0	21.0

Source: Value Line.

By any standards, these debt-equity ratios are high and, with a *Fortune* "500" average return on assets, coverage is low at about three times. The basis of Overseas' business, however, is the long-term chartering of vessels such that the length and terms of charter will cover all or a major part of the finance charges on each vessel. The operating strategy can be more or less conservative, depending upon how much of its fleet OSG wishes to charter long and safely or short and speculatively. To the extent that the operating strategy is conservative, financial strategy can be highly aggressive since the stability of cash flows is very high. For example, 97 percent of the foreign flag fleet, as of January 1975, was chartered through 1975, 93 percent through 1976, and 82 percent through 1977.

Clearly, liquidity risks are minimized and OSG is a superb example of the interface of business and financial risks and strategies. Equally clear, companies such as OSG are setting prices premised upon significant leverage. This means that managements with a debt aversion cannot compete in this industry without taking great operating risks; i.e., competing only in the short-term or "spot" market.

Even the chemical industry has analogous examples. Both *Airco* and *Air Products and Chemicals* maintain historical debt-equity ratios of close to 1 to 1 with returns, on assets in the 7 percent to 10 percent range—lower than the *Fortune* "500," on average. One characteristic of the industrial gas business is that oxygen plants are placed with steel mills on long-term contracts such that the annual cash flow can carry debt service of 100 percent—*or more*—of the cost of the equipment. Thus, while coverage is very low, stability is very high.

In both of these cases, the nature of the asset and terms of sale or lease determine the appropriate debt-equity ratio—not recourse to industry averages or standard financial ratios. Also in both cases, the true debt capacity is that of the ultimate consumer. In the maritime example, it is the oil companies and in the gas example, the steel companies.

It is an unusual testament to institutional analysis that companies such as OSG can maintain high debt ratios based on the capacity of their customers, while the customers (oil companies) avoid full integration back into tankers largely to keep the debt off their balance sheets.

Pragmatically, then, debt capacity truly arises from the nature of each business in which the corporation competes and deviations from average norms must be premised upon an analysis of each business, its return and its stability. The cost of deviation from conservative standards is usually in the bond rating and, hence, the interest rate, terms of repayment, and restrictive covenants otherwise.

Perhaps more poor decisions are made in this area than any other. A bond rating is important only to the extent that it does not fall so low that access to credit is wholly precluded. The interest rate is all but immaterial. When corporations can earn, on an average, 20 percent before taxes and borrow, on an average, at 10 percent, pretax, one or two points of interest have little impact relative to the earnings that could be generated by additional investment. More usually, interest rate ranges are within one point, and to discontinue borrowing because the rate would go from 10 percent to 10.75 percent means that the financial officer would prefer to save $0.75 on a $100 investment *pretax* than to earn $9.25, before taxes, on the same investment. The financial function is not a profit center; it is part of overall corporate direction. Good performance is supporting the goals of the firm, not minimizing interest costs.

Restrictive covenants and repayment terms can sharply reduce debt capacity by increasing the annual liquidity problem, either by a rapid repayment or an inability to refund if ratios drop below agreed-upon levels. The critical element is the management's willingness to give in on higher interest rates in favor of more generous terms. As with almost all decisions, there is a trade-off involved. Returning again to the coverage concept, a 15-year mortgage at 10 percent interest provides for annual payments of $13.15 per year per $100 of debt. Alternatively, a 20-year mortgage at 11 percent requires only $12.55, annually. Put another way, the corporation could borrow $105 at 11 percent over 20 years with the same annual commitment as borrowing $100 for 15 years at 10 percent. Debt capacity, then, orients much more closely to liquidity requirements than the actual cost of money, as long as that cost stays below the corporation's earning rate.

In summary, then, pragmatic constraints exist in terms of institutional perceptions and self-imposed perceptions or trade-offs. There is no definitive answer as to how far a company should go. Rather, the answer must be based on an analysis of the stability, return, and competitive characteristics of *each business* the corporation is in.

Conceptual Constraints. The most influential conceptual work written regarding capital structure has been that of Modigliani and Miller.[3] Writing in the late 1950s, Modigliani and Miller observed that leverage had no logical impact on share valuation. Simply stated, they had two basic arguments: first, that addition of debt had no impact on the basic return of the business. This means that borrowing more money results in higher earnings, but also higher financial risk. Second, they argued that the shareholder, in the aggregate, had a risk-return balance. If the company was underlevered, the shareholder would borrow personally to enhance his return on equity. If the corporation had too much debt, the share-

---

[3] F. Modigliani and M. H. Miller, "The Cost of Capital, Corporation Finance and the Theory of Investment," *The American Economic Review*, 48 (June 1958), pp. 261–97.

holder would undo the leverage by using less debt, personally, or demanding a higher equity return to compensate for the risk. The result, of course, would be to depress share prices as corporate debt increased in order to hold constant the ultimate shareholders' risk-return balance.

Their argument is totally sound and dominates the conceptual literature. The logic of this chapter suggests, however, that the Modigliani and Miller thesis operates within too narrow an environment.

The key impact of leverage is not simply on the shareholders' return on equity. More fundamentally, it impacts on how the corporation pursues its operating strategy and the rate at which the firm grows. Overseas Shipholding Group or Air Reduction, for example, premised debt upon a very safe asset deployment. As a result of that, aggressive debt policy could be pursued and adequate returns on equity could be earned with minimal operating risk. The low debt company, alternatively, could not pursue that business without taking a more speculative posture in the marketplace. The net result is that the *interaction* between operating and financial policies can lead to a higher return, lower overall risk balance than could be established by treating the operating decision and the investment decision as separate.

Further, there is significant evidence that the leading companies in each industry are also the most profitable. Consider, for example, General Motors, Ford, and Chrysler; Anheuser-Busch, Schlitz, and Pabst; Procter & Gamble, Colgate, and Lever Brothers. In each case, the largest company is the most profitable on trend—with profitability falling off as relative market share declines. The recent PIMS[4] work initiated by the General Electric Company and pursued by the Marketing Science Institute suggests strongly that the major determinant in relative corporate profitability is relative market share. If this is true, and strong evidence exists to support its validity, then the company gaining market share will improve its profitability relative to the company holding or losing share. This means that relative growth has an operating payout in excess of simply generating more size.

Again, corporate growth, operating strategy, and financial struc-

---

[4] Sidney Schoeffler, Robert D. Buzzell, and Donald F. Heany, "Impact of Strategic Planning on Profit Performance," *Harvard Business Review*, vol. 52, no. 2 (1974), p. 137.

TABLE 9
Relative Size and Relative Profitability

| | Cosmetics—Toiletries* | | | Brewing Industry† | |
| | 1973 | | | 1973 | |
Company	Sales ($ millions)	Operating Margin (percent)	Company	Sales ($ millions)	Operating Margin (percent)
Avon	$1,150	25.0%	Anheuser-Busch	$1,110	14.6%
Gillette	1,064	17.3	Schlitz	703	18.3
Revlon	506	17.4	Pabst	355	15.6
Chesebrough-Ponds	464	16.6	Carling	264	4.6
Alberto-Culver.	184	7.2	Schaefer	236	6.8
Faberge.	160	11.7	Falstaff.	174	1.9
Carter-Wallace‡	148	11.0			
Helene Curtis	78	1.1			

* Value Line data—omitting International Flavor & Fragrance, Swank, Tampax, which are highly specialized.
† Omitting Heilman due to recent acquisitions.
‡ 1972, 1974 data, not 1973 which was an extraordinary year.

ture are intimately related, not separate considerations. Table 9 lists the competitors in the brewing industry and cosmetics industry by size and operating margin. Note that while the correlation is not perfect, these companies do not compete with one another across the board and that, on an average, the larger firms are the most profitable. This suggests that while investors may, indeed, discount financial risk in valuing shares, performance over time may well modify their discount rate. The same phenomenon is apparent in viewing the brewing industry, as noted below:

Company	1973 Debt/Equity	1973 Operating Margin	1973 Price-Earnings
Anheuser-Busch	0.34	14.6%	30.4
Schlitz	0.22	18.3	32.0
Pabst	0.00	15.6	20.2
Schaefer	nmf*	6.8	13.1
Carling	0.24	4.6	nmf*
Falstaff.	0.69	3.0	nmf

* nmf = no meaningful figure.
Source: Value Line.

Finally, note Dow's price-earnings ratio versus Du Pont. This suggests that in at least one case, the greater use of debt has not depressed the market's valuation of earnings. In fact, Dow's price-earnings multiple versus Du Pont's has looked as follows:

	Price-Earnings Multiple	
Year	Dow	Du Pont
1964	22.9	25.7
1965	20.8	27.8
1966	16.6	22.7
1967	18.3	23.9
1968	17.6	20.6
1970	14.6	18.0
1971	15.4	16.9
1972	19.3	19.7
1973	22.3	20.0

Source: Value Line.

In summary, then, Modigliani and Miller have a powerful argument within traditional financial boundaries. Modigliani and Miller's premise that debt policy did not impact on the risk characteristics of the operating earnings stream is parallel to the traditional financial dictum that the decision to invest is separate from the decision as to how to finance the investment. The logic of this chapter is that the decision to invest and the financial decision interact in terms of overall corporate goals and derivative policies.

Conclusions: Optimal Capital Structure

In summary, the optimal capital structure is one which:

1. Supports corporate operating strategy.
2. Maximizes debt leverage and, therefore:
    a. Return on shareholders' equity.
    b. Corporate growth rate.
3. Minimizes short-term liquidity problems.

As was discussed earlier, the dividend decision had a significant impact on the corporate capital structure. A high dividend company, such as Du Pont, cannot sustain a high debt ratio without living within a very narrow coverage constraint.

The key decision relates to the stability of earnings, the return on assets and, as a resultant, the required coverage of fixed charges.

Fixed charges, of course, include interest, debt repayment when refinancing must be deferred, and dividends.

This means that the optimal capital structure is a mixture of corporate policies and the characteristics of each business which comprise the corporate portfolio. The key corporate policy impacting on capital structure is the dividend policy.

Beyond that, the corporate capital structure is the conglomeration of the proper capital structures of each business comprising the corporate portfolio. Traditionally, it is argued that the corporate portfolio generates debt capacity over and above the constituent businesses to the extent that these businesses are inversely correlated in terms of cash flows. That is, if a corporation had two businesses whose cash flows ranged from +$20 to −$5 each year *and* whose cash flows were perfectly out of phase, annual cash flows would look as follows:

Year	Business A	Business B	Corporation
1	$20	$−5	$15
2	−5	20	15
3	20	−5	15
4	−5	20	15

In this case, neither business has real debt capacity due to the recurring liquidity problem. The corporation, however, has perfect stability of earnings and great debt capacity.

Ideally, then, the capital structure analysis should embody a thorough analysis of each business, its cash flows, the degree to which maintenance can be deferred in favor of debt service in a bad year, and the extent to which depreciation is available for debt service when reported earnings are depressed. This should include, additionally, the degree to which each business phases with each other business in determining the corporate portfolio debt capacity.

In practice, I have not found a corporation of any complexity in which a determination of portfolio interactions can be done with a strong enough degree of confidence to support major financial decisions. Rather, the International Utilities model is one which this author feels will characterize the complex company of the future.

International Utilities has a variety of major businesses including electric utilities in Canada, an international shipping business, various industrial companies, water utilities, sugar, and real estate interests. International Utilities views itself as a holding company with a portfolio of operating companies and a portfolio of ventures. Each operating company establishes its own capital structure based upon the return, coverage, and stability characteristics discussed earlier. International Utilities finances the ventures until they reach a point of maturity where they develop debt capacity and can sustain their own growth.

The weakness in this structure is that International Utilities essentially gives up the corporate portfolio debt capacity on its total business. The strength is that each business can deal with an institution that understands the real characteristics of that business and who will view a capital structure in the light of what is appropriate for that single business.

Finally, it should be noted that the debt capacity of a business *on trend* far exceeds any debt capacity calculated on the basis of coverage of fixed charges in a bad year. A recent trend, and one with a great deal of logic, is to maintain a corporate portfolio of marketable securities. This portfolio serves as a surge tank against liquidity needs in an adverse business year. The concept is simply to borrow an additional 15 percent of assets as a surge tank. At the outside, the investment returns from that portfolio should be close to the cost of debt money. The average is simply the insurance cost of being able to sustain a high corporate leverage with protection against the short-term liquidity pressures.

Conclusions: The Financial Executive

Rather than restate the observations made thus far, this chapter will stress two points in conclusion. First, it was argued that the equity markets valued performance over and above financial parameters. In the few examples cited—Dow versus Du Pont and the brewing industry, performance outweighed financial risk. Other examples could be cited to indicate that high debt companies sold at lower price-earnings ratios than low debt companies. The problem, however, is that weak companies usually have more debt than strong companies. This is because managements tend to borrow when forced to, rather than as an aggressive, positive strategy.

Paradoxically, the strongest companies with the most debt capacity can grow with minimal leverage while the weakest companies *with the least debt* capacity must borrow to keep up with the industry growth.

The second, and derivative point, is that the key role of the financial executive is to develop a capital structure which is consistent with and which supports overall corporate goals and strategy. This chapter has stressed the role of financial strategy in corporate success. The financial executive cannot view his responsibility as *passive* in minimizing interest costs and raising money in support of operating decisions; rather, he must take an *active* role in meshing financial strategy with the operating goals of the business.

APPENDIX

Derivation of Interest Coverage Equation

1. $$\text{Coverage} = \frac{\text{Earnings}}{\text{Interest}}$$

2. $$\text{Earnings} = \text{Return on assets} \times \text{assets}$$
$$\text{Return on assets} = R$$
$$\text{Assets} = \text{Debt} + \text{equity}$$
$$= D + E$$
$$\text{Earnings} = R(D + E)$$

3. $$\text{Interest} = \text{Interest rate } (i) \times \text{Debt } (D)$$
$$= iD$$

4. $$\text{Coverage } (C) = \frac{R(D + E)}{iD}$$
$$C = \frac{RD + RE}{iD}$$
$$CiD = RD + RE$$
$$\frac{CiD}{E} = R\frac{D}{E} + R\frac{E}{E}$$

$$C = \frac{R\left(\dfrac{D}{E} + 1\right)}{\dfrac{iD}{E}}$$

Derivation of Sustainable Growth Equation

The rate of growth is equal to the firm's return on equity if no dividends are paid. We can define the return (profits) as the rate of return less interest on the debt. Symbolically, this is:

$$\text{Profit} = R(TA) - iD$$

where

$$
\begin{aligned}
R &= \text{After-tax return on assets} \\
TA &= \text{Total assets} \\
i &= \text{Interest rate} \\
D &= \text{Debt} \\
E &= \text{Equity}
\end{aligned}
$$

Since total assets are equal to the sum of debt and equity, we may rewrite the expression as:

$$\text{Profit} = R(D + E) - iD$$

or

$$\text{Profit} = RD + RE - iD$$

If the whole expression is divided through by E (equity), it becomes

$$\frac{\text{Profit}}{\text{Equity}} = R\frac{D}{E} + R\frac{E}{E} - i\frac{D}{E}$$

This can be rewritten as

$$\frac{\text{Profit}}{\text{Equity}} = \frac{D}{E}(R - i) + R$$

or

$$\text{Growth rate} = \frac{D}{E}(R - i) + R$$

Since dividend payments reduce this rate of growth, the effect of dividends may be introduced by multiplying the expression by p, the percent of earnings *retained*. The growth formula thus becomes

$$g = \frac{D}{E}(R - i)p + Rp,$$

where

$$g$$ = Rate of growth
$$D$$ = Debt
$$E$$ = Equity
$$R$$ = After-tax return on assets
$$i$$ = Interest rate
$$p$$ = Percent of earnings retained

ADDITIONAL SOURCES

See Additional Sources at end of Chapter 32.

Chapter 31

Effective Use of Financial Leverage

George E. Williams*

SINCE MONEY is an invention of man, nothing in connection with money is subject to natural or physical law. In the instance of the physical sciences, words are used to define or describe natural phenomena which themselves remain unchanged regardless of the words used to describe them. In contrast with this, financial relationships are strictly man-made and are subject to change. However, the word leverage as applied to finance has been borrowed from simple mechanics. In a mechanical sense it refers to the large force which may be directed to an object through the use of a beam with the fulcrum placed closer to the point where the work is to be performed on the object than it is to the end of the beam where the lesser, prime force is applied. Thus we multiply the effectiveness of an available force.

It was long ago discovered that an analogous situation could exist in financial affairs. Means were developed to multiply the effect of a given amount of investment. The published definitions of this financial phenomenon vary considerably and too often the definition is narrow in concept. For our purposes, it is useful to think of financial leverage as being simply the use of funds for a

---

* George E. Williams is senior vice president—Finance, Otis Elevator Company, New York, New York.

669

business enterprise which were obtained from two or more classes of investors with the expectation that the monetary return to the higher risk class of investor will be enhanced by use of funds from the lower risk class of investor. In the classical case, the owners of the business borrow money and expect that money to earn more than the interest cost. Such a residual would accrue to the owners and increase the return on their own investment. A larger amount of revenue-generating assets and, presumably more profits are attained without an increase in investment by the owners. Their investment is, therefore, said to have been leveraged. The owners have the higher risk, because lenders have a higher priority claim on company assets. However, this is balanced by the owners' potential for a higher return. On the other hand, the lenders have a lower risk but a more limited potential gain; i.e., the fixed interest payment. Pure debt, of course, has a fixed return, but the debt can be convertible or have other features such as warrants to buy common stock on some basis. Thus, an investment can have a mixture of debt and equity characteristics. There is an infinity of possible combinations and, consequently, it is not possible to discuss each variation. It is probably fair to say that the more complex instruments tend to be used when raising funds is difficult. In any event, the issuer of such securities should not only consider their salability but also their effect on leverage. Obviously, after conversion, a typical convertible debenture becomes common stock and the leverage derived from that security disappears.

It is possible also to have leverage within classes of equity holders. Voting preferred stock, for instance, certainly represents equity but the fixed dividend rate on preferred stock acts as a lever in respect to the earnings of the common shareholders.

Not generally recognized is the fact that sources of leverage include not only short- and long-term borrowings but also unpaid amounts for goods and services already received; i.e., accounts payable. Delaying payment of invoices for purchased goods or services as a source of operating funds is more prevalent in Europe than it is in the United States. In Europe it is not uncommon for the unpaid bills to be regularly many months old and since this seems to be accepted practice there, the credit rating of a firm does not suffer. In the United States, payments are generally considered delinquent if not received after some specified term, usually 30 days. Some observers have indicated a trend in the United States toward a slowing of payment in recent years to the point where 45 days or more are not uncommon periods. Thus, it can be said that leverage is the use by an owner or a class of owners of funds supplied by others for the purpose of increasing the net return to the owner or the particular class of owners.

Mathematics and General Application

In order to simplify the mathematical illustrations, we shall concentrate on the use of borrowed money as the source of leverage. The same principles would apply to other sources such as preferred stock.

The reason the use of leverage funds is attractive is that return on equity can be increased by the use of borrowed money if the earnings generated by the borrowed money exceed the cost of the borrowing. A brief description of the mathematics behind this thesis is the simplest way to describe it.

Let us define the following:

R_e = Return on equity
t = Average tax rate
R_b = Return on total investment (before tax and before cost of borrowings)
R_a = Return on total investment (after tax) = $R_b(1 - t)$
E = Equity
D = Debt
T = Total investment = $D + E$
L_T = Debt ratio, or proportion of investment supplied by borrowings = $\dfrac{D}{T}$
i_b = Average interest rate before tax
i_a = Average after-tax cost of borrowing = $i_b(1 - t)$

The mathematical expression for return on equity in terms of the above factors is:

$$R_e = \frac{(R_b T - i_b D)(1 - t)}{E} \tag{1}$$

or

$$R_e = \frac{(R_b - i_b L_T)(1 - t)}{E/T} \tag{2}$$

Since equity (E) is equal to total investment (T) less borrowings (D), or $E = T - D$, by substitution we see that

$$R_e = \frac{(R_b - i_b L_T)(1 - t)}{1 - L_T} \tag{3}$$

On an after-tax basis, that is:

$$R_e = \frac{R_a - i_a L_T}{1 - L_T} \tag{4}$$

For illustration, let return on total investment R_b be 20 percent and $R_a = 10$ percent. Let the cost of borrowing be 10 percent, or $i_a = 0.05$. Let the total investment be \$10 million and the borrowings be \$8 million, or $L_T = 0.8$. The resulting return on equity from this hypothetical situation is 30 percent:

$$R_e = \frac{.1 - (.05)(.8)}{1 - .8} = \frac{.1 - .04}{.2} = \frac{.06}{.2} = .3 \text{ or } 30\%$$

This example shows that it is theoretically possible for a firm earning 10 percent (after taxes) on the total assets employed to have a return on the owner's investment considerably in excess of the rate of return on total investment. Obviously the return on equity would have been only 10 percent without the leverage of the borrowings. By further increasing the proportion of the investment which is supplied by borrowings, the returns on equity of much larger percentages can be demonstrated. Table 1 and the graph in Figure 1 show the relationships.

Note, for example, the return on equity with a debt ratio of 95 percent and a return on assets of 10 percent equals 105 percent. Another significant point illustrated by the curves is the leverage from an increase in the return on total investment. At the condition of an 80 percent debt ratio and a 10 percent return on total assets we had a 30 percent return on equity. If the return on total investment is doubled to 20 percent, the return on equity goes to 80 percent— an increase of 167 percent in the return on equity from a 100 percent increase in the return on total investment.

While the theoretical possibilities may be intriguing, the extreme results would lead the prudent individual to question the practicality. The reasons why such extreme results are ordinarily not attainable will be discussed later. At this point, however, it is im-

TABLE 1
Return on Equity in Relation to Debt Ratio for
$i_a = 5$ **percent**

Debt/Total Investments (L_T)	Return on Total Assets after Tax*	
	= 10%	= 20%
	Return on Equity (R_e)*	Return on Equity (R_e)*
.10	10.6%	21.7%
.20	11.3	23.8
.30	12.1	26.4
.40	13.3	30.0
.50	15.0	35.0
.60	17.5	42.5
.70	21.7	55.0
.80	30.0	80.0
.90	55.0	155.0
.95	105.0	305.0

* The equation is: $R_e = \dfrac{R_a - i_a L_T}{1 - L_T}$

FIGURE 1
Return on Equity versus Debt Ratio for
$R_a = 10\%$ **and** $R_a = 20\%$; $i_a = 5\%$

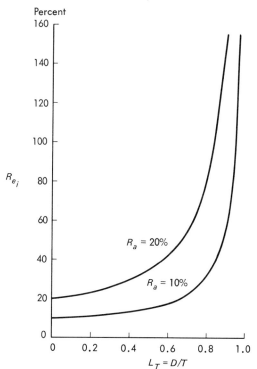

portant to note that high corporate tax rates tend to encourage the use of borrowed funds. With corporate tax rates at approximately 50 percent, the net cost of borrowings is just about half of the payments made to lenders. If tax rates were not so high, the attractiveness of borrowed money compared with equity funds would be far less. Some government officials are beginning to recognize the situation and current proposals include ideas for narrowing the gap such as through tax deductions for dividends.

The use of preferred stock as a source of leverage is generally not mentioned in the literature. It does not, of course, have the tax advantage that exists with debt. However, it is just as real a leverage possibility for the capital manager as is the use of borrowings. As an illustration, consider a company with 1 million common shares and 1 million shares of $10 preferred. If the after-tax profit is $20 million, there remains for the common shareholders $10 million after payment of the preferred dividends and this amounts to $10 per common share. However, if the earnings increase by 10 percent to $22 million, the result, after payment of the dividends on preferred stock, is a residual of $12 per common share or a 20 percent increase. On the other hand, if earnings decrease by 10 percent, the residual earnings per common share drop by 20 percent to only $8 per share. The fixed payment character of the preferred dividend, therefore, provides leverage in the same manner as the fixed interest payment associated with debt.

Another factor in considering the use of leverage in a capital structure is the company's price-earnings ratio for its common shares. This is not a simple matter because the price-earnings ratio might change if investors thought the company was exceeding prudent limits in its use of debt. Some stockholders might feel, on the other hand, that a company was not taking advantage of leverage opportunities if its debt was too small a part of its total capitalization. However, this latter opinion is not likely to have a depressing effect on the stock as long as the earnings are good and continue to grow. Because of possible effects on the market price of the stock, decisions on borrowing cannot be made solely from the mathematics based on the effect of price-earnings ratios, but they do need to be considered. For illustration, consider a company with 1 million shares and $10 million of earnings ($10 per share), with a 5 percent after-tax cost of money. The assumption is made that to buy its own stock, the firm will borrow money; and conversely it will retire debt when it sells stock. Table 2 shows the effect of the price-earnings ratio on leverage considerations.

The reciprocal of the 20 to 1 price-earnings ratio is 0.05. Therefore, at the 5 percent net cost of money and a 20 to 1 price-earnings

TABLE 2
Effect of Buying Shares and Adding Debt

Price-Earnings Ratio	10	20	30
Company action on:			
Stock.	Buy 100,000 shares	Buy 100,000 shares	Buy 100,000 shares
Debt	Add $10,000,000	Add $20,000,000	Add $30,000,000
Net interest cost.	Up $500,000	Up $1,000,000	Up $1,500,000
Result:			
Earnings	$9,500,000	$9,000,000	$8,500,000
Shares	900,000	900,000	900,000
Earnings per share . . .	$10.56	$10.00	$9.44

ratio, the earnings per share cannot be affected by adding debt because the cost of the debt equals the cost of the retired equity. If the price-earnings ratio is less than 20 to 1, the earnings per share can be increased by buying shares and replacing them with relatively cheaper debt. If the price-earnings ratio exceeds 20, the earnings per share would be decreased by buying stock and selling the relatively more costly debt.

The converse results (Table 3) follow when stock is sold to retire

TABLE 3
Effect of Selling Shares and Retiring Debt

Price-Earnings Ratio	10	20	30
Company action on:			
Stock.	Sell 100,000 shares	Sell 100,000 shares	Sell 100,000 shares
Debt	Retire $10,000,000	Retire $20,000,000	Retire $30,000,000
Net interest cost.	Down $500,000	Down $1,000,000	Down $1,500,000
Result:			
Earnings	$10,500,000	$11,000,000	$11,500,000
Shares	1,100,000	1,100,000	1,100,000
Earnings per share . . .	$9.54	$10.00	$10.45

5 percent after-tax debt. At a price-earnings ratio below 20, earnings per share are decreased. But at a price-earnings ratio above 20, earnings per share are increased by retiring the relatively more costly debt.

As noted earlier, an increase in leverage can result in a lower price-earnings ratio. Therefore, even if the earnings per share were to rise, the stock price may not. It could even decline. When this happens, the market has judged implicitly that the increase in returns provided by the leverage is not sufficient to compensate for the accompanying increase in risk. The stock market, therefore, tends to limit the amount of leverage which can be successfully used. These interactions suggest other interesting relationships. As interest rates go up, stock prices tend to go down and price-earnings ratios drop. At lower price-earnings ratios the break point between advantageous borrowing and advantageous selling of stock comes at a higher interest rate. If stock prices, price-earnings ratios and interest rates moved exactly proportionately, we see that the break point for a company would not change with changes in interest rates. Of course, actual relationships are not usually that neat, but awareness of these factors may help in financial planning.

Trading on the Equity

Trading on the equity is a term often applied to the use of leverage and the degree to which this is done varies from company to company and industry to industry. For manufacturing industries, however, there is usually a very narrow range of average leverage among different industries although there are significant differences from company to company. Recent data for manufacturing firms show the ratio of liabilities to net worth from one major industry to another is within the range of 0.4 to 1.2, with most industries falling in the narrow range of 0.6 to 0.8. When one looks at non-manufacturing companies, especially those in banking and insurance, we find the picture significantly different. Here we find ratios of total liabilities to net worth up to almost 30; and 10 is common. For example, one of the nation's leading banks has a ratio of liabilities to net worth of about 22. Yet we can safely assume that a manufacturing firm applying for a loan to this bank would be given little consideration if its ratio of liabilities to net worth was even half of 22. Banks are in the business of borrowing money to lend to others. This function implies a high degree of leverage. Financial institutions, in fact, differ from most other businesses in that their product and their raw materials consist of money, not goods. However, even with the special care and attention they get from the government, they are not without risk. It is felt that many banks today need a greater equity base. The preceding is intended to illustrate the point that there is no one acceptable degree of leverage, or trading on the equity. A firm should adopt that degree of leverage which is appropriate considering all factors, including the certainty of its profits.

Risk Assumption

The supplier of funds to a business has a degree of risk which depends in part on the terms under which he has supplied the funds. It is generally accepted that the common stockholder occupies the position of greatest risk and the lender of funds has the position of least risk. In-between, of course, is the preferred stockholder. Within a group of lenders of money, there may be a hierarchy with some loans being subordinate to others. There is established by law and contract a "pecking order" so that it is understood who gets hurt first and last in case the company encounters financial difficulties.

The pure lenders of money expect a constant rate of return without any benefit from an increase in profits and they expect to receive this return while cash is available even if the company is operating at a loss. The equity investment is looked upon as a reservoir from which payments can be made to debt holders in case of difficulty. Even with small amounts of leverage, this is not a perfect protection to the debt holders and they are theoretically faced with some risk. When the debt risk is significant, potential lenders demand higher interest rates as compensation for the risk. If leverage has increased to the point where the lender believes his risk is about the same as that assumed by the equity holders, he is likely to require an interest rate equal to or greater than the return which most equity holders would hope to receive. Thus, the money market places a limit on the degree of leverage by its cognizance of risk. The risk to the equity holders also increases as the degree of leverage increases. We have seen earlier that leverage can increase the return to the owners when the rate of return on total investment did not change. What happens if the rate of return drops? The leverage is still there, of course, and the drop in profit is multiplied in its effect on the equity holders. In a previous example we showed the potential gain to the owners of a company with $10 million of total investment of which $8 million was borrowed. With a pretax

cost of money of 10 percent and a return after taxes on total investment of 10 percent before interest charges, the owners made a return of 30 percent. For the purposes of this presentation we need
to consider the change in tax effect when there is no profit or when
a loss occurs. For simplicity, the tax rate is taken as 50 percent and
it is assumed that there is no benefit from a tax loss carry-back.
Table 4 and Figure 2 show the effects of changes in the rate of re-

TABLE 4
Calculations for the Graph in Figure 2

R_b	Case	$2.5\,R_b$	$5.0\,R_b$	R_e
.20.	1	.50	—	.30
.15.	1	.375	—	.175
.10.	1	.25	—	.05
.08.	1	.20	—	0
.05.	2	—	.25	−.15
0	2	—	0	−.40
−.05.	2	—	−.25	−.65
−.10.	2	—	−.50	−.90
−.12.	2	—	−.60	−1.00

turn to total investment on the return on equity. The relationships
are as follow:

Formulae:

Case 1.   Interest charges are covered

$$R_e = \frac{R_b(1 - t) - i_b(1 - t)L_T}{1 - L_T}$$

$$R_e = \frac{R_b(1 - .5) - (.1)(1 - .5)(.8)}{1 - (.8)} = \frac{.5R_b - .04}{.2}$$

$$R_e = 2.5R_b - .2$$

Case 2.   Interest charges not covered

$$R_e = \frac{R_b - i_b L_T}{1 - L_T}$$

$$R_e = \frac{R_b - (.1)(.8)}{1 - (.8)} = \frac{R_b - .08}{.2}$$

$$R_e = 5R_b - .40$$

The cutoff point occurs where operating income equals interest payments; i.e., $R_e = 0$. The corresponding value of R_b is calculated as follows:

$$R_e = 2.5R_b - .2$$
$$0 = 2.5R_b - .2$$
$$2.5R_b = .2$$
$$R_b = .08$$

In Figure 2 there is a change in the slope of the line when the

FIGURE 2
Return on Equity (R_e) as a Function of Return on Total Investment (R_b)

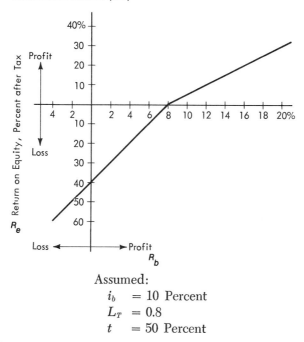

Assumed:
i_b = 10 Percent
L_T = 0.8
t = 50 Percent

dollar return on total investment is just equal to the dollar cost of interest. Under these circumstances the equity holders lose money if the total pretax return drops below 8 percent. This means that equity holders can lose money while the company is making a positive return on total investment. If there is zero operating profit during the year, the equity holders lose 40 percent of their investment. By extrapolation it can be seen that a 12 percent loss on total investment wipes out the equity. Leverage, therefore, works both ways; i.e., losses are magnified as well as profits. The degree of leverage which can be achieved will depend on the stability and certainty of future earnings. For example, it is well known that public utilities tend to a greater degree of leverage than most industrial groups. This is because lenders of money traditionally (before the recent inflation crunch) have had a relatively high confidence in their future stream of earnings.

It is worth taking a moment to consider this industry as an example of the need to be constantly alert to changing conditions when considering leverage. At the current time in the United States, there is a growing uncertainty as to the future of the utility industry. The growing uncertainty comes from the high rate of inflation and the public attitude. As regulated businesses, they are not free to increase prices, even under the condition of rising costs, without approval from the regulating authority. There may be sufficient anti-business sentiment among the population, reflected in the regulating bodies, to preclude utility prices rising at the same rate as their costs during periods of high inflation. Consequently, the old assumptions on which utility financing was based may need reappraisal. The ultimate result of utility earnings being below the level needed to attract private investment is government take over. Then the investment is no longer optional; it becomes required and is forced upon people through taxation. The point is that the probability of future earnings as a determinant of possible leverage within an industry will change from one period of time to another. Historical precedent is not a perfect guide.

It is not possible to establish an unchanging mathematical limit for a company's leverage. There are judgments which must be made as to the certainty of earnings and the reaction which is likely to occur within the money market as leverage increases. In recent years the proportion of capital which has been supplied by debt for industrial firms has increased. For the companies included in Moody's Industrial Average, the long-term debt increased from 14 percent of total capitalization in 1966 to 22 percent at the end of 1972.

The corporation's management will naturally give consideration to the effect on existing stockholders of the increased use of leverage. The decision to use borrowed funds arises from the belief that it will benefit the stockholders. Stock market prices may be down and the price-earnings ratio low. At some point, though, too much leverage will place the stockholders in a precarious position in terms of weathering the storm of decreased earnings. Balancing the risk and return trade-off from use of leverage is one of financial management's responsibilities. It is a responsibility which may be difficult to carry out under some circumstances. Such measures as the interest coverage ratio are commonly used to aid in making these judgments. In addition, the degree to which total operating costs, other than interest, are relatively fixed is a consideration. This latter factor might be considered the operating leverage as contrasted with financial leverage. The result of high operating leverage is to have large swings in operating earnings from relatively small changes in sales volume. The judgments as to the level of future earnings and cash flow, stock market reactions to further borrowings, and so on are almost always difficult and bound to be imprecise.

Actual Leverage Results

Proponents of high leverage point to the high corporate tax rates and say it is foolish not to use borrowed money. Some think the more the better. As discussed above, things are not that simple. If they were we should expect to see a general pattern of companies with high leverage having a higher return on equity than those companies having low leverage.

From an analysis of a *Fortune* "500" list of industrial firms a study was made in which those companies with the highest return on equity were compared to those with the lowest return on equity. A summary of the results is shown below.

	Companies with Highest Return on Equity	Companies with Lowest Return on Equity
Average total assets (in $ millions)	$1,406	$1,088
Average ratio liabilities to assets.	.40	.51
Average ratio equity to assets	.60	.49
Lowest ratio equity to assets	.32	.10
Highest ratio equity to assets	.80	.72
Average return on equity	18.8%	3.7%

The companies with the highest return on equity had the lowest leverage. The result of this investigation does not support the proponents of high leverage. Of course, one could argue that the high return companies could have done better with more leverage but certainly the argument is theoretical and without statistical support. It may be noted that companies with a loss were excluded from the data tabulated above.

There are several possible explanations for the anomaly that low leverage companies tend to have a higher return on equity than high leverage companies. One may be that companies with good earnings have less need to obtain outside financing because internal cash generation is sufficient for their needs. Another explanation may be that management who are skilled at making operating profits tend to be conservative in matters of risk such as leverage. Whatever the reason, it is clear that the recent experience of American industry does not show a correlation between high leverage and high return on equity.

Perspective

The preceding brief discussion touches on some aspects of financial leverage as known today. Man's imagination will continue to develop new relationships for which some of the details of this discourse will not apply. For example, the founding of a new business may well involve a mixture of debt and equity in its capital structure. The owners of the debt may also be owners of some of the equity. Certain of the owners of the equity may have invested relatively little cash. Perhaps they had the idea or product on which the company is based and their contribution is that idea or product plus the application of their time and energy. The mixture of debt and equity in this case is not determined from the identical leverage considerations which exist in a going business. For, in fact, the risk of loss may be very nearly the same for the debt portion of the capital as it is for the equity portion.

But a very important point on leverage is to keep its function in proper perspective. The primary objectives of a business manager include generating a profit for the owner-investors and avoiding the dissipation of the assets invested. Financial leverage does not generate operating profit. It only affects how the operating profits are distributed to various groups such as common shareholders, preferred shareholders, debt holders, and the tax collector. This can be a significant role, but must be secondary, since benefits of leverage will not occur if there are no operating profits to distribute.

Consequently, the first task of the financial officer is to aid in the production of an operating profit. Only then can he consider making use of financial leverage to increase the proportionate flow to equity holders.

The responsibility to avoid dissipation of assets also takes precedence over the fine points of leverage management. All financial officers recognize the responsibility to prevent theft of assets, but far greater losses occur from ineptness than from dishonesty. Consequently, first emphasis must be placed on making good management decisions. They are dependent upon the skills of the people involved and the aptness and validity of the data available. Among the important decisions which could result in dissipation of assets are those relating to financial leverage. As noted earlier, too much leverage with insufficient operating profits can quickly dissipate the assets of the equity owners. Bankruptcy is the ultimate threat. Restrictions on growth as the possible alternative to high-risk leverage when equity funds are hard to raise are naturally unpleasant, but not as unpleasant as bankruptcy. Even without reaching the extreme of bankruptcy, too much leverage can have the bad effect of diminishing the company's flexibility. Because of earlier decisions to finance with debt instead of equity, including retained earnings, a firm can find itself at some crucial moment not being able to raise funds to take advantage of a new opportunity or need. This can mean a deteriorating competitive position having long-term implications for the company.

In summary, it seems that the prudent company will emphasize operating profits, as measured by return on total assets. It will try to make any judgments as to degree of leverage in the direction of better too little than too much.

ADDITIONAL SOURCES

See Additional Sources at end of Chapter 32.

Chapter 32

Leverage and the Cost of Capital

J. Fred Weston[*]

THIS CHAPTER analyzes the effects of the use of debt on the firm's cost of capital.

The definitions of terms frequently used are first reviewed. Asset structure is the left-hand side of the balance sheet—the assets or investment of the firm which must be financed. Financial structure is the right-hand side of the balance sheet—all sources of financing. Capital structure (capitalization) is financing long-term sources, including long-term debt, preferred stock, and net worth. The capital structure or capitalization of the firm is therefore equal to total assets less current liabilities. Financial leverage is the ratio of total debt to net worth, called the debt-equity ratio. Business risk is the variability of the expected return resulting from the product-market mix activities of the firm. Operating risk reflects the degree of operating leverage employed by the firm—the relative proportion of fixed and variable costs in the firm's cost structure. Financial risk is the risk compounded on business and operating risk resulting from the use of financial leverage.

This chapter is taken from Chapter 14 in J. Fred Weston, *Programmed Learning Aid for Financial Management* (Homewood, Ill.: Learning Systems Company, 1975).

[*] J. Fred Weston is professor of business economics and finance, University of California, Los Angeles.

DESIGNING THE CAPITAL STRUCTURE OF THE FIRM

To determine the optimal capital structure of the firm requires an application of the theory of financial leverage. If the return on assets exceeds the cost of debt, leverage may increase the returns to equity. However, leverage also increases the degree of fluctuations in the returns to equity for any given degree of fluctuations in sales and the return on assets. Leverage increases the returns to owners if used successfully, but if leverage is unsuccessful, the result may be bankruptcy.

These generalizations are now illustrated, Table 1 provides data for calculating the return on equity under alternative leverage and profitability conditions.

TABLE 1
Return on Common Stock under Alternative Leverage and Profitability Conditions

	Profitability Conditions						
	Very Poor	*Poor*	*Marginal*	*Below Average*	*Normal*	*Good*	*Very Good*
Rate of return on total assets	2%	6%	8%	12%	18%	22%	25%
(EBIT)	$2	$6	$8	$12	$18	$22	$25
Firm A: Leverage factor 0%							
EBIT	$2	$6	$8	$12	$18	$22	$25
Less: Interest expense	0	0	0	0	0	0	0
Taxable income	$2	$6	$8.00	$12	$18	$22	$25
Taxes	1	3	4	6	9	11	12.5
Profit after taxes	$1	$3	$4	$ 6	$ 9	$11	$12.5
Return on equity	1%	3%	4%	6%	9%	11%	12.5%
Firm B: Leverage factor 50%							
EBIT	$2	$6	$8	$12	$18	$22	$25
Less: Interest expense	4	4	4	4	4	4	4
Taxable income	($2)	$2	$4	$ 8	$14	$18	$21
Taxes	(1)	1	2	4	7	9	10.5
Profit after taxes	($1)	$1	$2	$ 4	$ 7	$ 9	$10.5
Return on equity	(2%)	2%	4%	8%	14%	18%	21%
Firm C: Leverage factor 80%							
EBIT	$2	$6	$8	$12	$18	$22	$25
Less: Interest expense	6.40	6.40	6.40	6.40	6.40	6.40	6.40
Taxable income	($4.40)	($0.40)	$1.60	$ 5.60	$11.60	$15.60	$18.60
Taxes	(2.20)	(0.20)	0.80	2.80	5.80	7.80	9.30
Profit after taxes	($2.20)	($0.20)	$0.80	$ 2.80	$ 5.80	$ 7.80	$ 9.30
Return on equity	(11%)	(1%)	4%	14%	29%	39%	46.5%

In line 1 of Table 1, the rates of return on total assets before interest and taxes are set forth under alternative profitability conditions ranging from very poor to very good. It is assumed that the firm has total assets of 100, hence the second row, entitled earnings before interest and taxes (EBIT), represents the first row with the percentage translated into dollars. The rate of interest on debt is 8 percent, and the tax rate is 50 percent.

The first line for each firm, EBIT, represents the data from the profitability conditions. Since Firm A employs no leverage, the interest expense is zero. The rate of return on common stock would be one half the rate of return on total assets because income would be reduced 50 percent by taxes, and the firm's net worth is equal to its total assets.

Firm B has a leverage factor of 50 percent so that its debt is 50 percent of total assets. At an 8 percent interest rate, its interest expense would be $4. The percent return on equity for Firm B ranges from −2 percent to +21 percent. Its range is 23 percentage points as compared with the range of 11.5 percentage points for Firm A. For Firm C the leverage factor is 80 percent—the ratio of debt to equity is four times. Its interest expense would be 8 percent times $80, or $6.40. The percentage return on common stock ranges from −11.0 percent to +46.5 percent, a total range of 57.5 percent. This example shows how leverage increases the variability of the return on common stock, also illustrated in Figure 1. The return on net worth degrees of leverage intersect the zero leverage return on net worth lines at the return on asset rate equal to the before-tax interest cost of debt.

The effects of leverage on profitability are next expressed in terms of earnings per share under the assumption that at higher degrees of leverage, the cost of debt may increase. The data are set forth in Tables 2A and 2B. The right-hand side of the balance sheet is shown in Table 2A for four cases representing different degrees of leverage ranging from no leverage to a leverage ratio of 75 percent. In Table 2B, data are set forth for sales with the associated probabilities for achieving each indicated level of sales, and the total cost structure of the firm is also included. Sales less total operating costs would represent earnings before interest and taxes (EBIT). The effect on earnings per share of the four leverage situations is also developed in Table 2B. With no leverage, earnings per share range from a loss of $0.75 per share to a gain of $1 per share. With lever-

FIGURE 1

**Return on Net Worth as a Function of the Return on Assets
under Alternative Leverage Rates**

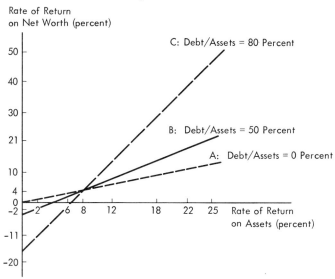

age of 75 percent the range is from a loss of $3.60 per share to a gain of $3.40 per share.

The variability of returns is greater under the higher leverage case. But what is the profitability in relation to the variations in returns? This question is analyzed in Table 3. The probabilities set forth in Table 2B are applied to indicated earnings per share for each of the four cases. Thus, it can be seen that the expected return is highest under the 50 percent leverage factor. In addition, the variance and standard deviation of the earnings per share results are also calculated, and as before, the variability of earnings per share increases with increased leverage. In each case, the coefficient of variation is calculated by dividing the standard deviation by average earnings per share, and it rises from 2.43 in Case I to 17.06 in Case IV.

In Case IV the expected earnings per share drop to $0.10 because the after-tax cost of debt capital is so high. Hence, we can rule Case IV out as a possible desired level of leverage. In Cases I through III, the expected earnings per share rises, but the standard deviation rises even more, so that the coefficient of variation increases as

TABLE 2A
Financial Structure from the Balance Sheet

	Case I		Case II		Case III		Case IV	
	No Leverage		Leverage 25%		Leverage 50%		Leverage 75%	
Total debt	0		$100		$200		$300	
Interest rate applicable. . . .	5%		5%		10%		20%	
Common stock, par $1	$200		$150		$100		$50	
Retained earnings.	200		150		100		50	
Total equity	$400		$300		$200		$100	
Total Assets.	$400		$400		$400		$400	

TABLE 2B
Analysis of Effects of Leverage

	Probability of Achieving Indicated Sales						
	5%	10%	30%	25%	15%	10%	5%
Sales	$ 200	$ 400	$800	$1,000	$1,200	$1,400	$1,600
Total costs (400 + 0.5 S).	$ 500	600	800	900	1,000	1,100	1,200
Earnings before Interest and Taxes. .	$(300)	$(200)	$ 0	$ 100	$ 200	$ 300	$ 400

Effects on earnings per share
Case I—no leverage:

Interest expense.	0	0	0	0	0	0	0
Profit before taxes	$(300)	$(200)	$ 0	$ 100	$ 200	$ 300	$ 400
Profit after taxes	(150)	(100)	0	50	100	150	200
Earnings per share (200*)	(.75)	(.50)	0	.25	.50	.75	1.00

Case II—leverage 25%:

Interest expense.	5	5	5	5	5	5	5
Profit before taxes	(305)	(205)	(5)	95	195	295	395
Profit after taxes	(152)	(102)	(2)	48	98	148	198
Earnings per share (150*)	(1.01)	(.68)	(.01)	.32	.65	.99	1.32

Case III—leverage 50%:

Interest expense.	20	20	20	20	20	20	20
Profit before taxes	(320)	(220)	(20)	80	180	280	380
Profit after taxes	(160)	(110)	(10)	40	90	140	190
Earnings per share (100*)	(1.60)	(1.10)	(.10)	.40	.90	1.40	1.90

Case IV—leverage 75%:

Interest expense.	60	60	60	60	60	60	60
Profit before taxes	(360)	(260)	(60)	40	140	240	340
Profit after taxes	(180)	(130)	(30)	20	70	120	170
Earnings per share (50*)	(3.60)	(2.60)	(.60)	.40	1.40	2.40	3.40

* Number of shares of common stock.

TABLE 3
Computation of Expected EPS and Measures of Dispersion

Probability	EPS	pEPS	$(EPS - \overline{EPS})$*	$(EPS - \overline{EPS})^2$	$p(EPS - \overline{EPS})^2$
Case I—no leverage					
.05	(.75)	(.0375)	(.925)	.8556	.0428
.10	(.50)	(.0500)	(.675)	.4556	.0456
.30	0	.0000	(.175)	.0306	.0092
.25	.25	.0625	.075	.0056	.0014
.15	.50	.0750	.325	.1056	.0158
.10	.75	.0750	.575	.3306	.0331
.05	1.00	.0500	.825	.6806	.0340
		E(EPS) = .1750	CV = σ/E(EPS) = 2.43		σ² = .1819 σ = .4260
Case II—leverage 25%					
.05	(1.01)	(.0505)	(1.231)	1.5150	.0758
.10	(0.68)	(.0680)	(0.901)	.8118	.0812
.30	(0.01)	(.0030)	(0.231)	.0534	.0160
.25	0.32	.0800	.099	.0098	.0025
.15	0.65	.0975	.429	.1840	.0276
.10	0.99	.0990	.769	.5914	.0591
.05	1.32	.0660	1.099	1.2078	.0604
		E(EPS) = .2210	CV = σ/E(EPS) = 2.57		σ² = .3226 σ = .5680
Case III—leverage 50%					
.05	(1.60)	(.080)	(1.85)	3.4225	.1711
.10	(1.10)	(.110)	(1.35)	1.8225	.1823
.30	(0.10)	(.030)	(0.35)	0.1225	.0368
.25	0.40	.100	0.15	0.0225	.0056
.15	0.90	.135	0.65	0.4225	.0634
.10	1.40	.140	1.15	1.3225	.1323
.05	1.90	.095	1.65	2.7225	.1361
		E(EPS) = .250	CV = σ/E(EPS) = 3.41		σ² = .7276 σ = .8530
Case IV—leverage 75%					
.05	(3.60)	(.18)	(3.70)	13.69	.6845
.10	(2.60)	(.26)	(2.70)	7.29	.7290
.30	(0.60)	(.18)	(0.70)	0.49	.1470
.25	0.40	.10	0.30	0.09	.0225
.15	1.40	.21	1.30	1.69	.2535
.10	2.40	.24	2.30	5.29	.5290
.05	3.40	.17	3.30	10.89	.5445
		E(EPS) = .10	CV = σ/E(EPS) = 17.06		σ² = 2.910 σ = 1.706

* $\overline{EPS}$ is the same as E(EPS).

well. The choice among the three remaining possibilities would depend upon the influence of greater risk per dollar of expected return on the firm's cost of capital. Therefore, the groundwork has been established for turning to a consideration of the fundamental relationship between these two variables.

THE EFFECTS OF LEVERAGE ON THE COST OF CAPITAL

Professors Modigliani and Miller (referred to as MM) set forth two propositions for a world of pure and perfect competition, with no taxes:

$$\rho = \frac{\bar{X}}{V_u} \text{ (MM proposition I)} \tag{1}$$

$$k = \rho + (\rho - i)\frac{D}{E} \text{ (MM proposition II)} \tag{2}$$

Symbols are explained in Table 4.

TABLE 4
Symbols Used in Discussion of Costs of Capital Theorems

ρ = The cost of capital of an unlevered firm.
$\bar{X}$ = Expected EBIT.
V = Total value of a levered firm = D + E = V_u + tD.
V_u = The value of an unlevered firm.
π = Net income available to common stock holders.
k = Cost of equity capital for a levered firm.
i = Cost of debt.
E = Equity value of a firm.
D = Value of the debt of a levered firm.
t = Tax rate.
(WACC) = Weighted average cost of capital = $k\left(\frac{E}{V}\right) + i\left(\frac{D}{V}\right)$.
$\wedge$ = Refers to after-tax measures.

Proposition I states that the cost of capital of an unlevered firm is equal to the net operating income (or earnings before interest and taxes) divided by the value of the firm. Proposition II states that the cost of equity capital rises linearly with the debt-to-equity ratio. These propositions are illustrated in Table 5.

Summary income statements and summary balance sheets for a levered and an unlevered firm are presented in Table 5. Proposition I is calculated by dividing EBIT by the total value of the firm to obtain 20 percent. Proposition II states that the return on equity is: Overall cost of capital of an unlevered firm plus the difference between this cost of capital and the cost of debt, weighted by the leverage ratio. This is 30 percent. Alternatively, the final profit term in the income statement of $60,000 can be divided by the equity value of $200,000 to again obtain 30 percent.

This illustration indicates the plausibility of the MM propositions: in a no-tax world, leverage has no influence on a firm's cost of capital. As shown in the table, the weighted average cost of capital remains constant regardless of the degree of leverage.

TABLE 5
Illustration of MM's Propositions—No Taxes

Facts	*No Leverage*	*50% Leverage*	*75% Leverage*
Income statement			
Sales	$800,000	$800,000	$800,000
Total costs.	720,000	720,000	720,000
EBIT = $\bar{X}$	$ 80,000	$ 80,000	$ 80,000
Interest.		20,000	30,000
Profit = π.	$ 80,000	$ 60,000	$ 50,000
Balance sheet (at market values)*			
Value of debt (D)	0	$200,000	$300,000
Equity value (E).	$400,000	$200,000	$100,000

Calculations:

No leverage

$$\rho = \frac{\$ \; 80,000}{\$400,000} = .20$$

50% leverage (i = 10%)

$$k = .20 + (.20 - .10)1$$
$$= .30$$
$$k = \frac{\pi}{E} = \frac{\$ \; 60,000}{\$200,000} = .30$$
$$(WACC) = .30(\tfrac{1}{2}) + .10(\tfrac{1}{2}) = .20$$

75% leverage (i = 10%)

$$k = .20 + (.20 - .10)3$$
$$= .50$$
$$k = \frac{\pi}{E} = \frac{\$ \; 50,000}{\$100,000} = .50$$
$$(WACC) = .50(\tfrac{1}{4}) + .10(\tfrac{3}{4}) = .125 + .075 = .20$$

* No leverage $\frac{D}{E}$ = 0; 50% leverage $\frac{D}{E}$ = 1; 75% leverage $\frac{D}{E}$ = 3.

THE COST OF CAPITAL WITH TAXES

The MM propositions for a world with taxes are set forth in Table 6 in equations (3) through (7). The facts are the same as in Table 5 with the addition of a corporate tax rate of 40 percent.

The calculation of the cost of equity capital for the unlevered firm begins with the relations between the value of an unlevered

TABLE 6
Illustration of MM's Propositions—With Taxes

Facts*	No Leverage	50% Leverage
Income statement:		
Sales	$800,000	$800,000
Total costs.	720,000	720,000
EBIT = $\overline{X}$	$ 80,000	$ 80,000
Interest.	0	20,000
PBT.	$ 80,000	$ 60,000
Taxes.	32,000	24,000
Profit after tax	$ 48,000	$ 36,000

Calculations:

MM II. Cost of equity capital

No leverage

$$V_u = V - tD \tag{3}$$
$$V_u = 400,000 - .4(200,000)$$
$$= 320,000$$

$$\hat{k} = \frac{\overline{X}(1-t)}{V_u} = \hat{p}_u \tag{4}$$

$$\hat{p}_u = \frac{(80,000)(.6)}{320,000} = \frac{48,000}{320,000} = .15$$

50% leverage

$$\hat{k} = \hat{p}_u + (\hat{p}_u - i)\frac{D(1-t)}{E} \tag{5}$$
$$= .15 + (.15 - .10)(0.6)$$
$$\hat{k} = .18$$

MM I. Cost of capital

No leverage

$$(\hat{WACC})_u = \frac{\overline{X}(1-t)}{V_u} = \hat{p}_u = .15 \tag{4}$$

50% leverage

$$(\hat{WACC})_L = \frac{\overline{X}(1-t)}{V} \tag{6}$$

$$= \frac{48,000}{400,000} = .12$$

$$(\hat{WACC})_L = i(1-t)\frac{D}{V} + \hat{k}\frac{E}{V} \tag{7}$$
$$= .10(.6)(.5) + (.18)(.5)$$
$$= .03 + .09 = .12$$

* Same as Table 5 plus $t = 40\%$.

firm and the value of the levered firm set forth in equation (3). The value of an unlevered firm is smaller than the value of a levered firm by the amount of the tax shelter lost by not using debt, as measured by the term: the tax rate times total debt. Since the value of a levered firm is $400,000, the value of the unlevered firm would be this amount, less 0.4 × $200,000, or $320,000. The cost of equity capital for the unlevered firm can then be calculated as set forth in equation (4), yielding 15 percent.

The after-tax cost of equity capital for the levered firm can then be calculated by equation (5). Inserting the appropriate information yields an after-tax cost of equity for the levered firm of 18 percent, 3 percentage points higher than the cost of equity capital for the unlevered firm. Equation (5) yields a result consistent with that of equation (4). Since the unlevered firm has no leverage, the second term of equation (5) becomes zero, and the cost of equity for the unlevered firm would be 15 percent.

Next, the overall cost of capital can be calculated. The overall cost of capital for the unlevered firm is the same as its cost of equity capital since the unlevered firm is all-equity financed. The weighted average cost of capital for the levered firm can first be calculated by using equation (6). This is the same as equation (4), except that the value of the levered firm is used in the denominator. The weighted average cost of capital for the levered firm is 12 percent, as shown in Table 6. A check on the calculation of the weighted average cost of capital for the levered firm can be achieved by using the weighted proportions of the cost of debt and the cost of equity capital. This is set forth in equation (7) in Table 6. Inserting the appropriate figures, the result confirms that the weighted average cost of capital is 12 percent. The weighted average cost of capital for the levered firm is lower than for the unlevered firm because of the tax shelter benefits achieved by the levered firm but not achieved by the unlevered firm.

The cost of capital comparisons for the levered and unlevered firms can be generalized under the alternative assumptions set forth in Figure 2. In panel 2A, the traditional view holds that the cost of

FIGURE 2
Alternative Theories of Cost of Capital Functions

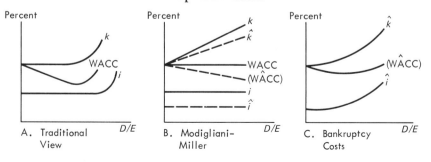

debt or equity does not rise until leverage becomes "excessive." The solid lines in panel 2B reflect the assumptions of no taxes and no bankruptcy costs, also in the original MM propositions. The cost of capital is the same as previously described. Under these assumptions "leverage does not matter." The broken lines in panel 2B depict a world with corporate taxes but no bankruptcy costs. In this world, the cost of capital for a levered firm decreases as compared with the cost of capital for an unlevered firm: the more leverage the lower the cost of capital for the leveraged firm. This implies extremely high leverage ratios not observed in the actual world.

The actual world appears to be reflected in Panel 2C. For small amounts of debt well within the margin of safety to creditors and owners, the cost of debt and cost of equity functions are approximately linear. In this range, the overall cost of capital is declining, as in Panel 2B, because it is a world with corporate taxes, but bankruptcy costs have not yet affected the relationships. At some leverage, however, the risks of bankruptcy costs increase to the point where both the cost of debt and the cost of equity begin to rise. During some range, two opposing forces are operative. The tax effect tends to pull down the overall cost of capital for the levered firm. At some point, however, the increased risk of bankruptcy costs causes the cost of debt function and the cost of equity function to rise with sufficient steepness to begin to pull up the cost of capital for the levered firm. The weighted average cost of capital curve is relatively flat in the area of its minimum level.

THE COST OF CAPITAL AS AN INVESMENT HURDLE RATE

The capital asset pricing model permits the criteria for asset expansion decisions to be set out unambiguously and compactly. It generalizes the more traditional weighted average cost of capital approach. In the case that follows, some illustrative materials for the application of the market price of risk (MPF) criteria, as compared with the WACC criteria, are provided.

Statement of the Mostin Company Case. The Mostin Company is considering four projects in a capital expansion program. The vice president of finance has estimated that the firm's weighted average cost of capital (WACC) is 12 percent. The economics staff projected the future course of the market portfolio over the estimated life span of the projects under each of the four states of the world (first three columns in Table 7); it recommended the use of a risk-free rate of return of 4 percent. The finance department provided the estimates of project returns conditional on the state of the world (columns 4 through 7 in Table 7). Each project involves an outlay of approximately $50,000.

TABLE 7
Summary of Information—Mostin Case

(1)	(2)	(3)	(4)	(5)	(6)	(7)
					Rates of Return	
State of World (s)	*Subjective Probability* (p_s)	*Market Return* R_{ms}	*Project 1*	*Project 2*	*Project 3*	*Project 4*
$s = 1$. 1		−.30	−.46	−1.00	−.40	−.40
$s = 2$. 2		−.10	−.26	−0.50	−.20	−.20
$s = 3$. 3		.10	.46	0.00	.00	.60
$s = 4$. 4		.30	.00	1.00	.70	.00

Assuming that the projects are independent and that the firm can raise sufficient funds to finance all four projects, which projects would be accepted using the WACC and MPR criteria?

Solution Procedure for the Mostin Company Case. The solution procedures for the Mostin case are as follows. The data provided by market relationships are utilized to calculate the expected return on the market along with its variance and standard deviation in Table 8. A similar procedure is followed in Table 9 for calculating

TABLE 8
Solution Procedure for Calculation of Market Parameters

(1) p	(2) R_m	(3) pR_m	(4) $R_m - E(R_m)$	(5) $[R_m - E(R_m)]^2$	(6) $p[(R_m - E(R_m)]^2$
.1.	−.30	−.03	−.40	.16	.016
.2.	−.10	−.02	−.20	.04	.008
.3.	.10	.03	0	0	0
.4.	.30	.12	.20	.04	.016
		$E(R_m) = .10$			Var $R_m = .040$
					$\sigma_m = .20$

the expected return and the covariance for each of the four individual projects.

In Table 10, the beta (β) for each project is calculated as the ratio of its covariance to the variance of the market return. The resulting betas in Table 10 range from a low of 0.60 to a high of 3.50.

Since the size of the beta is an index of the degree of risk or volatility of each individual investment project, it is used in Table

TABLE 9
Calculation of Expected Returns and Covariances for the Four Hypothetical Projects

(1) Project Number	(2) p	(3) R_j	(4) pR_j	(5) $[R_j - E(R_j)]$	(6) $[R_m - E(R_m)]$	(7) $[R_j - E(R_j)] \times [R_m - E(R_m)]$	(8) $p[R_j - E(R_j)] \times [R_m - E(R_m)]$
P1 . . .	.1	−.46	−.046	−.50	−.40	.200	.0200
	.2	−.26	−.052	−.30	−.20	.060	.0120
	.3	.46	.138	.42	.00	.000	.0000
	.4	.00	.000	−.04	.20	−.008	−.0032
			$E(R_1) = .040$				$\text{Cov}(R_1,R_m) = .0288$
P2 . . .	.1	−1.00	−.10	−1.20	−.40	.480	.0480
	.2	−.50	−.10	−0.70	−.20	.140	.0280
	.3	0	.00	−0.20	.00	.000	.0000
	.4	1.00	.40	0.80	.20	.160	.0640
			$E(R_2) = .20$				$\text{Cov}(R_2,R_m) = .1400$
P3 . . .	.1	−.40	−.04	−.60	−.40	.240	.0240
	.2	−.20	−.04	−.40	−.20	.080	.0160
	.3	.00	.00	−.20	.00	.000	.0000
	.4	+.70	.28	.50	.20	.100	.0400
			$E(R_3) = .20$				$\text{Cov}(R_3,R_m) = .0800$
P4 . . .	.1	−.40	−.04	−.50	−.40	.200	.0200
	.2	−.20	−.04	−.30	−.20	.060	.0120
	.3	.60	.18	.50	.00	.000	.0000
	.4	.00	.00	−.10	.20	−.020	−.0080
			$E(R_4) = .10$				$\text{Cov}(R_4,R_m) = .0240$

TABLE 10
Calculation of the Betas

$$\beta_1{}^0 = .0288/.04 = 0.72$$
$$\beta_2{}^0 = .1400/.04 = 3.50$$
$$\beta_3{}^0 = .0800/.04 = 2.00$$
$$\beta_4{}^(= .0240/.04 = 0.60$$

11 to estimate the required return $(E(R_j) = Rf + [E(Rm) - Rf]\beta_j)$ on each project in terms of the market line relationship, where the risk-free rate of return is assumed to be 4 percent; hence the market risk premium is 6 percent $(E(Rm) - Rf - .10 - .04 = .06)$. The market risk differential is multiplied by each individual

TABLE 11
Calculation of Excess Returns

(1) Project Number	(2) Measurement of Required Return	(3) Estimated Return	(4) Excess Return
P1	$E(R_j^\circ) = R_f + MRP(\beta.)$		
P1	$E(R_1^\circ) = .04 + .06(0.72) = .083$	.040	−.043
P2	$E(R_2^\circ) = .04 + .06(3.50) = .250$	.200	−.050
P3	$E(R_3^\circ) = .04 + .06(2.00) = .160$	.200	.040
P4	$E(R_4^\circ) = .04 + .06(0.60) = .076$	.100	.024

project beta and added to the pure rate of interest to obtain the required return on each project.

These required returns, as shown in column 2 of Table 11, are deducted from the estimated returns taken from column 4 of Table 9 for each individual project. The results, shown in column 4 of Table 11, are the estimated returns less the required returns, called the excess returns. These relations are depicted graphically in Figure 3.

FIGURE 3
Application of the Asset Expansion Criterion

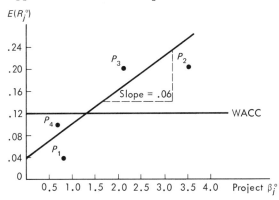

The MPR criterion accepts the projects with positive excess returns, which appear above the MPR line. It rejects those with negative excess returns (plotted below the MPR line). The WACC criterion as portrayed in Figure 3 accepts projects with returns above 12 percent and rejects those with returns of less than 12 percent. The two criteria give conflicting results for Project 2 and for Project 4. The MPR criterion rejects Project 2 because it falls below the MPR line; but the WACC accepts it because the return is in excess of 12 percent. In addition, the MPR criterion accepts Project 4 while the WACC criterion rejects it.

The above example illustrates that the MPR criterion directly adjusts for risk differences and develops the appropriate return-risk relations for making a determination of whether to accept or reject an individual project. However, the WACC criterion does not provide such a direct measure of the return-risk relation.

ADDITIONAL SOURCES

Adler, Michael. "On the Risk-Return Trade-Off in the Valuation of Assets." *Journal of Financial and Quantitative Analysis,* 25 (December 1969), 493–512.

Alberts, W. W., and Archer, S. H. "Some Evidence on the Effect of Company Size on the Cost of Equity Capital." *Journal of Financial and Quantitative Analysis,* 8 (March 1973), 229–45.

Archer, Stephen H., and Faerber, LeRoy G. "Firm Size and the Cost of Equity Capital." *Journal of Finance,* 21 (March 1966), 69–84.

Arditti, Fred D. "Risk and the Required Return on Equity." *Journal of Finance,* 22 (March 1967), 19–36.

Arditti, Fred D., and Tysseland, Milford S. "Three Ways to Present the Marginal Cost of Capital." *Financial Management,* 2 (Summer 1973), 63–67.

Barges, Alexander. *The Effect of Capital Structure on the Cost of Capital.* Englewood Cliffs, N.J.: Prentice-Hall, 1963.

Beranek, William. *The Effects of Leverage on the Market Value of Common Stocks.* Madison, Wis.: Bureau of Business Research and Service, University of Wisconsin, 1964.

Bierman, Harold, Jr. "Risk and the Addition of Debt to the Capital Structure." *Journal of Financial and Quantitative Analysis,* 3 (December 1968), 415–23.

Bierman, Harold, and Haas, Jerome. "Are High Cut-off Rates a Fallacy?" *Financial Executive,* 41 (June 1973), 88–91.

Bower, Richard S., and Bower, Dorothy H. "Risk and the Valuation of Common Stock." *Journal of Political Economy,* 77 (May–June 1969), 349–62.

Brennan, Michael J. "A New Look at the Weighted Average Cost of Capital." *Journal of Business Finance,* 5 (1973), 24–30.

Budd, A. P., and Litzenberger, R. H. "Changes in the Supply of Money:

The Firm's Market Value and Cost of Capital." *Journal of Finance,* 28 (March 1973), 49–58.

Burton, R. M., and Damon, W. W. "On the Existence of a Cost of Capital under Pure Capital Rationing." *Journal of Finance,* 29 (September 1974), 1165–74.

Donaldson, Gordon. *Corporate Debt Capacity.* Boston: Division of Research, Harvard Business School, 1961.

Donaldson, Gordon. "New Framework for Corporate Debt Capacity." *Harvard Business Review,* 40 (March–April 1962), 117–31.

Elton, Edwin J., and Gruber, Martin J. "The Cost of Retained Earnings—Implications of Share Repurchase." *Industrial Management Review,* 9 (Spring 1968), 87–104.

Fama, Eugene F. "Risk, Return, and Equilibrium: Some Clarifying Comments." *Journal of Finance,* 23 (March 1968), 29–40.

Foster, Earl M. "Price-Earnings Ratio and Corporate Growth." *Financial Analysts Journal,* January–February 1970, 96–99.

Hakansson, Nils H. "On the Dividend Capitalization Model under Uncertainty." *Journal of Financial and Quantitative Analysis,* 4 (March 1969), 65–87.

Haley, Charles W. "A Note on the Cost of Debt." *Journal of Financial and Quantitative Analysis,* 1 (December 1966), 72–93.

Hamada, Robert S. "Portfolio Analysis, Market Equilibrium and Corporation Finance." *Journal of Finance,* 24 (March 1969), 13–32.

Haugen, Robert A. "Expected Growth, Required Return, and the Variability of Stock Prices." *Journal of Financial and Quantitative Analysis,* 5 (September 1970), 297–308.

Haugen, Robert A., and Kumar, Prem. "The Traditional Approach to Valuing Levered-Growth Stocks: A Clarification." *Journal of Financial and Quantitative Analysis,* 9 (December 1974), 1031–44.

Hunt, Pearson. "A Proposal for Precise Definitions of 'Trading on the Equity' and 'Leverage.'" *Journal of Finance,* 16 (September 1961), 377–86.

Jensen, Michael C. "Risk, the Pricing of Capital Assets, and the Evaluation of Investment Portfolios." *Journal of Business,* 42 (April 1969), 167–247.

Keenan, Michael. "Models of Equity Valuation: The Great Serm Bubble." *Journal of Finance,* 25 (May 1970), 243–73.

Kraus, Alan, and Litzenberger, Robert. "A State-Preference Model of Optimal Financial Leverage." *Journal of Finance,* 28 (September 1973), 911–22.

Krouse, Clement G. "Optimal Financing and Capital Structure Programs for the Firm." *Journal of Finance,* 27 (December 1972), 1057–72.

Kumar, Prem. "Growth Stocks and Corporate Capital Structure Theory." *Journal of Finance,* 30 (May 1975), 532–47.

Lerner, Eugene M., and Carleton, Willard T. "Financing Decisions of the Firm." *Journal of Finance,* 21 (May 1966), 202–14.

Lev, Baruch. "On the Association between Operating Leverage and Risk." *Journal of Financial and Quantitative Analysis,* 9 (September 1974), 627–42.

Lev, Baruch, and Pekelman, Dov. "A Multiperiod Adjustment Model for the Firm's Capital Structure." *Journal of Finance,* 30 (March 1975), 75–92.

Lewellen, Wilbur G. *The Cost of Capital.* Belmont, Calif.: Wadsworth, 1969, chaps. 3–4.

Lewellen, Wilbur G. "A Conceptual Reappraisal of Cost of Capital." *Financial Management,* 3 (Winter 1974), 63–70.

Linke, Charles M., and Kim, Moon K. "More on the Weighted Average Cost of Capital: A Comment and Analysis." *Journal of Financial and Quantitative Analysis,* 9 (December 1974), 1069–80.

Logue, Dennis E., and Merville, Larry J. "Financial Policy and Market Expectations." *Financial Management,* 1 (Summer 1972), 37–44.

Long, Michael S., and Racette, George A. "Stochastic Demand, Output and the Cost of Capital." *Journal of Finance,* 19 (May 1974), 499–506.

Love, Douglas. "The Use and Abuse of Leverage." *Financial Analysts Journal,* 31 (March–April 1975), 51–59.

McDonald, John G. "Market Measures of Capital Cost." *Journal of Business Finance,* 2 (Autumn 1970), 27–36.

McEnally, Richard W. "A Note on the Return Behavior of High Risk Common Stocks." *Journal of Finance,* 29 (March 1974), 199–202.

Malkiel, Burton G. "Equity Yields, Growth, and the Structure of Share Prices." *American Economic Review,* 53 (December 1963), 467–94.

Mao, James C. T. "The Valuation of Growth Stocks: The Investment Opportunities Approach." *Journal of Finance,* 21 (March 1966), 95–102.

Miller, M. H., and Modigliani, Franco. "Cost of Capital to Electric Utility Industry." *American Economic Review,* 56 (June 1966), 333–91.

Modigliani, Franco, and Miller, M. H. "The Cost of Capital, Corporation Finance and the Theory of Investment." *American Economic Review,* 48 (June 1958), 261–97.

Myers, Stewart C. "A Time-State Preference Model of Security Valuation." *Journal of Financial and Quantitative Analysis,* 3 (March 1968), 1–34.

Pringle, John J. "Price/Earnings Ratios, Earnings per Share, and Financial Management." *Financial Management,* 2 (Spring 1973), 34–40.

Reilly, Raymond R., and Wecker, William E. "On the Weighted Average Cost of Capital." *Journal of Financial and Quantitative Analysis,* 8 (January 1973), 123–26.

Reilly, Raymond R., and Wecker, William E. "On the Weighted Average Cost of Capital: Reply." *Journal of Financial and Quantitative Analysis,* 10 (June 1975), 367–68.

Robichek, Alexander A.; Higgins, Robert C.; and Kinsman, Michael. "The Effect of Leverage on the Cost of Equity Capital of Electric Utility Firms." *Journal of Finance,* 28 (May 1973), 353–67.

Robichek, Alexander A., and Myers, Stewart C. *Optimal Financial Decisions.* Englewood Cliffs, N.J.: Prentice-Hall, 1965.

Scott, David. "Evidence on the Importance of Financial Structure." *Financial Management,* 1 (Summer 1972), 45–50.

Sharpe, William F. "Capital Asset Prices: A Theory of Market Equilibrium." *Journal of Finance,* 19 (September 1964), 425–42.

Solomon, Ezra. *The Theory of Financial Management.* New York: Columbia University Press, 1963.

Sullivan, Timothy G. "Market Power, Profitability and Financial Leverage." *Journal of Finance,* 29 (December 1974), 1407–14.

Tepper, Irwin. "Revealed Preference Methods and the Pure Theory of the Cost of Capital." *Journal of Finance,* 28 (March 1973), 35–48.

Walter, James E. "Investment Planning under Variable Price Change." *Financial Management,* 1 (Winter 1972), 36–50.

Williams, Edward E. "Cost of Capital Functions and the Firm's Optimal Level of Gearing." *Journal of Business Finance,* 4 (1972), 78–83.

PART IX

Managing Sources of Long-Term Capital

IN PART IX, alternative sources of long-term capital are discussed. Just as the commercial bank performs a pivotal role in working capital management and short-term financing, the investment banker is the key financial intermediary in the longer term capital markets. In Chapter 33, Paul K. Kelly describes how to work effectively with the investment banker. Mr. Kelly describes the types and functions of investment banking activities. The criteria he sets forth for ranking investment bankers include underwriting experience, specialized services offered, capital strength, reputation, and quality of investment banker personnel. He recommends that the selection of an investment banking firm should be based on an objective set of standards, tempered by subjective considerations related to the particular circumstances and needs of the company.

Since equity financing is the foundation to which all other forms of financing relate, in Chapter 34 Robert McGuinness discusses the role of equity capital financing. He points out that the equity market has had different characteristics at different periods of our economic history. He then demonstrates how equity financing is related to six different stages in the development of the firm and how these stages affect the firm's characteristics, sources of funds, the investment objectives of investors, uses of funds, and the forms of financing. The external factors affecting equity financing are the cost of capital, flotation costs, and timing. He shows how the question of control is related to both internal and external factors. The major sources of equity financing are systematically discussed. Mr. McGuinness discusses the present and prospective trends affecting the use of equity capital.

A major source of equity financing is retained earnings. Thus, dividend policy and retained earnings, discussed by David Vitale in Chapter 35, are topics directly related to the analysis of sources of equity financing. The theory and empirical studies relating to dividend policy are first presented. Mr. Vitale then describes market characteristics that affect the applicability of the theory. He places emphasis on corporate considerations that affect dividend policy, particularly the need for capital and for financial flexibility. Mr. Vitale presents a framework for choosing among dividend policy alternatives to develop a dividend strategy.

In Chapter 36, Edward Sheridan provides a comprehensive survey of debt financing. He describes the variables that determine the dimensions and characteristics of debt instruments. Mr. Sheridan discusses the different considerations influencing the pricing of a debt issue. He presents with good insights the rationale and nature of the covenants or restrictions in debt-financing agreements. He describes a wide range of forms and sources of debt, covering their leading characteristics, advantages, and limitations. He then develops the ingredients for developing a financial strategy for effectively combining the range of debt-financing alternatives and opportunities described.

In view of the increased role of leasing as a source of financing we are fortunate to have a comprehensive treatment of financial leases by Nathan Snyder in Chapter 37. The size of the leasing market is described, the nature of financial institutions in the market and the growing role of commercial banks in leasing activity are indicated. The distinction between leveraged leases, financial leases, and tax leases are explained. The Internal Revenue Service requirements for establishing a "true lease" are set forth. The 1975 modifications in the tax treatment of leases are covered in his presentation.

The economic considerations for a comparative analysis of the lease versus alternative methods of financing assets are developed fully by Mr. Snyder. Emphasis is placed on the assumptions with regard to tax benefits, the timing of tax benefits, tax rates, and depreciation methods reflected in the analysis. The comparative analysis is then made by the use of the discounted cash flow method.

Noneconomic considerations in the comparative analysis include accounting treatments and the possible benefits and limitations of leasing as a financing device.

With the foregoing as a background the considerations involved in negotiating the lease are then set forth. While the treasurer is not responsible for intricate legal considerations involved in a sophisticated lease transaction, material is presented to sensitize the treasurer to areas that may require legal counseling.

In recent years options have had a major impact on the theoretical finance literature and in financial market activity as well. In Chapter 38, Madison Haythe covers the basic ideas involved in his treatment of convertibles and warrants. He covers the fundamentals, the logic of option pricing formulas, and the basis for investor evaluations of warrants and convertibles. He then turns to an analysis of the use of convertibles and warrants from the standpoint of the corporate treasurer in financing. He covers all aspects of the terms of warrant issues including consideration of such matters as the trade-off between the size of the conversion premium and the required coupon rate. He calls attention to the use of warrants which provide for the purchase of stock in other companies, warrants used in the sale of common stock, and in reorganizations and exchange offers. The concepts are also treated in the framework of employee stock option plans.

Chapter 33

Working with Your Investment Banker

Paul K. Kelly[*]

INTRODUCTION

THE CHOICE of a proper investment banker is a crucial decision for any corporation, and is increasingly being treated as such by the corporate community. The "old school tie" choice of an investment banker has largely given way to an objective decision-making process administered by corporate professionals. In a close decision, personal relationships may often be a deciding factor but usually only where the contenders are otherwise deemed relatively comparable in terms of the quality and number of required investment banking services offered.

The choice of investment bankers based upon their merits, rather than personal relationships, results in several important benefits for a corporate chief executive officer. First, his delegation of the responsibility for evaluating and recommending investment bankers to those responsible for daily financial administration of the company assures that the corporate officers who will work closely with the investment banker have been instrumental in the final choice. Second, and not entirely facetiously, an objective group participa-

---

* Paul K. Kelly was formerly vice president, First Boston Corporation, New York, and is currently general partner, Prescott, Ball & Turben, Cleveland, Ohio.

tion decision can help a chief executive officer keep his personal relationships with Wall Street intact. This is particularly so in regard to chief executives of major corporations who may be acquainted personally with investment bankers from several firms. The choice of an investment banker based upon the objective recommendation of a company's financial staff indicates that the chief executive officer did not unduly influence the selection by favoring one investment banking acquaintance to the detriment of others. This objective standard of choosing investment bankers on a merit basis usually results in a more productive relationship in which investment bankers are continually seeking to justify the company's confidence on a performance basis.

There are objective criteria upon which a corporation can base the choice of an investment banker, although the importance attached to each individual criterion will vary between companies. In each instance, subjective criteria or subjective conceptions of objective criteria will also affect the final decision. In the course of this chapter we will consider the weightings of these varied criteria, but first we should establish a clear idea of the service business known as investment banking.

WHAT IS AN "INVESTMENT BANKER"?

An investment banker basically provides three types of services. He acts as an insurer underwriting the risk associated with the market reception of publicly issued securities, as an agent handling the private distribution of securities, and as a financial adviser to corporations. These services are available both separately and in various combinations. Advice and financial counsel, for example, may be obtained without employing the distribution services of an investment banker.

Any definition of an investment banker stresses his "middleman" role between borrowers and lenders (investors) in the long-term capital markets. In this capacity he may be either a "dealer" acting as a principal for his own account, or a "broker" who acts solely as an agent in bringing together buyers and sellers for a commission. A dealer making a capital commitment by purchasing securities with his own money for later resale to an investor thus bears the risk of (*underwrites*) future adverse price fluctuations. A broker, on the other hand, makes no financial capital outlay.

The strict definition of an investment banker stresses his "underwriting" function in which he acts as a dealer, particularly in the distribution of new issues of stocks and bonds. This definition is perhaps too limiting for our purposes in view of the great number of middlemen who act (or seek to act) as strictly agent intermediaries in the capital markets. It is not necessary in every situation for an investment banker to have capital at risk in order to satisfy the capital needs of a borrower, although most corporations would probably require that their investment banker have the ability to underwrite securities as required. This being so, the universe of "investment bankers," in the sense of financial middlemen, is a larger one which can be narrowed down and classified according to specific abilities and functions.

Some Investment Banking Statistics

According to the Securities and Exchange Commission (SEC), there were 4,229 domestic and 27 foreign broker-dealer organizations in the United States as of December 31, 1973, many of which might potentially serve as capital market middlemen under certain conditions. A relatively small proportion would have the necessary capital, however, to perform an underwriting function of any magnitude. Only 523 firms of the entire broker-dealer community were members of the New York Stock Exchange as of year-end 1973. The net worth, excluding capital debentures, of these member firms was $3.625 billion at that time. A similar net worth figure for the broker-dealer industry as a whole is not readily available, but a good guess is that the net worth of NYSE member firms constitutes a decidedly major portion.

Studies during the 1960s by the SEC and the Wharton School of Finance and Commerce found that less than 3 percent of the firms engaged in investment banking accounted for more than half of the capital of all securities firms and handled the vast majority of the corporate underwritings. This indicates the relatively high concentration of underwriting capability within a small number of firms in the broker-dealer community. It is this group of firms with a traditional underwriting capability which we will consider most closely, although the function of those who act in purely an agent capacity are also worth reviewing.

Functional Differences

Agent-brokers are the financial intermediaries with the most limited functions in raising new capital for corporations. Since they do not perform an underwriting function, they deal almost exclusively in the private placement of securities with institutional investors. They also perform certain other noncapital intensive financial services common to all investment bankers such as seeking suitable partners for corporate mergers and acquisitions.

The caliber of service performed by these agents varies greatly, as does the degree of sophistication of the corporations they serve. Those who perform no financial advisory service beyond introducing borrowers and investors are known, somewhat pejoratively, as "finders." These persons may or may not be registered broker-dealers and are often merely individuals with an opportunistic flair.

Corporate financial officers should be very discriminating when dealing with independent finders whether they come in the guise of lawyers, accountants, or businessmen. There is no code of ethics similar to that of the National Association of Securities Dealers (NASD) regulating the actions of broker-dealers which is in effect for nonbroker-dealer entrepreneurs. Many financial officers have found to their chagrin that there exists an element of finders who have misrepresented themselves to corporations as sole and exclusive representatives of certain institutional investors, or vice versa. The scenario often involves a finder approaching a company and indicating that he is sole agent for an enormous sum of available low rate money which, he hints, derives from Swiss banks, Arab oil money, or even more mysterious sources. Many corporate officials, unable to withstand the lure of ridiculously cheap money, have spent hours of wasted time dealing with such finders, only to find that their reputed money sources are phantom.

The reason that certain finders employ this exaggerated technique is to engage the attention of corporate financial officers who otherwise would not acknowledge their existence by giving them an appointment. Often the initial approach is to the chief executive officer who, particularly if he is not a conversant financial man, may order his financial staff to investigate the situation. Once again, the finder has accomplished his objective of attaining visibility. Having gained entrance, the finder will, as long as the financial staff humors him, begin a long series of follow-up contacts during which a series of excuses are presented as to why the proferred loan cannot be consummated at the original terms. The hope of the finder is that the company will accept his reasoning and end up doing the deal at the going market rate, paying him a commission in the process.

Seasoned financial officers have generally learned to avoid this type of unscrupulous finder. Common sense dictates that their reputedly sophisticated money sources would never consider lending money below the going market rate. For those, however, who are willing to consider any offer of funds at a low rate, the following procedure is offered as the least painless way to deal with finders of untested repute. Simply have your secretary distribute a standard prepared outline to any interested finder indicating the terms, including the finder's fee, under which the company is willing to borrow. The form should have a blank space in which you can insert a currently acceptable interest rate range on borrowings for which you would be willing to employ the finder's services. (It should be realized that finder's fees in this type of situation are almost always paid by the borrower, rather than the lender.) The outline should indicate that a meeting with the finder is necessary only after the lender has signed a loan agreement incorporating the terms outlined or otherwise signified directly to the borrower, either in writing or verbally, a willingness to lend upon acceptable terms. Requests for minor modifications in the outlined acceptable terms can be submitted by the finder in writing and acknowledged by the corporate financial officer in a similar manner. A procedure akin to the one suggested will minimize unnecessary expenditures of time by a corporate financial staff with finders of unknown caliber.

The foregoing recommendations do not, of course, apply to entities of established reputation which may seek to represent a company as agent in a financial transaction. Some commercial banks, for example, have recently established corporate finance departments which assist corporations in the areas of private placements and mergers and acquisitions. Banks are not, however, permitted to underwrite corporate securities as principal in a public offering. In a similar manner, there are reputable specialist firms which do excellent work in particular areas of corporate finance, such as mergers and acquisitions, often concentrating only on assisting companies within particular industries where they have a special expertise. Management consulting and accounting firms may offer similar services. In addition, there is the entire broker-dealer community whose members vary greatly in terms of experience and expertise in representing corporate borrowers in the private market. The leading investment banking firms are often retained by major corporations as much to represent them in the negotiation of terms with lenders as to actually place the issue. Even in those instances when a private lender, such as an insurance company, directly approaches a potential corporate borrower, the help and advice of the investment banker is often sought by the borrower in obtaining the best borrowing terms and covenants possible.

Structural Differences

Confining ourselves now to a stricter definition of "investment banker," i.e., the ability to underwrite securities, there are notable structural differences among the different types of firms. Some firms are *corporate finance specialists* dealing primarily with sophisticated corporate clients whose securities are readily marketable to institutional investors. The concentration of buying power represented by institutional investors usually means that these firms can distribute the securities of their clients with fewer offices and smaller sales forces than required by the wirehouses. Experience in a broad array of financial consulting and advisory work is also characteristic of this type of firm.

Wirehouses are so named because their offices, including branches and correspondents, are directly connected by wire to New York City. Since they have larger distribution systems, the wirehouses, in addition to their institutional business also deal in securities which have a more limited institutional appeal, either because of the smaller size of the issues involved, or the types of companies and industries represented. Since institutional interest is limited, securities of this kind require retail distribution to individual investors. Because of the smaller transaction size associated with individuals, as opposed to institutions, broad retail distribution requires many offices and individual salesmen.

The definitions given represent two extremes and there are, of course, various investment banking houses whose structures fall somewhere between these points. Generally, however, most firms will tend to have predominantly corporate finance specialist or wirehouse characteristics, and will be so considered by the corporate community and the investment banking fraternity itself.

Geographical Differences

In addition to the aforementioned structural differences, investment banking firms differ as to the geographical scope of their activities. Firms are generally classified as regional, national, or international in nature. These designations related to the types of clients served, the geographical areas from which a firm draws its clients, and to those areas in which it markets securities. The choice of the proper type of investment banking firm will vary greatly among corporations based upon their own structures and needs.

SELF-ANALYSIS OF CORPORATE FINANCIAL NEEDS

The first step in choosing an investment banker is a thorough self-analysis of a corporation's overall financial needs by its financial staff. This includes asking such questions as: Which investment banking services does the corporation require? Are such specialized services as foreign financing, leasing, real estate financing, commercial paper, and advisory work (either specific or general in nature) needed? Or perhaps all that is required is assistance in the underwriting or private placement of securities. The answer to these questions will determine whether or not a "full line" investment banker is needed.

Having determined the extent and variety of the corporation's investment banking needs, the next question is whether the securities of the corporation have a decided institutional interest. In asking this question, an analysis of the pattern of common stockholders of the corporation may be helpful. As a rule of thumb, a mature, sizable corporation can consider that it has an institutional following if about 10 percent or more of its outstanding shares are held by institutional investors such as mutual funds and trust departments. If an initial public offering is planned, and the corporation has no previous record of existing public stock-holdings, an examination of stockholders patterns for public companies in the same, or closely aligned, businesses may be helpful. Any competent investment banker can assist in obtaining this information and will supplement it with his own market judgments.

Limited institutional interest in a corporation's common stock does not necessarily mean, however, that a wirehouse would be the best choice as an investment banker for that company. Distribution of common equity is only one facet of an investment banking relationship. If the company is in need of other specialized investment banking services, then a corporate finance specialist firm may be a better overall choice. There are numerous examples of companies whose stock has limited institutional appeal but whose financial activity in other areas makes them highly desirable clients for corporate specialist firms. The key to such a relationship is whether it is mutually beneficial to both the client and the investment banking firm. There is no need to exclude the company from access to the most sophisticated investment banking advice available simply because its stock has a limited institutional following.

Some corporate financial officers might raise the question as to how institutionally oriented investment banking firms distribute securities of clients which lack an institutional following. First, let us clarify what is meant by institutional appeal. The term is generally applied to common stock of a company rather than its debt obligations. Many companies whose earnings growth, and so on, is not sufficient to generate institutional buying of their common stock, may nevertheless find a considerable institutional following for their senior debt obligations. This is because institutional bond buyers make investments based upon well-structured balance sheets and adequate fixed charge coverages, not upon relative earnings growth per se. Since a bondholder has limited price appreciation opportunities, his foremost consideration is safety of principal, rather than the higher risk/reward ratio which stockholders are willing to assume. The result is that the debt securities and preferred stock of most well-managed companies may have an institutional following which a corporate finance specialist firm will have no problem accommodating. As to distributing the common stock of a client with little institutional appeal, the corporate finance specialist firm has a ready answer and solution: the use of the *syndicate.*

The investment banker, as manager of a client corporation's financing, structures a syndicate group of other investment banking firms designed to accomplish the most effective distribution pattern among various types of buyers. For example, if a corporate finance specialist firm is managing a common stock deal for a company with a strong regional identification and a limited institutional following, it will structure the syndicate to include those wirehouses and regional brokers from that area which have the best retail distribution capability. In addition to the syndicate group, a *selling group* of local broker-dealers would be invited to participate in the sale, but not the underwriting, of the stock issue. The selling group is composed of small NASD members which generally do not have enough capital to commit themselves to the underwriting of an issue. The syndicate managers set aside a portion of a deal, called the "pot," which is allocated on a first-come, first-served basis to members of the selling group who are able to generate orders from investors.

While the proper structuring of a syndicate permits a corporate finance specialist firm to satisfy the distribution requirements of a client with retail-oriented securities, this does not provide an adequate basis for an investment banking relationship. As previously mentioned, a company of the type discussed should have additional financing requirements other than an occasional stock issue before deciding upon a specialist firm as opposed to a wirehouse or regional dealer. If such a company has little need for future debt issues or specialized financing services, then perhaps a relationship with a wirehouse or regional dealer might be more suitable. The choice between a national wirehouse or a regional dealer will be based in part upon the geographical breadth of individual interest in a company's stock.

When the general investment banking needs of a corporation are minimal, the choice of an investment banker has often been predicated upon which firm is willing to follow most actively the company's stock both from research and trading viewpoints. This may well be a meaningful consideration if the stock of a company is unlisted, has only limited appeal, and is not otherwise traded actively. In general, however, using a piece of business as leverage to extract from an investment banking firm a favorable research report on your company is frowned upon. Similarly, asking an investment banking firm to commit capital in making an "active" market in the company's stock may be asking too much, particularly when conditions in the securities markets are highly volatile and uncertain. A firm may, however, be willing to make a limited capital commitment to trading the stock, simply as a client service to monitor the market reaction in your stock. These points will be elaborated upon in the section "Subjective Considerations."

In summary, a self-analysis of the nature of the company's financial needs and the characteristics of its securities as seen by the investment community, will provide a guideline as to the choice of a proper investment banker. This analysis need not be made in a vacuum. Assistance on these questions from various types of investment banking houses is provided since they, as does the corporation, do not wish to become involved in an unprofitable relationship. The final choice of an investment banker should be based upon an objective assessment of which candidate firm best fulfills the company's individual financial service requirements.

OBJECTIVE CRITERIA FOR RANKING INVESTMENT BANKING FIRMS

The best way to compare investment banking firms is to establish a matrix which rates each candidate as to competence in certain defined categories. The rating system, might assign a rating of 1 to 10, the highest, for each category. Rather than simply totaling the ratings, a weighting system should also be devised to give greatest emphasis to those categories which are most germane to the particular needs of the corporation. Thus, while one firm may rate highly compared to its peers in the area of international finance, this factor should have relatively little effect upon the final choice if the company has no international operations or financing requirements.

There are many possible sets of criteria which might be established as a measure against which to compare investment banking firms. The following five categories are suggested as pertinent components of any ranking system which might be derived:

A. Underwriting experience.
B. Specialized services offered.
C. Capital strength.
D. Reputation.
E. Quality of personnel.

An elaboration on each of these criteria may be helpful.

Underwriting Experience. Under this category, the firm should be judged upon the dollar volume and number of taxable public issues which it has managed, or co-managed, during the past ten years.

Such data is readily available from the *Investment Dealers' Digest-Corporate Financing Directory.*

As the main point of interest here is in the ability of an investment banker to structure successful underwritings, not merely participate in deals structured by some other firm, it is important to concentrate on data concerning deals managed or co-managed and not merely on deals in which the firm has participated as a syndicate member. Distribution capabilities of a firm can be determined by asking what percentage of its underwriting commitments it has actually sold over a representative period, as opposed to turning back unsold securities to the syndicate for ultimate distribution by others in the group.

A final consideration to determine a firm's experience should be a client list of the companies for which it has managed underwritings in the previous ten years. Inspect this list in regard to the quality of the companies and the types of deals represented. Familiarity of the investment banker with companies in the same industry can also be established from such a list.

Specialized Services Offered.   This category covers a potentially broad array of services which are of interest to your firm currently, or may be at a future date. A particularly pertinent piece of information here is volume of private placements which the investment banker has handled for his clients. This is especially important because a corporation should always be in a position to tap the private market when the overall terms to be derived are relatively attractive compared to the public issuance of securities.

The types of financial advisory work performed by a firm and the clients involved should also be of interest. Merger and acquisition capability, for example, is one major area of advisory work which may be of interest to you. Other specialized services might include capabilities in international finance, commercial paper, real estate financing, pollution control financing, and leasing. In assessing the potential performance of an investment banker in these areas, attention should be paid to his existing market share, not merely the fact that he claims to offer the services mentioned.

Capital Strength.   This is a measure of the "staying power" of an investment banking firm in a business which has become increasingly volatile in terms of profitability. Certain ratios of capital adequacy are required for the daily unimpeded inventorying of securities by NASD and NYSE member firms. These ratios apply to both new issues which a firm may be underwriting as well as inventories of securities resulting from secondary market trading activities.

A prospective corporate client should make sure that the investment banking firm chosen has sufficient equity capital, in addition to subordinated debt, if any, to handle the underwriting needs of a group of clients simultaneously. A firm with a limited capital base may only be able to underwrite one or two deals at a time which could mean that its clients may have to queue up and wait for their respective turns. If such a queue were long enough, it is possible that some clients' deals might miss temporarily favorable market conditions, all because of the inflexibility of having chosen an investment banker with insufficient capital.

Reputation. When ranking investment banking firms according to reputation, one must differentiate between reputation based upon performance and "mystique." The latter has connotations of the prestige value of having the name of the corporation associated with a given Wall Street firm. If such a firm also satisfies best the individual investment banking needs of the company, then it is a logical choice. When prestige replaces expected performance in the choice of an investment banker, however, a corporation short-changes itself.

In gauging the reputation of a firm, a company may consult a firm's clients, major commercial banks, and even other investment banking firms. Again the performance reputation of a company should be weighted by the particular services the company requires. At the same time, some of the intangibles of a firm, such as professionalism and integrity should also be assessed. They may add to its performance reputation. This leads us directly into the final criterion of assessing the professional staff of each competing firm.

Quality of Personnel. It may seem rather hackneyed to use the oft-quoted phrase "our people are our finest recommendation." In investment banking, however, this is truly the case. Corporate finance officers of the major underwriting firms, in particular, are given a good deal of latitude by their managements in conducting overall relationships with corporate clients. This being so, it is wise to meet the individual investment banker who will be responsible for handling the company's needs, prior to retaining his firm. Consider also that in any investment banking firm there is the chance that the account officer in charge of handling the client corporation's account may someday be transferred or that he may even leave the firm entirely. This being so, it is important to also consider the breadth and depth of overall corporate finance personnel at the firms under consideration. It can be dangerous to count on the abilities of any single individual if his organization is not generally of high caliber.

In rating corporate finance personnel of an investment banking firm, it is fitting to consider their educational and previous business backgrounds. A legal or accounting background can be very valuable for an investment banker since so much of his work is involved with SEC procedures. An MBA is likewise an assurance that an investment banker has probably had formal training in the analytical skills which his position requires. As in many other professions, however, formalized educational training is no guarantee, in itself, that a person will be a competent, successful practitioner.

The ultimate test of an individual investment banker is the breadth of financing experience which he has personally experienced. This includes the number and size of financings which he has personally structured, the industries involved, and the type of deals; i.e., bonds, stocks, mergers, international, and so forth.

An analysis of personnel should not be limited solely to corporate finance personnel. It would also be beneficial to consider the head of the syndicate and the sales groups responsible for the pricing and distribution of the securities. A high quality of personnel should be evident throughout the organization.

SUBJECTIVE CONSIDERATIONS

Throughout this chapter we have stressed the importance of setting objective standards as a guide to choosing an investment banker. It would be foolish, however, not to also consider some subjective judgments in making such a decision.

The client should feel completely at ease in any investment banking relationship formed. If there is any dissatisfaction concerning personnel in the firm associated with the client's account; the simplest solution is to request that someone else at the firm handle the company's account. Most firms would rather change personnel on an account than risk losing a client completely. The client, in turn, will have removed a personal obstacle while still retaining the firm which was considered best in satisfying its corporate financial needs. Only if personal relationships cannot be altered should the client consider choosing, or changing to, an investment banker which was originally considered to be second best.

Another subjective judgment is whether it is felt that adequate attention will be received from the investment banking firm which, potentially, best suits the company's needs. If the firm which was considered first choice seems less enthusiastic about the business than desired, it may not be the best choice after all. The resources of an investment banking firm are of no help to a client if they are not willingly offered or easily mobilized by the client. A "prestige" firm loses its appeal if it neglects the company's needs in favor of those of other clients.

THE ETIQUETTE OF AN INVESTMENT BANKING RELATIONSHIP

A smoothly functioning investment banking relationship requires certain rules of mutual etiquette from both investment banker and client. An idea of what one can, and cannot, reasonably expect from an investment banker may be of some help in determining your company's own role as a client.

A question which is often asked is whether it is acceptable to "negotiate" with an investment banker. The answer is, very definitely, yes. Investment banking is a service business and hence either party should be free to terminate the relationship at will. Under these circumstances, neither party should feel restricted in negotiating with the other.

An investment banker represents its client. It is thus expected to advise on financial matters and prices on securities with the client company's interests foremost in mind. It is true that the investment banker must design a security which is attractive to the investor but, in pricing it, his first loyalty is to the client. A mispriced security may make many investors happy but it may also result in losing a client. The client has the final say in accepting or rejecting the new issue price on his securities, and he should expect the investment banker to justify his pricing recommendations in a logical fashion. There is, however, a practical limitation between what the client would like to receive for his securities and what the market will be willing to pay. Up to that point, however, the client should feel free to express his pricing ideas to his investment banker.

Another area of possible negotiation relates to fees and underwriting spread between the price paid to the corporate issuer by the investment banker and the price at which he offers it to investors. The client is well within his rights to ask the investment banker to justify the spread charged by furnishing him with underwriting spread information for issues of similar quality offered under similar market conditions. Gross underwriting spreads will vary with the type of security, the size of the issue, the credit rating of the issuer, the marketability of the securities, and general market conditions expected during the offering period.

Fees charged for advisory work, such as mergers and acquisitions, are also subject to negotiation. Unlike law firms, very few investment banking firms charge for their services on a per diem basis. The more general rule is that the fee charged relates to the benefit derived by the corporate client, rather than the time actually spent designing or refining the financing concept. The percentage fee charged tends to be smaller the larger the assignment, reflecting certain economies of scale which are possible in this regard. It is also common for an investment banker to be paid for his time spent on advisory work, such as evaluating a merger candidate, whether or not the client is successful in consummating the deal. The fee is often somewhat less in the case of an uncompleted project since the client does not realize any additional value, as it would if the project was successfully completed.

A final word on negotiating underwriting spreads and fees. While there is room for legitimate negotiation in these areas, this does not mean that haggling and attempts to extract something for nothing is an acceptable practice. Both parties, investment banker and corporation, are expected to conduct their negotiations in a businesslike, professional manner. Anything less in terms of decorum is sufficient reason to terminate a relationship.

Another question which is often raised by the corporate community is whether more than one investment banker is advisable for a company. Again, the question depends on whether it takes more than one firm to satisfy the company's investment banking requirements. It is certainly acceptable to use a firm with a specialized expertise (i.e., real estate financing) if your regular investment banker does not have a comparable quality service.

A corporation should also feel free to entertain financing concepts as they are submitted by sources other than its regular investment banker. It may be appropriate to reward a good financing idea submitted by another firm by permitting the firm to be involved in implementing that piece of business. This might be done by giving the other firm sole control of the financing, or by simply making it co-manager with the regular investment banker. If the regular investment banker is particularly lax compared to other firms in bringing up new financing ideas, it may be appropriate to consider changing firms. In any case, the fastest way to isolate the company from new financing ideas is to pick the brains of various investment bankers while continuing to give all the company's business to its regular investment banking firm. New financing concepts are the stock in trade of investment bankers and they will not long continue to share these ideas with companies that pirate them.

As in everything else, one gets only what one pays for in an investment banking relationship. This should be considered when deciding whether co-managers are appropriate for a company's security issues. If the company does not generate enough total investment banking revenues to compensate two or more co-managers adequately, it should consider retaining fewer investment banking firms. A corporate client experiences a good deal more service and attention when the relationship is profitable for the investment banking firms involved.

When a co-manager really adds something, in terms of advice or distribution, to the investment banking relationship, then he should be retained. If, however, a corporation is simply seeking to be the friend of every firm on Wall Street as a means of gaining support for its stock, then its intentions will be quickly realized and little meaningful investment banking service will be offered.

SUMMARY

The choice of a proper investment banker depends upon the particular needs of the company. The selection of an investment banking firm should be based upon as objective a set of standards as possible, tempered by some subjective factors. It is important here that personal relationships with the individual investment bankers assigned to the company's account be satisfactory. Such mutually satisfactory relationship with the company's investment banker, however, does not exclude the possibility of accepting valid ideas from other sources. Where meaningful contributions are made by these other firms, adequate compensation should be made. An investment banker that is treated as a professional will in turn serve the company as one.

ADDITIONAL SOURCES

Archer, Stephen H., and Faerber, LeRoy G. "Firm Size and the Cost of Equity Capital." *Journal of Finance,* 21 (March 1966), 69–84.

Bloch, Ernest. "Pricing a Corporate Bond Issue. A Look Behind the Scenes." In *Essays in Money and Credit.* New York: Federal Reserve Bank of New York (1964), 72–76.

Brown, J. Michael. "Post-Offering Experience of Companies Going Public." *Journal of Business,* (January 1970), 10–18.

Friend, Irwin; Hoffman, G. W.; and Winn, W. J. *The Over-the-Counter Securities Market.* New York: McGraw-Hill, 1958.

Goldsmith, Raymond W. *The Flow of Capital Funds in the Postwar Economy.* New York: National Bureau of Economic Research, 1965.

Hayes, Samuel L., III. "Investment Banking: Power Structure in Flux." *Harvard Business Review,* 49 (March–April 1971), 136–52.

Karna, Adi S. "The Cost of Private versus Public Debt Issues." *Financial Management,* 1 (Summer 1972), 65–67.

Logue, Dennis E., and Lindvall, John R. "The Behavior of Investment Bankers: An Econometric Investigation." *Journal of Finance,* 29 (March 1974), 203–15.

Chapter 34

Sources and Forms of
Equity Capital

Robert J. McGuinness[*]

THE NATURE OF THE EQUITY MARKET

EQUITY CAPITAL is a breed apart from other forms of financing. The equity market is dynamic, using the word "dynamic" in its true dictionary sense, to whit: "Active: marked by continuous unusual productive activity and change." It responds with greater sensitivity to a wider range of variables than other investment media.

One simply cannot pick out a specific point of time in history and sit down and describe the equity market at that moment and say, "There it is. That is what it's like." At any one time, it will not be as it was before, nor as it will be in the future.

For example, throughout the 1960s, the stock market enjoyed an almost unprecedented popularity. As a result, access to equity financing was remarkably free and easy, permitting corporations of all kinds to reach the marketplace, almost without regard to their age, size, or quality. Private placements and venture capital financing likewise boomed.

In the 1970s, precisely the opposite circumstances prevailed. We experienced the second worst stock market decline in this century. From the end of 1968 to the end of 1974, the *average* stock on the

* Robert J. McGuinness is vice president, Special Investment Services, Bateman Eichler, Hill Richards, Inc., Los Angeles, California.

New York Stock Exchange lost about 75 percent of its market value, a staggering loss by any standards. Prevailing price–earnings ratios ranged in the 5–6 times level. Yields hit historic highs. The underwriting of new equity issues came to a virtual standstill.

Which period is typical of the equity market, the 1960s or the 1970s? Probably neither. Is there such a thing as a typical period? Probably not. How, then, can we write significantly about the subject? We can do so in this manner. We can write about how equity financing has been done in the past and is being done in the present. Such description will encompass the majority of this chapter. Then we can conclude with some hypotheses about possible future developments.

The treatment of the subject will not be theoretical. Insofar as possible it will be presented as practically as possible, so that the reader might enjoy as close a view of the field as that of a practitioner, be the practitioner a venture capitalist, insurance company, or investment banker.

As the reader studies this chapter, he should bear a few concepts in mind: The equity market simply does not lend itself easily to formula approaches. Much as corporate planners might like to fine tune the equity market into their capitalization plans and structures, just so they will experience much frustration in the process. The price-earnings ratios, yields, and rates of growth that one might adopt as benchmarks for making judgments and plans in one era, can be swept away in another. Markets change now in a month as much as they did in a year some decades ago. We can deal with such a market only in broad brush strokes and rules.

The body of this chapter will have four parts. The first will deal with the *internal* factors affecting equity financing; that is, those factors indigenous to the firm itself. The second will cover external factors, those things over which the firm has little or no control. The third will provide a close-up view of the various institutional sources of equity capital. The concluding section will propose some views of the future.

INTERNAL FACTORS AFFECTING EQUITY FINANCING

In this section we will do two things. We will describe those characteristics which are internal to the business firm itself, and which determine the firm's ability to obtain equity capital at all. Then we will describe the natural evolution, the stages, that a firm passes through as it develops from a start-up to a publicly owned company. For each stage we will note: (1) the characteristics of the firm, (2) the sources of funds (investors) available, (3) the investment objectives of these investors, (4) the uses of the funds, and (5) the forms of financing.

Characteristics of Corporations Qualifying for Equity Financing

The following are the essential characteristics of companies capable of reaching the external equity capital market. These are not hard-and-fast criteria. There will always be exceptions. But they do represent a reasonable guide to the qualities looked for by the sources of equity capital:

Significant Sales Potential. The product or service involved should have already reached, or at least be projectable into, annual sales of $10 million or more. There is nothing magic about this figure. It is admittedly arbitrary, but it does represent a basic guide to the expectations of the institutions that work in the field. It might be lower for high technology companies, and higher for more mundane operations. An alternative criteria is $1 million net profit after taxes.

A Record of Sales and Earnings Growth. A company should show a history of sales growth, and more particularly, an earnings growth at an annualized rate of 10–15 percent or better during its most recent three- to five-year financial history. Preferably this growth should be continuous in nature, rather than erratic. If such a record has not already been established, at least the potential for creating such a performance should be present.

Value Added. A business should bring to its product a skill which adds a definable increase to its value. This value-added capability should reflect a 15 percent or higher rate of return on equity, exclusive of financial leverage. Firms which operate in rather well-established industries are generally characterized by low profit margins and limited returns on net worth. They are unattractive to suppliers of equity capital. These are the "unpopular industries" in which equity financing is difficult for all but the largest firms. *Typically, most retail businesses fall into this category.*

Management Capability. A subjective criteria, this can best be determined by asking the question "Does the present management possess the capacity to accomplish the three previous criteria?" Subjective though it might be, it will be raised inevitably by the suppliers of equity capital. The answer is a judgmental one and upon it may well depend the success or failure of any equity financing effort.

The large majority of business enterprises in this country do not possess the above characteristics and are thus virtually precluded from raising equity funds from external sources. Those firms that reasonably well meet these criteria, or at least hold forth the promise of doing so, are the subject of the rest of this chapter.

Financing the Stages of Development of the Corporation

We will now describe the stages of development of the firm from start-up to publicly held company. In doing so, we will note the following for each stage: the characteristics of the firm, the sources of funds available (the type of investors involved), the investment objectives of these investors, the uses of funds and the forms of investment.

We will distinguish six stages, or levels, of development:

First Level.   Start-up, or "Seed Capital."

Second Level.   Customer acceptance or credibility.

Third Level.   Market penetration.

Fourth Level.   Pre-public.

Fifth Level.   Going public.

Sixth Level.   The public company.

There is nothing particularly scientific in such a categorization. One might refine the development concept into more or less stages than these, or give them different names, but for practical purposes these are the stages which are generally recognized by the equity sources we will be describing.

First Level.   Start-up or Seed Capital

A.   Characteristics of firm.
     Companies at this stage have an idea or business plan, but not yet a product, plant, or proven success.

B. Source of funds.
    Private individuals, venture capitalists.
C. Objectives of investors.
    A return on investment of 10–20 times over a five- to seven-year period.
D. Uses of funds.
    To cover operating losses, purchase plant and equipment.
E. Form.
    Private placement of common stock.
F. Observations.

This is the most difficult of all stages at which to obtain equity capital. Sources are very limited. The entrepreneurs themselves, their associates and friends and private individuals are one source, and perhaps the best, if available. But this is fragmented and very individualized. It does not lend itself to meaningful discussion here.

From an institutional standpoint, some venture capitalists and, to a lesser degree, some SBICs (small business investment companies) provide equity at this stage. But they are few in number.

The requirements for obtaining external equity capital at this stage are rigorous and formidable in the extreme. It is seldom sufficient to have an attractive invention, idea, or plan. The entrepreneurs almost invariably must demonstrate a strong prior record of success or expertise in their field. In addition, the product must possess a high value-added capability with a significant market potential. This stage places intense strain on the entrepreneurial group as witnessed by the fact that about 75 percent of all founding groups break up in varying degrees within the first 18 months of the firm's existence.

Second Level. *Customer Acceptance or Credibility*

A. Characteristics of firm.
    Companies at this stage have already begun marketing their product and have developed something of a track record for sales and/or customer acceptance. Market credibility has been established. They are still unprofitable, or if profitable, only marginally so.
B. Source of funds.
    Some venture capitalists, some SBICs, and a few industrial companies.

C. Objectives of investors.

A return on investment of about 10 times over a five-year period.

D. Use of funds.

To cover operating losses, purchase plant and equipment, increase working capital. Should *not* be used for repayment of debt.

E. Form.

Private replacement of common stock. To a lesser degree, subordinated convertible notes.

F. Observations.

While most venture capitalists purport to do financing at this level, probably fewer do than do not. The same can be said for SBICs. In recent years, some industrial companies have begun to participate at this level, but these are few too. Proper financing at this stage is important, specifically in the effect it will have on future levels of financing. The most common failing is underfinancing and a premature reliance on borrowed money. Ideally, a firm should have no debt at this stage. Financing should be equity, or equity oriented.

Third Level.   Market Penetration

A. Characteristics of firm.

Companies at this stage have already established a definite market for their product and are making a significant profit. Typically, they are three to five years old. The emphasis is on increasing market penetration.

B. Source of funds.

Most venture capitalists and SBICs; some insurance companies; a few industrial companies.

C. Objectives of investors.

A return on investment of around five times over a three- to five-year period.

D. Uses of funds.

To increase working capital in order to finance a significantly higher level of accounts receivable and inventory as market penetration is expanded. Should *not* be used for debt repayment.

E. Form.
   Private placement. Common stock, convertible subordinated notes, notes with warrants attached.
F. Observations.

Equity financing at this stage should be designed to generate a geometric increase in sales volume by increasing the equity base, and should be structured to be used in combination with short-term debt financing, which can properly be initiated at this level. Such debt financing is generally short-term bank financing and usually takes the form of accounts receivable financing. The pattern is for the bank to finance around 80 percent of the receivables up to a certain percentage of net worth, normally around 50 percent but in exceptional cases up to 100 percent.

This stage is one of the most critical points in the financial life of a developing company. If the company's equity base was not adequately funded at prior levels, and equity capital has to be raised simply to repay borrowings, the company could be in serious financial trouble. Few suppliers of funds at this stage care to have these funds used to pay off prior creditors. Having to repay loans puts the company in a financial trap which at best knocks down the price at which the company might obtain additional equity capital or at worst could result in virtual loss of control through dilution or outright financial failure.

Fourth Level. Pre-Public

A. Characteristics of firm.
   Companies at this stage have already made the decision to go public. They have met the criteria for public companies given earlier, or are well on their way to doing so. They may be anywhere from three to ten years old.
B. Sources of funds.
   Venture capitalists, SBICs, some insurance companies, some investment bankers.
C. Objectives of investors.
   Variable, depending upon prevailing market conditions and the particular needs and budgets of the financial institutions involved. Probably two times investment over a two-year period.

D.   Use of funds.
     By definition, this stage is intended to "bridge" the financial gap until the company goes public, and as such, the funds may be used in a number of ways, all of which would classify under the general heading of increasing working capital.
E.   Forms.
     Private placement, mostly convertible notes, or notes with warrants attached.
F.   Observations.

   This stage is somewhat of an extension of the third level, and could perhaps be included in that section. The distinguishing point is that the decision to go public has already been made and plans in that direction have been initiated. This is usually the first stage at which the investment banker becomes interested, and at which his advice and help can be meaningful to the firm. Since his services will be needed in the near future, the company should begin making such contacts.

   Those insurance companies, who, by policy, make equity-oriented private placements, become more interested at this level.

   Not all companies need additional equity financing at this stage. Many are already adequately financed and simply proceed from the third to the fifth levels.

Fifth Level.   Going Public

A.   Characteristics of firm.
     Companies going public already demonstrate those characteristics described at the beginning of this chapter, or are well on their way to doing so.
B.   Sources of funds.
     Public investors through investment bankers.
C.   Objective of investors.
     Variable, whatever the investing public thinks it wants and the investment bankers think they can sell.
D.   Use of funds.
     To increase working capital by both retiring short-term debt and increasing the financing base for current assets. To add to plant and equipment. *Not* to cash out insiders.
E.   Form.
     An underwriting of common stock.
F.   Observations.

Chapter 33 in this book describes the underwriting process and the work of investment bankers. The reader is referred to that chapter for a detailed description of the process. Some points will be made here: The act of going public should not be considered an end in itself. Rather, it should be regarded as an integral part of a firm's long-term financing plan. More financing will be required after this point, and the initial public offering should be structured to facilitate future financing insofar as possible. Once a company has gone public, its common stock will become the principal vehicle for equity financing. It will also become an important instrument for external growth through acquisitions. Therefore, its price level and the regard in which it is held will become a critical determinant in pursuing these objectives. Hopefully, its history in the marketplace will become a help to that end and not a constraint.

A poorly conceived or executed initial offering, an ill-chosen investment banker, a bad timing decision, can well result in a significant decline in value after the offering. If such should be the case, all future financing may be seriously, if not permanently, impaired.

Also, management should be fully aware that running a publicly owned company is a new way of life. Public disclosure of all significant facts about the company must be made and maintained. Investors, brokers and regulatory agencies must be dealt with as an ongoing fact of life.

Minimum underwriting requirements by most reputable investment bankers are:

1. Sales of around $10 million and/or net profit after taxes of $1 million.
2. Average annual increases in earnings over the last three years of 15 percent or more.
3. An initial underwriting of at least $3 million or more, consisting of at least 300,000 shares. A reasonably liquid after-market is an essential element for a successful public offering, and these numbers are presently the minimum to achieve that.

Proceeds from the public offering should not properly be used to cash out insiders. This should wait for a subsequent secondary offering.

Sixth Level.   The Public Company

A.   Characteristics of firm.

There is only one characteristic that distinguishes companies at this stage. They are all publicly owned.

B.   Source of funds.

Primarily the public market through investment bankers: some insurance companies, and some venture capitalists.

C.   Objectives of investors.

Variable, depending upon market conditions and investor psychology.

D.   Use of funds.

All corporate purposes: plant and equipment, working capital, reduction of short- and long-term debt, acquisitions, cashing in selling stockholders.

E.   Form.

Public underwritings through investment bankers. To a much lesser degree private placements through insurance companies, some venture capitalists.

F.   Observations.

Once the initial offering has been made, the public market thus created becomes the primary vehicle for future equity financing. The major determinant of the cost of equity capital thereafter will be the market price of the stock.

This level is not so much a stage of development as it is a permanent way of life. Depending upon the particular fortunes of the firm, many types and forms of financing might take place. In the public marketplace the company may have occasion to sell more common stock, debentures, convertible debentures, and so on. In the private market it might affect private placements in the form of common stock, straight notes, convertible notes, and notes with warrants. The company probably continues to work closer with its investment banker than with any of the other sources of capital mentioned in this chapter.

EXTERNAL FACTORS AFFECTING EQUITY FINANCING

In this section, we will consider those factors influencing the equity capital markets which are external to the corporation and over which it has little, if any, control. In doing so, however, we will not get into a lengthy discussion of the economy, money supply, interest rate trends, and so on. These matters are covered elsewhere in this book. We confine our remarks here to observations about cost of capital, flotation costs, market timing, and the question of control.

Cost of Capital

It would indeed be delightful if we could fine tune the cost of capital concept for equity financing with formulas and devices that permit a close projection of such costs and an optimum capital structuring in relation to all other financing, both internal and external. In theory, this can be done, but in actuality it is most difficult. Equity financing has been, and probably will remain, an art rather than a science. This is not to say that a firm should not attempt to establish certain criteria and guidelines that become goals. They certainly should. Rather, the firm should recognize the practicality of leaving rather wider perimeters with respect to equity financing, wider probably than any other type of financing. Equity markets are more mercurial than debt markets and rather challenge one's ability to forecast with precision.

The principal determinant of the cost of equity financing is, of course, the price-earnings (P/E) ratios that prevail at any given time. Raising money at 20 times earnings puts the cost of capital at 5 percent. at 10 times earnings, 10 percent: at 5 times earnings, 20 percent. If the P/E ratio is lower than the company's *internal rate of return,* then the financing would have a negative or delusive effect on earnings.

The general level and direction of the stock market has a strong influence over P/E ratios. Therefore, we will have something to say about timing in a subsequent section.

Flotation Costs

In addition to the implied costs of financing attributable to varying price-earnings ratios, there are direct costs incurred in raising external capital. These are the flotation costs.

In underwritings they include the underwriter's fee or commission, quite often the underwriter's out-of-pocket expense (due diligence meetings, and so on) and "other" expenses, which encompass the legal, accounting, and printing costs. The underwriter's fee may be viewed as a semivariable cost, depending on such factors as size of offering and market receptivity. The other costs may be regarded as relatively fixed insofar as they will not vary appreciably with respect to size or marketability, but rather with the internal complexity of the issuer.

There is no precise percentage that can be applied to flotation costs. Each financing is an individual thing. A generalized picture, however, can be presented of such costs in the SEC table on underwritings (See Table 1).

TABLE 1
Flotation Costs Common Stock

Size of Issue (000 omitted)	Commissions (%)	Other Expenses (%)	Total Cost (%)
$ 500–$ 900	9.7	4.9	14.6
$ 1,000–$ 1,900	8.6	3.0	11.6
$ 2,000–$ 4,900	7.4	1.7	9.1
$ 5,000–$ 9,900	6.7	1.0	7.6
$10,000–$19,900	6.2	0.6	6.8
$20,000–$49,900	4.9	0.8	5.7
$50,000 and over	2.3	0.2	2.5

Private placement financing is generally cheaper than public underwriting especially in the lower dollar volume where it is most apt to occur. Again, each financing is an individual matter, but fees charged by investment banker or finders range somewhat between the following extremes:

	Percent	Percent
First million	5	5
Second million	1	4
Third million	1	3
Fourth million	1	2
Fifth million	1	1
Balance	1	1

"Other" expenses are generally lower in private placements than in public underwritings, often by substantial amounts.

In addition to the above direct costs, the investment banker may also negotiate for warrants as part of his fee. The amount can vary considerably from one situation to another, and from state to state, which have different rules. A reasonable figure might be about 5 percent of the offering, with an exercise price about 10–20 percent above the offering price.

Timing

Timing is the essence of the art of good equity financing. There are innumerable approaches and techniques for determining future stock prices. The scope and purpose of this chapter does not permit exploring them here.

Yet timing *is* important. Therefore, the writer would like to offer one technique or device that he has found both useful and profitable.

In 1962, an article appeared in *Barron's*[1] in which a technical indicator was described. It was developed by the Trendex Research Corporation.[2] Called the "Very Long-Term Buying Guide for Conservative Investors," the guide purports to signal or confirm a newly emerging bull market.

Throughout the last 50 years of stock market history this indicator does have a remarkable record for doing what it was designed to do. With very few exceptions, the general level of stock prices rose for at least 12 months *after* the indicator rendered its signal. The average advance has been around 24 months; some lasted longer.

Based on past probabilities, the period from 6 to 18 months after the signal occurs seems to be particularly appropriate for timing a public underwriting.

A period of generally rising stock prices does not guarantee that stocks in all industries will similarly rise. However, the overall odds of getting off an equity financing in a rising market are certainly much better than in a declining one.

The Question of Control

The question of control (i.e. the percentage of ownership given up by the entrepreneurs in obtaining equity financing, may be viewed by them as an internal, rather than an external factor. But in reality, it is dependent on the terms, or cost, of money, and that is an external factor.

The entrepreneurs of younger companies frequently get hung up on the question of control. They do not want to lose control of their

[1] "The Madness of Crowds," *Barron's*, October 15, 1962, p. 5.

[2] Trendex Research Corporation, Maverick Bldg., San Antonio, Texas.

company and, therefore, approach a prospective equity financing with a deep prejudice in this regard which distorts their objectivity to the realities of such financing. Institutional investors involved in equity financing do not predicate their terms with this factor specifically in mind. They simply determine what will be necessary to adequately and realistically finance the operation and bring the return on investment which they want and which is their objective. This may be 5 percent or 65 percent of the operation.

The point is this. Most institutional investors do not seek control for its own sake. They would much prefer not to get involved in management. The percentage of ownership they might require is simply a function of the terms of the financing itself, and those terms are essentially set by the degree of competition existing in the economy at any one time for funds of that type.

The issue of control, therefore, is really set or decided by prevailing external conditions, and is not simply a subjective judgment on the part of either owners or investors.

At levels one and two, venture capitalists rather often require that the entrepreneurs accept some performance criteria that must be met as a condition of the financing, regardless of the percentage of ownership involved. If the criteria are met by the management, they simply carry on. If the criteria are not met, the venture capitalist may have the right to remove the management or at least oversee their activities.

In publicly held companies, 35 percent of the stock owned by management is generally considered sufficient to retain effective control.

SOURCES OF FINANCING

There is at least one other chapter in this book describing in detail the sources of equity capital discussed here. Therefore, we will confine this section to certain highlights that may prove useful to the reader.

First, let us point out a truism that is so fundamental that oftentimes it is not considered by companies in need of equity financing. A basic concept of *equity* financing as practiced by all the institutional sources of capital described herewith is that of eventual liquidity. None of these sources make equity investments without the definite expectation that the investment will become marketable in the intermediate term, usually within five years or less. Thus, it is implicit in this type of financing that the investment eventuates in some form of publicly held security, either directly, or indirectly through merger.

Venture Capitalists

The concept of venture capital is probably pretty near as old as the human race. Certainly it enjoys a long and perhaps romantic history through the great merchant banks of Europe and the empire builders of this country.

Yet the practice has always been rather fragmented and individualized to the point that one could not really define venture capitalists as financial institutions.

Now, however, one gets the impression that this area of the financial spectrum has taken on a certain coalescence, a certain maturity and sophistication that it did not previously possess. There now exists, for example, a National Association of Venture Capitalists[3] with a present membership of about 100 firms. These firms represent about $500 million in invested funds.

Beyond this group, there are perhaps another 200 organizations involved to some degree in venture capital financing. Their names can be obtained from a publication entitled, *Venture Capital.*[4]

Venture capital firms are equity investors. Aside from wealthy individuals, they constitute the primary source of financing from the first through the third stages. They are not intermediaries. They are investors themselves. Therefore, they do not normally charge fees or commissions.

Venture capital firms represent a number of types of investors: private individuals, wealthy families, insurance companies, commercial banks, industrial companies, or various combinations thereof.

Some of the more prominent and successful venture capital firms are: Fred Adler (New York City); American Research & Development (Boston); Asset Management Company (Palo Alto); Bessemer Securities (New York); Greater Washington Investors, Inc. (Washington, D.C.); New Business Resources (Dallas); Arthur Rock & Co. (San Francisco); Rockefeller Family & Assoc.

---

[3] National Association of Venture Capitalists, 10 So. La Salle St., Chicago, Ill.

[4] *Venture Capital,* Technimetrics, Inc., 919 Third Ave., New York, New York 10022.

(New York); Sutter Hill Ventures (Palo Alto); West Ven (San Francisco); Morgenthaler Associates (Cleveland); Idanta Partners (San Diego).

Small Business Investment Companies

Much of what has been said of venture capitalists applies to SBICs. They tend to operate through about the same spectrum. The SBICs are somewhat more confined by law to the size of company they can invest in, and the percentage of their investment in that company.

When the Small Business Investment Company Act of 1958 was passed, it was widely hailed as a great new way to finance the younger company. Many SBICs were formed, often with insufficient financing to be really effective. This, together with a rather disappointing investment experience, caused many to leave the field or to cut back on new investments made.

The more successful and sizable SBICs now operating are those belonging to commercial banks, such as: Chase Manhattan Capital Corp. (Chase Manhattan Bank); Citicorp Venture Capital, Ltd. (First National City Bank New York City); 15 Broad Street Resources Corp. (Morgan Guaranty Trust, New York); Continental Illinois Venture Corp. (Continental Illinois Bank, Chicago); First Capital Corp. of Chicago (First National Bank of Chicago); Small Business Enterprises Co. (Bank of America, Los Angeles and San Francisco); First Small Business Investment Company (Security Pacific Bank, Los Angeles).

Like the Venture Capitalists, many of the SBICs have formed their own association.[5]

Insurance Companies

Relatively few insurance companies participate in venture capital financing. The ones that are active may do so in two different ways. Some have their own venture capital subsidiaries, such as Allstate and Massachusetts Mutual. Some invest directly from their own portfolios, such as Equitable Life Assurance and American General Insurance Company.

---

[5] National Association of Small Business Investment Companies, 512 Washington Building, Washington, D.C. 20005.

Those companies that are active in making equity-oriented private placements constitute a significant source of capital throughout all the stages. Their most common form of investment is the convertible note, or the note with warrants attached. They tend to work closely with selected investment bankers.

Investment Bankers

Investment bankers have long been the traditional source for the large majority of equity financing in this country, since they control the mechanism whereby corporations reach the public market place. They are the primary source of such capital at the fifth and sixth levels.

Investment bankers do not employ their own capital to make equity investments in other companies. Rather, they are intermediaries and perform their services for a fee.

Most investment bankers are not particularly interested in companies at the first three levels. They will become more interested at the fourth, and of course, are directly involved at the fifth and sixth stages.

One present trend among investment bankers should be noted here. Formerly, virtually all underwriting activity was dominated and controlled by the major New York houses. In recent years, however, we have seen the rise of the "Regional Firm" (headquartered outside of New York City) as a strong contributor to the initiating of new issues. It is now often more advisable for the smaller to medium-sized company to use the services of his regional investment banker than to go through a New York firm.

Some of the prominent regional firms are: Bateman Eichler, Hill Richards, Inc. (Los Angeles); Dain, Kalman & Quail (Minneapolis); Piper Jaffray & Hopwood, Inc. (Minnesota); The Robinson-Humphrey Co. Inc. (Atlanta); Rauscher Pierce (Dallas).

Industrial Companies

In recent years, we have begun to see the emergence of the industrial company in the field of equity financing. The trend is not significant yet, but it is noticable. It could well become more pronounced in the future.

The publication previously mentioned, *Venture Capital,* contains a special section that lists 50 industrial companies that purport to do equity capital financing.

The majority appear to be more interested in making acquisitions than anything else, but some do have formalized programs for making direct equity investments in younger companies. In doing this, however, their primary objective is different than all the other sources covered in this chapter. They are not particularly interested in making an investment to resell at a later date and thereby make a capital gain. Rather, they are interested in developing a subsidiary that can contribute to the income flow of the parent company on an ongoing basis. Some use the subsidiary approach to develop a new line of business, or to extend a present product line. They do not appear much at the first or second level, but rather at the third. Singer and Honeywell are two firms active in this area.

PRESENT AND FUTURE TRENDS

Throughout this chapter, we have viewed the sources and forms of equity financing much as they have been during the last decade or so. They still exist and function as described, but certain changes have occurred in recent years which suggest somewhat different trends for the future. This chapter cannot be properly closed without making note of some of these changes.

The areas we will look at are: (1) corporate liquidity; (2) stock market cycles; (3) option markets; (4) Rule 144; (5) foreign investors; (6) institutional investors; and (7) industrial companies.

Corporate Liquidity. Over the past several decades, the liquidity of American corporations in the aggregate has deteriorated to such a degree that it has become a matter of significance with respect to future equity financing.

America is supposed to be the land of the capitalist, of equity, but in fact we are really a debt-oriented society. Corporate growth in the last two decades has been financed much more by debt than by equity, to the point where balance sheets have deteriorated markedly. The statistics in Tables 2A and 2B (for all manufacturing firms) bear this out.

We cannot state precisely what the optimum debt load for an individual corporation, or for the entire system, should be. But we can state with certainty that there is some limit to indebtness, be-

TABLE 2A
Ratios for Years Indicated

	1947	1971
Current ratio.	2.67	2.03
Quick ratio.	0.83	0.25
Long-term debt as a percentage of total capital	27.8%	
Debt-equity ratio		44.4%
Debt coverage	24.2 times	4.4 times
Ratio of interest to profits and interest	8.6%	45.6%

TABLE 2B
Compound Annual Rates of Increase

	1947-71 (percent)	1965-71 (percent)
Corporate profits before taxes.	4.1%	1.2%
Corporate profits after taxes.	3.5	0.0
Total corporate debt	8.8	10.5
Total long-term corporate debt	9.2	10.4

yond which either individual corporations or the entire system could not function.

Just where the limit is, we do not know. That we have been brushing against it in recent years is testified by the periodic recurrence of credit crunches, liquidity crises, and currency alarms.

The fact is that a great debt structure has been superimposed upon an ever more fragile equity base. This will cause corporations to go to the equity market when, as, and if they are able. But in a stock market of high yields and low price-earnings ratios, only the better known and more mature companies can command a public underwriting. That companies will go to the equities market, if they can, regardless of cost, is testified to by the plethora of public utilities offerings in 1974–75 at prices well below book value and at dilutive price-earnings ratios. This suggests that many corporations will go to the public *when* they can, not if they should.

In this climate, the small- to medium-sized company will be hard-pressed to get through to the public equity market. Whether they can get through at all in the 1970s is problematical.

This problem is elemental in its foundations and will not shortly pass away. It is further intensified by other trends as described below.

The Stock Market.   In a previous section, we estimated that the members of the National Association of Venture Capitalists had invested around $500 million primarily in stage one to three companies. Of that amount, we would estimate that perhaps 75 percent to 85 percent is "locked in"; that is, the investee companies could not effectively register and distribute the shares.

Two routes are open to these investors seeking liquidity: either Rule 144 (about which we will say more), or selling out to a larger company which has stock already public. More and more the latter course is being taken.

Why are the venture investors locked in? For reasons cited in the previous section on corporate liquidity, and because the majority of these investments were made in the late 60s and early 70s, when underwritings on newer, smaller companies still had a market. Now they do not.

Many institutional investors have thus developed liquidity problems of their own as a result. And many have been "burned." So the amount of money going into stage one to three companies has been severely curtailed in recent years. This type of financing is simply noncompetitive.

Will we have another speculative period in the stock market? History indicates we will, but perhaps not until the 1980s. And even if and when we do, the speculation of the public may not manifest itself in the new issue market as it has in the past. The options market may take care of that.

Options Markets.   The Chicago Board Option Exchange first opened in 1973. Since that time, option volume has grown to 30 percent of New York Stock Exchange volume. The American Stock Exchange Option Market went on stream in 1975. Other regional exchanges followed. It may well be that these various option exchanges will go a long way toward satiating the public's desire for speculation. In this writer's opinion, the option markets pose a major competitor to the new issue market, and will compound the difficulties posed in a previous discussion.

Rule 144.   It is difficult to deal with this subject within the confines of a chapter like this. The rule is relatively simple; its application is a bit more complex than most practitioners will allow.

Rule 144 was first adopted by the Securities and Exchange Commission on April 15, 1972. Essentially, it permitted owners of restricted shares (corporate officers and directors, majority stockholders, and private placement investors) to sell an amount of shares equal to 1 percent of the total number of shares outstanding by the issuer in the case of unlisted companies, and an amount equal to this 1 percent or the average weekly trading volume, whichever is the lesser, if the company is listed.

The seller, the broker, and the issuer have to conform to certain SEC forms and rules in the state. This can be done once in every six-month period, provided the shares have been held for at least two years.

Rule 144 offers some liquidity to private placement investors, and could be said to enhance such investment. However, 1 percent of a company's outstanding shares does not represent a major investment. So while the Rule does offer some liquidity to institutional investors, it still cannot be considered significant enough to completely offset the circumstances described in previous sections.

Foreign Investors. A significant amount of the liquidity of the Western world has been flowing into the OPEC (Organization of Petroleum Exporting Countries) nations as the price for oil. The Arab nations could therefore represent one of the great potential markets for equity capital.

Have the Arabs shown an appetite for such investment? In real estate, to some degree; in corporate financing, almost not at all. Should they be looked to as a future source of equity financing for the smaller to medium-sized American company? It would not appear so from their interest to date.

Institutional Investors. We have already discussed the locked-in character of much of the institutional private placements of the 1960s and 1970s.

In recent years, most new financing done by these institutional sources has been into companies they had already sponsored, but were unable to fund externally through the various levels.

There are still venture capital firms making new investments. They were mentioned in previous sections. But the majority are not. As an aggregate, the resources, interest, and liquidity of venture capitalists preclude them from being a major answer to the equity crises of the American corporate community.

The SBICs are even more withdrawn. Most independent SBICs are relatively illiquid as of the mid 1970s. Those with liquidity are invariably sponsored by major banks, whose investments appear to be gravitating more and more to semidebt or debt instruments as the form of financing. The SBIC seems less a force now in equity financing than formerly.

Insurance companies would appear to be logical beneficiaries of the hiatus of the venture capitalists and the SBICs, but this has proven not quite to be the case. A number of insurance companies moved into the equity private placement field in the late 1960s, and had an uncomfortable experience in doing so. There are many locked-in situations in insurance portfolios.

The passage of the Fiduciary Responsibility Act in 1975 may have further ramifications in this area. Suffice to say, insurance companies as a whole have not moved in to supply the demand for equity capital on the part of medium to smaller sized companies.

Industrial Investors.   Here we have a more positive trend. The large industrial company in the United States has shown a growing interest in its smaller counterpart in the 1970s. More frequently now, the smaller company is bypassing the conventional system of venture capitalists, insurance companies, and investment bankers, to sell out directly to the large company with a well-established market for its common stock.

More and more, venture capitalists are making investments in companies without an intention of going public, but with the intention of selling out to a specific, larger firm.

This is much as it was in the late 1940s and in the 1950s, when price-earnings ratios were relatively low and the new issue market was quiet. There is one significant difference, however. Corporate liquidity was high then. It is low now. Regardless, the industrial investor appears to be the only real growing factor in the equity financing markets of the mid-1970s.

ADDITIONAL SOURCES

Alberts, W. W., and Archer, S. H. "Some Evidence on the Effect of Company Size on the Cost of Equity Capital." *Journal of Financial and Quantitative Analysis*, 8 (March 1973), 229–42.

Bacon, Peter W. "The Subscription Price in Rights Offerings." *Financial Management*, 1 (Summer 1972), 59–64.

Graham, Benjamin. "The Future of Common Stocks." *Financial Analysts Journal*, 30 (September–October 1974), 20–31.

Hettenhouse, George. "A Rationale for Restructuring Stock Plans." *Financial Management*, 1 (Summer 1972), 30–36.

Keane, Simon M. "The Significance of the Issue Price in Rights Issues." *Journal of Business Finance*, 4 (1972), 40–45.

Krouse, Clement G., and Lee, Wayne Y. "Optimal Equity Financing of the Corporation." *Journal of Financial and Quantitative Analysis*, 8 (September 1973), 539–64.

Logue, Dennis E. "On the Pricing of Unseasoned Equity Issues: 1965–1969." *Journal of Financial and Quantitative Analysis*, 8 (January 1973), 91–104.

Reilly, Frank K. "Further Evidence on Short-Run Results for New Issue Investors." *Journal of Financial and Quantitative Analysis*, 8 (January 1973), 83–90.

Stevenson, Harold W. *Common Stock Financing*. Ann Arbor, Mich.: University of Michigan, 1957.

Wakoff, Gary I. "On Shareholders' Indifference to the Proceeds Price in Preemptive Rights Offerings." *Journal of Financial and Quantitative Analysis*, 8 (December 1973), 835–36.

Chapter 35

Dividend Policy and Retained Earnings

David J. Vitale[*]

INTRODUCTION

MOST CORPORATE financial officers, looking back over the late 1960s and 1970s, would probably agree that the most significant development in the economic environment during that period was the quantum leap in the volatility of the financial markets. Interest rate cycles were closer together and the amplitude of the swings was much greater. The long-term debt markets were both very nervous and selective. The markets for new equity, when they existed at all, were receptive to only a small percentage of corporations. And the markets for existing equity were extremely volatile.

In this type of environment, the perceived value of financial flexibility is heightened. Staying power and reserve strength become important aspects of overall success in the corporate financial officer's ability to utilize the various financial markets. Although it is not certain that the future of the financial markets will continue on this erratic and volatile course, recent history has focused increased attention on retained earnings as a source of financing and, therefore, on the dividend policy decision. In fact, history suggests that the recurring need for capital is a primary factor in determining corporate dividend policy.

* David J. Vitale is vice president and treasurer of First Chicago Corporation, Chicago, Illinois.

A commonly used measure of dividend policy is the ratio of dividends to corporate profits. Statistics show that, between 1920 and 1947, dividends paid by U.S. corporations as a percentage of net profits dropped from 64.1 percent to 35.6 percent after rising to a high of 71.2 percent in 1929. Yet in the 13 years following 1947, this percentage rose again to 61.3 percent in 1960. Since then the ratio has declined erratically, dropping to a 20-year low of 38 percent in 1974.

These figures would seem to suggest an erratic need for capital. In fact, this is not so. In a study at the Brookings Institution, statistical techniques were used to isolate and measure the influence of various factors on the changes in historical dividend performance.[1] The most important determining factor in dividend payout was not corporate profits, but cash flow, defined as profits after taxes plus depreciation. Because of the liberalization of depreciation allowances over the period, the ratio of depreciation charges to profits rose from 30 percent in 1947 to over 100 percent in 1960. This factor more than accounts for the indicated change from 36 percent to 62 percent in the dividend to profit percentage during that period. With respect to the more recent decline, perhaps a portion can be attributed to the effect of "inventory" profits in a period of severe inflation. The U.S. Department of Commerce estimates that payouts in 1974 were about 52 percent of profits adjusted for these inventory profits.

All things being equal, corporations in the aggregate tend to maintain a ratio of dividends to cash flow, for cash flow represents one source of capital needed to finance future expansion. Although history suggests that dividends are a function of corporate cash flow and that retained earnings represent the most reliable source of capital, the impact of dividend policy on the cost of raising external capital cannot be overlooked. Dividend policy does, in fact, significantly affect the ability of corporations to raise capital externally. Because the potential for meeting the financial requirements of the firm from external sources is significantly greater than its internal potential, greater emphasis should be placed on the impact of a dividend decision on the marketplace.

Unfortunately, there are no empirical studies that prove that any given dividend policy will absolutely determine the market valua-

---

[1] John A. Brittain, *Corporate Dividend Policy* (Washington, D.C.: The Brookings Institution, 1966).

tion for the shares of a firm. However, building on basic financial theory, intuitive logic, and some recent analytical work, a reasonable conclusion can be reached: A dividend policy which reflects the underlying nature of the firm and which is *consistently* applied will minimize financing costs and provide adequate flexibility over time.

In this chapter, we will attempt to outline a framework for the dividend policy decision. We will look at the decision first from the point of view of shareholders, to see how their needs and preferences should impact the decision process. We will also look at the financial constraints and criteria facing an individual firm in establishing a dividend policy. Beginning with an idealized model, we will look in turn at each of the various factors that tend either to offset the general policies suggested by the model, or to influence systematically the direction of a dividend policy for an individual firm. With this as a base, we will try to construct a framework for making the dividend policy decision in an individual firm, and finally look at some recent trends that may also tend to influence the dividend policy decision.

Throughout this chapter the phrase "dividend policy decision" will be repeated. It is not an idle choice of words. The temptation to make a series of dividend decisions on a quarter-to-quarter basis should be avoided. Dividend policy is too important a tool for overall financial management and too valuable as a means for communicating with the investing world to be relegated to the role of a short-term option or tactic. A long-term focus is strongly advocated, not only because of the major impact of this policy decision on the company, but also because the market places a high value on consistency in the actual dividend policy. Throughout the chapter this theme will receive appropriate elaboration.

THE SHAREHOLDER'S VIEW—UNCERTAINTY AND THE VALUE OF CONSISTENCY

While at the most general level, both the firm and its shareholders share the same objective of optimum long-run return, shareholders have particular preferences for the form and predictability of that return and face complications such as taxes and transactions costs that must be recognized in formulating a responsive dividend policy. Unless these needs and preferences are satisfied, the firm will fail to achieve the objectives of its shareholder constituency.

Theoretical financial models, like most theoretical models, usually make the initial assumption of a perfect world. Here, perfect knowledge, foresight and capital markets make dividend policy irrelevant to the corporation. Secure in the knowledge that an equity issue in the perfect market would be available to satisfy future capital needs as they arise, corporations are free to pay shareholders whatever amounts might not be needed immediately by the company. Stockholders are also indifferent to the dividend policy of corporations in this perfect world. A stockholder in need of cash would just sell whatever percentage of his shares necessary to generate that cash.

The world is obviously not this perfect. It is thus necessary to examine some of the factors that cause these "imperfections" because they are ultimately the prime motivation for payment of dividends and because they strongly influence the dividend policy decision.

First, let us look at the "imperfections" which affect stockholders. Taxes are one of the more important influences on corporate stockholders. Dividends are taxable to recipients at normal income rates (after the dividend exclusion), whereas the capital gains on increases in share values are taxable at the lower capital gains rates. Thus, the effect of taxes should encourage the retention of earnings rather than the payment of dividends. In fact, the study by Brittain shows that this factor was substantial and accounted for part of the downward trend in dividend payout that occurred between the late 1920s and the early postwar years.[2]

However, this analysis erroneously implies that all stockholders face the same tax situation. For some stockholders tax considerations are not important. These include endowment funds and pension and retirement trusts. Also, for lower income individuals current income tax rates and capital gains tax rates may be nearly equal. Thus, although taxes create a tendency toward greater retention of earnings as opposed to increased dividends, there are a substantial number of investors for whom tax considerations are unimportant, and these investors are influenced by other factors in determining their preference for capital gains versus dividends.

---

[2] Ibid.

A second "imperfection" from the viewpoint of the stockholder is transactions costs. In the perfect world, a stockholder can sell shares to generate needed cash at no cost. In the real world, there are costs associated with the sale or transfer of shares which are typically borne by the stockholder. Although there are also costs associated with the payment of dividends, they are less than those incurred in the sale of stock (or at least less visible since they are borne by the company). This, in general, results in a preference for dividends over capital gains.

A third "imperfection" in the real-world marketplace, and one which also tends to favor dividend payments over retention of earnings, is legal or policy constraints on institutions that require investments to yield a certain amount of income on a current basis. For example, certain insurance companies or pension and trust funds are prohibited by law, by regulation, or by charter, from owning stocks that do not or have not paid regular dividends over a period of time.

But perhaps the most important, if least visible "imperfection" is the fact that, because the future and hence shareholders' total return is uncertain, there is a value placed on increased certainty or predictability of shareholders' potential return. Even ignoring the complications of taxes, transactions costs, and legal constraints, this "imperfection" implies that there is a positive value associated with a consistent dividend policy; i.e., one which is consistent with both the firm's operating results or financial condition and management's expectations for the future. These two aspects of consistency are equally important. Practically speaking, shareholders will use the past dividend history as one of the bases for prediction of future returns. If dividends are closely related to earnings or financial condition, one element of variability in future returns—namely, capricious managerial decisions—is eliminated from the prediction process, and shareholders can focus instead on the firm's likely performance. But if dividends are also an accurate reflection of management's expectations, predictions can be made with greater confidence, assuming that the expectations so expressed are likely to be realized. So from the shareholders' point of view, the greater the consistency in dividend policy, the less uncertainty he will perceive in total return, and consequently the greater the value he will attribute to his ownership.

CORPORATE CONSTRAINTS—THE NEED FOR CAPITAL AND FINANCIAL FLEXIBILITY

While the shareholders' view suggests that dividend policy does matter, and that there is a positive value to a consistent policy, it does not suggest what the policy should be. We have mentioned that historical analysis shows that, in the aggregate, corporate dividends tend to be directly related to cash flow. Attempts to apply this statistical analysis to individual firms proved much less satisfactory. Income and cash flow measures were much less able to predict the actual dividend policy for an individual firm than they were for firms in the aggregate. What this tends to suggest is that factors internal to the firm contribute significantly to dividend policy. Only in the aggregate, where these differences may tend to balance out, do dividends tend to have a proportional relationship to profits or cash flow. It is these internal factors and the firm's economic environment that, in addition to the basic shareholder considerations, will shape the policy decision in a particular direction.

The Need for Capital

Firms need capital to maintain their resources and to grow. The faster a firm wants to grow, the more capital it will need. Unless it raises new equity or increases its leverage by borrowing more funds, retained earnings are the principal source of this capital.

This general concept can also be expressed as a precise relationship—the growth rate in earnings will equal the rate of return on equity multiplied by the percentage of earnings that are retained. For example, a firm that earns a constant 15 percent after tax on its equity can grow at 9 percent per year if it pays out 40 percent of earnings as dividends. The formula:

$$G = R(1 - P)$$

where

G = Growth rate of earnings (annual percentage)
R = Return on equity (annual after-tax percentage)
P = Payout ratio (dividends/net income after taxes)

is more obvious at the extremes. If the company pays out all its earnings and its return on equity does not change, its earnings will not grow at all since its capital base remains constant $(.15(1-1) = .15(0) = 0)$; whereas, if dividends are zero, earnings growth will equal return on equity $(.15(1-0) = .15(1) = .15)$.

For firms that require capital as part of their mix of productive resources, this is an inescapable reality. By combining this constraint with the model of dividend policy in a perfect world and the factors that affect the assumption of perfection, we can examine a number of the considerations that are likely to affect the dividend policy of any particular corporation.

In a world without taxes and other irregularities, if the corporate management sees that their company has the capacity to expand (meaning capacity to expand in the sense of opportunity to employ capital productively at or above its normal rate of return) at a rate of 5 percent per year and its return on invested funds is 10 percent, then the decision is simple. The corporation retains half of its earnings, exactly what it needs to meet its capital requirements, and pays out the rest in dividends. Unfortunately, as we have suggested, the decision is not nearly this simple. There are a great number of other factors that will tend to influence the decision on the most appropriate payout ratio, and it is these factors that we will examine next.

The Need for Financial Flexibility

A number of specific factors that affect the dividend decision relate to the economic environment of the firm and its own needs to maintain financial flexibility while optimizing performance. Each has its own particular impact on the formulation of a dividend policy.

Imperfections and Access to the Capital Markets. While it is true that, in the long run, the company's annual need for increased capital will be approximately the earnings growth rate times the actual capital base (as derived from the formula for the basic constraint on corporate growth), for many corporations this may not be true in the short run. If a company cannot add to its productive capacity except in very large units, the ability to employ funds productively in the interim becomes a factor. An example would be a manufacturing company that finds that it cannot build an efficient plant below a certain size and can, therefore, only build one additional plant every five years. If the company has relatively uninter-rupted access to debt and equity markets, it might increase short-run payout and issue new securities when needed for expansion. However, if timing is critical and rates and access to the markets are uncertain, there is a high risk of possible disruption of financing for planned future expansion. A greater retention of earnings here might, therefore, be justified.

Interest Rate Expectations and Financial Flexibility. Another factor that can assume importance in the dividend policy decision is the expected behavior of interest rates and the consequent effect on the need for financial flexibility. Most corporations have sources of funds other than capital and retained earnings. The use of lever-age is common in industry and adds another dimension to the dividend policy decision. Most corporations find that in addition to equity capital, they can effectively employ long-term debt in the creation of additional productive capacity.

While optimum debt structure is an important topic that cannot be analyzed in sufficient detail here, it does have implications for the overall dividend policy decision.

Typically, most corporations feel that they have certain restric-tions on the overall mix of debt and equity funds that they can em-ploy. It is virtually impossible to define optimum debt structure as a single value of a particular ratio. There is probably a band of ratios of debt to capital and capital to various types of debt within which a given corporation can operate efficiently and comfortably. For example, if the optimal debt structure for a corporation sug-gested that the ratio of long-term debt to equity should always be between 30 percent and 40 percent, then in an environment where long-term interest rates were expected to be stable and access to the long-term debt market was expected to be fairly continuous, financing strategy is straightforward. Under these circumstances, the only impact of overall balance sheet proportion considerations on dividend policy arises from the size of the efficient unit of addi-tions to long-term debt. Thus, if the corporation has a 40 percent long-term debt to equity ratio, slightly more earnings than abso-lutely necessary to maintain that 40 percent ratio would be retained. Resulting increases in equity would reduce the ratio to, say, 35 percent, providing the opportunity to issue an efficient amount of additional debt. Note that an issue of 5 percent of equity capital structure would increase the debt equity ratio back to 40 percent.

On the other hand, if there were likely to be great variability in the level of long-term rates or perhaps periods when long-term debt was simply unavailable to the corporation, then the corporate dividend strategy might be altered appreciably. For example, in a relatively stable environment a company might normally expect to go to the long-term debt market once a year. They would then need to retain only the extra amount of earnings necessary to prevent exceeding a 40 percent ratio even immediately following a new debt issue. In an environment in which there might be two consecutive years in which an issue of long-term debt were either too expensive to be employed profitably, or simply unattainable, the appropriate policy might be an increase in the amount of earnings retained to a level that would allow the company to meet its total needs for funds without being required to use the debt markets. The analysis required is the same as that used to solve the problem of the efficient minimum issue size for long-term debt. The efficient minimum size now becomes the amount that would be needed over the longest period in which either rates would be too high or during which access might be prohibited.

Looking back over the past few years, a period during which interest rates fluctuated wildly and corporations had only intermittent access to various segments of capital markets, the price paid for the sacrifice of financial flexibility can be clearly seen. To the extent that this kind of economic volatility is expected to continue, treasurers may find that the increased flexibility resulting from higher retention rates will be a desirable goal. In any event, the overall considerations of financial flexibility will continue to play a major role in the formulation of dividend policy.

A FRAMEWORK FOR THE POLICY DECISION

Policy Alternatives

For almost all corporations it is useful and even necessary to express the cumulative analysis of those factors affecting the dividend decision in a policy form. To some extent, most current practices are merely variations on a theme but each has slight differences that might be more or less appropriate for any particular company.

One obvious extreme to be considered is no payout at all. As a practical matter, changing to this policy could be quite difficult for a firm with an established record of dividend payments. But if this course were desirable, interim steps such as partial payment of dividends in stock rather than cash or creation of a second class of shares which had dividends paid only in additional stock could be used to effect the transition.

A second alternative is a fixed level of payments with a clear policy of making one-time "special" payments as yearly performance warrants. For the company that can determine a base level of performance and reinvestment needs, with expected fluctuations occurring only above that level, this kind of policy could mesh nicely with the realities it faces.

A third alternative would be to establish a target of a regular percentage increase in the dividends paid that reflects the company's estimate of its long-run growth potential and to adhere to it regardless of fluctuations in year-to-year results.

A fourth choice would be to establish a percentage of earnings that would be paid out as dividends each year. If year-to-year fluctuations were not expected to be severe, or if maintaining a regular percentage increase during short-run fluctuations were deemed appropriate, this might be a suitable course.

Finally, combinations of policies could also be adopted. For example, combining the last two alternatives might result in a policy of paying out 40 percent of earnings in the long run but limiting the extent of year-to-year changes in the amount paid per share to no more than 8 percent but no less than 5 percent.

Consistency Rewarded

We have already discussed the positive value to shareholders of consistency in dividend policy. Investors look at dividends as a major indicator of the future prospects for the company. Because of this aspect of dividends as a signal to the investment community, as well as the fact that many stockholders have only limited flexibility to respond to changes in dividend income in the short run (for example, people on fixed incomes for whom dividends are a major source of current income and foundations and endowments who rely upon dividends for the maintenance of their operations), all the other considerations that infringe upon dividend policy must be balanced by a reasonable degree of consistency. This is why a long-term framework for dividend policy decisions must be established and periodically reviewed. Using these guidelines and others, once a formula for determining the corporation's appropriate dividend payout is established, an additional factor that must be considered is the extent to which a consistent dividend policy will be modified in the short run to reflect changes in any of the other considerations. We have, for example, discussed a policy which would dictate that under no circumstance would dividend levels themselves actually change by more than a certain percent a year, so that short-run unsustainable increases in profit growth are not totally reflected in higher dividends only to be followed by a period of dividend cuts or changes that could have an overall negative impact on the company's share price. But even this policy is largely consistent with management expectations if short-run jumps in profit are in fact viewed as unsustainable.

A Policy Framework

For the corporation, the establishment of a dividend policy is not an academic exercise, but a practical and ongoing necessity. And while in the short run, there are real limits on the extent to which an existing dividend policy can be modified, an overall evaluation of that policy is an activity which must be conducted regularly. The preceding discussion suggests that a number of steps must be employed in this evaluation of the dividend policy for a given firm. It begins with an estimation of the company's sustainable growth rate, and its relative profitability (return on equity). These two factors will suggest both the amount of capital that will be needed, and the relative desirability of retaining capital in the company as opposed to distributing it to shareholders for alternative uses. For example, a company may have a relatively high rate of growth, and may feel that its primary group of stockholders are those who would prefer capital gains to current income. Further, if its own performance is subject to substantial seasonal or secular variability and its access to the capital market will be at best intermittent, it may be likely to conclude that it should pay out as small a percentage of earnings in dividends as would be consistent with the company's ability to use the retained funds efficiently. On the other hand, a company in a mature market which sees that its own return on equity is likely to decline and that its prospects for growth are somewhat limited, but whose relative stability of earnings and performance are not likely to interrupt its reception by the capital market for long periods, and whose shareholders are more interested in steady current income, may conclude that a high dividend payout is appropriate.

Dividend policy cannot be determined by the arbitrary application of any mathematical formula. But a systematic evaluation of the company's needs, prospects, and overall characteristics can lead to the formulation of a dividend policy consistent with both the company's interests and the interests of its shareholders.

CONCLUSION

The dividend policy decision is difficult to make and difficult to change. As we have suggested, the environment demands a well-conceived and consistent policy as the basis on which individual dividend decisions are to be made. We have suggested that by reviewing its need for capital, its needs for flexibility, its economic environment and its stockholder constituency, the process of shaping such a policy can be rationalized for corporate management.

Putting a dividend policy in place is much like hanging the rudder on a ship. Once in place it can be used to make course corrections or to offset the pressures from changing winds and seas while helping to hold a steady path. And by looking at this rudder, others on the outside can see the direction that has been set. Similarly, without the rudder of policy in place, the course will be erratic and unpredictable, the result of immediate external pressures. The alternatives make the choice compelling.

ADDITIONAL SOURCES

Baumol, William J. "On Dividend Policy and Market Imperfection." *Journal of Business*, 36 (January 1963), 112–15.

Brittain, John A. *Corporate Dividend Policy*. Washington, D.C.: Brookings, 1966.

Chatlos, William; Creal, Richard; Doane-Dodge, Michael; and Hall, Warren. "Growth of Automatic Dividend Investment Plans." *Financial Executive*, 42 (October 1974), 38–43.

Elton, Edwin J., and Gruber, Martin J. "Marginal Stockholder Tax Rates and the Clientele Effect." *Review of Economics and Statistics*, 52 (February 1970), 68–74.

Fama, E. F. "The Empirical Relationships between the Dividend and Investment Decisions of Firms." *American Economic Review,* 64 (June 1974), 304–18.

Fama, E. F., and Babiak, Harvey. "Dividend Policy: An Empirical Analysis." *Journal of the American Statistical Association,* 63 (December 1968), 1132–61.

Friend, Irwin, and Puckett, Marshall. "Dividends and Stock Prices." *American Economic Review,* 54 (September 1964), 656–82.

Gordon, Myron J. "Dividends, Earnings and Stock Prices." *Review of Economics and Statistics,* 41 (May 1959), 99–105.

Higgins, Robert C. "The Corporate Dividend-Saving Decision." *Journal of Financial and Quantitative Analysis,* 7 (March 1972), 1527–42.

Higgins, Robert C. "Dividend Policy and Increasing Discount Rates: A Clarification." *Journal of Financial and Quantitative Analysis,* 7 (June 1972), 1757–62.

Lintner, John. "Distribution of Incomes of Corporations among Dividends, Retained Earnings, and Taxes." *American Economic Review,* 46 (May 1956), 97–113.

Millar, James, and Fielitz, Bruce. "Stock-Split and Stock-Dividend Decisions." *Financial Management,* 2 (Winter 1973), 35–46.

Miller, Merton H., and Modigliani, Franco. "Dividend Policy, Growth, and the Valuation of Shares." *Journal of Business,* 34 (October 1961), 411–33.

Pettit, R. Richardson. "Dividend Announcements, Security Performance, and Capital Market Efficiency." *Journal of Finance,* 27 (December 1972), 993–1008.

Pettway, Richard, and Malone, Phil. "Automatic Dividend Reinvestment-Plans of Nonfinancial Corporations." *Financial Management,* 2 (Winter 1973), 11–18.

Sanden, B. Kenneth, and Crawford, Charles T. "Dividend Tax Reform: Obtaining Relief from Double Taxation." *Financial Executive,* 63 (September 1975), 18–23.

Walter, James E. *Dividend Policy and Enterprise Valuation.* Belmont, Calif.: Wadsworth, 1967.

Watts, Ross. "The Information Content of Dividends." *Journal of Business,* 46 (April 1973), 191–211.

Chapter 36

Sources and Forms of
Debt Capital

Edward P. Sheridan[*]

INTRODUCTION

THE CAPITALIZATION of most companies is composed of two elements—equity and debt. The equity component is reasonably straightforward with the principal variations in classes of stock being the priority of dividend payments; the relative degree of preference in liquidation; and the extent of potential dilution as a result of future conversion of existing convertible securities. The debt element, however, is an altogether different matter and it is this source of capital that provides an opportunity for creativity that makes the corporate fiscal function an exciting challenge in the fulfillment of a company's financial goals. This chapter will review various forms of debt financing as well as prospective sources of funds that corporate financial officers might consider when assessing the capital needs of their own companies. It is not intended to be a review of all such alternatives, but rather to identify those most commonly employed to generate the substantial resources necessary to finance programs of larger borrowing corporations.

Direct sources of debt capital may be simply divided into two basic categories—public and private. The preponderance of long-

---

[*] Edward P. Sheridan is senior vice president and treasurer of the City Investing Company, New York, New York.

term corporate debt financing is done in the public market through securities firms which work together in underwriting syndicates. Issues of debt securities are subscribed to by institutions such as insurance companies, banks, various taxable and nontaxable funds as well as individual investors who purchase such issues for their own account. This is obviously a well-established market, with many investment banking firms having a high degree of competence in placing debt securities of prospective corporate issuers.

The private capital markets that exist are also substantial and these often represent an equally attractive, if not more so, alternative to public financing. These markets are dominated by commercial banks, which historically have loaned money on terms ranging from a demand note to ten years as well as both insurance companies and various state and local employee pension funds which typically provide longer term money out to 25 years. In addition, there is another more diversified and less precisely identifiable group of private lenders ranging from both captive and independent finance companies or basic suppliers on the one hand to governmental agencies on the other. Many private sources of capital are also active in the public market and consequently certain of the selling considerations to be subsequently reviewed have the same degree of applicability to those purchasers of debt securities that are active in both markets. Commercial bank lenders and certain other more specialized types of creditors are notable exceptions and these will be reviewed later.

PUBLIC FINANCING

There are several important and related considerations to be reviewed at the outset of any proposed financing. While these might appear to have greater applicability to the public markets, they are similarly relevant to private placements and include: (*a*) the nature of the issue itself; (*b*) the coupon and other related costs; (*c*) the term and average life; (*d*) the restrictive covenants that will be placed on the issuer; (*e*) the bond rating of the company issuing the security; and (*f*) general conditions of the money and capital markets both at the time the proposed issue is initiated as well as the best estimates of such market conditions at the time of distribution. Each of these items deserves additional comment.

Type of Issue

The form of the debt issue itself is the most basic consideration. Decisions such as whether the security should be short, medium, or long—senior or subordinated—convertible or straight debt— secured or unsecured—direct or indirect—must be made first and are usually dictated by such things as the purpose for which the proceeds will be used; the existing capital/liquidity structure of the issuer; total cost considerations; various indenture requirements; and the future need for additional debt or equity capital.

Pricing

The pricing of any debt issue is a composite of a number of different considerations. A straight debt issue will have a coupon attached which will reflect both the relative creditworthiness or strength of the issuing company as well as the existing market conditions. Naturally, a senior debt issue will have a lower coupon than a comparable subordinated debenture because of the relative priorities of the respective security holders with respect to the assets of the issuing company. A convertible security, while generally subordinated, should have a lower rate than either senior or subordinated issues inasmuch as the purchaser is also buying the right to convert the debt issue into an equity investment over the typical 15–25-year term of the debenture. Flexibility with respect to coupon pricing of a convertible subordinated debenture is usually a direct function of the conversion premium, which is the percentage above the present market value of the stock at which price the bonds may be converted into stock. A low premium will generally mean a lower interest rate, while a high premium will necessitate a greater cost. Typically, conversion premiums are in the 10–15 percent range, but may be higher or lower depending on the volatility of the stock and the future prospects for the issuing company. The interest rate on a convertible debenture thus becomes a direct reflection of the fundamental issue of the extent to which pricing considerations will be weighted in favor of either equity or debt.

As a nearly parallel alternative to a convertible debenture, one might consider a debenture with detachable warrants. While such an issue may seem to be nothing more than a convertible debenture, coupon pricing may be modestly different in that detachable warrants are more valuable than a straight conversion feature as they can be traded separately, thereby generating immediate cash for the investor. This assumption may be more theoretical than real, however, and most investment banking firms would probably insist that it was too immaterial a consideration to make a meaningful difference in the coupon. This notwithstanding, the use of warrants should be carefully analyzed inasmuch as they do generate additional cash resources when exercised. Further, the warrant term is often designed to expire well before there has been much amortization of the debt instrument and the exercise may provide somewhat of a self-liquidating feature in advance of the specific maturities. It should also be recognized that warrants, like a conversion feature on a bond, can provide for the purchase of an equity security of a company other than the direct issuer. The use of subsidiary stock for conversion or warrant exercise has been employed by many companies in situations where they wanted to avoid direct dilution or were prepared to distribute part of a subsidiary holding which might even be a more attractive equity than that of the parent.

Both the underwriting commission or placement fee—typically called the "spread"—and the actual issuing price of the security itself are other factors to be considered when trying to determine the total cost of a financing. Bonds sold at a discount from their face value are obviously more expensive, but such a discount may be an appropriate way to generate a marketable return for an investor while still preserving a coupon that management for one reason or another does not wish to exceed.

Basic to the pricing consideration is the yield of presently trading comparable debt securities of both the issuing company and other similarly rated issues. While there is obviously a relationship between the yield on existing securities and a new issue, the latter can rarely be sold at the then current market yield of outstanding issues and it may take 10–25 basis points to attract additional investor interest, depending on the size of the offering. Factors such as the breadth of the existing market in a given issue already outstanding and the basic strength or weakness of the market into which the issue is being sold will affect the amount of the premium needed to market the new securities.

There are many ways to price an issue and an astute financial officer has an opportunity to make an important contribution to future income statement benefits as a result of his judgment on this facet of the sale of debt securities. It is absolutely necessary, however, that a publicly issued debt security not be too thinly priced if an issuer has a future need to return to such markets. Both underwriters and purchasers are a lot more enthusiastic about future issues if prior sales were successful and did not result in a loss on the inventory while in syndicate or an immediate markdown of the value in a portfolio.

Maturity

The term of any issue and its average life are straightforward considerations. While the term of bank borrowings is often quite short, other more conventional maturities generally range between intermediate 5–7-year notes and 25-year bonds with varying moratoriums on the amortization of principal. Shorter term notes may have a single payment at maturity while bonds may have a ten-year or longer moratorium on repayment. Naturally, the longer the deferral of any principal amortization, the longer the average life of an issue. A 15-year issue with a 12½-year average life (maturities in years 11–15) may well be more beneficial to the issuer than a security of the same duration but amortizing from the outset with a resulting approximate 7½-year average life. Sinking-fund payments can also be "skewed" to provide a greater average life based on smaller payments in earlier years with larger payments in later years and/or large balloon payments at maturity. Interest rates again are partially a function of the life of the issue, with shorter termed issues generally having lower rates than longer maturities unless there happens to be a temporary inversion in the normal yield curve for the respective maturities.

While the term of bank lending arrangements has gone through cycles from the very short to ten-year nonamortizing credits, the current maximum maturity seems to be about seven years in the absence of extenuating circumstances. At the same time, many insurance company lenders have recently been inclined to telescope longer maturities back from 25 years to the 15-year range reflecting their interest in a shorter average life and greater turnover of funds.

Covenants

Other than bank credit lines to handle seasonal financing needs, both public and private senior debt offerings normally include certain restrictions on the issuer. Such restrictions are found in the affirmative and negative covenants that appear in the basic documentation relating to the financing transaction. These covenants are designed to preserve the creditworthiness of the borrower within the framework of certain historically accepted tests which are generally quantifiable as ratios or actual dollar limitations.

The typical covenants most often imposed on borrowing corporations seek to: (*a*) limit the maximum amount of debt that can be incurred relative to total assets or shareholder equity; (*b*) restrict amounts of dividends that can be paid relative to income; (*c*) maintain certain working capital minimums to assure future liquidity; (*d*) provide for the maintenance of certain historic relationships between income and prospective fixed interest charges as well as; (*e*) limitating the incurrence of lease rental obligations, sale leaseback transactions, and guarantees of debt. In addition, there are many other more specifically tailored kinds of tests that might be imposed on the borrowing company that are peculiar to either its business or the nature of the transaction itself.

While covenants in public indentures are usually less restrictive than those in private note agreements, it is essential that compliance with such tests be analyzed as carefully as possible to determine their effect on future corporate flexibility. While modifications to an overly restrictive credit test may be subsequently granted, this is often very time consuming and sometimes will require an upward adjustment in the interest rate as a "quid pro quo." While lenders in the private sector generally represent themselves as being reassuringly sympathetic to future changes, it is unwise to agree to a specific restriction if there is any reasonable chance that a violation will be incurred no matter how far into the financing it may occur. It is far better to take the time to negotiate the specifics before concluding the transaction than to be subject to the lender's attitudes later on when the circumstances surrounding both the financing and business relationships might be materially different.

Bond Ratings

These ratings are absolutely critical to the sale of straight debt securities to the public, but have been historically somewhat less important in private placements with institutional sources. While securities ratings are not nearly as important in the sale of an equity-related issue, such as a convertible debenture, they do have a certain influence nevertheless. Ratings affect both the actual interest rate as well as ultimate marketability. In particular, many prospective purchasers are regulated by state and local requirements with respect to guideline criteria on the composition of bond portfolios which criteria often relies in large part on the bond rating of an issuer. Consequently, a weaker grade issue might not qualify for acceptance by a certain class of purchaser which obviously reduces the potential market with an attendant effect on the success of the issue.

At present, the best known bond rating agencies are Standard & Poor's and Moody's. The bond rating process is one that is initiated by the issuer and/or managing underwriter of the syndicate and involves one or more meetings between the agency and management. Historic financial information is reviewed, and both present and future prospects are discussed. Visits may also be arranged for representatives of the rating agency to certain plant or manufacturing sites to provide greater insight into the basic operations. In the final analysis, however, the rating is based on a statistical review of current data highlighting various derivatives of: (*a*) the relationship of operating income to the coverage of interest and lease rental fixed charges; (*b*) tangible asset coverages of both senior and total debt; and (*c*) cash flow in relation to present aggregate long-term debt as well as projected maturities. The rating agencies arbitrarily set minimum coverages necessary to attain a specific rating, and the statistical analysis eventually becomes a series of simple quantitative measures.

Companies should be prepared to go to great lengths to protect higher quality ratings and those with lower ratings should covet an upgrading. While this is not to suggest that all debt financing be done to accommodate a bond rating, it is well to keep an eye on such a consideration as the differences in bond ratings will always affect the actual interest rate. More importantly, however, is the fact that the inability of a company to sustain an "investment grade" bond rating could mean the difference in whether or not it even has access to public markets under then existing money or capital market conditions.

Market Conditions

The conditions prevailing in the money and capital markets at the time of an offering of debt securities is perhaps the thread of commonality that runs through all other considerations previously reviewed. At the extremes, money can either be tight or there can be an abundance of liquidity competing for the yields of fixed-income investments. When there is an ample amount of cash for investment, interest rates are lower and prospective purchasers are often willing to compromise their standards to achieve a slightly better return than could otherwise be realized by staying with issues of higher quality. When money is tight, quality counts as the better issues will be priced to yield relatively attractive returns even compared to lower rated borrowers. More often than not, market conditions are somewhere in-between these two extremes and it is in this kind of environment that the necessary ingredients of relative seniority, pricing, convertibility, restrictive covenants, average life and bond rating must be considered in the order of their relative priorities to the issuer to assure a successful offering of debt securities.

Commercial Paper

While the comments relating to public financing have been limited to the medium- and long-term elements of the capital market, there is also a very important market for the sale of short-term notes called commercial paper. This market simply permits one corporation to borrow from another with the securities generally sold through a limited number of investment banking firms who are dealers in such instruments. Maturities can range from a few days to several months, but generally they do not exceed 270 days. Commercial paper is used to finance working capital needs similar to the application of bank lines of credit. While commercial paper is typically unsecured, it is customary for the issuer to have back-up bank lines available to refinance maturities that are not renewed. Some commercial paper has been issued with bank letters of credit attached to guarantee its repayment at maturity in which case credit facilities exist to refinance any drawings under these performance bonds. Commercial paper rates are usually somewhat lower than the bank prime rate even after attaching the normal one eighth of 1 percent fee payable to the dealer for selling the note. Circumstances under which commercial paper would be more expensive than short-term bank loans would normally be limited to periods when the bank prime lending rate was being held at an artificially low level for political or other reasons while the paper rate floated freely in the market. The selection of the range of maturities is a critical factor from the standpoint of portfolio runoff and interest savings and this should be reviewed carefully on a regular basis. A well-balanced commercial paper program used to supplement bank borrowings can be an important element of any debt financing program and may well result in worthwhile cost savings to the issuer. Ratings are given for commercial paper from the same agencies that rate longer term debt issues and these are clearly important in both the pricing and the selling effort.

PRIVATE SOURCES

While the long-term public debt market is bigger and considerations such as indenture covenants, sinking-fund installments, pricing and the like are somewhat more patterned, the individual sources of private financing are greater in number. Inasmuch as private financings are often the result of more specific negotiation over a broader range of topics and, therefore, potentially more suited to a given situation, it is important to review the principal elements of this market.

Banks

The most important source of short- and medium-term credit is the commercial banking system in the United States. The big domestic money center banks as a group have historically had the capacity and commitment to provide larger amounts of funds with greater expediency to the corporate borrower than any other comparable source throughout the world with the possible historic exception of the relationship of the Japanese banks and their trading company affiliates. Bank credit is generally well understood by corporate financial officers and used to (*a*) finance seasonal working capital requirements relating to the carrying of inventories or accounts receivable; (*b*) provide a balance of three- to seven-year medium-term money that will supplement the short- and long-term debt elements of a balance sheet; or (*c*) provide temporary financing for an acquisition or other particular project pending refinancing in the long-term market.

Bank loans are most often made at a rate of interest that fluctuates as the prime or base lending rates change. While fixed-rate loans have been made, the bank lender can find such arrangements having a distinctly negative impact on future earnings if the basic cost of money exceeds such fixed returns and, therefore, interest rates are fixed at present as an exception only. In addition to the normal pricing considerations bearing on customary bank lending transactions, banks in the past have been willing to negotiate out of the ordinary pricing arrangements as the basis for their entering into certain kinds of credits when money is generally easy. The proposals so financed may often result in a potentially large gain to the borrower and include acquisitions, repurchases of stock, or other specific projects. Extraordinary formula pricing for such financial support has generally taken the form of additional compensation, over and above a straight interest rate, related to equity appreciation during a period subsequent to the financing. Such arrangements have sought to equate return with the risk being incurred but these may well be a thing of the past inasmuch as bank lenders have become considerably more conscious of the quality of their loan portfolios during the last two years and have been less willing to accept greater risk regardless of the return.

The importance of banking relationships is a topic that cannot be overemphasized for any company that has an ongoing need for this source of financing. Commercial bankers can be extremely creative in the application of their product to a given borrower's needs and corporate financial officers should recognize the value of an equitable relationship with benefits accruing to both parties. As a practical matter, banks have become increasingly aware of profit considerations related to both individual transactions as well as overall relationships and this evolution during the past few years has not been without some startling effects on historic associations. The entire area of bank relations should be a high priority concern to most companies, and corporate financial officers as well as other members of senior management should be prepared to devote the necessary time to make sure that relationships are maintained on a sound basis.

In addition to straight bank borrowings, another source of bank credit might be available as a result of bank management of pension and other retirement funds. Bank investment managers have used private short-term vehicles for temporary investment of retirement funds to supplement the purchases of publicly traded money market instruments. Companies having a continuing need for short-term funds and wanting to develop a source in addition to bank line or commercial paper borrowings, have in some cases been able to issue so called "Master Notes" to bank investment groups under which retirement funds are temporarily invested pending other disposition. Rates on these notes are tied closely to other short-term money market yields and they provide the bank with an opportunity to commingle funds instead of having to make a lot of individual short-term purchases in the public market. From the issuer's standpoint, however, the dollars generated are more permanent than the clients for whom the bank may invest and, therefore, this is a source well worth exploring. It should be recognized, however, that the bank investment divisions have a fudiciary responsibility for the investment of such retirement funds and therefore only very creditworthy issuers will qualify and then only with the proper safeguards which may include unused back-up bank credit lines.

Institutional Lenders

Private placements of long-term debt are often preferable to comparable public offerings for companies who might be smaller in size or whose structure and prospects may be more complicated than can be effectively explained in a prospectus. On the other hand, large well-known names in the public market also use the private market to supplement their public offerings as another source of debt capital. There is a greater amount of direct borrower/lender contact in a private placement than a public offering which leads to a greater familiarity on the part of the debt purchasers with management and which can often translate itself into greater support and participation than would be the case for the same security offered through a syndicate to the public. An obvious advantage of a private financing is the ability to specifically tailor the transaction to a borrower's needs.

Private capital markets are made principally by the life insurance companies. This type of investment supplements the equity and publicly traded bond segments of large portfolios and can often enable these investors to generate higher yields than might otherwise be available. In addition, pension funds provide a creditable source of prospective debt capital and can be discussed as one with insurance company lenders except that often state retirement funds have more specifically inhibiting investment criteria in terms of bond ratings, liquidity, and so on than do the traditional insurance lenders.

In general, private placements of long-term debt are done through investment bankers for the simple reason that these firms maintain regular contact with the large institutions and know which are likely to be in the market at any given time. Investment banking firms also keep detailed up-to-date records on the entire spectrum of prospective participants and are able to round out a purchasing group in short order. It should be emphasized, however, that the ability to put together a private placement group is not necessarily contingent upon having an investment banker and there is no reason why financial officers of private corporations cannot make and maintain direct contact themselves. One specific advantage of such direct placements is the saving in the amount of fee which is typically charged on the basis of the size of the issue itself. Further, there should be no substitute for such direct contact by a well-informed financial officer and the abdication of this function to an outside agent could actually be detrimental to the outcome of the financing because of the latter's lack of total familiarity with all of the nuances of any particular company. The principal disadvantage of a corporate financial officer's trying to undertake such a program is the commitment of time and people required to identify prospective lenders and stay current on their interests as well as actually making the many contacts necessary to determine the degree of interest. A simple solution to what may appear to be a dilemma of sorts could be the use of an investment banker the first time a private placement is put together and then the corporate financial officer might take on the task for future financings using those purchasers participating in the first issue as the basis for subsequent direct placements.

The sequence in a private placement normally calls for the preparation of a private placement memorandum which reviews the prospective borrower's record as well as future prospects and incorporates a proposed summary of principal terms. This is somewhat comparable to the typical prospectus in a public offering and should also be considered as a liability type of disclosure document. The next step becomes one of finding a relatively major institution to commit to the financing proposal and assume the "lead" position. The more prestigious the principal lender, the easier the subsequent selling job to other participants as many medium and smaller investors place a great deal of weight on the investment judgment of the more experienced institutions. Once specific terms and conditions have been agreed upon with the lead lender, the proposal is then presented to others as a specific bond purchase with little, if any, future modification in the basic provisions. This is an important consideration inasmuch as it is virtually impossible for any issuer to be responsive to the various investment idiosyncracies of all potential purchasers which could necessitate continuing renegotiation over a protracted period of time.

Money market conditions and purchaser liquidity are important considerations that must be analyzed in every private placement. Institutional lenders are under pressure to invest their premium cash flow at the highest yields. In a tight credit market when rates are high, an insurance lender is anxious to make as many commitments as possible even though there may have to be a delay in the actual fundings based on availability of resources. Such a feature of a delayed funding is, of course, not inherent in a public offering as the proceeds of such a financing are paid to the borrowing company immediately. Delayed fundings may, however, provide a corporation with a certain measure of flexibility that enables it to secure forward commitments at fixed rates to which future capital requirements could be allocated. Such forward commitments are also beneficial because they eliminate financing uncertainties that could develop based on future market conditions.

A continuing concern among financial officers is the potential embarrassment of agreeing to a high-interest rate based on present conditions and then having the market ease considerably before the actual funding takes place. There is always the second guessing and wonder about whether the borrower should abandon the commitment in hopes of securing a comparable arrangement at lower rates. Obviously, markets can move in both directions and often a rate will actually be more favorable at the time of closing than when the financing was initially committed. A compulsion to constantly shop for the lowest possible rate should be suppressed as it will lead to general disenchantment on the part of long-term lenders. Corporate financial officers should be prepared to live with the agreements they negotiate or have their own credibility suffer with an attendant loss of effectiveness.

Interest rates on private placements under relatively normal circumstances should range from 50 to 100 basis points higher than those on public offerings for comparable credits. This premium rate is imposed because of the general lack of liquidity in a private issue as opposed to a public debt security traded on a national exchange. As in the case of public offerings, bond ratings play a role in determining the interest rate on a private placement, but they are not as compelling a consideration. Ratings are probably more appropriately described as a guideline to an individual institution's purchasing deliberations with other more subjective considerations such as evaluation of management, past record, and future prospects having greater influence. Assessments of each of these latter factors are made as a result of the private meetings held between representatives of the purchasers and corporate officers. While common in private placements, these kinds of meetings are not part of the marketing effort in a public debt issue as the participants in the underwriting syndicate usually only have an opportunity to discuss management's performance and future plans at a more formal "due diligence" meeting prior to the sale of an issue. This type of meeting does not readily lend itself to an in-depth review of many matters and as a result, the syndicate members depend quite heavily on the evaluation of the lead underwriter which has satisfied itself in greater detail.

Finance Companies

In addition to bank and institutional lenders, other private sources of capital are also provided by sales finance companies which often have a vested interest in concluding a sale and are willing to assist financially to assure the consummation of the transaction.

Finance companies that are wholly owned subsidiaries of major industrial companies have historically been utilized by the parent to assist in the marketing of the manufacturer's products. While these have typically focused on retail sales such as automobiles, appliances or other merchandise of a more general nature, many of the large captives have broadened their own loan portfolios in recent years beyond financing those products manufactured by their parent companies. As a result, a new, more flexible source of medium-term money in the seven- to ten-year range has developed. Debt investments of these large finance companies not related to the basic product of their parent company have generally been made through the medium of a private placement and have tended to cost more than a comparable medium-term issue that might have otherwise been placed with a bank directly or even sold to the public as a note issue. Collateral, in the form of a mortgage on real or personal property which may or may not have been financed with the loan proceeds is often required as security for such debt financings.

Independent finance companies, while also committing the bulk of their resources to financing the sale of retail goods that best lend themselves to an installment type of purchase, are also active in financing "bigger ticket" items on a debt basis for terms in the seven- to ten-year range. Generally, the credit and pricing criteria are much the same for both captives and independents and the only purpose in making a distinction is merely to identify the specific elements of this possible source of debt financing.

Leasing

Off-balance sheet sources of funds are often as responsive to given financing needs and can even be less expensive in certain circumstances than direct debt arrangements. This type of financing is typically generated through the vehicle of a direct lease or as a result of a sale leaseback transaction. In either event, funds are raised to finance the specific asset being acquired or to provide resources available for alternative investment. The independent leasing business while being very large in the aggregate, is somewhat fragmented in scope of operation with the result that the focus of this business has been on the so-called smaller ticket or more retail-oriented items. On the other hand, many large financial institutions have developed substantial leasing capabilities over the past decade and considerably expanded the breadth of this market as a source of funds to finance very large asset purchases as a consequence.

Transportation equipment such as aircraft has been ideally suited to a form of lease financing called a leverage lease. Under such an arrangement, a financial institution or other group would make a relatively modest equity investment in the asset and then employ the use of long-term senior debt on a secured but nonrecourse basis to finance the balance of the purchase price. The long-term debt is raised in either the private or public markets at then current interest rates for such funds. Security for the lenders includes a mortgage on the asset being financed and a lease with the end user typically written on a full payout basis to assure adequate coverge of debt service. The actual equity owner, having a relatively small amount invested, is able to recapture the bulk of its investment in a short period of time through both direct lease rentals and the use of tax benefits resulting from accelerated depreciation and investment tax credits which greatly enhance the overall return. Certain of the "soft dollar" tax savings may be passed along to the lessee with the result that the financing cost of the transaction is lower than it might otherwise have been assuming a constant interest factor for the long-term debt. Such a form of lease financing is particularly suited to companies that can forecast excessive depreciation expense and therefore cannot benefit directly from the potential tax savings but would like to realize a lower effective interest cost.

Vendor Financing

Many companies engaged in manufacturing heavy goods and equipment are also willing to assist directly with financing in an effort to promote the sale of their own products and, therefore, may also be regarded as a source of capital. Such companies generally sell products that cost substantial amounts of money and the concept of a typical finance subsidiary to help the sales effort is really not viable inasmuch as the financing for each sale is often negotiated as part of the sale order itself. The term of such an extension of credit may not necessarily relate directly to the useful life of the asset nor even to the buyer's own schedule of debt maturities. In addition, the financing cost will usually be higher than many of the other alternatives previously discussed, inasmuch as the seller will mark up its own cost of capital that must remain committed to the manufacturing and sale processes for the duration of the deferred payment. On the other hand, from the buyers' standpoint, the borrowing cost can be viewed as part of the purchase price and any other inhibiting aspects of a vendor financing program may be evaluated against the quality and need for the product. While manufacturer financed purchases may only represent an interim form of capital, it might be the best source available at the time and should always be considered. It is a simple truth that vendors have a vital interest in marketing their products and may, therefore, be willing to provide credit terms that are sufficient to enable the ultimate user to make a purchase when other sources of financing are limited.

Governmental Agencies

In addition to the private sources of capital reviewed to this point, various governmental agencies often play a vital role in the financing of individual projects or transactions. As an example, state and local governmental agencies assist in industrial revenue bond financing by raising funds to finance plant investment at relatively favorable interest costs. Proceeds of such bond issues are used to build a particular plant facility which is then leased over a long term to the end user. The lease represents the vehicle through which the "ultimate borrower" amortizes the debt at a predetermined rate of return. The tax-exempt nature of interest on these bonds assures the issuer of a relatively low cost while at the same time providing an adequate after-tax return to investors.

In addition, federal governmental agencies can often be helpful in generating funds either through direct credits or the issuance of guarantees. Corporate financial officers of companies engaged in raising money for overseas sales or foreign project investment may do well to consider the applicability of a government agency support as a means of minimizing political and other risks inherent in doing business in foreign countries. Such financing commitments, whether by way of loan or guarantee, are issued consistent with the government's view of the various economic, political, and social considerations in each country and may well have an attendantly beneficial effect on our trade position and overall balance of payments account.

Another example of government financial support is that accorded the domestic maritime industry. In the interest of maintaining a fleet of merchant vessels for use in national emergencies, the government is willing to guarantee publicly issued mortgage bonds to assist in the financing of vessel construction in U.S. shipyards. The government guarantee substitutes for the direct credit of the ship-owner with the result that interest rates are lower than they would otherwise be.

FOREIGN FINANCING

While the basic frame of reference in this chapter has been the U.S. capital market, it is important for any well-rounded corporate financial officer to be aware of the potential for raising money from offshore sources.

The Eurodollar market which flourishes in London and on the Continent is an established market and one which can be used to finance either domestic or foreign activities. This market is in the hands of the major banks who generate the dollar deposits and is largely a private, medium-term seven- to ten-year market even though public offerings of longer term Eurodollar as well as other Eurocurrency issues are also commonplace. Such offshore public financings have generally been for shorter periods than an issuer would sell bonds in the domestic capital market and the amounts are generally much smaller with a $50 million offering being at the upper end of the spectrum. For an issuer who wants to raise substantial amounts in the Eurodollar market, however, private sources are by far and away the preferable alternative as the public debt capital markets do not seem to have developed to the extent of in the United States.

Eurodollar pricing on private issues is generally based on a premium over a floating base called the London Inter-Bank Offered Rate which is the rate at which banks in the market are prepared to sell such funds to one another. The markup is intended to assure the lender an adequate profit margin although some financings have been done at ridiculously low premiums which are too thin to support any reasonable return. Public offerings are generally made at fixed rates which often bear a direct relationship to comparable bond yields in the U.S. market and the outlook for the dollar relative to other major currencies.

In addition to offshore dollar financings, local currency funds are often available in sufficient quantity and at low enough costs to make their exploration a worthwhile exercise. When dealing with potential foreign currency financings, however, one must keep in mind the potential exchange risk that is being undertaken. If a U.S.

company does not have access to internally generated funds in the borrowed currency, it will have to buy such foreign exchange to satisfy future principal and interest payments and may, therefore, end up paying substantial premiums depending on the vagaries of the international currency markets. While it is true that the borrowing of a potentially weak currency versus the dollar may eventually result in "profits" from such exchange transactions, these currencies are not typically available in sufficient amounts as a consequence of their weakness. More often, it is the potentially stronger currencies that are available at what may appear to be very attractive interest cost savings, but the corporate financial officer considering such a proposal would do well to assure a sufficient hedge against any potentially unfavorable movements in the given currency, or the financing could well become surprisingly expensive.

Another offshore market that has surfaced in the past year is in the Middle East and has its roots in the massive amounts of so-called petrodollars that have been sent to the Arab countries in payment of inflated oil prices. In 1975, the first major private dollar financing has been announced which was a $100 million medium-term credit for one of the largest companies in our country. The future evolution of the market is somewhat unpredictable inasmuch as much of the potential foreign currency inflow to the Middle Eastern countries may well be committed to internal development and therefore not be immediately available for re-lending in international markets for other than very short periods through banks in which the Arab central banks choose to keep their deposits awaiting ultimate reinvestment.

In addition to financings in a given currency, there have been some credits worked out in units composed of a number of currencies which diversification in theory is supposed to protect both investors and borrowers from excessive costs resulting from the fluctuations of specific currencies against each other. While these have perhaps been appropriately suited to the circumstances of the issuers, investors, and the market, they do not appear to have changed historic financing patterns up to this point. The concept, however, cannot be disregarded and may well translate itself sometime in the future into a conventional security denominated in Special Drawing Rights (SDR) which is the currency of the International Monetary Fund for settling international trade balances. A SDR is a unit representing a composite of 16 currencies with the relative weight of each based on each country's share of world exports. The U.S. dollar represents 33 percent of the basic unit and the value of a SDR expressed in dollars in 1975 was about $1.20. In anticipation of the SDR possibly becoming the international unit of account, a few major foreign borrowers have already ventured into the capital market with SDR denominated issues, but it is still too early to accurately judge the outcome of such a potential shift away from historic straight currency financings.

PREFERRED STOCK

While this chapter has been devoted to considerations relative to debt securities, it is important to recognize that preferred stock may be used in a similar manner to raise money at a fixed rate of return to the investor. Clearly, the dividend in a given preferred issue is subordinate to interest on both senior and subordinated debt, but the use of preferreds should be considered under appropriate circumstances. Preferred stock can be sold: (*a*) as a straight issue with a simple dividend; (*b*) as a convertible issue which would give the investor the right to participate in the appreciation of the common stock; (*c*) with warrants to combine both a fixed rate of return with an equity feature; (*d*) or with a dividend that is junior to other existing preferred issues, but senior to the common dividend. Preferreds intended to be used as a form of debt security can also be sold with sinking-fund provisions which will provide for scheduled amortization which will relieve the issuer of what might turn out to be a high fixed cost of capital at some future time. As a form of fixed-income security, preferred issues often have greater appeal to certain classes of investors who are permitted to deduct 85 percent of dividends received for tax purposes and therefore only pay the full rate on the 15 percent balance. This has a clear advantage over the ordinary tax liability on interest received from a debt issue and may be an important facet of the marketing effort.

FINANCING STRATEGY

While it is clear that there are many money and capital market sources of debt financing available to most borrowers, it is essential that the corporate financial officer develop a financing strategy that will permit the prudent pursuit of his capital requirements. Such a strategy should be conceived in a fashion to provide the company with sufficient inherent flexibility to adapt to changing market conditions without being unduly limited in the range of financing alternatives.

A financing strategy should address itself to both present and future cash needs with specific focus on such things as cost of capital, balance sheet flexibility, and the predictability with which internally generated cash flow can service aggregate debt.

Straight debt financing costs are readily quantifiable and as previously discussed, these basically reflect the liquidity in both the short- and long-term markets. For the company with a relatively simple capital structure, the most attractive financing opportunities may boil down to a simple difference in cost as to which type of debt instrument should be used to satisfy either short- or long-term needs. Unfortunately, however, most companies are unable to limit their financing considerations to the cost element alone and must analyze the impact of the debt to be incurred on other aspects of their overall financial condition.

Balance sheet flexibility is an essential consideration of any ongoing financing program both in terms of capital structure and liquidity. The decision to proceed with a debt financing instead of an equity offering is an example of a judgment that may have short-term shareholder benefits but could be detrimental to everyone's interests over the long term. While ultimate dilution in earnings per share is not a desirable result of any corporate endeavor, the opportunity to build up an equity base may not be present at a future date when it might be particularly appropriate. Convertible securities often offer an appropriate middle ground inasmuch as the coupon is lower and their "equity" feature may indeed be beneficial. The call feature inherent in this security preserves a certain amount of flexibility so long as the stock sells at a sufficient premium to assure conversion instead of redemption. Such conversion could well be an important factor in reestablishing a sounder capital structure which may then serve as the basis for additional debt financing that might be needed to satisfy a particularly pressing need. Balance sheet liquidity considerations are similarly important. Basically, short-term borrowings should be used to finance current assets and while there may be temporary exceptions, there should always be a refinancing capability to assure the continued preservation of adequate working capital. Longer lived assets should be financed with more permanent capital such as long-term debt or equity.

The ability to service debt repayment with internally generated funds is a guideline that will always result in a soundly conceived fiscal program. Various ranges of maturities with different sinking-fund provisions can be employed but the object should generally be the spreading of such fixed charges over a long enough time frame to assure adequate coverage from reasonably predictable cash flow. This is not to say that the use of single maturities or large balloon payments should be ignored, but there should always be adequate financing flexibility to anticipate such amounts well in advance of their actual maturities. A medium-term issue without any required sinking fund will have a beneficial effect on cash flow that might be reinvested in the business and for that reason, such a security may be particularly appropriate at a given point in time but the flexibility to refinance it at maturity must be considered as well. Many companies are disposed to have combination type offerings where both medium-term notes and longer term debentures are sold. Such financings can have both cost and cash flow advantages that either security might not have if issued alone.

Timing is an essential ingredient in the implementation of a financing program and corporate financial officers should be prepared to take advantage of markets when conditions appear to be favorable even though they may be anticipating particular needs and could therefore justify delaying. This is particularly true of long-term debt financing as both amounts and costs can be optimized in certain markets while other circumstances may be decidedly less favorable.

CONCLUSION

During the course of any analysis considering those sources and forms of financing that are most appropriate under the given circumstances, the many aspects heretofore reviewed should be assessed and assigned relative priorities. Clearly, there are many elements that will bear on the eventual decision to proceed with a specific proposal and it is important that these be considered in concert with the ultimate corporate financial goal of fiscal integrity combined with the retention of maximum financing flexibility. Those companies that are willing to maintain a disciplined commitment to achieving these results will sustain the ability to finance their corporate growth on both a stable and predictable basis which should be at the heart of the corporate financing endeavor.

ADDITIONAL SOURCES

Ang, James S. "The Two Faces of Bond Refunding." *Journal of Finance,* 30 (June 1975), 869–74.

Bierman, Harold. "The Bond Refunding Decision." *Financial Management,* 1 (Summer 1972), 27–29.

Bierman, Harold, and Barnea, Amir. "Expected Short-term Interest Rates in Bond Refunding." *Financial Management,* 3 (Spring 1974), 75–79.

Bierman, Harold, Jr., and Thomas, L. Joseph. "Ruin Considerations and Debt Issuance." *Journal of Financial and Quantitative Analysis,* 7 (January 1972), 1361–78.

Bullington, Robert. "How Corporate Debt Issues Are Rated." *Financial Executive,* 42 (September 1974), 28–37.

Ederington, Louis H. "The Yield Spread on New Issues of Corporate Bonds." *Journal of Finance,* 29 (December 1974), 1531–44.

Findlay, Chapman, III, and Williams, Edward. "Capital Allocation and the Nature of Ownership Equities." *Financial Management,* 1 (Summer 1972), 68–76.

Fisher, Lawrence. "Determinants of Risk Premiums on Corporate Bonds." *Journal of Political Economy,* 67 (June 1959), 217–37.

Handorf, William. "Flexible Debt Financing." *Financial Management,* 3 (Summer 1974), 17–23.

Jen, Frank C., and Wert, James E. "The Value of the Deferred Call Privilege." *National Banking Review,* 3 (March 1966), 369–78.

Johnson, Ramon E. "Term Structures of Corporate Bond Yields as a Function of Risk of Default." *Journal of Finance,* 22 (May 1967), 313–45.

Johnson, Robert W. "Subordinated Debentures: Debt That Serves as Equity." *Journal of Finance,* 10 (March 1955), 1–16.

Karna, Adi. "The Cost of Private Versus Public Debt Issues." *Financial Management,* 1 (Summer 1972), 65–67.

Kraus, Alan. "The Bond Refunding Decision in an Efficient Market." *Journal of Financial and Quantitative Analysis,* 8 (December 1973), 793–806.

Lewellen, Wilbur. "Finance Subsidiaries and Corporate Borrowing Capacity." *Financial Management,* 1 (Spring 1972), 21–32.

Litzenberger, Robert H., and Rutenberg, David P. "Size and Timing of Corporate Bond Flotations." *Journal of Financial and Quantitative Analysis,* 7 (January 1972), 1343–60.

Pye, Gordon. "Gauging the Default Premium." *Financial Analysis Journal,* 30 (January–February 1974), 49–52.

Remmers, Lee; Stonehill, Arthur; Wright, Richard; and Beekhuisen, Theo. "Industry and Size as Debt Ratio Determinants in Manufacturing Internationally." *Financial Management,* 3 (Summer 1974), 24–32.

Van Horne, James C. "Implied Fixed Costs of Long-Term Debt Issues." *Journal of Financial and Quantitative Analysis,* 8 (December 1973), 821–34.

White, William L. "Debt Management and the Form of Business Financing." *Journal of Finance,* 19 (May 1974), 565–78.

Zinbarg, Edward. "The Private Placement Loan Agreement." *Financial Analysts Journal,* 31 (July–August 1975), 33–35.

Chapter 37

Financial Leases

Nathan Snyder[*]

HISTORY AND EMERGENCE OF LEASING AS A FINANCING TOOL

General

HISTORICALLY, the most familiar commodity that had been the subject of leasing was real estate. The distinction between the use and the ownership of real property can be traced back to feudal times. However, the distinction between the use and ownership of personal property is a more recent phenomenon. After World War II, when the economy was rebuilding at a super accelerated pace, the need for new and expanded methods of financing was pressing and the leasing of personal property became an alternative means of financing. Many reasons for viewing leasing as something other than a variant of conventional debt financing have been offered to prospective lessees over the years. Some of these reasons are sound and have withstood careful scrutiny—others have been effectively decimated.

Where the rationale for the lease transaction is to obtain the use of the property for a period of time which is substantially less than the useful life of the property for an aggregate cost which is sub-

---

[*] Nathan Snyder is vice president, Acquisitions, CBS Inc., New York.

The author gratefully acknowledges the guidance and counsel of John M. Randolph, one of the pioneers in the equipment leasing industry.

stantially less than the acquisition cost, then the lessee is contracting for an *operating lease* where he is protected against the risk of obsolescence and where the lessor assumes the burden of maintenance, insurance, and taxes. This type of leasing has generally been limited to electronic data processing equipment, automobiles, and smaller aircraft. Indeed, where the lessee can look to the foregoing services being handled by the lessor and also, where he is protected against technological obsolescence by means of a right to terminate the lease on short notice, then lease payments generally carry a substantial premium over debt financing.

The short-term nature and flexibility of an operating lease does not exist in the *finance lease*. The finance lease is truly a method of financing a piece of equipment over a period that is related to the useful life of that property. The lessor is generally looking to recover his original investment plus an appropriate return on that investment. The source of that return is the combination of: (*a*) rental payments; (*b*) job development credit (investment tax credit) and accelerated depreciation; and (*c*) residual value upon expiration of the lease.

The lessors who are engaged in operating leases are often the manufacturers of the equipment as well as third parties who have a remarketing capability; i.e., who are able to place the equipment on rent to second and third users upon the expiration of the initial lease term. Finance leases, on the other hand, are usually entered into by financial institutions who are seeking rates of return on their investment that are related to the yields for conventional financing.

Lease Statistics

The present method of not reporting most lease transactions on corporate balance sheets makes it difficult to obtain exact information on the total volume of equipment that is currently under lease contracts. It is possible, however, to estimate the size of the market by determining the total equipment expenditures each year, by breaking this information down into product categories, and by finding evidence to substantiate what percent of each of these products is leased.

At the end of 1969, it was estimated that equipment with an original cost of approximately $58 billion was on lease. This included equipment leased by manufacturers, automobile lessors, and third-party lessors. Third-party lessors owned approximately $13 billion of this total (26 percent), banks approximately $2 billion (4 percent), manufacturers $27 billion (54 percent), and auto and truck lessors $8 billion (16 percent), totaling $50 billion of the $58 billion.

The National Planning Association Center for Economic Projections estimates that of the total $78.4 billion plant and equipment expenditures in 1969, $54.7 billion was for durable equipment (the balance nonresidential structures). Of this $54.7 billion, $11.3 billion (20 percent) was leased. Most of this leasing was dominated by the manufacturer, especially in computers and office equipment. Third-party lessors have historically been most prominent in aircraft, ships, railroad cars, and furniture and fixtures. This relationship is shown graphically in Figure 1. Of particular significance is the observation that while capital goods (including electrical machinery, instruments, fabricated metals, engines, turbines, and construction, mining, metalworking, special industrial and general

FIGURE 1
1969 Equipment Leased Related to Total Durable Equipment Expenditures (by type of equipment)

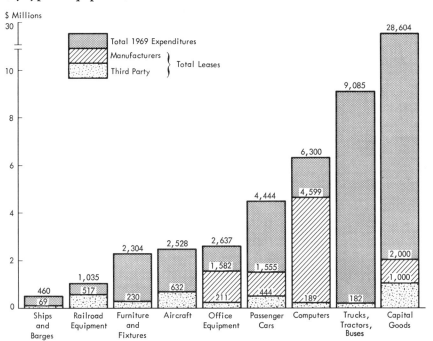

industrial machinery) represent over one-half of the total equipment expenditures, only $2 billion (7 percent) was leased. On the other hand, leasing's share of the computer market was 73 percent. Of course, included in the computer leasing figures are nonpayout, operating leases.

In updating these relationships (Figure 2) for the year 1972, the percentages remain fairly constant. Capital goods leasing gained

FIGURE 2
Equipment Purchases and Percent Leased, 1972 (billions of dollars)

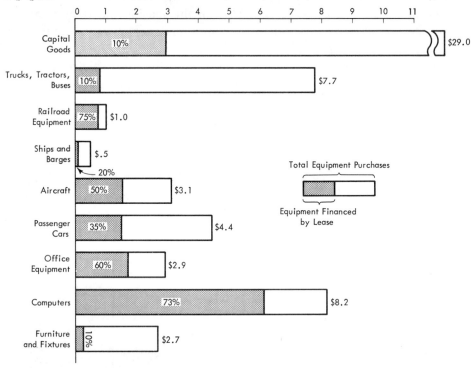

slightly (from 7 percent to 10 percent) while computers remained static at 73 percent of the market. Included in the 1972 figures, however, are finance contracts (conditional sales and chattel mortgages) which may distort the comparison slightly.

Total durable goods expenditures are estimated to grow with the economy at an annual rate of 5 percent. This should reach $77 billion by 1976. In 1976 it is projected that $19 billion (26 percent) of this total will be leased.

From these figures, provided by the National Planning Association, it can be determined that leasing is growing at a compounded rate in excess of 10 percent annually, while total equipment expenditures are growing at 5 percent. This increase suggests inroads made by leasing into other forms of financing; i.e., depreciation, retained earnings, bank term loans, long-term debt, and equity.

These forecasts for 1976 as outlined above were made by the National Planning Association prior to the reinstatement of the job development credit in the fall of 1971. Therefore, in all likelihood they have a conservative bias. It is estimated, however, that an anticipated Financial Accounting Standards Board opinion to require the capitalization of most leases would constrict leasing growth by 10 percent to 20 percent.

The Lease Market

The smaller "middle market" finance lease transactions ($25,000–$1,000,000 in asset value) are sought after by organizations of diverse sophistication, including the manufacturers, finance companies, banks, and third-party lessors. The larger tax-oriented lease (generally involving an investment of at least $1,000,000) is limited to a select cadre of transaction-oriented lessors who work for financial institutions or others who are in a position to utilize the tax benefits available from the ownership of equipment and at the same time have access to substantial amounts of low-cost funds.

Manufacturers generally look upon leasing as a method of moving the goods they produce or as a means of controlling certain markets, but not usually as a method of sheltering taxes. Finance companies and banks oftentimes look at leasing as just another method of employing funds for a financial rate of return, overlooking or minimizing the effects of residual values, accelerated depreciation, and job development credit. Certain banks on occasion have fully sheltered their taxes as a result of other activities and have been forced to participate in this market only as brokers.

Many finance companies, especially the smaller ones, lack the taxable income, expertise or incentive to structure tax leases. The same situation, similar to finance companies, carries through to include many of the independent leasing companies. Their marketing thrust often is geared to the middle market leases or conditional sale contracts which do not lend themselves to tax accounting. Competition for tax leases would be found with the following:

1. Banks or bank affiliated leasing companies.
2. Insurance companies.
3. Large independent lessors.
4. Large finance companies.
5. Individuals and tax-shelter partnerships.
6. Brokers and investment bankers seeking transactions for the accounts of third parties.

ROLE OF BANKS

The participation of banks in the leasing business has been a significant factor in the growth and development of this industry. The levels of sophistication of lessors and lessees has heightened over the years and the intricate balance between tax considerations, income statement results, and cash flow are consistently being orchestrated by the participants in a leasing transaction.

As of June 30, 1972, 469 national banks—more than 10 percent of all such banks—were engaged in the leasing business with $971.9 million invested in lease transactions. This represented a 12 percent growth in a one-year period. When these numbers are viewed in light of the total investment in 1965 being $150 million, this rate of growth is nothing short of spectacular.

Because the nature of the tax-oriented lease is such that each transaction is individually tailored to fit each situation with intangible variables such as tax consequences and credit and equipment evaluations, generalizations as to which lessors will seek out specific types of transactions are difficult to make. Some lessors are in and out of the market as their particular tax situation dictates and as external forces such as the withdrawal or reenactment of tax credits, or availability and cost of funds come into play.

TYPES OF LEASES

Tax and Nontax Leases

The three general types of full payout leases being offered by lessor institutions today are the leverage lease, the nonleverage tax lease, and the nontax finance lease. The first two utilize the tax-paying posture of the lessor when structuring the economics of the lease and may be grouped together and called the "tax" lease. The third, or "nontax" finance lease, does not rely on the tax-paying characteristics of the lessor in its structure, and is often most closely related to the conditional sales contract.

In order for a lessor to utilize the tax advantage in structuring a tax lease, the lease must meet the tests of trueness as set forth by the Internal Revenue Service and the accounting profession. These tests of trueness have varied from time to time and, in many cases, are not clearly and accurately defined. The results oftentimes are varied interpretations resulting in different lessors taking slightly different positions. The current position of the Internal Revenue Service as to leases is discussed in the following section.

The basic concept which underlies the position of the accountants and the Internal Revenue Service is that the lessor, not the lessee, must have the risk of ownership of the asset if it is to be deemed a true tax lease. This is the case with operating, as opposed to full payout, leases. With the operating lease, the lessee is obligated to pay rentals over an initial term of the lease which is generally too short in duration to cover the cost of the asset. The lessor must look for speculative renewals or residuals to recover his cost and make a profit. This, indeed, clearly places the risk of ownership on the lessor.

The economic advantages to the lessee of a tax lease as opposed to a nontax lease generally center around a considerably lower lease rate ("nominal rate"). The nominal rates on tax leases are often considerably lower than the lessee's alternative methods of long-term financing and, in many cases, lower than short-term borrowings at prime rate. The trade-off for these lower rates, however, must be considered in the lessee's economic analysis. Since the ownership of the equipment is with the lessor, the lessee forfeits the advantages of accelerated depreciation, job development credit (unless the lessor elects to pass it through to the lessee), and the residual values of the equipment.

The nontax lease, on the other hand, could easily be structured so the lessee would not lose these advantages. Since a nontax lease usually is not true, it should be considered a conditional sales contract and the "lessee" is really the owner of the equipment for tax purposes. He can then use the investment tax credit and accelerated depreciation. Also these types of leases are likely to have nominal purchase options thereby assuring the "lessee" that he will not have to give up the residual value of the equipment. Because he does not trade away these advantages, the "lessee" will pay a higher rate, more closely related to his regular long-term borrowing rate.

If the lessor is looking for a minimum of 5.5 percent after-tax return on an investment in a lease, this would be approximately 11 percent pretax (assuming a 50 percent tax rate). A nontax lease has only the nominal rate plus the anticipated residual (may be in the form of fixed price purchase option or renewal) to achieve the desired result. A typical five-year nontax lease would need a 9.5 percent nominal rate plus an anticipated 5 percent residual in order to approximate the 11 percent desired yield.

Tax leases, on the other hand, are made up of four yield-producing factors: (1) nominal rate; (2) accelerated depreciation; (3) investment tax credit; and (4) residual. A typical ten-year lease could achieve the overall 11 percent pretax yield to the lessor as follows:

	Percent
Nominal rate	4.47%
Enhanced by accelerated depreciation to	5.51
Enhanced by investment tax credit to	9.32
Enhanced by residual to	11.00

The nontax lease is quickly documented with standard documents and the total time necessary to complete a transaction is relatively short. The tax lease is much more complicated and requires tailor-made documents which, coupled with the longer time necessary to make credit analyses on larger transactions, results in longer lead times until the takedown.

The lessees likely to find nontax leases attractive are the smaller to medium-sized companies which are attracted to the cash flow advantages of the lease as opposed to a cash purchase financed by short-term bank borrowings. The tax leases find favor with the larger corporation, especially in capital intensive industries such as transportation and utilities. It is especially attractive to companies who are not in a tax-paying posture because of operating losses or tax loss carry-forwards.

In summary, most of the *transactions* done in leasing today are of the nontax variety. However, most of the *dollars* are found in tax leases.

Leveraged and Nonleveraged Leases

Since the enactment of the investment tax credit in 1971, considerable emphasis has been placed on the "leveraged" lease. A leveraged lease is one which brings a third party, the debt holder, into the normal lessor/lessee arrangement. This is not to imply that debt leverage is not an integral part of nonleverage lease transactions because most leasing companies are highly leveraged. However, in the leveraged lease, the debt holder looks through the lessor to the lessee for credit and security and is not relying on the credit of the lessor. In fact, an important ingredient to the leveraged lease is a structure in which the debt holder "lends" the major portion of the cost of the asset to the lessor on a nonrecourse basis. This structure is accomplished through trust arrangements, limited partnerships and/or nonrecourse notes.

By acquiring a large portion of the cost of the asset through this nonrecourse arrangement, a lessor has the benefit of accelerated depreciation and the investment tax credit on 100 percent of the asset with an investment and exposure of only a fraction of the total cost. Thus, he has "leveraged" his tax benefits. The lessee has the advantage of a lower than otherwise possible lease rate which is usually lower than his long-term borrowing rate. Most leverage leases are structured so that the lessor recovers his investment through the tax savings and anticipated residuals as opposed to contractual lease payments. Nearly the entire lease payment is earmarked to amortize the debt portion of the transaction at a rate generally comparable to the lessee's long-term borrowing or bond rate. This accomplishes the normal expected rate of return to the debt holder on his investment, but nearly no return of interest or principal to the lessor on his investment in the form of cash flow from rental payments. The result is a weighted overall dollar cost to the lessee on the entire asset being considerably less than his long-term borrowing rate. For example, a 70 percent debt lease transaction at an 8 percent long-term debt rate with all of the lease payments serving to amortize the debt would result in reducing the overall cost to the lessee from his normal 8 percent to less than 2 percent on a 12-year term. By adding a limited cash flow dollar return to the lessor plus the high front-end brokerage, the debt placement and legal fees generally associated with leverage leases, the more normal nominal lease rate of 3 percent to 4 percent is achieved.

Both the leveraged leases and the nonleveraged leases are "tax" leases and must meet the Internal Revenue Service tests of "true" leases in order to allow the tax benefits to be utilized by the lessor. The basic difference between the two is that in the nonleveraged lease the lessor is getting his entire investment returned to him through the rental payments and he uses the tax benefits merely to enhance his return on investment. The leveraged lessor looks almost entirely to the tax benefits for his return of his equity investment and profit. Both types of lessors must be in a tax-paying posture, and the income producing this tax liability must come from sources other than the lease itself. As a result, the tax "shelter" aspect is introduced. The leveraged lease is almost entirely a tax shelter while the nonleveraged lease can be a bona fide financing investment by the lessor, the "shelter" being utilized simply to enhance the return on that investment.

Three areas in the economic computations of both leveraged and nonleveraged leases can have a considerable impact on the final calculation of return on equity with very little input variation. They are: (1) residual values; (2) timing of tax advantages; and (3) modified sinking-fund rates.

As leasing transactions get longer and longer, it becomes more critical to assign accurate residual values to equipment. The conservative approach would be to assign zero or minimal value to residuals when computing the lease rate on the transaction. A sophisticated lessor would want residuals to be his hedge against increased costs of his funds, especially if, as is usually the case, the lease rate is fixed over the term. Competition, however, has forced lessors to look longer and harder at residual values and forces them to include some of this value in their calculations when pricing a lease transaction.

Considerable impact can be obtained on the calculation of a return on equity by accelerating the timing of the tax benefits. For instance, if the job development credit was computed to be utilized during the first month of the lease, this could result in a false value. Most taxpayers pay taxes quarterly and often after being granted extensions. Such timing should be considered in computing the return to the lessor.

In order for leveraged leases to work properly, a modified sinking-fund (theoretical or actual) arrangement is added to the computations. The lessor has large depreciation tax losses in early years which "cross over" to tax liabilities in later years. In order to provide the funds for these later tax liabilities, a lessor, in theory, should set aside some of the tax savings he received in earlier years. This fund is then "invested" at an after-tax rate of return which, when compounded at that rate until needed to pay those tax liabilities, will grow to the exact amount needed to pay those taxes at the times needed. The higher the sinking-fund rate utilized in the analysis, the less tax-saving dollars will have to be set aside in this fund, and consequently the more tax dollar savings left over to make up the return on equity the lessor is striving to attain. A small variance in this sinking-fund rate can have a major impact on return on equity.

From the lessor's viewpoint, the leveraged lease is more tax oriented than the nonleveraged lease. If the prime motivation of the lessor is to shelter taxes, he can do so much quicker by entering into leveraged lease transactions.

INTERNAL REVENUE CODE AND THE TRUE LEASE

General

To the extent that a lease transaction generates tax losses during its early years, such losses may be offset against taxable earnings generated by other activities of the lessor. A principal reason that substantial tax losses may be generated in the early years of a lease is the availability of accelerated depreciation deductions with respect to the leased property. Accordingly, it is essential that the lessor be eligible to depreciate the property which it leases in accordance with the accelerated methods of depreciation provided for under the Internal Revenue Code.

Property which is owned by a taxpayer is depreciable if it is subject to exhaustion, wear and tear, or obsolescence and is used by the taxpayer in a trade or business or is held by the taxpayer for the production of income. Accelerated depreciation may be used in the case of tangible property: (a) which is acquired after December 31, 1953, (b) the original use of which commences with the taxpayer, and (c) which has a useful life to the taxpayer of three years or more. To ensure that the "original use" of the property will commence with the lessor, care must be taken to ensure that in all cases property to be acquired by the lessor is acquired directly from the manufacturer and conversely that the intended lessee of the property does not take title and then engage in a sale and leaseback with the lessor. If the procedure suggested above is followed, the lessor will be considered to be the owner and original user of property which it leases and the taxpayer which places the property in service. A deviation from this procedure would cause the equipment to be "used," resulting in less advantageous depreciation allowances and loss of the investment tax credit, if it were otherwise available.

The True Lease

There are a variety of circumstances which may cause what is in form a lease transaction, nevertheless, to be characterized as a conditional sale or as a financing for federal income tax purposes because the purported lessor does not have sufficient ownership interest in the property subject to the "lease." Since the lessor would not be considered to be the owner of the property for federal income tax purposes if such a transaction is characterized as a conditional sale or as a financing, it would not be entitled to claim depreciation and investment tax credit with respect to the property. The proper characterization of a transaction which, although in form a lease, is not treated as such for tax purposes, is not clear. In such case the transaction might be treated either as a conditional sale or as a financing and the appropriate tax accounting treatment of such a transaction is set forth in Revenue Ruling 72-408 (August 28, 1972). In any event, if the transaction is not characterized as a lease some or all of the tax losses which are expected during the early years of the transaction would be lost.

The basic test for determining the proper income tax characterization of arrangements which purport to be a "lease" is whether at the time the agreement to lease is made (the "Date of Commitment) the parties thereto had an objective intent to enter into a lease rather than a conditional sale or financing. The touchstone for resolving this question of intent is whether at the Date of Commitment it was reasonable for the parties to believe that the lessor would have a substantial economic or proprietary interest in the leased property and not simply an interest which more closely resembles a creditor's security interest.

In general, in the absence of other contrary factors, a lease of property will be characterized as a lease for federal income tax purposes if, according to the best bona fide estimates available at the Date of Commitment, (a) the value of the property at the end of the lease term will not be insubstantial or nominal, and (b) the property at such time will have a remaining economic useful life which is not insubstantial or nominal. In making this determination, the lease term must be considered to include any terms for which the lease may be renewed at the option of one of the parties which, on the basis of present estimates, it appears likely will be exercised. Thus, where the lessee has the option to extend the lease for one or more renewal periods beyond the original term at a fixed rental which appears to be substantially less than the best present estimates of the fair rental value of such property during the renewal term, it is likely that such option will be exercised. Similarly, when the lessor has the option to require the lessee to renew for a term at a fixed rental, it is likely that such option will be exercised if the renewal term rent substantially exceeds the best present estimates of the fair rental value of the property during the renewal term. In either case, any renewal period would be considered as part of the lease term.

If the lessee has an option to acquire title to the property at a price which is nominal in relation to the fair market value of the property at the time the option may be exercised, as estimated at the Date of Commitment, the agreement will not be treated as a lease for federal income tax purposes, without regard to the lease term. Since it would be relatively certain that the lessee would exercise such option, the lessor would have retained no substantial economic or proprietary interest in the property subject to the lease other than in the nature of a secured creditor's interest. The greater the fixed option price the less likely it is that the option will be exercised and, accordingly, that the transaction will be treated other than as a lease. The existence of an option where the price is expressed as an amount equal to at least the fair market value of the property as determined at the time it may be exercised, rather than fixed dollar amount, will not in any way inhibit characterization of the transaction as a lease for tax purposes.

A lessor's option to sell the equipment to the lessee at a price significantly in excess of the estimate, at the Date of Commitment, of the fair market value of the property at the time such option may be exercised will also probably result in the transaction not being treated as a lease because of the relative certainty that such option will be exercised. Once again, the existence of an option in which the price is expressed as an amount equal to the fair market value of the property as determined at the time the option to sell may be exercised, rather than as a predetermined fixed price, will not cause the lease to be characterized as other than a lease.

Set forth below are guidelines based upon the foregoing discussion which, if followed in the negotiation of leasing transactions, should generally result in such transactions being characterized as leases for federal income tax purposes.

Minimum Unconditional "At Risk" Investment. The lessor must have made a minimum unconditional "at risk" investment in the property (the "Minimum Investment") when the lease begins, must maintain such *Minimum Investment throughout the entire lease term, and such Minimum Investment must remain at the end of the lease term.* The Minimum Investment must be an equity investment (the "Equity Investment") which includes only consideration paid and personal liability incurred by the lessor to purchase the property. The net worth of the lessor must be sufficient to satisfy any such personal liability. In determining the lessor's Minimum Investment, the following rules will be applied:

Initial Minimum Investment. When the property is first placed in service or use by the lessee, the Minimum Investment must be equal to at least *20 percent of the cost of the property.* The Minimum Investment must be unconditional. That is, after the property is first placed in service or use by the lessee, the lessor must not be entitled to a return of any portion of the Minimum Investment through any arrangement, directly or indirectly, with the lessee, a shareholder of the lessee, or any party related to the lessee (the "Lessee Group"). The lease transaction may include an arrangement with someone other than the foregoing parties that provides for such a return to the lessor if the property fails to satisfy written specifications for the supply, construction, or manufacture of the property.

Maintenance of Minimum Investment. The Minimum Investment *must remain equal to at least 20 percent of the cost of the property at all times throughout the entire lease term.* That is, the excess of the cumulative payments required to have been paid by the lessee to or on behalf of the lessor over the cumulative disbursements required to have been paid by or for the lessor in connection with the ownership of the property must never exceed the sum of (a) any excess of the lessor's initial Equity Investment over 20 percent of the cost of the property plus (b) the cumulative pro rata portion of the projected profit from the transaction (exclusive of tax benefits).

Residual Investment. The lessor must represent and demonstrate that an amount equal to at least 20 percent of the original cost of the property *is a reasonable estimate of what the fair market value of the property will be at the end of the lease term.* For this purpose, fair market value must be determined (a) without including in such value any increase or decrease for inflation or deflation during the lease term, and (b) after substracting from *such value any cost to the lessor for removal and delivery of possession of the property to the lessor at the end of the lease term.* In addition, the lessor must represent and demonstrate that a remaining useful life of *the longer of one year or 20 percent of the originally estimated useful life of the property is a reasonable estimate of what the remaining useful life of the property will be at the end of the lease term.*

Lease Term and Renewal Options. The lease term includes all renewal or extension periods except renewals or extensions at the option of the lessee at *fair rental value at the time of such renewal or extension.*

Purchase and Sale Rights. No member of the Lessee Group may have a contractual right to purchase the property from the lessor at a price *less than its fair market value at the time the right is exercised.* When the property is first placed in service or use by the lessee, the lessor *may not have a contractual right* to cause any party to purchase the property. The lessor must also represent that it does not have any present intention to acquire such a contractual right. The effect of any such right acquired at a subsequent time will be determined at that time based on all the facts and circumstances. A provision that permits the lessor to abandon the property to any party will be treated as a contractual right of the lessor to cause such party to purchase the property.

No Investment by Lessee. No part of the cost of the property may be furnished by any member of the Lessee Group. Nor may any such party furnish any part of the cost of improvements or additions to the property, except for improvements or additions that are owned by any member of the Lessee Group and are readily removable without causing material damage to the property. Any item that is so readily removable must not be subject to a contract or option for purchase or sale between the lessor and any member of the Lessee Group at a price other than its fair market value at the time of such purchase or sale. However:

Cost Overruns and Modifications. If the cost of the property exceeds the estimate on which the lease was based, the lease may provide for adjustment of the rents to compensate the lessor for such additional cost.

Maintenance and Repair. If the lease requires the lessee to maintain and keep the property in good repair during the term of the lease, ordinary maintenance and repairs performed by the lessee will not constitute an improvement or addition to the property.

No Lessee Loans or Guarantees. No member of the Lessee Group may lend to the lessor any of the funds necessary to acquire the property, *or guarantee any indebtedness created in connection with the acquisition of the property by the lessor.* A guarantee by any member of the Lessee Group of the lessee's obligation to pay rent, properly maintain the property, or pay insurance premiums or other similar conventional obligations of a net lease does not constitute the guarantee of the indebtedness of the lessor.

Profit Requirement. The lessor must represent and demonstrate that it expects to receive a profit from the transaction, apart from the value of or benefits obtained from the tax deductions, allowances, credits, and other tax attributes arising from such transaction. This requirement is met if the aggregate amount required to be paid by the lessee to or for the lessor over the lease term plus the value of the residual investment exceed an amount equal to the sum of the aggregate disbursements required to be paid by or for the lessor in connection with the ownership of the property and the lessor's Equity Investment in the property, including any direct costs to finance the Equity Investment, and the aggregate amounts required to be paid to or for the lessor over the lease term exceed by a reasonable amount the aggregate disbursements required to be paid by or for the lessor in connection with the ownership of the property.

Other Considerations. Leveraged lease transactions that satisfy the guidelines set forth, nevertheless, may contain uneven rent payments that result in prepaid or deferred rent. The Service ordinarily will not raise any question about prepaid or deferred rent if the an-

nual rent for any year (a) is not more than 10 percent above or below the amount calculated by dividing the total rent payable over the
lease term by the number of years in such term, or (b) during at
least the first two thirds of the lease term is not more than 10 percent above or below the amount calculated by dividing the total
rent payable over such initial portion of the lease term by the number of years in such initial portion of the lease term, and if the
annual rent for any year during the remainder of the lease term is
no greater than the highest annual rent for any year during the initial
portion of the lease term and no less than one half of the average
annual rent during such initial portion of the lease term.

Financing Considerations

If the putative "owner" finances so great a portion of the aggregate purchase price of an item of equipment that it makes only a
nominal equity investment in the equipment, under certain circumstances its ownership of such equipment might be called into
question.

If the entire purchase price of the equipment is borrowed
(whether on a recourse or nonrecourse basis) and the rental payments under the lease cover both principal and interest payments
due on such financing, there is a great risk that the IRS might
challenge the ownership of the equipment. The IRS may hold
that such an arrangement would not have been made unless in the
view of the parties to the lease, the lease grants the lessee use of
the equipment for a great part if its entire useful life and the equipment will have no substantial value at the end of the term of the
lease.

On the other hand, if the financing is on a nonrecourse basis,
and the lessee is not, in effect, obligated by the lease to make all
principal and interest payments due on the financing (or if so
obligated, is in a precarious financial condition such that there is
a substantial chance that it will not be able to meet such obligations), the IRS might contend that the lender, rather than the
would-be "owner," is the true owner of the equipment. In such a
case, since the "interest rate" on the "financing" would likely be
quite high, thus enhancing the possibility of default, the IRS
might well take the view that the putative lender is the owner of
the equipment since it has really assumed the risks and has secured
many of the potential benefits which usually accrue to the owner

of the equipment, while the "owner," with no real risk of loss and little possibility of gain, has no substantial proprietary interest in the equipment. If such financing is, however, on a full recourse basis, no matter what portion of the purchase price is so financed, there will be little risk that the IRS could successfully so contend because the "owner" will be obligated to pay the principal and interest on the financing in all events.

It is generally accepted that if the owner makes an equity investment in the equipment equal to at least 20 percent of the purchase price, its claim to ownership of the equipment will not be challenged from this standpoint.

ECONOMIC CONSIDERATIONS

The treasurer of a corporation, in evaluating a proposed lease transaction, must compare that method of financing with the alternative methods of financing that are available to him. Most often the appropriate method of determining the most desirable approach will be through an after-tax discounted cash flow analysis. This method of analysis permits the factor of timing of capital expenditures as well as the value of the tax benefits to be analyzed and evaluated through an objective comparative technique.

In any such comparative analysis of a lease as opposed to (*a*) cash purchase, (*b*) installment purchase, or (*c*) bank loan, the assumptions that are used are of critical importance. Before going through a sample analysis, a discussion of the assumptions to be made is in order.

Tax Qualification of the Lease. If the transaction is to be in the form of a lease with the consequent tax treatment to the lessor as owner and to the lessee as user, care must be taken to ensure that the transaction meets the Internal Revenue Service standards of a true lease.

Timing of Use of Tax Benefits. Whether the user elects to lease the equipment or own the equipment, a portion of his analysis will require an assumption as to when he will derive the tax benefit of: (*a*) job development credit and depreciation (if he is the owner); or (*b*) rental expense (if he is the lessee). First of all, if the user is not a current taxpayer because of current operating losses or because of a tax loss carry-forward, he must not include the benefit of the tax deductions that would have otherwise accrued to him during the current period. He should factor into his analysis the assumed timing for the realization of the tax consequences of the transaction.

Tax Rate. In assuming a tax rate, it is important to give effect to the state and local taxes which will impact the transaction. For example, although the federal tax rate may be 48 percent, a 6 percent state and local tax will result in an overall tax rate of 51.12 percent.

Depreciation Method. Under the asset depreciation range (ADR) guidelines, there are certain technical rules that should be followed in evaluating the impact of depreciation upon a transaction. Without the ADR considerations, an asset would be depreciated for tax purposes from the date of acquisition over a period equal to its useful life or over the class life of that asset. The method of depreciation might be straight line, double-declining balance, sum-of-the-years'-digits, or 150 percent declining balance (the latter being the most accelerated method available for used tangible personal property). The ADR is a statutory system which provides a range of years of 20 percent greater and 20 percent shorter than the class life of certain assets. This system, which may be elected by a taxpayer each year as to individual classes of assets placed in service that year, generally applies to all depreciable business property.

Under ADR a taxpayer may use the straight line, the sum-of-the-years'-digits or the double-declining balance method for new eligible property. In the case of used eligible assets, he may use the straight-line or 150 percent declining balance method. Straight-line depreciation is computed by dividing the depreciable value of the property by the number of years in the asset depreciation period. Sum-of-the-years'-digits depreciation is calculated by multiplying the same depreciable value of the asset by sum-of-the-years' digits fraction based upon the asset depreciation period. The double-declining balance method applies twice the straight-line rate to the undepreciated value of the asset. Thus, for a $1,000 asset with a five-year life, the first year's depreciation would be $400 (40% × $1,000), while the depreciation for the second year would be $240, obtained by multiplying 40 percent by the remaining undepreciated balance of $600 ($1,000 − $400 = $600).

Finally, consideration should be given as to whether one of the conventions relating to depreciation should be elected. In computing ADR depreciation, the taxpayer must use one of two first-year conventions:

The Half-Year Convention. A half year's depreciation is taken on all assets placed in service during the year. The assumption is made that the property is placed in service and extraordinary retirements occur on the first day of the second half of the tax year.

The Modified Half-Year Convention. First half additions get a full year's depreciation in the year first placed in service. Second half additions get a full year's depreciation in the year following the year they are placed in service. Correspondingly, first half extraordinary retirements get no depreciation while second half extraordinary retirements get a full year's depreciation in the year of retirement. The assumption is made that first half additions and extraordinary retirements are made on the first day of the year and second half additions and extraordinary retirements are made on the first day of the succeeding tax year.

Residual Value of Property. If the lease route is elected, the lessee will be relinquishing any rights to the residual value of the property. Obviously, if the loan or installment purchase approach is selected, then the residual value will be retained. In any discounted tax flow analysis, the value of this residual must be accurately estimated.

Cost of Borrowed Funds. Obviously, if the property is acquired via the bank loan or installment purchase route, then an accurate estimate of the term of the loan, the interest cost, any down payment, and any advance payments or compensating balances must be considered in the cash flow analysis. Any device which effectively deprives the user of cash must be factored in as a cost of the transaction.

Reinvestment Rate. One of the primary attractions of a lease transaction is the fact that it helps conserve cash. The amount of actual cash flow realized, however, depends on the reinvestment rate assumed. Obviously, the higher the reinvestment rate, the greater will be the benefit of cash which is conserved in the early years of the transaction.

LEASE VERSUS BORROW BY DISCOUNTED CASH FLOW

When costs of acquiring an asset or the use of an asset are being analyzed by tax-paying corporations, it is inappropriate to compare one method of acquisition with another merely on a *total cost* basis. First, an adjustment should be made to convert the total cost of each financing method from pretax to after-tax to equalize the differences caused by taxes. The result is called *after-tax cash flow*.

Furthermore, when costs of acquiring an asset or the use of an asset are being paid over varying periods of time, the time value of money should be considered. One dollar received today is worth more than $1 to be received five years from now. Conversely, $1 due to be paid by you five years from now has a value today of less than $1. This *present value* of the *cash flow* is called the *discounted cash flow*. By discounting the cash flows of alternative methods of financing back to their respective present values, a meaningful dollar cost comparison can be made because the differences caused by variations in timing are eliminated.

Example 1

Table 1 shows the discounted cash flow of a typical true lease and a typical borrowing. To make the comparison valid, the cost to the lessee of purchasing the equipment at fair market value at the end of the lease is included in the calculation and the most optimum method of depreciation (double-declining balance converted to sum-of-the-years' digits) is used. Interestingly enough, with this sample transaction, the lessor receives a pretax yield of 11 percent on the lease while charging only 7¼ percent to the lessee. The lender on the borrowed funds has no tax enhancement; therefore, his yield is limited to that charged, namely 8½ percent.

The total discounted cash flow cost to the lessee/borrower on the lease in this example is $61,229 while the borrowing is $61,617[1]. The following assumptions were used in arriving at these figures:

	Lease	*Borrowing*
Equipment cost	$100,000	$100,000
Term	10 years	5 years
Payments.	Level monthly, in arrears	Level monthly, in arrears
Simple interest rate	7¼%	8½%
Down payment	None	15%
Investment tax credit	Passed to lessee	Retained by lessee
Depreciation.		10 year to 15% salvage
Residual purchase.	15%	Not applicable
Tax bracket	50%	50%
Reinvestment rate (*after* tax)	6%	6%

---

[1] Even though the discounted cash flow cost of the lease is only slightly less than the borrowing, the lower periodic payments of the lease during the first five years may give a decided additional advantage.

TABLE 1
Comparison of Lease with Borrowing by Discounted Cash Flow

| | Lease | | Borrow | | | Discounted Cash Flow Analysis | | |
| | (1) | (2) | (3) | (4) | (5) | (6) | (7) | (8) |
Year	Total Rents and Residual Purchase	Net Cost after Tax (Cash Flow)	Total Payments	Tax Deduction from Interest and Depreciation	Net Cost after Tax (Cash Flow)	Present Value Factor at 6%	Discounted Cash Flow of Lease (col. 2 × col. 6)	Discounted Cash Flow of Borrowing (col. 5 × col. 6)
0	$ 14,088	$ 7,044	$ 15,000		$15,000	1.000		$15,000
1	14,088	7,044	20,926	$11,771	9,155	0.971	$ 6,840	8,890
2	14,088	7,044	20,926	9,418	11,508	0.914	6,438	10,518
3	14,088	7,044	20,926	8,006	12,920	0.861	6,065	11,124
4	14,088	7,044	20,926	6,596	14,330	0.811	5,713	11,622
5	14,088	7,044	20,926	5,189	15,737	0.763	5,375	12,007
6	14,088	7,044		3,778	(3,778)	0.719	5,065	(2,716)
7	14,088	7,044		3,022	(3,022)	0.677	4,769	(2,046)
8	14,088	7,044		2,265	(2,265)	0.638	4,494	(1,445)
9	14,088	7,044		1,513	(1,513)	0.601	4,233	(909)
10	14,088	7,044		756	(756)	0.566	3,987	(428)
11	15,000	15,000				0.550	8,250	
Total	$155,880	$85,440	$119,630	$52,314	$67,316		$61,229	$61,617

Example 1 evidenced less expense through the lease route than the loan route. Example 2 reflects a significantly higher lease rate (10 percent instead of 7¼ percent) and also reflects no down payment required on the loan transaction. In that situation, the loan transaction is a far more attractive alternative.

Example 2: Standard Input

1. Ten-year lease with level monthly payments payable in arrears.
2. 10 percent lease rate ("nominal" rate).
3. 10 percent residual purchase ($100,000).
4. 7 percent investment tax credit passed to lessee.
5. Five-year loan payable monthly in arrears in equal principal payments plus interest on unamortized balance.
6. 8 percent simple interest loan rate.
7. Ten-year double-declining balance converted to straight-line depreciation to zero residual value.
8. 50 percent income tax bracket.
9. 6 percent after-tax reinvestment rate.
10. $1,000,000 equipment cost.

Comparison of Present Values of Costs

	Lease	Buy	Loan
Present value.	$583,182	$529,138	$483,640
Index.	100	91	83

Total Cash (pretax)

Year	(1) Lease	(2) Buy	(3) Loan
1.	$ 158,580	$1,000,000	$ 272,000
2.	158,580	–	256,000
3.	158,580	–	240,000
4.	158,580	–	224,000
5.	158,580	–	208,000
6.	158,580	–	–
7.	158,580	–	–
8.	158,580	–	–
9.	158,580	–	–
10.	158,580	–	–
11.	100,000		
Total	$1,685,800	$1,000,000	$1,200,000

Cash Flow (after-tax)

	Lease		Buy				Loan		
Year	(1) Tax Deductible	(2) Cash Flow	(3) Depreciation (DDB to Straight Line)	(4) Tax Deductible	(5) Cash Flow	(6) Interest	(7) Depreciation Plus Interest	(8) Tax Deductible	(9) Cash Flow
1	$79,290	$ 9,290	$200,000	$100,000	$830,000	$72,000	$272,000	$136,000	$ 66,000
2	79,290	79,290	160,000	80,000	(80,000)	56,000	216,000	108,000	148,000
3	79,290	79,290	128,000	64,000	(64,000)	40,000	168,000	84,000	156,000
4	79,290	79,290	102,400	51,200	(51,200)	24,000	126,400	63,200	160,800
5	79,290	79,290	81,920	40,960	(40,960)	8,000	89,920	44,960	163,040
6	79,290	79,290	65,536	32,768	(32,768)	—	65,536	32,768	(32,768)
7	79,290	79,290	65,536	32,768	(32,768)	—	65,536	32,768	(32,768)
8	79,290	79,290	65,536	32,768	(32,768)	—	65,536	32,768	(32,768)
9	79,290	79,290	65,536	32,768	(32,768)	—	65,536	32,768	(32,768)
10	79,290	79,290	65,536	32,768	(32,768)	—	65,536	32,768	(32,768)
11	—	100,000	—	—	—	—	—	—	—
Total		$822,900			$430,000				$530,000

Discounted Cash Flow

	Lease			Buy			Loan		
Year	(1) Cash Flow	(2) 6 Percent Discount Factor*	(3) Discounted Cash Flow	(4) Cash Flow	(5) 6 Percent Discount Factor*	(6) Discounted Cash Flow	(7) Cash Flow	(8) 6 Percent Discount Factor*	(9) Discounted Cash Flow
0	$ —	1.0000	$ —	$1,000,000	1.0000	$1,000,000	$ —	1.0000	$ —
1	9,290	0.9706	9,017	(170,000)	0.9706	(165,002)	66,000	0.9706	64,060
2	79,290	0.9141	72,479	(80,000)	0.9141	(73,128)	148,000	0.9141	135,287
3	79,290	0.8608	68,253	(64,000)	0.8608	(55,091)	156,000	0.8608	134,285
4	79,290	0.8107	64,280	(51,200)	0.8107	(41,508)	160,800	0.8107	130,360
5	79,290	0.7635	60,538	(40,960)	0.7635	(31,273)	163,040	0.7635	124,481
6	79,290	0.7190	57,009	(32,768)	0.7190	(23,560)	(32,768)	0.7190	(23,560)
7	79,290	0.6772	53,695	(32,768)	0.6772	(22,190)	(32,768)	0.6772	(22,190)
8	79,290	0.6377	50,563	(32,768)	0.6377	(20,896)	(32,768)	0.6377	(20,869)
9	79,290	0.6006	47,622	(32,768)	0.6006	(19,680)	(32,768)	0.6006	(19,680)
10	79,290	0.5656	44,846	(32,768)	0.5656	(18,534)	(32,768)	0.5656	(18,533)
11	100,000	0.5488	54,880	—	—	—	—	—	—
Total			$583,182			$ 529,138			$483,661

* Based on mid-point between indicated year and prior year.

Schedule A

		Lease	*Buy*	*Loan*
1.	Standard input variations from standard	$583,182	$529,138	$483,614
2.	52% tax bracket.	559,328	513,021	464,872
3.	48% tax bracket.	607,035	545,376	503,351
4.	8-year ADR depreciation.	583,182	505,114	459,589
5.	12-year ADR depreciation.	583,182	535,419	489,893
6.	12% lease rate	634,348	529,138	483,614
7.	8% lease rate.	534,334	529,138	483,614
8.	10% loan rate	583,182	529,138	506,248
9.	6% loan rate	583,182	529,138	460,979
10.	5% residual purchase	559,742	529,138	483,614
11.	15% residual purchase	614,622	529,138	483,614
12.	9% reinvestment rate	496,524	564,557	402,316
13.	3% reinvestment rate	690,126	483,839	507,526
14.	ITC retained by lessor	651,124	529,138	483,614
15.	Depreciate to 10% salvage	583,182	569,431	523,905
16.	10-year loan	583,182	529,138	446,313
17.	Level payment loan.	583,182	529,138	482,155

In Schedule A, the sensitivity of various other inputs is reflected by showing the variations from the standard input.

NONECONOMIC CONSIDERATIONS RELATED TO THE LEASING DECISION
ACCOUNTING PRACTICES

In 1975, true leases were not required to be capitalized on the lessee's balance sheet. Thus, although the lessor, for book purposes, will probably report the earnings of the lease on the finance basis and will not capitalize the asset, the lessee is permitted to expense the rental payments each period and is not required to show the aggregate rental payment due over the life of the lease as a fixed obligation. This practice has evolved from the accountants' position that executory contracts (contracts where payment by one side does not become due until performance is completed by the other side) do not require that the aggregate obligation be capitalized.

Traditional accounting does not recognize assets or liabilities arising from executory-type contracts. One of the reasons for the failure to record these assets and liabilities is that their valuations are not easily estimated. Another reason is that the effect on income arises from later events rather than from the signing of the contract. However, in most cases, because the contracts represent commitments for the future, a disclosure of them is very relevant for investment and other decisions relying on some prediction of future income amounts. If this disclosure cannot be made appropriately in the formal statements, the information should be disclosed in footnotes.

Included in the executory-type contracts are long-term leases and purchase commitments. While the capitalization of these commitments and the inclusion of them among the assets and liabilities of the balance sheet may improve the statements, the nature of these contracts usually requires supplementary information also. In addition to the capitalized valuation, the reader of the report would probably be interested in knowing the terminal date of the contract, the amount of annual payment, the annual charge to expense, and other features. Therefore, footnote disclosure may be desirable to provide supplementary information regarding the long-term contracts; it should not be viewed only as an alternative to capitalization.

Based upon the foregoing treatment, any balance sheet analysis or ratio test which does not take the uncapitalized lease into consideration might be misleading. The argument that leasing improves the company's apparent financial position or improves ratios of profit to fixed assets by keeping debt off the balance sheet is basically discredited. Appropriate footnotes usually disclose the aggregate lease obligations and lenders expect an appropriate amount of equity to support these fixed obligations. Notwithstanding the acknowledgment that sophisticated analysts will factor in lease obligations which are not disclosed on the balance sheet, many potential lessees are still attracted to leasing because of the ability to treat that obligation as something other than fixed debt.

Financing Advantages

Because leasing companies are often knowledgeable in the used equipment market and are therefore prepared to evaluate the value of the equipment as part of the credit judgment in any transaction, certain desirable types of equipment should be considered as being particularly financeable through the leasing route. An informed judgment of the residual value of a piece of equipment will generally be reflected in the form of lower rental payments. Also, to the extent that the lessee's credit might be marginal on an unsecured basis, highly remarketable equipment may be decisive in having the lessee's credit approved. Certain lessors will even work closely with used equipment dealers and will pay them a fee in exchange for the right to "put" certain equipment to them in the event of a default.

One of the critical advantages of leasing as a form of financing is the fact that unless prepayments, or additional collateral, are required, leasing provides 100 percent financing of the acquisition cost of the asset. Most conditional sales, on the other hand, require that the buyer provide a substantial down payment.

Another financing advantage of leasing is the ability of the lessee to take down and pay for funds only as he uses them. In contrast, in a public financing, generally, funds are borrowed in substantial quantities with excess borrowings being used as compensating balances or to pay down bank debt or to be invested in short-term, liquid investments. If the temporary employment of these funds yields an amount equivalent to the interest cost of the borrowed funds, then the funds are being effectively managed. However, often these excess funds will yield far less than the cost of such funds, so an additional cost is incurred in "warehousing" these funds until they are invested in income-producing assets in the business. Most lessors will grant a lessee a "line" for a period of time and will advance the funds for equipment to the respective vendors, as the equipment is accepted and placed into service by the lessee.

Flexibility

As compared to the alternative methods of debt financing, leasing is generally considered to be the most flexible for a variety of reasons.

The use of operating leases permits the postponement of long-term debt financing in a period of abnormally high-interest rates. Only such amounts as are specifically allocable to the financing of certain pieces of equipment need be committed for and major long-term financing can be delayed until the interest market has overcome any temporary aberrations.

Lessors, in keeping with their relationship to specific pieces of equipment, are accustomed to make a commitment subject to the lessee having an opportunity to test the equipment and be assured that various performance levels are met. Thus, the lessor's advance of funds is customarily made directly to the vendor only upon the lessor's receipt of a delivery and acceptance certificate from the lessee. Indeed, any purchase order from the lessor to the vendor always spells out quite specifically that payment for the equipment is to be made by the lessor only after the lessee has designated his satisfaction with the equipment.

Lease agreements are usually very flexible. In larger lease transactions, lessors are generally prepared to negotiate special terms and conditions to accommodate the lessee. Similarly, leases generally can provide for renewal options or purchase options. Care should be taken to ensure that the Internal Revenue Service guidelines are not violated in these areas if it is critical that the lease qualify as a true lease for tax purposes.

To the extent that certain companies permit the final decision for smaller lease transactions to be made at lower managerial levels than the level at which the long-term debt decision is made, and further, since such leases can be entered into without going through the capital expenditure committee, many managers find the leasing route to be the most flexible from within the lessee's organization.

On occasion, a lessee is faced with a loan indenture which is restrictive about increasing additional debt, but may not restrict leasing. Alternatively, there may be balance sheet ratio tests that would be violated if any form of capitalized debt were to be increased. Although lenders can be approached for waivers to these limitations, waivers often have a price. Whether it would be an increase in the rate or an acceleration of the amortization schedule, a request for a waiver could be expensive. As long as the indenture does not restrict leasing and as long as the lease is not capitalized, it may be a very desirable alternative.

Questionable Benefits

The promotional argument of leasing companies that leasing frees working capital is illusory. Obviously, the same advantages attributable to a leasing transaction can be obtained with a borrowing which has a comparable term and amortization schedule. Similarly, any argument that leasing provides a hedge against inflation is equally applicable to long-term debt as well. The concept of paying back presently incurred obligations with future dollars is not peculiar to a long-term lease. Indeed, any long-term obligation, especially one with a balloon payment at the end will justifiably claim this advantage.

Because leasing permits a tax deduction of the entire lease payment, lessees are sometimes enticed by apparent tax savings. This is a simplistic argument because if the user borrows the funds to acquire the equipment, he will derive the tax benefits attributable to deductions for interest expense on the borrowing plus depreciation. If the lessee can negotiate the lease payments so that his rents will be higher during the early years and lower in the late years (assuming that on a discounted cash flow analysis the overall economics are not distorted as a result) then he may be able to shelter more taxes in the early years as a lessee than as an owner.

The one area where leasing does create a distinct tax advantage is with land. By leasing land the lessee is able to obtain a deduction for those rental payments, while as owner, because land is not subject to depreciation, he would derive no tax deduction. Of course, as lessee he would be denied the residual value of the land at the end of the lease which then accrues to the lessor.

Because the tax position and creditworthiness of each lessee is different, it is difficult to draw a profile of a company that is likely to find leasing to be a more desirable form of financing than borrowing. However, there are certain general situations where leasing may be less expensive than borrowing such as:

1. Where the lessor can pass on all or part of the benefit of the investment tax credit or job development credit to the lessee in the form of lower rentals.
2. Where low cost underlying financing is available to the lessor— as is usually the case with a lessor that is an industrial development agency.
3. Where the lease payments are tax free to the lessor—i.e., a lessor that is a foundation or a university.
4. Where the lease payments amortization, but not the lease term, is shorter than the allowable form of depreciation.
5. Where the lessor is an individual in a higher tax bracket and can derive a greater tax saving from the depreciation than can the corporate lessee.
6. Where there is a significant service and maintenance function performed by the lessor.
7. Where the interest rate required by the lessor is close to the

rate of direct borrowing and those costs of direct borrowing such as underwriting fees, legal fees and compensating balances are high and eliminated by the lease.

8. Where the interest rate a lessee would pay for borrowed funds is high because it can get funds only from a commercial finance company.

NEGOTIATING THE LEASE

General

In preparing to negotiate a lease transaction, the lessee must have a precise understanding of his objectives. In addition, he should clearly evaluate the marketplace to have an appreciation for the prevailing rates and terms available from lessors.

As to the lessee's objectives, he should evaluate his own tax position and how that is likely to impact the negotiation. In certain cases, the ultimate tax treatment of the transaction may be a negotiable issue and the ultimate use of the job development credit may be swappable for an adjustment to the rate. However, if the lessee is anxious to reflect the tax credit on his income statement, that may become an item of paramount importance and may impact the entire negotiation. Another area, as an example, that must be evaluated by the lessee may relate to the payment schedule under the lease. Based upon the cash flow projections of the lessee, he may be very rigid in requiring a balloon rental payment at the end of the lease or he may be anxious to front load the lease payments to maximize his tax deductions. Because each lessee may be faced with different economic priorities, he should prepare a checklist which at least covers the following items:

1. Has the economic need for facilities in the business been clearly established?
2. Has an alternative way of obtaining the equipment or facilities been considered?
3. Are all of the advantages or services which the lessor claims to offer needed by the lessee?
4. Have all tax and legal questions been examined by competent legal counsel?
5. Does the company wish to increase its fixed commitments at this time?

6. Will the company's total borrowing capacity be expanded by leasing?
7. Has the lease proposal been reviewed by the persons who screen the company's investment and financing decisions?
8. Has the lease been evaluated on a basis that would indicate quantitatively:
    a. The value of specialized services offered?
    b. The total cost or rate of lease financing compared with the total cost or rate of direct financing?
    c. The profit potential of the facilities to be leased?
9. Are residual values available for purchase at termination of the lease, or for continued use under a renewable lease? Does the purchase option price correspond with the anticipated market value of the facilities?
10. Has a decision been made about how the lease obligation would be recorded on the company's financial statement? Will financial ratios be affected?
11. Has the lessor been carefully screened and his financial position, capability, and reputation investigated?
12. Have comparable propositions from several lessors been evaluated?
13. Has every possible effort been made by those negotiating the lease to schedule lease payments to suit the company's convenience?

Cost of the Lease

In any negotiation, the ultimate concern to the lessee should be his total cost. Every area of give and take can be reduced to a cost factor. No lessor performs services for nothing. No arrangement for staggered lease payments will be available without impacting the ultimate cost of the transaction. The sophisticated lessor has his minimum rate objectives and must evaluate the ultimate profitability of every transaction by determining not only the yield of the lease transaction itself, but also the impact of that lease transaction upon his overall general and administrative expenses.

Residual Values

If the transaction is to be structured as a true lease, then the lessor is the owner of the equipment, and at the end of the lease term, the lessee will be deprived of further use of that asset unless he has negotiated a renewal option or purchase option. The lessor will readily grant a fair market rental or purchase option. This will assure favorable tax treatment to the lease. The lessee will attempt to fix the option price or renewal rental. Many lease negotiations have foundered in this area. Of course, in evaluating the overall cost of the lease transaction, the lessee must factor in the additional cost of the renewal or purchase option.

Deposits and Advance Payments

A lessor may request an escrow deposit, an advance payment or some form of additional collateral to support the transaction. This, of course, is generally a function of the credit standing of the lessee. If the creditworthiness of the lessee falls below a certain norm, then one or more of the foregoing forms of support man be sought by the lessor.

The Job Development Credit

The respective tax positions of the lessee and lessor will be critical in determining the value to each of any available tax credit. To the extent that one of the parties cannot use the tax credit, then the other party should be able to use that information to his advantage in negotiating the lease rate. Many independent lessors will often be in a negative tax position because of the depreciation generated by an ever increasing portfolio of acquired equipment—and, therefore, will not be able to currently use the tax credit to shelter taxes. However, the lessor may still wish to retain the tax credit to have a favorable impact on his income statement. (The investment tax credit may be shown as a reduction to taxes, even though those are actually deferred taxes.) On the other hand, lessors that are affiliated with large banks or manufacturing companies are often in a position to use all tax credits to shelter the income of their parent or affiliate—assuming that the tax return of both entities are consolidated.

Timing and Level of Lease Payments

Most lessors calculate their yields on transactions on an after-tax discounted cash flow basis. Thus, in the absence of credit con-

siderations, and assuming that the lessor has no unusual cash requirements, the lessor should be willing to entertain almost any
variation from the conventional pattern of level lease payments.
The rate at which the lessor receives his cash should be reflected in
his calculation of his overall yield. Of course, if payments are
heavily skewed toward the later years of a lease, the lessor might
be entitled to a higher overall yield because he may be taking a
greater credit risk by seeking the bulk of his return during a period
that is too far down the road to withstand detailed credit analysis.
Another reason for a higher yield with a payment schedule skewed
toward the later years is the more likely impact of inflation upon
these later payments.

Cancellation Rights

Unless the lessor is in the business of providing operating leases,
he will resist any provision which permits the lessee to terminate
the lease before the end of the term. Although most lessees view
a cancellation as being comparable to a prepayment privilege in
a loan agreement, the lessor will generally be unwilling to permit
a provision in the lease that authorizes the lessee to cancel the
lease upon the payment of a fixed fee which is equivalent to the
lessor's unamortized investment, plus a penalty. Just as in the purchase option area, tax considerations will generally result in the
lessor being willing to undertake to sell the equipment for its fair
market value if the lessee wishes to terminate and the lessee will
be held liable if such sale results in proceeds below an amount
that would return to the lessor his unamortized investment, plus a
penalty. If the proceeds of sale were in excess of this amount, the
excess would remain with the lessor. This approach, of course,
emphasizes that the true ownership of the property is with the
lessor.

Selecting a Lessor

Although the selection of a lessor might appear to be merely a
matter of choosing the company that offers the lowest lease rate,
there are countless standards that should be considered in addition
to the single economics of the rate. Set forth below are several
of the factors that a lessee should focus upon before making his
final commitment to any one lessor.

1. Is the investment tax credit passed to the lessee?
2. Is the investment tax credit passed on immediately to the lessee through an election, or through the technique of a rental adjustment with a resulting effect on cash flow?
3. Is a security deposit or down payment required?
4. Are trustee's fees payable over the lease term?
5. Does the lessor purchase the equipment and add a fee either with or without the lessee's knowledge?
6. Does the lease specify a "capitalized residual" or fee for the lessor paid at time of closing?
7. Does the lessor borrow from the banks of the lessee and diminish access to the lessee's own credit sources?
8. Are compensating balances required or imputed in the lessor's program?
9. Are premiums applicable upon involuntary loss or destruction of a leased asset?
10. What are the lessor's termination fees?
11. Does the lessor pay vendors' invoices promptly or does it obtain free financing by delaying payments? The cost to the vendor of carrying such financing is passed on to the lessee in a higher acquisition cost of equipment.
12. Does the lease have an amortization period of a sufficiently long term? The shorter the term, the lower the cost of money; but a shorter term may precipitate tax problems.
13. Is the quoted rate in fact a true simple interest rate or an add-on rate?
14. Does the lessor receive a full month's rent no matter when, during the month, the equipment is delivered?
15. Are finders' fees or commissions payable by the lessee?
16. What are the legal expenses payable by the lessee?
17. What are the renewal options?
18. What are the purchase options?
19. Are rental payments due and payable quarterly or semi-annually in advance?
20. Are commitment or "standby" fees required?
21. Are any interim rents, payable before amortization begins?
22. Are there additional "administrative fees" above and beyond the lease rate charge.
23. Are some of the competitive lessor's "operating services" mostly fictitious, enabling the lessor to obtain higher charges

and fees for services with little or no value to the lessee?

24. Is there any possibility of increased rent during a later period in the lease, or is the rent fully predetermined throughout?

25. Is the lessor financially stable?

26. Does the lessor have a firm commitment from his investors for the stated lease rate quotation?

27. Will the lease be treated as a true lease from the standpoint of the Internal Revenue Service, the Armed Services Procurement Regulations and loan agreement restrictions?

28. Are there any negative covenants or restrictive requirements in the lease?

29. Are any personal or corporate guarantees required by the lessor?

30. Does the lessor require any additional security by way of pledged collateral?

31. Is the lessor on secure ground from the standpoint of possible tax assessment by the Internal Revenue Service?

32. Will the lease be considered a debt transaction and capitalized under *Accounting Principles Board Opinion No. 5?*

33. Is there a "hell-or-high-water" clause in the lease agreement making the instrument effectively a debt obligation from the standpoint of the lessee's lenders?

LEGAL CONSIDERATIONS

The treasurer of a corporation is not likely to be responsible for the intricate legal considerations that are relevant to the sophisticated lease transaction. However, it is helpful to have a sensitivity to areas that may require legal counseling. In many instances, the areas that may require legal attention are not necessarily unique to leasing. They might be just as applicable to any contractual arrangement.

Doing Business in Various States

Use of equipment in a particular jurisdiction is likely to be related to the overall business activity of the lessee. In most jurisdictions, the combination of an active business activity with salesmen, telephone listings, offices and advertising are clearly sufficient for the company to qualify to do business in that jurisdiction. The leasing of equipment, as a part of the overall scheme of doing business, is merely another factor in the overall consideration of whether such qualification is necessary. On the other hand, as a lessor of equipment where the only relationship to a particular jurisdiction is the ownership of property located in that jurisdiction, there are genuine questions as to whether qualification to do business is necessary under the statutes of most states. However, consequences of not qualifying to do business within a jurisdiction where qualification would otherwise be necessary are generally the prohibition of using the courts of that jurisdiction to enforce contracts and, in addition, there may be certain penalties involved for such failure. In most states a corporation has the right to "cure" the failure to qualify before suing on a contract. In a few states the contract is void and unenforceable if the corporation did not properly qualify before the contract was entered into.

Personal Property and Real Property

In certain jurisdictions a lessor will require that the lessee obtain a waiver from the landlord or mortgagee of the real property upon which the personal property is located. The statutes vary from state to state in this area, but generally speaking, the statutes contemplate that personal property that is affixed to the premises will become a fixture and consequently be treated as an integral part of the real property. In other jurisdictions, a landlord or a mortgagee may have a claim upon all personal property located upon the premises in the event of a default by the lessee or mortgagor of the property. In Louisiana, for example, the property of third parties located on the premises of a defaulting tenant is susceptible to the claims of the landlord in satisfaction of any rental deficiencies. In addition, in Pennsylvania, the industrial plant doctrine generally gives a mortgagee of an industrial plant a claim to all of the property located within that plant.

Lessee and Loan Agreements

Any lessee who is contracting on behalf of his company should be cognizant of any restrictions that may be imposed upon his company by other lessors or lenders to that company. The negative covenants in various loan agreements or leases may seriously impact the terms and conditions of subsequent financing transactions.

Government Regulations

In negotiating a lease transaction with those banks that are subject to the Federal Reserve regulations, a lessee should be aware of the restrictions imposed by Federal Reserve Regulation Y. That regulation provides that the lessor must recover his investment plus a reasonable return on that investment from a combination of rentals, tax benefits (tax credits and accelerated depreciation), residuals and reasonably anticipated future transactions with the same lessee. Thus, a bank lessor will be most anxious to require that the lease be full payout in nature and not subject to early termination without a penalty sufficient in magnitude to meet the requirements of Regulation Y.

Passage of Title

Under the Uniform Commercial Code, the passage of title, which is a critical consideration in any lease transaction, is primarily a function of the intention of the parties. Some vendors state that title passes when the equipment leaves the vendor's factory. Obviously, in such instance, the risk of loss during transportation and shipment is upon the buyer. Most lessors will require that the lessee insure the property as of the moment title passes to the lessor with such insurance payable to the lessee or the lessor as their respective interests may appear. The lease itself will generally provide a table of payments specifically outlining the amount payable to the lessor in the event of the destruction of the equipment at any point during the life of the lease.

Filing

To the extent that a lease transaction is a true lease and not a financing transaction, the lessor owns the equipment and would not normally be expected to file a UCC financing statement. However, many lessors, reflecting an abundance of caution, will file such statements to avoid the risk or harassment of a trustee in bankruptcy challenging the trueness of the lease. A trustee in bankruptcy who sucessfully pursues such a challenge would then only be faced with the lessor's secured interest in the equipment.

There should be no concern regarding the possibility of the Internal Revenue Service viewing the filing of a financing statement as an admission that the transaction is not a true lease. Revenue Ruling 15-540 states that the filing or nonfiling of a financing statement will not determine the essential nature of the contract.

Sale-Leaseback

Where the existing owner of property enters into a contract to sell that property to a lessor and simultaneously leases back the property, certain specialized rules apply. Since the property is not being acquired from a vendor who is selling in the ordinary course of business, the buyer must be assured that there are no existing liens on the property or if such liens exist, they are released prior to the passage of title. Furthermore, the lessee and lessor should assure themselves that any existing loan agreements do not prohibit such a sale leaseback. In addition, if the property constitutes a substantial portion of the seller's assets, stockholder consent may be required and the bulk sale statutes of the jurisdiction may be applicable. In some jurisdictions, a sale leaseback, regardless of how the transaction is structured, will be deemed to be a loan and the usury statutes of that jurisdiction will apply. The sale leaseback is a transaction where professional expertise is essential.

ADDITIONAL SOURCES

Axelson, Kenneth S. "Needed: A Generally Accepted Method for Measuring Lease Commitments." *Financial Executive,* 39 (July 1971), 40–52.

Bower, Richard S. "Issues in Lease Financing." *Financial Management,* 2 (Winter 1973), 25–34.

Defliese, Philip. "Accounting for Leases: A Broader Perspective." *Financial Executive,* 42 (July 1974), 14–23.

Doenges, R. Conrad. "The Cost of Leasing." *Engineering Economist,* 17 (Fall 1971), 31–44.

Findlay, Chapman, III. "A Sensitivity Analysis of IRR Leasing Models." *The Engineering Economist,* 20 (Summer 1975), 231–42.

Fishbach, Karl. "A Look at Lease Disclosure Requirements." *Financial Executive,* 42 (April 1974), 24–41.

Gordon, Myron J. "A General Solution to the Buy or Lease Decision: A Pedagogical Note." *The Journal of Finance,* 29 (March 1974), 245–50.

Gustafson, George. "Computers-Lease or Buy?" *Financial Executive,* 41 (July 1973), 64–66.

Hill, William. "Should You Lease Company Cars?" *Financial Executive,* 41 (November 1973), 48–55.

Johnson, Robert W., and Lewellen, Wilbur G. "Analysis of the Lease-or-Buy Decision." *Journal of Finance,* 27 (September 1972), 815–23.

Nantell, Timothy J. "Equivalence of Lease Versus Buy Analyses." *Financial Management,* 2 (Autumn 1973), 61–65.

Randolph, John M. "Computer Leasing Today." *Financial Executive,* 62 (May 1974), 50–54, 56.

Roenfeldt, Rodney L., and Osteryoung, Jerome S. "Analysis of Financial Leases." *Financial Management,* 2 (Spring 1973), 74–87.

Sartoris, William L., and Paul, Ronda S. "Lease Evaluation—Another Capital Budgeting Decision." *Financial Management,* 2 (Summer 1973), 46–52.

Schall, Lawrence D. "The Lease-or-Buy and Asset Acquisition Decisions." *Journal of Finance,* 29 (September 1974), 1203–14.

Vancil, Richard F. "Lease or Borrow: New Method of Analysis." *Harvard Business Review,* 39 (September–October 1961), 122–36.

Wiar, Robert C. "Economic Implications of Multiple Rates of Return in the Leveraged Lease Context." *Journal of Finance,* 28 (December, 1973), 1275–86.

Chapter 38

Convertibles and Warrants

Madison H. Haythe[*]

INTRODUCTION

THE PURPOSES of this chapter are to explore in a general way how warrants and convertible securities are valued and to discuss how they are used in corporate finance. No attempt will be made to go into the mathematical theories of valuation.[1] Furthermore, detailed tax, legal, and accounting problems will be left to the lawyers and accountants, although some reference will be made to them. Finally, it is suggested that before any corporate treasurer embarks upon the use of these securities the investment banker be brought into the picture at an early date.

The use of options, such as warrants and convertible securities, is not new. A little known book, entitled *Confusion de Confusiones* and published in Amsterdam in 1688, is believed to be the first book written on the stock market. It was a practical guide to the rules and methods of the Amsterdam Stock Exchange and contains what may be the earliest description of an option:

---

[*] Madison H. Haythe is vice president, Morgan Stanley & Co. Incorporated, New York.

[1] See Robert C. Merton, "Theory of Rational Option Pricing," *Bell Journal of Economics and Management Science*, 4 (Spring 1973), 141–83; Hans R. Stoll, "The Relationship between Put and Call Option Price," *Journal of Finance*, 24 (December 1969), 802–824; and Fischer Black and Myron Scholes, "The Valuation of Option Contacts and a Test of Market Efficiency," *Journal of Finance*, 27 (May 1972), 399–417.

In 1602 a few Dutch merchants founded a company. The wealthiest people (in the country) took an interest in it, and a total capital of sixty-four and a third tons of gold (or more than 6.4 million florins) was raised. Several ships were built and in 1604 were sent out to seek adventure Quixote-like in the East Indies. The property of the Company was broken into several parts, and each part (called an actie [share], carrying the possibility of acting upon [or laying a claim to] the surplus or profits) amounted to 500 pounds [Flemish] or 3,000 florins. . . .

The price of the shares is now 580 [and let us assume that] it seems to me that they will climb to a much higher price because of the extensive cargoes that are expected from India, because of the good business of the Company, of the reputation of its goods, of the prospective dividends, and of the peace in Europe. Nevertheless I decide not to buy shares through fear that I might encounter a loss and might meet with embarrassment if my calculations should prove erroneous. I therefore turn to those persons who are willing to take options and ask them how much [premium] they demand for the obligation to deliver shares at 600 each at a certain later date. I come to an agreement about the premium, have it transferred [to the taker of the options] immediately at the Bank, and then I am sure that it is impossible to lose more than the price of the premium. And I shall gain the entire amount by which the price [of the stock] shall surpass the figure of 600.

In modern times options have become accepted financial instruments and have been traded in the principal financial markets of the world, particularly New York, Berlin, and London. It is therefore important to understand fully what an option is. An option may be defined as contractual privilege representing the right to buy or sell property, including securities, at a given price or prices within specified periods of time. Such an option obviously has value.

Probably everyone has tried to deal in options at one time or another in his life. When a potential purchaser asks a storekeeper to set aside an item while he tries to make up his mind whether he actually wishes to purchase the item or because he needs time to obtain the purchase price, he is asking that the storekeeper give him an option. The storekeeper recognizes immediately that he is being asked to give something of value because during the period in which the item is set aside he may miss a sale, the price might increase and he would forego additional profit, or the price might decline, leaving him with a diminished profit or an actual loss. If he feels that he is giving up considerable value, he will refuse. But if he feels that the option is of limited value and that he is running little risk by taking his product temporarily off the market, he will grant the option. There is one thing that he probably will do intuitively, however— restrict the period of the option. As will be discussed later the length of time during which an option may be exercised has an important bearing on its value.

The remainder of this chapter will discuss two of the main forms which options have taken in modern times. These are common stock purchase warrants and convertible debentures and convertible preferred stock. The determinants of their value will be discussed and examples of their applications will be presented.

WARRANTS

A common stock purchase warrant is a certificate representing an option or contractual right to purchase common stock at a specified price or prices during one or more specified periods. One warrant usually, but not always, gives the holder the right to acquire one share of common stock at any time on or before a fixed date (the expiration date). In some cases warrants are for fractions of a share or for more than one share. In order to exercise the option, the warrant must be surrendered to the issuer, together with a fixed sum of money (the exercise price), in exchange for a share of the specified common stock. In some cases a security can be used in lieu of cash, but the use of cash is more typical.

Most warrants are protected against dilution resulting from stock splits and certain other events and, as a result, many warrants that originally entitled the holder to purchase one share have been adjusted to give the holder the right to purchase a larger number of shares. The terms of some warrants provide for step-ups in the exercise price at certain dates. Normally, provided there is no change in the exercise price, warrants are not exercised (if at all) until just prior to the expiration date. Warrants are generally freely transferable, and in the United States they are traded either on the major and regional stock exchanges or on the over-the-counter market.

Warrants are similar to "calls," which are options to purchase securities ("puts" are options to sell securities). The main difference is in the method by which they are created. Calls ordinarily are issued by individuals or other investors against outstanding publicly traded securities in the United States and, consequently, are of interest to speculators and investors. Warrants, on the other hand, ordinarily are issued by corporations and are therefore of interest to corporate treasurers. They usually give the holder the right to purchase shares of the issuing corporation, although there have been a number of warrants created which entitle the holder to purchase shares in another corporation.

Another important difference between calls and warrants relates to the length of the exercise period. Until quite recently, most calls were for 30 days. However, since a six months' holding period differentiates a short-term from a long-term capital gain for purposes of tax liability under current U.S. tax legislation, interest in longer term calls has increased, and many are written today for six months or one year. Formerly, members of the Put and Call Brokers and Dealers Association, Inc. agreed not to deal in calls with a term longer than 13 months. The fact that they now deal in longer calls is indicative of the pressure generated by speculators and investors to increase the length of the exercise period. Lengthening the term could also be an attempt by the regular put and call brokers to enhance the competitive position of the calls in which they deal. A sizable amount of the total activity in calls is now centered in listed options traded on the relatively new Chicago Board Option Exchange (CBOE). Calls on the CBOE, it should be pointed out, are not guaranteed by a New York Stock Exchange member firm as is the case with the older type "puts" and "calls," but are backed by the Exchange. Warrants, in contrast to calls, usually have a much longer exercise period; most are issued initially with exercise periods of five to ten years.

Warrant Prices

The prices at which warrants sell fall within certain limits as shown in Figure 1. For a warrant to purchase one share of common stock for cash, these limits are as follows:

Minimum Price. The minimum price at which a warrant will sell is known as its "intrinsic value." The intrinsic value is the difference between the exercise price and the current common stock price. In other words, it is the amount which the holder of a warrant can obtain by exercising the warrant and selling the stock received. Obviously, the holder of the warrant would not accept a price less than this amount. Any time the common stock is selling below the exercise price, the intrinsic value of a warrant is zero.

Maximum Price. This is the price of the common stock itself. In the case of a warrant entitling the holder to purchase one share of stock, it is obvious that no rational investor would pay a price for the warrant which was higher than the price of the common stock.

FIGURE 1

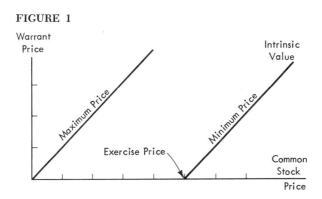

Warrant Premiums

Warrants can be expected to sell at prices which, after adding the exercise price, represent premiums over the current value of the common stock. Specifically, the price of a warrant at a given moment has two components, its intrinsic value, which can be positive or zero, and a positive premium.

The premium represents the value of what might be described as a "hedge" against uncertainty which the warrant represents to the purchaser. If, after the purchase of the warrant, the stock price falls drastically and stays low during the warrant period, the warrant holder avoids the significant capital losses which would have occurred had he purchased the stock. He loses as a maximum the purchase price of the warrant. On the other hand, if the stock price rises by a great amount, he may exercise the warrant or sell it, and obtain a profit (roughly) equal to at least the intrinsic value of the warrant at the time he chooses to exercise it, less the price he paid for it.

The prices at which warrants sell in relation to the prices of the common stock can be represented by a curve. Its shape is determined as follows: the price is zero when the common stock has no value. The price reflects a substantial premium (the maximum dollar premium) when the common stock price and the exercise price are the same. The price usually includes little or no premium over intrinsic value when the common stock sells at three to five times the exercise price. These relationships are illustrated in Figure 2.

FIGURE 2
A Warrant to Buy One Share of Common Stock for Five Years

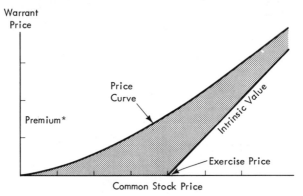

* Vertical distance between price curve and intrinsic value line or between the price curve and the horizontal axis is represented by shaded area. See text for method of computing "warrant premium."

What determines the size of the premium? The premium is attributable to the option privilege. It is the amount investors are willing to pay for the opportunity to purchase stock at a fixed price during the remaining life of a warrant, without having to make the larger initial investment in the stock. In other words, it is the price paid by the purchaser to obtain leverage; i.e., to use a little of his money to benefit from an anticipated rise in the value of a security of much greater value.

The leverage inherent in a typical warrant is just as important today in determining the premium as it was in 17th-century Amsterdam. Take, for example, a stock selling at $11 a share and a warrant to buy the stock at $10 a share for five years. The intrinsic value of the warrant is $1. If the common stock were to increase in price to

$16.50 a share, or by 50 percent, the intrinsic value of the warrant would become $6.50, or an increase of 550 percent. Obviously, with this leverage, and any probability of an increase in the price of the common stock, such a warrant would be a bargain at $1. No rational person, however, would sell the warrant at $1, a price which included no premium over the intrinsic value. Sellers strive to obtain maximum premiums over intrinsic value and buyers try to pay as little as possible, since the more they pay the less leverage they would obtain. The forces of supply and demand result in a price well above intrinsic value—perhaps in the area of $4 in this particular example.

Warrants have generally retained some market value even when the market price of the stock is substantially lower than the exercise price, because even under these circumstances the option privilege to purchase the stock in the future at a fixed price has a positive value, assuming there is a possibility, even though it may be remote, of the stock price rising above the exercise price. The greatest premiums (although not the maximum dollar amounts) prevail when the common stock is well below the exercise price. The premium declines as the intrinsic value rises, and largely disappears when the common stock price greatly exceeds the exercise price.

The premium at which a warrant sells can be calculated as follows:

$$\text{Premium} = \left(\frac{\text{Exercise price} + \text{warrant price}}{\text{Market price of common stock}} - 1\right) 100\%$$

Using the figures in the example just outlined, the premium would be computed as follows:

$$\text{Premium} = \left(\frac{10+4}{11} - 1\right) 100\% = \left(\frac{14}{11} - 1\right) 100\%$$
$$= (1.273 - 1)100\% = 27.3\%$$

As might be expected, the size of premiums differs among warrants to purchase different stocks. Premiums also reflect a number of other factors. Among the most important are:

1. *Term.* The most important single factor affecting the value of a warrant is the term. Maximum premiums are attached to warrants with terms that are five years or longer. Warrants with an expiration date of five years sell at premiums almost equivalent to

those that pertain in the case of a perpetual warrant. The above implies a planning horizon of no more than five years owing to the possibility that the terms of a warrant may be changed through merger or otherwise. As the exercise period shortens, premiums begin to decline, slowly at first, but rapidly when the remaining period of exercise is three years or less.

2. *Investor Expectations.* Although investor expectations as to the future of the common stock are difficult to measure, they are undoubtedly important.

3. *Volatility.* While investor expectations as to the future of the common stock are undoubtedly important, volatility is probably one of the most significant factors and can usually be measured with more accuracy than investor expectations. In the case of a stock which fluctuates widely in price, the related warrant tends to sell higher than a warrant connected with a stock whose market action tends to be only average or below average.

4. *Dividend on the Common Stock.* The higher the yield on the common stock, the lower the premium for the warrant. Warrant holders are foregoing large amounts of income in those cases where the dividend payments on the common stock are high; this loss of income is believed by many to have a most important effect on warrant premiums. Also, stocks with high yields usually lack the growth potentials of stocks paying low dividends, and investors may consider that high yielding stocks do not offer attractive appreciation possibilities. High dividends, which are a result of paying out a large proportion of earnings, mean that book value does not rise significantly. An examination of the premiums, usually low, of warrants to purchase REITs (real estate investment trusts), where practically all income must be distributed if the companies are to retain their favorable tax status, bears out this point.

5. *Interest Rates Generally.* The higher interest rates in general are, the higher the warrant premium. When interest rates are high, investors are either paying high rates of interest on loans to carry securities which they could avoid by investing smaller sums in highly leveraged warrants, or perhaps, are foregoing high yields on investible funds. Consequently, the advantage of investing a small amount in a leveraged warrant increases.

6. *Dilution.* The dilution which will take place when warrants are exercised has a bearing on the warrant premium. The greater the dilution, the more adverse the effect upon value. One theory

contends, however, that the price of the common stock reflects any potential dilution.

7. *Listing.* All things being equal, listed warrants appear to command higher prices than unlisted ones. In many cases, marketability is improved, and in some cases in the United States listed warrants may be acquired in margin accounts.

There is no hard and fast rule for determining warrant prices. Despite numerous attempts to develop formulae which include a number of variables, market prices usually differ from those arrived at mathematically. Nevertheless, a hypothetical warrant to purchase what was considered a promising common stock might sell at the following relationships to the common stock, depending upon the length of the exercise period (see table below).

Hypothetical Five-Year Warrant to Purchase One Share of Common Stock for $50

Price of Common Stock	Prices of Warrant in Years Remaining				
	5	4	3	2	1
$ 10	$ 1.50	$ 1.46	$ 1.26	$ 0.85	$ 0.40
20	3.50	3.43	3.05	2.28	0.87
30	7.00	6.85	6.36	5.08	2.48
40	11.75	11.58	10.88	9.10	5.25
50	17.50	17.28	16.39	14.18	9.31
60	23.50	23.23	22.23	19.73	14.42
70	30.25	29.97	28.94	26.28	21.06
80	37.00	36.72	35.64	33.07	30.25
90	44.75	44.46	43.41	40.99	40.00
100	52.50	52.21	51.16	50.75	50.00

CONVERTIBLE SECURITIES

Convertible debentures and convertible preferred stocks are securities which may be converted or exchanged at the option of the holder into common stock or another security. They can occupy senior or junior positions in a company's capitalization. In many cases, companies have issued subordinated convertible debentures or junior preferred stock or preference stock.

A convertible debenture or convertible preferred stock may be regarded as consisting of two components—a straight debenture or preferred stock, plus an option (which can be considered as representing a "latent warrant") to purchase another security, usually the common stock of the issuer. In order to exercise the latent warrant, the holder of the convertible must surrender the straight debenture or preferred stock portion of the holding. A holder of an ordinary warrant usually has to give up cash when he exercises his warrant. In other words, a convertible security is similar to a straight debenture (or a straight preferred stock) plus a warrant.

The main difference between a fixed-income security plus a warrant and a convertible is that, in the case of a convertible, the fixed-income portion and the conversion privilege (the latent warrant portion) cannot be separated. Consequently, a latent warrant tends to be worth less than an ordinary warrant. Two factors are primarily responsible: (1) warrants are normally, but not necessarily, purchased by speculators who have no interest in tying up their funds in the fixed-income portion; and (2) many convertible securities are callable at the option of the issuer. Since the period during which the latent warrant is exercisable is not, therefore, fixed, but can be ended through call, speculators naturally tend to be unwilling to pay as large premiums as they would for comparable regular unattached warrants with set exercise periods. This is particularly true when a convertible is selling well above the redemption price and, hence, when redemption of the issue is a distinct possibility.

Value of a Latent Warrant

To determine the value of a latent warrant in an outstanding convertible security, it is necessary first to determine the straight investment value of the security in question. It should be pointed out that this is not easy. Even a bond expert must analyze the security carefully to arrive at an estimate. Furthermore, investment values change during periods of rising or declining interest rates, or when developments take place which may affect the quality of the particular security. If a company has bonds outstanding which are not convertible and are publicly traded, thus giving the market's judgment as to investment value, the task is made much less difficult.

When the straight investment value of the convertible security is subtracted from the market value, the value of the conversion or latent option privilege is determined. When the value of the option privilege is divided by the number of shares into which the issue is convertible, the value of the latent warrant is ascertained. The effective exercise price is found by dividing the straight investment value by the number of shares into which the issue is convertible.

For example, assume that a 25-year debenture is convertible into common stock at $50 per share or into two shares per $100 of principal amount. Also, assume that the market price of the convertible is 116 percent and the straight investment value is 104 percent of the principal amount. Then,

$$
\begin{aligned}
\text{Option value (per \$100)} &= \$116 - \$104 = \$12 \\
\text{Value of latent warrant} &= \$12/2 \qquad\ \ = \$\ 6 \\
\text{Effective exercise price} &= \$104/2 \qquad = \$52
\end{aligned}
$$

The premium for a latent warrant can be computed like that of any other warrant. The formula is as follows:

$$
\text{Premium} = \left(\frac{\substack{\text{Exercise price (effec-} \\ \text{tive exercise price in} \\ \text{case of latent} \\ \text{warrant)}} + \substack{\text{warrant price} \\ \text{(latent} \\ \text{warrant} \\ \text{value)}}}{\text{Market price of common stock}} - 1 \right) 100\%
$$

Let it be assumed that the common stock in the above example has a market value of $46. The premium of the latent warrant would be as follows:

$$
\text{Premium} = \left(\frac{52 + 6}{46} - 1 \right) 100\% = \left(\frac{58}{46} - 1 \right) 100\% = 26.1\%
$$

This premium is the market value of the convertible security (in the example, $116) over the underlying value of the common stock (in the example, two shares at $46 per share, or $92):

$$
\text{Premium} = \left(\frac{\text{Market value}}{\text{Underlying common stock value}} - 1 \right) 100\%
$$

$$
\text{Premium} = \left(\frac{\text{Market value}}{\substack{\text{(Number of shares} \times \text{(market value of} \\ \text{into which issue} \qquad \text{common stock)} \\ \text{is convertible)}}} - 1 \right) 100\%
$$

$$
\text{Premium} = \left(\frac{116}{2 \times 46} - 1 \right) 100\% = \left(\frac{116}{92} - 1 \right) 100\% = 26.1\%
$$

Therefore, in attempting to value convertible securities, the premium of market value over underlying common stock value, commonly called the conversion premium, can be used as a proxy for the latent warrant premium.

This concept of latent warrants can probably be understood better if one compares a convertible debenture with a straight debenture with warrants attached, where the debenture, as is sometimes the case, may be used at 100 percent, in lieu of cash, when exercising the warrants. Assume that a convertible debenture is convertible into common stock at $50 a share or into two shares for each $100 principal amount. Let us make further assumptions that the convertible debenture's investment value—that is, the price at which it would sell were it not convertible—is $80, and that the common stock is selling at $70 a share. Therefore, the underlying value of the common stock is $140 for each $100 principal amount. For illustrative purposes, assume that the convertible debenture has been called for redemption at some modest premium over 100 percent. The difference between the investment value, $80, and the market price, $140, represents the value of the latent warrants, $60.

Now, let us compare this issue between a straight debenture with warrants attached entitling the holder to buy two shares of the same common stock at $50 a share for each $100 principal amount of debentures, and a convertible debenture using the same terms. The straight debenture would obviously be worth $80, its investment value. Assuming that the warrants are expiring, so that there is no premium over their intrinsic value, they would be worth $60, the same as the convertible latent warrants. This follows because the warrants plus the straight debenture worth $80 would entitle the holder, upon surrender of the warrants and the debenture at 100 percent in lieu of cash, to obtain two shares of common stock worth $140. In other words, a convertible debenture and a straight debenture—which may be used at 100 percent in lieu of cash with warrants attached—are comparable. It can be seen clearly that the value of the two components—straight investment value and the value of the latent warrants (representing the value of the conversion privilege) or actual warrants—is the same in both cases.

The price of a convertible cannot be less than its straight investment value or its underlying common stock value. It will always be at least the greater of the two. Since a convertible involves a latent warrant, its price, as might be expected, will also be represented by a curve, the shape of which depends upon the relationship of the components—the straight investment value and the value of the latent warrants. Figure 3 portrays the value of a typical convertible.

FIGURE 3
A Typical Convertible Curve

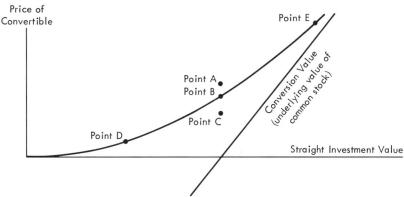

The maximum dollar premium over the higher of investment value or underlying common stock value exists when the straight investment value and the conversion value are equal. This can be seen easily from Figure 3. The height of the curve above the intersection point is based upon the premium at which the latent warrant or warrants are valued. The value of the latent warrant is determined by the same principal factors as apply in the case of an ordinary warrant.

Figure 3 portrays a convertible which sells at a reasonable premium. Depending upon those factors affecting latent warrant values, the price curves of convertibles will vary; some will be higher, going through point *A*, for example, and some lower, say, at point *C*.

USES OF CONVERTIBLES AND
OF WARRANTS

The preceding comments should have made it clear that premiums larger than intrinsic values are present in warrants and convertible securities. The effective use of these premiums can be of great assistance in designing certain financing plans. A number of types of securities utilizing premium values, such as convertible debentures and convertible preferred stock, are well tested and well known, but investment bankers are ever alert to new ideas, and from time to time some interesting new uses are developed. Some, but by no means all, possible uses are described in the following paragraphs.

Sale of Convertible Debentures for Cash

In recent years most convertible debentures have been sold for cash, although in the period following World War II, when many railroads were emerging from bankruptcy, reorganization plans employed convertibles extensively. Managements, or their investment banker advisers, undoubtedly have had many different objectives in mind when considering the use of convertible debentures and when arriving at the various terms. In some cases, there probably was a combination of objectives. Some of the principal reasons for the sale of convertible debentures for cash are discussed below:

1. In the vast majority of cases, companies have resorted to the sale of convertible debentures in order to reduce the coupon rate which would have been required to issue straight debt. It should be understood that it is the coupon rate which is reduced and not in a true sense the cost of money, since borrowers have to pay the going rate on the straight investment portion of the debentures. It is the sale of latent warrants, in addition, which enables the debentures to be issued with a lower coupon. S. S. Kresge Company probably would have had to pay in the area of 9½ percent if it had sold a straight subordinated debenture in the summer of 1974, but was able to borrow by means of a convertible issue which carried a coupon of only 6 percent.

2. In a number of cases, the companies simply could not raise the amount of money desired, at least on reasonable terms, without a "sweetener." The fact that the majority of convertible debentures issued in this country have been given a rating lower than single A by the rating agencies is indicative of the fact that most issues are not of investment quality. This suggests that at certain times a convertible was chosen because of the need for some kind of "equity kicker."

3. Some companies have sold convertible subordinated debentures in the expectation that the issues will be converted and that the use of convertibles will, therefore, prove to have been a means of selling common stock at a premium over the price prevailing at

the time of issuance. In some cases, this premium has been relatively small, as managements have hoped that the price of the common stock would rise moderately and that conversion would take place within a relatively short period of time. In other cases, managements may have felt that the common stock was unrealistically depressed and did not wish to sell common stock unless the price reflected what they considered the true value of the equity. In this case the conversion price would have been set well above the market price.

In other words, a convertible can be tailored to meet many objectives. When the primary objective is to obtain a low coupon, the conversion price must be set low; i.e., only slightly above the market. Whereas, if the primary objective is to sell common equity at a high price, the conversion price must be set high, and this high exercise price must be compensated for by a high coupon. Consequently, in arriving at the terms of any convertible, there is a trade-off between coupon and exercise price. It should also be evident that the market price actions of convertibles will differ, depending upon the terms.

Figure 3 shows that a convertible which sells at a much higher premium over investment value than over conversion value, for example at point *E*, will appreciate almost as much as the common stock in a rising market but will decline much less than the stock in a falling market. It appears that most investors like a convertible with such terms. On the other hand, if terms are such that an issue sells at a price represented by point *B*, where the issuer will obtain the maximum dollar premium (not percentage premium) over conversion value and investment value, the issue will tend both to rise and to fall considerably less than the related common stock. Depending upon the objectives of the issuer, terms which produce equal premiums over investment values and conversion 'values are probably the optimum ones.

An excellent example of the sale of a convertible debenture for cash is furnished by S. S. Kresge Company. In the summer of 1974, S. S. Kresge wished to raise a substantial amount of money. The stock market as a whole was very depressed, and the company's common stock had declined about 18 percent from its high for the year and almost 38 percent from its all-time high registered in the first quarter of 1973. Because of poor market conditions, it was not a good time to sell common stock, and the company decided to

raise the money it needed through the sale at a price of 100 percent
of $200 million of 6 percent convertible subordinated debentures
due 1999. These debentures were rated single A by the rating
services and therefore were of investment quality.

The debenture terms shed light on conditions prevailing in the
summer of 1974, and on what investors expected when purchasing
a good quality convertible issue of a company with an impressive
record of earnings growth. The debentures, which are callable at
any time on 30 days' notice, are convertible into common stock of
S. S. Kresge at a conversion price of $35½ a share (or into approxi-
mately 28.17 shares per $1,000 principal amount). This conversion
price represented a premium of 11.8 percent at time of issuance.
It is likely that a straight 25-year subordinated debenture of S. S.
Kresge would have required a coupon of approximately 9.5 percent
in order for it to sell at 100 percent. The 6 percent convertible debentures on a fully distributed basis probably had a straight investment value of about 68 percent, so that the offering price of 100
percent represented a substantial premium of approximately 47
percent over the straight investment value.

The terms, which were designed to meet conditions prevailing
at the time, bear out the point that investors are attracted to issues
whose terms are such that they sell at modest premiums over conversion values but at sizable premiums over straight investment
values. In the period immediately following the sale of the convertible debentures, which initially traded at a small premium,
interest rates rose only slightly, but S. S. Kresge common stock
declined to $24 a share; the debentures, with a low straight invest-
ment value, sold off to 90 percent.

Sale of Convertible Debentures Overseas

Beginning in 1963, in response to the continuing deficit in the
country's balance of payments, the U.S. government adopted a
series of moves, either by promulgation of regulations or by requests
for cooperation, that forced U.S. corporations to raise a significant
portion of any external funds needed for expansion or other purposes abroad through the sale of securities outside the United
States. A large amount of such financing for American companies
took place through the sale of dollar-denominated debentures of
subsidiaries usually located in countries with favorable tax laws,

such as Luxembourg, The Netherlands, and the Netherlands
Antilles. These debentures were guaranteed by the parent company
and were exchangeable into the common stock of the parent company. For reasons not germane to this discussion, the interest on the
debentures, in contrast to dividends on the parent company's common stock, was not subject to the U.S. withholding tax. Furthermore, even without tax considerations, the yields on the debentures
exceeded the returns on the related common stocks, and the debentures were considered very attractive by many foreign investors.
Large amounts of such convertible debentures were sold in the
Eurobond market. Among the major American companies that used
this method of financing were the following:

American Can	Gillette
American Express	Honeywell
American Brands	Mohasco
Borden	J. P. Morgan
Chesebrough-Pond's	Nabisco
Chrysler	Standard Oil (Indiana)
Clark Equipment	Texaco
Eastman Kodak	Union Carbide
Ford Motor	Warner Lambert
General Electric	Xerox
General Foods	

The J. P. Morgan Overseas Capital Corporation issue, which was
placed in June 1972, is typical of the generally high quality of the
convertible securities sold in the Eurobond market. The obligor was
a Delaware subsidiary of J. P. Morgan & Co. Incorporated, which
unconditionally guaranteed the payment of principal and interest.
The issue had a 4¼ percent coupon and was convertible, beginning
on June 15, 1973, into J. P. Morgan common stock at $52.25 a share,
or into approximately 19.13 shares for each $1,000 principal amount.
The issue, which matures on June 15, 1987, becomes callable under
certain conditions beginning July 15, 1975. At the time of issuance,
J. P. Morgan common stock was selling around 45½ (adjusted for
a subsequent 2-for-1 stock split in 1973), whereby the offering price
of 100 percent represented a premium of almost 15 percent over
the underlying value of the common stock. The offering price was
substantially above the estimated straight investment value of the
debentures. J. P. Morgan common stock advanced following the
offering, and in 1973 reached $73½ a share. Reflecting the rise in
the value of the underlying common shares, the debentures sold at

a substantial premium and at their peak price were quoted around 140 percent. J. P. Morgan common sold below $45 a share during the summer of 1974, and the J. P. Morgan Overseas convertibles dropped to around 88 percent. The decline was attributable not only to the decrease in the value of the underlying common shares, but also to a drop in the estimated straight investment value. The latter was adversely affected by the steep climb in interest rates which had taken place since June 1972.

Beginning in early 1974, the various government controls on the movements of funds abroad which had grown up in the preceding decade were dismantled in a series of steps. The result has been a cessation of financing by means of convertible issues by subsidiaries of American companies. While the use of convertible debentures to obtain funds abroad is no longer needed, a secondary market for the principal outstanding Eurodollar convertibles continues to exist. The market in most cases is a narrow one by American standards, but European investors, who are attracted in part by the absence of the U.S. withholding tax, and some American investors, who, as a result of the expiration of the Interest Equalization Tax, are no longer deterred from investing abroad, trade in these securities. Circumstances may change at some future time, and there is always a possibility that American corporations again will find the Euro-bond market an attractive one for raising capital.

Delayed Convertible Subordinated Debentures

Investment bankers are constantly seeking new financing ideas. One recent example involved an issue in the spring of 1973 of $60 million First Pennsylvania Corporation convertible subordinated debentures due 1993. These convertible debentures are unusual in two ways. First, they bear interest at the rate of 7 percent until June 1, 1978, and thereafter bear interest at the reduced rate of 5 percent until maturity. The second is a delay in the conversion privilege for five years until June 1, 1978, at which time the debentures become convertible at a price to be determined by formula as described below.

The First Pennsylvania Corporation debentures will be convertible on and after June 1, 1978, until maturity or redemption at a price per share equal to 87½ percent of the average of the daily mean between the high and low sales prices for the common stock on 10 trading days to be selected by the trustee within the 30-day trading period ending on the close of business on the fourth trading day prior to June 1, 1978. The conversion price, however, shall not be less than $43, nor more than $68½. At the time of issuance the last sale price of the common stock was $41.

As a method of corporate financing, this offering had some interesting aspects. It is estimated that a convertible debenture with customary terms would have borne an interest rate of about 5¼ percent and a conversion premium of approximately 10 percent. By paying a higher initial interest rate of 7 percent, which was probably ½ percent below the rate which would have been required on a straight five-year issue, the company was able to obtain a potentially higher conversion price and a lower interest rate after the fifth year.

Exchanging Convertible Debentures for Other Securities

There have been a number of cases in which companies have offered holders of their common stock, or other securities, convertible debentures in exchange. An example of this involved LTV Corporation. In December 1972, LTV made an exchange offer to holders of its outstanding 6½ percent debentures. The offer included cash and 7½ percent convertible subordinated notes due 1977.

Use of Convertible Preferred Stock in Mergers and Acquisitions

The 1960s were a period during which a large number of mergers and acquisitions took place, and convertible preferred stock played a prominent role. Companies were able to use this type of security (as well as common stock) to acquire other companies on a tax-free basis. It was possible to give the selling stockholders a security with a fixed income which maintained or increased their current income. If common stock of the acquiring company had been used, in some cases current income may have fallen, and the offer may have been unacceptable to the selling stockholders. Moreover, the selling stockholders were given an opportunity to share in any future growth by making the preferred stock convertible into the acquiring company's common stock. Hundreds of millions of dollars of such stock were issued.

Since 1970, however, accounting principles, as applied by the American Institute of Certified Public Accountants, have eliminated the pooling of interests basis of accounting when convertible preferred stock is used. While it is possible to use convertible preferred in a tax-free merger, the buyer has to write up all assets if the purchase price is above book value. But the higher asset values cannot be used for tax purposes. Moreover, the accounting rules state that unless the dividend on the convertible preferred stock is equivalent to two thirds of the existing bank prime rate the security must be treated as a common stock equivalent.

Thus, what was once one of the principal uses of convertible preferred stock has been largely eliminated. There are, of course, some special cases in which the new requirements have little effect and convertible preferred stock can be used. It is not possible to generalize, however, and if the use of convertible preferred stock in a merger is contemplated, any treasurer would do well to discuss the problems involved with his investment banker, his accountant, and his lawyer.

Sale of Convertible Preferred Stock for Cash

In contrast to the decline in the use of convertible preferred stocks in mergers and acquisitions, there is a continuing use of convertible preferred stocks to raise cash. While the volume has been high in recent years, the demand has tended to fluctuate, depending upon investors' expectations for the stock market and the profitability of certain institutional investors, such as insurance companies, which pay the corporate income tax and which historically have been buyers of preferred stock. The exclusion of 85 percent of dividend income paid on most preferred stocks from corporate income taxes gives almost all preferred stocks, whether they are convertible or not, a certain appeal to corporate buyers. A few industrial companies with special tax situations, or those whose managements may have felt their common stock did not reflect full value and have not wished to sell their common stock at prevailing prices, have sold convertible preferred stocks for cash. It is primarily the major regulated telephone and electric utility companies, however, which have accounted for the bulk of the recent sales of convertible preferred stocks for cash.

The regulated companies in their search for equity capital have resorted in part to the sale of convertible preferred stock in place of common stock, primarily because their common stocks have sold at unsatisfactory relationships to book values. The sale by telephone companies and electric utility companies of common stock below book value tends to dilute earnings per share and, therefore, to affect adversely the price of the common stock. Future sales of common stock, therefore, become more difficult, since those investors who purchased stock in earlier offerings have had disappointing investment experiences. Consequently, many regulated companies, when faced with the possibility of selling common stock below book value, have refrained from doing so and instead have resorted to borrowing. The amount of debt in their capitalizations, however, has increased in many cases to the point at which equity capital is necessary to prevent the quality of outstanding bonds from deteriorating in an unacceptable way. Since the prices of common stocks of electric utilities and telephone companies in most cases in recent years have continued to decline while book values have increased, sale of common stocks has become an even more unattractive method of financing. As an alternative way of raising needed equity capital, some companies have turned to preferred stock which is convertible at a price close to the book value of the common stock, thus avoiding dilution if the preferred is converted at a later date, and which has a dividend rate lower than would have been required for a straight preferred stock. In some cases the sale of convertible preferred stock was the only practical method of raising equity capital.

Among companies that have issued large amounts of convertible preferred or preference stock are American Telephone and Telegraph Company, Consumers Power Company, Detroit Edison Company, and Duke Power Company. The Consumers Power preference stock, for example, was issued on July 25, 1974, at a time when sale of common stock of electric utility companies was extremely difficult; a number of issues of utilities were canceled or postponed around that time. The $50 par value preference stock had a dividend of $6, which furnished a yield of 12 percent, and was convertible into four shares of common stock, or at a price which represented only a modest premium above the market at the time. Consumers Power serves communities in Michigan where the regulatory climate, in the view of many, has long been considered unsatisfactory, and the common stock prior to the offering of the preference stock, was selling at such a depressed price that the yield, based upon the indicated annual dividend of $2 a share, was approximately 17.2 percent. Investors were aware, of course, that in the 12 months ended May 31, 1974, earnings per share of common stock amounted to only $1.79, and many may have questioned the ability of the company to continue its $2 dividend. Obviously, it was an unpropitious time to sell common stock, and while the terms of the convertible preference stock appeared somewhat onerous at the time, the company was able to raise $30 million of needed equity.

The factors in 1971, which apparently resulted in the decision of AT&T to offer stockholders "rights" to buy more than $1.3 billion of $4 preferred stock ($50 par), convertible at a price of $47.50 per common share (equivalent to 1.05 common shares for each convertible preferred share), at $50 a share, were on the whole quite different. The conversion price was in the area of the book value per share. The use of a convertible preferred enabled the company to raise the large amount of equity capital needed. It could not have been done through the sale of a straight preferred stock. The largest straight preferred issue ever sold publicly for cash up to that time was $100 million, and even since then, the largest issues have been the two $500 million AT&T straight preferreds sold in 1973. The terms of the AT&T convertible preferred also were such that the stock was worth considerably more than $50 a share during the entire subscription period. Consequently, a "rights" value was created and maintained which induced stockholders to subscribe and, in addition, enabled the "dealer-manager" to "lay off" a large number of shares created through the exercise of purchased "rights." The premium over the subscription price was created largely by the value of the "latent" warrant.

Convertibles with Warrant Features

Before completing the discussion of convertibles and turning to warrants, it should be pointed out that some convertible securities incorporate features which are very close to warrants. For example, United Airlines issued convertible debentures which require cash payments when conversions take place; securities such as these are known as "cash-added" convertibles. One of these issues, the $4\frac{1}{4}$ percent convertible debentures due 1992, is convertible into 16.20 shares of United Airlines common stock upon surrender of $1,000 principal amount of debentures and a payment of $260. An example of a "cash-added" convertible preferred stock is an issue of R. J. Reynolds Industries. Each share of R. J. Reynolds Industries $2.25 convertible preferred stock, plus $22, is convertible into 1.5 shares of common stock. These types of convertible issues give the holders options, in effect, on additional shares without any initial payment. The purchase of that portion of the total number of shares into which such securities are convertible through the payment of cash is similar to the exercise of an ordinary warrant, which requires a cash payment. The issuing companies, of course, will receive additional cash if the securities are converted just as they would if warrants were being exercised.

The Rockwell International $1.35 convertible preferred, Series B, was issued in 1969 in connection with the merger of Miehle-Goss-Dexter. Each share of the preferred is convertible into 0.9 common shares at any time, or until June 30, 1979, upon payment of $10.125 into 1.125 common shares. At the time of issuance the $1.35 dividend was less than 90 percent of the dividend on the common stock, and the novel optional warrant feature was included so as to give the convertible preferred a value in excess of 90 percent of the value of the common stock and thereby prevent or slow down conversions.

THE USE OF WARRANTS

Warrants have been used for many purposes and it is probable that new uses will evolve in years ahead. Before discussing some of those which have been employed in the recent years, it seems desirable to point out that the use of debentures with warants—one of the major uses—in some circumstances can give rise to tax questions. It is appropriate, therefore, to discuss what we understand the tax problems to be, although any treasurer should receive advice from counsel and accountants when considering the use of warrants with debentures.

Debentures with Warrants: Tax Implications

First of all, in a package of debentures and warrants, where it is intended that the unit will sell at 100 percent, the debentures will necessarily be worth less than 100 percent, and there is a possibility that so-called original issue discount may be involved. Present IRS rules are that the sale of bonds or debentures with a discount greater than an amount represented by one fourth of the number of full years to maturity will result in original issue discount. Hence, a 25-year issue cannot be sold at a price equal to or below 93¾ percent (100 − (¼ × 25)), if original issue discount is to be avoided.

The tax consequences of original issue discount are relatively simple: the issuing corporation can add to the coupon each year a sum representing the discount divided by the number of years to maturity in computing the amount of interest to be used as an income tax deduction. This, of course, is favorable to the issuing corporation. On the other hand, the holder of the issue, assuming that he is a taxpayer, must include as income each year a portion of the discount. Thus, he is being taxed currently on an amount which he will not receive for many years and which is not discounted for present-day values. The holder cannot treat the difference between cost and 100 percent at maturity as a capital gain which presumably would be taxed at a lower rate than ordinary income and only at a future date.

The other tax question involved in the issuance of all warrants arises when a warrant expires without being exercised. The IRS holds (the matter has not been settled in the courts) that when a warrant expires unexercised, the value received by the issuer at the time of issuance—that is, the market's appraisal of the value of the warrant when the unit was sold—must be considered ordinary business income in the year in which the warrant expires. This is in contrast with the treatment if the warrant is exercised, where the exercise price plus the market value of the warrant at the time of issuance is included in the capital accounts.

Debentures with Warrants Attached: Uses

One of the most commonly used is in connection with an offering of debentures with stock purchase warrants attached to buy common stock of the issuer. The tax implications have just been discussed. Probably one or a combination of the reasons listed below was responsible for the decisions of the many companies which have adopted this form of financing:

1.   Bonds or debentures with warrants can be sold in a package at a price of 100 percent with a coupon rate lower than would be the case with a bond or debenture without warrants. Such financing conserves cash flow.

2.   The use of the "equity kicker" has enabled a larger amount

of bonds to be issued. The offering of AT&T debentures with warrants in 1970 would fall in this category. AT&T offered stockholders approximately $1.6 billion, 8¾ percent debentures with warrants attached which entitled holders to purchase shares of AT&T common stock at $52 a share until May 15, 1975. This was, and still is, the largest corporate debt issue ever sold.

3.   Another use is in those cases in which the quality of a company's debt is such that bonds cannot be sold on reasonable terms without warrants being attached, or without making the issue convertible. It would appear that quality and its effect upon terms is an important factor in management's decision to include warrants.

4.   Management may believe that the common stock is underpriced and that common stock can be sold at a higher price at a later date. This could result in a decision to defer the sale of common stock and to use, as an alternative financing plan, debentures with warrants. If the exercise price of the warrants is set well above the market at the time of issuance and the common stock does rise in price, the warrants may be exercised, and management will succeed in the sale of stock at a higher level. This wish to sell common stock at a higher price probably influences most managements.

5.   As pointed out in connection with convertible debentures, most buyers apparently like terms which set the conversion price at a modest premium. The market price of the convertible will naturally then represent a sizable premium over straight investment value. As discussed earlier, such terms do not result in a price at which the maximum premium in dollars over both straight investment value and conversion value is obtained. A warrant to buy common stock at the market, which appeals to speculators, on the other hand, gives the maximum dollar premium over intrinsic value. If maximum dollar premium is one of the qualities sought by management, the use of debentures with warrants to buy stock at the market may have appeal. This factor apparently has not been of any significance in influencing management to reach a decision to issue debentures with warrants, but it may be of greater importance in future financings.

Creating a "Rights" Value

When an offering of debentures and warrants is made to stockholders, the value of the warrant can be used to create a package which is worth considerably more than the subscription price and thereby create a "rights" value. This was an important ingredient in the successful sale in 1970 of the record sized $1.6 billion AT&T offering of debentures and warrants under very difficult market conditions. During the offering period, interest rates were rising and the stock market was declining. Nevertheless, throughout the subscription period the AT&T debenture with warrants traded on a "when issued" basis at prices well above the offering price of 100 percent. The value of the "rights" induced stockholders to subscribe or to sell their "rights." The "dealer-manager" was able to purchase large amounts of "rights" which permitted it, through their exercise, to create debentures with warrants and to "lay off" the debentures and warrants with the investing public.

This proved to be a most successful method to sell the largest corporate debt offering in history. Corporate treasurers might well consider the advisability of utilizing this way of raising large amounts of money in difficult times.

Stock in Other Companies

Many companies, as a result of a number of kinds of transactions, have become large holders of stock in another company. In many cases the blocks are large, and sale could be made only at some discount from the quoted market. Moreover, managements may have felt that future prospects for the companies involved were good and that the stocks would rise in price. By issuing debentures of their companies with warrants attached to purchase the shares in another company, they have accomplished, or hope to accomplish, two goals—they have obtained a lower coupon on the debentures of their company, and if the warrants are exercised, they will have sold the stock in the other company at a price higher than the market price of the stock at the time of issuance of the debenture with warrants attached. Companies that have utilized this type of financing include:

1. Amerada Hess—issued its debentures with warrants to purchase Louisiana Land & Exploration common stock.
2. Cities Service—issued its debentures with warrants to purchase Atlantic Richfield common stock.

3. Northern Natural Gas—issued its debentures with warrants to purchase Mobil Oil common stock.

Common Stock with Warrants

Warrants have also been used in conjunction with the sale of common stock and, in many cases, cash has been raised by the sale of packages consisting of shares of common stock and warrants. It should be pointed out again that warrants which expire unexercised may create tax problems for the issuing companies. The real estate investment trusts, a relatively new type of intermediary, utilized extensively the method of combining debentures or common stock with warrants to raise capital and a large number of the warrants currently outstanding are to buy the shares of REITs. As pointed out before, such warrants tend to sell at small premiums. In contrast, this was not the case with the warrants to buy Hamilton Brothers Exploration Company common stock, which were sold in 1972 in a package consisting of one share of common stock of Hamilton Brothers Exploration and one warrant to buy ¼ share of common stock. Investors, or probably more aptly termed, speculators, recognized that a major discovery of oil by the company could result in substantial appreciation in the price of the common stock. The warrants sold at the extreme upper range for warrant premiums. The use of warrants in a package probably enabled the company to raise more money on very satisfactory terms than could have been obtained through the sale of common stock alone.

Reorganizations and Exchange Offers

Warrants have been used to satisfy claims in reorganizations or to induce holders of securities to accept exchange offers. A good example of the former involved United Airlines a number of years ago. Capital Airlines had been in financial difficulty and was acquired by United Airlines. Prior to the acquisition, Vickers Armstrong Ltd., in settlement of large claims against Capital Airlines arising from the sale of equipment, accepted notes of Capital Airlines. When United acquired Capital Airlines, Vickers agreed to take warrants to buy United Airlines common stock as part of settlement of the notes. The common stock of United Airlines, and thus the warrants, appreciated in price and ultimately the warrants sold at many times their value at the time they were accepted by Vickers.

Litigation

Warrants have been used in various types of litigation, and a novel type of warrant is to be issued by Talley Industries, Inc. Certain stockholders of General Time Corporation, which was merged with Talley, alleged that there had been various violations of the provisions of the Securities Act of 1933 and other laws. In partial settlement of their claims, Talley will issue five-year term warrants to purchase the company's series B preferred stock which, in turn, is convertible into the company's common stock. Among the features of the warrant is a provision that if they are not exercised by the end of the five-year period, they may be "put" to the company at $4 a warrant.

Dividend Free Stock

The two issues of warrants which have been sold by Commonwealth Edison have interesting implications. The warrants, in addition to giving holders the right to purchase Commonwealth Edison common stock during a ten-year period, are convertible as long as they are outstanding into one-third share of Commonwealth Edison common stock. Thus, their value is dependent upon either the conversion value or the value attributable to the option feature. The exercise price was set below the market at the time of issuance, creating large intrinsic value for the warrants. Furthermore, regardless of the price level of Commonwealth Edison, there will always be a positive conversion value. The result has been that the warrants have sold and continue to sell at a high price relative to the common stock. From the standpoint of management, the warrants, which were sold for cash, might almost be considered a "dividend free" stock. Because Commonwealth Edison common stock has fallen in price to a level where the "warrant value" is far less than the conversion value, conversion has taken place at a rapid rate. It is possible that any company using this type of security in the future might be able to include some new features which would delay conversion.

A Long-Term "Right"

One of the newest uses of warrants has been announced by Ocean Oil & Gas Company. Ocean Oil has two classes of stock which are basically identical, one of which is owned by Ocean Drilling & Exploration Company and the other by the public. Ocean Oil wishes to raise funds to bid on offshore oil leases and apparently would have liked to sell stock in an amount that would have increased its capitalization by 66⅔ percent. This is a large increase in capitalization for any company, let alone one without any record of earnings. The financing plan involved a dividend to stockholders at the rate of one warrant for each share held, entitling the warrant holder to buy two-thirds share of common stock. The warrant has a term of less than a year, and includes one step-up in the exercise price. Ocean Drilling & Exploration plans to exercise its warrants as funds are required by Ocean Oil. Presumably, if the drilling on acquired leases is successful and the stock rises in price, other holders will exercise their warrants, thereby furnishing Ocean Oil with additional funds with which the company can bid for new leases.

EMPLOYEE STOCK OPTION PLANS

Treasurers may be involved in options granted to employees by corporations. Employee stock option plans generally provide an employee with an opportunity to purchase stock of the employer corporation at a price below the market value of the stock on the date the option is exercised. The granting of such options to employees have been considered desirable from the standpoint of the corporation on the theory that the potential gains, provided the stock of the issuing company does well, are strong incentives for an employee to exert his utmost efforts for the benefit of the corporation. An employee realizes that the better the company does, the more likely its stock will rise in price and his option will attain value. Tax factors also make certain options potentially very attractive as part of total compensation. Thus, options have been used extensively as means of retaining key employees and in enticing able personnel to join a company. Many options have been granted, however, when stocks were selling much higher in price than at the present time, and many employees have had disappointing experiences. With stocks at the lowest levels in years, options granted currently, when the Dow-Jones Industrial Average is in the area of 600, could prove in time to be very rewarding.

Primarily because of tax implications, it is very important that a corporate treasurer obtain legal advice in setting up any stock option plan. It is also important that he be aware of tax and reporting requirements and that employees who are granted options understand fully their position.

Types of Options

There are two categories of options and these are differentiated by their tax treatment: *Qualified* (within the meaning of the Internal Revenue Code of 1954 Section 422) and *Nonqualified* (all others).

Tax Considerations

Counsel should be consulted on tax matters and some of these are described below. The principal differences for tax purposes between the two categories of options are as follows:

1. Exercise Term. *Qualified options* cannot be exercised after five years from the date of grant. *Nonqualified* options have no such limit.

2. Sequential Exercise. *Qualified options* cannot be exercised while a qualified option previously granted to the same individual holder at a higher option price remains outstanding. *Non qualified options* have no such restrictions.

3. Tax Consequences upon Exercise. *Qualified options:* No taxable income is realized upon exercise unless the stock is sold within three years and one day of the date of exercise, although the difference between the option price and the market price of the stock on the date of exercise is an item included in the computation of an individual's tax preference income (TPI) under the 1969 Tax Reform Act and, to the extent such TPI exceeds $30,000, may also affect computation of the maximum tax on earned income and the minimum tax on tax preferences. *Nonqualified options:* Upon exercise, the spread between the option price and the market price of the stock on the exercise date is taxable as "earned income" in the year of exercise.

4. Tax Consequences upon Sale of Stock. *Qualified options:* If stock received pursuant to exercise of the option is sold: (*a*) after three years and one day from the date of exercise, then the difference between the option price and the sale price will be long-term capital gain or loss as the case may be; or (*b*) within three years and one day after the exercise date, then a "disqualifying disposition" has occurred, and to the extent that the lesser of (1) the market value at exercise and (2) the sale price exceeds the option price, such amount will be taxed as "earned income." If the stock is held for more than six months after exercise date, the excess, if any, of the sale price over the market value of the stock on the exercise date will be taxed as long-term capital gain; if the sale price is less than the option price, there is no "earned income" and the amount of difference is a capital loss. If the stock is sold within the tax year during which the option was exercised, any spread at exercise will not constitute TPI. *Nonqualified options:* The difference between the market value of the stock on the exercise date and the sale price is taxed as long-term capital gain or loss if the stock has been held more than six months after exercise.

5. Withholding Tax. *Qualified options:* No withholding is necessary. *Nonqualified options:* Since the difference between the market price and the option price is treated as a supplemental wage payment subject to federal (and possibly state and city) income tax withholding, the company should make appropriate arrangements for the payment of any withholding tax due upon exercise of the nonqualified option.

Other Tax, Reporting, and SEC Considerations

In certain circumstances, an employer will be allowed as a deduction an amount equal to any ordinary income reportable as compensation by an employee. The corporate treasurer should be aware that every corporation is required to file an information return with respect to any transfer of stock to any employee pursuant to his exercise of a qualified stock option.

The treasurer should see that employees are aware of Section 16(b) of the Securities Exchange Act of 1934 which relates to the repayment of profits to the employer when any purchase and sale or any sale and purchase are made within any period of less than six months. Any officer and director of a company should know that Section 16(b) of the Act requires that he file with the Securities and Exchange Commission a statement of equity securities of the company and thereafter a monthly statement of any change in beneficial ownership of equity securities of the company. The status of an officer's or director's options can have a bearing on these reporting requirements.

ADDITIONAL SOURCES

Some of the following references were published after completion of this chapter in 1974.

Bacon, Peter W., and Winn, Edward L., Jr. "The Impact of Forced Conversion on Stock Prices." *Journal of Finance,* 24 (December 1969), 871–74.

Baumol, William J.; Malkiel, Burton G.; and Quandt, Richard E. "The Valuation of Convertible Securities." *Quarterly Journal of Economics,* 80 (February 1966), 48–59.

Black, Fischer, and Scholes, Myron. "The Valuation of Option Contracts and a Test of Market Efficiency." *Journal of Finance,* 27 (May 1972), 399–417.

Black, Fischer, and Scholes, Myron. "The Pricing of Options and Corporate Liabilities." *Journal of Political Economy,* 81 (May–June 1973), 637–54.

Bierman, Harold Jr. "The Costs of Warrants." *Journal of Financial and Quantitative Analysis,* 8 (June 1973), 499–504.

Brigham, Eugene F. "An Analysis of Convertible Debentures: Theory and Some Empirical Evidence." *Journal of Finance,* 21 (March 1966), 35–54.

Chen, Andrew H. Y. "A Model of Warrant Pricing in a Dynamic Market." *Journal of Finance,* 25 (December 1970), 1041–59.

Cretien, Paul D., Jr. "Premiums on Convertible Bonds: Comment." *Journal of Finance,* 25 (September 1970), 917–22.

Dawson, Steven. "Timing Interest Payments for Convertible Bonds." *Financial Management,* 3 (Summer 1974), 14–16.

Frank, Werner, and Kroncke, Charles. "Classifying Conversions of Convertible Debentures over Four Years." *Financial Management,* 3 (Summer 1974), 33–42.

Frankle, Alan W. "An Estimate of Convertible Bond Premiums: Comment." *Journal of Financial and Quantitative Analysis,* 10 (June 1975), 375–76.

Frankle, A. W., and Hawkins, C. A. "Beta Coefficients for Convertible Bonds." *Journal of Finance,* 30 (March 1975), 207–10.

Groth, Stephen. "The Trouble with Convertibles." *Financial Analysts Journal,* 28 (November–December 1972), 92–95.

Jennings, Edward H. "An Estimate of Convertible Bond Premiums." *Journal of Financial and Quantitative Analysis,* 9 (January 1974), 33–56.

Jennings, Edward H. "Reply: An Estimate of Convertible Bond Premiums." *Journal of Financial and Quantitative Analysis,* 10 (June 1975), 375–76.

Leabo, Dick A., and Rogalski, Richard J. "Warrant Price Movements and the Efficient Market Model." *Journal of Finance,* 30 (March 1975), 163–78.

Leibowitz, Martin. "Understanding Convertible Securities." *Financial Analysts Journal,* 30 (November–December 1974), 57–67.

Lewellen, Wilbur G., and Racette, George A. "Convertible Debt Financing." *Journal of Financial and Quantitative Analysis,* 8 (December 1973), 777–92.

Miller, Alexander B. "How to Call Your Convertible." *Harvard Business Review,* 49 (May–June 1971), 66–70.

Miller, Roger. "Convertible Exchange Offers—Everyone Can Win." *Financial Executive,* 42 (February 1974), 25–35.

Pinches, George E. "Financing with Convertible Preferred Stock, 1960–1967." *Journal of Finance,* 25 (March 1970), 53–63.

Poensgen, Otto H. "The Valuation of Convertible Bonds," Parts I and II. *Industrial Management Review,* 6 and 7 (Fall 1965 and Spring 1966), 77–92 and 83–98.

Rush, David F., and Melicher, Ronald W. "An Empirical Examination of Factors Which Influence Warrant Prices." *Journal of Finance,* 29 (December 1974), 1449–66.

Samuelson, Paul A., and Merton, Robert C. "A Complete Model of Warrant Pricing That Maximizes Utility." *Industrial Management Review,* 10 (Winter 1969), 17–46.

Shelton, John P. "The Relation of the Price of a Warrant to the Price of Its Associated Stock." *Financial Analysts Journal,* 23 (May–June and July–August 1967), 143–151 and 88–99.

Sprecher, C. Ronald. "A Note on Financing Mergers with Convertible Preferred Stock." *Journal of Finance,* 26 (June 1971), 683–86.

Turov, Daniel. "Warrants of Dividend-Paying Stocks." *Financial Analysts Journal,* 29 (March–April 1973), 76–78.

Walter, James E., and Que, Agustin V. "The Valuation of Convertible Bonds." *Journal of Finance,* 28 (June 1973), 713–32.

Weil, Roman L., Jr.; Segall, Joel E.; and Green, David, Jr. "Premiums on Convertible Bonds." *Journal of Finance,* 23 (June 1968), 445–64.

PART X

Financing Growth

In Part X we take up dynamic aspects of the development of the firm and the treasurer's responsibilities in contributing to the growth and profitability of his firm. Some of the topics provide the function of integrating a number of threads of discussion presented previously in connection with individual aspects of financial operations.

In Chapter 39, Bruce Rossiter and Gene Miller provide a comprehensive and documented treatment of financing the new enterprise. They explain why problems of raising equity for the new enterprise may be encountered. They provide guidance to the treasurer to assist him in overcoming the obstacles that may be encountered. They provide a particularly valuable discussion of private placement procedures, including a step-by-step outline for developing a private placement memorandum to increase the probability that the new enterprise will be successful in obtaining funds.

After a survey of the wide range of potential sources of financing for the new enterprise, they treat at some length the role of venture capitalists. Again, a step-by-step consideration of all elements involved in the process are provided. The policies of venture capitalists are considered and the need to relate to the policies of particular venture capital sources is established. The important considerations involved in structuring the deal are covered. Finally, the requirements of continuing relationships with the venture capital source are described.

The emphasis of the preceding chapter in financing the new enterprise was on private transactions with venture capital forces. In Chapter 40, John Shad takes us to the next stage in the develop-

857

ment of the firm in which it is involved in "going public." The important considerations that require understanding by the treasurer in this important stage of the firm's development are set forth. The requirements for going public are described. Mr. Shad explains both the advantages and disadvantages of going public. He then provides a detailed and comprehensive treatment of how investment bankers appraise corporations in connection with the initial public offerings of their securities. The factors influencing the determination of pricing the initial public offering of the firm's securities are analyzed. The rationale and nature of the continuing relationship with the investment banking firm which brings out the initial public offering is explained.

The new financing turbulence and particularly the impacts of inflation have given rise to important financial innovations. Paul Kelly has written one of the few available comprehensive treatments of these developments in Chapter 41. He describes new financing techniques such as documented discount notes, leveraged leasing, pollution control bonds, floating rate securities, mutually redeemable preferred stock, and preferred stock with accelerated sinking-fund patterns. He also treats new variations that have been added to the older and more conventional methods of financing. He points out that the task of new financing vehicles is to adapt to a changing economic environment in such a way as to assist in the formation of investment capital throughout the world.

A new and important form of financing of relevance to corporate treasurers is "project financing," discussed by Robert Huston in Chapter 42. He explains that project financing applies to a wide range of different forms of financing. He sets forth seven characteristics which characterize what is most generally regarded as project financing. He provides illustrative examples of the use of project financing, indicating that over 100 major activities in more than 30 countries each involving costs in excess of $100 million have been identified. Mr. Huston describes the factors involved in project evaluation and their economic appraisal. He points out that major projects may be in the formative stage for two to three years and more than five years may pass from the germination of a project idea to the start of construction. He describes the special factors in the evaluation of projects in the raw materials area, plant construction and in plant operation. Thus a framework for understanding and participating in project financing is provided.

Another new development related to financing the growth of firms is represented by employee stock ownership plans (ESOPs). These developments are described by Joseph Taussig in Chapter 43. He first describes the nature of an ESOP. He then explains how ESOPs can be used as a vehicle for transactions of a number of different types. He shows how ESOP transactions can put pretax dollars to better use by providing for an immediate infusion of capital into the firm, increasing cash flow, increasing the growth rate of net worth, and meeting obligations without impairing net worth growth. He also explains the use of the ESOP as an alternative to going public or as a method of going private and in acquisitions as well as divestitures. Finally, he treats the legal foundations of the ESOP, particularly as strengthened in the new Pension Reform Act of 1974 and in the Tax Reform Act of 1975.

Mergers and acquisitions also have a useful function to perform in contributing to company growth. However, in recent years, the role of mergers and acquisitions has been discredited to some degree. The reason is that many mergers, particularly during the merger wave of the late 1960s, were aimed at the objective of using financial legerdemain to turn quick profits and were not based on well-formulated, long-range plans in the framework of carefully constructed business strategies. Two aspects of importance to corporate treasurers for utilizing mergers and acquisitions effectively in planning the healthy growth of their firms are developed in Chapters 44 and 45.

In Chapter 44, Roger Cope emphasizes the critical importance of proper planning as the basis for any acquisition program. He also points out that a merger and acquisition program is one among a number of alternative methods of growth and the relative advantages of each method should be fully evaluated for their proper use. Other prerequisites are that the company have a planned growth program and that this plan have the support of all levels of management, particularly the chief executive officer and his staff. With these prerequisites Mr. Cope sets forth a planning, analyzing, and acquiring program. He first considers the sources for acquisition candidates. Then initial review procedures are described. The key objective of the initial visit is to determine whether there will be a fit between the managements of the companies involved. The next step involves tours of the facilities, meetings with key managers, and covering a long check-list of factors. A comprehensive acquisition analysis can then be prepared, providing a basis for a decision of whether to go ahead. Mr. Cope then takes us through the subsequent important steps in the process including negotiations, the offer, the report to the board, the closing, and post-closing activities. Fewer mergers would have failed if the comprehensive planning process set forth by Mr. Cope had been followed by other companies in earlier periods.

In Chapter 45, Gary MacDougal treats a critical aspect of an acquisition program—the merger negotiations. The principles he sets forth are based on his earlier extensive experience as a management consultant in the mergers and acquisitions area and his knowledge of the literature of the subject. In this chapter he provides illustrations based on the experience of the company which he now heads. The fundamental approach in the merger negotiations he describes is the basic return on investment concept utilizing discounted cash flow techniques as described in Chapters 15 and 16.

First the company must lay some groundwork by thinking through its own corporate objectives and acquisition criteria as described in the previous chapter by Mr. Cope. The company should then determine the general financial relationships which will affect price, involving the interrelationship of factors such as earnings-per-share growth rates, capital requirements, purchase prices, and forms of payment. The kind of financial analysis of an acquisition that should be performed is set forth and illustrated. The framework of implementing a return on investment target is set forth. Careful consideration is given to (1) developing the seller interest and (2) resolving financial terms. Thus the emphasis of the chapter is on providing guidance in surmounting the most common obstacles to success in merger negotiations.

Chapter 39

Financing the New Enterprise

Bruce G. Rossiter[*]
Gene I. Miller[†]

THE FOREWORD to a recent government study best sums up the problem facing the entrepreneur seeking capital. It stated that there was a need "to remove some of the aura of 'black art' mysticism from the entrepreneurial process, especially the financing aspects."[1]

No universally accepted definition for "venture capital" exists. Common usage implies money at risk with potentially high return. It is money invested in situations where it cannot be borrowed prudently from a commercial bank. It is the hardest money for the new enterprise to find. While the general public has at times been a source of funds, venture capital raised from a public offering is unpredictable as a means of financing. Most often venture capital is provided by the privately managed funds of wealthy individuals and institutions.

As stated by Stanley Rubel, "Many venture capitalists occupy

---

[*] Bruce G. Rossiter is vice president for First Small Business Investment Company of California, and Security Pacific Capital Corporation, Los Angeles, California.

[†] Gene I. Miller is vice president for First Small Business Investment Company of California, and Security Pacific Capital Corporation, Los Angeles, California.

[1] *Venture Capital, A Guidebook for New Enterprises*, A U.S. Government Printing Office publication prepared for the New England Regional Commission by the Management Institute, School of Management, Boston College, March 22, 1972, p. v.

unmarked offices, have unlisted telephones, and shun publicity."[2]
The average entrepreneur will approach his banker, attorney, or
CPA for assistance in locating venture capital. These professionals,
even if they have worked in the past with a venture source, will
usually have only one or two references for the entrepreneur. The
few venture references given the entrepreneur may well be inappropriate in that these sources very likely will not have an interest
in the entrepreneur's industry or his company's stage of development. However, it has been estimated that over $3 billion is avail-
able from organized venture sources, and that 99.9 percent of the
venture industry will never see any specific entrepreneur's proposal.

This chapter concentrates on the basics of how to launch a successful fund-raising effort. It is organized from the institutional
point of view and is structured around the following subjects:

1. Looking at common fund-raising difficulties.
2. Determining the company's financial needs.
3. Preparing the private placement memorandum.
4. Locating sources of venture capital.
5. Dealing with the venture capitalist.

LOOKING AT COMMON FUND-RAISING DIFFICULTIES

Every entrepreneur who has raised money for his company knows
the frustrations of this process. The process is just as frustrating for
the investor. Months are spent screening and investigating scores
of proposals before a suitable investment is found. Most professional
venture capitalists invest in only 1 percent to 2 percent of the
opportunities afforded them.

A review of some of the common difficulties encountered by the
investor should help the entrepreneur to avoid the tremendous
waste of effort many experience in seeking financial support. Four
problems occur with regularity, as follows:

1. Mediocre company performance or concept.
2. Lack of business experience or acumen of the principal.
3. Unique preferences or policies of the venture capitalist.
4. Failure of the company to follow up.

----

[2] Stanley M. Rubel (ed.), *Guide to Venture Capital Sources* (Chicago: Capital
Publishing Corporation, 1972–73), p. 8, introduction.

Mediocre Company Performance or Concept

The greatest single reason for which existing or new companies are refused financing involves mediocre or worse performance or concept. Too often the management of a company has spent substantial time and money and achieved a very low level of sales, little if any profitability, and a situation that demands more funds. This picture is not appealing to an investor. Often the attempt is made to overcome this weakness by projecting a brilliant future. That future is usually based on heroic assumptions that ignore the detailed steps necessary to reach the sales goals—all the while being optimistic about the margins that will be achieved and the time it will take to achieve the business plan.

Viewed from another perspective two elements underlie the typical venture capitalist's disinterest. Either the company or concept involves too high a business risk; or, too low a profit or too low a return on investment.

High Risk. Investor risk is the risk of losing capital and not realizing expected returns. Factors causing risk are as myriad as there are companies. Some areas of risk are: the company's inability to withstand competition (lack of a proprietary product? ease of entry by competitors?); its inability to sustain changes in its economic environment (on its own and in comparison to those with which it must do battle for its revenue base); the strengths and weaknesses highlighted by the financial statements (too much inventory?, too many accumulated payables?, poor profit margins?); the difficulty for the investor in working with the investment (geographic distance?, management personalities?); significant pending litigation; or start-up nature of the company.

Entrepreneurs believe venture capital should be risk capital available for start-ups. Start-ups are the most risky investments. They entail unknown product acceptance; untested management, both individually and as a team; unknown production capability; and unknown expense levels. Having a wide choice, the venture capitalist will tend to invest in less risky ventures. He will avoid high risk situations even if there is a chance for high payoff when the probability of success is too low. Some investors will finance the beginning enterprise if they envision high returns and where a detailed business plan has been developed that can be reasonably attained, or if the funds are used for assets of an easily liquidable nature, or there is some other secondary source of repayment.

The entrepreneur can play a significant role in minimizing the risks he asks the venture capitalist to take. He can invest his own monies subordinated to or along with the venture capitalist. Most investors will require a significant investment by the entrepreneur to ensure commitment to the project. Although some entrepreneurs feel their time and "opportunities forgone" should be enough of a commitment, the investor knows that as ulcers start becoming a possibility because of the day-to-day pressure of running a business, a high salary job offer from an established company can become more attractive. This sense of commitment is important to the investor because it provides him with the reassurance that there will be someone in the daily operations of the company who will fight for its survival and that the investor will not be faced suddenly with the burden of trying to administer the company to save his investment. If the entrepreneur does not have a significant net worth, and cannot borrow his share of the initial investment, occasionally the investor may lend him the money, or ask for a personal loan guarantee. The entrepreneur now faces the loan liability as an incentive to stick with the company if the going gets rough. This compromise solution is used more by individual venture capitalists than by institutional venture groups.

The selection of the business to be funded is just as important in reducing risk as are monetary contributions and personal guarantees. If the entrepreneur is starting from scratch, seeking a business in an area that has less risk, such as a large market with few competitors, makes more sense than choosing one in a field replete with risk.

Another significant influence in reducing risk is reducing the unknown. The less the investor knows about the company the more risk he perceives. An investor may raise a number of general arguments concerning the risk of a particular deal, many of which can be mitigated by elaborating the facts. A venture group was recently requested by an oil production company to invest several million dollars in exploration. No historical record of past drilling successes was given. During initial screening this request was viewed as a high risk venture. There was little chance that it would be funded. Through probing for details on past drilling programs it was learned that this company had a much greater drilling success ratio than the average oil company. Further investigation showed that a large second position could exist behind the banks that were lending on already producing property. Thus a request for a high risk activity was later viewed as one of only moderate risk as more facts were developed about the company. The venture group funded the project and further reduced its risk by funding in stages. As performance bench marks were met, additional monies were released.

Low Profits or Low Return on Investment. Profit levels are important. If a company has low margins, as an example, returning 1 percent of $1,000,000 of sales, there is little to intrigue the investor. The time, trouble, and risk do not warrant a share of the company producing the miniscule profit of $10,000. Companies with low sales volumes after a long period of operation, for example, several hundred thousand dollars after five years of growth, low growth potential, insufficient backlog, or unrealistic projections also suffer from low absolute dollar returns. Companies with a long break even time horizon, historical losses with no demonstrable turnaround, negative cash flows, and requirements for large amounts of investment dollars are likely to be turned down as giving too low a return on investment. The investor will be looking instead for companies that can efficiently use capital and thus produce high returns.

In turn, the returns generated by the company will help determine the returns the investor can expect on his investment. The large number of companies that fall into the low profit, low return, or turnaround category may represent sound companies in which the entrepreneur can earn a respectable salary. But an investor needs more. A passive investor draws no salary and thus can invest only in those situations in which the returns are sufficient enough that they cover both rewards to the entrepreneur for his efforts and to the investor for his capital.

The rate of return sought by venture groups on their investment varies but will range from 25 percent compound return per year for low risk ventures, to very high returns such as 70, 80, 100 percent, or even more for high risk ventures. These profits are well within reach if the company generates good earnings on the assets employed, has good growth potential, and receives a satisfactory multiple on its stock in the market.

The entrepreneur may believe that the investor is seeking an extraordinary return on his investment. However, generally only a small number of the investor's portfolio are highly successful. The investor must make a sufficient return on his successful investments to achieve an acceptable overall return. An unpublished study showed the returns generated by nine public SBICs (small business investment companies) as a compound rate of return from 1965 to 1970 of only 19 percent. This result included unrealized gains in the calculation of return and covered a period when the stock market was kind to over-the-counter stocks. Every year the Small Business Administration (SBA) publishes an industry survey of SBIC returns on realized gains. The returns on investment fluctuate at break even for the industry as a whole, and the more successful institutional venture groups often average returns of only 10 to 12 percent.

Lack of Business Experience or Acumen of the Principal

A favorite truism among venture investors is that investments are made in men, not in companies or concepts. Some investors state that they "First and foremost . . . look at the management of a soliciting company. If it does not measure up, nothing else is likely to make them want to invest. . . ."[3] While the "man" in the equation "Man-idea-money"[4] is vital, because of the difficulty in measuring management performance apart from profit performance, this category is difficult to assess. Profit performance can be reviewed while management quality can only be guessed.

An investor will be concerned with the management team's individual successes prior to the proposed venture, experience in the particular business, and depth of management in key areas. Lack of confidence may arise from a feeling that management's talent is overly promotional, not operational; that management does not have a good grasp of the key factors for success in its business; that financial control skills are lacking; that management is not tough, not capable of rolling with the punches; that management is not honest; that management is not creative or imaginative; or that management is not realistic.

A willingness to work with the venture group in whatever ways practicable can do much to establish needed rapport. The investor group likewise needs to be in tune with the problems faced and overcome by management, and to view management's talents with openness. Unfortunately, some entrepreneurs and investors, flushed with past success, adopt a take-it-or-leave-it stance. In practice,

---

[3] "Venture Capital; What Is It/Where Is It/How to Get It," *Business Management*, 26 (July 1964), p. 32.

[4] *Venture Capital, A Guidebook for New Enterprises*, p. 6.

both sides need to establish bonds of respect. Each is asking the other to become a partner in a venture designed to produce high returns for both.

Unique Preferences or Policies of the Venture Capitalist

The difficulties previously described derive from the project or management. Not all deals fail because of internal defects. Problems unique to the venture group account for some. Some examples of these individual preferences are:

1. The deal is too small. A request for $30,000 requires as much investigation as one for $500,000. Because of the often limited return possible on the smaller investment, it may be classified as too small for consideration.
2. The use of proceeds is questionable in the eyes of the investor; e.g., a large portion of the investment capital is to be used to advertise an untested product.
3. The venture group has a general dislike for the investment area; e.g., the company is operating in a cyclical industry, the company is dependent on competitive bidding, the company operates in an industry the investor thinks unattractive, or the investor feels the company's operations are so unfamiliar to him as to be beyond his ability to make a contribution.
4. Too many problems need to be overcome. Some deals have so many intermediate steps that must be accomplished before the investment is made that it is not worth the herculean task to put the deal together.

Failure of the Company to Follow up

Some companies make their initial contact without any prepared private placement memorandum. The management seems to be testing the waters to see if they could receive an infusion of cash— only to drop their pursuit upon learning of the major educational effort required to instill enough confidence in the investor to risk his money. The entrepreneur is best advised not to approach investors in a casual fashion.

The search for funding should begin well in advance of the date it is required. It usually takes at least two to three months to locate a venture source, assist the investor in the analysis, and to structure a deal. Many companies underestimate this time necessary to carry through a successful negotiation.

DETERMINING THE COMPANY'S FINANCIAL NEEDS

To raise venture capital, one needs to know how much money is needed. Yet many entrepreneurs do not know the mechanics of estimating the financial needs of a company. Financial planning falls into two broad categories: planning for liquidity and planning for profit. Planning for liquidity centers in planning the company's cash flow. One element of the cash flow projection involves projecting the company's future sales and profits. The profit projection also has independent validity as a statement of future company income. It is the cash flow projection, supported by profit projections, that is of greatest utility in determining the company's financial needs. To better understand the mechanics of this process the cash needs for a start-up will be considered first, and then the cash needs for an existing business will be determined.

Determining Cash Needs for a Start-up

The cash needs for a starting venture may be projected in a number of ways. Kelley, Lawyer, and Baumback review several techniques for mechandising, manufacturing, and service businesses.[5] The "desired income" approach develops the amount of capital needed to produce a given amount of annual personal income. The "rental rate" approach determines the amount of sales and then the capital needed to support an assumed rental. The "cash available" approach starts with an amount of capital assumed to be available to determine the probable income resulting from its efficient use.

A standard method is to project an expected sales level, its associated expenses, and additional funds needed for capital assets. Several texts illustrate methods for sales projections.[6] Assuming sales

---

[5] Pearce Kelley, Kenneth Lawyer, and Clifford Baumback, *How to Organize and Operate a Small Business*, 3d ed. (Englewood Cliffs, N.J.: Prentice-Hall, Inc., 1961), pp. 175–84.

[6] See, for example, George Steiner, *Top Management Planning*, (New York: The Macmillan Company, 1969), chap. 8; pp, 217–29. J. Fred Weston and Eugene F. Brigham, *Managerial Finance*, 2d ed. (New York: Holt, Rinehart, and Winston, 1966), chap. 8.

for the year of $200,000, the following analysis can give a quick approximation of the amount of initial investment required for a typical merchandising store:

	Total Investment Needed
Operating expenses* (one month)	
General and administrative	$ 500
Rent (2,000 sq.ft. at $0.30 per sq.ft.)	600
Selling	1,500
Payroll	1,800
Subtotal	$ 4,400

Beginning inventory purchases (one month)

$$BI = \frac{S}{T} \times (CGS)$$

where:

BI = Beginning inventory
S = Sales ($200,000 per year or $16,666 per month)
T = Turnover (3)
CGS = Cost of goods sold as a percentage of sales (0.50)

$$BI = \frac{\$16,666}{3} \times (0.50) = \$2,777$$

Subtotal	$ 2,777
Down payment on fixtures and equipment	$ 4,000
Reserves	
One month inventory re-order	2,777
Operating expenses, one month	4,400
Miscellaneous (10% of operating expense)	440
Subtotal	$ 7,617
Total Initial Investment	$18,794

* Ratios of expenses to sales or actual expenses for various types of business may be obtained from *Financial Ratios,* Robert Morris & Associates, Research Department, Philadelphia National Bank Building, Philadelphia, Pennsylvania 19107; or the Small Business Administration for studies on various small businesses; or Dun and Bradstreet, Inc., Industry Studies Dept., New York, which publishes an annual report, *Key Business Ratios.*

After reviewing this simplified approach for determining the capital needs to start a business, several major flaws become apparent. No account is taken of the extra demands for cash necessitated by the buildup of sales to the required level. Also, cash needs for a growing sales base are not dealt with, but are assumed to be satisfied by normal cash flow from operations. This assumption can be fatal. The approach used to determine cash flow as if the business were ongoing helps solve these problems.

Determining the Cash Needs for an Existing Business

For an existing business, full income statement, balance sheet, and cash flow projections are helpful to both management and the investor. Management benefits from the discipline of thinking through each element of the company's growth and its profit and cash impact. The exact financial needs of the company given various assumptions and the various potential sources to fill these needs are pinpointed. A surprising number of companies seek amounts of venture capital that cannot be justified by projected operations. The entrepreneur and investor can come to agreement only from disciplined planning. The investor benefits since the sources and uses of cash are specified. He can observe what effect this cash infusion will have on the business. Finally, he can test the reasonableness of the various assumptions used in the projections.

There are various ways to project a company's cash needs.[7] Figures 1 through 5 present a helpful method in accomplishing this objective. It is a six-step procedure that will be outlined around a hypothetical company called Any Industries, Inc. The planning will be for a six-month period for illustrative purposes. However, a company should prepare at least a three-year forecast, on a monthly basis for the first year and quarterly for the last two years. Footnotes should be used for each forecast category, keying that category to a backup sheet specifying the underlying assumptions and calculations. Any Industries, Inc. is assumed to be a manufacturer in the recreational field. It has just received several orders that will cause it to double its sales within the next six months. The company is reviewing the profit and cash impact of accepting these orders, knowing that a capital expenditure of $500,000 for equipment will have to be made to allow increased production.

Step 1. Prepare Income Statement Projections. Figure 1. Sales were forecast on results projected by the sales force, validated by management, and with information on current backlog. The expected doubling in sales is the occasion for Any Industries, Inc.'s

---

[7] See Perry Mason *"Cash Flow" Analysis and the Funds Statement,* An Accounting Research Study, No. 2 (New York: American Institute of CPAs, 1961).

FIGURE 1

ANY INDUSTRIES, INC.
Pro Forma Income Statement Projections
(000s omitted)

	September	October	November	December	January	February	Totals
Net Sales.	$705	$1,079	$1,184	$1,304	$1,420	$1,500	$7,192
Cost of goods sold (CGS)							
Material	219	338	361	398	428	445	2,189
Labor.	244	375	401	443	477	498	2,438
Factory overhead	86	131	140	154	165	173	849
Subtotal	$549	$ 844	$ 902	$ 995	$1,070	$1,116	$5,476
Depreciation.	8	8	8	11	14	14	63
Total cost of goods sold	$557	$ 852	$ 910	$1,006	$1,084	$1,130	$5,539
Gross margin.	$148	$ 227	$ 274	$ 298	$ 336	$ 370	$1,653
Operating expenses	$108	$ 150	$ 191	$ 197	$ 198	$ 202	$1,046
Interest.	5	5	5	5	5	5	30
Profit before income taxes. . . .	$ 35	$ 72	$ 78	$ 96	$ 133	$ 163	$ 577
Income taxes at 50%	18	36	39	48	67	82	290
Net Profit after Taxes	$ 17	$ 36	$ 39	$ 48	$ 66	$ 81	$ 287

current financial needs, both to finance the increased receivables and to purchase fixed assets necessary to handle the expanded sales.

Cost of goods sold before depreciation was assumed to equal 78 percent of sales but would decline to 74 percent of sales from volume efficiencies in purchasing and labor efficiencies from the new fixed assets. Depreciation was treated as a separate expense so that all noncash items could be properly segregated in the cash flow. Operating expenses were projected at 13 to 16 percent of sales.

The results of the expansion for the six months would be revenues of $7,192,000 and net income of $287,000.

Step 2. Prepare Work Sheet for Cash Flow and Balance Sheet Items. Figure 2. This work sheet provides the detail necessary to recast a monthly balance sheet based on changes in operations, and to assist in the preparation of the cash flow. Cash is not treated in Step 2 work sheets since this amount is a result of the final cash flow. The first account updated was accounts receivable. Receivables were calculated as collected within 60 days and were updated as per the work sheet. Inventory cost input of material purchases, direct labor, and factory overhead are forecasted to increase directly with sales volume and to precede the sales increase by one month. Cost input would be based on historical data taking into consider-

FIGURE 2

ANY INDUSTRIES, INC.
Work Sheet for Cash Flow and Balance Sheet Items
(000s omitted)

Pro Forma Balance Sheet Detail	September	October	November	December	January	February
A. Accounts Receivable Detail:						
Beginning receivable balance	$1,090	$1,145	$1,524	$2,003	$2,228	$2,464
Add: Sales	705	1,079	1,184	1,304	1,420	1,500
Subtotal	$1,795	$2,224	$2,708	$3,307	$3,648	$3,964
Deduct: Cash receipts	650	700	705	1,079	1,184	1,304
Ending receivable balance	$1,145	$1,524	$2,003	$2,228	$2,464	$2,660
Change from Beginning to Ending	$ 55	$ 379	$ 479	$ 225	$ 236	$ 196
B. Inventory Flow/Cost of Goods Sold Detail:						
Beginning inventory	$1,112	$1,453	$1,515	$1,658	$1,763	$1,869
Add: Material purchases	360	380	452	484	521	562
Direct labor	390	385	440	458	485	525
Factory overhead	140	141	153	158	170	185
Subtotal	$2,002	$2,359	$2,560	$2,758	$2,939	$3,141
Deduct: material used	219	338	361	398	428	445
Direct labor used	244	375	401	443	477	498
Factory overhead used	86	131	140	154	165	173
Subtotal (Cost of Goods Sold)	$ 549	$ 844	$ 902	$ 995	$1,070	$1,116
Ending inventory	$1,453	$1,515	$1,658	$1,763	$1,869	$2,025
Change from Beginning to Ending	$ 341	$ 62	$ 143	$ 105	$ 106	$ 156
C. Accounts Payable Detail:						
Beginning payable balance	$1,492	$1,643	$1,741	$2,170	$2,386	$2,225
Add: Material purchases	360	380	452	484	521	562
Factory overhead*	128	128	135	139	147	160
Operating expenses*	73	110	132	136	140	144
Capital equipment items	–	–	250	250	–	–
Subtotal	$2,053	$2,261	$2,710	$3,179	$3,194	$3,091
Deduct: Cash Disbursements	410	520	540	793	969	810
Ending Accounts Payable Balance	$1,643	$1,741	$2,170	$2,386	$2,225	$2,281
Change from Beginning to Ending	$ 151	$ 98	$ 429	$ 216	$ (161)	$ 56

* Excludes payroll since this expense is assumed to be made by cash payments in the month incurred.

ation any anticipated production efficiencies. In this example, material purchases are forecasted at approximately 33 percent of each succeeding months' sales, while direct labor is forecasted at 32 percent and factory overhead at 11 percent. In updating accounts payable note that Any Industries, Inc. purchased $500,000 of fixed assets in November and December, in increments of $250,000. These assets were originally financed by increases in accounts payable. However, it was assumed that payment for these capital assets would have to be made within 30 days, thus giving rise to a cash need. Other payables were assumed paid in 60 days. The ending balances for each account are then used in the monthly balance sheet updates and cash flow projections.

FIGURE 3

ANY INDUSTRIES, INC.
Cash Flow Projections
(000s omitted)

Inflows:	September	October	November	December	January	February
Sales	$ 705	$1,079	$1,184	$ 1,304	$ 1,420	$ 1,500
Increase A/P.	151	98	429	216	0	56
Increase debt and equity*						
Total Inflows	$ 856	$1,177	$1,613	$ 1,520	$ 1,420	$ 1,556
Outflows:						
CGS (less depreciation)	$ 549	$ 844	$ 902	$ 995	$ 1,070	$ 1,116
Other expenses	113	155	196	202	203	207
Taxes.	18	36	39	48	67	82
Increase A/R	55	379	479	225	236	196
Increase inventory	341	62	143	105	106	156
Decrease A/P	0	0	0	0	161	0
Increase capital expenditures	0	0	250	250	0	0
Principal repayments on debt	0	0	0	0	0	0
Dividends	0	0	0	0	0	0
Total Outflows	$1,076	$1,476	$2,009	$ 1,825	$ 1,843	$ 1,757
Net Change in Cash:						
Inflows less outflows	$ (220)	$ (299)	$ (396)	$ (305)	$ (423)	$ (201)
Add: Beginning cash	25	(195)	(494)	(890)	(1,195)	(1,618)
Cumulative Cash (Needs).	$ (195)	$ (494)	$ (890)	$(1,195)	$(1,618)	$(1,819)

* To be determined by viewing Cumulative Cash (Needs).

Step 3. Prepare Cash Flow Projection. Figure 3. This step is the heart of the planning operation. For Any Industries, Inc., new debt or equity requirements will be determined by the cumulative cash needs from this projection. Inflows from operations and from balance sheet changes are accumulated and offset against operational and balance sheet outflows. Operational flows are taken from the income statement projections, Figure 1. Notice that noncash outflows are not used. Thus, cost of goods sold is taken from the income statement before depreciation. For balance sheet flows, recall that if an asset increases from one period to the next this represents a use of cash and thus an outflow. If an asset decreases, this represents a conversion of an asset to cash and thus an inflow. Likewise, if a liability increases, this represents a source of cash; or if it decreases a use of cash.

Finally, outflows are netted against inflows to arrive at a cumulative cash balance. Thus, $1,819,000 cumulative need in February represents Any Industries, Inc.'s greatest need for outside cash to finance its coming expansion. It is this amount that the company will work with in Step 6 in determining sources of new funds to supply the needed cash.

FIGURE 4

ANY INDUSTRIES, INC.
Pro Forma Balance Sheet
(000s omitted)

Assets:	Balance at Prior Month	September	October	November	December	January	February
Cash	$ 25	($ 195)	($ 494)	($ 890)	($1,195)	($1,618)	($1,819)
Accounts receivable.	1,090	1,145	1,524	2,003	2,228	2,464	2,660
Inventory	1,112	1,453	1,515	1,658	1,763	1,869	2,025
Fixed assets—net	522	514	506	748	987	973	959
Total Assets.	$2,749	$2,917	$3,051	$3,519	$3,783	$3,688	$3,825
Liabilities and Net Worth:							
Accounts payable.	$1,492	$1,643	$1,741	$2,170	$2,386	$2,225	$2,281
Notes payable	600	600	600	600	600	600	600
New debt/equity	—	—	—	—	—	—	—
Capital stock.	500	500	500	500	500	500	500
Retained earnings.	157	174	210	249	297	363	444
Total Liabilities and Net Worth.	$2,749	$2,917	$3,051	$3,519	$3,783	$3,688	$3,825

Step 4. Prepare Balance Sheet Projections. Figure 4. Starting with the company's current balance sheet (Figure 4, column 1, "Balance at Prior Month") various adjustments are made from the work sheet. Notes Payable and Capital Stock were assumed to remain unchanged. The balance sheet projection plays an important

role in allowing management to check the reasonableness of various assumptions, as reviewed below.

Step 5. Prepare Summary Sheet for Cash Needs and Uses. Figure 5. In order to approach an investor successfully, management

FIGURE 5
Summary Sheet for Cash Uses (000s omitted)

	Source	Use
Cash from operations.	$ 287	
Add back noncash deductions (depreciation)	63	
Increase in accounts receivable		$1,570
Increase in inventory		913
Increase in capital equipment		500
Increase in accounts payable.	789	
Add beginning cash	25	
	$1,164	$2,983
New Cash Needs.		$1,819

must specify the uses for the cash to be invested. The method advocated here allows management to pinpoint the uses of the cash. In Step 5, cash from operations is added as a source. Noncash deductions from operational results such as depreciation are added back. The sources and uses of cash are aggregated from the balance sheet by determining the change in each account, from the current balance (column 1, Balance at Prior Month in Figure 4) to the period-end balance (column 7, Figure 4). The net cumulative cash required is then totaled, $1,819,000 for Any Industries, Inc. Aside from the amount needed, management can specify the uses directly. Of the total $2,983,000 uses of cash, $1,570,000 will be used to support increased amounts receivable, $913,000 for increased inventory, and $500,000 for fixed asset expenditures.

Step 6. Determine Portion of Total Cash Needs to Be Financed by Venture Capital. Any Industries, Inc. had never utilized accounts receivable financing. Upon consultation with a bank officer, management was informed that because of the rapid increase of new accounts, many of a marginal credit nature, the bank would finance only 45 percent of the company's accounts receivables, to a maximum of $1,100,000. The bank informed the company that it would finance $100,000 of its new fixed asset needs of $500,000 on a long-term note. This combination of $1,200,000 of new bank debt was the limit for bank-supplied funds.

Further, this new debt, when combined with the company's existing notes payable of $600,000, gave the company a debt-to-equity ratio of 2 to 1. While the bank was willing to lend on this ratio, it recommended an increase of the company's equity (or subordinate debt) to provide a cushion against unexpected cash needs resulting from the rapid increase in company volume. The company, therefore, decided to seek $650,000 venture capital to supply the difference between bank-supplied financing and its cash needs, and further to seek these funds either as equity or subordinate long-term debt.

It would be helpful to review the advantages of the six-step procedure at this point. Through this procedure management and the investor can understand what factors give rise to the cash needs since specific uses are highlighted. Because the uses are tied to the balance sheet and income statement, different outside sources of financing can be considered in the light of the company's ability to handle various types of debt. The investor is able to check the reasonableness of the assumptions used in the forecast. He can determine and question the projected growth rate in sales, assumptions about various expenses as a percent of sales, aging of receivables and payables, working capital, and debt-to-equity ratios. As an example, the investor may question whether accounts payable can increase $789,000 as shown in Figure 5. If this increase is not reasonable, a greater amount than $1,819,000 may be needed. Checking the balance sheet, (Figure 4) accounts payable, the September balance is 90 days of cost of goods sold. At the end of the six-month period it has been reduced to 61 days. Thus, instead of the $789,000 increase being an unreasonable expansion, it represents an improved position, consistent with a bank's overall requirement for an accounts receivable loan. It would be wise for the entrepreneur to do two things: first, work the projection until a point in time is reached when the cumulative cash need declines; second, work the projections more than once varying one principal assumption each time in order to better understand the implication of that assumption on the cash needs of his company, and as a consequence, where he can best focus his efforts as a manager to most positively affect his cash needs.

PREPARING THE PRIVATE PLACEMENT MEMORANDUM

Having determined the company's investment needs, the entrepreneur should prepare a written presentation designed to do two things—interest an investor in exploring the investment opportunity, and provide the investor with sufficient information to gain an initial understanding of the company. The private placement memorandum is the typical document used for these purposes.

A private placement solicitation for funds is one in which a security such as stock, warrants, or a convertible debenture is offered for value. The private placement is exempted from legal registration requirements if the offer is confined to a limited number of sophisticated investors. Although an attorney should be consulted about individuals who may be safely approached, all venture institutions usually qualify as sophisticated investors.

The entrepreneur should consider the competing roles inherent in this presentation document. It is a selling document; it embodies the corporate business plan and thus is a document supposedly representing reality; and it is also a legal document. It is a legal document in that it is the basis for the investor's decision. Charges of fraud and security violations can arise from misleading statements or omissions in this document. The following should be reviewed with these several, and sometimes competing, needs in mind.

Outline for a Private Placement Memorandum

Summary of the Company
1. Description of products or services and company's function (manufacturer, retailer, wholesaler, or . . .).
2. Significant company history.
3. Capsule statement of financial history and operating statistics.
4. Statement of company goals.

Use of Proceeds
1. The amount of money needed, the timing of that need, and a description of where the funds will be disbursed.

The Offer
(This section is optional. It should be prepared and included if you have in mind a particular structure for the investment. Most venture capitalists have their own preferences for structuring which is not uniform throughout the industry and which changes from time to time. Nevertheless, the preparation of the materials that would be included in this section should prove invaluable in bet-

ter fixing within one's own mind what one is willing to give up to attract additional capital.)

1. Proposed structure of the deal.
    a. If convertible debt; assumed interest rate, term of loan, availability of collateral, subordination assumptions, and terms of conversion (see "If equity," following).
    b. If equity; number of shares, price per share given for the proceeds, and the percentage to the total shares outstanding this represents.
    c. If a start-up; investment contribution from entrepreneur toward total capital needs.
2. Range of potential returns to investor.
    a. Range of projected net income.
    b. Reasonable multiple range to assume in a public offering.
    c. Range of rates of return on the investor's capital based on valuation of company, investor's percentage of ownership, and timing of investment and returns (see "Structuring the Deal—Rate of Return Method," below).

Business

1. Company organization.
    a. Legal structure (date and state of incorporation, legal address, etc.).
    b. Organization of functional units (e.g., administration, production, R&D, etc.) with key management noted.
2. Company history.
3. Principal products or services—include sales analysis for several years, special competitive advantages and protections, and underlying factors influencing demand. Where technical in nature, describe uses for product or service.
4. Marketing methods.
    a. General description of marketing methods, including use or not of company sales personnel versus sales representatives, advertising methods, pricing, types of buyers.
    b. Principal distributors.
    c. Principal customers.
5. Competition.
    a. Structure of industry (e.g., fragmented competition among many "mom and pop" stores accounting for 75 percent of the volume).

     b. Direct and indirect competitors (e.g., direct competition, as Hertz Rent-A-Car is to Avis, indirect, as are airlines to buses).

     c. Nature of competitive practices within industry in pricing, quality, location, advertising, services, and other key items.

6. Industry.

     a. Sales and profit record, if available, for industry for the last three years.

     b. Growth prospects and projections for industry.

     c. Technological, marketing, or other trends that might advantageously or adversely affect subject's business.

7. Production and facilities.

     a. Production methods.

     b. Problem areas in the production cycle.

     c. Quality control and reject level experience for principal products.

     d. Facilities and capacities.

     e. Analysis of fixed costs versus variable production costs.

Management

1. Resumes of key managers.
2. Remuneration of key managers and copies of employment contracts, if any.
3. Number of employees in each functional area.
4. Stock option arrangements for key managers.

Principal Stockholders

1. Number of shares, prices paid per share, and percentage ownership.

Financial Statements

1. Sales/Net Income summary for last five years—include breakdown of cost of goods, selling, and general and administrative expenses.
2. Balance sheet and income statement for last fiscal year, plus interim statements.
3. Summary of sales backlog and comparison to prior year or years.
4. Aging of accounts receivable and payable.
5. Explanation of unusual fluctuations in both income statement and balance sheet accounts.

Financial Projections

(See discussion, "Determining the Company's Financial Needs.")

Risk Factors

1. General factors concerning industry.
2. Specific factors concerning company, including any litigation and any known health problems of managers. This section should be included at the end of the presentation from a presentation viewpoint. Unless some aspect of the presentation catches the interest of the investor quickly, he may tend to screen the deal by looking for the negative aspects. After having uncovered one or more significant negative aspect he may hurriedly complete his review. Much more to the advantage of the entrepreneur is to lead with strong points. If these have merit, the investor, when encountering the negative aspect, may be in a positive frame of mind, now interested in discovering factors that outweigh these obstacles.

Miscellaneous

(Name of principal accountants, attorneys, bank officers; special studies about company, and other pertinent data.)

A good write-up will not hide mediocre company performance or business concept, but will highlight these problems more quickly for both the entrepreneur and the investor. Treating the reality of the company in an open and detailed way builds the investor's confidence. The outline given here is a checklist, not a prescription for a thesis. The entrepreneur should use ingenuity in designing the presentation to fit his needs. To increase reader interest photographs, product brochures, advertising copy, or other pictorial highlights should be included.

Having reviewed and avoided the common pitfalls in raising venture capital, determined his financial needs, and prepared a private placement memorandum, the entrepreneur is now ready to locate sources of capital.

LOCATING SOURCES OF VENTURE CAPITAL

Before considering the sources of money, the entrepreneur should consider capital substitutes. Money has been viewed philosophically as the most flexible form of power. But its ability to cause results can be achieved in other ways.

A Los Angeles-based company was formed by leveraging the expertise of several teachers who were interested in developing educational products for gifted children. Immediate income in the form of salary was not the teachers' primary motive. All worked without salary to develop products; they received instead stock in the company. Offering stock to key individuals in return for assistance is a traditional way to start a company.

In some cases barter can be a powerful resource. A start-up corporation in the process of purchasing two radio stations in the northern California area reduced its equity capital needs by trading advertising air time for various offices and furnishings.

Suppliers of raw materials may sometimes agree to be paid after the finished product is sold. A small company that originated etched wood decorative wall panels made such an arrangement with a major plywood producer. This plywood producer believed that the uniqueness and attractiveness of the product offered a new way to market its plywood. It allowed the company to order plywood by the carload from its mill, process it into etched wood wall panels, and pay for the material after receipt of payment from the customer.

In another example, a new recreational vehicle manufacturer was paid within three to ten days by its newly established dealers (each dealer was financed by its local bank with a "flooring" line). However, the manufacturer did not pay its suppliers until 120 days after delivery, on the average. At one point, the net 110 days of supplier credit represented over $600,000 of "venture" financing.

Individual Sources of Financing

An entrepreneur has access to two sources of funding from individuals: personal funds and funds from the public at large. The entrepreneur's cash may well be the most significant, if not the only, source available to many starting ventures. Other personal resources include bank borrowings against collateral, borrowings against life insurance policies, or against the equity in a house, and loans or investments from friends and relatives. The willingness of friends and relatives to lend or invest lies in their knowledge of and confidence in the individual, his experience, character, and capabilities. This knowledge reduces the risks of the unknown faced by outside investors.

The public at large represents another source, and as used here means noninstitutional private placement investors and individuals willing to invest in franchising and distributorships. Many wealthy individuals desire to invest in starting ventures. The private placement is the vehicle used to attract these potential investors. Locating wealthy individuals who may be attracted to invest in a venture is not easy. Individuals who have an interest or expertise in the functional area of the enterprise are candidates. Reputable finders can be helpful. Finders make it their business to know many potential sources of investment capital, contacts built up over time. The previously mentioned company, formed in 1971 to purchase two radio stations in northern California, was financed by the board chairman of a large transportation company. A finder was aware of the investor's interest in broadcasting and arranged the introduction. Locating a finder of good reputation and quality might seem as difficult as locating the original source of capital. However, by inquiring of commercial loan bank officers, stockbrokers, institutional venture capital sources, and other service professionals who are involved with growing companies, a number of qualified referrals can be obtained.

Franchising and distributorships are valid and creative ways to harness the financial resources of individuals who share with the entrepreneur the desire to own a business. McDonald's has thousands of franchisees who have helped finance the company's expansion by purchasing an outlet. This type of financing is best applied when the company has something of value, as a trade name or a patented product, to offer the franchisee and the franchisee has the capability to run his own business. Many books exist on the subject of franchising, as a check in the index and catalog of any library will show.

Institutional Sources of Venture Capital

Significant sources of money available and diversity of investment interests have recently emerged with the advent of institutional venture capital. Some of the first institutional sources were corporations and partnerships formed in the 1940s. Until 1958 only a handful existed. With the enactment of the Small Business Investment Act of 1958, a surge of venture capital company formations occurred as small business investment companies (SBICs). Currently there are over 300 SBICs and at least that number of additional non-SBIC venture companies.

SBICs range in size from $150,000 paid-in capital to larger companies with over $40 million in assets. By law, SBICs can invest in only "small businesses" as defined by the Small Business Investment Act and the Small Business Administration (SBA). Non-SBIC sources have a much wider range of investment potential constrained only by self-imposed limitations.

All SBICs are readily identifiable at any Small Business Administration office. The National Association of Small Business Investment Companies (NASBIC)[8] publishes a membership directory of SBIC members including over 200 SBICs and MESBICs (minority enterprise small business investment companies), representing approximately 85 percent of the industry's resources.

On the West Coast several active associations of venture capitalists exist. The membership lists of these groups, or their geographical counterparts in various areas list localized sources for venture capital.[9]

Several excellent books have been published that include both non-SBICs and SBICs. *Venture Capital*[10] lists over 400 venture companies with a brief description of whom to contact, preferred areas for investment, approximate range of financings, special help provided to the company, and some examples of recent investments. *Venture Capital, A Guidebook for New Enterprises*[11] covers 99 venture firms in the New England and New York area. It includes whom to contact, general information about the company, and individual investment approaches. Another comprehensive directory is *Guide to Venture Capital Sources*.[12] Over 600 firms are listed geographically. Preferred investment limits and areas are listed as well as an extensive bibliography of articles, books, and published studies

---

[8] The National Association of Small Business Investment Companies, 512 Washington Building, Washington, D.C., 20005.

[9] Typical venture capital associations are the Western Association of Venture Capital Companies in San Francisco (244 California St., Suite 500, San Francisco, California 94111) and the Pacific Southwest Association of SBICs (Association Secretary at First Small Business Investment Company of California, 333 South Hope St., Los Angeles, California 90017).

[10] *Venture Capital* published by Technimetrics, Inc., 919 Third Avenue, New York, New York 10022.

[11] *Venture Capital, A Guidebook for New Enterprises.*

[12] Rubel (ed.), *Guide to Venture Capital Sources.*

about venture capital. This book is recommended to the serious fund seeker.

Corporations as a Source of Financing

Many operating corporations make venture investments for a variety of reasons: gaining access to emerging technologies, assisting in corporate diversification plans, or providing the potential for a high return on investment. Corporations active as investors at various times include Hercules, Borden, Dow Chemical, Singer, Alcoa, Boise Cascade, Coca-Cola, Du Pont, Ford, General Electric, International Paper, Mobil Oil, Standard Oil, General Mills, Exxon, and Union Carbide, to name a few. Corporations as a source are hard to categorize since some corporations that have gained a reputation for venturing in the past are no longer active, and many more are not visible as venture sources but will venture if an appropriate deal is shown to them. A rule of thumb can only suffice in this area —the entrepreneur should approach those corporations that could logically benefit from the venture. But he should be cautioned that ultimate acquisition of the venture may be a goal.

An Emerging Source of Venture Capital

A new source of quasi-venture capital may be emerging under the auspices of the SBA. Small businesses not qualifying for conventional long-term bank financing can seek an SBA-guaranteed loan. This is a regular loan funded by a bank, but guaranteed by the SBA. The company has to fall within the SBA's definition of a "small business." Roughly, the company would be eligible to be considered if it was in retailing or a service business and had less than $1 million in sales for the last fiscal year, or if in wholesaling or manufacturing, less than $5 million or less than 250 employees (manufacturing only). The business must not be in a prohibited area such as sale of alcoholic beverages. Based on the SBA's analysis and bank's recommendation, the SBA will guarantee up to $350,000, requiring the bank to risk at least 10 percent of the funding, for a total availability of $388,000. The bank can fund a greater amount than $388,000, but its percentage guarantee will be less.

This program is still evolving. In mid-1973, the SBA issued guidelines necessary for nonbank funding sources to receive the SBA's guarantee. Based on the large number of applicants seeking to become approved funding sources, we may witness an additional source of expansion capital in the coming years.

Investor Preferences

Locating sources of venture capital in itself is not enough since all sources will have investment preferences and dislikes. It is important to know at what stage of company development the venture capital company will invest. The process can be put in context by examining the stages of corporate development as delineated in *Venture Capital, A Guidebook for New Enterprises.*

> *Stage Zero.* Usually at Stage Zero some monies (usually the principal's own) have been invested, a great deal of effort (on a part-time basis) has been expended, and a prototype may have been developed. Or it is possible that only the time and effort required to organize and plan for the new enterprise have been expended prior to entering Stage I.
>
> *Stage I.* Stage I is the start-up phase. It is during this period that the operation is formalized and the product or service is developed and produced. This start is made with seed capital which can come from a number of diverse sources.
>
> *Stage II.* This stage occurs when the company has built up a bit of a track record. It has moved through the initial growth phase and some of the conventional techniques of investment analysis can be applied to it. At this point the company has developed capital equipment and can begin to plan for long-term growth.
>
> *Stage III.* Further expansion is warranted due to favorable indications regarding the company's potential. The quantities of funds required are much greater than those raised in the earlier stages and the early investors are seeking both realized gains and liquidity. It is at this point that the public equity offering is usually made for the dual purpose of raising additional funds for the company (primary offering) and enabling the initial investors to realize a gain by selling a portion of their shares (secondary offering).
>
> *Stage IV.* The mature company has established itself and become a viable corporation.[13]

The entrepreneur should approach venture capitalists who have a preference for the functional area of his interest. The NASBIC and Rubel guides give 12 preference codes for the listed venture

---

[13] *Venture Capital, A Guidebook for New Enterprises.*

capital companies. These lists are interesting in what they detail and what they treat generally. Below is the list in Rubel's guide.

Industry Preferences

1. Communications.
2. Construction and development.
3. Natural resources.
4. Hotels, motels, and restaurants.
5. Manufacturing and processing (general).
6. Medical products manufacturers and distributors.
7. Recreation and leisure time companies.
8. Research and technology (electronics).
9. Retailing, wholesaling, and distributing.
10. Service business.
11. Pollution control, ecology, and oceanography.
12. Diversified.[14]

In further determining a venture group's characteristics, reference should be made to their preferred investment amounts, both maximums and minimums. Rubel's guide distinguishes among investor's preferences as follows:

A—up to $100,000
B—up to $250,000
C—up to $500,000
D—up to $1,000,000
E—over $1,000,000[15]

The entrepreneur should cautiously screen venture sources with respect to their preferred limits for investment. Most clearly a request for $3 million would find little likelihood of success among "A" classified investors. However, "C" or "D" companies might prove good sources. First Small Business Investment Company of California is a good example. It has a house limit of investing up to $1 million in any one deal. However, if a $2 million request is made by a company in which it desires to invest, it will help introduce, at no cost, the remaining $1 million among interested institutional colleagues.

The liquidity of the venture group at the time of inquiry will influence its interest in the deal. The entrepreneur will have to determine this factor through inquiry of each venture firm.

---

[14] Rubel (ed.), *Guide to Venture Capital Sources.*
[15] Ibid.

Finally, many venture firms have developed an expertise in one or more functional areas such as high technology, retailing, or the construction industry. This existing understanding of an area can be invaluable. Lack of knowledge about an area tends to increase perceptions of risk. If the venture capitalist is familiar with the industry and its key factors, he will be more likely to accede to a strong contender's financial request. If the venture capitalist has in his portfolio similar investments to the one for which funds are being sought, it would be indicative of interest in the industry.

Once a number of appropriate sources have been identified, the entrepreneur encounters the critical procedure of dealing with the venture capitalist.

DEALING WITH THE VENTURE CAPITALIST

Making the Initial Contact

Having located the names of likely sources of venture capital, through the various directories or an intermediary, the entrepreneur may ask: What is the best approach for introduction—one of initial contact by the entrepreneur, or contact through an accountant, lawyer, finder, investment banker, or other person familiar with "whom to talk with" in any given firm? In many instances the benefit of an introduction is not worth the price. Value usually comes from locating sources of capital one would not otherwise have been aware of, or from assistance in preparing a presentation. Once the overtures have been made, an investor will consider the merits of the proposal regardless of who introduced the deal.

The entrepreneur with an ongoing business often seeks an initial meeting "at the plant" before submitting a written proposal. The entrepreneur is wise to push for such a meeting. Initial enthusiasm for the management team and a first-hand feeling for the results embodied in the financial statements may cause the investor to proceed further in his investigation. On the other hand, the investor will not make plant visits on every inquiry, for the sake of his own efficiency. The investor's acceptance of an invitation to visit the plant generally depends on his interest in a few key items such as product area, results to date, backlog, or other strengths of the proposal. The entrepreneur should be prepared to supply this information before a visit by the potential investor.

There are several reasons for and against approaching a number of venture capital sources at the same time. To increase the chances of funding, the entrepreneur should not initially rely on any one source. The investor, because of the large number of proposals he sees, tends to defer some deals. Knowledge that he is in competition, *within reasonable bounds,* may increase the chances of his giving the proposal early consideration. Although most investors will not willingly become involved in a bidding contest over a deal, the entrepreneur can benefit from having several different offers to choose among. Therefore, in making a selection of investors to approach it would be wise to select representatives of the different types: wealthy individuals, SBICs, private venture capitalists, and other large institutions. Fairness demands that the venturer be told that other sources are being considered when that is the case.

There are risks to "shopping" a deal. Depending on the opportunity and who is being consulted, the investor may wish to await the results of competing analyses before proceeding. Management also runs the risk of lack of investor enthusiasm if a financing deal may be completed by a competing venture capital source. The investor is not inclined to spend investigatory time where there is little hope for concluding a deal.

Analyzing the Deal

Most venture capital investors have a strong aversion to risk. Their screening and analysis procedure is designed to minimize two types of risks: (1) risk of the unknown that can cause loss of capital and (2) risk of loss of time spent on unproductive projects.

Risk of the unknown is both the risk of not perceiving those key elements for success in a business, and the risk of not knowing the outcome of events on issues raised. The investor can control the risk of uncovering all key factors for success and related issues by educating himself about the people, the company, and the industry. The risk of unknown outcomes from future events can only be hedged against over time through contingent planning by capable management.

Counterbalancing the need for extensive education is the risk that the investor may spend an inordinate amount of time investigating a deal that may not be consummated. This risk of time lost on unproductive projects causes the investor to educate himself efficiently, through screening out much information not considered immediately valuable. This tug-of-war between the need for extensive education and the need for intensive education has evolved the screening and analysis procedures of the institutional investor, typically as outlined here:

Conducting the Initial Screening. Much of the initial screening is done on an informal basis. A telephone conversation will qualify a large number of requests. Of those resulting in submission of a proposal, only a handful will intrigue the venture capitalist enough for the next stage of review.

Conducting the Secondary Screening. Here the venture capitalist has usually convinced himself that a fairly extensive investigation is warranted. An initial meeting with the management team will occur, either at the plant or in the venture capitalist's office. Extensive details will be requested covering such things outlined in the section "Preparing the Private Placement Memorandum." Back-up documents will be sought to verify key elements of the proposal. Supplemental information will be requested, such as the following:

1. Research reports on the industry.
2. Prospectuses and annual reports of competitors.
3. Internal control reports from auditors.
4. List of customers and creditors for reference checks.
5. IRS reports on any tax audits.
6. Names and phone numbers of former employers for reference checks.
7. Home address and social security number of managers for the purpose of credit checks.

In short, the secondary screening process encompasses the gathering and verification of information so that the investor can feel comfortable about making an offer.

Conducting the Final Analysis. Assuming a meeting of minds on both the proposal and the structure of the deal (to be discussed), the final analysis ensues. This analysis encompasses the completion of verifications started in the secondary process, the gathering of final documents such as certified statements to replace ones prepared by management, and the preparation of needed legal documents. If the venture group is an institutional one requiring board approval, a final presentation would be submitted to the board for approval.

A certain amount of irrationality exists in the process. Personality conflicts between the investor and entrepreneur can cause rejection of an otherwise good venture. If the venture organization is large, the personal dislikes of one investor may cause the premature rejection of a proposal that might have fared better had another individual been approached. It is hard to avoid this outcome. One can only try to present his best and be sensitive to the reactions he receives. If difficulties are perceived often they can be solved through further discussion.

Structuring the Deal

At some point the venture capitalist will have made a decision that if the company and management check out, if the problem areas uncovered can be corrected, and if no unforeseen problems arise, negotiations should be initiated toward structuring the deal. This process will usually start before the intensive analysis is much under way, since failure to reach agreement on basic terms will stop investigations before management and the venture capitalist waste inordinate amounts of time.

It is in structuring the deal that factors such as the amount of investment, the form of investment vehicle, required controls, the amount of stock required, and pricing will be negotiated.

Most venture sources have a ceiling on the amount they will invest in any one company. If the company's request exceeds this ceiling and analysis demonstrates that a smaller amount or combination of conventional financing and venture monies will not suffice, the venture group must decide whether or not to syndicate the deal to others in the venture capital community. This decision is based on the venture group's willingness to spend the time and make the effort to syndicate the deal (usually at no charge to the company), participate as part of a group, and assume partial responsibilities for analysis and follow-up. The company must decide whether the venture group is strong enough to attract other partners. The company must be concerned with the extra time and resources it now needs to bring several different groups to agree to invest. In some instances a syndicate will be to the company's advantage if the presence of several well-respected venture groups helps bring in other groups. On the other hand, flexibility in negotiating price is lost since interested venture groups will either join on the basis of the lead investor's structure of the deal or perhaps insist on more stringent terms.

The form of investment preferred by many venture capitalists is the convertible debenture. A debenture is a debt instrument containing protective provisions but usually without a specific lien on any asset. Conversion features provide that some or all of the debenture may be converted into some number of shares at a given conversion price. A nonconvertible debenture with warrants can also provide the equity needed, but suffers in that the time period of ownership before freely trading the underlying stock under Rule 144 (Securities Act of 1933) does not start running until the warrant is exercised.

The advantages to the venture capitalist of using a convertible debenture rather than common stock are many, including the ability to build in debenture controls without taking stock control, greater flexibility in determining the amount of equity and the pricing per share and better provision for the return of invested capital should the company not achieve all that was hoped for.

A minority shareholder has little leverage to influence management if the business starts to have significant problems. By structuring the investment in the form of a debenture, the investor can include those restrictions necessary to safeguard the investment. Typical restrictions might include one or more of the following:

1. Maintenance of a minimum net worth, working capital position, and certain "critical" ratios.
2. Restriction on dividend payments.
3. Restrictions on acquisition or disposition of fixed assets.
4. Restrictions on certain types of expenses, such as research and development.
5. Restrictions on mergers or acquisitions.
6. Provisions to limit salaries and benefits paid top management.
7. Restrictions on further pledges of assets as collateral.

These restrictions can be incorporated in the debenture in various forms, but are difficult to include in a stock purchase agreement because of the inability to provide an effective remedy for the breach of a provision.

If the company is a start-up, a pure equity investment in common stock might be more advantageous since no cash drain occurs for interest payments or debt amortization, and the equity base can be used for leverage to secure bank debt. However, the convertible debenture can be tailored to accomplish these goals through arrangements for a suspension of interest and payments on debt during the early critical periods, and long payout terms.

Determining the amount of stock to be exchanged or converted for the financing and its price hinges on expectations of return and risk. The following procedures may be used to determine the amount of ownership and pricing of stock to structure an attractive offer:

Method 1. Price/Earnings Multiple Method. First, compare the company to similar public companies. Such comparison should be conducted on the basis of similarity of balance sheet ratios, income statement margins and levels of expense, share of market served, gross sales per employee, assets per employee, asset turnover, and other generally accepted measures of efficiency. Then determine a comparable P/E (price to earnings ratio), assuming that a 25 to 50 percent discount should be given for letter stock. Apply this adjusted multiple to current earnings per share and divide the resulting stock price into the amount of funds sought to determine the number of shares to be issued. A comparison of this number of shares to the new total of shares outstanding (current outstanding plus this new amount to be issued to the investor) will show the percentage of the company that must be negotiated.

Method 2. Rate of Return Method. Estimate the rate of return range required. Most investors seek a 25 to 80+ percent compound rate of return depending upon the riskiness of the company.

Translate the desired return into the amount of ownership required by one of two ways: use an actual Rate of Return Range method; or use a Factor of Return method. The following illustrate the mechanics of determining ownership from these two methods.

Example 1. Rate of Return Range. Figure 6 illustrates this method, as well as other principles used in pricing a deal. In this example a company requested $1 million long-term debt at 10 percent interest. The company was agreeable to a convertible debenture but would look to the investor for guidance in establishing the amount of equity at conversion and the conversion price to make it an attractive investment. After studying the company and its management, the investor judged that a return between 35 and 50 percent would be acceptable in relation to risks assumed. Further, he assumed that the company would reach the position for a public

FIGURE 6
Deal Pricing Work Sheet—Rate of Return Range (000s omitted)

	(1) Percent of Forecast	(2) NPAT	(3) P/E	(4) Total Company Value	(5) Investor Owner- ship (percent)	(6) No. of Shares to Investor	(7) Cost of Conver- sion	(8) Investor's Share of Total Value	(9) Total Investor Return	(10) ROI (Per- cent)
1. NPAT with $1,000...........	100	$1,525	15	$22,875	8	69,565	$800	$1,830	$2,030	43
2. NPAT without $1,000...........	100	1,000	12	12,000						

offering within two years. The investor would charge a 10 percent interest, a rate above the then prime rate. Because interest rates were considered high at 10 percent, the investor believed that any portion of the remaining debt after cost of conversion would very likely be repaid, either from the proceeds of underwriting or from refinancing at a lower interest rate. The investor had requested that management prepare an income statement forecast for each of the next two years, including the effect of the $1 million financing, and without its effect.

An investor might utilize a work sheet as in Figure 6 to assist in structuring a conversion amount and price as follows. First, the investor must either reforecast net profit after tax (NPAT) based on assumptions he feels more comfortable with, or accept those given by management. Here NPAT the second year is of key concern since it is this year the company is aiming for a public offering. Column 2, line 1 shows forecasted income of $1,525,000 with the use of $1,000,000 debenture capital (and possibly additional bank leverage because of the subordination of the debenture to bank debt). Next the investor used a best guess as to a multiple the company could expect, here 15 times earnings as in column 3, line 1. Multiplying total earnings times the multiple gives the company's valuation of $22,875,000, column 4, line 3. The investor had been advised management would not accept dilution above 15 percent. Accepting a lower percentage, an 8 percent interest to the investor was tried to see its effect on the investor's return on investment. Eight hundred thousand shares are assumed to be outstanding. The investor must divide the shares outstanding (800,000) by 92 percent to find out the new total of shares of which he will receive 8 percent. Column 6, line 1 shows that the investor will receive 69,565 shares representing 8 percent of the new total shares after his dilution (800,000/.92 = 869,565 × .08 = 69,565).

Next the cost of conversion must be determined. Since the investor does not yet know his rate of return from owning 8 percent of the market value of the company, he can choose a cost of conversion somewhat at will to see the combined effect of number of shares and return of debt (corollary to cost of conversion) on his total return on investment. Taking into account the $200,000 interest earned on the $1,000,000, the net investment of $800,000 obtained 8 percent of the total number of shares which equals 69,565 shares. Hence the investor paid $800,000 ÷ 69,565 or $11.50 per share. The total market value of $22,875,000 divided by the total number of shares 869,565 indicates a market value of $26.31 per share for which the investor paid $11.50 per share.

At this point the investor can determine the rate of return. Column 8, line 1 shows he will receive $1,830,000 for his 8 percent share of the total value of $22,875,000. Adding the interest return of $200,000 on debt, the investor's total return is $2,030,000, column 9, line 1. Use present value tables or other convenient means to determine the rate of return as 42.5 or approximately 43 percent. Note that interest earned at 10 percent was excluded from returns since the investor's cost of capital and administration just about negate this return.

If the investor wishes, the formula to determine compound rate of return can be used as follows:

$$0 = I - \frac{R_1}{(1 + r_1)^1} + \cdots + \frac{R_N}{(1 + r_N)N}$$

where

R = Return in relevant time period
r = ROI
N = Number of time periods, starting with 1 and progressing by units to last period
I = Initial outlay

To use this formula, an r is guessed as to most probably being the true rate of return, and plugged through the formula. If the result is not 0, then r is re-guessed and reworked through to finally approach 0; e.g.,

$$0 = \$1,000,000 - \frac{0}{(1.43)^1} + \frac{2,030,000}{(1.43)^2}$$

The 43 percent return is well within the range acceptable to the investor. However, the investor will probably apply various other tests to determine whether the share number and cost is acceptable. The investor might ask what value the company must reach for the investor to break even on his 8 percent investment. By dividing the $800,000 cost of conversion by the 8 percent share interest to be received, the investor can determine that the company must reach a value of at least approximately $10,000,000 for his 8 percent to return $800,000. A variety of lesser net income or multiples (than assumed in the example yielding a $22,875,000 value) will produce a market value of $10,000,000, all of which may be highly attainable by the company if problems do occur. The company's current net worth can be matched against this $10,000,000 value to gauge how close to this value the company already is, just in current net worth.

Another test might be for the investor to match the share of the company he is receiving in relation to his contribution of cash to the new effective net worth. In this case, assume that the new effective net worth of the company is $4,000,000, $3,000,000 existing net worth plus the addition of the $1,000,000 "quasi-" equity (money effectively like equity since totally at risk since subordinate to all other debt, like shareholder's equity). Here the investor is contributing 25 percent of the new capital base, but only receiving 8 percent of the company. The investor may wish to adjust his percentage to more equitably align his reward to match his contribution.

The investor will be interested in noting the multiple he is to pay for his 8 percent share. To determine this the investor would divide his forecasted value of the company by the new number of shares outstanding, to give the implied value per share of the company. In this example it would be $26.30 per share ($22,875,000/869,565). Then by dividing this share price by the current earnings per share he can compare the resulting multiple with current market valuations. Here, assuming earnings per share of $0.80, the investor would be paying 33 times current earnings. This may be much too high a multiple and cause the investor to adjust his share of the company higher, or cost lower, or both.

After trying various ownership shares and costs given these various tests, a final percent and cost will be settled upon by the investor. He must now test to make sure that the company's shareholders are better off by taking his offer than not. By taking the forecast supplied by the investor as to the net income level of the company in two years without the infusion of $1,000,000, a value of the company based on some multiple can be determined. Assuming a multiple of 12x, column 3, line 2, a total company value of $12,000,000 is determined, column 4, line 2. Assume that the investor had finally chosen 15 percent of the company as the share necessary to meet his various criteria. By multiplying the $22,875,000 company value with the infusion of cash by 85 percent, the remaining amount owned by existing shareholders, the investor can see that shareholder's value is $19,443,750, or substantially above $12,000,000 they would have if they did not take the cash. In fact, the investor may use this type of analysis to show that the maximum acceptable dilution of 15 percent might be too restrictive, and that shareholders can accept more dilution and still be better off than in not doing any deal.

One final variation is worth mentioning. The investor may structure a deal in which the number of shares and cost is based on the achievement of various profit levels. In this way the investor may be able to accommodate the company's desire for lesser dilution if it reaches forecasted profit levels. However, if management falls far short, by receiving a greater number of shares at a lower cost, the investor is not penalized for accepting bad management forecasts. The investor provides management the incentive for achieving its own forecasts while achieving a more consistent rate of return over a broader range of earnings.

Example 2. Factor of Returns Method. This example is the same as the previous one except management assumed that an investor would seek a return of five times his investment within three to five years.

Investment required ($1,000,000) multiplied by factor of returns greater than investment (5) equals total return required ($5,000,000).

Total return required divided by projected value of company in third to fifth years equal percentage ownership needed to realize return.

Time	Total Return Value of Company	Percent of Owner-ship Given Up
3d year	$\dfrac{\$5,000,000}{\$34,312,000}$	15%
4th year	$\dfrac{\$5,000,000}{\$42,890,000}$	12%
5th year	$\dfrac{\$5,000,000}{\$49,323,500}$	10%

In Example 2 the range of rate of return was between 71 percent to 38 percent for an investment that returns five times itself in three to five years. One should note the substantial decline in return as time passes. Figure 7 illustrates the relationship between the factor of returns to rates of return, in effect emphasizing the relationship of timing of returns on the overall rate of return.

FIGURE 7
Translation of Factor of Returns Greater Than
Investment into a Rate of Return (percent)

Factor \ Year	1	2	3	4	5
1	0	–	–	–	–
2	100	41	26	19	15
3	200	73	44	32	25
4	300	100	59	41	32
5	400	124	71	50	38
6	500	145	82	57	43
7	600	165	91	63	48
8	700	183	100	68	52
9	800	200	108	73	55
10	900	216	115	78	58
11	1000	232	122	82	62
12	1100	246	129	86	64
13	1200	261	135	90	67
14	1300	274	141	93	70
15	1400	287	147	97	72

Continuing Relationships

Most venture groups prefer to play a passive role in the ongoing management of the company. If all is well with the company's progress, the venture group will monitor this performance by a monthly review of financial statements and other key data pertaining to the specific company and industry. The investor may advise the company on specific problems and contribute his thinking to the policy formation of the company. He is often well qualified, having seen numerous other businesses resolve similar problems. The venture capitalist may aid the business to increase its bank credit lines and other long-term debt, and establish relationships and assist in negotiations with underwriters to facilitate public offerings.

If performance falters, and especially if the investment falls into jeopardy, the venture capitalist may play a more active role in helping make key business decisions. As an example, if management is ineffective in areas of cost control, the investor may help the company find a competent chief financial officer. If current operations are not yielding satisfactory returns, the investor may help devise plans to curtail expansion, stop acquisitions or diversifications, or arrange divestments until current operations are in order. In the extreme, if the company is approaching insolvency, the investor may lead the effort to turn the situation around, or consolidate operations to effect a better yield from liquidation of assets. Some venture firms charge for consulting, but most do not, believing their just reward comes from stock appreciation.

It is important for the company to live up to the terms of agreement with the investor. Also important is the continuing effort to keep the investor informed and aware of the company's changing environment. Special care should be taken to supply all required information, observe the warranties and covenants, and avoid events that could precipitate a default in the debenture. If a breach of a provision should be imminent or actually occur, management should promptly counsel with the investor to gain his understanding and support. Surprisingly, many companies promptly forget these requirements after closing the deal. The ensuing breakdown in communication leads to discord between the investor and the company. In addition to the required information it is often wise to ask for an informal meeting with the investors at which the current developments of the company can be reviewed. This type of working relationship fosters mutual respect for the working style and needs of both groups and promotes accommodations on issues of mutual concern. If the company manages its relations well, the venture capitalist can be a source of informed and seasoned judgment in helping the company grow and prosper.

ADDITIONAL SOURCES

Archer, S. H., and Faerber, L. G. "Firm Size and the Cost of Externally Secured Equity Capital." *Journal of Finance,* 21 (March 1966), 69–83.

Brigham, E. F., and Smith, K. V. "The Cost of Capital to the Small Firm." *Engineering Economist,* 13 (Fall 1967), 1–26.

Davis, R. D. "Small Business in the Next Decade." *Advanced Management Journal,* 31 (January 1966), 5–8.

Dominguez, John R. *Venture Capital.* Lexington, Mass.: D. C. Heath, 1974.

Guttentag, J. M., and Herman, E. S. "Do Large Banks Neglect Small Business?" *Journal of Finance,* 21 (September 1966), 535–38.

Martin, D. "Can Edge Act Companies Have a Venture Capital Strategy?" *Columbia Journal of World Business,* 4 (November 1969), 73–80.

Nantell, Timothy. "Equivalence of Lease vs. Buy Analyses." *Financial Management,* 2 (Autumn 1973), 39–44.

Pfeffer, Irving. *The Financing of Small Business.* New York: Macmillan, 1967.

Rubel, S. M. "Important Changes Occur in Venture Capital Industry." *Bankers Monthly,* 87 (May 1970), 24–25.

Sholes, Stephen. "The Search for Venture Capital." *Financial Executive,* 42 (August 1974), 46–59.

Steiner, George. "Approaches to Long-Range Planning for Small Business." *California Management Review,* 10 (Fall 1967), 3–16.

Stoll, Hans R., and Curley, Anthony J. "Small Business and the New Issues Market for Equities." *Journal of Financial and Quantitative Analysis,* 5 (September 1970), 309–22.

Chapter 40

Going Public

John S. R. Shad[*]

THE MARKET for initial public offerings is more volatile than the stock market in general. In bear markets it is next to impossible to do initial public offerings on reasonable terms. For example, there was virtually no market for initial public offerings during the 1973–74 bear market.

This chapter describes the requirements, advantages, disadvantages, and cost of going public when market conditions are favorable. It also describes how investment bankers appraise corporations for public offerings, mergers, and acquisitions. It seeks to provide answers to such questions as how large should a company be before it can effectively make an initial public offering of its common stock? What are the advantages and disadvantages of "going public"? What are the costs involved? What is my company's stock worth? It is the purpose of this chapter to answer these and other questions commonly raised by officers, directors, and major stockholders of closely held companies.

THE REQUIREMENTS

There are two fundamental reasons for "going public." One is to raise cash. The other is to create a readily marketable security—a

---
[*] John S. R. Shad is vice chairman of the board of E. F. Hutton & Company, New York.

security which the investing public can buy or sell in reasonable quantity over a reasonable period of time without materially disrupting the market; a security the company can use to raise additional funds or to acquire other companies; and which can be used to attract and hold able executives through stock options.

Such a security should enjoy a *representative public market*—one that is sufficiently broad and active so that the price fairly reflects the investment merits of the security relative to comparable investment opportunities. Therefore, the company must have a sufficient following among stockbrokers and the investing public at large so that if the market price of the security falls below comparable investment opportunities, it will attract buyers and be brought back into line.

As a general rule, the minimum size initial offering necessary to establish a representative market is $5 million—typically 500,000 shares at $10 per share. Such an offering might of course only represent a small portion of the issuing company's total shares outstanding following the offering. The balance would continue to be held by the original stockholders. While a small offering, a $5 million issue should result in more than 2,500 public stockholders. National and leading regional underwriting firms should participate with the managing underwriter in the offering in order to assure a broad distribution and the continuing support and sponsorship of the securities by an important segment of the financial community. The offering should not be concentrated in the issuing company's "backyard," for it will not result in a representative market. Further, as the result of the activities of local security dealers and investors, the tendency is for the stock to gravitate back to the area in which the company is best known. This desirable after-issue market-buying support should not be dissipated by saturating the local market on the initial offering.

In order for a company to do a $5 million initial public offering, it must generally have an established position within its industry, clearly defined future prospects, capable management in reasonable depth and sufficient size, and financial resources reasonably to assure its continued successful operations in the face of possible economic adversities, competitive pressures, and the normal vicissitudes of business. While there are no absolute mathematical standards, such companies will generally have net income after taxes of over $1 million and a favorable operating experience of at least five years.

Of course, the larger and more successful a company, the more suitable it is for public finance, and the larger the offering, the broader the distribution, and the more active and representative the after-issue market.

If a company is not large enough to permit a national distribution of its shares, it would be well advised to exhaust alternative sources of finance, rather than do a limited public offering. Premature public offerings do not result in a representative market and the high effective costs (often in excess of 20 percent of the funds raised) seriously limit the benefits to be derived by the issuer from the offering. Desirable alternative sources of capital may include the sale and leaseback of fixed assets, loans from banks, insurance companies, pension funds and others, investments by business associates and venture capital groups, and mergers with related operations or companies which are already publicly owned. Leading investment banking firms assist both large and small companies in raising capital on a private placement basis and in mergers.

ADVANTAGES AND DISADVANTAGES OF GOING PUBLIC

A public offering might consist of: (a) authorized but unissued shares for the purpose of providing the company with funds to expand its operations or retire senior obligations; (b) shares held by the company's existing stockholders, in which case the proceeds would go to such stockholders, and not to the company; or (c) a combination of both unissued and selling-stockholders' shares.

Corporate Advantages of Public Ownership

Advantages which accrue to a company (and indirectly its stockholders) from a public offering and the establishment of a broad public market in the stock include the following:

1. Additional capital is obtained with which to expand the business or retire senior obligations.

2. By thus broadening its equity base, a company can generally increase its bank lines of credit and obtain substantial additional long-term loans from other institutional lenders on better terms than would otherwise be the case. It can also generally obtain better terms on leases, installment purchases, and similar contracts.

3. Once a representative public market has been established in the common stock of a company which does well over the years, substantial additional capital can generally be raised from the public and institutional investors on increasingly favorable terms, not only through the sale of common stock, but also through the sale of bonds, debentures, preferred stocks, and convertible securities. Thus, a marketable common stock substantially increases management's financing alternatives—both in terms of the needs of the business and the class of security which currently enjoys the most favorable market.

4. Able executives can be attracted and held with stock options—and often on better terms than with cash alone. Few medium-sized companies can compete with the nation's largest corporations on a straight salary basis for capable executives. They can, however, compete with stock options which afford executives the opportunity to build their estates. An able executive can have a dramatic impact upon the profits of a medium-sized company and, as a consequence, the market value of its stock—and his options. However, such an individual is not likely to have as dramatic an effect upon the profits or market value of a substantially larger corporation.

5. A company's growth can be accelerated through corporate acquisitions involving the issuance of securities, rather than cash. Such acquisitions can be effected through the issuance of debt or equity securities, and if effected through an exchange of shares, they are tax free. Although few company owners are willing to merge into closely held concerns and accept nonmarketable minority interests, they seldom object to becoming minority investors in publicly owned companies.

6. "Going public" is a major step in the corporate growth process. It enhances a company's image and public following.

7. A company's stock is often purchased by its customers, suppliers, officers, employees, and friends and business associates of the management. The interest of these important groups in a company's profits, products, and continued success is thus significantly stimulated.

8. Public stockholders are also an important element in supporting or opposing legislative and other measures affecting a company.

9. A public offering permits a company to do a broad national

public relations job with important segments of the economy. This includes the financial community, institutional investors, and the investing public at large. Thousands of copies of the company's prospectus are distributed to such individuals and concerns throughout the nation. The prospectus provides an effective means of projecting a company's image in well-documented facts. It becomes the basic reference document on the company. Statements it contains are incorporated in reports and write-ups on the company by investment firms, financial manuals (Moody's, Standard & Poor's, Dun and Bradstreet, and so on), the financial and trade press, and others.

10.   The ready availability of information on publicly owned companies generally results in greater exposure to business opportunities and better press relations and coverage.

Stockholder Advantages of Public Offerings

The advantages to a closely held company's stockholders of a public offering and the establishment of a broad public market in the stock include the following:

1.   Many contend that it is not prudent for the owner-managers of a company to have both their capital (as represented by their ownership of the company) and their employment income largely, if not entirely, dependent upon the fortunes of a single business. It often makes sense for them to sell a portion of their stock to the public and invest the proceeds in a diversified portfolio of high-quality stocks and bonds.

2.   A public market minimizes estate tax problems upon the untimely death of a principal. Such taxes can be met from the proceeds of a prior offering or the sale of a portion of the decedent's shares to the investing public at large, without withdrawing any funds from the business itself.

3.   A public market simplifies appraisal problems in connection with gift and inheritance taxes, mergers, and consolidations.

4.   A public market permits the existing stockholders to sell their shares at the most opportune times in terms of their personal needs, taxes, market conditions, and other considerations.

5.   A public market alleviates minority stockholder problems. When a company is closely held, minority stockholders sometimes harass management. Since such harassment, and sometimes litiga-

tion, diverts management's time from directing a company's profitable operations, both groups generally benefit from the establishment of a public market in which the minority shareholders can readily sell their shares.

6.   All other things being equal, the mere conversion of a nonmarketable interest into a marketable interest enhances its value.

Disadvantages of Public Ownership

The major disadvantages of becoming a publicly owned company include the following:

1.   Through family trusts, partnerships, multiple corporate and other arrangements, it is sometimes possible for the owner-managers of closely held companies to minimize their personal and corporate income taxes. However, careful analysis often discloses that such measures merely result in temporary deferment, rather than permanent avoidance of taxes. Consequently, this is an area in which owner-managers should proceed with caution so as not to work themselves into inextricable positions which preclude the greater long-term advantages of public ownership to themselves, members of their families, and their companies.

2.   Publicly owned companies have greater exposure to derivative suits by dissident stockholders if there is evidence of so-called insider dealings or conflicts of interest with the company's management. In addition to the legal exposure, such actions damage a company's public image and investors' confidence. For these reasons, all interests of the owner-managers and members of their families which are related to the company's operations should generally be consolidated into the prospective public company prior to the offering.

3.   Publicly owned companies, their officers, directors, and major stockholders, become subject to certain reporting, proxy, trading, and other regulations. For example, "controlling" stockholders (within the meaning of the Securities Act) are limited as to the number of shares they can sell on the open market at a given time without registering them with the Securities and Exchange Commission. Also, officers, directors, and individuals who own more than 10 percent of the outstanding shares are required to report their purchases and sales of the stock, and they can be required to

turn over to the company so-called short-swing profits (i.e., profits realized through the purchase and sale of the stock within a six-month period).

4. Closely held companies can be informally directed; whereas, public ownership entails more formal board and stockholders' meetings, annual and interim reports. Financial and other data must also be made public; however, a publicly owned company is not generally required to disclose information which could be used prejudicially against it by its competitors.

5. If over half of a company's shares are sold to the public, the original owners could lose control; however, initial public offerings seldom result in the public holding over half of a company's outstanding common stock, and even if such were the case, the shares sold to the public are very broadly distributed in small amounts. Many publicly owned companies are effectively controlled by managements which hold a negligible percentage of the outstanding shares. In most instances, it can be statistically demonstrated that it would be prohibitively expensive for an outside group to attempt to acquire control of a company.

The original stockholders receive the fair cash value of the shares sold, which can of course be invested in other securities which may enjoy even greater future appreciation in value than the shares sold. Further, a well-conceived public offering should result in the original stockholders retaining a smaller but more marketable interest in a company, with improved prospects. The original stockholders' total net worth should thus be enhanced in value.

THE COST

An additional disadvantage is the cost of "going public." Generally, the larger an underwriting, the lower the cost when expressed as a percentage of the principal amount of the offering. In the case of initial public offerings of $5 million to $20 million, the discount to the underwriters will generally range between 5 percent and 8 percent, depending upon the size and nature of the offering, the issuing company's operating record and capital structure, market conditions, and other considerations. The issuer also incurs legal, printing, and other expenses which vary with the size and nature of the offering. As a general rule, the total expenses to be borne by the issuer including the underwriting discount, will range from 7 percent to 10 percent of the principal amount of $5 million to $20 million initial public offerings.

HOW INVESTMENT BANKERS APPRAISE CORPORATIONS

It should be borne in mind that the investment banker and corporate issuer do not merely join forces for a single financing. Their relationship is a continuing one aimed at satisfying the common objectives of a successful initial public offering of the company's securities; a favorable after-issue market; sound financial planning; and the long-term success of the business. The investment banker's contribution to these objectives is a product of his ability to appraise his corporate client.

Evaluation of the Company's Financial Statements

The initial area of inquiry is typically a company's financial statements—its balance sheets and operating statements over a period of years. Such statements are generally accompanied by an auditor's certificate. If the certificate is without qualifications or exceptions—which is the strongest one an auditor can give—it may consist simply of a statement to the following effect:

> In our opinion, the accompanying statements present fairly the financial position of the company at June 30, 19XX and the results of its operations for the fiscal year then ended, in conformity with generally accepted accounting principles applied on a consistent basis with the preceding fiscal year.

Statements of Opinion. However, no matter how capable or reputable a company's auditors, its financial statements are only statements of opinion, based upon any one of a variety of generally accepted accounting principles which the company and its auditors are privileged to adopt at their discretion.

Consequently, two otherwise identical companies would be unrecognizable from their financial statements, if they adopted different accounting principles. For example, assume that Corporation A depreciates its plant and equipment on a straight-line basis, values its inventories under the first in, first out (Fifo) method and capitalizes its expenditures on plant improvements, intangibles (i.e., patents, trademarks, and so on), and other items to the maximum extent consonant with generally accepted accounting principles; and that Corporation B uses accelerated depreciation, last in, first out (Lifo) inventory valuation and expenses the foregoing items; A's audited financial statements would show substantially higher profits and a significantly higher net worth than B's, even though the two companies were in fact identical in all respects. The difference would be due solely to the different accounting principles which the two companies chose to adopt. In this example there were only three variations in the "generally accepted accounting principles" adopted by the two companies. There are, in fact, literally hundreds of possible variations in the accounting principles which companies and their auditors are privileged to adopt.

Further, even if two companies follow identical accounting principles and have identical balance sheets and operating statements, one's operations could involve highly speculative activities, while the other's might be extremely conservative.

Finally, it is a rare coincidence when the figures at which a company carries its assets correspond to their replacement, liquidation or fair market value—and the stated net worth of a corporation rarely bears a close relationship to its fair market value.

Thus, it may be concluded that corporate financial statements only provide meaningful clues to the historical size and profitability of a company's operations and the strength or weakness of its financial condition as of a given date.

Every company is unique in many respects. The investment banker must carefully appraise the quality of a company's earnings and assets, and its future prospects and requirements, in order to evolve a sound financing program which will serve the company's specific immediate and long-term objectives at the lowest effective cost.

Profit Manipulation. Regardless of the accounting principles a company adopts, there are a variety of things it could do to increase its earnings in anticipation of a public financing or merger, with a view to obtaining the highest possible price for its stock. A prospective issuer could reduce or temporarily defer various expenses, such as maintenance, advertising, insurance, research and development—to name a few. It could also increase its sales and

net income by accelerating shipments to customers, with the understanding that payment will be due in accord with usual delivery
schedules—accounts receivable will thus be created and sales and
earnings recorded. However, such measures seldom escape SEC
and State Security Commissioners' scrutiny, can interminably delay
an offering, and are in any case, extremely short-sighted, if not
fraudulent actions for a company to take in the face of a public
offering. The inevitable disillusionment will destroy investors' and
the financial communities' confidence in the company's management, which will preclude subsequent financings on attractive terms
for years to come.

Some Critical Areas of Consideration

The company is requested to provide the following information
which must be analyzed for inclusion in the prospectus. The investment banker's objective is to comply with the Securities Act
"full disclosure" requirements, while at the same time effectively
characterizing the company.

An Inventory of the Company. The historical development of
the company, its overall record of profitability, the date and state
of incorporation, and major changes in its ownership, management,
capitalization, operations and location over the years are material
considerations, both from a legal and a financial point of view.

A breakdown of its sales and gross profits by major product and
customer categories indicates the shifting product mix, sources of
profits and margins, the direction in which the company is moving,
its major areas of profit strength and weakness, and its potential
capital requirements.

A similar breakdown of its current and historical backlog figures
is reviewed for the same purposes.

A list of each of the major customers, suppliers and competitors,
with indications of the volume of business done with and by each,
and the company's relationship with each, is used to appraise the
company's competitive position and its dependency on any single
or group of customers or suppliers, which may require disclosure in
the prospectus.

In addition to the existing operating policies and physical facilities, recent and planned changes are analyzed. Emphasis is placed
on new marketing, production, distribution, personnel and other

policies, and facilities, as well as research and development, expansion and corporate acquisition plans which, in conjunction with the product mix and backlog data, provide an indication of the direction in which the company is moving and its future capital requirements.

The amounts spent on research and development and the amount of current sales and earnings accounted for by products introduced within the past ten years provide an indication of the success, relative to cost, of the research and development program, as well as the company's leadership within its industry.

Possible Conflicts of Interest. Those situations in which an officer or director has a direct or indirect interest outside of his official capacity must be carefully studied, since they may require disclosure and can result in conflicts of interest, and exposure to derivative stockholder suits. When derivative actions are brought, they make headlines in the financial press. When they are won by management a year or two later, they are lost among the obituaries—but unfortunately by then, the damage has been done to the company's public image.

The management compensation, bonus and profit sharing arrangements and stock option plans are reviewed to determine whether the company is competitive, and also as to whether such arrangements are equitable from the viewpoint of the prospective public stockholders. Although stock options do result in dilution of the public stockholders' interest in a company, reasonable stock option plans are regarded favorably.

The company's historical employee relations, its strike history, wage scales and whether or not it is unionized, are material considerations. Nonunionized companies may pay more in hourly wages than the union scales, but less in fringe benefits (i.e., pensions, insurance, hospitalization, and vacations). Their actual labor costs may, therefore, be appreciably lower than their unionized competitors. Cheap labor is a material competitive advantage, but abnormally wide wage scale differentials cannot generally be expected to persist indefinitely.

Contingent Liabilities

Material contingent liabilities not carried on the company's balance sheet or covered by insurance in the ordinary course of its business must be disclosed. This includes legal actions and state and federal agency proceedings threatened, pending or in process, guarantees and warranties, contract termination penalties and renegotiation provisions, and potential tax claims. The year through which a company has been audited by the Internal Revenue Service and its record of past tax deficiencies are reviewed. Also, by selling and leasing back its fixed assets a company can remove substantial debt from its balance sheets and strengthen its working capital position (which are desirable objectives), but the satisfaction of such lease obligations are usually just as fundamental to a company's survival as its debt obligations. Lease obligations must be disclosed and may be capitalized in appraising the leverage in a company's capitalization and its return on "invested capital."

If officers, directors, major stockholders, corporate affiliates or others have guaranteed or endorsed any of the company's obligations or vice versa, they must be reviewed. This includes so-called solvency agreements and stockholder undertakings, which may not be disclosed in the company's financial statements. If a company's past results are in part the product of such arrangements, it should be disclosed, for such arrangements are generally terminated when a company merges or "goes public." A publicly owned company must be capable of standing on its own feet as an independent entity—and should not be dependent upon others for its credit or similar essentials.

Projections are reviewed of the company's operating statements and balance sheets for the current and at least the following fiscal year, with explanations of any abnormal, nonrecurring or unusual items, and the facts and assumptions upon which they are based.

Legal Contractual and Voting Clauses. The company's charter, bylaws, loan agreements, and material contracts must be reviewed. Voting trusts, dividend restrictions, negative-pledge and after-acquired property clauses, net working capital maintenance and other requirements and restrictions in loan agreements and contracts sometimes have to be modified before the company can do a public offering on attractive terms.

With reference to cumulative versus noncumulative voting, most companies have noncumulative voting. Under noncumulative voting, 51 percent of the votes elect all the directors. Under cumulative voting it is possible for the minority to gain proportional representation on a company's board. There is something to be said for both approaches. The proponents of noncumulative voting contend that a board of directors is not a debating society and that it is in the best interest of all the stockholders for the board to function smoothly. In order to assure management continuity and inhibit "raiders" many companies stagger the election of directors (i.e., a third of the directors annually).

"Bailouts." Public offerings may consist solely of existing stockholders' interest in the company (none of the proceeds of which would go to the company), or of new money for the company, or both. In the case of new money offerings, the intended application of the proceeds is carefully reviewed in the light of the company's future prospects and less expensive alternative sources of finance.

The extent of the owner-manager's retained interest is significant—100 percent sellouts are rare. While selling-stockholder offerings are commonly referred to as "bailouts," there are many valid reasons why the owners of a company sell a portion of their shares to the public. For example, it may not be prudent for the owner-managers to have both their capital (as represented by their ownership of the company) and their employment income entirely dependent upon the fortunes of a single business. Other valid reasons include the liquidation of dissident minority interests and prospective estate taxes.

Biographical sketches of each officer director, and middle-management executive are reviewed and pertinent facts are included in the prospectus. This includes their ages, titles, compensation, equity and stock option interests in the company, past positions and associations, educational background, outside business, and other interests.

Copies are requested of studies, reports, and analyses of the company and material aspects of its operations, prepared by the company, management consultants, and others.

The foregoing are the major areas covered. Assemblage of this information is time consuming, but most of it is required in order to prepare the Registration Statement which must be filed with and reviewed by the Securites and Exchange Commission and the individual State Security Commissioners before the company's securities can be offered to the public.

Trade Checks

Following receipt of the foregoing information, the next steps are to digest it, study the immediate and long-term prospects for the company's industry, run statistical comparisons with comparable concerns, and make trade checks with the company's major customers, suppliers, competitors, and others.

There are sometimes incipient problems of which the management may not be aware, such as the impending departure of one or more key executives, a material change in the buying policies of a major customer, a prospective price increase or serious shortage in an essential raw material or the imminent introduction of major new lines or other moves by important competitors. Investment banking firms have broad industry associations through which they may be able to obtain this type of information, and assist their corporate clients in anticipating such problems.

Plant Inspection

The investment banking firm's "due diligence" review also includes visiting the company's facilities and interviewing its management.

Management Appraisals

Now we come to the most difficult area of corporate appraisals—that of evaluating management's ability to direct a company's future growth.

A company's relative performance within its industry, the speed of its adaptation to changing conditions (has it led or followed?), its sales and earnings record, profit margins, and return on invested capital, provide tangible evidence of management's abilities.

The officers', directors', and middle-management executives' past accomplishments, rates of advancement, training, and academic backgrounds are also reviewed.

PRICING CONSIDERATIONS

Following the appraisal of the quality of a company's earnings and assets, and its management's abilities to direct its future growth, such values must be equated to the prices which the investing public is currently paying for the most comparable investment opportunities. This is accomplished by preparing *comparative pricing schedules* which set forth the financial and other pertinent data on the most comparable publicly owned companies. Key considerations include the quality of their earnings and assets, their relative size and profitability, the amount of fixed charges (principally debt service and rent) ahead of the common stock, the debt-equity ratio, working capital position, net worth and book value per share, the rate and consistency of sales and earnings growth, profit margins, return on invested capital, the price-earnings ratios, and dividend yields at which their securities are selling, the number of shares in public hands and the market in which they are traded (i.e., the New York Stock Exchange, regional exchanges, or over-the-counter).

Just as a doctor's advice and treatment are no better than the diagnosis upon which they are based, so it is with the investment banker. In the absence of a thorough appraisal of the company, its future prospects and the market prices of comparable investment opportunities, it is evident that he would not be in a position to propose and implement a sound financing program.

In order to assure a successful offering and a favorable after-issue market, initial public offerings of securities are typically priced at a modest discount from the existing market prices of the most comparable seasoned securities. A portion—10 percent to 20 percent—of initial public offerings are purchased by speculators who hope to sell the shares at a profit shortly after the offering. These individuals tend to sell their shares within a matter of days to weeks. If the stock was overpriced on the offering and the market is not sufficiently broad and strong to absorb such selling at or above the issue price, the stock will go to a discount. This tends to attract additional selling from individuals who would otherwise have been long-term investors. If the stock is selling much below the issue price as the year-end approaches, it attracts still greater selling from individuals who wish to establish tax losses. When the stock recovers to the issue price, many of the individuals who have held on, become sellers when they see the opportunity to break even. Thus, there is a considerable supply of stock around the issue price level, which has to be absorbed before the stock can move higher.

As a result of this progressive selling, the stock will establish a low price-earnings ratio during its seasoning period (i.e., the year following the offering) and as a consequence, it will generally sell at an abnormally low multiple indefinitely thereafter. Once a stock has established a low price-earnings ratio, relative to other companies in its industry and the market in general, it is interminably difficult to improve its relative valuation.

This does not mean that a stock must go up during the months following an initial public offering, but if the offering was soundly conceived and executed, it should not decline more than the general market. With able management direction and sound financial planning, the capital resources available to a company will increase significantly over the years, and the relative terms will steadily improve.

CONTINUING RELATIONSHIP WITH THE INVESTMENT BANKER

After-Issue Market Support

As indicated above, 10 percent to 20 percent of the shares purchased on initial offerings are typically sold within a matter of weeks. If it appears that the market may not be sufficiently broad and strong to absorb such selling at or above the issue price, responsible managing underwriters will attempt to establish a short position on the offering. For example, if the offering consists of 500,000 shares, the underwriters may sell 550,000 shares, and then provide after-issue market support by buying back the extra 50,000 shares in the after-market. Their objective is to absorb the initial selling and stabilize the price of the stock. Underwriters commonly incur losses covering such short positions.

If the stock is traded over-the-counter following the offering, the managing underwriter should continue to make the primary market in the stock until it is listed on an exchange. The objective is to maintain an orderly market. Therefore, if the buy or sell orders from the public do not pair off at any given moment, the market makers will buy or sell stock for their own accounts and gradually raise or lower the bid and asked prices to a level at which the public's orders are in equilibrium.

After-Issue Market Sponsorship

The managing underwriter should also keep the financial community and investing public informed of a company's progress through timely research reports and bulletins. This does not mean indiscriminately recommending purchase of the stock regardless of its merits, but it does mean appraising and amplifying the company's current developments in the light of the general market conditions and the prospects for the economy and the company's industry.

Continuing Relationship

Leading investment banking firms would not be interested in handling a company's initial public offering but for the prospect of establishing a continuing relationship with the issuer. However, they do not request the right of first refusal to handle a company's subsequent public offerings, for the essence of their relationship with corporate clients is mutual confidence. A contractual relationship will not suffice in the absence of such confidence.

As previously indicated, investment bankers are in a position to make both an immediate and a continuing contribution to their corporate clients, particularly in such areas as after-issue market support and sponsorship, financial planning, mergers, corporate acquisitions, expansion and diversification plans, dividend, stock option and pension plans, board and top-management candidates, annual and interim reports to stockholders, bank and term loans, and listing the stock on a national securities exchange.

ADDITIONAL SOURCES

Furst, Richard W. "Does Listing Increase the Market Price of Common Stocks?" *Journal of Business,* 43 (April 1970), 174–80.

Goulet, Waldemar. "Price Changes, Managerial Actions and Insider Trading at the Time of Listing." *Financial Management,* 3 (Spring 1974), 30–36.

McDonald, J. G., and Fisher, A. K. "New Issue Stock Price Behavior." *Journal of Finance,* 27 (March 1972), 97–102.

Sears, Gerald A. "Public Offerings for Smaller Companies." *Harvard Business Review,* 46 (September–October 1968), 112–20.

Van Horne, James C. "New Listings and Their Price Behavior." *Journal of Finance,* 25 (September 1970), 783–94.

Chapter 41

New Financing Techniques on Wall Street[*]

Paul K. Kelly[†]

BACKGROUND

LIKE A PRO QUARTERBACK, Wall Street has had to scramble to stay healthy.

Current economic conditions have forced the nation's investment community to deviate from its traditional game plan—to improvise new techniques and modify long-established methods of operation in an attempt to satisfy corporate financing requirements. Necessity has truly been the mother of invention—investment bankers have probably been more creative and innovative in developing new financing techniques during the past five years than in any other period in history.

Although these new techniques have become increasingly important vehicles for raising capital, many of them are not necessarily widely employed by the corporate financial community. However, they do exist, both for equity and debt financing, and, if applied effectively, can ease or eliminate many of a corporation's financial pressures. Among the more notable of these new financing techniques are project financing, "documented discount notes" (DDNs), leveraged leasing, pollution control bonds, floating rate securities,

* This chapter first appeared in the *Financial Executive* of November 1974, from which it is reprinted with the permission of the Financial Executives Institute.
† Paul K. Kelly is a general partner with Prescott, Ball & Turben, Cleveland, Ohio.

mutually redeemable preferred stock, and preferred stock with accelerated sinking-fund patterns, as well as variations of other familiar financing vehicles.

Before describing how these new techniques work, let us consider the background against which they were developed and refined. First and foremost, the techniques were evolved because there was no other way to meet vast capital needs that could not be adequately serviced by traditional financing means.

It is also important to bear in mind that along with this tremendous increase in demand for capital during the past few years has come the practical realization that long-term capital is in finite supply.

For the first time in recent U.S. history, many creditworthy companies have found themselves unable to attract sufficient long-term capital—at any price. Public capital markets, both debt and equity, have been practically closed for certain industries in particular, and to small- and medium-sized companies in general. In a world of increasing uncertainty, our free market system has made a determination to allocate its limited supply of capital only to the largest, most creditworthy entities. Safety of principal and return, high enough to offset double-digit inflation, has become the predominant investor consideration, making it difficult for developing or hard-pressed corporations to raise funds.

These circumstances forced many companies to revert to various forms of higher cost bank financing as their sole source of capital funds. The result has been many instances in which banks have, in effect, become joint venturers with certain businesses, assuming a credit risk exposure which normally would be spread among a large group of capital market investors.

Aggravating the situation has been the continuation—and acceleration—of worldwide inflation, which has had an adverse impact upon the structure of our capital markets. The depressed state of the stock markets in recent years has obviously not been conducive to raising new equity capital. Investor concern with inflation has been reflected in declining price/earnings ratios for particularly vulnerable companies and industry groups and in sharply reduced investor interest in the stock market generally.

Inflation has also made it more difficult for corporations to turn to the debt markets for relief. In recent months, inflation's hot breath has considerably wilted the appeal of bonds as a corporate vehicle for raising capital. The U.S. capital market has responded to these inflationary pressures and increased capital demands by changing the traditional forms of long-term debt instruments. The results have been debt securities modified to counteract the effects of inflation and uncertain future outlooks, and designed to become more attractive to individual as well as institutional investors.

INNOVATIONS IN DEBT FINANCING

The major problem for capital-intensive corporations, such as those in the utility and petroleum industries, is how to keep their capitalization from becoming debt heavy, a condition which could result in a lowering of their bond ratings and general credit status. With common equities selling below book value, traditional sources of equity capital have become prohibitively expensive. This makes it increasingly difficult for companies to keep their traditional debt-equity ratios in historical perspective by relying solely upon retained earnings. Firms faced with this problem are increasingly resorting to off-balance sheet financing devices. This has opened a whole new area of innovative investment banking techniques, sometimes referred to generically as "project financing," to meet both interim and long-term requirements for funds. Project financing combines elements of new applications of traditional financing methods as well as entirely new techniques.

In recent years, several off-balance sheet, short-term or interim financing methods have been devised which make use of the commercial paper or short-term private placement markets. One such method involves the use of the documented discount note, or DDN. An example of how the DDN is used is the financing of items such as utility fuel supplies, particularly nuclear fuel cores. Generally, a trust is established by a third party; the trust has title to a nuclear core and leases it to a utility, thus keeping the dollar amount of the core off the utility's balance sheet. Typically the trust is financed with DDNs—commercial paper or other forms of short- and intermediate-term notes, supported by attached letters of credit from major banks. The letter of credit guarantees to the notes' buyers that payment of principal and interest will be made at maturity, by the bank if necessary. As a result, the trust obtains a credit status that permits it to sell its debt securities to institutional investors in large amounts.

Because DDNs are bank-guaranteed securities, they are exempt from the requirement, imposed upon ordinary commercial paper, that the proceeds be used for "current transactions purposes." Consequently, DDNs may be used for certain transactions of a long-term nature, such as plant construction, which cannot legally be financed with ordinary commercial paper. The use of DDNs as a construction financing device has often saved the issuing company as much as 2 percent compared to traditional bank construction loans.

Wall Street is exploring the use of similar trust arrangements to finance other corporate assets in an off-balance sheet manner. Oil inventories, for example, might be removed from a company's balance sheet and allocated back to the company as needed, on a contractual basis. And timber-cutting trusts can be established to permit paper companies access to timber-cutting rights without actually having to tie up capital in the ownership of timberlands. Also under study are construction financing trusts, which could be used to construct plants or other projects.

New intermediate- and long-term financing devices are also being developed. Many of these are simply new and creative applications of traditional leasing and leveraged leasing concepts. Utilities, for example, have financed peaking generators and even entire generating plants, on a joint basis, using leasing techniques. Recently, a group of five utilities began the joint development of a coal mining property under a leveraged lease arrangement that passes along tax benefits to the third-party equity holder.

Leveraged leasing concepts are also being applied to various projects undertaken by the petroleum industry and other heavy users of capital. The technique is particularly attractive to those industries that have low effective tax rates and therefore do not profit significantly from the retention of tax benefits. A fairly recent innovation is the application of the leveraged lease concept to a pollution control financing, wherein the investor received both tax-exempt income and tax benefits which could not be fully utilized by the issuing company.

In addition to adapting leasing techniques, corporations are making use of other off-balance sheet financing methods as a substitute for direct long-term debt obligations. This is again particularly notable in the energy-related industries, including utilities and petroleum companies, where long-term capital needs are expanding at an accelerating rate.

The petroleum industry has been particularly creative in developing new off-balance sheet financing methods and the utility industry recently has begun adopting some of these new methods. These techniques often relate to major energy-producing, refining, or transportation projects, both joint venture and wholly-owned. Certain projects, such as offshore oil ports and pipelines, often make use of "take-or-pay contracts" or "throughput and deficiency agreements." A take-or-pay contract guarantees that the taker will pay for the project's output at a rate that will adequately service the debt of the project and, moreover, that the taker will make these payments in a timely fashion even if the delivery of the output is interrupted. This type of contract, with a creditworthy taker or takers, is sufficient to obtain financing for the project since the lender is assured that funds will be provided to the project under all circumstances.

The throughput and deficiency agreement is similar to the take-or-pay contract in concept, although somewhat different in form. It is usually used in financing a pipeline project. The taker agrees to accept oil shipments at a certain flow rate and at a price that will adequately service the debt of the project. If for some reason the flow is interrupted, the taker continues to make timely payments sufficient to maintain uninterrupted debt service.

An important benefit of both take-or-pay contracts and throughput and deficiency agreements is that greater leverage can be achieved for projects employing these concepts than would be permissible if the projects were carried directly on the balance sheets of their equity sponsors. With these techniques debt leverage of up to 90 percent is not uncommon for major projects, depending upon the creditworthiness of the takers.

Some utilities have begun in recent years to integrate their operations vertically in order to assure their sources of fuel supply. The take-or-pay contract concept, which was pioneered by the petroleum industry, has proven particularly suitable in helping to finance the vertical integration of utilities back to sources of fuel supply. The utilities have, in at least one instance, adapted this concept to the construction and operation of a joint-venture utility plant.

Both the petroleum and utility industries have made use of "bareboat charters" to provide off-balance sheet financing of fuel carriers that otherwise they would be required to own outright. The bareboat charter is somewhat like a take-or-pay contract in effect, if not in form. It permits the financing of the vessel upon the strength of a company which agrees to charter the vessel at a certain dollar rate for a definite period of time rather than upon the credit of the third-party equity owner. If the dollar rate and the length of the charter are sufficient to service the debt necessary to finance the vessel, long-term lenders are willing to make the necessary capital commitment. New applications of techniques to float debt based on the credit of the taker, rather than of the issuer of the debt, will undoubtedly be developed as long as the taker is not required to capitalize the obligation on its balance sheet.

Because of the complexity of joint-venture financing techniques, most large projects are financed privately with sophisticated institutional investors. Moreover, because of the mammoth size of many energy-related projects, new sources of capital must be tapped. At this point, the Eurodollar market seems most promising.

Investment bankers are aware of the huge amount of investable funds that will be generated by the oil-producing nations in the forthcoming years. Still to be resolved, however, is how to convince these lenders to extend their commitments beyond short-term Euro-dollar deposits with major banking institutions. Because the depositors make short-term commitments, the banking institutions, in turn, lend on a short-term basis to finance long-term projects. The challenge to the financial community is to design a long-term Euro-dollar security that will adequately protect the lender against excessive risk from inflation and currency fluctuations.

While all of these financing techniques have been off the balance sheet, new direct-obligation debt instruments have also been developed in recent years to help ease the financial strain for corporate borrowers. A notable example is tax-exempt pollution control financing—an application of the industrial revenue bond structure by which a municipality, or municipal entity, issues tax-exempt bonds to finance pollution control facilities to be sold or leased to a private corporation. The lease or sale payments the corporation makes to the municipality must be sufficient to pay all costs of servicing the bonds. In case of default, the private corporation's credit is behind the bonds. With a tax-exempt financing, a corporation can currently save from 2 to $2\frac{1}{2}$ percent in interest when compared to taxable securities of similar quality. More than $3 billion of these bonds have been underwritten by investment banking firms since their inception in 1971.

A more recent innovation in debt financing has been the floating-rate note. This instrument has been developed in response to the reluctance of institutional investors to invest in fixed-rate bonds during a period of high inflation. The instrument protects the buyer against excessive price erosion due to higher rates. It has been particularly popular with individual investors because of the "put" feature which permits the investors, at their option, to redeem the note at par every six months. The floating-rate security is in its infancy and its potential attractiveness as a financing vehicle is tied almost entirely to the future rate of inflation. If the rate remains high, it can be expected that new modifications and refinements of floating rate securities will be introduced as a marketing device to attract investor interest. One example would be to tie the rates on such securities to money market or price indices other than the Treasury bill rate, which has been the pricing mechanism for the first group of floating rate issues.

Companies that are experiencing difficulty in floating straight debt issues may also attempt, in a better stock market environment, to improve the marketability of their obligations through the addition of "sweeteners"; i.e., warrants or convertibility features. These features are not being used as frequently now because the stocks of many companies are selling substantially below book value and the companies are reluctant to issue future calls upon their equity at these levels. To prevent substantial dilution when issuing additional shares, the premium on convertibles or warrants would have to be too high to have any real market value in the pricing of the underlying debt security. In an improved stock market environment, however, these equity-oriented debt instruments, or new variations of them, will once again become viable alternatives. The attraction to the issuer lies in the lower coupon generally available on debt issued with equity sweeteners, as well as the increased interest that such instruments may generate in the company's common stock.

TRENDS IN EQUITY FINANCING

Amassing a sufficient equity base is perhaps the greatest obstacle confronting many companies. It is obvious that retained earnings are not keeping pace with debt accumulation and that, at some point, most companies will be forced to resort to external sources of financing.

Several solutions to this problem have been suggested. Some observers contend that our historical concepts of appropriate debt-to-equity ratios have been outdated in a capital-short world, and that U.S. companies should be permitted greater leverage to compete with foreign companies, which generally have much higher debt ratios. While the argument may have a number of corporate supporters, neither the rating services nor American investors give a discernible indication that they are willing to accept this alternative.

A more acceptable approach might be to rely more on preferred stock when common equity is not available at a reasonable cost. If a company's earnings/price (E/P) ratio is considered to approximate the cost of capital of its common stock, the company can judge the approximate cost of using preferred stock by comparing the preferred dividend rate with its E/P. Obviously, the more depressed a company's price/earnings ratio, the more attractive the preferred stock alternative. The major drawback with preferred stock is that the cash flow requirement of the preferred dividend, at present market levels, is usually substantially greater than the common dividend.

A recent innovation has been the creation of mutually redeemable preferred stock. Unlike ordinary preferred stock, which has either a sinking fund or a redemption privilege limited exclusively to the issuer, this new instrument permits redemption by either the issuer or the holder of the stock after an initial, and relatively short, non-redemption period. These nonredemption periods have reputedly been as short as two years, but are usually three years or longer.

This type of preferred stock, essentially short-term in nature, permits the issuer to obtain equity at a slightly lower cost than ordinary preferred. It also gives the issuer the flexibility of refunding the preferred with a common issue if the stock market improves between the time of issuance and the end of the nonredemption period. The holder, in turn, receives a short-term investment which will pay out at par whenever he exercises his redemption privilege. And his investment is subject to the 85 percent intercorporate dividend exclusion for tax purposes. The result is a short-term investment with no market risk and a largely tax-sheltered return. Such issues to date have been negotiated only on a private placement basis.

Another equity variation has been the creation of a preferred stock with an accelerated sinking-fund pattern designed to retire the security within ten years of issuance and to produce an even shorter average life. Again, this innovation reflects the investor's unwillingness to commit to long-term preferred stock issues because of the uncertainties of the future, and the issuer's response to this trend.

A "near-equity" alternative which some companies may consider is the addition of a layer of subordinated debt to their capital structures. The benefit of this equity supplement is the deductibility of interest charges for tax purposes, unlike either preferred or common dividends. A negative aspect of subordinated debt is its lack of availability, at a reasonable price, under stringent money conditions when investors are barraged by high-quality senior debt issues at historically high-rate levels. In addition, the interest on subordinated debt is included in the calculation of fixed charges coverage of a company's debt position, even though it may be regarded as near-equity for capital base purposes.

The general lack of investor interest in new stock issues has led to various suggestions for providing equity money to good small- or medium-sized companies which no longer have sufficient access to the public market. The trust department of at least one major bank has undertaken, with certain discretionary funds, a program of providing equity to companies of this type. The program provides necessary equity funds to the companies involved and the possibility of an increased yield, based upon equity participation, for the trust funds involved.

Again, it should be stressed that these are good small companies with established operating records and not speculative venture capital situations. Seed capital for venture companies is currently relegated to SBICs (small business investment companies) and a decreasing number of venture capital organizations. In the absence of a bull market condition, equity sources for many smaller corporations will remain quite limited. Congress has entertained various tax incentives to attract the individual back into the stock market. Whether these benefits will have the desired effect, only time will tell.

CHALLENGE OF THE FUTURE

Wall Street's creative resources are being tested more today than at any other period in American economic history. The task is to structure new financing vehicles which, in a changing economic environment, will assist in the formation of investment capital for industry throughout the world. The futures of such industries as housing, transportation, and power generation will be determined in large measure by how well Wall Street meets the challenge.

ADDITIONAL SOURCES

Beizer, J. "Want to Make Workers More Productive? Give Them Stock." *Iron Age*, 215 (January 27, 1975), 22–24.

Bettinger, C. "ESOT and the Commerical Banker." *Journal of Commercial Bank Lending*, 57 (April 1975), 31–37.

Binns, W. Gordon, Jr. "ESOPs: A Joint Piece of the Action." *Financial Executive*, 63 (September 1975), 48–52, 54.

Bushman, R. M. "Employee Stock Ownership Plan." *Trusts and Estates*, 113 (September 1974), 580–83.

Business Week. "Can U.S. Industry Find the Money It Needs? (Special Report)," September 22, 1973, 43–54.

Business Week. "Financing 1974's Capital Spending Boom." November 17, 1973, 81–82.

Business Week. "Very Big Deals of Project Financing." February 2, 1974, 59.

Business Week. "Desperate Search for More Capital." September 14, 1974, 134–37.

Clipsham, M. "Overdraft: Flexible, Cheap and Simple (How to Match Capital Needs with Appropriate Sources)." *Industrial Management*, 4 (December 1974/January 1975), 16–17.

Diener, Royce. *How to Finance a Growing Business*. New York: F. Fell, 1974.

Elton, Edwin J., and Gruber, Martin J. *Finance as a Dynamic Process*. Englewood Cliffs, N.J.: Prentice Hall, 1975.

Ghee, W. K., and others. "Banker's Viewpoints on Financing Proposed Capital Expenditures." *Journal of Commercial Bank Lending*, 57 (February 1975), 51–64.

Gunton, M. "Striving for Worker Involvement." *International Management*, 30 (May 1975), 32–33.

Haverkampf, P. T. "Investing in Real Estate for Pension and Profit-Sharing Trusts." *Trusts and Estates*, 112 (September 1973), 638–39.

Kelly, Paul. "New Financing Techniques on Wall Street." *Financial Executive*, 41 (November 1974), 30–43.

Mason, R. "Borrowing Money—The Right Way." *Industry Week,* 184 (February 24, 1975), 46–47.

Mock, R. D. "Financing Plan Keyed to Pretax Dollars (Kelso Plan)." *Industry Week,* 179 (November 26, 1973), 50.

Morthland, R. J. "Capital Shortages in a Shortage Economy." *Journal of Commercial Bank Lending,* 56 (December 1973), 29–37.

Nadler, P. S. "Corporate Banking Relationships." *Bankers Monthly,* 92 (April 1975), 11–12; 92 (May 1972), 11–13.

Paulos, J. J. "Inflation and Capital Intensive Industries." *Financial Executive,* 43 (February 1975), 56–61.

Schwartz, Eli, and Aronison, J. Richard. "How to Integrate Corporate and Personal Income Taxation." *Journal of Finance,* 27 (December 1972), 1073–80.

Sholes, S. D. "Search for Venture Capital—Preparatory Steps." *Financial Executive,* 42 (August 1974), 46.

Sommer, D. W. "Enough Money to Go Around?" *Industry Week,* 178 (August 6, 1973), 26–31.

Thomas, D. L. "New Ways to Raise Money: Corporate Finance Will Never Be the Same Again." *Barrons,* 54 (July 1, 1974), 3.

Todd, J. O. "Employee Stock Ownership Trust—Opportunity for Banks." *Burroughs Clearing House,* 58 (August 1974), 17–19.

Williams, J. H. "Package of Finance (Bank Services for Business Capital)." *Industrial Management,* 5 (February 1975), 29–30.

Wright, K. M. "Corporate Long-Term Financing." *Conference Board Record,* 12 (April 1975), 62–64.

Chapter 42

Project Financing

Robert L. Huston[*]

INTRODUCTION

IN RECENT YEARS a series of developments has led to a form of raising debt called international project financing. The broadening search for raw materials and increases in construction costs, the formation of joint ventures between government and private enterprise, the magnitude of risks in a new project, and the partners' desire to restrict their financial exposure have all led to a somewhat new approach to raising debt funds for major new facilities.

The words "project finance" are used with different meanings, ranging from "cash flow lending" to "nonrecourse" finance, where the physical assets and cash flow of the project alone are the credit substance for the financing.

Since each project has unique characteristics, the use of any generality for its financing is not meaningful. There is in fact wide latitude in "project financing" as a debt-raising technique.

We will address project financing in the framework of real international transactions which have been financed, spelling out those broad factors which have been addressed by project partners and project lenders.

The process of arranging project debt finance is that of risk identification and resolving the risks in acceptable fashion for both lenders and owners.

---

[*] Robert L. Huston is senior vice president of White, Weld & Company, New York.

The type of projects we shall discuss have the following characteristics:

1. There is high debt leverage.
2. There is normally more than one equity owner in the project company.
3. The equity owners collectively have operating, technical, and marketing ability, as well as the financial strength, to see the project through to fruition.
4. Normal corporate guarantees of debt are not available throughout.
5. The project equity owners desire to shift some of the project risk to lenders.
6. Contracts among the equity owners and lenders are the core of the credit.
7. The project may be located anywhere in the world.

Two examples of such projects are presented below.

Example 1

Peru: Copper Mine (000 omitted)

Equity	$216,000	35%
Debt	404,000	65
Total.	$620,000	

On 11/21/75, it was announced that a cost increase of $35.7 million had been incurred for the project; additionally, $30 million for inventory and $40 million for start-up expenses have resulted in new financial requirements of $105.7 million.

Of the original $216 million equity in the project, ownership was as follows:

	Project Ownership (percent)
Southern Peru Copper Corp..	88.5
Owned by:	
Asarco 51.50	
Cerro Corp. 22.25	
Phelps Dodge 16.0	
Newmont Mining 10.25	
Billiton (owned by Shell Trading	
& Transport)	11.5
	100.0

Of the original $404 million debt structure, the components were as follows:

(000 omitted)

Eurodollar Bank Syndicate	$200,000
Export Agency Credits.	140,000
Purchasers of Copper.	54,000
International Finance Corp. (IFC)	10,000
	$404,000

Example 2

Brazil: Iron Ore Project (000 omitted)

Equity	$110,000	31%
Debt	242,000	69
Total.	$352,000	
Equity Ownership		
Samitri (Brazil)		51
Marcona International		49
Debit Capital		
Export Agency Credit	78,000	
Eurodollar Bank Syndicate	164,000	
	$242,000	

Additionally, banks have established a standby credit of $30 million, should costs exceed forecast.

HISTORY

Project financing can be viewed in a historical context, in current trends and its probable future. Since major projects generally occur in the capital-intensive industries, project financing has been practiced in the extractive industries, that is, the oil, gas and hard minerals businesses—primarily in the United States and Canada. Certain types of projects which were financed on the basis of asset and future product-price evaluations, explicit contractual obligations and extensive documentation.

Historically, oil pipelines in the United States and Canada were financed on a basis which some describe as project financing. While high debt ratios were achieved by the borrowing companies, the ultimate credit responsibility for the debt financing of such pipelines usually was that of the parent companies which owned and were utilizing the pipeline. The parent corporations were legally liable for the debt repayment and for operating costs of the borrowing company. In the case of a number of gas pipelines, term lenders relied not on creditworthy shipper-owners' corporate backstops, but rather on reserve estimates, pipeline economics and marketing contracts.

During the 1950s and 1960s, production payment financing in the oil and gas industry became commonplace. Without going into detail, companies were able to acquire producing properties through high debt leverage with no liability for repayment of the debt. There were at the time tax advantages, as well as balance sheet advantages, in utilizing the production payment technique for acquisitions. During the 1960s, production payment financing was adapted to the hard minerals industry, particularly to coal. The two largest coal companies in the United States were acquired by noncoal companies utilizing the production payment financing technique.

Lenders relied solely on the cash flow from the producing properties subject to the production payment; if reserves or economics were not as originally estimated, loans were not repaid.

A parallel type of production payment transaction known as carve-out financing became prominent, again for tax purposes. Tax law changes have subsequently reduced the incentives for production payment financing although it still exists to a limited extent today.

During the 1960s, several transactions, which are considered the forerunners of today's major international joint-venture project activity, took place outside the United States and Canada. Of particular interest were some Australian projects to develop iron ore for export shipment, primarily to Japan. These transactions involved a degree of cross-border exposure for lenders which added a new dimension of risk, and cash flow was dependent on third parties in a third country. In the first half of the decade of the 1970s there have been other transactions of size outside North America where bank lenders and export credit agencies have extended debt financing in excess of 50 percent of the capital costs of the project without corporate guarantees throughout.

Leasing, real estate, and ship financing grew to enormous magnitude in the post–World War II years. Owners have been able to obtain high debt leverage in a variety of asset-based transactions; lenders relied on evaluation of assets, usage agreements of a wide variety, and extensive legal documentation. Broadly speaking, there are fundamental similarities in financing in these areas to international project finance activity.

Recently a survey was undertaken of the announced industrial and extractive projects around the world, and well over 100 projects were identified. The minimum size for project cost was set at $100 million. Geographically these announced projects are located in more than 30 countries, spread from Asia through the Western Hemisphere to Africa and the Middle East. Perhaps not too surprisingly, the developed world is not commonly the location of major projects. The developing countries are the location of a large portion of the energy resources and mineral resources of the world, and processing as well as extractive facilities are being built in such countries. By type of project we find the following predominating:

LNG plants.
Refineries.
Hard minerals projects.
Petrochemical and fertilizer plants.
Oil and gas pipelines.
Transportation projects.
Steel mills/sponge iron plants.

The type of project participant follows logically:

Private oil companies.
Government companies.
Mining and metals companies.
Chemical companies.
Transportation companies.

It is not uncommon to find five or six equity partners in a $600 million project, and this in itself introduces problem areas, such as coming to common agreement on the structure of financing and the nature of the common contractual agreements critical to obtaining financing. Due to the complexities, experienced financial guidance is usually sought early in the project development stage.

There are new factors which have a bearing on the ability to raise debt funds, especially the sheer dollar size of project debt related to the degree of political risk in the project country. Outside the United States and Canada very few true project financings have actually closed of the type that are currently being undertaken in the oil, gas, hard minerals, metals and processing industries. Due to the relative lack of project financing experience outside the United States and Canada, and the introduction of new political/economic factors, there is an evolutionary process underway in the financing of major projects throughout the world. With that broad background, let us spell out project financing in practical terms.

PROJECT EVALUATION

As the first step, lenders and owners have to identify the risk areas which are of common concern. Resolving these risks determines the nature of the owners' contractual obligations on which project financing is based.

The risks in a project such as we have described can be summarized as follows:

Economic.
Raw materials.
Completion.
Operation.
Marketing.
Financial.
Political.

In addressing the risks, lenders seek protection in various ways, and equity owners seek to limit their credit responsibility. Evaluation of the risk factors by owners and lenders is time-consuming, especially in a global environment of inflation, commodity price fluctuations, rate swings, and political change. Many projects of size are in the formative stage for a minimum of two to three years; over five years may pass from the germination of a project to the commencing of construction. Change during that period is expected for nearly all the identified risk issues—costs may double, governments change, prices rise and fall, and borrowing rates gyrate regularly.

PROJECT ECONOMICS

An evaluation of a project initially includes an examination of the following:

Feasibility studies.
Cash flow projections.
Market studies.
Price competition.
Technology.
Labor availability/productivity.
Taxes.
Depreciation schedule.
Transportation.
Site location.
Infrastructure.
Sensitivity analysis.

Satisfaction on these basic factors is key to the initial acceptability of a project to owners and potential lenders. As the locus of projects shifts to the developing world, we see the cost, timing and availability of infrastructure as one of the most uncontrollable factors in a project's success.

Desirably, feasibility studies go well beyond an engineering study for the physical plant into the areas of raw materials, operations, and markets. In many cases, separate studies are required to be made to satisfy potential lenders that there has been competent third-party attention focused on the key project aspects. While owners' feasibility studies are useful, they rarely are sufficient to satisfy lenders in major project fundings.

RAW MATERIALS

The principal questions that arise in the raw materials area are: (1) size and quality of resources; (2) nature of contract for supply; (3) price; (4) escalation provision; (5) ability of supplier(s); (6) substitutability; (7) transportation; and (8) currency of contract.

In the case of extractive projects, a third-party study of the mineral deposit is normally required. The nature of the raw material contract between the project company and its suppliers (perhaps one or more of the project owners) has to be satisfactory to provide assurance that the project will have the material to process.

Parallel to this is an examination of the potential for substituting of other sources should the intended supplier not be able to deliver. In some cases there are cross-border aspects of the flow of materials to the project, which could introduce a compounding of the sovereign risks of the project.

PLANT COMPLETION

Major projects in the capital-intensive industries take an extensive time period to complete once construction has commenced. This is particularly true in the developing countries due to the lack of infrastucture and the logistics of supply of construction materials.

Lenders are intent on assuring that the project facility is completed by the owners on time, in operating condition, and producing in accordance with the technical and economic parameters originally forecast.

Overall, the major issues that all parties address in this area are: (1) time frame; (2) quantity; (3) quality; (4) cost; (5) start-up period; (6) overruns; (7) general contractor; (8) work permits; (9) pollution control; and (10) owners' obligation.

Accepting any risks of failure to complete in accordance with predetermined criteria is not normal for project lenders, for the risks of completion are equity risks and not lender risk.

Owners normally are corporately responsible for getting the project up to design capacity for an extended production period with costs and quality of output at agreed levels. Whether this is several- or joint-owner responsibility is a matter of negotiation, but owners are normally not able to lay this financial responsibility at the feet of the construction company.

Overruns are expected in major projects, and it is usual to have an overrun credit arranged, or at least have an agreed-upon ratio of permitted additional debt and equity to cope with any cost overruns.

Permits for construction and start-up are occasionally problems, and there is growing sensitivity globally to the necessity for high standards of control of atmospheric or water pollution, and terrain replacement.

PLANT OPERATION

Lenders and owners will have to come to agreement on a variety of issues concerning the actual project facility operation. The factors at issue include: (1) operating responsibility; (2) management contract; (3) board election; (4) dispute resolution process; (5) parent company involvement; (6) technical assistance; (7) labor force; (8) training programs; (9) work permits; and (10) insurance.

The major issues are: Who is going to run the facility? What agreements for technicians and management exist among the owners and the project company? How do any disputes get resolved among the partners? With governmental agencies as partners, this becomes a delicate issue, for economic or operating reality may not on all occasions suit political objectives.

Providing a continuity of technical skill is of concern to project lenders and they will seek satisfaction in advance from those owners who bring the greatest professional skill to the project. In nearly all countries, governments want to ensure a high percentage of national employees, including the management and technical staffs. A commitment from the project owners for training is common and, while costly, has to be included in the economic projections.

SALE OF PRODUCTS

While all the preceding risk areas involve analysis, negotiation, and resolution, the most difficult issue normally is the product offtake responsibility. Historically, a number of projects were based on airtight throughput and/or purchase agreements by owners which insured cash flow to the project borrower sufficient to pay off debt and operate the facility. In some international project transactions, lenders have accepted a degree of risk in the marketing area; the owners' obligation to purchase a product has either been qualified by force majeure, economic circumstances, or has been passed on to third parties unrelated to the project.

In all cases, the owners and lenders focus on the following:

Contracts.
Market studies.
Currency of sale.
Price.
Escalation.
Domicile of payments.
Assignability.
Enforceability.
Force majeure.

Lenders desire to have strong credits on a contractual take-or-pay basis for the project output; project owners want to put the market and price risk on other parties, or limit their responsibility to the project in specific ways.

Studies based on the market for the product can be helpful in the negotiations. In some circumstances, a minimum volume and price floor contract from project owners will satisfy lenders, even though the actual product purchasers are other than the project partners.

Cross-currency risks may be involved where the currency of the project loan differs from the currency of the product sales.

Lenders to international projects generally seek to ensure that the proceeds of sale of the project output are paid to a trustee account outside the project country.

Legal assignability of the product offtake contracts to lenders is also sought by those providing project debt.

In the developing world, there are some new legal matters being addressed, such as enforceability of contracts in countries where legal precedent does not provide guidelines. In certain Muslim countries, legal procedure may well provide new challenges to lenders and owners.

While force majeure clauses have implications for the entire breadth of the contracts on which project finance is based, they have particular significance in the product-marketing area. The clear disparity of interest among owner and lender comes to a head in addressing the unpredictable risks of the future when negotiating the marketing contracts.

In summary, the results of negotiation in this broad marketing area determine some of the fundamental issues of risk assumptions for project financing.

FINANCING MATTERS

Separate from the risk evaluation matters set forth above, there are a variety of issues to be addressed which we will cluster as follows:

Leverage—The ratio of debt to equity.
Currencies of debt.
Sources of debt.
Availability of funds.

Restrictive covenants.
Repayment provisions.
Cross default.
Security.
Financial statements.

While relatively high debt to equity relationships may be permitted in specific project financings, lenders seek substantial equity investment from project owners. Broadly speaking, the degree of corporate commitment by the partners through their contractual commitments determines the degree of debt leverage permitted. The more qualitative risk assumed by lenders, the higher the ratio of equity needed.

Since major international projects tend to provide output for international markets, there may be several currencies in which the debt is issued. To the extent several government export agencies may be guaranteeing or insuring debt, or lending directly, debt will usually be expressed in the currency of each lender country. Interest rate variations at the time of debt raising may induce the project owners to raise funds in more than one currency.

Local currencies may be available in the project country, and to the extent local cost component exists for construction and operation, it may be desirable to match this component with debt in that currency. Lenders desire to see project cash generation match as closely as practical with the currency(ies) of debt funds in order to avoid cross-currency rate changes which could impair the project's ability to repay its obligations.

Sources of international project debt are generally export credit agencies, commercial banks, suppliers and product purchasers. Other sources might include the International Finance Corporation, regional or local Development Banks and local government funds. In some cases, especially when cost overruns occur, owner advances are made, perhaps subordinate to other lenders in terms of maturity and/or security.

International investment bankers usually serve as project financial advisers, drawing on their knowledge of market sources to fit together the various types of financing needed to meet the project requirements.

Restrictions on the project borrower will be required by lenders, and each transaction will have various covenants related directly to the nature of the project. Due to the reliance of lenders on the contractual obligations of the project owners, the matter of cross-default will be negotiated. Project lenders desire to be assured that a weakening of a project partner's financial condition will be reflected in the terms and conditions of their project debt agreements.

Debt drawdown will be subject to a variety of conditions, especially engineering/construction certificates of progress. Equity drawdown may parallel debt borrowings or precede them.

Repayment will be geared to cash projections generally, and in normal circumstances earnings "recapture" provision will be made should cash flow exceed forecast.

Security in the form of mortgage liens will vary widely from project to project, as the value of the project facility will depend on the marketability of the assets and the mortgage or security provisions of local law. The necessity of mortgage security will be evaluated in the context of the strength of the various contracts entered into by the project owners. A mineral property will perhaps have value for lenders under certain countries' laws compared to a specialized plant in a country with little or no legal precedent as far as security liens are concerned.

There are a number of other matters to be agreed upon, including local exchange availability for debt repayment. Lenders and owners will view these risks in light of the past and probable future government policy of the host country. Resolution of these issues again draws out very clearly the degree of corporate backing that project owners will provide for major projects.

In turn, lenders have to resolve where the fine line exists between equity risk and lender risk. Rarely is a higher interest rate sufficient to induce lenders to assume what is considered equity risk for sizable projects.

Finally, lenders will require project financial and operating information of an unusual depth in project debt financing. Separately, the owners will also have to provide their normal financial information to project lenders.

OTHER FACTORS

There are some points which deserve mention: the partners, the overall legal framework, and sovereign issues. Project financing is sometimes viewed as a way to avoid incurrence of direct corporate debt. Lenders look primarily to the strengths of the partners from their management, operating, technical and marketing standpoints, as well as their financial strengths. The matter of the project partners' obligation to disclose and the effect on their balance sheets are corporate matters and will be debated as true project financing increases. There are some accounting questions surfacing currently in the leasing area, and as project financing grows, the matter of materiality of corporate contractural obligation will undoubtedly be scrutinized by appropriate regulators.

The legal framework for project activity and its financing varies from country to country; each project will have documentation and terms reflecting international legal standards as well as the legal setting of the project country.

About all one can say is that there are no two projects directly comparable, and the local regulatory and legal framework will lead to different forms of contracts, security and debt ratios for exactly the same type of project facility being built in two different countries.

Parallel to this reality, lenders will be more interested in lending to similar projects in some countries than in others, directly related to the strength of a country's economy and its perceived sovereign attitude, monetary reserve position, balance of payments, its record of payments, exchange controls, and political stability.

ADDITIONAL SOURCES

See Additional Sources at the end of Chapter 41.

Chapter 43

ESOPs—A Creative Financial Alternative

Joseph K. Taussig[*]

ESOPs (employee stock ownership plans) can have a tremendous impact on any corporation that uses it to (1) increase cash flow; (2) increase net worth; (3) provide immediate capital infusions; (4) repay debt with pretax dollars; (5) provide liquidity for large blocks or privately held stock; (6) serve as a vehicle to tender for stock or to go private at one half the normal bid price; (7) greatly enchance acquisitions and distributions; and (8) perform many additional financial transactions at a substantially reduced price. Unfortunately, they are such a recent innovation, that sheer unfamiliarity scares off many potential users without giving the vehicle a fair look.

Unequivocally, *any* treasurer who does not thoroughly investigate the use of an ESOP as an alternative to conventional financing has failed to do his job. ESOPs are by no means ideal for all corporate situations, but can have a major impact on the financial health of companies ranging from 25 employees to AT&T, whether privately or publicly held.

This chapter will illustrate both the advantages and disadvantages of ESOP financing and will give hard examples of current uses. However, there is no way that the article could serve as a substitute for an appropriate thorough investigation, nor would an

---

[*] Joseph K. Taussig is president, J. K. Taussig & Co., Los Angeles, California.

afternoon's conversation do it justice. The permutations and combinations, perpetrated by the number of variables involved, make an ESOP's impact on a given situation very wide—ranging. On the other hand, the dollars concerned are very significant and will invariably justify the frustration and time involved to thoroughly investigate the potential of the program for a given situation.

Most available literature on ESOPs extol the virtues of people's capitalism, giving the employee a piece of the action, life insurance benefits, and the like because they have a nice ring. Business writers do not admit to their lack of understanding of the financial significance of the program, nor do they want to expose themselves by even calling that shortcoming to the readers attention. While not wishing to underplay the value of the social virtues, they simply do not stimulate chief executive officers, chief financial officers, or top management to action. What does cause excitement is the hard-dollar financial power of the ESOP and this chapter will emphasize this fact in its fullest extent.

WHAT IS AN ESOP?

While ESOP stands for Employees Stock Ownership Plan, it is often referred to as a Kelso Plan (named after the brilliant San Francisco lawyer and economist who has pioneered them for several years). Essentially, an ESOP is nothing more than an Internal Revenue Service qualified profit sharing or pension plan (there can be both) whose *primary objective* is to invest in the securities of the employer company. (Caveat: any good law firm can execute an ESOP and get it qualified by the IRS. *But* there are so many variables involved that a plan could be suboptimally structured and percentages of large numbers of dollars can slip through the cracks, interminably, as an opportunity cost. Professional, experienced ESOP assistance will pay for itself many times over.) The full nature of an ESOP will be developed through a series of illustrative examples, presented after a few additional technical characteristics are summarized in the following five paragraphs and Figure 1.

FIGURE 1

The ESOP, because of its nature, is exempted from the restrictions of self-dealing in conventional benefit plans, and has been strengthened in this respect under the new Pension Reform Act of 1974. (See Chapter 51.) It must be emphasized that the ESOP is able to invest in the employer firm's securities, but is not limited to doing so. Thus, a very strong case can be made for having an ESOP just to have the flexibility it provides without altering the intention of any current or future employee benefit plan philosophies that the company might have or develop.

The employee stock ownership trust (ESOT) is owned by all those employees who are covered. Each portion is owned by employees in degrees that are dictated by the structuring of the plan, which is one of the critical aspects of the concept. Yet this is often underemphasized, because a plan can be put into effect with results that provide fewer dollars in the pockets of those that ownership and management want to favor. Management of the trust can remain in the hands of management and ownership, and thus they control the destiny of the funds and their application.

The basic transaction with an ESOP is an annual contribution, made by the company, that is tax deductible to the corporation and nontaxable to the employee until the benefits are distributed to him. This pool of dollars can then be applied in a myriad of transactions on behalf of the corporation that are, in effect, done with untaxed dollars. Figure 1 illustrates this feature.

The use of 100-cent dollars (versus taxed dollars) to make transactions happen makes the ESOP an incredibly powerful financial vehicle. However, in addition to the financial well-being of the company, ESOPs have other positive effects for the corporation. As will be seen, an employee benefit plan is established that is so substantial as to have *real* meaning for employees (many nonunion plans are token, at best). Thus, not only are the employees taken care of for the long term, to the benefit of the company, rather than to its detriment under conventional plans, but also personnel issues such as retention, productivity, and morale are strengthened.

Particularly, for highly compensated employees, to include salesmen on commission, the prospect of leaving the company can be very costly, depending on vesting and redemption provisions. Insiders at Sears fondly refer to their plan as "the Golden Handcuffs" for this reason. In addition, morale and productivity are strengthened and self-policed. What employee would strike if this benefit plan were tied to the company's stock, whose price is hurt by a strike. Also, the inclination to allow the inefficiency of others in the company dies when it comes out of the employees' own pockets.

USING THE ESOP AS THE VEHICLE FOR TRANSACTIONS

Sources of Money for the Transactions

The financing vehicle represented by an ESOP works because it takes in untaxed cash and can meet obligations with untaxed cash. Generally, its sources of cash are illustrated in Figure 2 as follows:

FIGURE 2

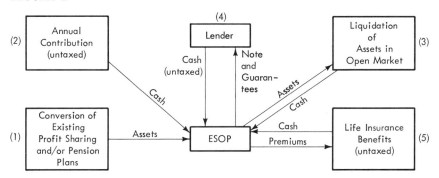

(1) Conversion of existing profit sharing and pension plans to ESOPs; (2) annual contributions from the corporation; (3) liquidation of assets in the trust; (4) direct input from a lender; and (5) insurance benefits.

Converting Existing Benefit Plans (1)

Conversion of existing plans is feasible and could provide, in many cases, an instantaneous source of much needed capital for the company. This, of course, raises several issues along the lines of all-the-eggs-in-one-basket and self-dealing that will be analyzed, later. A judgment must be made as to the trade-offs involved, but it is really frustrating to be a capital provider for IBM, Polaroid or Xerox (which any owner of their stock effectively is), when your own company desperately needs the capital infusion. Generally most of the existing plan will be owned by management who would most likely favor the move. It is possible that labor might even support the investment in corporate securities because it strengthens the company, making jobs more secure. If there are no jobs, there are no unions and no benefits to negotiate in the future.

Because there is the flexibility to invest in other companies' securities, the issue of conversion to an ESOP or starting one that runs parallel to other plans should not be a problem. However, not having one certainly lops off a major alternative for future use in times where alternatives are few and dear.

Corporate Contributions (2)

Annual contributions from the firm is the major source of funds over the years. However, they do not have the same immediate impact as the other four methods. Instead, they are "foundation" dollars as opposed to "opportunity" dollars. Because this source is fairly predictable over time, it can provide the means or credibility of obtaining dollars from the other sources when the need is immediate.

The contributions can be up to 25 percent of covered payroll in most cases or 30 percent in certain situations. This means that people-intensive corporations such as service companies and certain types of manufacturing and distribution businesses could contribute a significant portion of their revenue dollar. Depending on the structuring of the ESOPs, the company can have a good amount of flexibility so that it contributes mostly according to the needs or stresses that it has, and the ownership of the trust will generally accrue to whomever management and ownership desires to benefit, including themselves.

Some businesses, such as securities firms, are so people intensive and low in profit margin (as a return on sales) that they could conceivably shield every dollar of cash flow from operations from corporate taxes. This often has an additional effect of providing equity participations for partnership-type businesses, such as securities firms, law firms, and CPA firms without the economic burden placed on participants by the tax system.

Liquidating Assets (3)

The liquidation of assets is another source of cash. Whether they are assets acquired from the conversion of other plans or assets acquired in the normal course of business, the trust should sell them when cash or other investment opportunities seem more rewarding. Naturally, these assets would be sold in the open market in return for cash.

Borrowing (4)

Lenders should provide ESOPs a major source of money, particularly of the large amount, single-purpose, opportunistic variety. Lending to an ESOP, collaterized by stock in the company and guaranteed by the company and/or its officers, should offer the lender the same recourse as lending to the corporation itself. However, it is a better deal for the lender because the corporation needs only to perform half as well (assuming a 50 percent tax bracket) to repay the debt. (This will be illustrated later.) Since the earnings coverage is lower by 50 percent, the lender's risk is *greatly* reduced.

A lender that desires to lend to a corporation which has or might need an ESOP is foolish not to lend through an ESOP, instead, because the coverage and risk factors make it a higher quality loan. Unfortunately, it will take tremendous insight and understanding to see this and the banking community will probably respond unevenly. (Union Bank of California, a historically aggressive and innovative institution, is becoming very active in this area and has launched a major effort to educate their lending officers and customers.) On the other hand, venture capital firms and insurance companies will most likely recognize the tremendous value in short order and can be expected to become very active in this area.

Insurance Benefits (5)

Insurance can also play a role, but not so major as the others (although most of the merchandising of ESOPs have been done by insurance salesmen.) Essentially, ESOPs can purchase keyman insurance (or other life insurance) and use the proceeds, in the event of death, to purchase the deceased's stock from his estate. The value, here, is that keyman insurance is not deductible to the corporation, but the ESOP buys it with pretax dollars. Also, the ESOP comes up with the money to make liquid a block of stock of a deceased (particularly a large stockholder), without putting an undue strain on the company.

TRANSACTIONS THAT PUT PRETAX
DOLLARS TO BETTER USE

Numerous transactions are possible, because the ESOP can borrow, purchase or sell stock, obligate itself with notes, or lend money. The trick becomes identification of the types of transactions, pricing them, and determining what source of cash is logical. (Caveat: pricing is a major issue because the trustee has a fiduciary responsibility to insure that pricing is fair. The problems of pricing must be carefully looked at by the company, in order to keep the plan qualified. The ramifications of this problem are too great for the scope of this chapter, and generally, the assistance of an investment banking, accounting or appraisal firm is needed. An appraisal done by anyone who receives fees for services other than appraisal will be tainted and may cause disqualification.

Itemized below, are a series of deals that can use an ESOP. These are by no means all that can be done. They are simply typical examples and rearranging certain aspects or combining some of them will yield a number of variations.

Obtaining an Immediate Infusion of Capital

This objective is achieved if the corporation issues stock to the ESOP or borrows from it. Assuming that the source of money is a lender (it could come from the other sources previously mentioned), the transaction appears as shown in Figure 3.

FIGURE 3

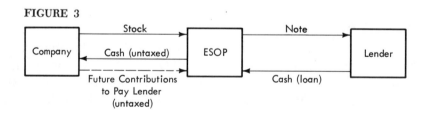

Depending upon the sources of cash, the ESOP provides the untaxed cash to the company, taking stock or a note in exchange. Later on, we will see how the debt can be repaid with pretax dollars. Recently, Steiger Tractor raised new capital in this manner.

Increasing Cash Flow and Doubling the Growth Rate of Net Worth

The contributions to the ESOP can immediately be recycled into the company by purchasing stock in the firm. Recognizing that all contributions reduce earnings, they also reduce tax liabilities. The transaction appears in Figure 4.

FIGURE 4

Normal Corporation		
1.	Earnings before taxes	$1,000,000
2.	Tax liability	500,000
3.	After tax retained earnings (net worth and cash flow growth)	500,000
ESOP Corporation		
1.	Earnings before taxes and contributions	$1,000,000
2.	Contributions	1,000,000
3.	Taxable earnings	0
4.	Taxes	0
5.	Increases in paid-in-capital when ESOP purchases stock (net worth and cash flow growth)	$1,000,000

The net effect is that the retained earnings account is reduced by one half the contribution (assuming a 50 percent tax rate). However, the earnings reduction *and* the tax liability of those earnings come back into the company as paid-in capital. Thus, the cash account grows by the amount equal to the reduction of taxes, and the rate of growth of net worth increases by the same amount (its paid-in capital). Robinson-Humphrey in Atlanta used the ESOP to achieve this end and greatly increased its net worth.

Two variations of the cash flow increase include (1) contributing more than pretax earnings to force a loss, which recaptures previously paid tax dollars, and (2) getting the ESOP installed well before the end of the year so that contributions can be accrued. Assuming that the current year is as good or better than the previous one, the accrual reduces the quarterly tax payment. This not only keeps cash in the company, it reduces interest expense if borrowings are reduced, or increases income if the cash is put to use. If the cost of debt is 10 percent, a company with a $4 million payroll would save (or earn) roughly $37,500 in interest expense while increasing its available cash by $250,000 a quarter. This interest expense saving will be more than the cost of installing an ESOP.

Another variation occurs through the additional 1 percent investment tax credit awarded to ESOP companies in the recently enacted Tax Reform Act of 1975. For most corporations capable of listing on the New York Stock Exchange, this is a significant number of dollars—in the hundreds of thousands or millions of dollars a year.

Using Tax Dollars to Meet Obligations without Impairing Net Worth Growth

This transaction is a variation of a previous one, but only half of the contribution is used to meet other obligations. Figure 5 illustrates this transaction.

FIGURE 5

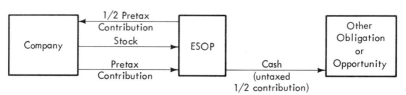

The ESOP in this case only buys stock in the amount that would normally have been applied to retained earnings. Thus, paid-in capital increases by the amount retained earnings failed to grow and net worth continues to grow as normal. However, all of the tax dollars can be applied to other transactions as outlined in other examples. Obviously the split can vary and does not need to be 50–50. The company should balance internal growth with obligations depending on its needs, and it is this ability that permits the other transactions to be done to the degree necessary.

Repaying Loans or Notes in Pretax Dollars

This transaction occurs when the pretax contributions are then utilized to meet obligations as shown in Figure 6. Whether only part of the contribution or the whole contribution is used, all dollars used in repayment are untaxed. The conventionally financed company pays its taxes prior to repaying its debt and not only has more difficulty in meeting the obligation, it is less healthy afterward. The obligation might have been created by a direct loan of cash from a

FIGURE 6

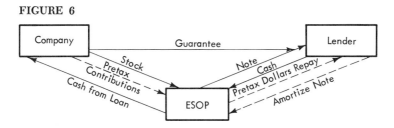

lender, as mentioned before, or by issuing a note in exchange for securities or other assets, as will be obtained later.

Because the loan is safer for a lender and cheaper for the corporation, most corporations and lenders *should consider* refinancing existing debt. Another variation might find a corporation making a strong case for obtaining more cash through an increase in borrowings, in exchange for an agreement to pay back through the ESOP, accelerating the repayment of the old debt, and increasing the interest rate. All of these conditions are still more attractive to both the borrower and the lender, if an ESOP is used. Ultra-Violet Products in California restructured its debt by this means.

The ESOP as a Market Maker

The ESOP may invest in the securities of the employer firm, but is not limited to purchasing them from the company. The trust of a public company can purchase (or sell) shares in the open market, while the trust of either a public or private company can buy from stockholders, who desire liquidity where it otherwise might not exist. Figure 7 shows the transactions that are possible. Effectively,

FIGURE 7

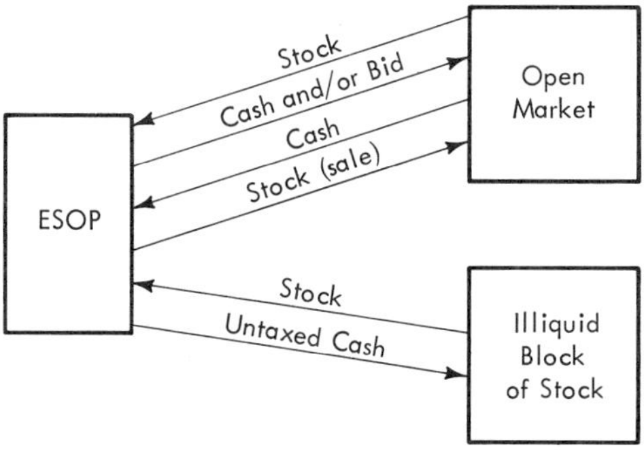

the trustees of the ESOP have an obligation to purchase the *same* security for the best price. At the same time, the company has no desire to issue stock at too cheap a price. Thus, if the best price comes from the company (to include transaction costs) then the stock will be purchased from the company; if not, it will be purchased elsewhere. For private companies, the choice will be between the company and any shareholder seeking liquidity. For the public company, all three entities could be involved. These basic transactions set the stage for numerous other types of deals.

Providing Liquidity for the Illiquid

As we saw before, the ESOP can buy from private sources other than the firm. Quite often, letter stock, control stock, unusual classes of securities, or large blocks have trouble getting liquid. The market won't or can't absorb them. In a privately held company, there is no market for the stock, unless there are buy-back agreements. However, buy-back agreements impair the net worth of the firm, especially if the stock is a major portion, and the dollars paid are after-tax dollars. (This is a common ailment of the securities brokerage industry.) An ESOP can purchase securities of all of these types, if the price is right. In addition, it does it with pretax dollars, which in effect, means it only pays one half the amount. In another case, the ESOP may not have the cash, but can simply buy on an installment note basis. Thus, the cash payments would match the contributions.

If the seller is an estate, the cash could come from a life insurance policy paid for by the ESOP, which, in turn, is the beneficiary. For many companies, buy-back provisions require that the company get the estate liquid, and the ESOP is by far the least painful way for all concerned. At Mulach Steel in Pittsburgh, the ESOP provided liquidity for some of the principal shareholders.

The Alternative to Going Public

The major reasons for going public are to raise equity capital and to provide liquidity. The ESOP does both of these, but the corporation has far more control over its destiny in view of its stock price, which can be pegged at a specific rate, rather than be subject to the vagaries of the marketplace. Smaller companies which are public have trouble, regardless of their performance, getting recognition during periods when the general equity market is weak as evidenced by seven to eight times multiples on the Dow or Standard & Poor's common stock indexes. Many small companies (as well as larger ones) are selling at significant discounts from book value during a weak equity market. For the company desiring to raise capital and provide liquidity in such an environment, an ESOP is a very attractive alternative.

In addition, the ESOP could be a prelude to going public. If the market timing is not right, an ESOP could be employed to meet the immediate capital need. Then, later, the ESOP could sell the stock to the public marketplace when timing and prices are better.

Going Private and Tender Offers

The ESOP can bring more sense to types of transactions such as tenders and going private which are otherwise carried out in after-tax dollars. When done through an ESOP they are accomplished in pretax dollars or at 50 percent of the cost. Figure 8 shows the basic transaction.

FIGURE 8

Korn/Ferry International and Certified Plans, Inc., two creative, aggressive service companies, used ESOPs to go private, in essence paying only half as much and, if done correctly, without impairing the net worth of the firm. In Korn/Ferry's case, their stock was $5 bid, they tendered at $7 per share, but Korn/Ferry's outlay was only $3.50 per share. A recent article in *Forbes* magazine complimented Mary Wells for her shrewdness in taking Wells, Rich & Greene private, thus enhancing her own interest in the company and net worth. The irony is that the company will pay $12 million more than it would have, if it had tendered through an ESOP (this also comes out of her net worth) and her interest in the firm might ultimately have increased by the same amount depending on the dynamics and structure of the ESOP. Since the deal was a package of cash and notes, there is still a chance to save almost $8 million if Wells, Rich & Greene installs an ESOP soon.

Currently, there is a lot of adverse publicity, potential lawsuits and SEC scrutiny regarding "going private." If the company can say "our employees bought it," then much of this flak should subside. It is unlikely that Mary Wells, for example, would have borne the criticism that she did.

All tenders can be done this way and the ESOP can often borrow to obtain the cash that may otherwise be lacking. One interesting variation of ESOP financing and a tender offer is the case of Hi-Shear. The victim of a "successful" hostile tender, the management of Hi-Shear installed an ESOP and by borrowing money from a bank, used it to sell the ESOP additional common stock to dilute the tender to a level below controlling interest.

Acquisition and Divestitures with Pretax Dollars

An acquisition can be done with an ESOP using either the acquiring company's money or using the acquired company's money. Essentially, a stock for stock transaction is executed whereby the acquiring company issues a new class of stock to the sellers of the acquisition in exchange for 100 percent of the acquisition. Then, the owners of the new class of stock sell the new class of stock to an

FIGURE 9

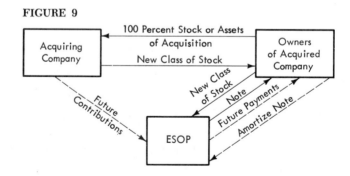

ESOP at whatever terms were prearranged. The transaction would appear as in Figure 9.

If it is desired to use the acquiring company's money, the ESOP covers employees of the acquiring company. But, it is desired to use the acquired company's money, then the ESOP would cover the acquired company's employees only. In some cases, recourse to the total company makes sense, and in others the sellers may trust the earning power of their division only.

Divestitures

Divestitures are simply the reverse process of an acquisition, which puts the parent company in the creditor status. This is a good way to spin-off a division to its employees and better ensure that payment will be made, as was done in the case of Monolith Portland Cement. The transaction would appear as in Figure 10.

FIGURE 10

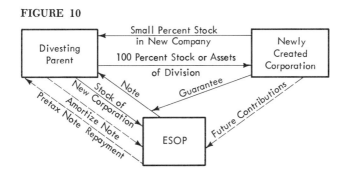

POSSIBLE DISADVANTAGES OF ESOPs

Despite the advantages of ESOPs, issues such as ownership dilution, earnings reductions, the future legality of ESOPs, and the propriety of self-dealing with benefit funds pose problems. Under some circumstances these may be significant disadvantages although some potential drawbacks are avoidable.

Ownership Dilution

Ownership dilution occurs when new shares are issued. Current owners do not see themselves as owning as great a percentage of the company as prior to institution of the ESOP. Assuming that the ESOP purchases voting common stock, this could be a valid complaint. However, the ESOP can purchase nonvoting stock, preferred stock or various types of debt (to include convertibles), so voting control need not be a problem.

In the case of common stock, dilution may or may not be a valid issue. If the stock sells at a premium over book value the ownership will often increase its net claim on the company (the number of shares they hold stays the same but book value/share increases). If the ownership is employed by the company, it also holds an interest through the trust. While his share of the annual contribution may not be proportionate to his ownership interest, he will almost always be made whole in the future, because the trust is 50 percent funded by U.S. dollars and the owner/employee recaptures forfeitures in proportion to his usually higher salary level.

The outside or nonemployee owner will see his interest reduced, unless he perceives that a better capitalized entity will yield him more value or that an ESOP also provides *his* liquidity. In the case of publicly held corporations this could be a problem, but could also enhance the price of the stock by putting buying pressure on the market.

Earnings Reductions

Earnings reductions occur because the contribution is tax deductible and must be reported as a reduction in earnings. This is particularly onerous for publicly held firms.

Because reported earnings per share are reduced by the after-tax value of the contribution and the additional dilution of new shares, many public companies may be reluctant to use an ESOP. The effect of earnings on a corporation's stock price varies from company to company, so it is not easy to generalize. However, in years such as the bear market of 1974, earnings have been erratic and prices so low, particularly for smaller companies, that it is unlikely that a further reduction in nominal earnings will affect many companies. On the other hand, we have seen how an ESOP can perform as a market maker. As such, it could be a continuous bidder for the corporation's stock. While limited to the greater of 100 shares or 15 percent of the daily trading volume (or block transactions), it can still impart a healthy boost to the demand function in a stock price. This could make the trade-off of earnings worth it. A small company should ask itself what it thinks its stock price would be if earnings were zero and what it would be if there was a 15 percent increase in demand. Often the rewards would justify the risks.

Another aspect for a public company occurs when its price is low, it desires to stay publicly held, and it wants to raise capital. In this case the company can issue a different class of security with different features to justify a higher price and can float it to the ESOP. This gives a corporation, particularly one selling below book value, an opportunity to go to the capital markets at a reasonable price, when none really exists in the traditional sense.

Another use of an ESOP for a public company would be a combination of controlling earnings and using the surplus to increase demand for the stock. A certain over-the-counter company on the West Coast could have truncated its earnings growth to successive 30 percent increases for 1973 and 1974, and used the excess dollars as an ESOP contribution. The ESOP could have purchased (within trading rules) all of the shares of stock that came to the market in 1974 at five times the current market price with the ESOP proceeds. Here the reduction of earnings could create the means to raise the demand for the stock fivefold.

For the privately held company, the earnings reduction should pose no problem at all, because net worth and cash-flow benefits should dictate practice.

For companies that put their contribution at 1 percent of capital investment, the earnings per share reduction is very small; it is limited to the additional dilution of the number of shares the 1 percent capital investment buys. For a company with an annual capital investment of $10 million, an ESOP provides $100,000 a year in additional cash flow and net worth. If that same company had 10 million shares outstanding at $10 per share, the resulting dilution in earning per share would only be one-tenth of 1 percent. ($100,000/$10 = 10,000 shares; 10,000/10,000,000 = .001.) Because the amount is so small relative to the company itself, the dilution factor and earnings reduction are usually negligible.

The issues of dilution and earnings reduction often look so adverse that resistance to the idea builds to the extent that a feasibility study is not even undertaken to see if structuring could ameliorate the problem or lay it to rest altogether. This is unfortunate, because given realistic objectives on the part of management and ownership, and reasonable assumptions as to the makeup of people in the company, their growth rate, and turnover rates, as well as other relevant inputs, the ESOP can almost always be structured to minimize the effects of dilution and earnings reduction that takes place.

The rules regarding the structuring of an ESOP are far too numerous and complex to cover in this chapter. Such issues as the desired degree of employee welfare, profit sharing versus pension ESOPs, integration with social security, eligibility, coverage, discrimination, contributions, allocations, vesting, forfeitures, redistributions, liquidity, and the pricing of transactions can all have a tremendous impact on the desired objectives. Because there are so many variables creating an infinite number of combinations to contend with, there is a significant amount of skill involved in optimally structuring the ESOP. In fact, the *opportunity cost* to ownership, management, and the company of suboptimally structuring the ESOP could run in the millions of dollars even in medium-sized corporations. Just one nuance or twist may mean thousands of dollars for any company, because everything recurs year after year and is done on such scale. But, because it is an opportunity cost, it may even go unrecognized forever.

THE LEGAL FOUNDATION OF ESOPs

The reasons the law provides for ESOPs are based on sound business principles. Heretofore, employee benefit plans were a full burden on the company. Thus, a decision had to be made between divergent goals of the short-term (and sometimes the long-term) financial health of the company and the long-term welfare of employees. The choice was often simple for the species of management who measure performance by short-term yardsticks. Many plans put into effect were due to either union pressures or were done as token fringe benefits that often had little meaning, but which would not be conspicuous by their absence. Needless to say, neither impetus yields the type of plan which earns employee gratitude or loyalty.

ESOP financing, on the other hand, puts the objectives of employee welfare and corporate financial health in concert with each other. In effect, the greater the contribution (within certain parameters) the more favorable the impact on the corporation's financial health. Thus, there is an incentive to the company to provide for the welfare of its employees.

Some of ESOPs' detractors claim it is only a tax dodge. The counterargument is that taxes are really only deferred until much later and shifted to the employees when they receive the benefits. Theoretically, the company could pay out the amount in bonuses, shifting the tax load from the company to the individual. The employee could then defer the tax in the new ERISA (Employee Retirement Income Security Act of 1974) plans and buy stock in his company with the untaxed dollars. (This is the same as partnership units for lawyers and CPAs). *But,* without the incentive of capital formation, the company has little motivation to take that course of action. Ideally, employees will have enough money to retire and do not burden the taxpayers, later. Without a doubt, such people aspects as morale, loyalty, productivity, and efficiency are better insured and it is conceivable that even the least skilled and lowest paid can accumulate wealth from this form of people's capitalism.

Because of the justifiable concern over pension reform, capital formation, unemployment and productivity, there is significant support in Washington (both bipartisan and biphilosophical) for ESOP financing. Senators Fannin and Percy have made public their views and Senator Long went on record proposing that any aid to Pan American or TWA be in the form of ESOP financing. He further regretted, on the record, that the Lockheed loan was not done through an ESOP. There is also wide speculation that any financing of the Northeast railroads will be done through this vehicle.

Given this type of support and the strengthening of ESOPs in the new Pension Reform Act of 1974 and in the Tax Reform Act of 1975, there is a strong basis for the conclusion that the ESOP is soundly established in a legal sense.

The Issue of Self-Dealing

The all-the-eggs-in-one-basket fear could be a valid one, in some cases. If the company no longer remains viable, the employees' benefit plan will own worthless assets. This has happened before and has also raised questions as to whether or not there are fiduciary and personal liabilities for officers and directors in these cases.

On the other hand, arguments can be made that an ESOP increases both the short- and long-term welfare of the employee. For example, one could argue that employees care more about today than tomorrow. Offer any employee $50 more in the paycheck each month or $100 more a month in a retirement plan; most will choose $50 today. "Today" is even more acute when it comes to having a job at all, especially in the face of the 8 to 9 percent national unemployment rates of 1974–75. The number of jobs which do not exist now that could exist, if the mechanisms of capital formation had not slowed down, is substantial. The capital formation capabilities of an ESOP guarantee more jobs for employees and most likely a higher quality of life in the later years. In addition, a company that fails when better capitalized, would be more likely to fail if undercapitalized. Thus, an ESOP gives the firm a chance it would not normally have to maintain jobs, particularly if survival is an issue.

Another argument against the all-the-eggs-in-one-basket fear is that in many cases there would not be any eggs (or basket, for that matter), without the incentive of reinvesting the benefit plan's funds into the employer company. One hundred percent of nothing is nothing. If there is little or no incentive to have benefit plans they will be token or nonexistent. How can people who currently have little or no assets in a retirement plan say they do not want their money in their own company? Maybe the trust assets will be lost if the company fails. But, in reality, the employees are no worse off than if they had a token plan or no plan at all. Instead, they gain the benefits of being employed by a more viable company, and have, in most cases, a *real* chance to acquire wealth.

CONCLUSIONS: THE USE OF ESOPs

The power of using tax dollars to make the business go should be sufficient incentive for any top officer in a company to explore ESOPs in greater depth. It simply takes the cost of most transactions and reduces it 50 percent (tax dollars underwrite the remaining cost).

The ABCs of the use of ESOPs can be summarized in a number of steps.

First, it is most important to define the objectives that a company wants to achieve by implementing an ESOP. Generally, these objectives should address the following issues:

1. What type of financial transaction is desired?
2. At what price should securities transact?
3. How many dollars can be spared or saved?
4. Who should own the trust?
5. What is the makeup of the company, and what reasonable assumptions about turnover and makeup in the future should be made?
6. What other objectives (i.e., earnings) are strongly held?

These issues should be answered *in detail*.

Next, a plan should be structured with the help of an experienced professional and a deal should be negotiated to achieve the ends desired. Third, a plan should be drawn up by an attorney and then adopted by the company. The plan must later be qualified by the IRS.

Fourth, the securities transacted should be independently appraised and the method of appraisal should not be taken lightly. A future problem could develop if the appraisal is made by someone who also receives sums for consulting or legal work. There is a real possibility that the appraisal would be less than fair or arm's length, if compensation for other services were tied to a prearranged value. This obvious conflict of interest could lose a challenge in court and cost a qualification of the plan.

The plan should be administered (paper work and score keeping) and trusteed by professionals. Some banks and insurance companies do either very well (rarely both). But, their fees are substantial and a company and its officers might want to look into the trade-offs of providing these services in house.

ADDITIONAL SOURCES

See Additional Sources at the end of Chapter 41.

Chapter 44

Evaluating Corporate Acquisitions

Roger W. Cope*

INTRODUCTION

It has become fairly evident to most people who are either working in the merger and acquisition field today or who have worked in the field in the past that numerous mistakes were made during the frantic acquisition activities in the 1960s and early 1970s. Many major U.S. companies were seeking growth but found that they acquired severe cases of corporate indigestion.

The current divestiture activities being carried out by many corporations have focused attention on some of the problems inherent in ill-advised, poorly planned acquisition programs and, we feel, have shown that making acquisitions is relatively easy; making successful acquisitions is not easy at all.

This chapter will focus on an acquisition evaluation process which should help in reducing the probability of making major mistakes in your company's acquisition activities.

The assumed need for continued increases in earnings per share has been the culprit in causing many acquisitions to be made which resulted in expansion rather than growth. As earnings per share as an investment analysis tool has declined in favor, many companies

---

* Roger W. Cope is corporate group vice president, planning and development, Dart Industries, Inc., Los Angeles, California.

that were acquired solely for their earnings are being sold.[1] When a corporation is asked why they are selling a division or subsidiary, the response is oftentimes, "It does not fit." If this is true now, it was probably true when the company was acquired, all of which points to the critical importance of proper planning as the base for any acquisition program.

Any merger and acquisition program should be looked upon as merely one avenue to growth. There are other methods such as increased spending on product development or perhaps venture management programs. Each of these activities should typically be examined in terms of their role in an overall corporate plan—a plan which one hopes would aim at, in a multicompany corporation, a balanced portfolio approach. The balanced portfolio can also be looked upon as another path to controlled growth. For the purposes of the discussion in this chapter, we will assume that acquisitions are one of your company's approved methods of growth, that you have a plan outlining the growth program for your company, and that this plan has been accepted and approved by those individuals responsible for its successful implementation. Typically, this would include operating management as well as the chief executive officer and his staff.

Now that we have made our assumptions, let us follow a step-by-step program for finding, analyzing, and acquiring viable acquisition candidates.

SOURCES FOR ACQUISITION CANDIDATES

Investment Bankers

Historically, the investment banking community has been the major source of large acquisition candidates. In order to make the most efficient use of investment bankers, it is necessary to provide them with guidelines as to the types of companies which you seek to acquire. This does not mean that you should provide very detailed criteria with close limits as to size and product range. One of the problems with being too definitive in your guidelines is that oftentimes companies in which you might have had an interest will

---

[1] See J. M. Stern, "Earnings per Share Don't Count," *Financial Analysts Journal,* July–August 1974.

be excluded because they cannot meet all the criteria. Typically, you would discuss with the investment banker your development plan and say, "We have an interest in expanding in the widget business and are looking for companies that have experienced management in place (who will remain) and that have sales of not less than a certain amount." By using such broad descriptions, you will ensure yourself the opportunity of looking at most of the known-to-be-available businesses in industries in which you have an interest.

Investment bankers, of course, provide other services, some of which are described in Chapter 33 of this *Handbook*. In the case of all these services, however, the investment banker does not take the role of a charitable institution. Therefore, if you utilize his services, you will end up paying the fee. As you proceed in establishing your acquisition program with the investment banking community, you will hear repeatedly over and over again, "We charge the standard fee . . . 5 percent on the first million dollars of the purchase price, 4 percent on the second million, 3 percent on the third million, 2 percent on the fourth million and 1 percent on everything over $4 million." This is a fictitious statement in that there is no "standard fee," and in each instance you will find yourself negotiating the amount you are willing to pay for the services rendered. Generally speaking, investment bankers expect to be compensated based upon the amount of work that they put in on a project. If you have identified the target company and have asked for the assistance of the investment banking firm, this situation would require a lesser fee than if the investment banking firm had brought you the target company as their idea. As in all businesses, some firms are better than others. This also holds true for investment bankers in the merger and acquisition business.

Business Brokers

The second source of acquisition candidates is a vast armada of independent "business brokers." This is a group whose integrity is spread across a broad spectrum from those who are totally honest and forthright individuals whose word you can trust to those who you make a mistake in taking a telephone call from in that you can always count on it being a problem. An example of what can happen if you don't "consider the source" carefully might be illustrated by the following. A business broker informs you that the

XYZ Company, a company you have identified in the past as being a potential acquisition candidate, had called and stated that they were ready to merge with a large company and had selected your company as the best potential partner for them. Naturally, you are flattered that they have sought you out. At this time, you request financial information and product brochures. The broker informs you that the owner of the company is prepared to deliver all of these things if you would meet with him.

As you have already identified this company as an acquisition candidate and knew that their product line fits with your plans, you agree to the meeting. The first part of the meeting, namely the plant tour and preliminary discussions of areas of mutual interest, go very well. The problems arise as you sit down to lunch and the owner of the company says to you, "Before we discuss my financial statements, could you please tell me how you reached the decision to ask Mr. A (the business broker) to contact me on your behalf?" It is at this point that you realize that you are the victim of a successful fishing expedition on the part of the broker. He called both of you and told each of you that the other had high regard for the other and wished to discuss the possibilities of a merger.

Brokers of this ilk can cause you to waste a great deal of time and effort because many companies will agree to talk only to be polite. This kind of broker just hopes something will click, and he will earn a fee.

Commercial Banks

During the past few years, various commercial banks have begun to take advantage of the vast potential of acquisition sources with which they deal every day; namely, their customers. In many instances, the first person to know of a company's activities, either in acquiring financing to grow or in having grown too fast for their capital base or for a myriad of other reasons that companies get in trouble, is the commercial lending officer. As a result of having successfully placed companies in the above-mentioned categories in touch with those who seek acquisitions, commercial bankers have gradually worked their way into an area previously reserved for investment bankers and brokers. As they discovered how lucrative the fees can be in acquisition work, many commercial banks have developed formal merger and acquisition departments who actively solicit business on behalf of the bank while acting as broker for either buyer or seller.

This area of potential candidates has not yet matured to its optimum efficiency mainly because of poor communications between the field lending officer and the bank's merger and acquisition staff. It will, however, continue to improve in the future, and acquiring companies will be getting more and more ideas from this potentially plentiful source.

Internal Sources

The fourth and last source of acquisition candidates to be discussed in this chapter are the internal sources of the acquiring corporation. Many large companies have formal acquisition departments who diligently search for companies which meet the criteria expressed in the corporation's growth plans. There are numerous financial services such as Standard & Poors, Moody's, and Dun & Bradstreet which provide information on the finances and product lines of both public and private companies. Many corporations have become quite sophisticated in the use of the information provided by these firms and have been successful in identifying and acquiring companies through their use.

There is also another internal source and that is the management and staff of your company's operating divisions. They are in contact with many companies each day in the course of conducting their business, and if you have made them aware of your company's acquisition requirements, they can be very helpful in providing ideas as to candidates which fulfill the requirements of your growth plans.

INITIAL REVIEW PROCEDURES

After one of your sources has submitted an acquisition candidate for your review, it is necessary that you have an established procedure which will allow you to quickly decide whether or not the candidate warrants continued analysis. The first screening step is to determine that the company submitted meets the criteria outlined in your corporation's plan for growth. As soon as this is established, you should ensure that the company meets your financial criteria. The next step is to present it for management review. In many instances, you will find that management is familiar with the company and its personnel. This is especially true if the acquisition is intended to supplement or complement one of your existing businesses.

If the candidate submitted is of sufficient size and/or does not supplement or complement one of your existing operations, then the second review step typically is conducted by senior corporate management rather than operating management. Once these appropriate initial approvals or expressions of interest have been established, this should be communicated to the acquisition candidate. The method by which you contact this company will be determined generally by the source from which it was submitted. In the case of investment bankers, commercial bankers or business brokers, in most instances the expression of your interest will be communicated through them.

In the case of internally generated candidates, however, a decision must be made on how to contact the company identified as a potential candidate. In some cases, a phone call to the chief executive officer is the acceptable route. However, in many instances this is not the case. The thing you must keep in mind is that independent companies are contacted frequently by brokers and others who wish to earn a fee by developing a salable commodity. It is, therefore, sometimes more productive to make your initial contact through someone the candidate knows and trusts. This can be a director, a banker, a friend, or a relative. Each case must be examined individually. If the company is a customer, supplier, or competitor, it may be that someone within your organization has developed contacts and can be used.

DETERMINING CANDIDATE INTEREST

In the case of an approach by a broker representing a client/ seller, you know that there is an interest on the part of the company to be purchased. In the case of the approach where you have no knowledge of interest on the part of the potential acquiree, the amount of information to be gained in the initial contact may be limited to a simple "Yes, I could be interested"; "No, I am definitely not interested"; or, as occurs in most cases, "I could be interested . . . convince me . . . everything is for sale at the right price."

In this latter case, it may be necessary to assume the role of the marketing man and sell the benefits of being a part of your company. You may be put in the position of assuming this selling role without really knowing the degree of your interest in the company to be acquired. For the purposes of this discussion, however, let us assume that you establish communications with the selling company, that he has an interest in selling, and that the general information at your disposal convinces you that he "fits" in with your plans. You should at this point arrange to visit him and begin the next step in the evaluation process.

THE INITIAL VISIT

In most cases, management of companies to be acquired have pride in the companies they manage and are not at all reluctant to give you a thorough and complete sales pitch describing in detail the virtues of their operation. Your role as investigator will be to sit back and listen, asking a few questions, most of which at this stage are designed to ensure that you have not erred in inferring that this company fits with your plans. The key accomplishment of these first few hours of discussion should be determining how the management of the potential acquiree will "fit" within your company. If your company's policy is to retain the management of the companies you acquire, you most certainly want to make sure that the management of this potential acquisition candidate will be people who will be happy within your organization and with whom you and your colleagues can work.

Typically, the next step is to tour the facilities, allowing the company to show off its accomplishments while at the same time you get a handle on their general housekeeping, some labor attitudes, equipment maintenance, OSHA (Occupational Safety and Health Administration) and EPA (Environmental Protection Agency) problems, and so on, keeping in mind that this first visit is designed only to provide for the establishment of communications and to reinforce your earlier favorable feelings about the acquisition potential of the company.

You should endeavor to meet and begin to evaluate key managers in the finance, marketing, and manufacturing areas. Depending upon the circumstances, this may be the time to begin trying to establish some price parameters. We could at this time put together a massive checklist of all the areas that need to be studied and the legal and financial implications of each. This would, however, require a book in itself, so let us at this point suggest that you refer to other books which deal specifically with this question.[2]

It is at this point generally that the very comprehensive acquisition analysis is prepared, providing an in-depth discussion of the acquisition candidate's financial history and forecasts, its marketing philosophy, market share, and future programs in terms of both product development and penetration. If there are any potential tax problems, they should be discussed at this time, as well as a full review of real estate, equipment, machinery, and so on. The aim of this report is to provide all the information required to make a decision as to whether or not your company should proceed with the time-consuming and costly investigation that will be required prior to seeking the board of directors' approval. The immediate goal will be the presentation of the report for management review and either rejection of the candidate or approval to negotiate. Each company will have a different system for the presentation of these company analyses.

NEGOTIATIONS

Once again we arrive at an area of discussion where numerous books have been written giving an in-depth analysis of the topic. For the purpose of this chapter, perhaps it would be sufficient to mention a few key factors. The first and paramount thing to remember is that *negotiations begin with the first conversation.* This includes the investment banker, whether he represents you or the seller, as well as the principal or principals in the company to be acquired. The acquisition of the company is a transaction of high value and as in all matters involving high values, great care must be exercised in every discussion. You must do your utmost to determine the attitude of the seller while he is doing his best to determine your degree of interest and the value you place on his company.

Once again, each potential acquisition must be examined individually to determine the negotiating style which will be most productive. It is extremely critical to determine the motivation of the seller

---

[2] As an example, see William Alberts and Joel Segall, *The Corporate Merger* (Chicago: The University of Chicago Press, 1966).

when deciding upon your negotiating posture. This seems to be a relatively self-evident statement; however, the emotional issues underlying this type of negotiation are very significant. You have one type of problem in the case of a seller who is a 70-year-old gentleman who has just taken a 25-year-old bride and is seeking the financial liquidity required to pursue his new interests, and you have another type of problem in the case of the 30-year-old MBA recently assuming command of the family business and desirous of "earning his spurs." In the first case, you have the relatively simple problem of arriving at a price acceptable to both parties. In the second case, you have the additional problem of satisfying the ambitions of a young man who sees his future before him. These are not unusual situations—rather they are fairly common (although a 25-year-old bride is not always involved).

In addition to different negotiating styles required due to age and life-style variations on the part of the sellers, there also appears to be a difference in the styles required by location. You will find that negotiations will be carried out differently in the New York City area than they are in Atlanta, Georgia. Portland, Oregon presents a different set of problems than Bangor, Maine. These geographic differences are generalizations on our part; however, we think that you should be aware of the potential problems in becoming too rigid in your negotiating style.

THE OFFER

In addition to purchase price differences due to life-style variations, sellers have many and varied requirements due to different tax treatments accorded the form of the purchase price. Some sellers will want stock, some will want cash, some will want notes, some will want deferred payment. Many ingenious methods of meeting the seller's demands have been developed.

The earnout was developed to solve the problem of sellers consistently feeling that "next year will be better," expecting the purchase price to reflect that feeling. It is our personal opinion that earn-outs cause more problems than they solve. In any event, once both parties have agreed to an acceptable price, a way can generally be found to structure the payment in a manner acceptable to both parties. Typically, the offer and the form of payment is made subject to both senior management and board approval and contingent upon a thorough investigation to confirm the statements made by the seller.

THE REPORT TO THE BOARD

After senior management has had an opportunity to review the offer and has determined its acceptability based upon information then in hand, work can begin on preparing the report for the board. It is at this point that some large expenditures may have to be made. You may wish, for example, to perform your own audit of the selling company's financial statements; you may require an appraisal; and there is a substantial amount of legal work to be performed including patent search, contract and lease analysis. Also, in the light of today's requirements, a thorough OSHA and EPA examination should be made. In short, all pertinent information required for your board report should be thoroughly investigated and substantiated. Some investigations may take weeks and even months. The important thing is not to be caught up in the momentum that seems to build as you approach a closing and, thereby, overlook salient points which could cause problems in the future.

The method by which a corporation's board of directors reviews acquisition candidates varies from company to company. In some cases, the corporate staff will make the presentation; in some cases the report described earlier is mailed to the board members which serves as the briefing; in some cases operating management which will have responsibility for the new company will make the board report. Whichever method you choose to use, the key thing to remember is that you must focus attention on the positive and important aspects of the acquisition. Your report should point out how the acquisition fits into your growth program and how it will be beneficial in helping to increase shareholder wealth. If there are negatives, and there always are, either the positives far outweigh them or there are solutions available. In any case, both the problems and the solutions should be fully explained in the board report.

THE CLOSING

The word "closing" has a finality about it which accurately describes the end of a long and arduous path begun during the initial planning process of your company. Unfortunately, it is easier to plan than it is to close, and the vast majority of acquisition investigations fail to reach this ultimate goal. Once your board has given authorization to make a formal offer and the offer has been accepted and your board has voted to confirm the agreement, you reach the last and sometimes the most difficult part of the acquisition process.

If you are acquiring a public company and paying cash, a proxy statement must be submitted to the SEC and shareholders of the selling corporation must vote their approval; if you are buying assets only, the selling corporation must be liquidated; if you are paying with stock, your shareholders must vote their approval in some cases, and so on.

In other words, the mechanics of the closing can easily become entangled in a giant web of legal and accounting complexities which may become increasingly frustrating for both buyer and seller. Therefore, you would be wise to establish a comprehensive closing procedure, with an accompanying timetable of implementation, to guide personnel of both companies to the closing date. As each closing presents a new set of problems, typically you will have to draft a new procedure for each acquisition.

POST-CLOSING ACTIVITIES

As the new division or subsidiary joins your company, there is a requirement, regardless of the degree of autonomy practiced in your company, to integrate many of the systems which will be common to both. This typically includes financial reporting systems, insurance programs, pension and/or profit sharing programs, personnel policies, and so forth. The length of the list depends upon the policies of each individual corporation. Things usually go more smoothly if an activity plan is established scheduling all the corporate personnel involved into the new division with a goal of making the transition as painless as possible. The smaller the company acquired, the greater the turmoil caused during the integration process. Once again, proper planning will ease the way.

The last item emphasized is the postacquisition audit program. During the initial phases of the analysis of your newly acquired company, many forecasts of future performance were made. You should endeavor to establish a program to monitor the progress of this new acquisition not so much to grade the people who made the forecasts, but rather with an eye to improving your analytical methods to try to avoid forecasting errors in the future.

It is sincerely hoped that this very broad, very general discussion has been helpful in delineating one acquisition process and has perhaps provided you with some ideas for your own program.

ADDITIONAL SOURCES

See Additional Sources at end of Chapter 45.

Chapter 45

Effective Merger Negotiations —An Analytical Approach

Gary E. MacDougal*

AT Mark Controls Corporation, successful acquisitions in related businesses have fueled the growth of the company from earnings of $300,000 in 1969 to $6 million in 1975, with sales growth from $16 million to $70 million during this period. The first acquisition was larger than Mark Controls, and acquisitions have accounted for one half of the total sales growth and more than half the profit growth.

Yet this was accomplished with only two acquisitions in about six years—out of literally hundreds which were reviewed. The lesson here to me is twofold: First, there are very few *good* acquisition candidates around, so it makes sense to have a financial evaluation process that will help spot the good ones. Second, when you think you have a good acquisition candidate, it makes sense to really plan an analytical approach to merger negotiations.

The approach used at Mark Controls has proven out well in practice, and it rests fundamentally on a very basic return on investment approach utilizing discounted cash flow. There is no reason why a new plant investment should be subjected to ROI (return on investment) analysis and not acquisitions—even an investment in dividends should be subjected to ROI analysis.[1] Yet

---

* Gary E. MacDougal is chairman of the board and chief executive officer of Mark Controls Corporation, Evanston, Illinois.

[1] Gary E. MacDougal, "Investing in a Dividend Boost," *Harvard Business Review*, July–August, 1967, pp. 87–92.

many sophisticated investment bankers use a straight "effect on earnings per share" approach, ignoring the ROI. Earnings per share impact should be looked at, but it confuses the ranking of investment alternatives since it is dramatically influenced by the type of financing which is assumed. Many of the famous conglomerators of the 60s were carried away by the positive short-term earnings per share impact of acquisitions. A number of them met their downfall when, inevitably, they ran out of debt capacity and interest rates rose.

Mergers and acquisitions still loom large in many companies' strategic growth plans as well they should. The pressures to acquire—whether to improve earnings growth and stability through diversification or to ward off possible take-overs—preoccupy many chief executives, and the financial officers who are their right arm. Very often, these pressures demand large amounts of top-management time.

If the chief executive officer's background happens to be in corporate finance, this may be time well spent. But more often he will have come up through the sales or manufacturing ranks perhaps with a tour of duty as a division manager.

Such cases, when the chief executive is not well prepared by experience for his vital role in acquisition analysis and negotiations, often follow a familiar pattern. Much effort goes into screening long lists of industries and companies, and into gathering published data on possible acquisition candidates, but not enough thought is given to developing an analytical approach to merger negotiations that can be understood and communicated effectively. This is where the astute financial officer can earn his keep many times over.

Without an analytical approach, two kinds of consequences may result: (*a*) through failure to "sell the seller" on some aspect of the acquisition, management may find itself unable to "close" or complete anything of substance. Or, worse yet, (*b*) faulty financial analysis may lead management to acquire a poor company, or to pay so much for a good one that it cannot hope to earn an acceptable return on the investment.

The approach to acquisition negotiations outlined in this chapter are designed to enhance the chances of success in merger negotiations. It shows negotiating executives, too often perplexed by the maze of technical, legal, and financial details surrounding a prospective acquisition, how to handle three critical aspects of the negotiating process:

1. Laying the groundwork by understanding the financial relationships that underlie any agreement between the two companies.
2. Developing the seller's interest in the nonfinancial aspects of the proposition.
3. Resolving the financial facts in a way that will make possible any early and realistic agreement on terms.

Laying the Groundwork

As the first step toward successful acquisition negotiations, the acquiring company should lay the groundwork in two areas: (*a*) it needs to think out carefully and express in specific terms its own corporate objectives and acquisition criteria; and (*b*) it needs to study and understand the basic financial relationships between itself and its potential acquisition.

Objectives and Criteria

Developing corporate objectives and acquisition criteria is too important and complex a subject to be covered thoroughly here. At a minimum, for acquisition evaluation purposes, corporate objectives should include such financial standards as earnings per share growth rate and annual return on investment. Without these yardsticks, there is no way of knowing whether a given acquisition would act as a spur or a brake on overall corporate performance. Consider the following factors:

1. An acquisition candidate that is showing an earnings per share growth rate of 9 percent a year compounded will look very good to a company that is currently growing at 5.5 percent a year compounded and aiming for an 8 percent growth rate.
2. However, that same acquisition candidate will (or should) hold little attraction for a would-be acquirer that is growing at 10 percent a year, and has set its sights on 14 percent.

The earnings growth rate and return on investment an acquirer should set as its goals depend on many factors that will emerge only from a thoughtful evaluation of internal corporate potential combined with a sound assessment of the business environment. Some companies regularly measure themselves on two counts: first, against their own industry; then, against a cross section of all manufacturing companies, such as that provided by *Fortune's* "500."

For example, an earnings per share growth rate of 12.5 percent a year compounded would equal the performance of companies at the bottom of the top quartile of *Fortune's* "500" during the past decade. A 15 percent return on shareholders' equity would also place a company at the bottom of the top quartile during this period. The end result should be performance goals that are challenging but attainable.

Criteria for the evaluation of investments should include, in addition to the type and size of business and other appropriate screening factors, a return on investment target that takes present-value considerations into account. The discounted cash flow method provides a good measurement of the return on investment. A typical company, then, might develop these yardsticks against which to measure prospective acquisitions:

1. Annual compound earnings per share (EPS) growth rate.
2. Annual return on shareholders' equity.
3. Prospective return on the investment, calculated on a discounted cash flow basis.

The buying company can then proceed to examine the financial characteristics of the acquisition candidate, evaluate them in the light of the corporate objectives and acquisition criteria it has established, and began to define the range of feasible purchase prices and terms.

Prenegotiation Homework

Once the buying company has spotted a promising acquisition candidate, has become acquainted with its principal characteristics, and is preparing for the first approach, the time has come to examine certain key relationships in order to determine what price can be paid—and in what form—without undermining corporate objectives. Management should at this point determine the following relationships:

1. The relationships of various selling-company EPS growth rates and new capital requirements to possible purchase prices and discounted cash flow ROI.

2. The impact that various earnings-growth rates of the acquisition candidate and various purchase prices and forms of payment will have on the parent company's earnings per share and annual ROI.

3. The maximum percentage of control the acquired company would retain at various purchase prices and under alternative forms of payment.

To determine these relationships, we recommend an analytical approach that has proven effective in practice and is relatively easy to use. A series of graphic guides such as those used in the accompanying simulated case history (see Figures 1 through 7) will quickly demonstrate the financial considerations involved in most acquisitions.

The graphs make it simpler for negotiating executives to grasp the essentials before talks begin. They provide a sound understanding of the true trade-offs involved and the limitations on purchase price and terms.

Management can thus proceed into negotiations with greater confidence, since the graphs can be used for quick assessment of the potential impact of changes in terms or prices. This increased flexibility helps to eliminate unnecessary roadblocks and prevent mistakes.

Finally, as we shall see, the graphs themselves become persuasive tools for the acquiring company's negotiating team: when shown to the seller, they help in moving talks on the crucial financial details from an emotional or intuitive level to a more objective plane where the facts convincingly speak for themselves.

Simulated Case History

How does this analytical approach work in practice? We have devised an example to illustrate both the financial analysis which management of the acquiring company should undertake and the graphic guides it could use as tools.

Mark Industries, a publicly owned (New York Stock Exchange) company with $125 million in sales, is preparing to commence negotiations with Historic Family Enterprise (HFE), a $12 million company closely held by the chairman of the board and his family. To provide a framework for its acquisition program, Mark Industries' board of directors has approved these corporate financial objectives and acquisition criteria:

1. All new capital investments, including acquisitions, must provide a discounted cash flow ROI of 12 percent or better after taxes.
2. The objective for Mark Industries' earnings per share growth is 10 percent a year.
3. The target for Mark Industries' annual return on shareholders' investment is 14 percent.
4. Dilution of earnings per share should be minimized, and any dilution which does result should be eliminated by the third year after acquisition.

The basic financial characteristics of Mark Industries and of HFE look like this (HFE's earnings per share are not known and there is no established market value for HFE's stock):

	Mark Industries	Historic Family Enterprise
Profits after taxes.	$5,000,000	$1,000,000
Earnings per share.	$5	—
Past growth rate.	6%	10%
Management growth projection	6%	12%
P/E ratio	12	

In preparing for negotiations, Mark Industries' management has two purposes in mind: (*a*) to understand the financial relationships that will exist between the two companies so that it will know what prices are reasonable under varying conditions—and why—and (*b*) to improve its ability to communicate purchase price limits which the HFE negotiating team will understand and consider reasonable.

At this point, Mark Industries' executives must clarify the basic financial issues. Because HFE is not publicly owned, there is no established market price, nor has HFE management indicated a preference for any particular exchange instrument. In addition, Mark Industries is uncertain what rate of earnings growth to expect from HFE. Therefore, Mark Industries is interested in analyzing these financial impacts:

1. The relationship among probable HFE earnings per share
    growth rates, purchase price levels, and Mark Industries' dis-
    counted cash flow return (e.g., with an HFE annual growth
    rate of 15 percent, what is the maximum feasible purchase
    price if the discounted cash flow ROI is to equal 12 percent or
    better).
2. The year-by-year impact on Mark Industries' earnings per share
    of various HFE growth rates and purchase prices (e.g., at
    what growth rate is dilution overcome within three years if
    HFE is purchased for $20 million in common stock).
3. At a given price, the year-by-year effect on earnings per share
    of alternate combinations of cash, common stock, and preferred
    stock (e.g., if the purchase price is $20 million, what is the
    effect on dilution of increasing the cash portion from 5 percent
    to 20).
4. The relationship of purchase price and type of exchange in-
    strument to the resulting degree of HFE control (e.g., if the
    price is $20 million and the terms are 25 percent cash and 75
    percent common stock, what percentage of the new, combined
    enterprise will be represented by former HFE shareholders).

Assessing ROI Target

Discounted-cash-flow return analysis, now in use by a number of
sophisticated companies, offers several important advantages. For
one thing, it provides a means of determining value that is independent of the financial terms involved. If only EPS impact is
measured, an all-cash acquisition of a slowly growing company, for
example, can be made to look good on a straight earnings per
share basis because the effect of leveraging the company, through
the use of cash, is confused with the acquisition evaluation.

For another thing, the present-value ROI approach also gives
full recognition to the fact that earnings received in, say, ten
years are less valuable than those received in two, three, or four
years. In addition, management can easily decide by assessing the
ROI in terms of present value whether acquiring a given company
is preferable to using the same capital for internal projects or for
other acquisitions.

The essence of this discounted-cash-flow ROI approach is to
estimate cash inflows for each year of a given period (often a ten-
year period is appropriate). These inflows include the capitalized

increases in earnings per share. In addition, cash outflows are estimated for the same period—outflows which include the initial purchase price of the acquisition and the amount by which capital investment exceeds depreciation. The initial value of the company acquired is then treated as a cash inflow in the final year of the period under consideration.

In the case of Mark Industries, assume that management's calculation's show that investing new capital at a discounted cash flow ROI rate of 12 percent or better will produce an annual return on shareholders' equity of 14 percent or better—thus meeting two of the goals approved by Mark Industries' board of directors. (Note that the 12 percent discounted cash flow is on total capital, whereas the 14 percent return on shareholders' equity covers only the equity portion.)

Therefore, in contemplating the purchase of HFE, the first task for Mark Industries' executives is to project a range of possible compound after-tax earnings per share growth rates for HFE, and then ask: What is the maximum price we can pay at each of the various HFE growth levels if we are going to meet our 12 percent discounted cash flow ROI targets?

Figure 1 shows graphically this relationship between purchase price, projected HFE growth rate, and Mark Industries' return on investment. (See Appendix at end of chapter which describes in detail the assumptions underlying Figure 1. A financial analyst familiar with basic present-value techniques can easily construct a similar chart.)

If an annual HFE growth rate of 10 percent seems probable, then Mark Industries can pay $20.75 million for the company and get a 12 percent return on investment. However, if HFE is expected to grow at a rate of 12 percent annually, a price as high as $25.25 million can be paid without falling below the ROI criterion set by Mark Industries' board of directors.

Mark Industries' management, therefore, knows that negotiations on the purchase price should stay within a range of $20 million to $25 million, and that the critical factor is the HFE projected earnings per share growth rate.

Effect on Earnings

A second question now confronts Mark Industries' executives: If we are to overcome dilution within three years, as our acquisi-

FIGURE 1
Mark Industries' ROI at Various
Growth Rates and Purchase Prices

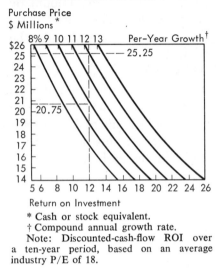

Return on Investment

* Cash or stock equivalent.
† Compound annual growth rate.
Note: Discounted-cash-flow ROI over a ten-year period, based on an average industry P/E of 18.

tion criteria specify, what is the appropriate purchase price, and should it be in cash, common stock, preferred stock, or some combination of these?

Using the range of estimated HFE growth rates, Mark Industries' executives decide to test the effect of offering a $20 million exchange of Mark Industries common stock for HFE common stock to determine both the impact on combined earnings per share and the year in which dilution can be replaced by appreciation.

It is immediately apparent from Figure 2 that even if HFE were to grow at a rate of 15 percent annually, Mark Industries' earnings would be diluted through the sixth year after acquisition with a $20 million common-for-common exchange. Lower HFE growth rates continue the dilution even longer. In other words, a common-for-common exchange at this price rules out hope of meeting Mark Industries' acquisition criteria.

Mark Industries' management then must work out purchase terms and a price that will allow dilution to be overcome by the third year. Again, various HFE projected growth rates of 10 percent, 12 percent, and 15 percent per year are evaluated.

As Figure 3 indicates, if dilution beyond the third year is to be avoided, the top price Mark Industries can offer HFE in a common-

FIGURE 2
Impact of Various HFE Growth
Rates on Mark Industries' Earnings

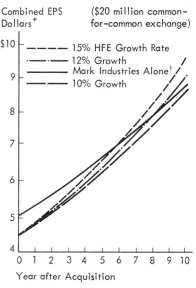

Combined EPS   ($20 million common-
Dollars*   for-common exchange)

* Assumes projected 6 percent after-tax
growth rate.
† Compound annual growth rates in
HFE after-tax earnings.

for-common exchange, assuming a projected HFE growth rate of
15 percent a year, is $15.32 million. With a more probable 12 per-
cent growth rate, no more than $14.16 million in common stock
can be paid.

Mark Industries knows that the owners of HFE would consider
a $15.32 million offer quite unrealistic. It would represent only
slightly over 15 times HFE's annual $1 million after-tax earnings,
and comparable companies in HFE's industry have been selling for
18 times earnings—which suggests what HFE's expectations will
be. The average price for all companies acquired in the past few
years has been in the range of 23 to 25 times earnings.[2]

With a modest 6 percent annual growth rate, Mark Industries
itself commands a price/earnings ratio of 12; HFE's growth rate
is expected to be nearly twice that of Mark Industries. Thus, if the
negotiations are to succeed, it is apparent that Mark Industries will

---

[2] *1968 Merger Study* (Chicago: W. T. Grimm & Co.)

FIGURE 3
Relationship of Purchase Prices and HFE
Growth Rates to Year in Which Dilution
Is Replaced by Appreciation

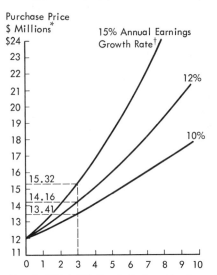

Year in Which Dilution Is Replaced by Appreciation

* Assumes common-for-common exchange.
† Compound annual growth in HFE after-tax
earnings.

have to put forth a better offer. The key question at this point then becomes: Is there any combination of exchange instruments that will make a $20 million purchase price consistent with Mark Industries' own objectives?

As Figure 4 shows, the introduction of cash into the acquisition package substantially affects the impact of the acquisition on Mark Industries' earnings per share. Assuming that the 12 percent projected growth rate for HFE is most likely, paying about 50 percent of a $20 million purchase price in cash will produce neither dilution nor appreciation within three years.

Figure 5, which covers a broader range, indicates the various purchase prices and the various mixes of cash and common stock that could start earnings per share appreciation after the third year. This exhibit shows that if Mark Industries wants to keep the cash input of the package below 50 percent for tax purposes, then its offer cannot go above $20 million.

FIGURE 4

**Impact on Mark Industries' Earnings of Alternate
Combinations of Cash and Common Stock**

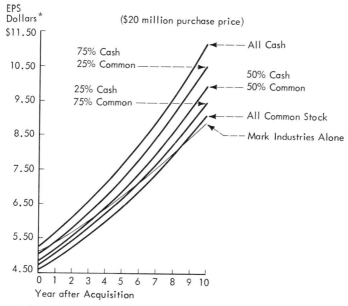

EPS
Dollars*   ($20 million purchase price)

* Assumes (*a*) Mark's EPS growth, 6 percent, and HFE EPS growth,
12 percent; (*b*) 8 percent interest expense on cash portion; and (*c*) no
goodwill amortization.

Figure 6 illustrates a similar family of curves, developed to show
the results of various combinations of cash and preferred stock.
Given a $20 million purchase price of 40 percent cash and 60 percent
convertible preferred, EPS appreciation will begin in the fourth
year, after conversion of the preferred.

By this time, Mark Industries' management realizes that it must
use a fairly high percentage of cash and/or preferred stock to effect
a deal that meets its criteria for acquisitions. During the negotiations ahead, the charts will help its team to move quickly from
discussion of one financial instrument and one purchase price to an
alternative, keeping a clear view of what the effect of each would
be on corporate objectives.

Impact on Control

Since HFE is a closely held company, the degree of control that
HFE shareholders can exert after the transaction becomes espe-

FIGURE 5
Relationship of Cash and Common Stock
Combinations at Various Purchase Prices to Year
in Which Dilution Is Replaced by Appreciation

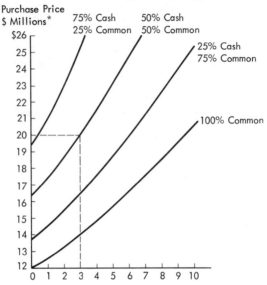

* Assumes (*a*) Mark's EPS growth, 6 percent, and HFE EPS growth, 12 percent; (*b*) 8 percent interest expense on cash portion; and (*c*) no goodwill amortization.

cially important. Hence, the natural question for Mark Industries' management is: What combinations of cash and stock would give HFE shareholders too much control of Mark Industries and at what purchase price would this occur?

Figure 7 illustrates how Mark Industries improves its own control as the purchase price is reduced and the percentage of cash or of preferred stock in the package is increased. This is the only exhibit of the series which Mark Industries' management would do well to keep to itself.

As we shall subsequently see in the final section of this chapter, Figures 1 through 6 can—and should—be shown to HFE's management when discussion of the financial terms begins. Actual experience has shown that charts such as these become a useful negotiating tool which help to guide both parties toward a reasonable and satisfactory agreement.

FIGURE 6

Relationship of Preferred Stock and Cash Combinations at Various Purchase Prices to Year in Which Dilution Is Replaced by Appreciation

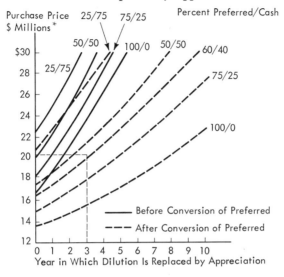

* Assumes (*a*) Mark's EPS growth, 6 percent, and HFE EPS growth, 12 percent; (*b*) 8 percent before-tax interest expense on cash portion; (*c*) no goodwill amortization; and (*d*) terms of preferred: 6 percent yield, priced 10 percent over underlying conversion value.

Developing Seller Interest

Having established the basic financial relationships which underlie the acquisition, Mark Industries' management must now turn its attention to other aspects of the coming discussions, with an eye toward the errors that so often result in unsuccessful negotiations.

It is not unusual to see a would-be buyer approach a company he knows is for sale—often with his investment banker in tow—and devote most of his time to discussing purchase prices, terms, and the financial advantages that selling shareholders can expect. By doing this he implicitly overlooks a major fact of life in today's merger-conscious business world: any attractive company known to be interested in selling (and most that are not interested) will have four or five—perhaps even dozens—of offers. Most of these will be reasonably attractive financially, with several offering to exchange securities which promise comparably attractive growth prospects.

FIGURE 7
**Relationship of Cash, Common, and Preferred
Stock Combinations and Various Purchase
Prices to Degree of Ownership by
Former HFE Shareholders**

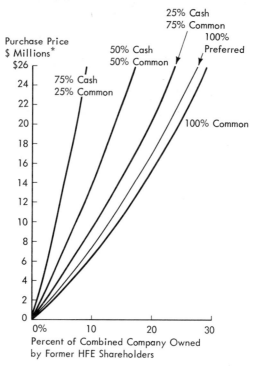

* Assumes preferred stock is priced 10 percent over conversion value.

In a situation like this, the prize often goes to the company that can offer the seller something more than money: a sound future for the business to which he has devoted years of hard work and personal commitment.

Both owners and managers of a selling company are normally extremely concerned about the future of their enterprise, whether or not they retain a continuing stock interest. Even if management does not hold substantial shares, the owners will feel a personal obligation to their executives and will usually want their support in any merger or sale.

In most cases, the buying company itself will hope to keep on the acquired company's management after the deal is closed. The would-be buyer who can arouse the seller's interest in the non-financial aspects of the acquisition has won an advantage that sets his company apart from the crowd of aspirants. This entails considerable work even before the negotiations commence.

To begin with, management of the acquiring company should gain a thorough understanding of the seller's business and industry. Elementary as this point may seem, executives of a would-be purchaser often enter negotiations armed with only the sketchiest knowledge of conditions in the business their company is seeking to enter. In such cases, it is not unusual for the seller to call off the deal before it really gets started.

Once the negotiators have familiarized themselves with the selling company's background, they must work out a strategy to activate the seller's strong, though sometimes latent, interest in the nonfinancial aspects of the merger. The key tasks at this point are as follows:

1. To identify, and then communicate, specific business advantages from which the selling company can benefit after the acquisition.
2. To map out a thoughtful and stimulating growth plan for the new combined enterprise.
3. To develop sound and continuing personal relationships.

Each of these factors will vary in importance according to the situation, but all of them should be completely thought through during the initial planning for negotiations and refined as discussions progress.

The essential thing to remember is that in most good companies top management is vitally interested in such goals as improving competitive position, capitalizing on new market opportunities, and investigating other major growth possibilities. A merger is likely to make substantially more sense to these men, regardless of purchase price, if it means they can achieve one or more of their primary objectives.

In each case, executives of the buying company should do their homework, thoroughly exploring the advantages they can offer, and then, early in the negotiations, beginning to work with the potential seller to determine their value. Discussing such opportunities in itself helps to form a strong link between the two companies during the period when they are getting to know one another.

Resolving Financial Terms

By the time discussions begin to evolve into true negotiations, there should be an atmosphere of warm goodwill between the executives of the buying and selling companies. The problem then is to be able to resolve financial terms in a way that allows the economic considerations to be communicated without diminishing this goodwill.

It is at this point that charts such as those used to illustrate the Mark Industries-HFE case history (Figures 1 through 6) can be shown to the seller and become effective negotiating tools. The buyer can use them to elicit initial reactions without actually proposing a price, knowing that they are concrete evidence of the acquiring company's thoughtful approach to the future. As such, they inspire a sense of respect for management's preparation and thoroughness.

The acquisition prospect can readily accept the logic of the buyer's need to obtain a return on investment equivalent to its target rate. The desire to avoid earnings dilution is equally understandable. In thus introducing a discussion of such basic financial relationships at an early stage in the talks, the acquiring company tends to appeal to the candidate's common sense and good judgment. In this way, the discussions can be based on objective considerations, and emotions cannot so easily enter.

Perhaps even more important—as actual experience has shown—is that by demonstrating clearly the financial relationships, and thus "opening the book" to the candidate, the acquiring company creates a feeling of mutual trust and understanding. Again, the focus is on the future and on the success of the new, combined enterprise which, by now, both the buying company and the seller can begin to see as a reality.

Conclusion

Our experience indicates that the approach to merger negotiations outlined in this chapter offers a good way of surmounting the two most common obstacles to success: inability to settle on a realistic price, and failure to "sell the seller" on the nonfinancial aspects of the acquisition. By first analyzing, then portraying graphically, the key relationships of various financial alternatives, management cannot fail to gain a solid grasp of the true trade-offs involved and the limitations of various purchase price levels and terms.

Equipped with this understanding, executives can enter into negotiations knowing that they can quickly assess the impact of alternative prices, financing methods and growth rate projections on the ROI and EPS performance of their company. This greater flexibility helps to eliminate unnecessary roadblocks, prevent mistakes and increase the chances of a successful acquisition. Finally, the charts that are developed provide an excellent basis for fact-founded "open book" discussion during the negotiations.

Persuading the selling company of the nonfinancial advantages of the acquisition will not, of course, be accomplished through good quantitative analysis or well-designed charts. Clearly identifiable business advantages, personal relationships and some sort of "need to sell" (i.e., potential estate problems, and so on) are also extremely important.

Admittedly, negotiation is not a science but an art. However, technical advances are possible in art as well as in science. Our experience indicates that an analytical approach to merger negotiations can materially improve any acquirer's prospects of success.

APPENDIX: NOTES TO FIGURE 1

In Figure 1, ROI on a discounted cash flow basis is used to evaluate the proposed acquisition. Any advantages which would result from new business opportunities are not included in the calculations. At a later point in the negotiations these can be taken into account by including any profit improvement in the performance of the company to be acquired.

It is also assumed that the candidate company will generate its projected earnings without additional capital investment from the parent: the only investment is the purchase price. Additional investment, however, can be included as a cash outflow if appropriate.

The principal inflow to the parent company consists of the assumed annual incremental increase (or decrease) in the total value of the candidate company. By including these changes in company value in the cash flow, traditional cash flow analysis is extended to include potential returns, even though the choice can be made not to realize them as they occur.

The total value of the candidate is assumed to be earnings after taxes multiplied by the P/E ratio typical for its industry. The P/E ratio must be estimated for future years; in this exhibit it is assumed to be constant during the next ten years and equal to the present industry P/E of 18.

Assuming that the candidate company is sold at the end of a ten-year period (the limit for a reasonable projection), the value of the potential return in the last year is calculated as the increase in value for that year plus the market value of the company at the time of purchase.

On this basis, the discount rate at which the present value of these inflows is equal to a given purchase price is the rate of return for the total investment.

To construct this chart, let the present profit of the company to be evaluated ($1 million in Figure 1) grow at alternative growth rates (8 percent, 9 percent, 10 percent, 11 percent, 12 percent, and 13 percent in Figure 1) over a period of ten years. Calculate the increments and multiply with the average industry P/E ratio (18 in Figure 1). Add to the tenth value the average market value in year 0; i.e., average industry P/E ratio times earnings in year 0. Then calculate the present value (purchase price) for various hypothetical rates of return. This can be expressed in the following equation:

$$P/E \left[E \, \frac{(q^{10} - q^9 + 1)}{g^{10}} \right] + P/E \times E \sum_{n=1}^{9} \frac{(q^n - q^{n-1})}{g^n} = P$$

where:

$$P/E = \text{Average industry } P/E \text{ ratio}$$
$$E = \text{Earnings in year 0}$$
$$P = \text{Purchase price}$$
$$q = 1 + \frac{\text{growth rate}}{100}$$
$$g = 1 + \frac{\text{rate of return}}{100}$$

ADDITIONAL SOURCES

Alberts, William W., and Segall, Joel E., eds. *The Corporate Merger.* Chicago: University of Chicago Press, 1966.

Austin, Douglas. "The Financial Management of Tender Offer Take-overs." *Financial Management*, 3 (Spring 1974), 37–43.

Balog, James. "Market Reaction to Merger Announcements." *Financial Analysts Journal*, 31 (March–April 1975), 84–88.

Cheney, Richard E. "Remedies for Tender-Offer Anxiety." *Financial Executive*, 63 (August 1975), 16–19.

Defliese, Philip L. "Business Combinations Revisited." *Financial Executive*, 63 (September 1975), 42–47.

Folz, David F., and Weston, J. Fred. "Looking Ahead in Evaluating Proposed Mergers." *NAA Bulletin*, 43 (April 1962), 17–27.

Foster, William. "The Illogic of Pooling." *Financial Executive*, 42 (December 1974), 16–21.

Gaskill, William. "Are You Ready for the New Merger Boom?" *Financial Executive*, 42 (September 1974), 38–41.

Gort, Michael. *Diversification and Integration in American Industry*. Princeton, N.J.: Princeton University Press, 1962.

Gort, Michael, and Hogarty, Thomas E. "New Evidence on Mergers." *Journal of Law and Economics*, 13 (April 1970), 167–84.

Goudzwaard, Maurice B. "Conglomerate Mergers, Convertibles, and Cash Dividends." *Quarterly Review of Business and Economics*, 9 (Spring 1969), 53–62.

Haugen, Robert A., and Udell, Jon G. "Rates of Return to Stockholders of Acquired Companies." *Journal of Financial and Quantitative Analysis*, 7 (January 1972), 1387–98.

Higgins, Robert C., and Schall, Lawrence D. "Corporate Bankruptcy and Conglomerate Merger." *Journal of Finance*, 30 (March 1975), 93–114.

Hogarty, Thomas F. "The Profitability of Corporate Mergers." *Journal of Business*, 44 (July 1970), 317–27.

Joehnk, Michael D., and Nielsen, James F. "The Effects of Conglomerate Merger Activity on Systematic Risk." *Journal of Financial and Quantitative Analysis* 9 (March 1974), 215–26.

Kitching, John. "Winning and Losing with European Acquisitions." *Harvard Business Review*, 52 (March–April 1974), 124–36.

Larson, Kermit D., and Gonedes, Nicholas J. "Business Combinations: An Exchange-Ratio Determination Model." *Accounting Review*, 44 (October 1969), 720–28.

Lev, Baruch, and Mandelker, Gershon. "The Microeconomic Consequences of Corporate Mergers." *Journal of Business*, 45 (January 1972), 85–104.

Lewellen, Wilbur G. "A Pure Financial Rationale for the Conglomerate Merger." *Journal of Finance,* 26 (May 1971), 521–37.

Lootens, Donald M. "Policing the Financial Marriage." *Business Horizons,* 17 (August 1974), 79–86.

Lorie, J. H., and Halpern, P. "Conglomerates: The Rhetoric and the Evidence." *Journal of Law and Economics,* 13 (April 1970), 149–66.

MacDougal, Gary E., and Malek, Fred V. "Master Plan for Merger Negotiations." *Harvard Business Review,* 48 (January–February 1970), 71–82.

Mason, R. Hal, and Goudzwaard, Maurice B. "Performance of Conglomerate Firms: A Portfolio Approach." *Journal of Finance,* 31 (March 1976), 39–48.

Melicher, Ronald W., and Harter, Thomas R. "Stock Price Movements of Firms Engaging in Large Acquisitions." *Journal of Financial and Quantitative Analysis,* 7 (March 1972), 1469–75.

Melicher, Ronald W., and Rush, David F. "The Performance of Conglomerate Firms: Recent Risk and Return Experience." *Journal of Finance,* 28 (May 1973), 381–87.

Melicher, Ronald W., and Rush, David F. "Evidence on the Acquisition-Related Performance of Conglomerate Firms." *Journal of Finance,* 29 (March 1974), 141–49.

Melnik, A., and Pollatschek, M. A. "Debt Capacity, Diversification and Conglomerate Mergers." *Journal of Finance,* 28 (December 1973), 1263–74.

Mueller, Dennis C. "A Theory of Conglomerate Mergers." *Quarterly Journal of Economics,* 83 (November 1969), 643–59.

Nielsen, James F., and Melicher, Ronald W. "A Financial Analysis of Acquisition and Merger Premiums." *Journal of Financial and Quantitative Analysis,* 8 (March 1973), 139–48.

Petty, William, and Walker, Ernest. "Optimal Transfer Pricing for the Multinational Firm." *Financial Management,* 1 (Winter 1972), 74–87.

Reid, Samuel R. "Reply." *Journal of Finance,* 29 (June 1974), 1013–15.

Reid, Samuel Richardson. *Mergers, Managers, and the Economy.* New York: McGraw-Hill, 1968.

Reinhardt, Uwe E. *Mergers and Consolidations: A Corporate-Finance Approach.* Morristown: General Learning Press, 1972.

Sauerhaft, Stan. "The 'New' Corporate Raiders." *Dun's Review,* 105 (April 1975), 70–73.

Seed, Allen, III. "Why Corporate Marriages Fail." *Financial Executive,* 42 (December 1974), 56–62.

Shad, John S. R. "The Financial Realities of Mergers," *Harvard Business Review,* 47 (November–December 1969), 133–46.

Shick, Richard, and Jen, Frank. "Merger Benefits to Shareholders of Acquiring Firms." *Financial Management,* 3 (Winter 1974), 45–53.

Silberman, Irwin H. "A Note on Merger Valuation." *Journal of Finance,* 23 (June 1968), 528–34.

Smith, David, and Goho, Thomas. "The 1968 Merger Guidelines: Do They Assist in Planning?" *Managerial Planning,* 22 (November–December 1973), 6–8.

Sprecher, C. Ronald. "A Note on Financing Mergers with Convertible Preferred Stock." *Journal of Finance,* 26 (June 1971), 683–86.

Stevens, Donald L. "Financial Characteristics of Merged Firms: A Multivariate Analysis." *Journal of Financial and Quantitative Analysis,* 8 (March 1973), 149–58.

Weston, J. Fred. *The Role of Mergers in the Growth of Large Firms.* Berkeley: University of California Press, 1953.

Weston, J. Fred, and Mansinghka, Surendra K. "Tests of the Efficiency of Conglomerate Firms." *Journal of Finance,* 26 (September 1971), 919–36.

Weston, J. Fred, and Mansinghka, Surendra K. "Conglomerate Performance Measurement: Comment." *Journal of Finance,* 29 (June 1974), 1011–12.

Weston, J. Fred, and Peltzman, Sam, eds. *Public Policy toward Mergers.* Pacific Palisades, Calif.: Goodyear, 1969.

Weston, J. Fred; Smith, Keith V.; and Shrieves, Ronald E. "Conglomerate Performance Using the Capital Asset Pricing Model." *Review of Economics and Statistics,* 54 (November 1972), 357–63.

Woods, Donald H., and Caverly, Thomas A. "Development of a Linear Programming Model for the Analysis of Merger/Acquisition Situations." *Journal of Financial and Quantitative Analysis,* 4 (January 1970), 627–42.

Wyatt, Arthur R., and Kieso, Donald E. *Business Combinations: Planning and Action.* Scranton: International Textbook Company, 1969.

PART XI

Financial Readjustments

DESPITE strong aspirations for corporate growth and sometimes because of them, reverses may be encountered which may confront the firm with financial readjustments—the subject of Part XI of the *Treasurer's Handbook*. In Chapter 46, Richard Broude describes the various aspects of financial reorganization. He divides the subject into out-of-court arrangements and in-court arrangements. Out-of-court arrangements involve the extension or composition of debt. In-court arrangements are under two main provisions of the bankruptcy laws. The bankruptcy Chapter XI proceedings are relatively informal and well controlled. But Chapter X proceedings are quite formal and include the full trappings of extensive court supervision and control.

Under any of the foregoing proceedings, if it is determined that the value of the firm, if liquidated, will be greater than if the firm were kept operating, liquidation will take place. Liquidation procedure may be relatively informal as in assignments or relatively formal through legal bankruptcy procedures under court supervision.

Mr. Broude emphasizes that the treasurer should be alert to early warning signals of financial distress. If prompt action is taken, informal arrangements made provide fully effective solutions. On the other hand, delay may entail extensive and time-consuming proceedings. Thus, even in the area of financial distress, there are opportunities for the treasurer to make substantial contributions to the value of his enterprise.

Two methods of financial readjustment have come into increased use in recent years. One is the stock reacquisition program covered in Chapter 47 and the other is "going private" described in Chapter 48. In stock reacquisition programs the company reduces a portion of its publicly held equity shares. In going private, all of the publicly held shares are eliminated.

In Chapter 47, John Shad provides a thorough treatment of stock acquisition programs. He sets out the benefits that may accrue from such programs. He also considers possible disadvantages. He then presents a case study illustrating the factors which determine the terms of a share tender or exchange offering attractive to stockholders. He also assesses the relative effectiveness of alternative methods of carrying out stock acquisition programs.

Steven Lee calls attention to recent stock price trends and the decline in price-earnings ratios. When share prices are at less than book value in spite of good earnings performance of the firm, the issue is raised of whether the treasurer's own company is the most attractive investment vehicle available. Mr. Lee then presents a number of examples illustrating the management's view of going private. He then considers the steps in going private, first emphasizing the regulatory considerations that must be taken into account. With illustrative examples, he indicates alternative methods of going private. Mr. Lee then faces up to the public policy issues posed by going private. He summarizes the business purposes that may be served by going private and develops a checklist of factors to provide guidance for managements in making the "going private" decisions.

Chapter 46

Financial Reorganization

Richard F. Broude[*]

THE SETTING

MOST CORPORATIONS faced with financial difficulties usually realize too late just how serious those problems are. Following some period of time in which the corporation has been suffering losses and the corresponding period of time in which the concomitant lack of cash flow has created its own problems, the corporation then seeks the advice of counsel.

The immediate precipitating factors which cause this to be done generally are the filing of a number of lawsuits by unsecured creditors of the corporation; the reluctance on the part of its secured creditors to advance any more money on inventory and receivables; and, in jurisdictions where permitted, the attaching of bank accounts or other property of the corporate debtor, or the placing upon the corporate premises of a keeper or other judicial officer. In more extreme cases, the secured creditor may inform the corporate debtor that it intends to foreclose upon its security interest in the collateral securing loans, and requests that the collateral be delivered peaceably to the secured creditor so that a foreclosure sale may be held. In a few cases, an involuntary petition in bankruptcy may be filed against the corporation, seeking its adjudication as a bankrupt.

---

[*] Richard F. Broude is a member of the law firm of Commons & Broude, Los Angeles, California.

It is unfortunate that the realization of the seriousness of such financial problems often comes when immediate short-term remedial action is imperative. Were the corporate officer to comprehend the seriousness of the financial situation at an early stage, the possibilities of a more relaxed atmosphere for out-of-court dealings with the corporation's creditors, both secured and unsecured, might be realized. However, there is always the hope that a big contract might be awarded the corporation, or that cash flow will improve, or that for any one of a number of reasons, the situation will work itself out. More often than not, these optimistic projections do not come about, and the facts of corporate financial distress will have to be faced and solutions found.

This chapter will explore various methods by which a corporation in financial distress can more effectively deal with the situation. Because of the cost and complexity of legal procedures, the corporation should first consider voluntary out-of-court settlements through *extension, composition* or *arrangement* with unsecured and secured creditors. Where such a settlement cannot be worked out, the debtor may then consider filing a petition initiating court proceedings for arrangement with unsecured creditors under Chapter XI of the Bankruptcy Act or resort to the more stringent corporate reorganization under Chapter X of the same act. If all else fails, the last resort would be liquidation proceedings through either *assignment* or *bankruptcy.*

OUT-OF-COURT ARRANGEMENTS

Out-of-court arrangements are a useful device by means of which formal reorganization proceedings may be avoided. They range in complexity from simple compositions or extensions with unsecured creditors to highly involved and sophisticated transactions with secured and unsecured creditors. The latter may involve the restructuring of secured debt or the issuance of preferred or common stock in exchange for forgiveness of debt. The complexity of the deal is probably a function of the size of the corporation, although the difficulty of the corporation's financial problems will obviously play a large part in determining the type of remedy needed. The following discussion will deal first with the simpler types of out-of-court arrangements through compositions and extensions of unsecured debt. Some attention will then be devoted to transactions of increased complexity.

General Procedures

The initiation of discussions with creditors should be preceded by consultation with counsel, who should be given a detailed picture of the corporate financial position. Counsel should be educated regarding the business of the corporation, its financial history, and the reasons for its problems. Extended consultation between counsel and the debtor's accountants is also warranted. With this information, a meeting of unsecured creditors can then be arranged. In some cases, it will be wise for the debtor's officers and counsel to meet first with a small group of the largest creditors. Their agreement and cooperation can be of substantial help in convincing smaller creditors to go along with the debtor's settlement plans.

At all times during this procedure, the secured creditors, if any, of the corporation should be kept informed with respect to the steps being taken to solve the debtor's financial problems. A secured creditor who learns third hand that a meeting with unsecured creditors has been called will in many cases overreact and take precipitous action without really considering the consequences. A little soothing of the secured creditor's concerns will be of enormous benefit.

At the meeting of unsecured creditors, a financial statement should be distributed so that creditors might comprehend the nature and extent of the corporation's financial problems. Counsel for the corporation and its officers who are in attendance at the meeting should then give a detailed explanation of the situation that faces the corporation and how that situation came about. The causes might include such things as lack of working capital, rising price of raw materials, unforeseen circumstances which resulted in sales not being as high as projected, and a multitude of other reasons which may have led the corporation into its financial problems. Counsel and the officers of the corporation must take care to be neither too pessimistic nor too optimistic about prospects for the future operations of the corporation. Too optimistic a point of view may cause creditors to take the position that they can be paid in full if only they wait long enough for the corporation to reach the rosy future projected for it. On the other hand, too much pessimism might cause creditors to throw up their hands and take the position that a bankruptcy proceeding resulting in liquidation of the corporation is the only feasible alternative. Creditors must be told that a bankruptcy petition, resulting in the forced liquidation of the corporate assets, would lead to the least possible return to creditors and that is an end no one desires.

Following the presentation by the corporate officers and counsel, the creditors will generally ask representatives of the debtor to leave the room so that they might discuss the situation among themselves. In many cases, those creditors in attendance will elect a committee to represent their interests in negotiating with the corporation of a moratorium, workout or composition of the unsecured debt, or a combination thereof. The committee, or its agents, including such accountants or attorneys as it may employ, will request and should be given free access to the books, records, and operations of the corporation so that they might become fully informed as to its present operations and future prospects.

Negotiating for an Extension or a Composition Agreement

The corporation should, during the entire procedure, have a plan in mind for dealing with its unsecured creditors. If the corporation is in fairly decent shape, it may wish nothing more than an *extension* of time within which to pay unsecured debts in full. The bleaker the picture looks, the less unsecured creditors can expect to realize upon their obligations. Because the creditors would rather settle for something than nothing, they may accept a *composition* wherein they voluntarily reduce their claims against the debtor on a pro rata basis. The unsecured creditors may get as little as 20 cents on the dollar owed from the corporation in return for full and complete releases from the remainder of its unsecured obligations. In many cases, this will be unacceptable to the creditors. The bargaining process will usually lead to a compromise *combination extension-composition* settlement. Thus, the creditors might be willing to accept 20 cents on the dollar at the present time with an additional 30 percent in installments of 5 percent each year over the next six years. These promised installments are often represented by notes. All sorts of combinations of timing and percentages may be negotiated with the creditors' committee in this rather simple form of extension or combination extension-composition agreement.

It should be remembered that the process being discussed is one of negotiation. The debtor's first offer will frequently be less than it is prepared to finally settle for. The uppermost limits of what the debtor can financially afford to do should be kept firmly in mind at all times. Too optimistic an agreement will do nothing more than prolong the agony.

If an agreement is reached with the creditors' committee, the committee members will notify their constituents of the proposal, and send along forms which will request each creditor to indicate the amount of his claim, and to sign the form if the proposal is acceptable. The consent form will also constitute an agreement on the part of the creditor to be bound by the terms of the composition or extension agreement if a predetermined number of their peers are so inclined. For example, the composition-extension contract agreed upon by the creditors committee and the corporation might be considered to be effective if 80 percent of unsecured debt accepts the agreement. Problems may be caused by the number of creditors who do not accept, but those may be dealt with either by some provision in the composition agreement for payment of smaller nonaccepting creditors, or by a Chapter XI proceeding under the Bankruptcy Act, to be discussed below. An out-of-court settlement will also provide that expenses incurred by the committee for professional advice will be paid by the debtor. These are ordinarily paid out of the first distribution to creditors, although in some cases installment payments are provided.

One of the disadvantages of an out-of-court composition or extension agreement is that no way exists to make the agreement binding upon creditors who do not consent. Even if 90 percent or 95 percent of unsecured creditors accept the agreement, and it has become binding on these parties, nonaccepting creditors are free to file suit upon or take other action to enforce their obligations. The plan may provide for payment in full of small creditors; e.g., those with claims of $100 or less. This will negate the nuisance which such creditors may cause. The debtor will have promised that no creditor will be preferred, and thus there is no way in which he may legally deal with the recalcitrant creditor who refuses to accept the settlement plan and sues. As indicated above, such creditors may have to be dealt with in an expedited Chapter XI proceeding.

Arrangements to Convert Unsecured Debt

Arrangements with unsecured creditors may also include the conversion of all or a portion of the unsecured debt into an equity position in the corporation. This relieves the debtor of the continued obligation to make installment payments to unsecured creditors that the extension-composition agreements entail. Also, creditors oftentimes are willing to settle for a combination cash-stock arrangement as it benefits them in two ways. First, it enables creditors to keep a valued customer. Second, it gives the unsecured creditor a participation in future profits of the corporation not tied to the amount of his debt.

Restructuring of Secured Debt

For some corporations arrangements must be made with secured as well as unsecured creditors. The willingness of the secured creditor to go along with the corporation in modifying the terms of the repayment schedule may depend in large part upon how adequately collateralized he is. The secured creditor will realize that if the corporation files bankruptcy proceedings, the values of his collateral (particularly accounts receivable and inventory) will dissipate quickly. Account debtors will inevitably find excuses not to pay their debts; inventory sold at a bankruptcy sale will realize only a fraction of its value; raw material inventory often has value only when transformed into work in process and finished goods. Bankruptcy will usually not permit this to be done, and the secured creditor will wind up with a large deficiency. The secured creditor who has security in real estate, machinery and equipment, and other hard assets might not be quite as willing to consider a restructuring of the obligation, however.

Nevertheless, many secured creditors realize the value of an ongoing relationship with a customer who, given proper financial incentive, will continue to repay its obligation. In most cases, participation of the creditors' committee in the negotiations between the debtor and its secured creditors can be of great value.

Both parties will realize that the cooperation of both is necessary for the continued viability of the debtor. They will see that they have the same goal. This will frequently overcome the antithetical nature of their positions, greatly enhancing the chances of the debtor's financial survival.

Arrangements with the secured creditor may include forgiveness of a portion of the indebtedness; an extension of the time of repayment; or a decision on the part of the secured creditor to expand its line of credit, assuming that it can be given new collateral in the form of assets previously free and clear. The willingness of the secured creditor to enter into such arrangements may very well depend upon its sophistication and its experience with other corporations faced with like situations.

There is no way to predict how any particular secured creditor will react to the financial problems being faced by his debtor, but no alternative may exist for the debtor except to restructure its secured debt. If the secured creditor is recalcitrant and unwilling to go along with the suggestions made by the debtor and the creditors' committee, so long as those suggestions are realistic, no alternative may exist for the debtor but to institute proceedings for reorganization or arrangement under Chapters X or XI of the Bankruptcy Act, respectively.

Infusion of New Capital

Finally, the debtor may be able to persuade a third party to make an infusion of new capital. The investor may require, in return for his money, an equity position in the corporation, or a secured position in its property, or both. Many times he will fund the agreed-upon payment to creditors. The agreement with the third party will have been the result of negotiations with both the debtor and the creditors' committee.

There are many permutations and combinations of ways in which arrangements with secured creditors and unsecured creditors may be obtained without the necessity of proceedings under the Bankruptcy Act. These are dependent upon the rapport established between management and the debtor's creditors, and the willingness of the unsecured creditors to believe in and trust management. If management is able to convince its creditors that the financial position of the corporation is not the result of dishonesty or incompetence on its part, the possibility of an out-of-court settlement is greatly enhanced. If, on the other hand, an atmosphere of distrust exists between the creditors and the corporation, bankruptcy proceedings of one sort or another may then be unavoidable.

ARRANGEMENT PROCEEDINGS UNDER
CHAPTER XI OF THE BANKRUPTCY ACT

Chapter XI of the Bankruptcy Act provides a means whereby arrangements with unsecured creditors may be obtained under the aegis of a formalized court proceedings with many protections not available to the corporate debtor in an out-of-court arrangement such as that discussed above.

In essence, Chapter XI is a device whereby a corporation in financial distress can, while continuing to operate its business, propose a composition or extension with its unsecured creditors. A Chapter XI proceeding can be instituted only by the debtor; it cannot be involuntary. Many times, the filing of a Chapter XI proceeding is precipitated by attachments, numerous civil lawsuits to collect debts, by the filing of an involuntary petition in bankruptcy seeking liquidation of the debtor's property, or by the action of a secured creditor informing the debtor of its intention to foreclose or in other way realize upon its collateral pledged to secure the obligation. The filing of a Chapter XI proceeding has the effect of staying the continuation or institution of suits to collect unsecured obligations and restraining all acts and proceedings to enforce liens upon the property of the debtor. The initiation of a Chapter XI proceeding gives the bankruptcy court jurisdiction over the debtor and all of its property, wherever located. While the stay against lien enforcement may not continue indefinitely, the filing of the Chapter XI petition will give management relief from the problem of harassing creditors, and the ability to devote more time to managing the company.

A Chapter XI proceeding is "debtor controlled." The management of the corporation remains operating the corporate business. It must report to the court in accordance with local court rules as to operations and prospects, but management and stock ownership, except insofar as affected by a plan of arrangement, remains undisturbed.

It is commonly said that Chapter XI proceedings cannot affect secured creditors. Nothing could be further from the truth. As indicated above, a Chapter XI proceeding has the effect of restraining the continuation of commencement of proceedings to enforce liens upon property of the debtor. The debtor will often be able to parlay this restraint into an agreement with its secured creditor whereby continued financing will be made available. If the secured creditor has been informed beforehand of the corporation's decision to file a Chapter XI proceeding, he may already have indicated a willingness to continue to finance the operations of the business during that proceeding.

Initial Stages

Once the Chapter XI petition is filed, the debtor may be continued in possession of its operations, or a receiver may be appointed. A presumption exists in favor of a debtor-in-possession but a receiver may be appointed for cause shown. In some cases, creditors may desire the presence of an independent third party to take a new look at the affairs and operations of the debtor and to retain day-to-day control over its business. If creditors have some reason to doubt the competency or honesty of present management, they will request the court to appoint a receiver. Even if a receiver is appointed, he generally will employ management and retain the nonmanagement employees of the company to continue its operations.

The presence of a receiver should not, however, be treated lightly. For example, where a receiver is appointed, he has sole discretion with respect to whether or not to employ current management and, if the decision is made to employ management, what salary they should receive. Many local court rules provide that officers cannot be employed by a receiver (or for that matter, by a debtor-in-possession) without specific court order authorizing the employment and fixing salaries.

The most difficult stage of a Chapter XI proceeding is the first few weeks after filing. The bankruptcy judge must immediately make a decision regarding whether or not he will permit the debtor (or receiver) to continue operations. As a rule of thumb, the bankruptcy judge will permit operations to continue if he is shown that the debtor has sufficient funds to meet its current and next week's payroll, enough funds to pay withholding and other trust fund taxes, and enough funds with which to purchase inventory or raw materials, to manufacture, and to sell its output. If this showing cannot be made to the bankruptcy judge, either at initial hearings following filing of the Chapter XI petition, or in the judge's consultations with the receiver if one is appointed, the court will order operations closed.

It is at this point that the pre-Chapter XI conversations with the secured creditor become most important. If the secured creditor has been informed of the corporation's intention to file a Chapter XI, and if that secured creditor (or some substitute secured creditor) has indicated a willingness to finance the operations of the debtor, the bankruptcy judge will generally be satisfied that he should permit operations to continue. The confidence displayed in the debtor by the secured creditor (whatever the reason for that confidence) will likewise persuade the bankruptcy judge. A court order will be needed in order to permit the new borrowing to go forward. A debtor-in-possession is not the same entity as the pre-Chapter XI debtor, so new documentation will be needed.

The Creditors' Committee

If the debtor gets over those first few weeks, and operations fall into a relatively successful pattern, the next step in the ordinary Chapter XI is the first meeting of creditors. At this meeting, a formal creditors' committee will oftentimes be elected. This creditors' committee may have been created either during informal meetings with creditors prior to the filing of the Chapter XI, or at a creditors' meeting called by the debtor after the filing of the Chapter XI and before the official first meeting of creditors held under the applicable provisions of the Bankruptcy Act.

The functions of the creditors' committee in Chapter XI are very similar to those in an out-of-court arrangement such as that discussed above. It will consult with the receiver or debtor-in-possession to ascertain the reason for the financial problems; it will retain counsel and accountants to make a thorough examination of the corporation's books and records to determine the reasons for the financial problems, and it will negotiate with the debtor's representatives for the formulation of a plan of arrangement.

The Plan of Arrangement

The plan of arrangement will many times be very similar to the out-of-court extension or composition agreement discussed above. However, one very important difference between a Chapter XI proceeding and an informal composition is that the Chapter XI plan of arrangement, if approved by the requisite number of creditors (a majority in number and amount of claims), will be binding on both consenting and nonconsenting creditors. It was mentioned above that a few recalcitrant creditors can upset an out-of-court arrangement. No such leverage is afforded in a Chapter XI proceeding. If a majority in number and amount of unsecured creditors who have filed claims consent to a plan of arrangement, nonconsenting creditors are bound and must abide by the terms of the plan.

The plan of arrangement will be the result of long and hard negotiations between the debtor and the creditors' committee. It may be a plan which contemplates the payment of so many cents on the dollar to unsecured creditors either at one time or over a period of time. It may contemplate issuance of stock in exchange for unsecured obligations. (There are certain exemptions contained in Chapter XI to the registration requirements of Securities Act of 1933 and the Securities Exchange Act of 1934, but those exemptions must be dealt with gingerly and only upon the advice of competent securities counsel.) The plan of arrangement can classify unsecured creditors into separate categories and creditors in different classes can be treated differently. For example, creditors with claims under a certain amount, such as $100, may be paid in full while all other creditors will receive 25 cents on the dollar. In addition, creditors who elect to reduce their claims to $100 may be paid in full. This has the effect of eliminating a large number of unsecured creditors. Because such creditors are being paid in full, they are not "affected" by the plan, and their consent to the plan need not be obtained. The task of soliciting consents to the plan is thus made that much easier.

It should be kept in mind that it is the debtor, and no one else, who may propose a plan of arrangement with its unsecured creditors. As contrasted with Chapter X proceedings, which will be discussed in the next section, the debtor remains in control of its plan at all times. One other great advantage of Chapter XI over Chapter

X is that consents may be solicited by the debtor before the Chapter XI is even filed or before the plan is presented to the court. No such versatility is available in Chapter X.

External Infusion of Funds

Many times, a plan of arrangement under Chapter XI will contemplate an infusion of capital by a new investor. In order to confirm, the debtor must pay into court what is known as the "deposit." The deposit is a sum of money which is necessary to pay the following expenses: all nondischargeable tax claims; all expenses of administration; all other priority claims (primarily wages) and enough money to make the initial payment to creditors under the plan of arrangement. Expenses of administration will include such things as fees for the debtor's attorney; professional fees incurred by the creditors' committee; fees for the receiver (if one has been appointed) and for his attorney. In a drawn-out Chapter XI proceeding, these fees might be extensive. Since the debtor will ordinarily not be able to generate enough profits for it to internally fund its own plan of arrangement, it needs to look for an outside investor to meet such needs. The investor might be a new secured creditor, who in addition to furnishing some funds for the deposit, will agree to make a working capital loan to the rehabilitated debtor. He might be a person who will receive, in return for his payment, an equity position in the debtor. The funder of the plan might also be a corporation seeking to merge or to expand its product line. In this case, the debtor's plan of arrangement might be nothing more than one which contemplates the sale of all of its assets to the purchasing corporation in return for cash or stock which would then be used to pay the expenses of administration and make a distribution to unsecured creditors.

Unless stock in the debtor is given to creditors or to the third-party funder, the debtor's stockholders will keep their equity position in what is now a corporation with an improved financial structure.

Confirmation of the Plan

Once the plan of arrangement has been agreed upon between the creditors' committee and the debtor, solicitation of consents will occur and creditors will be asked to file their claims and their consents with the bankruptcy court. The plan is filed with the court and a hearing date is set for confirmation. The plan will be confirmed if, among other things, the court finds that "it is for the best interests of the creditors and is feasible."

The "best interests of the creditors" test has been interpreted to mean that a plan should be confirmed if unsecured creditors will realize more from the plan than they would realize upon a liquidation of the debtor's assets in a straight bankruptcy proceeding. That this is true may be shown in the overwhelming majority of cases. Everyone experienced in sales upon liquidation knows that inventory, for example, brings little if it is sold at auction, as opposed to its value if it is converted into work in process and then into finished product. Likewise, accounts receivable are worth more to an ongoing business than they are in liquidation. Once account debtors know that their creditor is a *straight* bankrupt, collections fall off drastically. The same is true, although to a lesser extent, with respect to machinery, equipment, and real estate. Even these assets, although they sell for more realistic sums than does inventory, do not bring anything approaching their fair market value at a liquidation sale. And certainly, machinery and equipment have a much higher value as a part of an ongoing business operation than it would at any sale.

The second requirement for confirmation of a plan of arrangement is that it is "feasible." This means that there is some likelihood that the rehabilitated debtor will be able to consummate the plan and make a go of its operations. At the hearing on confirmation, the debtor might present evidence as to its restated balance sheet, what its business prospects look like, and how operations have been hardened by the Chapter XI and much of the flab removed.

Confirmation of a plan of arrangement has the effect of discharging the debtor corporation from all of its dischargeable debts. As mentioned above, nonconsenting creditors are bound by the terms of the confirmed plan of arrangement. In addition, one of the sections of the Bankruptcy Act provides that the debtor does not realize taxable income, either under the federal Internal Revenue Code or under the tax laws of any state, "in respect to the adjustment of the indebtedness of a debtor in a proceeding under this Chapter." That is, while forgiveness of indebtedness ordinarily results in taxable income to the debtor, such is not the case with a plan of arrangement confirmed under Chapter XI. The only exception to this rule is where Chapter XI has been used for the evasion of any income tax.

One last positive effect of a Chapter XI proceedings is the provision for the rejection of burdensome executory contracts. For example, if the debtor is the lessee under an onerous or burdensome lease, it may be rejected by the debtor in a Chapter XI proceedings. Such a rejection will have the effect of terminating the lease, and remitting the landlord to his claim for damages as an unsecured creditor in the proceeding. This claim may not exceed the sum of three years' rental reserved under the lease. Likewise, an onerous purchase contract or sales contract might be rejected as part of a Chapter XI plan.

If a Chapter XI proceeding is successful, the rehabilitated debtor will have undergone extensive surgery, resulting in the removal of a significant portion of its unsecured debt. The balance sheet will be greatly improved and, hopefully, so will the prospects of the rehabilitated corporate debtor.

PROCEEDINGS FOR REORGANIZATION OF A CORPORATION UNDER CHAPTER X

While Chapter XI proceedings may be thought of as relatively informal and debtor controlled, Chapter X proceedings are quite formal, rigid, and include the full trappings and panoply of extensive court supervision and control. While a Chapter XI can be of short duration, a Chapter X is usually a long, drawn-out and expensive procedure. It may be instituted either by voluntary or involuntary petition.

The Trustee's Role

A Chapter X is a trustee's proceeding. He is responsible for making all the corporate decisions. He is also the person who usually proposes the plan of reorganization. The debtor plays only a passive role. Thus when a Chapter X petition is approved by the judge, a disinterested trustee will be appointed to manage and completely control all of the debtor's operations. Disinterestedness in this context means having had no association of any kind with the debtor corporation. The trustee takes over for the management.

He may choose to employ some or all of old management, but often he will dismiss many management personnel. Chapter X proceedings are usually instituted for large publicly held corporations with widespread public holdings of either debt or equity securities. The disinterested trustee is charged with the task of making a thorough investigation of the corporation's affairs, the dealings of management with the corporation, its competency and the reasons for the financial collapse of the debtor. This report is then presented to the court.

The Securities and Exchange Commission

In addition, the Securities and Exchange Commission plays a vital and important role in Chapter X proceedings. While they have no mandated functions under Chapter XI, they have significant duties to fulfill in Chapter X proceedings. Generally speaking, the role of the SEC is to protect the public. In fulfilling this role, it will keep in close touch with the progress of the proceeding and will be consulted at all stages for its advice and guidance.

Normal Procedures

Chapter X provides that the judge is to fix a time within which the trustee is to prepare and file a plan, or state reasons why a plan cannot be effected. If the trustee does prepare and file a plan, it is sent to the Securities and Exchange Commission for its review and recommendations. The judge may not enter an order approving a plan until after the Securities and Exchange Commission has either filed its report or has notified the judge that it will not file a report. If the plan is approved by the judge, the trustee is to mail the plan to all creditors and stockholders who are affected by the plan.

Dealing with Secured Creditors

A major difference between Chapter XI and X is that under Chapter X, plans for reorganization of the corporation may modify, amend, or otherwise deal with the claims of secured creditors. Within constitutional limitations, the terms of payment may be stretched out, the interest rate may be adjusted, the nature of the collateral may be changed, or the secured debt may be modified in other ways to improve the prospects for the reorganized corporation.

Because a Chapter X plan will generally divide creditors into classes, there is a major practical problem dealing with secured creditors as each secured creditor is in a class by himself. This means that acceptance of the plan by each secured creditor whose debt is modified must be obtained before the plan can be confirmed. Thus, large secured creditors must be closely informed regarding the progress of events during the Chapter X proceeding and their cooperation secured. A plan will only work out with the concurrence and the help of the major secured creditors. A hostile secured creditor could possibly veto any plan of reorganization that the trustee presents to the court for acceptance.

The Absolute Priority Rule

Chapter X also enforces the absolute priority rule. This means that each class of creditors must be paid in full before a lower class of creditors can participate at all in the plan of reorganization. Thus, senior secured creditors must be paid in full before junior secured creditors can be paid. All secured creditors must be paid in full before unsecured creditors can receive anything. And, of course, all creditors must be paid in full before stockholders can participate in the plan of reorganization (unless their participation is in return for their contributing new cash to the corporation). Obviously, this means that if the corporation is insolvent, shareholders cannot participate in the plan; equity will be wiped out.

Chapter X contains its own mechanism for determining solvency. An insolvency hearing is held many months after the Chapter X has been filed. Generally, the interested parties project future earnings for the corporation, and then a multiplier is fixed by which the value of the corporation may be determined. The court arrives at a valuation for the corporation as a going concern that it, in its judgment, gives credence to all evidence which has been presented to it. If the value of the corporation as thus hypothesized is less than the amount of debt which the corporation has, the corporation is insolvent and shareholders cannot participate in the plan of reorganization without contributing new cash for their new shares. Likewise, insolvency generally means that the lowest class of creditors will receive little, if anything, on their claims. In any event, the fundamental result of a Chapter X, as opposed to a Chapter XI, is that old stockholders and old management generally disappear. The lowest class of creditors entitled to participate in the plan will become the debtor's new stockholders.

As can be seen from the foregoing discussion, the Chapter X proceeding results in a complete restructuring of the corporation; a revolution in its operations; and the displacement and replacement of management and shareholders. It constitutes major surgery for a dying corporation.

LIQUIDATION

If attempts at rehabilitation fail, or if it is determined that the value of the firm, if liquidated, will be greater than if an attempt is made to keep the firm operating, it should be liquidated. Liquidation procedures may be relatively informal, as in assignments, or formal, via a straight bankruptcy proceeding.

An assignment is an out-of-court liquidation procedure. The common law provides for an assignment whereby a debtor transfers title to his assets to a third person known as an assignee. The assignee liquidates the assets and distributes the proceeds among the unsecured creditors on a pro rata basis. The creditors may then sign a release of the debtor from all his unpaid obligations.

More formal procedures are involved in bankruptcy. A voluntary petition of bankruptcy may be filed by the debtor himself. Creditors may file an involuntary petition in bankruptcy if the following conditions are met:

1. The total debts must be $1,000 or more.
2. The creditors filing must be owed $500 or more.
3. Within the four preceding months the debtor must have committed one or more of the six acts of bankruptcy.
4. One creditor may file an involuntary petition unless the debtor has 12 or more creditors in which case 3 petitioning creditors are necessary.

The six acts of bankruptcy are: (1) concealment, or fraudulent conveyance of assets; (2) preferential transfer of assets to one or more creditors; (3) an insolvent debtor permits a creditor to obtain a lien or to seize property by legal or equitable proceedings; (4) the debtor makes a general assignment; (5) the insolvent debtor permits the appointment of a receiver or trustee; and (6) the debtor admits in writing his inability to pay his debts and his willingness to be adjudged a bankrupt.

Upon an adjudication of bankruptcy, the case is referred to a bankruptcy judge, who is the judicial officer in charge of the bankruptcy case. In addition, on petition of the creditors, the bankruptcy judge may appoint a receiver to serve as custodian of the property of the bankrupt until the election of a trustee at the first creditors' meeting. The trustee is charged with the task of converting all assets into cash.

When the assets have been converted into cash to the extent possible, the cash is paid out on a pro rata basis in the following order of priority:

1. Costs of administering the bankrupt estate.
2. Wages due workers if earned within three months prior to the filing of the petition in bankruptcy. The amount of wages is not to exceed $600 a person.
3. Taxes due the United States, state, county, or any other governmental agency.
4. General or unsecured creditors. This class includes remaining balances after payment to secured creditors from liquidation of their collateral, trade creditors, unsecured bank loans, and debenture bonds.

Studies of the proceeds in bankruptcy liquidation reveal that unsecured creditors receive a few cents on the dollar. Consequently, where an assignment for the benefit of creditors is likely to yield more, assignment is preferred to bankruptcy.

CONCLUSION

Early warning signals of financial distress must be recognized and acted upon as soon as possible by management. The longer the problem is allowed to fester, the more radical the solution will become. If prompt action is taken, there is every possibility that informal solutions will be sufficient, and that cumbersome, expensive and time-consuming proceedings will be unnecessary. Early recognition is management's function; diligent and serious prosecution of this function will result in a sounder corporation with substantially increased chances for future success.

ADDITIONAL SOURCES

Altman, Edward I. *Corporate Bankruptcy in America.* Lexington, Mass.: Heath Lexington Books, 1971.

Altman, Edward I. "Corporate Bankruptcy Potential, Stockholder Returns and Share Valuation." *Journal of Finance,* 24 (December 1969), 887–900.

Altman, Edward I. "Railroad Bankruptcy Propensity." *Journal of Finance,* 26 (May 1971), 333–45.

Beaver, William H. "Financial Ratios as Predictors of Failure." *Empirical Research in Accounting: Selected Studies* Supplement to *Journal of Accounting Research* (1966), 71–111.

Edmister, Robert O. "An Empirical Test of Financial Ratio Analysis for Small Business Failure Prediction." *Journal of Financial and Quantitative Analysis,* 7 (March 1972), 1477–93.

Murray, Roger F. "The Penn Central Debacle: Lessons for Financial Analysis." *Journal of Finance,* 26 (May 1971), 327–32.

Nicholson, Rupert. "The Bankrupt Bonanza." *Dun's Review,* 105 (March 1975), 76–77.

Weston, J. Fred. "The Industrial Economics Background of the Penn Central Bankruptcy." *Journal of Finance,* 26 (May 1971), 311–26.

Chapter 47

Stock Reacquisition Programs[*]

John S. R. Shad[†]

THIS CHAPTER describes: (1) the benefits to a company, its management and those shareholders who do not tender their shares, as well as to those who do; (2) the disadvantages of stock reacquisition programs; (3) the factors which determine the terms required to induce shareholders to tender or exchange their shares and to approve statutory mergers; and assesses the cost-time effectiveness of block purchases, open market accumulation, cash tender and exchange offers, statutory mergers and reverse splits.

Many chief financial officers are opposed to contracting their companies' equity capitalizations. Understandably so, for a company's entire capitalization rests on its equity base—the larger its equity base, the greater its financial stability and financing alternatives. However, many publicly owned companies can realize higher returns (and other major benefits) with greater certainty by reacquiring their own shares, than through conventional corporate commitments.

---

[*] This chapter is based on talks by Mr. Shad in 1974 under the auspices of the *New York Law Journal* and the Financial Communication Society.

[†] John S. R. Shad is vice chairman of the board, E. F. Hutton & Company, New York.

BENEFITS OF COMPANY STOCK
REACQUISITIONS

While few companies actually "go private," over 25 percent of
the companies listed on the New York Stock Exchange reacquired
some of their outstanding common shares in 1974 (and many are
continuing to do so). Most such purchases have been modest, but a
number of publicly owned companies have reacquired 10 percent
to more than 50 percent of their outstanding shares on terms which
confer major benefits to the companies, their managements and
those shareholders who do not tender their shares, *as well as those
who do.*

High Effective Returns

At times, many publicly owned companies' shares sell at low
price/earnings ratios (less than six times the estimated next 12
months' earnings; or in other words, at less than three times the
indicated earnings before taxes at a 50 percent rate) and at significant discounts from their *understated* book values per share.

If a company's indicated annual *pretax* earnings are $8 per share
and it pays $20 per share for a portion of its shares, the company's
indicated effective annual pretax earnings return on its investment
in its own shares is 40 percent ($8 ÷ $20). This is the rate of
return the company would have to earn on an internal commitment
or acquisition to produce a comparable improvement in its earnings per share. Figure 1 provides a scale of the pretax return on
shares reacquired.

More important, by reducing its outstanding shares, a company
can:

1. Not only increase the current level, but also the future growth
   rate, of its earnings and book value per share.
2. Enhance the intrinsic value and appreciation potentialities
   of the shares that remain outstanding.
3. Increase the return on its equity.
4. Improve its equity financing and acquisition-for-stock capabilities.
5. Reduce the future dilution of its outstanding shares under
   various stock issuance requirements and programs.

FIGURE 1
Pretax Return on Shares Reacquired

Multiple of Indicated Annual Earnings per Share	Earnings Multiple Paid per Share Reacquired (a 25% premium)	Effective Annual Pretax Return per Share Reacquired*
1	1.25	160.0%
2	2.50	80.0
3	3.75	53.3
4	5.00	40.0
5	6.25	32.0
6	7.50	26.7
7	8.75	22.9
8	10.00	20.0
9	11.25	17.8
10	12.50	16.0
11	13.75	14.5
12	15.00	13.3
13	16.25	12.3
14	17.50	11.4
15	18.75	10.7

* Before interest costs, as well as dividend savings, earnings per share enchancement and the other benefits of reacquiring the shares.

Note: Assumes that shares are reacquired at a 25 percent premium over the market and that the company pays taxes at a 50 percent rate.

6. Take potential sellers out of the stock without depressing the price.
7. Reduce the future supply of the shares on the market.
8. Increase the percentage interest in the shares that remain outstanding of management stock and option holders and other nontendering shareholders.
9. Tangibly evidence management's confidence in the company's future prospects.
10. Inhibit potential raiders from accumulating the shares in the open market and making tender offers.

   Dividend Savings. An added benefit to dividend paying companies is the dividend saving on the shares reacquired. For example, if the dividend yield on the cost of the shares to the company is 6 percent, the pretax dividend saving to the company is 12 percent. Thus, the dividend saving may exceed the interest on debt, if any, incurred to reacquire the shares. (See Figure 2 for a scale of the dividend savings on shares reacquired.)

   Exchange Offer Advantages. Further, if the shares are reacquired through an exchange offer, no cash is required. The company merely creates a new security—typically a subordinate de-

FIGURE 2
Dividend Savings on Shares Reacquired

Dividend Yield	Reacquired Yield (a 25% premium)	Portion of 10 Percent Interest Cost Covered by Dividend Saving
1%.	0.8%	16%
2.	1.6	32
3.	2.4	48
4.	3.2	64
5.	4.0	80
6.	4.8	96
7.	5.6	112
8.	6.4	128
9.	7.2	144
10.	8.0	160

Note: Assumes that shares are reacquired at a 25 percent premium over the market with funds borrowed at a 10 percent interest cost and that the company pays taxes at a 50 percent rate.

benture—which it offers in exchange for its common shares. Such nonconvertible debentures are usually subordinated to all present and future incurred debt, and callable immediately at a modest premium. When and if interest rates decline, or the stock's price recovers, the debentures can be refunded at a lower interest rate, or retired with the proceeds of a public offering of a *portion* of the shares reacquired—*possibly within a year or two.* If interest rates rise, the debentures will decline in market price and the company can reacquire them at a discount.

"Busted Convert" Exchanges. A company can also reduce its debt and potential common stock dilution through an exchange offer of nonconvertible debentures for so-called busted converts— convertible debentures that are selling for less than 60 percent of their maturity value.

Market Performance. During a period of generally declining stock prices, a tender or exchange offer may not stem the tide, but the stock should subsequently perform better than it would have otherwise performed. If the stock declines to an even lower earnings multiple and greater discount from book value, the company should consider reacquiring additional shares at the lower prices.

Benefits to Tendering Shareholders

Tendering shareholders have generally received 25 percent to 100 percent premiums (in cash or marketable securities) over the market price of their shares before announcement of the offer. The stocks have generally declined below the tender or exchange offer prices when the offers expire, and a tendering shareholder has been able to use the proceeds to repurchase a greater number of the company's shares than he tendered. He can also readily reinvest in other depressed securities.

Debenture-for-stock exchange offers generally enable shareholders to upgrade the quality, and increase the yield and *market value* of their investments without incurring any brokerage or other expenses in the process.

THE DISADVANTAGES OF STOCK REACQUISITION PROGRAMS

The principal disadvantages of stock reacquisition programs include the following:

1. They reduce a company's net worth and borrowing capacity, and they may increase its debt-equity ratio and fixed charges.
2. If the future earnings per share decline below the after-tax interest cost incurred per share reacquired, the earnings per share will be reduced, instead of enhanced.
3. Acquisitions cannot be effected on a pooling-of-interest accounting basis for two years, unless the reacquired shares are reissued earlier for qualified purposes.
4. If an opposition group has acquired a large interest in the shares, a tender or exchange offer could deliver effective control to them. Such offers can also be used to take such groups out of the stock.

Delisting Possibility

Relatively few stock reacquisition programs have resulted in delisting of the shares from the stock exchange or interdealer market in which they were traded, and if delisted from the New York Stock Exchange, they have usually been listed on the American or a regional stock exchange, or traded over the counter.

While stock reacquisition programs do reduce the liquidity of the market in the shares, *companies and shareholders generally prefer thinner, to lower, markets.* Sound stock reacquisition programs take potential sellers out of the stock without depressing the price, reduce the future supply of the shares on the market and enhance the intrinsic value and appreciation potentialities of the shares that remain outstanding.

Because of the depressed prices of their shares, companies that are willing to suffer delistings generally have no near-term intentions of doing common stock financings nor of using their shares for acquisitions.

However, the possibility of delisting is a negative inducement to shareholders to accept tender and exchange offers, and under proposed SEC Rule 13e–3, stock reacquisition programs which result in delisting will be unlawful unless the company has a valid business purpose and the terms are fair to the shareholders.

Public Criticism

Thousands of companies have reacquired some of their shares. The few that have been subject to criticism should not inhibit constructive stock reacquisition programs. Few critics would deny shareholders the right to decide whether to sell or exchange their shares—usually at significant premiums over the prior market price. Nor would it be in the national interest to revert to the old common-law principle that permitted minority shareholders to veto the desires of the majority (e.g., block statutory mergers).

Many shareholders believe their stocks will continue to decline in price (as well they may). If their only recourse is to sell in the open market, they will further depress the market, to their own detriment, as well as that of the majority of shareholders, corporations, and the nation. Companies that reacquire their shares accommodate potential sellers without depressing the market.

Also, some have criticized managements who employ corporate funds at lower rates of return and higher risks than under stock reacquisition programs.

To Minimize Possible Abuses

In order to minimize possible abuses, it is suggested that the SEC require:

1. Simpler and briefer, balanced disclosures of the negative, as well as the affirmative, facts shareholders should consider.

2. Formal opinions of qualified experts as to whether the terms are fair to the public shareholders (as suggested under proposed SEC Rule 13e–3).
3. Simpler descriptions of shareholders' legal remedies.

Voluminous, legalistic, disclaimer prospectuses limit companies' liabilities, but they are not very helpful to shareholders. Few institutional research reports exceed 20 pages. Similarly brief, balanced presentations, prepared by qualified experts would greatly facilitate informed shareholder decisions. The supporting documentation should be filed with the SEC and provided by the company to any shareholder (or others) who return a prepaid postcard requesting it.

Shareholders have extensive legal remedies (temporary restraining orders, injunctions, rights of appraisal, derivative, class and fraud actions). Such actions are often initiated in behalf of small shareholders by attorneys who have the incentive of the large legal fees awarded by the courts at the defendants' expense, if they win such suits.

How High a Premium Is Required?

Premiums of 25 percent to 100 percent over the market price, prior to announcement of cash tender and exchange offers, have historically induced acceptances by 25 percent to over 50 percent of the shares held by the public. Similar premiums have generally been paid in statutory mergers. The premiums in cash or marketable securities required to induce shareholders to accept tender and exchange offers and to approve statutory mergers are determined by the following factors.

Market Conditions. Smaller premiums are required in declining than in rising markets.

Portion of Float. The larger the percentage of the publicly held shares that the company seeks, the higher the premium.

Holder Characteristics. The number of shareholders and shares held in odd lots, round lots, small and large blocks, under investment letters, and registered in the names of brokers and institutions is important. Usually, the larger the investment letter, block and broker interests, the lower the premium.

Price Action. Generally, if the stock has been actively trading at a depressed price or declining over many months, the lower the premium. If the price has been rising over several months or has recently dropped sharply on low volume, the higher the premium.

Stock Price. Usually, the lower the dollar price of the stock, the higher the premium. A $1.50 offer for a stock trading at $1 will not induce as large a volume of tenders as a $45 offer for a stock trading at $30—even though the premium is 50 percent in both cases.

Comparative Value. If the stock is selling at a higher price/earnings ratio, lower dividend yield and small discount from book value than the stocks of other companies with comparable balance sheets, earnings records and prospects, the lower the premium.

Soliciting Dealers. The use of soliciting dealers increases the volume of acceptances and reduces the premium.

Latitude of the Offer. If the offer is unlimited as to the minimum and maximum number of shares the company will accept, the lower the premium.

Exchange Offers. Exchange offer premiums are based on the "when issued" market value of the new security. They depend on the foregoing factors, plus the marketability and quality of the security being offered in exchange for the shares. It is desirable for the new security to be traded in the same market as the shares. The quality of the new security depends principally on the company's historical and projected earnings, cash flows, debt/equity ratios and fixed-charge coverages.

STOCK REACQUISITION APPROACHES

The manner and cost-time effectiveness of the various means under which shares can be reacquired are described below.

By Majority Shareholder Approval

The most cost-time effective means of eliminating public shareholders and truly "going private" are through statutory mergers and reverse splits. Upon 51 percent to 67 percent shareholder approval (depending principally on the company's state of incorporation), the minority shareholders are bound (subject to their legal remedies) by the terms approved by the majority. Under proposed SEC Rule 13e–3, if such transactions are effected by controlling persons (as defined), they will be unlawful unless the terms are fair to the public shareholders and the company has a valid business purpose.

Statutory Mergers. Companies typically enter into statutory mergers to improve their financial alternatives, operations and competitive positions, and to eliminate duplications of effort and possible conflicts of interest. To date, the premiums over the prior market value of their shares received by the acquired company's shareholders (in cash or securities of the acquiring company) have been similar to those paid in comparable tender and exchange offers described above.

Reverse Splits. The principal purpose of reverse splits has been to bring a stock up into a more respectable price range. In times past, many investment banking and brokerage firms would not underwrite public offerings nor recommend purchases to their clients of so-called "cats and dogs"—stocks selling below $10 per share. Through a 1-for-10 share reverse split of a stock selling at $1, its market price will theoretically be increased from $1 to $10 per share.

By doing a large reverse split (e.g., 1-for-10,000 shares) and paying cash in lieu of fractional shares, the shares of all who held less than 10,000 shares will be retired. This may include substantially all of the shares held by the public. If the company pays a high enough price for such fractional shares, two qualified independent persons (as proposed under Rule 13e–3) might conclude that the terms are fair to the shareholders, but it may be difficult to demonstrate the valid business purpose of such splits.

Voluntary Reacquisitions

Companies can reacquire stock from their shareholders on a voluntary basis through block purchases, open-market accumulation, cash tender and exchange offers. The cost-time effectiveness of such voluntary programs are as follows.

Block Purchases. Block purchases are the least expensive approach. The effectiveness depends on the portion of the shares held in blocks. The New York Stock Exchange defines a block as having a market value of $200,000 or more.

The company publicly announces the number of shares it will purchase in blocks from time to time at prices related to the market. Institutions and other block holders (particularly those holding under investment letters) have been very receptive to such offers. In weak markets, it has seldom been necessary to pay premiums over the market for blocks, and the company's brokerage commissions are at volume discount rates. However, this approach requires cash, and it often takes more than a month to repurchase as little as 5 percent of the outstanding shares.

Open-Market Accumulation. Open-market accumulation is the next least expensive means of reacquiring shares. The company purchases the shares in the open market at prevailing prices, and pays conventional brokerage commissions. However, cash is required and it often takes over six months to accumulate as little as 5 percent of the outstanding shares.

Under proposed SEC Rule 13e–2, a company's daily purchases will be limited to 15 percent of the four preceding weeks' average daily volume of transactions in the security. The company may not execute the opening trade on any day, purchase any shares within 30 minutes of the close, nor at "up-tick" prices.

Cash Tender Offers. Cash tender offers are more expensive, but they are the fastest and most effective voluntary means of reacquiring over 10 percent of the shares held by the public. The company announces the maximum number of shares it will purchase at a certain price, if tendered typically within 30 days. The price is usually 25 percent to 100 percent higher than the market price before announcement of the offer. If an investment banking and brokerage firm assists in structuring the offer and acts as the dealer manager, the dealer manager and soliciting dealer fees typically aggregate 1½-to-2 stock exchange commissions per share purchased.

If the company lacks excess cash with which to make a tender offer, the funds must be raised by selling assets or obtaining a long-term loan. It is extremely risky to use bank loans for this purpose, unless long-term take-out financing is readily available.

ESOT Tender Offers. Cash tender offers can be financed through a company's *tax deductible* contributions to an employee stock ownership trust (ESOT). The trust must be formed for the benefit of a major cross section of the employees, not merely top management.

A loan against the company's guarantee and the stock to be acquired by the ESOT may be used to make the cash tender offer. The company's tax deductible contributions to the ESOT (of up to 15 percent of the participating employee's wages) are used to repay the loan. When an employee's association with the company ends, he receives his stock (based on the portion of the contributions for his benefit) at no cost. He pays a federal income tax at favorable rates, based on the lower of the ESOT's original cost of the shares or the then current market value (which becomes his cost basis for future capital gains taxes when he sells the shares).

However, the trust's stock purchases do not reduce the company's outstanding shares. Consequently, the current level and future growth rate of the earnings and book value per share are not increased, nor is the interest in the company of the nontendering shareholders. Actually, the company's contributions to the trust reduce the earnings per share at the expense of the nontendering shareholders, including employees who have substantial stock interests. The latter generally bear a greater derivative portion of the cost of the company's contributions to the trust than their interest in the shares acquired by the trust.

Exchange Offers.   Exchange offers are usually the most expensive, but also the most practical voluntary means for many companies to reacquire their shares, because no cash is required. The company usually creates a new security for the purpose, typically a subordinated debenture that is immediately callable at a modest premium.

The nonconvertible debentures (unsecured notes) offered in exchange for shares are typically subordinated to all present and future incurred debt and callable immediately at 105 percent of par, declining to par in five years. There may be no sinking fund for 5 years and 5 percent per annum over the next 10 years, leaving half the issue due in 15 years.

When and if interest rates decline or the stock's price recovers, the debentures can be refunded at a lower interest rate, or retired with the proceeds of a public offering of a portion of the shares reacquired—possibly within a year or two. If interest rates rise, the debentures will decline in market price and the company can reacquire them at a discount. If the company pays a dividend, the dividend saving on the shares reacquired will cover at least a portion of the debenture interest.

Exchange offers are more difficult to consummate than cash tender offers, because the shareholders are being offered a different security from the one they hold. Consequently, the premium and the other fees and expenses typically exceed those of a "comparable" cash tender offer.

XYZ CORPORATION MAKES AN EXCHANGE
OFFER: A COMPOSITE CASE STUDY

The following *realistic* example illustrates the terms and effects of an exchange offer. Many companies can effect cash tender and exchange offers at lower effective costs than assumed here.

Assume that XYZ's earnings per share are expected to decline from $5 in 1974 to $4 in 1975 and that the stock has a book value of $40, pays a $1.20 dividend, and is trading at $20. Thus, it is selling at five times estimated 1975 earnings, 50 percent of book value and yields 6 percent.

Assume that XYZ offers to exchange, for up to half of its outstanding shares, $30 in principal amount of a 15 percent, 15-year subordinated debenture per common share. Thus, exchanging shareholders will receive $4.50 a share in annual interest payments (i.e., 15 percent of $30), which is 3.75 times the $1.20 dividend they were previously receiving, and equivalent to a 22.5 percent yield, based on the $20 market price of the shares before the offer. If the debentures trade in the "when issued" market during the exchange period at par (to yield 15 percent), exchanging shareholders will receive $30 in market value of a senior security per common share exchanged, which is a 50 percent premium over the $20 prior market price of the shares.

The 15 percent debenture interest rate and the 50 percent premium bring XYZ's effective interest cost per share reacquired to 22.5 percent. If XYZ has excess cash or can borrow the funds at less than 15 percent on a comparably subordinated, 15-year unsecured note, which is callable immediately at a modest premium, XYZ should do so and make a cash tender offer. If the funds are borrowed at 10 percent and used to make a cash offer at a 50 percent premium, the effective interest cost would be 15 percent, instead of 22.5 percent.

However, even at a 22.5 percent effective interest cost, the $4.50 interest per reacquired share is tax deductible and equivalent to $2.25 after taxes at a 50 percent rate. Therefore, XYZ's incremental 1975 earnings benefit per share reacquired is $1.75 (i.e., $4.00 — $2.25).

All future earnings in excess of the $2.25 after-tax interest cost per share reacquired will enhance the earnings of the shares that remain outstanding. If (based on the pre-exchange capitalization) the 1975 earnings per share are not expected to decline more than

55 percent (from $5 to less than $2.25 per share), the exchange will increase the earnings per share of the shares that remain outstanding. If 50 percent of the outstanding shares are exchanged, the indicated 1975 earnings will be increased 44 percent, from $4 to $5.75 per share.

Reduction of the outstanding shares will also accelerate the future growth rate of the earnings and book value per share. The following exhibit illustrates the effect of a 50 percent reduction in XYZ's outstanding shares. It assumes continuation of the $1.20

FIGURE 3

A. If XYZ *does not do* the exchange offer.

	Assuming 1,000 Shares Outstanding					Percent Increase	
	1974(A)	*1975(E)*	*1976(E)*	*1977(E)*	*1978(E)*	*1974-78*	*1975-78*
Pretax income.	$10,000	$8,000	$8,800	$9,680	$10,648		
Taxes (50%).	(5,000)	(4,000)	(4,400)	(4,840)	(5,324)		
Net income	$ 5,000	$4,000	$4,400	$4,840	$ 5,324		
Less dividends.	1,200	1,200	1,200	1,200	1,200		
Retained earnings.	$ 3,800	$2,800	$3,200	$3,640	$ 4,124		
Per share:							
Earnings	$ 5.00	$ 4.00	$ 4.40	$ 4.84	$ 5.32	6%	33%
Book value.	40.00	42.80	46.00	49.64	53.76	34	26

A = Actual.
E = Estimated.

B. If XYZ *does do* the exchange offer (as of January 1, 1975).

	1,000 Shares Out- standing *1974(A)*	After 1/1/75 Exchange Offer 500 Shares Outstanding				Percent Increase	
		1975(E)	*1976(E)*	*1977(E)*	*1978(E)*	*1974-78*	*1975-78*
Pretax income.	$10,000	$8,000	$8,800	$9,680	$10,648		
Debenture interest	—	(2,250)	(2,250)	(2,250)	(2,250)		
Adjusted pretax income . .	$10,000	$5,750	$6,550	$7,430	$ 8,398		
Taxes (50%).	(5,000)	(2,875)	(3,275)	(3,715)	(4,199)		
Net income	$ 5,000	$2,875	$3,275	$3,715	$ 4,199		
Less dividends.	1,200	600	600	600	600		
Retained earnings.	$ 3,800	$2,275	$2,675	$3,115	$ 3,599		
Per share:							
Earnings	$ 5.00	$ 5.75	$ 6.55	$ 7.43	$ 8.40	68%	46%
Book value.	40.00	54.55*	59.90	66.13	73.33	83	34

* Reflects the $10 increase due to the exchange offer discussed below, plus $4.55 of retained earnings per share.

A = Actual.
E = Estimated.

dividend and that following the 1975 earnings decline, XYZ's pretax earnings are expected to grow at a 10 percent annual rate.

Note that despite the 20 percent decline in 1975 pretax earnings (from $10,000 to $8,000), the exchange *accelerates* XYZ's earnings and book value per share growth rate, *and improves the consistency of the earnings per share growth record.* Conversely, if XYZ's earnings decline below the $2.25 after-tax interest cost per reacquired share, it will adversely affect the comparative results. Also, the exchange reduces the company's net worth, future borrowing capacity, and retained earnings and increases its fixed charges.

The company's cost per share reacquired is the $30 market value of the debenture. Based on the pre-exchange indicated 1975 earnings per share of $4 ($8 before taxes), the company's pretax return on its investment in its own shares is 26.7 percent (i.e., $8 ÷ $30). This does not reflect the increase in the earnings per share, the dividend saving, nor the other benefits of the exchange itself.

The $1.20 dividend saving per reacquired share equals more than half the $2.25 after-tax interest cost. Thus the dividend saving reduces XYZ's annual carrying cost per share reacquired from $2.25 to $1.05. If the company raises the dividend in future years, the annual cost will be further reduced.

Since XYZ is reacquiring shares that have a $40 book value with $30 in market value of debentures, the incremental gain in book value per reacquired share is 25 percent (i.e., $10 ÷ $40). Exchange of 50 percent of the outstanding stock will increase the book value of the shares that remain outstanding by 25 percent, from $40 to $50 per share. In addition, future earnings in excess of the $1.05 annual carrying cost will enhance the book value of the shares that remain outstanding.

The percentage interest in the company of management stock and option holders and other nontendering shareholders increases more than the percentage of the outstanding shares reacquired. If management owns 5 percent of the outstanding shares and holds options on an additional 5 percent, and if 50 percent of the outstanding shares are reacquired, management's effective interest will be increased 100 percent from 10 percent to 20 percent.

The increase in the current level and future growth rate of the earnings and book value per share, raises the intrinsic value and appreciation potentialities of the shares that remain outstanding. If the shares sell at the same price/earnings ratio as before the exchange, the market price will be increased by five times the gain in the earnings per share. Generally, the higher and the more consistent the earnings per share growth rate, the higher the price/earnings ratio; and therefore, the market price.

Stock reacquisition programs also enable a company to reduce the future dilution of its outstanding shares by using the reacquired shares for employee stock purchase and option plans, to cover the shares issuable upon exercise of warrants and options, the conversion of convertible securities and under acquisition "earn-outs," as well as for future equity financing and acquisitions.

SOUNDLY STRUCTURED PROGRAMS: CONCLUSIONS

Whether a company should reacquire its own shares (and if so, the amount and manner of doing so) depend on, among other things, its past and projected earnings, sources and applications of funds, debt/equity ratios, fixed-charge coverages, the terms of its existing loan agreements and how the stock is held—as well as the price/earnings ratio, price/book value ratio, and dividend yield at which the stock is selling.

While block and open-market purchases are the least expensive means of reacquiring shares, they are very slow, cumbersome approaches that not only require cash, but also tend to increase the price that must ultimately be paid to induce significant acceptances of cash tender or exchange offers. Statutory mergers and reverse splits are the most effective means of truly "going private," provided that they are effected for valid business purposes and on fair terms to the shareholders.

Soundly structured and executed stock reacquisition programs confer substantial benefits to the company, its management, and those shareholders who do not tender their shares, as well as to those who do.

ADDITIONAL SOURCES

Austin, Douglas V. "Treasury Stock Reacquisition by American Corporations: 1961–67." *Financial Executive*, 37 (May 1969), 41–49.

Bierman, Harold, Jr., and West, Richard. "The Acquisition of Common Stock by the Corporate Issuer." *Journal of Finance,* 21 (December 1966), 687–96.

Guthart, Leo A. "More Companies Are Buying Back Their Stock." *Harvard Business Review*, 43 (March–April 1965), 40–45.

Guthart, Leo A. "Why Companies Are Buying Back Their Own Stock." *Financial Analysts Journal*, 23 (April–May 1967), 105–10.

Hershman, Arlene. "Going Private—Or How to Squeeze Investors." *Dun's Review*, 105 (January 1975), 36–38, 64.

Hettenhouse, George W. "A Rationale for Restructuring Stock Plans." *Financial Management*, 1 (Summer 1972), 30–35.

Lee, Steven James. "Going Private." *Financial Executive*, 42 (December 1974), 10–15.

Norgaard, Richard, and Norgaard, Corine. "A Critical Examination of Share Repurchase." *Financial Management*, 3 (Spring 1974), 44–50.

Weinraub, Herbert, and Austin, Douglas. "Treasury Stock Reacquisition: 1971–1973." *Financial Executive*, 42 (August 1974), 28–35.

Chapter 48

Going Private

Steven James Lee[*]

Recent Stock Price Trends

WHEN THE Dow Jones Industrial Average slipped to close at 584.56 in the autumn of 1974 this marked a price/earnings (P/E) ratio of 6.3 times the $93.26 per share earnings of its 30 component stocks for the 12 months ended June 28, 1974. Only a year earlier, at 971.25, the Dow Jones was 12.5 times the per share earnings of $77.56 for the 12 months ended June 28, 1973. Translating this discouraging news into corporate language is simple. While corporate profits may have increased, the decline in price to earnings ratios has eroded any benefit to stock prices.

As Figure 1 illustrates, there has been a relatively consistent downward trend in the price/earnings ratio of stocks on the New York Stock Exchange since 1957. The scandalously high multiples of the early 60s have gone the way of Edsels, 3 percent savings accounts, and ducktail haircuts. Such a dismal decline in P/E ratios has by no means been unique to the New York Stock Exchange. Just about all public stocks seem to have fallen into the sinking spiral.

During the same period that the P/E kept losing steam, nominal corporate profits before tax showed substantial upward movement. In 1958, corporate profits before tax showed substantial upward movement. In 1958, corporate profits before tax were $41.4 billion

---

* Steven James Lee is a financial consultant, Bankers Trust Company, New York.

FIGURE 1
Price/Earnings Ratios and Nominal Profits

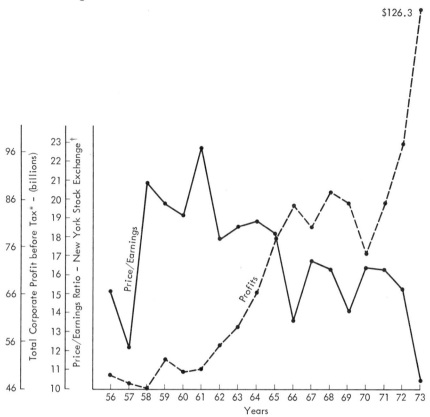

* *Survey of Current Business; Business Statistics*, 1973 ed.
† *New York Stock Exchange Fact Book*, 1966 and 1974.

and they jumped 305 percent in 15 years to reach $126.3 billion in 1973. After-tax profit in this same time span rose from $22.3 billion in 1958 to $40.4 billion in 1973. Even if we take out the toll of inflation, that still is an impressive record.

The reward for such outstanding growth and achievement was the Dow Jones Industrial Average began selling below the book value of its 30 components for the first time since 1942. In fact, in October 1974 on a price/earnings basis stocks were the cheapest since 1949. Some executives have begun to reflect on active participation in that kind of market environment. Performance, at least for them, has not been associated with stock appreciation.

Where to best utilize cash in a healthy company once was a difficult choice. Today, if your common shares are being valued at a lower level than book value and performance has been consistently good it makes sense to consider your own company as a likely investment vehicle. The near all-time bargain basement stock prices naturally led to the question of how to utilize available funds most effectively.

The Company View of Going Private

Globe Security Systems Inc., a subsidiary of Walter Kidde & Company, Inc. tendered for all of the 335,450 shares of its common stock. Common shares of Globe traded once at 31½ on the American Stock Exchange, but at the time of the tender offer sold at 3⅞. The per share book value of the company was $5.99 and the cash tender was made at $5 per share which was a 38 percent premium over the market. Globe management stated in its offer that they had no plans to liquidate the company, sell its assets, or merge the corporate entity other than becoming a wholly owned subsidiary of Walter Kidde & Company, Inc. One can infer the principal reasons for the transaction were disappointment in public recognition of the value of the company and a desire to be relieved of the substantial expenses inherent in continued status as a public company.

When Mr. Wiggs Department Stores, Inc., tendered for its common stock at a 40 percent premium above the market price in February 1974, management issued a statement as to why it wanted to go private. Officers and directors let the public know that they had been dissatisfied with the market performance of the company's stock for a considerable period of time. Contrary to their expectations when they went public, the limited amount of outstanding shares proved insufficient to generate institutional or dealer interest, the market for small over-the-counter companies became demoralized, and public ownership inhibited management flexibility to make decisions and policies it felt vitally important.

Another deserter of the public market is McCaffrey and McCall, Inc., which in February 1974, offered to purchase any and all shares of its common stock. Its board of directors maintained a unanimous opinion that the underlying value of the company's business exceeded the value ascribed to it by the market. The company first exposed itself to the public in October 1969, when it sold 185,000 shares of common at a price of $14.50. The bid price for the common in February 1974, was only $5.25. Average trading volume in the stock had been approximately 1,400 shares per week so large shareholders found themselves illiquid as a practical matter. It is interesting to note that the tender was set at $9.25 per share, which was the audited book value as of December 31, 1973.

Air Industries Corporation was a public company that chose to become private through the merger route. In November 1973, Sam Higgins, the president and owner of 76 percent of the common stock, transferred his interest in these shares into AIC Investment Company, which was wholly owned by himself. He then issued a notice which pointed out that a two-thirds vote of stockholders would be necessary to merge Air Industries into AIC. Since Sam Higgins owned 76 percent of the common, and intended to vote in favor of the merger, it was suggested that the best interests of other stockholders would lie in accepting a $2.50 per share cash payment. Company stock had been sold to the public in 1967 for $16 per share but the bid price had plummeted to 1⅝ during the week prior to the announcement of the merger.

In arriving at an equitable valuation of what price should be paid to stockholders, the company hired an investment banker to appraise its financial condition and future prospects. On the date of the proposed merger it was concluded that $2.50 should reflect what a willing buyer would pay to a willing seller. Under California law, shareholders who felt that $2.50 was not a fair price could enforce their rights of appraisal in the courts. Air Industries escaped the transformation process without any of the dissenting shareholders taking legal action for a court determined independent appraisal.

On July 19, 1974, Barbara Lynn Stores, Inc. announced its intention to return to private status through a proposed merger into a corporate shell called Lynbar Corporation which became the surviving entity. The outstanding shares of Barbara Lynn common stock held by Lynbar would be canceled with each holder receiving $4 in cash. Barbara Lynn common stock had traded as high as 30⅛ in 1969 on the American Stock Exchange but on the last sale before announcement of the merger had fallen to 2⅜. Management hired an independent consultant to recommend a cash merger price that would be fair and equitable to the public stockholders. Under court order this report was distributed to shareholders to give them additional information about the transaction.

Wells, Rich, Greene Inc., in its controversial exchange offer attempted to swap all of its 1,405,008 common shares owned by the public for $3 cash and $8 principal amount of a new 10 percent subordinated sinking-fund debenture due in 1984. Wells, Rich stock traded on the New York Stock Exchange at a high of 27⅞ but the last reported sale before announcement of the exchange offer was 5½. According to the Prospectus, White, Weld & Co., the Dealer Manager, intended to make an over-the-counter market if the common shares had to be delisted because of insufficient float. No independent market appraisal was used to substantiate the price offered to outside stockholders and management could not be certain that its method of determining value would be held appropriate and proper in a court of law. Wells, Rich was one of about a dozen ad agencies which went public during the last ten years. Through this offer they became the third agency in recent years to attempt to reverse that decision.

The Regulatory Considerations

Any publicly held corporation venturing into the area of purchasing its own securities must tread around the maze of anti-fraud and anti-manipulative provisions of the Securities Exchange Act of 1934 ("Exchange Act"). Manipulation is an activity that is calculated to affect the investment judgment of others. The deception in a manipulation must have been purposely calculated or contrived to affect investors in a way that they would not have been influenced through the normal exercise of free judgment.

Proposed Rule 13e–2 under the Exchange Act is an attempt to codify some of the more specific anti-manipulation requirements drawn from cases and SEC market experience. Although the formal adoption of Rule 13e–2 has been bandied around the bureaucratic pyramids for nearly three years, it is safe to say that most of the provisions are used as guidelines by the commission's staff. Figure 2 compares some of the provisions for repurchase of listed and non-listed securities by the issuer. This is a good starting point for the executive who needs to become somewhat familiar with the terrain before actually considering an open-market repurchase method of going back into the private womb.

Few believers will doubt that the number of other more technical

FIGURE 2
Provisions for Repurchase of Listed and Nonlisted Securities

Listed Securities Guidelines	Nonlisted Securities Guidelines
1. Only one broker may be used on any one day.	1. Only one broker may be used on any one day.
2. No purchases until after an independent person makes opening transaction.	2. If purchases are made by issuer may buy from several dealers if volume and price restrictions are met.
3. No purchases in last half hour of trading.	3. No purchase can be made above the mean between the highest current independent bid and offering.
4. No purchases at a bid higher than the last independent bid price or current highest independent bid price.	4. The number of shares purchased in any week cannot exceed $\frac{1}{25}$ of 1 percent of the shares of the outstanding class. An exception is made for $250,000 block purchases.
5. Amount of shares purchased in any day may not exceed 15 percent of average daily volume in four previous calendar weeks.	

details goes on ad nauseum. The escape from Rule 13e–2 lies in issuer-solicited private transactions that do not involve a broker or a dealer. In such cases, there are no volume limitations, but the issuer must comply with open-market price restrictions.

If the transaction is not solicited in any way by the issuer, such as an approach from an institutional stockholder, then it is exempted from the regulations of proposed Rule 13e–2. The issuer is free to purchase its shares from the independent offeror at a mutually agreeable price and in any volume offered.

The major thrust of anti-fraud regulation is contained in Rule 10b–5. It basically requires a duty of full disclosure prior to repurchases. Theoretically, the small investor may consider it a material fact that the issuer is in the market buying his own shares. All information supplied by the company must be accurate and adequate to inform the public of the issuer's intent and financial position. A company is also required to file monthly reports on Form 8-K after purchases exceed 5 percent of the number of shares of the class outstanding.

One of the great bits of irony in the whole situation is that the weavers of the high-flying hot issue market are most deeply entangled in their own web. The publicly held dealers are required to use an independent agent to purchase securities in the open market. This means that the agent must have unfettered discretion on amount, price (within a reasonable variance set by the purchaser), and market conditions. In addition, a good argument can be made that broker-dealers cannot take advantage of escape clauses in the proposed rule, which frees public companies from volume and price restrictions when in private negotiations that do not involve a "broker or dealer." It has been argued that private negotiations by a broker-dealer with an outside party cannot exist without a "broker or dealer" because of the very character of the issuer.

With this brief background in the dynamics of SEC regulation we shall now consider the methods of converting back to old-time religion. The plight of the medium-sized company whose management wishes to purge itself of cantankerous shareholders and the SEC is not hopeless. In fact, there have been some significant success stories to date.

Methods of Going Private

The cheapest and most obvious method of going private is to offer all of the holders of public stock a new nonconvertible debenture. With a lot of work on the prayer beads and an attractively conceived financial benefit to shareholders, there may be a full subscription. When this happens, the firm is once again sailing on private waters. An example of this concept is American Financial Leasing & Service which offered roughly $14.8 million of new nonconvertibles. If all common shares are handed over, AFS will return to the status of a wholly owned subsidiary.

The most commonly used ploy to pry shares out of the safety deposit boxes of the investing public has been the tender offer. This is a widely ballyhooed announcement by the company that it will guarantee to accept and pay for a certain number of shares, at a stipulated price, if they are presented by a certain expiration date.

Two of the down-to-earth problems of such a move are the stipulated price and the source of the funds to pay shareholders.

Merle Norman ran afoul of its shareholders with a tender offer that was 40 percent above the current market quote the day previous to its announcement. During the gun-slinging days of 1969 Merle Norman came out at $25 per share and went up to $32.75. It offered $13 a share and received all but 90,000 of the original 740,000 shares held by the public. Unfortunately, certain dissidents felt the stock was worth more and have instituted a class action suit for independent appraisal. Besides the expense of defending the suit, Merle Norman would have to pay additional sums if the scales of justice tip against it.

Sources of funds for the purchase of shares in a tender offer are a prime consideration. These must generally come as a new inflow from family interests who owned the company before its public debut or from management that is willing to supplement the corporate coffers and be rid of the "stockholder smile" (dusted off and worn at annual meetings). It may be considered unjust for the corporation to use its own cash to buy out minority interests.

One of the blessings of a tender offer is that the issuer does not have to entice all shareholders to give up their ownership. The SEC exempts a firm with less than 300 outside stockholders from the majority of its reporting and filing regulations. Brokers realize that when this happens the market for shares is considerably reduced. In addition, if less than 100,000 common shares are in the hands of persons other than officers and directors of the company and members of their families, the remaining common stock does not qualify for National Association of Securities Dealers Automatic Quotation (NASDAQ) to carry a price quotation. This adds some fuel to the urge to give unto the company that which once belonged to the company.

After a tender offer, the issuer who has managed to regain 90 percent or more of its subsidiary can merge the subsidiary into itself, or vice versa, under Delaware law. In doing so, minority interest can be forced to take cash and thus be eliminated. Delaware has even gone so far as to allow shifting domicile of a corporation to that state in anticipation of such a freeze out of minority interests. This has been euphemistically called a short-form merger. In other states, such as New York, the percentage needed to do a short-form merger is 95 percent.

Another way to approach the problem is to have a dilution merger. This means that the smaller company merges into a much larger private company. To accomplish this task, the python swallowing the pig must have the requisite stockholder voting strength and generally the board of each corporation proposing to participate must approve the plan. Under New York law, merger plans need to be authorized by a two-thirds vote of all outstanding shares. (See BCL Section 903.) Delaware law requires that a majority of outstanding stock entitled to vote must be in favor of adoption of such a plan. (See General Corporation Law of the State of Delaware Section 251.)

Public Policy Issues

There have been a myriad of press releases about corporate stock repurchases which imply that it is a freshly discovered phenomena. It should be plainly understood that going private is not really the newest and most exciting game in town. The truth is that companies have been doing it for a very long time and what we are presently observing is an enlightened rethinking about its utility. Going private has been taken from under the cloak of the financial whiz kids and placed in the arsenal of responsible corporate planning. There is no stampede to go private. Facts show that fewer companies have successfully returned to private status in the last year than went public in a single week of the hot-issue markets.

There is, by its inherent nature, a distasteful aura attached to corporate contraction which runs contrary to the instinct of those of us interested in the American equity markets. The overwhelming proclivity of financial advisors is toward expansion and continual growth. American industry has maintained a vitality that is envied by the rest of the world. But we do make mistakes in our desire to broaden the base and scope of corporate enterprise. These must be corrected to sustain an orderly process of expansion. Going private is one such correction that has been given unusual attention because it puts the reins on a company and contracts overreached development.

We have seen fit in the past to erect a framework of laws enforced by public agencies to guide the practices employed in corporate expansion through public shareholders. We are all aware that along the road to our current equity markets many techniques were inappropriately applied by individuals for their personal advantage. Abuse has been met with civil and criminal sanctions that correct unfair practices in light of equity and our concepts of fair dealings. A constriction of the corporation is also available to perversion and requires enlightened regulation. The only real difference is that we have more experience in dealing with companies seeking to go public than with those going private. The problem before us now is to balance the justifiable interests of directors, shareholders, management, and creditors in guidelines which will not overtax legitimate purposes.

Management's View of Its Relationship to Shareholders

Equity markets originally promised publicly traded companies a widespread following of rational, eager investors. The attractiveness of shareholders was interpreted as meaning ever-increasing price to earnings ratios and limitless pool of participation as the corporation prospered. With continued good fortune management believed long-term funds would readily pour into the hands of consistent profit makers. There was also the lure of the liquidity derived from paper certificates and stock options to reward a job well done. Everyone presumed that when it came time to cash in and retire, or pass control to the new generation, the equity market was the most sensible solution.

Unfortunately, the erosion of the Dow Jones has caused a spasm among Big Board investors; and the devastation of smaller company quotes has caused virtual paralysis. The drop in stock prices has been so dramatic that a high percentage of all public issues are currently trading below book value. This makes it strikingly evident that stock options are really of dubious value and principal shareholders will not enjoy their sought after liquidity. As for mergers, the exchange of earning assets for paper certificates in the current economic environment makes little sense.

In many cases when management went public they looked forward to a secondary offering to reward them for their achievements. Windfall profits were not made by selling insider stock positions to strangers. Management stayed on board to continue development and expansion of the company. Today, very few secondary issues can be successfully marketed to the public. From the point of view of many founders, they have not and cannot realize proper benefits. When they decide to go private it is a retraction of what they consider premature steps. To them it is not a breach of their relationship with their public shareholders.

Times change—a management drafting its prospectus in one economic environment, although well intended, can hardly be held to its absolute letter in an enormously differentiated and turmoiled future. There is a valid question as to who amongst us has the ability of infallible prognostication. Wild claims or promises in a prospectus which were misleading at issuance of a security should have been eliminated or given rise to a cause of action at that time. The duty of courts and regulatory agencies is to supervise and protect the public from outlandish claims before shareholders begin to participate in the corporation. We must separate the reversal of expectations and goals in the offering document which may be legitimately shifted as times and circumstances dictate.

Minority Shareholders

When the minority shareholders acquired their interest in the corporate entity they should have been aware that they were not in control. In fact, it was a free and open choice on their part to become the surrogates of another group. Such a financial decision has at its nexus a sound basis. The shareholder will contribute his capital in an enterprise of his choice and rely on the competency of others to increase his investment. The hope and expectation of the minority is to earn a profit passively.

Management, on the other hand, also commits itself to give up a part of its earned return in exchange for the use of shareholder funds. They are aware that others will gain through the application of their expertise but this is part of the mechanism of corporate participation. We have addressed much attention to the duty of management, and over the years there has been an evolution of state and federal laws based on the presumption of propriety in actions. The body of federal standards has emerged through the application and extension of the securities acts. Liability to the minority has been construed to arise from the public purpose of protecting investors. But we should not overextend the rights of the minority to obfuscate the true facts of their original investment decision.

It is in the common interest of justice and organized growth that we balance the scale between the majority and minority correctly. Our national strength bears witness to the fact that their viewpoints often converge in common interest and good, still management has a unique *role* and duty to the corporation itself. It is to this area that will now be discussed.

The Role of Management Is to Manage

Public or private, the task of management is to optimize the chances for corporate survival. Their position of leadership holds them accountable for the development of the corporation in a competitive marketplace. Where management is also the majority equity interest, their commitment to the future of the company is that much more intense. Decisions adverse to the prosperity of the enterprise impact on them proportionately greater than on the minority interest.

There is an underlying soundness in select companies purchasing common shares in a program to go private. When the business purpose is real it can be the decision to go private itself that will secure the viability of the corporation. Our laws dealing with security transactions initiated by management are based on the concept that parties will act in good faith, deal fairly, and disclose properly. Technical requirements that are satisfied as to the absolute letter cannot (and must not) circumvent such an equitable dictum. Circuit Court Judge Tuttle in the case against Brock & Blevins Co. Inc. applies this concept in "equity and state law grounds" to prevent a company from confiscating a minority shareholder's investment at less than its true value.

Such decisions help corporations who approach the going private area with good business purpose and the attitude of dealing fairly with the public. No outside motives, hidden from shareholders and secretly known to management should be the underlying forces in the transformation from public to private ownership. Some of the business reasons given by management in the course of our dealings with companies involved in a program of going private which may or may not meet the valid corporate purposes test are as follows (not necessarily in order of importance):

A. To alter the focus of management from concentration on cosmetic goals which are brought to the public attention, such as earnings per share, to the planning of a sound cash flow.

B. To end the use of scarce cash and manpower resources for purposes unrelated to basic corporate goals.

C. To prevent low stock prices resulting from cyclical markets from placing a ceiling on the realizable value of a company should the majority wish to sell.

D. To reduce the possibility of being confronted with unreasonable, protracted stockholder lawsuits in the present litigious climate.

E. To avoid increasing restraints on public corporations that have inhibited actions which may benefit the corporation and its stockholders.

F. To halt the erosion of morale of key employees because of valueless options and losses of investments in corporate stock.

G. To eliminate the increasing costs of reporting procedures for public companies.

Implicit in the business judgments presented here is a management understanding of its role to guide the corporation through the attacks of competition. Weakness and vulnerability will produce the eventual demise of the company with loss to majority and minority interests alike.

Optimism is always based on historical recovery and yet no one can be certain at what point the reversal will come. I have very real problems rationalizing some statements that we should categorically cut off a shareholder's access to a company-sponsored premium on his securities because they will be worth more in the future. In the case of going private, such excess payments on the companies we studied averaged 44 percent over the last market bid. Who can state with certainty the level a particular security will fetch in the marketplace at a finite future time? Do we not perform a disservice by instituting protection that will deprive minority interests of the highest price they will see for some time? What if the turmoil of our equity markets persists and shareholders pile up still greater losses because they were locked in?

The world has certainly lost its limitless supply of cheap energy and each day we feel the impact of resource scarcity. Doubtless new industries will develop and many established companies will undergo readjustment to the new environment. When minority investors, who planned their participation in a radically differentiated market, can recoup a premium over current bid prices on their holdings they have a fresh opportunity to redeploy funds in other investments.

Much controversy has centered on the use of involuntary methods for eliminating minority interest and reduced markets produced under other techniques. These are troublesome problems, but we cannot lose sight of the voluntary subordination these minority investors chose. Protection should only extend as far as forcing management to furnish external evidence for the reasonableness of its actions. Not all circumstances in which shareholders are compelled directly or indirectly to sell stock will pass the test of responsible corporate posture. Where there is abuse we must move to correct it. Where there is ample justification, we must be prepared to accept a valid financial process that has a long-standing precedent.

The amount given to the shareholder faced with the prospect of a going private situation is not justifiably compared to the original offering price. Often, after the company went public, the quote on its shares rose dramatically in response to the market environment. We did not then call for a corporate right to redeem its equity at the original price and deprive investors of their profit. Share prices for good or worse are established by independent forces. We cannot now scrutinize lower quotations and associate a going private offer with issuance price. This would produce unrealistically high premiums.

One solution to this dilemma is the use of an outside independent agent to do an appraisal or evaluation which clearly furnishes external evidence of the reasonableness of management's offer. Such an agent should construct a written record which could be used to establish the merits of criticism in a particular going private situation. The expertise of the outside party adds a new dimension to shareholder protection and supplements legal or regulatory measures.

Attrition from the Market

There is nothing permanent except change. The equity markets are constantly active because of older companies that fail to survive in the face of new innovation or altered business circumstance. Progress, the base of our prosperity, means the efficient utilization of all industrial resources—including capital. The Federal Advisory Council, a statutory body established under the Federal Reserve

Act, as recently as September 16, 1974, recognized that the supply of lendable funds is finite.

Allocation of capital takes many forms. Between 1952 and 1962 equity markets blossomed with a large number of new issues. In 1963, the SEC made a sample of these companies which went public and found that approximately 37 percent either could not be located or were inactive, liquidated, dissolved, in receivership, or in reorganization. Capital, once deployed in these spent enterprises was absorbed in new ones. Again, in the period from 1967 to 1972 some 3,000 companies filed first time registration statements with the SEC. We must expect that competition will again exact its toll and companies shall continue to leave the equity markets.

This time around, however, a select group of basically sound corporations have realized the painful impact of a premature debut. For them, a wise management decision might be to go private and concentrate on strengthening their business and financial base. Management should see that they survive and continue to offer employment, goods, and services. In the long run abandonment of shareholder participation could be the intelligent solution that best balances the interest of an enlightened management and disgruntled stockholders.

Helpful Regulation

The key difficulty in dealing with the unsophisticated investor is communication. Over the years financial experts, lawyers, accountants, regulatory agencies, analysts, and many other groups have arranged a language of carefully chosen jargon that escapes the grasp of the public. The present format for public offering documents, proxy statements, and tender offers has wandered into a complex form that far outstrips the ability of the average individual to understand. Perhaps, as professionals in the field, we communicate well with each other. I submit that this does not aid the investor.

How often, when we construct documents to be distributed to the public, do we rely on the so-called boiler plate language of others? All this succeeds in doing is perpetuating the clouds over our basic goal of full disclosure in the light of fair dealings. Our task is clearly to reverse the evolutionary trend toward complexity in language and format. We should not be so naïve as to believe that this can be accomplished overnight. Such a problem is slow in resolving itself. We might, however, consider adding several introductory pages written in layman language to public documents.

In the midst of confusion investors will rely on the reputation of certain advisors. Large financial institutions, including commercial banks, will perform an important mediation function. They have a concentrated number of skilled employees who are equipped to review distributed material and explain it to those seeking their counsel. For them, a long-standing reputation is more important than any immediately realized gain. This is where the independent market appraisal or evaluation becomes important in the going private context. The independent agent can evaluate an equitable balance between shareholders and management without any direct interest.

A separate dilemma that confronts the unsophisticated investor is the difficulty of availing himself of so-called appraisal rights. Even when the shareholder is aware of this remedy, and many are not, the cost and effort loom as prohibitive. It would be helpful to have a streamlined set of guidelines drawn up by a caucus of state and federal parties. This could bring some uniformity to actions critical of management considering going private.

As a relatively inexpensive first step we might also have an independent body that could initially analyze the nature and basis of shareholder claims before the entire jury process is invoked. In such an informal environment the special interests of parties might be resolved among themselves without costly legal confrontation. Participation must be voluntary, but reasonable groups acting in good faith would probably welcome such an opportunity.

One final action that could prove useful when companies decide to go private is retention of an adviser available to answer shareholder questions about the transaction. Information supplied to shareholders often provokes questions and sometimes promotes misunderstanding when management is not able to personally answer inquiries. A full-time expert at the company could increase the communication flow so necessary for arriving at a proper decision.

The Outlook

On the best of assumptions that equity markets will break with the current tide and begin to recover it still makes sense for certain corporations to consider going private. We are, after all, speaking of companies who went public when the new-issue market looked very promising. The lack of liquidity in such shares makes them less desirable and the real benefits of public shareholders cannot be appreciated at the present time. While public ownership might be useful at some later date, these smaller firms now suffer serious inhibitions on risk-taking and deployment of assets that would not be present if they were private.

A score of six "yes" answers to the questions in Figure 3 should provoke management to inquire about the benefits of going private. Some of the obvious advantages of private companies are elimination of printing and mailing costs of various reports, the ability to increase ownership without individual cash outlay, flexibility, and, of course, intelligent estate planning. The situation of any specific company is unique and dozens of other ramifications can be waiting in the eaves.

It is not a simple matter to return to private ownership, but it can be done. The help of financial specialists will ease the burdens, and it goes without saying that counsel and qualified accountants should be consulted at an early stage. Your company will require a systematic plan that undoubtedly shall take many months to be fully successful. Management will have to be prepared to cope with some difficulties if it believes the end result is worth the expense of time and money.

Just as Alice passed through the looking glass into a world in

FIGURE 3
Can You Go Private?

	Yes	No
1. Is the money you spend on glossy annuals and interim reports significant by company standards?	—	—
2. Did principals of your company fail to realize cash through sale of their stock when you went public?	—	—
3. Do SEC requirements add heavy extra expense over and above customary financial reporting when you were private?	—	—
4. Did you go public more than three years ago?	—	—
5. Were all the claims in your original offering prospectus conservative?	—	—
6. Is your cash position strong?	—	—
7. Is your current stock quotation less than 60 percent of the issue price?	—	—
8. Would you run your company differently and more advantageously if it were private?	—	—
9. Have stock options that you gave key employees proved to be of little value to them?	—	—
10. Is less than 55 percent of your company in public hands?	—	—

which she did not belong, many companies have become public when it was truly to their advantage to stay private. These enterprises are suffering the same space and time distortions that Alice found in her wonderland. Return to reality is still a matter of waking up and bringing everything back into proper perspective.

ADDITIONAL SOURCES

Donath, Bob. "WRG's Private Bid Seen Good For Shop, Not Stockholders." *Advertising Age,* 45 (September 9, 1974), 1.

Donath, Bob. "Private Bid: Can Mary Pull It Off?" *Advertising Age,* 45 (October 14, 1974), 114–16.

"Fair Shares in Corporate Mergers and Takeovers." *Harvard Law Review,* 88 (December 1974), 297–346.

Freeman, R. G. "Going Private: Corporate Insiders Move to Eliminate Outside Shareholders." *The Wall Street Journal* (October 18, 1974).

"Going Private—Old Tort or No Tort?" *New York University Law Review,* 49 (December 1974), 987–1042.

Hershman, Arlene. "Going Private—or How to Squeeze Investors." *Dun's Review,* (January 1975), 36.

Lee, Steven James. "Going Private." *Financial Executive,* 43 (December 1974), 10–15.

Malley, Robert J. "Corporate Repurchase of Stock and the SEC Rules: An Overview." *The Business Lawyer,* 29 (November 1973), 117–31.

Malley, Robert J. "Corporate Repurchases of Stock: Proposed Rule 13e-2 Revisited." *The Business Lawyer,* 29 (April 1974), 879–82.

Pacey, Margaret D. "Going Private: More Firms Are Turning Their Backs on Wall Street." *Barron's,* 54 (March 4, 1974), 3.

"The Urge to go Private Spreads to a Retailer." *Business Week* (November 30, 1974), 32.

PART XII

Overall Corporate Responsibilities

As a final integrating section, Part XII covers subjects involving a wide range of corporate activities or overall corporate responsibilities. Certainly tax considerations must be taken into account in a number of business decision areas. In Chapter 49, Frederic White provides a framework for taking tax factors into account in business decisions. He explains and illustrates a number of tax deferral techniques. These include the use of Lifo depreciation methods, accelerated depreciation, the asset depreciation range system, expensing research and development costs, the use of the installment method of reporting income and the use of the domestic international sales corporation in international business operations. The tax avoidance category includes allocations of the excess purchase price to amortizable assets, tax-free transactions, converting ordinary income into capital gains, the use of a Western Hemisphere Trade Corporation or Possessions Corporations in international business, and the utilization of the expiring tax loss carry-forward. Mr. White observes that since these methods are followed to defer or avoid taxes, any apparent reduction in reported income is illusory.

Another area which impacts management decisions in most areas of the business are considerations of insurance and risk management. Since the insurance manager may report to the treasurer, this is a particularly important area for the treasurer. In Chapter 50, F. X. McCahill presents a systematic treatment of the subject. He covers three major areas: (1) Identifying exposures to loss, (2) eliminating exposures to loss and minimizing those that cannot be eliminated, and (3) developing programs for absorbing losses or transferring the risk of losses.

In Chapter 51, Peter Vermilye and Frank Husic present a valuable treatise on managing pension funds. As they point out, the corporate pension fund has become one of the treasurer's major responsibilities. They point to some dramatic developments. Annual contributions of pension and profit sharing plans are currently running at an average of about 20 percent of pretax profits. In a number of companies, the value of their pension fund accumulations are greater than their net worth.

Mr. Vermilye and Mr. Husic provide a history of the growth of pension funds both in dollar amounts and the development of the goals and objectives of pension funds. They then turn to the fundamental problems of designing a pension fund plan. This leads to the development of a planning framework that integrates many parts of the process and evaluates the net impact of their interaction. This framework is summarized in a one-page exhibit and provides useful guidelines for obtaining an understanding of the many factors in pension fund planning. A full and insightful treatment is presented in the development of investment policy and in the selection of the money managers. The critical area of the measurement of investment performance is set forth. Finally, the total relationship with the money manager and possibilities of changing money managers is treated.

Chapter 52 covers investor relations in a broader sense. Robert Savage begins by emphasizing the needs and benefits of involving the small stockholder in investor relations. He points out some practical considerations for motivating a well-managed investor relations program. He surveys effective methods of communicating, emphasizing the use of the press and company reports. He discusses the role of the investor-relations function within a company and the required qualifications for executives who occupy the position. His conclusion emphasizes the critical importance of maintaining communication and an effective working relationship with the security analyst and the exchange specialist in the company stock.

The capstone chapter on overall corporate responsibilities is the corporation's social responsibilities and the role of the treasurer in carrying out the corporation's social obligations. William Mobraaten reviews the divergent views on defining the corporation's social responsibility, emphasizing the importance of constructively re-examining its social and economic role. While important questions may remain regarding the kinds of activities which should be undertaken by the corporation, a number of the areas relate uniquely to the responsibilities of the treasurer. Those that particularly involve the treasurer include the financing of a social responsibility program and the ongoing measurement of the social programs, and their impact on cost, benefits, and profits.

Social responsibility in financial management includes managing financial assets, managing pension funds and encouraging minority enterprise through minority banking and the use of minority suppliers. In Chapter 53, Mr. Mobraaten observes that speaking out on issues of social concern is a part of the treasurer's obligation to achieve a continuing dialogue with the general public in terms of social priorities. The fact that resources are limited requires that critical choices be made in terms of priorities and trade-offs. Here the treasurer's particularly important responsibility is to provide carefully assembled evidence for making the trade-off to avoid the tendency of responding to the demands of the most insistent and vocal groups. The treasurer can potentially make a significant contribution in this area by being sensitive to real public needs in the social responsibility area, and also related to the necessary analysis of trade-offs. In this way the company's social responsibility efforts can be more than a public relations exercise. Rather, the aim is progress toward defining and achieving social goals concurrent with the goals of the growth of profits and stockholder wealth.

With Part XII, we come to the end of over 50 chapters dealing with a wide range of responsibilities of the treasurer. Clearly, his potential role is major and significant. Hopefully, the materials in this *Handbook* will contribute to the ability of treasurers to carry out these responsibilities effectively.

Chapter 49

Tax Deferral Techniques, Cash Flow, and Tax Planning

Frederic Enoch White[*]

INTRODUCTION

TAX PLANNING is often thought of as an exercise in devising ways to avoid or minimize the impact of taxation. Although very little can be done to avoid income taxes permanently, a great deal can be achieved by deferring taxes for a period of time.

As the term implies, tax deferral is a technique for delaying the payment of an inevitable tax liability. The result of deferral is that cash which would currently be paid out to the government is retained in the business for varying lengths of time during which it may be used to finance operations. Tax which is deferred represents a temporary interest-free loan from the government that must ultimately be repaid. In addition to the impact on cash flow, deferred tax can also affect reported net income depending upon how it is handled for financial statement purposes. The various tax deferral and avoidance techniques discussed below illustrate the effect of tax planning on cash flow and financial statement reporting.

---

[*] Frederic Enoch White is a CPA, attorney, and tax manager, Arthur Andersen & Co., San Francisco, California.

TAX DEFERRAL TECHNIQUES

Depreciation Methods

The depreciation of fixed assets often provides one of the most fruitful opportunities for achieving substantial tax deferral. Depreciation is an accounting technique for systematically allocating the cost of an asset over its economic useful life. Most corporations use straight-line depreciation in their published financial reports but many employ some form of accelerated depreciation for tax purposes.[1] It is these latter methods which generate valuable tax deferrals. In fact, there seems little justification for a profitable firm to forego the use of accelerated depreciation.

For example, assume that a corporation acquires an asset that costs $1 million and has an estimated ten-year life. The company decides to depreciate the asset on a straight-line basis for financial reporting purposes resulting in a yearly depreciation book charge of $100,000. On the other hand, the firm uses double-declining balance for tax purposes with the option of switching to straight line in the year when it produces a bigger tax deduction. The total depreciation charged off under any method cannot exceed asset cost so that after ten years, the total written off under both straight-line and double-declining balance equals $1 million. This is illustrated in Table 1. The table also demonstrates that in the early part of the asset's life, accelerated depreciation provides differentially higher tax deductions which are exactly offset by lower write-offs in later years. Thus during the first year accelerated depreciation provides an extra $50,000 in cash by way of deferred taxes. By the fourth year, however, the differential stream has declined to $1,200.

Although the stream of cash savings net out to zero over the ten-year period, the fact that money has a time value means that the earlier use of the extra cash made available by the higher tax depreciation yields a present value that far exceeds the negative value of the lower charge-offs in the later years. In this particular case, discounting the entire stream of cash savings over the ten-year period by a 10 percent rate yields a present value of $37,819. This

---

[1] Internal Revenue Code, Section 167 allows (1) the straight-line method, (2) the declining-balance method, (3) the sum-of-the-years'-digits method, and (4) any other consistent method (as long as it does not exceed double-declining balance).

TABLE 1

Present Value Obtained by Using Accelerated Depreciation

	1	2	3	4	5	6
Book depreciation	$100,000	$100,000	$100,000	$100,000	$100,000	$100,000
Tax depreciation	200,000	160,000	128,000	102,400	68,266	68,266
Excess depreciation.	100,000	60,000	28,000	2,400	(31,734)	(31,734)
Deferred taxes at 50% . . .	50,000	30,000	14,000	1,200	(15,867)	(15,867)
Present value of deferred taxes at 10%.	50,000	27,270	11,564	901	(10,837)	(9,853)

	7	8	9	10	Total
Book depreciation	$100,000	$100,000	$100,000	$100,000	$1,000,000
Tax depreciation	68,266	68,266	68,266	68,270	1,000,000
Excess depreciation.	(31,734)	(31,734)	(31,734)	(31,730)	0
Deferred taxes at 50% . . .	(15,867)	(15,867)	(15,867)	(15,865)	0
Present value of deferred taxes at 10%.	(8,949)	(8,140)	(7,410)	(6,727)	37,819

present value figure represents the benefits of deferring the tax that would have been payable had a straight-line method been used.

To the extent that the same method is used for both book and income tax purposes, the accounting treatment is relatively simple. However, the difficulty arises in the usual case where the corporation wants the best of both worlds by using straight-line depreciation for financial statement purposes and accelerated depreciation for income tax purposes. The resulting "timing differences" between book income and taxable income gives rise to interperiod tax accounting adjustments. Until recently, there was substantial disagreement (especially among public utilities) regarding how these timing differences should be properly treated for accounting purposes.

There are currently two major accounting treatments used: the flow-through and the normalizing method. Flow-through reports net income on the books in accordance with the cash accounting concept; that is, book income is reduced by the amount of income tax that is actually payable for the year. Consequently, depreciation expense on the books is shown on a straight-line basis but tax expense is determined by deducting accelerated depreciation. In effect, the tax benefits of accelerated depreciation are "flowed through" to reported income.

Normalizing, on the other hand, reduces book income by a provision for income tax based on book income rather than taxable income. This is achieved by setting up a deferred tax liability account for taxes not currently payable. Where the tax advantage of accelerated over straight-line depreciation in the early years results in a current tax liability that is less than the book tax provision, a credit to the deferred tax reserve account offsets the corresponding debit entry to the tax provision. Later in the asset's life when accelerated depreciation falls below straight-line depreciation, and tax depreciation is less than book depreciation, the reserve for deferred taxes is reduced (debited) and the current liability is increased (credited). The normalizing method is required by the Accounting Principles Board.[2]

Asset Depreciation Range System

For years beginning after 1970, a company may elect to use the Asset Depreciation Range system (ADR) which will allow it, for tax purposes, to use useful lives 20 percent shorter than "guideline lives."[3] If a company is conservative in determining the economic useful life of its depreciable assets, ADR may provide an excellent method of deferring federal income tax.

For example, if an asset falls within Asset Guideline Class 79.0 (recreation and amusement), the depreciation range is 8 to 12 years. If a 12-year life (straight-line depreciation) is used for financial statement purposes, and an 8-year life (double-declining balance) for tax purposes, the effect on cash flow is as shown in Table 2.

ADR offers additional benefits as well, one of which is that the Internal Revenue Service will not attack the useful lives of assets under the system. If a company does not elect ADR, it must justify the useful lives it uses by reference to facts and circumstances.

Lifo versus Fifo

In periods of a high rate of inflation, the method of accounting for inventory costs can dramatically affect the earnings and the current tax liability of a corporation. Generally, a corporate taxpayer uses one of the two more popular methods of accounting for

---

[2] *Accounting for Income Taxes,* Accounting Principles Board Opinion No. 11, December 1967; *Accounting for Income Taxes—Special Areas,* Accounting Principles Board Opinion No. 23, April 1972.

[3] Internal Revenue Code, Section 167 (m).

TABLE 2
Present Value by Using ADR (years 1–10)

	1	2	3	4	5	6	7
Book depreciation	$100,000	$100,000	$100,000	$100,000	$100,000	$100,000	$100,000
Tax (ADR) depreciation	300,000	225,000	168,750	126,562	94,922	94,922	94,922
Excess depreciation	200,000	125,000	68,750	26,562	(5,078)	(5,078)	(5,078)
Income tax deferrals at 50%	100,000	62,500	34,375	13,281	(2,539)	(2,539)	(2,539)
Present value of tax deferrals (cost) at 10% rate of interest	100,000	56,813	28,352	9,974	(1,734)	(1,577)	(1,432)

	8	9	10	11	12	Total
Book depreciation	$100,000	$100,000	$100,000	$100,000	$100,000	$1,200,000
Tax (ADR) depreciation	94,922	–	–	–	–	1,200,000
Excess depreciation	(5,078)	(100,000)	(100,000)	(100,000)	(100,000)	0
Income tax deferrals at 50%	(2,539)	(50,000)	(50,000)	(50,000)	(50,000)	0
Present value of tax deferrals (cost) at 10% rate of interest	(1,303)	(23,350)	(21,200)	(19,300)	(17,500)	107,743

its inventory costs: Fifo where the oldest inventory is deemed to be sold first (first in, first out), and Lifo where inventories are charged to the income statement of the basis of last in, first out.

Table 3 indicates that the pretax earnings of a company using

TABLE 3
Comparison of Lifo with Fifo

	Lifo		Fifo	
	Amount per Unit	*$ Amount*	*Amount per Unit*	*$ Amount*
Beginning inventory				
50,000 units....................	$2	$100,000	$2	$100,000
Purchases				
20,000 units....................	3	60,000	3	60,000
		$160,000		$160,000
Ending inventory				
20,000 units....................	2	40,000	3	60,000
10,000 units....................	2	20,000	2	20,000
Total.....................		$ 60,000		$ 80,000
Cost of goods sold		$100,000		$ 80,000

Fifo would be $20,000 greater than if Lifo were used. This is because cost of goods sold is charged with the lower cost of the earlier inventories. As the same inventory method must be used for both book and tax purposes, the current tax liability of the company is accelerated.[4] Consequently, Fifo has two great shortcomings. First, it overstates profits by including inventory profits (which are arguably not true operating profits) and second, it accelerates a tax liability that could be deferred with the use of Lifo.[5]

The emphasis on earnings per share, however, often makes management reluctant to convert to an inventory method which will reduce earnings. On the other hand, it should be kept in mind that a corporation using Lifo may, by footnote, indicate the effect on earnings if Fifo were used in the year of change.[6] Also, there is some question as to whether the reduction in earnings as a result of switching to Lifo affects the price of the corporation's stock.[7] The

[4] Income Tax Regulations, Sec. 1.472-2(h).

[5] Henry C. Wallich and Mable I. Wallich, "Profits Aren't as Good as They Look," *Fortune,* March 1974, p. 128.

[6] Revenue Ruling 73–66, IRB 1973. See also Rev. Proc. 75–10, Rev. Rul. 75–49, and Rev. Rul. 75–50.

[7] Wallich, "Profits Aren't as Good as They Look," p. 128.

sophisticated investor realizes that in a period of rising prices, inflated inventory values artificially inflate profits. As the investing public becomes more sophisticated the emphasis will increasingly be on the quality of profits rather than quantity. Accordingly, Lifo may continue to gain as the more popular inventory method.

The company that charges current inventory costs against current sales benefits by deferring income taxes and more correctly stating its income statement. Its balance sheet, on the other hand, suffers in that inventories are stated at amounts substantially below current costs. Lifo, thus, represents price-level accounting for the income statement, but not for the balance sheet. No one method represents "the" answer. The best alternative is to allow Lifo for tax purposes and Fifo for book purposes, with any difference being reflected in an interperiod tax allocation. Unfortunately, this alternative is not currently available.

Research and Development Costs

In an age of rapid technological advances, most manufacturing companies have found that to be competitive they must incur substantial amounts of research and development costs. There was for some time no uniformity in accounting for these costs. A company had the alternative, from a financial statement standpoint, of (1) expensing the costs currently, (2) deferring and amortizing the costs, or (3) charging income in advance of the time when the costs are incurred.[8] Despite the acceptability of any of these methods, most companies expense research costs as incurred. In 1974, the FASB (Financial Accounting Standards Board) proposed the use of the current expense method.[9]

For federal income tax purposes, a taxpayer may elect to (1) expense research costs currently, or (2) defer and amortize the costs over a period not less than 60 months.[10] Unlike inventory accounting methods, it is not necessary to use the same method for book and tax purposes. A company will be tempted initially to expense research costs currently for tax purposes, but this may prove

---

[8] Arthur Andersen & Co., *Accounting and Reporting Problems of the Accounting Profession,* 4th ed., August 1973, p. 103.

[9] *Accounting for Research and Development Costs,* Statement of Financial Accounting Standards, No. 2, October 1974.

[10] Internal Revenue Code, Section 174.

to be ill-advised if the company anticipates substantial net operating losses.

In Table 4, assume that XYZ Corporation elects, in the first year, to expense research costs currently. Unless XYZ Corporation gen-

TABLE 4

THE XYZ CORPORATION
Accounting for Research and Development Costs

	1974	1975	1976	1977	1978
Gross income	$ 0	$ 0	$ 0	$ 50,000	$100,000
Cost of goods sold	$ 0	$ 0	$ 0	(20,000)	(40,000)
Gross profit	$ 0	$ 0	$ 0	$ 30,000	$ 60,000
Administrative and					
selling expenses	(20,000)	(20,000)	(20,000)	(20,000)	(20,000)
Research and development expenses.	(30,000)	(40,000)	(50,000)	(50,000)	(50,000)
Profit (loss)	($50,000)	($60,000)	($70,000)	($40,000)	($10,000)

erates $50,000 of profit in 1979, the research costs expensed in 1974 will generate no tax benefit. This is because net operating losses may only be carried forward for five years for federal income tax purposes.[11] Also, once a corporation elects to expense or defer research costs, it may not change its method unless the Internal Revenue Service grants permission to do so. It is doubtful whether permission would be granted where the primary reason for the request is to save a net operating loss from expiring.

A company should also consider using different methods for different projects, an approach which is allowable under the Internal Revenue Code. Those projects which are projected to ripen early could be expensed currently. Those which are long term or of uncertain duration could be deferred with amortization beginning, for tax purposes, in the first year in which benefits are realized.

In several states, net operating loss carry-overs are not recognized for income or franchise tax purposes.[12] Accordingly, it may be advisable, where allowable, to use a different method of accounting for research costs for state purposes. For example, in Table 4, even if XYZ Corporation was profitable in 1979, it should have considered deferring research costs for state purposes if there was no net operating loss carry-over provision under state law.

---

[11] Internal Revenue Code, Section 172.

[12] The law in California, for example, has no provision for carry-back or carry-forward of net operating losses.

Installment Method of Reporting

As a general rule, profit from a sale is reported for financial statement purposes in the year in which the sale is consummated. For tax purposes, a company may elect to defer the gain on an installment sale of property and report it over the period of collection.[13] A common use of this provision is in the sale of real property or the casual sale of personal property. In addition, a "dealer" may report the sale of inventory using the installment method.

Often overlooked is the availability of this method to manufacturing companies who may be classified as a dealer for tax purposes. The ability to defer tax by electing the installment method provides yet another means for a company to finance its operations via deferred tax cash flow. For example, assume that a manufacturing company has $2 million in year-end receivables, earns 40 percent on gross sales and is in the 50 percent tax bracket. By merely reporting sales on the installment method the firm can increase its working capital by $400,000 ($50\% \times 40\% \times \$2,000,000$). These benefits are further enhanced if the receivables are long term due to the type of business transacted.

If a company does not generally sell on the installment basis, it can change its modus operandi by requiring the distributor or retailer to pay 10 percent down. A dealer may elect the installment method without securing the permission of the Internal Revenue Service. Where a company has been on the accrual basis and changes to the installment method, it may subject prior years' sales to partial double taxation.[14] This potential for double taxation has been one reason why few companies have switched from the accrual basis. The potential benefits, however, may be substantially in excess of any toll required for the switch.

Taxation of International Business Operations

The corporate taxpayer that expands its business activities outside of the United States confronts unusual tax problems and tax

---

[13] Internal Revenue Code, Section 453.

[14] Ibid., Section 453(c) provides that if a taxpayer changes from the accrual to the installment method, installment collections on sales reported in prior periods will be taxed again in the year of receipt. The double tax is partially eliminated by reducing the tax in the year of receipt by a pro rata portion of the prior year's tax.

opportunities. Historically, Congress has sought to encourage expansion of U.S. business in foreign countries and, accordingly, legislation has been enacted which confers tax benefits on certain types of international business activities.

In 1971, Congress enacted the 1971 Tax Reform Act which provided for the creation of a new tax creature, the Domestic International Sales Corporation (DISC).[15] The primary purpose of this legislation was to encourage U.S. corporations to export U.S. manufactured goods. It was hoped that by creating an inducement to export in the form of an income tax deferral, fewer corporations would transfer production facilities outside of the United States, and more would export U.S. manufactured goods.

By exporting through a DISC, a U.S. corporation can defer the tax on one half of the profit earned by the DISC. As a general rule, a DISC may earn one half of the profit that its manufacturing parent currently earns on foreign exports by selling directly. Therefore, if the manufacturing parent currently earns $1 million on export sales (net, after general and administrative and selling expenses), $500,000 may be allocated to the DISC, of which $250,000 is taxed currently at a rate of 48 percent. The $120,000 of deferred tax creates additional working capital which the DISC may make available to the manufacturing parent through "producer loans."

The tax deferred on accumulated DISC earnings is not required to be charged to earnings currently.[16] Therefore, a DISC will help not only cash flow, but earnings as well. This is one of the exceptions that the Accounting Principles Board carved out of the general rule requiring interperiod tax allocation. Earnings are charged with the tax due on accumulated DISC profits only when they are distributed (actually or constructively) to the parent. It should be noted that most states do not recognize the DISC, and state taxes on DISC profits are payable currently.

A foreign base company is a foreign corporation incorporated in a low-tax rate country. Generally, base companies buy from related parties and sell to unrelated third parties. Since the base company is a foreign corporation, its earnings are generally not subject to U.S. tax currently. If a substantial portion of the sales are outside of the country of incorporation, the Subpart F rules may subject

---

[15] Internal Revenue Code, Section 991. The Tax Reduction Act of 1975 eliminated DISC benefits for all energy products.

[16] Accounting Principles Board Opinion No. 23.

the earnings of the base company to tax currently in the United States.[17] However, in the absence of the application of the Subpart F rules (and the inapplicability of any other statutory weapons the IRS has at its disposal),[18] the earnings of the foreign subsidiary will not be taxed currently.

The use of a base company is, in effect, a deferral technique since the foreign subsidiary earnings will ultimately be taxed in the United States when they are repatriated in the form of dividends. However, as in the case of DISC earnings, deferred taxes need not be provided currently.[19]

TAX AVOIDANCE TECHNIQUES

Can an operating company create permanent tax deductions or nontaxable income without reducing earnings? As a general rule, excepting certain specific statutory provisions such as municipal bond interest, it cannot. However, to forego tax benefits merely to avoid the reduction in earnings may be a dubious decision.

Allocation of Excess Purchase Price to Amortizable Assets

The accounting profession has established two basic ways to account for the acquisition by one business entity of another entity. An acquisition transaction will be treated as a "pooling" if the acquiring company acquires the stock or assets of the acquired company for common stock.[20] No goodwill is created as a result of the pooling. If the acquisition is not a "pooling," it will be treated as a "purchase." If the acquiring entity pays more in a purchase for the

---

[17] Internal Revenue Code, Section 951. These rules were enacted by Congress in 1962 to discourage U.S. corporations from using tax haven countries as a base of operation. There are innumerable exceptions to the general rule and the foreign base company is still therefore an attractive tax deferral vehicle. These rules were substantially revised under the Tax Reduction Act of 1975.

[18] The Internal Revenue Service will generally attack foreign-based companies using Section 482 by attempting to reallocate income back to the U.S. parent company.

[19] Accouncting Principles Board Opinion No. 23.

[20] *Business Combinations*, Accounting Principles Board Opinion No. 16, August 1970. The Financial Accounting Standards Board (the successor to the APB) is currently considering the withdrawal of Opinion No. 16.

acquired entity than the fair market value of its underlying tangible assets, any excess must be allocated to intangibles.[21]

Historically, an account called "goodwill" was the repository for excess purchase price. The major attribute of goodwill was that it had no useful life, and therefore, it would not have to be amortized and charged against earnings. The Accounting Principles Board changed the ground rules to now require corporations to amortize goodwill over a maximum of 40 years.[22]

The tax rules for accounting for acquisitions, mergers, consolidations, and amalgamations are unlike the accounting rules. For example, a pooling or a purchase may or may not be a tax-free reorganization, depending upon the character of the items exchanged.[23]

Taking one type of transaction which is clearly a purchase for accounting purposes and a taxable acquisition for tax purposes, permanent tax benefits may be realized if the management of the acquiring entity is not blinded by earnings myopia. If XYZ Corporation buys all of the assets of ABC Corporation for $5 million and the underlying fair market value of the tangible assets is $4 million, the $1 million excess represents, presumably, something of value.[24] XYZ may be motivated, purely from an earnings standpoint to allocate the entire $1 million to goodwill so that it can be amortized for book purposes over a 40-year period. From a tax standpoint, goodwill is not deductible currently, and if the acquired business is continued indefinitely, no tax benefit will ever be realized for this part of XYZ's investment.[25]

XYZ may be able to identify certain amortizable assets which can be segregated from goodwill, given a short useful life and amortized for tax purposes. The list of potential intangibles is almost endless, ranging from customer lists, trade accounts, patents, covenants not to compete, licenses, and franchises. The Internal

---

[21] Ibid.

[22] *Intangible Assets,* Accounting Principles Board Opinion No. 17, August 1970.

[23] For example, a tax-free Section 368(a)(1)(B) reorganization may be effectuated with voting preferred stock of the acquiring company. For accounting purposes, the acquisition would be treated as a purchase.

[24] If, in fact, ABC Corporation's assets generate losses in the future periods an argument could be made that the $1,000,000 constitutes something other than goodwill. It may, in fact, represent bad judgment on the part of XYZ's management. The subsequent realization of losses should bolster an argument that the $1,000,000 should not be allocated to nonamortizable going concern value.

[25] Goodwill may be deducted if the business to which it relates is abandoned. If the business is sold, the seller could reduce the gain by the amount paid for the goodwill.

Revenue Service has taken the position that many intangibles are not separable from goodwill, but the Service has not been uniformly successful. The best approach is to allocate the excess purchase price to various intangibles, including goodwill, on some reasonable basis and determine a useful life for each asset.[26]

It should be kept in mind that if the $1 million excess purchase price is being amortized for tax purposes over a short period of time, the same method generally must be used for book purposes. The facts cannot be different for each purpose.

If XYZ Corporation bought ABC stock for cash, the excess purchase price would only generate a current tax benefit if the acquired company was liquidated within two years.[27]

Tax-Free Transactions

I have categorized certain transactions which are tax free as avoidance techniques when, in fact, they should be properly categorized as potential long-term deferral techniques. The most common tax-free transaction (in the corporate tax world) is the trading of one business asset (a trade-in of a computer) for another.[28] Although an economic gain may be realized, it is deferred until a future date by adjusting the tax cost basis of the asset acquired in exchange.

The same concept prevails in corporate reorganizations. XYZ Corporation can transfer an appreciated asset to ABC Corporation tax free if it owns at least 80 percent of the stock of ABC after the exchange.[29] XYZ can subsequently liquidate ABC tax free.[30] XYZ may acquire EFG Corporation tax free by statutory merger[31] or by transferring its voting stock for 80 percent of EFG's voting stock,[32]

---

[26] The most difficult determination will be the useful life of an intangible. The taxpayer will be required to show that, in fact, the asset to which the cost was assigned is a wasting asset. For example, if the excess purchase price is assigned to retail store outlets, presumably a deduction could be taken as the store is closed down, although the Service would argue to the contrary.

[27] Internal Revenue Code, Section 334(b) (2), provides, in essence, that the purchase of stock for cash followed by a liquidation under Section 332 within two years will be treated as a purchase of assets.

[28] Internal Revenue Code, Section 1031.

[29] Internal Revenue Code, Section 351.

[30] Internal Revenue Code, Section 332.

[31] Internal Revenue Code, Section 368(a)(1)(A).

[32] Internal Revenue Code, Section 368 (a)(1)(B).

or most of EFG's assets.[33] The shareholders of EFG can effectively sell their business and avoid (defer) tax. If EFG shareholders hold onto the XYZ shares until death, no income tax will ever have to be paid on the gain.[34] If the XYZ shares are sold prior to death, the total deferred gain will be reorganized at that time.

Converting Ordinary Income into Capital Gains

The capital gains rate for corporate taxpayers is ordinarily lower than the tax rate on ordinary income. To the extent ordinary income can be converted to capital gain, taxes are reduced.

Congress has given certain types of transactions special treatment by categorizing them as capital gain transactions.[35] In the absence of special statutory authority, a corporate taxpayer, must fit the gain within the general capital gains rules in order to receive capital gain treatment on a particular transaction. Generally, there must be a "sale or exchange" of a "capital asset" as defined in the Code.[36]

The sale of capital stock,[37] and land,[38] will generally create capital gains unless the seller is a dealer.[39] Dispositions of depreciable buildings and other fixed assets may generate capital gains if the gain is greater than any depreciation recaptured.[40]

---

[33] Internal Revenue Code, Section 368(a)(1)(C).

[34] At the present time, no gain is realized on the death of an individual, and his heirs obtain a step-up in basis equal to the fair market value of the assets at the date of death.

[35] For example, Section 631 of the Internal Revenue Code provides that the cutting of timber constitutes a capital gain transaction.

[36] Internal Revenue Code, Section 1221 defines capital assets by specifying those assets which are not included within the definition.

[37] The issuance of capital stock by a corporation is not a taxable transaction under Internal Revenue Code, Section 1032. The sale by a corporation of stock in another corporation is generally a taxable event.

[38] If the land was used for farming there may be some ordinary income on the sale due to the Section 1251 recapture rules if the corporation elected to deduct certain expenses under Section 175 (relating to soil and water conservation expenditures) and 182 (relating to expenditures by farmers for clearing land).

[39] If a seller is a dealer, the property sold will be treated as inventory and ordinary income will be generated. It is not clear at what point a taxpayer becomes a dealer if there are more than a few isolated sales over a period of years.

[40] Internal Revenue Code, Sections 1245 and 1350 provide for the recapture of depreciation on the sale of Section 1231 assets. Any gain in excess of the recapture will generally be Section 1231 gain which is capital gain if Section 1231 gains exceed Section 1231 losses. By timing Section 1231 gains and losses, a taxpayer may be able to maximize tax benefits if gains are reported in a different year than losses.

One type of transaction which has caused a substantial amount of litigation is the licensing of intangibles. The transfer of the right to use a trademark, tradename, patent,[41] franchise,[42] or trade secret may be treated as a capital gain. The Internal Revenue Service has argued successfully on various occasions that if less than all the rights of an intangible are transferred (as may be the case where a license to use is granted) there has not been a sale or exchange, and therefore the capital gains rules do not apply.[43] The Service has also argued successfully that an intangible may not be a capital asset under certain circumstances.[44] The licensing of intangibles continues to be a fertile area of tax planning, but it also remains an area of uncertainty.

Special Statutory Avoidance Vehicles

A Western Hemisphere Trade Corporation is a U.S. corporation which is entitled, by statute, to a reduced federal income tax rate of 34 percent. The 14 percent decrease is a permanent benefit.[45] The special rate is available to a domestic corporation engaged in the active conduct of a trade or business which derives most of its income from within the Western Hemisphere, but outside of the United States.

The Section 931 "possessions" corporation is a U.S. corporation which, by statute, is entitled to exclude all of its income from U.S. tax.[46] The Possessions Corporation is essentially one which does most of its business in Puerto Rico. Currently, Puerto Rico allows a "tax holiday" for certain U.S. manufacturing companies, and therefore, the company does not pay any corporate income tax.

Both of these vehicles produce tax benefits which generate cash flow and increase earnings. They are unique in this respect and are

---

[41] Individual taxpayers may rely on Section 1235 to obtain capital gain treatment, but this Code section does not apply to corporations.

[42] In 1969, Congress attempted to establish guidelines for capital gain treatment of the transfer of franchises, trademarks, and tradenames. Code Section 1253 addresses itself mainly to the problem of "sale or exchange."

[43] *C. A. Norgren Co.* v. *U.S.*, D.C. Colo., May 3, 1967.

[44] The primary attack has been that the intangibles were inventory items and the seller was a dealer.

[45] Internal Revenue Code, Section 921.

[46] The Section 931 benefit is available to domestic corporations doing business in a "possession of the United States." "Possession" for purposes of this section does not include the Virgin Islands.

representative of a limited number of special statutory tax avoidance vehicles.

The Expiring Carry-Forward

It is not unusual, particularly for a company in a start-up situation, to have net operating loss, investment tax credit, charitable contribution, or foreign tax credit carry-forwards. From an accounting standpoint, generally, the benefits cannot be recorded and taken into income until they are realized.[47] Proper planning will help assure realization thus benefiting both earnings and cash flow.

If a net operating loss is due to expire, the obvious solution is to defer deductions and accelerate income. This is not a simple task from a tax standpoint. Techniques sometimes used are the sale-leaseback of appreciated assets,[48] the receipt of prepaid income such as royalties from unrelated parties or unconsolidated subsidiaries,[49] the deferral of research and development costs,[50] and the capitalization of interest and taxes on unproductive realty.[51]

A classic example is XYZ Corporation which discovered in December 1974 that a $100,000 foreign tax credit carry-forward was to expire at the end of their 1974 calendar year because it was to realize a $200,000 net operating loss. The carry-forward had been created as a result of domestic losses incurred by XYZ being offset against dividends paid by foreign subsidiaries in prior years. To create taxable income XYZ used various techniques as shown in Table 5.

The interesting aspect of the approaches taken was that all were effectuated in the last month of the year. It is not recommended, however, that planning for carry-over utilization wait until the last minute.

---

[47] Accounting Principles Board Opinion No. 11.

[48] The Internal Revenue Service will carefully scrutinize a sale-leaseback if the purchaser is a related party or if the lessee has an option to repurchase the property at the end of the lease.

[49] Even though the recipient of the prepaid income is an accrual basis taxpayer, the income will generally be taxable when received as opposed to when earned. See Regulation Section 1.451-5.

[50] A taxpayer may request a change in accounting for research and experimental expenditures and it will be effective if granted for the year in which the change is requested. See Regulation Section 1.174-4(b)(2).

[51] Internal Revenue Code, Section 266.

TABLE 5
Creating Taxable Income to Absorb a Carry-Forward

Net operating loss	$(200,000)
1. Foreign subsidiaries prepaid 1975 royalties	50,000
2. XYZ contributed appreciated real property (basis $150,000, FMV = $250,000) to its employee profit-sharing plan	100,000
3. XYZ requested permission to defer research and development costs incurred in 1974	100,000
4. XYZ made a Section 963 minimum distribution the effect of which was to include in XYZ's income a pro rata share of exchange gains realized by XYZ's subsidiaries that paid dividends in 1974*	250,000
Revised Taxable Income	$ 300,000
U.S. Tax	$ 150,000
Foreign tax credit:	
Current year	(50,000)
Carry-forward	(100,000)
Net U.S. tax†	$ 0

* The Tax Reduction Act of 1975 repealed Section 963 for years beginning after 1975.
† Internal Revenue Code, Section 904, provides for limitations on the use of claiming foreign tax credits. For purposes of the example, it is assumed that there is no limitation.

CONCLUSION

Planning for the reduction of income tax may involve both deferral and avoidance techniques. A financial officer should be primarily concerned with attempting to quantify the value of the economic benefit to be derived. Although there may be an effect on earnings if an avoidance technique is used, the effect may be, in fact, illusory. Unfortunately, with the emphasis today on earnings multiples only privately traded companies may have the motivation to use every tax planning technique available.

ADDITIONAL SOURCES

Bastable, C. W., and Merriwether, J. D. "Fifo in an Inflationary Environment." *Journal of Accounting*, 139 (March 1975), 49–55.

Beghe, R. "Tax Planning for the Financially Troubled Corporation." *Taxes*, 52 (December 1974), 795–820.

Bierman, H. "Regulation, Implied Revenue Requirements and Methods of Depreciation." *Accounting Review*, 49 (July 1974), 448–54.

Blau, J. D. "Tax Incentives or Tax Shelters." *Commercial and Financial Chronicle*, 219 (November 25, 1974), 6.

Brinner, R. "Inflation, Deferral and Neutral Taxation of Capital Gains." *National Tax Journal*, 26 (December 1973), 565–73.

Bullock, C. L. "Reconciling Economic Depreciation with Tax Allocation." *Accounting Review,* 49 (January 1974), 98–103.

Calkins, H. "Tax Sheltering in Perspective." *Taxes,* 51 (December 1973), 758–69.

Coen, R. M. "Investment Behavior, the Measurement of Depreciation and Tax Policy." *American Economic Review,* 65 (March 1975), 59–74.

Comiskey, Eugene, and Hasselback, James. "Analyzing the Profit-Tax Relationship." *Financial Management,* 2 (Winter 1973), 57–62.

Corman, J. C. "Tax Shelters for Capital Investment—A View on Their Reform." *Management Accounting,* 55 (January 1974), 15–17.

Edwards, C. E., and Goodwin, J. S. "Tax Shields from Depreciation Allowances: A Further Examination." *Quarterly Review of Economics and Business,* 14 (Winter 1974), 116–22.

Edwards, J. D., and Barrack, J. B. "Last-in, First-out Inventory Valuation as a Way to Control Illusory Profits." *Michigan State University Business Topics,* 23 (Winter 1975), 19–27.

Faust, G. R., and Garland, W. D. "Capital Recovery Dilemma." *Public Utilities Fortnightly,* 94 (August 29, 1974), 19–22.

Feinschreiber, R. "Computing Depreciation under the Class Life System." *Certified Public Accountant Journal,* 43 (October 1973), 857–62.

Fisher, A., et al. "With Proper Planning, Deferred Ordinary Income of a DISC Need Never Be Recaptured." *Journal of Taxation,* 40 (March 1974), 138–42.

Gaskins, J. P. "Taxation of Foreign Source Income." *Financial Analysts Journal,* 29 (September 1973), 55–58.

Lenrow, G. I., and Halpern, E. "ADR and Class Life Systems—Another Dimension of Depreciation." *Best's Review Property/Liability Edition,* 74 (February 1974), 70.

Lyons, J. F. "Tax Shelters: A New Approach." *Financial World,* 141 (May 29, 1974), 28–30.

Priest, A. L. "Tax Shelters: Myths and Facts." *Commercial and Financial Chronicle,* 219 (July 8, 1974), 1.

Raby, W. L., and Richter, E. D. "Conformity of Tax and Financial Accounting." *Journal of Accounting,* 139 (March 1975), 42–48.

Revsine, L., and Weygandt, J. J. "Accounting for Inflation: The Controversy." *Journal of Accounting,* 138 (October 1974), 72–78.

Rollin, A. S., and Michi, R. A. "Outlook for Tax Shelters." *Certified Public Accountants Journal,* 43 (December 1973), 1063–66.

Rossback, L. B. "The Role of Tax-Incentive Investments in Sheltering Substantial Capital Gains." *Trusts and Estates*, 113 (June 1974), 362–63.

Scholler, T. P., et al. "ADR System: An Analysis of the Final Regs and How Practitioners Should Use Them." *Journal of Taxation*, 39 (July 1973), 16–22.

Schwartz, Eli, and Aronison, J. Richard. "How to Integrate Corporate and Personal Income Taxation," *Journal of Finance*, 27 (December 1972), 1073–80.

Chapter 50

Insurance and Risk Management

F. X. McCahill, Jr. [*]

RISK MANAGEMENT primarily concerns the protection of the company's assets. This involves both the prevention of accidental losses as well as the installation and maintenance of optimum conditions to meet those accidental losses that are not preventable or that occur despite preventive measures. Various methods are evaluated toward this end. Where a more economic means of protecting these assets does not exist, the company resorts to ensuring assets against losses as a last step.

Specifically, the job of risk management can be considered in three facets—each of which will be discussed in turn:

1. Finding exposures to loss.
2. Eliminating exposures to loss and minimizing those that cannot be eliminated.
3. Instituting and administering programs for absorbing losses or transferring the risk of losses.

FINDING EXPOSURES

A company is exposed to a countless variety of potential losses from the small crack in the pavement that can stub toes to the

---

[*] F. X. McCahill, Jr., is director of insurance and safety, Bristol-Myers Company, New York.

large plant that can be leveled by a fire. Some exposures are obvious; some have a way of becoming apparent only after the damage has occurred. Nevertheless, effort to identify exposures can never be relaxed unless the company is prepared to gamble in an area where even its survival may be at stake.

Effective loss avoidance cannot depend upon the sporadic efforts at risk exposure identification by employees in a company's various departments. Although their aid in identification is important, a program of continued surveillance by a specialist (we'll call him a risk manager) whose primary duty is loss prevention is critically needed.

Now, how does this risk manager go about the job? Does he merely make sure that every plant is completely fitted with fire-prevention facilities, that a shotgun is carried on every trailer-load of merchandise and that every employee is encased in impenetrable plastic? Obviously not. Essentially, he should recognize that the unexpected can, and often does, happen: the ammonium nitrate fertilizer that blew up Texas City in 1947, killing 561 persons, had at least a 25-year history of perfect behavior. He should recognize that loss possibilities do not remain static: the sprinklers that could have contained the fire yesterday in the tubed shaving cream plant are inadequate today after its conversion to aerosol cans; criminal techniques somehow keep abreast of the newest safeguards; employees get rashes even from safety clothing. New interpretation of laws, new legislation, new technology, and new products make novel exposures inevitable.

Checklists

The company's exposures to loss may be classified under three general headings: property, income, and legal liability.

In regard to property loss, more obvious questions include:

1. What are the fire exposures?
2. What are the cigarette smoking practices? (In 1970, careless smoking accounted for 107,200 out of 992,000 building fires.)
3. What are solvent use and storage practices? (Solvents caused 58,800 of those fires in 1970.)
4. Are hazardous operations segregated?
5. Is good housekeeping to reduce fire and other property losses in constant demand?

6. Is trash buildup kept to a minimum?
7. Are stockpiling and empty pallet storage kept within prescribed limits?
8. What are the earthquake, flood, explosion, and windstorm possibilities?

Checklists to augment and detail perils are readily available—but, despite their value, it remains for the risk manager to supplement them by constantly seeking out exposures not yet listed. Since loss of income is usually the consequence of property loss, the same checklists apply, with some additions such as:

1. How dependable are the supply sources of product components, power, and other services?
2. If one source fails, is there an alternative source?
3. Can access to a plant be cut off by snow or by damage to a bridge or roadway?
4. How long would it take to replace vital machinery?
5. What are the guarantees that the company's labor force would return after even a brief shutdown period?

Again, checklists are available and must be supplemented as well.

Exposures to legal liability losses go beyond reckless driving, slippery floors, and defective products. In this area, questions of interest include:

1. What responsibilities—even to the extent of paying for the negligence of others—is the company assuming in construction, acquisition, lease, and other agreements?
2. Do vapors being discharged into the air or effluents into rivers offend the new ecology?
3. What legal action can be anticipated from a public alerted to windfalls by lawyers' associations, by sales campaigns for new types of legal liability insurance, and by munificent court awards?

Exposure Flow Charts

To effectively anticipate loss exposures is to prepare flow charts with checklists. These exposure flow charts must be drafted well in advance to cover all the questions that require answers bearing upon impending corporate developments such as plant construction, execution of an acquisition agreement, or signing a lease contract.

Reconstruction: Will the design incorporate the optimum loss-prevention features of built-in protection and availability of public services? Do the persons authorizing the capital expenditure know whether full consideration has been given to safeguards which best assure uninterrupted operations?

Are they aware of the differential in insurance rates applicable to protected and unprotected property—a differential which often pays for the installation of loss-prevention devices within a two- or three-year period? Have they considered whether a revision in plans could accomplish an interchange of the proposed facility with present operations at other plants—so that a single-source-of-supply situation or a loss potential for one line of products is avoided?

Re an acquisition: Do those who approve the acquisition know that the property is insurable or whether it can be made insurable at reasonable cost through installation of minimum protection standards? Are they dependent upon title insurance purchased some 50 years ago which may reflect only a percentage of the present-day value of the property? Do they know which party to the merger agreement will sustain any property loss which occurs before closing date? Do they know whether the unknown insurable liabilities which they are agreeing to assume are adequately insured?

Re a lease agreement: Do those who will execute the agreement know whether the other party has shifted the risk of loss to their company—even if the other party's negligence causes the loss? Are they aware that they may have invalidated their company's insurance on its own property through a provision in the agreement that exonerates the other party from damages to their company's property? (A standard insurance policy provides that the insurer after payment of a loss acquires any rights the insured may have against the party responsible for the loss. If the insured has waived those rights without the insurer's permission, the policy does not cover the loss.) Do they know whether there is double insurance, both premiums to be paid by their company, on the subject of the agreement, or whether the lease doubles up on their company in other ways? For example, if the premises they lease are destroyed, they may be obliged to rebuild and to continue full rental payments during the period of rebuilding. Have they investigated whether some of the liabilities they assume in the agreement are unlimited in dollar amount? Even insurance companies limit their liability.

In drafting the various checklists, the risk manager must keep in mind that, if he does not assume that there is a loss exposure waiting around every corner and in every facet of company activities, he will be ineffective in his job. While others in the company strive to find reasons for the success of their projects, the risk manager strives to arrive at reasons for failure, in order to ensure success. While this may not be a popular role, if in its course just one substantial monetary loss (to say nothing of loss of life) is avoided, any periodic unpopularity is quite endurable.

In short, finding exposures to loss has a requisite: one must incessantly seek them.

MINIMIZING EXPOSURES

While the best facilities and most stringent policies can nearly eliminate loss potentials (no one has yet succeeded in totally eliminating losses due to hurricanes, earthquakes, and floods), the costs of complete elimination, in many cases, cannot be justified. Risk management seeks to arrive at the optimum combination of maximum loss prevention and reasonable cost.

Unfortunately, it is all too true that countless people in the company are not the least bit reluctant, because of their lack of understanding of the insurance function, to give away the "company jewels." The risk manager must recognize these people in the same light that he views alcohol operations in a room containing a gas-fired boiler. A few examples are stated below.

The corporate counsel sends up an agreement for instant approval. It includes an indemnification clause that makes the company responsible for everybody's and anybody's negligence, but, he says, "We've got insurance, haven't we?"

A corporation president keeps a wonderful acquisition so secret that the risk manager gets to read the agreement only after it has been executed. "We are undertaking all your liabilities," it states, in effect.

"No problem in your area," says the president to the risk manager. "They have a complete insurance program." True enough, the acquired company did maintain every kind of insurance, but the product liability policy contained a coverage limitation of $500,000 for all payments in any one year. "This is adequate, isn't it," the president asks, "since the worst open case in litigation has been forecast by the insurance company to settle out at $100,000? And, besides, we ourselves have $25 million in product liability coverage that can take care of any shortfalls."

"No," the risk manager explains, "our policy would cover only if we were responsible as of the date that the injury occurred. For instance, there is at least one case on record where $500,000 in coverage was about $700,000 light."

A purchasing manager orders a $200,000 piece of intricate machinery and agrees to terms of f.o.b. seller's plant. The machinery arrives heavily damaged—to the tune of about $200,000—but the purchasing manager laughs it off with: "we've got insurance. And, besides, it's the carrier's responsibility." Unhappily, the carrier blames the manufacturer for inadequate loading, and the manufacturer stands on his f.o.b. plant terms.

As part of a drive to retain his company's share of a market, a vice president in charge of customer relations dreams up a great gimmick: he arranges to fly 150 representatives of the company's leading customers to Paris for four days. The representatives, of course, are highly paid executives.

"We've chartered a plane," he tells the risk manager, "but don't you fret. Look at the charter agreement! The airline has a $50 million legal liability insurance policy in which we are named as additional insured. Please put your stamp of approval on the agreement quickly; we're taking off from JFK tomorrow morning!"

The risk manager looks at the document. Yes, the airline does have the $50 million policy, and the charterer is named as additional insured. But there are two hitches:

First, the aircraft hull alone is worth $7 million. Unless the charterer is also named in the airline's hull policy as an additional insured, the company is left to its own devices for protection against damage to the aircraft.

Second, the $50 million policy contains a seemingly innocuous provision that limits coverage to amounts payable under the Warsaw Convention. But the Warsaw Convention limits only the airline's liability; it has no relevance to whatever company charters the aircraft. It does not take much imagination to guess what the survivors of the 150 customers who went down with the ship would do. If the return from the airline is limited, why not sue the charterer for an additional $500,000 per head?

A corporate financial officer believes he has adequate protection in his custody agreement with the bank, under which the bank keeps substantial amounts of the company's securities. He is also well satisfied with the certificates of insurance, furnished him by the bank, that cover losses of the securities up to $50 million. The trouble is, the insurance would apply only if the bank could be held legally liable for the loss. And if the bank had performed well as a custodian, it would not be liable.

Do the possibilities of loss sound remote in most of these "people areas"? Of course they do. Just as remote, before the fact, as General Motors' loss in the Livonia, Michigan fire in 1953, Monsanto's Texas City loss in 1947, and the thalidomide, the MER 29, the Cutter vaccine losses—all counted in millions of dollars.

Keeping the Company Informed

However, business must go on. Acquisitions cannot be discontinued, machinery must be purchased, customers need incentives, banking arrangements are indispensable. But none of these realities makes a case for overlooking reasonable efforts to reduce such loss exposures.

A primary function of the risk manager then, is to keep the company informed of facts about commercial insurance; for instance, the fact that insurance represents a net cost to the company. Even if the premium paid represents the maximum corporate contribution for certain agreed-upon losses that the company may incur over a specific period of time, this is calculated by the insurance company to more than cover the expected losses: the loss pattern of any insurance applicant is first determined, then the level of premium is set to equal expected losses plus estimated expenses and profits. One should remember that insurance companies operate as much as a business as do their client companies. The record has shown that over the past ten years, insurance companies have maintained break-even points of between 45 cents and 70 cents in loss payments out of each premium dollar. This means that the company that insures against its normally expected losses is in a position to collect 45 percent to 70 percent of the premium it has paid during a normal loss year. These figures should interest many corporate executives who breathe a sigh of relief when the risk manager assures them that the $1,500 theft is covered by insurance.

It is obvious that there is no such thing as a free lunch. Total premiums paid will always exceed benefits received on the average. It follows that any insurance is a net cost to the insured. This outlay can be minimized by intelligent preventative measures that anticipate as many contingencies as possible.

The Role of People

In "selling" his company's risks, the risk manager must consider the emphasis an insurer places on a prospective client's personnel. A property insurer is less impressed by the best equipped manufacturing plant operated by under-paid, disgruntled, ill-trained individuals under sloppy management than by a wood-frame un-sprinkled plant staffed by employees and management who take pride in operating a clean shop and in observing all the sound principles of loss prevention such as fire brigades, safety committees, and the rest. An auto liability insurer considers few things more important when accepting a risk than a fleet of intelligent drivers. A products liability insurer is more concerned about a low-hazard product turned out by a fast-buck, low quality-control company, than about a high-hazard product put out by a company headed by responsible management aware of its duty to the public.

Of course, the risk manager himself is not always a paragon. Since this fellow is usually the only one in the company who has read the insurance policy, he can give false assurance to others that their undertakings are secure against loss. Although he generally understands the normal exclusions in a policy, he may realize too late that the standard policy obscures many more exclusions. For example, if the valuation-of-loss clause in a policy provides that finished stock be covered only at factory cost, the policyholder sustaining a loss of finished stock will find that any resulting drop in sales will not be compensated.

The chief item in replacing records often is the cost of labor, which could be sad news if the company insured valuable papers only for their value as blank sheets plus transcription costs.

A crime policy clearly covering losses that arise out of the infidelity of employees may cause great disappointment to the corporation whose risk manager failed to notice that the policy differentiates between an employee and an agent, before $600,000 disappeared simultaneously with the agent.

The risk manager who does not deign to read his insurance coverages, in anticipation of the day following a loss, is as dangerous as the hazards he seeks to expose and remove.

In fairness to employees, it must be said that they are the most reliable tool for revealing exposures. Internal auditors, for instance, can be invaluable to the risk manager, since they are constantly visiting company locations and are concerned not only with the company's books but also with its entire operations. They can help him by observing safekeeping and storage practices in connection with accounts receivable, EDP tapes, and valuable papers; by noting unhealthy accumulations of combustibles, such as paper cards in the computer room or wooden crates on a shipping dock; by reporting any dangerous egress conditions; and even by enforcing action to reduce high stockpiling and to clean sprinkler heads.

People sources are indispensable to the risk manager because when it comes to furnishing information that can cure conditions leading to loss, the boiler room trainee does not take a back seat to the chairman of the board.

TRANSFERRING RISK

When the company has done, and continues to do, everything possible to remove exposures to loss, what preparations should it make to minimize the effects on the profit and loss statement of those losses unavoidably sustained?

Not much effort is required to estimate the dollar value of the losses that a company can expect to incur in the coming year. The amount is projected out of the company's past experience, supplemented by a close reading of inflation factors, legal decisions and new legislation, changes in company operations, and new loss-prevention facilities.

The end figure—call it normally expected losses—is just as easily computed by an insurance company which uses it as the base for the premium charge. The insurer's procedure here, however, is unlike that accorded the individual homeowner, whose premium level is primarily a function of the combined loss experience of millions of policyholders. While a company's premium does include an increment for overall industry loss experience, its own experience and desirability as a risk outweighs all other factors.

Although corporate insureds know that the cost of insuring

normally expected losses also includes the insurer's expected profit, they have not yet reached the point where they can take the obvious course and self-insure or assume the risk of the normally expected loss. The reason is, corporate insureds continue to be subject to "tie-in" sales—that is, if they want commercial insurance where it really counts—(in the catastrophe category)—they can buy it only as part of a policy that covers the routine losses. In fairness to some insurers, however, there has been progress in the deductible coverage field, so corporate insureds can realize some savings in absorbing the low-level losses themselves.

What is the utopian program for a company, knowing as it does that it will experience losses large and small, however good its loss-prevention program? Simply this: a program that unequivocally sets the maximum dollar amount it will pay for losses in the coming year—a figure no less budgetable than the cost of raw materials. Its components are: (1) The cost of installation and maintenance of loss-prevention facilities; (2) the dollar amount of normally expected losses; and (3) the cost of insuring or spreading the risk of those losses that exceed the normally expected ones.

It is simple to compute the first and second items. It is very difficult to compute the third for the simple reason that insurance companies have not yet arrived at a pricing formula. Here is where we enter the most valid realm of insurance from the corporate insured's point of view because we are dealing with the catastrophe losses which, without the proper hedging arrangements, can affect a company's financial viability. This is the area which commercial insurers are beginning to research—an area in which they must become competent unless they are prepared to watch industry seek out new vehicles for spreading the risk.

Captive Insurance

The idea of a captive insurance company emerged largely out of commercial insurers' unwillingness (some of them say "inability") to meet the real spreading-of-risk needs of corporations. Today, many captives owe their existence to the unavailability, or to the exhorbitant cost, of forms of commercial coverage—coverage which one way or another had to be maintained by a corporation interested in its survival.

However, while the captive insurance company appeared to be the risk manager's oasis, it has for many turned out to be a mirage. Briefly, a captive insurance company is one that is created by the company seeking insurance protection. The most popular captive to date is the one set up in Bermuda because of its attractive insurance and tax regulations. But, an obvious truth is that a captive can only generate income through premiums paid into it and the investment return on that portion of premiums not paid in expenses or in losses. It has the advantage of immediate tax deductibility for the parent on premiums paid into it. Amounts paid into a self-insured reserve do not qualify, of course, for such deductibility. Under self-insurance, deductibility must await the actual expenditure for the loss. A further advantage is the parent's avoidance of having to pay the brokerage commission that comprises a percentage of the premiums paid to the commercial insurer.

However, there are some limitations too. To the extent that the captive cannot justify its reserves for losses and its expenses, it has income—even in Bermuda—under U.S. tax laws. So it is not the same clear case of premium tax deductibility that the parent enjoys through commercial insurance. In fact, when the tax advantages of maintaining a captive rather than a self-insurance account are viewed over a long term, they must diminish to just one small effect: the parent's net deductibility is on the amount set up by the captive as a legitimate reserve for losses. This deductibility is no greater than the amount the parent would enjoy on losses paid out of a self-insured account; it is merely available at an earlier date.

Furthermore, the reinsurance market—to which all captives must resort if they intend to follow the spread-of-risk principle—is no different nor broader than that available to commercial insurers. Certainly, there is no reason to believe that a captive can negotiate reinsurance more advantageously than the commercial insurer—who may well believe that his accounts were driven to captives because of the reinsurers' withdrawals.

However, a captive designed to service not just one company but an entire segment of industry (such as a drug group, an oil group, and an airline group), could obtain the resources necessary to meet its sponsors' needs and spread the risk.

Establishing the club rules and dues, though, requires answers to many difficult questions. For instance:

1. What form of insurance company—a mutual, a stock, or a reciprocal—will be used?
2. What limits will be set on the individual member's liability?
3. What minimum loss-prevention standards will be required for membership?
4. What activities will disqualify a company, and what will be the policing arrangements?
5. What will be the maximum amount available for any one loss?

This kind of captive could provide the potential for the utopian risk program mentioned earlier. Under such a program, the individual member would absorb the normally expected losses as well as others up to the point of extreme discomfort. But the member would be protected in the event of a severe loss. Furthermore, the captive would be competitive with commercial insurers for reinsurance business.

Another advantage of the group captive, not found in the present system, could be the breadth of its coverage. A loss is a loss is a loss! A manufacturing plant carried off in a flood has no more value to its owner than if it had burned to the ground. The company that sustains a million-dollar business interruption loss because of power failure does not suffer a trifle less than the company that sustains a million-dollar loss because a supplier's facilities exploded. A captive company's insurance policy could provide coverage for all accidental losses, not just those that happen to fall within the purview of a commercial insurance policy.

Foreign Assets

It would be presumptuous for anyone to suggest that he had all the insurance answers for the U.S. company with assets abroad. Company A is content to rest with the forms of coverage available in the foreign (local) countries; Company B purchases such local coverage, but makes up for the inadequacies, which are many, by maintaining a "gap-filling" U.S. policy; Company C purchases only the insurance (at times, less than) required by local laws and depends almost entirely on a U.S. blanket policy covering all foreign assets.

Company A will not face tax or legal problems. It will face archaic policies—in many countries 30 years behind the U.S. standards—with limited coverages and onerous conditions; it will face overpriced (in some cases outrageously so) insurance; it will face a dearth of the services—loss-prevention engineering, safety counselling—that accompany the U.S. insurance policy.

Company B, through its U.S. "gap" policy will overcome some of A's problems, but will face tax problems: the premium paid in the United States to insure the losses of a foreign entity, subsidiary though it is, may not be deductible; losses collected in the United States for insured losses of the foreign entity may be taxable income. There is more to be said on this taxability question—but answers will have to come from the tax experts.

Company C will have the same tax problem as Company B, and may, in addition, face legal problems within the local country. These legal problems could result from C's overzealousness in avoiding purchases of local insurance.

Regardless of the approach taken, the U.S. company should have full knowledge of the implications. Some countries positively forbid insurance on the assets within those countries unless it is purchased from an admitted insurance company. Some countries positively require certain insurances to be maintained while others regulate the forms of coverage, the price of coverage, and brokerage commissions. Some countries imprison the "illegal" purchaser of insurance.

Today, sizable portions of U.S. companys' income are from foreign countries. Today, loss prevention, as we know it, is in its infancy abroad. Today, the main thrust of many of these U.S. companies is directed properly to engineering their foreign properties to the U.S. degree of protection. In the wake of these efforts toward conservation of property and protection of personnel, their insurance coverage problems are gradually receding. American insurance companies are more fully recognizing that the results of fires in foreign countries bear a striking resemblance to those in the United States.

The Commercial Insurance Policy

Having reached the point where we have reduced loss exposures to the absolute minimum, and having determined just how many dollars we want to pay for uninsured losses, we are ready to transfer the residue of risk to an insurance company.

But standard forms of insurance policies too often fall short of the corporation's transfer needs. That a policy can supply coverage in bold print and negate it in fine print is no fable. Double negatives, circuitous references, specialized language (Greek to the unitiated) remain "proud" parts of many policies.

The closest approach, then, that a corporation can make to a satisfactory transfer of risk must be accomplished through either: (a) a manuscript insurance policy (one that is drafted as a combined effort, usually, of the buyer, the broker and the underwriter); or (b) a standard form of policy endorsed to eliminate the unwanted and to include the wanted.

Either way, here are some of the questions the corporation should raise with respect to policy coverage:

1. Is the name of the insured property spelled out? (For example, ABC Company's subsidiaries are not covered unless the policy says so.)
2. Is the stated insurance value or the limits of insurer's liability clearly understood? (Can a coinsurance penalty clause be overcome by an "agreed amount" endorsement?)
3. Are the reporting requirements fully understood? (For example, values, claims, potential claims, and changes in exposures.)
4. Does the valuation clause for collection of loss meet the insured's intent? (For example, replacement cost new, actual cash value, cost at time and sight of loss, selling price, and cost plus a percentage.)
5. Does the policy cover all perils except those specifically excluded or does it cover only named perils?
6. Does the policy contain an errors and omissions clause so that the intent of the policy will not be negated by honest mistakes of the insured?
7. Does it contain an automatic coverage clause which will apply to new property or other expansions—subject to the insured's reporting within a reasonable time?
8. Are the deductibles fully understood? (There are per loss deductibles, combined deductibles, aggregate annual deductibles, disappearing deductibles, and reimbursing deductibles.)

Here is another area where the checklist could fill a good-sized book—but we still must arrive at the position where there is no substitute for the insured being satisfied that the insurance contract spells out in unambiguous English the full intentions of the two parties.

Finally, the risk manager can ill afford to be either bashful or independent if he hopes to fulfill his function. He must use all conceivable aids: outside people and fellow employees such as internal auditors, referred to earlier. These sources should help him keep a constantly updated checklist in effectively carrying out his risk management function. Another invaluable source which is often overlooked are the insurance brokers who are paid part of the insured's premium dollars for their services. Good brokers have a wealth of both information and talent, there for the picking, to help eliminate risks. They have engineering, legal, claim, insurance experts who are paid, to repeat, out of premium dollars. The insured who neglects or is distrustful of these fringe benefits has not grasped the full meaning of commercial insurance. That same premium dollar contains an increment for insurance company services. Again, to bypass these facilities is to leave part of the order on the counter.

To end where we began, insuring assets against loss is the last step in the risk management process. However, it is not the last in importance because the day will never come where risk elimination will be refined enough to eliminate risk transfer.

ADDITIONAL SOURCES

Finding Exposures

Daenzer, B. J. *Fact Finding Techniques in Risk Management.* New York: American Management Association, Inc., 1970.

Identifying and Controlling the Risks of Accidental Loss. New York: American Management Association, Inc., 1962.

Minimizing Exposures

Bests' Safety Maintenance Directory. New York: Alfred M. Best Company, Inc., 1976.

Handbook of Industrial Loss Prevention (Factory Mutual). New York: McGraw-Hill, 1967.

Keeping the Company Informed

Blum, A. A. *Company Organization of Insurance Management.* New York: American Management Association, Inc., 1961.

The Growing Job of Risk Management. New York: American Management Association, Inc., 1962.

Transferring Risk

The Growing Job of Risk Management. New York: American Management Association, Inc., 1962.

McDonald, D. L. *Corporate Risk Control.* New York: Ronald Press, 1966.

Mehr, R. I., and Hedges, B. A. *Risk Management in the Business Enterprise.* Homewood, Ill.: Richard D. Irwin, Inc., 1974.

Williams, C. A., and Heins, R. M. *Risk Management and Insurance,* New York: McGraw-Hill, 1964.

Captive Insurers

Daenzer, B. J. "More Captives." *International Insurance Monitor* (April 1969).

Hare, W. A. *Captive Insurance Companies.* New York: American Management Association, Inc., 1972.

Foreign Assets

Sourcebook of International Corporate Insurance and Employee Benefit Management. Vol. I, C. S. Hart; Vol. II, R. Wells. New York: American Management Association, Inc., 1967–68.

The Commercial Insurance Policy

Fire, Casualty and Surety (FCS) Bulletins. Cincinnati, Ohio: The National Underwriter Company.

General

Hershman, Arlene. "Insurance—New Headache for Executives." *Dun's,* 104 (December 1974), 73–74.

O'Meara, Robert, and Koralik, Susan. "Cutting Group Insurance Costs." *Financial Executive,* 42 (July 1974), 70–75.

Paul, Robert. "Self-Insurance under the Microscope." *Financial Executive,* 41 (August 1973), 32–35.

Chapter 51

Managing Pension Funds

Peter H. Vermilye*
Frank J. Husic†

INTRODUCTION

THE CORPORATE PENSION FUND has become one of the financial officer's major responsibilities. A 1973 survey of the country's largest corporations showed that contributions to pension and profit sharing plans are currently running at an average rate of about 20 percent of pretax profits.[1] In addition while profits fluctuate, pension costs tend to grow steadily and many corporations have had the unhappy experience of making sizable contributions even in loss years. Those companies that are highly automated, have a young work force, a high turnover or less liberal employee benefits may not feel the full weight of their obligations as keenly, but for many others the burden of contributions is considerable and pension liabilities are a continuing concern. Some pension funds are now larger than the net worth of the sponsoring corporation. In most instances, the fund is at least as large as a major division of the corporation. These assets and the levels of return they generate can be as important to the financial officer as any other division or department obligation. If pension assets do not generate the kind of return

* Peter H. Vermilye is chairman and chief investment officer, Alliance Capital Management Corporation, New York.

† Frank J. Husic is vice president, Alliance Capital Management Corporation, New York.

[1] P. J. Davey, *Financial Management of Company Pension Plans.* Report No. 611 (New York: The Conference Board, Inc. 1973).

that has been actuarially assumed, the shortfall must come from company profits—and the impact can be severe.

Viewed from one perspective, these pressures have had their beneficial effects. Corporate management has been forced into paying more attention to pension plan management. The plan is being looked at more realistically. Actuaries and consultants have been called into spell out not only what the liabilities of the plan are now but also what it is likely to cost the corporation in the future. Companies have hired or trained staff personnel to monitor the fund and its managers. In short, the importance of the plan to the company's profits is being recognized and the pension plan is getting the attention it deserves. Along with this trend has come increasing pressure on the chief financial officer to oversee the pension fund administration function.

Despite these developments, little has been written to aid the financial manager assigned to the task. Corporate management courses in business schools deal with questions such as capital budgeting, cost of capital and cash management but generally ignore pension fund administration. The smattering of articles in journals attack the issue on a piecemeal basis with little attempt to develop an overview. Below we discuss pension fund administration for the financial executive and offer guidelines for decision making.

It is important to note that there are a number of subjects we do not intend to emphasize in our presentation. Actuarial and accounting considerations as well as the entire question of appropriate benefit mix will be mentioned only briefly. Provisions of the recently enacted Employee Retirement Income Security Act of 1974 (ERISA) are described where applicable, but we do not discuss all aspects of the act in detail. Our purpose will be to provide a general description of the function of the financial manager in pension fund administration with a focus on the financial aspects of this responsibility. If the company's pension administration program is well conceived and organized, broad issues such as fund investment policy, changing economic conditions, and government legislation and regulation can be dealt with effectively.

HISTORY

The private pension system had an unspectacular start with the establishment of the first private plan by the American Express

Company in 1875. By 1930 about 3 million workers were covered by such plans. Industry distribution was far from uniform with rails, utilities, and oil companies participating most actively. Many of the trade unions provided their own pension plans.[2]

As shown in Table 1, development in both number of plans and

TABLE 1
Annual Rates of Growth of Assets and Benefits Paid, Private
Pension Plans, 1920–1972

| Period | Average Annual Rate of Growth | |
	In Assets (at book value) (percent)	In Benefits Paid (percent)
1920–1930.	27.1%	—
1930–1940.	7.2	—
1940–1950.	17.3	10.2%
1950–1960.	19.8	16.8
1960–1970.	11.3	16.3
1970–1972.	10.1	17.3

Source: Roger F. Murray, *Economic Aspects of Pensions: A Summary Report* (New York: National Bureau of Economic Research, 1968), pp. 72–85; Patrick J. Davey, *Financial Management of Company Pension Plans*, Report No. 611 (New York: The Conference Board, Inc., 1973).

depth of coverage slowed markedly through the 1930s, no doubt a reflection of the difficulty of the times. Offsetting this, at least to some extent, was the growth of public pension plans through the introduction of social security in 1935. If nothing else, this legislation reinforced the view that pension plans would be a permanent part of the social and economic fabric of this country.

As our table of growth rates indicates, starting in 1940 the development of private pension plans began to accelerate. The 20-year period from 1940 to 1960 was the period of development and rapid growth for pension plans. The principal stimuli behind this growth were fourfold:

1. The desire for economic security resulting from the depression and the massive economic dislocation which accompanied it.
2. The imposition of wage controls and exemption of retirement benefits from those controls during World War II encouraged

---

[2] For a very readable and more detailed history of the growth of pension plans, see Roger F. Murray, *Economic Aspects of Pensions: A Summary Report* (New York: National Bureau of Economic Research, 1968), pp. 72–85.

the establishment of new or expansion of old retirement plans as a competitive tactic by employers.

3. The high corporate income tax rates along with the excess profits tax levied during the war lowered the net cost of tax-deductible pension contributions.

4. To all of this was added governmental pressure principally through two major findings: (*a*) the National Labor Relations Board decision in 1948 requiring employers to bargain on pension issues, and (*b*) the Steel Industry Fact Finding Board conclusions in 1949 supporting the human depreciation concept of pension benefits.

In the period since 1960 private plans have expanded further, benefits have been enlarged and increasing numbers of employees have received retirement payments. To a greater extent in the future, pension plans will be providing benefits instead of just expectations. This is quite clear from Table 1 which shows benefits paid growing rapidly over time while the growth of assets has clearly begun to slow by 1965.

The projected slowdown in the rate of growth of assets reflects the fact that a high proportion of potentially eligible employees has already come under coverage. Of all employees on nonagricultural payrolls, excluding government, 47.5 percent had been covered by the end of 1960 compared with only 25 percent at the end of 1950. If this group of employees is further reduced to exclude part-time workers and those under 25, the coverage ratio approximates 65 percent. High coverage already prevails in transportation, public utilities, finance and insurance, mining, and many sectors of manufacturing.[3] In short, the large groups most readily covered by group plans have already been included.

A number of factors can influence the rate at which pension plans mature; that is, reach the point where benefits paid out tend to be larger than new money contributed to the plan. The most important factor in delaying maturity is an acceleration in the rate of increase in wages which increases pension contributions per employee. A second factor is the trend toward relating benefits to final average compensation. Finally, the inclusion of larger death, disability, survivor, and early retirement benefits in the plan increases con-

---

[3] David M. Holland, *Private Pension Funds: Protected Growth* (New York, National Bureau of Economic Research, 1966).

tribution rates and slows maturation. Eventually these all have the effect of increasing benefit payments, but in the meantime, the pace of the maturing process can be slowed.

Along with the spectacular growth in the size of pension assets, have come important shifts in the manner of investing these assets. Prior to the 1950s, pension commitments were generally funded on an annuity basis by premium payments or deposits with life insurance companies. Pension funds, like other insurance company assets, were invested primarily in marketable fixed-income securities, privately placed long-term loans to business and mortgages on commercial and industrial property. These "insured plans" were essentially the sinking fund that resulted from a calculation of the payments needed at an assumed rate of interest to meet a future fixed liability.

In the mid- and late-1940s came change, however. Government bond yields were in the area of 2.5 percent and high-grade corporate bonds provided about 2.6 percent to 3 percent yield while common stocks were providing a dividend return of over 5 percent. For corporations facing increasing pension costs, the attraction of equities was apparent. Life insurance companies, handicapped by tax and legal constraints, could not easily compete with the banks and trust companies who became the predominant managers of the separately trusteed retirement plans. By 1950, insured pension reserves were $5.6 billion while trusteed plans were $6.5 billion. By 1972 trusteed assets of $117.5 billion were more than double the $52.3 billion insured pension reserves.[4]

The growth of trusteed plans was encouraged by broader legal interpretations of the "prudent man" rule to permit significant holdings of common stock in personal trust accounts. While these rulings did not directly affect pension plan monies, they nonetheless provided a more favorable atmosphere for increasing commitments to equity investment.

Most importantly, the growth of trusteed plans and the dialogue between managers and corporate trustees led gradually to a change in the concept of the pension trust fund itself. Rather than the notion of meeting a known liability, the company was funding a distant retirement benefit which, along with public benefits, would be "suitable" to the standard of living that the employee would be

---

[4]Data from *Pension Facts 1974* (New York: Institute of Life Insurance), pp. 16–17, 22.

enjoying at retirement. From this perspective, the commitment of the plan could not be determined by a precise mathematical formula that one calculated today and never changed. Rather, the pension fund was a set of assets to be invested as productively as possible on a long-range basis for the purpose of generating a level of benefits which would carry out its broad retirement objective. The most important implication of such rethinking was to change the problem of investment management from earning a fixed return to earning the best possible rate that available investment opportunities would permit.

As a consequence, common stock investments began to grow in importance as an investment vehicle for pension funds. This is clearly illustrated in Figure 1. From under 20 percent in 1950,

FIGURE 1

Holdings of Private Pension Funds in the United States, 1950–1972
(assets stated in book value)

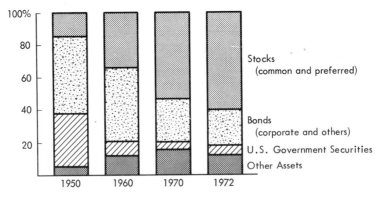

Source: Patrick J. Davey, *Financial Management of Company Pension Plans* (The Conference Board Inc., 1973), p. 34.

equities had grown to well over 60 percent of private noninsured pension monies by 1972 on a book value basis. These overall statistics are confirmed by a Conference Board Survey of 113 major corporate pension plans done in 1973. All of the companies reporting included equity securities in their pension fund portfolios. Stockholdings ranged from a low of 35 percent to a high of 98 percent of pension fund assets at market, with 95 percent of the reporting companies having at least half of their total pension fund investments invested in equities. Bond holdings accounted for

50 percent or more of trust assets for only five companies with just over half of the companies indicating that bond investments accounted for between 10 percent and 25 percent of total trust investments. In the majority of companies, real estate, short-term securities, and other investments, where they were included at all, accounted for 10 percent or less of total pension assets.

The process of rethinking the nature of pension plans has had other results worth noting. As the desire to increase investment returns on pension assets grew, a new set of investment managers, the nonbank managers, arose within the investment community. The principal marketing arguments of these companies were, first, that the banks were too narrow in their investment approach, and second, that they were too large to provide maximum service and attention. It is too soon to know the extent of the impact to be made ultimately by nonbank management groups. There is little question, however, that many of these firms have become important members of the pension fund investment management business. We will consider the question of bank and nonbank managers later in the section on "Selection of Money Managers."

The desire to increase pension fund returns has also led to the use of other investment vehicles by corporations such as participation in either real estate or venture capital pools. In overall dollars, the commitments to either of these vehicles by pension plans is still small. In the Conference Board study of 113 plans, however, a few companies held as much as 20 percent of their assets in real estate. It is too soon to tell whether there will be more attractive vehicles in the future for pension fund investment. We shall take up the question of these alternative investment forms later.

THE DESIGN AND PLANNING OF PENSION FUNDS

Considerations in the Design of Pension Plans

Pension plans are custom-tailored to meet the needs of specific companies and their employees. Furthermore, the task is not finished when the original design is developed. Few pension programs that have been in existence for any length of time are still in their original form. Conditions and needs change and pension plans are typically revised from time to time in order to adapt to the changing environment, particularly employee demands for increased benefits. Because of this and because our main concern is with the financial management aspects of pension plans, the discussion in this section will be confined to a brief outline of the major considerations in plan design and the features which are typically found in plans today.

Who Are Involved?

Pension plan design involves top management, personnel and labor relations people in addition to the financial officer. The company will also require advice from its actuaries, lawyers, and public accountants. Since contributions to pension plans are deductible for corporate income tax purposes, pension plans and changes in plans must be approved in advance by the Internal Revenue Service which has set up standards for acceptable pension plans. In addition to working with actuaries on plan design the company's attorneys must be sure that all requirements of the Internal Revenue Service are met.

It is also the responsibility of the financial officer and the trustees of the pension plan to select the custodian. Insurance companies perform this function for insured pension plans. Normally a bank trust department or a trust company performs this function for trusteed plans. The functions of the custodian include: keeping the actual securities in safe storage; seeing that investment transactions are properly executed regardless of who makes the investment decision; keeping the basic financial records for the trustees; and finally, making payments to retired persons after proper authorization by the trustees.

The two considerations in selecting a custodian are the efficiency of the operation and the cost to the pension trust. Some banks are willing to serve as custodians even though they are not managing all or part of the trust; other banks are unwilling to do so. Rates for these services are usually negotiable, particularly for sizable pension trusts. A study should be made of local and money center banks. Useful information can usually be obtained from clients of the banks in which the company is interested. It is worth making a reasonably thorough study because the level of efficiency and the costs vary considerably.

Major considerations that influence the design of pension plans include work force characteristics, economic conditions, the long-term outlook for the company, the adequacy of existing benefits, and the plans of others, especially competitors. An ideal plan may prove to be a practical impossibility because of financial and other constraints. Therefore, a trade-off between the features desired and the costs involved must be made.

A Checklist

Although individual pension plans differ from one another in such respects as benefit formulas and qualification requirements, they also have much in common. In structuring their pension programs, companies must give consideration to the minimum requirements under ERISA and to the following elements, all of which have financial implications.

1. Participation Requirements. These requirements most frequently take the form of the following:

a. Age or service requirements before becoming eligible for coverage.
b. Limits on maximum age at which employees can join the plan.
c. Establishment of normal retirement age and provisions for retirement before or after the normal retirement age.

2. Funding. Pensions may be funded entirely by the company or jointly by the company and employee contributions. We will not deal here with the special problems of profit sharing plans whose contributions and benefits depend on company profits. These seem to have declined in popularity because they failed to motivate the average employee as hoped and employees seem to prefer fixed dollar pensions to uncertain benefits determined not only by the varying level of company profits but the fluctuation in the value of invested assets. The added cost burdens implied in the Employee Retirement Income Security Act of 1974 could revive an interest in profit sharing plans.

Contributory plans may permit more liberal benefits. The combined contributions will be higher than those of the employer alone and so will support larger benefits. Employee contributions are returned with interest should termination of employment occur prior to the vesting of the pension rights. Contributions from two sources obviously build more protection into the pension plan and tend to discourage abandonment of the plan during economic hard times.

On the other hand, *noncontributory pension plans* provide some advantages. These include:

a. Greater Flexibility. Noncontributory plans means the company has more leeway in establishing a retirement program and in setting the benefits under the program.
b. Easier Administration. There are some cost savings in not being required to persuade workers to participate and not being required to handle payroll deductions and records relating to employee contributions.
c. Tax Benefits. Employer contributions are deductible for income tax purposes whereas employee contributions to pension plans are made from their income after taxes. Added to this is the fact that mounting deductions from workers' gross income for social security taxes make it more difficult for employees to afford contributory retirement programs.

3. Retirement Benefits. The diverse formulas employed by firms to determine their pension benefits can be divided into two major categories—defined contribution and defined benefit.

Under *defined contribution* or *money-purchase* plans which are less common today, a specified percentage of an employee's compensation is contributed by the employer and invested until retirement or termination when it is used to buy whatever it can in the way of retirement benefits. The variable factor in this kind of arrangement is the pension benefit. Identical contributions will produce smaller benefits for older employees than younger ones because of cost considerations. The contributions for the younger worker would be invested over a much longer period than those for the older and would, as a result, accumulate through interest and dividend payments to an amount that would support a larger benefit level.

Defined benefit plans, unlike money-purchase arrangements specify the benefits to be paid out. Contributions, therefore, are the variable in such plans amounting to whatever is needed to produce the defined level of benefits.

The benefits associated with these types of plans are generally determined by one of two computational methods. The first, a percent of pay scheme, provides benefits computed by multiplying a fixed percentage of earnings by years of participation in the plan. For example, an employee with 30 years of service earning a career average of $600 monthly under a plan providing 1.5 percent compensation per year of service would receive $270 monthly (.015 × 30 × 600). A more generous variant of this approach is to base compensation on some average of final years' pay (perhaps the last ten years) rather than career average. The second defined benefit approach is called flat-sum formulas. These provide a flat monthly benefit to all workers who fulfill basic length of service requirements. Probably the most common flat-sum pension plans are those for hourly paid employees where the formula provides a flat dollar amount per month in pension payments for each year of credit at service. For example, the plan may provide $5 per month per year of credit at service. Under such a plan an employee with 30 years of service would receive $150 a month in a pension payment—($5 × 30 = $150).

Many other kinds of benefit formulas also exist. Perhaps the most important of these in the future will be plans that provide for integration of benefits with those offered under social security benefits. Our purpose here has merely been to describe the major methods of computation utilized in pension plans today.

4. Vesting. To date, private pension plans generally fall somewhere between the two extremes of terminal and full immediate vesting. However, ERISA has gone a considerable distance toward constraining the freedom of employers to determine vesting of pension plans. The act essentially specifies that every employee benefit plan must meet one of three minimum vesting rules. First, a ten-year service rule provides 100 percent vesting after ten years of service. Second, a graded 15-year service rule provides 25 percent vesting after 5 years of service, then 5 percent additional vesting for each year of service from year 6 through 10, then 10 percent additional vesting for every year of service from year 11 through 15 so that an employee is 100 percent vested after 15 years of service. Third, the Rule of 45 provides 45 percent to 50 percent vesting after five years' service or, if later, when age plus service equals 45, such percentage increasing by 10 percent each year until 100 percent is reached. Additionally, a participant under the Rule of 45 must be 50 percent vested after 10 years of covered service with the percentage increasing by 10 percent each additional year of covered service so that an employee is 100 percent vested after 15 years regardless of his age.

THE PENSION PLANNING PROCESS

In the early history of pension plans when insured plans were popular, pension planning was a relatively simple process. The firm typically contracted with an insurance carrier to provide a stipulated retirement benefit for covered employees. The benefits were funded by means of fixed, annual premium payments. Modifications and improvements in benefits could be negotiated with the carrier and revised premiums would be paid by the employer. The question of the actuarial rate of return assumption was a simple one since the investments of insurance companies produced quite predictable rates of return.

With the advent of noninsured plans, corporations themselves assumed responsibility for meeting benefit obligations and investing assets. Benefit levels were no longer fixed liabilities but increased with wages and employee needs. As assets were invested in common stocks, higher returns were often achieved by pension funds. In some cases, actuarial assumptions were increased because of increased returns but remained conservative through the early 1960s. Then investment return assumptions began to rise, due in part to the Internal Revenue Service's position that low-interest rate assumptions were an attempt to avoid taxes and due in part to company recognition that increasing the investment return assumption reduced the required pension contribution. Some firms employed this as a cost-cutting tool. Reducing contributions would also add to profits, a maneuver used by the conglomerates in the late 1960s. Finally, increases in investment return assumptions were used to help balance the rising costs of increased benefits.[5]

The major shift from insured to trusteed plans has made the problem of pension planning more formidable. Such apparently unrelated variables as the rate of growth of the work force, government legislation, the rate of inflation, and the return on stocks and bonds, all influence the decisions of the financial officer. Moreover,

---

[5] For some interesting observations on the question of realistic rates of return, see C. Ellis, "Cautions on Pension ROI Assumptions," *Harvard Business Review*, July–August 1972.

the net effect of changes in combinations of these factors may in some cases be cumulative and in others offsetting.

A Planning Framework

Successful pension planning begins with the development of a framework that logically integrates these many parts of the process and evaluates the net impact of their interaction. Figure 2 outlines one such overview.

Before any investment decisions can be made, the corporation must first study its plan to determine just what the needs of the corporation are and how these might change in the future. The goal is to arrive at a model which will project into the future the benefits to be paid out and the accrued liabilities generated by those benefits. The firm's actuary usually has the job of building such a model based on three sets of inputs.

First, from the firm itself, the actuary will receive information that is unique to the company. This consists of such factors as the specific provisions of the pension plan, projections for growth or change in the work force and expected benefit revision and liberalization. To this information the actuary adds assumptions about mortality rates, employee turnover, and investment return. Finally, to make the model as realistic as possible, it is important to include the impact of changes in the external environment. This will include revisions necessary to comply with present or prospective legislation, revisions required to remain competitive with other companies in the same industry or geographic area, realistic inflation assumptions, trends in social security benefits, and so on.

Once the firm has developed a realistic model, it is possible to establish a schedule of projected benefit payouts and accrued liabilities. Using this, the company can first make a judgment about what percentage of the assets of the plan should be kept in conservative, highly marketable securities to meet liquidity needs. The next job is to compare the corporation's needs, as defined by this schedule of benefits and liabilities, with different investment strategies in order to estimate possible contribution levels. A dialogue with present or possible future investment managers can be of help here. There is a trade-off between the cost of funding the plan, return on investment, and the riskiness of any investment strategy. Investment managers can be helpful in assessing the degree of risk

FIGURE 2
The Pension Problem in Perspective

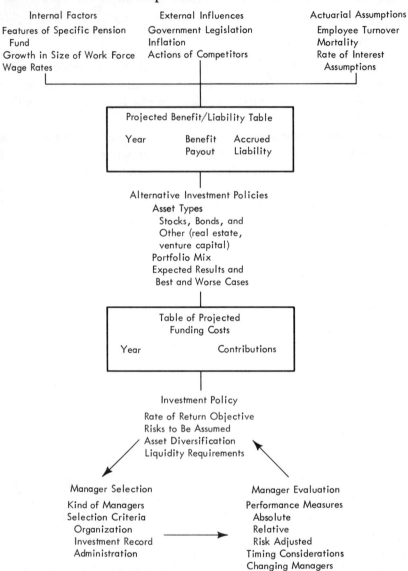

involved. Through such a dialogue, an investment policy can be developed that best meets the needs of the specific plan.

It is also possible to hire one of several firms that have developed computerized pension planning models. These computer programs can test different assumptions about the returns to be received from different investment strategies and assess the effects on the projected contribution schedules. Some of the models that have been developed go a step further and permit various inputs to the planning model as probability distributions. For example, one can specify that while a best guess for inflation in the next five years is 7 percent or 8 percent, it could be as low as 5 percent and as high as 10 percent. With data like this, models can generate the probability distribution of projected contributions.

This would provide an estimate of the magnitude of the reduction or increase in contributions that would occur in the event of either good or bad investment results.

The Development of an Investment Policy Statement

Once the firm has decided what its goals are and has arrived at a general investment policy, the next task is to prepare an accurate and logically consistent statement of the investment policy. This will serve as a focus for ongoing discussions with both existing and potential new managers. It is important that the statement be written as carefully and precisely as possible.

Policy statements appear in as many different forms as there are different companies and no one structure is better than another. Regardless of form, however, there are topics that should be included in any complete policy statement.

The first element to be considered is a statement of the rate of return expectations for the funds. This may be stated in either absolute or relative terms. Because the funding of the plan is predicated in part upon an assumed rate of interest, there is a tendency to think of an investment return objective in absolute terms such as "a target rate of 9 percent compounded annually over a period of five years." This approach, while convenient for planning purposes, is not as practical from an investment point of view. The rate of return on any portfolio is related to the investment markets which fluctuate over any period of time, thus making an absolute rate of return a questionable investment objective. Nonetheless, a minimum acceptable return based on dividends and long-term bond notes may not be unreasonable. A second approach is a goal relative to some market index such as the Standard & Poor's "500." This has value since it accounts for whatever conditions prevail in the general marketplace. The final commonly used specification is a goal relative to other pension funds. For example, a company could specify that it wanted its managers to be consistently in the top 25th percentile of pension funds monitored by one of several firms who monitor and measure investment performance. This third approach has the virtue of accounting not only for conditions in the general market but also results obtained by managers with similar objectives. When grouped with funds managed with similar investment risk, the approach has added value in cases where there is reason to believe that the money is being managed either very conservatively or very aggressively—that is, in a fashion quite different from the general market.

The second area to be considered in the policy statement should be some indication of the risk levels the firm has determined to be acceptable. This is a difficult characteristic to describe due to a lack of any wholly satisfactory definition of risk. Thus, this portion of the investment policy statement can vary from general statements such as "management should follow the prudent man rule" or "management should not take undue risk" to more quantitative considerations. The latter generally fall into one of three categories. The first approaches risk from the point of view of the risk inherent in any individual investment. For example, the policy statement could say that the risk inherent in a 15 to 25 percent expected rate of return on an individual security acceptable, while those inherent in returns of less than 10 percent are too conservative and more than 25 percent too risky. This method suffers from many shortcomings, the most important of which is a concentration on individual securities and not the portfolio itself. A second quantitative measure characterizes risk in terms of the variability of period rates of return. For example, a company may specify as acceptable risk a certain maximum percentage fluctuation in the annual rates of return. A final approach can look at risk in terms of the volatility of the overall portfolio. This is the so-called Beta theory which has gained some popularity in recent years, in which portfolio volatility is measured relative to the market in general.

More quantitively oriented people often use an approach such as Beta analysis while the more qualitative attempt to define verbally, as carefully as possible, the desired risk level. The only thing to remember is the basic law of capital markets that risk and return go hand in hand. If a manager is expected to outperform the market by 20 percent or 30 percent, it must be expected that he will assume more portfolio risk than if his objective were to only equal the market. Moreover, despite all of our better wishes, the odds are that managers who can outperform the market on the upside will also do worse than the market during declines. The reverse would, of course, hold true for conservative investment managers. In laying out an investment policy, then, it is important to always bear in mind the improbability of achieving at the same time the highest return and the lowest risk.

A third area of concern in the policy statement should be the allocation of funds to different types of assets. The most important consideration is the ratio between equity and fixed-income investments. This may be left to the discretion of the investment manager, or the company may specify the percentage of stocks and bonds to be held at any time and may also indicate the process by which that ratio should be reviewed and possibly changed. Some companies also include in their policy statements specification of the maximum percentage of the portfolio to be invested in any single industry group or security. Obviously, any or all of these issues may be left to the discretion of the portfolio manager, or they may be specified in detail.

A fourth consideration of the policy statement should be the liquidity objectives of the plan. This includes specification of the percentage of the assets of the fund that are to be kept in short-term, highly marketable securities. Future benefit payout needs will be a major determinant of the level of reserves held.

A fifth area to be included should be a statement of any limitations on the kinds of investment vehicles or types of transaction prohibited by the plan. Typically, this would include forbidding short sales, option trading, margin transactions, use of letter stock, or private placements. Less common would be limitations on foreign securities and over-the-counter securities. Most policy instructions prohibit investment in securities of the corporation itself.

Finally, the statement should include some indication of the kinds of information the company will require. A detailed statement would describe such items as the desired frequency and content of reports, requests for copies of all transactions and a description of the frequency and content of the regular meetings to be held between the manager and the company. On the other hand, it is common for companies to be more general and simply agree to accept the standard reporting practices of their investment manager.

SELECTION OF MONEY MANAGERS

An Overview

Once the firm has articulated its objectives by means of the investment policy statement, it can turn its attention to the selection of investment managers. Moreover, the firm can evaluate the investment style and approach of management organizations in the context of its own needs rather than just by comparing performance numbers.

Investment managers have different styles. They can stress selection of securities or timing of purchases and sales; they can have low or high turnover rates; they can specialize in large growth companies or special situations; they can have bond as well as stock expertise; and so on. It is most important at the outset to understand that studies show that no one style is clearly superior to any other. There is no "best" way to manage money, and there are no two or three top firms with a corner on investment management skill. Rather one should match investment style with the needs of the plan.

It is also important to resist the temptation to view the investment process like an operating division of a corporation which has certain inputs and designated costs which will produce predictable results at some consistent rate. Instead, investment management should be compared with the professions. Flesh and blood people possessing intellectual skills and a body of knowledge are trying their best to practice the profession in a professional manner. Like doctors and lawyers, the investment professional is devoted to his clients' interest, spends a lifetime learning as well as practicing in a field where no one can know all and realizes that each "case" or "situation" is unique. If there is an "art" to investing, it is so to the same degree that a good doctor seems to have an "intuition" about his diagnosis or a good lawyer a "feel" for the law. One wonders if this sensitivity is not itself a result of accumulated and assimilated professional experience.

But investment management is changing rapidly, perhaps more rapidly than law or medicine. Changes in the world economy dictate adjustments in the traditional financial outlook, and, what is most difficult, the investment manager feels he is shooting at a moving target whose gyrations are powered by the emotions of millions of investors. Yet, the success of one's marksmanship is measureable each and every moment.

Criteria for Selection

In spite of the intangible nature of the investment process, the selection of investment managers should be a rational process. There are common denominators—basic characteristics and qualities—that distinguish the better money managers from those of lesser quality. We would divide these into three major parts—organization, performance record, and administrative management. Each of these can be subdivided, and our purpose will be to highlight some of the more important aspects. Unfortunately, the imprecise nature of the process prevents placing exact weightings on each piece of information or impression which could then be tallied systematically with the manager scoring the most points being selected. Our approach will be rather to deal with each of these three parts separately, briefly discussing the important considerations in each.

Organization. It has been said repeatedly that the investment management business is a people business. Therefore, the decision of manager selection must be weighted heavily toward an evaluation of the organization and the people within it.

Professionalism must begin at the top since the leaders lend direction to the entire organization and are responsible for its success. One dimension of this is an assessment of the investment skills of the firm's senior management. One useful measure is the investment backgrounds of the principals and their prior success in the investment business. A second is the extent to which they can articulate a logically consistent philosophy of investment to which they have adhered through adverse as well as favorable market cycles. Finally, there should be depth and scope to leadership both to step in should one of the principals leave and, also, to present divergent styles and contrary opinions.

It is not sufficient, however, that the senior personnel display superior investment skills. They are also responsible for the management of the people resources of the firm. There are a number of considerations to be evaluated in this regard. One important measure is the extent to which less senior individuals are being groomed for positions of greater responsibility as opposed to bringing in outsiders to fill vacancies. A negative indication is high personnel turnover at lower levels.

Another measure of the quality of the firm's leadership is the ability to balance successfully the discipline required to maintain a consistent investment philosophy with an environment that encourages individual talent and initiative. To assess this, one must examine the firm's portfolio review system. Accounts should be reviewed regularly to monitor the performance of each manager and to ensure that the firm's overall strategy is being carried out. These reviews should include senior personnel. Another plus for top management is the encouragement of peer review through an open forum where the investment decisions and portfolios of each individual manager are subject to the scrutiny of fellow managers. This is a strong sign that top management has created a positive, healthy environment that can benefit the firm and its clients.

Another characteristic of a professional organization is the structure or mechanism by which information and ideas flow from analyst to portfolio manager and among portfolio managers. There are firms where analysts and portfolio managers seldom get together except on structured occasions. There are firms where portfolio managers do not share ideas among themselves because of an overly competitive environment. High-quality investment managers have a planned system for circulating internal and external information. In such firms there will not only be formal information-gathering systems but there will be an open and informal work atmosphere which encourages the free exchange of ideas.

The final measure of the high quality investment management firm is the most difficult to specify in tangible terms, yet it is an extremely significant one. Essentially, it involves distinguishing between whether the people view their activities as simply a job or, instead, a way of life. It is the difference between people being highly motivated and really enjoying their work and simply filling up time and space in order to earn a living. While maintaining an exciting environment is not sufficient in itself to guarantee success, it is probably one of the necessary ingredients.

Investment Management Record. In addition to organizational characteristics, one must analyze performance records to see if they confirm one's impression of quality. But, again, to look superficially is to invite trouble. There are many ways to measure past investment performance and each investment manager will have shaped the data to make his own record more attractive. Thus, while judgments are possible, one should not expect to obtain exact comparisons among various potential money managers. One has to consider where the market was at the starting and ending point of the time span under consideration. Performance cannot be judged realistically without relating it to broad-based indices such as the Standard & Poor's "500." One must relate it also to the record of other institutional investors and one has to look at a meaningful time span to see how the firm has performed in a full market cycle, through a down as well as an up market, usually a minimum of three years. Moreover, it is well to remember that an outstanding past record is no guarantee of future results. For this reason, it is important to understand how the performance results relate to the investment philosophy and strategies of the particular manager.

One of the characteristics that separates the successful investment manager from his less successful counterpart is the quality of research. At least as important as examining the past investment record is the determination that the potential money manager has a continuing source of quality investment ideas. Measures that are of use in making such an assessment would include the size of the in-house research staff, the manner in which they are organized, the track records of the analysts, the size of the universe of companies followed—too large a list can dilute quality, the amount of research received for directed brokerage and the mechanism by which this research is merged with the in-house research effort.

This is only a partial list and is intended to be suggestive of the types of measures that are useful. What one is after is the determination of the degree to which the firm has a well-planned research-gathering system that takes maximum advantage of all internal and external information sources.

A final area that sometimes is useful as a selection criterion is the number and types of accounts managed by the individual portfolio manager. There can be no rule as to the number of accounts one individual should manage, but fewer accounts permit more attention per account. Size, level of activity, investment objectives, and the ability of each portfolio manager makes any fixed rule regarding account load impossible. However, some general principles do exist. An account manager should have responsibility for accounts which have similar investment objectives. Growth-oriented accounts should not be mixed with those which stress preservation of capital. Tax-exempt accounts should not be mixed with taxable accounts. The decision-making process is different in each of those cases.

Administrative Considerations. A more mundane though no less important area of concern involves administrative matters. Here there are two major considerations, the first of which is the fee schedule of the investment firm. While high fee levels are certainly no guarantee of superior results, it is generally true that you get what you pay for in the investment business. There is a limited supply of talented people in the business, and compensation levels reflect the quality of those individuals. A firm must have a fee schedule sufficient to support a high caliber staff and provide a reasonable return on shareholders' investment.

It is important to determine that the firm's fee schedule is generally in line with the rest of the investment industry. However, contrary to the usual concern, one should be more apprehensive about a schedule out of line on the low rather than the high side. It is well to remember that it takes only a small improvement in performance to offset higher fees.

The second major consideration relates to reporting and record-keeping. There will be various reports that must be prepared for agement. This is a less glamorous area but it is nonetheless essential that the prospective manager has the capability to meet these requirements. Above all, it is well to be certain that the firm has devoted sufficient attention to the operational side of money management. This is a less glamorous area but it is nonetheless essential that the firm have an up-to-date accounting system, a smooth-running back office, an efficient trading desk, and the ability to meet whatever deadlines are required for reporting purposes.

The Search Process

The next step is to conduct a search for appropriate pension fund managers. If the financial officer should decide to do the work with the staff he has available, the first step is to translate the above criteria into a questionnaire which can be mailed to potential pension fund managers. Many lists of pension fund managers are available which provide information on present clients, size, personnel, organizational affiliations, and so on.

In choosing a manager, the most important options available are: large bank trust departments; regional bank trust departments; mutual fund manager affiliates; independent investment advisors, insurance companies, and in-house management. In our discussions, we shall ignore the in-house management alternative. A few firms such as General Electric and U.S. Steel have managed their own pension funds successfully for many years but the costs of maintaining a competent, competitive staff, particularly in research, are so great that this is not an attractive alternative for most firms.

Performance data reveals no consistent differences in investment performance between types of managers so there is little reason for preferring one group to the exclusion of another. There are some important considerations worthy of note, however. First, some people feel that it is wise for a company with a relatively small portfolio (that is, up to $20–$25 million) to avoid the very largest management firms. In an organization managing $5, $10, or more billion dollars, a small account may receive less attention than it would at a smaller investment management organization. Second, the company is probably wise to avoid an investment management firm without a substantial in-house research organization. In the competitive world of investment management, such firms probably will have trouble surviving in the future.

Third, a misconception that many financial officers labor under when choosing managers is that banks are still more staid and inflexible than, say, an investment counseling firm. There need not be differences between the two. A large counseling firm may operate in a fashion identical to that of a trust department, except that the firm cannot act as trustee and hold the assets. And a smaller bank might look very much like a smaller counseling firm. Many old shibboleths about banks have not been true for years. Many banks now pay competitively so that they can attract and retain talent, and systems have evolved that allow individual portfolio managers more discretion within guidelines and directives set down by department heads that are no different from the checks and balances operative at large counseling firms. What one should look for in considering any investment group is how it meets the selection criteria rather than attaching stereotypes to any one kind of manager.

It is true that most investment management organizations have some other affiliation. Trust departments are affiliated with the commercial side of banks and investment managers are usually associated with an insurance company, mutual fund group, or brokerage firm. Conflicts of interest are possible because of these affiliations. However, dishonest games can be played by any organization. The only assurance of honesty is to deal with honest people. It should be mentioned, too, that there are advantages to these affiliations. The officers of the bank will try to make sure the trust department is well run; the brokerage firm or mutual fund group can lend economic and security research strength to the investment arm; and so on. Access to further professionalism should be an advantage in bettering performance.

Once the questionnaires have been returned, the most attractive candidates should be interviewed personally and in depth, probably over a period of time. Regardless of the objective criteria set up, an important part of the decision will be the subjective opinion of the people who will be actively involved in the administration of the funds. These opinions should be formed carefully and slowly. It is quite important to visit the offices of the investment manager to form an impression of the kind of organization involved and to meet a larger number of people than normally make sales calls. Time spent on home ground with a management firm will allow corporate officers to identify professionalism. The top professionals have an inherent sense of quality in all that they do, and that quality is usually discernable.

In light of the obviously imprecise and time-consuming process that has been described, it is hardly surprising that a few firms have specialized in aiding pension plan administrators in the selection and evaluation of investment managers. The outside consultant can make a good deal of sense, particularly for a firm with neither the time nor the resources to conduct a search of its own. Moreover, the consulting firm can make the process less painful. For example, the high-quality consulting firm will have already developed and tested a useful questionnaire for screening candidates. The development of such a questionnaire involves a good deal of time and resources and is expensive for the small firm to develop. Second, on the basis of an investment policy statement, the consulting firm can reduce the universe of managers to a small number. Doing the job alone generally means seeing and hearing from many managers, a large percentage of whom are simply not right for the particular plan under consideration. Third, the consultant can handle the tedious detail of scheduling the presentations for the final set of candidates.

One disadvantage of using a consultant is that the firm does not gain first-hand experience in the selection process. This kind of "black-box" approach means the firm may have to hire a consultant each time it selects another manager. The consultant gains experience through the search process, not the company's staff.

Most of the consulting firms that are well known in the business will do an adequate job. An obvious caveat is to avoid the firm with the reputation for recommending managers with whom it has less than an arm's-length relationship. As in many other business activities, one is well served to check with other financial managers who have used consultants in the past allowing one's self to be guided by their recommendations or complaints in building an initial list of possible candidate consultants.

Other Considerations

Multiple Management. To this point we have confined our discussions to the criteria for selecting a particular manager. There is the further question of the appropriate number of managers to employ. Splitting funds among managers has become popular within recent years. Three main reasons (other than the obvious one of size—for example, American Telephone and Telegraph simply could not let only one manager handle its assets) have spurred interest in the use of multiple managers. The first is that managers competing against one another will try harder and so do better. While such a strategy may be successful in a rising market, it carries with it great risk. With each manager striving aggressively to outperform the others, the total portfolio could be particularly vulnerable during a market decline. For this reason, it may be useful to measure performance on a risk adjusted basis.

The second reason for multiple management is to diversify across different investment styles. Since no investment style is superior for all market conditions, it seems reasonable to diversify by dividing assets among more than one investment style. This does not refer to dividing funds between bond managers and common stock managers. The company may decide to hire one or more firms solely for the management of bonds, or it may decide to hire firms with capabilities in both areas. Rather, this refers to various styles of common stock investment. As the firms specializing in pension fund management grow larger and as the business becomes more competitive, there is a tendency for the differences in investment style to diminish. Nevertheless, some firms frankly represent themselves as growth stock investors. Others put more emphasis on cash management in an effort to call stock market cycles hoping to achieve investment performance by increasing cash at the top of markets and investing it at the bottom. Some firms place great emphasis on "fundamental value" and basic assets investing. Some firms attempt to adjust their investment strategy to business cycles while others try to minimize exposure to the business cycle, and so on. Without commenting on the appropriateness of any of these investment styles, it would not be wise for a corporation to hire all managers who profess to follow the same investment style. Rather, diversification by investment style could well be one of the most worthwhile forms of diversification for the pension fund.

Finally, splitting managers also permits the firm to diversify across different risk levels. For example, one may elect to have equal portions of the total portfolio run by three separate managers—the first, aggressive; the second, moderate; and the third, conservative so that the overall risk profile of the entire fund would be a fairly moderate one. For those who are inclined to beta analysis, control on overall risk levels can be achieved by requiring each manager over time to keep his portfolio within a predetermined beta range.

Using split management to control risk and diversify across styles has implications also for allocating additional cash flows to the fund. As long as the corporate trustees are satisfied with their desired risk exposure, new cash flows should be allocated in a balanced way to keep the percentage of funds being handled by each manager approximately constant. It is only when there is agreement that the objectives of the fund should be altered or that a manager has shown clearly superior long-term performance that the balance should be changed. Above all, allocation of monies on the basis of short-term performance is a risky strategy. Not only is performance not correlated over short periods, but such an allocation scheme leads managers to be overly aggressive in an attempt to secure the additional cash flows.

Bond Management. Regardless of whether the corporation decides to employ firms specializing in bond management only or firms with the dual capability of managing equity and bond port-folios, it is important to select a manager organized to manage bond portfolios actively. In the past, efforts to increase returns on fixed-income portfolios were concentrated to a large extent in efforts to obtain higher than market yields through the purchase of bonds with somewhat higher yields because of acceptable but higher credit risks or participation in private placements. This strategy sacrificed marketability and made it difficult to switch the portfolio during times of change. The intention usually was to hold any bond purchased to maturity. Modern bond management has concentrated on efforts to outperform the long-term bond market over an ex-tended period of time by: first, varying the average maturity de-pending upon the direction of long-term interest rates; second, emphasizing market sectors which currently appear undervalued; and, finally to the extent possible in the current market, taking advantage of short-term market aberrations through bond "swaps." The management of such a portfolio requires a high level of marketability. This kind of portfolio might vary from an average maturity of 10–12 years to an average maturity of 22–24 years depending upon the judgment as to whether long-term interest rates over the coming months are likely to increase or decrease. Short-term fluctuations are, of course, extremely hard to predict and so these movements in average maturities are likely to be gradual.

In selecting money managers, the process by which assets get allocated between stocks and bonds must be carefully developed. If managers who specialize either in bond or stock investment are chosen, the corporation will have to make the asset allocation decision. The alternative is to use a manager who is competent to manage both equities and fixed-income securities. Such a firm should display historically the economic skills and disciplines to make bond/stock ratio decisions on a timely basis.

RELATIONSHIP WITH MANAGERS

Introduction

Effective communications between the corporation and its in-vestment manager is an important element of all successful invest-ment programs. Quite often little attention is paid to the steps that can be taken to aid in building a sound relationship with the manager. After the pension fund managers have been selected, it is appropriate to schedule a meeting with each of the new managers to be sure that everyone has a common understanding of the objectives of the fund and the performance expectations of the corporate trustees. While these items should have been discussed during the presentations and meetings with the selection committee, various points may have been overlooked or misunderstood due to the nature of the selection process. Another purpose of this meeting is to settle the numerous accounting and operational questions such as responsibility for the transfer of securities, reporting deadlines and requirements for future meetings with the board or committee.

If the company intends to employ an outside consultant to help in monitoring performance, this relationship should be made clear. When appropriate, brokerage to pay such consultants must be arranged. Finally, during this meeting there should be a clear understanding as to how investment results are to be measured. It is also important to be sure that the managers clearly understand the time horizon which will be utilized for determining their success or failure. These are the final responsibilities remaining in the pension fund administration area, and we now turn our attention to them.

The development of a system for evaluating investment managers must relate to the nature of the assets being invested. Since pension plans are intended to provide benefits for employees 20 and 30 years into the future, their assets are being invested for the long term. Above all, focusing on short-term performance results is not appropriate. What must be stressed is that it takes time for a manager to structure a portfolio, that no group can be a manager for all seasons and all markets and that performance must be judged in the context of what the market as a whole and other managers have done. Corporate officers may become too concerned with short-term performance. Too often managers are compared to other managers as though the management of the fund were a horse race, manager pitted against manager. Managers who sense this attitude, or are openly informed of it, may try to outshine others every quarter by deviating from their own investment philosophy in favor of the "hot game" of the moment. Or, if they have not been doing well and know they face being fired because of a few poor quarters, they may take inappropriate risks in the hope they will catch up by the next quarterly reporting time.

Some of the pressure for this kind of investment behavior comes, as has been mentioned, from top management of corporations. Chief executive officers in some cases have become so alarmed by the quarterly figures that they have leaped into decision making without knowing enough about the nature of investment management. They have asked that an investment manager be fired because of poor performance over even a short term and have wanted to hire a manager whose record superficially looks good without considering the time frame of that record, the quality of that firm, the degree of risks it takes, the consistency of its approach and performance, and other key matters. One danger of this tendency to think in terms of short-term performance is that it has corroded the investment arena by encouraging portfolio managers to dump blocks of stocks because a company has one or two bad quarters and to flock into groups of stocks currently in favor. This is what, more than anything else, has created the volatility and illiquidity of the market, the huge drops in stocks when a number of institutional investors try to get out of big positions all at once, the public's fear of and disillusionment with the market and even the doubts of many business people about the rationality of the financial marketplace. This is what happened to mutual funds that played the short-term performance game in order to attract public savings. Their performance mania led to speculation and the collapse of many of the funds and the public's eventual disillusionment with them. Since pension funds own many times as many securities as mutual funds, they can do even more harm by following a course that those who care about a free market deplore.

While such an approach is harmful to the security markets generally, it has important implications for the fund itself. Opportunism cannot work over any extended period. Instead, it encourages the tendency to play the game of the moment—be it growth stocks, shortage stocks, cyclicals, reversion to cash or whatever is in vogue—but such managers will make a misstep sooner or later. These managers in attempting to follow the course that is currently successful will end up adopting an approach that worked well in the last market—for example, going into bonds or cash just before a bull market in stocks or making large commitments to high growth stocks at the tops of markets—so that they are always out of synchronization with the market.

What the corporate officer should look for instead is consistency of approach and consistency of performance. Studies have shown that the investment managers that have done better than average but have not been at the top every year have produced the best results for their clients over the long run. While the system for evaluating managers we describe in the following section includes the calculation of quarterly measures of performance, it is important to keep in mind that the purpose of the system is not to create a stick with which to whip the manager but rather a focal point around which can revolve the ongoing dialogue between investment manager and corporate officers.

The corporate officer and the investment manager should agree on a reasonable time period over which to measure performance. For the poorly performing manager, any time period is too short. Probably a full market cycle (three to four years) should be sufficient.

The Measurement of Investment Performance

The basic component of any system for evaluating investment managers is a calculation of rate of return for any particular time period. There are two different calculations for measuring portfolio performance, internal rate of return, and time-weighted rate of return.

An internal rate of return is the equivalent of the discount rate which is applied in the calculation to determine the present value of a dollar. As applied to calculating the rate of return in a portfolio, it is the constant growth rate at which the beginning assets of a portfolio must grow to equal the ending value adjusted for capital changes that occur during the time period. The internal rate of return computed over long time periods is an essential measure for it shows what the actual return has been on the capital employed. Thus, it can readily be compared to the actuarially required rate of return.

However, the internal rate of return calculation is dependent upon the specific contributions (cash flows) in and out of a portfolio. Since the portfolio manager has no control over such cash flows, the internal rate of return should not be used to measure his performance. The appropriate measure for evaluating investment performance is the time-weighted rate of return. This problem may be seen in the following simplified example:

On the first day of the month, a portfolio is worth $100. It rises to $200 by the end of the month partially because of a contribution of $90 made at mid-month. Using the approximation of the internal rate of return calculation developed by Peter Dietz[6] which is ending market value minus one-half cash flow divided by beginning market value plus one-half cash flow, the internal rate of return calculation would indicate a 6.9 percent rate of return.

$$\frac{\$200 - \frac{1}{2} \times \$90}{\$100 + \frac{1}{2} \times \$90} = 6.9\%$$

The internal rate of return of 6.9 percent is that constant growth rate at which $100 plus $90 (weighted for the number of days it was in the portfolio) would have to grow to equal $200 at the end of the period.

However, in the above example, suppose we had known that just before the contribution of $90 was made, that is at mid-month, our portfolio was already worth $110. This means that by mid-month, the portfolio manager has invested in stocks that have risen by 10 percent. Further, suppose that the entire portfolio remained flat for the last half of the month. Under these circumstances the manager's performance for the whole month would be 10 percent, not 6.9 percent.

Calculated on this basis, a time-weighted rate of return seeks to minimize the distorting effects of dollar flows by computing performance for each subperiod in which there was a capital flow and then linking subperiods in computing the total period return. In the above example, we show that the rate of return for the first half of the month was 10 percent and 0 percent for the last half. Linking these subperiod returns and weighting each return by the period of time for which it applies yields the more correct performance of the manager of the portfolio. The time-weighted return is 10 percent determined by the simple computation: $(1.1) \times (1.0) = 1.10$ or 10%.

It is this weighted averaging of subperiod rates, where the weights are not dollars but time periods, that is basic to the time-weighted rate. Since cash flow dollars were not permitted to affect portfolio value, any distortion caused by them is eliminated. The result is that time-weighted rates respond only to changes in value of the assets in which the manager has invested and not to changes

---

[6] Peter O. Dietz, *Pension Funds Measuring Investment Performance* (New York: Free Press, 1966).

in the level of invested capital over which the manager may not have control. This feature makes time-weighted rates of return more valid for measuring portfolio manager performance. It should be recognized, of course, that if there are no cash flows into or out of the portfolio, both time-weighted and internal rates will give the same measured result.

Ideally, to compute time-weighted rates, one must (1) determine the market value of a portfolio at the instant the cash flow occurs, (2) compute the subperiod rate, and (3) link subperiod rates using weighted averages. The costs of computing rates on this basis are prohibitive, and in the mid-1960s, the Bank Administration Institute developed two alternative computational procedures which closely approximate the exact rate, are less costly and therefore have become widely accepted. These two approximation techniques, the regression method and the linked internal rate of return method, have gained about equal popularity although we would prefer the latter on the basis of ease of understanding and computation. This method operates as follows. First, we divide the desired period of time (for example, a quarter) into equal subperiods (for example, months). Second, we compute the approximate internal rate of return for each of the equal subperiods. Extensive testing has shown that for short periods of time such as months, the internal and time-weighted rates of return will not differ substantially unless there have been cash contributions greater than 15 percent of the market value of the portfolio. Therefore, using these monthly internal rates of return as approximations for the monthly time-weighted rates of return, one links together those subperiod returns to form the time-weighted rate of return for the quarter. In its study on pension fund performance measurement, the Bank Administration Institute recommended that time-weighted rates of return be calculated quarterly.[7]

In addition to computing absolute rates of return, any reasonable assessment of performance will include comparisons to other types of funds or market indices. The most common practice is to compare equity results to the Dow Jones Industrial Average, the Standard & Poor's "500," the New York Stock Exchange Composite or some combination of these. While helpful in evaluating performance,

[7] Bank Administration Institute, Kalman J. Cohen, et al., _Measuring the Investment Performance of Premium Funds_ (Park Ridge, Ill.: Bank Administration Institute, 1968).

it is important to recognize that such a comparison presents only a partial picture of events in the marketplace. Both those popular indices are value weighted. Thus, a 1 percent move in IBM will have a much greater impact on the S&P "500," for example, than an identical percent change in a smaller issue. Attention to only value-weighted indices can be misleading. For example, in the first quarter of 1974 while the S&P was down over 5 percent, a number of unweighted indices were actually ahead slightly. The general market had outperformed the larger issues. There are a number of unweighted indices available on a regular basis. It appears the most popular of these are the Indicator Digest Index and the Value Line Index. As far as the fixed-income portion of the portfolio is concerned, several market indices are also available. The most popular of these currently are probably the Solomon Brothers or Kuhn, Loeb indexes.

Expanding comparative analysis to encompass both weighted and unweighted averages still only focuses on unmanaged portfolios. To round out the analysis, the company should compare performance of its managers to that of others responsible for similar kinds of portfolios. The best sources for comparative evaluation would be A. G. Becker, Merrill Lynch, Frank Russell Co., Inc., Callan Associates, Inc., Blyth Eastman Dillon, among others.

Any quality investment management organization will have incorporated the concepts discussed above into some sort of computerized system for reporting to clients on a regular basis, usually quarterly. If funds have been split among managers, there are two choices available for achieving comparable results across managers. First, the company can carefully check that each manager is using the same computations in measuring performance. Differences usually occur in the approximation technique used to measure time-weighted returns or in the assumption about the exact timing of cash flows in and out of the portfolio. Even if calculation techniques are identical, there is still the job of accepting input—usually in differing formats—from each manager and then organizing this data in a meaningful way for the pension committee. Because this approach entails considerable staff time, many companies prefer to engage the services of one of a set of outside firms (this work is often done by consultants who also aid in manager selection) who will assume the dual chores of securing comparability of results across managers and organizing performance data in appropriate formats. These services often include a verification of securities purchased and sold, dividends and interest received, and so on.

Currently, only a small percentage of corporations employ quantitative estimates of risk for performance measurement purposes although the number is probably up substantially from a few years ago. In the Conference Board Study dated 1973, only 41 out of 117 companies surveyed made any attempt at quantifying risk levels. As discussed in an earlier section on investment policy formulation, the entire area of risk definition, and therefore quantification, is one of controversy.

The Total Relationship

In addition to expecting its investment managers to report the rate of return accurately along with comparative performance figures, the corporation has a right to expect to be kept informed on the investment thinking and portfolio strategy of the manager. At least quarterly the corporation should receive from each investment manager a summary of its current economic thinking, an analysis of strategic investment changes which are planned for the future, a summary of changes which have been made in the portfolio since the last review and, of course, an accurate listing of the current portfolio. In addition to these regularly written reports, a good investment manager will keep in regular contact with his clients. Formal meetings with the corporate trustees should be scheduled at least once a year—quarterly may be too often. The staff people responsible for pension fund management have a right to expect regular phone calls from their investment managers as matters of particular importance arise. Those responsible at the corporate level for pension fund investments should feel very free to insist that their investment managers provide an adequate, continuous flow of information.

This kind of ongoing dialogue allows the corporation to judge the managers on two counts—their performance measured on a quantitative basis and the professional quality evident on an ongoing basis in the conduct of their business. The corporation can understand why performance was as it was and decide if the managers have been and are in command of the situation, even if recent short-term performance has been disappointing. If the corporation has a pension officer, this monitoring can be continuous. That does not mean that he is judging performance on a daily basis. What he can do is be certain that the guidelines given to the managers are not being abrogated. It does not mean that the officer will continually question and second-guess the managers which would be an impossible situation for those managers. It is the responsibility of the pension officer to see that the managers operate according to the strategies and follow the investment philosophy they espoused when retained. If they are buying cyclicals, which implies an ability at timing the market's turns, when they said their strength was picking growth stocks, or if they are buying third-rate companies whose stocks are "hot" when they were hired to buy quality companies, the pension officer should ask for and receive an explanation. If turnover becomes excessive in terms of the expected approach to the market, again an explanation is necessary. The pension officer can also watch for turnover in personnel which can be crucial considering the fact that it is professional expertise the company has hired. What the officer gains from his dialogue with his managers is not the imposition of his own investment judgment, whether explicit or implied, but a feeling of whether or not the investment managers are indeed following a consistent approach.

Changing Investment Managers

One can never be entirely right in making a series of decisions no matter how much care is taken in the decision-making process. From time to time, circumstances of one type or another force corporations to change their advertising agencies, law firms, and even their public accounting firms. Certainly, mistakes and misjudgments are made in hiring employees at any level. Pension fund investment managers are no different. The primary caution is the same as that with public accountants and law firms. If the original selection has been made after extended study and with care, a good deal of time, and perhaps patience, will be necessary to see how the choice will work out. Unless there is some serious deterioration in the firm which has been selected, at least three years, and perhaps five, are needed to evaluate the abilities of an investment manager. Some investment managers perform well in one type of economic or investment environment and not in another so that a full market cycle is essential. The manager who did poorly last year can well be the one that does best this year.

Since change is sometimes necessary, however, it might be advisable to mention danger signals or signs that should make the corporation particularly cautious. One of these is a lack of continuity in the investment personnel at all levels. Unusual turnover in the research department, frequent changes in top management or portfolio management are certainly indications that all is not well. Normally a corporation employs an investment manager because that manager's investment style fits in with the needs of the corporation. Signs that the manager's approach to investments changes rapidly or under stress are certainly danger signals. Finally, difficulty in communicating with the investment manager and a lack of regular attention to the corporation's problems bear immediate investigation.

OTHER TYPES OF INVESTMENT VEHICLES

Investment Vehicles Other Than Marketable Fixed-Income and Equity Investments

The company with less than $50 million or even $100 million in pension funds would in most cases be wise to limit its pension fund investments to marketable securities, debt instruments of various maturities, and U.S. common stocks. Broader diversification into real estate, a variety of foreign securities or venture capital pools should be supported by a fairly sophisticated corporate staff with the time and experience to make and supervise such investments. Since the larger pension plans to whom this type of investment will be of interest will have an experienced investment staff, there is little point in our spending too much time in this area other than to caution against this kind of diversification without a most serious study. For example, investment in real estate, like other investments, can be divided into debt instruments, mortgages and equity investments. Investment in mortgages requires a staff to evaluate individual investments and offers little advantage to the corporation over marketable bonds. The yields over a period of time must be roughly comparable. Equity investments in real estate have in the past been structured largely for the taxable investor. Thus, real estate investments with appeal to pension plans must be specially structured. There are some investment firms specializing in real estate investments for pension plans, and such firms should be consulted. Unfortunately, in real estate as in any other form of investment, higher reward carries higher risk. Real estate offers no magic answer to the desire for better pension fund returns.

The same reasoning applies to venture capital pools. Some competent, experienced firms run venture capital pools designed for pension fund investment. The risks are high but the rewards can be high. A large pension plan with a staff competent to follow such investments might well consider putting 2 percent or 3 percent of its funds in such vehicles.

One argument which is sometimes used against pension plan investments in real estate and venture capital pools does not usually have validity. This is the argument that such investments are not liquid. Contrary to some casual thinking, pension plans in general have a very high level of liquidity and can tolerate a small portion of their assets being committed to less liquid investments. Assuming that the work of actuaries has been properly done, it is relatively easy to forecast when cash outflows begin. Normal corporate contributions and normal planning should take care of any liquidity need. Most bonds and common stocks held in pension plans are relatively liquid. Thus, for a pension plan of any size to have 5 percent or 10 percent of its investments in a nonliquid form such as real estate should not in itself present a problem.

CONCLUSION

The proper management of pension fund assets is serious business and the Corporate Treasurer should give it serious attention. The fiduciary responsibilities required under ERISA are substantial. In this chapter we have provided some general guidelines which the treasurer can use. No longer can he make pension payments to a local bank trust department and consider his responsibilities fulfilled. Investment objectives must be set, managers selected with care, and their performance maintained on an ongoing basis.

ADDITIONAL SOURCES

Bagehot, Walter. "Risk in Corporate Pension Funds." *Financial Analysts Journal,* 28 (January–February 1972), 80–84.

Carson, Donald G. "Responding to the Pension Reform Law." *Harvard Business Review,* 52 (November–December 1974), 133–44.

Christiansen, Beric M.; Ekeblad, Raymond E.; and Woods, William S., Jr. "Pension Fund Management: A View from the Inside." *Financial Executive,* 63 (July 1975), 24–27.

Doyle, Allan M. Jr. "Pension Fund Assets: Help for the Small Corporation?" *Financial Executive,* 63 (August 1975), 28–31.

Driscoll, Robert S. "Evaluating Your Outside Investment Manager." *Financial Executive,* 63 (January 1975), 10–13.

Hershman, Arlene. "The Big Pension Fund Drain." *Dun's Review,* 106 (July 1975), 31–35.

McKee, James W., and Hindenach, Lee P. "The Corporation and ERISA: For Now and for the Future." *Financial Executive,* 63 (June 1975), 16–22.

McLaughlin, Frank C. "Investing as a Prudent Expert." *Financial Executive,* 63 (June 1975), 23–29.

Paul, Robert D. "Can Private Pension Plans Deliver?" *Harvard Business Review,* 51 (September–October 1974), 22–34, 165–66.

Shapiro, Max. "Can Companies Afford Pensions?" *Dun's,* 103 (June 1974), 72–75, 139–40.

Tepper, Irwin. "Optimal Financial Strategies for Trusteed Pension Plans." *Journal of Financial and Quantitative Analysis,* 9 (June 1974), 357–76.

Tepper, Irwin, and Affleck, A. R. P. "Pension Plan Liabilities and Corporate Financial Strategies." *Journal of Finance,* 29 (December 1974), 1549–64.

Chapter 52

Communicating with the Investing Public

Robert H. Savage[*]

STOCKHOLDER RELATIONS

A LITTLE OLD LADY who owns six shares of a company's stock and an institution which owns 600,000 shares have a common denominator—both are stockholders. Yet practical considerations dictate that both cannot be treated exactly alike. Generally speaking, the individual investor's contact with his company is via the printed word, with perhaps a once-in-a-while viewing of management at an annual meeting of stockholders. By contrast, the institutional holder relies heavily on personal contact with management, usually through investor relations.

The Need and Benefits of Involving the Small Stockholder

The widespread attention often given to the institutional investor should not, however, be at the expense of maintaining excellent relations with and attention to the private investor who may have at his command significant funds to put into equity securities.

[*] Robert H. Savage is vice president and director of investor relations, International Telephone and Telegraph Corporation, New York.

I wish to thank my associate, Victor A. Liston, formerly manager of investor relations, International Telephone and Telegraph Corporation, for his contributions to the preparation of this chapter.

Since the stock market as a whole and each company's stock compete with a vast array of alternative investment mediums, a company must exert extra effort in this area of stockholder relations to achieve its share of the consumer savings dollar.

The end result can be highly rewarding, since the individual investor in quality stocks typically is a long-term, committed shareholder. This commitment can also be expressed in a loyalty to and preference for a company's products and services. The confidence by a host of individual investors in a company can help to create a positive and healthy image of the company's place in the community.

For all of the above reasons, a company should consider the individual investor as its most treasured shareholder. No feasible effort should be overlooked to provide good communication on a timely and accurate basis. The small stockholder should receive a steady flow of printed material from the company including the annual and interim reports, talks before analysts' groups and special reports on major items in the news. In addition, this stockholder's inquiries to the company should be answered promptly, in depth and candidly, by a senior officer of the corporation. Any extra expenses and efforts in this area will be generously rewarded by public confidence.

Because the principal means employed by management to keep individual stockholders informed is the written word, it is important that the investor relations executive play an active part in the preparation of all material to be distributed to stockholders. He is, in a real sense, the representative of the investor within the management. As such, he is eminently qualified to view matters from the perspective of the investor, to weigh and evaluate the impact of the written message on the investing community.

The small investor buys shares because he welcomes those dividend checks. He naturally hopes that the price of the shares will rise so that he may, if he wishes, sell them later at a nice profit. With the exception of that bête noire of all publicly held companies—the professional publicity seeker whose obvious purpose in owning one share is to go on ego trips at annual meetings—most holders of relatively small amounts of shares seem quite content to let management run the show, just so long as that price shows a steady appreciation and those dividends keep rolling along. Should these perfectly reasonable objectives not be met, the smaller investor simply sells his shares and quietly disappears. Contrary to a widely held impression, most individual investors do not write "Dear Sir, You Cur" letters to managements of companies whose stocks have failed to live up to the individual's expectations. Such stockholders tend to buy—and sell—without ever getting in touch with the companies.

Because most small stockholders tend to be modest in their demands for corporate attention, it is quite difficult to get acquainted with them in order to discover their attitudes and predispositions. Some companies as a matter of policy send every new stockholder a welcoming letter. Other companies pour enormous amounts of money and time into stockholder profiling programs. And there are companies which write the selling stockholder a where-did-we-go-wrong? letter. The responses generated by such letters sometimes elicit useful information as to how management can avoid a continuing exodus. More often, however, those who bother to reply indicate a sharp desire that management mind its own business.

Whatever the merits or flaws of such attempts to get a reading on stockholders, it is always sound policy for management to know as much about its stockholders as can be reasonably ascertained. Analysis of stockholder lists will disclose, among other useful data, size of holdings, geographical location and density, the number of male and female owners, joint accounts, fiduciaries, institutions, brokers, and nominees. Such statistical information is particularly useful to companies engaged in manufacturing consumer products or offering consumer services. Leaflets drawing the attention of stockholders to those products or services can be enclosed with dividend checks or other correspondence from the company, thereby helping to build sales and earnings.

These are some of the functions the investor relations officer can initiate in his continuing effort to provide an open link between the company and the investment community. A great part of such a program, however, involves proper coordination with the company's other divisions. The end result in sustaining investor confidence can clearly be seen to translate directly into investor support for the company's products.

A Legal Responsibility

Entirely apart from the benefits accruing to a company which institutes and maintains a sound investor relations program, there is the ethical—not to mention legal—responsibility of every publicly held corporation to keep its stockholders informed. The magnitude, scope, and diversity of any program to meet this responsibility will, of course, depend on the size of the company. A multibillion dollar corporation may have a fairly large staff performing the investor relations functions, while a much smaller company may require the services of only one person, or designate an officer of the company to take care of the investor relations function. The point is that, regardless of size, every company ought to recognize that investor relations is an essential service to which its stockholders and, by extension, the financial community, are entitled. Doubting Thomases, if there be any, are urged to communicate with the Securities and Exchange Commission!

If it is agreed that a publicly held company has an ethical and legal obligation to maintain clear and open channels of communication with those who have bought its securities, then surely common sense dictates that we convert this necessity into a virtue by providing the best investor relations service we can develop. If we *must* do something, we might as well do it with grace and competence!

Which brings us to what I consider to be the most important aspect of an investor relations program—commitment from the top. A program which is instituted reluctantly, is foredoomed to failure. Management must believe that the program is essential to the health of the company and that continuity of the program is vital to the company's future.

Some Practical Considerations

There are some extremely practical reasons why a publicly owned company should maintain a carefully planned, consistently applied investor relations program. Among these are the following factors:

1. Future expansion of a company usually depends on its ability to raise additional equity capital. A well-informed financial community makes this task that much easier.
2. There are just so many investment dollars to go around, so those companies with an established record for open communication with investors have an edge on less-communicative competitors for those dollars.

3. A company whose stock is held in good esteem in the market-place tends to attract—and keep—key executives because their stock options have real potential under normal market conditions.

4. Acquisition-minded companies are keenly aware that their stock must command strong investor interest if an exchange-of-shares is programmed.

5. In the event of a take-over threat, management's record and reputation as a communicator in the financial community can prove to be a formidable weapon in fending off corporate raiders.

At some point in its existence, every company has been or will be exposed to one or more of these conditions. Those who have practiced good investor relations have generally weathered the tides and storms. Others have not.

THE ROLE OF INVESTOR RELATIONS

The primary objective of investor relations is to achieve—and try to maintain—a fair market value for the company's securities. Investor relations seeks to achieve this objective by serving as a direct communications link between a publicly held company and the financial community which embraces stockholders (both actual and potential), fund managers, security analysts, the investment trust departments of banks and insurance companies, advisory services and consultants. The investor relations executive not only acts as management's spokesman in "The Street"; he also reports back to management on the attitudes, views, commendations, and criticisms of those with whom he deals in the financial community.

At this point, let me anticipate a question: "Can an investor relations program really influence the price of a company's stock?" All other factors being equal, I am convinced that the answer is "Yes." By itself, investor relations means little or nothing. The most skillful investor relations executive cannot make a weak management dynamic and strong. He cannot fashion an investor's silk purse out of a corporate sow's ear!

Assume that you have a dozen companies in a given industry whose records of sales and earnings are more or less comparable. Let us further assume that two of those companies maintain a strong, provenly reliable investor relations program, while the remaining ten companies lack such a program. I submit that the market performances of the two investor-oriented companies will tend to surpass those of the other ten. The basis for this assertion is rather simple: there are so many thousands of companies from which the financial community can pick and choose, why should a security analyst struggle to extract information from a company whose top management is tight-lipped and studiously uncooperative, when so many equally good or better companies are unabashedly seeking to catch the analyst's attention?

Based on experience, the key to successful investor relations is to have someone in the company who is knowledgeable about its operations and always available to discuss them.

Most Effective Methods of Communicating

In 1972, an interesting report made by the well-known firm of Georgeson & Co., entitled "Informing the Investor," ranked in order of importance four effective methods of keeping the security analysts informed:

1. Management meetings.
2. Analyst meetings—not necessarily in the formalized setting of analyst society meetings which can sometimes yield mixed results, ranging from extremely good to disastrous.
3. Annual reports.
4. 10–Ks and registration statements.

I propose to discuss in some detail the first two of these four techniques—management meetings and analysts meetings. By management meetings I mean sessions where management is host. Conversely, analyst's meetings are sessions hosted by analyst groups.

Before discussing these two approaches to maintaining financial communications, I want to emphasize that—above all else—companies must engage in financial communications on a continuous basis—in good times and in bad times. Even in these days when management likes to be thought of as sophisticated, it is incredible how often a management will start a love affair with the financial community when everything's coming up roses—only to scurry into hiding as soon as the going gets rough. Increasingly, the financial community resents this summer soldier approach. And rightly so.

At ITT we have an inflexible policy—we are *always* available. We may not always have the answer on hand, but we do not duck the question either. We try our best to find the answer and get back to the analyst as soon as possible.

Continuous Rapport with Key Analysts

Over the years we have established a valued rapport with some 15 to 20 key analysts who are, in turn, regarded by the financial community as being most knowledgeable about our company. While we devote a great deal of time to these acknowledged experts on ITT, this is not to say that we ignore or short-change other analysts. We are quite conscious that the analytical experts of the future are going to come from today's newcomers.

At least once a month we meet with, or are in touch with, every one of these key analysts. We may sit down with them in small groups, or perhaps, just one or two at a time. Whatever the means employed, we make it our business to keep these individuals informed. I might comment that they are equally determined to be informed. They stay close to the day-to-day operations and developments. For example, we arrange sessions after each quarterly report to give them an opportunity to go over financial results with us.

In addition, we have what are known in newspaper circles as "backgrounders." These are small group meetings at which a product group executive, or a technical expert will explain to the analysts the activities of his group, division, or area of operations. These are usually nonfinancial type meetings, designed to give the audience a better understanding of specific areas of our diversified operations.

In addition to the key analysts, another 40–50 analysts are contacted on a regular basis (at least quarterly) if our transfer sheets show significant buying or selling activities in our securities. We are our own transfer agent, and screen the transfer reports weekly, with special interest in large buying or selling—10,000 shares or more.

We also contact each of the major institutions holding our stock, at least once a quarter, to update them on company developments and ask for their opinions and comments.

Another 150–200 analysts are on our mailing list to receive quarterly earnings reports, major speeches, and news releases. A word of caution—do not flood the analysts with trivial releases. We mail financial statements to analysts on the day following newspaper releases, since they prefer to see earnings releases and financial tabulations rather than to rely on newspaper coverage.

We have another rule or policy insofar as these and all other contacts with analysts are concerned: "Let your experts do the talking!" One learns over the years that the really qualified, sharp, knowledgeable analyst is not impressed by corporate titles. He wants to talk with someone who is an expert on the subject at hand. His total preoccupation is with gaining deeper insights into what the company is doing and where it is going. He usually knows what he is talking about. So a word of advice—make certain that the individuals who speak for your company really know what they are talking about.

Should your company wait for analysts to call, or initiate contact? Analysts appreciate having companies contact them. I have never known an analyst who objected to being called. Some analysts cover as many as 50 different companies, and tend to focus on "problem" companies, thereby ignoring major companies where earnings growth has been relatively predictable.

ITT has three individuals in its investor relations department who have responsibility for:

1. Contacts with major institutional holders and analysts in New York and other major metropolitan financial centers.
2. Contacts with out-of-town analysts and institutions.
3. Contacts with brokerage firms and writing assignments.

At ITT, we do not forecast earnings. We believe that is the analyst's job—not ours. Key analysts almost always get in touch with us to check if their estimates are "in the ball park." It is important that their estimates be neither too high nor too low, so some guidance from the company is important.

The SEC suggests that companies have responsibilities to tone down earnings estimates which are too optimistic. This is easier said than done. For instance, in industries such as steel and autos there are factors beyond the company's control which can significantly affect a company's financial results. Even utilities are subject to fluctuations in interest rates and changes in regulatory climate.

Meetings with Analysts' Societies

The investor relations executive has a leading role in all meetings between the financial community and top management. His chief executive, and to a lesser extent, those close to the president's office, receive more invitations to address analysts' societies than they can accept. Not the least of investor relations responsibilities is to decide which invitations ought to be accepted by the chief executive, and which can be delegated to other officers.

Investor relations usually is involved in the preparation of the chief executive's formal remarks. While the actual speechwriting may be done elsewhere—in the public relations department, for example—investor relations will still be deeply involved as to the speech's content as well as the form of presentation.

Experience has established that the time given to making sure that the chief executive covers all major points of interest in his speech is time well spent. This is particularly true when a delicate or complicated subject will almost certainly be raised during the question-and-answer session. If the chief executive has covered the point as carefully as circumstances permit, then he can always refer to his formal remarks, and thus avoid being drawn into saying more than he had intended. Worse, in the give-and-take of debate, he may inadvertently make a statement which is not entirely correct.

While most meetings with security analysts' societies are full dress parades, less formal gatherings are frequently arranged by the investor relations executive. Often the chief executive sits down informally with a group of investment analysts who are quite sophisticated in their knowledge of the company and its industry. They will wish to go beyond generalities. While such sessions are of great value to management and analysts alike, care must be exercised to avoid even the appearance of giving company information only to selected audiences; otherwise, the "full disclosure" rules may be violated.

For the smaller, newer companies, appearances before analysts' societies provide a forum at which management can gain a much-needed exposure. However, it is my personal conviction that the value of such forums to established, widely known companies is quite limited. The most frequently heard complaint is that these formalized sessions are heavily sales oriented at which lengthy presentations leave insufficient time for the give-and-take of the question-and-answer period.

While they unquestionably have their uses, such sessions cannot substitute for the one-on-one meetings, nor for those occasions when management presents its story to a group, large or small, of selectively chosen guest analysts.

Communicating through the Press

Should the press be invited? Admittedly, this is a touchy subject, with strong feelings being expressed pro and con. My own opinion is that common sense should dictate the answer. The SEC rule on all matters of disclosure is our guide. If any information which might have a material effect on the price of the stock is to be disclosed at the meeting, then certainly the press must be invited. If information of this sort is unexpectedly disclosed—usually in the confusion of answering the barrage of questions—then a press release giving this information should be immediately sent out over the Dow Jones and other wire services.

Press releases, while an essential tool in communications with stockholders and the financial community, are limited in their usefulness though. Subject as they are to editing, revision, and interpretation by the newspapers, it is not uncommon for a reader to obtain from the financial pages of his favorite daily an impression of his company's condition or prospects quite contrary to that contained in the original press release.

The Message through Company Reports

The role of the investor relations executive is to augment, to expand, and where necessary, to clarify, on a day-to-day basis, media communications between a company and the financial community. Most companies, as a matter of course, issue annual reports, interim or quarterly reports, as well as a variety of press releases dealing with financial matters. Valuable as these communications are, they are by their nature limited. No matter how diligently an annual report has been prepared, the company issuing that report has absolutely no way of compelling its stockholders to read the report. Continuing surveys have established that a discouragingly small percent of stockholders ever bother to read annual reports. One plausible reason is that because so many companies operate on a calendar year basis, stockholders find their mailboxes suddenly crammed with company reports, each simultaneously vying for their attention, during a relatively brief period—usually during the months of March and April.

In between annual reports, management also employs interim or quarterly reports to keep stockholders informed. Such reports usually are brief, concise, and transitory. Later developments frequently render their content out-of-date, no longer an accurate reflection of the corporation's condition.

These considerations support the contention that the written word alone cannot be relied upon to keep stockholders and the financial community fully informed.

Useful as the written word unquestionably is, its limitations are clear. To the extent possible, it is the function of investor relations to extend the life-span of the written word by maintaining a day-to-day dialogue with the financial community. Whether, as in some companies, the written word originated in investor relations, or, as in many major corporations, was submitted in advance to investor relations for comment and/or revision, the fact is that investor relations must be prepared by foreknowledge as well as by professional qualifications to carry on the communication between the company and the financial community. Investor relations must be qualified to expand on, to explain and, when needed, to correct any erroneous impressions.

INVESTOR RELATIONS QUALIFICATIONS

The investor relations function with a major company, including most of the *Fortune* "500" companies, is—or certainly ought to be—a full-time job. Its importance is being increasingly recognized in the corporate status and compensation for such executives. It is essential to have the right persons in this role. They must have complete knowledge of the company's operations, and also the experience to know what can be said and what should not be said.

Probably because they do not fully appreciate the importance of the function, some companies will assign investor relations responsibility to an executive solely because his regular position has been swallowed up in a realignment of duties. Other companies whose top management is somewhat hazy as to just what investor relations is all about, decide the function belongs in public relations. While obviously there must be close collaboration between investor relations and public relations, the concept that they are interchangeable is not sound. Fairly or not, many security analysts prefer not to deal with public relations.

At the other extreme are companies whose chief executives assume that the best candidate for the investor relations slot is to be found in their comptroller's or treasurer's departments. They reason that since security analysts deal in statistical data, who could be better qualified to take care of investor relations than an accountant? Unfortunately, familiarity with statistical data does not necessarily qualify an executive as an effective communicator of that knowledge.

The solution is to be found somewhere between these extremes. The best candidate for the investor relations post will have had experience in both public relations and also in the financial phases of a company's operations. Their careers invariably include several years' experience as financial news writers for the daily press or business news magazines. It is likely that they took special courses in finance and security analysis. They may have worked as security analysts in the research department of a brokerage firm, or performed the same function in the investment department of a bank or an insurance company. They are on familiar ground when talking with security analysts. They empathize with the analysts. They know what he is talking about and can appreciate the nuances of the sophisticated analyst's comments or inquiries.

Generally speaking, the person assigned to investor relations reports directly to the president or, if the company is a major one, to the chief financial officer. The investor relations executive must have direct and ready access to top management. He must be fully informed on top-level policy and planning. His advice ought to be asked for and given careful consideration on any program or policy change which has a direct effect on the company's standing and its relationships with the financial community. These requirements should be self-evident.

RELATIONSHIPS WITH THE SECURITY ANALYST

The successful conduct of the investor relations functions depends to a large extent on the response and cooperation of one of its largest and certainly more influential group of recipients— the *security analyst*. An attempt to understand his role and code of conduct is necessary in order to establish the kind of working relationship desired.

The profession of security analysis is both a science and an art. It has come a long way from its origins. Time was when the security analyst was low man on the Wall Street totem pole. His function then was closer to that of a reporter rather than an investigator. He gratefully accepted whatever crumbs of corporate information fell from the board room table. More often than not, corporations exploited him by feeding him information which had only the most tenuous relationship with truth. He was not trained to search out facts and come to independent conclusions. Sources of information were meager, at best, and his own employers were not likely to implore their lowly hired hand to give them the benefit of his sagacity and insight.

Today's security analyst is a professional. Educated and trained in the craft of his trade, he enjoys the respect which enlightened management accords to his profession. He is expected to demonstrate an independence not only in his dealings with corporate management but also with his own firm. He usually is a member of a regional analysts' society and, by extension, a member of The Financial Analysts Federation.

In common with all professional organizations, his society provides him with a code of standards governing the relationship of the security analyst and corporate managements. In the belief that familiarity with the content of one such code will assist management in its dealings with financial analysts, we offer as an example the standards of The New York Society of Security Analysts:

1. The analyst must conduct himself at all times in accordance with the standards set down by the Constitution of the NYSSA. He must bear in mind that his department will be judged as a reflection on the profession.
2. Upon initiating a corporate contact, the analyst should identify himself, the nature of his interest, and whether the information is intended for publication and in what form.

3. It is deemed of the greatest importance that the security analyst perform his homework in a thorough manner beforehand. The implications of insufficient preparation for an interview should be readily apparent. Corporate officials are able to determine quickly the extent to which an analyst has prepared himself for the interview and treat him accordingly. Company officials have corporate responsibilities which extend far beyond their obligation to the financial community.

4. It is assumed, as a matter of course, that prior to the interview the analyst will have reviewed company data including annual reports, quarterly reports, prospectuses, file clippings, company brochures of various sorts including sales and product descriptions, and the usual statistical manuals. These should be supplemented by reports filed with regulatory agencies and by transcripts of management's previous appearances before various analysts' societies. It is also assumed that the analyst is generally familiar with the industry, and that his studies are based on industry files, trade publications and industry surveys by statistical organizations.

5. The working interview itself should be organized to save the time of corporate officials. Management's loudest complaints are (*a*) poor preparation and (*b*) overlengthy interviews. The preparation of an outline of the information already available would permit a more efficient utilization of time which can then be devoted to filling obvious gaps and obtaining elaboration where needed.

6. Security analysts generally find that tours of facilities including plants, research laboratories, production fields and mines, among others, may be desirable in determining the "personality" of each company. However, these visits should be selective and, if possible, not in such frequency as to strain management's hospitality.

7. Analysts are to be cautioned about making idle visits and calls on management. Once contact is established with a company, subsequent visits should be held to a minimum. Analysts should also try to space their inquiries and avoid calling at the time of impact when good or bad news has inspired the contact. As much as possible, the security analyst should act as his firm's spokesman for calls to management, as it is essential to maintenance of good relations to eliminate unnecessary calls on corporate management. Conversely, an analyst favorably known to management can obtain the most efficient replies to inquiries.

8. Managements normally prefer a single contact in each organization. Analysts should, therefore, determine whether an associate in their own organization has already established a line of communication and to avoid unnecessary duplication.

9. The analyst should not seek to obtain information which the company is not prepared to make available to other analysts and to the public. By the same token, the corporate manager can be expected not to withhold information which is known in the trade or to the public.

10. If an analyst, in the course of his communication with a company, becomes the recipient of what he considers to be "material information" not in public domain, he is advised to consult with counsel on its use and dissemination.

CONCLUSIONS

Managements of publicly held companies have an ethical, as well as legal obligation to keep their stockholders and the financial community informed. Enlightened management discharges this obligation, willingly, consistently, and cheerfully, recognizing that an obligation can be transformed into an opportunity. Investor relations provides management with the ways and means to make the most of that opportunity.

ADDITIONAL SOURCES

Barrett, Edgar, and Werner, Jeffrey. "Seven Steps to Better Investor Relations." *Financial Executive*, 42 (August 1974), 60–65.

Chatlos, William. "Informing the Analysts." *Trends* (February–March 1972), 226–27.

Chatlos, William. "Investor Relations Needs a Bibliography . . . Here's a Start." *Trends* (December 1972–January 1973), 234–35.

Lewis, Richard A. "Is Investor Relations Worth Saving?" *The Corporate Communications Report*, 6 (January 1975).

Malley, Francis. "How the SEC May Change Your Annual Report." *Financial Executive*, 42 (October 1974), 44–47.

Chapter 53

Social Responsibility of
the Treasurer

William L. Mobraaten[*]

. . . in an age which demands more than goods and services, the insistence of corporations on being nothing but producers of goods and services threatens to force corporations increasingly out of the mainstream of American life and into irrelevance.[1]

. . . there is one and only one social responsibility of business—to use its resources and engage in activities designed to increase its profits so long as it stays within the rules of the game. . . .[2]

THE ACADEMIC DEBATE over the social responsibility of the corporation continues. The basic issues are complex and their ultimate resolution will indeed exert a profound impact on the role of the corporation in our society. In the meantime, demands for expanded corporate activity in areas of social concern mount. And with these mounting demands, the pressure increases for the corporate executive to "do something." Such pressures can no longer be prudently

---

[*] William L. Mobraaten is vice president and treasurer, American Telephone and Telegraph, New York.

[1] Henry G. Manne and Henry C. Wallich, *The Modern Corporation and Social Responsibility* (Washington, D.C.: American Enterprise Institute for Public Policy Research, 1972), p. 59.

[2] Milton Friedman, *Capitalism and Freedom* (Chicago: University of Chicago Press, 1962), p. 133.

1144

ignored—they are a fact of corporate life and must be dealt with constructively.

The prospect of an expanded role for business forces us to broaden our view of the social responsibility of the treasurer. Participation in community activities, although important, no longer seems to suffice in light of the pervasive impact of the corporation on the American life-style. This chapter will, therefore, attempt to examine some aspects of the treasurer's corporate role in terms of its social impact.

WHAT *IS* THE CORPORATION'S SOCIAL RESPONSIBILITY?

Overview

A cursory examination of some of the basic issues will set the stage for discussion. Volumes have been written on the social responsibility of the corporation, and while it may be somewhat dangerous to generalize, the multitude of sometimes conflicting demands conveys one message clearly: *corporate legitimacy is being questioned as the public places increased emphasis on the quality of life for all.*[3] Expressions of this emphasis are found in demands for pollution control, new opportunities for disadvantage minorities and women, job enrichment, product safety, health standards, urban renewal, and so on.

These items on the public agenda are questioned by few who have entered the fray over corporate social responsibility. The significant problems are widely recognized, but the question remains: Who should tackle them? The public has turned to business, perhaps out of recognition that it can get things done with relative efficiency. Many in business have picked up the gauntlet, ignoring those who question this extension of the corporation's role. Perhaps this is as it should be. Times have indeed changed and a persuasive case can be made to justify activities related to social objectives under the cloak of enlightened self-interest, if no other. Indeed, the long-run profitability and perhaps the continued existence of the corporation may depend on the extent of its support of broad, long-

---

[3] Edwin M. Epstein, "The Historical Enigma of Corporate Legitimacy," *California Law Review*, vol. 60 (November 1972), pp. 1701–17.

range social objectives. But the critics should not be dismissed too lightly, for they raise fundamental questions which society must face lest its economic system be unalterably changed by the cumulative effects of many small decisions made without regard to their long-run implications.

Critics Position.   Milton Friedman and Henry G. Manne rightly question the appropriate role of government and the corporation, including the capacity of businessmen educationally and financially to tackle the problems. Friedman does not reject activities which are entirely justified in the firm's self-interest. He does, however, object to placing the social responsibility label on such efforts.[4] In his view, the general public has a responsibility to establish a framework of law such that individuals and corporations, each pursuing their own selfish goals, will be led by Adam Smith's "invisible hand" to achieve the best good for all.[5] The problem with corporate executives' exercising social responsibility is that they are spending someone else's funds for a general social purpose—the shareowner's funds if returns are reduced; the employee's, if wages are lowered; the consumer's, if prices are raised. To Friedman this is a form of taxation without representation. If executives are to impose taxes and make expenditures for social programs, then they ought to be elected through a political process. Friedman thus concludes that the notion of corporate social responsibility "involves the acceptance of the socialist view that political mechanisms, not market mechanisms, are the appropriate way to determine the allocation of scarce resources to alternative uses."[6]

Manne's analysis of the issue leads him to a similar conclusion and a disheartening paradox: the doctrine of corporate social responsibility "offered by many as a scheme to popularize and protect free enterprise, can only succeed if the free market is abandoned in favor of greater government controls." He identifies three elements to a working definition of corporate responsibility: (1) the activity must be one for which "the marginal returns are less than those for an alternative expenditure," (2) the activity must be voluntary, and (3) the activity must not be a conduit for individual largess. Manne doubts that voluntary, independent corporate

---

[4] Milton Friedman, "The Social Responsibility of Business Is to Increase Its Profits," *The New York Times Magazine*, September 13, 1970, p. 124.

[5] Friedman, *Capitalism and Freedom*, p. 133.

[6] Friedman, *New York Times Magazine*, p. 122.

action will be of a magnitude sufficient to increase social welfare. Hence, the paradox.[7]

Advocate View. Henry Wallich, on the other hand, bases his case for social responsibility on what he calls functional considerations. The advantage of corporate exercise of social responsibility is found in "shifting from the public to the private sector activities that should be performed with maximum economy rather than maximum bureaucracy." He too recognizes that little can be accomplished by individual corporate action especially in a competitive industry where the higher costs would force a firm to price itself out of the market. Such cases may call for cooperative action if antitrust laws permit. Alternatively, corporate social responsibility may require efforts to bring about changes in laws, taxes and regulation in order that social welfare increase.[8]

Need for Debate

Serious debate on the fundamental issues has unfortunately been confined largely to academia. Some businessmen, partly in response to the precipitous decline in public confidence, have initiated social programs without giving sufficient thought to the long-run implications of their actions. The debate needs to be continued in the public forum so that the choice of appropriate roles will be a deliberate one. If business is to assume a major responsibility for achieving social objectives, then priorities must be clarified and measurement techniques developed. If the obligation falls on government, corporate responsibility can be exercised by bringing to the public sector the business "know-how" needed to assure the efficient allocation of society's scarce resources.

Treasurer's Unique Role

The debate over the social responsibility of the corporation will not be easily resolved and will, no doubt, continue for years to come. Viewed as part of a democratic society's need to periodically question and redefine the role of its major institutions, the controversy poses a threat to the business community only if it refuses to

---

[7] Manne and Wallich, *Modern Corporation and Social Responsibility,* pp. 1–34.

[8] Ibid, pp. 37–62.

participate constructively in the reexamination of its social and economic role. The major challenge to corporate managers is that of establishing a continuing dialogue with the general public so that intelligent policies can be established to support social goals. Conflict is an inevitable part of this process. But continuing dialogue will assure that the divergence between what corporate behavior is and what society demands can be more quickly reconciled. A real threat to the private business sector lies in an incomplete appreciation by the public of complex trade-offs between economic and social goals; potentially crippling legal requirements may result.

The purpose of the following sections might best be described as "consciousness raising." Regardless of labels, the notion that business should be held accountable for a wider range of its activities and responsive to a wider range of demands has been fairly well established. In Peter Drucker's view:

> The great new fact is that a society of organizations holds institutions and their executives not only accountable for quantities. . . . It holds its institutions collectively accountable for the quality of life. This is above all new opportunity for the organization and its executives, a new dimension of performance and results. . . .[9]

While important questions remain regarding the kinds of activities which should be undertaken and the extent of business' involvement, treasurers must nonetheless become watchful of those aspects of their role which require a sensitivity to social issues. This discussion should suggest some areas that might be examined for potential change so that corporations will be a net contributor to the achievement of social goals. *Many areas of contribution relate to the treasurer's capacity as an officer of the company, a manager of people, and a member of the community. These areas are beyond the scope of this chapter: we will focus only on those areas of corporate operation unique to the treasurer.*

While the discussion will include some specific activities and choices which a treasurer must face, it is important to recognize that issues relevant in today's social environment may be less so in the years to come. Indeed one of the major difficulties in dealing with social pressures is the speed with which they change. The frustration of some is indicated by their characterization of social responsibility as a "moving target."

---

[9] Peter F. Drucker, *The Age of Discontinuity* (New York: Harper & Row, 1969), p. 207.

The key to dealing effectively with social requirements is not, however, to be found in any catalog of activities and issues. Instead the treasurer should focus on the development of methods to evaluate social issues and programs with the same vigor applied to other aspects of the firm's operation. Henry C. Wallich has identified three basic steps required in the exercise of social responsibility: "(1) the setting of objectives, (2) the decision whether or not to pursue given objectives, and (3) the financing of these objectives."[10]

A fourth step should be added: the ongoing measurement of the impact of social programs in terms of costs, benefits, and profits. For the responsibility of using limited resources efficiently is no less important in the production of social goods than it is in the production of private goods and services.

SOCIAL RESPONSIBILITY TO INVESTORS

Owner Representative

More than any other corporate officer, the treasurer must represent in all corporate councils the interests and expectations of the company's stock and bond investors. If this fundamental and continuing responsibility is not successfully fulfilled, then the business may fail, and all of its contributions to society in the form of goods and services, jobs, purchases, wages, pensions, dividends, and taxes may be forfeited.

Allocation of Resources

A primary concern of the treasurer has traditionally focused on the protection and enhancement of the shareowner's investment. The responsibility includes the financial management of corporate growth as well as the prudent use of existing funds. The exercise of this obligation may place the treasurer at variance with other corporate officers who advocate growth for its own sake. But expansion can only be justified if the anticipated return on the investment exceeds other alternatives available to the shareowner. If adequate returns cannot be expected within a reasonable period, then the treasurer's fiduciary responsibility requires him to advise that earnings be distributed to the shareholders as cash dividends.

---

[10] Manne and Wallich, *Modern Corporation and Social Responsibility*, p. 41.

In addition to a misallocation of society's scarce resources, expansion for expansion's sake increases the risk of business failure.

Full Disclosure

A treasurer's fiduciary responsibility to investors derives in part from his day-to-day relations with them. Efforts to raise corporate funds bring him into frequent contact with both individual and institutional investors. It, therefore, is incumbent upon the treasurer to demonstrate responsibility and leadership in establishing an adequate and continuing flow of useful financial information to the public.

Purpose. The purpose of a full disclosure policy is to assure a fair market price for the company's stock based on facts, not a high price based on rumor, speculation or elaborate campaigns to persuade rather than inform. The efficient functioning of the capital market is vitally dependent on the flow of accurate information. Attempts to disrupt this flow can only be counterproductive in the long run as investor confidence is eroded.

The impact of investor confidence on the functioning of capital markets is evident today. Poll after poll shows a precipitous drop of the public's confidence in its major institutions, particularly business. This skepticism has undoubtedly contributed to the flight of the individual from the stock market. The exit of the individual is particularly serious for small- and medium-sized firms who look to the nation's 25 million individual investors for their new equity capital. But the impact is not limited to small corporations, for a shrinking ownership base diminishes the liquidity of the market as a whole. The decline of individual ownership coupled with a sagging economy has led to problems so severe that many are questioning the potence of the market in performing its basic function of equity capital formation. As a result of this concern, congressmen, academicians, lawyers, and corporate managers have joined members of the Securities and Exchange Commission, the Financial Accounting Standards Board, and the stock exchanges in the search for ways to bolster the capital market. Indeed, the social cost of a breakdown in society's mechanism for allocating capital resources would be enormous; and the impact, far-reaching.

Requirements. A policy of full disclosure requires a periodic flow of information which investors need to properly assess the financial condition and prospects of the company. Such a policy necessarily excludes material information withheld for legitimate business reasons. Standards for public disclosure are set by the Securities and Exchange Commission. The treasurer has a legal obligation to meet these standards; but he has a social obligation to determine for his own business exactly where SEC standards fail to meet particular needs and to provide the information required to fill the gap. Publication of financial statements which are complete and easily understood is a good place to start. Most shareowners need clarifying background beyond the basic facts. The tendency to emphasize the favorable and explain away the unfavorable should, however, be kept in check if credibility is to be maintained and the responsibility discharged.

Accounting Practices. Full disclosure implies the use of good accounting practices to avoid misleading the public. The resolution of important issues such as treatment of deferred income taxes, interest during construction, leases, pension fund liability, and inflation cannot, with all due respect, be relegated solely to professional accountants. Treasurers can, and must, provide an input based on their unique perspective.

Guidelines for Security Analysts. Another aspect of promoting a full disclosure policy is the articulation of guidelines for dealing with security analysts. Standards for establishing materiality are also required. Such guidelines will help to assure that professional investors are not given an advantage over the small investor. As noted before, the emphasis should be placed on facts not persuasion.

Public Contact. Full disclosure extends beyond financial statements. In daily contacts with the investment community and the general public, the treasurer becomes an important spokesman on other issues many of which relate to social concerns. He must articulate the company's policies to audiences whose concern and understanding vary widely. The vehicles at his disposal are numerous: printed material, speeches, seminars, letters, and shareowner visits.

Evaluation of Owner Concerns

A wise corporate position on social matters will be developed from many inputs. The treasurer's special contribution will stem from his reading of the pulse of the investing public. For this reason, the treasurer will want to listen to and discuss with share-owners their opinion and concerns about social issues.

The development of an effective organization to respond to calls and letters is a prerequisite for two-way shareholder communication. The exact organizational requirements depend, of course, on the size of the company. Visiting owners in their homes is another way of identifying owner concerns and provides an opportunity for a more extensive discussion of their opinions. Shareholder surveys may also be useful in evaluating priorities.

Institutional views on social matters can be explored through ordinary business channels: organized meetings with investor groups, individual interviews, telephone conversations with portfolio managers and analysts, professional society memberships, and client relationships with underwriters and pension fund managers.

Evaluation of voting patterns on proxy proposals relating to social issues can also provide insight regarding the strength and breadth of owner interest. Several institutions have used the proxy vehicle to express their position on social issues. Aetna Life & Casualty, for example, has cast its vote against the management of companies in their portfolio which in their opinion fail to meet social obligations.[11] The issues have been varied: publication of minority hiring and promotion data, strip mining, political contributions, production of military weapons, energy policies, environmental impacts, business activities in Latin America, Ireland, Middle East, South Africa, and Rhodesia. The proxy is limited, however, as a means of identifying all the social issues of import to owners: SEC regulations limit proposals on social issues to matters related to the company's business and within its control.

In all of these relationships with individual investors and professional money managers, the treasurer should remain conscious of the need to assess their reaction to the firm's social commitment: for market signals are frequently absent as guides to appropriate corporate activity.

Communication with Top Management

The treasurer's responsibility to investors has been viewed as a two-way communication process. Exercise of social responsibility in

---

[11] Institutions That Balk at Antisocial Management," *Business Week* (January 19, 1974), p. 66.

speaking to the investment community dictates a policy of complete and continuing disclosure. The primary purpose of *listening* to members of the investment community is to provide an input in the development of corporate policy. If the social concerns of institutions and individuals are to play an important part in the formulation of company policy, they must be conveyed to the policy makers. The obligation of the treasurer includes not only the identification of important issues but also an assessment of the relative strength of the concerns so that priorities can be established. Such information can signal needed change in corporate policy. It may also point to an information gap and the need for more effective shareowner education.

SOCIAL RESPONSIBILITY IN FINANCIAL MANAGEMENT

Managing Financial Assets

Management of company financial assets involves the treasurer more than most officers in activities which may have direct impact on individuals outside the company. In all these relationships he has a responsibility to anticipate the consequences of his actions and to limit any negative impact on people.

One example is the relationship with company suppliers and customers. Conventional cash management policy would dictate deferral of payments and minimization of accounts receivable. But such policies could easily jeopardize fledgling companies. Small local suppliers, for example, may depend primarily on a single corporation for their survival and, thus, lack the necessary bargaining strength for improving their own cash flow positions.

A similar case can be made for the prompt payment of local taxes. During periods of tight money, interest rates may exceed delinquency charges. The temptation to take advantage of this difference ought to be resisted in those cases where corporate taxes represent a major source of local revenue. If not, the payment lag could cause disruption of community services. Such cases require a balance to be struck between the interests of the corporation, those of its suppliers/clients, and the community of which they are a part.

Managing Pension Funds

The treasurer's traditional responsibility in the area of pension funds has been that of a fiduciary to employees both current and past. To meet this obligation, the treasurer must see that adequate funding is obtained and that prudent investment practices are followed. Flagrant violations of this trust by some organizations led to the passage of "The Employee Retirement Income Security Act of 1974." The law, however, does not absolve the treasurer of his social responsibility on pension issues—it merely sets the minimum standard of performance. In short, investment guidelines must be articulated and effectively enforced.

The selection of pension fund investments provides another means of effecting social change. Funds can be withdrawn from companies judged to be socially irresponsible. Corporations might also consider exercising the prerogatives of a stockholder by retaining the right to cast proxy votes.

Encouraging Minority Enterprise

Minority Banking.   Banks owned and operated by minority business people offer the treasurer an opportunity to help establish, broaden, and strengthen the economic base of disadvantaged communities. While these banks obviously cannot solve all the problems of poverty, they do create jobs and aid the financing of new businesses in their neighborhoods. In 1971, for instance, minority banks, with combined assets less than one tenth of 1 percent of all commercial banks extended $60 million in loans to minority entrepreneurs compared to $150 million granted by nonminority banks.[12] The multiplier effect resulting from the Federal Reserve's fractional reserve requirement adds to the attractiveness of using minority banks as a vehicle for channeling funds to disadvantaged communities: with a 20 percent reserve requirement, each dollar deposited can support $5 in loans to the community.

One typical example, is the program developed at AT&T which encompasses substantially all minority-owned banks located in communities served by Bell System companies. The project was

---

[12] David I. Fisher, "Minority Banks: A Progress Report," *The Conference Board Record*, December 1973, p. 37.

initiated in 1971 in support of a one-year, federal government program aimed at boosting minority bank deposits. At that time, a number of large national companies agreed to increase corporate deposits in minority banks substantially. The Bell System committed itself to maintaining at least $5 million in balances or equivalent balances with a major part in the form of time and demand deposits. The original commitment was met with AT&T providing around $2.5 million primarily in CDs (certificates of deposit) and the Associated Operating Companies contributing the remainder in demand deposits and tax deposit equivalent balances. Each company's share was initially related to the number and size of minority banks in its territory. The program continues today and has grown from 8 banks in early 1971 to more than 55 in 1975. More will be added as new minority banks open.

Another important aspect of a minority bank undertaking is the relationship developed through greater use of minority bank services. For example, the banks can be used as collection agents for company bills and as a source for corporate loans. Large corporate clients are often important to minority banks which are attempting to establish their presence and reputation in the local community.

Such programs do, however, involve extra administrative effort. First, care must be taken lest large and/or untimely withdrawals disrupt the operations of the banks. Second, the value of tax deposits from corporations fluctuates widely as the U.S. Treasury changes the retention periods for such deposits. Thus, these deposits must be closely monitored to assure that the value of them remains relatively constant. Third, while we know of no depositor who has lost money in minority banks, added risk is assumed in dealing with some of them which are still in a formative stage and as such, undercapitalized.

In our view, the benefits of this type of program more than justify the added administrative effort. Evaluation of such programs should, however, be made on an individual company basis. The treasurer's obligation to assure the financial integrity of his company and to use shareowners' funds prudently must be weighed against the benefits, often intangible, of such programs. There are no easy solutions: the balance which is struck will depend on the size and financial condition of a particular corporation.

Minority Suppliers. Minority supplier development programs are another way to bring minority groups into the economic mainstream. Although primarily a function of the purchasing department, the treasurer can help in several ways, including credit checks and financial advice.

Western Electric, the manufacturing arm of the Bell System, has developed one such program. This continuing effort is designed to identify and develop minority-owned and operated suppliers who are capable of meeting the company's procurement needs. The commitment of management was explicitly made in 1969 when the following set of purchasing goals were formulated:

1. To seek out minority businesses that can provide the goods and services necessary to Bell System operations.
2. To use resources and capabilities to help expand existing minority businesses, and to develop new minority businesses, particularly those that could provide goods rather than services.
3. To encourage other major U.S. firms to join in cooperative efforts aimed at accomplishing these goals.

The treasurer's most direct role in the program is in support of goal two. The company often does what is needed to help put minority firms in a position to compete for its business. On occasion they have collaborated in the establishment of new business. Such efforts may require financial counseling and aid in setting up cost systems.

Goal three deserves some comment in passing. The need for corporations to collaborate on matters relating to social responsibility becomes increasingly apparent as these programs expand. Encouraging participation of other corporations and sharing experiences both good and bad provides new ideas and an added measure of assurance that the goals of these programs will actually be met.

Support of Community Redevelopment

From time to time a corporation may be presented with an opportunity to invest either equity or debt money in local community redevelopment projects. The wide variety of local problems and projects designed to meet them precludes any detailed discussion. Suffice it to say, many corporations find that "seed money" is one effective way to exercise social responsibility.

SOCIAL RESPONSIBILITY AS
COMPANY SPOKESMAN

A dialogue is an *exchange* of ideas and opinions. Speaking out on issues of social concern is, therefore, an implicit requirement of the treasurer's obligation to foster a continuing dialogue with the general public to assure that business actions are not in conflict with social priorities. Critical examination of social demands is of paramount importance for the issues seldom have simple solutions. The fact that resources are limited requires that critical choices be made in terms of priorities and in terms of goods which society must forego if social goals are to be realized. Blind response to the demands of the most vocal group can in no way be viewed as an exercise in social responsibility.

Defining the Role of Business

In addition to the public's reaching a consensus on specific social goals and programs which will support these objectives, fundamental decisions must be reached on the role which each segment of society should play. The call for business to shoulder greater responsibility in meeting social goals seems to imply, on the one hand, an expansion of business' role with a concomitant increase in its power. On the other hand, much of the public distrust of business appears to stem from the juxtaposition of economic concentration and democratic tradition. Clearly the public ambivalence toward the corporation needs to be aired.

Roles assigned to the public and private sectors ought to reflect their comparative advantages. The responsibility of identifying social goals and establishing priorities should ideally reside in the public sector, for the process is a political one. While business can contribute to this process by helping to sharpen the issues and encouraging alternative policy analysis with an eye to the future, it should not attempt to impose its priorities on the general public.

The strength of business lies in its capacity to manage resources efficiently, spawn innovation and thus increase productivity. The American standard of living is a testament of this strength. Thus, the task of developing the mechanics to carry out social policies might well be assigned to business. The pricing mechanism can provide the proper signals to business if the government makes it profitable to do what the public wants; unprofitable to do what it does not want. This division of responsibility is not without snags, for conceptual problems still exist with regard to delineation of objectives and measuring progress toward these objectives. Such problems present challenges to American business ingenuity which are perhaps unparalleled. Much basic research and development needs to be undertaken if social objectives are to be met efficiently.

Treasurer's Contribution

The treasurer's contact with investors both large and small provides opportunity for a positive contribution to the clarification of objectives and roles. As mentioned previously, complete and accurate disclosure on a continuing basis will do much to restore public confidence—the foundation of meaningful dialogue—in the integrity of American business. Speeches, letters, and meetings with various groups offer other opportunities to increase the understanding of the public—for the strengths of the American business system in providing society's needs should be brought to the public's attention.

The tendency of many to dwell on the negative aspects of the capitalist system has disturbing long-run implications. Much criticism reflects a lack of knowledge about the system. The treasurer can do much to fill this gap. A quick review of Samuelson's *Economics* is highly recommended, however, lest we be caught in the untenable position of defending the status quo instead of the principles of our free enterprise system. For one is being less than candid if he denies the imperfections of the system.

The extent of public hostility toward profits is one item worthy of note. A discussion of social goals must not omit the most obvious goal of all: providing goods and services that people need and want at a decreasing real cost. An increasing standard of living is probably society's oldest social issue. It is still paramount. What the treasurer needs to make clear is that the opportunity to earn a profit is what motivates business to accept the risks involved in trying to "build a better mousetrap." Perhaps, we should stop speaking in terms of "a profit system" for as Samuelson reminds us:

> Ours is a profit-and-loss system. Profits are the carrots held out as
> an incentive to efficiency, and losses are the kicks that penalize

using inefficient methods of devoting resources to uses not desired by spending consumers.[13]

He also points out that "much of the hostility toward profit is really hostility toward the extremes of inequality in the distribution of money income that come from unequal factor ownership; this should be kept distinct from hostility toward profit created by imperfections of competition."[14]

In addition to lack of knowledge, the public's attitude toward business mirrors a certain callousness toward the public on the part of business. Too often we lack candor and assume a defensive attitude which serves only to confirm the widespread notion that business motives are sinister. Indeed, we might learn from the activists who challenge business today. They select an issue of importance to them and gather enough information to convince the public—the ultimate source of their authority—that improper activity is taking place.

MANAGING SOCIAL RESPONSIBILITY

We started by noting the importance of focusing on the basic activities involved in the exercise of social responsibility: selecting objectives; establishing and financing programs; and measuring the impact of these programs. We have suggested that the selection of broad social goals is within the domain of the public sector. The priority placed on these goals is most clearly expressed through the law. Given these directives, the treasurer must settle on more specific objectives and programs taking into account the capacity of his organization to meet them in terms of financing and skills. The discussion of Western Electric's Minority Suppliers Program provides an example of some of these aspects of managing social responsibility.

Measuring the impact of specific programs is, however, a more troublesome problem; more often than not, the benefits cannot be readily translated into dollars and cents. But this difficulty does not absolve one of responsibility, for the resources which are necessarily diverted from other uses must be accounted for. Treasurers need to develop appropriate control mechanisms for those social

---

[13] Paul A. Samuelson, *Economics* (New York: McGraw-Hill Book Company, 1970), p. 599.

[14] Ibid., p. 600.

programs they undertake and to work toward the addition of social considerations to the regular decision-making process.

The treasurer's interest in measuring the effectiveness of social programs extends beyond activities under his direct control. The job requires him to inform shareowners of the company's progress in meeting all social objectives. Where yardsticks are lacking, the treasurer may need to encourage the development of appropriate measures or audit procedures.

CONCLUSION

The message seems clear—the treasurer has a leading role in assuring that business is responsive to society's newly urgent aims: the preservation of the environment, the salvation of our cities, the protection of the consumer, the expansion of opportunity and the elevation of the quality of our national life. Based on pragmatic grounds if no other, few fail to recognize that over the long run the corporation will be judged and its freedom to manage determined on the basis of the degree to which it meets society's expectations.[15]

We have tried to examine ways in which a treasurer can respond to these expectations through his unique role within the corporation. There are limitations to this response posed by skills and resources. These constraints cannot be overlooked lest resources—human, financial, material—be diverted to the extent that the basic economic needs of society cannot be effectively met.

In terms of specific programs, it seems that the treasurer has a comparative advantage in expanding economic opportunities for disadvantaged groups. He is also in a position to listen and speak to many outside groups and, thus, to elevate the level of national debate on important social issues.

But the obligation extends beyond specific programs. The treasurer should build a management framework to provide the requisite flexibility and responsiveness as social goals change. If scarce resources are to be used wisely, management techniques, used in other areas of operation, may require modification to handle the special problems presented by social programs—particularly those of measurement.

Difficult times lie ahead. But with sensitivity to limitations and

---

[15] J. D. deButts, "Citizen Business," Speech, North Carolina Citizens Association, Raleigh, North Carolina, March 21, 1973.

to real public requirements, the treasurer can, in most companies, make social responsibility efforts more than a public relations exercise.

ADDITIONAL SOURCES

Andrews, Kenneth R. "Can the Best Corporations Be Made Moral?" *Harvard Business Review*, 51 (May–June 1973), 57–64.

Baker, Henry G. "Identity and Social Responsibility Policies." *Business Horizons*, 14 (April 1973), 23–28.

Bauer, Raymond A. "A Practical Approach to Corporate Responsiveness." Lecture presented at the College of Business Administration, University of Minnesota, May 10, 1974.

Bauer, Raymond A., and Fenn, Dan H., Jr. "What *Is* a Corporate Social Audit?" *Harvard Business Review*, 51 (January–February, 1973), 37–48.

Blake, David H. "The Management of Corporate Social Policy." Lecture presented at the College of Business Administration, University of Minnesota, May 10, 1974.

Bowman, Edward H. *University Investing and Corporate Responsibility.* Cambridge, Mass.: Massachusetts Institute of Technology, August 31, 1971.

Burck, Gilbert. "The Hazards of Corporate Responsibility." *Fortune*, 87 (June 1973), 114.

Business Week. "The First Attempts at a Corporate 'Social Audit'." (September 23, 1972), 88.

Business Week. "Institutions That Balk at Antisocial Management." (January 19, 1974), 66–67.

Davis, Keith. "Five Propositions for Social Responsibility." *Business Horizons*, 18 (June 1975), 19–24.

Drucker, Peter F. *The Age of Discontinuity.* chap. 9. New York: Harper & Row, 1969.

Epstein, Edwin M. "Dimensions of Corporate Power Pt. 1." *California Management Review*, 16 (Winter 1973), 9–23.

Epstein, Edwin M. "Dimensions of Corporate Power, Pt. 2." *California Management Review*, 16 (Summer 1974), 32–47.

Epstein, Edwin M. "The Historical Enigma of Corporate Legitimacy." *California Law Review*, 60 (November 1972), 1701–17.

Fisher, David I. "Minority Banks: A Progress Report." *The Conference Board Record*, 10 (December 1973), 37–41.

Ford, Robert N. "Job Enrichment Lessons from AT&T." *Harvard Business Review,* 51 (January–February 1973), 96–114.

Friedman, Milton. *Capitalism and Freedom.* Chicago: University of Chicago Press, 1962.

Friedman, Milton. "The Social Responsibility of Business Is to Increase Its Profits." *The New York Times Magazine* (September 13, 1970), 32.

Gaskill, William J. "What's Ahead for Corporations in Social Responsibility?" *Financial Executive,* 39 (July 1971), 10–18.

Gray, Daniel. "Corporate Standards are Changing." *Financial Analysts Journal,* 27 (September–October 1971), 28–29.

Harlan, Ridge L. "A Chief Executive's Responsibilities in Financial Communications Today." Address at the Annual Educational Seminar of the National Investor Relations Institute, May 20–21, 1974, New York City.

Heyne, Paul. "The Market System Is the Best Guide." *Financial Analysts Journal,* 27 (September–October 1971), 26–27.

Jacoby, Neil H. *Corporate Power and Social Responsibility.* New York: Macmillan 1973.

Kastenholz, Francis. "An Accountant's View of Social Responsibility." *Financial Executive,* 42 (April 1974), 68–79.

Kristol, Irving. "The Corporation and the Dinosaur." *Wall Street Journal* (February 4, 1974), 20.

Lodge, George Cabot. "Business and the Changing Society." *Harvard Business Review,* 52 (March–April 1974), 59–72.

Lowes, Bryan, and Sparkes, John R. "Fitting Accounting to Social Goals." *Business Horizons,* 17 (June 1974), 53–60.

McColough, C. Peter. "The Corporation and Its Obligations." *Harvard Business Review,* 53 (May–June 1975), 127–38.

Manne, Henry G., and Wallich, Henry C. *The Modern Corporation and Social Responsibility.* Washington D.C.: American Enterprise Institute for Public Policy Research, 1972.

Moskowitz, Milton. "Emergence of the Corporate Conscience." *The New York Times* (January 6, 1974), sec. F, 73.

Parket, I. Robert, and Eilbirt, Henry. "The Practice of Business Social Responsibility: The Underlying Factors." *Business Horizons,* 18 (August 1975), 5–11.

Raffalovich, Hilda. "Corporate Planning for Social Responsibility." *Managerial Planning,* 24 (July–August 1975), 24–29.

Samuelson, Paul A. *Economics.* 8th ed. New York: McGraw-Hill, 1970.

Siegel, Barry. "Minding the Corporate Conscience." *Mainliner* (August, 1974), 32–34.

Simon, John G.; Powers, Charles W.; and Gunnemann, Jon P. *The Ethical Investor*. New Haven, Conn.: Yale University Press, 1972.

Steiner, George A. *Business and Society*, 2d ed. New York: Random House, 1971.

Van Arsdell, Paul M. *Education in Finance: Final Objectives and Problems of Disciplinary Integration*. Working Paper no. 24, Virginia Polytechnic Institute, 1969.

Appendix: Compound Interest Tables

TABLE A–1. Compound Sum of \$1; $S_n = P(1 + r)^n$

Year	1%	2%	3%	4%	5%	6%	7%	8%
1.	1.010	1.020	1.030	1.040	1.050	1.060	1.070	1.080
2.	1.020	1.040	1.081	1.082	1.102	1.124	1.145	1.166
3.	1.030	1.061	1.093	1.125	1.158	1.191	1.225	1.260
4.	1.041	1.082	1.126	1.170	1.216	1.262	1.311	1.360
5.	1.051	1.104	1.159	1.217	1.276	1.338	1.403	1.469
6.	1.062	1.126	1.194	1.265	1.340	1.419	1.501	1.587
7.	1.072	1.149	1.230	1.316	1.407	1.504	1.606	1.714
8.	1.083	1.172	1.267	1.369	1.477	1.594	1.718	1.851
9.	1.094	1.195	1.305	1.423	1.551	1.689	1.838	1.999
10.	1.105	1.219	1.344	1.480	1.629	1.791	1.967	2.159
11.	1.116	1.243	1.384	1.539	1.710	1.898	2.105	2.332
12.	1.127	1.268	1.426	1.601	1.796	2.012	2.252	2.518
13.	1.138	1.294	1.469	1.665	1.886	2.133	2.410	2.720
14.	1.149	1.319	1.513	1.732	1.980	2.261	2.579	2.937
15.	1.161	1.346	1.558	1.801	2.079	2.397	2.759	3.172
16.	1.173	1.373	1.605	1.873	2.183	2.540	2.952	3.426
17.	1.184	1.400	1.653	1.948	2.292	2.693	3.159	3.700
18.	1.196	1.428	1.702	2.026	2.407	2.854	3.380	3.996
19.	1.208	1.457	1.754	2.107	2.527	3.026	3.617	4.316
20.	1.220	1.486	1.806	2.191	2.653	3.207	3.870	4.661

Year	9%	10%	11%	12%	13%	14%	15%	16%
1.	1.090	1.100	1.110	1.120	1.130	1.140	1.150	1.160
2.	1.188	1.210	1.232	1.254	1.277	1.300	1.322	1.346
3.	1.295	1.331	1.368	1.405	1.443	1.482	1.521	1.561
4.	1.412	1.464	1.518	1.574	1.631	1.689	1.749	1.811
5.	1.539	1.611	1.685	1.762	1.842	1.925	2.011	2.100
6.	1.677	1.772	1.870	1.974	2.082	2.195	2.313	2.436
7.	1.828	1.949	2.076	2.211	2.353	2.502	2.660	2.826
8.	1.993	2.144	2.305	2.476	2.658	2.853	3.059	3.278
9.	2.172	2.358	2.558	2.773	3.004	3.252	3.518	3.803
10.	2.367	2.594	2.839	3.106	3.395	3.707	4.046	4.411
11.	2.580	2.853	3.152	3.479	3.836	4.226	4.652	5.117
12.	2.813	3.138	3.499	3.896	4.335	4.818	5.350	5.936
13.	3.066	3.452	3.883	4.363	4.898	5.492	6.153	6.886
14.	3.342	3.797	4.310	4.887	5.535	6.261	7.076	7.988
15.	3.642	4.177	4.785	5.474	6.254	7.138	8.137	9.266
16.	3.970	4.595	5.311	6.130	7.067	8.137	9.358	10.748
17.	4.328	5.054	5.895	6.866	7.986	9.276	10.761	12.468
18.	4.717	5.560	6.544	7.690	9.024	10.575	12.375	14.463
19.	5.142	6.116	7.263	8.613	10.197	12.056	14.232	16.777
20.	5.604	6.728	8.062	9.646	11.523	13.743	16.367	19.461

TABLE A-2
Present Value of $1; $P = S_n(1 + r)^{-n}$

Periods until Payment	1%	2%	2½%	3%	4%	5%	6%	8%	10%	12%	14%	15%	16%	18%	20%	22%	24%	25%	26%	30%	40%	50%
1	0.990	0.980	0.976	0.971	0.962	0.952	0.943	0.926	0.909	0.893	0.877	0.870	0.862	0.847	0.833	0.820	0.806	0.800	0.794	0.769	0.714	0.667
2	0.980	0.961	0.952	0.943	0.925	0.907	0.890	0.857	0.826	0.797	0.769	0.756	0.743	0.718	0.694	0.672	0.650	0.640	0.630	0.592	0.510	0.444
3	0.971	0.942	0.929	0.915	0.889	0.864	0.840	0.794	0.751	0.712	0.675	0.658	0.641	0.609	0.579	0.551	0.524	0.512	0.500	0.455	0.364	0.296
4	0.961	0.924	0.906	0.888	0.855	0.823	0.792	0.735	0.683	0.636	0.592	0.572	0.552	0.516	0.482	0.451	0.423	0.410	0.397	0.350	0.260	0.198
5	0.951	0.906	0.884	0.863	0.822	0.784	0.747	0.681	0.621	0.567	0.519	0.497	0.476	0.437	0.402	0.370	0.341	0.328	0.315	0.269	0.186	0.132
6	0.942	0.888	0.862	0.837	0.790	0.746	0.705	0.630	0.564	0.507	0.456	0.432	0.410	0.370	0.335	0.303	0.275	0.262	0.250	0.207	0.133	0.088
7	0.933	0.871	0.841	0.813	0.760	0.711	0.665	0.583	0.513	0.452	0.400	0.376	0.354	0.314	0.279	0.249	0.222	0.210	0.198	0.159	0.095	0.059
8	0.923	0.853	0.821	0.789	0.731	0.677	0.627	0.540	0.467	0.404	0.351	0.327	0.305	0.266	0.233	0.204	0.179	0.168	0.157	0.123	0.068	0.039
9	0.914	0.837	0.801	0.766	0.703	0.645	0.592	0.500	0.424	0.361	0.308	0.284	0.263	0.225	0.194	0.167	0.144	0.134	0.125	0.094	0.048	0.026
10	0.905	0.820	0.781	0.744	0.676	0.614	0.558	0.463	0.386	0.322	0.270	0.247	0.227	0.191	0.162	0.137	0.116	0.107	0.099	0.073	0.035	0.017
11	0.896	0.804	0.762	0.722	0.650	0.585	0.527	0.429	0.350	0.287	0.237	0.215	0.195	0.162	0.135	0.112	0.094	0.086	0.079	0.056	0.025	0.012
12	0.887	0.788	0.744	0.701	0.625	0.557	0.497	0.397	0.319	0.257	0.208	0.187	0.168	0.137	0.112	0.092	0.076	0.069	0.062	0.043	0.018	0.008
13	0.879	0.773	0.725	0.681	0.601	0.530	0.469	0.368	0.290	0.229	0.182	0.163	0.145	0.116	0.093	0.075	0.061	0.055	0.050	0.033	0.013	0.005
14	0.870	0.758	0.708	0.661	0.577	0.505	0.442	0.340	0.263	0.205	0.160	0.141	0.125	0.099	0.078	0.062	0.049	0.044	0.039	0.025	0.009	0.003
15	0.861	0.743	0.690	0.642	0.555	0.481	0.417	0.315	0.239	0.183	0.140	0.123	0.108	0.084	0.065	0.051	0.040	0.035	0.031	0.020	0.006	0.002
16	0.853	0.728	0.674	0.623	0.534	0.458	0.394	0.292	0.218	0.163	0.123	0.107	0.093	0.071	0.054	0.042	0.032	0.028	0.025	0.015	0.005	0.002
17	0.844	0.714	0.657	0.605	0.513	0.436	0.371	0.270	0.198	0.146	0.108	0.093	0.080	0.060	0.045	0.034	0.026	0.023	0.020	0.012	0.003	0.001
18	0.836	0.700	0.641	0.587	0.494	0.416	0.350	0.250	0.180	0.130	0.095	0.081	0.069	0.051	0.038	0.028	0.021	0.018	0.016	0.009	0.002	0.001
19	0.828	0.686	0.626	0.570	0.475	0.396	0.331	0.232	0.164	0.116	0.083	0.070	0.060	0.043	0.031	0.023	0.017	0.014	0.012	0.007	0.002	
20	0.820	0.673	0.610	0.554	0.456	0.377	0.312	0.215	0.149	0.104	0.073	0.061	0.051	0.037	0.026	0.019	0.014	0.012	0.010	0.005	0.002	
21	0.811	0.660	0.595	0.538	0.439	0.359	0.294	0.199	0.135	0.093	0.064	0.053	0.044	0.031	0.022	0.015	0.011	0.009	0.008	0.004	0.001	
22	0.803	0.647	0.581	0.522	0.422	0.342	0.278	0.184	0.123	0.083	0.056	0.046	0.038	0.026	0.018	0.013	0.009	0.007	0.006	0.003	0.001	
23	0.795	0.634	0.567	0.507	0.406	0.326	0.262	0.170	0.112	0.074	0.049	0.040	0.033	0.022	0.015	0.010	0.007	0.006	0.005	0.002		
24	0.788	0.622	0.553	0.492	0.390	0.310	0.247	0.158	0.102	0.066	0.043	0.035	0.028	0.019	0.013	0.008	0.006	0.005	0.004	0.002		
25	0.780	0.610	0.539	0.478	0.375	0.295	0.233	0.146	0.092	0.059	0.038ᵃ	0.030	0.024	0.016	0.010	0.007	0.005	0.004	0.003	0.001		
26	0.772	0.598	0.526	0.464	0.361	0.281	0.220	0.135	0.084	0.053	0.033	0.026	0.021	0.014	0.009	0.006	0.004	0.003	0.002	0.001		
27	0.764	0.586	0.513	0.450	0.347	0.268	0.207	0.125	0.076	0.047	0.029	0.023	0.018	0.011	0.007	0.005	0.003	0.002	0.002	0.001		
28	0.757	0.574	0.501	0.437	0.333	0.255	0.196	0.116	0.069	0.042	0.026	0.020	0.016	0.010	0.006	0.004	0.002	0.002	0.001	0.001		
29	0.749	0.563	0.489	0.424	0.321	0.243	0.185	0.107	0.063	0.037	0.022	0.017	0.014	0.008	0.005	0.003	0.002	0.002	0.001			
30	0.742	0.552	0.477	0.412	0.308	0.231	0.174	0.099	0.057	0.033	0.020	0.015	0.012	0.007	0.004	0.003	0.002	0.001	0.001			
40	0.672	0.453	0.372	0.307	0.208	0.142	0.097	0.046	0.022	0.011	0.005	0.004	0.003	0.001	0.001							
50	0.608	0.372	0.291	0.228	0.141	0.087	0.054	0.021	0.009	0.003	0.001	0.001	0.001									

TABLE A-3

Present Value of $1 Received Annually; $A_{\overline{n}|r} = \$1\left[\dfrac{1-(1+r)^{-n}}{r}\right] = \$1P_{m,r}$

Periods to Be Paid	1%	2%	2½%	3%	4%	5%	6%	8%	10%	12%	14%	15%	16%	18%	20%	22%	24%	25%	26%	30%	40%	50%
1	0.990	0.980	0.976	0.971	0.962	0.952	0.943	0.926	0.909	0.893	0.877	0.870	0.862	0.847	0.833	0.820	0.806	0.800	0.794	0.769	0.714	0.667
2	1.970	1.942	1.927	1.914	1.886	1.859	1.833	1.783	1.736	1.690	1.647	1.626	1.605	1.566	1.528	1.492	1.457	1.440	1.424	1.361	1.224	1.111
3	2.941	2.884	2.856	2.829	2.775	2.723	2.673	2.577	2.487	2.402	2.322	2.283	2.246	2.174	2.106	2.042	1.981	1.952	1.923	1.816	1.589	1.407
4	3.902	3.808	3.762	3.717	3.630	3.546	3.465	3.312	3.170	3.037	2.914	2.855	2.798	2.690	2.589	2.494	2.404	2.362	2.320	2.166	1.849	1.605
5	4.853	4.713	4.646	4.580	4.452	4.330	4.212	3.993	3.791	3.605	3.433	3.352	3.274	3.127	2.991	2.864	2.745	2.689	2.635	2.436	2.035	1.737
6	5.795	5.601	5.508	5.417	5.242	5.076	4.917	4.623	4.355	4.111	3.889	3.784	3.685	3.498	3.326	3.167	3.020	2.951	2.885	2.643	2.168	1.824
7	6.728	6.472	6.349	6.230	6.002	5.786	5.582	5.206	4.868	4.564	4.288	4.160	4.039	3.812	3.605	3.416	3.242	3.161	3.083	2.802	2.263	1.883
8	7.652	7.325	7.170	7.020	6.733	6.463	6.210	5.747	5.335	4.968	4.639	4.487	4.344	4.078	3.837	3.619	3.421	3.329	3.241	2.925	2.331	1.922
9	8.566	8.162	7.971	7.786	7.435	7.108	6.802	6.247	5.759	5.328	4.946	4.772	4.607	4.303	4.031	3.786	3.566	3.463	3.366	3.019	2.379	1.948
10	9.471	8.983	8.752	8.530	8.111	7.722	7.360	6.710	6.145	5.650	5.216	5.019	4.833	4.494	4.192	3.923	3.682	3.571	3.465	3.092	2.414	1.965
11	10.368	9.787	9.514	9.253	8.760	8.306	7.887	7.139	6.495	5.938	5.453	5.234	5.029	4.656	4.327	4.035	3.776	3.656	3.544	3.147	2.438	1.977
12	11.255	10.575	10.258	9.954	9.385	8.863	8.384	7.536	6.814	6.194	5.660	5.421	5.197	4.793	4.439	4.127	3.851	3.725	3.606	3.190	2.456	1.985
13	12.134	11.348	10.983	10.635	9.986	9.394	8.853	7.904	7.103	6.424	5.842	5.583	5.342	4.910	4.533	4.203	3.912	3.780	3.656	3.223	2.468	1.990
14	13.004	12.106	11.691	11.296	10.563	9.899	9.295	8.244	7.367	6.628	6.002	5.724	5.468	5.008	4.611	4.265	3.962	3.824	3.695	3.249	2.478	1.993
15	13.865	12.849	12.381	11.938	11.118	10.380	9.712	8.559	7.606	6.811	6.142	5.847	5.576	5.092	4.676	4.315	4.001	3.859	3.726	3.268	2.484	1.995
16	14.718	13.578	13.055	12.561	11.652	10.838	10.106	8.851	7.824	6.974	6.265	5.954	5.668	5.162	4.730	4.357	4.033	3.887	3.751	3.283	2.488	1.997
17	15.562	14.292	13.712	13.166	12.166	11.274	10.477	9.122	8.022	7.120	6.373	6.047	5.749	5.222	4.775	4.391	4.059	3.910	3.771	3.295	2.492	1.998
18	16.398	14.992	14.353	13.754	12.659	11.690	10.828	9.372	8.201	7.250	6.467	6.128	5.818	5.273	4.812	4.419	4.080	3.928	3.786	3.304	2.494	1.999
19	17.226	15.678	14.979	14.324	13.134	12.085	11.158	9.604	8.365	7.366	6.550	6.198	5.878	5.316	4.844	4.442	4.097	3.942	3.799	3.311	2.496	1.999
20	18.046	16.351	15.589	14.877	13.590	12.462	11.470	9.818	8.514	7.469	6.623	6.259	5.929	5.353	4.870	4.460	4.110	3.954	3.808	3.316	2.497	1.999
21	18.857	17.011	16.185	15.415	14.029	12.821	11.764	10.017	8.649	7.562	6.687	6.312	5.973	5.384	4.891	4.476	4.121	3.963	3.816	3.320	2.498	2.000
22	19.660	17.658	16.765	15.937	14.451	13.163	12.042	10.201	8.772	7.645	6.743	6.359	6.011	5.410	4.909	4.488	4.130	3.970	3.822	3.323	2.498	2.000
23	20.456	18.292	17.332	16.444	14.857	13.489	12.303	10.371	8.883	7.718	6.792	6.399	6.044	5.432	4.924	4.499	4.137	3.976	3.827	3.325	2.499	2.000
24	21.243	18.914	17.885	16.936	15.247	13.799	12.550	10.529	8.985	7.784	6.835	6.434	6.073	5.451	4.937	4.507	4.143	3.981	3.831	3.327	2.499	2.000
25	22.023	19.523	18.424	17.413	15.622	14.094	12.783	10.675	9.077	7.843	6.873	6.464	6.097	5.467	4.948	4.514	4.147	3.985	3.834	3.329	2.499	2.000
26	22.795	20.121	18.951	17.877	15.983	14.375	13.003	10.810	9.161	7.896	6.906	6.491	6.118	5.480	4.956	4.520	4.151	3.988	3.837	3.330	2.500	2.000
27	23.560	20.707	19.464	18.327	16.330	14.643	13.211	10.935	9.237	7.943	6.935	6.514	6.136	5.492	4.964	4.524	4.154	3.990	3.839	3.331	2.500	2.000
28	24.316	21.281	19.965	18.764	16.663	14.898	13.406	11.051	9.307	7.984	6.961	6.534	6.152	5.502	4.970	4.528	4.157	3.992	3.840	3.331	2.500	2.000
29	25.066	21.844	20.454	19.188	16.984	15.141	13.591	11.158	9.370	8.022	6.983	6.551	6.166	5.510	4.975	4.531	4.159	3.994	3.841	3.332	2.500	2.000
30	25.808	22.396	20.930	19.600	17.292	15.372	13.765	11.258	9.427	8.055	7.003	6.566	6.177	5.517	4.979	4.534	4.160	3.995	3.842	3.332	2.500	2.000
40	32.835	27.355	25.103	23.115	19.793	17.159	15.046	11.925	9.779	8.244	7.105	6.642	6.234	5.548	4.997	4.544	4.166	3.999	3.846	3.333	2.500	2.000
50	39.196	31.424	28.362	25.730	21.482	18.256	15.762	12.233	9.915	8.304	7.133	6.660	6.246	5.554	4.999	4.545	4.167	4.000	3.846	3.333	2.500	2.000

TABLE A–4

Sum of an Annuity of $1 for n Years; $S_{\overline{n}|r} = \$1 \left[\dfrac{(1+r)^n - 1}{r} \right] = \$1C_{n,r}$

Year	1%	2%	3%	4%	5%	6%	7%	8%
1..........	1.000	1.000	1.000	1.000	1.000	1.000	1.000	1.000
2..........	2.010	2.020	2.030	2.040	2.050	2.080	2.070	2.080
3..........	3.030	3.060	3.091	3.122	3.152	3.184	3.215	3.246
4..........	4.060	4.122	4.184	4.246	4.310	4.375	4.440	4.506
5..........	5.101	5.204	5.309	5.416	5.526	5.637	5.751	5.867
6..........	6.152	6.308	6.468	6.633	6.802	6.975	7.153	7.336
7..........	7.214	7.434	7.662	7.898	8.142	8.394	8.654	8.923
8..........	8.286	8.583	8.892	9.214	9.549	9.897	10.260	10.637
9..........	9.369	9.755	10.159	10.583	11.027	11.491	11.978	12.488
10..........	10.462	10.950	11.464	12.006	12.578	13.181	13.816	14.487
11..........	11.567	12.169	12.808	13.846	14.207	14.972	15.784	16.645
12..........	12.683	13.412	14.192	15.026	15.917	16.870	17.888	18.977
13..........	13.809	14.680	15.818	16.627	17.713	18.882	20.141	21.495
14..........	14.947	15.974	17.086	18.292	19.599	21.051	22.550	24.215
15..........	16.097	17.293	18.599	20.024	21.579	23.276	25.129	27.152

Year	9%	10%	11%	12%	13%	14%	15%	16%
1..........	1.000	1.000	1.000	1.000	1.000	1.000	1.000	1.000
2..........	2.090	2.100	2.110	2.120	2.130	2.140	2.150	2.160
3..........	3.278	3.310	3.342	3.374	3.407	3.440	3.473	3.506
4..........	4.573	4.641	4.710	4.779	4.850	4.921	4.993	5.066
5..........	5.985	6.105	6.228	6.353	6.480	6.610	6.742	6.877
6..........	7.523	7.716	7.913	8.115	8.323	8.536	8.754	8.977
7..........	9.200	9.487	9.783	10.089	10.405	10.730	11.067	11.414
8..........	11.028	11.436	11.859	12.300	12.757	13.233	13.727	14.240
9..........	13.021	13.579	14.164	14.776	15.416	16.085	16.786	17.518
10..........	15.193	15.937	16.772	17.549	18.420	19.337	20.304	21.321
11..........	17.560	18.531	19.561	20.655	21.814	23.044	24.349	25.733
12..........	20.141	21.384	22.713	24.133	25.650	27.271	29.002	30.850
13..........	22.953	24.523	26.212	28.029	29.985	32.089	34.352	36.786
14..........	26.019	27.975	30.095	32.393	34.883	37.581	40.505	43.672
15..........	29.361	31.772	34.405 ·	37.286	40.417	43.842	47.580	51.659

INDEX

Index